# A SELECT LIBRARY

OF THE

# NICENE AND POST-NICENE FATHERS

OF

# THE CHRISTIAN CHURCH

EDITED BY

## PHILIP SCHAFF, D.D., LL.D.,

PROFESSOR IN THE UNION THEOLOGICAL SEMINARY, NEW YORK,

*IN CONNECTION WITH A NUMBER OF PATRISTIC SCHOLARS OF EUROPE AND AMERICA*

## VOLUME V

### SAINT AUGUSTIN:

ANTI-PELAGIAN WRITINGS.

## T&T CLARK
EDINBURGH

## WM. B. EERDMANS PUBLISHING COMPANY
GRAND RAPIDS, MICHIGAN

**British Library Cataloguing in Publication Data**

Nicene & Post-Nicene Fathers. — 1st series
1. Fathers of the church
I. Title   II.  Schaff, Philip
230′.11     BR60.A62

T&T Clark ISBN 0 567 09394 8


Eerdmans ISBN 0-8028-8102-5

*Reprinted, November 1987*

# SAINT AUGUSTIN'S ANTI-PELAGIAN WORKS.

*TRANSLATED BY*

## PETER HOLMES, D.D., F.R.A.S.,

DOMESTIC CHAPLAIN TO THE RIGHT HONORABLE THE COUNTESS OF ROTHES,
AND CURATE OF PENNYCROSS, PLYMOUTH;

AND

## REV. ROBERT ERNEST WALLIS, Ph.D.,

INCUMBENT OF CHRIST CHURCH, COXLEY, SOMERSET.

*THE TRANSLATION REVISED, AND AN INTRODUCTION PREFIXED, BY*

## BENJAMIN B. WARFIELD, D.D.,

PROFESSOR IN THE THEOLOGICAL SEMINARY AT PRINCETON, N.J.

# CONTENTS.

Note. — The treatises marked with an asterisk above were translated by Dr. Wallis; the others by Dr. Holmes.

# PREFACE TO THE AMERICAN EDITION.

"THIS volume contains all the Anti-Pelagian writings of Augustin, collected by the Benedictine editors in their tenth volume, with the exception only of the two long works *Against Julian*, and *The Unfinished Work*, which have been necessarily excluded on account of their bulk. The translation here printed is that of the English version of Augustin's works, published by Messrs. T. and T. Clark at Edinburgh. This translation has been carefully compared with the Latin throughout, and corrected on every page into more accurate conformity to its sense. But this has not so altered its character that it ceases to be the Edinburgh translation, — bettered somewhat, but still essentially the same. The excellent translation of the three treatises, *On the Spirit and the Letter*, *On Nature and Grace*, and *On the Proceedings of Pelagius*, published in the early summer of this year by two Oxford scholars, Messrs. Woods and Johnston (London: David Nutt), was unfortunately too late in reaching America to be of any service to the editor.

"What may be called the explanatory matter of the Edinburgh translation, has been treated here even more freely than the text. The headings to the chapters have been added to until nearly every chapter is now provided with a caption. The brackets which distinguished the notes added by the translator from those which he translated from the Benedictine editor, have been generally removed, and the notes themselves often verbally changed, or otherwise altered. A few notes have been added, — chiefly with the design of rendering the allusions in the text intelligible to the uninstructed reader; and the more lengthy of these have been enclosed in brackets, and signed with a W. The result of all this is, that it is unsafe to hold the Edinburgh translators too closely responsible for the unbracketed matter; but that the American editor has not claimed as his own more than is really his.

"In preparing an *Introductory Essay* for the volume, two objects have been kept in view: to place the necessary Prolegomena to the following treatises in the hands of the reader, and to furnish the English reader with some illustrations of the Anti-Pelagian treatises from the other writings of Augustin. In the former interest, a brief sketch of the history of the Pelagian controversy and of the Pelagian and Augustinian systems has been given, and the occasions, objects, and contents of the several treatises have been briefly stated. In the latter, Augustin's letters and sermons have been as copiously extracted as the limits of space allowed. In the nature of the case, the sources have been independently examined for these materials; but those who have written of Pelagianism and of Augustin's part in the controversy with it, have not been neglected. Above others, probably special obligations ought to be acknowledged to the Benedictine preface to their tenth volume, and to Canon Bright's Introduction to his edition of *Select Anti-Pelagian Treatises*. The purpose of this essay will be subserved if it enables the reader to attack the treatises themselves with increased interest and readiness to assimilate and estimate their contents.

"References to the treatises in the essay, and cross-references in the treatises themselves, have been inserted wherever they seemed absolutely necessary; but they have been often omitted where otherwise they would have been inserted because it has been thought that the *Index of Subjects* will suffice for all the needs of comparison of passages that are likely to arise. In the *Index of Texts*, an asterisk marks some of those places where a text is fully explained; and students of the history of Biblical Interpretation may find this feature helpful to them. It will not be strange, if, on turning up a few passages, they will find their notion of the power, exactness, and devout truth of Augustin as an interpreter of Scripture very much raised above what the current histories of interpretation have taught them."

The above has been prepared by Dr. Warfield. I need only add that the present volume contains the most important of the doctrinal and polemical works of Augustin, which exerted a powerful influence upon the Reformers of the sixteenth century and upon the Jansenists in the seventeenth. They constitute what is popularly called the Augustinian system, though they only represent one side of it. Enough has been said on their merits in the Prolegomena to the first volume, and in the valuable Introductory Essay of Dr. WARFIELD, who has been called to fill the chair of systematic theology once adorned by the learning and piety of the immortal HODGES, father and son.

The remaining three volumes will contain the exegetical writings of the great Bishop of Hippo.

PHILIP SCHAFF.

NEW YORK, September, 1887.

# INTRODUCTORY ESSAY ON AUGUSTIN AND THE PELAGIAN CONTROVERSY,

*BY PROFESSOR BENJAMIN B. WARFIELD, D.D.*

# A SELECT BIBLIOGRAPHY OF THE PELAGIAN CONTROVERSY.

*(Adapted from Dr. Schaff's Church History, vol. iii.)*

I. THREE works of PELAGIUS, printed among the works of Jerome (Vallarsius' edition, vol. xi.): viz., the *Expositions on Paul's Epistles*, written before 410 (but somewhat, especially in Romans, interpolated); the *Epistle to Demetrias*, 413; and the *Confession of Faith*, 417, addressed to Innocent I. Copious fragments of other works (*On Nature, In Defence of Free Will, Chapters, Letter to Innocent*) are found quoted in Augustin's refutations; as also of certain works by CŒLESTIUS (e.g., his *Definitions, Confession to Zosimus*), and of the writings of JULIAN. Here also belong CASSIAN's *Collationes Patrum*, and the works of the other semi-Pelagian writers.

II. AUGUSTIN'S anti-Pelagian treatises; also his work *On Heresies*, 88, 428; many of his letters, as e.g., those numbered by the Benedictines, 140, 157, 178, 179, 190, 191, 193, 194; and many of his sermons, as e.g., 155, 163, 165, 168, 169, 174, 176, 293, 294, etc. JEROME'S *Letter to Ctesiphon* (133), and his three books of *Dialogue against the Pelagians* (vol. ii. of Vallarsius); PAULUS OROSIUS' *Apology against Pelagius*; MARIUS MERCATOR'S *Commonitoria*; PROSPER OF AQUITAINE'S writings, as also those of such late writers as AVITUS, CÆSARIUS, FULGENTIUS, who bore the brunt of the semi-Pelagian controversy.

III. The collections of *Acta* of the councils and other public documents, in MANSI and in the appendix to the Benedictine edition of Augustin's anti-Pelagian writings (vol. x.).

IV. LITERATURE. — A. Special works on the subject: GERH. JOH. VOSSIUS, *Hist. de Controversiis quas Pelagius ejusque reliquiæ moverunt*, 1655; HENR. NORISIUS, *Historia Pelagiana*, etc., 1673; GARNIER, *Dissert. vii. quibus integra continuentur Pelagianorum Hist.* (in his edition of Marius Mercator, I. 113); the PRÆFATIO to vol. x. of the Benedictine edition of Augustin's works; CORN. JANSENIUS, *Augustinus sive doctrina S. Augustini, etc., adversus Pelagianos et Massilienses*, 1640; JAC. SIRMOND, *Historia Prædestinatiana*, 1648; TILLEMONT, *Mémoires* xiii. 1-1075; CH. WILH. FR. WALCH, *Ketzerhistorie*, Bd. iv. and v., 1770; JOHANN GEFFKEN, *Historia semi-pelagianismi antiquissima*, 1826; G. F. WIGGERS, *Versuch einer pragmatischen Darstellung des Augustinismus und Pelagianismus*, 1821-1833 (Part I. dealing with Pelagianism proper, in an E. T. by Professor Emerson, Andover, 1840); J. L. JACOBI, *Die Lehre des Pelagius*, 1842; P. SCHAFF, *The Pelagian Controversy*, in the *Bibliotheca Sacra*, May, 1884; THEOD. GANGAUF, *Metaphysische Psychologie des Heiligen Augustinus*, 1852; JULIUS MÜLLER, *Die Christliche Lehre von der Sünde*, 5th edition 1866 (E. T. by Urwick, Edinburgh); Do., *Der Pelagianismus*, 1854; F. WÖRTER, *Der Pelagianismus u. s. w.* 1866; MOZLEY, *On the Augustinian Doctrine of Predestination*, 1855; NOURRISSON, *La philosophie de S. Augustin*, 1868; BRIGHT, *Select anti-Pelagian Treatises of St. Augustine*, 1880; WILLIAM CUNNINGHAM (not to be confounded with the Scotch professor of that name), *S. Austin and his Place in the History of Christian Thought*, being the Hulsean Lectures for 1885; JAMES FIELD SPALDING, *The Teaching and Influence of St. Augustine*, 1886; HERMANN REUTER, *Augustinische Studien*, 1887.

B. The appropriate section in the Histories of Doctrine, as for example those of MÜNCHNER, BAUMGARTEN-CRUSIUS, HAGENBACH (also E. T.), NEANDER (also E. T.), BAUR, BECK, THOMASIUS, HARNACK (vol. ii. in the press); and in English, W. CUNNINGHAM, SHEDD, etc.

C. The appropriate chapters in the various larger church histories, e.g., those of SCHRÖCKH, FLEURY, GIESELER (also E. T.), NEANDER (also E. T.), HEFELE (*History of the Councils*, also E. T.), KURTZ (also E. T.); and in English, SCHAFF, MILMAN, ROBERTSON, etc.

# INTRODUCTORY ESSAY ON AUGUSTIN AND THE PELAGIAN CONTROVERSY.

## BY PROFESSOR B. B. WARFIELD, D.D.

### I. THE ORIGIN AND NATURE OF PELAGIANISM.

IT was inevitable that the energy of the Church in intellectually realizing and defining its doctrines in relation to one another, should first be directed towards the objective side of Christian truth. The chief controversies of the first four centuries and the resulting definitions of doctrine, concerned the nature of God and the person of Christ; and it was not until these theological and Christological questions were well upon their way to final settlement, that the Church could turn its attention to the more subjective side of truth. Meanwhile she bore in her bosom a full recognition, side by side, of the freedom of the will, the evil consequences of the fall, and the necessity of divine grace for salvation. Individual writers, or even the several sections of the Church, might exhibit a tendency to throw emphasis on one or another of the elements that made up this deposit of faith that was the common inheritance of all. The East, for instance, laid especial stress on free will: and the West dwelt more pointedly on the ruin of the human race and the absolute need of God's grace for salvation. But neither did the Eastern theologians forget the universal sinfulness and need of redemption, or the necessity, for the realization of that redemption, of God's gracious influences; nor did those of the West deny the self-determination or accountability of men. All the elements of the composite doctrine of man were everywhere confessed; but they were variously emphasized, according to the temper of the writers or the controversial demands of the times. Such a state of affairs, however, was an invitation to heresy, and a prophecy of controversy; just as the simultaneous confession of the unity of God and the Deity of Christ, or of the Deity and the humanity of Christ, inevitably carried in its train a series of heresies and controversies, until the definitions of the doctrines of the Trinity and of the person of Christ were complete. In like manner, it was inevitable that sooner or later some one should arise who would so one-sidedly emphasize one element or the other of the Church's teaching as to salvation, as to throw himself into heresy, and drive the Church, through controversy with him, into a precise definition of the doctrines of free will and grace in their mutual relations.

This new heresiarch came, at the opening of the fifth century, in the person of the British monk, Pelagius. The novelty of the doctrine which he taught is repeatedly asserted by Augustin,[1] and is evident to the historian; but it consisted not in the emphasis that he laid on free will, but rather in the fact that, in emphasizing free will, he denied the ruin of the race and the necessity of grace. This was not only new in Christianity; it was even anti-Christian. Jerome,

---

[1] *On the Merits and Remission of Sins*, iii. 6, 11, 12; *Against Two Letters of the Pelagians*, iv. 32; *Against Julian*, i. 4; *On Heresies*, 88; and often elsewhere. Jerome found *roots* for the theory in Origen and Rufinus (*Letter* 133, 3), but this is a different matter. Compare *On Original Sin*, 25.

as well as Augustin, saw this at the time, and speaks of Pelagianism as the "heresy of Pythagoras and Zeno;"[1] and modern writers of the various schools have more or less fully recognized it. Thus Dean Milman thinks that "the greater part" of Pelagius' letter to Demetrias "might have been written by an ancient academic;"[2] Dr. De Pressensé identifies the Pelagian idea of liberty with that of Paganism;[3] and Bishop Hefele openly declares that their fundamental doctrine, "that man is virtuous entirely of his own merit, not of the gift of grace," seems to him "to be a rehabilitation of the general heathen view of the world," and compares with it Cicero's words :[4] "For gold, lands, and all the blessings of life, we have to return thanks to the Gods; but no one ever returned thanks to the Gods for virtues."[5] The struggle with Pelagianism was thus in reality a struggle for the very foundations of Christianity; and even more dangerously than in the previous theological and Christological controversies, here the practical substance of Christianity was in jeopardy. The real question at issue was whether there was any need for Christianity at all; whether by his own power man might not attain eternal felicity; whether the function of Christianity was to save, or only to render an eternity of happiness more easily attainable by man.[6]

Genetically speaking, Pelagianism was the daughter of legalism; but when it itself conceived, it brought forth an essential deism. It is not without significance that its originators were "a certain sort of monks;" that is, laymen of ascetic life. From this point of view the Divine law is looked upon as a collection of separate commandments, moral perfection as a simple complex of separate virtues, and a distinct value as a meritorious demand on Divine appro- bation is ascribed to each good work or attainment in the exercises of piety. It was because this was essentially his point of view that Pelagius could regard man's powers as sufficient to the attainment of sanctity, — nay, that he could even assert it to be possible for a man to do more than was required of him. But this involved an essentially deistic conception of man's relations to his Maker. God had endowed His creature with a capacity (*possibilitas*) or ability (*posse*) for action, and it was for him to use it. Man was thus a machine, which, just because it was well made, needed no Divine interference for its right working; and the Creator, having once framed him, and endowed him with the *posse*, henceforth leaves the *velle* and the *esse* to him.

At this point we have touched the central and formative principle of Pelagianism. It lies in the assumption of the plenary ability of man; his ability to do all that righteousness can demand, — to work out not only his own salvation, but also his own perfection. This is the core of the whole theory; and all the other postulates not only depend upon it, but arise out of it. Both chronologically and logically this is the root of the system.

When we first hear of Pelagius, he is already advanced in years, living in Rome in the odour of sanctity,[7] and enjoying a well-deserved reputation for zeal in exhorting others to a good life, which grew especially warm against those who endeavoured to shelter themselves, when charged with their sins, behind the weakness of nature.[8] He was outraged by the universal excuses on such occasions, — "It is hard!" "it is difficult!" "we are not able!" "we are men!" — "Oh, blind madness!" he cried: "we accuse God of a twofold ignorance, — that He does not seem to know what He has made, nor what He has commanded, — as if forgetting the human weakness of which He is Himself the Author, He has imposed laws on man which He cannot endure."[9] He himself tells us[10] that it was his custom, therefore, whenever he had to speak on moral improve- ment and the conduct of a holy life, to begin by pointing out the power and quality of human nature, and by showing what it was capable of doing. For (he says) he esteemed it of small use to exhort men to what they deemed impossible: hope must rather be our companion, and all longing and effort die when we despair of attaining. So exceedingly ardent an advocate was he

[1] Preface to Book iv. of his work on Jeremiah.   [2] *Latin Christianity*, i. 166, note 2.   [3] *Trois Prem. Siècles*, ii. 375.
[4] *De Natura Deorum*, iii. 36.   [5] *History of the Councils of the Church* (E. T.), ii. 446, note 3.
[6] Compare the excellent statement in Thomasius' *Dogmengeschichte*, i. 483.
[7] *On the Proceedings of Pelagius*, 46; *On the Merits and Remission of Sins*, iii. 1; *Epistle* 186, etc.
[8] *On Nature and Grace*, 1.   [9] *Epistle to Demetrias*, 16.   [10] Do. 2 and 19.

of man's unaided ability to do all that God commanded, that when Augustin's noble and entirely scriptural prayer — "Give what Thou commandest, and command what Thou wilt " — was repeated in his hearing, he was unable to endure it; and somewhat inconsistently contradicted it with such violence as almost to become involved in a strife.[1] The powers of man, he held, were gifts of God; and it was, therefore, a reproach against Him as if He had made man ill or evil, to believe that they were insufficient for the keeping of His law. Nay, do what we will, we cannot rid ourselves of their sufficiency: "whether we will, or whether we will not, we have the capacity of not sinning."[2]  "I say," he says, "that man is able to be without sin, and that he is able to keep the commandments of God;" and this sufficiently direct statement of human ability is in reality the hinge of his whole system.

There were three specially important corollaries which flowed from this assertion of human ability, and Augustin himself recognized these as the chief elements of the system.[3] It would be inexplicable on such an assumption, if no man had ever used his ability in keeping God's law; and Pelagius consistently asserted not only that all might be sinless if they chose, but also that many saints, even before Christ, had actually lived free from sin. Again, it follows from man's inalienable ability to be free from sin, that each man comes into the world without entailment of sin or moral weakness from the past acts of men; and Pelagius consistently denied the whole doctrine of original sin. And still again, it follows from the same assumption of ability that man has no need of supernatural assistance in his striving to obey righteousness; and Pelagius consistently denied both the need and reality of divine grace in the sense of an inward help (and especially of a prevenient help) to man's weakness.

It was upon this last point that the greatest stress was laid in the controversy, and Augustin was most of all disturbed that thus God's grace was denied and opposed. No doubt the Pelagians spoke constantly of "grace," but they meant by this the primal endowment of man with free will, and the subsequent aid given him in order to its proper use by the revelation of the law and the teaching of the gospel, and, above all, by the forgiveness of past sins in Christ and by Christ's holy example.[4] Anything further than this external help they utterly denied; and they denied that this external help itself was absolutely necessary, affirming that it only rendered it easier for man to do what otherwise he had plenary ability for doing. Chronologically, this contention seems to have preceded the assertion which must logically lie at its base, of the freedom of man from any taint, corruption, or weakness due to sin. It was in order that they might deny that man needed help, that they denied that Adam's sin had any further effect on his posterity than might arise from his bad example. "Before the action of his own proper will," said Pelagius plainly, " that only is in man which God made."[5]  "As we are procreated without virtue," he said, " so also without vice."[5]  In a word, "Nothing that is good and evil, on account of which we are either praiseworthy or blameworthy, is born with us, — it is rather done by us; for we are born with capacity for either, but provided with neither."[5]  So his later follower, Julian, plainly asserts his " faith that God creates men obnoxious to no sin, but full of natural innocence, and with capacity for voluntary virtues."[6]  So intrenched is free will in nature, that, according to Julian, it is "just as complete after sins as it was before sins;"[7] and what this means may be gathered from Pelagius' definition in the " Confession of Faith," that he sent to Innocent: " We say that man is always able both to sin and not to sin, so as that we may confess that we have free will." That sin in such circumstances was so common as to be well-nigh universal, was accounted for by the bad example of Adam and the power of habit, the latter being simply the

---

[1] On the Gift of Perseverance, 53.                    [2] On Nature and Grace, 49.

[3] On the Gift of Perseverance, 4; Against Two Letters of the Pelagians, iii. 24; iv. 2 sq.

[4] On the Spirit and Letter, 4; On Nature and Grace, 53; On the Proceedings of Pelagius, 20, 22, 38; On the Grace of Christ, 2, 3, 8, 31, 42, 45; Against Two Letters of the Pelagians, iv. 11; On Grace and Free Will, 23–26, and often.

[5] On Original Sin, 14.                    [6] The Unfinished Work, iii. 82.

[7] Do. i. 91; compare do. i. 48, 60; ii. 20.  " There is nothing of sin in man, if there is nothing of his own will."  " There is no original sin in infants at all."

result of imitation of the former. "Nothing makes well-doing so hard," writes Pelagius to Demetrias, "as the long custom of sins which begins from childhood and gradually brings us more and more under its power until it seems to have in some degree the force of nature (*vim naturæ*)." He is even ready to allow for the force of habit in a broad way, on the world at large ; and so divides all history into progressive periods, marked by God's (external) grace. At first the light of nature was so strong that men by it alone could live in holiness. And it was only when men's manners became corrupt and tarnished nature began to be insufficient for holy living, that by God's grace the Law was given as an addition to mere nature ; and by it " the original lustre was restored to nature after its blush had been impaired." And so again, after the habit of sinning once more prevailed among men, and " the law became unequal to the task of curing it," [1] Christ was given, furnishing men with forgiveness of sins, exhortations to imitation of the example and the holy example itself. [2] But though thus a progressive deterioration was confessed, and such a deterioration as rendered desirable at least two supernatural interpositions (in the giving of the law and the coming of Christ), yet no corruption of nature, even by growing habit, is really allowed. It was only an ever-increasing facility in imitating vice which arose from so long a schooling in evil ; and all that was needed to rescue men from it was a new explanation of what was right (in the law), or, at the most, the encouragement of forgiveness for what was already done, and a holy example (in Christ) for imitation. Pelagius still asserted our continuous possession of " a free will which is unimpaired for sinning and for not sinning ; " and Julian, that " our free will is just as full after sins as it was before sins ; " although Augustin does not fail to twit him with a charge of inconsistency. [3]

The peculiar individualism of the Pelagian view of the world comes out strongly in their failure to perceive the effect of habit on nature itself. Just as they conceived of virtue as a complex of virtuous acts, so they conceived of sin exclusively as an act, or series of disconnected acts. They appear not to have risen above the essentially heathen view which had no notion of holiness apart from a series of acts of holiness, or of sin apart from a like series of sinful acts. [4] Thus the will was isolated from its acts, and the acts from each other, and all organic connection or continuity of life was not only overlooked but denied. [5] After each act of the will, man stood exactly where he did before : indeed, this conception scarcely allows for the existence of a " man " — only a willing machine is left, at each click of the action of which the spring regains its original position, and is equally ready as before to reperform its function. In such a conception there was no place for character : freedom of will was all. Thus it was not an unnatural mistake which they made, when they forgot the man altogether, and attributed to the faculty of free will, under the name of "*possibilitas*" or "*posse*," the ability that belonged rather to the man whose faculty it is, and who is properly responsible for the use he makes of it. Here lies the essential error of their doctrine of free will : they looked upon freedom in its *form* only, and not in its *matter;* and, keeping man in perpetual and hopeless equilibrium between good and evil, they permitted no growth of character and no advantage to himself to be gained by man in his successive choices of good. It need not surprise us that the type of thought which thus dissolved the organism of the man into a congeries of disconnected voluntary acts, failed to comprehend the solidarity of the race. To the Pelagian, Adam was a man, nothing more ; and it was simply unthinkable that any act of his that left his own subsequent acts uncommitted, could entail sin and guilt upon other men. The same alembic that dissolved the individual into a succession of voluntary acts, could not fail to separate the race into a heap of unconnected units. If sin, as Julian declared, is nothing but will, and the will itself remained intact after each act, how could the individual act of an individual will condition the acts of men as yet unborn? By "imitation" of his act alone could

---

[1] *On Original Sin*, 30.    [2] *On the Grace of Christ*, 43.    [3] *The Unfinished Work*, i. 91; compare 69.

[4] Dr. Matheson finely says (*Expositor*, i. ix. 21), "There is the same difference between the Christian and Pagan idea of prayer as there is between the Christian and Pagan idea of sin. Paganism knows nothing of sin, it knows only sins: it has no conception of the principle of evil, it comprehends only a succession of sinful acts." This is Pelagianism too.

[5] Compare Schaff, *Church History*, iii. 804; and Thomasius' *Dogmengeschichte*, i. 487-8.

(under such a conception) other men be affected. And this carried with it the corresponding view of man's relation to Christ. He could forgive us the sins we had committed; He could teach us the true way; He could set us a holy example; and He could exhort us to its imitation. But He could not touch us to enable us to will the good, without destroying the absolute equilibrium of the will between good and evil; and to destroy this was to destroy its freedom, which was the crowning good of our divinely created nature. Surely the Pelagians forgot that man was not made for will, but will for man.

In defending their theory, as we are told by Augustin, there were five claims that they especially made for it.[1] It allowed them to praise as was their due, the creature that God had made, the marriage that He had instituted, the law that He had given, the free will which was His greatest endowment to man, and the saints who had followed His counsels. By this they meant that they proclaimed the sinless perfection of human nature in every man as he was brought into the world, and opposed this to the doctrine of original sin; the purity and holiness of marriage and the sexual appetites, and opposed this to the doctrine of the transmission of sin; the ability of the law, as well as and apart from the gospel, to bring men into eternal life, and opposed this to the necessity of inner grace; the integrity of free will to choose the good, and opposed this to the necessity of divine aid; and the perfection of the lives of the saints, and opposed this to the doctrine of universal sinfulness. Other questions, concerning the origin of souls, the necessity of baptism for infants, the original immortality of Adam, lay more on the skirts of the controversy, and were rather consequences of their teaching than parts of it. As it was an obvious fact that all men died, they could not admit that Adam's death was a consequence of sin lest they should be forced to confess that his sin had injured all men; they therefore asserted that physical death belonged to the very nature of man, and that Adam would have died even had he not sinned.[2] So, as it was impossible to deny that the Church everywhere baptized infants, they could not refuse them baptism without confessing themselves innovators in doctrine; and therefore they contended that infants were not baptized for forgiveness of sins, but in order to attain a higher state of salvation. Finally, they conceived that if it was admitted that souls were directly created by God for each birth, it could not be asserted that they came into the world soiled by sin and under condemnation; and therefore they loudly championed this theory of the origin of souls.

The teachings of the Pelagians, it will be readily seen, easily welded themselves into a system, the essential and formative elements of which were entirely new in the Christian Church; and this startlingly new reading of man's condition, powers, and dependence for salvation, it was, that broke like a thunderbolt upon the Western Church at the opening of the fifth century, and forced her to reconsider, from the foundations, her whole teaching as to man and his salvation.

## II. The External History of the Pelagian Controversy.

Pelagius seems to have been already somewhat softened by increasing age when he came to Rome about the opening of the fifth century. He was also constitutionally averse to controversy; and although in his zeal for Christian morals, and in his conviction that no man would attempt to do what he was not persuaded he had natural power to perform, he diligently propagated his doctrines privately, he was careful to rouse no opposition, and was content to make what progress he could quietly and without open discussion. His methods of work sufficiently appear in the pages of his " Commentary on the Epistles of Saint Paul," which was written and published during these years, and which exhibits learning and a sober and correct but somewhat shallow exegetical skill. In this work, he manages to give expression to all the main elements of his system, but always introduces them indirectly, not as the true exegesis, but by way of objections to the ordinary teaching, which were in need of discussion. The most important fruit of his residence in Rome

---

[1] *Against Two Letters of the Pelagians*, iii. 25, and iv. at the beginning.
[2] This belongs to the earlier Pelagianism; Julian was ready to admit that death came from Adam, but not sin.

was the conversion to his views of the Advocate Cœlestius, who brought the courage of youth and the argumentative training of a lawyer to the propagation of the new teaching. It was through him that it first broke out into public controversy, and received its first ecclesiastical examination and rejection. Fleeing from Alaric's second raid on Rome, the two friends landed together in Africa (A.D. 411), whence Pelagius soon afterwards departed for Palestine, leaving the bolder and more contentious [1] Cœlestius behind at Carthage. Here Cœlestius sought ordination as a presbyter. But the Milanese deacon Paulinus stood forward in accusation of him as a heretic, and the matter was brought before a synod under the presidency of Bishop Aurelius.[2]

Paulinus' charge consisted of seven items,[3] which asserted that Cœlestius taught the following heresies : that Adam was made mortal, and would have died, whether he sinned or did not sin ; that the sin of Adam injured himself alone, not the human race ; that new-born children are in that state in which Adam was before his sin ; that the whole human race does not, on the one hand, die on account of the death or the fall of Adam, nor, on the other, rise again on account of the resurrection of Christ ; that infants, even though not baptized, have eternal life ; that the law leads to the kingdom of heaven in the same way as the gospel ; and that, even before the Lord's coming, there had been men without sin. Only two fragments of the proceedings of the synod in investigating this charge have come down to us ;[4] but it is easy to see that Cœlestius was contumacious, and refused to reject any of the propositions charged against him, except the one which had reference to the salvation of infants that die unbaptized, — the sole one that admitted of sound defence. As touching the transmission of sin, he would only say that it was an open question in the Church, and that he had heard both opinions from Church dignitaries ; so that the subject needed investigation, and should not be made the ground for a charge of heresy. The natural result was, that, on refusing to condemn the propositions charged against him, he was himself condemned and excommunicated by the synod. Soon afterwards he sailed to Ephesus, where he obtained the ordination which he sought.

Meanwhile Pelagius was living quietly in Palestine, whither in the summer of 415 a young Spanish presbyter, Paulus Orosius by name, came with letters from Augustin to Jerome, and was invited, near the end of July in that year, to a diocesan synod, presided over by John of Jerusalem. There he was asked about Pelagius and Cœlestius, and proceeded to give an account of the condemnation of the latter at the synod of Carthage, and of Augustin's literary refutation of the former. Pelagius was sent for, and the proceedings became an examination into his teachings. The chief matter brought up was his assertion of the possibility of men living sinlessly in this world ; but the favour of the bishop towards him, the intemperance of Orosius, and the difficulty of communication between the parties arising from difference of language, combined so to clog proceedings that nothing was done ; and the whole matter, as Western in its origin, was referred to the Bishop of Rome for examination and decision.[5]

Soon afterwards two Gallic bishops, — Heros of Arles, and Lazarus of Aix, — who were then in Palestine, lodged a formal accusation against Pelagius with the metropolitan, Eulogius of Cæsarea ; and he convened a synod of fourteen bishops which met at Lydda (Diospolis), in December of the same year (415), for the trial of the case. Perhaps no greater ecclesiastical farce was ever enacted than this synod exhibited.[6] When the time arrived, the accusers were prevented from being present by illness, and Pelagius was confronted only by the written accusation. This was both unskilfully drawn, and was written in Latin which the synod did not understand. It was, therefore, not even consecutively read, and was only head by head rendered into Greek by an interpreter. Pelagius began by reading aloud several letters to himself from various men of reputation

---

[1] *On Original Sin*, 13.    [2] Early in 412, or, less probably, according to the Ballerini and Hefele 411.
[3] See *On Original Sin*, 2, 3, 12; *On the Proceedings of Pelagius*, 23. They are also given by Marius Mercator (Migne, **xlviii.** 69, 70), and the fifth item (on the salvation of unbaptized infants) omitted, — though apparently by an error.
[4] Preserved by Augustin, *On Original Sin*, 3, 4.
[5] An account of this synod is given by Orosius himself in his *Apology for the Freedom of the Will*.
[6] A full account and criticism of the proceedings are given by Augustin in his *On the Proceedings of Pelagius*.

in the Episcopate,—among them a friendly note from Augustin.  Thoroughly acquainted with both Latin and Greek, he was enabled skillfully to thread every difficulty, and pass safely through the ordeal.  Jerome called this a " miserable synod," and not unjustly : at the same time it is suffi- cient to vindicate the honesty and earnestness of the bishops' intentions, that even in such circum- stances, and despite the more undeveloped opinions of the East on the questions involved, Pelagius escaped condemnation only by a course of most ingenious disingenuousness, and only at the cost both of disowning Cœlestius and his teachings, of which he had been the real father, and of leading the synod to believe that he was anathematizing the very doctrines which he was himself proclaiming.  There is really no possibility of doubting, as any one will see who reads the pro- ceedings of the synod, that Pelagius obtained his acquittal here either by a " lying condemnation or a tricky interpretation " [1] of his own teachings ; and Augustin is perfectly justified in asserting that the "heresy was not acquitted, but the man who denied the heresy," [2] and who would him- self have been anathematized had he not anathematized the heresy.

However obtained, the acquittal of Pelagius was yet an accomplished fact.  Neither he nor his friends delayed to make the most widely extended use of their good fortune.  Pelagius himself was jubilant.  Accounts of the synodal proceedings were sent to the West, not altogether free from uncandid alterations ; and Pelagius soon put forth a work *In Defence of Free-Will*, in which he triumphed in his acquittal and "explained his explanations" at the synod.  Nor were the champions of the opposite opinion idle.  As soon as the news arrived in North Africa, and before the authentic records of the synod had reached that region, the condemnation of Pela- gius and Cœlestius was re-affirmed in two provincial synods, — one, consisting of sixty-eight bishops, met at Carthage about midsummer of 416 ; and the other, consisting of about sixty bishops, met soon afterwards at Mileve (Mila).  Thus Palestine and North Africa were arrayed against one another, and it became of great importance to obtain the support of the Patriarchal See of Rome.  Both sides made the attempt, but fortune favored the Africans.  Each of the North- African synods sent a synodal letter to Innocent I., then Bishop of Rome, engaging his assent to their action : to these, five bishops, Aurelius of Carthage and Augustin among them, added a third " familiar" letter of their own, in which they urged upon Innocent to examine into Pelagius' teach- ing, and provided him with the material on which he might base a decision.  The letters reached Innocent in time for him to take advice of his clergy, and send favorable replies on Jan. 27, 417.  In these he expressed his agreement with the African decisions, asserted the necessity of inward grace, rejected the Pelagian theory of infant baptism, and declared Pelagius and Cœles- tius excommunicated until they should return to orthodoxy.  In about six weeks more he was dead : but Zosimus, his successor, was scarcely installed in his place before Cœlestius appeared at Rome in person to plead his cause ; while shortly afterwards letters arrived from Pelagius addressed to Innocent, and by an artful statement of his belief and a recommendation from Praylus, lately become bishop of Jerusalem in John's stead, attempting to enlist Rome in his favour.  Zosimus, who appears to have been a Greek and therefore inclined to make little of the merits of this Western controversy, went over to Cœlestius at once, upon his profession of willingness to anathe- matize all doctrines which the pontifical see had condemned or should condemn ; and wrote a sharp and arrogant letter to Africa, proclaiming Cœlestius "catholic," and requiring the Africans to appear within two months at Rome to prosecute their charges, or else to abandon them.  On the arrival of Pelagius' papers, this letter was followed by another (September, 417), in which Zosimus, with the approbation of the clergy, declared both Pelagius and Cœlestius to be orthodox, and severely rebuked the Africans for their hasty judgment.  It is difficult to understand Zosimus' action in this matter : neither of the confessions presented by the accused teachers ought to have deceived him, and if he was seizing the occasion to magnify the Roman see, his mistake was dreadful. Late in 417, or early in 418, the African bishops assembled at Carthage, in number more than two

---

[1] *On Original Sin*, 13, at the end.          [2] Augustin's *Sermons* (Migne, v. 1511).

hundred, and replied to Zosimus that they had decided that the sentence pronounced against Pelagius and Cœlestius should remain in force until they should unequivocally acknowledge that "we are aided by the grace of God, through Christ, not only to know, but to do what is right, in each single act, so that without grace we are unable to have, think, speak, or do anything pertaining to piety." This firmness made Zosimus waver. He answered swellingly but timidly, declaring that he had maturely examined the matter, but it had not been his intention finally to acquit Cœlestius; and now he had left all things in the condition in which they were before, but he claimed the right of final judgment to himself. Matters were hastening to a conclusion, however, that would leave him no opportunity to escape from the mortification of an entire change of front. This letter was written on the 21st of March, 418; it was received in Africa on the 29th of April; and on the very next day an imperial decree was issued from Ravenna ordering Pelagius and Cœlestius to be banished from Rome, with all who held their opinions; while on the next day, May 1, a plenary council of about two hundred bishops met at Carthage, and in nine canons condemned all the essential features of Pelagianism. Whether this simultaneous action was the result of skillful arrangement, can only be conjectured: its effect was in any case necessarily crushing. There could be no appeal from the civil decision, and it played directly into the hands of the African definition of the faith. The synod's nine canons part naturally into three triads.[1] The first of these deals with the relation of mankind to original sin, and anathematizes in turn those who assert that physical death is a necessity of nature, and not a result of Adam's sin; those who assert that new-born children derive nothing of original sin from Adam to be expiated by the laver of regeneration; and those who assert a distinction between the kingdom of heaven and eternal life, for entrance into the former of which alone baptism is necessary. The second triad deals with the nature of grace, and anathematizes those who assert that grace brings only remission of past sins, not aid in avoiding future ones; those who assert that grace aids us not to sin, only by teaching us what is sinful, not by enabling us to will and do what we know to be right; and those who assert that grace only enables us to do more easily what we should without it still be able to do. The third triad deals with the universal sinfulness of the race, and anathematizes those who assert that the apostles' (1 John i. 8) confession of sin is due only to their humility; those who say that "Forgive us our trespasses" in the Lord's Prayer, is pronounced by the saints, not for themselves, but for the sinners in their company; and those who say that the saints use these words of themselves only out of humility and not truly. Here we see a careful traversing of the whole ground of the controversy, with a conscious reference to the three chief contentions of the Pelagian teachers.[2]

The appeal to the civil power, by whomsoever made, was, of course, indefensible, although it accorded with the opinions of the day, and was entirely approved by Augustin. But it was the ruin of the Pelagian cause. Zosimus found himself forced either to go into banishment with his wards, or to desert their cause. He appears never to have had any personal convictions on the dogmatic points involved in the controversy, and so, all the more readily, yielded to the necessity of the moment. He cited Cœlestius to appear before a council for a new examination; but that heresiarch consulted prudence, and withdrew from the city. Zosimus, possibly in the effort to appear a leader in the cause he had opposed, not only condemned and excommunicated the men whom less than six months before he had pronounced "orthodox" after a 'mature consideration of the matters involved,' but, in obedience to the imperial decree, issued a stringent paper which condemned Pelagius and the Pelagians, and affirmed the African doctrines as to corruption of nature, true grace, and the necessity of baptism. To this he required subscription from all bishops as a test of orthodoxy. Eighteen Italian bishops refused their signature, with Julian of Eclanum, henceforth to be the champion of the Pelagian party, at their head, and were therefore deposed, although several of them afterwards recanted, and were restored. In Julian, the

---

[1] Compare Canon Bright's *Introduction* in his *Select Anti-Pelagian Treatises*, p. xli.

[2] See above, p xv., and the passages in Augustin cited in note 3.

heresy obtained an advocate, who, if aught could have been done for its re-instatement, would surely have proved successful. He was the boldest, the strongest, at once the most acute and the most weighty, of all the disputants of his party. But the ecclesiastical standing of this heresy was already determined. The policy of Zosimus' test act was imposed by imperial authority on North Africa in 419. The exiled bishops were driven from Constantinople by Atticus in 424; and they are said to have been condemned at a Cilician synod in 423, and at an Antiochian one in 424. Thus the East itself was preparing for the final act in the drama. The exiled bishops were with Nestorius at Constantinople in 429; and that patriarch unsuccessfully interceded for them with Cœlestine, then Bishop of Rome. The conjunction was ominous. And at the ecumenical synod at Ephesus in 431, we again find the "Cœlestians" side by side with Nestorius, sharers in his condemnation.

But Pelagianism did not so die as not to leave a legacy behind it. "Remainders of Pelagianism"[1] soon showed themselves in Southern Gaul, where a body of monastic leaders attempted to find a middle ground on which they could stand, by allowing the Augustinian doctrine of assisting grace, but retaining the Pelagian conception of our self-determination to good. We first hear of them in 428, through letters from two laymen, Prosper and Hilary, to Augustin, as men who accepted original sin and the necessity of grace, but asserted that men began their turning to God, and God helped their beginning. They taught[2] that all men are sinners, and that they derive their sin from Adam; that they can by no means save themselves, but need God's assisting grace; and that this grace is gratuitous in the sense that men cannot really deserve it, and yet that it is not irresistible, nor given always without the occasion of its gift having been determined by men's attitude towards God; so that, though not given on account of the merits of men, it is given according to those merits, actual or foreseen. The leader of this new movement was John Cassian, a pupil of Chrysostom (to whom he attributed all that was good in his life and will), and the fountain-head of Gallic monasticism; and its chief champion at a somewhat later day was Faustus of Rhegium (Riez).

The Augustinian opposition was at first led by the vigorous controversialist, Prosper of Aquitaine, and, in the next century, by the wise, moderate, and good Cæsarius of Arles, who brought the contest to a conclusion in the victory of a softened Augustinianism. Already in 431 a letter was obtained from Pope Cœlestine, designed to close the controversy in favor of Augustinianism, and in 496 Pope Gelasius condemned the writings of Faustus in the first index of forbidden books; while, near the end of the first quarter of the sixth century, Pope Hormisdas was appealed to for a renewed condemnation. The end was now in sight. The famous second Synod of Orange met under the presidency of Cæsarius at that ancient town on the 3d of July, 529, and drew up a series of moderate articles which received the ratification of Boniface II. in the following year. In these articles there is affirmed an anxiously guarded Augustinianism, a somewhat weakened Augustinianism, but yet a distinctive Augustinianism; and, so far as a formal condemnation could reach, semi-Pelagianism was suppressed by them in the whole Western Church. But councils and popes can only decree; and Cassian and Vincent and Faustus, despite Cæsarius and Boniface and Gregory, retained an influence among their countrymen which never died away.

### III. Augustin's Part in the Controversy.

Both by nature and by grace, Augustin was formed to be the champion of truth in this controversy. Of a naturally philosophical temperament, he saw into the springs of life with a vividness of mental perception to which most men are strangers; and his own experiences in his long life of resistance to, and then of yielding to, the drawings of God's grace, gave him a clear apprehension of the great evangelic principle that God seeks men, not men God, such as no sophistry could cloud. However much his philosophy or theology might undergo change in other particu-

---

[1] Prosper's phrase.   [2] Augustin gives their teaching carefully in his *On the Predestination of the Saints*, 2.

lars, there was one conviction too deeply imprinted upon his heart ever to fade or alter, — the conviction of the ineffableness of God's grace. Grace, — man's absolute dependence on God as the source of all good, — this was the common, nay, the *formative* element, in all stages of his doctrinal development, which was marked only by the ever growing consistency with which he built his theology around this central principle. Already in 397, — the year after he became bishop, — we find him enunciating with admirable clearness all the essential elements of his teaching, as he afterwards opposed them to Pelagius.[1] It was inevitable, therefore, that although he was rejoiced when he heard, some years later, of the zealous labours of this pious monk in Rome towards stemming the tide of luxury and sin, and esteemed him for his devout life, and loved him for his Christian activity, he yet was deeply troubled when subsequent rumours reached him that he was "disputing against the grace of God." He tells us over and over again, that this was a thing no pious heart could endure ; and we perceive that, from this moment, Augustin was only biding his time, and awaiting a fitting opportunity to join issue with the denier of the Holy of holies of his whole, I will not say theology merely, but life. "Although I was grieved by this," he says, "and it was told me by men whom I believed, I yet desired to have something of such sort from his own lips or in some book of his, so that, if I began to refute it, he would not be able to deny it."[2] Thus he actually excuses himself for not entering into the controversy earlier. When Pelagius came to Africa, then, it was almost as if he had deliberately sought his fate. But circumstances secured a lull before the storm. He visited Hippo ; but Augustin was absent, although he did not fail to inform himself on his return that Pelagius while there had not been heard to say "anything at all of this kind." The controversy against the Donatists was now occupying all the energies of the African Church, and Augustin himself was a ruling spirit in the great conference now holding at Carthage with them. While there, he was so immersed in this business, that, although he once or twice saw the face of Pelagius, he had no conversation with him ; and although his ears were wounded by a casual remark which he heard, to the effect "that infants were not baptized for remission of sins, but for consecration to Christ," he allowed himself to pass over the matter, "because there was no opportunity to contradict it, and those who said it were not such men as could cause him solicitude for their influence."[3]

It appears from these facts, given us by himself, that Augustin was not only ready for, but was looking for, the coming controversy. It can scarcely have been a surprise to him when Paulinus accused Cœlestius (412) ; and, although he was not a member of the council which condemned him, it was inevitable that he should at once take the leading part in the consequent controversy. Cœlestius and his friends did not silently submit to the judgment that had been passed upon their teaching : they could not openly propagate their heresy, but they were diligent in spreading their plaints privately and by subterraneous whispers among the people.[4] This was met by the Catholics in public sermons and familiar colloquies held everywhere. But this wise rule was observed, — to contend against the erroneous teachings, but to keep silence as to the teachers, that so (as Augustin explains [5]) "the men might rather be brought to see and acknowledge their error through fear of ecclesiastical judgment than be punished by the actual judgment." Augustin was abundant in these oral labours ; and many of his sermons directed against Pelagian error have come down to us, although it is often impossible to be sure as to their date. For one of them (170) he took his text from Phil. iii. 6–16, "as touching the righteousness which is by the law blameless ; howbeit what things were gain to me, those have I counted loss for Christ." He begins by asking how the apostle could count his blameless conversation according to the righteousness which is from the law as dung and loss, and then proceeds to explain the purpose for which the law was given, our state by nature and under law, and the kind of blamelessness that the law

---

[1] Compare his work written this year, *On Several Questions to Simplicianus*. For the development of Augustin's theology, see the admirable statement in Neander's *Church History*, E. T., ii. 625 sq.

[2] *On the Proceedings of Pelagius,* 46.       [3] *On the Merits and Remission of Sins,* iii. 12.       [4] *Epistle* 157, 22.

[5] *On the Proceedings of Pelagius,* 46.

could produce, ending by showing that man can have no righteousness except from God, and no perfect righteousness except in heaven. Three others (174, 175, 176) had as their text 1 Tim. i. 15, 16, and developed its teaching, that the universal sin of the world and its helplessness in sin constituted the necessity of the incarnation ; and especially that the necessity of Christ's grace for salvation was just as great for infants as for adults. Much is very forcibly said in these sermons which was afterwards incorporated in his treatises. "There was no reason," he insists, "for the coming of Christ the Lord except to save sinners. Take away diseases, take away wounds, and there is no reason for medicine. If the great Physician came from heaven, a great sick man was lying ill through the whole world. That sick man is the human race" (175, 1). "He who says, 'I am not a sinner,' or 'I was not,' is ungrateful to the Saviour. No one of men in that mass of mortals which flows down from Adam, no one at all of men is not sick : no one is healed without the grace of Christ. Why do you ask whether infants are sick from Adam? For they, too, are brought to the church ; and, if they cannot run thither on their own feet, they run on the feet of others that they may be healed. Mother Church accommodates others' feet to them so that they may come, others' heart so that they may believe, others' tongue so that they may confess ; and, since they are sick by another's sin, so when they are healed they are saved by another's confession in their behalf. Let, then, no one buzz strange doctrines to you. *This* the Church has always had, has always held ; this she has received from the faith of the elders ; this she will perseveringly guard until the end. Since the whole have no need of a physician, but only the sick, what need, then, has the infant of Christ, if he is not sick? If he is well, why does he seek the physician through those who love him? If, when infants are brought, they are said to have no sin of inheritance ( *peccatum propaginis* ) at all, and yet come to Christ, why is it not said in the church to those that bring them, 'Take these innocents hence ; the physician is not needed by the well, but by the sick ; Christ came not to call the just, but sinners'? It never has been said, and it never will be said. Let each one therefore, brethren, speak for him who cannot speak for himself. It is much the custom to intrust the inheritance of orphans to the bishops ; how much more the grace of infants ! The bishop protects the orphan lest he should be oppressed by strangers, his parents being dead. Let him cry out more for the infant who, he fears, will be slain by his parents. Who comes to Christ has something in him to be healed ; and he who has not, has no reason for seeking the physician. Let parents choose one of two things : let them either confess that there is sin to be healed in their infants, or let them cease bringing them to the physician. This is nothing else than to wish to bring a well person to the physician. Why do you bring him? To be baptized. Whom? The infant. To whom do you bring him? To Christ. To Him, of course, who came into the world? Certainly, he says. Why did He come into the world? To save sinners. Then he whom you bring has in him that which needs saving?"[1] So again : "He who says that the age of infancy does not need Jesus' salvation, says nothing else than that the Lord Christ is not *Jesus* to faithful infants ; i.e., to infants baptized in Christ. For what is *Jesus?* *Jesus* means saviour. He is not Jesus to those whom He does not save, who do not need to be saved. Now, if your hearts can bear that Christ is not *Jesus* to any of the baptized, I do not know how you can be acknowledged to have sound faith. They are infants, but they are made members of Him. They are infants, but they receive His sacraments. They are infants, but they become partakers of His table, so that they may have life."[2] The preveniency of grace is explicitly asserted in these sermons. In one he says, "Zaccheus was seen, and saw ; but unless he had been seen, he would not have seen. For 'whom He predestinated, them also He called.' In order that we may see, we are seen ; that we may love, we are loved. 'My God, may His pity prevent me!'"[3] And in another, at more length : "His calling has preceded you, so that you may have a good will. Cry out, 'My God, let Thy mercy prevent me' (Ps. lviii. 11). That you may be, that you may feel, that you may hear, that you may consent,

---

[1] *Sermon* 176, 2.  [2] *Sermon* 174.  [3] Do.

His mercy prevents you. It prevents you in all things; and do you too prevent His judgment in something. In what, do you say? In what? In confessing that you have all these things from God, whatever you have of good; and from yourself whatever you have of evil" (176, 5). "We owe therefore to Him that we are, that we are alive, that we understand: that we are men, that we live well, that we understand aright, we owe to Him. Nothing is ours except the sin that we have. For what have we that we did not receive?" (1 Cor. ix. 7) (176, 6).

It was not long, however, before the controversy was driven out of the region of sermons into that of regular treatises. The occasion for Augustin's first appearance in a written document bearing on the controversy, was given by certain questions which were sent to him for answer by "the tribune and notary" Marcellinus, with whom he had cemented his intimacy at Carthage, the previous year, when this notable official was presiding, by the emperor's orders, over the great conference of the catholics and Donatists. The mere fact that Marcellinus, still at Carthage, where Cœlestius had been brought to trial, wrote to Augustin at Hippo for written answers to important questions connected with the Pelagian heresy, speaks volumes for the prominent position he had already assumed in the controversy. The questions that were sent, concerned the connection of death with sin, the transmission of sin, the possibility of a sinless life, and especially infants' need of baptism.[1] Augustin was immersed in abundant labours when they reached him:[2] but he could not resist this appeal, and that the less as the Pelagian controversy had already grown to a place of the first importance in his eyes. The result was his treatise, *On the Merits and Remission of Sins and on the Baptism of Infants,* consisting of two books, and written in 412. The first book of this work is an argument for original sin, drawn from the universal reign of death in the world (2–8), from the teaching of Rom. v. 12–21 (9–20), and chiefly from the baptism of infants (21–70).[3] It opens by exploding the Pelagian contention that death is of nature, and Adam would have died even had he not sinned, by showing that the penalty threatened to Adam included physical death (Gen. iii. 19), and that it is due to him that we all die (Rom. viii. 10, 11; 1 Cor. xv. 21) (2–8). Then the Pelagian assertion that we are injured in Adam's sin only by its bad example, which we imitate, not by any propagation from it, is tested by an exposition of Rom. v. 12 sq. (9–20). And then the main subject of the book is reached, and the writer sharply presses the Pelagians with the universal and primeval fact of the baptism of infants, as a proof of original sin (21–70). He tracks out all their subterfuges, — showing the absurdity of the assertions that infants are baptized for the remission of sins that they have themselves committed since birth (22), or in order to obtain a higher stage of salvation (23–28), or because of sin committed in some previous state of existence (31–33). Then turning to the positive side, he shows at length that the Scriptures teach that Christ came to save sinners, that baptism is for the remission of sins, and that all that partake of it are confessedly sinners (34 sq.); then he points out that John ii. 7, 8, on which the Pelagians relied, cannot be held to distinguish between ordinary salvation and a higher form, under the name of "the kingdom of God" (58 sq.); and he closes by showing that the very manner in which baptism was administered, with its exorcism and exsufflation, implied the infant to be a sinner (63), and by suggesting that the peculiar helplessness of infancy, so different not only from the earliest age of Adam, but also from that of many young animals, may possibly be itself penal (64–69). The second book treats, with similar fulness, the question of the perfection of human righteousness in this life. After an exordium which speaks of the will and its limitations, and of the need of God's assisting grace (1–6), the writer raises four questions. First, whether it may be said to be possible, by God's grace, for a man to attain a condition of entire sinlessness in this life (7). This he answers in the affirmative. Secondly, he asks, whether any one has ever done this, or

---

[1] *On the Merits and Remission of Sins,* iii. 1.          [2] *On the Merits and Remission of Sins,* i. 1. Compare *Epistle* 139.

[3] On the prominence of infant baptism in the controversy, and why it was so, see *Sermon* 165, 7 sq. "What do you say? 'Just this,' he says, 'that God creates every man immortal.' Why, then, do infant children die? For if I say, 'Why do adult men die?' you would say to me, 'They have sinned.' Therefore I do not argue about the adults: I cite infancy as a witness against you," and so on, eloquently developing the argument.

may ever be expected to do it, and answers in the negative on the testimony of Scripture (8–25). Thirdly, he asks why not, and replies briefly because men are unwilling, explaining at length what he means by this (26–33). Finally, he inquires whether any man has ever existed, exists now, or will ever exist, entirely without sin, — this question differing from the second inasmuch as that asked after the attainment in this life of a state in which sinning should cease, while this seeks a man who has never been guilty of sin, implying the absence of original as well as of actual sin. After answering this in the negative (34), Augustin discusses anew the question of original sin. Here after expounding from the positive side (35–38) the condition of man in paradise, the nature of his probation, and of the fall and its effects both on him and his posterity, and the kind of redemption that has been provided in the incarnation, he proceeds to answer certain cavils (39 sq.), such as, "Why should children of baptized people need baptism?" — "How can a sin be remitted to the father and held against the child?" — "If physical death comes from Adam, ought we not to be released from it on believing in Christ?" — and concludes with an exhortation to hold fast to the exact truth, turning neither to the right nor left, — neither saying that we have no sin, nor surrendering ourselves to our sin (57 sq.).

After these books were completed, Augustin came into possession of Pelagius' *Commentary on Paul's Epistles*, which was written while he was living in Rome (before 410), and found it to contain some arguments that he had not treated, — such arguments, he tells us, as he had not imagined could be held by any one.[1] Unwilling to re-open his finished argument, he now began a long supplementary letter to Marcellinus, which he intended to serve as a third and concluding book to his work. He was some time in completing this letter. He had asked to have the former two books returned to him; and it is a curious indication of his overworked state of mind, that he forgot what he wanted with them:[2] he visited Carthage while the letter was in hand, and saw Marcellinus personally; and even after his return to Hippo, it dragged along, amid many distractions, slowly towards completion.[3] Meanwhile, a long letter was written to Honoratus, in which a section on the grace of the New Testament was incorporated. At length the promised supplement was completed. It was professedly a criticism of Pelagius' Commentary, and therefore naturally mentioned his name; but Augustin even goes out of his way to speak as highly of his opponent as he can,[4] — although it is apparent that his esteem is not very high for his strength of mind, and is even less high for the moral quality that led to his odd, oblique way of expressing his opinions. There is even a half sarcasm in the way he speaks of Pelagius' care and circumspection, which was certainly justified by the event. The letter opens by stating and criticising in a very acute and telling dialectic, the new arguments of Pelagius, which were such as the following: "If Adam's sin injured even those who do not sin, Christ's righteousness ought likewise to profit even those who do not believe" (2–4); "No man can transmit what he has not; and hence, if baptism cleanses from sin, the children of baptized parents ought to be free from sin;" "God remits one's own sins, and can scarcely, therefore, impute another's to us; and if the soul is created, it would certainly be unjust to impute Adam's alien sin to it" (5). The stress of the letter, however, is laid upon two contentions, — 1. That whatever else may be ambiguous in the Scriptures, they are perfectly clear that no man can have eternal life except in Christ, who came to call sinners to repentance (7); and 2. That original sin in infants has always been, in the Church, one of the fixed facts, to be used as a basis of argument, in order to reach the truth in other matters, and has never itself been called in question before (10–14). At this point, the writer returns to the second and third of the new arguments of Pelagius mentioned above, and discusses them more fully (15–20), closing with a recapitulation of the three great points that had been raised; viz., that both death and sin are derived from Adam's sin by all his posterity; that infants need salvation,

---

[1] *On the Merits and Remission of Sins*, iii. 1.   [2] *Letter* 139, 3.   [3] *Letter* 140.
[4] See chaps. 1 and 5.

and hence baptism ; and that no man ever attains in this life such a state of holiness that he cannot truly pray, " Forgive us our trespasses."

Augustin was now to learn that one service often entails another. Marcellinus wrote to say that he was puzzled by what had been said in the second book of this work, as to the possibility of man's attaining to sinlessness in this life, while yet it was asserted that no man ever had attained, or ever would attain, it. How, he asked, can that be said to be possible which is, and which will remain, unexampled? In reply, Augustin wrote, during this same year (412), and sent to his noble friend, another work, which he calls *On the Spirit and the Letter,* from the prominence which he gives in it to the words of 2 Cor. iii. 6.[1] He did not content himself with a simple, direct answer to Marcellinus' question, but goes at length into a profound disquisition into the roots of the doctrine, and thus gives us, not a mere explanation of a former contention, but a new treatise on a new subject, — the absolute necessity of the grace of God for any good living. He begins by explaining to Marcellinus that he has affirmed the possibility while denying the actuality of a sinless life, on the ground that all things are possible to God, — even the passage of a camel through the eye of a needle, which nevertheless has never occurred (1, 2). For, in speaking of man's perfection, we are speaking really of a work of God, — and one which is none the less His work because it is wrought through the instrumentality of man, and in the use of his free will. The Scriptures, indeed, teach that no man lives without sin, but this is only the proclamation of a matter of fact ; and although it is thus contrary to fact and Scripture to assert that men may be found that live sinlessly, yet such an assertion would not be fatal heresy. What is unbearable, is that men should assert it to be possible for man, unaided by God, to attain this perfection. This is to speak against the grace of God : it is to put in man's power what is only possible to the almighty grace of God (3, 4). No doubt, even these men do not, in so many words, exclude the aid of grace in perfecting human life, — they affirm God's help ; but they make it consist in His gift to man of a perfectly free will, and in His addition to this of commandments and teachings which make known to him what he is to seek and what to avoid, and so enable him to direct his free will to what is good. / What, however, does such a " grace " amount to? (5). Man needs something more than to know the right way : he needs to love it, or he will not walk in it ; and all mere teaching, which can do nothing more than bring us knowledge of what we ought to do, is but the letter that killeth. What we need is some inward, Spirit-given aid to the keeping of what by the law we know ought to be kept. Mere knowledge slays : while to lead a holy life is the gift of God, — not only because He has given us will, nor only because He has taught us the right way, but because by the Holy Spirit He sheds love abroad in the hearts of all those whom He has predestinated, and will call and justify and glorify (Rom. viiii. 29, 30). To prove this, he states to be the object of the present treatise ; and after investigating the meaning of 2 Cor. iii. 6, and showing that "the letter" there means the law as a system of precepts, which reveals sin rather than takes it away, points out the way rather than gives strength to walk in it, and therefore slays the soul by shutting it up under sin, — while "the Spirit" is God's Holy Ghost who is shed abroad in our hearts to give us strength to walk aright, — he undertakes to prove this position from the teachings of the Epistle to the Romans at large. This contention, it will be seen, cut at the very roots of Pelagianism : if all mere teaching slays the soul, as Paul asserts, then all that what they called "grace" could, when alone, do, was to destroy ; and the upshot of "helping" man by simply giving him free will, and pointing out the way to him, would be the loss of the whole race. Not that the law is sin : Augustin teaches that it is holy and good, and God's instrument in salvation. Not that free will is done away : it is by free will that men are led into holiness. But the purpose of the law (he teaches) is to make men so feel their lost estate as to seek the help by which alone they may be saved ; and will is only then liberated to do good when grace has

---

[1] *Sermon* 163 treats the text similarly.

made it free. "What the law of works enjoins by menace, that the law of faith secures by faith. What the law of works does is to say, 'Do what I command thee;' but by the law of faith we say to God, 'Give me what thou commandest.'" (22).[1] In the midst of this argument, Augustin is led to discuss the differentiating characteristics of the Old and New Testaments; and he expounds at length (33–42) the passage in Jer. xxxi. 31–34, showing that, in the prophet's view, the difference between the two covenants is that in the Old, the law is an external thing written on stones; while in the New, it is written internally on the heart, so that men now wish to do what the law prescribes. This writing on the heart is nothing else, he explains, than the shedding abroad by the Holy Spirit of love in our hearts, so that we love God's will, and therefore freely do it. Towards the end of the treatise (50–61), he treats in an absorbingly interesting way of the mutual relations of free will, faith, and grace, contending that all co-exist without the voiding of any. It is by free will that we believe; but it is only as grace moves us, that we are able to use our free will for believing; and it is only after we are thus led by grace to believe, that we obtain all other goods. In prosecuting this analysis, Augustin is led to distinguish very sharply between the faculty and use of free will (58), as well as between ability and volition (53). Faith is an act of the man himself; but only as he is given the power from on high to will to believe, will he believe (57, 60).

By this work, Augustin completed, in his treatment of Pelagianism, the circle of that triad of doctrines which he himself looked upon as most endangered by this heresy,[2] — original sin, the imperfection of human righteousness, the necessity of grace. In his mind, the last was the kernel of the whole controversy; and this was a subject which he could never approach without some heightened fervour. This accounts for the great attractiveness of the present work, — through the whole fabric of which runs the golden thread of the praise of God's ineffable grace. In Canon Bright's opinion, it "perhaps, next to the 'Confessions,' tells us most of the thoughts of that 'rich, profound, and affectionate mind' on the soul's relations to its God."[3]

After the publication of these treatises, the controversy certainly did not lull; but it relapsed for nearly three years again, into less public courses. Meanwhile, Augustin was busy, among other most distracting cares (Ep. 145, 1), still defending the grace of God, by letters and sermons. A fair illustration of his state of mind at this time, may be obtained from his letter to Anastasius (145), which assuredly must have been written soon after the treatise *On the Spirit and the Letter*. Throughout this letter, there are adumbrations of the same train of thought that filled this treatise; and there is one passage which may almost be taken as a summary of it. Augustin is so weary of the vexatious cares that filled his life, that he is ready to long for the everlasting rest, and yet bewails the weakness which allowed the sweetness of external things still to insinuate itself into his heart. Victory over, and emancipation from, this, he asserts, "cannot, without God's grace, be achieved by the human will, which is by no means to be called free so long as it is subject to enslaving lusts." Then he proceeds: "The law, therefore, by teaching and commanding what cannot be fulfilled without grace, demonstrates to man his weakness, in order that the weakness, thus proved, may resort to the Saviour, by whose healing the will may be able to do what it found impossible in its weakness. So, then, the law brings us to faith, faith obtains the Spirit in fuller measure, the Spirit sheds love abroad in us, and love fulfils the law. For this reason the law is called a schoolmaster, under whose threatening and severity 'whosoever shall call on the name of the Lord shall be delivered.' But 'how shall they call on Him in whom they have not believed?' Wherefore, that the letter without the Spirit may not kill, the life-giving Spirit is given to those that believe and call upon Him; but the love of God is poured out into our hearts by the Holy Spirit who is given to us, so that the words of the same apostle, 'Love is the fulfilling of the law,' may be realized. Thus the law is good to him that uses it lawfully; and he uses it lawfully, who, understanding wherefore it was given, betakes himself, under the pressure of its threatening,

---

[1] See this prayer beautifully illustrated from Scripture in *On the Merits and Remission of Sins*, ii. 5.  [2] See above, p. xv.
[3] As quoted above, p. xx.

to liberating grace. Whoever ungratefully despises this grace by which the ungodly is justified, and trusts in his own strength for fulfilling the law, being ignorant of God's righteousness, and going about to establish his own righteousness, is not submitting himself to the righteousness of God; and therefore the law is made to him not a help to pardon, but the bond of guilt; not because the law is evil, but because 'sin,' as it is written, 'works death to such persons by that which is good.' For by the commandment, he sins more grievously, who, by the commandment, knows how evil are the sins which he commits." Although Augustin states clearly that this letter is written against those "who arrogate too much to the human will, imagining that, the law being given, the will is, of its own strength, sufficient to fulfil the law, though not assisted by any grace imparted by the Holy Ghost, in addition to instruction in the law," — he refrains still from mentioning the names of the authors of this teaching, evidently out of a lingering tenderness in his treatment of them. This will help us to explain the courtesy of a note which he sent to Pelagius himself at about this time, in reply to a letter he had received some time before from him; of which Pelagius afterwards (at the Synod of Diospolis) made, to say the least of it, an ungenerous use. This note,[1] Augustin tells us, was written with "tempered praises" (wherefrom we see his lessening respect for the man), and so as to admonish Pelagius to think rightly concerning grace, — so far as could be done without raising the dregs of the controversy in a formal note. This he accomplished by praying from the Lord for him, those good things by which he might be good forever, and might live eternally with Him who is eternal; and by asking his prayers in return, that he, too, might be made by the Lord such as he seemed to suppose he already was. How Augustin could really intend these prayers to be understood as an admonition to Pelagius to look to God for what he was seeking to work out for himself, is fully illustrated by the closing words of this almost contemporary letter to Anastasius: "Pray, therefore, for us," he writes, "that we may be righteous, — an attainment wholly beyond a man's reach, unless he know righteousness, and be willing to practise it, but one which is immediately realized when he is perfectly willing; but this cannot be in him unless he is healed by the grace of the Spirit, and aided to be able." The point had already been made in the controversy, that, by the Pelagian doctrine, so much power was attributed to the human will, that no one ought to pray, "Lead us not into temptation, but deliver us from evil."

If he was anxious to avoid personal controversy with Pelagius himself in the hope that he might even yet be reclaimed, Augustin was equally anxious to teach the truth on all possible occasions. Pelagius had been intimate, when at Rome, with the pious Paulinus, bishop of Nola; and it was understood that there was some tendency at Nola to follow the new teachings. It was, perhaps, as late as 414, when Augustin made reply in a long letter,[2] to a request of Paulinus' for an exposition of certain difficult Scriptures, which had been sent him about 410.[3] Among them was Rom. xi. 28; and, in explaining it, Augustin did not withhold a tolerably complete account of his doctrine of predestination, involving the essence of his whole teaching as to grace: "For when he had said, 'according to the election they are beloved for their father's sake,' he added, 'for the gifts and calling of God are without repentance.' You see that those are certainly meant who belong to the number of the predestinated. . . . 'Many indeed are called, but few chosen;' but those who are elect, these are called 'according to His purpose;' and it is beyond doubt that in them God's foreknowledge cannot be deceived. These He foreknew and predestinated to be conformed to the image of His Son, in order that He might be the first born among many brethren. But 'whom He predestinated, them He also called.' This calling is 'according to His purpose,' this calling is 'without repentance,'" etc., quoting Rom. v. 28–31. Then continuing, he says, "Those are not in this vocation, who do not persevere unto the end in the faith that worketh by love, although they walk in it a little while. . . . But the reason why some belong to it, and some do not, can easily be hidden, but cannot be unjust. For is there injustice

---

[1] *Epistle* 146. See *On the Proceedings of Pelagius*, 50, 51, 52.    [2] *Epistle* 149. See especially 18 sq.    [3] *Epistle* 121.

with God? God forbid! For this belongs to those high judgments which, so to say, terrified the wondering apostle to look upon."

Among the most remarkable of the controversial sermons that were preached about this time, especial mention is due to two that were delivered at Carthage, midsummer of 413. The former of these [1] was preached on the festival of John the Baptist's birth (June 24), and naturally took the forerunner for its subject. The nativity of John suggesting the nativity of Christ, the preacher spoke of the marvel of the incarnation. He who was in the beginning, and was the Word of God, and was Himself God, and who made all things, and in whom was life, even this one "came to us. To whom? To the worthy? Nay, but to the unworthy! For Christ died for the ungodly, and for the unworthy, though He was worthy. We indeed were unworthy whom He pitied; but He was worthy who pitied us, to whom we say, 'For Thy pity's sake, Lord, free us!' Not for the sake of our preceding merits, but 'for Thy pity's sake, Lord, free us;' and 'for Thy name's sake be propitious to our sins,' not for our merit's sake. . . . For the merit of sins is, of course, not reward, but punishment." He then dwelt upon the necessity of the incarnation, and the necessity of a mediator between God and "the whole mass of the human race alienated from Him by Adam." Then quoting 1 Cor. iv. 7, he asserts that it is not our varying merits, but God's grace alone, that makes us differ, and that we are all alike, great and small, old and young, saved by one and the same Saviour. "What then, some one says," he continues, "even the infant needs a liberator? Certainly he needs one. And the witness to it is the mother that faithfully runs to church with the child to be baptized. The witness is Mother Church herself, who receives the child for washing, and either for dismissing him [from this life] freed, or nurturing him in piety. . . . Last of all, the tears of his own misery are witness in the child himself. . . . Recognize the misery, extend the help. Let all put on bowels of mercy. By as much as they cannot speak for themselves, by so much more pityingly let us speak for the little ones," — and then follows a passage calling on the Church to take the grace of infants in their charge as orphans committed to their care, which is in substance repeated from a former sermon.[2] The speaker proceeded to quote Matt. i. 21, and apply it. If Jesus came to save from sins, and infants are brought to Him, it is to confess that they, too, are sinners. Then, shall they be withheld from baptism? "Certainly, if the child could speak for himself, he would repel the voice of opposition, and cry out, 'Give me Christ's life! In Adam I died: give me Christ's life; in whose sight I am not clean, even if I am an infant whose life has been but one day in the earth.'" "No way can be found," adds the preacher, "of coming into the life of this world except by Adam; no way can be found of escaping punishment in the next world except by Christ. Why do you shut up the one door?" Even John the Baptist himself was born in sin; and absolutely no one can be found who was born apart from sin, until you find one who was born apart from Adam. "'By one man sin entered into the world, and by sin, death; and so it passed through upon all men.' If these were my words, could this sentiment be expressed more expressly, more clearly, more fully?"

Three days afterwards,[3] on the invitation of the Bishop of Carthage, Augustin preached a sermon professedly directed against the Pelagians,[4] which takes up the threads hinted at in the former discourse, and develops a full polemic with reference to the baptism of infants. He began, formally enough, with the determination of the question in dispute. The Pelagians concede that infants should be baptized. The only question is, for what are they baptized? We say that they would not otherwise have salvation and eternal life; but they say it is not for salvation, not for eternal life, but for the kingdom of God. . . . "The child, they say, although not baptized, by the desert of his innocence, in that he has no sin at all, either actual or original, either from him-

---

[1] *Sermon* 293.         [2] *Sermon* 176, 2.

[3] The inscription says, " V Calendas Julii," i.e., June 27: but it also says, " *In natalis martyris Guddentis*," whose day appears to have been July 18. Some of the martyrologies assign 28th of June to Gaudentius (which some copies read here), but possibly none to Guddene.

[4] *Sermon* 294.

self or contracted from Adam, necessarily has salvation and eternal life even if not baptized;
but is to be baptized for this reason, — that he may enter into the kingdom of God, i.e., into the
kingdom of heaven." He then shows that there is no eternal life outside the kingdom of
heaven, no middle place between the right and left hand of the judge at the last day, and that,
therefore, to exclude one from the kingdom of God is to consign him to the pains of eternal fire ;
while, on the other side, no one ascends into heaven unless he has been made a member of Christ,
and this can only be by faith, — which, in an infant's case, is professed by another in his stead.
He then treats, at length, some of the puzzling questions with which the Pelagians were wont to
try the catholics ; and then breaking off suddenly, he took a volume in his hands. " I ask you,"
he said, " to bear with me a little : I will read somewhat. It is St. Cyprian whom I hold in my
hand, the ancient bishop of this see. What he thought of the baptism of infants, — nay, what
he has shown that the Church always thought, — learn in brief. For it is not enough for them to
dispute and argue, I know not what impious novelties : they even try to charge us with asserting
something novel. It is on this account that I read here St. Cyprian, in order that you may perceive that the orthodox understanding and catholic sense reside in the words which I have been
just now speaking to you. He was asked whether an infant ought to be baptized before he was
eight days old, seeing that by the ancient law no infant was allowed to be circumcised unless he
was eight days old. A question arose from this as to the day of baptism, — for concerning the
origin of sin there was no question ; and therefore from this thing of which there was no question,
that question that had arisen was settled." And then he read to them the passage out of
Cyprian's letter to Fidus, which declared that he, and all the council with him, unanimously
thought that infants should be baptized at the earliest possible age, lest they should die in their
inherited sin, and so pass into eternal punishment.[1] The sermon closed with a tender warning
to the teachers of these strange doctrines : he might call them heretics with truth, but he will not ;
let the Church seek still their salvation, and not mourn them as dead ; let them be exhorted as
friends, not striven with as enemies. " They disparage us," he says, " we will bear it ; let them
not disparage the rule [of faith], let them not disparage the truth ; let them not contradict the
Church, which labours every day for the remission of infants' original sin. This thing is settled.
The errant disputer may be borne with in other questions that have not been thoroughly canvassed,
that are not yet settled by the full authority of the Church, — their error should be borne with :
it ought not to extend so far, that they endeavour to shake even the very foundation of the Church !"
He hints that although the patience hitherto exhibited towards them is " perhaps not blameworthy," yet patience may cease to be a virtue, and become culpable negligence : in the mean
time, however, he begs that the catholics should continue amicable, fraternal, placid, loving,
long suffering.

Augustin himself gives us a view of the progress of the controversy at this time in a letter
written in 414.[2] The Pelagians had everywhere scattered the seeds of their new error ; and
although some, by his ministry and that of his brother workers, had, " by God's mercy," been
cured of their pest, yet they still existed in Africa, especially about Carthage, and were everywhere
propagating their opinions in subterraneous whispers, for fear of the judgment of the Church.
Wherever they were not refuted, they were seducing others to their following ; and they were so
spread abroad that he did not know where they would break out next. Nevertheless, he was still
unwilling to brand them as heretics, and was more desirous of healing them as sick members
of the Church than of cutting them off finally as too diseased for cure. Jerome also tells us that
the poison was spreading in both the East and the West, and mentions particularly as seats where
it showed itself the islands of Rhodes and Sicily. Of Rhodes we know nothing further ; but
from Sicily an appeal came to Augustin in 414 from one Hilary,[3] setting forth that there were

---

[1] The passage is quoted at length in *On the Merits and Remission of Sins*, iii. 10. Compare *Against Two Letters of the Pelagians*, iv. 23.

[2] *Epistle* 157, 22.   [3] *Epistle* 156, among Augustin's *Letters*.

certain Christians about Syracuse who taught strange doctrines, and beseeching Augustin to help him in dealing with them. The doctrines were enumerated as follows : " They say (1) that man can be without sin, (2) and can easily keep the commandments of God if he will; (3) that an unbaptized infant, if he is cut off by death, cannot justly perish, since he is born without sin ; (4) that a rich man that remains in his riches cannot enter the kingdom of God, except he sell all that he has ; . . . (5) that we ought not to swear at all ; " (6) and, apparently, that the Church is to be in this world without spot or blemish. Augustin suspected that these Sicilian disturbances were in some way the work of Cœlestius, and therefore in his answer[1] informs his correspondent of what had been done at the Synod of Carthage (412) against him. The long letter that he sent back follows the inquiries in the order they were put by Hilary. To the first he replies, in substance, as he had treated the same matter in the second book of the treatise, *On the Merits and Forgiveness of Sins*, that it was opposed to Scripture, but was less a heresy than the wholly unbearable opinion that this state of sinlessness could be attained without God's help. " But when they say that free will suffices to man for fulfilling the precepts of the Lord, even though unaided to good works by God's grace and the gift of the Holy Spirit, it is to be altogether anathematized and detested with all execrations. For those who assert this are inwardly alien from God's grace, because being ignorant of God's righteousness, like the Jews of whom the apostle speaks, and wishing to establish their own, they are not subject to God's righteousness, since there is no fulfilment of the law except love ; and of course the love of God is shed abroad in our hearts, not by ourselves, nor by the force of our own will, but by the Holy Ghost who is given to us." Dealing next with the second point, he drifts into the matter he had more fully developed in his work *On the Spirit and the Letter.* " Free will avails for God's works," he says, " if it be divinely aided, and this comes by humble seeking and doing ; but when deserted by divine aid, no matter how excellent may be its knowledge of the law, it will by no means possess solidity of righteousness, but only the inflation of ungodly pride and deadly arrogance. This is taught us by that same Lord's Prayer ; for it would be an empty thing for us to ask God 'Lead us not into temptation,' if the matter was so placed in our power that we would avail for fulfilling it without any aid from Him. For this free will is free in proportion as it is sound, but it is sound in proportion as it is subject to divine pity and grace. For it faithfully prays, saying, 'Direct my ways according to Thy word, and let no iniquity reign over me.' For how is that free over which iniquity reigns ? But see who it is that is invoked by it, in order that it may not reign over it. For it says not, 'Direct my ways according to free will because no iniquity shall rule over me,' but 'Direct my ways according to Thy *word, and let no iniquity rule over me.*' It is a prayer, not a promise ; it is a confession, not a profession ; it is a wish for full freedom, not a boast of personal power. For it is not every one 'who confides in his own power,' but 'every one who calls on the name of God, that shall be saved.' 'But how shall they call upon Him,' he says, 'in whom they have not believed?' Accordingly, then, they who rightly believe, believe in order to call on Him in whom they have believed, and to avail for doing what they receive in the precepts of the law ; since what the law commands, faith prays for." " God, therefore, commands continence, and gives continence ; He commands by the law, He gives by grace ; He commands by the letter, He gives by the spirit : for the law without grace makes the transgression to abound, and the letter without the spirit kills. He commands for this reason, — that we who have endeavoured to do what He commands, and are worn out in our weakness under the law, may know how to ask for the aid of grace ; and if we have been able to do any good work, that we may not be ungrateful to Him who aids us." The answer to the third point traverses the ground that was fully covered in the first book of the treatise *On the Merits and Forgiveness of Sins*, beginning by opposing the Pelagians to Paul in Rom. v. 12–19 : " But when they say that an infant, cut off by death, unbaptized, cannot perish since he is born without sin, — it is not this that the apostle says ; and

---

[1] *Epistle*, 157, 22.

I think that it is better to believe the apostle than them." The fourth and fifth questions were new in this controversy ; and it is not certain that they belong properly to it, though the legalistic asceticism of the Pelagian leaders may well have given rise to a demand on all Christians to sell what they had, and give to the poor. This one of the points, Augustin treats at length, pointing out that many of the saints of old were rich, and that the Lord and His apostles always so speak that their counsels avail to the right use, not the destruction, of wealth. Christians ought so to hold their wealth that they are not held by it, and by no means prefer it to Christ. Equal good sense and mildness are shown in his treatment of the question concerning oaths, which he points out were used by the Lord and His apostles, but advises to be used as little as possible lest by the custom of frequent oaths we learn to swear lightly. The question as to the Church, he passes over as having been sufficiently treated in the course of his previous remarks.

To the number of those who had been rescued from Pelagianism by his efforts, Augustin was now to have the pleasure of adding two others, in whom he seems to have taken much delight. Timasius and James were two young men of honorable birth and liberal education, who had, by the exhortation of Pelagius, been moved to give up the hope that they had in this world, and enter upon the service of God in an ascetic life.[1] Naturally, they had turned to him for instruction, and had received a book to which they had given their study. They met somewhere with some of Augustin's writings, however, and were deeply affected by what he said as to grace, and now began to see that the teaching of Pelagius opposed the grace of God by which man becomes a Christian. They gave their book, therefore, to Augustin, saying that it was Pelagius', and asking him for Pelagius' sake, and for the sake of the truth, to answer it. This was done, and the resulting book, *On Nature and Grace*, sent to the young men, who returned a letter of thanks[2] in which they professed their conversion from their error. In this book, too, which was written in 415, Augustin refrained from mentioning Pelagius by name,[3] feeling it better to spare the man while not sparing his writings. But he tells us, that, on reading the book of Pelagius to which it was an answer, it became clear to him beyond any doubt that his teaching was distinctly anti-Christian ;[4] and when speaking of his own book privately to a friend, he allows himself to call it " a considerable book against *the heresy* of Pelagius, which he had been constrained to write by some brethren whom he had persuaded to adopt his fatal error, denying the grace of Christ."[5] Thus his attitude towards the persons of the new teachers was becoming ever more and more strained, in despite of his full recognition of the excellent motives that might lie behind their " zeal not according to knowledge." This treatise opens with a recognition of the zeal of Pelagius, which, as it burns most ardently against those who, when reproved for sin, take refuge in censuring their nature, Augustin compares with the heathen view as expressed in Sallust's saying, " The human race falsely complains of its own nature,"[6] and which he charges with not being according to knowledge, and proposes to oppose by an equal zeal against all attempts to render the cross of Christ of none effect. He then gives a brief but excellent summary of the more important features of the catholic doctrine concerning nature and grace (2–7). Opening the work of Pelagius, which had been placed in his hands, he examines his doctrine of sin, its nature and effects. Pelagius, he points out, draws a distinction, sound enough in itself, between what is " possible " and what is " actual," but applies it unsoundly to sin, when he says that every man has the *possibility* of being without sin (8–9), and therefore without condemnation. Not so, says Augustin ; an infant who dies unbaptized has no possibility of salvation open to him ; and the man who has lived and died in a land where it was impossible for him to hear the name of Christ, has had no possibility open to him of becoming righteous by nature and free will. If this be not so, Christ is dead in vain, since all men then might have accomplished their salvation, even if Christ had never died (10). Pelagius, moreover, he shows, exhibits a tendency to deny the sinful character of all sins

---

[1] *Epistles* 177, 6; and 179, 2.  
[2] *Epistle* 168. *On the Proceedings of Pelagius*, 48.  
[3] *On the Proceedings of Pelagius*, 47; and *Epistle* 186, 1.  
[4] Compare *On Nature and Grace*, 7; and *Epistle* 186, 1.  
[5] *Epistle* 169, 13.  
[6] *On Nature and Grace*, 1. Sallust's *Jugurtha*, prologue.

that are impossible to avoid, and so treats of sins of ignorance as to show that he excuses them (13-19). When he argues that no sin, because it is not a substance, can change nature, which is a substance, Augustin replies that this destroys the Saviour's work, — for how can He save from sins if sins do not corrupt? And, again, if an act cannot injure a substance, how can abstention from food, which is a mere act, kill the body? In the same way sin is not a substance; but God is a substance, — yea, the height of substance, and only true sustenance of the reasonable creature; and the consequence of departure from Him is to the soul what refusal of food is to the body (22). To Pelagius' assertion that sin cannot be punished by more sin, Augustin replies that the apostle thinks differently (Rom. i. 21-31). Then putting his finger on the main point in controversy, he quotes the Scriptures as declaring the present condition of man to be that of spiritual death. "The truth then designates as *dead* those whom this man declares to be unable to be damaged or corrupted by sin, — because, forsooth, he has discovered sin to be no substance!" (25). It was by free will that man passed into this state of death; but a dead man needs something else to revive him, — he needs nothing less than a Vivifier. But of vivifying grace, Pelagius knew nothing; and by knowing nothing of a Vivifier, he knows nothing of a Saviour; but rather by making nature of itself able to be sinless, he glorifies the Creator at the expense of the Saviour (39). Next is examined Pelagius' contention that many saints are enumerated in the Scriptures as having lived sinlessly in this world. While declining to discuss the question of fact as to the Virgin Mary (42), Augustin opposes to the rest the declaration of John in 1 John i. 8, as final, but still pauses to explain why the Scriptures do not mention the sins of all, and to contend that all who ever were saved under the Old Testament or the New, were saved by the sacrificial death of Christ, and by faith in Him (40-50). Thus we are brought, as Augustin says, to the core of the question, which concerns, not the fact of sinlessness in any man, but man's ability to be sinless. This ability Pelagius affirms of all men, and Augustin denies of all "unless they are justified by the grace of God through our Lord Jesus Christ and Him crucified" (51). Thus, the whole discussion is about grace, which Pelagius does not admit in any true sense, but places only in the nature that God has made (52). We are next invited to attend to another distinction of Pelagius', in which he discriminates sharply between the nature that God has made, the crown of which is free will, and the use that man makes of this free will. The endowment of free will is a "capacity;" it is, because given by God in our making, a necessity of nature, and not in man's power to have or not have. It is the right use of it only, which man has in his power. This analysis, Pelagius illustrates at length, by appealing to the difference between the possession and use of the various bodily senses. The ability to see, for instance, he says, is a necessity of our nature; we do not make it, we cannot help having it; it is ours only to use it. Augustin criticises this presentation of the matter with great sharpness (although he is not averse to the analysis itself), — showing the inapplicability of the illustrations used, — for, he asks, is it not possible for us to blind ourselves, and so no longer have the ability to see? and would not many a man like to control the "use" of his "capacity" to hear when a screechy saw is in the neighbourhood? (55); and as well the falsity of the contention illustrated, since Pelagius has ignored the fall, and, even were that not so, has so ignored the need of God's aid for all good, in any state of being, as to deny it (56). Moreover, it is altogether a fallacy, Augustin argues, to contend that men have the "ability" to make every use we can conceive of our faculties. We *cannot* wish for unhappiness; God *cannot* deny Himself (57); and just so, in a corrupt nature, the mere possession of a *faculty of choice* does not imply the ability to use that faculty for not sinning. "Of a man, indeed, who has his legs strong and sound, it may be said admissibly enough, 'whether he will or not, he has the capacity of walking;' but if his legs be broken, however much he may wish, he has not the 'capacity.' The nature of which our author speaks is corrupted" (57). What, then, can he mean by saying that, whether we will or not, we have the capacity of not sinning, — a statement so opposite to Paul's in Rom. vii. 15? Some space is next given to an attempted rebuttal by Pelagius of the testimony of Gal. v. 17, on the ground that the "flesh" there does not refer to the baptized (60–70) ; and then the passages are examined which Pelagius had quoted against Augustin out of earlier writers, — Lactantius (71), Hilary (72), Ambrose (75), John of Constantinople (76), Xystus, — a blunder of Pelagius, who quoted from a Pythagorean philosopher, mistaking him for the Roman bishop Sixtus (57), Jerome (78), and Augustin himself (80). All these writers, Augustin shows, admitted the universal sinfulness of man, — and especially he himself had confessed the necessity of grace in the immediate context of the passage quoted by Pelagius. The treatise closes (82 sq.) with a noble panegyric on that love which God sheds abroad in the heart, by the Holy Ghost, and by which alone we can be made keepers of the law.

The treatise *On Nature and Grace* was as yet unfinished, when the over-busy [1] scriptorium at Hippo was invaded by another young man seeking instruction. This time it was a zealous young presbyter from the remotest part of Spain, "from the shore of the ocean," — Paulus Orosius by name, whose pious soul had been afflicted with grievous wounds by the Priscillianist and Origenist heresies that had broken out in his country, and who had come with eager haste to Augustin, on hearing that he could get from him the instruction which he needed for confuting them. Augustin seems to have given him his heart at once ; and, feeling too little informed as to the special heresies which he wished to be prepared to controvert, persuaded him to go on to Palestine to be taught by Jerome, and gave him introductions which described him as one "who is in the bond of catholic peace a brother, in point of age a son, and in honour a fellow-presbyter, — a man of quick understanding, ready speech, and burning zeal." His departure to Palestine gave Augustin an opportunity to consult with Jerome on the one point that had been raised in the Pelagian controversy on which he had not been able to see light. The Pelagians had early argued,[2] that, if souls are created anew for men at their birth, it would be unjust in God to impute Adam's sin to them. And Augustin found himself unable either to prove that souls are transmitted (*traduced*, as the phrase is), or to show that it would not involve God in injustice to make a soul only to make it subject to a sin committed by another. Jerome had already put himself on record as a believer in both original sin and the creation of souls at the time of birth. Augustin feared the logical consequences of this assertion, and yet was unable to refute it. He therefore seized this occasion to send a long treatise on the origin of the soul to his friend, with the request that he would consider the subject anew, and answer his doubts.[3] In this treatise he stated that he was fully persuaded that the soul had fallen into sin, but by no fault of God or of nature, but of its own free will ; and asked when could the soul of an infant have contracted the guilt, which, unless the grace of Christ should come to its rescue by baptism, would involve it in condemnation, if God (as Jerome held, and as he was willing to hold with him, if this difficulty could be cleared up) makes each soul for each individual at the time of birth? He professed himself embarrassed on such a supposition by the penal sufferings of infants, the pains they endured in this life, and much more the danger they are in of eternal damnation, into which they actually go unless saved by baptism. God is good, just, omnipotent : how, then, can we account for the fact that "in Adam all die," if souls are created afresh for each birth? "If new souls are made for men," he affirms, "individually at their birth, I do not see, on the one hand, that they could have any sin while yet in infancy ; nor do I believe, on the other hand, that God condemns any soul which He sees to have no sin ; " "and yet, whoever says that those children who depart out of this life without partaking of the sacrament of baptism, shall be made alive in Christ, certainly contradicts the apostolic declaration," and " he that is not made alive in Christ must necessarily remain under the condemnation of which the apostle says that by the offence of one, judgment came upon all men to condemnation." "Wherefore," he adds to his correspondent, "if that

---

[1] For Augustin's press of work just now, see *Epistle* 169, 1 and 13.

[2] The argument occurs in Pelagius' *Commentary on Paul*, written before 410, and is already before Augustin in *On the Merits and Forgiveness of Sins*, etc., iii. 5.

[3] *Epistle* 166.

opinion of yours does not contradict this firmly grounded article of faith, let it be mine also; but if it does, let it no longer be yours."[1] So far as obtaining light was concerned, Augustin might have spared himself the pain of this composition: Jerome simply answered[2] that he had no leisure to reply to the questions submitted to him. But Orosius' mission to Palestine was big with consequences. Once there, he became the accuser of Pelagius before John of Jerusalem, and the occasion, at least, of the trials of Pelagius in Palestine during the summer and winter of 415 which issued so disastrously, and ushered in a new phase of the conflict.

Meanwhile, however, Augustin was ignorant of what was going on in the East, and had his mind directed again to Sicily. About a year had passed since he had sent thither his long letter to Hilary. Now his conjecture that Cœlestius was in some way at the bottom of the Sicilian outbreak, received confirmation from a paper which certain catholic brethren brought out of Sicily, and which was handed to Augustin by two exiled Spanish bishops, Eutropius and Paul. This paper bore the title, *Definitions Ascribed to Cœlestius*, and presented internal evidence, in style and thought, of being correctly so ascribed.[3] It consisted of three parts, in the first of which were collected a series of brief and compressed "definitions," or "ratiocinations" as Augustin calls them, in which the author tries to place the catholics in a logical dilemma, and to force them to admit that man can live in this world without sin. In the second part, he adduced certain passages of Scripture in defence of his doctrine. In the third part, he undertook to deal with the texts that had been quoted against his contention, not, however, by examining into their meaning, or seeking to explain them in the sense of his theory, but simply by matching them with others which he thought made for him. Augustin at once (about the end of 415) wrote a treatise in answer to this, which bears the title of *On the Perfection of Man's Righteousness*. The distribution of the matter in this work follows that of the treatise to which it is an answer. First of all (1–16), the "ratiocinations" are taken up one by one and briefly answered. As they all concern sin, and have for their object to prove that man cannot be accounted a sinner unless he is able, in his own power, wholly to avoid sin, — that is, to prove that a plenary natural ability is the necessary basis of responsibility, — Augustin argues *per contra* that man can entail a sinfulness on himself for which and for the deeds of which he remains responsible, though he is no longer able to avoid sin; thus admitting that for the race, plenary ability must stand at the root of sinfulness. Next (17–22) he discusses the passages which Cœlestius had advanced in defence of his teachings, viz., (1) passages in which God commands men to be without sin, which Augustin meets by saying that the point is, whether these commands are to be fulfilled *without God's aid*, in the body of this death, while absent from the Lord (17–20); and (2) passages in which God declares that His commandments are not grievous, which Augustin meets by explaining that all God's commandments are fulfilled only by *Love*, which finds nothing grievous; and that this love is shed abroad in our hearts by the Holy Ghost, without whom we have only fear, to which the commandments are not only grievous, but impossible. Lastly, Augustin patiently follows Cœlestius through his odd "oppositions of texts," explaining carefully all that he had adduced, in an orthodox sense (23–42). In closing, he takes up Cœlestius' statement, that "it is quite possible for man not to sin even in word, if God so will," pointing out how he avoids saying "if God give him His help," and then proceeds to distinguish carefully between the differing assertions of sinlessness that may be made. To say that any man ever lived, or will live, without needing forgiveness, is to contradict Rom. v. 12, and must imply that he does not need a Saviour, against Matt. ix. 12, 13. To say that after his sins have been forgiven, any one has ever remained without sin, contradicts 1 John i. 8 and Matt. vi. 12. Yet, if God's help be allowed, this contention is not so wicked as the other; and the great heresy is to deny the necessity of God's constant grace, for which we pray when we say, "Lead us not into temptation."

---

[1] An almost contemporary letter to Oceanus (*Epistle* 180, written in 416) adverts to the same subject and in the same spirit, showing how much it was in Augustin's thoughts. Compare *Epistle* 180, 2 and 5.

[2] *Epistle* 172.  [3] See *On the Perfection of Man's Righteousness*, 1.

Tidings were now (416) beginning to reach Africa of what was doing in the East. There was diligently circulated everywhere, and came into Augustin's hands, an epistle of Pelagius' own " filled with vanity," in which he boasted that fourteen bishops had approved his assertion that " man can live without sin, and easily keep the commandments if he wishes," and had thus " shut the mouth of opposition in confusion," and " broken up the whole band of wicked conspirators against him." Soon afterwards a copy of an " apologetical paper," in which Pelagius used the authority of the Palestinian bishops against his adversaries, not altogether without disingenuousness, was sent by him to Augustin through the hands of a common acquaintance, Charus by name. It was not accompanied, however, by any letter from Pelagius; and Augustin wisely refrained from making public use of it. Towards midsummer Orosius came with more authentic information, and bearing letters from Jerome and Heros and Lazarus. It was apparently before his coming that a controversial sermon was preached, only a fragment of which has come down to us.[1] So far as we can learn from the extant part, its subject seems to have been the relation of prayer to Pelagianism; and what we have, opens with a striking anecdote : " When these two petitions — ' Forgive us our debts as we also forgive our debtors,' and ' Lead us not into temptation ' — are objected to the Pelagians, what do you think they reply? I was horrified, my brethren, when I heard it. I did not, indeed, hear it with my own ears; but my holy brother and fellow-bishop Urbanus, who used to be presbyter here, and now is bishop of Sicca," when he was in Rome, and was arguing with one who held these opinions, pressed him with the weight of the Lord's Prayer, and " what do you think he replied to him? ' We ask God,' he said, ' not to lead us into temptation, lest we should suffer something that is not in our power, — lest I should be thrown from my horse; lest I should break my leg; lest a robber should slay me, and the like. For these things,' he said, ' are not in my power; but for overcoming the temptations of my sins, I both have ability if I wish to use it, and am not able to receive God's help.'[2] You see, brethren," the good bishop adds, " how malignant this heresy is : you see how it horrifies all of you. Have a care that you be not taken by it." He then presses the general doctrine of prayer as proving that all good things come from God, whose aid is always necessary to us, and is always attainable by prayer; and closes as follows : " Consider, then, these things, my brethren, when any one comes to you and says to you, ' What, then, are we to do if we have nothing in our power, unless God gives all things? God will not then crown us, but He will crown Himself.' You already see that this comes from that vein : it is a vein, but it has poison in it; it is stricken by the serpent; it is not sound. For what Satan is doing to-day is seeking to cast out from the Church by the poison of heretics, just as he once cast out from Paradise by the poison of the serpent. Let no one tell you that this one was acquitted by the bishops : there was an acquittal, but it was his confession, so to speak, his amendment, that was acquitted. For what he said before the bishops seemed catholic; but what he wrote in his books, the bishops who pronounced the acquittal were ignorant of. And perchance he was really convinced and amended. For we ought not to despair of the man who perchance preferred to be united to the catholic faith, and fled to its grace and aid. Perchance this was what happened. But, in any event, it was not the heresy that was acquitted, but the man who denied the heresy."[3]

The coming of Orosius must have dispelled any lingering hope that the meaning of the council's finding was that Pelagius had really recanted. Councils were immediately assembled at Carthage and Mileve, and the documents which Orosius had brought were read before them. We know nothing of their proceedings except what we can gather from the letters which they sent[4] to Innocent at Rome, seeking his aid in their condemnation of the heresy now so nearly approved in Palestine. To these two official letters, Augustin, in company with four other bishops, added a

---

[1] Migne's Edition of Augustin's Works, vol. v. pp. 1719-1723.     [2] Compare the words of Cicero quoted above, p. xiv.

[3] Compare the similar words in *Epistle* 177, 3, which was written, not only after what had occurred in Palestine was known, but also after the condemnatory decisions of the African synods.

[4] *Epistles* 175 and 176 in Augustin's *Letters*.

third private letter,[1] in which they took care that Innocent should be informed on all the points necessary to his decision.   This important letter begins almost abruptly with a characterization of Pelagianism as inimical to the grace of God, and has grace for its subject throughout.   It accounts for the action of the Palestinian synod, as growing out of a misunderstanding of Pelagius' words, in which he seemed to acknowledge grace, which these catholic bishops understood naturally to mean that grace of which they read in the Scriptures, and which they were accustomed to preach to their people, — the grace by which we are justified from iniquity, and saved from weakness; while he meant nothing more than that by which we are given free will at our creation.   " For if these bishops had understood that he meant only that grace which we have in common with the ungodly and with all, along with whom we are men, while he denied that by which we are Christians and the sons of God, they not only could not have patiently listened to him, — they could not even have borne him before their eyes."   The letter then proceeds to point out the difference between grace and natural gifts, and between grace and the law, and to trace out Pelagius' meaning when he speaks of grace, and when he contends that man can be sinless without any really inward aid.   It suggests that Pelagius be sent for, and thoroughly examined by Innocent, or that he should be examined by letter or in his writings; and that he be not cleared until he unequivocally confessed the grace of God in the catholic sense, and anathematized the false teachings in the books attributed to him.   The book of Pelagius which was answered in the treatise *On Nature and Gráce* was enclosed, with this letter, with the most important passages marked: and it was suggested that more was involved in the matter than the fate of one single man, Pelagius, who, perhaps, was already brought to a better mind; the fate of multitudes already led astray, or yet to be deceived by these false views, was in danger.

At about this same time (417), the tireless bishop sent a short letter[2] to a Hilary, who seems to be Hilary of Norbonne, which is interesting from its undertaking to convey a characterization of Pelagianism to one who was as yet ignorant of it.   It thus brings out what Augustin conceived to be its essential features.   " An effort has been made," we read, " to raise a certain new heresy, inimical to the grace of Christ, against the Church of Christ.   It is not yet openly separated from the Church.   It is the heresy of men who dare to attribute so much power to human weakness that they contend that this only belongs to God's grace, — that we are created with free will and the possibility of not sinning, and that we receive God's commandments which are to be fulfilled by us; but, for keeping and fulfilling these commandments, we do not need any divine aid.   No doubt, the remission of sins is necessary for us; for we have no power to right what we have done wrong in the past.   But for avoiding and overcoming sins in the future, for conquering all temptations with virtue, the human will is sufficient by its natural capacity without any aid of God's grace.   And neither do infants need the grace of the Saviour, so as to be liberated by it through His baptism from perdition, seeing that they have contracted no contagion of damnation from Adam."[3]   He engages Hilary in the destruction of this heresy, which ought to be " concordantly condemned and anathematized by all who have hope in Christ," as a " pestiferous impiety," and excuses himself for not undertaking its full refutation in a brief letter.   A much more important letter was sent off, at about the same time, to John of Jerusalem, who had conducted the first Palestinian examination of Pelagius, and had borne a prominent part in the synod at Diospolis.   He sent with it a copy of Pelagius' book which he had examined in his treatise *On Nature and Grace*, as well as a copy of that reply itself, and asked John to send him an authentic copy of the proceedings at Diospolis.   He took this occasion seriously to warn his brother bishop against the wiles of Pelagius, and begged him, if he loved Pelagius, to let men see that he did not so love him as to be deceived by him.   He pointed out that in the book sent with the letter, Pelagius called nothing the grace of God except nature; and that he affirmed, and even vehemently contended, that by free will alone, human nature was able to suffice for itself for working righteousness and keeping

---

[1] *Epistle* 177.   The other bishops were Aurelius, Alypius, Evodius, and Possidius.          [2] *Epistle* 178.          [3] *Epistle* 179.

all God's commandments; whence any one could see that he opposed the grace of God of which the apostles spoke in Rom. vii. 24, 25, and contradicted, as well, all the prayers and benedictions of the Church by which blessings were sought for men from God's grace. "If you love Pelagius, then," he continued, "let him, too, love you as himself, — nay, more than himself; and let him not deceive you. For when you hear him confess the grace of God and the aid of God, you think he means what you mean by it. But let him be openly asked whether he desires that we should pray God that we sin not; whether he proclaims the assisting grace of God, without which we would do much evil; whether he believes that even children who have not yet been able to do good or evil are nevertheless, on account of one man by whom sin entered into the world, sinners in him, and in need of being delivered by the grace of Christ." If he openly denies such things, Augustin would be pleased to hear of it.

Thus we see the great bishop sitting in his library at Hippo, placing his hands on the two ends of the world. That nothing may be lacking to the picture of his universal activity, we have another letter from him, coming from about this same time, that exhibits his care for the individuals who had placed themselves in some sort under his tutelage. Among the refugees from Rome in the terrible times when Alaric was a second time threatening the city, was a family of noble women, — Proba, Juliana, and Demetrias,[1] — grandmother, mother, and daughter, — who, finding an asylum in Africa, gave themselves to God's service, and sought the friendship and counsel of Augustin. In 413 the granddaughter "took the veil" under circumstances that thrilled the Christian world, and brought out letters of congratulation and advice from Augustin and Jerome, and also from Pelagius. This letter of Pelagius seems not to have fallen into Augustin's way until now (416): he was so disturbed by it that he wrote to Juliana a long letter warning her against its evil counsels.[2] It was so shrewdly phrased, that, at first sight, Augustin was himself almost persuaded that it did somehow acknowledge the grace of God; but when he compared it with others of Pelagius' writings, he saw that here, too, he was using ambiguous phrases in a non-natural sense. The object of his letter (in which Alypius is conjoined, as joint author) to Juliana is to warn her and her holy daughter against all opinions that opposed the grace of God, and especially against the covert teaching of the letter of Pelagius to Demetrias.[3] "In this book," he says, "were it lawful for such an one to read it, a virgin of Christ would read that her holiness and all her spiritual riches are to spring from no other source than herself; and thus before she attains to the perfection of blessedness, she would learn — which may God forbid! — to be ungrateful to God." Then, after quoting the words of Pelagius, in which he declares that "earthly riches came from others, but your spiritual riches no one can have conferred on you but yourself; for these, then, you are justly praised, for these you are deservedly to be preferred to others, — for they can exist only from yourself and in yourself," he continues: " Far be it from any virgin to listen to statements like these. Every virgin of Christ understands the innate poverty of the human heart, and therefore declines to be adorned otherwise than by the gifts of her spouse. . . . Let her not listen to him who says, 'No one can confer them on you but yourself, and they cannot exist except from you and in you:' but to him who says, 'We have this treasure in earthen vessels, that the excellency of the power may be of God, and not of us.' And be not surprised that we speak of these things as yours, and not from you; for we speak of daily bread as 'ours,' but yet add 'give it to us,' lest it should be thought it was from ourselves." Again, he warns her that grace is not mere knowledge any more than mere nature; and that Pelagius, even when using the word "grace," means no inward or efficient aid, but mere nature or knowledge or forgiveness of past sins; and beseeches her not to forget the God of all grace from whom (Wisdom i. 20, 21) Demetrias had that very virgin continence which was so justly her boast.

---

[1] See vol. i. of this series, p. 459, and the references there given. Compare Canon Robertson's vivid account of them in his *History of the Christian Church*, ii. 18, 145.

[2] *Epistle* 188.

[3] Compare *On the Grace of Christ*, 40. In the succeeding sections, some of its statements are examined.

With the opening of 417, came the answers from Innocent to the African letters.[1] And although they were marred by much boastful language concerning the dignity of his see, which could not but be distasteful to the Africans, they admirably served their purpose in the satisfactory manner in which they, on the one hand, asserted the necessity of the "daily grace, and help of God," for our good living, and, on the other, determined that the Pelagians had denied this grace, and declared their leaders Pelagius and Cœlestius deprived of the communion of the Church until they should "recover their senses from the wiles of the Devil by whom they are held captive according to his will." Augustin may be pardoned for supposing that a condemnation pronounced by two provincial synods in Africa, and heartily concurred in by the Roman bishop, who had already at Jerusalem been recognized as in some sort the fit arbiter of this Western dispute, should settle the matter. If Pelagius had been before jubilant, Augustin found this a suitable time for his rejoicing.

About the same time with Innocent's letters, the official proceedings of the synod of Diospolis at last reached Africa, and Augustin lost no time (early in 417) in publishing a full account and examination of them, thus providing us with that inestimable boon, a full contemporary history of the chief events connected with the controversy up to this time. This treatise, which is addressed to Aurelius, bishop of Carthage, opens with a brief explanation of Augustin's delay heretofore, in discussing Pelagius' defence of himself in Palestine, as due to his not having received the official copy of the Proceedings of the Council at Diospolis (1–2a). Then Augustin proceeds at once to discuss at length the doings of the synod, point by point, following the official record step by step (2b–45). He treats at large here eleven items in the indictment, with Pelagius' answers and the synod's decision, showing that in all of them Pelagius either explained away his heresy, taking advantage of the ignorance of the judges of his books, or else openly repudiated or anathematized it. When the twelfth item of the indictment was reached (41b–43), Augustin shows that the synod was so indignant at its character (it charged Pelagius with teaching that men cannot be sons of God unless they are sinless, and with condoning sins of ignorance, and with asserting that choice is not free if it depends on God's help, and that pardon is given according to merit), that, without waiting for Pelagius' answer, it condemned the statement, and Pelagius at once repudiated and anathematized it (43). How could the synod act in such circumstances, he asks, except by acquitting the man who condemned the heresy? After quoting the final judgment of the synod (44), Augustin briefly characterizes it and its effect (45) as being indeed all that could be asked of the judges, but of no moral weight to those better acquainted than they were with Pelagius' character and writings. In a word, they approved his answers to them, as indeed they ought to have done ; but they by no means approved, but both they and he condemned, his heresies as expressed in his writings. To this statement, Augustin appends an account of the origin of Pelagianism, and of his relations to it from the beginning, which has the very highest value as history (46–49) ; and then speaks of the character and doubtful practices of Pelagius (50–58), returning at the end (59–65) to a thorough canvass of the value of the acquittal which he obtained by such doubtful practices at the synod. He closes with an indignant account of the outrages which the Pelagians had perpetrated on Jerome (66).

This valuable treatise is not, however, the only account of the historical origin of Pelagianism that we have, from Augustin's hands. Soon after the death of Innocent (March 12, 417), he found occasion to write a very long letter[2] to the venerable Paulinus of Nola, in which he summarized both the history of and the arguments against this "worldly philosophy." He begins by saying that he knows Paulinus has loved Pelagius as a servant of God, but is ignorant in what way he now loves him. For he himself not only has loved him, but loves him still, but in different ways. Once he loved him as apparently a brother in the true faith : now he loves him in the longing that God will by His mercy free him from his noxious opinions against God's grace.

---

[1] *Epistles* 181, 182, 183, among Augustin's *Letters.*    [2] *Epistle* 186, written conjointly with Alypius.

He is not merely following report in so speaking of him: no doubt report did for a long time represent this of him, but he gave the less heed to it because report is accustomed to lie. But a book of his[1] at last came into his hands, which left no room for doubt, since in it he asserted repeatedly that God's grace consisted of the gift to man of the capacity to will and act, and thus reduced it to what is common to pagans and Christians, to the ungodly and godly, to the faithful and infidels. He then gives a brief account of the measures that had been taken against Pelagius, and passes on to a treatment of the main matters involved in the controversy, — all of which gather around the one magic word of "the grace of God." He argues first that we are all lost, — in one mass and concretion of perdition, — and that God's grace alone makes us to differ. It is therefore folly to talk of deserving the beginnings of grace. Nor can a faithful man say that he merits justification by his faith, although it is given to faith; for at once he hears the words, "What hast thou that thou didst not receive?" and learns that even the deserving faith is the gift of God. But if, peering into God's inscrutable judgments, we go farther, and ask why, from the mass of Adam, all of which undoubtedly has fallen from one into condemnation, this vessel is made for honor, that for dishonor, — we can only say that we do not know more than the fact; and God's reasons are hidden, but His acts are just. Certain it is that Paul teaches that all die in Adam; and that God freely chooses, by a sovereign election, some out of that sinful mass, to eternal life; and that He knew from the beginning to whom He would give this grace, and so the number of the saints has always been fixed, to whom he gives in due time the Holy Ghost. Others, no doubt, are called; but no others are elect, or "called according to his purpose." On no other body of doctrines, can it be possibly explained that some infants die unbaptized, and are lost. Is God unjust to punish innocent children with eternal pains? And are they not innocent if they are not partakers of Adam's sin? And can they be saved from that, save by the undeserved, and that is the gratuitous, grace of God? The account of the Proceedings at the Palestinian synod is then taken up, and Pelagius' position in his latest writings is quoted and examined. "But why say more?" he adds. . . . "Ought they not, since they call themselves Christians, to be more careful than the Jews that they do not stumble at the stone of offence, while they subtly defend nature and free will just like philosophers of this world who vehemently strive to be thought, or to think themselves, to attain for themselves a happy life by the force of their own will? Let them take care, then, that they do not make the cross of Christ of none effect by the wisdom of word (1 Cor. i. 17), and thus stumble at the rock of offence. For human nature, even if it had remained in that integrity in which it was created, could by no means have served its own Creator without His aid. Since then, without God's grace it could not keep the safety it had received, how can it without God's grace repair what it has lost?" With this profound view of the Divine immanence, and of the necessity of His moving grace in all the acts of all his creatures, as over against the heathen-deistic view of Pelagius, Augustin touched in reality the deepest point in the whole controversy, and illustrated the essential harmony of all truth.[2]

The sharpest period of the whole conflict was now drawing on.[3] Innocent's death brought Zosimus to the chair of the Roman See, and the efforts which he made to re-instate Pelagius and Cœlestius now began (September, 417). How little the Africans were likely to yield to his remarkable demands, may be seen from a sermon[4] which Augustin preached on the 23d of September, while Zosimus' letter (written on the 21st of September) was on its way to Africa. The preacher took his text from John vi. 54–66. "We hear here," he said, "the true Master, the

---

[1] The book given him by Timasius and James, to which *On Nature and Grace* is a reply.

[2] Compare also Innocent's letter (*Epistle* 181) to the Carthaginian Council, chap. 4, which also Neander, *History of the Christian Church*, E. T., ii. 646, quotes in this connection, as showing that Innocent "perceived that this dispute was connected with a different way of regarding the relation of God's providence to creation." As if Augustin did not see this too!

[3] The book addressed to Dardanus, in which the Pelagians are confuted, but not named, belongs about at this time. Compare *Retractations*, ii. 49.

[4] *Sermon* 131, preached at Carthage.

Divine Redeemer, the human Saviour, commending to us our ransom, His blood. He calls His body food, and His blood drink; and, in commending such food and drink, He says, 'Unless you eat My flesh, and drink My blood, ye shall have no life in you.' What, then, is this eating and drinking, but to live? Eat life, drink life; you shall have life, and life is whole. This will come, — that is, the body and blood of Christ will be life to every one, — if what is taken visibly in the sacrament is in real truth spiritually eaten and spiritually drunk. But that He might teach us that even to believe in Him is of gift, not of merit, He said, 'No one comes to Me, except the Father who sent Me draw him.' *Draw* him, not *lead* him. This violence is done to the *heart*, not the flesh. Why do you marvel? Believe, and you come; love, and you are drawn. Think not that this is harsh and injurious violence; it is soft, it is sweet; it is sweetness itself that draws you. Is not the sheep drawn when the succulent herbage is shown to him? And I think that there is no compulsion of the body, but an assembling of the desire. So, too, do you come to Christ; wish not to plan a long journey, — when you believe, then you come. For to Him who is everywhere, one comes by loving, not by taking a voyage. No doubt, if you come not, it is your work; but if you come, it is God's work. And even after you have come, and are walking in the right way, become not proud, lest you perish from it: 'happy are those that confide in Him,' not in *themselves*, but in *Him*. We are saved by grace, not of ourselves: it is the gift of God. Why do I continually say this to you? It is because there are men who are ungrateful to grace, and attribute much to unaided and wounded nature. It is true that man received great powers of free will at his creation; but he lost them by sinning. He has fallen into death; he has been made weak; he has been left half dead in the way, by robbers; the good Samaritan has lifted him up upon his ass, and borne him to the inn. Why should we boast? But I am told that it is enough that sins are remitted in baptism. But does the removal of sin take away weakness too? What! will you not see that after pouring the oil and the wine into the wounds of the man left half dead by the robbers, he must still go to the inn where his weakness may be healed? Nay, so long as we are in this life we bear a fragile body; it is only after we are redeemed from corruption that we shall find no sin, and receive the crown of righteousness. Grace, that was hidden in the Old Testament, is now manifest to the whole world. Even though the Jew may be ignorant of it, why should Christians be enemies of grace? why presumptuous of themselves? why ungrateful to grace? For, why did Christ come? Was not nature already here, — that very nature by the praise of which you are beguiled? Was not the law here? But the apostle says, 'If righteousness is of the law, then is Christ dead in vain.' What the apostle says of the law, that we say to these men about nature: if righteousness is by nature, then Christ is dead in vain. What then was said of the Jews, this we see repeated in these men. They have a zeal for God: I bear them witness that they have a zeal for God, but not according to knowledge. For, being ignorant of God's righteousness, and wishing to establish their own, they are not subject to the righteousness of God. My brethren, share my compassion. Where you find such men, wish no concealment; let there be no perverse pity in you: where you find them, wish no concealment at all. Contradict and refute, resist, or persuade them to us. For already two councils have, in this cause, sent letters to the Apostolic See, whence also rescripts have come back. The cause is ended: would that the error might some day end! Therefore we admonish so that they may take notice, we teach so that they may be instructed, we pray so that their way be changed." Here is certainly tenderness to the persons of the teachers of error; readiness to forgive, and readiness to go all proper lengths in recovering them to the truth. But here is also absolute firmness as to the truth itself, and a manifesto as to policy. Certainly, on the lines of the policy here indicated, the Africans fought out the coming campaign. They met in council at the end of this year, or early in the next (418); and formally replied to Zosimus, that the cause had been tried, and was finished, and that the sentence that had been already pronounced against Pelagius and Cœlestius should remain in force until they should unequivocally acknowledge that "we are aided by the grace of God through Christ, not only to know, but to do, what is right, and that in each single act; so that without grace we are unable to have, think, speak, or do anything belonging to piety." As we may see Augustin's hand in this, so, doubtless, we may recognize it in that remarkable piece of engineering which crushed Zosimus' plans within the next few months. There is, indeed, no direct proof that it was due to Augustin, or to the Africans under his leading, or to the Africans at all, that the State interfered in the matter; it is even in doubt whether the action of the Empire was put forth as a rescript, or as a self-moved decree: but surely it is difficult to believe that such a *coup de théâtre* could have been prepared for Zosimus by chance; and as it is well known, both that Augustin believed in the righteousness of civil penalty for heresy, and invoked it on other occasions, and defended and used it on this, and that he had influential friends at court with whom he was in correspondence, it seems, on internal grounds, altogether probable that he was the *Deus ex machinâ* who let loose the thunders of ecclesiastical and civil enactment simultaneously on the poor Pope's devoted head.

The "great African Council" met at Carthage, on the 1st of May, 418; and, after its decrees were issued, Augustin remained at Carthage, and watched the effect of the combination of which he was probably one of the moving causes. He had now an opportunity to betake himself once more to his pen. While still at Carthage, at short notice, and in the midst of much distraction, he wrote a large work, in two books which have come down to us under the separate titles of *On the Grace of Christ*, and *On Original Sin*, at the instance of another of those ascetic families which formed so marked a feature in those troubled times. Pinianus and Melania, the daughter of Albina, were husband and wife, who, leaving Rome amid the wars with Alaric, had lived in continence in Africa for some time, but now in Palestine had separated, he to become head of a monastery, and she an inmate of a convent. While in Africa, they had lived at Sagaste under the tutelage of Alypius, and in the enjoyment of the friendship and instruction of Augustin. After retiring to Bethlehem, like the other holy ascetics whom he had known in Africa, they kept up their relations with him. Like the others, also, they became acquainted with Pelagius in Palestine, and were well-nigh deceived by him. They wrote to Augustin that they had begged Pelagius to condemn in writing all that had been alleged against him, and that he had replied in the presence of them all, that " he anathematized the man who either thinks or says that the grace of God whereby Christ Jesus came into the world to save sinners is not necessary, not only for every hour and for every moment, but also for every act of our lives," and asserted that " those who endeavor to disannul it are worthy of everlasting punishment." [1] Moreover, they wrote that Pelagius had read to them, out of his book that he had sent to Rome,[2] his assertion " that infants ought to be baptized with the same formula of sacramental words as adults." [3] They wrote that they were delighted to hear these words from Pelagius, as they seemed exactly what they had been desirous of hearing; and yet they preferred consulting Augustin about them, before they were fully committed regarding them.[4] It was in answer to this appeal, that the present work was written; the two books of which take up the two points in Pelagius' asseveration, — the theme of the first being " the assistance of the Divine grace towards our justification, by which God co-operates in all things for good to those who love Him, and whom He first loved, giving to them that He may receive from them," — while the subject of the second is " the sin which by one man has entered the world along with death, and so has passed upon all men." [5]

The first book, *On the Grace of Christ*, begins by quoting and examining Pelagius' anathema of all those who deny that grace is necessary for every action (2 sq.). Augustin confesses that this would deceive all who were not fortified by knowledge of Pelagius' writings; but asserts that in the light of them it is clear that he means that grace is always necessary, because we need continually to remember the forgiveness of our sins, the example of Christ, the teaching of the law, and the like. Then he enters (4 sq.) upon an examination of Pelagius' scheme of human

---

[1] *On the Grace of Christ*, 2.
[2] The so-called *Confession of Faith* sent to Innocent after the Synod of Diospolis, but which arrived after Innocent's death.
[3] *On Original Sin*, 1.          [4] Do., 5.          [5] *On the Grace of Christ*, 55.

faculties, and quotes at length his account of them given in his book, *In Defence of Free Will*, wherein he distinguishes between the *possibilitas* (*posse*), *voluntas* (*velle*), and *actio* (*esse*), and declares that the first only is from God and receives aid from God, while the others are entirely ours, and in our own power.  Augustin opposes to this the passage in Phil. ii. 12, 13 (6), and then criticises (7 sq.) Pelagius' ambiguous acknowledgment that God is to be praised for man's good works, " because the capacity for any action on man's part is from God," by which he reduces all grace to the primeval endowment of nature with " capacity " (*possibilitas*, *posse*), and the help afforded it by the law and teaching.  Augustin points out the difference between law and grace, and the purpose of the former as a pedagogue to the latter (9 sq.), and then refutes Pelagius' further definition of grace as consisting in the promise of future glory and the revelation of wisdom, by an appeal to Paul's thorn in the flesh, and his experience under its discipline (11 sq.). Pelagius' illustrations from our senses, of his theory of natural faculty, are then sharply tested (16) ; and the criticism on the whole doctrine is then made and pressed (17 sq.), that it makes God equally sharer in our blame for evil acts as in our praise for good ones, since if God does help, and His help is only His gift to us of ability to act in either part, then He has equally helped to the evil deeds as to the good.  The assertion that this " capacity of either part " is the fecund root of both good and evil is then criticised (19 sq.), and opposed to Matt. vii. 18, with the result of establishing that we must seek two roots in our dispositions for so diverse results, — covetousness for evil, and love for good, — not a single root for both in nature.  Man's " capacity," it is argued, is the root of nothing ; but it is capable of both good and evil according to the moving cause, which, in the case of evil, is man-originated, while, in the case of good, it is from God (21).  Next, Pelagius' assertion that grace is given according to our merits (23 sq.) is taken up and examined.  It is shown, that, despite his anathema, Pelagius holds to this doctrine, and in so extreme a form as explicitly to declare that man comes and cleaves to God by his freedom of will alone, and without God's aid.  He shows that the Scriptures teach just the opposite (24–26) ; and then points out how Pelagius has confounded the functions of knowledge and love (27 sq.), and how he forgets that we cannot have merits until we love God, while John certainly asserts that *God loved us first* (1 John iv. 10).  The representation that what grace does is to render obedience *easier* (28–30), and the twin view that prayer is only relatively necessary, are next criticised (32).  That Pelagius never acknowledges real grace, is then demonstrated by a detailed examination of all that he had written on the subject (31–45).  The book closes (46–80) with a full refutation of Pelagius' appeal to Ambrose, as if he supported him ; and exhibition of Ambrose's contrary testimony as to grace and its necessity.

The object of the second book — *On Original Sin* — is to show, that, in spite of Pelagius' admissions as to the baptism of infants, he yet denies that they inherit original sin and contends that they are born free from corruption.  The book opens by pointing out that there is no question as to Cœlestius' teaching in this matter (2–8), as he at Carthage refused to condemn those who say that Adam's sin injured no one but himself, and that infants are born in the same state that Adam was in before the fall, and openly asserted at Rome that there is no sin *ex traduce*. As for Pelagius, he is simply more cautious and mendacious than Cœlestius : he deceived the Council at Diospolis, but failed to deceive the Romans (5–13), and, as a matter of fact (14–18), teaches exactly what Cœlestius does.  In support of this assertion, Pelagius' *Defence of Free Will* is quoted, wherein he asserts that we are born neither good nor bad, " but with a capacity for either," and " as without virtue, so without vice ; and previous to the action of our own proper will, that that alone is in man which God has formed " (14).  Augustin also quotes Pelagius' explanation of his anathema against those who say Adam's sin injured only himself, as meaning that he has injured man by setting a bad " example," and his even more sinuous explanation of his anathema against those who assert that infants are born in the same condition that Adam was in before he fell, as meaning that they are *infants* and he was a *man!* (16–18).  With this introduction to them, Augustin next treats of Pelagius' subterfuges (19–25), and then animadverts on the importance of the issue (26–37), pointing out that Pelagianism is not a mere error, but a deadly heresy, and strikes at the very centre of Christianity. A counter argument of the Pelagians is then answered (38–45), " Does not the doctrine of original sin make marriage an evil thing?" No, says Augustin, marriage is ordained by God, and is good; but it is a diseased good, and hence what is born of it is a good nature made by God, but this good nature in a diseased condition, — the result of the Devil's work. Hence, if it be asked why God's gift produces any thing for the Devil to take possession of, it is to be answered that God gives his gifts liberally (Matt. v. 45), and makes men; but the Devil makes these men sinners (46). Finally, as Ambrose had been appealed to in the former book, so at the end of this it is shown that he openly proclaimed the doctrine of original sin, and here too, before Pelagius, condemned Pelagius (47 sq.).

What Augustin means by writing to Pinianus and his family that he was more oppressed by work at Carthage than anywhere else, may perhaps be illustrated from his diligence in preaching while in that capital. He seems to have been almost constantly in the pulpit, during this period " of the sharpest conflict with them," [1] preaching against the Pelagians. There is one series of his sermons, of the exact dates of which we can be pretty sure, which may be adverted to here, —Sermons 151 and 152, preached early in October, 418; Sermon 155 on Oct. 14, 156 on Oct. 17, and 26 on Oct. 18; thus following one another almost with the regularity of the days. The first of these was based on Rom. vii. 15–25, which he declares to contain dangerous words if not properly understood; for men are prone to sin, and when they hear the apostle so speaking they do evil, and think they are like him. They are meant to teach us, however, that the life of the just in this body is a war, not yet a triumph: the triumph will come only when death is swallowed up in victory. It would, no doubt, be better not to have an enemy than even to conquer. It would be better not to have evil desires: but we have them; therefore, let us not go after them. If they rebel against us, let us rebel against them; if they fight, let us fight; if they besiege, let us besiege: let us look only to this, that they do not conquer. With some evil desires we are born: others we make, by bad habit. It is on account of those with which we are born, that infants are baptized; that they may be freed from the guilt of inheritance, not from any evil of custom, which, of course, they have not. And it is on account of these, too, that our war must be endless: the concupiscence with which we are born cannot be done away as long as we live; it may be diminished, but not done away. Neither can the law free us, for it only reveals the sin to our greater apprehension. Where, then, is hope, save in the superabundance of grace? The next sermon (152) takes up the words in Rom. viii. 1–4, and points out that the inward aid of the Spirit brings all the help we need. " We, like farmers in the field, work from without: but, if there were no one who worked from within, the seed would not take root in the ground, nor would the sprout arise in the field, nor would the shoot grow strong and become a tree, nor would branches and fruit and leaves be produced. Therefore the apostle distinguishes between the work of the workmen and of the Creator (1 Cor. iii. 6, 7). If God give not the increase, empty is this sound within your ears; but if he gives, it avails somewhat that we plant and water, and our labor is not in vain." He then applies this to the individual, striving against his lusts; warns against Manichean error; and distinguishes between the three laws, — the law of sin, the law of faith, and the law of deeds, — defending the latter, the law of Moses, against the Manicheans; and then he comes to the words of the text, and explains its chief phrases, closing thus: " What other do we read here than that Christ is a sacrifice for sin? . . . Behold by what 'sin' he condemned sin: by the sacrifice which he made for sins, he condemned sin. This is the law of the Spirit of life which has freed you from the law of sin and death. For that other law, the law of the letter, the law that commands, is indeed good; 'the commandment is holy and just and good:' but 'it was weak by the flesh,' and what it commanded it could not

---

[1] *On the Gift of Perseverance*, 55.

bring about in us. Therefore there is one law, as I began by saying, that reveals sin to you, and another that takes it away: the law of the letter reveals sin, the law of grace takes it away." Sermon 155 covers the same ground, and more, taking the broader text, Rom. viii. 1–11, and fully developing its teaching, especially as discriminating between the law of sin and the law of Moses and the law of faith; the law of Moses being the holy law of God written with His finger on the tables of stone, while the law of the Spirit of life is nothing other than the same law written in the heart, as the prophet (Jer. xxx. 1, 33) clearly declares. So written, it does not terrify from without, but soothes from within. Great care is also taken, lest by such phrases as, "walk in the Spirit, not in the flesh," "who shall deliver me from the body of this death?" a hatred of the body should be begotten. "Thus you shall be freed from the body of this death, not by having no body, but by having another one and dying no more. If, indeed, he had not added, 'of this death,' perchance an error might have been suggested to the human mind, and it might have been said, 'You see that God does not wish us to have a body.' But He says, 'the body of this death.' Take away death, and the body is good. Let our last enemy, death, be taken away, and my dear flesh will be mine for eternity. For no one can ever 'hate his own flesh.' Although the 'spirit lusts against the flesh, and the flesh against the spirit,' although there is now a battle in this house, yet the husband is seeking by his strife not the ruin of, but concord with, his wife. Far be it, far be it, my brethren, that the spirit should hate the flesh in lusting against it! It hates the vices of the flesh; it hates the wisdom of the flesh; it hates the contention of death. This corruption shall put on incorruption, — this mortal shall put on immortality; it is sown a natural body; it shall rise a spiritual body; and you shall see full and perfect concord, — you shall see the creature praise the Creator." One of the special interests of such passages is to show, that, even at this early date, Augustin was careful to guard his hearers from Manichean error while proclaiming original sin. One of the sermons which, probably, was preached about this time (153), is even entitled, "Against the Manicheans openly, but tacitly against the Pelagians," and bears witness to the early development of the method that he was somewhat later to use effectively against Julian's charges of Manicheanism against the catholics.[1] Three days afterwards, Augustin preached on the next few verses, Rom. viii. 12–17, but can scarcely be said to have risen to the height of its great argument. The greater part of the sermon is occupied with a discussion of the law, why it was given, how it is legitimately used, and its usefulness as a pedagogue to bring us to Christ; then of the need of a mediator; and then, of what it is to live according to the flesh, which includes living according to merely human nature; and the need of mortifying the flesh in this world. All this, of course, gave full opportunity for opposing the leading Pelagian errors; and the sermon is brought to a close by a direct polemic against their assertion that the function of grace is only to make it more easy to do what is right. "With the sail more easily, with the oar with more difficulty: nevertheless even with the oar we can go. On a beast more easily, on foot with more difficulty: nevertheless progress can be made on foot. It is not true! For the true Master who flatters no one, who deceives no one, — the truthful Teacher and very Saviour to whom the most grievous pedagogue has led us, — when he was speaking about good works, i.e., about the fruits of the twigs and branches, did not say, 'Without me, indeed, you can do something, but you will do it more easily with me;' He did not say, 'You can make your fruit without me, but more richly with me.' He did not say this! Read what He said: it is the holy gospel, — bow the proud necks! Augustin does not say this: the Lord says it. What says the Lord? 'Without me you can do *nothing'!*" On the very next day, he was again in the pulpit, and taking for his text chiefly the ninety-fourth Psalm.[2] The preacher began[3] by quoting the sixth verse, and laying stress on the words "our Maker." 'No Christian,' he said, 'doubted that God had made him, and that in such a sense that God created not only the

---

[1] Compare, below, pp. lv-lviii. Neander, in the second volume (E. T.) of his *History of the Christian Church*, discusses the matter in a very fair spirit.

[2] English version, xcv.; see verse 6.          [3] *Sermon* 26.

first man, from whom all have descended, but that God to-day creates every man, — as He said to one of His saints, " Before that I formed thee in the womb, I knew thee." At first He created man apart from man ; now He creates man from man : nevertheless, whether man apart from man, or man from man, " it is He that made us, and not we ourselves." Nor has He made us and then deserted us ; He has not cared to make us, and not cared to keep us. Will He who made us without being asked, desert us when He is besought? But is it not just as foolish to say, as some say or are ready to say, that God made them men, but they make themselves righteous? Why, then, do we pray to God to make us righteous? The first man was created in a nature that was without fault or flaw. He was made righteous : he did not make himself righteous ; what he did for himself was to fall and break his righteousness. This God did not do : He permitted it, as if He had said, " Let him desert Me ; let him find himself; and let his misery prove that he has no ability without Me." In this way God wished to show man what free will was worth without God. O evil free will without God ! Behold, man was made good ; and by free will man was made evil ! When will the evil man make himself good by free will? When good, he was not able to keep himself good ; and now that he is evil, is he to make himself good? Nay, behold, He that made us has also made us " His people " (Ps. xciv. 7). This is a distinguishing gift. Nature is common to all, but grace is not. It is not to be confounded with nature ; but if it were, it would still be gratuitous. For certainly no man, before he existed, deserved to come into existence. And yet God has made him, and that not like the beasts or a stock or a stone, but in His own image. Who has given this benefit? He gave it who was in existence : he received it who was not. And only He could do this, who calls the things that are not as though they were : of whom the apostle says that " He chose us before the foundation of the world." We have been made in this world, and yet the world was not when we were chosen. Ineffable ! wonderful ! They are chosen who are not : neither does He err in choosing, nor choose in vain. He chooses, and has elect whom He is to create to be chosen : He has them in Himself, not indeed in His nature, but in His prescience. Let us not, then, glory in ourselves, or dispute against grace. If we are men, He made us. If we are believers, He made us this too. He who sent the Lamb to be slain has, out of wolves, made us sheep. This is grace. And it is an even greater grace than that grace of nature by which we were all made men.' " I am continually endeavouring to discuss such things as these," said the preacher, "against a new heresy which is attempting to rise ; because I wish you to be fixed in the good, untouched by the evil. . . . For, disputing against grace in favor of free will, they became an offence to pious and catholic ears. They began to create horror ; they began to be avoided as a fixed pest ; it began to be said of them, that they argued against grace. And they found such a device as this : . . . ' Because I defend man's free will, and say that free will is sufficient in order that I may be right-eous,' says one, ' I do not say that it is without the grace of God.' The ears of the pious are pricked up, and he who hears this, already begins to rejoice : ' Thanks be to God ! He does not defend free will without the grace of God ! There is free will, but it avails nothing without the grace of God.' If, then, they do not defend free will without the grace of God, what evil do they say? Expound to us, O teacher, what grace you mean? ' When I say,' he says, ' the free will of man, you observe that I say " of man "?' What then? 'Who created man?' God. 'Who gave him free will?' God. ' If, then, God created man, and God gave man free will, whatever man is able to do by free will, to whose grace does he owe it, except to His who made him with free will?' And this is what they think they say so acutely ! You see, nevertheless, my brethren, how they preach that general grace by which we were created and by which we are men ; and, of course, we are men in common with the ungodly, and are Christians apart from them. It is this grace by which we are Christians, that we wish them to preach, this that we wish them to acknowledge, this that we wish, — of which the apostle says, ' I do not make void the grace of God, for if righteousness is by the law, Christ is dead in vain.' " Then the true function of the law is explained, as a revealer of our sinfulness, and a pedagogue to lead us to Christ : the Manichean view of the Old-Testament law is attacked, but its insufficiency for salvation is pointed out; and so we are brought back to the necessity of grace, which is illustrated from the story of the raising of the dead child in 2 Kings iv. 18–37, — the dead child being Adam; the ineffective staff (by which we ought to walk), the law; but the living prophet, Christ with his grace, which we must preach. "The prophetic staff was not enough for the dead boy: would dead nature itself have been enough? Even this, by which we are made, although we nowhere read of it under this name, we nevertheless, because it is given gratuitously, confess to be grace. But we show to you a greater grace than this, by which we are Christians. . . . This is the grace by Jesus Christ our Lord: it was He that made us, — both before we were at all, it was He that made us, and now, after we are made, it is He that has made us all righteous, — and not we ourselves." There was but one mass of perdition from Adam, to which nothing was due but punishment; and from that mass vessels have been made unto honor. "Rejoice because you have escaped; you have escaped the death that was due, — you have received the life that was not due. 'But,' you ask, 'why did He make me unto honor, and another unto dishonor?' Will you who will not hear the apostle saying, 'O man, who art thou that repliest against God?' hear Augustin? . . . Do you wish to dispute with me? Nay, wonder with me, and cry out with me, 'Oh the depth of the riches!' Let us both be afraid, — let us both cry out, 'Oh the depth of the riches!' Let us both agree in fear, lest we perish in error."

Augustin was not less busy with his pen, during these months, than with his voice. Quite a series of letters belong to the last half of 418, in which he argues to his distant correspondents on the same themes which he was so iterantly trying to make clear to his Carthaginian auditors. One of the most interesting of these was written to a fellow-bishop, Optatus, on the origin of the soul.[1] Optatus, like Jerome, had expressed himself as favoring the theory of a special creation of each at birth; and Augustin, in this letter as in the paper sent to Jerome, lays great stress on so holding our theories on so obscure a matter as to conform to the indubitable fact of the transmission of sin. This fact, such passages as 1 Cor. xv. 21 sq., Rom. v. 12 sq., make certain; and in stating this, Augustin takes the opportunity to outline the chief contents of the catholic faith over against the Pelagian denial of original sin and grace: that all are born under the contagion of death and in the bond of guilt; that there is no deliverance except in the one Mediator, Christ Jesus; that before His coming men received him as promised, now as already come, but with the same faith; that the law was not intended to save, but to shut up under sin and so force us back upon the one Saviour; and that the distribution of grace is sovereign. Augustin pries into God's sovereign counsels somewhat more freely here than is usual with him. "But why those also are created who, the Creator foreknew, would belong to damnation, not to grace, the blessed apostle mentions with as much succinct brevity as great authority. For he says that God, 'wishing to show His wrath and demonstrate His power,' etc. (Rom. ix. 22). Justly, however, would he seem unjust in forming vessels of wrath for perdition, if the whole mass from Adam were not condemned. That, therefore, they are made on birth vessels of anger, belongs to the punishment due to them; but that they are made by re-birth vessels of mercy, belongs to the grace that is not due to them. God, therefore, shows his wrath, — not, of course, perturbation of mind, such as is called wrath among men, but a just and fixed vengeance. . . . He shows also his power, by which he makes a good use of evil men, and endows them with many natural and temporal goods, and bends their evil to admonition and instruction of the good by comparison with it, so that these may learn from them to give thanks to God that they have been made to differ from them, not by their own deserts which were of like kind in the same mass, but by His pity. . . . But by creating so many to be born who, He foreknew, would not belong to his grace, so that they are more by an incomparable multitude than those whom he deigned to predestinate as children of the promise into the glory of His Kingdom, — He wished to show by this very

---

[1] *Epistle* 190.

multitude of the rejected how entirely of no moment it is to the just God what is the multitude of those most justly condemned. And that hence also those who are redeemed from this condemnation may understand, that what they see rendered to so great a part of the mass was the due of the whole of it, — not only of those who add many others to original sin, by the choice of an evil will, but as well of so many children who are snatched from this life without the grace of the Mediator, bound by no bond except that of original sin alone." With respect to the question more immediately concerning which the letter was written, Augustin explains that he is willing to accept the opinion that souls are created for men as they are born, if only it can be made plain that it is consistent with the original sin that the Scriptures so clearly teach. In the paper sent to Jerome, the difficulties of creationism are sufficiently urged ; this letter is interesting on account of its statement of some of the difficulties of traducianism also, — thus evidencing Augustin's clear view of the peculiar complexity of the problem, and justifying his attitude of balance and uncertainty between the two theories. 'The human understanding,' he says, 'can scarcely comprehend how a soul arises from a parent's soul in the offspring ; or is transmitted to the offspring as a candle is lighted from a candle and thence another fire comes into existence without loss to the former one. Is there an incorporeal seed for the soul, which passes, by some hidden and invisible channel of its own, from the father to the mother, when it is conceived in the woman? Or, even more incredible, does it lie enfolded and hidden within the corporeal seed? He is lost in wonder over the question whether, when conception does not take place, the immortal seed of an immortal soul perishes ; or, does the immortality attach itself to it only when it lives? He even expresses the doubt whether traducianism will explain what it is called in to explain, much better than creationism ; in any case, who denies that God is the maker of every soul? Isaiah (lvii. 16) says, "I have made every breath ; " and the only question that can arise is as to method, — whether He "makes every breath from the one first breath, just as He makes every body of man from the one first body ; or whether he makes new bodies indeed, from the one body, but new souls out of nothing." Certainly nothing but Scripture can determine such a question ; but where do the Scriptures speak unambiguously upon it? The passages to which the creationists point only affirm the admitted fact that God makes the soul ; and the traducianists forget that the word "soul" in the Scriptures is ambiguous, and can mean "man," and even a "dead man." What more can be done, then, than to assert what is certain, viz., that sin is propagated, and leave what is uncertain in the doubt in which God has chosen to place it?

This letter was written not long after the issue of Zosimus' *Tractoria*, demanding the signature of all to African orthodoxy ; and Augustin sends Optatus "copies of the recent letters which have been sent forth from the Roman see, whether specially to the African bishops or generally to all bishops," on the Pelagian controversy, "lest perchance they had not yet reached" his correspondent, who, it is very evident, he was anxious should thoroughly realize "that the authors, or certainly the most energetic and noted teachers," of these new heresies, "had been condemned in the whole Christian world by the vigilance of episcopal councils aided by the Saviour who keeps His Church, as well as by two venerable overseers of the Apostolical see, Pope Innocent and Pope Zosimus, unless they should show repentance by being convinced and reformed." To this zeal we owe it that the letter contains an extract from Zosimus' *Tractoria*, one of the two brief fragments of that document that have reached our day.

There was another ecclesiastic in Rome, besides Zosimus, who was strongly suspected of favoring the Pelagians, — the presbyter Sixtus, who afterwards became Pope Sixtus III. But when Zosimus sent forth his condemnation of Pelagianism, Sixtus sent also a short letter to Africa addressed to Aurelius of Carthage, which, though brief, indicated a considerable vigor against the heresy which he was commonly believed to have before defended,[1] and which claimed him as its own.[2] Some months afterwards, he sent another similar, but longer, letter to Augustin and Alypius, more fully

---

[1] See *Epistle* 194, 1.   [2] See *Epistle* 191, 1.

expounding his rejection of "the fatal dogma" of Pelagius, and his acceptance of "that grace of God freely given by Him to small and great, to which Pelagius' dogma was diametrically opposed." Augustin was overjoyed with these developments. He quickly replied in a short letter [1] in which he expresses the delight he has in learning from Sixtus' own hand that he is not a defender of Pelagius, but a preacher of grace. And close upon the heels of this he sent another much longer letter,[2] in which he discusses the subtler arguments of the Pelagians with an anxious care that seems to bear witness to his desire to confirm and support his correspondent in his new opinions. Both letters testify to Augustin's approval of the persecuting measures which had been instituted by the Roman see in obedience to the emperor; and urge on Sixtus his duty not only to bring the open heretics to deserved punishment, but to track out those who spread their poison secretly, and even to remember those whom he had formerly heard announcing the error before it had been condemned, and who were now silent through fear, and to bring them either to open recantation of their former beliefs, or to punishment. It is pleasanter to recall our thoughts to the dialectic of these letters. The greater part of the second is given to a discussion of the gratuitousness of grace, which, just because grace, is given to no preceding merits. Many subtle objections to this doctrine were brought forward by the Pelagians. They said that "free will was taken away if we asserted that man did not have even a good will without the aid of God;" that we made "God an accepter of persons, if we believed that without any preceding merits He had mercy on whom He would, and whom He would He called, and whom He would He made religious;" that "it was unjust, in one and the same case, to deliver one and punish another;" that, if such a doctrine is preached, "men who do not wish to live rightly and faithfully, will excuse themselves by saying that they have done nothing evil by living ill, since they have not received the grace by which they might live well;" that it is a puzzle "how sin can pass over to the children of the faithful, when it has been remitted to the parents in baptism;" that "children respond truly by the mouth of their sponsors that they believe in remission of sins, but not because sins are remitted to *them*, but because they believe that sins are remitted in the church or in baptism to those in whom they are found, not to those in whom they do not exist," and consequently they said that "they were unwilling that infants should be so baptized unto remission of sins as if this remission took place in them," for (they contend) "they have no sin; but they are to be baptized, although without sin, with the same rite of baptism through which remission of sins takes place in any that are sinners." This last objection is especially interesting,[3] because it furnishes us with the reply which the Pelagians made to the argument that Augustin so strongly pressed against them from the very act and ritual of baptism, as implying remission of sins.[4] His rejoinder to it here is to point to the other parts of the same ritual, and to ask why, then, infants are exorcised and exsufflated in baptism. "For, it cannot be doubted that this is done fictitiously, if the Devil does not rule over them; but if he rules over them, and they are therefore not falsely exorcised and exsufflated, why does that prince of sinners rule over them except because of sin?" On the fundamental matter of the gratuitousness of grace, this letter is very explicit. "If we seek for the deserving of hardening, we shall find it. . . . But if we seek for the deserving of pity, we shall not find it; for there is none, lest grace be made a vanity if it is not given gratis, but rendered to merits. But, should we say that faith preceded and in it there is desert of grace, what desert did man have before faith that he should receive faith? For, what did he have that he did not receive? and if he received it, why does he glory as if he received it not? For as man would not have wisdom, understanding, prudence, fortitude, knowledge, piety, fear of God, unless he had received (according to the prophet) the spirit of wisdom and understanding, of prudence and fortitude, of knowledge and piety and the fear of God; as he would not have justice, love, continence, except the spirit was received of whom the apostle says, 'For you did not receive the spirit of fear, but of

---

[1] *Epistle* 191.    [2] *Epistle* 194.

[3] It appears to have been first reported to Augustin, by Marius Mercator, in a letter received at Carthage. See *Epistle* 193, 3.

[4] As, for example, in *On the Merits and Remission of Sins*, etc., i.

virtue, and love, and continence : ' so he would not have faith unless he received the spirit of faith of whom the same apostle says, ' Having then the same spirit of faith, according to what is written, " I believed and therefore spoke," we too believe and therefore speak.' But that He is not received by desert, but by His mercy who has mercy on whom He will, is manifestly shown where he says of himself, ' I have obtained mercy to be faithful.' " " If we should say that the merit of prayer precedes, that the gift of grace may follow, . . . even prayer itself is found among the gifts of grace " (Rom. viii. 26). " It remains, then, that faith itself, whence all righteousness takes beginning ; . . . it remains, I say, that even faith itself is not to be attributed to the human will which they extol, nor to any preceding merits, since from it begin whatever good things are merits : but it is to be confessed to be the gratuitous gift of God, since we consider it true grace, that is, without merits, inasmuch as we read in the same epistle, ' God divides out the measure of faith to each ' (Rom. xii. 3). Now, good works are done by man, but faith is wrought in man, and without it these are not done by any man. For all that is not of faith is sin " (Rom. xiv. 23).

By the same messenger who carried this important letter to Sixtus, Augustin sent also a letter to Mercator,[1] an African layman who was then apparently at Rome, but who was afterwards (in 429) to render service by instructing the Emperor Theodosius as to the nature and history of Pelagianism, and so preventing the appeal of the Pelagians to him from being granted. Now he appears as an inquirer : Augustin, while at Carthage, had received a letter from him in which he had consulted him on certain questions that the Pelagians had raised, but in such a manner as to indicate his opposition to them. Press of business had compelled the postponement of the reply until this later date. One of the questions that Mercator had put concerned the Pelagian account of infants sharing in the one baptism unto remission of sins, which we have seen Augustin answering when writing to Sixtus. In this letter he replies : " Let them, then, hear the Lord (John iii. 36). Infants, therefore, who are made believers by others, by whom they are brought to baptism, are, of course, unbelievers by others, if they are in the hands of such as do not believe that they should be brought, inasmuch as they believe they are nothing profited ; and accordingly, if they believe by believers, and have eternal life, they are unbelievers by unbelievers, and shall not see life, but the wrath of God abideth on them. For it is not said, ' it comes on them,' but ' it abideth on them,' because it was on them from the beginning, and will not be taken from them except by the grace of God through Jesus Christ, our Lord. . . . Therefore, when children are baptized, the confession is made that they are believers, and it is not to be doubted that those who are not believers are condemned : let them, then, dare to say now, if they can, that they contract no evil from their origin to be condemned by the just God, and have no contagion of sin." The other matter on which Mercator sought light concerned the statement that universal death proved universal sin :[2] he reported that the Pelagians replied that not even death was universal, — that Enoch, for instance, and Elijah, had not died. Augustin adds those who are to be found living at the second advent, who are not to die, but be " changed ; " and replies that Rom. v. 12 is perfectly explicit that there is no death in the world except that which comes from sin, and that God is a Saviour, and we cannot at all " deny that He is able to do that, now, in any that he wishes, without death, which we undoubtingly believe is to be done in so many after death." He adds that the difficult question is not why Enoch and Elijah did not die, if death is the punishment of sin ; but why, such being the case, the justified ever die ; and he refers his correspondent to his book *On the Baptism of Infants*[3] for a resolution of this greater difficulty.

It was probably at the very end of 418 that Augustin wrote a letter of some length[4] to Asellicus, in reply to one which he had written on " avoiding the deception of Judaism," to the primate of the Bizacene province, and which that ecclesiastic had sent to Augustin for answering. He discusses in this the law of the Old Testament. He opens by pointing out that the apostle forbids Christians to Judaize (Gal. ii. 14–16), and explains that it is not merely the ceremonial

---

[1] *Epistle* 193.
[3] That is, *On the Merits and Remission of Sins*, etc., ii. 30 sq
[2] Compare *On Dulcitius' Eight Questions*, 3.
[4] *Epistle* 196.

law that we may not depend upon, "but also what is said in the law, 'Thou shalt not covet' (which no one, of course, doubts is to be said to Christians too), does not justify man, except by faith in Jesus Christ and the grace of God through Jesus Christ our Lord." He then expounds the use of the law: "This, then, is the usefulness of the law: that it shows man to himself, so that he may know his weakness, and see how, by the prohibition, carnal concupiscence is rather increased than healed. . . . The use of the law is, thus, to convince man of his weakness, and force him to implore the medicine of grace that is in Christ." "Since these things are so," he adds, "those who rejoice that they are Israelites after the flesh, and glory in the law apart from the grace of Christ, these are those concerning whom the apostle said that 'being ignorant of God's righteousness, and wishing to establish their own, they are not subject to God's righteousness;' since he calls 'God's righteousness' that which is from God to man; and 'their own,' what they think that the commandments suffice for them to do without the help and gift of Him who gave the law. But they are like those who, while they profess to be Christians, so oppose the grace of Christ, that they suppose that they fulfil the divine commands by human powers, and, 'wishing to establish their own,' are 'not subject to the righteousness of God,' and so, not indeed in name, but yet in error, Judaize. This sort of men found heads for themselves in Pelagius and Cœlestius, the most acute asserters of this impiety, who by God's recent judgment, through his diligent and faithful servants, have been deprived even of catholic communion, and, on account of an impenitent heart, persist still in their condemnation."

At the beginning of 419, a considerable work was published by Augustin on one of the more remote corollaries which the Pelagians drew from his teachings. It had come to his ears, that they asserted that his doctrine condemned marriage: "if only sinful offspring come from marriage," they asked, "is not marriage itself made a sinful thing?" The book which Augustin composed in answer to this query, he dedicated to, and sent along with an explanatory letter to, the Comes Valerius, a trusted servant of the Emperor Honorius, and one of the most steady opponents at court of the Pelagian heresy. Augustin explains[1] why he has desired to address the book to him: first, because Valerius was a striking example of those continent husbands of which that age furnishes us with many instances, and, therefore, the discussion would have especial interest for him; secondly, because of his eminence as an opponent of Pelagianism; and, thirdly, because Augustin had learned that he had read a Pelagian document in which Augustin was charged with condemning marriage by defending original sin.[2] The book in question is the first book of the treatise *On Marriage and Concupiscence.* It is, naturally, tinged, or rather stained, with the prevalent ascetic notions of the day. Its doctrine is that marriage is good, and God is the maker of the offspring that comes from it, although now there can be no begetting and hence no birth without sin. Sin made concupiscence, and now concupiscence perpetuates sinners. The specific object of the work, as it states it itself, is "to distinguish between the evil of carnal concupiscence, from which man, who is born therefrom, contracts original sin, and the good of marriage" (I. 1). After a brief introduction, in which he explains why he writes, and why he addresses his book to Valerius (1–2), Augustin points out that conjugal chastity, like its higher sister-grace of continence, is God's gift. Thus copulation, but only for the propagation of children, has divine allowance (3–5). Lust, or "shameful concupiscence," however, he teaches, is not of the essence, but only an accident, of marriage. It did not exist in Eden, although true marriage existed there; but arose from, and therefore only after, sin (6–7). Its addition to marriage does not destroy the good of marriage: it only conditions the character of the offspring (8). Hence it is that the apostle allows marriage, but forbids the "disease of desire" (1 Thess. iv. 3–5); and hence the Old-Testament saints were even permitted more than one wife, because, by multiplying wives, it was not lust, but offspring, that was increased (9–10). Nevertheless, fecundity is not to be thought the only good of marriage: true

---

[1] *On Marriage and Concupiscence,* i. 2.     [2] Compare the Benedictine Preface to *The Unfinished Work.*

marriage can exist without offspring, and even without cohabitation (11-13), and cohabitation is now, under the New Testament, no longer a duty as it was under the Old Testament (14-15), but the apostle praises continence above it. We must, then, distinguish between the goods of marriage, and seek the best (16-19). But thus it follows that it is not due to any inherent and necessary evil in marriage, but only to the presence, now, of concupiscence in all cohabitation, that children are born under sin, even the children of the regenerate, just as from the seed of olives only oleasters grow(20-24). And yet again, concupiscence is not itself sin in the regenerate; it is remitted as guilt in baptism: but it is the daughter of sin, and it is the mother of sin, and in the unregenerate it is itself sin, as to yield to it is even to the regenerate (25-39). Finally, as so often, the testimony of Ambrose is appealed to, and it is shown that he too teaches that all born from cohabitation are born guilty (40). In this book, Augustin certainly seems to teach that the bond of connection by which Adam's sin is conveyed to his offspring is not mere descent, or heredity, or mere inclusion in him, in a realistic sense, as partakers of the same numerical nature, but concupiscence. Without concupiscence in the act of generation, the offspring would not be a partaker of Adam's sin. This he had taught also previously, as, e.g., in the treatise *On Original Sin*, from which a few words may be profitably quoted as succinctly summing up the teaching of this book on the subject: " It is, then, manifest, that that must not be laid to the account of marriage, in the absence of which even marriage would still have existed. . . . Such, however, is the present condition of mortal men, that the connubial intercourse and lust are at the same time in action. . . . Hence it follows that infants, although incapable of sinning, are yet not born without the contagion of sin, . . . not, indeed, because of what is lawful, but on account of that which is unseemly : for, from what is lawful, nature is born ; from what is unseemly, sin " (42).

Towards the end of the same year (419), Augustin was led to take up again the vexed question of the origin of the soul, — both in a new letter to Optatus,[1] and by the zeal of the same monk, Renatus, who had formerly brought Optatus' inquiries to his notice, — in an elaborate treatise entitled *On the Soul and its Origin*, by way of reply to a rash adventure of a young man named Vincentius Victor, who blamed him for his uncertainty on such a subject, and attempted to determine all the puzzles of the question, though, as Augustin insists, on assumptions that were partly Pelagian and partly worse. Optatus had written in the hope that Augustin had heard by this time from Jerome, in reply to the treatise he had sent him on this subject. Augustin, in answering his letter, expresses his sorrow that he has not yet been worthy of an answer from Jerome, although five years had passed away since he wrote, but his continued hope that such an answer will in due time come. For himself, he confesses that he has not yet been able to see how the soul can contract sin from Adam and yet not itself be contracted from Adam ; and he regrets that Optatus, although holding that God creates each soul for its birth, has not sent him the proofs on which he depends for that opinion, nor met its obvious difficulties. He rebukes Optatus for confounding the question of whether God makes the soul, with the entirely different one of how he makes it, whether *ex propagine* or *sive propagine*. No one doubts that God makes the soul, as no one doubts that He makes the body. But when we consider how he makes it, sobriety and vigilance become necessary lest we should unguardedly fall into the Pelagian heresy. Augustin defends his attitude of uncertainty, and enumerates the points as to which he has no doubt : viz., that the soul is spirit, not body ; that it is rational or intellectual ; that it is not of the nature of God, but is so far a mortal creature that it is capable of deterioration and of alienation from the life of God, and so far immortal that after this life it lives on in bliss or punishment forever ; that it was not incarnated because of, or according to, preceding deserts acquired in a previous existence, yet that it is under the curse of sin which it derives from Adam, and therefore in all cases alike needs redemption in Christ.

---

[1] *Epistle* 202, *bis*. Compare *Epistle* 190.

The whole subject of the nature and origin of the soul, however, is most fully discussed in the four books which are gathered together under the common title of *On the Soul and its Origin*. Vincentius Victor was a young layman who had recently been converted from the Rogatian heresy; on being shown by his friend Peter, a presbyter, a small work of Augustin's on the origin of the soul, he expressed surprise that so great a man could profess ignorance on a matter so intimate to his very being, and, receiving encouragement, wrote a book for Peter in which he attacked and tried to solve all the difficulties of the subject. Peter received the work with transports of delighted admiration; but Renatus, happening that way, looked upon it with distrust, and, finding that Augustin was spoken of in it with scant courtesy, felt it his duty to send him a copy of it, which he did in the summer of 419. It was probably not until late in the following autumn that Augustin found time to take up the matter; but then he wrote to Renatus, to Peter, and two books to Victor himself, and it is these four books together which constitute the treatise that has come down to us. The first book is a letter to Renatus, and is introduced by an expression of thanks to him for sending Victor's book, and of kindly feeling towards and appreciation for the high qualities of Victor himself (1–3). Then Victor's errors are pointed out, — as to the nature of the soul (4–9), including certain far-reaching corollaries that flow from these (10–15), as well as, as to the origin of the soul (16–30); and the letter closes with some remarks on the danger of arguing from the silence of Scripture (31), on the self-contradictions of Victor (34), and on the errors that must be avoided in any theory of the origin of the soul that hopes to be acceptable, — to wit, that souls become sinful by an alien original sin, that unbaptized infants need no salvation, that souls sinned in a previous state, and that they are condemned for sins which they have not committed but would have committed had they lived longer. The second book is a letter to Peter, warning him of the responsibility that rests on him as Victor's trusted friend and a clergyman, to correct Victor's errors, and reproving him for the uninstructed delight he had taken in Victor's crudities. It opens by asking Peter what was the occasion of the great joy which Victor's book brought him? could it be that he learned from it, for the first time, the old and primary truths it contained? (2–3); or was it due to the new errors that it proclaimed, — seven of which he enumerates? (4–16). Then, after animadverting on the dilemma in which Victor stood, of either being forced to withdraw his violent assertion of creationism, or else of making God unjust in His dealings with new souls (17), he speaks of Victor's unjustifiable dogmatism in the matter (18–21), and closes with severely solemn words to Peter on his responsibility in the premises (22–23). In the third and fourth books, which are addressed to Victor, the polemic, of course, reaches its height. The third book is entirely taken up with pointing out to Victor, as a father to a son, the errors into which he has fallen, and which, in accordance with his professions of readiness for amendment, he ought to correct. Eleven are enumerated: 1. That the soul was made by God out of Himself (3–7); 2. That God will continuously create souls forever (8); 3. That the soul has desert of good before birth (9); 4. (contradictingly), That the soul has desert of evil before birth (10); 5. That the soul deserved to be sinful before any sin (11); 6. That unbaptized infants are saved (12); 7. That what God predestinates may not occur (13); 8. That Wisd. iv. 1 is spoken of infants (14); 9. That some of the mansions with the Father are outside of God's kingdom (15–17); 10. That the sacrifice of Christ's blood may be offered for the unbaptized (18); 11. That the unbaptized may attain at the resurrection even to the kingdom of heaven (19). The book closes by reminding Victor of his professions of readiness to correct his errors, and warning him against the obstinacy that makes the heretic (20–23). The fourth book deals with the more personal elements of the controversy, and discusses the points in which Victor had expressed dissent from Augustin. It opens with a statement of the two grounds of complaint that Victor had urged against Augustin; viz., that he refused to express a confident opinion as to the origin of the soul, and that he affirmed that the soul was not corporeal, but spirit (1–2). These two complaints are then taken up at length (2–16 and 17–37). To the first, Augustin replies that man's knowledge is at best limited, and often most limited about the things nearest to him ; we do not know the constitution of our bodies ; and, above most others, this subject of the origin of the soul is one on which no one but God is a competent witness. Who remembers his birth? Who remembers what was before birth? But this is just one of the subjects on which God has not spoken unambiguously in the Scriptures. Would it not be better, then, for Victor to imitate Augustin's cautious ignorance, than that Augustin should imitate Victor's rash assertion of errors? That the soul is not corporeal, Augustin argues (18–35) from the Scriptures and from the phenomena of dreams ; and then shows, in opposition to Victor's trichotomy, that the Scriptures teach the identity of " soul " and " spirit " (36–37). The book closes with a renewed enumeration of Victor's eleven errors (38), and a final admonition to his rashness (39). It is pleasant to know that Augustin found in this case, also, that righteousness is the fruit of the faithful wounds of a friend. Victor accepted the rebuke, and professed his better instruction at the hands of his modest but resistless antagonist.

The controversy now entered upon a new stage. Among the evicted bishops of Italy who refused to sign Zosimus' *Epistola Tractoria*, Julian of Eclanum was easily the first, and at this point he appears as the champion of Pelagianism. It was a sad fate that arrayed this beloved son of his old friend against Augustin, just when there seemed to be reason to hope that the controversy was at an end, and the victory won, and the plaudits of the world were greeting him as the saviour of the Church.[1] But the now fast-aging bishop was to find, that, in this " very confident young man," he had yet to meet the most persistent and most dangerous advocate of the new doctrines that had arisen. Julian had sent, at an earlier period, two letters to Zosimus, one of which has come down to us as a " Confession of Faith," and the other of which attempted to approach Augustinian forms of speech as much as possible ; the object of both being to gain standing ground in the Church for the Italian Pelagians. Now he appears as a Pelagian controversialist ; and in opposition to the book *On Marriage and Concupiscence*, which Augustin had sent Valerius, he published an extended work in four thick books addressed to Turbantius. Extracts from the first of these books were sent by some one to Valerius, and were placed by him in the hands of Alypius, who was then in Italy, for transmission to Augustin. Meanwhile, a letter had been sent to Rome by Julian,[2] designed to strengthen the cause of Pelagianism there ; and a similar one, in the names of the eighteen Pelagianizing Italian bishops, was addressed to Rufus, bishop of Thessalonica, and representative of the Roman see in that portion of the Eastern Empire which was regarded as ecclesiastically a part of the West, the design of which was to obtain the powerful support of this important magnate, perhaps, also, a refuge from persecution within his jurisdiction. These two letters came into the hands of the new Pope, Boniface, who gave them also to Alypius for transmission to Augustin. Thus provided, Alypius returned to Africa. The tactics of all these writings of Julian were essentially the same ; he attempted not so much to defend Pelagianism, as to attack Augustinianism, and thus literally to carry the war into Africa. He insisted that the corruption of nature which Augustin taught was nothing else than Manicheism ; that the sovereignty of grace, as taught by him, was only the attribution of " acceptance of persons," and partiality, to God ; and that his doctrine of predestination was mere fatalism. He accused the anti-Pelagians of denying the goodness of the nature that God had created, of the marriage that He had ordained, of the law that He had given, of the free will that He had implanted in man, as well as the perfection of His saints.[3] He insisted that this teaching also did dishonour to baptism itself which it professed so to honour, inasmuch as it asserted the continuance of concupiscence after baptism, — and thus taught that baptism does not take away sins, but only shaves them off as one shaves his beard, and leaves the roots whence the sins may grow anew, and need cutting down again. He complained bitterly of the way in which Pelagianism had been condemned, — that bishops had been compelled to sign a definition of dogma, not in council

---

[1] Compare *Epistle* 195.

[2] Julian afterwards repudiated this letter, perhaps because of some falsifications it had suffered; it seems to have been certainly his.

[3] Compare *Against Two Letters of the Pelagians*, iii. 24: and see above, p. xv.

assembled, but sitting at home ; and he demanded a rehearing of the whole case before a lawful council, lest the doctrine of the Manichees should be forced upon the acceptance of the world.

Augustin felt a strong desire to see the whole work of Julian against his book *On Marriage and Concupiscence* before he undertook a reply to the excerpts sent him by Valerius ; but he did not feel justified in delaying obedience to that officer's request, and so wrote at once two treatises, one an answer to these excerpts, for the benefit of Valerius, constituting the second book of his *On Marriage and Concupiscence;* and the other, a far more elaborate examination of the letters sent by Boniface, which bears the title, *Against Two Letters of the Pelagians.* The purpose of the second book of *On Marriage and Concupiscence*, Augustin himself states, in its introductory sentences, to be " to reply to the taunts of his adversaries with all the truthfulness and scriptural authority he could command." He begins (2) by identifying the source of the extracts forwarded to him by Valerius, with Julian's work against his first book, and then remarks upon the garbled form in which he is quoted in them (3–6), and passes on to state and refute Julian's charge that the catholics had turned Manicheans (7–9). At this point, the refutation of Julian begins in good earnest, and the method that he proposes to use is stated ; viz., to adduce the adverse statements, and refute them one by one (10). Beginning at the beginning, he quotes first the title of the paper sent him, which declares that it is directed against " those who condemn matrimony, and ascribe its fruit to the Devil " (11), which certainly, says Augustin, does not describe him or the catholics. The next twenty chapters (10–30), accordingly, following Julian's order, labour to prove that marriage is good, and ordained by God, but that its good includes *fecundity* indeed, but not *concupiscence*, which arose from sin, and contracts sin. It is next argued, that the doctrine of original sin does not imply an evil origin for man (31–51) ; and in the course of this argument, the following propositions are especially defended : that God makes offspring for good and bad alike, just as He sends the rain and sunshine on just and unjust (31–34) ; that God makes everything to be found in marriage except its *flaw*, concupiscence (35–40) ; that marriage is not the cause of original sin, but only the channel through which it is transmitted (41–47) ; and that to assert that evil cannot arise from what is good leaves us in the clutches of that very Manicheism which is so unjustly charged against the catholics — for, if evil be not eternal, what else was there from which it could arise but something good? (48–51). In concluding, Augustin recapitulates, and argues especially, that shameful concupiscence is of sin, and the author of sin, and was not in paradise (52–54) ; that children are made by God, and only marred by the Devil (55) ; that Julian, in admitting that Christ died for infants, admits that they need salvation (56) ; that what the Devil makes in children is not a substance, but an injury to a substance (57–58) ; and that to suppose that concupiscence existed in any form in paradise introduces incongruities in our conception of life in that abode of primeval bliss (59–60).

The long and important treatise, *Against Two Letters of the Pelagians*, consists of four books, the first of which replies to the letter sent to Rome, and the other three to that sent to Thessalonica. After a short introduction, in which he thanks Boniface for his kindness, and gives reasons why heretical writings should be answered (1–3), Augustin begins at once to rebut the calumnies which the letter before him brings against the catholics (4–28). These are seven in number : 1. That the catholics destroy free will ; to which Augustin replies that none are " forced into sin by the necessity of their flesh," but all sin by free will, though no man can have a rightous will save by God's grace, and that it is really the Pelagians that destroy free will by exaggerating it (4–8) ; 2. That Augustin declares that such marriage as now exists is not of God (9) ; 3. That sexual desire and intercourse are made a device of the Devil, which is sheer Manicheism (10–11) ; 4. That the Old-Testament saints are said to have died in sin (12) ; 5. That Paul and the other apostles are asserted to have been polluted by lust all their days ; Augustin's answer to which includes a running commentary on Rom. vii. 7 sq., in which (correcting his older exegesis) he shows that Paul is giving here a transcript of his own experience as a typical Christian (13–24) ; 6. That Christ is said not to have been free from sin (25) ; 7. That baptism does not give complete remission of sins, but leaves roots from which they may again grow ; to which Augustin replies that baptism does remit all sins, but leaves concupiscence, which, although not sin, is the source of sin (26–28). Next, the positive part of Julian's letter is taken up, and his profession of faith against the catholics examined (29–41). The seven affirmations that Julian makes here are designed as the obverse of the seven charges against the catholics. He believed : 1. That free will is in all by nature, and could not perish by Adam's sin (29) ; 2. That marriage, as now existent, was ordained by God (30) ; 3. That sexual impulse and virility are from God (31–35) ; 4. That men are God's work, and no one is forced to do good or evil unwillingly, but are assisted by grace to good, and incited by the Devil to evil (36–38) ; 5. That the saints of the Old Testament were perfected in righteousness here, and so passed into eternal life (39) ; 6. That the grace of Christ (ambiguously meant) is necessary for all, and all children — even those of baptized parents — are to be baptized (40) ; 7. And that baptism gives full cleansing from all sins ; to which Augustin pointedly asks, " What does it do for infants, then ? " (41). The book concludes with an answer to Julian's conclusion, in which he demands a general council, and charges the catholics with Manicheism.

The second, third, and fourth books deal with the letter to Rufus in a somewhat similar way, the second and third books being occupied with the calumnies brought against the catholics, and the fourth with the claims made by the Pelagians. The second begins by repelling the charge of Manicheism brought against the catholics (1–4), to which the pointed remark is added, that the Pelagians cannot hope to escape condemnation because they are willing to condemn another heresy ; and then defends (with less success) the Roman clergy against the charge of prevarication in their dealing with the Pelagians (5–8), in the course of which all that can be said in defence of Zosimus' wavering policy is said well and strongly. Next the charges against catholic teaching are taken up and answered (9–16), especially the two important accusations that they maintain fate under the name of grace (9–12), and that they make God an " accepter of persons " (13–16). Augustin's replies to these charges are in every way admirable. The charge of "fate " rests solely on the catholic denial that grace is given according to preceding merits ; but the Pelagians do not escape the same charge when they acknowledge that the " fates " of baptized and unbaptized infants do differ. It is, in truth, not a question of " fate," but of *gratuitous bounty ;* and " it is not the catholics that assert fate under the name of grace, but the Pelagians that choose to call divine grace by the name of ' fate ' " (12). As to " acceptance of persons," we must define what we mean by that. God certainly does not accept one's " person " above another's ; He does not give to one rather than to another because He sees something to please Him in one rather than another : quite the opposite. He gives of His bounty to one while giving all their due to all, as in the parable (Matt. xx. 9 sq.) To ask why He does this, is to ask in vain : the apostle answers by not answering (Rom. ix.) ; and before the dumb infants, who are yet made to differ, all objection to God is dumb. From this point, the book becomes an examination of the Pelagian doctrine of prevenient merit (17–23), concluding that God gives all by grace from the beginning to the end of every process of doing good. 1. He commands the good ; 2. He gives the desire to do it ; and, 3. He gives the power to do it : and all, of His gratuitous mercy. The third book continues the discussion of the calumnies of the Pelagians against the catholics, and enumerates and answers six of them : viz., that the catholics teach, 1. That the Old-Testament law was given, not to justify the obedient, but to serve as cause of greater sin (2–3) ; 2. That baptism does not give entire remission of sins, but the baptized are partly God's and partly the Devil's (4–5) ; 3. That the Holy Ghost did not assist virtue in the Old Testament (6–13) ; 4. That the Bible saints were not holy, but only less wicked than others (14–15) ; 5. That Christ was a sinner by necessity of His flesh (doubtless, Julian's inference from the doctrine of race-sin) (16) ; 6. That men will begin to fulfil God's commandments only after the resurrection (17–23). Augustin shows that at the basis of all these calumnies lies either misapprehension or misrepresentation ; and, in concluding the book, enumerates the three chief points in the

Pelagian heresy, with the five claims growing out of them, of which they most boasted, and then elucidates the mutual relations of the three parties, catholics, Pelagians, and Manicheans, with reference to these points, showing that the catholics stand asunder from both the others, and condemn both (24–27). This conclusion is really a preparation for the fourth book, which takes up these five Pelagian claims, and, after showing the catholic position on them all in brief (1–3), discusses them in turn (4–19) : viz., the praise of the creature (4–8), the praise of marriage (9), the praise of the law (10–11), the praise of free will (12–16), and the praise of the saints (17–18). At the end, Augustin calls on the Pelagians to cease to oppose the Manicheans, only to fall into as bad heresy as theirs (19) ; and then, in reply to their accusation that the catholics were proclaiming novel doctrine, he adduces the testimony of Cyprian and Ambrose, both of whom had received Pelagius' praise, on each of the three main points of Pelagianism (20–32),[1] and then closes with the declaration that the " impious and foolish doctrine," as they called it, of the catholics, is immemorial truth (33), and with a denial of the right of the Pelagians to ask for a general council to condemn them (34). All heresies do not need an ecumenical synod for their condemnation ; usually it is best to stamp them out locally, and not allow what may be confined to a corner to disturb the whole world.

These books were written late in 420, or early in 421, and Alypius appears to have conveyed them to Italy during the latter year. Before its close, Augustin, having obtained and read the whole of Julian's attack on the first book of his work *On Marriage and Concupiscence*, wrote out a complete answer to it,[2] — a task that he was all the more anxious to complete, on perceiving that the extracts sent by Valerius were not only all from the first book of Julian's treatise, but were somewhat altered in the extracting. The resulting work, *Against Julian*, one of the longest that he wrote in the whole course of the Pelagian controversy, shows its author at his best : according to Cardinal Noris's judgment, he appears in it "almost divine," and Augustin himself clearly set great store by it. In the first book of this noble treatise, after professing his continued love for Julian, "whom he was unable not to love, whatever he [Julian] should say against him " (35), he undertakes to show that in affixing the opprobrious name of Manicheans on those who assert original sin, Julian is incriminating many of the most famous fathers, both of the Latin and Greek Churches. In proof of this, he makes appropriate quotations from Irenæus, Cyprian, Reticius, Olympius, Hilary, Ambrose, Gregory Nazianzenus, Basil, John of Constantinople.[3] Then he argues, that, so far from the catholics falling into Manichean heresy, Julian plays, himself, into the hands of the Manicheans in their strife against the catholics, by many unguarded statements, such as, e.g., when he says that an evil thing cannot arise from what is good, that the work of the Devil cannot be suffered to be diffused by means of a work of God, that a root of evil cannot be placed within a gift of God, and the like. The second book advances to greater detail, and adduces the five great arguments which the Pelagians urged against the catholics, in order to test them by the voice of antiquity. These arguments are stated as follows (2) : " For you say, ' That we, by asserting original sin, affirm that the Devil is the maker of infants, condemn marriage, deny that all sins are remitted in baptism, accuse God of the guilt of sin, and produce despair of perfection.' You contend that all these are consequences, if we believe that infants are born bound by the sin of the first man, and are therefore under the Devil unless they are born again in Christ. For, ' It is the Devil that creates,' you say, ' if they are created from that wound which the Devil inflicted on the human nature that was made at first.' ' And marriage is condemned, you say, ' if it is to be believed to have something about it whence it produces those worthy of condemnation.' ' And all sins are not remitted in baptism,' you say, ' if there remains any evil in baptized couples whence evil offspring are produced.' ' And how is God,' you ask, ' not unjust, if He, while remitting their own sins to baptized persons, yet condemns their offspring,

---

[1] To wit: Cyprian's testimony on original sin (20–24), on gratuitous grace (25–26), on the imperfection of human righteousness (27–28), and Ambrose's testimony on original sin (29), on gratuitous grace (30), and on the imperfection of human righteousness (31).

[2] Compare *Epistle* 207, written probably in the latter half of 421.          [3] That is, Chrysostom.

inasmuch as, although it is created by Him, it yet ignorantly and involuntarily contracts the sins of others from those very parents to whom they are remitted?' 'Nor can men believe,' you add, 'that virtue — to which corruption is to be understood to be contrary — can be perfected, if they cannot believe that it can destroy the inbred vices, although, no doubt, these can scarcely be considered vices, since he does not sin, who is unable to be other than he was created.'" These arguments are then tested, one by one, by the authority of the earlier teachers who were appealed to in the first book, and shown to be condemned by them. The remaining four books follow Julian's four books, argument by argument, refuting him in detail. In the third book it is urged that although God is good, and made man good, and instituted marriage which is, therefore, good, nevertheless concupiscence is evil, and in it the flesh lusts against the spirit. Although chaste spouses use this evil well, continent believers do better in not using it at all. It is pointed out, how far all this is from the madness of the Manicheans, who dream of matter as essentially evil and co-eternal with God; and shown that evil concupiscence sprang from Adam's disobedience and, being transmitted to us, can be removed only by Christ. It is shown, also, that Julian himself confesses lust to be evil, inasmuch as he speaks of remedies against it, wishes it to be bridled, and speaks of the continent waging a glorious warfare. The fourth book follows the second book of Julian's work, and makes two chief contentions: that unbelievers have no true virtues, and that even the heathen recognize concupiscence as evil. It also argues that grace is not given according to merit, and yet is not to be confounded with fate; and explains the text that asserts that 'God wishes all men to be saved,' in the sense that 'all men' means 'all that are to be saved, since none are saved except by His will.[1] The fifth book, in like manner, follows Julian's third book, and treats of such subjects as these: that it is due to sin that any infants are lost; that shame arose in our first parents through sin; that sin can well be the punishment of preceding sin; that concupiscence is always evil, even in those who do not assent to it; that true marriage may exist without intercourse; that the "flesh" of Christ differs from the "sinful flesh" of other men; and the like. In the sixth book, Julian's fourth book is followed, and original sin is proved from the baptism of infants, the teaching of the apostles, and the rites of exorcism and exsufflation incorporated in the form of baptism. Then, by the help of the illustration drawn from the olive and the oleaster, it is explained how Christian parents can produce unregenerate offspring; and the originally voluntary character of sin is asserted, even though it now comes by inheritance.

After the completion of this important work, there succeeded a lull in the controversy, of some years duration; and the calm refutation of Pelagianism and exposition of Christian grace, which Augustin gave in his *Enchiridion*,[2] might well have seemed to him his closing word on this all-absorbing subject. But he had not yet given the world all he had in treasure for it, and we can rejoice in the chance that five or six years afterwards drew from him a renewed discussion of some of the more important aspects of the doctrine of grace. The circumstances which brought this about are sufficiently interesting in themselves, and open up to us an unwonted view into the monastic life of the times. There was an important monastery at Adrumetum, the metropolitan city of the province of Byzacium,[3] from which a monk named Florus went out on a journey of charity to his native country of Uzalis about 426. On the journey he met with Augustin's letter to Sixtus,[4] in which the doctrines of gratuitous and prevenient grace were expounded. He was much delighted with it, and, procuring a copy, sent it back to his monastery for the edification of his brethren, while he himself went on to Carthage. At the monastery, the letter created great disturbance: without the knowledge of the abbot, Valentinus, it was read aloud to the monks, many of whom were unskilled in theological questions; and some five or more were greatly offended, and declared that free will was destroyed by it. A secret strife arose among the brethren, some taking extreme grounds on both sides. Of all this, Valentinus remained ignorant until the return of Florus, who was attacked as the author of all the trouble, and who felt it his duty to inform the abbot of the state of affairs. Valentinus applied first to the bishop, Evodius, for such instruction as would make Augustin's letter clear to the most simple. Evodius replied, praising their zeal and deprecating their contentiousness, and explaining that Adam had full free will, but that it is now wounded and weak, and Christ's mission was as a physician to cure and recuperate it. "Let them read," is his prescription, "the words of God's elders. . . . And when they do not understand, let them not quickly reprehend, but pray to understand." This did not, however, cure the malecontents, and the holy presbyter Sabrinus was appealed to, and sent a book with clear interpretations. But neither was this satisfactory ; and Valentinus, at last, reluctantly consented that Augustin himself should be consulted, — fearing, he says, lest by making inquiries he should seem to waver about the truth. Two members of the community were consequently permitted to journey to Hippo, but they took with them no introduction and no commendation from their abbot. Augustin, nevertheless, received them without hesitation, as they bore themselves with too great simplicity to allow him to suspect them of deception. Now we get a glimpse of life in the great bishop's monastic home. The monks told their story, and were listened to with courtesy and instructed with patience ; and, as they were anxious to get home before Easter, they received a letter for Valentinus[1] in which Augustin briefly explains the nature of the misapprehension that had arisen, and points out that both grace and free will must be defended, and neither so exaggerated as to deny the other. The letter of Sixtus, he explains, was written against the Pelagians, who assert that grace is given according to merit, and briefly expounds the true doctrine of grace as necessarily gratuitous and therefore prevenient. When the monks were on the point of starting home, they were joined by a third companion from Adrumetum, and were led to prolong their visit. This gave him the opportunity he craved for their fuller instruction : he read with them and explained to them not only his letter to Sixtus, from which the strife had risen, but much of the chief literature of the Pelagian controversy,[2] copies of which also were made for them to take home with them ; and when they were ready to go, he sent by them another and longer letter to Valentinus, and placed in their hands a treatise composed for their especial use, which, moreover, he explained to them. This longer letter is essentially an exhortation " to turn aside neither to the right hand nor to the left," — neither to the left hand of the Pelagian error of upholding free will in such a manner as to deny grace, nor to the right hand of the equal error of so upholding grace as if we might yield ourselves to evil with impunity. Both grace and free will are to be proclaimed ; and it is true both that grace is not given to merits, and that we are to be judged at the last day according to our works. The treatise which Augustin composed for a fuller exposition of these doctrines is the important work *On Grace and Free Will.* After a brief introduction, explaining the occasion of his writing, and exhorting the monks to humility and teachableness before God's revelations (1), Augustin begins by asserting and proving the two propositions that the Scriptures clearly teach that man has free will (2–5), and, as clearly, the necessity of grace for doing any good (6–9). He then examines the passages which the Pelagians claim as teaching that we must first turn to God, before He visits us with His grace (10–11), and then undertakes to show that grace is not given to merit (12 sq.), appealing especially to Paul's teaching and example, and replying to the assertion that forgiveness is the only grace that is not given according to our merits (15–18), and to the query, "How can eternal life be both of grace and of reward?" (19–21). The nature of grace, what it is, is next explained (22 sq.). It is not the law, which gives only knowledge of sin (22–24), nor nature, which would render Christ's death needless (25), nor mere forgiveness of sins, as the Lord's Prayer (which should be read with Cyprian's comments on it) is enough to show (26). Nor will it do to say that it is given to the merit of a good will, thus distinguishing the good work which is of grace from the good will which precedes grace (27–30) ; for the Scrip-

---

[1] *Epistle* 214.     [2] *Epistle* 215, 2 sq.

tures oppose this, and our prayers for others prove that we expect God to be the *first mover*, as indeed both Scripture and experience prove that He is. It is next shown that both free will and grace are concerned in the heart's conversion (31–32), and that love is the spring of all good in man (33–40), which, however, we have only because God first loved us (38), and which is certainly greater than knowledge, although the Pelagians admit only the latter to be from God (40). God's sovereign government of men's wills is then proved from Scripture (41–43), and the wholly gratuitous character of grace is illustrated (44), while the only possible theodicy is found in the certainty that the Lord of all the earth will do right. For, though no one knows why He takes one and leaves another, we all know that He hardens judicially and saves graciously, — that He hardens none who do not deserve hardening, but none that He saves deserve to be saved (45). The treatise closes with an exhortation to its prayerful and repeated study (46).

The one request that Augustin made, on sending this work to Valentinus, was that Florus, through whom the controversy had arisen, should be sent to him, that he might converse with him and learn whether he had been misunderstood, or himself had misunderstood Augustin. In due time Florus arrived at Hippo, bringing a letter [1] from Valentinus which addresses Augustin as "Lord Pope" (*domine papa*), thanks him for his "sweet" and "healing" instruction, and introduces Florus as one whose true faith could be confided in. It is very clear, both from Valentinus' letter and from the hints that Augustin gives, that his loving dealing with the monks had borne admirable fruit: "none were cast down for the worse, some were built up for the better." [2] But it was reported to him that some one at the monastery had objected to the doctrine he had taught them, that "no man ought, then, to be rebuked for not keeping God's commandments; but only God should be besought that he might keep them." [3] In other words, it was said that if all good was, in the last resort, from God's grace, man ought not to be blamed for not doing what he could not do, but God ought to be besought to do for man what He alone could do: we ought, in a word, to apply to the source of power. This occasioned the composition of yet another treatise *On Rebuke and Grace*,[4] the object of which was to explain the relations of grace to human conduct, and especially to make it plain that the sovereignty of God's grace does not supersede our duty to ourselves or our fellow-men. It begins by thanking Valentinus for his letter and for sending Florus (whom Augustin finds well instructed in the truth), thanking God for the good effect of the previous book, and recommending its continued study, and then by briefly expounding the Catholic faith concerning grace, free-will, and the law (1–2). The general proposition that is defended is that the gratuitous sovereignty of God's grace does not supersede human means for obtaining and continuing it (3 sq.) This is shown by the apostle's example, who used all human means for the prosecution of his work, and yet confessed that it was "God that gave the increase" (3). Objections are then answered (4 sq.), — especially the great one that "it is not my fault if I do not do what I have not received grace for doing" (6); to which Augustin replies (7–10), that we deserve rebuke for our very unwillingness to be rebuked, that on the same reasoning the prescription of the law and the preaching of the gospel would be useless, that the apostle's example opposes such a position, and that our consciousness witnesses that we deserve rebuke for not persevering in the right way. From this point an important discussion arises, in this interest, of the gift of perseverance (11–19), and of God's election (20–24); the teaching being that no one is saved who does not persevere, and all that are predestinated or "called according to the purpose" (Augustin's phrase for what we should call "effectual calling") will persevere, and yet that we co-operate by our will in all good deeds, and deserve rebuke if we do not. Whether Adam received the gift of perseverance, and, in general, the difference between the grace given to him, which was that grace by which he could stand) and

---

[1] *Epistle* 216.  [2] *On Rebuke and Grace*, 1.
[3] *Retractions*, ii. 67. Compare *On Rebuke and Grace*, 5 sq.
[4] On the importance of this treatise for Augustin's doctrine of predestination, see Wiggers' *Augustinianism and Pelagianism*, E. T. p. 236, where a sketch of the history of this doctrine in Augustin's writings may be found.

that now given to God's children (which is that grace by which we are actually made to stand), are next discussed (26–38), with the result of showing the superior greatness of the gifts of grace now to those given before the fall. The necessity of God's mercy at all times, and our constant dependence on it, are next vigorously asserted (39–42) ; even in the day of judgment, if we are not judged "with mercy" we cannot be saved (41). The treatise is brought to an end by a concluding application of the whole discussion to the special matter in hand, *rebuke* (43–49). Seeing that rebuke is one of God's means of working out his gracious purposes, it cannot be inconsistent with the sovereignty of that grace ; for, of course, God predestinates the means with the end (43). Nor can we know, in our ignorance, whether our rebuke is, in any particular case, to be the means of amendment or the ground of greater condemnation. How dare we, then, withhold it? Let it be, however, graduated to the fault, and let us always remember its purpose (46–48). Above all, let us not dare hold it back, lest we hold back from our brother the means of his recovery, and, as well, disobey the command of God (49).

It was not long afterwards (about 427) when Augustin was called upon to attempt to reclaim a Carthaginian brother, Vitalis by name, who had been brought to trial on the charge of teaching that the beginning of faith was not the gift of God, but the act of man's own free will (*ex propria voluntatis*). This was essentially the semi-Pelagian position which was subsequently to make so large a figure in history ; and Augustin treats it now as necessarily implying the basal idea of Pelagianism. In the important letter which he sent to Vitalis,[1] he first argues that his position is inconsistent with the prayers of the church. He, Augustin, prays that Vitalis may come to the true faith ; but does not this prayer ascribe the origination of right faith to God? The Church so prays for all men : the priest at the altar exhorts the people to pray God for unbelievers, that He may convert them to the faith ; for catechumens, that He may breathe into them a desire for regeneration ; for the faithful, that by His aid they may persevere in what they have begun : will Vitalis refuse to obey these exhortations, because, forsooth, faith is of free will and not of God's gift? Nay, will a Carthaginian scholar array himself against Cyprian's exposition of the Lord's Prayer? for he certainly teaches that we are to ask of God what Vitalis says is to be had of ourselves. We may go farther : it is not Cyprian, but Paul, who says, "Let us pray to God that we do no evil" (2 Cor. xiii. 7) ; it is the Psalmist who says, "The steps of man are directed by God" (Ps. xxxvi. 23). "If we wish to defend free will, let us not strive against that by which it is made free. For he who strives against grace, by which the will is made free for refusing evil and doing good, wishes his will to remain captive. Tell us, I beg you, how the apostle can say, 'We give thanks to the Father who made us fit to have our lot with the saints in light, who delivered us from the power of darkness, and translated us into the kingdom of the Son of His love' (Col. i. 12, 13), if not He, but itself, frees our choice? It is, then, a false rendering of thanks to God, as if He does what He does not do ; and he has erred who has said that 'He makes us fit, etc.' 'The grace of God,' therefore, does not consist in the nature of free-will, and in law and teaching, as the Pelagian perversity dreams ; but it is given for each single act by His will, concerning whom it is written," — quoting Ps. lxvii. 10. About the middle of the letter, Augustin lays down twelve propositions against the Pelagians, which are important as communicating to us what he thought, at the end of the controversy, were the chief points in dispute. "Since, therefore," he writes, "we are catholic Christians : 1. We know that new-born children have not yet done anything in their own lives, good or evil, neither have they come into the miseries of this life according to the deserts of some previous life, which none of them can have had in their own persons ; and yet, because they are born carnally after Adam, they contract the contagion of ancient death, by the first birth, and are not freed from the punishment of eternal death (which is contracted by a just condemnation, passing over from one to all), except they are by grace born again in Christ. 2. We know that the grace of God is

---

[1] *Epistle* 217.

given neither to children nor to adults according to our deserts. 3. We know that it is given to adults for each several act. 4. We know that it is not given to all men; and to those to whom it is given, it is not only not given according to the merits of works, but it is not even given to them according to the merits of their will; and this is especially apparent in children. 5. We know that to those to whom it is given, it is given by the gratuitous mercy of God. 6. We know that to those to whom it is not given, it is not given by the just judgment of God. 7. We know that we shall all stand before the tribunal of Christ, and each shall receive according to what he has done through the body, — not according to what he would have done, had he lived longer, — whether good or evil. 8. We know that even children are to receive according to what they have done through the body, whether good or evil. But according to what "they have done" not by their own act, but by the act of those by whose responses for them they are said both to renounce the Devil and to believe in God, wherefore they are counted among the number of the faithful, and have part in the statement of the Lord when He says, "Whosoever shall believe and be baptized, shall be saved." Therefore also, to those who do not receive this sacrament, belongs what follows, "But whosoever shall not have believed, shall be damned" (Mark xvi. 16). Whence these too, as I have said, if they die in that early age, are judged, of course, according to what they have done through the body, i.e., in the time in which they were in the body, when they believe or do not believe by the heart and mouth of their sponsors, when they are baptized or not baptized, when they eat or do not eat the flesh of Christ, when they drink or do not drink His blood, — according to those things, then, which they have done through the body, not according to those which, had they lived longer, they would have done. 9. We know that blessed are the dead that die in the Lord; and that what they would have done had they lived longer, is not imputed to them. 10. We know that those that believe, with their own heart, in the Lord, do so by their own free will and choice. 11. We know that we who already believe act with right faith towards those who do not wish to believe, when we pray to God that they may wish it. 12. We know that for those who have believed out of this number, we both ought and are rightly and truly accustomed to return thanks to God, as for his benefits." Certainly such a body of propositions commends their author to us as Christian both in head and heart: they are admirable in every respect; and even in the matter of the salvation of infants, where he had not yet seen the light of truth, he expresses himself in a way as engaging in its hearty faith in God's goodness as it is honorable in its loyalty to what he believed to be truth and justice. Here his doctrine of the Church ran athwart and clouded his view of the reach of grace; but we seem to see between the lines the promise of the brighter dawn of truth that was yet to come. The rest of the epistle is occupied with an exposition and commendation of these propositions, which ranks with the richest passages of the anti-Pelagian writings, and which breathes everywhere a yearning for his correspondent which we cannot help hoping proved salutary to his faith.

It is not without significance, that the error of Vitalis took a semi-Pelagian form. Pure Pelagianism was by this time no longer a living issue. Augustin was himself, no doubt, not yet done with it. The second book of his treatise *On Marriage and Concupiscence*, which seems to have been taken to Italy by Alypius, in 421, received at once the attention of Julian, and was elaborately answered by him, during that same year, in eight books addressed to Florus. But Julian was now in Cilicia, and his book was slow in working its way westward. It was found at Rome by Alypius, apparently in 427 or 428, and he at once set about transcribing it for his friend's use. An opportunity arising to send it to Africa before it was finished, he forwarded to Augustin the five books that were ready, with an urgent request that they should receive his immediate attention, and a promise to send the other three as soon as possible. Augustin gives an account of his progress in his reply to them in a letter written to Quodvultdeus, apparently in 428.[1] This deacon was urging Augustin to give the Church a succinct account of all heresies;

---

[1] *Epistle* 224.

and Augustin excuses himself from immediately undertaking that task by the press of work on his hands. He was writing his *Retractations*, and had already finished two books of them, in which he had dealt with two hundred and thirty-two works. His letters and homilies remained, and he had given the necessary reading to many of the letters. Also, he tells his correspondent, he was engaged on a reply to the eight books of Julian's new work. Working night and day, he had already completed his response to the first three of Julian's books, and had begun on the fourth while still expecting the arrival of the last three which Alypius had promised to send. If he had completed the answer to the five books of Julian which he already had in hand, before the other three reached him, he might begin the work which Quodvultdeus so earnestly desired him to undertake. In due time, whatever may have been the trials and labours that needed first to be met, the desired treatise *On Heresies* was written (about 428), and the eighty-eighth chapter of it gives us a welcome compressed account of the Pelagian heresy, which may be accepted as the obverse of the account of catholic truth given in the letter to Vitalis.[1] But the composition of this work was not the only interruption which postponed the completion of the second elaborate work against Julian. It was in the providence of God that the life of this great leader in the battle for grace should be prolonged until he could deal with semi-Pelagianism also. Information as to the rise of this new form of the heresy at Marseilles and elsewhere in Southern Gaul was conveyed to Augustin along with entreaties, that, as "faith's great patron," he would give his aid towards meeting it, by two laymen with whom he had already had correspondence,—Prosper and Hilary.[2] They pointed out[3] the difference between the new party and thorough-going Pelagianism; but, at the same time, the essentially Pelagianizing character of its formative elements. Its representatives were ready, as a rule, to admit that all men were lost in Adam, and no one could recover himself by his own free will, but all needed God's grace for salvation. But they objected to the doctrines of prevenient and of irresistible grace; and asserted that man could initiate the process of salvation by turning first to God, that all men could resist God's grace, and no grace could be given which they could not reject, and especially they denied that the gifts

---

[1] The account given of Pelagianism is as follows: "They are in such degree enemies of the grace of God, by which we have been predestinated into the adoption of sons by Jesus Christ unto Himself (Eph. i. 5), and by which we are delivered from the power of darkness so as to believe in Him, and be translated into His kingdom (Col. i. 13) —'wherefore He says, 'No man comes to Me, except it be given him of My Father' (John vi. 66) — and by which love is shed abroad in our hearts (Rom. v. 5), so that faith may work by love: that they believe that man is able, without it, to keep all the Divine commandments, — whereas, if this were true, it would clearly be an empty thing that the Lord said, 'Without Me ye can do nothing' (John xv. 5). When Pelagius was at length accused by the brethren, because he attributed nothing to the assistance of God's grace towards the keeping of His commandments, he yielded to their rebuke, so far as not to place this grace above free will, but with faithless cunning to subordinate it, saying that it was given to men for this purpose; viz., that they might be able more easily to fulfil by grace, what they were commanded to do by free will. By saying, 'that they might be able more easily,' he, of course, wished it to be believed that, although with more difficulty, nevertheless men were able without divine grace to perform the divine commands. But that grace of God, without which we can do nothing good, they say does not exist except in free will, which without any preceding merits our nature received from Him; and that He adds His aid only in that by His law and teaching we may learn what we ought to do, but not in that by the gift of His Spirit we may do what we have learned ought to be done. Accordingly, they confess that knowledge by which ignorance is banished is divinely given to us, but deny that love by which we may live a pious life s given; so that, forsooth, while knowledge, which, without love, puffeth up, is the gift of God, love itself, which edifieth so that knowledge nay not puff up, is not the gift of God (1 Cor. viii. 11). They also destroy the prayers which the Church offers, whether for those that are unbelieving and resisting God's teaching, that they may be converted to God; or for the faithful, that faith may be increased in them, and .hey may persevere in it. For they contend that men do not receive these things from Him, but have them from ourselves, saying, that the grace of God, by which we are freed from impiety, is given according to our merits. Pelagius was compelled, no doubt, to condemn this by his fear of being condemned by the episcopal judgment in Palestine; but he is found to teach it still in his later writings. They also advanced so far as to say that the life of the righteous in this world is without sin, and the Church of Christ is perfected by them in this mortality, to the point of being entirely without spot or wrinkle (Eph. v. 27); as if it were not the Church of Christ, that, in the whole world, cries to God, 'Forgive us our debts.' They also deny that children, who are carnally born after Adam, contract the contagion of ancient death from their first birth. For they assert that they are born so without any bond of original sin, that there is absolutely nothing that ought to be remitted to them in the second birth, yet they are to be baptized; but for this reason, that, adopted in regeneration, they may be admitted to the kingdom of God, and thus be translated from good into better, — not that they may be washed by that renovation from any evil of the old bond. For although they be not baptized, they promise to them, outside the kingdom of God indeed, but nevertheless, a certain eternal and blessed life of their own. They also say that Adam himself, even had he not sinned, would have died in the body, and that this death would not have come as a desert to a fault, but as a condition of nature. Certain other things also are objected to them, but these are the chief, and also either all, or nearly all, the others may be understood to depend on these "

[2] Compare *Epistles* 225, 1, and 156. It is, of course, not certain that this is the same Hilary that wrote to Augustin from Sicily, but it seems probable.

[3] In *Letters* 225 and 226.

of grace came irrespective of merits, actual or foreseen. They said that what Augustin taught as to the calling of God's elect according to His own purpose was tantamount to fatalism, was contrary to the teaching of the fathers and the true Church doctrine, and, even if true, should not be preached, because of its tendency to drive men into indifference or despair. Hence, Prosper especially desired Augustin to point out the dangerous nature of these views, and to show that prevenient and co-operating grace is not inconsistent with free will, that God's predestination is not founded on foresight of receptivity in its objects, and that the doctrines of grace may be preached without danger to souls.

Augustin's answer to these appeals was a work in two books, *On the Predestination of the Saints*, the second book of which is usually known under the separate title of *The Gift of Perseverance.* The former book begins with a careful discrimination of the position of his new opponents : they have made a right beginning in that they believe in original sin, and acknowledge that none are saved from it save by Christ, and that God's grace leads men's wills, and without grace no one can suffice for good deeds. These things will furnish a good starting-point for their progress to an acceptance of predestination also (1–2). The first question that needs discussion in such circumstances is, whether God gives the very beginnings of faith (3 sq.) ; since they admit that what Augustin had previously urged sufficed to prove that faith was the gift of God so far as that the increase of faith was given by Him, but not so far but that the beginning of faith may be understood to be man's, to which, then, God adds all other gifts (compare 43). Augustin insists that this is no other than the Pelagian assertion of grace according to merit (3), is opposed to Scripture (4–5), and begets arrogant boasting in ourselves (6). He replies to the objection that he had himself once held this view, by confessing it, and explaining that he was converted from it by 1 Cor. iv. 7, as applied by Cyprian (7–8), and expounds that verse as containing in its narrow compass a sufficient answer to the present theories (9–11). He answers, further, the objection that the apostle distinguishes faith from works, and works alone are meant in such passages, by pointing to John vi. 28, and similar statements in Paul (12–16). Then he answers the objection that he himself had previously taught that God acted on foresight of faith, by showing that he was misunderstood (17–18). He next shows that no objection lies against predestination that does not lie with equal force against grace (19–22), — since predestination is nothing but God's foreknowledge of and preparation for grace, and all questions of sovereignty and the like belong to grace. Did God not know to whom he was going to give faith (19)? or did he promise the results of faith, works, without promising the faith without which, as going before, the works were impossible? Would not this place God's fulfilment of his promise out of His power, and make it depend on man (20)? Why are men more willing to trust in their weakness than in God's strength? do they count God's promises more uncertain than their own performance (22)? He next proves the sovereignty of grace, and of predestination, which is but the preparation for grace, by the striking examples of infants, and, above all, of the human nature of Christ (23–31), and then speaks of the twofold calling, one external and one " according to purpose," — the latter of which is efficacious and sovereign (32–37). In closing, the semi-Pelagian position is carefully defined and refuted as opposed, alike with the grosser Pelagianism, to the Scriptures of both Testaments (38–42).

The purpose of the second book, which has come down to us under the separate title of *On the Gift of Perseverance*, is to show that that perseverance which endures to the end is as much of God as the beginning of faith, and that no man who has been " called according to God's purpose," and has received this gift, can fall from grace and be lost. The first half of the treatise is devoted to this theme (1–33). It begins by distinguishing between temporary perseverance, which endures for a time, and that which continues to the end (1), and affirms that the latter is certainly a gift of God's grace, and is, therefore, asked from God : which would otherwise be but a mocking petition (2–3). This, the Lord's Prayer itself might teach us, as under Cyprian's exposition it does teach us, — each petition being capable of being read as a prayer for perseverance (4–9). Of course, moreover, it cannot be lost, otherwise it would not be " to the end." If man forsakes God, of course it is he that does it, and he is doubtless under continual temptation to do so; but if he abides with God, it is God who secures that, and God is equally able to *keep* one when drawn to Him, as He is to *draw* him to Him (10–15). He argues anew at this point, that grace is not according to merit, but always in mercy; and explains and illustrates the unsearchable ways of God in His sovereign but merciful dealing with men (16–25), and closes this part of the treatise by a defence of himself against adverse quotations from his early work on *Free Will*, which he has already corrected in his *Retractations*. The second half of the book discusses the objections that were being urged against the preaching of predestination (34–62), as if it opposed and enervated the preaching of the Gospel. He replies that Paul and the apostles, and Cyprian and the fathers, preached both together; that the same objections will lie against the preaching of God's foreknowledge and grace itself, and, indeed, against preaching any of the virtues, as, e.g., obedience, while declaring them God's gifts. He meets the objections in detail, and shows that such preaching is food to the soul, and must not be withheld from men; but explains that it must be given gently, wisely, and prayerfully. The whole treatise ends with an appeal to the prayers of the Church as testifying that all good is from God (63–65), and to the great example of unmerited grace and sovereign predestination in the choice of one human nature without preceding merit, to be united in one person with the Eternal Word, — an illustration of his theme of the gratuitous grace of God which he is never tired of adducing (66–67).

These books were written in 428–429, and after their completion the unfinished work against Julian was resumed. Alypius had sent the remaining three books, and Augustin slowly toiled on to the end of his reply to the sixth book. But he was to be interrupted once more, and this time by the most serious of all interruptions. On the 28th of August, 430, with the Vandals thundering at the gates of Hippo, full of good works and of faith, he turned his face away from the strifes — whether theological or secular — of earth, and entered into rest with the Lord whom he loved. The last work against Julian was already one of the most considerable in size of all his books; but it was never finished, and retains until to-day the significant title of *The Unfinished Work*. Augustin had hesitated to undertake this work, because he found Julian's arguments too silly either to deserve refutation, or to afford occasion for really edifying discourse. And certainly the result falls below Augustin's usual level, though this is not due, as is so often said, to failing powers and great age; for nothing that he wrote surpasses in mellow beauty and chastened strength the two books, *On the Predestination of the Saints*, which were written after four books of this work were completed. The plan of the work is to state Julian's arguments in his own words, and follow it with his remarks; thus giving it something of the form of a dialogue. It follows Julian's work, book by book. The first book states and answers certain calumnies which Julian had brought against Augustin and the catholic faith on the ground of their confession of original sin. Julian had argued, that, since God is just, He cannot impute another's sins to inno- cent infants; since sin is nothing but evil will, there can be no sin in infants who are not yet in the use of their will; and, since the freedom of will that is given to man consists in the capacity of both sinning and not sinning, free will is denied to those who attribute sin to nature. Augustin replies to these arguments, and answers certain objections that are made to his work *On Mar- riage and Concupiscence*, and then corrects Julian's false explanations of certain Scriptures from John viii., Rom. vi., vii., and 2 Timothy. The second book is a discussion of Rom. v. 12, which Julian had tried, like the other Pelagians, to explain by the "imitation" of Adam's bad example. The third book examines the abuse by Julian of certain Old-Testament passages — in Deut. xxiv., 2 Kings xiv., Ezek. xviii. — in his effort to show that God does not impute the father's sins to the children; as well as his similar abuse of Heb. xi. The charge of Manicheism, which was so repetitiously brought by Julian against the catholics, is then examined and refuted. The fourth book treats of Julian's strictures on Augustin's *On Marriage and Concupiscence* ii. 4–11, and proves from 1 John ii. 16 that concupiscence is evil, and not the work of God, but of the Devil. He argues that the shame that accompanies it is due to its sinfulness, and that there was none of it in Christ; also, that infants are born obnoxious to the first sin, and proves the corruption of their origin from Wisd. x. 10, 11. The fifth book defends *On Marriage and Concupiscence* ii. 12 sq., and argues that a sound nature could not have shame on account of its members, and the need of regeneration for what is generated by means of shameful concupiscence. Then Julian's abuse of 1 Cor. xv., Rom. v., Matt. vii. 17 and 33, with reference to *On Marriage and Concupiscence* ii. 14, 20, 26, is discussed; and then the origin of evil, and God's treatment of evil in the world. The sixth book traverses Julian's strictures on *On Marriage and Concupiscence* ii. 34 sq., and argues that human nature was changed for the worse by the sin of Adam, and thus was made not only sinful, but the source of sinners; and that the forces of free will by which man could at first do rightly if he wished, and refrain from sin if he chose, were lost by Adam's sin. He attacks Julian's definition of free will as "the capacity for sinning and not sinning" (*possibilitas peccandi et non peccandi*); and proves that the evils of this life are the punishment of sin, — including, first of all, physical death. At the end, he treats of 1 Cor. xv. 22.

Although the great preacher of grace was taken away by death before the completion of this book, yet his work was not left incomplete. In the course of the next year (431) the Œcumenical Council of Ephesus condemned Pelagianism for the whole world; and an elaborate treatise against the pure Pelagianism of Julian was already in 430 an anachronism. Semi-Pelagianism was yet to run its course, and to work its way so into the heart of a corrupt church as not to be easily displaced; but Pelagianism was to die with the first generation of its advocates. As we look back now through the almost millennium and a half of years that has intervened since Augustin lived and wrote, it is to his *Predestination of the Saints,* — a completed, and well-completed, treatise, — and not to *The Unfinished Work,* that we look as the crown and completion of his labours for grace.

### IV. THE THEOLOGY OF GRACE.

The theology which Augustin opposed, in his anti-Pelagian writings, to the errors of Pelagianism, is, shortly, the theology of grace. Its roots were planted deeply in his own experience, and in the teachings of Scripture, especially of that apostle whom he delights to call "the great preacher of grace," and to follow whom, in his measure, was his greatest desire. The grace of God in Jesus Christ, conveyed to us by the Holy Spirit and evidenced by the love that He sheds abroad in our hearts, is the centre around which this whole side [1] of His system revolves, and the germ out of which it grows. He was the more able to make it thus central because of the harmony of this view of salvation with the general principle of his whole theology, which was theocentric and revolved around his conception of God as the immanent and vital spirit in whom all things live and move and have their being. [2] In like manner, God is the absolute good, and all good is either Himself or from Him; and only as God makes us good, are we able to do anything good.

The *necessity of grace* to man, Augustin argued from the condition of the race as partakers of Adam's sin. God created man upright, and endowed him with human faculties, including free

---

[1] This is a necessary limitation, for there is another side — a churchly side — of Augustin's theology, which was only laid alongside of, and artificially combined with, his theology of grace. This was the *traditional* element in his teaching, but was far from the determining or formative element. As Thomasius truly points out (*Dogmengeschichte*, i. 495), both his experience and the Scriptures stood with him above tradition.

[2] It is only one of the strange assertions in Professor Allen's *Continuity of Christian Thought*, that he makes "the Augustinian theology rest upon the transcendence of Deity as its controlling principle" (p. 3), which is identified with "a tacit assumption of deism" (p. 171), and explained to include a "localization of God as a physical essence in the infinite remoteness," "separated from the world by infinite reaches of space." As a matter of mere fact, Augustin's conception of God was that of an immanent Spirit, and his tendency was consequently distinctly towards a pantheistic rather than a deistic view of His relation to His creatures. Nor is this true only "at a certain stage of his career" (p. 6), which is but Professor Allen's attempt to reconcile fact with his theory, but of his whole life and all his teaching. He, no doubt, did not so teach the Divine immanence as to make God the author of the *form* as well as the *matter* of all acts of His creatures, or to render it impossible for His creatures to turn from Him; this would be to pass the limits that separate the conception of Christian immanence from pure pantheism, and to make God the author of sin, and all His creatures but manifestations of Himself.

will ;[1] and gave to him freely that grace by which he was able to retain his uprightness.[2] Being thus put on probation,[3] with divine aid to enable him to stand if he chose, Adam used his free choice for sinning, and involved his whole race in his fall.[3] It was on account of this sin that he died physically and spiritually, and this double death passes over from him to us.[4] That all his descendants by ordinary generation are partakers in Adam's guilt and condemnation, Augustin is sure from the teachings of Scripture ; and this is the fact of original sin, from which no one generated from Adam is free, and from which no one is freed save as regenerated in Christ.[5] But how we are made partakers of it, he is less certain : sometimes he speaks as if it came by some mysterious unity of the race, so that we were all personally present in the individual Adam, and thus the whole race was the one man that sinned ;[6] sometimes he speaks more in the sense of modern realists, as if Adam's sin corrupted the nature, and the nature now corrupts those to whom it is communicated ;[7] sometimes he speaks as if it were due to simple heredity ;[8] sometimes, again, as if it depended on the presence of shameful concupiscence in the act of procreation, so that the propagation of guilt depends on the propagation of offspring by means of concupiscence.[9] However transmitted, it is yet a fact that sin is propagated, and all mankind became sinners in Adam. The result of this is that we have lost the divine image, though not in such a sense that no lineaments of it remain to us ;[10] and, the sinning soul making the flesh corruptible, our whole nature is corrupted, and we are unable to do anything of ourselves truly good.[11] This includes, of course, an injury to our will. Augustin, writing for the popular eye, treats this subject in popular language. But it is clear that he distinguished, in his thinking, between will as a faculty and will in a broader sense. As a mere faculty, will is and always remains an indifferent thing,[12] — after the fall, as before it, continuing poised in indifferency, and ready, like a weathercock, to be turned whithersoever the breeze that blows from the heart ("will," in the broader sense) may direct.[13] It is not the faculty of willing, but the man who makes use of that faculty, that has suffered change from the fall. In paradise man stood in full ability : he had the *posse non peccare*, but not yet the *non posse peccare ;*[14] that is, he was endowed with a capacity for either part, and possessed the grace of God by which he was able to stand if he would, but also the power of free will by which he might fall if he would. By his fall he has suffered a change, is corrupt, and under the power of Satan ; his will (in the broader sense) is now injured, wounded, diseased, enslaved, — although the faculty of will (in the narrow sense) remains indifferent.[12] Augustin's criticism of Pelagius' discrimination[15] of "capacity" (*possibilitas, posse*), "will" (*voluntas, velle*), and "act" (*actio, esse*), does not turn on the discrimination itself, but on the incongruity of placing the *power, ability* in the mere capacity or possibility, rather than in the living agent who "wills" and "acts." He himself adopts an essentially similar distribution, with only this correction ;[16] and thus keeps the faculty of will indifferent, but places the power of using it in the active agent, man. According, then, to the character of this *man*, will the use of the free will be. If the man be holy he will make a holy use of it, and if he be corrupt he will make a sinful use of it : if he be essentially holy, he cannot (like God Himself) make a sinful use of his will ; and if he be enslaved to sin, he cannot make a good use of it. The last is the present condition of men by nature. They have free will ;[17] the faculty by which they act remains in indifferency, and they are allowed to use it just as they choose : but such as they cannot desire and therefore cannot choose anything but evil ;[18] and therefore they, and therefore their choice, and therefore their willing, is always

---

[1] *On Rebuke and Grace*, 27, 28.  [2] *On Rebuke and Grace*, 29, 31 sq.  [3] *On Rebuke and Grace*, 28.
[4] *On the City of God*, xiii. 2, 12, 14; *On the Trinity*, iv. 13.  [5] *On the Merits and Remission of Sins*, i. 15, and often.
[6] *Against Two Letters of the Pelagians*, iv. 7; *On the Merits and Forgiveness of Sins*, iii. 14, 15.
[7] *On Marriage and Concupiscence*, ii. 57; *On the City of God*, xiv. 1.  [8] *Against Two Letters of the Pelagians*, iv. 7.
[9] *On Original Sin*, 42.  [10] *Retractations*, ii. 24.
[11] *Against Julian*, iv. 3, 25, 26. Compare Thomasius' *Dogmengeschichte*, i. 501 and 507.
[12] *On the Spirit and Letter*, 58.  [13] *On the Merits and Forgiveness of Sins*, ii. 30.  [14] *On Rebuke and Grace*, 11.
[15] *On the Grace of Christ*, 4 sq.  [16] *On the Predestination of the Saints*, 10.
[17] *Against Two Letters of the Pelagians*, i. 5. *Epistle* 215, 4 and often.
[18] *Against Two Letters of the Pelagians*, i. 7. Compare i. 5, 6.

evil and never good. They are thus the slaves of sin, which they obey; and while their free will avails for sinning, it does not avail for doing any good unless they be first freed by the grace of God. It is undeniable that this view is in consonance with modern psychology: let us once conceive of "the will" as simply the whole man in the attitude of willing, and it is immediately evident, that, however abstractly free the "will" is, it is conditioned and enslaved in all its action by the character of the willing agent: a bad man does not cease to be bad in the act of willing, and a good man remains good even in his acts of choice.

*In its nature,* grace is assistance, help from God; and all divine aid may be included under the term, — as well what may be called natural, as what may be called spiritual, aid.[1] Spiritual grace includes, no doubt, all external help that God gives man for working out his salvation, such as the law, the preaching of the gospel, the example of Christ, by which we may learn the right way; it includes also forgiveness of sins, by which we are freed from the guilt already incurred; but above all it includes that help which God gives by His Holy Spirit, working within, not without, by which man is enabled to choose and to do what he sees, by the teachings of the law, or by the gospel, or by the natural conscience, to be right.[2] Within this aid are included all those spiritual exercises which we call regeneration, justification, perseverance to the end, — in a word, all the divine assistance by which, in being made Christians, we are made to differ from other men. Augustin is fond of representing this grace as in essence the writing of God's law (or of God's will) on our hearts, so that it appears hereafter as our own desire and wish; and even more prevalently as the shedding abroad of love in our hearts by the Holy Ghost, given to us in Christ Jesus; therefore, as a change of disposition, by which we come to love and freely choose, in co-operation with God's aid, just the things which hitherto we have been unable to choose because in bondage to sin. Grace, thus, does not make void free will:[3] it acts through free will, and acts upon it only by liberating it from its bondage to sin, i.e., by liberating the agent that uses the free will, so that he is no longer enslaved by his fleshly lusts, and is enabled to make use of his free will in choosing the good; and thus it is only by grace that free will is enabled to act in good part. But just because grace changes the disposition, and so enables man, hitherto enslaved to sin, for the first time to desire and use his free will for good, it lies in the very nature of the case that it is *prevenient.*[4] Also, as the very name imports, it is necessarily *gratuitous;*[5] since man is enslaved to sin until it is given, all the merits that he can have prior to it are bad merits, and deserve punishment, not gifts of favour. When, then, it is asked, *on the ground of what,* grace is given, it can only be answered, "on the ground of God's infinite mercy and undeserved favour."[6] There is nothing in man to merit it, and it first gives merit of good to man. All men alike deserve death, and all that comes to them in the way of blessing is necessarily of God's free and unmerited favour. This is equally true of all grace. It is pre-eminently clear of that grace which gives faith, the root of all other graces, which is given of God, not to merits of good-will or incipient turning to Him, but of His sovereign good pleasure.[7] But equally with faith, it is true of all other divine gifts: we may, indeed, speak of "merits of good" as succeeding faith; but as all these merits find their root in faith, they are but "grace on grace," and men need God's mercy always, throughout this life, and even on the judgment day itself, when, if they are judged without mercy, they must be condemned.[8] If we ask, then, why God gives grace, we can only answer that it is of His unspeakable mercy; and if we ask why He gives it to one rather than to another, what can we answer but that it is of His will? The *sovereignty* of grace results from its very gratuitousness:[9] where none deserve it, it can be given only of the sovereign good pleasure of the great Giver, — and this is necessarily inscrutable, but cannot be unjust. We can faintly perceive, indeed, some reasons why God may be supposed not

---

[1] *Sermon 26.*  [2] *On Nature and Grace,* 62. *On the Grace of Christ,* 13. *On Rebuke and Grace,* 2 sq.
[3] *On the Spirit and Letter,* 52; *On Grace and Free Will,* 1 sq.   [4] *On the Spirit and Letter,* 60, and often.
[5] *On Nature and Grace,* 4, and often.   [6] *On the Grace of Christ,* 27, and often.
[7] *On the Grace of Christ,* 34, and often.   [8] *On Grace and Free Will,* 21.   [9] *On Grace and Free Will,* 30, and often.

to have chosen to give His saving grace to all,[1] or even to the most;[2] but we cannot understand why He has chosen to give it to just the individuals to whom He has given it, and to withhold it from just those from whom He has withheld it. Here we are driven to the apostle's cry, " Oh the depth of the riches both of the mercy and the justice of God !"[3]

The *effects of grace* are according to its nature. Taken as a whole, it is the recreative principle sent forth from God for the recovery of man from his slavery to sin, and for his reformation in the divine image. Considered as to the time of its giving, it is either *operating* or *co-operating* grace, i.e., either the grace that first enables the will to choose the good, or the grace that co-operates with the already enabled will to do the good ; and it is, therefore, also called either *prevenient* or *subsequent* grace.[4] It is not to be conceived of as a series of disconnected divine gifts, but as a constant efflux from God ; but we may look upon it in the various steps of its operation in men, as bringing forgiveness of sins, faith, which is the beginning of all good, love to God, progressive power of good working, and perseverance to the end.[5] In any case, and in all its operations alike, just because it is power from on high and the living spring of a new and re-created life, it is *irresistible* and *indefectible*.[6] Those on whom the Lord bestows the gift of faith working from within, not from without, of course, have faith, and cannot help believing. Those to whom perseverance to the end is given must persevere to the end. It is not to be objected to this, that many seem to begin well who do not persevere : this also is of God, who has in such cases given great blessings indeed, but not *this* blessing, of perseverance to the end. Whatever of good men have, that God has given ; and what they have not, why, of course, God has not given it. Nor can it be objected, that this leaves all uncertain : it is only unknown to us, but this is not uncertainty ; we cannot know that we are to have any gift which God sovereignly gives, of course, until it is given, and we therefore cannot know that we have perseverance unto the end until we actually persevere to the end;[7] but who would call what God does, and knows He is to do, uncertain, and what man is to do certain? Nor will it do to say that thus nothing is left for us to do : no doubt, all things are in God's hands, and we should praise God that this is so, but we must co-operate with Him ; and it is just because it is He that is working in us the willing and the doing, that it is worth our while to work out our salvation with fear and trembling. God has not determined the end without determining the appointed means.[8]

Now, Augustin argues, since grace certainly is gratuitous, and given to no preceding merits, — prevenient and antecedent to all good, — and, therefore, sovereign, and bestowed only on those whom God selects for its reception ; we must, of course, believe that the eternal God has foreknown all this from the beginning. He would be something less than God, had He not foreknown that He intended to bestow this prevenient, gratuitous, and sovereign grace on some men, and had He not foreknown equally the precise individuals on whom He intended to bestow it. To foreknow is to prepare beforehand. And this is *predestination*.[9] He argues that there can be no objection to predestination, in itself considered, in the mind of any man who believes in a God : what men object to is the gratuitous and sovereign grace to which no additional difficulty is added by the necessary assumption that it was foreknown and prepared for from eternity. That predestination does not proceed on the foreknowledge of good or of faith,[10] follows from its being nothing more than the foresight and preparation of grace, which, in its very idea, is gratuitous and not according to any merits, sovereign and according only to God's purpose, prevenient and in order to faith and good works. It is the sovereignty of grace, not its foresight or the preparation for it, which places men in God's hands, and suspends salvation absolutely on his unmerited

[1] *On the Gift of Perseverance*, 16; *Against Two Letters of the Pelagians*, ii. 15.  [2] *Epistle to Optatus*, 190.
[3] *On the Predestination of the Saints*, 17, 18.
[4] *On Grace and Free Will*, 17; *On the Proceedings of Pelagius*, 34, and often.
[5] Compare Thomasius' *Dogmengeschichte*, i. 510.
[6] *On Rebuke and Grace*, 40, 45; *On the Predestination of the Saints*, 13.  [7] *On Rebuke and Grace*, 40.
[8] *On the Gift of Perseverance*, 56.  [9] *On the Predestination of the Saints*, 36 sq.
[10] *On the Gift of Perseverance*, 41 sq., 47.

mercy. But just because God is God, of course, no one receives grace who has not been fore-known and afore-selected for the gift; and, as much of course, no one who has been foreknown and afore-selected for it, fails to receive it. Therefore the number of the predestinated is fixed, and fixed by God.[1] Is this fate? Men may call God's grace fate if they choose; but it is not fate, but undeserved love and tender mercy, without which none would be saved.[2] Does it paralyze effort? Only to those who will not strive to obey God because obedience is His gift. Is it unjust? Far from it: shall not God do what He will with His own undeserved favour? It is nothing but gratuitous mercy, sovereignly distributed, and foreseen and provided for from all eternity by Him who has selected us in His Son.

When Augustin comes to speak of *the means of grace*, i.e., of the channels and circumstances of its conference to men, he approaches the meeting point of two very dissimilar streams of his theology, — his doctrine of grace and his doctrine of the Church, — and he is sadly deflected from the natural course of his theology by the alien influence. He does not, indeed, bind the conference of grace to the means in such a sense that the grace must be given at the exact time of the application of the means. He does not deny that "God is able, even when no man rebukes, to correct whom He will, and to lead him on to the wholesome mortification of repentance by the most hidden and most mighty power of His medicine."[3] Though the Gospel must be known in order that man may be saved[4] (for how shall they believe without a preacher?), yet the preacher is nothing, and the preachment is nothing, but God only that gives the increase,[5] He even has something like a distant glimpse of what has since been called the distinction between the visible and invisible Church, — speaking of men not yet born as among those who are " called according to God's purpose," and, therefore, of the saved who constitute the Church,[6] — asserting that those who are so called, even before they believe, are " already children of God, enrolled in the memorial of their Father with unchangeable surety,"[7] and, at the same time, allowing that there are many already in the visible Church who are not of it, and who can there-fore depart from it. But he teaches that those who are thus lost out of the visible Church are lost because of some fatal flaw in their baptism, or on account of post-baptismal sins; and that those who are of the " called according to the purpose " are predestinated not only to salvation, but to salvation by baptism. Grace is not tied to the means in the sense that it is not conferred save in the means; but it is tied to the means in the sense that it is not conferred without the means. Baptism, for instance, is absolutely necessary for salvation: no exception is allowed except such as save the principle, — baptism of blood (martyrdom),[8] and, somewhat grudgingly, baptism of intention. And baptism, when worthily received, is absolutely efficacious: " if a man were to die immediately after baptism, he would have nothing at all left to hold him liable to punishment."[9] In a word, while there are many baptized who will not be saved, there are none saved who have not been baptized; it is the grace of God that saves, but baptism is a channel of grace without which none receive it.[10]

The saddest corollary that flowed from this doctrine was that by which Augustin was forced to assert that all those who died unbaptized, including infants, are finally lost and depart into eter-nal punishment. He did not shrink from the inference, although he assigned the place of lightest punishment in hell to those who were guilty of no sin but original sin, but who had departed this life without having washed this away in the " laver of regeneration." This is the dark side of his soteriology; but it should be remembered that it was not his theology of grace, but the universal and traditional belief in the necessity of baptism for remission of sins, which he inherited in common with all of his time, that forced it upon him. The theology of grace was destined in

[1] *On Rebuke and Grace*, 39. Compare 14.
[2] *On the Gift of Perseverance*, 29; *Against Two Letters of the Pelagians*, ii. 9 sq.     [3] *On Rebuke and Grace*, 1.
[4] *On the Predestination of the Saints*, 17, 18; if the gospel is not preached at any given place, it is proof that God has no elect there.
[5] *On the Merits and Forgiveness of Sins*, etc., ii. 37.     [6] *On Rebuke and Grace*, 23.     [7] Do., 20.
[8] *On the Soul and its Origin*, i. 11; ii. 17.     [9] *On the Merits and Forgiveness of Sins*, etc., ii. 46.
[10] On Augustin's teaching as to baptism, see Rev. James Field Spalding's *The Teaching and Influence of Augustin*, pp. 39 sq.

the hands of his successors, who have rejoiced to confess that they were taught by him, to remove this stumbling-block also from Christian teaching; and if not to Augustin, it is to Augustin's theology that the Christian world owes its liberation from so terrible and incredible a tenet. Along with the doctrine of infant damnation, another stumbling-block also, not so much of Augustinian, but of Church theology, has gone. It was not because of his theology of grace, or of his doctrine of predestination, that Augustin taught that comparatively few of the human race are saved. It was, again, because he believed that baptism and incorporation into the visible Church were necessary for salvation. And it is only because of Augustin's theology of grace, which places man in the hands of an all-merciful Saviour and not in the grasp of a human institution, that men can see that in the salvation of all who die in infancy, the invisible Church of God embraces the vast majority of the human race, — saved not by the washing of water administered by the Church, but by the blood of Christ administered by God's own hand outside of the ordinary channels of his grace. We are indeed born in sin, and those that die in infancy are, in Adam, children of wrath even as others; but God's hand is not shortened by the limits of His Church on earth, that it cannot save. In Christ Jesus, all souls are the Lord's, and only the soul that itself sinneth shall die (Ezek. xviii. 1–4); and the only judgment wherewith men shall be judged proceeds on the principle that as many as have sinned without law shall also perish without law, and as many as have sinned under law shall be judged by the law (Rev. ii. 12).

Thus, although Augustin's theology had a very strong churchly element within it, it was, on the side that is presented in the controversy against Pelagianism, distinctly anti-ecclesiastical. Its central thought was the absolute dependence of the individual on the grace of God in Jesus Christ. It made everything that concerned salvation to be of God, and traced the source of all good to Him. "Without me ye can do nothing," is the inscription on one side of it; on the other stands written, "All things are yours." Augustin held that he who builds on a human foundation builds on sand, and founded all his hope on the Rock itself. And there also he founded his teaching; as he distrusted man in the matter of salvation, so he distrusted him in the form of theology. No other of the fathers so conscientiously wrought out his theology from the revealed Word; no other of them so sternly excluded human additions. The subjects of which theology treats, he declares, are such as "we could by no means find out unless we believed them on the testimony of Holy Scripture."[1] "Where Scripture gives no certain testimony," he says, "human presumption must beware how it decides in favor of either side."[2] "We must first bend our necks to the authority of Scripture," he insists, "in order that we may arrive at knowledge and understanding through faith."[3] And this was not merely his theory, but his practice.[4] No theology was ever, it may be more broadly asserted, more conscientiously wrought out from the Scriptures. Is it without error? No; but its errors are on the surface, not of the essence. It leads to God, and it came from God; and in the midst of the controversies of so many ages it has shown itself an edifice whose solid core is built out of material "which cannot be shaken."[5]

---

[1] *On the Soul and its Origin,* iv. 14.  
[2] *On the Merits and Forgiveness of Sins,* etc., ii. 59.  
[3] *On the Merits and Forgiveness of Sins,* i. 29.  
[4] Compare *On the Spirit and the Letter,* 63.  
[5] On the subject of this whole section, compare Reuter's *Augustinische Studien,* which has come to hand only after the whole was already in type, but which in all essential matters — such as the formative principle, the sources, and the main outlines of Augustin's theology — is in substantial agreement with what is here said.

# TABLE OF MATTERS TREATED IN THE PRECEDING ESSAY.

# DEDICATION OF VOLUME I. OF THE EDINBURGH EDITION.

## TO THE RIGHT REVEREND THE LORD BISHOP OF EXETER.

My dear Lord, — I gladly avail myself of your permission to dedicate this volume to you. In the course of a professional life of nearly the third of a century, which has not been idly spent, I have never failed to find pleasure in theological pursuits. In the intervals of most pressing labour, these have often tended to refresh and comfort one's wearied spirit. If this confession of my own experience should have any weight with any one in our sacred calling to combine the hard work which we owe to others while ministering to their wants, with " that diligent attendance to read-ing" which we require for ourselves, to inform our minds and refresh our spirits, I shall have accomplished my only purpose in making it. Your Lordship, I am sure, will entirely approve of such a combination of employments in your clergy. I well remember your recommendation of theological study to us at the opening of Bishop Phillpott's Library at Truro ; and how you coun-selled us the more earnestly to pursue it, from the danger there is, in these busy times, of merging the acquisition of sacred learning in the active labours of our holy vocation. That the divine blessing may crown the work which you are so diligently prosecuting in the several functions of your high office, is the earnest wish, my dear Lord, of your faithful servant,

PETER HOLMES.

Mannamead, .Plymouth, March 10, 1872.

# DEDICATION OF VOLUME II. OF THE EDINBURGH EDITION.

## TO THE REV. C. T. WILKINSON, M.A.,
### VICAR OF ST. ANDREWS WITH PENNYCROSS, PLYMOUTH.

My DEAR VICAR, —I have great pleasure in associating your name with my own in this volume. We are officially connected in the sacred ministry of the Church, and I think I may, not unsuitably, extend our relations in this little effort to strengthen the defences of the great doctrine of GRACE committed to our care and advocacy. Never was this portion of revealed truth more formidably assailed than at the present day. Rationalism, as its primary dogma, asserts the perfectibility of our nature, out of its own resources; and with a versatility and power of argument and illustration, which gathers help from every quarter in literature and philosophy, it opposes "the truth as it is in Jesus." This truth, which implies, as its cardinal points, the ruin of man's nature in the sin of the first Adam, and its recovery in the obedience of the second Adam, is vindicated with admirable method and convincing force in the Anti-Pelagian treatises of the great Doctor of the Western Church. Some of these treatises appear for the first time in our language in this volume; and you will, I am sure, admire the acuteness with which Saint Augustin tracks out and refutes the sophistries of the rationalists of his own day, as well as the profound knowledge and earnest charity with which he enforces and recommends the Catholic verity.

In identifying you thus far with myself in this undertaking, I not only gratify my own feelings of sincere friendship, but with a confidence which I believe I do not over-estimate, I assume, what I highly prize, your agreement with me in accepting and furthering the principles set forth in this volume.

With sincere sympathy for you in your important work at Plymouth, and best wishes for the divine blessing upon it, believe me, yours very faithfully,

PETER HOLMES.

MANNAMEAD, PLYMOUTH, June 24, 1874.

2

# PREFACE TO VOLUME I. OF THE EDINBURGH EDITION.

§ 1. THE reader has in this volume, translated for the first time in English, five of the fifteen treatises of St. Augustin on the Pelagian heresy. They are here arranged in the same order (the chronological one) in which they are placed in the tenth volume of the Benedictine edition, and are therefore St. Augustin's earliest contributions to the great controversy. These are their Latin titles :

*De peccatorum meritis et remissione, et de baptismo parvulorum ad Marcellinum;* libri tres, scripti anno Christi 412.

*De Spiritu et littera ad eumdem;* liber unus, scriptus sub finem anni 412.

*De natura et gratia contra Pelagium, ad Timasium et Jacobum;* liber unus, scriptus anno Christi 415.

*De perfectione justitiæ hominis;* [Epistola seu] liber ad Eutropium et Paulum, scriptus circiter finem anni 415.

*De gestis Pelagii ad Aurelium episcopum;* liber unus, scriptus sub initium anni 417.

The Benedictine editors have enriched their edition with prefaces (" Admonitiones ") and critical and explanatory notes, and, above all, with the appropriate extracts from St. Augustin's *Retractations,*[1] in which we have the author's own final revision and correction of his works. All these have been reproduced in a translated form in this volume ; and they will, it is believed, afford the reader sufficient guidance for an intelligent apprehension of at least the special arguments of the several treatises. The Benedictine editors, however, prefixed to this detailed information an elaborate and lengthy preface, in which they reviewed the general history of the Pelagian discussions and their authors, with especial reference to the part which St. Augustin played throughout it. This historical introduction it was at first intended to present to the reader in English at the head of this volume. In consideration, however, of the length of the document, we have so far changed our purpose as to substitute a shorter statement of certain facts and features of the Pelagian controversy, which it is hoped may contribute to a better understanding of the general subject.

§ 2. The Pelagian heresy is so designated after Pelagius, a British monk. (Augustin calls him *Brito,* so do Prosper and Gennadius ; by Orosius he is called *Britannicus noster,* and by Mercator described as *gente Britannus.* This wide epithet is somewhat restricted by Jerome, who says of him, *Habet progeniem Scotiæ gentis de Britannorum vicinia;* leaving it uncertain, however, whether he deemed Scotland his native country, or Ireland. His monastic character is often referred to both by Augustin and other writers, and Pope Zosimus describes him as *Laicum virum ad bonam frugem longa erga Deum servitute nitentem.* It is, after all, quite uncertain what part of " Britain " gave him birth ; among other conjectures, he has been made a native of Wales, attached to a monastery at Bangor, and gifted with the Welsh name of *Morgan,* of which his usual designation of *Pelagius* is supposed to be simply the Greek version, Πελαγίος.) It was at the beginning of the fifth century that he became conspicuous. He then resided at Rome, known by many as an honourable and earnest man, seeking in a

---

[1] It is satisfactory to observe how brief and scanty are his " retractations " on the topics treated in the present volume.

corrupt age to reform the morals of society. (In the present volume the reader will not fail to observe the eulogistic language which Augustin often uses of Pelagius; see *On the Merits of Sin*, iii. 1, 5, 6.) Sundry theological treatises are even attributed to him; among them one *On the Trinity*, of unquestionable orthodoxy, and showing great ability. Unfavourable reports, however, afterwards began to be circulated, charging him with opening, in fact, entirely new ground in the fields of heresy. During the previous centuries of Christian opinion the speculations of active thinkers had been occupied on *Theology* properly so called, or the doctrine of God as to His nature and personal attributes, including *Christology*, which treated of Christ's divine and human natures. This was objective divinity. With Pelagius, however, a fresh class of subjects was forced on men's attention: in his peculiar system of doctrine he deals with what is subjective in man, and reviews the whole of his relation to God. His heresy turns mainly upon two points — the assumed incorruptness of human nature, and the denial of all supernatural influence upon the human will.

§ 3. He had an early associate in Cœlestius, a native of Campania, according to some, or as others say, of Ireland or of Scotland. This man, who is said to have been highly connected, began life as an advocate, but, influenced by the advice and example of Pelagius, soon became a monk. He excelled his master in boldness and energy; and thus early precipitated the new doctrine into a formal dogmatism, from which the caution and subtler management of Pelagius might have saved it. In the year A.D. 412 (Pelagius having just left him at Carthage to go to Palestine), Cœlestius was accused before the bishop Aurelius of holding and teaching the following opinions:

1. Adam was created mortal, and must have died, even if he had not sinned; 2. Adam's sin injured himself only, and not mankind; 3. Infants are born in the state of Adam before he fell; 4. Mankind neither died in Adam, nor rose again in Christ; 5. The Law, no less than the Gospel, brings men to the kingdom of heaven; 6. There were sinless men before the coming of Christ.[1] What Cœlestius thus boldly propounded, he had the courage to maintain. On his refusal to retract, he was excommunicated. He threatened, or perhaps actually though ineffectually made, an appeal to Rome, and afterwards quitted Carthage for Ephesus.

§ 4. Augustin, who had for some time been occupied in the Donatist controversy, had as yet taken no personal part in the proceedings against Cœlestius. Soon, however, was his attention directed to the new opinions, and he wrote the first two treatises contained in this volume, in the year when Cœlestius was excommunicated. At first he treated Pelagius, as has been said, with deference and forbearance, hoping by courtesy to recall him from danger. But as the heresy developed, Augustin's opposition was more directly and vigorously exhibited. The gospel was being fatally tampered with, in its essential facts of human sin and divine grace; so, in the fulness of his own absolute loyalty to the entire volume of evangelical truth, he concentrated his best efforts in opposition to the now formidable heresy. It is perhaps not too much to say, that St. Augustin, the greatest doctor of the Catholic Church, effected his greatness mainly by his labours against Pelagianism. Other Christian writers besides Augustin have achieved results of decisive influence on the Church and its deposit of the Christian faith. St. Athanasius, "alone against the world," has often been referred to as a splendid instance of what constancy, aided by God's grace and a profound knowledge of theology, could accomplish; St. Cyril of Alexandria, and St. Leo of Rome, might be also quoted as signal proofs of the efficacy of catholic truth in opposition to popular heresy: these men, under God, saved the Creed from the ravages of Arianism, and the subtler injuries of Nestorius and Eutyches. Then, again, in the curious learning of the primitive Irenæus; in the critical skill, and wide knowledge, and indomitable labours of Origen; in the catechetical teaching of the elder Cyril; in the chaste descriptive power of Basil; in the simplicity and self-denial of Ambrose; in the fervid eloquence of the "golden-mouthed" Chrysostom; in the great learning of Jerome; in the scholastic accuracy of Damascene; and in the varied sacred gifts of other Christian worthies, from the impetuous Tertullian and the gentle Cyprian, with all the Gregories of manifold endowments, down to the latest period of patristic wisdom, graced by our own Anselm and the unrivalled preacher Bernard, — in all these converging lines of diverse yet compatible accomplishments, the Church of Christ has found, from age to age, ample reinforcements against the attacks of heretical hostility. And in our great Bishop of Hippo one may trace, operating on various occasions in his various works, the manifold characteristics which we have just enumerated of his brother saints, — with this difference, that in no one of them are found combined the many traits which constitute *his* greatness. We have here to do only with his anti-Pelagian writings. Upon the whole, perhaps, these exhibit most of his wonderful resources of Christian character. In many respects, one is reminded by him of the great apostle, whom he reverenced, and whose profound doctrines he republished and vindicated. He has himself, in several of his works, especially in his *Confessions*, admitted us to a view of the sharp convulsions and bitter conflicts through which he passed, before his regeneration, into the Christian life, animated by the free and sovereign grace of God, and adorned with his unflagging energies in works of faith and love. From the depths of his own consciousness he instinctively felt the dangers of Pelagianism, and he put forth his strength, as God enabled him, to meet the evil; and the reader has in this volume samples in great variety of the earnestness of his conflict with

---

[1] Marius Mercator mentions a seventh opinion broached by Cœlestius, to the effect that "infants, though they be unbaptized, have everlasting life."

the new heresy and its leaders. These leaders he has himself characterized: " *Ille* [nempe Cœlestius] *apertior, iste* [scilicet Pelagius] *occultior fuit; ille pertinacior, iste mendacior; vel certe ille liberior, hic astutior;* "[1] and illustrations of the general correctness of this estimate will be forthcoming, especially in the fourth treatise of this volume, where Cœlestius is dealt with, and in the fifth, which relates to the subterfuges and pretexts practised by Pelagius in his proceedings in Palestine.

§ 5. The difference in the characters of the two leaders in this heresy contributed to different results in their earlier proceedings. We have seen the disastrous issue to Cœlestius at Carthage, from his outspoken and unyielding conduct. The more reserved Pelagius, resorting to a dexterous management of sundry favourable circumstances, obtained a friendly hearing on two public occasions — at Jerusalem, in the summer of A.D. 415, and again at the end of that year, in a council of fourteen bishops, at Diospolis, the ancient Lydda. In the last treatise of this volume,[2] the reader has a characteristic narrative of these events from St. Augustin's own pen. The holy man's disappointment at the untoward results of these two inquiries is apparent; but he struggles to maintain his respect for the bishops concerned in the affair, and comforts himself and all Catholics with the assurance, which he thinks is warranted by the proceedings, that the acquittal obtained by Pelagius, through the concealment of his real opinions, amounted in fact to a condemnation of them. This volume terminates with these transactions in Palestine; so that any remarks on the decline and fall of Pelagianism proper must be postponed to a subsequent volume.

§ 6. St. Jerome as well as St. Augustin engaged in this controversy, and experienced in the East some loss and much danger from the rougher followers of Pelagius.[3] It is not without interest that one observes the difference of view entertained by these eminent men on the general question of the Pelagian heresy. Augustin had but an imperfect acquaintance with either the language or the writings of the Greek Fathers, and had treated the Pelagian opinions as unheard-of novelties. Jerome, however, who had acquired a competent knowledge of the Christian literature of Greece during his long residence in the East, traced these heretical opinions to the school of Origen, for whose memory he entertained but scant respect. There is, no doubt, extravagance in Jerome's censure, but withal a foundation of truth. For from the beginning there was a tendency at least to divergent views between the Eastern and the Western sections of Christendom, on the relation of the human will to the grace of God in the matter of man's conversion and salvation. On the general question, indeed, there was always substantial agreement in the Catholic Church; — man, as he is born into the world, is not in his originally perfect state; in order to be able to live according to his original nature and to do good, he requires an inward change by the almighty power of God. But this general agreement did not hinder specific differences of opinion, which having been developed with considerable regularity, in East and West respectively, admit of some classification. The chief writers of the West, especially Tertullian and Cyprian in the third century, and Hilary of Poitiers and (notably) Ambrose in the fourth century, prominently state the doctrine of man's corruption, and the consequent necessity of a change of his nature by divine grace; whilst the Alexandrian Fathers (especially Clement), and other Orientals (for instance, Chrysostom), laid great stress upon human freedom, and on the indispensable co-operation of this freedom with the grace of God. By the fifth century these tendencies were ready to culminate; they were at length precipitated to a decisive controversy. In the Pelagian system, the liberty which had been claimed for man was pushed to the heretical extreme of independence of God's help; while Augustin, in resisting this heresy, found it hard to keep clear of the other extreme, of the absorption of human responsibility into the divine sovereignty. Our author, no doubt, moves about on the confines of a deep insoluble mystery here; but, upon the whole, it must be apparent to the careful reader how earnestly he tries to maintain and vindicate man's responsibility even amidst the endowments of God's grace.

§ 7. Much has been written on the conduct of the two leading opponents in this controversy. Sides (as usual) have been taken, and extreme opinions of praise and of blame have been freely bestowed on both Augustin and Pelagius. It is impossible, even were it desirable, in this limited space to enter upon a question which, after all, hardly rises above the dignity of mere *personalities*. The orthodox bishop and the heretical monk have had their share of censure as to their mode of conducting the controversy. Augustin has been taxed with intolerance, Pelagius with duplicity. We are perhaps not in a position to form an impartial judgment on the case. To begin with, the evidence comes all from one side; and then the critics pass their sentence according to the suggestions of modern prejudice, rather than by the test of ancient contemporary facts, motives, and principles of action. A good deal of obloquy has been cast on Augustin, as if he were responsible for the Rescript of Honorius and its penalties; but this is (to say the least) a conclusion which outruns the premises. We need say nothing of the peril which seriously threatened true religion when the half-informed bishops of Palestine, and the vacillating Pope, all gave their hasty and ill-grounded approval to Pelagius, as a justification of Augustin. He deeply felt the seriousness of the crisis, and he unsheathed "the sword of the Spirit," and dealt with it trenchant blows, every one of which struck home with admirable precision; but it is not proved that he ever wielded the civil sword of pains and penalties. Of all theological writers in ancient, medieval, or earlier modern times,

---

[1] *De Peccato originali,* [xii.] 13. See below.     [2] [i.e. *On the Proceedings of Pelagius.*]
[3] See the *Proceedings of Pelagius,* c. 66.

it may be fairly maintained that St. Augustin has shown himself the most considerate, courteous, and charitable towards opponents. The reader will trace with some interest the progress of his criticism on Pelagius. From the forbearance and love which he gave him at first,[1] he passes slowly and painfully on to censure and condemnation, but only as he detects stronger and stronger proofs of insincerity and bad faith.

§ 8. But whatever estimate we may form on the score of their personal conduct, there can be no doubt of the bishop's superiority over the monk, when we come to gauge the value of their principles and doctrines, whether tested by Scripture or by the great facts of human nature. Concerning the test of Scripture, our assertion will be denied by no one. No ancient Christian writer approaches near St. Augustin in his general influence on the opinions and belief of the Catholic Church, in its custody and interpretation of Holy Scripture; and there can be no mistake either as to the Church's uniform guardianship of the Augustinian doctrine, taken as a whole, or as to its invariable resistance to the Pelagian system, whenever and however it has been reproduced in the revolutions of human thought. There cannot be found in all ecclesiastical history a more remarkable fact than the deference shown to the great Bishop of Hippo throughout Christendom, on all points of salient interest connected with his name. Whatever basis of doctrine exists in common between the great sections of Catholicism and Protestantism, was laid at first by the genius and piety of St. Augustin. In the conflicts of the early centuries he was usually the champion of Scripture truth against dangerous errors. In the Middle Ages his influence was paramount with the eminent men who built up the scholastic system. In the modern Latin Church he enjoys greater consideration than either Ambrose, or Hilary, or Jerome, or even Gregory the Great; and lastly, and perhaps most strangely, he stands nearest to evangelical Protestantism, and led the van of the great movement in the sixteenth century, which culminated in the Reformation. How unique the influence which directed the minds of Anselm, and Bernard, and Aquinas, and Bonaventure, with no less power than it swayed the thoughts of Luther, and Melanchthon, and Zuingle, and Calvin!

§ 9. The key to this wonderful influence is Augustin's knowledge of Holy Scripture, and its profound suitableness to the facts and experience of our entire nature. Perhaps to no one, not excepting St. Paul himself, has it been ever given so wholly and so deeply to suffer the manifold experiences of the human heart, whether of sorrow and anguish from the tyranny of sin, or of spiritual joy from the precious consolations of the grace of God. Augustin speaks with authority here; he has traversed all the ground of inspired writ, and shown us how true is its portraiture of man's life. And, to pass on to our last point, he has threaded the mazes of human consciousness; and in building up his doctrinal system, has been, in the main, as true to the philosophy of fact as he is to the statements of revelation. He appears in as favourable a contrast to his opponent in his philosophy as in his Scripture exegesis. We cannot, however, in the limits of this Preface, illustrate this criticism with all the adducible proofs; but we may quote one or two weak points which radically compromise Pelagius as to the scientific bearings of his doctrine. By science we mean accurate knowledge, which stands the test of the widest induction of facts. Now, it has been frequently remarked that Pelagius is scientifically defective in the very centre of his doctrine, — on the freedom of the will. His theory, especially in the hands of his vigorous followers, Cœlestius and Julianus,[2] ignored the influence of habit on human volition, and the development of habits from action, isolating human acts, making man's power of choice (his *liberum arbitrium*) a mere natural faculty, of physical, not moral operation. How defective this view is, — how it impoverishes the moral nature of man, strips it of the very elements of its composition, and drops out of consideration the many facts of human life, which interlace themselves in our experience as the very web and woof of moral virtue, — is manifest to the students of Aristotle and Butler.[3] Acts are not mere insulated atoms, merely done, and then done with; but they have a relation to the will, and an influence upon subsequent acts: and so acts generate habits, and habits produce character, the formal cause of man's moral condition. The same defect runs through the Pelagian system. Passing from the subject of human freedom, and the effect of action upon conduct and habit, we come to Pelagius' view of sin. According to him, Adam's transgression consisted in an isolated act of disobedience to God's command; and our sin now consists in the mere repetition and imitation of his offence. There was no "original sin," and consequently no hereditary guilt. Adam stood alone in his transgression, and transmitted no evil taint to his posterity, much less any tendency or predisposition to wrong-doing: there was no doubt a bad example, but against this Pelagius complacently set the happier examples of good and prudent men. *Isolation*, then, is the principle of Pelagius and his school; *organization* is the principle of true philosophy, as tested by the experience and observation of mankind.

---

[1] For some time Augustin abstained from mentioning the name of Pelagius, to save him as much as he could from exposure, and to avoid the irritation which might urge him to heresy from obstinacy. Augustin recognised fairly enough the motive which influenced Pelagius at first. The latter dreaded the Antinomianism of the day, and concentrated his teaching in a doctrine which was meant as a protest against it. "We would rather not do injustice to our friends," says Augustin, as he praises their "strong and active minds;" and he goes on to commend Pelagius anonymously for "the zeal which he entertains against those *who find a defence for their sins in the infirmity of human nature.*" See the third treatise of this volume, *On Nature and Grace*, ch. 6, 7.

[2] We make this qualification, because Pelagius himself seems to have recognised to some extent the power of habit and its effect upon the will, in his Letter to Demetrias, 8. See Dr. Philip Schaff's *History of the Christian Church*, vol. iii. p. 804.

[3] Aristotle, *Ethic. Nicom.* ii. 2, 3, 6; Butler, *Analogy*, i. 5.

§ 10. We have said enough, and we hope not unfairly said it, to show that Pelagius was radically at fault in his deductions, whether tested by divine revelation or human experience. How superior to him in all essential points his great opponent was, will be manifest to the reader of this volume. Not a statement of Scripture, nor a fact of nature, does Augustin find it necessary to soften, or repudiate, or ignore. Hence his writings are valuable in illustrating the harmony between revelation and true philosophy ; we have seen how much of his far-seeing and eminent knowledge was owing to his own deep convictions and discoveries of sin and grace ; perhaps we shall not be wrong in saying, that even to his opponents is due something of his excellence. There can be no doubt that in Pelagius and Cœlestius, and his still more able follower Julianus, of whom we shall hear in a future volume, he had very able opponents — men of earnest character, acute in observation and reasoning, impressed with the truth of their convictions, and deeming it a fit occupation to rationalize the meaning of Scripture in its bearings on human experience. There is a remarkable peculiarity in this respect in the opinions of Pelagius. He accepted the mysteries of *theology*, properly so called, with the most exemplary orthodoxy. Nothing could be better than his exposition of the doctrine of the Holy Trinity. But again we find him hemmed in with a perverse isolation. The doctrine of the Trinity, according to him, stands alone ; it sheds no influence on man and his eternal interests ; but in the blessed Scripture, as read by Augustin, there is revealed to man a most intimate relation between himself and God, the Father, the Son, and the Holy Ghost, as his Creator, his Redeemer, and his Sanctifier. In Pelagianism, then, we see a disjointed and unconnected theory, — a creed which stands apart from practical life, and is not allowed to shape man's conduct, — a system, in short, which falls to pieces for want of the coherence of the true "analogy of the faith" which worketh by love. By exposing, therefore, this incompatibility in the doctrine of his opponents, Augustin shows how irreconcilable are the deductions of their Rationalism with the statements of Revelation. But Rationalism is not confined to any one period. We live to see a bolder Rationalism, which, unlike Pelagius', is absolutely uncompromising in its aims, and (as must be admitted) more consistent in its method. To institute the supremacy of Reason, it destroys more or less the mysteries of Religion. All the miraculous element of the gospel is discarded ; God's personal relation to man in the procedures of grace, and man's to God in the discipline of repentance, faith, and love, are abolished : nay, the Divine Personality itself merges into an impalpable, uninfluential Pantheism ; while man's individual responsibility is absorbed into a mythical personification of the race. The only sure escape from such a desolation as this, is to recur to the good old paths of gospel faith — "*stare super antiquas vias.*" Our directory for life's journey through these is furnished to us in Holy Scripture ; and if an interpreter is wanted who shall be able by competent knowledge and ample experience to explain to us any difficulties of direction, we know none more suited for the purpose than our St. Augustin.

§ 11. But Rationalism is not always so exaggerated as this : in its ordinary development, indeed, it stops short of open warfare with Revelation, and (at whatever cost of logical consistency) it will accommodate its discussions to the form of Scripture. This adaptation gives it double force : there is its own intrinsic principle of uncontrolled liberty in will and action, and there is "the form of godliness," which has weight with unreflective Christians. Hence Pelagianism was undoubtedly popular : it offered dignity to human nature, and flattered its capacity ; and this it did without virulence and with sincerity, under the form of religion. This acquiescence of matter and manner gave it strength in men's sympathies, and has secured for it durability, seeing that there is plenty of it still amongst us ; as indeed there always has been, and ever will be, so long as the fatal ambition of Eden (Gen. iii. 5, 6) shall seduce men into a temper of rivalry with God. Writers like Paley (in his *Evidences*) have treated of the triumph of Christianity over difficulties of every kind. Of all the stumbling-blocks to the holy religion of our blessed Saviour, not one has proved so influential as its doctrine of GRACE ; the prejudice against it, by what St. Paul calls "the natural man" (1 Cor. ii. 14), is ineradicable — and, it may be added, inevitable : for in his independence and self-sufficiency he cannot admit that in himself he is nothing, but requires external help to rescue him from sin, and through imparted holiness to elevate him to the perfection of the blessed. How great, then, is the benefit which Augustin has accomplished for the gospel, in probing the grounds of this natural prejudice against it, and showing its ultimate untenableness — the moment it is tested on the deeper principles of the divine appreciation ! No, the ultimate effect of the doctrine and operation of grace is not to depreciate the true dignity of man. If there be the humbling process first, it is only that out of the humility should emerge the exaltation at last (1 Pet. v. 6). I know nothing in the whole range of practical or theoretical divinity more beautiful than Augustin's analysis of the procedures of grace, in raising man from the depths of his sinful prostration to the heights of his last and eternal elevation in the presence and fellowship of God. The most ambitious, who thinks "man was not made for meanness," might be well content with the noble prospect. But his ambition must submit to the conditions ; and his capacity both for the attainment and the fruition of such a destiny is given to him and trained by God Himself. "It is so contrived," says Augustin, "in the discipline of the present life, that the holy Church shall arrive at last at that condition of unspotted purity which all holy men desire ; and that it may in the world to come, and in a state unmixed with all soil of evil men, and undisturbed by any law of sin resisting the law of the mind, lead the purest life in a divine eternity. . . . But in whatever place and at what time soever the love which animates the good shall reach that state of absolute perfection which shall admit of no increase, it is certainly not 'shed abroad in our hearts' by any energies either of the nature or the volition that are within us, but ' by the Holy Ghost which is given unto us' (Rom. v. 5), and which both helps our infirmity and co-operates with our strength " (*On Nature and Grace*, chs. 74 and 84).

§ 12. This translation has been made from the (Antwerp) Benedictine edition of the works of St. Augustin, tenth volume, compared with the beautiful reprint by Gaume, Although left to his own resources in making his version, the Translator has gladly availed himself of the learned aid within his reach. He may mention the *Kirchengeschichte* both of Gieseler and Neander [Clark's transl. vol. iv.]; Wiggers' *Versuch einer pragmatischen Darstellung des Augustinismus und Pelagianismus* [1st part]; Shedd's *Christian Doctrine;* Cunningham's *Historical Theology;* Short's *Bampton Lectures* for 1846 [Lect. vii.]; Professor Bright's *History of the Church* from A.D. 313 to A.D. 451; Bishop Forbes' *Explanation of the Thirty-nine Articles* [vol. i.]; Canon Robertson's *History of the Christian Church*, vol. i. pp. 376–392; and especially Professor Mozley's *Treatise on the Augustinian Doctrine of Predestination*, ch. iii. iv. vi.; and Dr. Philip Schaff's excellent *History of the Christian Church* [Clark, Edinburgh 1869 [1]], vol. iii. pp. 783–1028; of which work Dr. Dorner's is by no means exaggerated commendation: "It is," says he, "on account of the beauty of its descriptions, the lucid arrangement of its materials, and the moderation of its decisions, a very praiseworthy work" (Dorner's *History of Protestant Theology* [Clark's translation], vol. ii. p. 449, note 2). This portion of Dr. Schaff's work is an expansion of his able and interesting article on the *Pelagian Controversy* in the American *Bibliotheca Sacra* of May 1848.

PETER HOLMES.

1 [Revised edition.   Charles Scribner's Sons, New York, and T. Clark, Edinburgh, 1884.]

# PREFACE TO VOLUME II. OF THE EDINBURGH EDITION.

THIS volume contains a translation of the three following treatises by St. Augustin on the Pelagian controversy : —

*De Gratia Christi, et De Peccato originali contra Pelagium et Cœlestium, ad Albinam, Pinianum, et Melaniam;* libri duo, scripti anno Christi 418.

*De Nuptiis et Concupiscentiâ ad Valerium Comitem ;* libri duo, scriptus alter circiter initium anni 419; alter anno Christi 420.

*De Animâ et ejus origine, contra Vincentium Victorem ;* libri quatuor, scriptus sub finem anni Christi 419.

These, with the contents of our former volume, comprise eight of the fifteen works contributed by the great author to the defence of the Catholic faith against Pelagius and his most conspicuous followers. The préfaces and chapter headings, which have been, as heretofore, transferred to their proper places in this volume from the Benedictine edition of the original, will afford the reader preliminary help enough, and thus render more than a few general prefatory remarks unnecessary here.

The second book in the first of these treatises adds some facts to the historical information contained in our preceding volume; Pelagius is shown to be at one, in the main, with Cœlestius, the bolder but less specious heretic. They were condemned everywhere — even at Rome by Pope Zosimus, who had at first shown some favour to them. These authoritative proceedings against them gave a sensible check to their progress in public ; there is, however, reason to believe that the opinions, which the Pelagian teachers had with great industry, and with their varied ability, propounded, had created much interest and even anxiety in private society. The early part of the first of the following treatises throws some light on this point, and on the artful methods by which the heretics sought to maintain and extend their opinions; it affords some evidence also of the widespread influence of St. Augustin. The controversy had engaged the attention of a pious family in Palestine ; Pelagius was in the neighbourhood; and when frankly questioned by the friends, he strongly protested his adherence to the doctrine of GRACE. "I anathematize," he exclaimed with suspicious promptitude, "the man who holds that the grace of God is not necessary for us at every moment and in every act of our lives: and all who endeavour to disannul it, deserve everlasting punishment." It was an act of astonishing duplicity, which Augustin, to whom the case was referred, soon detected and exposed. It is satisfactory to find that the worthy Christians to whom the Saint addressed his loving labour were confirmed in their simple faith; and in one of the last of his extant letters, towards the close of his days on earth, the venerable St. Jerome, in the course of the following year, united the gratitude of Albina, Pinianus, and Melania, with his own to his renowned brother in the west, whom he saluted as "the restorer of the ancient faith." "*Macte virtute*," said the venerable man, "*in orbe celebraris ; et, quod signum majoris est gloriæ, omnes heretici detestantur.*" [Go on and prosper; the whole world endows thee with its praise, and all heretics with their hatred.]

In the latter part of the first treatise in this volume, one of the most formidable of the Pelagian objections to the Catholic doctrine of original sin is thrown out against marriage: "Surely that could not be a holy state, instituted of God, which produced human beings in sin!" Augustin in a few weighty chapters removes the doubts of his perplexed correspondents, and reserves his strength for the full treatment of the subject in the second treatise, here translated, *On Marriage and Concupiscence.* It is a noble monument of his firm grasp of Scripture truth, his loyal adherence to its plain meaning, and his delicate and, at the same time, intrepid handling of a subject, which could only be touched by a man whose mind possessed a deep knowledge of human nature — both in its moral and its physiological aspects, and in its relations to God as affected by its creation, its fall, and its redemption.

This treatise introduces us to a change of circumstances. The preceding one was, as we have seen, addressed to a small group of simple believers in sacred truth, who were not personally known to the author, and, though zealous in the maintenance of the faith, occupied only a private place in society; but the present work was written at the urgent request of a nobleman in high office as a minister of state, and well known to the writer. It is pleasant to trace a similar earnestness, in such dissimilar ranks, in the defence of the assailed faith : and it illustrates the wide stretch of mind and comprehensive love of Augustin, that he could so promptly sympathize with the anxieties of all classes and conditions in the Christian life; and, what is more, so administer comfort and conviction out of the treasures of his wisdom, as to settle their doubts and reassure them in faith. Nor does the change end here. Instead of Pelagius and Cœlestius, Augustin has in this work to confute the powerful argument of Julianus, bishop of Celanum, the ablest of his Pelagian opponents. This man was really the mainstay of the heresy; he had greater resources of mind and a firmer character than either of his associates; — more candid and sincere than Pelagius, and less ambitious and impatient than Cœlestius, he seemed to contend for truth for its own sake, and this disposition found a complete response in the Church's earnest and accomplished champion. Notwithstanding the difficulty and delicacy of the subject, which removes, no doubt, the treatise *De Nuptiis et Concupiscentiâ* out of the category of what is called "general reading," the great author never did a higher service to the faith than when he provided for it this defence of a fundamental point. The venerable Jerome rejoiced at the good service, and longed to embrace his brother Saint from his distant retreat of Bethlehem. "*Testem invoco Deum,*" he wrote to Augustin, and his dear friend and helper Alypius, "*quod si posset fieri, assumptis alis columbæ, vestris amplexibus implicarer.*"

In the last and longest work, translated for this volume, we come upon a change, both of subject and circumstances, as complete as that we have just noticed. Vincentius Victor, whose unsafe opinions are reviewed, was a young African of great ability and rhetorical accomplishment. His fluent tongue had fairly bewitched not only crowds of thoughtless hearers, but staid persons, whose faith should have been proof against a seductive influence which was soon shown to be transient and flimsy. The young disputant seems to have been more of a schismatic in the Donatist party, than a heretic with Pelagius; showy, however, and unstable, and hardly weighing the consequence of his own opinions, he began to air his metaphysics, and soon fell into strange errors about the nature and origin of the human soul. In his youthful arrogance he happened to censure Augustin for his cautious teaching on so profound a subject; kindly does the aged bishop receive the criticism, show its unreasonableness, and point out to his rash assailant some serious errors which he was propounding at random. He also reproves one of Victor's friends, who happened to be a presbyter, for allowing himself to be misled by the young man's eloquent sophistry; and in the latter half of his treatise, with fatherly love and earnestness, he advises Victor to renounce his dangerous errors, some of which were rankly Pelagian, and something worse. The result of Augustin's admonitions — adorned as they were with great depth and width of reflection and knowledge (extending this time even to physical science, on some facts of which he playfully comments with the ease of a modern experimenter), with loving consideration for his opponent's inexperience, kindly deference to his undoubted abilities, and a pious desire to win him over to the cause of truth and godliness — was entirely satisfactory. We find from the *Retractations* (ii. 56), that Victor in time abjured all his errors, and doubtless, like another Apollos, ably employed his best powers in the service of true religion. This was a real trophy, great among the greatest of Augustin's achievements for faith and charity. For so great a soul to stoop to the level of so captious a spirit, and with industrious love and patience to trace out and refute all its ambitious error, was "a labour of love" indeed. He remembered the wise counsel of the apostle: "Count him not as an enemy, but admonish him as a brother;" and he reaped the victory the Saviour promised: "Thou hast gained thy brother."

The translation, as in the former volume of the Anti-Pelagian writings of our author, has been made from the tenth volume of the Antwerp reprint of the Benedictine edition of St. Augustin's works.

PETER HOLMES.

[Volume III. of the Edinburgh edition appeared without dedication or preface, in 1876. It contained translations of Augustin's treatises on *Grace and Free-Will, Rebuke and Grace, The Predestination of the Saints, The Gift of Perseverance,* and of his work *Against Two Letters of the Pelagians.* Of these, only the first was from the pen of Dr. Holmes, the rest being the work of Dr. Robert Ernest Wallis, whose name has been accordingly placed on the general titlepage of this revision. — W.]

A TREATISE ON THE MERITS AND FORGIVENESS OF SINS,
AND ON THE BAPTISM OF INFANTS.

# EXTRACT FROM AUGUSTIN'S "RETRACTATIONS,"

## BOOK II. CHAP. 23,

### ON THE FOLLOWING TREATISE,

## "DE PECCATORUM MERITIS ET REMISSIONE."

---

A NECESSITY arose which compelled me to write against the new heresy of Pelagius. Our previous opposition to it was confined to sermons and conversations, as occasion suggested, and according to our respective abilities and duties; but it had not yet assumed the shape of a controversy in writing. Certain questions were then submitted to me [by our brethren] at Carthage, to which I was to send them back answers in writing: I accordingly wrote first of all three books, under the title, "On the Merits and Forgiveness of Sins," in which I mainly discussed the baptism of infants because of original sin, and the grace of God by which we are justified, that is, made righteous; but [I remarked] no man in this life can so keep the commandments which prescribe holiness of life, as to be beyond the necessity of using this prayer for his sins: "Forgive us our trespasses."[1] It is in direct opposition to these principles that they have devised their new heresy. Now throughout these three books I thought it right not to mention any of their names, hoping and desiring that by such reserve they might the more readily be set right; nay more, in the third book (which is really a letter, but reckoned amongst *the books,* because I wished to connect it with the two previous ones) I actually quoted Pelagius' name with considerable commendation, because his conduct and life were made a good deal of by many persons; and those statements of his which I refuted, he had himself adduced in his writings, not indeed in his own name, but had quoted them as the words of other persons. However, when he was afterwards confirmed in heresy, he defended them with most persistent animosity. Cœlestius, indeed, a disciple of his, had already been excommunicated for similar opinions at Carthage, in a council of bishops, at which I was not present. In a certain passage of my second book I used these words: "Upon some there will be bestowed this blessing at the last day, that they shall not perceive the actual suffering of death in the suddenness of the change which shall happen to them;"[2] — reserving the passage for a more careful consideration of the subject; for they will either die, or else by a most rapid transition from this life to death, and then from death to eternal life, as in the twinkling of an eye, they will not undergo the feeling of mortality. This work of mine begins with this sentence: "*However absorbing and intense the anxieties and annoyances.*"

---

[1] See Matt. vi. 12.

[2] See Book ii. ch. 50.

# CONTENTS OF THE TREATISE "ON THE MERITS AND FOR-GIVENESS OF SINS, AND ON THE BAPTISM OF INFANTS."

## BOOK I.

# BOOK II.

# BOOK III.

# A TREATISE ON THE MERITS AND FORGIVENESS OF SINS, AND ON THE BAPTISM OF INFANTS,

## BY AURELIUS AUGUSTIN, BISHOP OF HIPPO;

### IN THREE BOOKS,

### ADDRESSED TO MARCELLINUS, A.D. 412.

---

## BOOK I.

IN WHICH HE REFUTES THOSE WHO MAINTAIN, THAT ADAM MUST HAVE DIED EVEN IF HE HAD NEVER SINNED; AND THAT NOTHING OF HIS SIN HAS BEEN TRANSMITTED TO HIS POSTERITY BY NATURAL DESCENT. HE ALSO SHOWS, THAT DEATH HAS NOT ACCRUED TO MAN BY ANY NECESSITY OF HIS NATURE, BUT AS THE PENALTY OF SIN; HE THEN PROCEEDS TO PROVE THAT IN ADAM'S SIN HIS ENTIRE OFFSPRING IS IMPLICATED, SHOWING THAT INFANTS ARE BAPTIZED FOR THE EXPRESS PURPOSE OF RECEIVING THE REMISSION OF ORIGINAL SIN.

CHAP. 1 [I.] — INTRODUCTORY, IN THE SHAPE OF AN INSCRIPTION TO HIS FRIEND MARCELLINUS.

HOWEVER absorbing and intense the ·anxieties and annoyances in the whirl and warmth of which we are engaged with sinful men [1] who forsake the law of God, — even though we may well ascribe these very evils to the fault of our own sins, — I am unwilling, and, to say the truth, unable, any longer to remain a debtor, my dearest Marcellinus,[2] to that zealous affection of yours, which only enhances my own grateful and pleasant estimate of yourself. I am under the impulse [of a twofold emotion]: on the one hand, there is that very love which makes us unchangeably one in the one hope of a change for the better; on the other

hand, there is the fear of offending God in yourself, who has given you so earnest a desire, in gratifying which I shall be only serving Him who has given it to you. And so strongly has this impulse led and attracted me to solve, to the best of my humble ability, the questions which you have submitted to me in writing, that my mind has gradually admitted this inquiry to an importance transcending that of all others; [and it will now give me no rest] until I accomplish something which shall make it manifest that I have yielded, if not a sufficient, yet at any rate an obedient, compliance with your own kind wish and the desire of those to whom these questions are a source of anxiety.

CHAP. 2 [II.] — IF ADAM HAD NOT SINNED, HE WOULD NEVER HAVE DIED.

They who say that Adam was so formed that he would even without any demerit of sin have died, not as the penalty of sin, but from the necessity of his being, endeavour indeed to refer that passage in the law, which says: "On the day ye eat thereof ye shall surely die," [3] not to the death of

---

[1] This is probably an allusion to the Donatists, who were then fiercely assailing the Catholics; [and over the conference between whom and the Catholics, Marcellinus had presided the previous year (411). — W.]

[2] [Flavius Marcellinus, a "tribune and notary," a Christian man of high character and devout mind, who was much interested in theological discussions. He was appointed by Honorius to preside over the commission of inquiry into the disputes between the Catholics and Donatists in 411, and held the famous conference between the parties, that met in Carthage on the 1st, 3d, and 8th of June, 411. He discharged this whole business with singular patience, moderation, and good judgment; which appears to have cemented the intimate friendship between him and Augustin. Augustin's treatise on *The Spirit and Letter* is also addressed to him, and he undertook the *City of God* on his suggestion. See below, p. 80. — W.]

[3] Gen. ii. 17.

the body, but to that death of the soul which takes place in sin. It is the unbelievers who have died this death, to whom the Lord pointed when He said, " Let the dead bury their dead."[1] Now what will be their answer, when we read that God, when reproving and sentencing the first man after his sin, said to him, " Dust thou art, and unto dust shalt thou return?"[2] For it was not in respect of his soul that he was " dust," but clearly by reason of his body, and it was by the death of the self-same body that he was destined to " return to dust." Still, although it was by reason of his body that he was dust, and although he bare about the natural body in which he was created, he would, if he had not sinned, have been changed into a spiritual body, and would have passed into the incorruptible state, which is promised to the faithful and the saints, without the peril of death.[3] And for this issue we not only are conscious in ourselves of having an earnest desire, but we learn it from the apostle's intimation, when he says : " For in this we groan, longing to be clothed upon with our habitation which is from heaven ; if so be that being clothed we shall not be found naked. For we that are in this tabernacle do groan, being burdened ; not for that we would be unclothed, but clothed upon, that mortality may be swallowed up of life."[4] Therefore, if Adam had not sinned, he would not have been divested of his body, but would have been clothed upon with immortality and incorruption, that "mortality might have been swallowed up of life ; " that is, that he might have passed from the natural body into the spiritual body.

CHAP. 3 [III.] — IT IS ONE THING TO BE MORTAL, ANOTHER THING TO BE SUBJECT TO DEATH.

Nor was there any reason to fear that if he had happened to live on here longer in his natural body, he would have been oppressed with old age, and have gradually, by increasing age, arrived at death. For if God granted to the clothes and the shoes of the Israelites that "they waxed not old" during so many years,[5] what wonder if for obedience it had been by the power of the same [God] allowed to man, that although he had a natural and mortal body, he should have in it a certain condition, in which he might grow full of years without decrepitude, and, whenever God pleased, pass from mortality to immortality without the medium of death? For even as this very flesh of ours, which we now possess, is not therefore invulnerable, because it is not necessary that it should be wounded ; so also was his not therefore immortal, because there was no necessity for its dying. Such a condition, whilst

still in their natural and mortal body, I suppose, was granted even to those who were translated hence without death.[6] For Enoch and Elijah were not reduced to the decrepitude of old age by their long life. But yet I do not believe that they were then changed into that spiritual kind of body, such as is promised in the resurrection, and which the Lord was the first to receive ; only they probably do not need those aliments, which by their use minister refreshment to the body ; but ever since their translation they so live, as to enjoy such a sufficiency as was provided during the forty days in which Elijah lived on the cruse of water and the cake, without substantial food ;[7] or else, if there be any need of such sustenance, they are, it may be, sustained in Paradise in some such way as Adam was, before he brought on himself expulsion therefrom by sinning. And he, as I suppose, was supplied with sustenance against decay from the fruit of the various trees, and from the tree of life with security against old age.

CHAP. 4 [IV.] — EVEN BODILY DEATH IS FROM SIN.

But in addition to the passage where God in punishment said, " Dust thou art, unto dust shalt thou return,"[2] — a passage which I cannot understand how any one can apply except to the death of the body, — there are other testimonies likewise, from which it most fully appears that by reason of sin the human race has brought upon itself not spiritual death merely, but the death of the body also. The apostle says to the Romans : " But if Christ be in you, the body is dead because of sin, but the spirit is life because of righteousness. If therefore the Spirit of Him that raised up Jesus from the dead dwell in you, He that raised up Christ Jesus from the dead shall quicken also your mortal bodies by His Spirit that dwelleth in you."[8] I think that so clear and open a sentence as this only requires to be read, and not expounded. *The body*, says he, *is dead*, not because of earthly frailty, as being made of the dust of the ground, but *because of sin;* what more do we want? And he is most careful in his words : he does not say " is *mortal*," but " *dead*."

CHAP. 5 [V.] — THE WORDS, MORTALE (CAPABLE OF DYING), MORTUUM (DEAD), AND MORITURUS (DESTINED TO DIE).

Now previous to the change into the incorruptible state which is promised in the resurrection of the saints, the body could be *mortal* (capable of dying), although not destined to die (*moriturus*) ; just as our body in its present state can, so to speak, be capable of sickness, although not destined to be sick. For whose is the flesh which is

[1] Matt. viii. 22; Luke ix. 60.
[2] Gen. iii. 19.
[3] 1 Cor. xv. 52, 53.
[4] 2 Cor. v. 2-4.
[5] Deut. xxix. 5.
[6] Gen. v. 24; 2 Kings ii. 11.
[7] 1 Kings xix. 8.
[8] Rom. viii. 10, 11.

incapable of sickness, even if from some accident it die before it ever is sick? In like manner was man's body then mortal; and this mortality was to have been superseded by an eternal incorruption, if man had persevered in righteousness, that is to say, obedience: but even what was mortal (*mortale*) was not made dead (*mortuum*), except on account of sin. For the change which is to come in at the resurrection is, in truth, not only not to have death incidental to it, which has happened through sin, but neither is it to have mortality, [or the very possibility of death,] which the natural body had before it sinned. He does not say: "He that raised up Christ Jesus from the dead shall quicken also your *dead* bodies" (although he had previously said, "the body is dead"[1]); but his words are: "He shall quicken also your *mortal* bodies;"[2] so that they are not only no longer dead, but no longer mortal [or capable of dying], since the natural is raised spiritual, and this mortal body shall put on immortality, and mortality shall be swallowed up in life.[3]

### CHAP. 6 [VI.] — HOW IT IS THAT THE BODY IS DEAD BECAUSE OF SIN.

One wonders that anything is required clearer than the proof we have given. But we must perhaps be content to hear this clear illustration gainsaid by the contention, that we must understand "the dead body" here[1] in the sense of the passage where it is said, "Mortify your members which are upon the earth."[4] But it is *because of righteousness* and not because of sin that the body is in this sense mortified; for it is to do the works of righteousness that we mortify our bodies which are upon the earth. Or if they suppose that the phrase, "because of sin," is added, not that we should understand "because sin has been committed," but "in order that sin may not be committed" — as if it were said, "The body indeed is dead, in order to prevent the commission of sin:" what then does he mean in the next clause by adding the words, "because of righteousness," to the statement, "The spirit is life?"[1] For it would have been enough simply to have adjoined "the spirit is life," to have secured that we should supply here too, "in order to prevent the commission of sin;" so that we should thus understand the two propositions to point to one thing — that both "the body is dead," and "the spirit is life," for the one common purpose of "preventing the commission of sin." So likewise if he had merely' meant to say, "because of righteousness," in the sense of "for the purpose of doing righteousness," the two clauses might possibly be referred to this

one purpose — to the effect, that both "the body is dead," and "the spirit is life," "for the purpose of doing righteousness." But as the passage actually stands, it declares that "the body is dead because of sin," and "the spirit is life because of righteousness," attributing different merits to different things — the demerit of sin to the death of the body, and the merit of righteousness to the life of the spirit. Wherefore if, as no one can doubt, "the spirit is life because of righteousness," that is, as the desert, of righteousness; how ought we, or can we, understand by the statement, "The body is dead because of sin," anything else than that the body is dead as the desert of sin, unless indeed we try to pervert or wrest the plainest sense of Scripture to our own arbitrary will? But besides this, additional light is afforded by the words which follow. For it is with limitation to the present time, when he says, that on the one hand "the body is dead because of sin," since, whilst the body is unrenovated by the resurrection, there remains in it the desert of sin, that is, the necessity of dying; and on the other hand, that "the spirit is life because of righteousness," since, notwithstanding the fact of our being still burdened with "the body of this death,"[5] we have already by the renewal which is begun in our inner man, new aspirations[6] after the righteousness of faith. Yet, lest man in his ignorance should fail to entertain hope of the resurrection of the body, he says that the very body which he had just declared to be "dead because of sin" in this world, will in the next world be made alive "because of righteousness," — and that not only in such a way as to become alive from the dead, but immortal from its mortality.

### CHAP. 7 [VII.] — THE LIFE OF THE BODY THE OBJECT OF HOPE, THE LIFE OF THE SPIRIT BEING A PRELUDE TO IT.

Although I am much afraid that so clear a matter may rather be obscured by exposition, I must yet request your attention to the luminous statement of the apostle. "But if Christ," says he, "be in you, the body indeed is dead because of sin, but the spirit is life because of righteousness."[1] Now this is said, that men may not suppose that they derive no benefit, or but scant benefit, from the grace of Christ, seeing that they must needs die in the body. For they are bound to remember that, although their body still bears that desert of sin, which is irrevocably bound to the condition of death, yet their spirit has already begun to live because of the righteousness of faith, although it had actually become extinct by the death, as it were, of unbelief. No small gift, therefore, he says, must you suppose to have been conferred

---

[1] Rom. viii. 10.
[2] Rom. viii. 11.
[3] 1 Cor. xv. 44, 53, 55.
[4] Col. iii. 5.

[5] Rom. vii. 24.
[6] Respiramus.

upon you, by the circumstance that Christ is in you ; inasmuch as in the body, which is dead because of sin, your spirit is even now alive because of righteousness ; so that therefore you should not despair of the life even of your body. " For if the Spirit of Him that raised up Christ from the dead dwell in you, He that raised up Christ from the dead shall quicken also your mortal bodies by His Spirit that dwelleth in you." [1] How is it that fumes of controversy still darken so clear a light ? The apostle distinctly tells you, that although the body is dead because of sin within you, yet even your mortal bodies shall be made alive because of righteousness, because of which even now your spirit is life, — the whole of which process is to be perfected by the grace of Christ, that is, by His Spirit dwelling in you : and men still contradict ! He goes on to tell us how it comes to pass that life converts death into itself by mortifying it. "Therefore, brethren," says he, "we are debtors, not to the flesh, to live after the flesh ; for if ye live after the flesh, ye shall die ; but if ye through the spirit do mortify the deeds of the flesh, ye shall live." [2] What else does this mean but this : If ye live according to death, ye shall wholly die ; but if by living according to life ye mortify death, ye shall wholly live ?

CHAP. 8 [VIII.] — BODILY DEATH FROM ADAM'S SIN.

When to the like purport he says : " By man came death, by man also the resurrection of the dead," [3] in what other sense can the passage be understood than of the death of the body ; for having in view the mention of this, he proceeded to speak of the resurrection of the body, and affirmed it in a most earnest and solemn discourse ? In these words, addressed to the Corinthians : " By man came death, and by man came also the resurrection of the dead ; for as in Adam all die, even so in Christ shall all be made alive," [4] — what other meaning is indeed conveyed than in the verse in which he says to the Romans, " By one man sin entered into the world, and death by sin ? " [5] Now they will have it, that the death here meant is the death, not of the body, but of the soul, on the pretence that another thing is spoken of to the Corinthians, where they are quite unable to understand the death of the soul, because the subject there treated is the resurrection of the body, which is the antithesis of the death of the body. The reason, moreover, why only death is here mentioned as caused by man, and not sin also, is because the point of the discourse is not about righteousness, which is the antithesis of sin, but about the resurrection of the body, which is contrasted with the death of the body.

CHAP. 9 [IX.] — SIN PASSES ON TO ALL MEN BY NATURAL DESCENT, AND NOT MERELY BY IMITATION.

You tell me in your letter, that they endeavour to twist into some new sense the passage of the apostle, in which he says : " By one man sin entered into the world, and death by sin ; " [5] yet you have not informed me what they suppose to be the meaning of these words. But so far as I have discovered from others, they think that the death which is here mentioned is not the death of the body, which they will not allow Adam to have deserved by his sin, but that of the soul, which takes place in actual sin ; and that this actual sin has not been transmitted from the first man to other persons by natural descent, but by imitation. Hence, likewise, they refuse to believe that in infants original sin is remitted through baptism, for they contend that no such original sin exists at all in people by their birth. But if the apostle had wished to assert that sin entered into the world, not by natural descent, but by imitation, he would have mentioned as the first offender, not Adam indeed, but the devil, of whom it is written, [6] that " he sinneth from the beginning ; " of whom also we read in the Book of Wisdom : " Nevertheless through the devil's envy death entered into the world." [7] Now, forasmuch as this death came upon men from the devil, not because they were propagated by him, but because they imitated his example, it is immediately added : " And they that do hold of his side do imitate him." [8] Accordingly, the apostle, when mentioning sin and death together, which had passed by natural descent from one upon all men, set him down as the introducer thereof from whom the propagation of the human race took its beginning.

CHAP. 10. — THE ANALOGY OF GRACE.

No doubt all they imitate Adam who by disobedience transgress the commandment of God ; but he is one thing as an example to those who sin because they choose ; and another thing as the progenitor of all who are born with sin. All His saints, also, imitate Christ in the pursuit of righteousness ; whence the same apostle, whom we have already quoted, says : " Be ye imitators of me, as I am also of Christ." [9] But besides this imitation, His grace works within us our illumination and justification, by that operation concerning which the same preacher of His [name] says : " Neither is he that planteth anything, nor he that watereth, but God that giveth the

---

[1] Rom. viii. 11.
[2] Rom. viii. 12, 13.
[3] 1 Cor. xv. 21.
[4] 1 Cor. xv. 21, 22.
[5] Rom. v. 12.

[6] 1 John iii. 8.
[7] Wisd. ii. 24.
[8] Ver. 25.
[9] 1 Cor. xi. 1.

increase." [1] For by this grace He engrafts into His body even baptized infants, who certainly have not yet become able to imitate any one. As therefore He, in whom all are made alive, besides offering Himself as an example of righteousness to those who imitate Him, gives also to those who believe on Him the hidden grace of His Spirit, which He secretly infuses even into infants ; so likewise he, in whom all die, besides being an example for imitation to those who wilfully transgress the commandment of the Lord, depraved also in his own person all who come of his stock by the hidden corruption of his own carnal concupiscence. It is entirely on this account, and for no other reason, that the apostle says : " By one man sin entered into the world, and death by sin, and so passed upon all men ; in which all have sinned." [2] Now if *I* were to say this, they would raise an objection, and loudly insist that I was incorrect both in expression and sense ; for they would perceive no sense in these words when spoken by an ordinary man, except that sense which they refuse to see in the apostle. Since, however, these are the words of him to whose authority and doctrine they submit, they charge us with slowness of understanding, while they endeavour to wrest to some unintelligible sense words which were written in a clear and obvious purport. " By one man," says he, " sin entered into the world, and death by sin." This indicates propagation, not imitation ; for if imitation were meant, he would have said, " By the devil." But as no one doubts, he refers to that first man who is called Adam : " And so," says he, " it passed upon all men."

CHAP. 11 [X.] — DISTINCTION BETWEEN ACTUAL AND ORIGINAL SIN. [3]

Again, in the clause which follows, " In which all have sinned," how cautiously, rightly, and unambiguously is the statement expressed ! For if you understand that sin to be meant which by one man entered into the world, " In which [sin] all have sinned," it is surely clear enough, that the sins which are peculiar to every man, which they themselves commit and which belong simply to them, mean one thing ; and that the one sin, in and by which all have sinned, means another thing ; since all were that one man. If, however, it be not the sin, but that one man that is understood, " In which [one man] all have sinned," what again can be plainer than even this clear statement ? We read, indeed, of those being justified in Christ who believe in Him, by reason of the secret communion and inspiration of that spiritual grace which makes every one who cleaves to the Lord " one spirit " with

Him,[4] although His saints also imitate His example ; can I find, however, any similar statement made of those who have imitated His saints ? Can any man be said to be justified in Paul or in Peter, or in any one whatever of those excellent men whose authority stands high among the people of God ? We are no doubt said to be blessed in Abraham, according to the passage in which it was said to him, " In thee shall all nations be blessed " [5] — for Christ's sake, who is his seed according to the flesh ; which is still more clearly expressed in the parallel passage : " In thy seed shall all nations be blessed." I do not believe that any one can find it anywhere stated in the Holy Scriptures, that a man has ever sinned or still sins " in the devil," although all wicked and impious men " imitate " him. The apostle, however, has declared concerning the first man, that " in him all have sinned ;" [2] and yet there is still a contest about the propagation of sin, and men oppose to it I know not what nebulous theory of " imitation." [6]

CHAP. 12. — THE LAW COULD NOT TAKE AWAY SIN.

Observe also what follows. Having said, " In which all have sinned," he at once added, " For until the law, sin was in the world." [7] This means that sin could not be taken away even by the law, which entered that sin might the more abound,[8] whether it be the law of nature, under which every man when arrived at years of discretion only proceeds to add his own sins to original sin, or that very law which Moses gave to the people. " For if there had been a law given which could have given life, verily righteousness should have been by the law. But the Scripture hath concluded all under sin, that the promise by faith in Jesus Christ might be given to them that believe.[9] But sin is not imputed where there is no law." [7] Now what means the phrase " *is not imputed*," but " *is ignored*," or " *is not reckoned as sin ?* " Although the Lord God does not Himself regard it as if it had never been, since it is written : " As many as have sinned without law shall also perish without law." [10]

CHAP. 13 [XI.] — MEANING OF THE APOSTLE'S PHRASE " THE REIGN OF DEATH."

" Nevertheless," says he, " death reigned from Adam even unto Moses," [11] — that is to say, from

---

[1] 1 Cor. iii. 7.
[2] Rom. v. 12.
[3] See below, Book iii. c. vii.; also in the *De Nuptiis*, c. v.; also *Epist* 186, and *Serm.* 165.
[4] 1 Cor. vi. 17.
[5] Gal iii. 8: comp. Gen. xii. 3, xviii. 18, xxii. 18.
[6] This was the Pelagian term, expressive of their dogma that original sin stands in the following [or " imitation "] of Adam, instead of being the fault and corruption of the nature of every man who is naturally engendered of Adam's offspring; which doctrine is expressed by Augustin's word, *propagatio,* " propagation."
[7] Rom. v. 13.
[8] Rom. v. 20.
[9] Gal. iii. 21, 22.
[10] Rom. ii. 12.
[11] Rom. v. 14.

the first man even to the very law which was promulged by the divine authority, because even it was unable to abolish the reign of death. Now death must be understood "to reign," whenever the guilt of sin [1] so dominates in men that it prevents their attainment of that eternal life which is the only true life, and drags them down even to the second death which is penally eternal. This reign of death is only destroyed in any man by the Saviour's grace, which wrought even in the saints of the olden time, all of whom, though previous to the coming of Christ in the flesh, yet lived in relation to His assisting grace, not to the letter of the law, which only knew how to command, but not to help them. In the Old Testament, indeed, that was hidden (conformably to the perfectly just dispensation of the times) which is now revealed in the New Testament. Therefore "death reigned from Adam unto Moses," in all who were not assisted by the grace of Christ, that in them the kingdom of death might be destroyed, "even in those who had not sinned after the similitude of Adam's transgression," [2] that is, who had not yet sinned of their own individual will, as Adam did, but had drawn from him original sin, "who is the figure of him that was to come," [2] because in him was constituted the form of condemnation to his future progeny, who should spring from him by natural descent; so that from one all men were born to a condemnation, from which there is no deliverance but in the Saviour's grace. I am quite aware, indeed, that several Latin copies of the Scriptures read the passage thus: "Death reigned from Adam to Moses over them who have sinned after the similitude of Adam's transgression;" [3] but even this version is referred by those who so read it to the very same purport, for they understood those who have sinned in him to have sinned after the similitude of Adam's transgression; so that they are created in his likeness, not only as men born of a man, but as sinners born of a sinner, dying ones of a dying one, and condemned ones to a condemned one. However, the Greek copies from which the Latin version was made, have all, without exception or nearly so, the reading which I first adduced.

CHAP. 14. — SUPERABUNDANCE OF GRACE.

"But," says he, "not as the offence so also is the free gift. For if, through the offence of one, many be dead, much more the grace of God, and the gift by grace, which is by One Man, Jesus Christ, hath abounded unto many." [4]

[1] *Reatus peccati.*
[2] Rom. v. 14.
[3] Comp. *Epist.* 157, n. 19. [Some few Greek copies have come down to us (e.g. 67**) which omit the "not," but no Latin copy (unless *d*\* be an exception), although other Latin writers (e.g. Ambrosiaster) testify to their former existence. — W.]
[4] Rom. v. 15.

Not *many more*, that is, many more men, for there are not more persons justified than condemned; but it runs, *much more hath abounded;* inasmuch as, while Adam produced sinners from his one sin, Christ has by His grace procured free forgiveness even for the sins which men have of their own accord added by actual transgression to the original sin in which they were born. This he states more clearly still in the sequel.

CHAP. 15 [XII.] — THE ONE SIN COMMON TO ALL MEN.

But observe more attentively what he says, that "through the offence of one, many are dead." For why should it be on account of the sin of one, and not rather on account of their own sins, if this passage is to be understood of *imitation*, and not of *propagation?* [5] But mark what follows: "And not as it was by one that sinned, so is the gift; for the judgment was by one to condemnation, but the grace is of many offences unto justification." [6] Now let them tell us, where there is room in these words for *imitation*. "By one," says he, "to condemnation." By one what except one sin? This, indeed, he clearly implies in the words which he adds: "But the grace is of many offences unto justification." Why, indeed, is the judgment from one offence to condemnation, while the grace is from many offences to justification? If original sin is a nullity, would it not follow, that not only grace withdraws men from many offences to justification, but judgment leads them to condemnation from many offences likewise? For assuredly grace does not condone many offences, without judgment in like manner having many offences to condemn. Else, if men are involved in condemnation because of one offence, on the ground that all the offences which are condemned were committed in imitation of that one offence; there is the same reason why men should also be regarded as withdrawn from one offence unto justification, inasmuch as all the offences which are remitted to the justified were committed in imitation of that one offence. But this most certainly was not the apostle's meaning, when he said: "The judgment, indeed, was from *one* offence unto condemnation, but the grace was from *many* offences unto justification." We on our side, indeed, can understand the apostle, and see that judgment is predicated of one offence unto condemnation entirely on the ground that, even if there were in men nothing but original sin, it would be sufficient for their condemnation. For however much heavier will be their condemnation who have added their own sins to

[5] See note to last word of ch. 11.
[6] Rom. v. 16.

the original offence (and it will be the more severe in individual cases, in proportion to the sins of individuals) ; still, even that sin alone which was originally derived unto men not only excludes from the kingdom of God, which infants are unable to enter (as they themselves allow), unless they have received the grace of Christ before they die, but also alienates from salvation and everlasting life, which cannot be anything else than the kingdom of God, to which fellowship with Christ alone introduces us.

CHAP. 16 [XIII.] — HOW DEATH IS BY ONE AND LIFE BY ONE.

And from this we gather that we have derived from Adam, in whom we all have sinned, not all our actual sins, but only original sin ; whereas from Christ, in whom we are all justified, we obtain the remission not merely of that original sin, but of the rest of our sins also, which we have added. Hence it runs : "Not as by the one that sinned, so also is the free gift." For the judgment, certainly, from one sin, if it is not remitted — and that the original sin — is capable of drawing us into condemnation ; whilst grace conducts us to justification from the remission of many sins, — that is to say, not simply from the original sin, but from all others also whatsoever.

CHAP. 17. — WHOM SINNERS IMITATE.

"For if by one man's offence death reigned by one ; much more they which receive abundance of grace and of righteousness shall reign in life by one, even Jesus Christ." [1] Why did death reign on account of the sin of one, unless it was that men were bound by the chain of death in that one man in whom all men sinned, even though they added no sins of their own? Otherwise it was not on account of the sin of one that death reigned through one ; rather it was on account of the manifold offences of many, [operating] through each individual sinner. For if the reason why men have died for the transgression of another be, that they have imitated him by following him as their predecessor in transgression, it must even result, and *that* " much more," that that one died on account of the transgression of another, whom the devil so preceded in transgression as himself to persuade him to commit the transgression. Adam, however, used no influence to persuade his followers ; and the many who are said to have imitated him have, in fact, either not heard of his existence at all or of his having committed any such sin as is ascribed to him, or altogether disbelieve it. How much more correctly, therefore, as I have already remarked,[2] would the apostle have set

forth the devil as the author, from which "one" he would say that sin and death had passed upon all, if he had in this passage meant to speak, not of propagation, but of imitation? For there is much stronger reason for saying that Adam is an imitator of the devil, since he had in *him* an actual instigator to sin ; if one may be an imitator even of him who has never used any such persuasion, or of whom he is absolutely ignorant. But what is implied in the clause, "They which receive abundance of grace and righteousness," but that the grace of remission is given not only to that sin in which all have sinned, but to those offences likewise which men have actually committed besides ; and that on these [men] so great a righteousness is freely bestowed, that, although Adam gave way to him who persuaded him to sin, they do not yield even to the coercion of the same tempter? Again, what mean the words, "Much more shall they reign in life," when the fact is, that the reign of death drags many more down to eternal punishment, unless we understand those to be really mentioned in both clauses, who pass from Adam to Christ, in other words, from death to life ; because in the life eternal they shall reign without end, and thus exceed the reign of death which has prevailed within them only temporarily and with a termination?

CHAP. 18. — ONLY CHRIST JUSTIFIES.

"Therefore as by the offence of one upon all men to condemnation, even so by the justification of One upon all men unto justification of life." [3] This "offence of one," if we are bent on "imitation," can only be the devil's offence. Since, however, it is manifestly spoken in reference to Adam and not the devil, it follows that we have no other alternative than to understand the principle of natural propagation, and not that of imitation, to be here implied. [XIV.] Now when he says in reference to Christ, "By the *justification* of one," he has more expressly stated our doctrine than if he were to say, "By the *righteousness* of one ; " inasmuch as he mentions that justification whereby Christ justifies the ungodly, and which he did not propose as an object of imitation, for He alone is capable of effecting this. Now it was quite competent for the apostle to say, and to say rightly : "Be ye imitators of me, as I also am of Christ ; " [4] but he could never say : Be ye justified by me, as I also am by Christ ; — since there may be, and indeed actually are and have been, many who were righteous and worthy of imitation ; but no one is righteous and a justifier but Christ alone. Whence it is said : "To the man that believeth on him that justifieth the ungodly, his faith is counted

---

[1] Rom. v. 17.
[2] See above, ch. 9.

[3] Rom. v. 18.
[4] 1 Cor. iv. 16; xi. 1.

for righteousness." [1]   Now if any man had it in his power confidently to declare, " I justify you," it would necessarily follow that he could also say, " Believe in me."   But it has never been in the power of any of the saints of God to say this except the Saint of saints,[2] who said : " Ye believe in God, believe also in me ; " [3] so that, inasmuch as it is He that justifies the ungodly, to the man who believes in him that justifieth the ungodly his faith is imputed for righteousness.

CHAP. 19 [XV.] — SIN IS FROM NATURAL DESCENT, AS RIGHTEOUSNESS IS FROM REGENERATION ; HOW " ALL " ARE SINNERS THROUGH ADAM, AND " ALL " ARE JUST THROUGH CHRIST.

Now if it is imitation only that makes men sinners through Adam, why does not imitation likewise alone make men righteous through Christ ?   " For," he says, " as by the offence of one upon all men to condemnation ; even so by the justification of one upon all men unto justification of life." [4]   [On the theory of imitation], then, the " one " and the " one," here, must not be regarded as Adam and Christ, but Adam and Abel.   For although many sinners have preceded us in the time of this present life, and have been imitated in their sin by those who have sinned at a later date, yet they will have it, that only Adam is mentioned as he in whom all have sinned by imitation, since he was the first of men who sinned.   And on the same principle, Abel ought certainly to have been mentioned, as he " in which one " all likewise are justified by imitation, inasmuch as he was himself the first man who lived justly.   If, however, it be thought necessary to take into the account some critical period having relation to the beginning of the New Testament, and Christ be taken as the leader of the righteous and the object of their imitation, then Judas, who betrayed Him, ought to be set down as the leader of the class of sinners.   Moreover, if Christ alone is He in whom all men are justified, on the ground that it is not simply the imitation of His example which makes men just, but His grace which regenerates men by the Spirit, then also Adam is the only one in whom all have sinned, on the ground that it is not the mere following of his evil example that makes men sinners, but the penalty which generates through the flesh.   Hence the terms " *all men* " and " *all men.*"   For not they who are generated through Adam are actually the very same as those who are regenerated through Christ ; but yet the language of the apostle is strictly correct, because as none partakes of carnal generation except through Adam, so no one shares in the spiritual except through Christ.

For if any could be generated in the flesh, yet not by Adam ; and if in like manner any could be generated in the Spirit, and not by Christ ; clearly " *all* " could not be spoken of either in the one class or in the other.   But these " *all* " [5] the apostle afterwards describes as " *many ; *" [6] for obviously, under certain circumstances, the " all " may be but a few.   The carnal generation, however, embraces " *many*," and the spiritual generation also includes " *many ;* " although the " many " of the spiritual are less numerous than the " many " of the carnal.   But as the one embraces *all* men whatever, so the other includes *all* righteous men ; because as in the former case none can be a man without the carnal generation, so in the other class no one can be a righteous man without the spiritual generation ; in both instances, therefore, there are " many : " " For as by the disobedience of one man *many* were made sinners, so by the obedience of one shall *many* be made righteous." [7]

CHAP. 20. — ORIGINAL SIN ALONE IS CONTRACTED BY NATURAL BIRTH.

" Moreover the law entered, that the offence might abound." [8]   This addition to original sin men now made of their own wilfulness, not through Adam ; but even this is done away and remedied by Christ, because " where sin abounded, grace did much more abound ; that as sin hath reigned unto death " [9] — even that sin which men have not derived from Adam, but have added of their own will — " even so might grace reign through righteousness unto eternal life." [9]   There is, however, other righteousness apart from Christ, as there are other sins apart from Adam.   Therefore, after saying, " As sin hath reigned unto death," he did not add in the same clause " *by one*," or " *by Adam*," because he had already spoken of that sin which was abounding when the law entered, and which, of course, was not original sin, but the sin of man's own wilful commission.   But after he has said : " Even so might grace also reign through righteousness unto eternal life," he at once adds, " through Jesus Christ our Lord ; " [9] because, whilst by the generation of the flesh only that sin is contracted which is original ; yet by the regeneration of the Spirit there is effected the remission not of original sin only, but also of the sins of man's own voluntary and actual commission.

CHAP. 21 [XVI.] — UNBAPTIZED INFANTS DAMNED, BUT MOST LIGHTLY ; [10] THE PENALTY OF ADAM'S SIN, THE GRACE OF HIS BODY LOST.

It may therefore be correctly affirmed, that

---

[1] Rom. iv. 5.
[2] Sanctus sanctorum.
[3] John xiv. 1.
[4] Rom. v. 18.

[5] The word is " *all* " in ver. 18.
[6] See ver. 19.
[7] Rom. v. 19.
[8] Rom. v. 20.
[9] Rom. v. 21.
[10] See Augustin's *Enchirid.* c. 93, and *Contra Julianum,* v. 11.

such infants as quit the body without being baptized will be involved in the mildest condemnation of all. That person, therefore, greatly deceives both himself and others, who teaches that they will not be involved in condemnation; whereas the apostle says: "Judgment from one offence to condemnation,"[1] and again a little after: "By the offence of one upon all persons to condemnation."[2] When, indeed, Adam sinned by not obeying God, then his body — although it was a natural and mortal body — lost the grace whereby it used in every part of it to be obedient to the soul. Then there arose in men affections common to the brutes which are productive of shame, and which made man ashamed of his own nakedness.[3] Then also, by a certain disease which was conceived in men from a suddenly injected and pestilential corruption, it was brought about that they lost that stability of life in which they were created, and, by reason of the mutations which they experienced in the stages of life, issued at last in death. However many were the years they lived in their subsequent life, yet they began to die on the day when they received the law of death, because they kept verging towards old age. For that possesses not even a moment's stability, but glides away without intermission, which by constant change perceptibly advances to an end which does not produce perfection, but utter exhaustion. Thus, then, was fulfilled what God had spoken: "In the day that ye eat thereof, ye shall surely die."[4] As a consequence, then, of this disobedience of the flesh and this law of sin and death, whoever is born of the flesh has need of spiritual regeneration — not only that he may reach the kingdom of God, but also that he may be freed from the damnation of sin. Hence men are on the one hand born in the flesh liable to sin and death from the first Adam, and on the other hand are born again in baptism associated with the righteousness and eternal life of the second Adam; even as it is written in the book of Ecclesiasticus: "Of the woman came the beginning of sin, and through her we all die."[5] Now whether it be said of the woman or of Adam, both statements pertain to the first man; since (as we know) the woman is of the man, and the two are one flesh. Whence also it is written: "And they twain shall be one flesh; wherefore," the Lord says, "they are no more twain, but one flesh."[6]

CHAP. 22 [XVII.] — TO INFANTS PERSONAL SIN IS NOT TO BE ATTRIBUTED.

They, therefore, who say that the reason why infants are baptized, is, that they may have the remission of the sin which they have themselves committed in their life, not what they have derived from Adam, may be refuted without much difficulty. For whenever these persons shall have reflected within themselves a little, uninfluenced by any polemical spirit, on the absurdity of their statement, how unworthy it is, in fact, of serious discussion, they will at once change their opinion. But if they will not do this, we shall not so completely despair of men's common sense, as to have any fears that they will induce others to adopt their views. They are themselves driven to adopt their opinion, if I am not mistaken, by their prejudice for some other theory; and it is because they feel themselves obliged to allow that sins are remitted to the baptized, and are unwilling to allow that the sin was derived from Adam which they admit to be remitted to infants, that they have been obliged to charge infancy itself with actual sin; as if by bringing this charge against infancy a man could become the more secure himself, when accused and unable to answer his assailant! However, let us, as I suggested, pass by such opponents as these; indeed, we require neither words nor quotations of Scripture to prove the sinlessness of infants, so far as their conduct in life is concerned; this life they spend, such is the recency of their birth, within their very selves, since it escapes the cognizance of human perception, which has no data or support whereon to sustain any controversy on the subject.

CHAP. 23 [XVIII.] — HE REFUTES THOSE WHO ALLEGE THAT INFANTS ARE BAPTIZED NOT FOR THE REMISSION OF SINS, BUT FOR THE OBTAINING OF THE KINGDOM OF HEAVEN.[7]

But those persons raise a question, and appear to adduce an argument deserving of consideration and discussion, who say that new-born infants receive baptism not for the remission of sin, but that, since their procreation is not spiritual, they may be created in Christ, and become partakers of the kingdom of heaven, and by the same means children and heirs of God, and joint-heirs with Christ. And yet, when you ask them, whether those that are not baptized, and are not made joint-heirs with Christ and partakers of the kingdom of heaven, have at any rate the blessing of eternal life in the resurrection of the dead, they are extremely perplexed, and find no way out of their difficulty. For what Christian is there who would allow it to be said, that any one could attain to eternal salvation without being born again in Christ, — [a result] which He meant to be effected through baptism, at the very time when such a sacrament

---

[1] Rom. v. 16.
[2] Ver. 18.
[3] Gen. iii. 10.
[4] Gen. ii. 17.
[5] Ecclus. xxv. 24.
[6] Matt. xix. 5, 6.

[7] See below, c. 26; also *De Peccato orig.* c. 19-24; also *Serm.* 294.

was purposely instituted for regenerating in the hope of eternal salvation? Whence the apostle says: "Not by works of righteousness which we have done, but according to His mercy He saved us by the laver[1] of regeneration."[2] This salvation, however, he says, consists in hope, while we live here below, where he says, "For we are saved by hope: but hope that is seen is not hope; for what a man seeth, why doth he yet hope for? But if we hope for that we see not, then do we with patience wait for it."[3] Who then could be so bold as to affirm, that without the regeneration of which the apostle speaks, infants could attain to eternal salvation, as if Christ died not for them? For "Christ died for the ungodly."[4] As for them, however, who (as is manifest) never did an ungodly act in all their own life, if also they are not bound by any bond of sin in their original nature, how did He die for them, who died for *the ungodly?* If they were hurt by no malady of original sin, how is it they are carried to the Physician Christ, for the express purpose of receiving the sacrament of eternal salvation, by the pious anxiety of those who run to Him? Why rather is it not said to them in the Church: Take hence these innocents: "they that are whole need not a physician, but they that are sick;"—Christ "came not to call the righteous, but sinners?"[5] There never has been heard, there never is heard, there never will be heard in the Church, such a fiction concerning Christ.

CHAP. 24 [XIX.] — INFANTS SAVED AS SINNERS.

And let no one suppose that infants ought to be brought to baptism, on the ground that, as they are not sinners, so they are not righteous; how then do some remind us that the Lord commends this tender age as meritorious; saying, "Suffer the little children to come unto me, and forbid them not, for of such is the kingdom of heaven?"[6] For if this ["of such"] is not said because of likeness in humility (since humility makes [us] children), but because of the laudable life of children, then of course infants must be righteous persons; otherwise, it could not be correctly said, "Of such is the kingdom of heaven," for heaven can only belong to the righteous. But perhaps, after all, it is not a right opinion of the meaning of the Lord's words, to make Him commend the life of infants when He says, "Of such is the kingdom of heaven;" inasmuch as *that* may be their true sense, which makes Christ adduce the tender age of infancy as a likeness of humility. Even so, however,

perhaps we must revert to the tenet which I mentioned just now, that infants ought to be baptized, because, although they are not sinners, they are yet not righteous. But when He had said: "I came not to call the righteous," as if responding to this, Whom, then, didst Thou come to call? immediately He goes on to say: "—but sinners to repentance." Therefore it follows, that, however righteous they may be, if also they are not sinners, He came not to call them, who said of Himself: "I came not to call the righteous, but sinners." They therefore seem, not vainly only, but even wickedly to rush to the baptism of Him who does not invite them, — an opinion which God forbid that we should entertain. He calls them, then, as a Physician who is not needed for those that are whole, but for those that are sick; and who came not to call the righteous, but sinners to repentance. Now, inasmuch as infants are not held bound by any sins of their own actual life, it is the guilt of original sin which is healed in them by the grace of Him who saves them by the laver of regeneration.

CHAP. 25. — INFANTS ARE DESCRIBED AS BELIEVERS AND AS PENITENTS. SINS ALONE SEPARATE BETWEEN GOD AND MEN.

Some one will say: How then are mere infants called to repentance? How can such as they repent of anything? The answer to this is: If they must not be called penitents because they have not the sense of repenting, neither must they be called believers, because they likewise have not the sense of believing. But if they are rightly called believers,[7] because they in a certain sense profess faith by the words of their parents, why are they not also held to be before that penitents when they are shown to renounce the devil and this world by the profession again of the same parents? The whole of this is done in hope, in the strength of the sacrament and of the divine grace which the Lord has bestowed upon the Church. But yet who knows not that the baptized infant fails to be benefited from what he received as a little child, if on coming to years of reason he fails to believe and to abstain from unlawful desires? If, however, the infant departs from the present life after he has received baptism, the guilt in which he was involved by original sin being done away, he shall be made perfect in that light of truth, which, remaining unchangeable for evermore, illumines the justified in the presence of their Creator. For sins alone separate between men and God; and these are done away by Christ's grace, through whom, as Mediator, we are reconciled, when He justifies the ungodly.

---

[1] Lavacrum.
[2] Tit. iii. 5.
[3] Rom. viii. 24, 25.
[4] Rom. v. 6.
[5] Luke v. 31, 32.
Matt. xix. 14.

[7] See below, c. 26 and 40; also Book iii. c. 2; also *Epist.* 98, and *Serm.* 294.

CHAP. 26 [XX.] — NO ONE, EXCEPT HE BE BAP- TIZED, RIGHTLY COMES TO THE TABLE OF THE LORD.

Now they take alarm from the statement of the Lord, when He says, " Except a man be born again, he cannot see the kingdom of God ; " [1] because in His own explanation of the passage He affirms, " Except a man be born of water and of the Spirit, he cannot enter into the kingdom of God." [2] And so they try to ascribe to unbap- tized infants, by the merit of their innocence, the gift of salvation and eternal life, but at the same time, owing to their being unbaptized, to exclude them from the kingdom of heaven. But how novel and astonishing is such an assumption, as if there could possibly be salvation and eternal life without heirship with Christ, without the king- dom of heaven ! Of course they have their refuge, whither to escape and hide themselves, because the Lord does not say, Except a man be born of water and of the Spirit, he cannot have life, but — " he cannot enter into the kingdom of God." If indeed He had said the other, there could have risen not a moment's doubt. Well, then, let us remove the doubt ; let us now listen to the Lord, and not to men's notions and conjectures ; let us, I say, hear what the Lord says — not indeed con- cerning the sacrament of the laver, but concern- ing the sacrament of His own holy table, to which none but a baptized person has a right to approach : " Except ye eat my flesh and drink my blood, ye shall have no life in you." [3] What do we want more ? What answer to this can be adduced, unless it be by that obstinacy which ever resists the constancy of manifest truth ?

CHAP. 27. — INFANTS MUST FEED ON CHRIST.

Will, however, any man be so bold as to say that this statement has no relation to infants, and that they can have life in them without partak- ing of His body and blood — on the ground that He does not say, Except one eat, but " Ex- cept ye eat ; " as if He were addressing those who were able to hear and to understand, which of course infants cannot do ? But he who says this is inattentive ; because, unless all are em- braced in the statement, that without the body and the blood of the Son of man men cannot have life, it is to no purpose that even the elder age is solicitous of it. For if you attend to the mere words, and not to the meaning, of the Lord as He speaks, this passage may very well seem to have been spoken merely to the people whom He happened at the moment to be addressing ; because He does not say, Except one eat ; but Except ye eat. What also becomes of the state-

ment which He makes in the same context on this very point : " The bread that I will give is my flesh, for the life of the world ? " [4] For, it is according to this statement, that we find that that sacrament pertains also to us, who were not in existence at the time the Lord spoke these words ; for we cannot possibly say that we do not belong to " the world," for the life of which Christ gave His flesh. Who indeed can doubt that in the term *world* all persons are indicated who enter the world by being born ? For, as He says in another passage, " The children of this world beget and are begotten." [5] From all this it follows, that even for the life of *infants* was His flesh given, which He gave for the life of the world ; and that even they will not have life if they eat not the flesh of the Son of man.

CHAP. 28. — BAPTIZED INFANTS, OF THE FAITH- FUL ; UNBAPTIZED, OF THE LOST.

Hence also that other statement : " The Father loveth the Son, and hath given all things into His hand. He that believeth on the Son hath everlasting life ; while he that believeth not the Son shall not see life, but the wrath of God abideth on him." [6] Now in which of these classes must we place infants — amongst those who believe on the Son, or amongst those who believe not the Son ? In neither, say some, be- cause, as they are not yet able to believe, so must they not be deemed unbelievers. This, however, the rule of the Church does not indi- cate, for it joins baptized infants to the number of the faithful. Now if they who are baptized are, by virtue of the excellence and administra- tion of so great a sacrament, nevertheless reck- oned in the number of the faithful, although by their own heart and mouth they do not literally perform what appertains to the action of faith and confession ; surely they who have lacked the sacrament must be classed amongst those who do not believe on the Son, and therefore, if they shall depart this life without this grace, they will have to encounter what is written con- cerning such — they shall not have life, but the wrath of God abideth on them. Whence could this result to those who clearly have no sins of their own, if they are not held to be obnoxious to original sin ?

CHAP. 29 [XXI.] — IT IS AN INSCRUTABLE MYS- TERY WHY SOME ARE SAVED, AND OTHERS NOT.

Now there is much significance in that He does not say, " The wrath of God *shall come* upon him," but " *abideth* on him." For from this wrath (in which we are all involved under sin, and of which the apostle says, " For we too were once by nature

---

[1] John iii. 3.
[2] Ver. 5.
[3] John vi. 53.

[4] John vi. 51.
[5] Generant et generantur; Luke xx. 34.
[6] John iii. 35, 36.

the children of wrath, even as others"[1]) nothing delivers us but the grace of God, through Jesus Christ our Lord. The reason why this grace comes upon one man and not on another may be hidden, but it cannot be unjust. For "is there unrighteousness with God? God forbid."[2] But we must first bend our necks to the authority of the Holy Scriptures, in order that we may each arrive at knowledge and understanding through faith. For it is not said in vain, "Thy judgments are a great deep."[3] The profundity of this "deep" the apostle, as if with a feeling of dread, notices in that exclamation: "O the depth of the riches both of the wisdom and the knowledge of God!" He had indeed previously pointed out the meaning of this marvellous depth, when he said: "For God hath concluded them all in unbelief, that He might have mercy upon all."[4] Then struck, as it were, with a horrible fear of this deep: "O the depth of the riches both of the wisdom and the knowledge of God! how unsearchable are His judgments, and His ways past finding out! For who hath known the mind of the Lord? or who hath been His counsellor? or who hath first given to Him, and it shall be recompensed unto him again? For of Him, and through Him, and in Him, are all things: to whom be glory for ever. Amen."[5] How utterly insignificant, then, is our faculty for discussing the justice of God's judgments, and for the consideration of His gratuitous grace, which, as men have no prevenient merits for deserving it, cannot be partial or unrighteous, and which does not disturb us when it is bestowed upon unworthy men, as much as when it is denied to those who are equally unworthy!

CHAP. 30. — WHY ONE IS BAPTIZED AND ANOTHER NOT, NOT OTHERWISE INSCRUTABLE.

Now those very persons, who think it unjust that infants which depart this life without the grace of Christ should be deprived not only of the kingdom of God, into which they themselves admit that none but such as are regenerated through baptism can enter, but also of eternal life and salvation, — when they ask how it can be just that one man should be freed from original sin and another not, although the condition of both of them is the same, might answer their own question, in accordance with their own opinion of how it can be so frequently just and right that one should have baptism administered to him whereby to enter into the kingdom of God, and another not be so favoured, although the case of both is alike. For if the question disturbs him, why, of the two persons, who are both equally sinners by nature, the one is loosed from that bond, on whom baptism is conferred, and the other is not released, on whom such grace is not bestowed; why is he not similarly disturbed by the fact that of two persons, innocent by nature, one receives baptism, whereby he is able to enter into the kingdom of God, and the other does not receive it, so that he is incapable of approaching the kingdom of God? Now in both cases one recurs to the apostle's outburst of wonder, "O the depth of the riches!" Again, let me be informed, why out of the body of baptized infants themselves, one is taken away, so that his understanding undergoes no change from a wicked life,[6] and the other survives, destined to become an impious man? Suppose both were carried off, would not both enter the kingdom of heaven? And yet there is no unrighteousness with God.[2] How is it that no one is moved, no one is driven to the expression of wonder amidst such depths, by the circumstance that some children are vexed by the unclean spirit, while others experience no such pollution, and others again, as Jeremiah, are sanctified even in their mother's womb;[7] whereas all men, if there is original sin, are equally guilty; or else equally innocent if there is no original sin? Whence this great diversity, except in the fact that God's judgments are unsearchable, and His ways past finding out?

CHAP. 31 [XXII.] — HE REFUTES THOSE WHO SUPPOSE THAT SOULS, ON ACCOUNT OF SINS COMMITTED IN ANOTHER STATE, ARE THRUST INTO BODIES SUITED TO THEIR MERITS, IN WHICH THEY ARE MORE OR LESS TORMENTED.

Perhaps, however, the now exploded and rejected opinion must be resumed, that souls which once sinned in their heavenly abode, descend by stages and degrees to bodies suited to their deserts, and, as a penalty for their previous life, are more or less tormented by corporeal chastisements. To this opinion Holy Scripture indeed presents a most manifest contradiction; for when recommending divine grace, it says: "For the children being not yet born, neither having done any good or evil, that the purpose of God according to election might stand, not of works, but of Him that calleth, it was said, The elder shall serve the younger."[8] And yet they who entertain such an opinion are actually unable to escape the perplexities of this question, but, embarrassed and straitened by them, are compelled to exclaim like others, "O the depth!" For whence does it come to pass that a person shall from his earliest boyhood show greater moderation, mental excellence, and temperance, and shall to a great extent conquer

---

[1] Eph. ii. 3.
[2] Rom. ix. 14.
[3] Ps. xxxvi. 6.
[4] Rom. xi. 32.
[5] Rom. xi 33–36.

[6] Wisdom iv. 11.
[7] Jer. i. 5.
[8] Rom. ix. 11, 12.

lust, shall hate avarice, detest luxury, and rise to a greater eminence and aptitude in the other virtues, and yet live in such a place as to be unable to hear the grace of Christ preached?— for "how shall they call on Him in whom they have not believed? or how shall they believe in Him of whom they have not heard? and how shall they hear without a preacher?"[1] While another man, although of a slow mind, addicted to lust, and covered with disgrace and crime, shall be so directed as to hear, and believe, and be baptized, and be taken away,—or, if permitted to remain longer here, lead the rest of his life in a manner that shall bring him praise? Now where did these two persons acquire such diverse deserts,—I do not say, that the one should believe and the other not believe, for that is a matter for a man's own will; but that the one should hear in order to believe, and that the other should not hear, for this is not within man's power? Where, I say, did they acquire diverse deserts? If they had indeed passed any part of their life in heaven, so as to be thrust down, or to sink down, to this world, and to tenant such bodily receptacles as are congruous to their own former life, then of course that man ought to be supposed to have led the better life previous to his present mortal body, who did not much deserve to be burdened with it, so as both to have a good disposition, and to be importuned by milder desires which he could easily overcome; and yet he did not deserve to have that grace preached to him whereby alone he could be delivered from the ruin of the second death. Whereas the other, who was hampered with a grosser body, as a penalty—so they suppose—for worse deserts, and was accordingly possessed of obtuser affections, whilst he was in the violent ardour of his lust succumbing to the snares of the flesh, and by his wicked life aggravating his former sins, which had brought him to such a pass, by a still more abandoned course of earthly pleasures,—either heard upon the cross, "To-day shalt thou be with me in paradise,"[2] or else joined himself to some apostle, by whose preaching he became a changed man, and was saved by the washing of regeneration,—so that where sin once abounded, grace did much more abound. I am at a loss to know what answer they can give to this who wish to maintain God's righteousness by human conjectures, and, knowing nothing of the depths of grace, have woven webs of improbable fable.

CHAP. 32.—THE CASE OF CERTAIN IDIOTS AND SIMPLETONS.

Now a good deal may be said of men's strange vocations,—either such as we have read about,

or have experienced ourselves,—which go to overthrow the opinion of those persons who think that, previous to the possession of their bodies, men's souls passed through certain lives peculiar to themselves, in which they must come to this, and experience in the present life either good or evil, according to the difference of their individual deserts. My anxiety, however, to bring this work to an end does not permit me to dwell longer on these topics. But on one point, which among many I have found to be a very strange one, I will not be silent. If we follow those persons who suppose that souls are oppressed with earthly bodies in a greater or a less degree of grossness, according to the deserts of the life which had been passed in celestial bodies previous to the assumption of the present one, who would not affirm that those had sinned previous to this life with an especial amount of enormity, who deserve so to lose all mental light, that they are born with faculties akin to brute animals,—who are (I will not say most slow in intellect, for this is very commonly said of others also, but) so silly as to make a show of their fatuity for the amusement of clever people, even with idiotic gestures,[3] and whom the vulgar call, by a name derived from the Greek, *Moriones*?[4] And yet there was once a certain person of this class, who was so Christian, that although he was patient to the degree of strange folly with any amount of injury to himself, he was yet so impatient of any insult to the name of Christ, or, in his own person, to the religion with which he was imbued, that he could never refrain, whenever his gay and clever audience proceeded to blaspheme the sacred name, as they sometimes would in order to provoke his patience, from pelting them with stones; and on these occasions he would show no favour even to persons of rank. Well, now, such persons are predestinated and brought into being, as I suppose, in order that those who are able should understand that God's grace and the Spirit, "which bloweth where it listeth,"[5] does not pass over any kind of capacity in the sons of mercy, nor in like manner does it pass over any kind of capacity in the children of Gehenna, so that "he that glorieth, let him glory in the Lord."[6] They, however, who affirm that souls severally receive different earthly bodies, more or less gross according to the merits of their former life, and that their abilities as men vary according to the self-same merits, so that some minds are sharper and others more obtuse, and that the grace of God is also dispensed for

---

[1] Rom. x. 14.
[2] Luke xxiii. 43.

[3] We here follow the reading *cerriti;* other readings are,— *curati* (with studied folly), *cirrati* (with effeminate foppery), and *citrati* (decking themselves with *citrus* leaves).
[4] That is, "fools," from the Greek μωρός.
[5] John iii. 8.
[6] 1 Cor. i. 31.

the liberation of men from their sins according to the deserts of their former existence : — what will they have to say about this man? How will they be able to attribute to him a previous life of so disgraceful a character that he deserved to be born an idiot, and at the same time of so highly meritorious a character as to entitle him to a preference in the award of the grace of Christ over many men of the acutest intellect?

CHAP. 33. — CHRIST IS THE SAVIOUR AND RE- DEEMER EVEN OF INFANTS.

Let us therefore give in and yield our assent to the authority of Holy Scripture, which knows not how either to be deceived or to deceive ; and as we do not believe that men as yet unborn have done any good or evil for raising a differ- ence in their moral deserts, so let us by no means doubt that all men are under sin, which came into the world by one man and has passed through unto all men ; and from which nothing frees us but the grace of God through our Lord Jesus Christ. [XXIII.] His remedial advent is needed by those that are sick, not by the whole : for He came not to call the righteous, but sin- ners ; and into His kingdom shall enter no one that is not born again of water and the Spirit ; nor shall any one attain salvation and eternal life except in His kingdom, — since the man who believes not in the Son, and eats not His flesh, shall not have life, but the wrath of God remains upon him. Now from this sin, from this sickness, from this wrath of God (of which by nature they are children who have original sin, even if they have none of their own on account of their youth), none delivers them, ex- cept the Lamb of God, who takes away the sins of the world ;[1] except the Physician, who came not for the sake of the sound, but of the sick ; except the Saviour, concerning whom it was said to the human race : "Unto you there is born this day a Saviour ;"[2] except the Redeemer, by whose blood our debt is blotted out. For who would dare to say that Christ is not the Saviour and Redeemer of infants? But from what does He save them, if there is no malady of original sin within them? From what does He redeem them, if through their origin from the first man they are not sold under sin? Let there be then no eternal salvation promised to infants out of our own opinion, without Christ's baptism ; for none is promised in that Holy Scripture which is to be preferred to all human authority and opinion.

CHAP. 34 [XXIV.] — BAPTISM IS CALLED SALVA- TION, AND THE EUCHARIST, LIFE, BY THE CHRISTIANS OF CARTHAGE.

The Christians of Carthage have an excellent

name for the sacraments, when they say that baptism is nothing else than "salvation," and the sacrament of the body of Christ nothing else than "life." Whence, however, was this de- rived, but from that primitive, as I suppose, and apostolic tradition, by which the Churches of Christ maintain it to be an inherent principle, that without baptism and partaking of the supper of the Lord it is impossible for any man to at- tain either to the kingdom of God or to salva- tion and everlasting life? So much also does Scripture testify, according to the words which we already quoted. For wherein does their opinion, who designate baptism by the term *salvation*, differ from what is written : "He *saved us* by the washing of regeneration?"[3] or from Peter's statement : "The like figure where- unto even baptism doth also *now save us?*"[4] And what else do they say who call the sacra- ment of the Lord's Supper *life*, than that which is written : "I am the *living* bread which came down from heaven ;"[5] and "The bread that I shall give is my flesh, for *the life* of the world ;"[5] and "Except ye eat the flesh of the Son of man, and drink His blood, ye shall have no life in you?"[6] If, therefore, as so many and such divine witnesses agree, neither salvation nor eternal life can be hoped for by any man with- out baptism and the Lord's body and blood, it is vain to promise these blessings to infants with- out them. Moreover, if it be only sins that separate man from salvation and eternal life, there is nothing else in infants which these sac- raments can be the means of removing, but the guilt of sin, — respecting which guilty nature it is written, that "no one is clean, not even if his life be only that of a day."[7] Whence also that exclamation of the Psalmist : "Behold, I was shapen in iniquity ; and in sin did my mother conceive me !"[8] This is either said in the per- son of our common humanity, or if of himself only David speaks, it does not imply that he was born of fornication, but in lawful wedlock. We therefore ought not to doubt that even for in- fants yet to be baptized was that precious blood shed, which previous to its actual effusion was so given, and applied in the sacrament, that it was said, "This is my blood, which shall be shed for many for the remission of sins."[9] Now they who will not allow that they are under sin, deny that there is any liberation. For what is there that men are liberated from, if they are held to be bound by no bondage of sin?

---

[1] John. i. 29.
[2] Luke ii. 11.

[3] Tit. iii. 5.
[4] 1 Pet. iii. 21
[5] John vi. 51.
[6] John vi. 53.
[7] Job xiv. 4.
[8] Ps. li. 5.
[9] Matt. xxvi. 28.

CHAP. 35. — UNLESS INFANTS ARE BAPTIZED, THEY
REMAIN IN DARKNESS.

" I am come," says Christ, " a light into the
world, that whosoever believeth on me should
not abide in darkness." [1]　Now what does this
passage show us, but that every person is in
darkness who does not believe on Him, and that
it is by believing on Him that he escapes from
this permanent state of darkness? What do we
understand by the *darkness* but sin? And whatever else it may embrace in its meaning, at any
rate he who believes not in Christ will " abide in
darkness," — which, of course, is a penal state,
not, as the darkness of the night, necessary for
the refreshment of living beings. [xxv.] So that
infants, unless they pass into the number of believers through the sacrament which was divinely
instituted for this purpose, will undoubtedly remain in this darkness.

CHAP. 36. — INFANTS NOT ENLIGHTENED AS SOON
AS THEY ARE BORN.

Some, however, understand that as soon as
children are born they are enlightened ; and they
derive this opinion from the passage : " That
was the true Light, which lighteth every one that
cometh into the world." [2]　Well, if this be the
case, it is quite astonishing how it can be that
those who are thus enlightened by the only-begotten Son, who was in the beginning the Word
with God, and [Himself] God, are not admitted
into the kingdom of God, nor are heirs of God
and joint-heirs with Christ. For that such an
inheritance is not bestowed upon them except
through baptism, even they who hold the opinion
in question do acknowledge. Then, again, if
they are (though already illuminated) thus unfit
for entrance into the kingdom of God, they at
all events ought gladly to receive the baptism,
by which they are fitted for it ; but, strange to
say, we see how reluctant infants are to submit
to baptism, resisting even with strong crying.
And this ignorance of theirs we think lightly of
at their time of life, so that we fully administer
the sacraments, which we know to be serviceable
to them, even although they struggle against
them. And why, too, does the apostle say, " Be
not children in understanding," [3] if their minds
have been already enlightened with that true
Light, which is the Word of God?

CHAP. 37. — HOW GOD ENLIGHTENS EVERY PERSON.

That statement, therefore, which occurs in the
gospel, " That was the true Light, which lighteth
every one that cometh into the world," [2] has this
meaning, that no man is illuminated except with

that Light of the truth, which is God ; so that
no person must think that he is enlightened by
him whom he listens to as a learner, although
that instructor happen to be — I will not say, any
great man — but even an angel himself. For
the word of truth is applied to man externally
by the ministry of a bodily voice, but yet
" neither is he that planteth any thing, neither
he that watereth ; but God that giveth the increase." [4]　Man indeed hears the speaker, be he
man or angel, but in order that he may perceive
and know that what is said is true, his mind is
internally besprinkled with that light which remains for ever, and which shines even in darkness. But just as the sun is not seen by the
blind, though they are clothed as it were with
its rays, so is the light of truth not understood
by the darkness of folly.

CHAP. 38. — WHAT " LIGHTETH " MEANS.

But why, after saying, " which lighteth every
man," should he add, " that cometh into the
world," [2] — the clause which has suggested the
opinion that He enlightens the minds of newly-
born babes while the birth of their bodies from
their mother's womb is still a recent thing? The
words, no doubt, are so placed in the Greek,
that they may be understood to express that the
light itself " cometh into the world." [5]　If, nevertheless, the clause must be taken as expressing
the man who cometh into this world, I suppose
that it is either a simple phrase, like many others
one finds in the Scriptures, which may be removed without impairing the general sense ; or
else, if it is to be regarded as a distinctive addition, it was perhaps inserted in order to distinguish spiritual illumination from that bodily one
which enlightens the eyes of the flesh either by
means of the luminaries of the sky, or by the
lights of ordinary fire. So that he mentioned
the inner man as coming into the world, because
the outward man is of a corporeal nature, just as
this world itself ; as if he said, " Which lighteth
every man that cometh into the body," in accordance with that which is written : " I obtained
a good spirit, and I came in a body undefiled." [6]
Or again, the passage, " Which lighteth every
one that cometh into the world," — if it was
added for the sake of expressing some distinction, — might perhaps mean : Which lighteth
every inner man, because the inner man, when
he becomes truly wise, is enlightened only by
Him who is the true Light. Or, once more, if
the intention was to designate reason herself,
which causes the human soul to be called rational (and this reason, although as yet quiet
and as it were asleep, for all that lies hidden in

---

[1] John xii. 46.
[2] John i. 9.
[3] 1 Cor. xiv. 20.

[4] 1 Cor. iii. 7.
[5] Ὁ [*scil.* τὸ φῶς] φωτίζει πάντα ἄνθρωπον ἐρχόμενον εἰς τὸν κόσμον.
[6] Wisd. viii. 19, 20.

infants, innate and, so to speak, implanted), by the term *illumination*, as if it were the creation of an inner eye, then it cannot be denied that it is made when the soul is created; and there is no absurdity in supposing this to take place when the human being comes into the world. But yet, although his eye is now created, he himself must needs remain in darkness, if he does not believe in Him who said: "I am come a a Light into the world, that whosoever believeth on me should not abide in darkness."[1] And that this takes place in the case of infants, through the sacrament of baptism, is not doubted by mother Church, which uses for them the heart and mouth of a mother, that they may be imbued with the sacred mysteries, seeing that they cannot as yet with their own heart "believe unto righteousness," nor with their own mouth make "confession unto salvation."[2] There is not indeed a man among the faithful, who would hesitate to call such infants *believers* merely from the circumstance that such a designation is derived from the act of believing; for although incapable of such an act themselves, yet others are sponsors for them in the sacraments.

CHAP. 39 [XXVI.] — THE CONCLUSION DRAWN, THAT ALL ARE INVOLVED IN ORIGINAL SIN.

It would be tedious, were we fully to discuss, at similar length, every testimony bearing on the question. I suppose it will be the more convenient course simply to collect the passages together which may turn up, or such as shall seem sufficient for manifesting the truth, that the Lord Jesus Christ came in the flesh, and, in the form of a servant, became obedient even to the death of the cross,[3] for no other reason than, by this dispensation of His most merciful grace, to give life to all those to whom, as engrafted members of His body, He becomes Head for laying hold upon the kingdom of heaven: to save, free, redeem, and enlighten them, — who had aforetime been involved in the death, infirmities, servitude, captivity, and darkness of sin, under the dominion of the devil, the author of sin: and thus to become the Mediator between God and man, by whom (after the enmity of our ungodly condition had been terminated by His gracious help) we might be reconciled to God unto eternal life, having been rescued from the eternal death which threatened such as us. When this shall have been made clear by more than sufficient evidence, it will follow that those persons cannot be concerned with that dispensation of Christ which is executed by His humiliation, who have no need of life, and salvation,

and deliverance, and redemption, and illumination. And inasmuch as to this belongs baptism, in which we are buried with Christ, in order to be incorporated into Him as His members (that is, as those who believe in Him): it of course follows that baptism is unnecessary for them, who have no need of the benefit of that forgiveness and reconciliation which is acquired through a Mediator. Now, seeing that they admit the necessity of baptizing infants, — finding themselves unable to contravene that authority of the universal Church, which has been unquestionably handed down by the Lord and His apostles, — they cannot avoid the further concession, that infants require the same benefits of the Mediator, in order that, being washed by the sacrament and charity of the faithful, and thereby incorporated into the body of Christ, which is the Church, they may be reconciled to God, and so live in Him, and be saved, and delivered, and redeemed, and enlightened. But from what, if not from death, and the vices, and guilt, and thraldom, and darkness of sin? And, inasmuch as they do not commit any sin in the tender age of infancy by their actual transgression, original sin only is left.

CHAP. 40 [XXVII.] — A COLLECTION OF SCRIPTURE TESTIMONIES. FROM THE GOSPELS.

This reasoning will carry more weight, after I have collected the mass of Scripture testimonies which I have undertaken to adduce. We have already quoted: "I came not to call the righteous, but sinners."[4] To the same purport [the Lord] says, on entering the home of Zaccheus: "To-day is salvation come to this house, forsomuch as he also is a son of Abraham; for the Son of man is come to seek and to save that which was lost."[5] The same truth is declared in the parable of the lost sheep and the ninety and nine which were left until the missing one was sought and found;[6] as it is also in the parable of the lost one among the ten silver coins.[7] Whence, as He said, "it behoved that repentance and remission of sins should be preached in His name among all nations, beginning at Jerusalem."[8] Mark likewise, at the end of his Gospel, tells us how that the Lord said: "Go ye into all the world, and preach the gospel to every creature. He that believeth, and is baptized, shall be saved; but he that believeth not shall be damned."[9] Now, who can be unaware that, in the case of infants, being baptized is to believe, and not being baptized is not to believe? From the Gospel of John we have already ad-

---

[1] John xii. 46.
[2] Rom. x. 10.
[3] Phil. ii 8.

[4] Luke v. 32.
[5] Luke xix. 9, 10.
[6] Luke xv. 4.
[7] Luke xv. 8.
[8] Luke xxiv. 46, 47.
[9] Mark xvi. 15, 16.

duced some passages. However, I must also request your attention to the following : John Baptist says of Christ, " Behold the Lamb of God, Behold Him which taketh away the sin of the world ; " [1] and He too says of Himself, " My sheep hear my voice, and I know them, and they follow me : and I give unto them eternal life ; and they shall never perish." [2] Now, inasmuch as infants are only able to become His sheep by baptism, it must needs come to pass that they perish if they are not baptized, because they will not have that eternal life which He gives to His sheep. So in another passage He says : " I am the way, the truth, and the life ; no man cometh unto the Father, but by me." [3]

### CHAP. 41. — FROM THE FIRST EPISTLE OF PETER.

See with what earnestness the apostles declare this doctrine, when they received it. Peter, in his first Epistle, says : " Blessed be the God and Father of our Lord Jesus Christ, according to His abundant mercy, who hath regenerated us unto the hope of eternal life, by the resurrection of Jesus Christ, to an inheritance immortal, and undefiled, flourishing, reserved in heaven for you, who are kept by the power of God through faith unto salvation, ready to be revealed in the last time." [4] And a little afterwards he adds : " May ye be found unto the praise and honour of Jesus Christ : of whom ye were ignorant ; but in whom ye believe, though now ye see Him not ; and in whom also ye shall rejoice, when ye shall see Him, with joy unspeakable and full of glory : receiving the end of your faith, even the salvation of your souls." [5] Again, in another place he says : " But ye are a chosen generation, a royal priesthood, a holy nation, a peculiar people ; that ye should show forth the praises of Him who hath called you out of darkness into His marvellous light." [6] Once more he says : " Christ hath once suffered for our sins, the just for the unjust, that He might bring us to God : " [7] and, after mentioning the fact of eight persons having been saved in Noah's ark, he adds : " And by the like figure baptism saveth you." [8] Now infants are strangers to this salvation and light, and will remain in perdition and darkness, unless they are joined to the people of God by adoption, holding to Christ who suffered the just for the unjust, to bring them unto God.

### CHAP. 42. — FROM THE FIRST EPISTLE OF JOHN.

Moreover, from John's Epistle I meet with the following words, which seem indispensable to the solution of this question : " But if," says he, " we walk in the light, as He is in the light, we have fellowship one with another, and the blood of Jesus Christ His Son cleanseth us from all sin." [9] To the like import he says, in another place : " If we receive the witness of men, the witness of God is greater : for this is the witness of God, which is greater because He hath testified of His Son. He that believeth on the Son of God hath the witness in himself : he that believeth not God hath made Him a liar ; because he believed not in the testimony that God testified of His Son. And this is the testimony, that God hath given to us eternal life ; and this life is in His Son. He that hath the Son hath life ; and he that hath not the Son of God hath not life." [10] It seems, then, that it is not only the kingdom of heaven, but life also, which infants are not to have, if they have not the Son, whom they can only have by His baptism. So again he says : " For this cause the Son of God was manifested, that He might destroy the works of the devil." [11] Therefore infants will have no interest in the manifestation of the Son of God, if He do not in them destroy the works of the devil.

### CHAP. 43. — FROM THE EPISTLE TO THE ROMANS.

Let me now request your attention to the testimony of the Apostle Paul on this subject. And quotations from him may of course be made more abundantly, because he wrote more epistles, and because it fell to him to recommend the grace of God with especial earnestness, in opposition to those who gloried in their works, and who, ignorant of God's righteousness, and wishing to establish their own, submitted not to the righteousness of God. [12] In his Epistle to the Romans he writes : " The righteousness of God is upon all them that believe ; for there is no difference ; since all have sinned, and come short of the glory of God ; being justified freely by His grace, through the redemption that is in Christ Jesus ; whom God hath set forth as a propitiation through faith in His blood, to declare His righteousness for the remission [13] of sins that are past, through the forbearance of God ; to declare, I say, at this time His righteousness ; that He might be just, and the justifier of him which believeth in Jesus." [14] Then in another passage he says : " To him that worketh is the reward not reckoned of grace, but of debt. But to him that worketh not, but believeth on Him that justifieth the ungodly, his faith is counted for righteousness. Even as David also describeth

---

[1] John i. 29.
[2] John x. 27, 28.
[3] John xiv. 6.
[4] 1 Pet. i. 3-5.
[5] 1 Pet. i. 7-9.
[6] 1 Pet. ii. 9.
[7] 1 Pet. iii. 18.
[8] 1 Pet. iii. 21.

[9] 1 John i. 7.
[10] 1 John v. 9-12.
[11] 1 John iii. 8.
[12] Rom. x. 3.
[13] [This is the reading of the Vulgate, as well as of the Greek: but Augustin, following an Old Latin reading, actually has *propositum*, instead of *remissionem.* — W.]
[14] Rom. iii. 22-26.

the blessedness of the man, unto whom God imputeth righteousness without works, saying, Blessed are they whose iniquities are forgiven, and whose sins are covered. Blessed is the man to whom the Lord imputeth no sin." [1] And then after no long interval he observes: " Now, it was not written for his sake alone, that it was imputed to him; but for us also, to whom it shall be imputed, if we believe on Him that raised up Jesus Christ our Lord from the dead; who was delivered for our offences, and was raised again for our justification." [2] Then a little after he writes: " For when we were yet without strength, in due time Christ died for the ungodly." [3] In another passage he says: " We know that the law is spiritual; but I am carnal, sold under sin. For that which I do I know not: for what I would, that I do not; but what I hate, that I do. If then I do that which I would not, I consent unto the law that it is good. Now then, it is no more I that do it, but sin that dwelleth in me. For I know that in me (that is, in my flesh) dwelleth no good thing; for to will is present with me; but how to perform that which is good I find not. For the good that I would I do not; but the evil which I would not, that I do. Now if I do that I would not, it is no more I that do it, but sin that dwelleth in me. I find then a law, that, when I would do good, evil is present with me. For I delight in the law of God after the inward man: but I see another law in my members warring against the law of my mind, and bringing me into captivity to the law of sin which is in my members. O wretched man that I am! who shall deliver me from the body of this death? The grace of God, through Jesus Christ our Lord." [4] Let them, who can, say that men are not born in the body of this death, that so they may be able to affirm that they have no need of God's grace through Jesus Christ in order to be delivered from the body of this death. Therefore he adds, a few verses afterwards: " For what the law could not do, in that it was weak through the flesh, God, sending His own Son in the likeness of sinful flesh, and for sin, condemned sin in the flesh." [5] Let them say, who dare, that Christ must have been born in the likeness of sinful flesh, if we were not born in sinful flesh.

### CHAP. 44. — FROM THE EPISTLES TO THE CORINTHIANS.

Likewise to the Corinthians he says: " For I delivered to you first of all that which I also received, how that Christ died for our sins according to the Scriptures." [6] Again, in his Second Epistle to these Corinthians: " For the love of Christ constraineth us; because we thus judge, that if One died for all, then all died: and for all did Christ die, that they which live should no longer live unto themselves, but unto Him which died for them, and rose again. Wherefore, henceforth know we no man after the flesh; yea, though we have known Christ after the flesh, yet from henceforth know we Him so no more. Therefore if any man be in Christ, he is a new creature; old things are passed away; behold, all things are become new. And all things are of God, who hath reconciled us to Himself by Jesus Christ, and hath given unto us the ministry of reconciliation. To what effect? That God was in Christ, reconciling the world unto Himself, not imputing their trespasses unto them, and putting on us the ministry of reconciliation. Now then are we ambassadors for Christ, as though God did beseech you by us; we pray you in Christ's stead, to be reconciled to God. For He hath made Him to be sin for us, who knew no sin; that we might become the righteousness of God in Him.[7] We then, as workers together with Him, beseech you also that ye receive not the grace of God in vain. (For He saith, I have heard thee in an acceptable time, and in the day of salvation have I succoured thee: behold, now is the acceptable time; behold, now is the day of salvation.)" [8] Now, if infants are not embraced within this reconciliation and salvation, who wants them for the baptism of Christ? But if they are embraced, then are they reckoned as among the dead for whom He died; nor can they be possibly reconciled and saved by Him, unless He remit and impute not unto them their sins.

### CHAP. 45. — FROM THE EPISTLE TO THE GALATIANS.

Likewise to the Galatians the apostle writes: " Grace be to you, and peace, from God the Father, and from our Lord Jesus Christ, who gave Himself for our sins, that He might deliver us from this present evil world." [9] While in another passage he says to them: " The law was added because of transgressions, until the seed should come to whom the promise was made; and it was ordained by angels in the hand of a mediator. Now a mediator belongs not to one party; but God is one. Is the law then against the promises of God? God forbid: for if there had been a law given which could have given life, verily righteousness should have been by the law. But the scripture hath concluded all under sin, that the promise by faith of Jesus Christ might be given to them that believe." [10]

---

1 Rom. iv. 4-8.
2 Rom. iv. 23-25.
3 Rom. v. 6.
4 Rom. vii. 14-25.
5 Rom. viii. 3.
6 1 Cor. xv. 3.

7 2 Cor. v. 14-21.
8 2 Cor. vi. 1, 2.
9 Gal. i. 3, 4.
10 Gal. iii. 19-22.

CHAP. 46.—FROM THE EPISTLE TO THE
EPHESIANS.

To the Ephesians he addresses words of the same import: "And you when ye were dead in trespasses and sins; wherein in time past ye walked according to the course of this world, according to the prince of the power of the air, the spirit of him that now worketh in the children of disobedience; among whom also we all had our conversation in times past in the lusts of our flesh, fulfilling the desires of the flesh and of the mind; and were by nature the children of wrath, even as others. But God, who is rich in mercy, for His great love wherewith He loved us, even when we were dead in sins, hath quickened us together with Christ; by whose grace ye are saved."[1] Again, a little afterwards, he says: "By grace are ye saved through faith; and that not of yourselves: it is the gift of God: not of works, lest any man should boast. For we are His workmanship, created in Christ Jesus unto good works, which God hath before ordained that we should walk in them."[2] And again, after a short interval: "At that time ye were without Christ, being aliens from the commonwealth of Israel, and strangers from the covenants of promise, having no hope, and without God in the world: but now, in Christ Jesus, ye who were sometimes far off are made nigh by the blood of Christ. For He is our peace, who hath made both one, and hath broken down the middle wall of partition between us; having abolished in His flesh the enmity, even the law of commandments contained in ordinances; for to make in Himself of twain one new man, so making peace; and that He might reconcile both unto God in one body by the cross, having in Himself slain the enmity; and He came and preached peace to you which were afar off, and to them that were nigh. For through Him we both have access by one Spirit unto the Father."[3] Then in another passage he thus writes: "As the truth is in Jesus: that ye put off, concerning the former conversation, the old man, which is corrupt according to the deceitful lusts; and be renewed in the spirit of your mind; and that ye put on the new man, which after God is created in righteousness and true holiness."[4] And again: "Grieve not the Holy Spirit of God, whereby ye are sealed unto the day of redemption."[5]

CHAP. 47.—FROM THE EPISTLE TO THE
COLOSSIANS.

To the Colossians he addresses these words: "Giving thanks unto the Father, which hath made us meet to be partakers of the inheritance of the saints in light: who hath delivered us from the power of darkness, and hath translated us into the kingdom of His dear Son; in whom we have redemption in the remission of our sins."[6] And again he says: "And ye are complete in Him, which is the head of all principality and power: in whom also ye are circumcised with the circumcision made without hands, in putting off the body of the flesh by the circumcision of Christ; buried with Him in baptism, wherein also ye are risen with Him through the faith of the operation of God, who hath raised Him from the dead. And you, when ye were dead in your sins and the uncircumcision of your flesh, hath He quickened together with Him, having forgiven you all trespasses; blotting out the handwriting of the decree that was against us, which was contrary to us, and took it out of the way, nailing it to His cross; and putting the flesh off Him,[7] He made a show of principalities and powers, confidently triumphing over them in Himself."[8]

CHAP. 48.—FROM THE EPISTLES TO TIMOTHY.

And then to Timothy he says: "This is a faithful saying,[9] and worthy of all acceptation, that Christ Jesus came into the world to save sinners; of whom I am chief. Howbeit for this cause I obtained mercy, that in me first Jesus Christ might show forth all long-suffering, for a pattern to them which should hereafter believe on Him to life everlasting."[10] He also says: "For there is one God and one Mediator between God and men, the man Christ Jesus; who gave Himself a ransom for all."[11] In his second Epistle to the same Timothy, he says: "Be not thou therefore ashamed of the testimony of our Lord, nor of me His prisoner: but be thou a fellowlabourer for the gospel, according to the power of God; who hath saved us, and called us with a holy calling, not according to our works, but according to His own purpose and grace, which was given us in Christ Jesus before the world began; but is now manifested by the coming of our Lord Jesus Christ, who hath abolished death, and hath brought life and immortality to light through the gospel."[12]

CHAP. 49.—FROM THE EPISTLE TO TITUS.

Then again he writes to Titus as follows: "Looking for that blessed hope, and the glorious appearing of the great God and our Saviour Jesus Christ; who gave himself for us, that He might redeem us from all iniquity, and purify unto Himself a peculiar people, zealous of good

---

[1] Eph. ii. 1–5.
[2] Eph. ii. 8–10.
[3] Eph. ii. 12–18.
[4] Eph. iv. 21–24.
[5] Eph. iv. 30.

[6] Col. i. 12–14.
[7] Exuens se carnem.
[8] Col. ii. 10–15.
[9] Humanus sermo.
[10] 1 Tim. i. 15, 16.
[11] 1 Tim. ii. 5, 6.
[12] 2 Tim. i. 8–10.

works." [1] And to the like effect in another passage : "But after that the kindness and love of God our Saviour toward man appeared, not by works of righteousness which we have done, but according to His mercy He saved us, by the washing of regeneration, and renewing of the Holy Ghost ; which He shed on us abundantly through Jesus Christ our Saviour ; that, being justified by His grace, we should be made heirs according to the hope of eternal life." [3]

CHAP. 50. — FROM THE EPISTLE TO THE HEBREWS.

Although the authority of the Epistle to the Hebrews is doubted by some,[3] nevertheless, as I find it sometimes thought by persons, who oppose our opinion touching the baptism of infants, to contain evidence in favour of their own views, we shall notice the pointed testimony it bears in our behalf ; and I quote it the more confidently, because of the authority of the Eastern Churches, which expressly place it amongst the canonical Scriptures. In its very exordium one thus reads : "God, who at sundry times, and in divers manners, spake in time past unto the fathers by the prophets, hath in these last days spoken to us by His Son, whom He hath appointed heir of all things, by whom also He made the worlds ; who, being the brightness of His glory, and the express image of His person, and upholding all things by the word of His power, when He had by Himself purged our sins, sat down on the right hand of the Majesty on high." [4] And by and by the writer says : "For if the word spoken by angels was stedfast, and every transgression and disobedience received a just recompense of reward, how shall we escape if we neglect so great salvation ? " [5] And again in another passage : "Forasmuch then," says he, "as the children are partakers of flesh and blood, He also Himself likewise took part of the same ; that through death He might destroy him that had the power of death, that is, the devil ; and deliver them who through fear of death were all their lifetime subject to bondage." [6] Again, shortly after, he says : "Wherefore in all things it behoved Him to be made like unto His brethren, that He might be a merciful and faithful High Priest in things pertaining

to God, to make reconciliation for the sins of the people." [7] And in another place he writes : "Let us hold fast our profession. For we have not a high priest which cannot be touched with the feeling of our infirmities ; but was in all points tempted like as we are, yet without sin." [8] Again he says : "He hath an unchangeable priesthood. Wherefore He is able also to save them to the uttermost that come unto God by Him, seeing He ever liveth to make intercession for them. For such a High Priest became us, who is holy, harmless, undefiled, separate from sinners, and made higher than the heavens ; who needeth not daily (as those high priests) to offer up sacrifice, first for His own sins, and then for the people's : for this He did once, when He offered up Himself." [9] And once more : "For Christ is not entered into the holy places made with hands, which are the figures of the true ; but into heaven itself, now to appear in the presence of God for us : nor yet that He should offer Himself often, as the high priest entereth into the holy place every year with blood of others ; (for then must He often have suffered since the foundation of the world ;) but now once, in the end of the world, hath He appeared to put away sin by the sacrifice of Himself. And as it is appointed unto men once to die, but after this the judgment ; so Christ was once offered to bear the sins of many : and unto them that look for Him shall He appear the second time, without sin, unto salvation." [10]

CHAP. 51. — FROM THE APOCALYPSE.

The Revelation of John likewise tells us that in a new song these praises are offered to Christ : "Thou art worthy to take the book, and to open the seals thereof : for Thou wast slain, and hast redeemed us to God by Thy blood out of every kindred, and tongue, and people, and nation." [11]

CHAP. 52. — FROM THE ACTS OF THE APOSTLES.

To the like effect, in the Acts of the Apostles, the Apostle Peter designated the Lord Jesus as "the Author of life," upbraiding the Jews for having put Him to death in these words : "But ye dishonoured and denied the Holy One and the Just, and desired a murderer to be granted unto you, and ye killed the Author of life." [12] While in another passage he says : "This is the stone which was set at nought by you builders, which is become the head of the corner. Neither is there salvation in any other : for there is none other name under heaven given among men whereby we must be saved." [13] And again, else-

---

[1] Tit. ii. 13, 14.
[2] Tit. iii. 3-7.
[3] Amongst the Latins, as Jerome tells us in more than one passage (see his *Commentaries*, on Isa. vi., viii.; on Zech. viii.; on Matt. xxvi.; also, in his *Catal. Script. Eccles.*, c. xvi. [ad Paulum], and lxx. [ad Gaium], etc.). The Greeks, however, held that the epistle was the work of St. Paul. In his *Epistle* cxxix. [ad Dardanum] he thus writes: "We must admit that the epistle written to the Hebrews is regarded as the Apostle Paul's, not only by the churches of the East, but by all church writers who have from the beginning *(retro)* written in Greek." — NOTE OF THE BENEDICTINE EDITOR. [See Augustin's *City of God*, xvi. 22, and *Christian Doctrine*, ii. (8), 13. The matter is fairly stated by Augustin, after whose day the Epistle was not doubted even in the West. — W.]
[4] Heb. i. 1-3.
[5] Heb. ii. 2, 3.
[6] Heb. ii. 14, 15.

[7] Heb. ii 17.
[8] Heb. iv. 14, 15.
[9] Heb. vii. 24-27.
[10] Heb. ix. 24-28.
[11] Rev. v. 9.
[12] Acts iii. 14, 15.
[13] Acts iv. 11, 12.

where: "The God of our fathers raised up Jesus, whom ye slew, by hanging on a tree. Him hath God exalted with His right hand to be a Prince and a Saviour, for to give repentance to Israel, and forgiveness of sins."[1] Once more: "To Him give all the prophets witness, that, through His name, whosoever believeth in Him shall receive remission of sins."[2] Whilst in the same Acts of the Apostles Paul says: "Be it known therefore unto you, men and brethren, that through this Man is preached unto you the forgiveness of sins: and by Him every one that believeth is justified from all things, from which ye could not be justified by the law of Moses."[3]

CHAP. 53. — THE UTILITY OF THE BOOKS OF THE OLD TESTAMENT.

Under so great a weight of testimony, who would not be oppressed that should dare lift up his voice against the truth of God? And many other testimonies might be found, were it not for my anxiety to bring this tract to an end, — an anxiety which I must not slight. I have deemed it superfluous to quote from the books of the Old Testament, likewise, many attestations to our doctrine in inspired words, since what is concealed in them under the veil of earthly promises is clearly revealed in the preaching of the New Testament. Our Lord Himself briefly demonstrated and defined the use of the Old Testament writings, when He said that it was necessary that what had been written concerning Himself in the Law, and the Prophets, and the Psalms, should be fulfilled, and that this was that Christ must suffer, and rise from the dead the third day, and that repentance and remission of sins should be preached in His name among all nations, beginning at Jerusalem.[4] In agreement with this is that statement of Peter which I have already quoted, how that all the prophets bear witness to Christ, that at His hands every one that believes in Him receives remission of his sins.[2]

CHAP. 54. — BY THE SACRIFICES OF THE OLD TESTAMENT, MEN WERE CONVINCED OF SINS AND LED TO THE SAVIOUR.

And yet it is perhaps better to advance a few testimonies out of the Old Testament also, which ought to have a supplementary, or rather a cumulative value. The Lord Himself, speaking by the Psalmist, says: "As for my saints which are upon earth, He hath caused all my purposes to be admired in them."[5] Not *their merits*, but "*my purposes*." For what is theirs except that which is afterwards mentioned, —

"their weaknesses are multiplied,"[6] — above the weakness that they had? Moreover, the law also entered, that the offence might abound. But why does the Psalmist immediately add: "They hastened after?"[6] When their sorrows and infirmities multiplied (that is, when their offence abounded), they then sought the Physician more eagerly, in order that, where sin abounded, grace might much more abound. He then says: "I will not gather their assemblies together [with their offerings] of blood;" for by their many sacrifices of blood, when they gathered their assemblies into the tabernacle at first, and then into the temple, they were rather convicted as sinners than cleansed. I shall no longer, He says, gather their assemblies of blood-offerings together; because there is one blood-shedding given for many, whereby they may be truly cleansed. Then it follows: "Neither will I make mention of their names with my lips," as if they were the names of renewed ones. For these were their names at first: children of the flesh, children of the world, children of wrath, children of the devil, unclean, sinners, impious; but afterwards, children of God, — a new name to the new man, a new song to the singer of what is new, by means of the New Testament. Men must not be ungracious with God's grace, mean with great things; [but be ever rising] from the less to the greater. The cry of the whole Church is, "I have gone astray like a lost sheep."[7] From all the members of Christ the voice is heard: "All we, as sheep, have gone astray; and He hath Himself been delivered up for our sins."[8] The whole of this passage of prophecy is that famous one in Isaiah which was expounded by Philip to the eunuch of Queen Candace, and he believed in Jesus.[9] See how often he commends this very subject, and, as it were, inculcates it again and again on proud and contentious men: "He was a man under misfortune, and one who well knows to bear infirmities; wherefore also He turned away His face, He was dishonoured, and was not much esteemed. He it is that bears our weaknesses, and for us is involved in pains: and we accounted Him to be in pains, and in misfortune, and in punishment. But it was He who was wounded for our sins, was weakened for our iniquities; the chastisement of our peace was upon Him; and by His bruise we are healed. All we, as sheep, have gone astray; and the Lord delivered Him up for our sins. And although He was evilly entreated, yet He opened not His mouth: as a sheep was He led to the slaughter, and as a lamb is dumb before the shearer, so He opened not His mouth. In

---

[1] Acts v. 30, 31.
[2] Acts x. 43.
[3] Acts xiii. 38, 39.
[4] See Luke xxiv. 44-47.
[5] Ps. xvi. 3.

[6] Ps. xvi. 4.
[7] Ps. cxix. 176.
[8] Isa. liii. 6.
[9] Acts viii. 30-37.

His humiliation His judgment was taken away: His generation who shall declare? For His life shall be taken away from the earth, and for the iniquities of my people was He led to death. Therefore I will give the wicked for His burial, and the rich for His death; because He did no iniquity, nor deceit with His mouth. The Lord is pleased to purge Him from misfortune. If you could yourselves have given your soul on account of your sins, ye should see a seed of a long life. And the Lord is pleased to rescue His soul from pains, to show Him light, and to form it through His understanding; to justify the Just One, who serves many well; and He shall Himself bear their sins. Therefore He shall inherit many, and He shall divide the spoils of the mighty; and He was numbered amongst the transgressors; and Himself bare the sins of many, and He was delivered for their iniquities."[1] Consider also that passage of this same prophet which Christ actually declared to be fulfilled in Himself, when He recited it in the synagogue, in discharging the function of the reader:[2] "The Spirit of the Lord is upon me, because He hath anointed me: to preach glad tidings to the poor hath He sent me, that so I may refresh all who are broken-hearted, — to preach deliverance to the captives, and to the blind sight."[3] Let us then all acknowledge Him; nor should there be one exception among persons like ourselves, who wish to cleave to His body, to enter through Him into the sheepfold, and to attain to that life and eternal salvation which He has promised to His own. — Let us, I repeat, all of us acknowledge Him who did no sin, who bare our sins in His own body on the tree, that we might live with righteousness separate from sins; by whose scars we are healed, when we were weak[4] — like wandering sheep.

CHAP. 55 [XXVIII.] — HE CONCLUDES THAT ALL MEN NEED THE DEATH OF CHRIST, THAT THEY MAY BE SAVED. UNBAPTIZED INFANTS WILL BE INVOLVED IN THE CONDEMNATION OF THE DEVIL. HOW ALL MEN THROUGH ADAM ARE UNTO CONDEMNATION; AND THROUGH CHRIST UNTO JUSTIFICATION. NO ONE IS RECONCILED WITH GOD, EXCEPT THROUGH CHRIST.

In such circumstances, no man of those who have come to Christ by baptism has ever been regarded, according to sound faith and the true doctrine, as excepted from the grace of forgiveness of sins; nor has eternal life been ever thought possible to any man apart from His kingdom. For this [eternal life] is ready to be revealed at the last time,[5] that is, at the resurrection of the dead who are reserved not for that eternal death which is called "the second death," but for the eternal life which God, who cannot lie, promises to His saints and faithful servants. Now none who shall partake of this life shall be made alive except in Christ, even as all die in Adam.[6] For as none whatever, of all those who belong to the generation according to the will of the flesh, die except in Adam, in whom all sinned; so, out of these, none at all who are regenerated by the will of the Spirit are endowed with life except in Christ, in whom all are justified. Because as through one all to condemnation, so through One all to justification.[7] Nor is there any middle place for any man, and so a man can only be with the devil who is not with Christ. Accordingly, also the Lord Himself (wishing to remove from the hearts of wrong-believers[8] that vague and indefinite middle condition, which some would provide for unbaptized infants, — as if, by reason of their innocence, they were embraced in eternal life, but were not, because of their unbaptized state, with Christ in His kingdom) uttered that definitive sentence of His, which shuts their mouths: "He that is not with me is against me."[9] Take then the case of any infant you please: If he is already in Christ, why is he baptized? If, however, as the Truth has it, he is baptized just that he may be with Christ, it certainly follows that he who is not baptized is not with Christ; and because he is not "with" Christ, he is "against" Christ; for He has pronounced His own sentence, which is so explicit that we ought not, and indeed cannot, impair it or change it. And how can he be "against" Christ, if not owing to sin? for it cannot possibly be from his soul or his body, both of these being the creation of God. Now if it be owing to sin, what sin can be found at such an age, except the ancient and original sin? Of course that sinful flesh in which all are born to condemnation is one thing, and that Flesh which was made "after the likeness of sinful flesh," whereby also all are freed from condemnation, is another thing. It is, however, by no means meant to be implied that all who are born in sinful flesh are themselves actually cleansed by that Flesh which is "like" sinful flesh; "for all men have not faith;"[10] but that all who are born from the carnal union are born entirely of sinful flesh, whilst all who are born from the spiritual union are cleansed only by the Flesh which is in the likeness of sinful flesh.

---

[1] Isa. liii. 3-12.
[2] See Luke iv. 16-21.
[3] Isa. lxi. 1.
[4] There seems to be here some omission. — BENEDICTINE NOTE.
[5] 1 Pet. i. 5.
[6] 1 Cor. xv. 22.
[7] Rom. v. 18.
[8] Malè credentium.
[9] Matt. xii. 30.
[10] 2 Thess. iii. 2.

In other words, the former class are in Adam unto condemnation, the latter are in Christ unto justification. This is as if we should say, for example, that in such a city there is a certain midwife who delivers all; and in the same place there is an expert teacher who instructs all. By all, in the one case, only those who are born can possibly be understood; by all, in the other, only those who are taught: and it does not follow that all who are born also receive the instruction. But it is obvious to every one, that in the one case it is correctly said, "she delivers all," since without her aid no one is born; and in the other, it is rightly said, "he teaches all," since without his tutoring, no one learns.

CHAP. 56. — NO ONE IS RECONCILED TO GOD EXCEPT THROUGH CHRIST.

Taking into account all the inspired statements which I have quoted, — whether I regard the value of each passage one by one, or combine their united testimony in an accumulated witness or even include similar passages which I have not adduced, — there can be nothing discovered, but that which the catholic Church holds, in her dutiful vigilance against all profane novelties: that every man is separated from God, except those who are reconciled to God through Christ the Mediator; and that no one can be separated from God, except by sins, which alone cause separation; that there is, therefore, no reconciliation except by the remission of sins, through the one grace of the most merciful Saviour, — through the one sacrifice of the most veritable Priest; and that none who are born of the woman, that trusted the serpent and so was corrupted through desire,[1] are delivered from the body of this death, except by the Son of the virgin who believed the angel and so conceived without desire.[2]

CHAP. 57 [XXIX.] — THE GOOD OF MARRIAGE; FOUR DIFFERENT CASES OF THE GOOD AND THE EVIL USE OF MATRIMONY.

The good, then, of marriage lies not in the passion of desire, but in a certain legitimate and honourable measure in using that passion, appropriate to the propagation of children, not the gratification of lust.[3] That, therefore, which is disobediently excited in the members of the body of this death, and endeavours to draw into itself our whole fallen soul, (neither arising nor subsiding at the bidding of the mind), is that evil of sin in which every man is born. When, however, it is curbed from unlawful desires, and

is permitted only for the orderly propagation and renewal of the human race, this is the good of wedlock, by which man is born in the union that is appointed. Nobody, however, is born again in Christ's body, unless he be previously born in the body of sin. But inasmuch as it is evil to make a bad use of a good thing, so is it good to use well a bad thing. These two ideas therefore of *good* and *evil,* and those other two of a *good use* and an *evil use,* when they are duly combined together, produce four different conditions : — [1.] A man makes a good use of a good thing, when he dedicates his continence to God ; [2.] He makes a bad use of a good thing, when he dedicates his continence to an idol; [3.] He makes a bad use of an evil thing, when he loosely gratifies his concupiscence by adultery ; [4.] He makes a good use of an evil thing, when he restrains his concupiscence by matrimony. Now, as it is better to make good use of a good thing than to make good use of an evil thing, — since both are good, — so " he that giveth his virgin in marriage doeth well ; but he that giveth her not in marriage doeth better."[4] This question, indeed, I have treated at greater length, and more sufficiently, as God enabled me according to my humble abilities, in two works of mine, — one of them, *On the Good of Marriage,* and the other, *On Holy Virginity.* They, therefore, who extol the flesh and blood of a sinful creature, to the prejudice of the Redeemer's flesh and blood, must not defend the evil of concupiscence through the good of marriage ; nor should they, from whose infant age the Lord has inculcated in us a lesson of humility,[5] be lifted up into pride by the error of others. He only was born without sin whom a virgin conceived without the embrace of a husband, — not by the concupiscence of the flesh, but by the chaste submission of her mind.[6] She alone was able to give birth to One who should heal our wound, who brought forth the germ of a pure offspring without the wound of sin.

CHAP. 58 [XXX.] — IN WHAT RESPECT THE PELAGIANS REGARDED BAPTISM AS NECESSARY FOR INFANTS.

Let us now examine more carefully, so far as the Lord enables us, that very chapter of the Gospel where He says, " Except a man be born again, — of water and the Spirit, — he shall not enter into the kingdom of God."[7] If it were not for the authority which this sentence has with them, they would not be of opinion that infants ought to be baptized at all. This is their comment on the passage : " Because He does not say, ' Except a man be born again of water

---

[1] Gen. iii. 6.
[2] Luke i. 38.
[3] [The editions, but apparently no MSS., add here the somewhat sententious words: " Voluntas ista, non voluptas illa, nuptialis est," —which may, perhaps, be rendered: " Wedded desire is willingness, not wantonness." — W.]

[4] 1 Cor. vii. 38.
[5] Matt. xviii. 4.
[6] Luke i. 34, 38.
[7] John iii. 3, 5.

and the Spirit, he shall not have salvation or eternal life,' but He merely said, ' he shall not enter into the kingdom of God,' therefore infants are to be baptized, in order that they may be with Christ in the kingdom of God, where they will not be unless they are baptized. Should infants die, however, even without baptism, they will have salvation and eternal life, seeing that they are bound with no fetter of sin." Now in such a statement as this, the first thing that strikes one is, that they never explain *where the justice is* of separating from the kingdom of God that " image of God " which has no sin. Next, we ought to see whether the Lord Jesus, the one only good Teacher, has not in this very passage of the Gospel intimated, and indeed shown us, that it only comes to pass through the remission of their sins that baptized persons reach the kingdom of God; although to persons of a right understanding, the words, as they stand in the passage, ought to be sufficiently explicit: " Except a man be born again, he cannot see the kingdom of God;" [1] and: "Except a man be born of water and of the Spirit, he cannot enter into the kingdom of God." [2] For why should he be born again, unless to be renewed? From what is he to be renewed, if not from some old condition? From what old condition, but that in which " our old man is crucified with Him, that the body of sin might be destroyed?" [3] Or whence comes it to pass that " the image of God " enters not into the kingdom of God, unless it be that the impediment of sin prevents it? However, let us (as we said before) see, as earnestly and diligently as we are able, what is the entire context of this passage of the Gospel, on the point in question.

CHAP. 59.—THE CONTEXT OF THEIR CHIEF TEXT.

" Now there was," we read, " a man of the Pharisees, named Nicodemus, a ruler of the Jews: the same came to Jesus by night, and said unto Him, Rabbi, we know that thou art a teacher come from God: for no man can do these miracles that thou doest, except God be with him. Jesus answered and said unto him, Verily, verily, I say unto thee, Except a man be born again, he cannot see the kingdom of God. Nicodemus saith unto Him, How can a man be born when he is old? can he enter the second time into his mother's womb, and be born? Jesus answered, Verily, verily, I say unto thee, Except a man be born of water and of the Spirit, he cannot enter into the kingdom of God. That which is born of the flesh is flesh; and that which is born of the Spirit is spirit. Marvel not that I said unto thee, Ye must be born again.

The wind bloweth where it listeth, and thou hearest the sound thereof, but canst not tell whence it cometh, and whither it goeth: so is every one that is born of the Spirit. Nicodemus answered and said unto Him, How can these things be? Jesus answered and said unto him, Art thou a master of Israel, and knowest not these things? Verily, verily, I say unto thee, We speak that we do know, and testify that we have seen; and ye receive not our witness. If I have told you earthly things, and ye believe not, how shall ye believe if I tell you of heavenly things? And no man hath ascended up to heaven, but He that came down from heaven, even the Son of man which is in heaven. And as Moses lifted up the serpent in the wilderness,[4] even so must the Son of man be lifted up; that whosoever believeth in Him should not perish, but have eternal life. For God so loved the world, that He gave His only-begotten Son, that whosoever believeth in Him should not perish, but have everlasting life. For God sent not His Son into the world to condemn the world, but that the world through Him might be saved. He that believeth on Him is not condemned; but he that believeth not is condemned already, because he hath not believed in the name of the only-begotten Son of God. And this is the condemnation, that light is come into the world, and men loved darkness rather than light, because their deeds were evil. For every one that doeth evil hateth the light, neither cometh to the light, lest his deeds should be reproved. But he that doeth truth cometh to the light, that his deeds may be made manifest, that they are wrought in God." [5] Thus far the Lord's discourse wholly relates to the subject of our present inquiry; from this point the sacred historian digresses to another matter.

CHAP. 60 [XXXI.] — CHRIST, THE HEAD AND THE BODY; OWING TO THE UNION OF THE NATURES IN THE PERSON OF CHRIST, HE BOTH REMAINED IN HEAVEN, AND WALKED ABOUT ON EARTH; HOW THE ONE CHRIST COULD ASCEND TO HEAVEN; THE HEAD, AND THE BODY, THE ONE CHRIST.

Now when Nicodemus understood not what was being told him, he inquired of the Lord how such things could be. Let us look at what the Lord said to him in answer to his inquiry; for of course, as He deigns to answer the question, How can these things be? He will in fact tell us how spiritual regeneration can come to a man who springs from carnal generation. After noticing briefly the ignorance of one who assumed a superiority over others as a teacher, and having blamed the unbelief of all such, for not

---

[1] John iii. 3.
[2] John iii. 5.
[3] Rom. vi. 6.

[4] Num. xxi. 9.
[5] John iii. 1–21.

accepting His witness to the truth, He went on to inquire and wonder whether, as He had told them about earthly things and they had not believed they would believe heavenly things. He nevertheless pursues the subject, and gives an answer such as others should believe — though these refuse — to the question that he was asked, How these things can be? " No man," says He, " hath ascended up to heaven, but He that came down from heaven, even the Son of man which is in heaven." [1]  Thus, He says, shall come the spiritual birth, — men, from being earthly, shall become heavenly ; and this they can only obtain by being made members of me ; so that he may ascend who descended, since no one ascends who did not descend. All, therefore, who have to be changed and raised must meet together in a union with Christ, so that the Christ who descended may ascend, reckoning His body (that is to say, His Church) as nothing else than Himself, because it is of Christ and the Church that this is most truly understood : "And they twain shall be one flesh ; " [2] concerning which very subject He expressly said Himself, " So then they are no more twain, but one flesh." [3] To ascend, therefore, they would be wholly unable, since " no man hath ascended up to heaven, but He that came down from heaven, even the Son of man which is in heaven." [1]  For although it was on earth that He was made the Son of man, yet He did not deem it unworthy of that divinity, in which, although remaining in heaven, He came down to earth, to designate it by the name of the Son of man, as He dignified His flesh with the name of Son of God : that they might not be regarded as if they were two Christs, — the one God, the other man,[4] — but one and the same God and man, — God, because " in the beginning was the Word, and the Word was with God, and the Word was God ; " [5] and man, inasmuch as " the Word was made flesh and dwelt among us." [6]  By this means — by the difference between His divinity and His humiliation — He remained in heaven as Son of God, and as Son of man walked on earth ; whilst, by that unity of His person which made His two natures one Christ, He both walked as Son of God on earth, and at the same time as the very Son of man remained in heaven. Faith, therefore, in more credible things arises from the belief of such things as are more incredible. For if His divine nature, though a far more distant object, and more sublime in its incomparable diversity, had ability so to take upon itself

the nature of man on our account as to become one Person, and whilst appearing as Son of man on earth in the weakness of the flesh, was able to remain all the while in heaven in the divinity which partook of the flesh, how much easier for our faith is it to suppose that other men, who are His faithful saints, become one Christ with the Man Christ, so that, when all ascend by His grace and fellowship, the one Christ Himself ascends to heaven who came down from heaven? It is in this sense that the apostle says, " As we have many members in one body, and all the members of the body, being many, are one body, so likewise is Christ." [7]  He did not say, " So also is Christ's " — meaning Christ's body, or Christ's members — but his words are, " So likewise is Christ," thus calling the head and body one Christ.

CHAP. 61 [XXXII.] — THE SERPENT LIFTED UP IN THE WILDERNESS PREFIGURED CHRIST SUSPENDED ON THE CROSS ; EVEN INFANTS THEMSELVES POISONED BY THE SERPENT'S BITE.

And since this great and wonderful dignity can only be attained by the remission of sins, He goes on to say, " And as Moses lifted up the serpent in the wilderness, even so must the Son of man be lifted up ; that whosoever believeth in Him should not perish, but have eternal life." [8] We know what at that time happened in the wilderness. Many were dying of the bite of serpents : the people then confessed their sins, and, through Moses, besought the Lord to take away from them this poison ; accordingly, Moses, at the Lord's command, lifted up a brazen serpent in the wilderness, and admonished the people that every one who had been serpent-bitten should look upon the uplifted figure. When they did so they were immediately healed.[9]  What means the uplifted serpent but the death of Christ, by that mode of expressing a sign, whereby the thing which is effected is signified by that which effects it?  Now death came by the serpent, which persuaded man to commit the sin, by which he deserved to die. The Lord, however, transferred to His own flesh not sin, as the poison of the serpent, but He did transfer to it death, that the penalty without the fault might transpire in the likeness of sinful flesh, whence, in the sinful flesh, both the fault might be removed and the penalty. As, therefore, it then came to pass that whoever looked at the raised serpent was both healed of the poison and freed from death, so also now, whosoever is conformed to the likeness of the death of Christ by faith in Him and His baptism, is freed both from sin by justification, and from death by resurrection. For this

---

[1] John iii. 13.
[2] Gen. ii. 24.
[3] Mark x. 8.
[4] This was the error which was subsequently condemned in the heresy of Nestorius.
[5] John i. 1.
[6] John i. 14.

[7] 1 Cor. xii. 12.
[8] John iii. 14, 15.
[9] Numb. xxi. 6–9.

is what He says : "That whosoever believeth in Him should not perish, but have eternal life." [1] What necessity then could there be for an infant's being conformed to the death of Christ by baptism, if he were not altogether poisoned by the bite of the serpent?

CHAP. 62 [XXXIII.] — NO ONE CAN BE RECONCILED TO GOD, EXCEPT BY CHRIST.

He then proceeds thus, saying : "God so loved the world, that He gave His only-begotten Son, that whosoever believeth in Him should not perish, but have everlasting life." [2] Every infant, therefore, was destined to perish, and to lose everlasting life, if through the sacrament of baptism he believed not in the only-begotten Son of God ; while nevertheless, He comes not so that he may judge the world, but that the world through Him may be saved. This especially appears in the following clause, wherein He says, "He that believeth in Him is not condemned ; but he that believeth not is condemned already, because he hath not believed in the name of the only-begotten Son of God." [3] In what class, then, do we place baptized infants but amongst believers, as the authority of the catholic Church everywhere asserts? They belong, therefore, among those who have believed ; for this is obtained for them by virtue of the sacrament and the answer of their sponsors. And from this it follows that such as are not baptized are reckoned among those who have not believed. Now if they who are baptized are not condemned, these last, as not being baptized, are condemned. He adds, indeed : "But this is the condemnation, that light is come into the world, and men loved darkness rather than light." [4] Of what does He say, "Light is come into the world," if not of His own advent? and without the sacrament of His advent, how are infants said to be in the light? And why should we not include this fact also in "men's love of darkness," that as they do not themselves believe, so they refuse to think that their infants ought to be baptized, although they are afraid of their incurring the death of the body? "In God," however, he declares are the "works of him wrought, who cometh to the light," [5] because he is quite aware that his justification results from no merits of his own, but from the grace of God. "For it is God," says the apostle, "who worketh in you both to will and to do of His own good pleasure." [6] This then is the way in which spiritual regeneration is effected in all who come to Christ from their carnal generation. He explained it

Himself, and pointed it out, when He was asked, How these things could be? He left it open to no man to settle such a question by human reasoning, lest infants should be deprived of the grace of the remission of sins. There is no other passage leading to Christ ; no man can be reconciled to God, or can come to God otherwise, than through Christ.

CHAP. 63 [XXXIV.] — THE FORM, OR RITE, OF BAPTISM. EXORCISM.

What shall I say of the actual form of this sacrament? I only wish some one of those who espouse the contrary side would bring me an infant to be baptized. What does my exorcism work in that babe, if he be not held in the devil's family? The man who brought the infant would certainly have had to act as sponsor for him, for he could not answer for himself. How would it be possible then for him to declare that he renounced the devil, if there was no devil in him? that he was converted to God, if he had never been averted from Him? that he believed, besides other articles, in the forgiveness of sins, if no sins were attributable to him? For my own part, indeed, if I thought that his opinions were opposed to this faith, I could not permit him to bring the infant to the sacraments. Nor can I imagine with what countenance before men, or what mind before God, he can conduct himself in this. But I do not wish to say anything too severe. That a false or fallacious form of baptism should be administered to infants, in which there might be the sound and semblance of something being done, but yet no remission of sins actually ensue, has been seen by some amongst them to be as abominable and hateful a thing as it was possible to mention or conceive. Then, again, in respect of the necessity of baptism to infants, they admit that even infants stand in need of redemption, — a concession which is made in a short treatise written by one of their party, — but yet there is not found in this work any open admission of the forgiveness of a single sin. According, however, to an intimation dropped in your letter to me, they now acknowledge, as you say, that a remission of sins takes place even in infants through baptism. No wonder ; for it is impossible that *redemption* should be understood in any other way. Their own words are these : "It is, however, not originally, but in their own actual life, after they have been born, that they have begun to have sin."

CHAP. 64. — A TWOFOLD MISTAKE RESPECTING INFANTS.

You see how great a difference there is amongst those whom I have been opposing at such length and persistency in this work, — one of whom has

[1] John iii. 15.
[2] John iii. 16.
[3] John iii. 18.
[4] John iii. 19.
[5] John iii. 21.
[6] Phil. ii. 13.

written the book which contains the points I have refuted to the best of my ability. You see, as I was saying, the important difference existing between such of them as maintain that infants are absolutely pure and free from all sin, whether original or actual; and those who suppose that so soon as born infants have contracted actual sins of their own, from which they need cleansing by baptism. The latter class, indeed, by examining the Scriptures, and considering the authority of the whole Church as well as the form of the sacrament itself, have clearly seen that by baptism remission of sins accrues to infants; but they are either unwilling or unable to allow that the sin which infants have is original sin. The former class, however, have clearly seen (as they easily might) that in the very nature of man, which is open to the consideration of all men, the tender age of which we speak could not possibly commit any sin whatever in its own proper conduct; but, to avoid acknowledging original sin, they assert that there is no sin at all in infants. Now in the truths which they thus severally maintain, it so happens that they first of all mutually agree with each other, and subsequently differ from us in material aspect. For if the one party concede to the other that remission of sins takes place in all infants which are baptized, whilst the other concedes to their opponents that infants (as infant nature itself in its silence loudly proclaims) have as yet contracted no sin in their own living, then both sides must agree in conceding to us, that nothing remains but original sin, which can be remitted in baptism to infants.

## CHAP. 65 [XXXV.] — IN INFANTS THERE IS NO SIN OF THEIR OWN COMMISSION.

Will this also be questioned, and must we spend time in discussing it, in order to prove and show how that by their own will — without which there can be no sin in their own life — infants could never commit an offence, whom all, for this very reason, are in the habit of calling *innocent?* Does not their great weakness of mind and body, their great ignorance of things, their utter inability to obey a precept, the absence in them of all perception and impression of law, either natural or written, the complete want of reason to impel them in either direction, — proclaim and demonstrate the point before us by a silent testimony far more expressive than any argument of ours? The very palpableness of the fact must surely go a great way to persuade us of its truth; for there is no place where I do not find traces of what I say, so ubiquitous is the fact of which we are speaking, — clearer, indeed, to perceive than any thing we can say to prove it.

## CHAP. 66. — INFANTS' FAULTS SPRING FROM THEIR SHEER IGNORANCE.

I should, however, wish any one who was wise on the point to tell me what sin he has seen or thought of in a new-born infant, for redemption from which he allows baptism to be already necessary; what kind of evil it has in its own proper life committed by its own mind or body. If it should happen to cry and to be wearisome to its elders, I wonder whether my informant would ascribe this to iniquity, and not rather to unhappiness. What, too, would he say to the fact that it is hushed from its very weeping by no appeal to its own reason, and by no prohibition of any one else? This, however, comes from the ignorance in which it is so deeply steeped, by reason of which, too, when it grows stronger, as it very soon does, it strikes its mother in its little passion, and often her very breasts which it sucks when it is hungry. Well, now, these small freaks are not only borne in very young children, but are actually loved, — and this with what affection except that of the flesh,[1] by which we are delighted by a laugh or a joke, seasoned with fun and nonsense by clever persons, although, if it were understood literally, as it is spoken, they would not be laughed with as facetious, but at as simpletons? We see, also, how those simpletons whom the common people call *Moriones*[2] are used for the amusement of the sane; and that they fetch higher prices than the sane when appraised for the slave market. So great, then, is the influence of mere natural feeling, even over those who are by no means simpletons, in producing amusement at another's misfortune. Now, although a man may be amused by another man's silliness, he would still dislike to be a simpleton himself; and if the father, who gladly enough looks out for, and even provokes, such things from his own prattling boy, were to foreknow that he would, when grown up, turn out a fool, he would without doubt think him more to be grieved for than if he were dead. While, however, hope remains of growth, and the light of intellect is expected to increase with the increase of years, then the insults of young children even to their parents seem not merely not wrong, but even agreeable and pleasant. No prudent man, doubtless, could possibly approve of not only not forbidding in children such conduct in word or deed as this, as soon as they are able to be forbidden, but even of exciting them to it, for the vain amusement of their elders. For as soon as children are of an age to know their father and mother, they dare not use wrong words to either, unless permitted or bidden by either, or both.

[1] Carnali.
[2] See above, ch. 32.

But such things can only belong to such young children as are just striving to lisp out words, and whose minds are just able to give some sort of motion to their tongue. Let us, however, consider the depth of the ignorance rather of the new-born babes, out of which, as they advance in age, they come to this merely temporary stuttering folly, — on their road, as it were, to knowledge and speech.

### CHAP. 67 [XXXVI.] — ON THE IGNORANCE OF INFANTS, AND WHENCE IT ARISES.

Yes, let us consider that darkness of their rational intellect, by reason of which they are even completely ignorant of God, whose sacraments they actually struggle against, while being baptized. Now my inquiry is, When and whence came they to be immersed in this darkness? Is it then the fact that they incurred it all *here*, and in this their own proper life forgat God through too much negligence, after a life of wisdom and religion in their mother's womb? Let those say so who dare; let them listen to it who wish to; let them believe it who can. I, however, am sure that none whose minds are not blinded by an obstinate adherence to a foregone conclusion can possibly entertain such an opinion. Is there then no evil in ignorance, — nothing which needs to be purged away? What means that prayer: "Remember not the sins of my youth and of my ignorance?"[1] For although those sins are more to be condemned which are knowingly committed, yet if there were no sins of ignorance, we should not have read in Scripture what I have quoted, "Remember not the sins of my youth and of my ignorance." Seeing now that the soul of an infant fresh from its mother's womb is still the soul of a human being, — nay, the soul of a rational creature, — not only untaught, but even incapable of instruction, I ask why, or when, or whence, it was plunged into that thick darkness of ignorance in which it lies? If it is man's nature thus to begin, and that nature is not already corrupt, then why was not Adam created thus? Why was he capable of receiving a commandment? and able to give names to his wife, and to all the animal creation? For of her he said, "She shall be called Woman;"[2] and in respect of the rest we read: "Whatsoever Adam called every living creature, that was the name thereof."[3] Whereas this one, although he is ignorant where he is, what he is, by whom created, of what parents born, is already guilty of offence, incapable as yet of receiving a commandment, and so completely involved and overwhelmed in a thick cloud of ignorance, that he cannot be aroused out of his sleep, so as to recognize even

these facts; but a time must be patiently awaited, until he can shake off this strange intoxication, as it were, (not indeed in a single night, as even the heaviest drunkenness usually can be, but) little by little, through many months, and even years; and until this be accomplished, we have to bear in little children so many things which we punish in older persons, that we cannot enumerate them. Now, as touching this enormous evil of ignorance and weakness, if in this present life infants have contracted it as soon as they were born, where, when, how, have they by the perpetration of some great iniquity become suddenly implicated in such darkness?

### CHAP. 68 [XXXVII.] — IF ADAM WAS NOT CREATED OF SUCH A CHARACTER AS THAT IN WHICH WE ARE BORN, HOW IS IT THAT CHRIST, ALTHOUGH FREE FROM SIN, WAS BORN AN INFANT AND IN WEAKNESS?

Some one will ask, If this nature is not pure, but corrupt from its origin, since Adam was not created thus, how is it that Christ, who is far more excellent, and was certainly born without any sin of a virgin, nevertheless appeared in this weakness, and came into the world in infancy? To this question our answer is as follows: Adam was not created in such a state, because, as no sin from a parent preceded him, he was not created in sinful flesh. We, however, are in such a condition, because by reason of his preceding sin we are born in sinful flesh. While Christ was born in such a state, because, in order that He might for sin condemn sin, He assumed the likeness of sinful flesh.[4] The question which we are now discussing is not about Adam in respect of the size of his body, why he was not made an infant but in the perfect greatness of his members. It may indeed be said that the beasts were thus created likewise, — nor was it owing to their sin that their young were born small. Why all this came to pass we are not now asking. But the question before us has regard to the vigor of man's mind and his use of reason, by virtue of which Adam was capable of instruction, and could apprehend God's precept and the law of His commandment, and could easily keep it if he would; whereas man is now born in such a state as to be utterly incapable of doing so, owing to his dreadful ignorance and weakness, not indeed of body, but of mind, — although we must all admit that in every infant there exists a rational soul of the self-same substance (and no other) as that which belonged to the first man. Still this great infirmity of the flesh, clearly, in my opinion, points to a something, whatever it may be, that is penal. It raises the doubt whether, if the first human beings had not sinned, they would have had children who could use neither tongue, nor hands, nor feet. That they should be born children was perhaps necessary, on account of the limited capacity of the womb. But, at the same time, it does not follow, because a rib is a small part of a man's body, that God made an infant wife for the man, and then built her up into a woman. In like manner, God's almighty power was competent to make her children also, as soon as born, grown up at once.

CHAP. 69 [XXXVIII.] — THE IGNORANCE AND THE INFIRMITY OF AN INFANT.

But not to dwell on this, that was at least possible to them which has actually happened to many animals, the young of which are born small, and do not advance in mind (since they have no rational soul) as their bodies grow larger, and yet, even when most diminutive, run about, and recognize their mothers, and require no external help or care when they want to suck, but with remarkable ease discover their mothers' breasts themselves, although these are concealed from ordinary sight. A human being, on the contrary, at his birth is furnished neither with feet fit for walking, nor with hands able even to scratch ; and unless their lips were actually applied to the breast by the mother, they would not know where to find it ; and even when close to the nipple, they would, notwithstanding their desire for food, be more able to cry than to suck. This utter helplessness of body thus fits in with their infirmity of mind ; nor would Christ's flesh have been " in the likeness of sinful flesh," unless that sinful flesh had been such that the rational soul is oppressed by it in the way we have described, — whether this too has been derived from parents, or created in each case for the individual separately, or inspired from above, — concerning which I forbear from inquiring now.

CHAP. 70 [XXXIX.] — HOW FAR SIN IS DONE AWAY IN INFANTS BY BAPTISM, ALSO IN ADULTS, AND WHAT ADVANTAGE RESULTS THEREFROM.

In infants it is certain that, by the grace of God, through *His* baptism who came in the likeness of sinful flesh, it is brought to pass that the sinful flesh is done away. This result, however, is so effected, that the concupiscence which is diffused over and innate in the living flesh itself is not removed all at once, so as to exist in it no longer ; but only that that might not be injurious to a man at his death, which was inherent at his birth. For should an infant live after baptism, and arrive at an age capable of obedience to a law, he finds there somewhat to fight against, and, by God's help, to overcome, if he has not received His grace in vain, and if he is not willing to be a reprobate. For not even to those who are of riper years is it given in baptism (except, perhaps, by an unspeakable miracle of the almighty Creator), that *the law of sin* which is in their members, warring against the law of their mind, should be entirely extinguished, and cease to exist ; but that *whatever of evil has been done, said, or thought* by a man whilst he was servant to a mind subject to its concupiscence, should be abolished, and regarded as if it had never occurred. The concupiscence itself, however, (notwithstanding the loosening of the bond of guilt in which the devil, by it, used to keep the soul, and the destruction of the barrier which separated man from his Maker,) remains in the contest in which we chasten our body and bring it into subjection, whether to be relaxed for lawful and necessary uses, or to be restrained by continence.[1] But inasmuch as the Spirit of God, who knows so much better than we do all the past, and present, and future of the human race, foresaw and foretold that the life of man would be such that " no man living should be justified in God's sight," [2] it happens that through ignorance or infirmity we do not exert all the powers of our will against it, and so yield to it in the commission of sundry unlawful things, — becoming worse in proportion to the greatness and frequency of our surrender ; and better, in proportion to its unimportance and infrequency. The investigation, however, of the point in which we are now interested — whether there could possibly be (or whether in fact there is, has been, or ever will be) a man without sin in this present life, except Him who said, " The prince of this world cometh, and hath nothing in me " [3] — requires a much fuller discussion ; and the arrangement of the present treatise is such as to make us postpone the question to the commencement of another book.

---

[1] 1 Cor. ix. 27.
[2] Ps. cxliii. 2.
[3] John xiv. 30.

# BOOK II.

IN WHICH AUGUSTIN ARGUES AGAINST SUCH AS SAY THAT IN THE PRESENT LIFE THERE ARE, HAVE BEEN, AND WILL BE, MEN WHO HAVE ABSOLUTELY NO SIN AT ALL. HE LAYS DOWN FOUR PROPOSITIONS ON THIS HEAD: AND TEACHES, FIRST, THAT A MAN MIGHT POSSIBLY LIVE IN THE PRESENT LIFE WITHOUT SIN, BY THE GRACE OF GOD AND HIS OWN FREE WILL; HE NEXT SHOWS THAT NEVERTHELESS IN FACT THERE IS NO MAN WHO LIVES QUITE FREE FROM SIN IN THIS LIFE; THIRDLY, HE SETS FORTH THE REASON OF THIS, — BECAUSE THERE IS NO MAN WHO EXACTLY CONFINES HIS WISHES WITHIN THE LIMITS OF THE JUST REQUIRE-MENT OF EACH CASE, WHICH JUST REQUIREMENT HE EITHER FAILS TO PERCEIVE, OR IS UNWILLING TO CARRY OUT IN PRACTICE; IN THE FOURTH PLACE, HE PROVES THAT THERE IS NOT, NOR HAS BEEN, NOR EVER WILL BE, A HUMAN BEING — EXCEPT THE ONE MEDIATOR, CHRIST — WHO IS FREE FROM ALL SIN.

CHAP. 1 [I.] — WHAT HAS THUS FAR BEEN DWELT ON; AND WHAT IS TO BE TREATED IN THIS BOOK.

WE have, my dearest Marcellinus, discussed at sufficient length, I think, in the former book the baptism of infants, — how that it is given to them not only for entrance into the kingdom of God, but also for attaining salvation and eternal life, which none can have without the kingdom of God, or without that union with the Saviour Christ, wherein He has redeemed us by His blood. I undertake in the present book to dis-cuss and explain the question, Whether there lives in this world, or has yet lived, or ever will live, any one without any sin whatever, except "the one Mediator between God and man, the Man Christ Jesus, who gave Himself a ransom for all;" [1] — with as much care and ability as He may Himself vouchsafe to me. And should there occasionally arise in this discussion, either inevitably or casually from the argument, any question about the baptism or the sin of infants, I must neither be surprised nor must I shrink from giving the best answer I can, at such emer-gencies, to whatever point challenges my atten-tion.

CHAP. 2 [II.] — SOME PERSONS ATTRIBUTE TOO MUCH TO THE FREEDOM OF MAN'S WILL; IGNO-RANCE AND INFIRMITY.

A solution is extremely necessary of this ques-tion about a human life unassailed by any de-ception or preoccupation of sin, in consequence even of our daily prayers. For there are some persons who presume so much upon the free determination of the human will, as to suppose that it need not sin, and that we require no divine assistance, — attributing to our nature, once for all, this determination of free will. An inevitable consequence of this is, that we ought not to pray "not to enter into temptation," — that is, not to be overcome of temptation, either when it deceives and surprises us in our *igno-rance*, or when it presses and importunes us in our *weakness*. Now how hurtful, and how per-nicious and contrary to our salvation in Christ, and how violently adverse to the religion itself in which we are instructed, and to the piety whereby we worship God, it cannot but be for us not to beseech the Lord for the attainment of such a benefit, but be rather led to think that petition of the Lord's Prayer, "Lead us not into temptation," [2] a vain and useless insertion, — it is beyond my ability to express in words.

CHAP. 3 [III.] — IN WHAT WAY GOD COMMANDS NOTHING IMPOSSIBLE. WORKS OF MERCY, MEANS OF WIPING OUT SINS.

Now these people imagine that they are acute (as if none among us knew it) when they say, that "if we have not the will, we commit no sin; nor would God command man to do what was impossible for human volition." But they do not see, that in order to overcome certain things, which are the objects either of an evil desire or an ill-conceived fear, men need the

---

[1] 1 Tim. ii. 5, 6.  [2] Matt. vi. 13.

strenuous efforts, and sometimes even all the energies, of the will; and that we should only imperfectly employ these in every instance, He foresaw who willed so true an utterance to be spoken by the prophet: "In Thy sight shall no man living be justified."[1] The Lord, therefore, foreseeing that such would be our character, was pleased to provide and endow with efficacious virtue certain healthful remedies against the guilt and bonds even of sins committed after baptism, — for instance, the works of mercy, — as when he says: "Forgive, and ye shall be forgiven; give, and it shall be given unto you."[2] For who could quit this life with any hope of obtaining eternal salvation, with that sentence impending: "Whosoever shall keep the whole law, and yet offend in one point, he is guilty of all,"[3] if there did not soon after follow: "So speak ye, and so do, as they that shall be judged by the law of liberty: for he shall have judgment without mercy that hath showed no mercy; and mercy rejoiceth against judgment?"[4]

CHAP. 4 [IV.] — CONCUPISCENCE, HOW FAR IN US; THE BAPTIZED ARE NOT INJURED BY CONCUPISCENCE, BUT ONLY BY CONSENT THEREWITH.

Concupiscence, therefore, as the law of sin which remains in the members of this body of death, is born with infants. In baptized infants, it is deprived of guilt, is left for the struggle [of life],[5] but pursues with no condemnation, such as die before the struggle. Unbaptized infants it implicates as guilty and as children of wrath, even if they die in infancy, draws into condemnation. In baptized adults, however, endowed with reason, whatever consent their mind gives to this concupiscence for the commission of sin is an act of their own will. After all sins have been blotted out, and that guilt has been cancelled which by nature[6] bound men in a conquered condition, it still remains, — but not to hurt in any way those who yield no consent to it for unlawful deeds, — until death is swallowed up in victory,[7] and, in that perfection of peace, nothing is left to be conquered. Such, however, as yield consent to it for the commission of unlawful deeds, it holds as guilty; and unless, through the medicine of repentance, and through works of mercy, by the intercession in our behalf of the heavenly High Priest, they be healed, it conducts us to the second death and utter condemnation. It was on this account that the Lord, when teaching us to pray, advised us, besides other petitions, to say: "Forgive us

our debts, as we forgive our debtors; and lead us not into temptation, but deliver us from evil."[8] For evil remains in our flesh, not by reason of the nature in which man was created by God and wisdom, but by reason of that offence into which he fell by his own will, and in which, since its powers are lost, he is not healed with the same facility of will as that with which he was wounded. Of this evil the apostle says: "I know that in my flesh dwelleth no good thing;"[9] and it is likewise to the same evil that he counsels us to give no obedience, when he says: "Let not sin therefore reign in your mortal body, to obey the lusts thereof."[10] When, therefore, we have by an unlawful inclination of our will yielded consent to these lusts of the flesh, we say, with a view to the cure of this fault, "Forgive us our debts;"[11] and we at the same time apply the remedy of a work of mercy, in that we add, "As we forgive our debtors." That we may not, however, yield such consent, let us pray for assistance, and say, "And lead us not into temptation;" — not that God ever Himself tempts any one with such temptation, "for God is not a tempter to evil, neither tempteth He any man;"[12] but in order that whenever we feel the rising of temptation from our concupiscence, we may not be deserted by His help, in order that thereby we may be able to conquer, and not be carried away by enticement. We then add our request for that which is to be perfected at the last, when mortality shall be swallowed up of life:[13] "But deliver us from evil."[14] For then there will exist no longer a concupiscence which we are bidden to struggle against, and not to consent to. The whole substance, accordingly, of these three petitions may be thus briefly expressed: "Pardon us for those things in which we have been drawn away by concupiscence; help us not to be drawn away by concupiscence; take away concupiscence from us."

CHAP. 5 [V.] — THE WILL OF MAN REQUIRES THE HELP OF GOD.

Now for the commission of sin we get no help from God; but we are not able to do justly, and to fulfil the law of righteousness in every part thereof, except we are helped by God. For as the bodily eye is not helped by the light to turn away therefrom shut or averted, but is helped by it to see, and cannot see at all unless it help it; so God, who is the light of the inner man, helps our mental sight, in order that we may do some good, not according to our own, but according to His righteousness. But if we turn

---

[1] Ps. cxliii. 2.
[2] Luke vi. 37, 38.
[3] Jas. ii. 10.
[4] Jas. ii. 12.
[5] See above, Book i. chap. 70 (xxxix.)
[6] Originaliter, i.e. owing to birth-sin.
[7] 1 Cor. xv. 54.

[8] Matt. vi. 12, 13.
[9] Rom. vii. 18.
[10] Rom. vi. 12.
[11] Matt. vi. 12.
[12] Jas. i. 13.
[13] 2 Cor. v. 4.
[14] Matt. vi. 13.

away from Him, it is our own act; we then are wise according to the flesh, we then consent to the concupiscence of the flesh for unlawful deeds. When we turn to Him, therefore, God helps us; when we turn away from Him, He forsakes us. But then He helps us even to turn to Him; and this, certainly, is something that light does not do for the eyes of the body. When, therefore, He commands us in the words, "Turn ye unto me, and I will turn unto you," [1] and we say to Him, "Turn us, O God of our salvation," [2] and again, "Turn us, O God of hosts;" [3] what else do we say than, "Give what Thou commandest?" [4] When He commands us, saying, "Understand now, ye simple among the people," [5] and we say to Him, "Give me understanding, that I may learn Thy commandments;" [6] what else do we say than, "Give what Thou commandest?" When He commands us, saying, "Go not after thy lusts," [7] and we say to Him, "We know that no man can be continent, except God gives it to him;" [8] what else do we say than, "Give what Thou commandest?" When He commands us, saying, "Do justice," [9] and we say, "Teach me Thy judgments, O Lord;" [10] what else do we say than, "Give what Thou commandest?" In like manner, when He says: "Blessed are they which hunger and thirst after righteousness; for they shall be filled," [11] from whom ought we to seek for the meat and drink of righteousness, but from Him who promises His fulness to such as hunger and thirst after it?

CHAP. 6. — WHEREIN THE PHARISEE SINNED WHEN HE THANKED GOD; TO GOD'S GRACE MUST BE ADDED THE EXERTION OF OUR OWN WILL.

Let us then drive away from our ears and minds those who say that we ought to accept the determination of our own free will and not pray God to help us not to sin. By such darkness as this even the Pharisee was not blinded; for although he erred in thinking that he needed no addition to his righteousness, and supposed himself to be saturated with abundance of it, he nevertheless gave thanks to God that he was not "like other men, unjust, extortioners, adulterers, or even as the publican; for he fasted twice in the week, he gave tithes of all that he possessed." [12] He wished, indeed, for no addition

to his own righteousness; but yet, by giving thanks to God, he confessed that all he had he had received from Him. Notwithstanding, he was not approved, both because he asked for no further food of righteousness, as if he were already filled, and because he arrogantly preferred himself to the publican, who was hungering and thirsting after righteousness. What, then, is to be said of those who, whilst acknowledging that they have no righteousness, or no fulness thereof, yet imagine that it is to be had from themselves alone, not to be besought from their Creator, in whom is its store and its fountain? And yet this is not a question about prayers alone, as if the energy of our will also should not be strenuously added. God is said to be "our Helper;" [13] but nobody can be helped who does not make some effort of his own accord. For God does not work our salvation in us as if he were working in insensate stones, or in creatures in whom nature has placed neither reason nor will. Why, however, He helps one man, but not another; or why one man so much, and another so much; or why one man in one way, and another in another, — He reserves to Himself according to the method of His own most secret justice, and to the excellency of His power.

CHAP. 7 [VI.] — FOUR QUESTIONS ON THE PERFECTION OF RIGHTEOUSNESS: (1.) WHETHER A MAN CAN BE WITHOUT SIN IN THIS LIFE.

Now those who aver that a man can exist in this life without sin, must not be immediately opposed with incautious rashness; for if we should deny the possibility, we should derogate both from the free will of man, who in his wish desires it, and from the power or mercy of God, who by His help effects it. But it is one question, whether he *could* exist; and another question, whether he *does* exist. Again, it is one question, if he does not exist when he could exist, *why* he does not exist; and another question, *whether* such a man as had never sinned at all, not only is in existence, but also could ever have existed, or can ever exist. Now, if in the order of this fourfold set of interrogative propositions, I were asked, [1st,] Whether it be possible for a man in this life to be without sin? I should allow the possibility, through the grace of God and the man's own free will; not doubting that the free will itself is ascribable to God's grace, in other words, to the gifts of God, — not only as to its existence, but also as to its being good, that is, to its conversion to doing the commandments of God. Thus it is that God's grace not only shows what ought to be done, but also helps to the possibility of doing what it shows. "What

1 Zech. i. 3.
2 Ps. lxxxv. 4.
3 Ps. lxxx. 3, 4.
4 Da quod jubes; *see* the *Confessions*, Book x. chap. 26.
5 Ps. xciv. 8.
6 Ps. cxix. 73.
7 Ecclus. xviii. 30.
8 Wisd. viii. 21.
9 Isa. lvi. 1.
10 Ps. cxix. 108.
11 Matt. v. 6.
12 Luke xviii. 11, 12.

13 Ps. xl. 17, lxx. 5.

indeed have we that we have not received?"[1] Whence also Jeremiah says: "I know, O Lord, that the way of man is not in himself; it is not in man to walk and direct his steps."[2]  Accordingly, when in the Psalms one says to God, "Thou hast commanded me to keep Thy precepts diligently,"[3] he at once adds not a word of confidence concerning himself but a wish to be able to keep these precepts: "O that my ways," says he, "were directed to keep Thy statutes!  Then should I not be ashamed, when I have respect to all Thy commandments."[4] Now who ever wishes for what he has already so in his own power, that he requires no further help for attaining it?  To whom, however, he directs his wish, — not to fortune, or fate, or some one else besides God, — he shows with sufficient clearness in the following words, where he says: "Order my steps in Thy word; and let not any iniquity have dominion over me."[5]  From the thraldom of this execrable dominion they are liberated, to whom the Lord Jesus gave power to become the sons of God.[6]  From so horrible a domination were they to be freed, to whom He says, " If the Son shall make you free, then shall ye be free indeed."[7]  From these and many other like testimonies, I cannot doubt that God has laid no impossible command on man; and that, by God's aid and help, nothing is impossible, by which is wrought what He commands.  In this way may a man, if he pleases, be without sin by the assistance of God.

### CHAP. 8 [VII.] — (2) WHETHER THERE IS IN THIS WORLD A MAN WITHOUT SIN.

[*2nd.*] If, however, I am asked the second question which I have suggested, — whether there be a sinless man, — I believe there is not. For I rather believe the Scripture, which says: "Enter not into judgment with Thy servant; for in Thy sight shall no man living be justified."[8] There is therefore need of the mercy of God, which " exceedingly rejoiceth against judgment,"[9] and which that man shall not obtain who does not show mercy.[9]  And whereas the prophet says, " I said, I will confess my transgressions unto the Lord, and Thou forgavest the iniquity of my heart,"[10] he yet immediately adds, " For this shall every saint pray unto Thee in an acceptable time."[11]  Not indeed every sinner, but " every saint;" for it is the voice of saints which says, "If we say that we have no sin, we

deceive ourselves, and the truth is not in us."[12] Accordingly we read, in the Apocalypse of the same Apostle, of " the hundred and forty and four thousand " saints, " which were not defiled with women; for they continued virgins: and in their mouth was found no guile; for they are without fault."[13]  " Without fault," indeed, they no doubt are for this reason, — because they truly found fault with themselves; and for this reason, " in their mouth was discovered no guile," — " because if they said they had no sin, they deceived themselves, and the truth was not in them."[12]  Of course, where the truth was not, there would be guile; and when a righteous man begins a statement by accusing himself, he verily utters no falsehood.

### CHAP. 9. — THE BEGINNING OF RENEWAL; RESURRECTION CALLED REGENERATION; THEY ARE THE SONS OF GOD WHO LEAD LIVES SUITABLE TO NEWNESS OF LIFE.

And hence in the passage, " Whosoever is born of God doth not sin, and he cannot sin, for His seed remaineth in him,"[14] and in every other passage of like import, they much deceive themselves by an inadequate consideration of the Scriptures.  For they fail to observe that men severally become sons of God when they begin to live in newness of spirit, and to be renewed as to the inner man after the image of Him that created them.[15]  For it is not from the moment of a man's baptism that all his old infirmity is destroyed, but renovation begins with the remission of all his sins, and so far as he who is now wise is spiritually wise.  All things else, however, are accomplished in hope, looking forward to their being also realized in fact,[16] even to the renewal of the body itself in that better state of immortality and incorruption with which we shall be clothed at the resurrection of the dead.  For this too the Lord calls a regeneration, — though, of course, not such as occurs through baptism, but still a regeneration wherein that which is now begun in the spirit shall be brought to perfection also in the body.  " In the regeneration," says He, " when the Son of man shall sit in the throne of His glory, ye also shall sit upon twelve thrones, judging the twelve tribes of Israel."[17] For however entire and full be the remission of sins in baptism, nevertheless, if there was wrought by it at once, an entire and full change of the man into his everlasting newness, — I do not mean change in his body, which is now most clearly tending evermore to the old corruption and to death, after which it is to be renewed into

---

1 1 Cor. iv. 7.
2 Jer. x. 23.
3 Ps. cxix. 4.
4 Ps. cxix. 5, 6.
5 Ps. cxix. 133.
6 John i. 12.
7 John viii. 36.
8 Ps. cxliii. 2.
9 Jas. ii. 13.
10 Ps. xxxii. 5.
11 Ps. xxxii. 6.

12 1 John i. 8.
13 Rev. xiv. 3–5.
14 1 John iii. 9.
15 See Col. iii. 10.
16 *Donec etiam in re fiant.*
17 Matt. xix. 28.

a total and true newness, — but, the body being excepted, if in the soul itself, which is the inner man, a perfect renewal was wrought in baptism, the apostle would not say : "Even though our outward man perishes, yet the inward man is renewed day by day."[1] Now, undoubtedly, he who is still renewed day by day is not as yet wholly renewed ; and in so far as he is not yet wholly renewed, he is still in his old state. Since, then, men, even after they are baptized, are still in some degree in their old condition, they are on that account also still children of the world ; but inasmuch as they are also admitted into a new state, that is to say, by the full and perfect remission of their sins, and in so far as they are spiritually-minded, and behave correspondingly, they are the children of God. Internally we put off the old man and put on the new ; for we then and there lay aside lying, and speak truth, and do those other things wherein the apostle makes to consist the putting off of the old man and the putting on of the new, which after God is created in righteousness and true holiness.[2] Now it is men who are already baptized and faithful whom he exhorts to do this, — an exhortation which would be unsuitable to them, if the absolute and perfect change had been already made in their baptism. And yet made it was, since we were then actually *saved;* for "He saved us by the laver of regeneration."[3] In another passage, however, he tells us how this took place. "Not they only," says he, "but ourselves also, which have the first-fruits of the Spirit, even we ourselves groan within ourselves, waiting for the adoption, to wit, the redemption of our body. For we are saved by hope : but hope that is seen is not hope ; for what a man seeth, why doth he yet hope for ? But if we hope for that we see not, then do we with patience wait for it."[4]

CHAP. 10 [VIII.] — PERFECTION, WHEN TO BE REALIZED.

Our full adoption, then, as children, is to happen at the redemption of our body. It is therefore the first-fruits of the Spirit which we now possess, whence we are already really become the children of God ; for the rest, indeed, as it is by hope that we are saved and renewed, so are we the children of God. But inasmuch as we are not yet actually saved, we are also not yet fully renewed, nor yet also fully sons of God, but children of the world. We are therefore advancing in renewal and holiness of life, — and it is by this that we are children of God, and by this also we cannot commit sin ; — until at last the whole of that by which we are kept as yet children of this world is changed into this ; — for it is owing to this that we are as yet able to sin. Hence it comes to pass that "whosoever is born of God doth not commit sin ; "[5] and as well, "if we were to say that we have no sin, we should deceive ourselves, and the truth would not be in us."[6] There shall be then an end put to that within us which keeps us children of the flesh and of the world ; whilst that other shall be perfected which makes us the children of God, and renews us by His Spirit. Accordingly the same John says, "Beloved, now are we the sons of God ; and it doth not yet appear what we shall be."[7] Now what means this variety in the expressions, "*we are*," and "*we shall be*," but this — *we are* in hope, *we shall be* in reality ? For he goes on to say, "We know that when He shall appear, we shall be like Him, for we shall see Him as He is."[7] We have therefore even now begun to be like Him, having the first-fruits of the Spirit ; but yet we are still unlike Him, by reason of the remainders of the old nature. In as far, then, as we are like Him, in so far are we, by the regenerating Spirit, sons of God ; but in as far as we are unlike Him, in so far are we the children of the flesh and of the world. On the one side, we cannot commit sin ; but, on the other, if we say that we have no sin, we only deceive ourselves, — until we pass entirely into the adoption, and the sinner be no more, and you look for his place and find it not.[8]

CHAP. 11 [IX.] — AN OBJECTION OF THE PELAGIANS : WHY DOES NOT A RIGHTEOUS MAN BEGET A RIGHTEOUS MAN ?[9]

In vain, then, do some of them argue : "If a sinner begets a sinner, so that the guilt of original sin must be done away in his infant son by his receiving baptism, in like manner ought a righteous man to beget a righteous son." Just as if a man begat children in the flesh by reason of his righteousness, and not because he is moved thereto by the concupiscence which is in his members, and the law of sin is applied by the law of his mind to the purpose of procreation. His begetting children, therefore, shows that he still retains the old nature among the children of this world ; it does not arise from the fact of his promotion to newness of life among the children of God. For "the children of this world beget and are begotten."[10] Hence also what is born of them is like them ; for "that which is born of the flesh is flesh."[11] Only the children

---

[1] 2 Cor. iv. 16.
[2] Eph. iv. 24.
[3] Tit. iii. 5.
[4] Rom. viii. 23–25.

[5] 1 John iii. 9.
[6] 1 John i. 8.
[7] 1 John iii. 2.
[8] Ps. xxxvi. 10.
[9] [See below, c. 25; also *De Nuptiis,* i. 18; also *contra Julianum,* vi. 5.]
[10] Luke xx. 34.
[11] John iii. 6.

of God, however, are righteous ; but in so far as they are the children of God, they do not carnally beget, because it is of the Spirit, and not of the flesh, that they are themselves begotten. But as many of them as become parents, beget children from the circumstance that they have not yet put off the entire remains of their old nature in exchange for the perfect renovation which awaits them. It follows, therefore, that every son who is born in this old and infirm condition of his father's nature, must needs himself partake of the same old and infirm condition. In order, then, that he may be begotten again, he must also himself be renewed by the Spirit through the remission of sin ; and if this change does not take place in him, his righteous father will be of no use to him. For it is by the Spirit that he is righteous, but it is not by the Spirit that he begat his son. On the other hand, if this change does accrue to him, he will not be damaged by an unrighteous father : for it is by the grace of the Spirit that he has passed into the hope of the eternal newness ; whereas it is owing to his carnal mind that his father has wholly remained in the old nature.

### CHAP. 12 [X.] — HE RECONCILES SOME PASSAGES OF SCRIPTURE.

The statement, therefore, "He that is born of God sinneth not,"[1] is not contrary to the passage in which it is declared by those who are born of God, " If we say that we have no sin, we deceive ourselves, and the truth is not in us."[2] For however complete may be a man's present hope, and however real may be his renewal by spiritual regeneration in that part of his nature, he still, for all that, carries about a body which is corrupt, and which presses down his soul ; and so long as this is the case, one must distinguish even in the same individual the relation and source of each several action. Now, I suppose it is not easy to find in God's Scripture so weighty a testimony of holiness given of any man as that which is written of His three servants, Noah, Daniel, and Job, whom the Prophet Ezekiel describes as the only men able to be delivered from God's impending wrath.[3] In these three men he no doubt prefigures three classes of mankind to be delivered : in Noah, as I suppose, are represented righteous leaders of nations, by reason of his government of the ark as a type of the Church ; in Daniel, men who are righteous in continence ; in Job, those who are righteous in wedlock ; — to say nothing of any other view of the passage, which it is unnecessary now to consider. It is, at any rate, clear from this testimony of the prophet, and from other inspired statements, how eminent were these worthies in righteousness. Yet no man must be led by their history to say, for instance, that drunkenness is not sin, although so good a man was overtaken by it ; for we read that Noah was once drunk,[4] but God forbid that it should be thought that he was an habitual drunkard.

### CHAP. 13. — A SUBTERFUGE OF THE PELAGIANS.

Daniel, indeed, after the prayer which he poured out before God, actually says respecting himself, " Whilst I was praying and confessing my sins, and the sins of my people, before the Lord my God."[5] This is the reason, if I am not mistaken, why in the above-mentioned Prophet Ezekiel a certain most haughty person is asked, " Art thou then wiser than Daniel ? "[6] Nor on this point can that be possibly said which some contend for in opposition to the Lord's Prayer : " For although," they say, " that prayer was offered by the apostles, after they became holy and perfect, and had no sin whatever, yet it was not in behalf of their own selves, but of imperfect and still sinful men that they said, ' Forgive us our debts, as we also forgive our debtors.' They used the word *our*," they say, " in order to show that in one body are contained both those who still have sins, and themselves, who were already altogether free from sin." Now this certainly cannot be said in the case of Daniel, who (as I suppose) foresaw as a prophet this presumptuous opinion, when he said so often in his prayer, " We have sinned ;" and explained to us why he said this, not so as that we should hear from him, Whilst I was praying and confessing the sins of my people to the Lord, my God ; nor yet confounding distinction, so as that it would be uncertain whether he had said, on account of the fellowship of one body, While I was confessing *our* sins to the Lord my God ; but he expresses himself in language so distinct and precise, as if he were full of the distinction himself, and wanted above all things to commend it to our notice : " *My sins*," says he, " *and the sins of my people.*" Who can gainsay such evidence as this, but he who is more pleased to defend what he thinks than to find out what he ought to think ?

### CHAP. 14. — JOB WAS NOT WITHOUT SIN.

But let us see what Job has to say of himself, after God's great testimony of his righteousness. " I know of a truth," he says, " that it is so : for how shall a mortal man be just before the Lord ? For if He should enter into judgment with him, he would not be able to obey Him."[7] And shortly afterwards he asks : " Who shall resist His judgment ? Even if I should seem righteous,

---

[1] 1 John iii. 9.
[2] 1 John i. 8.
[3] Ezek. xiv. 14.

[4] Gen. ix. 21.
[5] Dan. ix. 20.
[6] Ezek. xxviii. 3.
[7] Job ix. 2, 3.

my mouth will speak profanely." [1]  And again, further on, he says : " I know He will not leave me unpunished.  But since I am ungodly, why have I not died?  If I should wash myself with snow, and be purged with clean hands, thou hadst thoroughly stained me with filth." [2]  In another of his discourses he says : " For Thou hast written evil things against me, and hast compassed me with the sins of my youth ; and Thou hast placed my foot in the stocks.  Thou hast watched all my works, and hast inspected the soles of my feet, which wax old like a bottle, or like a moth-eaten garment.  For man that is born of a woman hath but a short time to live, and is full of wrath ; like a flower that hath bloomed, so doth he fall ; he is gone like a shadow, and continueth not.  Hast Thou not taken account even of him, and caused him to enter into judgment with Thee?  For who is pure from uncleanness?  Not even one ; even should his life last but a day." [3]  Then a little afterwards he says : " Thou hast numbered all my necessities ; and not one of my sins hath escaped Thee.  Thou hast sealed up my transgressions in a bag, and hast marked whatever I have done unwillingly." [4]  See how Job, too, confesses his sins, and says how sure he is that there is none righteous before the Lord.  So he is sure of this also, that if we say we have no sin, the truth is not in us.  While, therefore, God bestows on him His high testimony of righteousness, according to the standard of human conduct, Job himself, taking his measure from that rule of righteousness, which, as well as he can, he beholds in God, knows of a truth that so it is ; and he goes on at once to say, " How shall a mortal man be just before the Lord?  For if He should enter into judgment with him, he would not be able to obey Him ; " in other words, if, when challenged to judgment, he wished to show that nothing could be found in him which He could condemn, " he would not be able to obey him," since he misses even that obedience which might enable him to obey Him who teaches that sins ought to be confessed.  Accordingly [the Lord] rebukes certain men, saying, " Why will ye contend with me in judgment?" [5]  This [the Psalmist] averts, saying, " Enter not into judgment with Thy servant ; for in Thy sight shall no man living be justified." [6]  In accordance with this, Job also asks : " For who shall resist his judgment?  Even if I should seem righteous, my mouth will speak profanely ; " which means : If, contrary to His judgment, I should call myself righteous, when His perfect

rule of righteousness proves me to be unrighteous, then of a truth my mouth would speak profanely, because it would speak against the truth of God.

CHAP. 15. — CARNAL GENERATION CONDEMNED ON ACCOUNT OF ORIGINAL SIN.

He sets forth that this absolute weakness, or rather condemnation, of carnal generation is from the transgression of original sin, when, treating of his own sins, he shows, as it were, their causes, and says that " man that is born of a woman hath but a short time to live, and is full of wrath."  Of what wrath, but of that in which all are, as the apostle says, " by nature," that is, by origin, " children of wrath," [7] inasmuch as they are children of the concupiscence of the flesh and of the world?  He further shows that to this same wrath also pertains the death of man.  For after saying, " He hath but a short time to live, and is full of wrath," he added, " Like a flower that hath bloomed, so doth he fall ; he is gone like a shadow, and continueth not."  He then subjoins : " Hast Thou not caused him to enter into judgment with Thee?  For who is pure from uncleanness?  Not even one ; even should his life last but a day."  In these words he in fact says, Thou hast thrown upon man, short-lived though he be, the care of entering into judgment with Thee.  For how brief soever be his life, — even if it last but a single day, — he could not possibly be clean of filth ; and therefore with perfect justice must he come under Thy judgment.  Then, when he says again, " Thou hast numbered all my necessities, and not one of my sins hath escaped Thee : Thou hast sealed up my transgressions in a bag, and hast marked whatever I have done unwillingly ; " is it not clear enough that even those sins are justly imputed which are not committed through allurement of pleasure, but for the sake of avoiding some trouble, or pain, or death?  Now these sins, too, are said to be committed under some necessity, whereas they ought all to be overcome by the love and pleasure of righteousness.  Again, what he said in the clause, " Thou hast marked whatever I have done unwillingly," may evidently be connected with the saying : " For what I would, that I do not ; but what I hate, that do I." [8]

CHAP. 16. — JOB FORESAW THAT CHRIST WOULD COME TO SUFFER ; THE WAY OF HUMILITY IN THOSE THAT ARE PERFECT.

Now it is remarkable [9] that the Lord Himself, after bestowing on Job the testimony which is expressed in Scripture, that is, by the Spirit of

---

[1] Job ix. 19, 20.
[2] Job ix. 30.
[3] Job xiii. 26, to xiv. 5.
[4] Job xiv. 16, 17.
[5] Jer. ii. 29.
[6] Ps. cxliii. 2.

[7] Eph. ii. 3.
[8] Rom. vii. 15.
[9] Quid quod.

God, " In all the things which happened to him he sinned not with his lips before the Lord,"[1] did yet afterwards speak to him with a rebuke, as Job himself tells us: " Why do I yet plead, being admonished, and hearing the rebukes of the Lord?"[2]  Now no man is justly rebuked unless there be in him something which deserves rebuke.  [XI.]  And what sort of rebuke is this, —which, moreover, is understood to proceed from the person of Christ our Lord?  He recounts to him all the divine operations of His power, rebuking him under this idea, — that He seems to say to him, " Canst thou effect all these mighty works as I can?"  But to what purpose is all this but that Job might understand (for this instruction was divinely inspired into him, that he might foreknow Christ's coming to suffer), — that he might understand how patiently he ought to endure all that he went through, since Christ, although, when He became man for us, He was absolutely without sin, and although as God He possessed so great power, did for all that by no means refuse to obey even to the suffering of death?  When Job understood this with a purer intensity of heart, he added to his own answer these words: " I used before now to hear of Thee by the hearing of the ear; but behold now mine eye seeth Thee: therefore I abhor myself and melt away, and account myself but dust and ashes."[3]  Why was he thus so deeply displeased with himself?  God's work, in that he was man, could not rightly have given him displeasure, since it is even said to God Himself, " Despise not Thou the work of Thine own hands."[4]  It was indeed in view of that righteousness, in which he had discovered his own unrighteousness,[5] that he abhorred himself and melted away, and deemed himself dust and ashes, — beholding, as he did in his mind, the righteousness of Christ, in whom there could not possibly be any sin, not only in respect of His divinity, but also of His soul and His flesh. It was also in view of this righteousness which is of God that the Apostle Paul, although as " touching the righteousness which is of the law he was blameless," yet " counted all things " not only as loss, but even as dung.[6]

CHAP. 17 [XII.] — NO ONE RIGHTEOUS IN ALL THINGS.[7]

That illustrious testimony of God, therefore, in which Job is commended, is not contrary to the passage in which it is said, " In Thy sight shall no man living be justified;"[8] for it does not lead us to suppose that in him there was nothing at all which might either by himself truly or by the Lord God rightly be blamed, although at the same time he might with no untruth be said to be a righteous man, and a sincere worshipper of God, and one who keeps himself from every evil work.  For these are God's words concerning him: " Hast thou diligently considered my servant Job?  For there is none like him on the earth, blameless, righteous, a true worshipper of God, who keeps himself from every evil work."[9]  First, he is here praised for his excellence in comparison with all men on earth.  He therefore excelled all who were at that time able to be righteous upon earth; and yet, because of this superiority over others in righteousness, he was not therefore altogether without sin.  He is next said to be " *blameless* " — no one could fairly bring an accusation against him in respect of his life; " *righteous* " — he had advanced so greatly in moral probity, that no man could be mentioned on a par with him; " *a true worshipper of God* " — because he was a sincere and humble confessor of his own sins; " *who keeps himself from every evil work* " — it would have been wonderful if this had extended to every evil word and thought.  How great a man indeed Job was, we are not told; but we know that he was a just man; we know, too, that in the endurance of terrible afflictions and trials he was great; and we know that it was not on account of his sins, but for the purpose of demonstrating his righteousness, that he had to bear so much suffering.  But the language in which the Lord commends Job might also be applied to him who " delights in the law of God after the inner man, whilst he sees another law in his members warring against the law of his mind; "[10] especially as he says, " The good that I would I do not: but the evil which I would not, that I do.  Now, if I do that I would not, it is no more I that do it, but sin that dwelleth in me."[11]  Observe how he too after the inward man is separate from every evil work, because such work he does not himself effect, but the evil which dwells in his flesh; and yet, since he does not have even that ability to delight in the law of God except from the grace of God, he, as still in want of deliverance, exclaims, " O wretched man that I am! who shall deliver me from the body of this death?  God's grace, through Jesus Christ our Lord!"[12]

CHAP. 18 [XIII.] — PERFECT HUMAN RIGHTEOUSNESS IS IMPERFECT.

There are then on earth righteous men, there are great men, brave, prudent, chaste, patient,

[1] Job i. 22.
[2] Job xxxix. 34.
[3] Job xlii. 5, 6.
[4] Ps. cxxxviii. 8.
[5] Qua se noverat *injustum*.  Several MSS. have *justum* [*q. d.* " had discovered what his own righteousness was," — *i.e.* nothing].
[6] Phil. iii. 6-8.
[7] See below, chap. 23.
[8] Ps. cxliii. 2.

[9] Job i. 8.
[10] Rom. vii. 22, 23.
[11] Rom. vii. 19, 20.
[12] Rom. vii. 24, 25.

pious, merciful, who endure all kinds of temporal evil with an even mind for righteousness' sake. If, however, there is truth — nay, because there is truth — in these words, " If we say we have no sin, we deceive ourselves," [1] and in these, " In Thy sight shall no man living be justified," they are not without sin ; nor is there one among them so proud and foolish as not to think that the Lord's Prayer is needful to him, by reason of his manifold sins.

### CHAP. 19. — ZACHARIAS AND ELISABETH, SINNERS.

Now what must we say of Zacharias and Elisabeth, who are often alleged against us in discussions on this question, except that there is clear evidence in the Scripture [2] that Zacharias was a man of eminent righteousness among the chief priests, whose duty it was to offer up the sacrifices of the Old Testament? We also read, however, in the Epistle to the Hebrews, in a passage which I have already quoted in my previous book,[3] that Christ was the only High Priest who had no need, as those who were called high priests, to offer daily a sacrifice for his own sins first, and then for the people. " For such a High Priest," it says, " became us, righteous, harmless, undefiled, separate from sinners, and made higher than the heavens ; who needeth not daily, as those high priests, to offer up sacrifice, first for his own sins." [4] Amongst the priests here referred to was Zacharias, amongst them was Phinehas, yea, Aaron himself, from whom this priesthood had its beginning, and whatever others there were who lived laudably and righteously in this priesthood ; and yet all these were under the necessity, first of all, of offering sacrifice for their own sins,— Christ, of whose future coming they were a type, being the only one who, as an incontaminable priest, had no such necessity.

### CHAP. 20. — PAUL WORTHY TO BE THE PRINCE OF THE APOSTLES, AND YET A SINNER.

What commendation, however, is bestowed on Zacharias and Elisabeth which is not comprehended in what the apostle has said about himself before he believed in Christ? He said that, " as touching the righteousness which is in the law, he had been blameless." [5] The same is said also of them : "They were both righteous before God, walking in all the commandments and ordinances of the Lord blameless." [6] It was because whatever righteousness they had in them was not a pretence before men that it is said accordingly, "They walked *before the Lord.*"

But that which is written of Zacharias and his wife in the phrase, *in all the commandments and ordinances of the Lord*, the apostle briefly expressed by the words, *in the law*. For there was not one law for him and another for them previous to the gospel. It was one and the same law which, as we read, was given by Moses to their fathers, and according to which, also, Zacharias was priest, and offered sacrifices in his course. And yet the apostle, who was then endued with the like righteousness, goes on to say : " But what things were gain to me, those I counted loss for Christ. Yea doubtless, and I count all things but loss for the excellency of the knowledge of our Lord Jesus Christ ; for whose sake I have not only thought all things to be only detriments, but I have even counted them as dung, that I may win Christ, and be found in Him, not having my own righteousness, which is of the law, but that which is through the faith of Christ, the righteousness which is of God by faith : that I may know Him, and the power of His resurrection, and the fellowship of His suffering, being made comformable unto His death ; if by any means I might attain unto the resurrection of the dead." [7] So far, then, is it from being true that we should, from the words in which Scripture describes them, suppose that Zacharias and Elisabeth had a perfect righteousness without any sin, that we must even regard the apostle himself, according to the self-same rule, as not perfect, not only in that righteousness of the law which he possessed in common with them, and which he counts as loss and dung in comparison with that most excellent righteousness which is by the faith of Christ, but also in the very gospel itself, wherein he deserved the pre-eminence of his great apostleship. Now I would not venture to say this if I did not deem it very wrong to refuse credence to himself. He extends the passage which we have quoted, and says : " Not as though I had already attained, or were already perfect ; but I follow after, if I may comprehend that for which also I am apprehended in Christ Jesus. Brethren, I count not myself to have apprehended : but this one thing I do, forgetting those things which are behind, and reaching forth unto those things which are before, I press toward the mark, for the prize of the high calling of God in Christ Jesus." [8] Here he confesses that he has not yet attained, and is not yet perfect in that plenitude of righteousness which he had longed to obtain in Christ ; but that he was as yet pressing towards the mark, and, forgetting what was past, was reaching out to the things which are before him. We are sure, then, that what he says elsewhere is true even of himself : " Al-

---

[1] 1 John i. 8.
[2] Luke i. 6–9.
[3] See above, Book i. c. 50.
[4] Heb. vii. 26, 27.
[5] Phil. iii. 6.
[6] Luke i. 6. [See also his work, *De Gratia Christi*, 53.]

[7] Phil. iii. 7–11.
[8] Phil. iii. 12–14.

though our outward man is perishing, yet the inward man is renewed day by day." [1]  Although he was already a perfect [2] traveller, he had not yet attained the perfect end of his journey.  All such he would fain take with him as companions of his course.  This he expresses in the words which follow our former quotation : " Let as many, then, of us as are perfect, be thus minded : and if ye be yet of another mind, God will reveal even this also to you.  Nevertheless, whereunto we have already attained, let us walk by that rule." [3]  This " walk " is not performed with the legs of the body, but with the affections of the soul and the character of the life, so that they who possess righteousness may arrive at perfection, who, advancing in their renewal day by day along the straight path of faith, have by this time become perfect as travellers in the self-same righteousness.

CHAP. 21 [XIV.] — ALL RIGHTEOUS MEN SINNERS.

In like manner, all who are described in the Scriptures as exhibiting in their present life good will and the actions of righteousness, and all who have lived like them since, although lacking the same testimony of Scripture ; or all who are even now so living, or shall hereafter so live : all these are great, they are all righteous, and they are all really worthy of praise, — yet they are by no means without sin : inasmuch as, on the authority of the same Scriptures which make us believe in their virtues, we believe also that in " God's sight no man living is justified," [4] whence all ask that He will " not enter into judgment with His servants : " [4] and that not only to all the faithful in general, but to each of them in particular, the Lord's Prayer is necessary, which He delivered to His disciples. [5]

CHAP. 22 [XV.] — AN OBJECTION OF THE PELA-GIANS ; PERFECTION IS RELATIVE ; HE IS RIGHTLY SAID TO BE PERFECT IN RIGHTEOUSNESS WHO HAS MADE MUCH PROGRESS THEREIN.

" Well, but," they say, " the Lord says, ' Be ye perfect even as your Father which is in heaven is perfect,' [6] — an injunction which He would not have given, if He had known that what He enjoined was impracticable."  Now the present question is not whether it be possible for any men, during this present life, to be without sin if they receive that perfection for the purpose ; for the question of possibility we have already discussed : [7] — but what we have now to consider is, whether any man in fact achieves perfection.

We have, however, already recognised the fact that no man wills as much as the duty demands, as also the testimony of the Scriptures, which we have quoted so largely above, declares. When, indeed, perfection is ascribed to any particular person, we must look carefully at the thing in which it is ascribed.  For I have just above quoted a passage of the apostle, wherein he confesses that he was not yet perfect in the attainment of righteousness which he desired ; but still he immediately adds, " Let as many of us as are perfect be thus minded."  Now he would certainly not have uttered these two sentences if he had not been perfect in one thing, and not in another.  For instance, a man may be perfect as a scholar in the pursuit of wisdom : and this could not yet be said of those to whom [the apostle] said, " I have fed you with milk, and not with meat : for hitherto ye have not been able to bear it, neither are ye yet able ; " [8] whereas to those of whom it could be said he says, " Howbeit we speak wisdom among them that are perfect," — meaning, of course, " perfect pupils " to be understood.  It may happen, therefore, as I have said, that a man may be already perfect as a scholar, though not as yet perfect as a teacher of wisdom ; may be perfect as a learner, though not as yet perfect as a doer of righteousness ; may be perfect as a lover of his enemies, though not as yet perfect in bearing their wrong. [9]  Even in the case of him who is so far perfect as to love all men, inasmuch as he has attained even to the love of his enemies, it still remains a question whether he be perfect in that love, — in other words, whether he so loves those whom he loves as is prescribed to be exercised towards those to be loved, by the unchangeable love of truth.  Whenever, then, we read in the Scriptures of any man's perfection, it must be carefully considered in what it is asserted, since a man is not therefore to be understood as being entirely without sin because he is described as perfect in some particular thing ; although the term may also be employed to show, not, indeed, that there is no longer any point left for a man to reach his way to perfection, but that he has in fact advanced a very great way, and on that account may be deemed worthy of the designation.  Thus, a man may be said to be perfect in the science of the law, even if there be still something unknown to him ; and in the same manner the apostle called men perfect, to whom he said at the same time, " Yet if in anything ye be otherwise minded, God shall reveal even this to you.  Nevertheless, whereto we have already attained, let us walk by the same rule." [10]

[1] 2 Cor. iv. 16.
[2] [Augustin plays on the word " perfect." — W.]
[3] Phil. iii. 15, 16.
[4] Ps. cxliii. 2.
[5] Matt. vi. 12; Luke xi. 4.
[6] Matt. v. 48.
[7] See above, chap. 7.

[8] 1 Cor. iii. 2.
[9] Ut sufferat is his antithesis here to ut diligat.
[10] Phil. iii. 15.

CHAP. 23 [XXI.] — WHY GOD PRESCRIBES WHAT HE KNOWS CANNOT BE OBSERVED.

We must not deny that God commands that we ought to be so perfect in doing righteousness, as to have no sin at all. Now that cannot be sin, whatever it may be, unless God has enjoined that it shall not be. Why then, they ask, does He command what He knows no man living will perform? In this manner it may also be asked, Why He commanded the first human beings, who were only two, what He knew they would not obey? For it must not be pretended that He issued that command, that some of us might obey it, if they did not; for, that they should not partake of the fruit of the particular tree, God commanded them, and none besides. Because, as He knew what amount of righteousness they would fail to perform, so did He also know what righteous measures He meant Himself to adopt concerning them. In the same way, then, He orders all men to commit no sin, although He knows beforehand that no man will fulfil the command; in order that He may, in the case of all who impiously and condemnably despise His precepts, Himself do what is just in their condemnation; and, in the case of all who while obediently and piously pressing on in his precepts, though failing to observe to the utmost all things which He has enjoined, do yet forgive others as they wish to be forgiven themselves, Himself do what is good in their cleansing. For how can forgiveness be bestowed by God's mercy on the forgiving, when there is no sin? or how prohibition fail to be given by the justice of God, when there is sin?

CHAP. 24. — AN OBJECTION OF THE PELAGIANS. THE APOSTLE PAUL WAS NOT FREE FROM SIN SO LONG AS HE LIVED.

"But see," say they, "how the apostle says, 'I have fought a good fight, I have kept the faith, I have finished my course : henceforth there is laid up for me a crown of righteousness ;'[1] which he would not have said if hè had any sin." It is for them, then, to explain how he could have said this, when there still remained for him to encounter the great conflict, the grievous and excessive weight of that suffering which he had just said awaited him.[2] In order to finish his course, was there yet wanting only a small thing, when that in fact was still left to suffer wherein would be a fiercer and more cruel foe? If, however, he uttered such words of joy feeling sure and secure, because he had been made sure and secure by Him who had revealed to him the imminence of his suffering, then he spoke these words, not in the fulness of realiza-tion, but in the firmness of hope, and represents what he foresees is to come as if it had already been done. If, therefore, he had added to those words the further statement, "I have no longer any sin," we must have understood him as even then speaking of a perfection arising from a future prospect, not from an accomplished fact. For his having no sin, which they suppose was completed when he spoke these words, pertained to the finishing of his course; just in the same way as his triumphing over his adversary in the decisive conflict of his suffering had also reference to the finishing of his course, although this they must needs themselves allow remained yet to be effected, when he was speaking these words. The whole of this, therefore, *we* declare to have been as yet awaiting its accomplishment, at the time when the apostle, with his perfect trust in the promise of God, spoke of it all as having been already realized. For it was in reference to the finishing of his course that he forgave the sins of those who sinned against him, and prayed that his own sins might in like manner be forgiven him ; and it was in his most certain confidence in this promise of the Lord, that he believed he should have no sin in that last end, which was still future, even when in his trustfulness he spoke of it as already accomplished. Now, omitting all other considerations, I wonder whether, when he uttered the words in which he is thought to imply that he had no sin, that "thorn of the flesh" had been already removed from him, for the taking away of which he had three times entreated the Lord, and had received this answer: "My grace is sufficient for thee; for my strength is made perfect in weakness."[3] For bringing so great a man to perfection, it was needful that that "messenger of Satan" should not be taken away by whom he was therefore to be buffeted, "lest he should be unduly exalted by the abundance of his revelations,"[4] and is there then any man so bold as either to think or to say, that any one who has to bend beneath the burden of this life is altogether clean from all sin whatever?

CHAP. 25. — GOD PUNISHES BOTH IN WRATH AND IN MERCY.

Although there are some men who are so eminent in righteousness that God speaks to them out of His cloudy pillar, such as "Moses and Aaron among His priests, and Samuel among them that call upon His name,"[5] the latter of whom is much praised for his piety and purity in the Scriptures of truth, from his earliest childhood, in which his mother, to accomplish her vow, placed him in God's temple, and devoted

---

[1] 2 Tim. iv. 7.
[2] 2 Tim. iv. 6.

[3] 2 Cor. xii. 8, 9.
[4] 2 Cor. xii. 7.
[5] Ps. xcix. 6.

him to the Lord as His servant; — yet even of such men it is written, " Thou, O God, wast propitious unto them, though Thou didst punish all their devices." [1]  Now the children of wrath God punishes in anger; whereas it is in mercy that He punishes the children of grace; since " whom He loveth He correcteth, and scourgeth every son whom He receiveth." [2]  However, there are no punishments, no correction, no scourge of God, but what are owing to sin, except in the case of Him who prepared His back for the smiter, in order that He might experience all things in our likeness without sin, in order that He might be the saintly Priest of saints, making intercession even for saints, who with no sacrifice of truth say each one even for himself, " Forgive us our trespasses, even as we also forgive them that trespass against us." [3]  Wherefore even our opponents in this controversy, whilst they are chaste in their life, and commendable in character, and although they do not hesitate to do that which the Lord enjoined on the rich man, who inquired of Him about the attainment of eternal life, after he had told Him, in answer to His first question, that he had already fully kept every commandment in the law, — that " if he wished to be perfect, he must sell all that he had and give to the poor, and transfer his treasure to heaven; " [4] yet they do not in any one instance venture to say that they are without sin.  But this, as we believe, they refrain from saying, with deceitful intent; but if they are lying, in this very act they begin either to augment or commit sin.

CHAP. 26 [XVII.] — (3) [5] WHY NO ONE IN THIS LIFE IS WITHOUT SIN.

[3d.] [5] Let us now consider the point which I mentioned as our third inquiry.  Since by divine grace assisting the human will, man may possibly exist in this life without sin, why does he not?  To this question I might very easily and truthfully answer: Because men are unwilling.  But if I am asked why they are unwilling, we are drawn into a lengthy statement.  And yet, without prejudice to a more careful examination, I may briefly say this much: Men are unwilling to do what is right, either because what is right is unknown to them, or because it is unpleasant to them.  For we desire a thing more ardently in proportion to the certainty of our knowledge of its goodness, and the warmth of our delight in it.  Ignorance, therefore, and infirmity are faults which impede the will from moving either for doing a good work, or for refraining from an evil one.  But that what was hidden may come to

light, and what was unpleasant may be made agreeable, is of the grace of God which helps the wills of men; and that they are not helped by it, has its cause likewise in themselves, not in God, whether they be predestinated to condemnation, on account of the iniquity of their pride, or whether they are to be judged and disciplined contrary to their very pride, if they are children of mercy.  Accordingly Jeremiah, after saying, " I know, O Lord, that the way of man is not in himself, and that it belongeth not to any man to walk and direct his steps," [6] immediately adds, " Correct me, O Lord, but with judgment, and not in Thine anger; " [7] as much as to say, I know that it is for my correction that I am too little assisted by Thee, for my footsteps to be perfectly directed : but yet do not in this so deal with me as Thou dost in Thine anger, when Thou dost determine to condemn the wicked; but as Thou dost in Thy judgment whereby Thou dost teach Thy children not to be proud.  Whence in another passage it is said, " And Thy judgments shall help me." [8]

CHAP. 27.[9] — THE DIVINE REMEDY FOR PRIDE.

You cannot therefore attribute to God the cause of any human fault.  For of all human offences, the cause is pride.  For the conviction and removal of this a great remedy comes from heaven.  God in mercy humbles Himself, descends from above, and displays to man, lifted up by pride, pure and manifest grace in very manhood, which He took upon Himself out of vast love for those who partake of it.  For, not even did even this One, so conjoined to the Word of God that by that conjunction he became at once the one Son of God and the same One the one Son of man, act by the antecedent merits of His own will.  It behoved Him, without doubt, to be one ; had there been two, or three, or more, if this could have been done, it would not have come from the pure and simple gift of God, but from man's free will and choice.[10]  This, then, is especially commended to us; this, so far as I dare to think, is the divine lesson especially taught and learned in those treasures of wisdom and knowledge which are hidden in Christ.  Every one of us, therefore, now knows, now does not know — now rejoices, now does not rejoice — to begin, continue, and complete our good work, in order that he may know that it is due not to his own will, but to the gift of God, that he either knows or rejoices ; and thus he is cured

---

[1] Ps. xcix. 8.
[2] Prov. iii. 12; Heb. xii. 6.
[3] Matt. vi. 12, 14; Luke xi. 4.
[4] Matt. xix. 12.
[5] See above, chs. 7 and 8.

[6] Jer. x. 23.
[7] Jer. x. 24.
[8] Ps. cxix. 175.
[9] See below, in ch. 33; also *De Naturâ et Gratiâ*, 29–32; and *De Corrept. et Gratia*, 10.
[10] [Augustin appears to say, in this obscure passage, that had there been two *persons*, instead of two *natures* only, in our blessed Lord's person, then no doubt salvation would have been due partly to a human cause. — W.]

of vanity which elated him, and knows how truly it is said not of this earth of ours, but spiritually, "The Lord will give kindness and sweet grace, and our land shall yield her fruit." [1] A good work, moreover, affords greater delight, in proportion as God is more and more loved as the highest unchangeable Good, and as the Author of all good things of every kind whatever. And that God may be loved, "His love is shed abroad in our hearts," not by ourselves, but "by the Holy Ghost that is given unto us." [2]

### CHAP. 28 [XVIII.] — A GOOD WILL COMES FROM GOD.

Men, however, are laboring to find in our own will some good thing of our own, — not given to us by God; but how it is to be found I cannot imagine. The apostle says, when speaking of men's good works, "What hast thou that thou didst not receive? now, if thou didst receive it, why dost thou glory, as if thou hadst not received it?" [3] But, besides this, even reason itself, which may be estimated in such things by such as we are, sharply restrains every one of us in our investigations so as that we may not so defend grace as to seem to take away free will, or, on the other hand, so assert free will as to be judged ungrateful to the grace of God, in our arrogant impiety. [4]

### CHAP. 29. — A SUBTERFUGE OF THE PELAGIANS.

Now, with reference to the passage of the apostle which I have quoted, some would maintain it to mean that "whatever amount of good will a man has, must be attributed to God on this account, — namely, because even this amount could not be in him if he were not a human being. Now, inasmuch as he has from God alone the capacity of being any thing at all, and of being human, why should there not be also attributed to God whatever there is in him of a good will, which could not exist unless he existed in whom it is?" But in this same manner it may also be said that a bad will also may be attributed to God as its author; because even it could not exist in man unless he were a man in whom it existed; but God is the author of his existence as man; and thus also of his bad will, which could have no existence if it had not a man in whom it might exist. But to argue thus is blasphemy.

### CHAP. 30. — ALL WILL IS EITHER GOOD, AND THEN IT LOVES RIGHTEOUSNESS, OR EVIL, WHEN IT DOES NOT LOVE RIGHTEOUSNESS.

Unless, therefore, we obtain not simply deter-

mination of will, which is freely turned in this direction and that, and has its place amongst those natural goods which a bad man may use badly; but also a good will, which has its place among those goods of which it is impossible to make a bad use: — unless the impossibility is given to us from God, I know not how to defend what is said: "What hast thou that thou didst not receive?" For if we have from God a certain free will, which may still be either good or bad; but the good will comes from ourselves; then that which comes from ourselves is better than that which comes from Him. But inasmuch as it is the height of absurdity to say this, they ought to acknowledge that we attain from God even a good will. It would indeed be a strange thing if the will could so stand in some mean as to be neither good nor bad; for we either love righteousness, and it is good, and if we love it more, more good, — if less, it is less good; or if we do not love it at all, it is not good. And who can hesitate to affirm that, when the will loves not righteousness in any way at all, it is not only a bad, but even a wholly depraved will? Since therefore the will is either good or bad, and since of course we have not the bad will from God, it remains that we have of God a good will; else, I am ignorant, since our justification is from it, in what other gift from Him we ought to rejoice. Hence, I suppose, it is written, "The will is prepared of the Lord;" [5] and in the Psalms, "The steps of a man will be rightly ordered by the Lord, and His way will be the choice of his will;" [6] and that which the apostle says, "For it is God who worketh in you both to will and to do of His own good pleasure." [7]

### CHAP. 31. — GRACE IS GIVEN TO SOME MEN IN MERCY; IS WITHHELD FROM OTHERS IN JUSTICE AND TRUTH.

Forasmuch then as our turning away from God is our own act, and this is evil will; but our turning to God is not possible, except He rouses and helps us, and this is good will, — what have we that we have not received? But if we received, why do we glory as if we had not received? Therefore, as "he that glorieth must glory in the Lord," [8] it comes from His mercy, not their merit, that God wills to impart this to some, but from His truth that He wills not to impart it to others. For to sinners punishment is justly due, because "the Lord God loveth mercy and truth," [9] and "mercy and truth are met together;" [10] and "all the paths of the Lord are

1 Ps. lxxxv. 12.
2 Rom. v. 5.
3 1 Cor. iv. 7.
4 See *De Gratiâ Christi*, 52; and *De Gratiâ et Libero Arbi-*

5 Prov. viii. 35.
6 Ps. xxxvii. 23.
7 Phil. ii. 13.
8 Isa. xlv. 25; Jer. ix. 23, 24; 1 Cor. i. 31.
9 Ps. lxxxiv. 11.
10 Ps. lxxxv. 10.

mercy and truth."¹ And who can tell the numberless instances in which Holy Scripture combines these two attributes? Sometimes, by a change in the terms, *grace* is put for *mercy*, as in the passage, " We beheld His glory, the glory as of the Only-begotten of the Father, full of grace and truth."² Sometimes also *judgment* occurs instead of *truth*, as in the passage, " I will sing of mercy and judgment unto Thee, O Lord."³

### CHAP. 32. — GOD'S SOVEREIGNTY IN HIS GRACE.

As to the reason why He wills to convert some, and to punish others for turning away, — although nobody can justly censure the merciful One in conferring His blessing, nor can any man justly find fault with the truthful One in awarding His punishment (as no one could justly blame Him, in the parable of the labourers, for assigning to some their stipulated hire, and to others unstipulated largess⁴), yet, after all, the purpose of His more hidden judgment is in His own power. [XIX.] So far as it has been given us, let us have wisdom, and let us understand that the good Lord God sometimes withholds even from His saints either the certain knowledge or the triumphant joy of a good work, just in order that they may discover that it is not from themselves, but from Him that they receive the light which illuminates their darkness, and the sweet grace which causes their land⁵ to yield her fruit.

### CHAP. 33. — THROUGH GRACE WE HAVE BOTH THE KNOWLEDGE OF GOOD, AND THE DELIGHT WHICH IT AFFORDS.

But when we pray Him to give us His help to do and accomplish righteousness, what else do we pray for than that He would open what was hidden, and impart sweetness to that which gave no pleasure? For even this very duty of praying to Him we have learned by His grace, whereas before it was hidden; and by His grace have come to love it, whereas before it gave us no pleasure, — so that " he who glorieth must glory not in himself, but in the Lord." To be lifted up, indeed, to pride, is the result of men's own will, not of the operation of God; for to such a thing God neither urges us nor helps us. There first occurs then in the will of man a certain desire of its own power, to become disobedient through pride. If it were not for this desire, indeed, there would be nothing difficult; and whenever man willed it, he might refuse without difficulty. There ensued, however, out of the penalty which was justly due such a defect, that henceforth it became difficult

to be obedient unto righteousness; and unless this defect were overcome by assisting grace, no one would turn to holiness; nor unless it were healed by efficient grace would any one enjoy the peace of righteousness. But whose grace is it that conquers and heals, but His to whom the prayer is directed: " Convert us, O God of our salvation, and turn Thine anger away from us?"⁶ And both if He does this, He does it in mercy, so that it is said of Him, " Not according to our sins hath He dealt with us, nor hath He recompensed us according to our iniquities;"⁷ and when He refrains from doing this to any, it is in judgment that He refrains. And who shall say to Him, " What hast Thou done?" when with pious mind the saints sing to the praise of His mercy and judgment? Wherefore even in the case of His saints and faithful servants He applies to them a tardier cure in certain of their failings, in order that, while they are involved in these, a less pleasure than is sufficient for the fulfilling of righteousness in all its perfection may be experienced by them at any good they may achieve, whether hidden or manifest; so that in respect of His most perfect rule of equity and truth " no man living can be justified in His sight."⁸ He does not in His own self, indeed, wish us to fall under condemnation, but that we should become humble; and He displays to us all the self-same grace of His own. Let us not, however, after we have attained facility in all things, suppose that to be our own which is really His; for that would be an error most antagonistic to religion and piety. Nor let us think that we should, because of His grace, continue in the same sins as of old; but against that very pride, on account of which we are humiliated in them, let us, above all things, both vigilantly strive and ardently pray Him, knowing at the same time that it is by His gift that we have the power thus to strive and thus to pray; so that in every case, while we look not at ourselves, but raise our hearts above, we may render thanks to the Lord our God, and whenever we glory, glory in Him alone.

### CHAP. 34 [XX.] — (4) THAT NO MAN, WITH THE EXCEPTION OF CHRIST, HAS EVER LIVED, OR CAN LIVE WITHOUT SIN.⁹

[4*th.*] There now remains our fourth point, after the explanation of which, as God shall help us, this lengthened treatise of ours may at last be brought to an end. It is this: Whether the man who never has had sin or is to have it, not merely is now living as one of the sons of men, but even could ever have existed at any time, or will yet in time to come exist? Now it is altogether most

---

¹ Ps. xxv. 10.
² John i. 14.
³ Ps. ci. 1.
⁴ Matt. xx. 1–16.
⁵ i.e., the soil of their hearts; see above, at the end of ch. 27.

⁶ Ps. lxxxv. 4.
⁷ Ps. ciii. 10.
⁸ Ps. cxliii. 2.
⁹ See above, chs. 7, 8, 26.

certain that such a man neither does now live, nor has lived, nor ever will live, except the one only Mediator between God and men, the Man Christ Jesus. We have already said a good deal on this subject in our remarks on the baptism of infants; for if these have no sin, not only are there at present, but also there have been, and there will be, persons innumerable without sin. Now if the point which we treated of under the second head be truly substantiated, that there is in fact no man without sin,[1] then of course not even infants are without sin. From which the conclusion arises, that even supposing a man could possibly exist in the present life so far advanced in virtue as to have reached the perfect fulness of holy living which is absolutely free from sin, he still must have been undoubtedly a sinner previously, and have been converted from the sinful state to this subsequent newness of life. Now when we were discussing the second head, a different question was before us from that which is before us under this fourth head. For then the point we had to consider was, Whether any man in this life could ever attain to such perfection as to be absolutely without sin by the grace of God, by the hearty desire of his own will? whereas the question now proposed in this fourth place is, Whether there be among the sons of men, or could possibly ever have been, or yet ever can be, a man who has not indeed emerged out of sin and attained to perfect righteousness, but has never, at any time whatever, been under the bondage of sin? If, therefore, the remarks are true which we have made at so great length concerning infants, there neither is, has been, nor will be, among the sons of men any such man, except the one Mediator, in whom there accrues to us propitiation and justification through which we have reconciliation with God, by the termination of the enmity produced by our sins. It will therefore be not unsuitable to retrace a few considerations, so far as the present subject seems to require, from the very commencement of the human race, in order that they may inform and strengthen the reader's mind in answer to some objections which may possibly disturb him.

CHAP. 35 [XXI.] — ADAM AND EVE; OBEDIENCE MOST STRONGLY ENJOINED BY GOD ON MAN.

When the first human beings — the one man Adam, and his wife Eve who came out of him — willed not to obey the commandment which they had received from God, a just and deserved punishment overtook them. The Lord had threatened that, on the day they ate the forbidden fruit, they should surely die.[2] Now, inasmuch as they had received the permission of using for food every tree that grew in Paradise, among which God had planted the tree of life, but had been forbidden to partake of one only tree, which He called the tree of knowledge of good and evil, to signify by this name the consequence of their discovering whether what good they would experience if they kept the prohibition, or what evil if they transgressed it: they are no doubt rightly considered to have abstained from the forbidden food previous to the malignant persuasion of the devil, and to have used all which had been allowed them, and therefore, among all the others, and before all the others, the tree of life. For what could be more absurd than to suppose that they partook of the fruit of other trees, but not of that which had been equally with others granted to them, and which, by its especial virtue, prevented even their animal bodies from undergoing change through the decay of age, and from aging into death, applying this benefit from its own body to the man's body, and in a mystery demonstrating what is conferred by wisdom (which it symbolized) on the rational soul, even that, quickened by its fruit, it should not be changed into the decay and death of iniquity? For of her it is rightly said, "She is a tree of life to them that lay hold of her."[3] Just as the one tree was for the bodily Paradise, the other is for the spiritual; the one affording a vigour to the senses of the outward man, the other to those of the inner man, such as will abide without any change for the worse through time. They therefore served God, since that dutiful obedience was committed to them, by which alone God can be worshipped. And it was not possible more suitably to intimate the inherent importance of obedience, or its sole sufficiency securely to keep the rational creature under the Creator, than by forbidding a tree which was not in itself evil. For God forbid that the Creator of good things, who made all things, "and behold they were very good,"[4] should plant anything evil amidst the fertility of even that material Paradise. Still, however, in order that he might show man, to whom submission to such a Master would be very useful, how much good belonged simply to obedience (and this was all that He had demanded of His servant, and this would be of advantage not so much for the lordship of the Master as for the profit of the servant), they were forbidden the use of a tree, which, if it had not been for the prohibition, they might have used without suffering any evil result whatever; and from this circumstance it may be clearly understood, that whatever evil they brought on themselves because they made use of it in spite of the prohibition, the tree did not produce from any noxious or pernicious quality

---

[1] See above, chs. 8, 9.
[2] Gen. ii. 17.
[3] Prov. iii. 18.
[4] Gen. i. 31.

in its fruit, but entirely on account of their violated obedience.

## CHAP. 36 [XXII.] — MAN'S STATE BEFORE THE FALL.

Before they had thus violated their obedience they were pleasing to God, and God was pleasing to them; and though they carried about an animal body, they yet felt in it no disobedience moving against themselves. This was the righteous appointment, that inasmuch as their soul had received from the Lord the body for its servant, as it itself obeyed the Lord, even so its body should obey Him, and should exhibit a service suitable to the life given it without resistance. Hence "they were both naked, and were not ashamed." [1] It is with a natural instinct of shame that the rational soul is now indeed affected, because in that flesh, over whose service it received the right of power, it can no longer, owing to some indescribable infirmity, prevent the motion of the members thereof, notwithstanding its own unwillingness, nor excite them to motion even when it wishes. Now these members are on this account, in every man of chastity, rightly called "*pudenda*," [2] because they excite themselves, just as they like, in opposition to the mind which is their master, as if they were their own masters; and the sole authority which the bridle of virtue possesses over them is to check them from approaching impure and unlawful pollutions. Such disobedience of the flesh as this, which lies in the very excitement, even when it is not allowed to take effect, did not exist in the first man and woman whilst they were naked and not ashamed. For not yet had the rational soul, which rules the flesh, developed such a disobedience to its Lord, as by a reciprocity of punishment to bring on itself the rebellion of its own servant the flesh, along with that feeling of confusion and trouble to itself which it certainly failed to inflict upon God by its own disobedience to Him; for God is put to no shame or trouble when we do not obey Him, nor are we able in any wise to lessen His very great power over us; but we are shamed in that the flesh is not submissive to our government, — a result which is brought about by the infirmity which we have earned by sinning, and is called " the sin which dwelleth in our members." [3] But this sin is of such a character that it is the punishment of sin. As soon, indeed, as that transgression was effected, and the disobedient soul turned away from the law of its Lord, then its servant, the body, began to cherish a law of disobedience against it; and then the man and the woman grew ashamed of their nakedness, when they perceived the rebellious motion of the flesh, which they had not felt before, and which perception is called " the opening of their eyes;" [4] for, of course, they did not walk about among the trees with closed eyes. The same thing is said of Hagar: " Her eyes were opened, and she saw a well." [5] Then the man and the woman covered their parts of shame, which God had made for them as members, but they had made parts of shame.

## CHAP. 37 [XXIII.] — THE CORRUPTION OF NATURE IS BY SIN, ITS RENOVATION IS BY CHRIST.

From this law of sin is born the flesh of sin, which requires cleansing through the sacrament of Him who came in the likeness of sinful flesh, that the body of sin might be destroyed, which is also called " the body of this death," from which only God's grace delivers wretched man through Jesus Christ our Lord. [6] For this law, the origin of death, passed on from the first pair to their posterity, as is seen in the labour with which all men toil in the earth, and the travail of women in the pains of childbirth. For these sufferings they merited by the sentence of God, when they were convicted of sin; and we see them fulfilled not only in them, but also in their descendants, in some more, in others less, but nevertheless in all. Whereas, however, the primeval righteousness of the first human beings consisted in obeying God, and not having in their members the law of their own concupiscence against the law of their mind; now, since their sin, in our sinful flesh which is born of them, it is obtained by those who obey God, as a great acquisition, that they do not obey the desires of this evil concupiscence, but crucify in themselves the flesh with its affections and lusts, in order that they may be Jesus Christ's, who on His cross symbolized this, and who gave them power through His grace to become the sons of God. For it is not to all men, but to as many as have received Him, that He has given to be born again to God of the Spirit, after they were born to the world by the flesh. Of these indeed it is written: " But as many as received Him, to them gave He power to become the sons of God; which were born, not of the flesh, nor of blood, nor of the will of man, nor of the will of the flesh, but of God." [7]

## CHAP. 38 [XXIV.] — WHAT BENEFIT HAS BEEN CONFERRED ON US BY THE INCARNATION OF THE WORD; CHRIST'S BIRTH IN THE FLESH, WHEREIN IT IS LIKE AND WHEREIN UNLIKE OUR OWN BIRTH.

He goes on to add, "And the Word was made

---

[1] Gen. ii 25.
[2] i.e. " Parts of shame."
[3] Rom. vii. 17, 23.

[4] Gen. iii. 7.
[5] Gen. xxi. 19.
[6] Rom. vii. 24, 25.
[7] John i. 12, 13.

flesh, and dwelt among us;"[1] as much as to say, A great thing indeed has been done among them, even that they are born again to God of God, who had before been born of the flesh to the world, although created by God Himself; but a far more wonderful thing has been done, that, although it accrued to them by nature to be born of the flesh, but by the divine goodness to be born of God, — in order that so great a benefit might be imparted to them, He who was in His own nature born of God, vouchsafed in mercy to be also born of the flesh; — no less being meant by the passage, "And the Word was made flesh, and dwelt among us." Hereby, he says in effect, it has been wrought that we who were born of the flesh as flesh, by being afterwards born of the Spirit, may be spirit and dwell in God; because also God, who was born of God, by being afterwards born of the flesh, became flesh, and dwelt among us. For the Word, which became flesh, was in the beginning, and was God with God.[2] But at the same time His participation in our inferior condition, in order to our participation in His higher state, held a kind of medium[3] in His birth of the flesh; so that we indeed were born in sinful flesh, but He was born in the likeness of sinful flesh, — we not only of flesh and blood, but also of the will of man, and of the flesh, but He was born only of flesh and blood, not of the will of man, nor of the will of the flesh, but of God: we, therefore, to die on account of sin, He, to die on our account without sin. So also, just as His inferior circumstances, into which He descended to us, were not in every particular exactly the same with our inferior circumstances, in which He found us here; so our superior state, into which we ascend to Him, will not be quite the same with His superior state, in which we are there to find Him. For we by His grace are to be made the sons of God, whereas He was evermore by nature the Son of God; we, when we are converted, shall cleave to God, though not as His equals; He never turned from God, and remains ever equal to God; we are partakers of eternal life, He is eternal life. He, therefore, alone having become man, but still continuing to be God, never had any sin, nor did he assume a flesh of sin, though born of a maternal[4] flesh of sin. For what He then took of flesh, He either cleansed in order to take it, or cleansed by taking it. His virgin mother, therefore, whose conception was not according to the law of sinful flesh (in other words, not by the excitement of carnal concupiscence), but who merited by her faith that the holy seed should be framed within her, He formed in order to choose her, and chose in order to be formed from her. How much more needful, then, is it for sinful flesh to be baptized in order to escape the judgment, when the flesh which was untainted by sin was baptized to set an example for imitation?

## CHAP. 39 [XXV.] — AN OBJECTION OF THE PELAGIANS.

The answer, which we have already given,[5] to those who say, "If a sinner has begotten a sinner, a righteous man ought also to have begotten a righteous man," we now advance in reply to such as argue that one who is born of a baptized man ought himself to be regarded as already baptized. "For why," they ask, "could he not have been baptized in the loins of his father, when, according to the Epistle to the Hebrews, Levi,[6] was able to pay tithes in the loins of Abraham?" They who propose this argument ought to observe that Levi did not on this account subsequently not pay tithes, because he had paid tithes already in the loins of Abraham, but because he was ordained to the office of the priesthood in order to receive tithes, not to pay them; otherwise neither would his brethren, who all contributed their tithes to him, have been tithed — because they too, whilst in the loins of Abraham, had already paid tithes to Melchisedec.

## CHAP. 40. — AN ARGUMENT ANTICIPATED.

And let no one contend that the descendants of Abraham might fairly enough have paid tithes, although they had already paid tithes in the loins of their forefather, seeing that paying tithes was an obligation of such a nature as to require constant repetition from each several person, just as the Israelites used to pay such contributions every year all through life to their Levites, to whom were due various tithes from all kinds of produce; whereas baptism is a sacrament of such a nature as is administered once for all, and if one had already received it when in his father, he must be considered as no other than baptized, since he was born of a man who had been himself baptized. Well, whoever thus argues (I will simply say, without discussing the point at length,) should look at circumcision, which was administered once for all, and yet was administered to each person separately and individually. Just as therefore it was necessary in the time of that ancient sacrament for the son of a circumcised man to be himself circumcised, so now the son of one who has been baptized must himself also receive baptism.

---

[1] John i. 14.
[2] John i. 1.
[3] Medietatem.
[4] De *maternâ* carne peccati, which is the reading of the best and oldest MSS. Another reading has, De *naturâ* carnis peccati (" of the nature of sinful flesh "); and a third, De *materiâ* carnis peccati (" of the matter of sinful flesh "). Compare *Contr. Julianum*, v. 9, and *De Gen. ad. Lit.* x. 18–20.

[5] See above, c. 11.
[6] The allusion is to Heb. vii. 9.

CHAP. 41. — CHILDREN OF BELIEVERS ARE CALLED "CLEAN" BY THE APOSTLE.[1]

The apostle indeed says, "Else were your children unclean, but now are they holy;"[2] and "therefore" they infer "there was no necessity for the children of believers to be baptized." I am surprised at the use of such language by persons who deny that original sin has been transmitted from Adam. For, if they take this passage of the apostle to mean that the children of believers are born in a state of holiness, how is it that even they have no doubt about the necessity of their being baptized? Why, in fine, do they refuse to admit that any original sin is derived from a sinful parent, if some holiness is received from a holy parent? Now it certainly does not contravene our assertion, even if from the faithful "holy" children are propagated, when we hold that unless they are baptized those go into damnation, to whom our opponents themselves shut the kingdom of heaven, although they insist that they are without sin, whether actual or original.[3] Or, if they think it an unbecoming thing for "holy ones" to be damned, how can it be a becoming thing to exclude "holy ones" from the kingdom of God? They should rather pay especial attention to this point, How can something sinful help being derived from sinful parents, if something holy is derived from holy parents, and uncleanness from unclean parents? For the twofold principle was affirmed when he said, "*Else were your children unclean,* but *now* are they *holy.*" They should also explain to us how it is right that the holy children of believers and the unclean children of unbelievers are, notwithstanding their different circumstances, equally prohibited from entering the kingdom of God, if they have not been baptized. What avails that sanctity of theirs to the one? Now if they were to maintain that the unclean children of unbelievers are damned, but that the holy children of believers are unable to enter the kingdom of heaven unless they are baptized, — but nevertheless are not damned, because they are "holy," — that would be some sort of a distinction; but as it is, they equally declare respecting the holy children of holy parents and the unclean offspring of unclean parents, that they are not damned, since they have not any sin; and that they are excluded from the kingdom of God because they are unbaptized. What an absurdity! Who can suppose that such splendid geniuses do not perceive it?

CHAP. 42. — SANCTIFICATION MANIFOLD; SACRAMENT OF CATECHUMENS.

Our opinions on this point are strictly in uni-son with the apostle's himself, who said, "From one all to condemnation," and "from one all to justification of life."[4] Now how consistent these statements are with what he elsewhere says, when treating of another point, "Else were your children unclean, but now are they holy," consider a while. [XXVI.] Sanctification is not of merely one measure; for even catechumens, I take it, are sanctified in their own measure by the sign of Christ, and the prayer of imposition of hands; and what they receive is holy, although it is not the body of Christ, — holier than any food which constitutes our ordinary nourishment, because it is a sacrament.[5] However, that very meat and drink, wherewithal the necessities of our present life are sustained, are, according to the same apostle, "sanctified by the word of God and prayer,"[6] even the prayer with which we beg that our bodies may be refreshed. Just as therefore this sanctification of our ordinary food does not hinder what enters the mouth from descending into the belly, and being ejected into the draught,[7] and partaking of the corruption into which everything earthly is resolved, whence the Lord exhorts us to labour for the other food which never perishes:[8] so the sanctification of the catechumen, if he is not baptized, does not avail for his entrance into the kingdom of heaven, nor for the remission of his sins. And, by parity of reasoning, that sanctification likewise, of whatever measure it be, which, according to the apostle, is in the children of believers, has nothing whatever to do with the question of baptism and of the origin or the remission of sin.[9] The apostle, in this very passage which has occupied our attention, says that the unbeliever of a married couple is sanctified by a believing partner: "For the unbelieving husband is sanctified by the wife, and the unbelieving wife is sanctified by the husband. Else were your children unclean, but now are they holy."[2] Now, I should say, there is not a man whose mind is so warped by unbelief, as to suppose that, whatever sense he gives to these words, they can possibly mean that a husband who is not a Christian should not be baptized, because his wife is a Christian, and that he has already obtained remission of his sins, with the certain prospect of entering the kingdom of heaven, because he is described as being sanctified by his wife.

---

[1] [See Gelasius, in his *Treatise against the Pelagians.*]
[2] 1 Cor. vii. 14.
[3] See above, Book i. chs 21–23.

[4] See Rom. v. 18.
[5] Catechumens received the *sacramentum salis* — salt placed in the mouth — with other rites, such as exorcism and the sign of the cross; the Lord's Prayer and other invocations concluding the ceremony. See Canon 5 of the third Council of Carthage; also Augustin's *De Catechiz. Rud.* 50; and his *Confessions,* i. 11, where (speaking of his own catechumenical course) he says: "I was now signed with the sign of His cross, and was *seasoned with His salt.*"
[6] 1 Tim. iv. 5.
[7] Mark vii. 19.
[8] John vi. 27.
[9] See below, Book iii. ch. 21; and his *Sermons,* xxix. 4.

CHAP. 43 [XXVII.] — WHY THE CHILDREN OF THE BAPTIZED SHOULD BE BAPTIZED.

If any man, however, is still perplexed by the question why the children of baptized persons are baptized, let him briefly consider this : Inasmuch as the generation of sinful flesh through the one man, Adam, draws into condemnation all who are born of such generation, so the generation of the Spirit of grace through the one man Jesus Christ, draws to the justification of eternal life all who, because predestinated, partake of this regeneration. But the sacrament of baptism is undoubtedly the sacrament of regeneration: Wherefore, as the man who has never lived cannot die, and he who has never died cannot rise again, so he who has never been born cannot be born again. From which the conclusion arises, that no one who has not been born could possibly have been born again in his father. Born again, however, a man must be, after he has been born ; because, " Except a man be born again, he cannot see the kingdom of God " [1] Even an infant, therefore, must be imbued with the sacrament of regeneration, lest without it his would be an unhappy exit out of this life ; and this baptism is not administered except for the remission of sins. And so much does Christ show us in this very passage ; for when asked, How could such things be? He reminded His questioner of what Moses did when he lifted up the serpent. Inasmuch, then, as infants are by the sacrament of baptism conformed to the death of Christ, it must be admitted that they are also freed from the serpent's poisonous bite, unless we wilfully wander from the rule of the Christian faith. This bite, however, they did not receive in their own actual life, but in him on whom the wound was primarily inflicted.

CHAP. 44. — AN OBJECTION OF THE PELAGIANS.

Nor do they fail to see this point, that his own sins are no detriment to the parent after his conversion ; they therefore raise the question : " How much more impossible is it that they should be a hinderance to his son? " But they who thus think do not attend to this consideration, that as his own sins are not injurious to the father for the very reason that he is born again of the Spirit, so in the case of his son, unless he be in the same manner born again, the sins which he derived from his father will prove injurious to him. Because even renewed parents beget children, not out of the first-fruits of their renewed condition, but carnally out of the remains of the old nature ; and the children who are thus the offspring of their parents' remaining old nature, and are born in sinful flesh, escape from the condemnation which is due to the old man by the sacrament of spiritual regeneration and renewal. Now this is a consideration which, on account of the controversies that have arisen, and may still arise, on this subject, we ought to keep in our view and memory, — that a full and perfect remission of sins takes place only in baptism, that the character of the actual man does not at once undergo a total change, but that the first-fruits of the Spirit in such as walk worthily change the old carnal nature into one of like character by a process of renewal, which increases day by day, until the entire old nature is so renovated that the very weakness of the natural body attains to the strength and incorruptibility of the spiritual body.

CHAP. 45 [XXVIII.] — THE LAW OF SIN IS CALLED SIN ; HOW CONCUPISCENCE STILL REMAINS AFTER ITS EVIL HAS BEEN REMOVED IN THE BAPTIZED.

This law of sin, however, which the apostle also designates " sin," when he says, " Let not *sin* therefore reign in your mortal body, that ye should obey it in the lusts thereof," [2] does not so remain in the members of those who are born again of water and the Spirit, as if no remission thereof has been made, because there is a full and perfect remission of our sins, all the enmity being slain, which separated us from God ; but it remains in our old carnal nature, as if overcome and destroyed, if it does not, by consenting to unlawful objects, somehow revive, and recover its own reign and dominion. There is, however, so clear a distinction to be seen between this old carnal nature, in which the law of sin, or sin, is already repealed, and that life of the Spirit, in the newness of which they who are baptized are through God's grace born again, that the apostle deemed it too little to say of such that they were not in sin ; unless he also said that they were not in the flesh itself, even before they departed out of this mortal life. " They that are in the flesh," says he, " cannot please God ; but ye *are not in the flesh*, but in the Spirit, if so be that the Spirit of God dwell in you." [3] And indeed, as they turn to good account the flesh itself, however corruptible it be, who apply its members to good works, and no longer are in that flesh, since they do not mould their understanding nor their life according to its principles ; and as they in like manner make even a good use of death, which is the penalty of the first sin, who encounter it with fortitude and patience for their brethren's sake, and for the faith, and in defence of whatever is true and holy and just, — so also do all " true yokefellows " in the faith turn to good account that very law of sin which still remains, though remitted, in their old

---

[1] John iii. 3.

[2] Rom. vi. 12.
[3] Rom viii. 8, 9.

carnal nature, who, because they have the new life in Christ, do not permit lust to have dominion over them. And yet these very persons, because they still carry about Adam's old nature, mortally generate children to be immortally regenerated, with that propagation of sin, in which such as are born again are not held bound, and from which such as are born are released by being born again. As long, then, as the law by concupiscence [1] dwells in the members, although it remains, the guilt of it is released; but it is released only to him who has received the sacrament of regeneration, and has already begun to be renewed. But whatsoever is born of the old nature, which still abides with its concupiscence, requires to be born again in order to be healed. Seeing that believing parents, who have been both carnally born and spiritually born again, have themselves begotten children in a carnal manner, how could their children by any possibility, previous to their first birth, have been born again?

### CHAP. 46.[2] — GUILT MAY BE TAKEN AWAY BUT CONCUPISCENCE REMAIN.

You must not be surprised at what I have said, that although the law of sin remains with its concupiscence, the guilt thereof is done away through the grace of the sacrament. For as wicked deeds, and words, and thoughts have already passed away, and cease to exist, so far as regards the mere movements of the mind and the body, and yet their guilt remains after they have passed away and no longer exist, unless it be done away by the remission of sins; so, contrariwise, in this law of concupiscence, which is not yet done away but still remains, its guilt is done away, and continues no longer, since in baptism there takes place a full forgiveness of sins. Indeed, if a man were to quit this present life immediately after his baptism, there would be nothing at all left to hold him liable, inasmuch as all which held him is released. As, on the one hand, therefore, there is nothing strange in the fact that the guilt of past sins of thought, and word, and deed remains before their remission; so, on the other hand, there ought to be nothing to create surprise, that the guilt of remaining concupiscence passes away after the remission of sin.

### CHAP. 47 [XXIX.] — ALL THE PREDESTINATED ARE SAVED THROUGH THE ONE MEDIATOR CHRIST, AND BY ONE AND THE SAME FAITH.

This being the case, ever since the time when by one man sin thus entered into this world and death by sin, and so it passed through to all men, up to the end of this carnal generation and perishing world, the children of which beget and are begotten, there never has existed, nor ever will exist, a human being of whom, placed in this life of ours, it could be said that he had no sin at all, with the exception of the one Mediator, who reconciles us to our Maker through the forgiveness of sins. Now this same Lord of ours has never yet refused, at any period of the human race, nor to the last judgment will He ever refuse, this His healing to those whom, in His most sure foreknowledge and future loving-kindness, He has predestinated to reign with Himself to life eternal. For, previous to His birth in the flesh, and weakness in suffering, and power in His own resurrection, He instructed all who then lived, in the faith of those then *future* blessings, that they might inherit everlasting life; whilst those who were alive when all these things were being accomplished in Christ, and who were witnessing the fulfilment of prophecy, He instructed in the faith of these then *present* blessings; whilst again, those who have since lived, and ourselves who are now alive, and all those who are yet to live, He does not cease to instruct, in the faith of these now *past* blessings. It is therefore "one faith" which saves all, who after their carnal birth are born again of the Spirit, and it terminates in Him, who came to be judged for us and to die, — the Judge of quick and dead. But the sacraments of this "one faith" are varied from time to time in order to its suitable signification.

### CHAP. 48. — CHRIST THE SAVIOUR EVEN OF INFANTS; CHRIST, WHEN AN INFANT, WAS FREE FROM IGNORANCE AND MENTAL WEAKNESS.

He is therefore the Saviour at once of infants and of adults, of whom the angel said, "There is born unto you this day a Saviour;" [3] and concerning whom it was declared to the Virgin Mary,[4] "Thou shalt call His name Jesus, for He shall save His people from their sins," where it is plainly shown that He was called Jesus because of the salvation which He bestows upon us, — Jesus being tantamount to the Latin *Salvator*, "Saviour." Who then can be so bold as to maintain that the Lord Christ is *Jesus* only for adults and not for infants also? who came in the likeness of sinful flesh, to destroy the body of sin, with infants' limbs fitted and suitable for no use in the extreme weakness of such body, and His rational soul oppressed with miserable ignorance! Now that such entire ignorance existed, I cannot suppose in the infant in whom the Word was made flesh, that He might dwell among us; nor can I imagine that such weakness of the mental faculty ever existed in the

---

[1] We follow the reading, *lex* [*scil*. peccati] *concupiscentialiter*, etc.

[2] Compare Augustin's *Contra Julianum*, vi. c. 22.

[3] Luke ii. 11.

[4] Rather to Joseph, Mary's husband; Matt. i. 21.

infant Christ which we see in infants generally. For it is owing to such infirmity and ignorance that infants are disturbed with irrational affections, and are restrained by no rational command or government, but by pains and penalties, or the terror of such; so that you can quite see that they are children of that disobedience, which excites itself in the members of our body in opposition to the law of the mind, — and refuses to be still, even when the reason wishes; nay, often is either repressed only by some actual infliction of bodily pain, as for instance by flogging; or is checked only by fear, or by some such mental emotion, but not by any admonishing of the will. Inasmuch, however, as in Him there was the likeness of sinful flesh, He willed to pass through the changes of the various stages of life, beginning even with infancy, so that it would seem as if even His flesh might have arrived at death by the gradual approach of old age, if He had not been killed while young. Nevertheless, the death is inflicted in sinful flesh as the due of disobedience, but in the likeness of sinful flesh it was undergone in voluntary obedience. For when He was on His way to it, and was soon to suffer it, He said, "Behold, the prince of this world cometh, and hath nothing in me. But that all may know that I am doing my Father's will, arise, let us go hence." [1] Having said these words, He went straightway, and encountered His undeserved death, having become obedient even unto death.

### CHAP. 49 [XXX.] — AN OBJECTION OF THE PELAGIANS.

They therefore who say, "If through the sin of the first man it was brought about that we must die, by the coming of Christ it should be brought about that, believing in Him, we shall not die;" and they add what they deem a reason, saying, "For the sin of the first transgressor could not possibly have injured us more than the incarnation or redemption of the Saviour has benefited us." But why do they not rather give an attentive ear, and an unhesitating belief, to that which the apostle has stated so unambiguously: "Since by man came death, by Man came also the resurrection of the dead; for as in Adam all die, even so in Christ shall all be made alive?" [2] For it is of nothing else than of the resurrection of the body that he was speaking. Having said that the bodily death of all men has come about through one man, he adds the promise that the bodily resurrection of all men to eternal life shall happen through one, even Christ. How can it therefore be that "the one has injured us more by sinning than the other has benefited us by redeeming," when by the

sin of the former we die a temporal death, but by the redemption of the latter we rise again not to a temporal, but to a perpetual life? Our body, therefore, is dead because of sin, but Christ's body only died without sin, in order that, having poured out His blood without fault, "the bonds" [3] which contain the register of all faults "might be blotted out," by which they who now believe in Him were formerly held as debtors by the devil. And accordingly He says, "This is my blood, which is shed for many for the remission of sins." [4]

### CHAP. 50 [XXXI.] — WHY IT IS THAT DEATH ITSELF IS NOT ABOLISHED, ALONG WITH SIN, BY BAPTISM.

He might, however, have also conferred this upon believers, that they should not even experience the death of their body. But if He had done this, there might no doubt have been added a certain felicity to the flesh, but the fortitude of faith would have been diminished; for men have such a fear of death, that they would declare Christians happy, for nothing else than their mere immunity from dying. And no one would, for the sake of that life which is to be so happy after death, hasten to the grace of Christ by the power of his contempt of death itself; but with a view to remove the trouble of death, would rather resort to a more delicate mode of believing in Christ. More grace, therefore, than this has He conferred on those who believe on Him; and a greater gift, undoubtedly, has He vouchsafed to them! What great matter would it have been for a man, on seeing that people did not die when they became believers, himself also to believe that he was not to die? How much greater a thing is it, how much braver, how much more laudable, so to believe, that although one is sure to die, he can still hope to live hereafter for evermore! At last, upon some there will be bestowed this blessing at the last day, that they shall not feel death itself in sudden change, but shall be caught up along with the risen in the clouds to meet Christ in the air, and so shall they ever live with the Lord. [5] And rightly shall it be these who receive this grace, since there will be no posterity after them to be led to believe, not by the hope of what they see not, but by the love of what they see. This faith is weak and nerveless, and must not be called faith at all, inasmuch as faith is thus defined: "Faith is the firmness of those who hope, [6] the clear proof of things which they do not see." [7] Accordingly, in the same Epistle to the Hebrews,

---

[1] John xiv. 30, 31.
[2] 1 Cor. xv. 21, 22.

[3] Col. ii. 14. Chirographa, i.e. "handwritings."
[4] Matt. xxvi. 28.
[5] 1 Thess. iv. 17. Compare *Retrac.* ii. 33 and Letter 193.
[6] Augustin constantly quotes this text with the active participle *sperantium*, instead of *sperandorum*. The Greek ἐλπιζομένων is not always construed passively in the passage; some regard it as of the middle voice.
[7] Heb. xi. 1.

where this passage occurs, after enumerating in subsequent sentences certain worthies who pleased God by their faith, he says : "These all died in faith, not having received the promises, but seeing them afar off, and hailing them, and confessing that they were strangers and pilgrims on the earth."[1]  And then afterwards he concluded his eulogy on faith in these words : "And these all, having obtained a good report through faith, did not indeed receive God's promises ; for they foresaw better things for us, and that without us they could not themselves become perfect."[2]  Now this would be no praise for faith, nor (as I said) would it be faith at all, were men in believing to follow after rewards which they could see, — in other words, if on believers were bestowed the reward of immortality in this present world.

## CHAP. 51. — WHY THE DEVIL IS SAID TO HOLD THE POWER AND DOMINION OF DEATH.

Hence the Lord Himself willed to die, "in order that," as it is written of Him, "through death He might destroy him that had the power of death, that is, the devil ; and deliver them who through fear of death were all their lifetime subject to bondage."[3]  From this passage it is shown with sufficient clearness that even the death of the body came about by the instigation and work of the devil, — in a word, from the sin which he persuaded man to commit ; nor is there any other reason why he should be said in strictness of truth to hold the power of death. Accordingly, He who died without any sin, original or actual, said in the passage I have already quoted : "Behold, the prince of this world," that is, the devil, who had the power of death, "cometh and findeth nothing in me," — meaning, he shall find no sin in me, because of which he has caused men to die.  As if the question were asked Him : Why then should you die? He says, "That all may know that I am doing the will of my Father, arise, let us go hence ;"[4] that is, that I may die, though I have no cause of death from sin under the author of sin, but only from obedience and righteousness, having become obedient unto death.  Proof is likewise afforded us by this passage, that the fact of the faithful overcoming the fear of death is a part of the struggle of faith itself ; for all struggle would indeed be at an end, if immortality were at once to become the reward of them that believe.

## CHAP. 52 [XXXII.] — WHY CHRIST, AFTER HIS RESURRECTION, WITHDREW HIS PRESENCE FROM THE WORLD.

Although, therefore, the Lord wrought many visible miracles in order that faith might sprout at first and be fed by infant nourishment, and grow to its full strength by and by out of this softness (for as faith becomes stronger the less does it seek such help) ; He nevertheless wished us to wait quietly, without visible inducements, for the promised hope, in order that "the just might live by faith ;"[5] and so great was this wish of His, that though He rose from the dead the third day, He did not desire to remain among men, but, after leaving a proof of his resurrection by showing Himself in the flesh to those whom He deigned to have for His witnesses of this event, He ascended into heaven, withdrawing Himself thus from their sight, and conferring no such thing on the flesh of any one of them as He had displayed in His own flesh, in order that they too "might live by faith," and in the present world might wait in patience and without visible inducements for the reward of that righteousness in which men live by faith, — a reward which should hereafter be visibly and openly bestowed.  To this signification I believe that passage must be referred which He speaks concerning the Holy Ghost : "He will not come, unless I depart."[6]  For this was in fact saying Ye shall not be able to live righteously by faith, which ye shall have as a gift of mine, — that is, from the Holy Ghost, — unless I withdraw from your eyes that which ye now gaze upon, in order that your heart may advance in spiritual growth by fixing its faith on invisible things.  This righteousness of faith He constantly commends to them.  Speaking of the Holy Ghost, He says, "He shall reprove the world of sin, and of righteousness, and of judgment : of sin, because they have not believed on me : of righteousness, because I go to the Father, and ye shall see me no more."[7]  What is that righteousness, whereby men were not to see Him, except that "the just is to live by faith," and that we, not looking at the things which are seen, but at those which are not seen, are to wait in the Spirit for the hope of the righteousness that is by faith?

## CHAP. 53 [XXXIII.] — AN OBJECTION OF THE PELAGIANS.

But those persons who say, "If the death of the body has happened by sin, we of course ought not to die after that remission of sins which the Redeemer has bestowed upon us," do not understand how it is that some things, whose guilt God has cancelled in order that they may not stand in our way after this life, He yet permits to remain for the contest of faith, in order that they may become the means of instructing and exercising those who are advancing in the

[1] Heb. xi. 13.
[2] Heb. xi. 39, 40.
[3] Heb. ii. 14.
[4] John xiv. 30, 31.

[5] Hab. ii. 4.
[6] John xvi. 7.
[7] John xvi. 8-10.

struggle after holiness. Might not some man, by not understanding this, raise a question and ask, If God has said to man because of his sin, " In the sweat of thy brow thou shalt eat thy bread : thorns also and thistles shall the ground bring forth to thee," [1] how comes it to pass that this labour and toil continues since the remission of sins, and that the ground of believers yields them this rough and terrible harvest? Again, since it was said to the woman in consequence of her sin, " In sorrow shalt thou bring forth children," [2] how is it that believing women, not-withstanding the remission of their sins, suffer the same pains in the process of parturition? And nevertheless it is an incontestable fact, that by reason of the sin which they had committed, the primeval man and woman heard these sentences pronounced by God, and deserved them ; nor does any one resist these words of the sacred volume, which I have quoted about man's labour and woman's travail, unless some one who is utterly hostile to the catholic faith, and an adversary to the inspired writings.

CHAP. 54 [XXXIV.] — WHY PUNISHMENT IS STILL INFLICTED, AFTER SIN HAS BEEN FORGIVEN.

But, inasmuch as there are not wanting persons of such character, just as we say in answer to those who raise this question, that those things are punishments of sins before remission, which after remission become contests and exercises of the righteous ; so again to such persons as are similarly perplexed about the death of the body, our answer ought to be so drawn as to show both that we acknowledge it to have accrued because of sin, and that we are not discouraged by the punishment of sins having been bequeathed to us for an exercise of discipline, in order that our great fear of it may be overcome by us as we advance in holiness. For if only small virtue accrued to " the faith which worketh by love " in conquering the fear of death, there would be no great glory for the martyrs ; nor could the Lord say, " Greater love hath no man than this, that he lay down his life for his friends ; " [3] which John in his epistle expresses in these terms : " As He laid down His life for us, so ought we to lay down our lives for the brethren." [4]   In vain, therefore, would commendation be bestowed on the most eminent suffering in encountering or despising death for righteousness' sake, if there were not in death itself a really great and very severe trial.   And the man who overcomes the fear of it by his faith, procures a great glory and just recompense for his faith itself.   Wherefore it ought to surprise no one, either that the death of the body

could not possibly have happened to man unless sin had been previously committed, since it was of this that it was to become the punishment ; nor that after the remission of their sins it comes to the faithful, in order that in their triumphing over the fear of it, the fortitude of righteousness may be exercised.

CHAP. 55. — TO RECOVER THE RIGHTEOUSNESS WHICH HAD BEEN LOST BY SIN, MAN HAS TO STRUGGLE, WITH ABUNDANT LABOUR AND SORROW.

The flesh which was originally created was not that sinful flesh in which man refused to maintain his righteousness amidst the delights of Paradise, wherefore God determined that sinful flesh should propagate itself after it had sinned, and struggle for the recovery of holiness, in many toils and troubles.   Therefore, after Adam was driven out of Paradise, he had to dwell over against Eden, — that is, over against the garden of delights, — to indicate that it is by labours and sorrows, which are the very contraries of delights, that sinful flesh had to be educated, after it had failed amidst its first pleasures to maintain its holiness, previous to its becoming sinful flesh. As therefore our first parents, by their subsequent return to righteous living, by which they are supposed to have been released from the worst penalty of their sentence through the blood of the Lord, were still not deemed worthy to be recalled to Paradise during their life on earth, so in like manner our sinful flesh, even if a man lead a righteous life in it after the remission of his sins, does not deserve to be immediately exempted from that death which it has derived from its propagation of sin.[5]

CHAP. 56. — THE CASE OF DAVID, IN ILLUSTRATION.

Some such thought has occurred to us about the patriarch David, in the Book of Kings. After the prophet was sent to him, and threatened him with the evils which were to arise from the anger of God on account of the sin which he had committed, he obtained pardon by the confession of his sin, and the prophet replied that the shame and crime had been remitted to him ; but yet, for all that, the evils with which God had threatened him followed in due course, so that he was brought low by his son.   Now why is not an objection at once raised here : " If it was on account of his sin that God threatened him, why, when the sin was forgiven, did He fulfil His threat?" except because, if the cavil had been raised, it would have been most correctly answered, that the remission of the sin was given that the man

---

[1] Gen. iii. 18, 19.
[2] Gen. iii. 16.
[3] John xv. 13.
[4] 1 John iii. 16.

[5] See also his treatise, *De Naturâ et Gratiâ*, ch. xxiii.

might not be hindered from gaining the life eternal, but the threatened evil was still carried into effect, in order that the man's piety might be exercised and approved in the lowly condition to which he was reduced. Thus also God has both inflicted on man the death of his body, because of his sin, and, after his sins are forgiven, has not released him in order that he may be exercised in righteousness.

## CHAP. 57 [XXXV.] — TURN TO NEITHER HAND.

Let us hold fast, then, the confession of this faith, without faltering or failure. One alone is there who was born without sin, in the likeness of sinful flesh, who lived without sin amid the sins of others, and who died without sin on account of our sins. " Let us turn neither to the right hand nor to the left." [1] For to turn to the right hand is to deceive oneself, by saying that we are without sin ; and to turn to the left is to surrender oneself to one's sins with a sort of impunity, in I know not how perverse and depraved a recklessness. "God indeed knoweth the ways on the right hand," [2] even He who alone is without sin, and is able to blot out our sins ; "but the ways on the left hand are perverse," [3] in friendship with sins. Of such inflexibility were those youths of twenty years, [4] who foretokened in figure God's new people ; they entered the land of promise ; they, it is said, turned neither to the right hand nor to the left. [5] Now this age of twenty is not to be compared with the age of children's innocence, but if I mistake not, this number is the shadow and echo of a mystery. For the Old Testament has its excellence in the five books of Moses, while the New Testament is most refulgent in the authority of the four Gospels. These numbers, when multiplied together, reach to the number twenty : four times five, or five times four, are twenty. Such a people (as I have already said), instructed in the kingdom of heaven by the two Testaments — the Old and the New — turning neither to the right hand, in a proud assumption of righteousness, nor to the left hand, in a reckless delight in sin, shall enter into the land of promise, where we shall have no longer either to pray that sins may be forgiven to us, or to fear that they may be punished in us, having been freed from them all by that Redeemer, who, not being "sold under sin," [6] "hath redeemed Israel out of all his iniquities," [7] whether committed in the actual life, or derived from the original transgression.

## CHAP. 58 [XXXVI.] — "LIKENESS OF SINFUL FLESH" IMPLIES THE REALITY.

It is no small concession to the authority and truthfulness of the inspired pages which those persons have made, who, although unwilling to admit openly in their writings that remission of sins is necessary for infants, have yet confessed that they need redemption. Nothing that they have said differs indeed from another word, even that which is derived from Christian instruction. Whilst by those who faithfully read, faithfully hear, and faithfully hold fast the Holy Scriptures, it cannot be doubted that from that flesh, which first became sinful flesh by the choice of sin, and which has been subsequently transmitted to all through successive generations, there has been propagated a sinful flesh, with the single exception of that "likeness of sinful flesh," [8] — which likeness, however, there could not have been, had there not been also the reality of sinful flesh.

## CHAP. 59. — WHETHER THE SOUL IS PROPAGATED ; ON OBSCURE POINTS, CONCERNING WHICH THE SCRIPTURES GIVE US NO ASSISTANCE, WE MUST BE ON OUR GUARD AGAINST FORMING HASTY JUDGMENTS AND OPINIONS ; THE SCRIPTURES ARE CLEAR ENOUGH ON THOSE SUBJECTS WHICH ARE NECESSARY TO SALVATION.

Concerning the soul, indeed, the question arises, whether it, too, is propagated in the same way [as the flesh,] and bound by the same guilt, which is forgiven to it — for we cannot say that it is only the flesh of the infant, and not his soul also, which requires the help of a Saviour and Redeemer, or that the latter must not be included in that thanksgiving in the Psalms, where we read and repeat, " Bless the Lord, O my soul, and forget not all His benefits ; who forgiveth all thine iniquities ; who healeth all thy diseases ; who redeemeth thy life from destruction." [9] Or if it be not likewise propagated, we may ask, whether, by the very fact of its being mingled with and weighed down by the sinful flesh, it still has need of the remission of its own sin, and of a redemption of its own, God being judge, in the height of His foreknowledge, [10] what infants do not deserve [11] to be absolved from that guilt, even before they are born, or have in any instance ever done anything good or evil. The question also arises, how God (even if He does not create souls by natural propagation) can yet not be the Author of that very guilt, on account of which redemption by the sacrament is necessary to the infant's soul. The subject is a wide and important one, [12]

---

[1] Prov. iv. 27.
[2] Same verse [in the Latin and Septuagint; the clause does not occur in the Hebrew].
[3] [See the last note.]
[4] Num. xiv. 29, 31.
[5] Josh. xxiii. 6, 8.
[6] Rom. vii. 14.
[7] Ps. xxv. 22.

[8] Rom. viii. 3.
[9] Ps. ciii. 2-4.
[10] We follow the reading, per summam præscientiam.
[11] Non mereantur.
[12] He treats it in his Epistle, 166; in his work, De Animâ et ejus Origine; and in his De Libero Arbitrio, 42.

and requires another treatise. The discussion, however, so far as I can judge, ought to be conducted with temper and moderation, so as to deserve the praise of cautious inquiry, rather than the censure of headstrong assertion. For whenever a question arises on an unusually obscure subject, on which no assistance can be rendered by clear and certain proofs of the Holy Scriptures, the presumption of man ought to restrain itself; nor should it attempt anything definite by leaning to either side. But if I must indeed be ignorant concerning any points of this sort, as to how they can be explained and proved, this much I should still believe, that from this very circumstance the Holy Scriptures would possess a most clear authority, whenever a point arose which no man could be ignorant of, without imperilling the salvation which has been promised him. You have now before you, [my dear Marcellinus,] this treatise, worked out to the best of my ability. I only wish that its value equalled its length; for its length I might probably be able to justify, only I should fear that, by adding the justification, I should stretch the prolixity beyond your endurance.

# BOOK III.,

*IN THE SHAPE OF A LETTER ADDRESSED TO THE SAME MARCELLINUS.*

IN WHICH AUGUSTIN REFUTES SOME ERRORS OF PELAGIUS ON THE QUESTION OF THE MERITS OF SINS AND THE BAPTISM OF INFANTS — BEING SUNDRY ARGUMENTS OF HIS WHICH HE HAD INTERSPERSED AMONG HIS EXPOSITIONS OF SAINT PAUL, IN OPPOSITION TO ORIGINAL SIN.

*To his beloved son Marcellinus, Augustin, bishop and servant of Christ and of the servants of Christ, sendeth greeting in the Lord.*

CHAP. 1 [I.] — PELAGIUS ESTEEMED A HOLY MAN ; HIS EXPOSITIONS ON SAINT PAUL.

THE questions which you proposed that I should write to you about, in opposition to those persons who say that Adam would have died even if he had not sinned, and that nothing of his sin has passed to his posterity by natural transmission ; and especially on the subject of the baptism of infants, which the universal Church, with most pious and maternal care, maintains in constant celebration ; and whether in this life there are, or have been, or ever will be, children of men without any sin at all — I have already discussed in two lengthy books. And I venture to think that if in them I have not met all the points which perplex all men's minds on such matters (an achievement which, I apprehend, — nay, which I have no doubt, — lies beyond the power either of myself, or of any other person), I have at all events prepared something in the shape of a firm ground on which those who defend the faith delivered to us by our fathers, against the novel opinions of its opponents, may at any time take their stand, not unarmed for the contest. However, within the last few days I have read some writings by Pelagius, — a holy man, as I am told, who has made no small progress in the Christian life, — containing some very brief expository notes on the epistles of the Apostle Paul ;[1] and therein I found, on coming to the passage where the apostle says, " By one man sin entered into the world, and death by sin ; and so it passed upon all men,"[2] an argument which is used by those who say that infants are not burdened with original sin. Now I confess that I have not refuted this argument in my lengthy treatise, because it did not indeed once occur to me that anybody was capable of thinking such sentiments. Being, however, unwilling to add to that work, which I had concluded, I have thought it right to insert in this epistle both the argument itself in the very words in which I read it, and the answer which it seems to me proper to give to it.

CHAP. 2 [II.] — PELAGIUS' OBJECTION ; INFANTS RECKONED AMONG THE NUMBER OF BELIEVERS AND THE FAITHFUL.

In these terms, then, the argument is stated : — " But they who deny the transmission of sin endeavour to impugn it thus : If (say they) Adam's sin injured even those who do not sin, therefore Christ's righteousness also profits even those who do not believe ; because ' In like manner, nay, much more,' he says, ' are men saved by one, than they had previously perished by one.' " Now to this argument, I repeat, I advanced no reply in the two books which I previously addressed to you ; nor, indeed, had I proposed to myself such a task. But now I beg you first of all to observe, when they say, " If Adam's sin injures even those who do not sin, then Christ's righteousness also profits even those who do not believe," how absurd and false they judge it to be, that the righteousness of Christ should profit even those who do not believe ; and that thence they think to put together such an argument as this : That no more could the first man's sin possibly do injury to infants who commit no sin, than the righteousness of Christ can benefit any who do not believe. Let them therefore tell us what is the benefit of Christ's

---

[1] [This commentary is also made known to us by Marius Mercator's *Commonitoria*, cap. 2, and has been preserved for us among the works of Jerome (Vallarsius' ed., tom. xi.), although probably not without alterations. It seems to have been composed before A.D. 410, at Rome. — W.]
[2] Rom. v. 12.

righteousness to baptized infants; let them by all means tell us what they mean. For of course, since they do not forget that they are Christians themselves, they have no doubt that there is some benefit. But whatever be this benefit, it is incapable (as they themselves assert) of benefiting those who do not believe. Whence they are compelled to class baptized infants in the number of believers, and to assent to the authority of the Holy Universal Church, which does not account those unworthy of the name of believers, to whom the righteousness of Christ could be, according to them, of no use except as believers. As, therefore, by the answer of those, through whose agency they are born again, the Spirit of righteousness transfers to them that faith which, of their own will, they could not yet have; so the sinful flesh of those, through whose agency they are born, transfers to them that injury, which they have not yet contracted in their own life. And even as the Spirit of life regenerates them in Christ as believers, so also the body of death had generated them in Adam as sinners. The one generation is carnal, the other Spiritual; the one makes children of the flesh, the other children of the Spirit; the one children of death, the other children of the resurrection; the one the children of the world, the other the children of God; the one children of wrath, the other children of mercy; and thus the one binds them under original sin, the other liberates them from the bond of every sin.

### CHAP. 3. — PELAGIUS MAKES GOD UNJUST.

We are driven at last to yield our assent on divine authority to that which we are unable to investigate with even the clearest intellect. It is well that they remind us themselves that Christ's righteousness is unable to profit any but believers, while they yet allow that it somewhat profits infants; according to this (as we have already said) they must, without evasion, find room for baptized infants among the number of believers. Consequently, if they are not baptized, they will have to rank amongst those who do not believe; and therefore they will not even have life, but "the wrath of God abideth on them," inasmuch as "he that believeth not the Son shall not see life; but the wrath of God abideth on him;"[1] and they are under judgment, since "he that believeth not is condemned already;"[2] and they shall be condemned, since "he that believeth, and is baptized, shall be saved; but he that believeth not shall be damned."[3] Let them, now, then see to it with what justice they can hold or strive to maintain that human beings have no part in eternal life, but in the wrath of God, and incur the divine judgment and condemnation, who are without sin; if, that is, as they cannot have any actual sin, so also they have within them no original sin.

### CHAP. 4.

To the other points which Pelagius makes them urge who argue against original sin, I have already, I think, sufficiently and clearly replied in the two former books of my lengthy treatise. Now if my reply should seem to any persons to be brief or obscure, I beg their pardon, and request the favour of their coming to terms with those who perhaps censure my treatise, not for being too brief, but rather as being too long; whilst any who still do not understand the points which I cannot help thinking I have explained as clearly as the nature of the subject allowed me, shall certainly hear no blame or reproach from me for indifference, or want of understanding me.[4] I would rather that they should pray God to give them intelligence.

### CHAP. 5 [III.] — PELAGIUS PRAISED BY SOME; ARGUMENTS AGAINST ORIGINAL SIN PROPOSED BY PELAGIUS IN HIS COMMENTARY.

But we must not indeed omit to observe that this good and praiseworthy man (as they who know him describe him to be) has not advanced this argument against the natural transmission of sin in his own person, but has reproduced what is alleged by those persons who disapprove of the doctrine, and this, not merely so far as I have just quoted and confuted the allegation, but also as to those other points on which I have now further undertaken to furnish a reply. Now, after saying, "If (they say) Adam's sin injured even those who do not sin, therefore Christ's righteousness also profits even those who do not believe," — which sentence, you will perceive from what I have said in answer to it, is not only not repugnant to what we hold, but even reminds us what we ought to hold, — he at once goes on to add, "Then they contend, if baptism cleanses away that old sin, those children who are born of two baptized parents must needs be free from this sin, for they could not have transmitted to their children what they did not possess themselves. Besides," says he, "if the soul is not of transmission, but only the flesh, then only the latter has the transmission of sin, and it alone deserves punishment; for they allege that it would be unjust for the soul, which is only now born, and comes not of the lump of Adam, to bear the burden of so old an alien sin. They say, likewise," says Pelagius, "that it cannot by any means be conceded that God, who remits to a man his own sins, should impute to him another's."

---

[1] John iii. 36.
[2] John iii. 18.
[3] Mark xvi. 16.

[4] [Or, "because they lack my own faculty of understanding the subject."]

CHAP. 6. — WHY PELAGIUS DOES NOT SPEAK IN HIS OWN PERSON.

Pray, don't you see how Pelagius has inserted the whole of this paragraph in his writings, not in his own person, but in that of others, knowing so well the novelty of this unheard-of doctrine, which is now beginning to raise its voice against the ancient ingrafted opinion of the Church, that he was ashamed or afraid to acknowledge it himself? And perhaps he does not himself think that a man is born without sin for whom he confesses that baptism to be necessary by which comes the remission of sins; or that the man is condemned without sin who must be reckoned, when unbaptized, in the class of non-believers, since the gospel of course cannot deceive us, when it most clearly asserts, "He that believeth not shall be damned;"[1] or, lastly, that the image of God, when without sin, is not admitted into the kingdom of God, forasmuch as "except a man be born of water and of the Spirit, he cannot enter into the kingdom of God,"[2] — and so must either be precipitated into eternal death without sin, or, what is still more absurd, must have eternal life outside the kingdom of God; for the Lord, when foretelling what He should say to His people at last, — "Come, ye blessed of my Father, inherit the kingdom prepared for you from the beginning of the world,"[3] — also clearly indicated what the kingdom was of which He was speaking, by concluding thus: "So these shall go away into everlasting punishment; but the righteous into life eternal."[4] These opinions, then, and others which spring from the central error, I believe so worthy a man, and so good a Christian, does not at all accept, as being too perverse and repugnant to Christian truth. But it is quite possible that he may, by the very arguments of those who deny the transmission of sin, be still so far distressed as to be anxious to hear or know what can be said in reply to them; and on this account he was both unwilling to keep silent the tenets propounded by them who deny the transmission of sin, in order that he might get the question in due time discussed, and, at the same time, declined to report the opinions in his own person, lest he should be supposed to entertain them himself.

CHAP. 7 [IV.] — PROOF OF ORIGINAL SIN IN INFANTS.

Now, although I may not be able myself to refute the arguments of these men, I yet see how necessary it is to adhere closely to the clearest statements of the Scriptures, in order that the obscure passages may be explained by help of these, or, if the mind be as yet unequal to either perceiving them when explained, or investigating them whilst abstruse, let them be believed without misgiving. But what can be plainer than the many weighty testimonies of the divine declarations, which afford to us the clearest proof possible that without union with Christ there is no man who can attain to eternal life and salvation; and that no man can unjustly be damned, — that is, separated from that life and salvation, — by the judgment of God? The inevitable conclusion from these truths is this, that, as nothing else is effected when infants are baptized except that they are incorporated into the church, in other words, that they are united with the body and members of Christ, unless this benefit has been bestowed upon them, they are manifestly in danger of[5] damnation. Damned, however, they could not be if they really had no sin. Now, since their tender age could not possibly have contracted sin in its own life, it remains for us, even if we are as yet unable to understand, at least to believe that infants inherit original sin.

CHAP. 8. — JESUS IS THE SAVIOUR EVEN OF INFANTS.

And therefore, if there is an ambiguity in the apostle's words when he says, "By one man sin entered into the world, and death by sin; and so it passed upon all men;"[6] and if it is possible for them to be drawn aside, and applied to some other sense, — is there anything ambiguous in this statement: "Except a man be born again of water and of the Spirit, he cannot enter into the kingdom of God?"[2] Is this, again, ambiguous: "Thou shalt call His name Jesus, for He shall save His people from their sins?"[7] Is there any doubt of what this means: "The whole need not a physician, but they that are sick?"[8] — that is, Jesus is not needed by those who have no sin, but by those who are to be saved from sin. Is there anything, again, ambiguous in this: "Except men eat the flesh of the Son of man," that is, become partakers of His body, "they shall not have life?"[9] By these and similar statements, which I now pass over, — absolutely clear in the light of God, and absolutely certain by His authority, — does not truth proclaim without ambiguity, that unbaptized infants not only cannot enter into the kingdom of God, but cannot have everlasting life, except in the body of Christ, in order that they may be incorporated into which they are washed

[1] Mark xvi. 16.
[2] John iii. 5.
[3] Matt. xxv. 34.
[4] Matt. xxv. 46.
[5] Pertinere ad.
[6] Rom. v. 12.
[7] Matt. i. 21.
[8] Matt. ix. 12.
[9] See John vi. 53.

in the sacrament of baptism? Does not truth, without any dubiety, testify that for no other reason are they carried by pious hands to Jesus (that is, to Christ, the Saviour and Physician), than that they may be healed of the plague of their sin by the medicine of His sacraments? Why then do we delay so to understand the apostle's very words, of which we perhaps used to have some doubt, that they may agree with these statements of which we can have no manner of doubt?

CHAP. 9. — THE AMBIGUITY OF "ADAM IS THE FIGURE OF HIM TO COME."

To me, however, no doubt presents itself about the whole of this passage, in which the apostle speaks of the condemnation of many through the sin of one, and the justification of many through the righteousness of One, except as to the words, "Adam is the figure of Him that was to come."[1] For this phrase in reality not only suits the sense which understands that Adam's posterity were to be born of the same form as himself along with sin, but the words are also capable of being drawn out into several distinct meanings. For we have ourselves perhaps actually contended for various senses from the words in question at different times,[2] and very likely we shall propound yet another view, which, however, will not be incompatible with the sense here mentioned; and even Pelagius has not always expounded the passage in one way. All the rest, however, of the passage in which these doubtful words occur, if its statements are carefully examined and treated, as I have tried my best to do in the first book of this treatise, will not (in spite of the obscurity of style necessarily engendered by the subject itself) fail to show the incompatibility of any other meaning than that which has secured the adhesion of the universal Church from the earliest times — that believing infants have obtained through the baptism of Christ the remission of original sin.

CHAP. 10 [V.] — HE SHOWS THAT CYPRIAN HAD NOT DOUBTED THE ORIGINAL SIN OF INFANTS.

Accordingly, it is not without reason that the blessed Cyprian[3] carefully shows how from the very first the Church has held this as a well understood article of faith. When he was asserting the fitness of infants only just born to receive Christ's baptism, on a certain occasion when he was consulted whether this ought to be administered before the eighth day, he endeavoured, as far as he could, to prove that they were per-

fect,[4] lest any one should suppose, from the number of the days (because it was on the eighth day that infants were before circumcised), that they so far lacked perfection. However, after bestowing upon them the full support of his argument, he still confessed that they were not free from original sin; because if he had denied this, he would have removed all reason for the very baptism which he was maintaining their fitness to receive. You can, if you wish, read for yourself the epistle of the illustrious martyr On the Baptism of Little Children; for it cannot fail to be within reach at Carthage. But I have deemed it right to transcribe some few statements of it into this letter of mine, so far as applies to the question before us; and I pray you to mark them carefully. "Now with respect," says he, "to the case of infants, whom you declared it would be improper to baptize if presented within the second and third day after their birth, since that due regard ought to be paid to the law of circumcision of old, so that you thought that the infant should not be baptized and sanctified before the eighth day after its birth, — a far different view has been formed of the question in our council. Not a man there assented to what you thought ought to be done; but the whole of us rather determined that to no one born of men ought God's mercy and grace to be denied. For since the Lord in His gospel says, 'The Son of man is not come to destroy men's lives, but to save them,'[5] so far as in us lies, not a soul ought, if possible, to be lost." You observe how in these words he supposes that it is fraught with ruin and death, not only to the flesh, but also to the soul, for one to depart this life without that saving sacrament. Wherefore, if he said nothing else, it was competent to us to conclude from his words that without sin the soul could not perish. See, however, what (when he shortly afterwards maintains the innocence of infants) he at the same time allows concerning them in the plainest terms: "But if," says he, "anything could hinder men from the attainment of grace, then their heavier sins might rather hinder those who have reached the stages of adults, and advanced life, and old age. Since, however, remission of sins is given even to the greatest sinners after they have believed, however much they have previously sinned against God, and since nobody is forbidden baptism and grace, how much more ought an infant not to be forbidden who newborn has done no sin, except that from having been born carnally after Adam he has contracted from his very birth the contagion of the primeval death! How, too, does this fact contribute in itself the more easily to their reception of the forgiveness of sins, that the remission which

[1] "Adam formam futuri;" see Rom. v. 14.
[2] Comp. above, Book i. c. 13; Epist. 157; De Nuptiis, ii. 44; and Contra Julianum, vi. 8.
[3] See Cyprian's Epistle, 64 (ad Fidum); also Augustin. Epist. 166; De Nuptiis, ii. 49; Contra Julianum, ii. 5; Ad Bonifacium, iv. 3; Sermons, 294.
[4] The word implies "of ripe age;" i.e., for "baptism."
[5] Luke ix. 56.

they have is not of their own sins, but of those of another!"

## CHAP. 11.—THE ANCIENTS ASSUMED ORIGINAL SIN.

You see with what confidence this great man expresses himself after the ancient and undoubted rule of faith. In advancing such very certain statements, his object was by help of these firm conclusions to prove the uncertain point which had been submitted to him by his correspondent, and concerning which he informs him that a decree of a council had been passed, to the effect that, if an infant were brought even before the eighth day after his birth, no one should hesitate to baptize him. Now it was not then determined or confirmed by the council that infants were held bound by original sin as if it were new, or as if it were attacked by the opposition of some one ; but when another controversy was being conducted, and the question was discussed, in reference to the law of the circumcision of the flesh, whether they ought to be baptized before the eighth day. None agreed with the person who denied this ; because it was not an open question admitting of discussion, but was fixed and unassailable, that the soul would forfeit eternal salvation if it ended this life without obtaining the sacrament of baptism : but at the same time infants fresh from the womb were held to be affected only by the guilt of original sin. On this account, although remission of sins was easier in their case, because the sins were derived from another, it was nevertheless indispensable. It was on sure grounds like these that the uncertain question of the eighth day was solved, and the council decided that after a man was born, not a day ought to be lost in rendering him that succour which should prevent his perishing for ever. When also a reason was given for the circumcision of the flesh as being itself a shadow of what was to be, its purport was not that we should understand that baptism ought to be administered on the eighth day after birth, but rather that we are spiritually circumcised in the resurrection of Christ, who rose from the dead on the third day, indeed, after His passion, but among the days of the week, by which time is counted, on the eighth, that is, on the first day after the Sabbath.

## CHAP. 12 [VI.]—THE UNIVERSAL CONSENSUS RESPECTING ORIGINAL SIN.

And now, again, with a strange boldness in new controversy, certain persons are endeavouring to make us uncertain on a point which our forefathers used to bring forward as most certainly fixed, whenever they would solve such questions as seemed uncertain to some. When this controversy, indeed, first began, I am unable to say ; but one thing I know, that even the holy Jerome, who is in our own day renowned for great industry and learning in ecclesiastical literature, for the solution of sundry questions treated in his writings, makes use of the same most certain assumption without exhibition of proofs. For instance, in his commentary on the prophet Jonah, when he comes to the passage where the infants were mentioned as chastened by the fast, he says : [1] "The greatest age comes first, and then all the rest is pervaded down to the least.[2] For there is no man without sin, whether the span of his age be but that of a single day, or he reckon many years to his life. For if the very stars are unclean in the sight of God,[3] how much more is a worm and corruption, such as are they who are held subject to the sin of the offending Adam?" If, indeed, we could readily interrogate this most learned man, how many authors who have treated of the divine Scriptures in both languages,[4] and have written on Christian controversies, would he mention to us, who have never held any other opinion since the Church of Christ was founded,—who neither received any other from their forefathers, nor handed down any other to their posterity? My own reading, indeed, has been far more limited, but yet I do not recollect ever having heard of any other doctrine on this point from Christians, who accept the two Testaments, whether established in the Catholic Church, or in any heretical or schismatic body whatever. I do not remember, I say, that I have at any time found any other doctrine in such writers as have contributed anything to literature of this kind, whether they have followed the canonical Scriptures, or have supposed that they have followed them, or had wished to be so supposed. From what quarter this question has suddenly come upon us I know not. A short time ago,[5] in a passing conversation with certain persons while we were at Carthage, my ears were suddenly offended with such a proposition as this : "That infants are not baptized for the purpose of receiving remission of sin, but that they may be sanctified in Christ." Although I was much disturbed by so novel an opinion, still, as there was no opportunity afforded me for gainsaying it, and as its propounders were not persons whose influence gave me anxiety, I readily let the subject slip into neglect and oblivion. And lo ! it is now maintained with burning zeal against the Church ; lo ! it is committed to our permanent notice by writing ; nay, the matter is brought to such a pitch of distracting influence, that we are even consulted on it by

---

[1] St. Jerome, on Jon. iii.
[2] Ver. 3.
[3] Job xxv. 4.
[4] Or "who have treated of both languages of the divine Scriptures."
[5] Probably in the year 411, when a conference was held at Carthage with the Donatists. Augustin says that he then saw Pelagius; see his work, *De Gestis Pelagii*, c. 46.

our brethren; and we are actually obliged to oppose its progress both by disputation and by writing.

### CHAP. 13 [VII.] — THE ERROR OF JOVINIANUS DID NOT EXTEND SO FAR.

A few years ago there lived at Rome one Jovinian,[1] who is said to have persuaded nuns of even advanced age to marry, — not, indeed, by seduction, as if he wanted to make any of them his wife, but by contending that virgins who dedicated themselves to the ascetic life had no more merit before God than believing wives. It never entered his mind, however, along with this conceit, to venture to affirm that children of men are born without original sin. If, indeed, he had added such an opinion, the women might have more readily consented to marry, to give birth to such pure offspring. When this man's writings (for he dared to write) were by the brethren forwarded to Jerome to refute, he not only discovered no such error in them, but, while looking out his conceits for refutation, he found among other passages this very clear testimony to the doctrine of man's original sin, from which Jerome indeed felt satisfied of the man's belief of that doctrine.[2] These are his words when treating of it: "He who says that he abides in Christ, ought himself also to walk even as He walked.[3] We give our opponent the option to choose which alternative he likes. Does he abide in Christ, or does he not? If he does, then, let him walk like Christ. If, however, it is a rash thing to undertake to resemble the excellences of Christ, he abides not in Christ, because he walks not as Christ did. He did no sin, neither was any guile found in His mouth;[4] who, when He was reviled, reviled not again; and as a lamb before its shearer is dumb, so He opened not His mouth;[5] to whom the prince of this world came, and found nothing in Him;[6] whom, though He had done no sin, God made sin for us.[7] We, however, according to the Epistle of James, all commit many sins;[8] and none of us is pure from uncleanness, even if his life should be but of one day.[9] For who shall boast that he has a clean heart? Or who shall be confident that he is pure from sins? We are held guilty according to the likeness of Adam's transgression. Accordingly David also says: 'Behold,

I was shapen in iniquity; and in sin did my mother conceive me.'"[10]

### CHAP. 14. — THE OPINIONS OF ALL CONTROVERSIALISTS WHATEVER ARE NOT, HOWEVER, CANONICAL AUTHORITY; ORIGINAL SIN, HOW ANOTHER'S; WE WERE ALL ONE MAN IN ADAM.

I have not quoted these words as if we might rely upon the opinions of every disputant as on canonical authority; but I have done it, that it may be seen how, from the beginning down to the present age, which has given birth to this novel opinion, the doctrine of original sin has been guarded with the utmost constancy as a part of the Church's faith, so that it is usually adduced as most certain ground whereon to refute other opinions when false, instead of being itself exposed to refutation by any one as false. Moreover, in the sacred books of the canon, the authority of this doctrine is vigorously asserted in the clearest and fullest way. The apostle exclaims: "By one man sin entered into the world, and death by sin; and so it passed upon all men, in which all have sinned."[11] Now from these words it cannot certainly be said, that Adam's sin has injured even those *who commit no sin*, for the Scripture says, "*In which all have sinned.*" Nor, indeed, are those sins of infancy so said to be *another's*, as if they did not belong to the infants at all, inasmuch as all then sinned in Adam, when in his nature, by virtue of that innate power whereby he was able to produce them, they were all as yet the one Adam; but they are called *another's*,[12] because as yet they were not living their own lives, but the life of the one man contained whatsoever was in his future posterity.

### CHAP. 15 [VIII.] — WE ALL SINNED ADAM'S SIN.

"It is," they say, "by no means conceded that God who remits to a man his own sins imputes to him another's." He remits, indeed, but it is to those regenerated by the Spirit, not to those generated by the flesh; but He imputes to a man no longer the sins of another, but only his own. They were no doubt the sins of another, whilst as yet they were not in existence who bore them when propagated; but now the sins belong to them by carnal generation, to whom they have not yet been remitted by spiritual regeneration.

### CHAP. 16. — ORIGIN OF ERRORS; A SIMILE SOUGHT FROM THE FORESKIN OF THE CIRCUMCISED, AND FROM THE CHAFF OF WHEAT.

"But surely," say they, "if baptism cleanses the primeval sin, they who are born of two bap-

---

[1] [This "Christian Epicurus," as he is called by the intemperate zeal of the asceticism of his day, was condemned as a heretic by councils at Rome and Milan in 390. According to Jerome, who wrote a book against him, he not only opposed asceticism, but also contended for the essential equality of all sins and of the punishments and rewards of the next world, and for the sinlessness of those baptized by the Spirit. — W.]
[2] See Jerome's work *Against Jovinian*, ii. near the beginning.
[3] John ii. 6.
[4] Isa. liii. 9.
[5] Isa. liii. 7.
[6] John xiv. 30.
[7] 2 Cor. v. 21.
[8] Jas iii. 2.
[9] Job xiv. 5.

[10] Ps. li. 5.
[11] Rom. v. 12.
[12] Aliena.

tized parents ought to be free from this sin; for these could not have transmitted to their children that thing which they did not themselves possess." Now observe whence error usually thrives: it is when persons are able to start subjects which they are not able to understand. For before what audience, and in what words, can I explain how it is that sinful mortal beginnings bring no obstacle to those who have inaugurated other, immortal, beginnings, and at the same time prove an obstacle to those whom those very persons, against whom it was not an obstacle, have begotten out of the self-same sinful beginnings? How can a man understand these things, whose labouring mind is impeded both by its own prejudiced opinions and by the chain of its own stolid obstinacy? If indeed I had undertaken my cause in opposition to those who either altogether forbid the baptism of infants, or else contend that it is superfluous to baptize them, alleging that as they are born of believing parents, they must needs enjoy the merit of their parents; then it would have been my duty to have roused myself perhaps to greater labour and effort for the purpose of refuting their opinion. In that case, if I encountered a difficulty before obtuse and contentious men in refuting error and inculcating truth, owing to the obscurity which besets the nature of the subject, I should probably resort to such illustrations as were palpable and at hand; and I should in my turn ask them some questions, — how, for instance, if they were puzzled to know in what way sin, after being cleansed by baptism, still remained in those who were begotten of baptized parents, they would explain how it is that the foreskin, after being removed by circumcision, should still remain in the sons of the circumcised? or again, how it happens that the chaff which is winnowed off so carefully by human labour still keeps its place in the grain which springs from the winnowed wheat?

CHAP. 17 [IX.] — CHRISTIANS DO NOT ALWAYS BEGET CHRISTIAN, NOR THE PURE, PURE CHILDREN.

With these and such like palpable arguments, should I endeavour, as I best could, to convince those persons who believed that sacraments of cleansing were superfluously applied to the children of the cleansed, how right is the judgment of baptizing the infants of baptized parents, and how it may happen that to a man who has within him the twofold seed — of death in the flesh, and of immortality in the spirit — that may prove no obstacle, regenerated as he is by the Spirit, which is an obstacle to his son, who is generated by the flesh; and that that may be cleansed in the one by remission, which in the other still requires cleansing by like remission, just as in the case supposed of circumcision, and as in the case of the winnowing and thrashing.

But now, when we are contending with those who allow that the children of the baptized ought to be baptized, we may much more conveniently conduct our discussion, and can say: You who assert that the children of such persons as have been cleansed from the pollution of sin ought to have been born without sin, why do you not perceive that by the same rule you might just as well say that the children of Christian parents ought to have been born Christians? Why, therefore, do you rather maintain that they ought to become Christians? Was there not in their parents, to whom it is said, "Know ye not that your bodies are the members of Christ?"[1] a Christian body? Perhaps you suppose that a Christian body may be born of Christian parents, without having received a Christian soul? Well, this would render the case much more wonderful still. For you would think of the soul one of two things as you pleased, — because, of course, you hold with the apostle, that before birth it had done nothing good or evil:[2] — either that it was derived by transmission, and just as the body of Christians is Christian, so should also their soul be Christian; or else that it was created by Christ, either in the Christian body, or for the sake of the Christian body, and it ought therefore to have been created or given in a Christian condition. Unless perchance you shall pretend that, although Christian parents had it in their power to beget a Christian body, yet Christ Himself was not able to produce a Christian soul. Believe then the truth, and see that, as it has been possible (as you yourselves admit) for one who is not a Christian to be born of Christian parents, for one who is not a member of Christ to be born of members of Christ, and (that we may answer all, who, however falsely, are yet in some sense possessed with a sense of religion) for a man who is not consecrated to be born of parents who are consecrated; so also it is quite possible for one who is not cleansed to be born of parents who are cleansed. Now what account will you give us, of why from Christian parents is born one who is not a Christian, unless it be that not generation, but regeneration makes Christians? Resolve therefore your own question with a like reason, that cleansing from sin comes to no one by being born, but to all by being born again. And thus any child who is born of parents who are cleansed, because born again, must himself be born again, in order that he too may be cleansed. For it has been quite possible for parents to transmit to their children that which they did not possess themselves, — thus resembling not only the wheat which yielded the chaff, and the circumcised the foreskin, but also the

[1] 1 Cor. vi. 15.
[2] Rom. ix. 11.

instance which you yourselves adduce, even that of believers who convey unbelief to their posterity ; which, however, does not accrue to the faithful as regenerated by the Spirit, but it is owing to the fault of the mortal seed by which they have been born of the flesh. For in respect of the infants whom you judge it necessary to make believers by the sacrament of the faithful, you do not deny that they were born in unbelief, although of believing parents.

### CHAP. 18 [X.] — IS THE SOUL DERIVED BY NATURAL PROPAGATION?

Well, but "if the soul is not propagated, but the flesh alone, then the latter alone has propagation of sin, and it alone deserves punishment :" this is what they think, saying "that it is unjust that the soul which is only recently produced, and that not out of Adam's substance, should bear the sin of another committed so long ago." Now observe, I pray you, how the circumspect Pelagius felt the question about the soul to be a very difficult one, and acted accordingly, — for the words which I have just quoted are copied from his book. He does not say absolutely, "Because the soul is not propagated," but hypothetically, *If the soul is not propagated*, rightly determining on so obscure a subject (on which we can find in Holy Scriptures no certain and obvious testimonies, or with very great difficulty discover any) to speak with hesitation rather than with confidence. Wherefore I too, on my side, answer this proposition with no hasty assertion : If the soul is not propagated, where is the justice that, what has been but recently created and is quite free from the contagion of sin, should be compelled in infants to endure the passions and other torments of the flesh, and, what is more terrible still, even the attacks of evil spirits? For never does the flesh so suffer anything of this kind that the living and feeling soul does not rather undergo the punishment. If this, indeed, is shown to be just, it may be shown, on the same terms, with what justice original sin comes to exist in our sinful flesh, to be subsequently cleansed by the sacrament of baptism and God's gracious mercy. If the former point cannot be shown, I imagine that the latter point is equally incapable of demonstration. We must therefore either bear with both positions in silence, and remember that we are human, or else we must prepare, at some other time, another work on the soul, if it shall appear necessary, discussing the whole question with caution and sobriety.

### CHAP. 19 [XI.] — SIN AND DEATH IN ADAM, RIGHTEOUSNESS AND LIFE IN CHRIST.

What the apostle says : "By one man sin entered into the world, and death by sin ; and so it passed upon all men, in which all have sinned ; " [1] we must, however, for the present so accept as not to seem rashly and foolishly to oppose the many great passages of Holy Scripture, which teach us that no man can obtain eternal life without that union with Christ which is effected in Him and with Him, when we are imbued with His sacraments and incorporated with the members of His body. Now this statement which the apostle addresses to the Romans, "By one man sin entered into the world, and death by sin ; and so it passed upon all men, in which all have sinned," tallies in sense with his words to the Corinthians : "Since by man came death, by Man came also the resurrection of the dead. For as in Adam all die, even so in Christ shall all be made alive." [2] For nobody doubts that the subject here referred to is the death of the body, because the apostle was with much earnestness dwelling on the resurrection of the body ; and he seems to be silent here about sin for this reason, namely, because the question was not about righteousness. Both points are mentioned in the Epistle to the Romans, and both points are, at very great length, insisted on by the apostle, — sin in Adam, righteousness in Christ ; and death in Adam, life in Christ. However, as I have observed already, I have thoroughly examined and opened, in the first book of this treatise, all these words of the apostle's argument, as far as I was able, and as much as seemed necessary.

### CHAP. 20. — THE STING OF DEATH, WHAT?

But even in the passage to the Corinthians, where he had been treating fully of the resurrection, the apostle concludes his statement in such a way as not to permit us to doubt that the death of the body is the result of sin. For after he had said, "This corruptible must put on incorruption, and this mortal must put on immortality : so when this corruptible shall have put on incorruption, and this mortal immortality, then," he added, "shall be brought to pass the saying which is written, Death is swallowed up in victory. O death, where is thy victory? O death, where is thy sting?" and at last he subjoined these words : "The sting of death is sin ; and the strength of sin is the law." [3] Now, because (as the apostle's words most plainly declare) death shall then be swallowed up in victory when this corruptible and mortal shall have put on incorruption and immortality, — that is, when "God shall quicken even our mortal bodies by His Spirit that dwelleth in us," — it manifestly follows that the sting of the body of this death, which is the contrary of the resur-

---

[1] Rom. v. 12.
[2] 1 Cor. xv. 21, 22.
[3] 1 Cor. xv. 53-56.

rection of the body, is sin. The sting, however, is that by which death was made, and not that which death made, since it is by sin that we die, and not by death that we sin. It is therefore called "the sting of death" on the principle which originated the phrase "the tree of life," — not because the life of man produced it, but because by it the life of man was made. In like manner "the tree of knowledge" was that whereby man's knowledge was made, not that which man made by his knowledge. So also "the sting of death" is that by which death was produced, not that which death made. We similarly use the expression "the cup of death," since by it some one has died, or might die, — not meaning, of course, a cup made by a dying or dead man.[1] The sting of death is therefore sin, because by the puncture of sin the human race has been slain. Why ask further: the death of what, — whether of the soul, or of the body? Whether the first which we are all of us now dying, or the second which the wicked hereafter shall die? There is no occasion for plying the question so curiously; there is no room for subterfuge. The words in which the apostle expresses the case answer the questions: "When this mortal," says he, "shall have put on immortality, then shall be brought to pass the saying which is written, Death is swallowed up in victory. O death, where is thy victory? O death, where is thy sting? The sting of death is sin, and the strength of sin is the law." He was treating of the resurrection of the body, wherein death shall be swallowed up in victory, when this mortal shall have put on immortality. Then over death itself shall be raised the shout of triumph, when at the resurrection of the body it shall be swallowed up in victory; then shall be said to it, "O death, where is thy victory? O death, where is thy sting?" To the death of the body, therefore, is this said. For victorious immortality shall swallow it up, when this mortal shall put on immortality. I repeat it, to the death of the body shall it be said, "Where is thy victory?" — that victory in which thou didst conquer all, so that even the Son of God engaged in conflict with thee, and by not shrinking but grappling with thee overcame. In these that die thou hast conquered; but thou art thyself conquered in these that rise again. Thy victory was but temporal, in which thou didst swallow up the bodies of them that die. Our victory will abide eternal, in which thou art swallowed up in the bodies of them that rise again. "Where is thy sting?" — that is, the sin wherewithal we are punctured and poisoned, so

that thou didst fix thyself in our very bodies, and for so long a time didst hold them in possession. "The sting of death is sin, and the strength of sin is the law." We all sinned in one, so that we all die in one; we received the law, not by amendment according to its precepts to put an end to sin, but by transgression to increase it. For "the law entered that sin might abound;"[2] and "the Scripture hath concluded all under sin;"[3] but "thanks be to God, who hath given us the victory through our Lord Jesus Christ,"[4] in order that "where sin abounded, grace might much more abound;"[2] and "that the promise by faith of Jesus Christ might be given to them that believe;"[3] and that we might overcome death by a deathless resurrection, and sin, "the sting" thereof, by a free justification.

CHAP. 21 [XII.] — THE PRECEPT ABOUT TOUCHING THE MENSTRUOUS WOMAN NOT TO BE FIGURATIVELY UNDERSTOOD; THE NECESSITY OF THE SACRAMENTS.

Let no one, then, on this subject be either deceived or a deceiver. The manifest sense of Holy Scripture which we have considered, removes all obscurities. Even as death is in this our mortal body derived from the beginning, so from the beginning has sin been drawn into this sinful flesh of ours, for the cure of which, both as it is derived by propagation and augmented by wilful transgression, as well as for the quickening of our flesh itself, our Physician came in the likeness of sinful flesh, who is not needed by the sound, but only by the sick, — and who came not to call the righteous, but sinners.[5] Therefore the saying of the apostle, when advising believers not to separate themselves from unbelieving partners: "For the unbelieving husband is sanctified by the wife, and the unbelieving wife is sanctified by the husband: else were your children unclean; but now are they holy,"[6] must be either so understood as both we ourselves elsewhere,[7] and as Pelagius in his notes on this same Epistle to the Corinthians,[8] has expounded it, according to the purport of the passages already mentioned, that sometimes wives gained husbands to Christ, and sometimes husbands converted wives, whilst the Christian will of even one of the parents prevailed towards making their children Christians; or else (as the apostle's words seem rather to indicate, and to a certain degree compel us) some particular sanctification is to be here understood, by which

---

[1] [This is only one of many examples of the care with which Augustin, writing for the popular eye, illustrates his exegetical points. "Of death" he thus shows is genitive of the object, not of the subject; giving to the phrase the meaning of "the sting which slays man." — W.]

[2] Rom. v. 20.
[3] Gal. iii. 22.
[4] 1 Cor. xv. 57.
[5] Mark ii. 17.
[6] 1 Cor. vii. 14.
[7] See Augustin's work *On the Sermon on the Mount*, i. 16.
[8] See the *Commentaries on St. Paul* in Jerome's works, vol. xi. (Vallarsius), the work of either Pelagius or one of his followers.

an unbelieving husband or wife was sanctified by the believing partner, and by which the children of the believing parents were sanctified, — whether it was that the husband or the wife, during the woman's menstruation, abstained from cohabiting, having learned that duty in the law (for Ezekiel classes this amongst the precepts which were not to be taken in a metaphorical sense [1] ), or on account of some other voluntary sanctification which is not there expressly prescribed, — a sprinkling of holiness arising out of the close ties of married life and children. Nevertheless, whatever be the sanctification meant, this must be steadily held : that there is no other valid means of making Christians and remitting sins, except by men becoming believers through the sacrament according to the institution of Christ and the Church. For neither are unbelieving husbands and wives, notwithstanding their intimate union with holy and righteous spouses, cleansed of the sin which separates men from the kingdom of God and drives them into condemnation, nor are the children who are born of parents, however just and holy, absolved from the guilt of original sin, unless they have been baptized into Christ ; and in behalf of these our plea should be the more earnest, the less able they are to urge one themselves.

#### CHAP. 22 [XIII.] — WE OUGHT TO BE ANXIOUS TO SECURE THE BAPTISM OF INFANTS.

For this is the point aimed at by the controversy, against the novelty of which we have to struggle by the aid of ancient truth : that it is clearly altogether superfluous for infants to be baptized. Not that this opinion is avowed in so many words, lest so firmly established a custom of the Church should be unable to endure its assailants. But if we are taught to render help to orphans, how much more ought we to labour in behalf of those children who, though under the protection of parents, will still be left more destitute and wretched than orphans,

should that grace of Christ be denied them, which they are all unable to demand for themselves?

#### CHAP. 23. — EPILOGUE.

As for what they say, that some men, by the use of their reason, have lived, and do live, in this world without sin, we should wish that it were true, we should strive to make it true, we should pray that it be true ; but, at the same time, we should confess that it is not yet true. For to those who wish and strive and worthily pray for this result, whatever sins remain in them are daily remitted because we sincerely pray, " Forgive us our debts, as we forgive our debtors." [2] Whosoever shall deny that this prayer is in this life necessary for every righteous man who knows and does the will of God, except the one Saint of saints, greatly errs, and is utterly incapable of pleasing Him whom he praises. Moreover, if he supposes himself to be such a character, " he deceives himself, and the truth is not in him," [3] — for no other reason than that he thinks what is false. That Physician, then, who is not needed by the sound, but by the sick, knows how to heal us, and by healing to perfect us unto eternal life ; and He does not in this world take away death, although inflicted because of sin, from those whose sins He remits, in order that they may enter on their conflict, and overcome the fear of death with full sincerity of faith. In some cases, too, He declines to help even His righteous servants, so long as they are capable of still higher elevation, to the attainment of a perfect righteousness, in order that (while in His sight no man living is justified [4]) we may always feel it to be our duty to give Him thanks for mercifully bearing with us, and so, by holy humility, be healed of that first cause of all our failings, even the swellings of pride. This letter, as my intention first sketched it, was to have been a short one ; it has grown into a lengthy book. Would that it were as perfect as it has at last become complete !

---

[1] Ezek. xviii. 6.

[2] Matt. vi. 12.
[3] 1 John i. 8.
[4] Ps. cxliii. 2.

A TREATISE ON THE SPIRIT AND THE LETTER.

# EXTRACT FROM AUGUSTIN'S "RETRACTATIONS,"

## BOOK II. CHAP. 37,

### *ON THE FOLLOWING TREATISE,*

# "DE SPIRITU ET LITTERA."

---

THE person[1] to whom I had addressed the three books entitled *De Peccatorum Meritis et Remissione,* in which I carefully discussed also the baptism of infants, informed me, when acknowledging my communication, that he was much disturbed because I declared it to be possible that a man might be without sin, if he wanted not the will, by the help of God, although no man either had lived, was living, or would live in this life so perfect in righteousness. He asked how I could say that was possible of which no example could be adduced. Owing to this inquiry on the part of this person, I wrote the treatise entitled *De Spiritu et Littera,* in which I considered at large the apostle's statement, "The letter killeth, but the spirit giveth life."[2] In this work, so far as God enabled me, I earnestly disputed with those who oppose that grace of God which justifies the ungodly. While treating, however, of the observances of the Jews, who abstain from sundry meats and drinks in accordance with their ancient law, I mentioned "the ceremonies of certain meats" [*quarumdam escarum cerimoniæ*][3] — a phrase which, though not used in Holy Scripture, seemed to me very convenient, because I remembered that *cerimoniæ* is tantamount to *carimoniæ,* as if from *carere,* to be without, and expresses the abstinence of the worshippers from certain things. If, however, there is any other derivation of the word, which is inconsistent with the true religion, I meant no reference whatever to it; I confined my use to the sense above indicated. This work of mine begins thus: "After reading the short treatises which I lately drew up for you, my beloved son Marcellinus," etc.

---

[1] The Tribune Marcellinus, with whose name are connected many other treatises of Augustin. In this work the author informs us that the occasion of its composition was furnished by this person, who mooted an inquiry touching a statement in the preceding books *Concerning the Merits and the Remission of Sins.* Those books, as we have already indicated, were published A.D. 412. Now in the *Retractations* there is placed after these very books the present work *Concerning the Spirit and the Letter,*—not, indeed, immediately next, but in the fourth place after, — so that it was written, no doubt, about the end of the same year, A.D. 412, some time previous to the death of Marcellinus, who was killed in the month of September of the following year, 413. This present work is also mentioned in the book *On Faith and Works,* c. 14; and in that *On Christian Doctrine,* iii. 33. Compare the notes on p. 15 and p. 130.

[2] 2 Cor. iii. 6.
[3] See chap. 36 [xxi.].

# CONTENTS OF THE TREATISE "ON THE SPIRIT AND THE LETTER."

# A TREATISE ON THE SPIRIT AND THE LETTER,

## *IN ONE BOOK,*

## ADDRESSED TO MARCELLINUS, A.D. 412.

---

MARCELLINUS, IN A LETTER TO AUGUSTIN, HAD EXPRESSED SOME SURPRISE AT HAVING READ, IN THE PRECEDING WORK, OF THE POSSIBILITY BEING ALLOWED OF A MAN CONTINUING IF HE WILLED IT, BY GOD'S HELP, WITHOUT SIN IN THE PRESENT LIFE, ALTHOUGH NOT A SINGLE HUMAN EXAMPLE ANYWHERE OF SUCH PERFECT RIGHTEOUSNESS HAS EVER EXISTED. AUGUSTIN TAKES THE OPPORTUNITY OF DISCUSSING, IN OPPOSITION TO THE PELAGIANS, THE SUBJECT OF THE AID OF GOD'S GRACE; AND HE SHOWS THAT THE DIVINE HELP TO THE WORKING OF RIGHTEOUSNESS BY US DOES NOT LIE IN THE FACT OF GOD'S HAVING GIVEN US A LAW WHICH IS FULL OF GOOD AND HOLY PRECEPTS; BUT IN THE FACT THAT OUR WILL ITSELF, WITHOUT WHICH WE CAN DO NOTHING GOOD, IS ASSISTED AND ELEVATED BY THE SPIRIT OF GRACE BEING IMPARTED TO US, WITHOUT THE AID OF WHICH THE TEACHING OF THE LAW IS "THE LETTER THAT KILLETH," BECAUSE INSTEAD OF JUSTIFYING THE UNGODLY, IT RATHER HOLDS THEM GUILTY OF TRANSGRESSION. HE BEGINS TO TREAT OF THE QUESTION PROPOSED TO HIM AT THE COMMENCEMENT OF THIS WORK, AND RETURNS TO IT TOWARDS ITS CONCLUSION; HE SHOWS THAT, AS ALL ALLOW, MANY THINGS ARE POSSIBLE WITH GOD'S HELP, OF WHICH THERE OCCURS INDEED NO EXAMPLE; AND THEN CONCLUDES THAT, ALTHOUGH A PERFECT RIGHTEOUSNESS IS UNEXAMPLED AMONG MEN, IT IS FOR ALL THAT NOT IMPOSSIBLE.

CHAP. I [I.] — THE OCCASION OF WRITING THIS WORK; A THING MAY BE CAPABLE OF BEING DONE, AND YET MAY NEVER BE DONE.

AFTER reading the short treatises which I lately drew up for you, my beloved son Marcellinus, about the baptism of infants, and the perfection of man's righteousness, — how that no one in this life seems either to have attained or to be likely to attain to it, except only the Mediator, who bore humanity in the likeness of sinful flesh, without any sin whatever, — you wrote me in answer that you were embarrassed by the point which I advanced in the second book,[1] that it was possible for a man to be without sin, if he wanted not the will, and was assisted by the aid of God; and yet that except One in whom "all shall be made alive,"[2] no one has ever lived or will live by whom this perfection has been attained whilst living here. It appeared to you absurd to say that anything was possible of which no example ever occurred, — although I suppose you would not hesitate to admit that no camel ever passed through a needle's eye,[3] and yet He said that even this was possible with God; you may read, too, that twelve thousand legions[4] of angels could possibly have fought for Christ and rescued Him from suffering, but in fact did not; you may read that it was possible for the nations to be exterminated at once out of the land which was given to the

---

[1] *On the Merits of Sins*, etc., ii. 6, 7, 20.

[2] 1 Cor. xv. 22.
[3] Matt. xix. 24, 26.
[4] Matt. xxvi. 53, but observe the "thousand" inserted.

children of Israel,[1] and yet that God willed it to be gradually effected.[2] And one may meet with a thousand other incidents, the past or the future possibility of which we might readily admit, and yet be unable to produce any proofs of their having ever really happened. Accordingly, it would not be right for us to deny the possibility of a man's living without sin, on the ground that amongst men none can be found except Him who is in His nature not man only, but also God, in whom we could prove such perfection of character to have existed.

### CHAP. 2 [II.] — THE EXAMPLES APPOSITE.

Here, perhaps, you will say to me in answer, that the things which I have instanced as not having been realized, although capable of realization, are *divine* works; whereas a man's being without sin falls in the range of a man's own work, — that being indeed his very noblest work which effects a full and perfect righteousness complete in every part; and therefore that it is incredible that no man has ever existed, or is existing, or will exist in this life, who has achieved such a work, if the achievement is possible for a human being. But then you ought to reflect that, although this great work, no doubt, belongs to human agency to accomplish, yet it is also a divine gift, and therefore, not doubt that it is a divine work; " for it is God who worketh in you both to will and to do of His good pleasure."[3]

### CHAP. 3. — THEIRS IS COMPARATIVELY A HARMLESS ERROR, WHO SAY THAT A MAN LIVES HERE WITHOUT SIN.

They therefore are not a very dangerous set of persons and they ought to be urged to show, if they are able, that they are themselves such, who hold that man lives or has lived here without any sin whatever. There are indeed passages of Scripture, in which I apprehend it is definitely stated that no man who lives on earth, although enjoying freedom of will, can be found without sin; as, for instance, the place where it is written, " Enter not into judgment with Thy servant, for in Thy sight shall no man living be justified."[4] If, however, anybody shall have succeeded in showing that this text and the other similar ones ought to be taken in a different sense from their obvious one, and shall have proved that some man or men have spent a sinless life on earth, — whoever does not, not merely refrain from much opposing him, but also does not rejoice with him to the full, is afflicted by extraordinary goads of envy. Moreover, if there neither is, has been, nor will be any man endowed with such perfection of purity (which I am more inclined to believe), and yet it is firmly set forth and thought there is or has been, or is to be, — so far as I can judge, no great error is made, and certainly not a dangerous one, when a man is thus carried away by a certain benevolent feeling; provided that he who thinks so much of another, does not think himself to be such a being, unless he has ascertained that he really and clearly is such.

### CHAP. 4. — THEIRS IS A MUCH MORE SERIOUS ERROR, REQUIRING A VERY VIGOROUS REFUTATION, WHO DENY GOD'S GRACE TO BE NECESSARY.

They, however, must be resisted with the utmost ardor and vigor who suppose that without God's help, the mere power of the human will in itself, can either perfect righteousness, or advance steadily towards it; and when they begin to be hard pressed about their presumption in asserting that this result can be reached without the divine assistance, they check themselves, and do not venture to utter such an opinion, because they see how impious and insufferable it is. But they allege that such attainments are not made without God's help on this account, namely, because God both created man with the free choice of his will, and, by giving him commandments, teaches him, Himself, how man ought to live; and indeed assists him, in that He takes away his ignorance by instructing him in the knowledge of what he ought to avoid and to desire in his actions : and thus, by means of the free-will naturally implanted within him, he enters on the way which is pointed out to him, and by persevering in a just and pious course of life, deserves to attain to the blessedness of eternal life.

### CHAP. 5 [III.] — TRUE GRACE IS THE GIFT OF THE HOLY GHOST, WHICH KINDLES IN THE SOUL THE JOY AND LOVE OF GOODNESS.

We, however, on our side affirm that the human will is so divinely aided in the pursuit of righteousness, that (in addition to man's being created with a free-will, and in addition to the teaching by which he is instructed how he ought to live) he receives the Holy Ghost, by whom there is formed in his mind a delight in, and a love of, that supreme and unchangeable good which is God, even now while he is still " walking by faith " and not yet " by sight;"[5] in order that by this gift to him of the earnest, as it were, of the free gift, he may conceive an ardent desire to cleave to his Maker, and may burn to enter upon the participation in that true light, that it may go well with him from Him to whom he owes his existence. A man's free-will, indeed, avails for nothing except to sin, if he

---

[1] Deut. xxxi. 3.
[2] Judg. ii. 3.
[3] Phil. ii. 13.
[4] Ps. cxliii. 2.

[5] 2 Cor. v. 7.

knows not the way of truth; and even after his duty and his proper aim shall begin to become known to him, unless he also take delight in and feel a love for it, he neither does his duty, nor sets about it, nor lives rightly. Now, in order that such a course may engage our affections, God's "love is shed abroad in our hearts," not through the free-will which arises from ourselves, but "through the Holy Ghost, which is given to us." [1]

CHAP. 6 [IV.] — THE TEACHING OF LAW WITHOUT THE LIFE-GIVING SPIRIT IS "THE LETTER THAT KILLETH."

For that teaching which brings to us the command to live in chastity and righteousness is "the letter that killeth," unless accompanied with "the spirit that giveth life." For that is not the sole meaning of the passage, "The letter killeth, but the spirit giveth life,[2] which merely prescribes that we should not take in the literal sense any figurative phrase which in the proper meaning of its words would produce only nonsense, but should consider what else it signifies, nourishing the inner man by our spiritual intelligence, since "being carnally-minded is death, whilst to be spiritually-minded is life and peace." [3] If, for instance, a man were to take in a literal and carnal sense much that is written in the Song of Solomon, he would minister not to the fruit of a luminous charity, but to the feeling of a libidinous desire. Therefore, the apostle is not to be confined to the limited application just mentioned, when he says, "The letter killeth, but the spirit giveth life;" [2] but this is also (and indeed especially) equivalent to what he says elsewhere in the plainest words: "I had not known lust, except the law had said, Thou shalt not covet;" [4] and again, immediately after: "Sin, taking occasion by the commandment, deceived me, and by it slew me." [5] Now from this you may see what is meant by "the letter that killeth." There is, of course, nothing said figuratively which is not to be accepted in its plain sense, when it is said, "Thou shalt not covet;" but this is a very plain and salutary precept, and any man who shall fulfil it will have no sin at all. The apostle, indeed, purposely selected this general precept, in which he embraced everything, as if this were the voice of the law, prohibiting us from all sin, when he says, "Thou shalt not covet;" for there is no sin committed except by evil concupiscence; so that the law which prohibits this is a good and praiseworthy law. But, when the Holy Ghost withholds His help, which inspires us with a good desire instead of this evil desire (in other words, diffuses love in our hearts), that law, however good in itself, only augments the evil desire by forbidding it. Just as the rush of water which flows incessantly in a particular direction, becomes more violent when it meets with any impediment, and when it has overcome the stoppage, falls in a greater bulk, and with increased impetuosity hurries forward in its downward course. In some strange way the very object which we covet becomes all the more pleasant when it is forbidden. And this is the sin which by the commandment deceives and by it slays, whenever transgression is actually added, which occurs not where there is no law.[6]

CHAP. 7 [V.] — WHAT IS PROPOSED TO BE HERE TREATED.

We will, however, consider, if you please, the whole of this passage of the apostle and thoroughly handle it, as the Lord shall enable us. For I want, if possible, to prove that the apostle's words, "The letter killeth, but the spirit giveth life," do not refer to figurative phrases, — although even in this sense a suitable signification might be obtained from them, — but rather plainly to the law, which forbids whatever is evil. When I shall have proved this, it will more manifestly appear that to lead a holy life is the gift of God, — not only because God has given a free-will to man, without which there is no living ill or well; nor only because He has given him a commandment to teach him how he ought to live; but because through the Holy Ghost He sheds love abroad in the hearts [4] of those whom he foreknew, in order to predestinate them; whom He predestinated, that He might call them; whom He called, that he might justify them; and whom he justified, that He might glorify them.[7] When this point also shall be cleared, you will, I think, see how vain it is to say that those things only are unexampled possibilities, which are the works of God, — such as the passage of the camel through the needle's eye, which we have already referred to, and other similar cases, which to us no doubt are impossible, but easy enough to God; and that man's righteousness is not to be counted in this class of things, on the ground of its being properly man's work, not God's; although there is no reason for supposing, without an example, that his perfection exists, even if it is possible. That these assertions are vain will be clear enough, after it has been also plainly shown that even man's righteousness must be attributed to the operation of God, although not taking place without man's will; and we therefore cannot deny that his perfection is possible even in this life, because

---

[1] Rom. v. 5.
[2] 2 Cor. iii. 6.
[3] Rom. viii. 6.
[4] Rom. vii. 7.
[5] Rom. vii. 11.

[6] Rom. iv. 15.
[7] Rom. viii. 29, 30.

all things are possible with God,[1] — both those which He accomplishes of His own sole will, and those which He appoints to be done with the co-operation with Himself of His creature's will. Accordingly, whatever of such things He does not effect is no doubt without an example in the way of accomplished facts, although with God it possesses both in His power the cause of its possibility, and in His wisdom the reason of its ,unreality. And should this cause be hidden from man, let him not forget that he is a man ; nor charge God with folly simply because he cannot fully comprehend His wisdom.

### CHAP. 8. — ROMANS INTERPRETS CORINTHIANS.

Attend, then, carefully, to the apostle while in his Epistle to the Romans he explains and clearly enough shows that what he wrote to the Corinthians, "The letter killeth, but the spirit giveth life,"[2] must be understood in the sense which we have already indicated, — that the letter of the law, which teaches us not to commit sin, kills, if the life-giving spirit be absent, forasmuch as it causes sin to be known rather than avoided, and therefore to be increased rather than diminished, because to an evil concupiscense there is now added the transgression of the law.

### CHAP. 9 [VI.] — THROUGH THE LAW SIN HAS ABOUNDED.

The apostle, then, wishing to commend the grace which has come to all nations through Jesus Christ, lest the Jews should extol themselves at the expense of the other peoples on account of their having received the law, first says that sin and death came on the human race through one man, and that righteousness and eternal life came also through one, expressly mentioning Adam as the former, and Christ as the latter ; and then says that "the law, however, entered, that the offence might abound : but where sin abounded, grace did much more abound : that as sin hath reigned unto death, even so might grace reign through righteousness unto eternal life by Jesus Christ our Lord."[3] Then, proposing a question for himself to answer, he adds, "What shall we say then? Shall we continue in sin, that grace may abound? God forbid."[4] He saw, indeed, that a perverse use might be made by perverse men of what he had said : "The law entered, that the offence might abound : but where sin abounded, grace did much more abound,"—as if he had said that sin had been of advantage by reason of the abundance of grace. Rejecting this, he answers his question with a "God forbid!" and at once

adds : "How shall we, that are dead to sin, live any longer therein?"[5] as much as to say, When grace has brought it to pass that we should die unto sin, what else shall we be doing, if we continue to live in it, than showing ourselves ungrateful to grace? The man who extols the virtue of a medicine does not contend that the diseases and wounds of which the medicine cures him are of advantage to him ; on the contrary, in proportion to the praise lavished on the remedy are the blame and horror which are felt of the diseases and wounds healed by the much-extolled medicine. In like manner, the commendation and praise of grace are vituperation and condemnation of offences. For there was need to prove to man how corruptly weak he was, so that against his iniquity, the holy law brought him no help towards good, but rather increased than diminished his iniquity ; seeing that the law entered, that the offence might abound ; that being thus convicted and confounded, he might see not only that he needed a physician, but also God as his helper so to direct his steps that sin should not rule over him, and he might be healed by betaking himself to the help of the divine mercy ; and in this way, where sin abounded grace might much more abound, — not through the merit of the sinner, but by the intervention of his Helper.

### CHAP. 10. — CHRIST THE TRUE HEALER.

Accordingly, the apostle shows that the same medicine was mystically set forth in the passion and resurrection of Christ, when he says, "Know ye not, that so many of us as were baptized into Jesus Christ were baptized into His death? Therefore we were buried with Him by baptism into death ; that like as Christ was raised up from the dead by the glory of the Father, even so we also should walk in newness of life. For if we have been planted together in the likeness of His death, we shall be also in the likeness of His resurrection : knowing this, that our old man is crucified with Him, that the body of sin might be destroyed, that henceforth we should not serve sin. For he that is dead is justified from sin. Now, if we be dead with Christ, we believe that we shall also live with Him : knowing that Christ, being raised from the dead, dieth no more ; death hath no more dominion over Him. For in that He died, He died unto sin once ; but in that He liveth, He liveth unto God. Likewise reckon ye also yourselves to be dead indeed unto sin, but alive unto God through Jesus Christ our Lord."[6] Now it is plain enough that here by the mystery of the Lord's death and resurrection is figured the death of our old sinful life, and the rising of the new ; and that here is

---

[1] Mark x. 27.
[2] 2 Cor. iii. 6.
[3] Rom. v. 20, 21.
[4] Rom. vi. 1, 2.

[5] Rom. vi. 2.
[6] Rom. vi. 3-11.

shown forth the abolition of iniquity and the renewal of righteousness. Whence then arises this vast benefit to man through the letter of the law, except it be through the faith of Jesus Christ?

### CHAP. 11 [VII.] — FROM WHAT FOUNTAIN GOOD WORKS FLOW.

This holy meditation preserves "the children of men, who put their trust under the shadow of God's wings,"[1] so that they are "drunken with the fatness of His house, and drink of the full stream of His pleasure. For with Him is the fountain of life, and in His light shall they see light. For He extendeth His mercy to them that know Him, and His righteousness to the upright in heart."[2] He does not, indeed, extend His mercy to them because they know Him, but that they may know Him; nor is it because they are upright in heart, but that they may become so, that He extends to them His righteousness, whereby He justifies the ungodly.[3] This meditation does not elevate with pride: this sin arises when any man has too much confidence in himself, and makes himself the chief end of living. Impelled by this vain feeling, he departs from that fountain of life, from the draughts of which alone is imbibed the holiness which is itself the good life, — and from that unchanging light, by sharing in which the reasonable soul is in a certain sense inflamed, and becomes itself a created and reflected luminary; even as "John was a burning and a shining light,"[4] who notwithstanding acknowledged the source of his own illumination in the words, "Of His fulness have all we received."[5] Whose, I would ask, but His, of course, in comparison with whom John indeed was no light at all? For "that was the true light, which lighteth every man that cometh into the world."[6] Therefore, in the same psalm, after saying, "Extend Thy mercy to them that know Thee, and Thy righteousness to the upright in heart,"[7] he adds, "Let not the foot of pride come against me, and let not the hands of sinners move me. There have fallen all the workers of iniquity: they are cast out, and are not able to stand."[8] Since by that impiety which leads each to attribute to himself the excellence which is God's, he is cast out into his own native darkness, in which consist the works of iniquity. For it is manifestly these works which he does, and for the achievement of such alone is he naturally fit. The works of righteousness he never does, except as he receives ability from that fountain and that light, where the life is that wants for nothing,

and where is "no variableness, nor the shadow of turning."[9]

### CHAP. 12. — PAUL, WHENCE SO CALLED; BRAVELY CONTENDS FOR GRACE.

Accordingly Paul, who, although he was formerly called Saul,[10] chose this new designation, for no other reason, as it seems to me, than because he would show himself *little*,[11] — the "least of the apostles,"[12] — contends with much courage and earnestness against the proud and arrogant, and such as plume themselves on their own works, in order that he may commend the grace of God. This grace, indeed, appeared more obvious and manifest in his case, inasmuch as, while he was pursuing such vehement measures of persecution against the Church of God as made him worthy of the greatest punishment, he found mercy instead of condemnation, and instead of punishment obtained grace. Very properly, therefore, does he lift voice and hand in defence of grace, and care not for the envy either of those who understood not a subject too profound and abstruse for them, or of those who perversely misinterpreted his own sound words; whilst at the same time he unfalteringly preaches that gift of God, whereby alone salvation accrues to those who are the children of the promise, children of the divine goodness, children of grace and mercy, children of the new covenant. In the salutation with which he begins every epistle, he prays: "Grace be to you, and peace, from God the Father, and from the Lord Jesus Christ;"[13] whilst this forms almost the only topic discussed for the Romans, and it is plied with so much persistence and variety of argument, as fairly to fatigue the reader's attention, yet with a fatigue so useful and salutary, that it rather exercises than breaks the faculties of the inner man.

### CHAP. 13 [VIII.] — KEEPING THE LAW; THE JEWS' GLORYING; THE FEAR OF PUNISHMENT; THE CIRCUMCISION OF THE HEART.

Then comes what I mentioned above; then he shows what the Jew is, and says that he is called a Jew, but by no means fulfils what he promises to do. "But if," says he, "thou callest thyself a Jew, and restest in the law, and makest thy boast of God, and knowest His will, and triest the things that are different, being instructed out of the law; and art confident that thou art thyself a guide of the blind, a light of them that are in darkness, an instructor of the foolish, a teacher of babes, which hast the form of knowledge and of the truth in the law. Thou therefore who teachest another, teachest thou not

---

1 Ps. xxxvi. 7.
2 Ps. xxxvi. 8-10.
3 Rom. iv. 5.
4 John v. 35.
5 John i. 16.
6 John i. 9.
7 Ps. xxxvi. 10.
8 Ps. xxxvi. 11, 12.

9 Jas. i. 17.
10 Acts. xiii. 9.
11 See Augustin's *Confessions*, viii. 4.
12 1 Cor. xv. 9.
13 See Rom i. 7, 1 Cor. i. 3, and Gal. i. 3.

thyself? thou that preachest a man should not steal, dost thou steal? thou that sayest a man should not commit adultery, dost thou commit adultery? thou that abhorrest idols, dost thou commit sacrilege? thou that makest thy boast of the law, through breaking the law dishonorest thou God? For the name of God is blasphemed among the Gentiles through you, as it is written. Circumcision verily profiteth, if thou keep the law; but if thou be a breaker of the law, thy circumcision is made uncircumcision. Therefore, if the uncircumcision keep the righteousness of the law, shall not his uncircumcision be counted for circumcision? And shall not uncircumcision which is by nature, if it fulfil the law, judge thee, who by the letter and circumcision dost transgress the law? For he is not a Jew who is one outwardly; neither is that circumcision which is outward in the flesh: but he is a Jew who is one inwardly; and circumcision is that of the heart, in the spirit, and not in the letter; whose praise is not of men, but of God." [1] Here he plainly showed in what sense he said, "Thou makest thy boast of God." For undoubtedly if one who was truly a Jew made his boast of God in the way which grace demands (which is bestowed not for merit of works, but gratuitously), then his praise would be of God, and not of men. But they, in fact, were making their boast of God, as if they alone had deserved to receive His law, as the Psalmist said: "He did not the like to any nation, nor His judgments has He displayed to them." [2] And yet, they thought they were fulfilling the law of God by their righteousness, when they were rather breakers of it all the while! Accordingly, it "wrought wrath" [3] upon them, and sin abounded, committed as it was by them who knew the law. For whoever did even what the law commanded, without the assistance of the Spirit of grace, acted through fear of punishment, not from love of righteousness, and hence in the sight of God that was not in the will, which in the sight of men appeared in the work; and such doers of the law were held rather guilty of that which God knew they would have preferred to commit, if only it had been possible with impunity. He calls, however, "the circumcision of the heart" the will that is pure from all unlawful desire; which comes not from the *letter*, inculcating and threatening, but from the *Spirit*, assisting and healing. Such doers of the law have their praise therefore, not of men but of God, who by His grace provides the grounds on which they receive praise, of whom it is said, "My soul shall make her boast of the Lord;" [4] and to whom it is said, "My praise

shall be of Thee:" [5] but those are not such who would have God praised because they are men; but themselves, because they are righteous.

CHAP. 14. — IN WHAT RESPECT THE PELAGIANS ACKNOWLEDGE GOD AS THE AUTHOR OF OUR JUSTIFICATION.

"But," say they, "we do praise God as the Author of our righteousness, in that He gave the law, by the teaching of which we have learned how we ought to live." But they give no heed to what they read: "By the law there shall no flesh be justified in the sight of God." [6] This may indeed be possible before men, but not before Him who looks into our very heart and inmost will, where He sees that, although the man who fears the law keeps a certain precept, he would nevertheless rather do another thing if he were permitted. And lest any one should suppose that, in the passage just quoted from him, the apostle had meant to say that none are justified by that law, which contains many precepts, under the figure of the ancient sacraments, and among them that circumcision of the flesh itself, which infants were commanded to receive on the eighth day after birth; he immediately adds what law he meant, and says, "For by the law is the knowledge of sin." [6] He refers then to that law of which he afterwards declares, "I had not known sin but by the law; for I had not known lust except the law had said, Thou shalt not covet." [7] For what means this but that "by the law comes the knowledge of sin?".

CHAP. 15 [IX.] — THE RIGHTEOUSNESS OF GOD MANIFESTED BY THE LAW AND THE PROPHETS.

Here, perhaps, it may be said by that presumption of man, which is ignorant of the righteousness of God, and wishes to establish one of its own, that the apostle quite properly said, "For by the law shall no man be justified," [6] inasmuch as the law merely shows what one ought to do, and what one ought to guard against, in order that what the law thus points out may be accomplished by the will, and so man be justified, not indeed by the power of the law, but by his free determination. But I ask your attention, O man, to what follows. "But now the righteousness of God," says he, "without the law is manifested, being witnessed by the law and the prophets." [8] Does this then sound a light thing in deaf ears? He says, "The righteousness of God is manifested." Now this righteousness they are ignorant of, who wish to establish one of their own; they will not submit themselves to it. [9] His words are, "*The righteousness of God*

---

[1] Rom. ii. 17-29.
[2] Ps. cxlvii. 20.
[3] Rom. iv. 15.
[4] Ps. xxxiv. 2.

[5] Ps. xxii. 25.
[6] Rom. iii 20.
[7] Rom. vii. 7.
[8] Rom. iii. 21.
[9] Rom. x. 3.

is manifested : " he does not say, the righteousness of man, or the righteousness of his own will, but the " righteousness *of God*," — not that whereby He is Himself righteous, but that with which He endows man when He justifies the ungodly. This is witnessed by the law and the prophets ; in other words, the law and the prophets each afford it testimony. The law, indeed, by issuing its commands and threats, and by justifying no man, sufficiently shows that it is by God's gift, through the help of the Spirit, that a man is justified ; and the prophets, because it was what they predicted that Christ at His coming accomplished. Accordingly he advances a step further, and adds, " But righteousness of God by faith of Jesus Christ," [1] that is, by the faith wherewith one believes in Christ ; for just as there is not meant the faith with which Christ Himself believes, so also there is not meant the righteousness whereby God is Himself righteous. Both no doubt are ours, but yet they are called God's, and Christ's, because it is by their bounty that these gifts are bestowed upon us. The righteousness of God then is without the law, but not manifested without the law ; for if it were manifested without the law, how could it be witnessed by the law ? That righteousness of God, however, is without the law, which God by the Spirit of grace bestows on the believer without the help of the law, — that is, when not helped by the law. When, indeed, He by the law discovers to a man his weakness, it is in order that by faith he may flee for refuge to His mercy, and be healed. And thus concerning His wisdom we are told, that " she carries law and mercy upon her tongue," [2] — the " *law*," whereby she may convict the proud, the " *mercy*," wherewith she may justify the humbled. " The righteousness of God," then, " by faith of Jesus Christ, is unto all that believe ; for there is no difference, for all have sinned, and come short of the glory of God " [3] — not of their own glory. For what have they, which they have not received ? Now if they received it, why do they glory as if they had not received it ? [4] Well, then, they come short of the glory of God ; now observe what follows : " Being justified freely by His grace." [5] It is not, therefore, by the law, nor is it by their own will, that they are justified ; but they are justified *freely by His grace*, — not that it is wrought without our will ; but our will is by the law shown to be weak, that grace may heal its infirmity ; and that our healed will may fulfil the law, not by compact under the law, nor yet in the absence of law.

## CHAP. 16 [X.] — HOW THE LAW WAS NOT MADE FOR A RIGHTEOUS MAN.

Because " for a righteous man the law was not made ; " [6] and yet " the law is good, if a man use it lawfully." [7] Now by connecting together these two seemingly contrary statements, the apostle warns and urges his reader to sift the question and solve it too. For how can it be that " the law is good, if a man use it lawfully," if what follows is also true : " Knowing this, that the law is not made for a righteous man ? " [7] For who but a righteous man lawfully uses the law ? Yet it is not for him that it is made, but for the unrighteous. Must then the unrighteous man, in order that he may be justified, — that is, become a righteous man, — lawfully use the law, to lead him, as by the schoolmaster's hand,[8] to that grace by which alone he can fulfil what the law commands ? Now it is freely that he is justified thereby, — that is, on account of no antecedent merits of his own works ; " otherwise grace is no more grace," [9] since it is bestowed on us, not because we have done good works, but that we may be able to do them, — in other words, not because we have fulfilled the law, but in order that we may be able to fulfil the law. Now He said, " I am not come to destroy the law, but to fulfil it," [10] of whom it was said, " We have seen His glory, the glory as of the only-begotten of the Father, full of grace and truth." [11] This is the glory which is meant in the words, " All have sinned, and come short of the glory of God ; " [12] and this the grace of which he speaks in the next verse, " Being justified freely by His grace." [5] The unrighteous man therefore lawfully uses the law, that he may become righteous ; but when he has become so, he must no longer use it as a chariot, for he has arrived at his journey's end, — or rather (that I may employ the apostle's own simile, which has been already mentioned) as a schoolmaster, seeing that he is now fully learned. How then is the law not made for a righteous man, if it is necessary for the righteous man too, not that he may be brought as an unrighteous man to the grace that justifies, but that he may use it lawfully, now that he is righteous ? Does not the case perhaps stand thus, — nay, not *perhaps*, but rather *certainly*, — that the man who is become righteous thus lawfully uses the law, when he applies it to alarm the unrighteous, so that whenever the disease of some unusual desire begins in them, too, to be augmented by the incentive of the law's prohibition and an increased

[1] Rom. iii. 22.
[2] Prov. iii. 16.
[3] Rom. iii. 22, 23.
[4] 1 Cor. iv. 7.
[5] Rom. iii. 24.

[6] 1 Tim. i. 8.
[7] 1 Tim. i. 9.
[8] Gal. iii. 24.
[9] Rom. xi. 6.
[10] Matt. v. 17.
[11] John i. 14.
[12] Rom. iii. 23.

amount of transgression, they may in faith flee for refuge to the grace that justifies, and becoming delighted with the sweet pleasures of holiness, may escape the penalty of the law's menacing letter through the spirit's soothing gift? In this way the two statements will not be contrary, nor will they be repugnant to each other: even the righteous man may lawfully use a good law, and yet the law be not made for the righteous man; for it is not by the law that he becomes righteous, but by the law of faith, which led him to believe that no other resource was possible to his weakness for fulfilling the precepts which " the law of works "[1] commanded, except to be assisted by the grace of God.

CHAP. 17. — THE EXCLUSION OF BOASTING.

Accordingly he says, "Where is boasting then? It is excluded. By what law? of works? Nay; but by the law of faith."[1]    He may either mean, the laudable boasting, which is in the Lord; and that it is *excluded*, not in the sense that it is driven off so as to pass away, but that it is clearly manifested so as to stand out prominently. Whence certain artificers in silver are called "*exclusores*."[2]   In this sense it occurs also in that passage in the Psalms: "That they may be *excluded*, who have been proved with silver,"[3] — that is, that they may stand out in prominence, who have been tried by the word of God. For in another passage it is said: "The words of the Lord are pure words, as silver which is tried in the fire."[4]   Or if this be not his meaning, he must have wished to mention that vicious boasting which comes of pride — that is, of those who appear to themselves to lead righteous lives, and boast of their excellence as if they had not received it, — and further to inform us, that by the law of faith, not by the law of works, this boasting was *excluded*, in the other sense of shut out and driven away; because by the law of faith every one learns that whatever good life he leads he has from the grace of God, and that from no other source whatever can he obtain the means of becoming perfect in the love of righteousness.

CHAP. 18 [XI.] — PIETY IS WISDOM; THAT IS CALLED THE RIGHTEOUSNESS OF GOD, WHICH HE PRODUCES.

Now, this meditation makes a man godly, and this godliness is true wisdom. By godliness I mean that which the Greeks designate θεοσέβεια, — that very virtue which is commended to man

in the passage of Job, where it is said to him, "Behold, godliness is wisdom."[5]   Now if the word θεοσέβεια be interpreted according to its derivation, it might be called " *the worship of God;* "[6] and in this worship the essential point is, that the soul be not ungrateful to Him. Whence it is that in the most true and excellent sacrifice we are admonished to " give thanks unto our Lord God."[7]   Ungrateful, however, our soul would be, were it to attribute to itself that which it received from God, especially the righteousness, with the works of which (the especial property, as it were, of itself, and produced, so to speak, by the soul itself for itself) it is not puffed up in a vulgar pride, as it might be with riches, or beauty of limb, or eloquence, or those other accomplishments, external or internal, bodily or mental, which wicked men too are in the habit of possessing, but, if I may say so, in a wise complacency, as of things which constitute in an especial manner the good works of the good. It is owing to this sin of vulgar pride that even some great men have drifted from the sure anchorage of the divine nature, and have floated down into the shame of idolatry. Whence the apostle again in the same epistle, wherein he so firmly maintains the principle of grace, after saying that he was a debtor both to the Greeks and to the Barbarians, to the wise and to the unwise, and professing himself ready, so far as to him pertained, to preach the gospel even to those who lived in Rome, adds: " I am not ashamed of the Gospel of Christ: for it is the power of God unto salvation to every one that believeth; to the Jew first, and also to the Greek. For therein is the righteousness of God revealed from faith to faith: as it is written, The just shall live by faith."[8]   This is the righteousness of God, which was veiled in the Old Testament, and is revealed in the New; and it is called *the righteousness of God*, because by His bestowal of it He makes us righteous, just as we read that " salvation is the Lord's,"[9] because He makes us safe. And this is the faith " from which " and " to which " it is revealed, — *from the faith* of them who preach it, *to the faith* of those who obey it. By this faith of Jesus Christ — that is, the faith which Christ has given to us — we believe it is from God that we now have, and shall have more and more, the ability of living righteously; wherefore we give Him thanks with that dutiful worship with which He only is to be worshipped.

---

[1] Rom. iii. 27.
[2] [The allusion appears to be to the special workmen engaged in producing hammered or beaten (*repoussé*) work. For other special classes of silver workers, see Guhl and Koner: *The Life of the Greeks and Romans*, p. 449. — W.]
[3] Ps. lxviii. 30.
[4] Ps. xii. 6.

[5] Job xxviii. 28.
[6] *Cultus Dei* is Augustin's Latin expression for the synonym.
[7] One of the suffrages of the *Sursum Corda* in the Communion Service [preserved also in the English service, which reads as follows: " *Priest.* Lift up your hearts. *Answer.* We lift them up to the Lord. *Priest.* Let us give thanks unto our Lord God. *Answer.* It is meet and right so to do." — W.]
[8] Rom. i. 14-17.
[9] Ps. iii. 8.

CHAP. 19 [XII.] — THE KNOWLEDGE OF GOD
THROUGH THE CREATION.

And then the apostle very properly turns from this point to describe with detestation those men who, light-minded and puffed up by the sin which I have mentioned in the preceding chapter, have been carried away of their own conceit, as it were, through empty space where they could find no resting-place, only to fall shattered to pieces against the vain figments of their idols, as against stones. For, after he had commended the piety of that faith, whereby, being justified, we must needs be pleasing to God, he proceeds to call our attention to what we ought to abominate as the opposite. " For the wrath of God," says he, " is revealed from heaven against all ungodliness and unrighteousness of men, who hold down the truth in unrighteousness; because that which may be known of God is manifest in them : for God hath showed it unto them. For the invisible things of Him are clearly seen from the creation of the world, being understood through the things that are made, even His eternal power and divinity; so that they are without excuse : because, knowing God, they yet glorified Him not as God, neither were thankful; but became vain in their imaginations, and their foolish heart was darkened. Professing themselves to be wise, they became fools; and they changed the glory of the uncorruptible God into an image made like to corruptible man, and to birds, and to four footed beasts, and to creeping things." [1] Observe, he does not say that they were ignorant of the truth, but that they held down the truth in unrighteousness. For it occurred to him, that he would inquire whence the knowledge of the truth could be obtained by those to whom God had not given the law; and he was not silent on the source whence they could have obtained it : for he declares that it was through the visible works of creation that they arrived at the knowledge of the invisible attributes of the Creator. And, in very deed, as they continued to possess great faculties for searching, so they were able to find. Wherein then lay their impiety? Because " when they knew God, they glorified Him not as God, nor gave Him thanks, but became vain in their imaginations." Vanity is a disease especially of those who mislead themselves, and " think themselves to be something, when they are nothing." [2] Such men, indeed, darken themselves in that swelling pride, the foot of which the holy singer prays that it may not come against him, [3] after saying, " In Thy light shall we see light;" [4] from which very light of unchanging truth they turn aside, and " their fool-

ish heart is darkened." [5] For theirs was not a wise heart, even though they knew God; but it was foolish rather, because they did not glorify Him as God, or give Him thanks; for " He said unto man, Behold, the fear of the Lord, that is wisdom." [6] So by this conduct, while " professing themselves to be wise " (which can only be understood to mean that they attributed this to themselves), " they became fools." [7]

CHAP. 20. — THE LAW WITHOUT GRACE.

Now why need I speak of what follows? For why it was that by this their impiety those men — I mean those who could have known the Creator through the creature — fell (since " God resisteth the proud " [8]) and whither they plunged, is better shown in the sequel of this epistle than we can here mention. For in this letter of mine we have not undertaken to expound this epistle, but only mainly on its authority, to demonstrate, so far as we are able, that we are assisted by divine aid towards the achievement of righteousness,— not merely because God has given us a law full of good and holy precepts, but because our very will, without which we cannot do any good thing, is assisted and elevated by the importation of the Spirit of grace, without which help mere teaching is " the letter that killeth," [9] forasmuch as it rather holds them guilty of transgression, than justifies the ungodly. Now just as those who come to know the Creator through the creature received no benefit towards salvation, from their knowledge, — because " though they knew God, they glorified Him not as God, nor gave Him thanks, although professing themselves to be wise; " [5] — so also they who know from the law how man ought to live, are not made righteous by their knowledge, because, " going about to establish their own righteousness, they have not submitted themselves unto the righteousness of God." [10]

CHAP. 21 [XIII.] — THE LAW OF WORKS AND
THE LAW OF FAITH.

The law, then, of deeds, that is, the law of works, whereby this boasting is not excluded, and the law of faith, by which it is excluded, differ from each other; and this difference it is worth our while to consider, if so be we are able to observe and discern it. Hastily, indeed, one might say that the law of works lay in Judaism, and the law of faith in Christianity; forasmuch as circumcision and the other works prescribed by the law are just those which the Christian system no longer retains. But there is a fallacy

---

[1] Rom. i. 18–23.
[2] Gal. vi. 3.
[3] Ps. xxxvi. 11.
[4] Ps. xxxvi. 9.

[5] Rom. i. 21.
[6] Job xxviii. 28.
[7] Rom. i. 22.
[8] Jas. iv. 6.
[9] 2 Cor. iii. 6.
[10] Rom. x. 3.

in this distinction, the greatness of which I have for some time been endeavoring to expose ; and to such as are acute in appreciating distinctions, especially to yourself and those like you, I have possibly succeeded in my effort. Since, however, the subject is an important one, it will not be unsuitable, if with a view to its illustration, we linger over the many testimonies which again and again meet our view. Now, the apostle says that that law by which no man is justified,[1] entered in that the offence might abound,[2] and yet in order to save it from the aspersions of the ignorant and the accusations of the impious, he defends this very law in such words as these : " What shall we say then? Is the law sin? God forbid. Nay, I had not known sin but by the law : for I had not known concupiscence, except the law had said, Thou shalt not covet. But sin, taking occasion, wrought, by the commandment, in me all manner of concupiscence."[3]  He says also : " The law indeed is holy, and the commandment is holy, and just, and good ; but sin, that it might appear sin, worked death in me by that which is good."[4]  It is therefore the very letter that kills which says, " Thou shalt not covet," and it is of this that he speaks in a passage which I have before referred to : " By the law is the knowledge of sin. But now the right-eousness of God without the law is manifested, being witnessed by the law and the prophets ; even the righteousness of God, which is by faith of Jesus Christ upon all them that believe ; for there is no difference : seeing that all have sinned, and come short of the glory of God : being justified freely by His grace, through the redemption that is in Christ Jesus ; whom God hath set forth to be a propitiation through faith in His blood, to declare His righteousness for the remission of sins that are past, through the forbearance of God ; to declare His righteousness at this time ; that He might be just, and the justifier of him which believeth in Jesus."[5]  And then he adds the passage which is now under consideration : " Where, then, is your boasting? It is excluded. By what law? of works? Nay ; but by the law of faith."[6]  And so it is the very law of works itself which says, " Thou shalt not covet ; " because thereby comes the knowledge of sin. Now I wish to know, if anybody will dare to tell me, whether the law of faith does not say to us, " Thou shalt not covet "? For if it does not say so to us, what reason is there why we, who are placed under it, should not sin in safety and with impunity? Indeed, this is just what those people thought the apostle meant, of whom

he writes : " Even as some affirm that we say, Let us do evil, that good may come ; whose damnation is just."[7]  If, on the contrary, it too says to us, " Thou shalt not covet " (even as numerous passages in the gospels and epistles so often testify and urge), then why is not this law also called the law of works? For it by no means follows that, because it retains not the " works " of the ancient sacraments, — even circumcision and the other ceremonies, — it therefore has no " works " in its own sacraments, which are adapted to the present age ; unless, indeed, the question was about sacramental works, when mention was made of the law, just because by it is the knowledge of sin, and therefore nobody is justified by it, so that it is not by it that boasting is excluded, but by the law of faith, whereby the just man lives. But is there not by it too the knowledge of sin, when even it says, " Thou shalt not covet ? "

CHAP. 22. — NO MAN JUSTIFIED BY WORKS.

What the difference between them is, I will briefly explain. What the law of works enjoins by menace, that the law of faith secures by faith. The one says, " Thou shalt not covet ; "[8] the other says, " When I perceived that nobody could be continent, except God gave it to him ; and that this was the very point of wisdom, to know whose gift she was ; I approached unto the Lord, and I besought Him."[9]  This indeed is the very wisdom which is called *piety*, in which is worshipped " the Father of lights, from whom is every best giving and perfect gift."[10]  This worship, however, consists in the sacrifice of praise and giving of thanks, so that the worshipper of God boasts not in himself, but in Him.[11]  Accordingly, by the law of works, God says to us, Do what I command thee ; but by the law of faith we say to God, Give me what Thou commandest. Now this is the reason why the law gives its command, — to admonish us what faith ought to do, that is, that he to whom the command is given, if he is as yet unable to perform it, may know what to ask for ; but if he has at once the ability, and complies with the command, he ought also to be aware from whose gift the ability comes. " For we have received not the spirit of this world," says again that most constant preacher of grace, " but the Spirit which is of God, that we might know the things that are freely given to us of God."[12]  What, however, " is the spirit of this world," but the spirit of pride? By it their foolish heart is darkened, who, although knowing God, glorified Him not as

1 Rom. iii. 20.
2 Rom. v. 20.
3 Rom. vii. 7, 8.
4 Rom. vii. 12, 13.
5 Rom. iii. 20-26.
6 Rom. iii. 27.

7 Rom. iii. 8.
8 Ex. xx. 17.
9 Wisdom viii. 21.
10 Jas. i. 17.
11 2 Cor. x. 17.
12 1 Cor. ii. 12.

God, by giving Him thanks.[1]  Moreover, it is really by this same spirit that they too are deceived, who, while ignorant of the righteousness of God, and wishing to establish their own righteousness, have not submitted to God's righteousness.[2]  It appears to me, therefore, that he is much more "a child of faith" who has learned from what source to hope for what he has not yet, than he who attributes to himself whatever he has; although, no doubt, to both of these must be preferred the man who both has, and at the same time knows from whom he has it, if nevertheless he does not believe himself to be what he has not yet attained to.  Let him not fall into the mistake of the Pharisee, who, while thanking God for what he possessed, yet failed to ask for any further gift, just as if he stood in want of nothing for the increase or perfection of his righteousness.[3]  Now, having duly considered and weighed all these circumstances and testimonies, we conclude that a man is not justified by the precepts of a holy life, but by faith in Jesus Christ, — in a word, not by the law of works, but by the law of faith; not by the letter, but by the spirit; not by the merits of deeds, but by free grace.

CHAP. 23 [XIV.] — HOW THE DECALOGUE KILLS, IF GRACE BE NOT PRESENT.

Although, therefore, the apostle seems to reprove and correct those who were being persuaded to be circumcised, in such terms as to designate by the word "*law*" circumcision itself and other similar legal observances, which are now rejected as shadows of a future substance by Christians who yet hold what those shadows figuratively promised; he at the same time nevertheless would have it to be clearly understood that the law, by which he says no man is justified, lies not merely in those sacramental institutions which contained promissory figures, but also in those works by which whosoever has done them lives holily, and amongst which occurs this prohibition: "Thou shalt not covet."  Now, to make our statement all the clearer, let us look at the Decalogue itself.  It is certain, then, that Moses on the mount received the law, that he might deliver it to the people, written on tables of stone by the finger of God.  It is summed up in these ten commandments, in which there is no precept about circumcision, nor anything concerning those animal sacrifices which have ceased to be offered by Christians.  Well, now, I should like to be told what there is in these ten commandments, except the observance of the Sabbath, which ought not to be kept by a Christian, — whether it prohibit the making and worshipping

of idols and of any other gods than the one true God, or the taking of God's name in vain; or prescribe honour to parents; or give warning against fornication, murder, theft, false witness, adultery, or coveting other men's property?  Which of these commandments would any one say that the Christian ought not to keep?  Is it possible to contend that it is not the law which was written on those two tables that the apostle describes as "the letter that killeth," but the law of circumcision and the other sacred rites which are now abolished?  But then how can we think so, when in the law occurs this precept, "Thou shalt not covet," by which very commandment, notwithstanding its being holy, just, and good, "sin," says the apostle, "deceived me, and by it slew me?"[4]  What else can this be than "the letter" that "killeth"?

CHAP. 24. — THE PASSAGE IN CORINTHIANS.

In the passage where he speaks to the Corinthians about the letter that kills, and the spirit that gives life, he expresses himself more clearly, but he does not mean even there any other "letter" to be understood than the Decalogue itself, which was written on the two tables.  For these are His words: "Forasmuch as ye are manifestly declared to be the epistle of Christ ministered by us, written not with ink, but with the Spirit of the living God; not in tables of stone, but in fleshy tables of the heart.  And such trust have we through Christ to God-ward: not that we are sufficient of ourselves to think anything as of ourselves; but our sufficiency is of God; who hath made us fit, as ministers of the new testament; not of the letter, but of the spirit: for the letter killeth, but the spirit giveth life.  But if the ministration of death, written and engraven in stones, was glorious, so that the children of Israel could not stedfastly behold the face of Moses for the glory of his countenance, which was to be done away; how shall not the ministration of the Spirit be rather glorious?  For if the ministration of condemnation be glory, much more shall the ministration of righteousness abound in glory."[5]  A good deal might be said about these words; but perhaps we shall have a more fitting opportunity at some future time.  At present, however, I beg you to observe how he speaks of the letter that killeth, and contrasts therewith the spirit that giveth life.  Now this must certainly be "the ministration of death written and engraven in stones," and "the ministration of condemnation," since the law entered that sin might abound.[6]  But the commandments themselves are so useful and salutary to the doer of them,

[1] Rom. i. 21.
[2] Rom. x. 3.
[3] Luke xviii. 11, 12.

[4] See Rom. vii. 7-12.
[5] 2 Cor. iii. 3-9.
[6] Rom. v. 20.

that no one could have life unless he kept them. Well, then, is it owing to the one precept about the Sabbath-day, which is included in it, that the Decalogue is called "the letter that killeth?" Because, forsooth, every man that still observes that day in its literal appointment is carnally wise, but to be carnally wise is nothing else than death? And must the other nine commandments, which are rightly observed in their literal form, not be regarded as belonging to the law of works by which none is justified, but to the law of faith whereby the just man lives? Who can possibly entertain so absurd an opinion as to suppose that "the ministration of death, written and engraven in stones," is not said equally of all the ten commandments, but only of the solitary one touching the Sabbath-day? In which class do we place that which is thus spoken of: "The law worketh wrath: for where no law is, there is no transgression?"[1] and again thus: "Until the law sin was in the world: but sin is not imputed when there is no law?"[2] and also that which we have already so often quoted: "By the law is the knowledge of sin?"[3] and especially the passage in which the apostle has more clearly expressed the question of which we are treating: "I had not known lust, except the law had said, Thou shalt not covet?"[4]

### CHAP. 25. — THE PASSAGE IN ROMANS.

Now carefully consider this entire passage, and see whether it says anything about circumcision, or the Sabbath, or anything else pertaining to a foreshadowing sacrament. Does not its whole scope amount to this, that the letter which forbids sin fails to give man life, but rather "killeth," by increasing concupiscence, and aggravating sinfulness by transgression, unless indeed grace liberates us by the law of faith, which is in Christ Jesus, when His love is "shed abroad in our hearts by the Holy Ghost, which is given to us?"[5] The apostle having used these words: "That we should serve in newness of spirit, and not in the oldness of the letter,"[6] goes on to inquire, "What shall we say then? Is the law sin? God forbid. Nay; I had not known sin, but by the law: for I had not known lust, except the law had said, Thou shalt not covet. But sin, taking occasion by the commandment, wrought in me all manner of concupiscence. For without the law sin was dead. For I was alive without the law once; but when the commandment came, sin revived, and I died. And the commandment, which was ordained to life, I found to be unto death.

For sin, taking occasion by the commandment deceived me, and by it slew me. Wherefore the law is holy, and the commandment holy, and just, and good. Was then that which is good made death unto me? God forbid. But sin, that it might appear sin, worked death in me by that which is good; that sin by the commandment might become exceeding sinful. For we know that the law is spiritual; whereas I am carnal, sold under sin. For that which I do I allow not: for what I would, that I do not; but what I hate, that I do. If then I do that which I would not, I consent unto the law that it is good. But then it is no longer I that do it, but sin that dwelleth in me. For I know that in me (that is, in my flesh) dwelleth no good thing. To will, indeed, is present with me; but how to perform that which is good I find not. For the good that I would, I do not; but the evil which I would not, that I do. Now, if I do that which I would not, it is no more I that do it, but sin that dwelleth in me. I find then a law, that, when I would do good, evil is present with me. For I delight in the law of God after the inward man: but I see another law in my members warring against the law of my mind, and bringing me into captivity to the law of sin which is in my members. O wretched man that I am! who shall deliver me from the body of this death? The grace of God, through Jesus Christ our Lord. So then with the mind I myself serve the law of God, but with the flesh the law of sin."[7]

### CHAP. 26. — NO FRUIT GOOD EXCEPT IT GROW FROM THE ROOT OF LOVE.

It is evident, then, that the oldness of the letter, in the absence of the newness of the spirit, instead of freeing us from sin, rather makes us guilty by the knowledge of sin. Whence it is written in another part of Scripture, "He that increaseth knowledge, increaseth sorrow,"[8] — not that the law is itself evil, but because the commandment has its good in the demonstration of the letter, not in the assistance of the spirit; and if this commandment is kept from the fear of punishment and not from the love of righteousness, it is servilely kept, not freely, and therefore it is not kept at all. For no fruit is good which does not grow from the root of love. If, however, that faith be present which worketh by love,[9] then one begins to delight in the law of God after the inward man,[10] and this delight is the gift of the spirit, not of the letter; even though there is another law in our members still warring against the law of the mind, until the old state is changed, and passes into that newness which increases from day to day in the

---

[1] Rom. iv. 15.
[2] Rom. v. 13.
[3] Rom. iii. 20.
[4] Rom. vii. 7.
[5] Rom. v. 5
[6] Rom. vii. 6.

[7] Rom. vii. 7–25.
[8] Eccles. i. 18.
[9] Gal. v. 6.
[10] Rom. vii. 22.

inward man, whilst the grace of God is liberating us from the body of this death through Jesus Christ our Lord.

### CHAP. 27 [XV.] — GRACE, CONCEALED IN THE OLD TESTAMENT, IS REVEALED IN THE NEW.

This grace hid itself under a veil in the Old Testament, but it has been revealed in the New Testament according to the most perfectly ordered dispensation of the ages, forasmuch as God knew how to dispose all things. And perhaps it is a part of this hiding of grace, that in the Decalogue, which was given on Mount Sinai, only the portion which relates to the Sabbath was hidden under a prefiguring precept. The Sabbath is a day of sanctification; and it is not without significance that, among all the works which God accomplished, the first sound of sanctification was heard on the day when He rested from all His labours. On this, indeed, we must not now enlarge. But at the same time I deem it to be enough for the point now in question, that it was not for nothing that the nation was commanded on that day to abstain from all servile work, by which sin is signified; but because not to commit sin belongs to sanctification, that is, to God's gift through the Holy Spirit. And this precept alone among the others, was placed in the law, which was written on the two tables of stone, in a prefiguring shadow, under which the Jews observe the Sabbath, that by this very circumstance it might be signified that it was then the time for concealing the grace, which had to be revealed in the New Testament by the death of Christ, — the rending, as it were, of the veil.[1] "For when," says the apostle, "it shall turn to the Lord, the veil shall be taken away."[2]

### CHAP. 28 [XVI.] — WHY THE HOLY GHOST IS CALLED THE FINGER OF GOD.

"Now the Lord is that Spirit: and where the Spirit of the Lord is, there is liberty."[3] Now this Spirit of God, by whose gift we are justified, whence it comes to pass that we delight not to sin, — in which is liberty; even as, when we are without this Spirit, we delight to sin, — in which is slavery, from the works of which we must abstain; — this Holy Spirit, through whom love is shed abroad in our hearts, which is the fulfilment of the law, is designated in the gospel as "the finger of God."[4] Is it not because those very tables of the law were written by the finger of God, that the Spirit of God by whom we are sanctified is also *the finger of God*, in order that, living by faith, we may do good works through love? Who is not touched by this congruity,

and at the same time diversity? For as fifty days are reckoned from the celebration of the Passover (which was ordered by Moses to be offered by slaying the typical lamb,[5] to signify, indeed, the future death of the Lord) to the day when Moses received the law written on the tables of stone by the finger of God,[6] so, in like manner, from the death and resurrection of Him who was led as a lamb to the slaughter,[7] there were fifty complete days up to the time when the finger of God — that is, the Holy Spirit — gathered together in one[8] perfect company those who believed.

### CHAP. 29 [XVII.] — A COMPARISON OF THE LAW OF MOSES AND OF THE NEW LAW.

Now, amidst this admirable correspondence, there is at least this very considerable diversity in the cases, in that the people in the earlier instance were deterred by a horrible dread from approaching the place where the law was given; whereas in the other case the Holy Ghost came upon them who were gathered together in expectation of His promised gift. *There* it was on tables of stone that the finger of God operated; *here* it was on the hearts of men. *There* the law was given outwardly, so that the unrighteous might be terrified;[9] *here* it was given inwardly, so that they might be justified.[10] For this, "Thou shalt not commit adultery, Thou shalt not kill, Thou shalt not covet; and if there be any other commandment," — such, of course, as was written on those tables, — "it is briefly comprehended," says he, "in this saying, namely, Thou shalt love thy neighbour as thyself. Love worketh no ill to his neighbour: therefore love is the fulfilling of the law."[11] Now this was not written on the tables of stone, but "is shed abroad in our hearts by the Holy Ghost, which is given unto us."[12] God's law, therefore, is love. "To it the carnal mind is not subject, neither indeed can be;"[13] but when the works of love are written on tables to alarm the carnal mind, there arises the law of works and "the letter which killeth" the transgressor; but when love itself is shed abroad in the hearts of believers, then we have the law of faith, and the spirit which gives life to him that loves.

### CHAP. 30. — THE NEW LAW WRITTEN WITHIN.

Now, observe how consonant this diversity is with those words of the apostle which I quoted not long ago in another connection, and which

---

[1] Matt. xxvii. 51.
[2] 2 Cor. iii. 16.
[3] 2 Cor. iii. 17.
[4] Luke xi. 20.

[5] Ex. xii. 3.
[6] Ex. xxxi. 18.
[7] Isa. liii. 7.
[8] Acts ii. 2.
[9] Ex. xix. 12, 16.
[10] Acts ii. 1-47.
[11] Rom. xiii. 9, 10.
[12] Rom. v. 5.
[13] Rom. viii. 7.

I postponed for a more careful consideration afterwards : " Forasmuch," says he, " as ye are manifestly declared to be the epistle of Christ ministered by us, written not with ink, but with the Spirit of the living God ; not in tables of stone, but in fleshy tables of the heart." [1] See how he shows that the one is written without man, that it may alarm him from without ; the other within man himself, that it may justify him from within. He speaks of the " fleshy tables of the heart," not of the carnal mind, but of a living agent possessing sensation, in comparison with a stone, which is senseless. The assertion which he subsequently makes, — that " the children of Israel could not look stedfastly on the end of the face of Moses," and that he accordingly spoke to them through a veil,[2] — signifies that the letter of the law justifies no man, but that rather a veil is placed on the reading of the Old Testament, until it shall be turned to Christ, and the veil be removed ; — in other words, until it shall be turned to grace, and be understood that from Him accrues to us the justification, whereby we do what He commands. And He commands, in order that, because we lack in ourselves, we may flee to Him for refuge. Accordingly, after most guardedly saying, " Such trust have we through Christ to God-ward," [3] the apostle immediately goes on to add the statement which underlies our subject, to prevent our confidence being attributed to any strength of our own. He says : " Not that we are sufficient of ourselves to think anything as of ourselves ; but our sufficiency is of God ; who also hath made us fit to be ministers of the New Testament ; not of the letter, but of the spirit : for the letter killeth, but the spirit giveth life." [4]

CHAP. 31 [XVIII.] — THE OLD LAW MINISTERS DEATH ; THE NEW, RIGHTEOUSNESS.

Now, since, as he says in another passage, " the law was added because of transgression," [5] meaning the law which is written externally to man, he therefore designates it both as " the ministration of death," [6] and " the ministration of condemnation ; " [7] but the other, that is, the law of the New Testament, he calls " the ministration of the Spirit " [8] and " the ministration of righteousness," [7] because through the Spirit we work righteousness, and are delivered from the condemnation due to transgression. The one, therefore, vanishes away, the other abides ; for the terrifying schoolmaster will be dispensed with, when love has succeeded to fear. Now " where

the Spirit of the Lord is, there is liberty." [9] But that this ministration is vouchsafed to us, not on account of our deserving, but from His mercy, the apostle thus declares : " Seeing then that we have this ministry, as we have received mercy, let us faint not ; but let us renounce the hidden things of dishonesty, not walking in craftiness, nor adulterating the word of God with deceit." [10] By this " craftiness " and " deceitfulness " he would have us understand the hypocrisy with which the arrogant would fain be supposed to be righteous. Whence in the psalm, which the apostle cites in testimony of this grace of God, it is said, " Blessed is the man to whom the Lord will not impute sin, and in whose mouth is no guile." [11] This is the confession of lowly saints, who do not boast to be what they are not. Then, in a passage which follows not long after, the apostle writes thus : " For we preach not ourselves, but Christ Jesus the Lord ; and ourselves your servants for Jesus' sake. For God, who commanded the light to shine out of darkness, hath shined in our hearts, to give the light of the knowledge of the glory of God in the face of Jesus Christ." [12] This is the knowledge of His glory, whereby we know that He is the light which illumines our darkness. And I beg you to observe how he inculcates this very point : " We have," says he, " this treasure in earthen vessels, that the excellency of the power may be of God, and not of us." [13] When further on he commends in glowing terms this same grace, in the Lord Jesus Christ, until he comes to that vestment of the righteousness of faith, " clothed with which we cannot be found naked," and whilst longing for which " we groan, being burdened " with mortality, " earnestly desiring to be clothed upon with our house which is from Heaven," " that mortality might be swallowed up of life ; " [14] — observe what he says : " Now He that hath wrought us for the self-same thing is God, who also hath given unto us the earnest of the Spirit ; " [15] and after a little he thus briefly draws the conclusion of the matter : " That we might be made the righteousness of God in Him." [16] This is not the righteousness whereby God is Himself righteous, but that whereby we are made righteous by Him.

CHAP. 32 [XIX.] — THE CHRISTIAN FAITH TOUCHING THE ASSISTANCE OF GRACE.

Let no Christian then stray from this faith, which alone is the Christian one ; nor let any one, when he has been made to feel ashamed to

1 2 Cor. iii. 3.
2 2 Cor. iii. 13.
3 2 Cor. iii. 4.
4 2 Cor. iii. 5, 6.
5 Gal. iii. 19.
6 2 Cor. iii. 7.
7 2 Cor. iii. 9.
8 2 Cor. iii. 8.

9 2 Cor. iii. 17.
10 2 Cor. iv. 1, 2.
11 Ps. xxxii. 2.
12 2 Cor. iv. 5, 6.
13 2 Cor. iv. 7.
14 See 2 Cor. v. 1-4.
15 2 Cor. v. 5.
16 2 Cor. v. 21.

say that we become righteous through our own selves, without the grace of God working this in us, — because he sees, when such an allegation is made, how unable pious believers are to endure it, — resort to any subterfuge on this point, by affirming that the reason why we cannot become righteous without the operation of God's grace is this, that He gave the law, He instituted its teaching, He commanded its precepts of good. For there is no doubt that, without His assisting grace, the law is "the letter which killeth;" but when the life-giving spirit is present, the law causes that to be loved as written within, which it once caused to be feared as written without.

### CHAP. 33. — THE PROPHECY OF JEREMIAH CONCERNING THE NEW TESTAMENT.

Observe this also in that testimony which was given by the prophet on this subject in the clearest way: "Behold, the days come, saith the Lord, that I will consummate a new covenant with the house of Israel, and with the house of Judah; not according to the covenant which I made with their fathers, in the day that I took them by the hand, to bring them out of the land of Egypt. Because they continued not in my covenant, I also have rejected them, saith the Lord. But this shall be the covenant that I will make with the house of Israel; After those days, saith the Lord, I will put my law in their inward parts, and write it in their hearts; and I will be their God, and they shall be my people. And they shall teach no more every man his neighbour, and every man his brother, saying, Know the Lord: for they shall all know me, from the least unto the greatest of them, saith the Lord: for I will forgive their iniquity, and I will remember their sin no more." [1] What say we to this? One nowhere, or hardly anywhere, except in this passage of the prophet, finds in the Old Testament Scriptures any mention so made of the New Testament as to indicate it by its very name. It is no doubt often referred to and foretold as about to þe given, but not so plainly as to have its very name mentioned. Consider then carefully, what difference God has testified as existing between the two testaments — the old covenant and the new.

### CHAP. 34. — THE LAW; GRACE.

After saying, "Not according to the covenant which I made with their fathers in the day that I took them by the hand, to bring them out of the land of Egypt," observe what He adds: "Because they continued not in my covenant." He reckons it as their own fault that they did not continue in God's covenant, lest the law, which

they received at that time, should seem to be deserving of blame. For it was the very law that Christ "came not to destroy, but to fulfil." [2] Nevertheless, it is not by that law that the ungodly are made righteous, but by grace; and this change is effected by the life-giving Spirit, without whom the letter kills. "For if there had been a law given which could have given life, verily righteousness should have been by the law. But the Scripture hath concluded all under sin, that the promise by faith of Jesus Christ might be given to them that believe." [3] Out of this promise, that is, out of the kindness of God, the law is fulfilled, which without the said promise only makes men transgressors, either by the actual commission of some sinful deed, if the flame of concupiscence have greater power than even the restraints of fear, or at least by their mere will, if the fear of punishment transcend the pleasure of lust. In what he says, "The Scripture hath concluded all under sin, that the promise by faith of Jesus Christ might be given to them that believe," it is the benefit of this "*conclusion*" itself which is asserted. For what purposes "*hath it concluded*," except as it is expressed in the next sentence: "Before, indeed, faith came, we were kept under the law, *concluded* for the faith which was afterwards revealed?" [4] The law was therefore given, in order that grace might be sought; grace was given, in order that the law might be fulfilled. Now it was not through any fault of its own that the law was not fulfilled, but by the fault of the carnal mind; and this fault was to be demonstrated by the law, and healed by grace. "For what the law could not do, in that it was weak through the flesh, God sending His own Son in the likeness of sinful flesh, and for sin, condemned sin in the flesh; that the righteousness of the law might be fulfilled in us, who walk not after the flesh, but after the Spirit." [5] Accordingly, in the passage which we cited from the prophet, he says, "I will consummate a new covenant with the house of Israel, and with the house of Judah," [6] — and what means *I will consummate* but *I will fulfil?* — "not, according to the covenant which I made with their fathers, in the day that I took them by the hand, to bring them out of the land of Egypt." [7]

### CHAP. 35 [XX.] — THE OLD LAW; THE NEW LAW.

The one was therefore old, because the other is new. But whence comes it that one is old and the other new, when the same law, which said in the Old Testament, "Thou shalt not

---

[1] Jer. xxxi. 31-34.

[2] Matt. v. 17.
[3] Gal. iii. 21, 22.
[4] Gal. iii. 23.
[5] Rom. viii. 3, 4.
[6] Jer. xxxi. 31.
[7] Jer. xxxi. 32.

covet," [1] is fulfilled by the New Testament? "Because," says the prophet, "they continued not in my covenant, I have also rejected them, saith the Lord." [2] It is then on account of the offence of the old man, which was by no means healed by the letter which commanded and threatened, that it is called the old covenant; whereas the other is called the new covenant, because of the newness of the spirit, which heals the new man of the fault of the old. Then consider what follows, and see in how clear a light the fact is placed, that men who have faith are unwilling to trust in themselves: "Because," says he, "this is the covenant which I will make with the house of Israel; After those days, saith the Lord, I will put my law in their inward parts, and write it in their hearts." [3] See how similarly the apostle states it in the passage we have already quoted: "Not in tables of stone, but in fleshy tables of the heart," [4] because "not with ink, but with the Spirit of the living God." [4] And I apprehend that the apostle in this passage had no other reason for mentioning "the New Testament" ("who hath made us able ministers of *the New Testament;* not of the letter, but of the spirit"), than because he had an eye to the words of the prophet, when he said, "Not in tables of stone, but in fleshy tables of the heart," inasmuch as in the prophet it runs: "I will write it in their hearts." [3]

### CHAP. 36 [XXI.] — THE LAW WRITTEN IN OUR HEARTS.

What then is God's law written by God Himself in the hearts of men, but the very presence of the Holy Spirit, who is "the finger of God," and by whose presence is shed abroad in our hearts the love which is the fulfilling of the law, [5] and the end of the commandment? [6] Now the promises of the Old Testament are earthly; and yet (with the exception of the sacramental ordinances which were the shadow of things to come, such as circumcision, the Sabbath and other observances of days, and the ceremonies of certain meats, [7] and the complicated ritual of sacrifices and sacred things which suited "the oldness" of the carnal law and its slavish yoke) it contains such precepts of righteousness as we are even now taught to observe, which were especially expressly drawn out on the two tables without figure or shadow: for instance, "Thou shalt not commit adultery," "Thou shalt do no murder," "Thou shalt not covet," [8] "and whatsoever other commandment is briefly comprehended in the saying, Thou shalt love thy neighbour as thyself." [9] Nevertheless, whereas as in the said Testament earthly and temporal

promises are, as I have said, recited, and these are goods of this corruptible flesh (although they prefigure those heavenly and everlasting blessings which belong to the New Testament), what is now promised is a good for the heart itself, a good for the mind, a good of the spirit, that is, an intellectual good; since it is said, "I will put my law in their inward parts, and in their hearts will I write them," [3] — by which He signified that men would not fear the law which alarmed them externally, but would love the very righteousness of the law which dwelt inwardly in their hearts.

### CHAP. 37 [XXII.] — THE ETERNAL REWARD.

He then went on to state the reward: "I will be their God, and they shall be my people." [3] This corresponds to the Psalmist's words to God: "It is good for me to hold me fast by God." [10] "I will be," says God, "their God, and they shall be my people." What is better than this good, what happier than this happiness, — to live to God, to live from God, with whom is the fountain of life, and in whose light we shall see light? [11] Of this life the Lord Himself speaks in these words: "This is life eternal, that they may know Thee the only true God, and Jesus Christ whom Thou hast sent," [12] — that is, "Thee and Jesus Christ whom Thou hast sent," the one true God. For no less than this did Himself promise to those who love Him: "He that loveth me, keepeth my commandments; and he that loveth me shall be loved of my Father, and I will love him, and will manifest myself unto him," [13] — in the form, no doubt, of God, wherein He is equal to the Father; not in the form of a servant, for in this He will display Himself even to the wicked also. Then, however, shall that come to pass which is written, "Let the ungodly man be taken away, that he see not the glory of the Lord." [14] Then also shall "the wicked go into everlasting punishment, and the righteous into life eternal." [15] Now this eternal life, as I have just mentioned, has been defined to be, that they may know the one true God. [12] Accordingly John again says: "Beloved, now are we the sons of God; and it doth not yet appear what we shall be: but we know that, when He shall appear, we shall be like Him; for we shall see Him as He is." [16] This likeness begins even now to be re-formed in us, while the inward man is being renewed from day to day, according to the image of Him that created him. [17]

### CHAP. 38 [XXIII.] — THE RE-FORMATION WHICH IS NOW BEING EFFECTED, COMPARED WITH THE PERFECTION OF THE LIFE TO COME.

But what is this change, and how great, in

---

[1] Ex. xx. 17.    [2] Jer. xxxi. 32.    [3] Jer. xxxi. 33.
[4] 2 Cor. iii. 3.    [5] Rom. xiii. 10.    [6] 1 Tim. i. 5.
[7] See *Retractations*, ii. 37, printed at the head of this treatise.
[8] Ex. xx. 13, 14, 17.    [9] Rom. xiii 9.

[10] Ps. lxxiii. 28.    [11] Ps. xxxvi. 9.    [12] John xvii. 3.
[13] John xiv. 21.    [14] Isa xxvi. 10.    [15] Matt. xxv. 46.
[16] 1 John iii. 2.    [17] Col. iii. 10.

comparison with the perfect eminence which is then to be realized? The apostle applies some sort of illustration, derived from well-known things, to these indescribable things, comparing the period of childhood with the age of manhood. "When I was a child," says he, "I used to speak as a child, to understand as a child, to think as a child; but when I became a man, I put aside childish things."[1] He then immediately explains why he said this in these words: "For now we see by means of a mirror, darkly; but then face to face: now I know in part; but then shall I know even as also I am known."[2]

CHAP. 39 [XXIV.] — THE ETERNAL REWARD WHICH IS SPECIALLY DECLARED IN THE NEW TESTAMENT, FORETOLD BY THE PROPHET.

Accordingly, in our prophet likewise, whose testimony we are dealing with, this is added, that in God is the reward, in Him the end, in Him the perfection of happiness, in Him the sum of the blessed and eternal life. For after saying, "I will be their God, and they shall be my people," he at once adds, "And they shall no more teach every man his neighbour, and every man his brother, saying, Know the Lord: for they shall all know me, from the least even unto the greatest of them."[3] Now, the present is certainly the time of the New Testament, the promise of which is given by the prophet in the words which we have quoted from his prophecy. Why then does each man still say even now to his neighbour and his brother, "Know the Lord?" Or is it not perhaps meant that this is everywhere said when the gospel is preached, and when this is its very proclamation? For on what ground does the apostle call himself "a teacher of the Gentiles,"[4] if it be not that what he himself implies in the following passage becomes realized: "How shall they call on Him in whom they have not believed? and how shall they believe in Him of whom they have not heard? and how shall they hear without a preacher?"[5] Since, then, this preaching is now everywhere spreading, in what way is it the time of the New Testament of which the prophet spoke in the words, "And they shall not every man teach his neighbour, and every man his brother, saying, Know the Lord; for they shall all know me, from the least of them unto the greatest of them,"[3] unless it be that he has included in his prophetic forecast the eternal reward of the said New Testament, by promising us the most blessed contemplation of God Himself?

CHAP. 40. — HOW THAT IS TO BE THE REWARD OF ALL; THE APOSTLE EARNESTLY DEFENDS GRACE.

What then is the import of the "*All*, from the

least unto the greatest of them," but all that belong spiritually to the house of Israel and to the house of Judah, — that is, to the children of Isaac, to the seed of Abraham? For such is the promise, wherein it was said to him, "In Isaac shall thy seed be called; for they which are the children of the flesh are not the children of God: but the children of the promise are counted for the seed. For this is the word of promise, At this time will I come, and Sarah shall have a son. And not only this; but when Rebecca also had conceived by one, even by our father Isaac, (for the children being not yet born, neither having done any good or evil, that the purpose of God according to election might stand, not of works, but of Him that calleth,) it was said unto her, "The elder shall serve the younger."[6] This is the house of Israel, or rather the house of Judah, on account of Christ, who came of the tribe of Judah. This is the house of the children of promise, — not by reason of their own merits, but of the kindness of God. For God promises what He Himself performs: He does not Himself promise, and another perform; which would no longer be promising, but prophesying. Hence it is "not of works, but of Him that calleth,"[7] lest the result should be their own, not God's; lest the reward should be ascribed not to His grace, but to their due; and so grace should be no longer grace which was so earnestly defended and maintained by him who, though the least of the apostles, laboured more abundantly than all the rest, — yet not himself, but the grace of God that was with him.[8] "They shall all know me,"[3] He says, — "*All*," the house of Israel and house of Judah. "All," however, "are not Israel which are of Israel,"[9] but they only to whom it is said in "the psalm concerning the morning aid"[10] (that is, concerning the new refreshing light, meaning that of the new testament), "All ye the seed of Jacob, glorify Him; and fear Him, all ye the seed of Israel."[11] All the seed, without exception, even the entire seed of the promise and of the called, but only of those who are the called according to His purpose.[12] "For whom He did predestinate, them He also called; and whom He called, them He also justified; and whom He justified, them He also glorified."[13] "Therefore it is of faith, that it might be by grace; to the end the promise might be sure to all the seed: not to that only which is of the law," — that is, which comes from the Old Testament into the New, — "but to that also which is of faith," which was indeed prior to the law, even "the faith of Abraham," — meaning those who imitate the faith of Abraham, — "who is the father of us all; as it is written, I have made

---

[1] 1 Cor. xiii. 11.    [2] 1 Cor. xiii. 12.    [3] Jer. xxxi. 34.
[4] 1 Tim. ii. 7.    [5] Rom. x. 14.

[6] Rom. ix. 7-12.    [7] Rom. ix. 11.    [8] 1 Cor. xv. 9, 10.
[9] Rom. ix. 6.
[10] See title of Ps. xxii. (xxi. Sept.) in the Sept. and Latin.
[11] Ps. xxii. 23.    [12] Rom. viii. 28.    [13] Rom. viii. 30.

thee the father of many nations." [1]  Now all these predestinated, called, justified, glorified ones, shall know God by the grace of the new testament, from the least to the greatest of them.

CHAP. 41. — THE LAW WRITTEN IN THE HEART, AND THE REWARD OF THE ETERNAL CONTEMPLATION OF GOD, BELONG TO THE NEW COVENANT; WHO AMONG THE SAINTS ARE THE LEAST AND THE GREATEST.

As then the law of works, which was written on the tables of stone, and its reward, the land of promise, which the house of the carnal Israel after their liberation from Egypt received, belonged to the old testament, so the law of faith, written on the heart, and its reward, the beatific vision which the house of the spiritual Israel, when delivered from the present world, shall perceive, belong to the new testament. Then shall come to pass what the apostle describes: "Whether there be prophecies, they shall fail; whether there be tongues, they shall cease; whether there be knowledge, it shall vanish away," [2] — even that imperfect knowledge of "the child" [3] in which this present life is passed, and which is but "in part," "by means of a mirror darkly." [4]  Because of this, indeed, "prophecy" is necessary, for still to the past succeeds the future; and because of this, too, "tongues" are required, — that is, a multiplicity of expressions, since it is by different ones that different things are suggested to him who does not as yet contemplate with a perfectly purified mind the everlasting light of transparent truth. "When that, however, which is perfect is come, then that which is in part shall be done away," [5] then, what appeared to the flesh in assumed flesh shall display Itself as It is in Itself to all who love It; then, there shall be eternal life for us to know the one very God; [6] then shall we be like Him, [7] because "we shall then know, even as we are known;" [8] then "they shall teach no more every man his neighbour, and every man his brother, saying, Know the Lord; for they shall all know me, from the least unto the greatest of them." [9]  Now this may be understood in several ways: Either, that in that life the saints shall differ one from another in glory, as star from star. It matters not how the expression runs, — whether (as in the passage before us) it be, "From the least unto the greatest of them," or the other way, From the greatest unto the least. And, in like manner, it matters not even if we understand "the least" to mean those who simply believe, and "the greatest" those who have been further able to understand — so far as may be in this

world — the light which is incorporeal and unchangeable. Or, "the least" may mean those who are later in time; whilst by "the greatest" He may have intended to indicate those who were prior in time. For they are all to receive the promised vision of God hereafter, since it was for us that they foresaw the future which would be better than their present, that they without us should not arrive at complete perfection. [10]  And so the earlier are found to be the lesser, because they were less deferred in time; as in the case of the gospel "penny a day," which is given for an illustration. [11]  This penny they are the first to receive who came last into the vineyard. Or, "the least and the greatest" ought perhaps to be taken in some other sense, which at present does not occur to my mind.

CHAP. 42 [XXV.] — DIFFERENCE BETWEEN THE OLD AND THE NEW TESTAMENTS.

I beg of you, however, carefully to observe, as far as you can, what I am endeavouring to prove with so much effort. When the prophet promised a new covenant, not according to the covenant which had been formerly made with the people of Israel when liberated from Egypt, he said nothing about a change in the sacrifices or any sacred ordinances, although such change, too, was without doubt to follow, as we see in fact that it did follow, even as the same prophetic scripture testifies in many other passages; but he simply called attention to this difference, that God would impress His laws on the mind of those who belonged to this covenant, and would write them in their hearts, [12] whence the apostle drew his conclusion, — "not with ink, but with the Spirit of the living God; not in tables of stone, but in fleshy tables of the heart;" [13] and that the eternal recompense of this righteousness was not the land out of which were driven the Amorites and Hittites, and other nations who dwelt there, [14] but God Himself, "to whom it is good to hold fast," [15] in order that God's good that they love, may be the God Himself whom they love, between whom and men nothing but sin produces separation; and this is remitted only by grace. Accordingly, after saying, "For all shall know me, from the least to the greatest of them," He instantly added, "For I will forgive their iniquity, and I will remember their sin no more." [9]  By the law of works, then, the Lord says, "Thou shalt not covet;" [16] but by the law of faith He says, "Without me ye can do nothing;" [17] for He was treating of good works, even the fruit of the vine-branches. It is therefore apparent what dif-

---

[1] Rom. iv. 16, 17.   [2] 1 Cor. xiii. 8.   [3] Ib. ver. 11.
[4] Ib. ver. 12.   [5] 1 Cor. xiii. 10.   [6] John xvii. 3.
[7] 1 John iii. 2.   [8] 1 Cor. xiii. 12.   [9] Jer. xxxi. 34.

[10] Heb. xi. 40.   [11] Matt. xx. 8.   [12] Jer. xxxi. 32, 33.
[13] 2 Cor. iii. 3.   [14] Josh. xii.   [15] Ps. lxxiii. 28.
[16] Ex. xx. 17.   [17] John xv. 5.

ference there is between the old covenant and the new,—that in the former the law is written on tables, while in the latter on hearts; so that what in the one alarms from without, in the other delights from within; and in the former man becomes a transgressor through the letter that kills, in the other a lover through the life-giving spirit. We must therefore avoid saying, that the way in which God assists us to work righteousness, and "works in us both to will and to do of His good pleasure," [1] is by externally addressing to our faculties precepts of holiness; for He gives His increase internally, [2] by shedding love abroad in our hearts by the Holy Ghost, which is given to us." [3]

CHAP. 43 [XXVI.] — A QUESTION TOUCHING THE PASSAGE IN THE APOSTLE ABOUT THE GENTILES WHO ARE SAID TO DO BY NATURE THE LAW'S COMMANDS, WHICH THEY ARE ALSO SAID TO HAVE WRITTEN ON THEIR HEARTS.

Now we must see in what sense it is that the apostle says, " For when the Gentiles, which have not the law, do by nature the things contained in the law, these, having not the law, are a law unto themselves, which show the work of the law written in their hearts," [4] lest there should seem to be no certain difference in the new testament, in that the Lord promised that He would write His laws in the hearts of His people, inasmuch as the Gentiles have this done for them naturally. This question therefore has to be sifted, arising as it does as one of no inconsiderable importance. For some one may say, " If God distinguishes the new testament from the old by this circumstance, that in the old He wrote His law on tables, but in the new He wrote them on men's hearts, by what are the faithful of the new testament discriminated from the Gentiles, which have the work of the law written on their hearts, whereby they do by nature the things of the law, [5] as if, forsooth, they were better than the ancient people, which received the law on tables, and before the new people, which has that conferred on it by the new testament which nature has already bestowed on them?"

CHAP. 44. — THE ANSWER IS, THAT THE PASSAGE MUST BE UNDERSTOOD OF THE FAITHFUL OF THE NEW COVENANT.

Has the apostle perhaps mentioned those Gentiles as having the law written in their hearts who belong to the new testament? We must look at the previous context. First, then, referring to the gospel, he says, " It is the power of God unto salvation to every one that believeth;

to the Jew first, and also to the Greek. For therein is the righteousness of God revealed from faith to faith: as it is written, The just shall live by faith." [6] Then he goes on to speak of the ungodly, who by reason of their pride profit not by the knowledge of God, since they did not glorify Him as God, neither were thankful.[7] He then passes to those who think and do the very things which they condemn, — having in view, no doubt, the Jews, who made their boast of God's law, but as yet not mentioning them expressly by name; and then he says, " Indignation and wrath, tribulation and anguish, upon every soul of man that doeth evil, of the Jew first, and also of the Gentile: but glory, honour, and peace, to every soul that doeth good; to the Jew first, and also to the Gentile: for there is no respect of persons with God. For as many as have sinned without law, shall also perish without law; and as many as have sinned in the law, shall be judged by the law; for not the hearers of the law are just before God, but the doers of the law shall be justified." [8] Who they are that are treated of in these words, he goes on to tell us: " For when the Gentiles, which have not the law, do by nature the things contained in the law," [5] and so forth in the passage which I have quoted already. Evidently, therefore, no others are here signified under the name of Gentiles than those whom he had before designated by the name of " Greek " when he said, " To the Jew first, and also to the Greek." [9] Since then the gospel is " the power of God unto salvation to every one that believeth, to the Jew first, and also to the Greek; " [9] and since " indignation and wrath, tribulation and anguish, are upon every soul of man that doeth evil, of the Jew first, and also of the Greek: but glory, honour, and peace, to every man that doeth good; to the Jew first, and also to the Greek; " since, moreover, the Greek is indicated by the term " Gentiles " who do by nature the things contained in the law, and which have the work of the law written in their hearts: it follows that such Gentiles as have the law written in their hearts belong to the gospel, since to them, on their believing, it is the power of God unto salvation. To what Gentiles, however, would he promise glory, and honour, and peace, in their doing good works, if living without the grace of the gospel? Since there is no respect of persons with God, [10] and since it is not the hearers of the law, but the doers thereof, that are justified, [11] it follows that any man of any nation, whether Jew or Greek, who shall believe, will equally have salvation under the gospel. " For there is no difference," as he says afterwards; " for all have sinned, and come short

---

[1] Phil. ii. 13.    [2] 1 Cor. iii. 7.    [3] Rom. v. 5.
[4] Rom. ii. 14, 15.    [5] Rom. ii. 14.

[6] Rom. i. 16, 17.    [7] Rom. i. 21.    [8] Rom ii. 8-13.
[9] Rom. i. 16.    [10] Rom. ii. 11.    [11] Rom. ii. 13.

of the glory of God : being justified freely by His grace." [1]　How then could he say that any Gentile person, who was a doer of the law, was justified without the Saviour's grace?

CHAP. 45. — IT IS NOT BY THEIR WORKS, BUT BY GRACE, THAT THE DOERS OF THE LAW ARE JUSTIFIED ; GOD'S SAINTS AND GOD'S NAME HALLOWED IN DIFFERENT SENSES.

Now he could not mean to contradict himself in saying, " The doers of the law shall be justified," [2] as if their justification came through their works, and not through grace ; since he declares that a man is justified freely by His grace without the works of the law, [3] intending by the term "*freely*" nothing else than that works do not precede justification.　For in another passage he expressly says, " If by grace, then is it no more of works ; otherwise grace is no longer grace." [4]　But the statement that " the doers of the law shall be justified " [2] must be so understood, as that we may know that they are not otherwise doers of the law, unless they be justified, so that justification does not subsequently accrue to them as doers of the law, but justification precedes them as doers of the law. For what else does the phrase " being justified " signify than "being made righteous," — by Him, of course, who justifies the ungodly man, that he may become a godly one instead?　For if we were to express a certain fact by saying, " The men will be liberated," the phrase would of course be understood as asserting that the liberation would accrue to those who were men already ; but if we were to say, The men will be created, we should certainly not be understood as asserting that the creation would happen to those who were already in existence, but that they became men by the creation itself.　If in like manner it were said, The doers of the law shall be honoured, we should only interpret the statement correctly if we supposed that the honour was to accrue to those who were already doers of the law : but when the allegation is, " The doers of the law shall be justified," what else does it mean than that the just shall be justified? for of course the doers of the law are just persons.　And thus it amounts to the same thing as if it were said, The doers of the law shall be created, — not those who were so already, but that they may become such ; in order that the Jews who were hearers of the law might hereby understand that they wanted the grace of the Justifier, in order to be able to become its doers also.　Or else the term " They shall be justified " is used in the sense of, They shall be deemed, or reckoned as just, as it is predicated of a certain man in the Gospel, " But he, willing to jus-

tify himself," [5] — meaning that he wished to be thought and accounted just.　In like manner, we attach one meaning to the statement, " God sanctifies His saints," and another to the words, " Sanctified be Thy name ; " [6] for in the former case we suppose the words to mean that He makes those to be saints who were not saints before, and in the latter, that the prayer would have that which is always holy in itself be also regarded as holy by men, — in a word, be feared with a hallowed awe.

CHAP. 46. — HOW THE PASSAGE OF THE LAW AGREES WITH THAT OF THE PROPHET.

If therefore the apostle, when he mentioned that the Gentiles do by nature the things contained in the law, and have the work of the law written in their hearts, [7] intended those to be understood who believed in Christ, — who do not come to the faith like the Jews, through a precedent law, — there is no good reason why we should endeavour to distinguish them from those to whom the Lord by the prophet promises the new covenant, telling them that He will write His laws in their hearts, [8] inasmuch as they too, by the grafting which he says had been made of the wild olive, belong to the self-same olive-tree, [9] — in other words, to the same people of God.　There is therefore a good agreement of this passage of the apostle with the words of the prophet ; so that belonging to the new testament means having the law of God not written on tables, but on the heart, — that is, embracing the righteousness of the law with innermost affection, where faith works by love. [10]　Because it is by faith that God justifies the Gentiles ; " and the Scripture foreseeing this, preached the gospel before to Abraham, saying, " In thy seed shall all nations be blessed," [11] in order that by this grace of promise the wild olive might be grafted into the good olive, and believing Gentiles might be made children of Abraham, " in Abraham's seed, which is Christ," [12] by following the faith of him who, without receiving the law written on tables, and not yet possessing even circumcision, " believed God, and it was counted to him for righteousness." [13]　Now what the apostle attributed to Gentiles of this character, — how that " they have the work of the law written in their hearts ; " [14] must be some such thing as what he says to the Corinthians : " not in tables of stone, but in fleshy tables of the heart." [15]　For thus do they become of the house of Israel, when their uncircumcision is accounted circumcision, by the fact that they do not exhibit the righteousness of the law by the excis-

---

[1] Rom. iii. 22–24.　[2] Rom. ii. 13.　[3] Rom. iii. 24, 28.
[4] Rom. xi. 6.

[5] Luke x. 29.　[6] Matt. vi. 9.　[7] Rom. ii. 14, 15.
[8] Jer. xxxii. 32.　[9] Rom. xi. 24.　[10] Gal. v. 6.
[11] Gal. iii. 8; Gen. xxii. 18.　[12] Gal. iii. 16.
[13] Gen. xv. 6; Rom. iv. 2.　[14] Rom. ii. 15.
[15] 2 Cor. iii. 3.

ion of the flesh, but keep it by the charity of the heart. "If," says he, "the uncircumcision keep the righteousness of the law, shall not his uncircumcision be counted for circumcision?"[1] And therefore in the house of the true Israel, in which is no guile,[2] they are partakers of the new testament, since God puts His laws into their mind, and writes them in their hearts with his own finger, the Holy Ghost, by whom is shed abroad in them the love[3] which is the "fulfilling of the law."[4]

### CHAP. 47 [XXVII.] — THE LAW "BEING DONE BY NATURE" MEANS, DONE BY NATURE AS RESTORED BY GRACE.

Nor ought it to disturb us that the apostle described them as doing that which is contained in the law "*by nature*," — not by the Spirit of God, not by faith, not by grace. For it is the Spirit of grace that does it, in order to restore in us the image of God, in which we were naturally created.[5] Sin, indeed, is contrary to nature, and it is grace that heals it, — on which account the prayer is offered to God, "Be merciful unto me: heal my soul; for I have sinned against Thee."[6] Therefore it is by nature that men do the things which are contained in the law;[7] for they who do not, fail to do so by reason of their sinful defect. In consequence of this sinfulness, the law of God is erased out of their hearts; and therefore, when, the sin being healed, it is written there, the prescriptions of the law are done "*by nature*," — not that by nature grace is denied, but rather by grace nature is repaired. For "by one man sin entered into the world, and death by sin, and so death passed upon all men; in which all have sinned;"[8] wherefore "there is no difference: they all come short of the glory of God, being justified freely by His grace."[9] By this grace there is written on the renewed inner man that righteousness which sin had blotted out; and this mercy comes upon the human race through our Lord Jesus Christ. "For there is one God, and one Mediator between God and men, the Man Christ Jesus."[10]

### CHAP. 48. — THE IMAGE OF GOD IS NOT WHOLLY BLOTTED OUT IN THESE UNBELIEVERS; VENIAL SINS.

According to some, however, they who do by nature the things contained in the law must not be regarded as yet in the number of those whom Christ's grace justifies, but rather as among those some of whose actions (although they are those of ungodly men, who do not truly and rightly worship the true God) we not only cannot

blame, but even justly and rightly praise, since they have been done — so far as we read, or know, or hear — according to the rule of righteousness; though at the same time, were we to discuss the question with what motive they are done, they would hardly be found to be such as deserve the praise and defence which are due to righteous conduct. [XXVIII.] Still, since God's image has not been so completely erased in the soul of man by the stain of earthly affections, as to have left remaining there not even the merest lineaments of it whence it might be justly said that man, even in the ungodliness of his life, does, or appreciates, some things contained in the law; if this is what is meant by the statement that "the Gentiles, which have not the law" (that is, the law of God), "do by nature the things contained in the law,"[7] and that men of this character "are a law to themselves," and "show the work of the law written in their hearts," — that is to say, what was impressed on their hearts when they were created in the image of God has not been wholly blotted out: — even in this view of the subject, that wide difference will not be disturbed, which separates the new covenant from the old, and which lies in the fact that by the new covenant the law of God is written in the hearts of believers, whereas in the old it was inscribed on tables of stone. For this writing in the heart is effected by renovation, although it had not been completely blotted out by the old nature. For just as that image of God is renewed in the mind of believers by the new testament, which impiety had not quite abolished (for there had remained undoubtedly that which the soul of man cannot be except it be rational), so also the law of God, which had not been wholly blotted out there by unrighteousness, is certainly written thereon, renewed by grace. Now in the Jews the law which was written on tables could not effect this new inscription, which is justification, but only transgression. For they too were men, and there was inherent in them that power of nature, which enables the rational soul both to perceive and do what is lawful; but the godliness which transfers to another life happy and immortal has "a spotless law, converting souls,"[11] so that by the light thereof they may be renewed, and that be accomplished in them which is written, "There has been manifested over us, O Lord, the light of Thy countenance."[12] Turned away from which, they have deserved to grow old, whilst they are incapable of renovation except by the grace of Christ, — in other words, without the intercession of the Mediator; there being "one God and one Mediator between God and men, the Man Christ Jesus, who gave Himself

---

[1] Rom. ii. 26.  [2] See John i. 47.  [3] Rom. v. 5.
[4] Rom. xiii. 10.  [5] Gen. i. 27.  [6] Ps. xli. 4.
[7] Rom. ii. 14.  [8] Rom. v. 12.  [9] Rom. iii. 22–24.
[10] 1 Tim. ii. 5.

[11] Ps. xix. 7.  [12] Ps. iv. 6.

a ransom for all." [1]  Should those be strangers to His grace of whom we are treating, and who (after the manner of which we have spoken with sufficient fulness already) "do by nature the things contained in the law," [2] of what use will be their "excusing thoughts" to them "in the day when God shall judge the secrets of men," [3] unless it be perhaps to procure for them a milder punishment?  For as, on the one hand, there are certain venial sins which do not hinder the righteous man from the attainment of eternal life, and which are unavoidable in this life, so, on the other hand, there are some good works which are of no avail to an ungodly man towards the attainment of everlasting life, although it would be very difficult to find the life of any very bad man whatever entirely without them.  But inasmuch as in the kingdom of God the saints differ in glory as one star does from another, [4] so likewise, in the condemnation of everlasting punishment, it will be more tolerable for Sodom than for that other city ; [5] whilst some men will be twofold more the children of hell than others. [6] Thus in the judgment of God not even this fact will be without its influence, — that one man will have sinned more, or less, than another, even when both are involved in the ungodliness that is worthy of damnation.

### CHAP. 49. — THE GRACE PROMISED BY THE PROPHET FOR THE NEW COVENANT.

What then could the apostle have meant to imply by, — after checking the boasting of the Jews, by telling them that "not the hearers of the law are just before God, but the doers of the law shall be justified," [7] — immediately afterwards speaking of them "which, having not the law, do by nature the things contained in the law," [2] if in this description not they are to be understood who belong to the Mediator's grace, but rather they who, while not worshipping the true God with true godliness, do yet exhibit some good works in the general course of their ungodly lives?  Or did the apostle perhaps deem it probable, because he had previously said that "with God there is no respect of persons," [8] and had afterwards said that "God is not the God of the Jews only, but also of the Gentiles," [9] — that even such scanty little works of the law, as are suggested by nature, were not discovered in such as received not the law, except as the result of the remains of the image of God ; which He does not disdain when they believe in Him, with whom there is no respect of persons?  But whichever of these views is accepted, it is evident that the grace of God was promised to the new testament even by the prophet, and that

this grace was definitively announced to take this shape, — God's laws were to be written in men's hearts ; and they were to arrive at such a knowledge of God, that they were not each one to teach his neighbour and brother, saying, Know the Lord ; for all were to know Him, from the least to the greatest of them. [10]  This is the gift of the Holy Ghost, by which love is shed abroad in our hearts, [11] — not, indeed, any kind of love, but the love of God, "out of a pure heart, and a good conscience, and an unfeigned faith," [12] by means of which the just man, while living in this pilgrim state, is led on, after the stages of "the glass," and "the enigma," and "what is in part," to the actual vision, that, face to face, he may know even as he is known. [13]  For one thing has he required of the Lord, and that he still seeks after, that he may dwell in the house of the Lord all the days of his life, in order to behold the pleasantness of the Lord. [14]

### CHAP. 50 [XXIX.] — RIGHTEOUSNESS IS THE GIFT OF GOD.

Let no man therefore boast of that which he seems to possess, as if he had not received it ; [15] nor let him think that he has received it merely because the external letter of the law has been either exhibited to him to read, or sounded in his ear for him to hear.  For "if righteousness is by the law, then Christ has died in vain." [16]  Seeing, however, that if He has not died in vain, He has ascended up on high, and has led captivity captive, and has given gifts to men, [17] it follows that whosoever has, has from this source.  But whosoever denies that he has from Him, either has not, or is in great danger of being deprived of what he has. [18]  "For it is one God which justifies the circumcision by faith, and the uncircumcision through faith ; " [19] in which clauses there is no real difference in the sense, as if the phrase "*by faith*" meant one thing, and "*through faith*" another, but only a variety of expression.  For in one passage, when speaking of the Gentiles, — that is, of the uncircumcision, — he says, "The Scripture, foreseeing that God would justify the heathen *by faith ;*" [20] and again, in another, when speaking of the circumcision, to which he himself belonged, he says, "We who are Jews by nature, and not sinners of the Gentiles, knowing that a man is not justified by the works of the law, but *through faith* in Jesus Christ, even we believed in Jesus Christ." [21]  Observe, he says that both the uncircumcision are justified by

---

[10] Jer. xxxi. 33, 34.     [11] Rom. v. 5.     [12] 1 Tim. i. 5.
[13] 1 Cor. xiii. 12.     [14] Ps. xxvii. 4.     [15] 1 Cor. iv. 7.
[16] Gal. ii. 21.     [17] Ps. lxviii. 18 ; Eph. iv. 8.
[18] Luke viii. 18 ; xix. 26.     [19] Rom. iii. 30.
[20] Gal. iii. 8.
[21] Gal ii. 15, 16. [The discussion turns on the difference in the Latin prepositions *ex* and *per*, representing the Greek ἐκ and διὰ. — W.]

---

[1] 1 Tim. ii. 5, 6.     [2] Rom. ii. 14.     [3] Rom. ii. 15, 16.
[4] 1 Cor. xv. 41.     [5] Luke x. 12.     [6] Matt. xxiii. 15.
[7] Rom. ii. 13.     [8] Rom. ii. 11.     [9] Rom. iii. 29.

faith, and the circumcision through faith, if, indeed, the circumcision keep the righteousness of faith. For the Gentiles, which followed not after righteousness, have attained to righteousness, even the righteousness which is by faith,[1] — by obtaining it of God, not by assuming it of themselves. But Israel, which followed after the law of righteousness, hath not attained to the law of righteousness. And why? Because they sought it not by faith, but as it were by works[2] — in other words, working it out as it were by themselves, not believing that it is God who works within them. "For it is God which worketh in us both to will and to do of His own good pleasure."[3] And hereby "they stumbled at the stumbling-stone."[4] For what he said, "not by faith, but as it were by works,"[4] he most clearly explained in the following words: "They, being ignorant of God's righteousness, and going about to establish their own righteousness, have not submitted themselves unto the righteousness of God. For Christ is the end of the law for righteousness to every one that believeth."[5] Then are we still in doubt what are those works of the law by which a man is not justified, if he believes them to be his own works, as it were, without the help and gift of God, which is "by the faith of Jesus Christ?" And do we suppose that they are circumcision and the other like ordinances, because some such things in other passages are read concerning these sacramental rites too? In this place, however, it is certainly not circumcision which they wanted to establish as their own righteousness, beeause God established this by prescribing it Himself. Nor is it possible for us to understand this statement, of those works concerning which the Lord says to them, "Ye reject the commandment of God, that ye may keep your own tradition;"[6] because, as the apostle says, Israel, which followed after the law of righteousness, hath not attained to the law of righteousness."[7] He did not say, Which followed after their own traditions, framing them and relying on them. This then is the sole distinction, that the very precept, "Thou shalt not covet,"[8] and God's other good and holy commandments, they attributed to themselves; whereas, that man may keep them, God must work in him through faith in Jesus Christ, who is "the end of the law for righteousness to every one that believeth."[9] That is to say, every one who is incorporated into Him and made a member of His body, is able, by His giving the increase within, to work righteousness. It is of such a man's works that Christ Himself has said, "Without me ye can do nothing."[10]

## CHAP. 51.—FAITH THE GROUND OF ALL RIGHTEOUSNESS.

The righteousness of the law is proposed in these terms, — that whosoever shall do it shall live in it; and the purpose is, that when each has discovered his own weakness, he may not by his own strength, nor by the letter of the law (which cannot be done), but by faith, conciliating the Justifier, attain, and do, and live in it. For the work in which he who does it shall live, is not done except by one who is justified. His justification, however, is obtained by faith; and concerning faith it is written, "Say not in thine heart, Who shall ascend into heaven? (that is, to bring down Christ therefrom;) or, Who shall descend into the deep? (that is, to bring up Christ again from the dead.) But what saith it? The word is nigh thee, even in thy mouth, and in thy heart: that is (says he), the word of faith which we preach: That if thou shalt confess with thy mouth the Lord Jesus, and shalt believe in thine heart that God hath raised Him from the dead, thou shalt be saved."[11] As far as he is saved, so far is he righteous. For by this faith we believe that God will raise even us from the dead, — even now in the spirit, that we may in this present world live soberly, righteously, and godly in the renewal of His grace; and by and by in our flesh, which shall rise again to immortality, which indeed is the reward of the Spirit, who precedes it by a resurrection which is appropriate to Himself, — that is, by justification. "For we are buried with Christ by baptism unto death, that like as Christ was raised up from the dead by the glory of the Father, even so we also should walk in newness of life."[12] By faith, therefore, in Jesus Christ we obtain salvation, — both in so far as it is begun within us in reality, and in so far as its perfection is waited for in hope; "for whosoever shall call on the name of the Lord shall be saved."[13] "How abundant," says the Psalmist, "is the multitude of Thy goodness, O Lord, which Thou hast laid up for them that fear Thee, and hast perfected for them that hope in Thee!"[14] By the law we fear God; by faith we hope in God: but from those who fear punishment grace is hidden. And the soul which labours under this fear, since it has not conquered its evil concupiscence, and from which this fear, like a harsh master, has not departed, — let it flee by faith for refuge to the mercy of God, that He may give it what He commands, and may, by inspiring into it the sweetness of His grace through His Holy Spirit, cause the soul to delight more in what He teaches it, than it delights in what opposes His instruction. In this manner it is that the great abundance of His sweet-

---

[1] Rom. ix. 30.　　[2] Rom. ix. 31, 32.　　[3] Phil. ii. 13.
[4] Rom. ix. 32.　　[5] Rom. x. 3, 4.　　[6] Mark vii. 9.
[7] Rom. ix. 31.　　[8] Ex. xx. 17.　　[9] Rom. x. 4.
[10] John xv. 5.

[11] Rom. x. 6–9.　　　　[12] Rom. vi. 4.
[13] Rom. x. 13; Joel ii. 32.　　[14] Ps. xxxi. 19.

ness, — that is, the law of faith, — His love which is in our hearts, and shed abroad, is perfected in them that hope in Him, that good may be wrought by the soul, healed not by the fear of punishment, but by the love of righteousness.

### CHAP. 52 [XXX.] — GRACE ESTABLISHES FREE WILL.

Do we then by grace make void free will? God forbid! Nay, rather we establish free will. For even as the law by faith, so free will by grace, is not made void, but established.[1] For neither is the law fulfilled except by free will; but by the law is the knowledge of sin, by faith the acquisition of grace against sin, by grace the healing of the soul from the disease of sin, by the health of the soul freedom of will, by free will the love of righteousness, by love of righteousness the accomplishment of the law. Accordingly, as the law is not made void, but is established through faith, since faith procures grace whereby the law is fulfilled; so free will is not made void through grace, but is established, since grace cures the will whereby righteousness is freely loved. Now all the stages which I have here connected together in their successive links, have severally their proper voices in the sacred Scriptures. The law says: "Thou shalt not covet."[2] Faith says: "Heal my soul, for I have sinned against Thee."[3] Grace says: "Behold, thou art made whole: sin no more, lest a worse thing come unto thee."[4] Health says: "O Lord my God, I cried unto Thee, and Thou hast healed me."[5] Free will says: "I will freely sacrifice unto Thee."[6] Love of righteousness says: "Transgressors told me pleasant tales, but not according to Thy law, O Lord."[7] How is it then that miserable men dare to be proud, either of their free will, before they are freed, or of their own strength, if they have been freed? They do not observe that in the very mention of free will they pronounce the name of liberty. But "where the Spirit of the Lord is, there is liberty."[8] If, therefore, they are the slaves of sin, why do they boast of free will? For by what a man is overcome, to the same is he delivered as a slave.[9] But if they have been freed, why do they vaunt themselves as if it were by their own doing, and boast, as if they had not received? Or are they in such sort that they do not choose to have Him for their Lord who says to them: "Without me ye can do nothing;"[10] and "If the Son shall make you free, ye shall be free indeed?"[11]

### CHAP. 53 [XXXI.] — VOLITION AND ABILITY.

Some one will ask whether the faith itself, in which seems to be the beginning either of salvation, or of that series leading to salvation which I have just mentioned, is placed in our power. We shall see more easily, if we first examine with some care what "our power" means. Since, then, there are two things, — will and ability; it follows that not every one that has the will has therefore the ability also, nor has every one that possesses the ability the will also; for as we sometimes will what we cannot do, so also we sometimes can do what we do not will. From the words themselves when sufficiently considered, we shall detect, in the very ring of the terms, the derivation of volition from willingness, and of *ability* from ableness.[12] Therefore, even as the man who wishes has volition, so also the man who can has ability. But in order that a thing may be done by ability, the volition must be present. For no man is usually said to do a thing with ability if he did it unwillingly. Although, at the same time, if we observe more precisely, even what a man is compelled to do unwillingly, he does, if he does it, by his volition; only he is said to be an unwilling agent, or to act against his will, because he would prefer some other thing. He is compelled, indeed, by some unfortunate influence, to do what he does under compulsion, wishing to escape it or to remove it out of his way. For if his volition be so strong that he prefers not doing this to not suffering that, then beyond doubt he resists the compelling influence, and does it not. And accordingly, if he does it, it is not with a full and free will, but yet it is not without will that he does it; and inasmuch as the volition is followed by its effect, we cannot say that he lacked the ability to do it. If, indeed, he willed to do it, yielding to compulsion, but could not, although we should allow that a coerced will was present, we should yet say that ability was absent. But when he did not do the thing because he was unwilling, then of course the ability was present, but the volition was absent, since he did it not, by his resistance to the compelling influence. Hence it is that even they who compel, or who persuade, are accustomed to say, Why don't you do what you have in your ability, in order to avoid this evil? While they who are utterly unable to do what they are compelled to do, because they are supposed to be able usually answer by excusing themselves, and say, I would do it if it were in my ability. What then do we ask more, since we call that ability when to the volition is added the faculty of doing? Accordingly, every one is said to have that in his ability which he does if he likes, and does not if he dislikes.

[1] Rom. iii. 31.    [2] Ex. xx. 17.    [3] Ps. xli. 4.
[4] John v. 14.    [5] Ps. xxx. 2.    [6] Ps. liv. 6.
[7] Ps. cxix. 85.    [8] 2 Cor. iii. 17.    [9] 2 Pet. ii. 19.
[10] John xv. 5.    [11] John viii. 36.

[12] [That is, in the Latin, "voluntas" (*choice, will, volition*) comes from "velle" (to *wish, desire, determine*), and "potestas" *power, ability*) from "posse" (*to be able*). — W.]

## CHAP. 54. — WHETHER FAITH BE IN A MAN'S OWN POWER.

Attend now to the point which we have laid down for discussion : whether faith is in our own power? We now speak of that faith which we employ when we believe anything, not that which we give when we make a promise ; for this too is called *faith*.[1] We use the word in one sense when we say, " He had no faith in me," and in another sense when we say, " He did not keep faith with me." The one phrase means, " He did not believe what I said ; " the other, " He did not do what he promised." According to the faith by which we believe, we are faithful to God ; but according to that whereby a thing is brought to pass which is promised, God Himself even is faithful to us ; for the apostle declares, " God is faithful, who will not suffer you to be tempted above that ye are able."[2] Well, now, the former is the faith about which we inquire, Whether it be in our power? even the faith by which we believe God, or believe on God. For of this it is written, " Abraham believed God, and it was counted unto him for righteousness."[3] And again, " To him that believeth on Him that justifieth the ungodly, his faith is counted for righteousness."[4] Consider now whether anybody believes, if he be unwilling ; or whether he believes not, if he shall have willed it. Such a position, indeed, is absurd (for what is believing but consenting to the truth of what is said? and this consent is certainly voluntary) : faith, therefore, is in our own power. But, as the apostle says : " There is no power but comes from God,"[5] what reason then is there why it may not be said to us even of this : " What hast thou which thou hast not received? "[6] — for it is God who gave us even to believe. Nowhere, however, in Holy Scripture do we find such an assertion as, There is no volition but comes from God. And rightly is it not so written, because it is not true : otherwise God would be the author of even of sins (which Heaven forbid !), if there were no volition except what comes from Him ; inasmuch as an evil volition alone is already a sin, even if the effect be wanting, — in other words, if it has not ability. But when the evil volition receives ability to accomplish its intention, this proceeds from the judgment of God, with whom there is no unrighteousness.[7] He indeed punishes after this manner ; nor is His chastisement unjust because it is secret. The ungodly man, however, is not aware that he is being punished, except when he unwillingly discovers by an open penalty how much evil he has willingly committed. This is just what the apostle says of certain men : " God hath given them up to the evil desires of their own hearts, . . . to do those things that are not convenient."[8] Accordingly, the Lord also said to Pilate : " Thou couldest have no power at all against me, except it were given thee from above."[9] But still, when the ability is given, surely no necessity is imposed. Therefore, although David had received ability to kill Saul, he preferred sparing to striking him.[10] Whence we understand that bad men receive ability for the condemnation of their depraved will, while good men receive ability for trying of their good will.

## CHAP. 55 [XXXII.] — WHAT FAITH IS LAUDABLE.

Since faith, then, is in our power, inasmuch as every one believes when he likes, and, when he believes, believes voluntarily ; our next inquiry, which we must conduct with care, is, What faith it is which the apostle commends with so much earnestness? For indiscriminate faith is not good. Accordingly we find this caution : " Brethren, believe not every spirit, but try the spirits whether they are of God."[11] Nor must the clause in commendation of love, that it " believeth all things,"[12] be so understood as if we should detract from the love of any one, if he refuses to believe at once what he hears. For the same love admonishes us that we ought not readily to believe anything evil about a brother ; and when anything of the kind is said of him, does it not judge it to be more suitable to its character not to believe? Lastly, the same love, " which believeth all things," does not believe every spirit. Accordingly, charity *believes* all things no doubt, but it *believes in* God. Observe, it is not said, Believes *in* all things. It cannot therefore be doubted that the faith which is commended by the apostle is the faith whereby we believe in God.[13]

## CHAP. 56. — THE FAITH OF THOSE WHO ARE UNDER THE LAW DIFFERENT FROM THE FAITH OF OTHERS.

But there is yet another distinction to be observed, — since they who are under the law both attempt to work their own righteousness through fear of punishment, and fail to do God's righteousness, because this is accomplished by the love to which only what is lawful is pleasing, and never by the fear which is forced to have in its work the thing which is lawful, although it has something else in its will which would prefer, if it were only possible, that to be lawful

---

[1] [That is, in Latin, *faith* (" fides ") is both active and passive, and means both *trust* and *trustworthiness*, both *faith* and *faithfulness*. This is also true in English, as Augustin's own examples illustrate. — W.]
[2] 1 Cor. x. 13.      [3] Rom. iv. 3; comp. Gen. xv. 6.
[4] Rom. iv. 5.      [5] Rom. xiii. 1.      [6] 1 Cor. iv. 7.
[7] Rom. ix. 14.

[8] Rom. i. 24, 28.      [9] John xix. 11.
[10] 1 Sam. xxiv. 7, and xxvi. 9.      [11] 1 John iv. 1.
[12] 1 Cor. xiii. 7.      [13] Rom. iv. 3.

which is not lawful. These persons also believe in God; for if they had no faith in Him at all, neither would they of course have any dread of the penalty of His law. This, however, is not the faith which the apostle commends. He says: "Ye have not received the spirit of bondage again to fear; but ye have received the spirit of adoption, whereby we cry, Abba, Father." [1] The fear, then, of which we speak is slavish; and therefore, even though there be in it a belief in the Lord, yet righteousness is not loved by it, but condemnation is feared. God's children, however, exclaim, "Abba, Father," — one of which words they of the circumcision utter; the other, they of the uncircumcision, — the Jew first, and then the Greek; [2] since there is "one God, which justifieth the circumcision by faith, and the uncircumcision through faith." [3] When indeed they utter this call, they seek something; and what do they seek, but that which they hunger and thirst after? And what else is this but that which is said of them, "Blessed are they which do hunger and thirst after righteousness, for they shall be filled?" [4] Let, then, those who are under the law pass over hither, and become sons instead of slaves; and yet not so as to cease to be slaves, but so as, while they are sons, still to serve their Lord and Father freely. For even this have they received; for the Only-begotten "gave them power to become the sons of God, even to them that believe on His name;" [5] and He advised them to ask, to seek, and to knock, in order to receive, to find, and to have the gate opened to them, [6] adding by way of rebuke, the words: "If ye, being evil, know how to give good gifts to your children, how much more shall your Father which is in heaven give good things to them that ask Him?" [7] When, therefore, that strength of sin, the law, [8] inflamed the sting of death, even sin, to take occasion and by the commandment, work all manner of concupiscence in them, [9] of whom were they to ask for the gift of continence but of Him who knows how to give good gifts to His children? Perhaps, however, a man, in his folly, is unaware that no one can be continent except God give him the gift. To know this, indeed, he requires Wisdom herself. [10] Why, then, does he not listen to the Spirit of his Father, speaking through Christ's apostle, or even Christ Himself, who says in His gospel, "Seek and ye shall find;" [11] and who also says to us, speaking by His apostle: "If any one of you lack wisdom, let him ask of God, that giveth to all men liberally, and upbraideth not, and it shall be given to him. Let him, however, ask in faith, nothing wavering?" [12] This is the faith by which

the just man lives; [13] this is the faith whereby he believes on Him who justifies the ungodly; [14] this is the faith through which boasting is excluded, [15] either by the retreat of that with which we become self-inflated, or by the rising of that with which we glory in the Lord. This, again, is the faith by which we procure that largess of the Spirit, of which it is said: "We indeed through the Spirit wait for the hope of righteousness by faith." [16] But this admits of the further question, Whether he meant by "the hope of righteousness" that by which righteousness hopes, or that whereby righteousness is itself hoped for? For the just man, who lives by faith, hopes undoubtedly for eternal life; and the faith likewise, which hungers and thirsts for righteousness, makes progress therein by the renewal of the inward man day by day, [17] and hopes to be satiated therewith in that eternal life, where shall be realized that which is said of God by the psalm: "Who satisfieth thy desire with good things." [18] This, moreover, is the faith whereby they are saved to whom it is said: "By grace are ye saved through faith; and that not of yourselves: it is the gift of God: not of works, lest any man should boast. For we are His workmanship, created in Christ Jesus unto good works, which God hath before ordained that we should walk in them." [19] This, in short, is the faith which works not by fear, but by love; [20] not by dreading punishment, but by loving righteousness. Whence, therefore, arises this love, — that is to say, this charity, — by which faith works, if not from the source whence faith itself obtained it? For it would not be within us, to what extent soever it is in us, if it were not diffused in our hearts by the Holy Ghost who is given to us. [21] Now "*the love of God*" is said to be shed abroad in our hearts, not because He loves us, but because He makes us lovers of Himself; just as "*the righteousness of God*" [22] is used in the sense of our being made righteous by His gift; and "*the salvation of the Lord*," [23] in that we are saved by Him; and "*the faith of Jesus Christ*," [24] because He makes us believers in Him. This is that righteousness of God, which He not only teaches us by the precept of His law, but also bestows upon us by the gift of His Spirit.

CHAP. 57 [XXXIII.] — WHENCE COMES THE WILL TO BELIEVE?

But it remains for us briefly to inquire, Whether the will by which we believe be itself the gift of God, or whether it arise from that free will which is naturally implanted in us? If we say that it is not the gift of God, we must

---

| 1 Rom. viii. 15. | 2 Rom. ii. 9. | 3 Rom. iii. 30. |
| 4 Matt. v. 6. | 5 John i. 12. | 6 See Matt. vii. 7. |
| 7 Matt. vii. 11. | 8 1 Cor. xv. 56. | 9 Rom. vii. 8. |
| 10 Wisd. viii. 21. | 11 Matt. vii. 7. | 12 Jas. i. 5, 6. |

| 13 Rom. i. 17. | 14 Rom. iv. 5. | 15 Rom. iii. 27. |
| 16 Gal. v. 5. | 17 2 Cor. iv. 16. | 18 Ps. ciii. 5. |
| 19 Eph. ii. 8-10. | 20 Gal. v. 6. | 21 Rom. v. 5. |
| 22 Rom. iii. 21. | 23 Ps. iii. 8. | 24 Gal. ii. 16. |

then incur the fear of supposing that we have discovered some answer to the apostle's reproachful appeal : "What hast thou that thou didst not receive? Now, if thou didst receive it, why dost thou glory, as if thou hadst not received it?"[1] — even some such an answer as this : 'See, we have the will to believe, which we did not receive. See in what we glory, — even in what we did not receive !' If, however, we were to say that this kind of will is nothing but the gift of God, we should then have to fear lest unbelieving and ungodly men might not unreasonably seem to have some fair excuse for their unbelief, in the fact that God has refused to give them this will. Now this that the apostle says, "It is God that worketh in you both to will and to do of His own good pleasure,"[2] belongs already to that grace which faith secures, in order that good works may be within the reach of man, — even the good works which faith achieves through the love which is shed abroad in the heart by the Holy Ghost which is given to us. If we believe that we may attain this grace (and of course believe voluntarily), then the question arises, whence we have this will? — if from nature, why it is not at everybody's command, since the same God made all men? if from God's gift, then again, why is not the gift open to all, since " He will have all men to be saved, and to come unto the knowledge of the truth?"[3]

## CHAP. 58. — THE FREE WILL OF MAN IS AN INTER-MEDIATE POWER.

Let us then, first of all, lay down this proposition, and see whether it satisfies the question before us : that free will, naturally assigned by the Creator to our rational soul, is such a neutral[4] power, as can either incline towards faith, or turn towards unbelief. Consequently a man cannot be said to have even that will with which he believes in God, without having received it ; since this rises at the call of God out of the free will which he received naturally when he was created. God no doubt wishes all men to be saved[3] and to come into the knowledge of the truth ; but yet not so as to take away from them free will, for the good or the evil use of which they may be most righteously judged. This being the case, unbelievers indeed do contrary to the will of God when they do not believe His gospel ; nevertheless they do not therefore overcome His will, but rob their own selves of the great, nay, the very greatest, good, and implicate themselves in penalties of punishment, destined to experience the power of Him in punishments whose mercy in His gifts they despised. Thus God's will is for ever invincible ;

but it would be vanquished, unless it devised what to do with such as despised it, or if these despises could in any way escape from the retribution which He has appointed for such as they. Suppose a master, for example, who should say to his servants, I wish you to labour in my vineyard, and, after your work is done, to feast and take your rest ; but who, at the same time, should require any who refused to work to grind in the mill ever after. Whoever neglected such a command would evidently act contrary to the master's will ; but he would do more than that, — he would vanquish that will, if he also escaped the mill. This, however, cannot possibly happen under the government of God. Whence it is written, "God hath spoken once," — that is, irrevocably, — although the passage may refer also to His one only Word.[5] He then adds what it is which He had irrevocably uttered, saying : "Twice have I heard this, that power belongeth unto God. Also unto Thee, O Lord, doth mercy belong : because Thou wilt render to every man according to his work."[6] He therefore will be guilty unto condemnation under God's power, who shall think too contemptuously of His mercy to believe in Him. But whosoever shall put his trust in Him, and yield himself up to Him, for the forgiveness of all his sins, for the cure of all his corruption, and for the kindling and illumination of his soul by His warmth and light, shall have good works by his grace ; and by them[7] he shall be even in his body redeemed from the corruption of death, crowned, satisfied with blessings, — not temporal, but eternal, — above what we can ask or understand.

## CHAP. 59. — MERCY AND PITY IN THE JUDGMENT OF GOD.

This is the order observed in the psalm, where it is said : " Bless the Lord, O my soul, and forget not all His recompenses ; who forgiveth all thine iniquities ; who healeth all thy diseases ; who redeemeth thy life from destruction ; who crowneth thee with loving-kindness and tender mercy ; who satisfieth thy desire with good things."[8] And lest by any chance these great blessings should be despaired of under the deformity of our old, that is, mortal condition, the Psalmist at once says, "Thy youth shall be renewed like the eagle's ; "[9] as much as to say, All that you have heard belongs to the new man and to the new covenant. Now let us consider together briefly these things, and with delight contemplate the praise of mercy, that is, of the grace of God. " Bless the Lord, O my soul," he says, " and forget not all His recompenses." Observe, he does not say blessings, but *recompenses;*[10] be-

[1] 1 Cor. iv. 7.    [2] Phil. ii. 13.    [3] 1 Tim. ii. 4.
[4] [" *Media vis*," a " midway power," as Dr. Bright translates it; i.e., it is indifferent in itself, and neither good nor bad, but may be *used* for either. — W.]

[5] John i. 1.    [6] Ps. lxii. 11, 12.    [7] Ex quibus.
[8] Ps. ciii. 2-5.    [9] Ps. ciii. 5.
[10] Non tributiones, sed retributiones.

cause He recompenses evil with good. " Who forgiveth all thine iniquities:" this is done in the sacrament of baptism. "Who healeth all thy diseases:" this is effected by the believer in the present life, while the flesh so lusts against the spirit, and the spirit against the flesh, that we do not the things we would;[1] whilst also another law in our members wars against the law of our mind;[2] whilst to will is present indeed to us, but not how to perform that which is good.[3] These are the diseases of a man's old nature, which, however, if we only advance with persevering purpose, are healed by the growth of the new nature day by day, by the faith which operates through love.[4] "Who redeemeth thy life from destruction;" this will take place at the resurrection of the dead in the last day. "Who crowneth thee with loving-kindness and tender mercy;" this shall be accomplished in the day of judgment; for when the righteous King shall sit upon His throne to render to every man according to his works, who shall then boast of having a pure heart? or who shall glory of being clean from sin? It was therefore necessary to mention God's loving-kindness and tender mercy there, where one might expect debts to be demanded and deserts recompensed so strictly as to leave no room for mercy. He crowns, therefore, with loving-kindness and tender mercy; but even so according to works. For he shall be separated to the right hand, to whom, it is said, "I was an hungered, and ye gave me meat."[5] There will, however, be also "judgment without mercy;" but it will be for him "that hath not showed mercy."[6] But "blessed are the merciful: for they shall obtain mercy"[7] of God. Then, as soon as those on the left hand shall have gone into eternal fire, the righteous, too, shall go into everlasting life,[8] because He says: "This is life eternal, that they may know Thee the only true God, and Jesus Christ whom Thou hast sent."[9] And with this knowledge, this vision, this contemplation, shall the desire of their soul be satisfied; for it shall be enough for it to have this and nothing else, — there being nothing more for it to desire, to aspire to, or to require. It was with a craving after this full joy that his heart glowed who said to the Lord Christ, "Show us the Father, and it sufficeth us;" and to whom the answer was returned, "He that hath seen me hath seen the Father."[10] Because He is Himself the eternal life, in order that men may know the one true God, Thee and whom Thou hast sent, Jesus Christ. If, however, he that has seen the Son has also seen the Father, then assuredly he who sees the Father and the Son sees also the Holy Spirit of the Father and the Son. So we

do not take away free will, whilst our soul blesses the Lord and forgets not all His recompenses;[11] nor does it, in ignorance of God's righteousness, wish to set up one of its own;[12] but it believes in Him who justifies the ungodly,[13] and until it arrives at sight, it lives by faith, — even the faith which works by love.[4] And this love is shed abroad in our hearts, not by the sufficiency of our own will, nor by the letter of the law, but by the Holy Ghost who has been given to us.[14]

CHAP. 60 [XXXIV.] — THE WILL TO BELIEVE IS FROM GOD.

Let this discussion suffice, if it satisfactorily meets the question we had to solve. It may be, however, objected in reply, that we must take heed lest some one should suppose that the sin would have to be imputed to God which is committed by free will, if in the passage where it is asked, "What hast thou which thou didst not receive?"[15] the very will by which we believe is reckoned as a gift of God, because it arises out of the free will which we received at our creation. Let the objector, however, attentively observe that this will is to be ascribed to the divine gift, not merely because it arises from our free will, which was created naturally with us; but also because God acts upon us by the incentives of our perceptions, to will and to believe, either externally by evangelical exhortations, where even the commands of the law also do something, if they so far admonish a man of his infirmity that he betakes himself to the grace that justifies by believing; or internally, where no man has in his own control what shall enter into his thoughts, although it appertains to his own will to consent or to dissent. Since God, therefore, in such ways acts upon the reasonable soul in order that it may believe in Him (and certainly there is no ability whatever in free will to believe, unless there be persuasion or summons towards some one in whom to believe), it surely follows that it is God who both works in man the willing to believe, and in all things prevents us with His mercy. To yield our consent, indeed, to God's summons, or to withhold it, is (as I have said) the function of our own will. And this not only does not invalidate what is said, "For what hast thou that thou didst not receive?"[15] but it really confirms it. For the soul cannot receive and possess these gifts, which are here referred to, except by yielding its consent. And thus whatever it possesses, and whatever it receives, is from God; and yet the act of receiving and having belongs, of course, to the receiver and possessor. Now, should any man be for constraining us to examine into this profound mystery, why this person is so per-

[1] Gal. v. 17.        [2] Rom. vii. 23.        [3] Rom. vii. 18.
[4] Gal. v. 6.        [5] Matt. xxv. 35.        [6] Jas. ii. 13.
[7] Matt. v. 7.        [8] Matt. xxv. 46.        [9] John xvii. 3.
[10] John xiv. 8, 9.

[11] Ps. ciii. 2.        [12] Rom. x. 3.        [13] Rom. iv. r
[14] Rom. v. 5.        [15] 1 Cor. iv. 7.

suaded as to yield, and that person is not, there are only two things occurring to me, which I should like to advance as my answer: "O the depth of the riches!"[1] and "Is there unrighteousness with God?"[2] If the man is displeased with such an answer, he must seek more learned disputants; but let him beware lest he find presumptuous ones.

CHAP. 61 [XXXV.] — CONCLUSION OF THE WORK.

Let us at last bring our book to an end. I hardly know whether we have accomplished our purpose at all by our great prolixity. It is not in respect of you, [my Marcellinus,] that I have this misgiving, for I know your faith; but with reference to the minds of those for whose sake you wished me to write, — who so much in opposition to my opinion, but (to speak mildly, and not to mention Him who spoke in His apostles) certainly against not only the opinion of the great Apostle Paul, but also his strong, earnest, and vigilant conflict, prefer maintaining their own views with tenacity to listening to him, when he "beseeches them by the mercies of God," and tells them, "through the grace of God which was given to him, not to think of themselves more highly than they ought to think, but to think soberly, according as God had dealt to every man the measure of faith."[3]

CHAP. 62. — HE RETURNS TO THE QUESTION WHICH MARCELLINUS HAD PROPOSED TO HIM.

But I beg of you to advert to the question which you proposed to me, and to what we have made out of it in the lengthy process of this discussion. You were perplexed how I could have said that it was possible for a man to be without sin, if his will were not wanting, by the help of God's aid, although no man in the present life had ever lived, was living, or would live, of such perfect righteousness. Now, in the books which I formerly addressed to you, I set forth this very question. I said: "If I were asked whether it be possible for a man to be without sin in this life, I should allow the possibility, by the grace of God, and his own free will; for I should have no doubt that the free will itself is of God's grace, — that is, has its place among the gifts of God, — not only as to its existence, but also in respect of its goodness; that is, that it applies itself to doing the commandments of God. And so, God's grace not only shows what ought to be done, but also helps to the possibility of doing what it shows."[4] You seemed to think it absurd, that a thing which was possible should be unexampled. Hence arose the subject treated of in this book; and thus did it devolve on me to show that a thing was possible although no example of it could be found. We accordingly adduced certain cases out of the gospel and of the law, at the beginning of this work, — such as the passing of a camel through the eye of a needle;[5] and the twelve thousand legions of angels, who could fight for Christ, if He pleased;[6] and those nations which God said He could have exterminated at once from the face of His people,[7] — none of which possibilities were ever reduced to fact. To these instances may be added those which are referred to in the Book of Wisdom,[8] suggesting how many are the strange torments and troubles which God was able to employ against ungodly men, by using the creature which was obedient to His beck, which, however, He did not employ. One might also allude to that mountain, which faith could remove into the sea,[9] although, nevertheless, it was never done, so far as we have ever read[10] or heard. Now you see how thoughtless and foolish would be the man who should say that any one of these things is impossible with God, and how opposed to the sense of Scripture would be his assertion. Many other cases of this kind may occur to anybody who reads or thinks, the possibility of which with God we cannot deny, although an example of them be lacking.

CHAP. 63. — AN OBJECTION.

But inasmuch as it may be said that the instances which I have been quoting are divine works, whereas to live righteously is a work that belongs to ourselves, I undertook to show that even this too is a divine work. This I have done in the present book, with perhaps a fuller statement than is necessary, although I seem to myself to have said too little against the opponents of the grace of God. And I am never so much delighted in my treatment of a subject as when Scripture comes most copiously to my aid; and when the question to be discussed requires that "he that glorieth should glory in the Lord;"[11] and that we should in all things lift up our hearts and give thanks to the Lord our God, from whom, "as the Father of lights, every good and every perfect gift cometh down."[12] Now if a gift is not God's gift, because it is wrought by us, or because we act by His gift, then it is not a work of God that "a mountain should be removed into the sea," inasmuch as, according to the Lord's statement, it is by the faith of men that this is possible. Moreover, He attributes the deed to their actual operation: "If ye have faith

1 Rom. xi. 33. 2 Rom. ix. 14. 3 Rom. xii. 1, 3.
4 See his work preceding this, *De Peccat. Meritis*, ii. 7.

5 Matt. xix 24. 6 Matt. xxvi. 53.
7 Deut. xxxi. 3; comp. Judg. ii. 3.
8 Wisdom xvi. 9 Matt. xxi. 21.
10 Augustin, it would then seem, had not met with the statement of Eusebius, as translated by Rufinus (*Hist.* vi. 24), to the effect that Gregory, bishop of Neocæsarea, in Pontus, once performed the miracle of removing a mountain or rock from its place; which Bede also mentions, *Comment.* on Mark xi., Book iii.
11 2 Cor. x. 17. 12 Jas. i. 17.

in yourselves as a grain of mustard-seed, ye shall say unto this mountain, "Be thou removed, and be thou cast into the sea; and it shall be done, and nothing shall be impossible *to you*."[1] Observe how He said "to you," not "to Me" or "to the Father;" and yet it is certain that no man does such a thing without God's gift and operation. See how an instance of perfect righteousness is unexampled among men, and yet is not impossible. For it might be achieved if there were only applied so much of will as suffices for so great a thing. There would, however, be so much will, if there were hidden from us none of those conditions which pertain to righteousness; and at the same time these so delighted our mind, that whatever hindrance of pleasure or pain might else occur, this delight in holiness would prevail over every rival affection. And that this is not realized, is not owing to any intrinsic impossibility, but to God's judicial act. For who can be ignorant, that what he should know is not in man's power; nor does it follow that what he has discovered to be a desirable object is actually desired, unless he also feel a delight in that object, commensurate with its claims on his affection? For this belongs to health of soul.

CHAP. 64 [XXXVI.] — WHEN THE COMMANDMENT TO LOVE IS FULFILLED.

But somebody will perhaps think that we lack nothing for the knowledge of righteousness, since the Lord, when He summarily and briefly expounded His word on earth, informed us that the whole law and the prophets depend on two commandments;[2] nor was He silent as to what these were, but declared them in the plainest words: "Thou shalt love," said He, "the Lord thy God, with all thy heart, and with all thy soul, and with all thy mind;" and "Thou shalt love thy neighbour as thyself."[3] What is more surely true than that, if these be fulfilled, all righteousness is fulfilled? But the man who sets his mind on this truth must also carefully attend to another, — in how many things we all of us offend,[4] while we suppose that what we do is pleasant, or, at all events, not unpleasing, to God whom we love; and afterwards, having (through His inspired word, or else by being warned in some clear and certain way) learned what is not pleasing to Him, we pray to Him that He would forgive us on our repentance. The life of man is full of examples of this. But whence comes it that we fall short of knowing what is pleasing to Him, if it be not that He is to that extent unknown to us? "For now we see through a glass, darkly; but then face to face."[5] Who,

however, can make so bold, on arriving far enough, to say: "Then shall I know even as also I am known,"[5] as to think that they who shall see God will have no greater love towards Him than they have who now believe in Him? or that the one ought to be compared to the other, as if they were very near to each other? Now, if love increases just in proportion as our knowledge of its object becomes more intimate, of course we ought to believe that there is as much wanting now to the fulfilment of righteousness as there is defective in our love of it. A thing may indeed be known or believed, and yet not loved; but it is an impossibility that a thing can be loved which is neither known nor believed. But if the saints, in the exercise of their faith, could arrive at that great love, than which (as the Lord Himself testified) no greater can possibly be exhibited in the present life, — even to lay down their lives for the faith, or for their brethren,[6] — then after their pilgrimage here, in which their walk is by "faith," when they shall have reached the "sight" of that final happiness[7] which we hope for, though as yet we see it not, and wait for in patience,[8] then undoubtedly love itself shall be not only greater than that which we here experience, but far higher than all which we ask or think;[9] and yet it cannot be possibly more than "with all our heart, and with all our soul, and with all our mind." For there remains in us nothing which can be added to the whole; since, if anything did remain, there would not be the whole. Therefore the first commandment about righteousness, which bids us love the Lord with all our heart, and soul, and mind[10] (the next to which is, that we love our neighbour as ourselves), we shall completely fulfil in that life when we shall see face to face.[5] But even now this commandment is enjoined upon us, that we may be reminded what we ought by faith to require, and what we should in our hope look forward to, and, "forgetting the things which are behind, reach forth to the things which are before."[11] And thus, as it appears to me, that man has made a far advance, even in the present life, in the righteousness which is to be perfected hereafter, who has discovered by this very advance how very far removed he is from the completion of righteousness.

CHAP. 65. — IN WHAT SENSE A SINLESS RIGHTEOUS-NESS IN THIS LIFE CAN BE ASSERTED.

Forasmuch, however, as an inferior righteousness may be said to be competent to this life, whereby the just man lives by faith[12] although absent from the Lord, and, therefore, walking

---

[1] Compare Matt. xvii. 20, Mark xi. 23, Luke xvii. 6.
[2] Matt. xxii. 40.    [3] Matt. xxii. 37, 39.    [4] Jas. iii. 2.
[5] 1 Cor. xiii. 12.

[6] John xv. 13.    [7] 2 Cor. v. 7.    [8] Rom. viii. 23.
[9] Eph. iii. 20.    [10] Matt. xxii. 37.    [11] Phil. iii. 13.
[12] Rom. i. 17.

by faith and not yet by sight,[1] — it may be without absurdity said, no doubt, in respect of it, that it is free from sin ; for it ought not to be attributed to it as a fault, that it is not as yet sufficient for so great a love to God as is due to the final, complete, and perfect condition thereof. It is one thing to fail at present in attaining to the fulness of love, and another thing to be swayed by no lust. A man ought therefore to abstain from every unlawful desire, although he loves God now far less than it is possible to love Him when He becomes an object of sight ; just as in matters connected with the bodily senses, the eye can receive no pleasure from any kind of darkness, although it may be unable to look with a firm sight amidst refulgent light. Only let us see to it that we so constitute the soul of man in this corruptible body, that, although it has not yet swallowed up and consumed the motions of earthly lust in that super-eminent perfection of the love of God, it nevertheless, in that inferior righteousness to which we have referred, gives no consent to the aforesaid lust for the purpose of effecting any unlawful thing. In respect, therefore, of that immortal life, the commandment is even now applicable : "Thou shalt love the Lord thy God with all thine heart, and with all thy soul, and with all thy might ; "[2] but in reference to the present life the following : "Let not sin reign in your mortal body, that ye should obey it in the lusts thereof."[3] To the one, again, belongs, "Thou shalt not covet ; "[4] to the other, "Thou shalt not go after thy lusts."[5] To the one it appertains to seek for nothing more than to continue in its perfect state ; to the other it belongs actively to do the duty committed to it, and to hope as its reward for the perfection of the future life, — so that in the one the just man may live forevermore in the sight of that happiness which in this life was his object of desire ; in the other, he may live by that faith whereon rests his desire for the ultimate blessedness as its certain end. (These things being so, it will be sin in the man who lives by faith ever to consent to an unlawful delight, — by committing not only frightful deeds and crimes, but even trifling faults ; sinful, if he lend an ear to a word that ought not to be listened to, or a tongue to a phrase which should not be uttered ; sinful, if he entertains a thought in his heart in such a way as to wish that an evil pleasure were a lawful one, although known to be unlawful by the commandment, — for this amounts to a consent to sin, which would certainly be carried out in act, unless fear of punishment deterred.)[6] Have such just men,

while living by faith, no need to say : "Forgive us our debts, as we forgive our debtors?"[7] And do they prove this to be wrong which is written, "In Thy sight shall no man living be justified?"[8] and this : "If we say that we have no sin, we deceive ourselves, and the truth is not in us?"[9] and, "There is no man that sinneth not ;"[10] and again, "There is not on the earth a righteous man, who doeth good and sinneth not"[11] (for both these statements are expressed in a general future sense, — "sinneth not," "will not sin," — not in the past time, "has not sinned")? — and all other places of this purport contained in the Holy Scripture? Since, however, these passages cannot possibly be false, it plainly follows, to my mind, that whatever be the quality or extent of the righteousness which we may definitely ascribe to the present life, there is not a man living in it who is absolutely free from all sin ; and that it is necessary for every one to give, that it may be given to him ;[12] and to forgive, that it may be forgiven him ;[13] and whatever righteousness he has, not to presume that he has it of himself, but from the grace of God, who justifies him, and still to go on hungering and thirsting for righteousness[14] from Him who is the living bread,[15] and with whom is the fountain of life ;[16] who works in His saints, whilst labouring amidst temptation in this life, their justification in such manner that He may still have somewhat to impart to them liberally when they ask, and something mercifully to forgive them when they confess.

CHAP. 66. — ALTHOUGH PERFECT RIGHTEOUSNESS BE NOT FOUND HERE ON EARTH, IT IS STILL NOT IMPOSSIBLE.

But let objectors find, if they can, any man, while living under the weight of this corruption, in whom God has no longer anything to forgive ; unless nevertheless they acknowledge that such an individual has been aided in the attainment of his good character not merely by the teaching of the law which God gave, but also by the infusion of the Spirit of grace — they will incur the charge of ungodliness itself, not of this or that particular sin. Of course they are not at all able to discover such a man, if they receive in a becoming manner the testimony of the divine writings. Still, for all that, it must not by any means be said that the possibility is lacking to God whereby the will of man can be so assisted, that there can be accomplished in every respect even now in a man, not that righteousness only which is of faith,[17] but that also in accordance with which we shall by and by have to live for ever in the very vision of God. For if he should now

---

[1] 2 Cor. v. 7.    [2] Deut. vi. 5.    [3] Rom. vi. 12.
[4] Ex. xx. 17.    [5] Ecclus. xviii. 30.
[6] The Benedictine editor is not satisfied with the place of the lines in the parenthesis. He would put them in an earlier position, perhaps before the clause beginning with, "Only let us see to it," etc.

[7] Matt. vi. 12.    [8] Ps. cxliii. 2.    [9] 1 John i. 8.
[10] 1 Kings viii. 46.    [11] Ecclus. vii. 21.    [12] Luke vi. 30, 38.
[13] Luke xi. 4.    [14] Matt. v. 6.    [15] John vi. 51.
[16] Ps. xxxvi. 9.    [17] Rom. x. 6.

wish even that this corruptible in any particular man should put on incorruption,[1] and to command him so to live among mortal men (not destined himself to die) that his old nature should be wholly and entirely withdrawn, and there should be no law in his members warring against the law of his mind,[2] — moreover, that he should discover God to be everywhere present, as the saints shall hereafter know and behold Him, — who will madly venture to affirm that this is impossible? Men, however, ask why He does not do this; but they who raise the question consider not duly the fact that they are human. I am quite certain that, as nothing is impossible with God,[3] so also there is no iniquity with Him.[4] Equally sure am I that He resists the proud, and gives grace to the humble.[5] I know also that to him who had a thorn in the flesh, the messenger of Satan to buffet him, lest he should be exalted above measure, it was said, when he besought God for its removal once, twice, nay thrice: " My grace is sufficient for thee; for my strength is made perfect in weakness." [6] There is, therefore, in the hidden depths of God's judgments, a certain reason why every mouth even of the righteous should be shut in its own praise, and only opened for the praise of God. But what this certain reason is, who can search, who investigate, who know? So "unsearchable are His judgments, and His ways past finding out! For who hath known the mind of the Lord? or who hath been his counsellor? or who hath first given to Him, and it shall be recompensed unto him again? For of Him, and through Him, and to Him, are all things: to whom be glory for ever. Amen." [7]

---

[1] 1 Cor. xv. 53.    [2] Rom. vii. 23.    [3] Luke i. 37.
[4] Rom. ix. 14.    [5] Jas. iv. 6.

[6] 2 Cor. xii. 7–9.      [7] Rom. xi. 33–36.

# A TREATISE ON NATURE AND GRACE.

# EXTRACT FROM AUGUSTIN'S "RETRACTATIONS,"

## Book II. Chap. 42,

### *ON THE FOLLOWING TREATISE,*

## "DE NATURA ET GRATIA."

---

"At that time also there came into my hands a certain book of Pelagius', in which he defends, with all the argumentative skill he could muster, the nature of man, in opposition to the grace of God whereby the unrighteous is justified and we become Christians. The treatise which contains my reply to him, and in which I defend grace, not indeed as in opposition to nature, but as that which liberates and controls nature, I have entitled *On Nature and Grace*. In this work sundry short passages, which were quoted by Pelagius as the words of the Roman bishop and martyr, Xystus, were vindicated by myself[1] as if they really were the words of this Sixtus. For this I thought them at the time; but I afterwards discovered, that Sextus the heathen philosopher, and not Xystus the Christian bishop, was their author. This treatise of mine begins with the words: 'The book which you sent me.'"

---

[1] In chap. 77.

# NOTE ON THE FOLLOWING WORK.

In a letter (169th [1]) to Evodius, written in the course of the year A.D. 415, Augustin assigned to this work, *On Nature and Grace*, the last place of several treatises written in that year. "I have also written," says he, "an extensive book in opposition to the heresy of Pelagius, at the request of some brethren, whom he had persuaded to accept a very pernicious opinion against the grace of Christ." The work had been begun, but was not completed, when Orosius sailed from Africa to Palestine, in the spring of this year of 415; for, shortly after his arrival there, at a council in Jerusalem, where Pelagius was present, he expressly affirmed, "that the blessed Augustin had prepared a very complete answer to Pelagius' book, two of whose followers had presented the work to him, and requested him to reply to it." Jerome, also, at this time mentioned a certain production of Augustin's, which he had not yet seen, wherein it was said that he had expressly opposed Pelagius. His words, which occur in his third dialogue against the heresy of Pelagius, are these: "It is said that he is preparing other treatises likewise, especially against your name." Augustin, however, did not actually employ in this work of his the *name* of Pelagius, whose book he was refuting, in order that (as he says in his letter [186th] to Paulinus) he might not by personal irritation drive him into a more incurable degree of opposition; for he hoped to be of some service to his opponent, if by still maintaining friendly terms with him he might be able to spare his feelings, although he could not in duty show leniency to his writings. Thus, at least, he expresses his mind, in his book *On the Proceedings of Pelagius*, ch. xxiii. No. 47. In this latter passage he subjoins a letter which he had received from Timasius and Jacobus, containing the expression of great gratitude to Augustin on receiving his volume *On Nature and Grace*, in which they expressed "their agreeable surprise" at the answers he had furnished to them "on every point" of the Pelagian controversy.

In the following year Augustin despatched this work, along with Pelagius' own book, to John, bishop of Jerusalem, in order that that prelate might at length become acquainted with the views of the new heresiarch, accompanying the books with a letter to the bishop [179th]. In the course of this year 416, he had the same two treatises (his own and Pelagius') forwarded to Pope Innocent, with a letter [177th] sent in the name of five bishops, to which Innocent returned an answer [183d]. It may be here stated, that in this last-mentioned letter [183, n. 5], and in the foregoing epistle [177, n. 6], there is honourable mention made of Timasius and Jacobus, as "conscientious and honourable young men, servants of God, who had relinquished the hope which they had in the world, and continued diligently to serve God." The same persons are described in another epistle [179, n. 2] as "young men of very honourable birth, and highly educated;" and in the work *On the Proceedings of Pelagius*, ch. xxiii. No 47, they are called "servants of God, good, and honourable men."

Julianus [who espoused the side of Pelagius], in his work addressed to Florus (book iv. n. 112, of the Imperfect Work),[2] quotes this treatise of Augustin's as addressed to Timasius, and calumniously pronounces it to be written "against free will"

---

[1] See vol. i. p. 543.

[2] [i.e., the work of Augustin against Julianus, which was left incomplete at his death, and hence is called the Imperfect Work. — W.]

# CONTENTS OF THE TREATISE "ON NATURE AND GRACE."

# A TREATISE ON NATURE AND GRACE, AGAINST PELAGIUS;

## *BY AURELIUS AUGUSTIN, BISHOP OF HIPPO;*

### CONTAINED IN ONE BOOK, ADDRESSED TO TIMASIUS AND JACOBUS.

#### WRITTEN IN THE YEAR OF OUR LORD 415.

---

HE BEGINS WITH A STATEMENT OF WHAT IS TO BE INVESTIGATED CONCERNING NATURE AND GRACE; HE SHOWS THAT NATURE, AS PROPAGATED FROM THE FLESH OF THE SINFUL ADAM, BEING NO LONGER WHAT GOD MADE IT AT FIRST, — FAULTLESS AND SOUND, — REQUIRES THE AID OF GRACE, IN ORDER THAT IT MAY BE REDEEMED FROM THE WRATH OF GOD AND REGULATED FOR THE PERFECTION OF RIGHTEOUSNESS: THAT THE PENAL FAULT OF NATURE LEADS TO A MOST RIGHTEOUS RETRIBUTION: WHILST GRACE ITSELF IS NOT RENDERED TO ANY DESERTS OF OURS, BUT IS GIVEN GRATUITOUSLY; AND THEY WHO ARE NOT DELIVERED BY IT ARE JUSTLY CONDEMNED. HE AFTERWARDS REFUTES, WITH ANSWERS ON EVERY SEVERAL POINT, A WORK BY PELAGIUS, WHO SUPPORTS THIS SELF-SAME NATURE IN OPPOSITION TO GRACE; AMONG OTHER THINGS ESPECIALLY, IN HIS DESIRE TO RECOMMEND THE OPINION THAT A MAN CAN LIVE WITHOUT SIN, HE CONTENDED THAT NATURE HAD NOT BEEN WEAKENED AND CHANGED BY SIN; FOR, OTHERWISE, THE MATTER OF SIN (WHICH HE THINKS ABSURD) WOULD BE ITS PUNISHMENT, IF THE SINNER WERE WEAKENED TO SUCH A DEGREE THAT HE COMMITTED MORE SIN. HE GOES ON TO ENUMERATE SUNDRY RIGHTEOUS MEN BOTH OF THE OLD AND OF THE NEW TESTAMENTS: DEEMING THESE TO HAVE BEEN FREE FROM SIN, HE ALLEGED THE POSSIBILITY OF NOT SINNING TO BE INHERENT IN MAN; AND THIS HE ATTRIBUTED TO GOD'S GRACE, ON THE GROUND THAT GOD IS THE AUTHOR OF THAT NATURE IN WHICH IS INSEPARABLY INHERENT THIS POSSIBILITY OF AVOIDING SIN. TOWARDS THE END OF THIS TREATISE THERE IS AN EXAMINATION OF SUNDRY EXTRACTS FROM OLD WRITERS, WHICH PELAGIUS ADDUCED IN SUPPORT OF HIS VIEWS, AND EXPRESSLY FROM HILARY, AMBROSE, AND EVEN AUGUSTIN HIMSELF.

CHAP. I [I.] — THE OCCASION OF PUBLISHING THIS WORK; WHAT GOD'S RIGHTEOUSNESS IS.

THE book which you sent to me, my beloved sons, Timasius and Jacobus, I have read through hastily, but not indifferently, omitting only the few points which are plain enough to everybody; and I saw in it a man inflamed with most ardent zeal against those, who, when in their sins they ought to censure human will, are more forward in accusing the nature of men, and thereby endeavour to excuse themselves. He shows too great a fire against this evil, which even authors of secular literature have severely censured with the exclamation: "The human race falsely complains of its own nature!"[1] This same senti-ment your author also has strongly insisted upon, with all the powers of his talent. I fear, however, that he will chiefly help those "who have a zeal for God, but not according to knowledge," who, "being ignorant of God's righteousness, and going about to establish their own righteousness, have not submitted themselves to the righteousness of God."[2] Now, what the righteousness of God is, which is spoken of here, he immediately afterwards explains by adding: "For Christ is the end of the law for righteousness to every one that believeth."[3] This righteousness of God, therefore, lies not in the commandment of the law, which excites fear, but in the aid afforded by the grace of Christ,

---

[1] See Sallust's Prologue to his *Jugurtha*.

[2] Rom. x. 2, 3.

[3] Rom. x. 4.

to which alone the fear of the law, as of a schoolmaster,[1] usefully conducts. Now, the man who understands this understands why he is a Christian. For " If righteousness came by the law, then Christ is dead in vain." [2]  If, however, He did not die in vain, in Him only is the ungodly man justified, and to him, on believing in Him who justifies the ungodly, faith is reckoned for righteousness.[3]  For all men have sinned and come short of the glory of God, being justified freely by His blood.[4]  But all those who do not think themselves to belong to the " all who have sinned and fall short of the glory of God," have of course no need to become Christians, because "they that be whole need not a physician, but they that are sick ; " [5] whence it is, that He came not to call the righteous, but sinners to repentance.[6]

### CHAP. 2 [II.] — FAITH IN CHRIST NOT NECESSARY TO SALVATION, IF A MAN WITHOUT IT CAN LEAD A RIGHTEOUS LIFE.

Therefore the nature of the human race, generated from the flesh of the one transgressor, if it is self-sufficient for fulfilling the law and for perfecting righteousness, ought to be sure of its reward, that is, of everlasting life, even if in any nation or at any former time faith in the blood of Christ was unknown to it.  For God is not so unjust as to defraud righteous persons of the reward of righteousness, because there has not been announced to them the mystery of Christ's divinity and humanity, which was manifested in the flesh.[7]  For how could they believe what they had not heard of; or how could they hear without a preacher? [8]  For " faith cometh by hearing, and hearing by the word of Christ." But I say (adds he) : Have they not heard? " Yea, verily ; their sound went out into all the earth, and their words unto the ends of the world." [9]  Before, however, all this had been accomplished, before the actual preaching of the gospel reaches the ends of all the earth — because there are some remote nations still (although it is said they are very few) to whom the preached gospel has not found its way, — what must human nature do, or what has it done — for it had either not heard that all this was to take place, or has not yet learnt that it was accomplished — but believe in God who made heaven and earth, by whom also it perceived by nature that it had been itself created, and lead a right life, and thus accomplish His will, uninstructed with any faith in the death and resurrection of Christ?  Well, if this could have been done, or can still be done, then for my part I have to say what the apostle said in regard to

the law : " Then Christ died in vain." [2]  For if he said this about the law, which only the nation of the Jews received, how much more justly may it be said of the law of nature, which the whole human race has received, " If righteousness come by nature, then Christ died in vain."  If, however, Christ did not die in vain, then human nature cannot by any means be justified and redeemed from God's most righteous wrath — in a word, from punishment — except by faith and the sacrament of the blood of Christ.

### CHAP. 3 [III.] — NATURE WAS CREATED SOUND AND WHOLE ; IT WAS AFTERWARDS CORRUPTED BY SIN.

Man's nature, indeed, was created at first faultless and without any sin ; but that nature of man in which every one is born from Adam, now wants the Physician, because it is not sound. All good qualities, no doubt, which it still possesses in its make, life, senses, intellect, it has of the Most High God, its Creator and Maker. But the flaw, which darkens and weakens all those natural goods, so that it has need of illumination and healing, it has not contracted from its blameless Creator — but from that original sin, which it committed by free will.  Accordingly, criminal nature has its part in most righteous punishment.  For, if we are now newly created in Christ,[10] we were, for all that, children of wrath, even as others,[11] " but God, who is rich in mercy, for His great love wherewith He loved us, even when we were dead in sins, hath quickened us together with Christ, by whose grace we were saved." [12]

### CHAP. 4 [IV.] — FREE GRACE.

This grace, however, of Christ, without which neither infants nor adults can be saved, is not rendered for any merits, but is given *gratis*, on account of which it is also called *grace*.  " Being justified," says the apostle, " freely through His blood." [13]  Whence they, who are not liberated through grace, either because they are not yet able to hear, or because they are unwilling to obey ; or again because they did not receive, at the time when they were unable on account of youth to hear, that bath of regeneration, which they might have received and through which they might have been saved, are indeed justly condemned ; because they are not without sin, either that which they have derived from their birth, or that which they have added from their own misconduct.  " For all have sinned " — whether in Adam or in themselves — " and come short of the glory of God." [14]

---

1 Gal. iil. 24.
2 Gal. ii. 21.
3 Rom. iv. 5.
4 Rom. iii 23, 24.
5 Matt. ix. 12.
6 Matt ix. 13.
7 1 Tim. iii. 16.
8 Rom. x. 14.
9 Rom. x. 17, 18.
10 2 Cor. v. 17.
11 Eph. ii. 3.
12 Eph. ii. 4, 5.
13 Rom. iii. 24.
14 Rom. iii. 23.

## CHAP. 5 [V.] — IT WAS A MATTER OF JUSTICE THAT ALL SHOULD BE CONDEMNED.

The entire mass, therefore, incurs penalty; and if the deserved punishment of condemnation were rendered to all, it would without doubt be righteously rendered. They, therefore, who are delivered therefrom by grace are called, not vessels of their own merits, but "vessels of mercy."[1] But of whose mercy, if not His who sent Christ Jesus into the world to save sinners, whom He foreknew, and foreordained, and called, and justified, and glorified?[2] Now, who could be so madly insane as to fail to give ineffable thanks to the Mercy which liberates whom it would? The man who correctly appreciated the whole subject could not possibly blame the justice of God in wholly condemning all men whatsoever.

## CHAP. 6 [VI.] — THE PELAGIANS HAVE VERY STRONG AND ACTIVE MINDS.

If we are simply wise according to the Scriptures, we are not compelled to dispute against the grace of Christ, and to make statements attempting to show that human nature both requires no Physician, — in infants, because it is whole and sound; and in adults, because it is able to suffice for itself in attaining righteousness, if it will. Men no doubt seem to urge acute opinions on these points, but it is only word-wisdom,[3] by which the cross of Christ is made of none effect. This, however, "is not the wisdom which descendeth from above."[4] The words which follow in the apostle's statement I am unwilling to quote; for we would rather not be thought to do an injustice to our friends, whose very strong and active minds we should be sorry to see running in a perverse, instead of an upright, course.

## CHAP. 7 [VII.] — HE PROCEEDS TO CONFUTE THE WORK OF PELAGIUS; HE REFRAINS AS YET FROM MENTIONING PELAGIUS' NAME.

However ardent, then, is the zeal which the author of the book you have forwarded to me entertains against those who find a defence for their sins in the infirmity of human nature; not less, nay even much greater, should be our eagerness in preventing all attempts to render the cross of Christ of none effect. Of none effect, however, it is rendered, if it be contended that by any other means than by Christ's own sacrament it is possible to attain to righteousness and everlasting life. This is actually done in the book to which I refer — I will not say by its author wittingly, lest I should express the judgment that he ought not to be accounted even a

Christian, but, as I rather believe, unconsciously. He has done it, no doubt, with much power; I only wish that the ability he has displayed were sound and less like that which insane persons are accustomed to exhibit.

## CHAP. 8. — A DISTINCTION DRAWN BY PELAGIUS BETWEEN THE POSSIBLE AND ACTUAL.

For he first of all makes a distinction: "It is one thing," says he, "to inquire whether a thing can be, which has respect to its possibility only; and another thing, whether or not it is." This distinction, nobody doubts, is true enough; for it follows that whatever is, was able to be; but it does not therefore follow that what is able to be, also is. Our Lord, for instance, raised Lazarus; He unquestionably was able to do so. But inasmuch as He did not raise up Judas,[5] must we therefore contend that He was unable to do so? He certainly was able, but He would not. For if He had been willing, He could have effected this too. For the Son quickeneth whomsoever He will.[6] Observe, however, what he means by this distinction, true and manifest enough in itself, and what he endeavours to make out of it. "We are treating," says he, "of possibility only; and to pass from this to something else, except in the case of some certain fact, we deem to be a very serious and extraordinary process." This idea he turns over again and again, in many ways and at great length, so that no one would suppose that he was inquiring about any other point than the possibility of not committing sin. Among the many passages in which he treats of this subject, occurs the following: "I once more repeat my position: I say that it is possible for a man to be without sin. What do you say? That it is impossible for a man to be without sin? But I do not say," he adds, "that there is a man without sin; nor do you say, that there is not a man without sin. Our contention is about what is possible, and not possible; not about what is, and is not." He then enumerates certain passages of Scripture,[7] which are usually alleged in opposition to them, and insists that they have nothing to do with the question, which is really in dispute, as to the possibility or impossibility of a man's being without sin. This is what he says: "No man indeed is clean from pollution; and, There is no man that sinneth not; and, There is not a just man upon the earth; and, There is none that doeth good. There are these and similar passages in Scripture," says he, "but they testify to the point of not being, not of not being able; for by testimonies of this sort it is shown what kind of per-

---

[1] Rom. ix. 23.　　　[2] Rom. viii. 29, 30.　　　[3] 1 Cor. i. 17.
[4] Jas. iii. 15.

[5] Peter Lombard refers to this passage of Augustin, to show that God can do many things which He will not do. See his 1 *Sent. Dist.* 43, last chapter.
[6] John v. 21.
[7] Job xiv. 2; 1 Kings viii. 46; Eccles. vii. 21; Ps. xiv. 1.

sons certain men were at such and such a time, not that they were unable to be something else. Whence they are justly found to be blameworthy. If, however, they had been of such a character, simply because they were unable to be anything else, they are free from blame."

though a man could not be justified at all without the grace of Christ, he would absolve him, if he dared, in accordance with his words, to the effect that, "if a man were of such a character, because he could not possibly have been of any other, he would be free from all blame."

## CHAP. 9 [VIII.] — EVEN THEY WHO WERE NOT ABLE TO BE JUSTIFIED ARE CONDEMNED.

See what he has said. I, however, affirm that an infant born in a place where it was not possible for him to be admitted to the baptism of Christ, and being overtaken by death, was placed in such circumstances, that is to say, died without the bath of regeneration, because it was not possible for him to be otherwise. He would therefore absolve him, and, in spite of the Lord's sentence, open to him the kingdom of heaven. The apostle, however, does not absolve him, when he says: "By one man sin entered into the world, and death by sin; by which death passed upon all men, for that all have sinned." [1] Rightly, therefore, by virtue of that condemnation which runs throughout the mass, is he not admitted into the kingdom of heaven, although he was not only not a Christian, but was unable to become one.

## CHAP. 10 [IX.] — HE COULD NOT BE JUSTIFIED, WHO HAD NOT HEARD OF THE NAME OF CHRIST; RENDERING THE CROSS OF CHRIST OF NONE EFFECT.

But they say: " He is not condemned; because the statement that all sinned in Adam, was not made because of the sin which is derived from one's birth, but because of imitation of him." If, therefore, Adam is said to be the author of all the sins which followed his own, because he was the first sinner of the human race, then how is it that Abel, rather than Christ, is not placed at the head of all the righteous, because he was the first righteous man? But I am not speaking of the case of an infant. I take the instance of a young man, or an old man, who has died in a region where he could not hear of the name of Christ. Well, could such a man have become righteous by nature and free will; or could he not? If they contend that he could, then see what it is to render the cross of Christ of none effect, [2] to contend that any man without it, can be justified by the law of nature and the power of his will. We may here also say, then is Christ dead in vain, [3] forasmuch as all might accomplish so much as this, even if He had never died; and if they should be unrighteous, they would be so because they wished to be, not because they were unable to be righteous. But even

## CHAP. 11 [X.] — GRACE SUBTLY ACKNOWLEDGED BY PELAGIUS.

He then starts an objection to his own position, as if, indeed, another person had raised it, and says: " ' A man,' you will say, ' may possibly be [without sin]; but it is by the grace of God.'" He then at once subjoins the following, as if in answer to his own suggestion: " I thank you for your kindness, because you are not merely content to withdraw your opposition to my statement, which you just now opposed, or barely to acknowledge it; but you actually go so far as to approve it. For to say, ' A man may possibly, but by this or by that,' is in fact nothing else than not only to assent to its possibility, but also to show the mode and condition of its possibility. Nobody, therefore, gives a better assent to the possibility of anything than the man who allows the condition thereof; because, without the thing itself, it is not possible for a condition to be." After this he raises another objection against himself: " ' But, you will say, ' you here seem to reject the grace of God, inasmuch as you do not even mention it;'" and he then answers the objection: " Now, is it I that reject grace, who by acknowledging the thing must needs also confess the means by which it may be effected, or you, who by denying the thing do undoubtedly also deny whatever may be the means through which the thing is accomplished?" He forgot that he was now answering one who does not deny the thing, and whose objection he had just before set forth in these words: " A man may possibly be [without sin]; but it is by the grace of God." How then does that man deny the possibility, in defence of which his opponent earnestly contends, when he makes the admission to that opponent that " the thing is possible, but only by the grace of God?" That, however, after he is dismissed who already acknowledges the essential thing, he still has a question against those who maintain the impossibility of a man's being without sin, what is it to us? Let him ply his questions against any opponents he pleases, provided he only confesses this, which cannot be denied without the most criminal impiety, that without the grace of God a man cannot be without sin. He says, indeed: " Whether he confesses it to be by grace, or by aid, or by mercy, whatever that be by which a man can be without sin, — every one acknowledges the thing itself."

---

[1] Rom. v. 12.    [2] 1 Cor. i. 1.    [3] Gal. ii. 21.

CHAP. 12 [XI.] — IN OUR DISCUSSIONS ABOUT GRACE, WE DO NOT SPEAK OF THAT WHICH RELATES TO THE CONSTITUTION OF OUR NATURE, BUT TO ITS RESTORATION.

I confess to your love, that when I read those words I was filled with a sudden joy, because he did not deny the grace of God by which alone a man can be justified; for it is this which I mainly detest and dread in discussions of this kind. But when I went on to read the rest, I began to have my suspicions, first of all, from the similes he employs. For he says: "If I were to say, man is able to dispute; a bird is able to fly; a hare is able to run; without mentioning at the same time the instruments by which these acts can be accomplished — that is, the tongue, the wings, and the legs; should I then have denied the conditions of the various offices, when I acknowledged the very offices themselves?" It is at once apparent that he has here instanced such things as are by nature efficient; for the members of the bodily structure which are here mentioned are created with natures of such a kind — the tongue, the wings, the legs. He has not here posited any such thing as we wish to have understood by *grace*, without which no man is justified; for this is a topic which is concerned about the cure, not the constitution, of natural functions. Entertaining, then, some apprehensions, I proceeded to read all the rest, and I soon found that my suspicions had not been unfounded.

CHAP. 13 [XII.] — THE SCOPE AND PURPOSE OF THE LAW'S THREATENINGS; "PERFECT WAYFARERS."

But before I proceed further, see what he has said. When treating the question about the difference of sins, and starting as an objection to himself, what certain persons allege, "that some sins are light by their very frequency, their constant irruption making it impossible that they should be all of them avoided;" he thereupon denied that it was "proper that they should be censured even as light offences, if they cannot possibly be wholly avoided." He of course does not notice the Scriptures of the New Testament, wherein we learn [1] that the intention of the law in its censure is this, that, by reason of the transgressions which men commit, they may flee for refuge to the grace of the Lord, who has pity upon them — "the schoolmaster" [2] "shutting them up unto the same faith which should afterwards be revealed;" [3] that by it their transgressions may be forgiven, and then not again be committed, by God's assisting grace. The road indeed belongs to all who are progressing in it; although it is they who make a good advance that are called "perfect travellers." That, however, is the height of perfection which admits of no addition, when the goal to which men tend has begun to be possessed.

CHAP. 14 [XIII.] — REFUTATION OF PELAGIUS.

But the truth is, the question which is proposed to him — "Are you even yourself without sin?" — does not really belong to the subject in dispute. What, however, he says, — that "it is rather to be imputed to his own negligence that he is not without sin," is no doubt well spoken; but then he should deem it to be his duty even to pray to God that this faulty negligence get not the dominion over him, — the prayer that a certain man once put up, when he said: "Order my steps according to Thy word, and let not any iniquity have dominion over me," [4] — lest, whilst relying on his own diligence as on strength of his own, he should fail to attain to the true righteousness either by this way, or by that other method in which, no doubt, perfect righteousness is to be desired and hoped for.

CHAP. 15 [XIV.] — NOT EVERYTHING [OF DOCTRINAL TRUTH] IS WRITTEN IN SCRIPTURE IN SO MANY WORDS.

That, too, which is said to him, "that it is nowhere written in so many words, A man can be without sin," he easily refutes thus: "That the question here is not in what precise words each doctrinal statement is made." It is perhaps not without reason that, while in several passages of Scripture we may find it said that men are without excuse, it is nowhere found that any man is described as being without sin, except Him only, of whom it is plainly said, that "He knew no sin." [5] Similarly, we read in the passage where the subject is concerning priests: "He was in all points tempted like as we are, only without sin," [6] — meaning, of course, in that flesh which bore the likeness of sinful flesh, although it was not sinful flesh; a likeness, indeed, which it would not have borne if it had not been in every other respect the same as sinful flesh. How, however, we are to understand this: "Whosoever is born of God doth not commit sin; neither can he sin, for his seed remaineth in him;" [7] while the Apostle John himself, as if he had not been born of God, or else were addressing men who had not been born of God, lays down this position: "If we say that we have no sin, we deceive ourselves, and the truth is not in us," [8] — I have already explained, with such care as I was able, in those books which I wrote to Marcellinus on this very subject. [9] It seems,

---

[1] We have read *discimus*, not *dicimus*.
[2] Gal. iii. 24.     [3] Gal. iii. 23.
[4] Ps. cxix. 133.     [5] 2 Cor. v. 21.     [6] Heb. iv. 15.
[7] 1 John iii. 9.     [8] 1 John i. 8.
[9] See the *De Peccat. Meritis et Remissione*, ii. 8-10.

moreover, to me to be an interpretation worthy of acceptance to regard the clause of the above quoted passage: "Neither can he sin," as if it meant: *He ought not to commit sin.* For who could be so foolish as to say that sin ought to be committed, when, in fact, sin is sin, for no other reason than that it ought not to be committed?

### CHAP. 16 [XV.] — PELAGIUS CORRUPTS A PASSAGE OF THE APOSTLE JAMES BY ADDING A NOTE OF INTERROGATION.

Now that passage, in which the Apostle James says: "But the tongue can no man tame,"[1] does not appear to me to be capable of the interpretation which he would put upon it, when he expounds it, "as if it were written by way of reproach; as much as to say: Can no man, then, tame the tongue? As if in a reproachful tone, which would say: You are able to tame wild beasts; cannot you tame the tongue? As if it were an easier thing to tame the tongue than to subjugate wild beasts." I do not think that this is the meaning of the passage. For, if he had meant such an opinion as this to be entertained of the facility of taming the tongue, there would have followed in the sequel of the passage a comparison of that member with the beasts. As it is, however, it simply goes on to say: "The tongue is an unruly evil, full of deadly poison,"[1] — such, of course, as is more noxious than that of beasts and creeping things. For while the one destroys the flesh, the other kills the soul. For, "The mouth that belieth slayeth the soul."[2] It is not, therefore, as if this is an easier achievement than the taming of beasts that St. James pronounced the statement before us, or would have others utter it; but he rather aims at showing what a great evil in man his tongue is — so great, indeed, that it cannot be tamed by any man, although even beasts are tameable by human beings. And he said this, not with a view to our permitting, through our neglect, the continuance of so great an evil to ourselves, but in order that we might be induced to request the help of divine grace for the taming of the tongue. For he does not say: "None can tame the tongue;" but "*No man;*" in order that, when it is tamed, we may acknowledge it to be effected by the mercy of God, the help of God, the grace of God. The soul, therefore, should endeavour to tame the tongue, and while endeavouring should pray for assistance; the tongue, too, should beg for the taming of the tongue, — He being the tamer who said to His disciples: "It is not ye that speak, but the Spirit of your Father which speaketh in you."[3] Thus, we are warned by the precept to do this, — namely, to make the attempt, and, failing

in our own strength, to pray for the help of God.

### CHAP. 17 [XVI.] — EXPLANATION OF THIS TEXT CONTINUED.

Accordingly, after emphatically describing the evil of the tongue — saying, among other things: "My brethren, these things ought not so to be"[4] — he at once, after finishing some remarks which arose out of his subject, goes on to add this advice, showing by what help those things would not happen, which (as he said) ought not: "Who is a wise man and endowed with knowledge among you? Let him show out of a good conversation his works with meekness of wisdom. But if ye have bitter envying and strife in your hearts, glory not and lie not against the truth. This wisdom descendeth not from above, but is earthly, sensual, devilish. For where there is envying and strife, there is confusion and every evil work. But the wisdom that is from above is first pure, then peaceable, gentle, and easy to be entreated, full of mercy and good fruits, without partiality, and without hypocrisy."[5] This is the wisdom which tames the tongue; it descends from above, and springs from no human heart. Will any one, then, dare to divorce it from the grace of God, and with most arrogant vanity place it in the power of man? Why should I pray to God that it be accorded me, if it may be had of man? Ought we not to object to this prayer lest injury be done to free will which is self-sufficient in the possibility of nature for discharging all the duties of righteousness? We ought, then, to object also to the Apostle James himself, who admonishes us in these words: "If any of you lack wisdom, let him ask of God, that giveth to all men liberally, and upbraideth not, and it shall be given him; but let him ask in faith, nothing doubting."[6] This is the faith to which the commandments drive us, in order that the law may prescribe our duty and faith accomplish it.[7] For through the tongue, which no man can tame, but only the wisdom which comes down from above, "in many things we all of us offend."[8] For this truth also the same apostle pronounced in no other sense than that in which he afterwards declares: "The tongue no man can tame."[1]

### CHAP. 18 [XVII.] — WHO MAY BE SAID TO BE IN THE FLESH.

There is a passage which nobody could place against these texts with the similar purpose of showing the impossibility of not sinning: "The wisdom of the flesh is enmity against God; for it is not subject to the law of God, neither indeed

---

[1] Jas. iii. 8.    [2] Wisd. i. 11.    [3] Matt. x. 20.

[4] Jas. iii. 10.    [5] Jas. iii. 13-17.    [6] Jas. i. 5, 6.
[7] Ut lex imperet et fides impetret.    [8] Jas. iii. 2.

can be ; so then they that are in the flesh cannot please God ; "[1] for he here mentions the wisdom of the flesh, not the wisdom which cometh from above : moreover, it is manifest, that in this passage, by the phrase, "being in the flesh," are signified, not those who have not yet quitted the body, but those who live according to the flesh. The question, however, we are discussing does not lie in this point. But what I want to hear from him, if I can, is about those who live according to the Spirit, and who on this account are not, in a certain sense, in the flesh, even while they still live here, — whether they, by God's grace, live according to the Spirit, or are sufficient for themselves, natural capability having been bestowed on them when they were created, and their own proper will besides. Whereas the fulfilling of the law is nothing else than love ;[2] and God's love is shed abroad in our hearts, not by our own selves, but by the Holy Ghost which is given to us.[3]

### CHAP. 19.—SINS OF IGNORANCE ; TO WHOM WISDOM IS GIVEN BY GOD ON THEIR REQUESTING IT.

He further treats of sins of ignorance, and says that "a man ought to be very careful to avoid ignorance ; and that ignorance is blameworthy for this reason, because it is through his own neglect that a man is ignorant of that which he certainly must have known if he had only applied diligence ; " whereas he prefers disputing all things rather than to pray, and say : " Give me understanding, that I may learn Thy commandments."[4] It is, indeed, one thing to have taken no pains to know what sins of negligence were apparently expiated even through divers sacrifices of the law ; it is another thing to wish to understand, to be unable, and then to act contrary to the law, through not understanding what it would have done. We are accordingly enjoined to ask of God wisdom, "who giveth to all men liberally ; "[5] that is, of course, to all men who ask in such a manner, and to such an extent, as so great a matter requires in earnestness of petition.

### CHAP. 20 [XVIII.] — WHAT PRAYER PELAGIUS WOULD ADMIT TO BE NECESSARY.

He confesses that "sins which have been committed do notwithstanding require to be divinely expiated, and that the Lord must be entreated because of them," — that is, for the purpose, of course, of obtaining pardon ; "because that which has been done cannot," it is his own admission, "be undone," by that "power of nature and will of man" which he talks about so much. From this necessity, therefore, it follows that a man must pray to be forgiven. That

a man, however, requires to be helped not to sin, he has nowhere admitted ; I read no such admission in this passage ; he keeps a strange silence on this subject altogether ; although the Lord's Prayer enjoins upon us the necessity of praying both that our debts may be remitted to us, and that we may not be led into temptation, — the one petition entreating that past offences may be atoned for ; the other, that future ones may be avoided. Now, although this is never done unless our will be assistant, yet our will alone is not enough to secure its being done ; the prayer, therefore, which is offered up to God for this result is neither superfluous nor offensive to the Lord. For what is more foolish than to pray that you may do that which you have it in your own power to do.

### CHAP. 21 [XIX.] — PELAGIUS DENIES THAT HUMAN NATURE HAS BEEN DEPRAVED OR CORRUPTED BY SIN.

You may now see (what bears very closely on our subject) how he endeavours to exhibit human nature, as if it were wholly without fault, and how he struggles against the plainest of God's Scriptures with that "wisdom of word "[6] which renders the cross of Christ of none effect. That cross, however, shall certainly never be made of none effect ; rather shall such wisdom be subverted. Now, after we shall have demonstrated this, it may be that God's mercy may visit him, so that he may be sorry that he ever said these things : "We have," he says, "first of all to discuss the position which is maintained, that our nature has been weakened and changed by sin. I think," continues he, "that before all other things we have to inquire what sin is, — some substance, or wholly a name without substance, whereby is expressed not a thing, not an existence, not some sort of a body, but the doing of a wrongful deed." He then adds : "I suppose that this is the case ; and if so," he asks, "how could that which lacks all substance have possibly weakened or changed human nature?" Observe, I beg of you, how in his ignorance he struggles to overthrow the most salutary words of the remedial Scriptures : "I said, O Lord, be merciful unto me ; heal my soul, for I have sinned against Thee."[7] Now, how can a thing be healed, if it is not wounded nor hurt, nor weakened and corrupted? But, as there is here something to be healed, whence did it receive its injury? You hear [the Psalmist] confessing the fact ; what need is there of discussion? He says : "Heal my soul." Ask him how that which he wants to be healed became injured, and then listen to his following words : "Because I have sinned against Thee."

---

[1] Rom. viii. 7, 8　　[2] Rom. xiii. 10.　　[3] Rom. v. 5.
[4] Ps. cxix. 73.　　[5] Jas. i. 5.

[6] 1 Cor. i. 17.　　　　　　[7] Ps. xli. 4.

Let him, however, put a question, and ask what he deemed a suitable inquiry, and say : " O you who exclaim, Heal my soul, for I have sinned against Thee ! pray tell me what sin is ?  Some substance, or wholly a name without substance, whereby is expressed, not a thing, not an existence, not some sort of a body, but merely the doing of a wrongful deed ? "  Then the other returns for answer : " It is even as you say ; sin is not some substance ; but under its name there is merely expressed the doing of a wrongful deed."  But he rejoins : " Then why cry out, Heal my soul, for I have sinned against Thee ?  How could that have possibly corrupted your soul which lacks all substance ? "  Then would the other, worn out with the anguish of his wound, in order to avoid being diverted from prayer by the discussion, briefly answer and say : " Go from me, I beseech you ; rather discuss the point, if you can, with Him who said : ' They that are whole need no physician, but they that are sick ; I am not come to call the righteous, but sinners,' " [1] — in which words, of course, He designated the righteous as the whole, and sinners as the sick.

### CHAP. 22 [XX.] — HOW OUR NATURE COULD BE VITIATED BY SIN, EVEN THOUGH IT BE NOT A SUBSTANCE.

Now, do you not perceive the tendency and direction of this controversy ?  Even to render of none effect the Scripture where it is said : " Thou shalt call His name Jesus, for He shall save His people from their sins." [2]  For how is He to save where there is no malady ?  For the sins, from which this gospel says Christ's people have to be saved, are not substances, and according to this writer are incapable of corrupting.  O brother, how good a thing it is to remember that you are a Christian !  To believe, might perhaps be enough ; but still, since you persist in discussion, there is no harm, nay there is even benefit, if a firm faith precede it ; let us not suppose, then, that human nature cannot be corrupted by sin, but rather, believing, from the inspired Scriptures, that it is corrupted by sin, let our inquiry be how this could possibly have come about.  Since, then, we have already learnt that sin is not a substance, do we not consider, not to mention any other example, that not to eat is also not a substance ?  Because such abstinence is withdrawal from a substance, inasmuch as food is a substance.  To abstain, then, from food is not a substance ; and yet the substance of our body, if it does altogether abstain from food, so languishes, is so impaired by broken health, is so exhausted of strength, so weakened and broken with very weariness, that even if it

be in any way able to continue alive, it is hardly capable of being restored to the use of that food, by abstaining from which it became so corrupted and injured.  In the same way sin is not a substance ; but God is a substance, yea the height of substance and only true sustenance of the reasonable creature.  The consequence of departing from Him by disobedience, and of inability, through infirmity, to receive what one ought really to rejoice in, you hear from the Psalmist, when he says : " My heart is smitten and withered like grass, since I have forgotten to eat my bread." [3]

### CHAP. 23 [XXI.] — ADAM DELIVERED BY THE MERCY OF CHRIST.

But observe how, by specious arguments, he continues to oppose the truth of Holy Scripture.  The Lord Jesus, who is called Jesus because He saves His people from their sins,[2] in accordance with this His merciful character, says : " They that be whole need not a physician, but they that are sick ; I am come not to call the righteous, but sinners to repentance." [4]  Accordingly, His apostle also says : " This is a faithful saying, and worthy of all acceptation, that Christ Jesus came into the world to save sinners." [5]  This man, however, contrary to the " faithful saying, and worthy of all acceptation," declares that " this sickness ought not to have been contracted by sins, lest the punishment of sin should amount to this, that more sins should be committed."  Now even for infants the help of the Great Physician is sought.  This writer asks : " Why seek Him ?  They are whole for whom you seek the Physician.  Not even was the first man condemned to die for any such reason, for he did not sin afterwards."  As if he had ever heard anything of his subsequent perfection in righteousness, except so far as the Church commends to our faith that even Adam was delivered by the mercy of the Lord Christ.  " As to his posterity also," says he, " not only are they not more infirm than he, but they actually fulfilled more commandments than he ever did, since he neglected to fulfil one," — this posterity which he sees so born (as Adam certainly was not made), not only incapable of commandment, which they do not at all understand, but hardly capable of sucking the breast, when they are hungry !  Yet even these would He have to be saved in the bosom of Mother Church by His grace who saves His people from their sins ; but these men gainsay such grace, and, as if they had a deeper insight into the creature than ever He possesses who made the creature, they pronounce [these infants] sound with an assertion which is anything but sound itself.

---

[1] Matt. ix. 12, 13.          [2] Matt. i. 21.          [3] Ps. cii. 4.          [4] Matt. ix. 12.          [5] 1 Tim. i. 15.

CHAP. 24 [XXII.] — SIN AND THE PENALTY OF SIN THE SAME.

"The very matter," says he, "of sin is its punishment, if the sinner is so much weakened that he commits more sins." He does not consider how justly the light of truth forsakes the man who transgresses the law. When thus deserted, he of course becomes blinded, and necessarily offends more ; and by so falling is embarrassed, and being embarrassed fails to rise, so as to hear the voice of the law, which admonishes him to beg for the Saviour's grace. Is no punishment due to them of whom the apostle says : "Because that, when they knew God, they glorified Him not as God, neither were thankful; but became vain in their imaginations, and their foolish heart was darkened?"[1] This darkening was, of course, already their punishment and penalty ; and yet by this very penalty — that is, by their blindness of heart, which supervenes on the withdrawal of the light of wisdom — they fell into more grievous sins still. "For giving themselves out as wise, they became fools." This is a grievous penalty, if one only understands it ; and from such a penalty only see to what lengths they ran : "And they changed," he says, "the glory of the uncorruptible God into an image made like to corruptible man, and to birds, and four-footed beasts, and creeping things."[2] All this they did owing to that penalty of their sin, whereby "their foolish heart was darkened." And yet, owing to these deeds of theirs, which, although coming in the way of punishment, were none the less sins (he goes on to say) : "Wherefore God also gave them up to uncleanness, through the lusts of their own hearts."[3] See how severely God condemned them, giving them over to uncleanness in the very desires of their heart. Observe also the sins they commit owing to such condemnation : "To dishonour," says he, "their own bodies among themselves."[3] Here is the punishment of iniquity, which is itself iniquity ; a fact which sets forth in a clearer light the words which follow : "Who changed the truth of God into a lie, and worshipped and served the creature more than the Creator, who is blessed for ever. Amen." "For this cause," says he, "God gave them up unto vile affections."[4] See how often God inflicts punishment; and out of the self-same punishment sins, more numerous and more severe, arise. "For even their women did change the natural use into that which is against nature ; and likewise the men also, leaving the natural use of the woman, burned in their lust one toward another ; men with men working that which is unseemly."[5] Then, to show that these things were so sins themselves, that they were also the penalties of sins, he further says : "And receiving in themselves that recompense of their error which was meet."[6] Observe how often it happens that the very punishment which God inflicts begets other sins as its natural offspring. Attend still further : "And even as they did not like to retain God in their knowledge," says he, "God gave them over to a reprobate mind, to do those things which are not convenient ; being filled with all unrighteousness, fornication, wickedness, covetousness, maliciousness ; full of envy, murder, debate, deceit, malignity ; whisperers, backbiters, odious to God, despiteful, proud, boasters, inventors of evil things, disobedient to parents, without understanding, covenant-breakers, without natural affection, implacable, unmerciful."[7] Here, now, let our opponent say : "Sin ought not so to have been punished, that the sinner, through his punishment, should commit even more sins."

CHAP. 25 [XXIII.] — GOD FORSAKES ONLY THOSE WHO DESERVE TO BE FORSAKEN. WE ARE SUFFICIENT OF OURSELVES TO COMMIT SIN ; BUT NOT TO RETURN TO THE WAY OF RIGHTEOUSNESS. DEATH IS THE PUNISHMENT, NOT THE CAUSE OF SIN.

Perhaps he may answer that God does not compel men to do these things, but only forsakes those who deserve to be forsaken. If he does say this, he says what is most true. For, as I have already remarked, those who are forsaken by the light of righteousness, and are therefore groping in darkness, produce nothing else than those works of darkness which I have enumerated, until such time as it is said to them, and they obey the command : "Awake thou that sleepest, and arise from the dead, and Christ shall give thee light."[8] The truth designates them as dead ; whence the passage : "Let the dead bury their dead." The truth, then, designates as *dead* those whom this man declares to have been unable to be damaged or corrupted by sin, on the ground, forsooth, that he has discovered sin to be no substance ! Nobody tells him that "man was so formed as to be able to pass from righteousness to sin, and yet not able to return from sin to righteousness." But that free will, whereby man corrupted his own self, was sufficient for his passing into sin ; but to return to righteousness, he has need of a Physician, since he is out of health ; he has need of a Vivifier, because he is dead. Now about such grace as this he says not a word, as if he were able to cure himself by his own will, since this alone was able to ruin him. We do not tell him that the death of the body is of efficacy for sinning, because it is only its

---

[1] Rom. i. 21.       [2] Rom. i. 23.       [3] Rom. i. 24.
[4] Rom. i. 25, 26.   [5] Rom. i. 26, 27.

[6] Rom. i. 27.       [7] Rom. i. 28-31.       [8] Eph. v. 14.

punishment; for no one sins by undergoing the death of his body; but the death of the soul is conducive to sin, forsaken as it is by its life, that is, its God; and it must needs produce dead works, until it revives by the grace of Christ. God forbid that we should assert that hunger and thirst and other bodily sufferings necessarily produce sin. When exercised by such vexations, the life of the righteous only shines out with greater lustre, and procures a greater glory by overcoming them through patience; but then it is assisted by the grace, it is assisted by the Spirit, it is assisted by the mercy of God; not exalting itself in an arrogant will, but earning fortitude by a humble confession. For it had learnt to say unto God: "Thou art my hope; Thou art my trust."[1] Now, how it happens that concerning this grace, and help and mercy, without which we cannot live, this man has nothing to say, I am at a loss to know; but he goes further, and in the most open manner gainsays the grace of Christ whereby we are justified, by insisting on the sufficiency of nature to work righteousness, provided only the will be present. The reason, however, why, after sin has been released to the guilty one by grace, for the exercise of faith, there should still remain the death of the body, although it proceeds from sin, I have already explained, according to my ability, in those books which I wrote to Marcellinus of blessed memory.[2]

CHAP. 26 [XXIV.] — CHRIST DIED OF HIS OWN POWER AND CHOICE.

As to his statement, indeed, that "the Lord was able to die without sin;" His being born also was of the ability of His mercy, not the demand of His nature: so, likewise, did He undergo death of His own power; and this is our price which He paid to redeem us from death. Now, this truth their contention labours hard to make of none effect; for human nature is maintained by them to be such, that with free will it wants no such ransom in order to be translated from the power of darkness and of him who has the power of death,[3] into the kingdom of Christ the Lord.[4] And yet, when the Lord drew near His passion, He said, "Behold, the prince of this world cometh and shall find nothing in me,"[5] — and therefore no sin, of course, on account of which he might exercise dominion over Him, so as to destroy Him. "But," added He, "that the world may know

that I do the will of my Father, arise, let us go hence;"[6] as much as to say, I am going to die, not through the necessity of sin, but in voluntariness of obedience.

CHAP. 27. — EVEN EVILS, THROUGH GOD'S MERCY, ARE OF USE.

He asserts that "no evil is the cause of anything good;" as if punishment, forsooth, were good, although thereby many have been reformed. There are, then, evils which are of use by the wondrous mercy of God. Did that man experience some good thing, when he said, "Thou didst hide Thy face from me, and I was troubled?"[7] Certainly not; and yet this very trouble was to him in a certain manner a remedy against his pride. For he had said in his prosperity, "I shall never be moved;"[8] and so was ascribing to himself what he was receiving from the Lord. "For what had he that he did not receive?"[9] It had, therefore, become necessary to show him whence he had received, that he might receive in humility what he had lost in pride. Accordingly, he says, "In Thy good pleasure, O Lord, Thou didst add strength to my beauty."[7] In this abundance of mine I once used to say, "I shall not be moved;" whereas it all came from Thee, not from myself. Then at last Thou didst turn away Thy face from me, and I became troubled.

CHAP. 28 [XXV.] — THE DISPOSITION OF NEARLY ALL WHO GO ASTRAY. WITH SOME HERETICS OUR BUSINESS OUGHT NOT TO BE DISPUTATION, BUT PRAYER.

Man's proud mind has no relish at all for this; God, however, is great, in persuading even *it* how to find it all out. We are, indeed, more inclined to seek how best to reply to such arguments as oppose our error, than to experience how salutary would be our condition if we were free from error. We ought, therefore, to encounter all such, not by discussions, but rather by prayers both for them and for ourselves. For we never say to them, what this opponent has opposed to himself, that "sin was necessary in order that there might be a cause for God's mercy." Would there had never been misery to render that mercy necessary! But the iniquity of sin, — which is so much the greater in proportion to the ease wherewith man might have avoided sin, whilst no infirmity did as yet beset him, — has been followed closely up by a most righteous punishment; even that [offending man] should receive in himself a reward in kind of his sin, losing that obedience of his body which had been in some degree put under his own control, which he had despised when it

1 Ps. lxxi. 5.
2 The tribune Marcellinus had been put to death in the September of 413, "having, though innocent, fallen a victim to the cruel hatred of the tyrant Heraclius," as Jerome writes in his book iii. against the Pelagians. Honorius mentions him as a "man of conspicuous renown," in a law enacted August 30, in the year 414, contained in the *Cod Theod.* xvi. 5 (de hæreticis), line 55. Compare the notes above, pp. 15 and 80.
3 Heb. ii. 14.     4 Col. i. 13.     5 John xiv. 30.
6 John xiv. 31.     7 Ps. xxx. 7.     8 Ps. xxx. 8.
9 1 Cor. iv. 7.

was the right of his Lord. And, inasmuch as we are now born with the self-same law of sin, which in our members resists the law of our mind, we ought never to murmur against God, nor to dispute in opposition to the clearest fact, but to seek and pray for His mercy instead of our punishment.

CHAP. 29 [XXVI.] — A SIMILE TO SHOW THAT GOD'S GRACE IS NECESSARY FOR DOING ANY GOOD WORK WHATEVER. GOD NEVER FORSAKES THE JUSTIFIED MAN IF HE BE NOT HIMSELF FORSAKEN.[1]

Observe, indeed, how cautiously he expresses himself : " God, no doubt, applies His mercy even to this office, whenever it is necessary ; because man after sin requires help in this way, not because God wished there should be a cause for such necessity." Do you not see how he does not say that God's grace is necessary to prevent us from sinning, but because we have sinned ? Then he adds : " But just in the same way it is the duty of a physician to be ready to cure a man who is already wounded ; although he ought not to wish for a man who is sound to be wounded." Now, if this simile suits the subject of which we are treating, human nature is certainly incapable of receiving a wound from sin, inasmuch as sin is not a substance. As therefore, for example's sake, a man who is lamed by a wound is cured in order that his step for the future may be direct and strong, its past infirmity being healed, so does the Heavenly Physician cure our maladies, not only that they may cease any longer to exist, but in order that we may ever afterwards be able to walk aright, — to which we should be unequal, even after our healing, except by His continued help. For after a medical man has administered a cure, in order that the patient may be afterwards duly nourished with bodily elements and aliments, for the completion and continuance of the said cure by suitable means and help, he commends him to God's good care, who bestows these aids on all who live in the flesh, and from whom proceeded even those means which [the physician] applied during the process of the cure. For it is not out of any resources which he has himself created that the medical man effects any cure, but out of the resources of Him who creates all things which are required by the whole and by the sick. God, however, whenever He — through " the one mediator between God and men, the man Christ Jesus " — spiritually heals the sick or raises the dead, that is, justifies the ungodly, and when He has brought him to perfect health, in other words, to the fulness of life and righteousness, does not forsake, if He is not

forsaken, in order that life may be passed in constant piety and righteousness. For, just as the eye of the body, even when completely sound, is unable to see unless aided by the brightness of light, so also man, even when most fully justified, is unable to lead a holy life, if he be not divinely assisted by the eternal light of righteousness. God, therefore, heals us not only that He may blot out the sin which we have committed, but, furthermore, that He may enable us even to avoid sinning.

CHAP. 30 [XXVII.] — SIN IS REMOVED BY SIN.

He no doubt shows some acuteness in handling, and turning over and exposing, as he likes, and refuting a certain statement, which is made to this effect, that " it was really necessary to man, in order to take from him all occasion for pride and boasting, that he should be unable to exist without sin." He supposes it to be " the height of absurdity and folly, that there should have been sin in order that sin might not be ; inasmuch as pride is itself, of course, a sin." As if a sore were not attended with pain, and an operation did not produce pain, that pain might be taken away by pain. If we had not experienced any such treatment, but were only to hear about it in some parts of the world where these things had never happened, we might perhaps use this man's words, and say, It is the height of absurdity that pain should have been necessary in order that a sore should have no pain.

CHAP. 31. — THE ORDER AND PROCESS OF HEALING OUR HEAVENLY PHYSICIAN DOES NOT ADOPT FROM THE SICK PATIENT, BUT DERIVES FROM HIMSELF. WHAT CAUSE THE RIGHTEOUS HAVE FOR FEARING.

" But God," they say, " is able to heal all things." Of course His purpose in acting is to heal all things ; but He acts on His own judgment, and does not take His procedure in healing from the sick man. For undoubtedly it was His wish to endow His apostle with very great power and strength, and yet He said to him : " My strength is made perfect in weakness ; "[2] nor did He remove from him, though he so often entreated Him to do so, that mysterious " thorn in the flesh," which He told him had been given to him " lest he should be unduly exalted through the abundance of the revelation."[3] For all other sins only prevail in evil deeds ; pride only has to be guarded against in things that are rightly done. Whence it happens that those persons are admonished not to attribute to their own power the gifts of God, nor to plume themselves thereon, lest by so doing they should perish with a

---

[1] See the treatise *De Peccatorum Meritis*, ii. 22.  [2] 2 Cor. xii. 9.  [3] 2 Cor. xii. 7, 8.

heavier perdition than if they had done no good at all, to whom it is said: "Work out your own salvation with fear and trembling, for it is God which worketh in you, both to will and to do of His good pleasure." [1] Why, then, must it be with fear and trembling, and not rather with security, since God is working; except it be because there so quickly steals over our human soul, by reason of our will (without which we can do nothing well), the inclination to esteem simply as our own accomplishment whatever good we do; and so each one of us says in his prosperity: "I shall never be moved?" [2] Therefore, He who in His good pleasure had added strength to our beauty, turns away His face, and the man who had made his boast becomes troubled, because it is by actual sorrows that the swelling pride must be remedied.

### CHAP. 32 [XXVIII.] — GOD FORSAKES US TO SOME EXTENT THAT WE MAY NOT GROW PROUD.

Therefore it is not said to a man: "It is necessary for you to sin that you may not sin;" but it is said to a man: "God in some degree forsakes you, in consequence of which you grow proud, that you may know that you are 'not your own,' but are His,[3] and learn not to be proud." Now even that incident in the apostle's life, of this kind, is so wonderful, that were it not for the fact that he himself is the voucher for it whose truth it is impious to contradict, would it not be incredible? For what believer is there who is ignorant that the first incentive to sin came from Satan, and that he is the first author of all sins? And yet, for all that, some are "delivered over unto Satan, that they may learn not to blaspheme." [4] How comes it to pass, then, that Satan's work is prevented by the work of Satan? These and such like questions let a man regard in such a light that they seem not to him to be too acute; they have somewhat of the sound of acuteness, and yet when discussed are found to be obtuse. What must we say also to our author's use of similes whereby he rather suggests to us the answer which we should give to him? "What" (asks he) "shall I say more than this, that we may believe that fires are quenched by fires, if we may believe that sins are cured by sins?" What if one cannot put out fires by fires: but yet pains can, for all that, as I have shown, be cured by pains? Poisons can also, if one only inquire and learn the fact, be expelled by poisons. Now, if he observes that the heats of fevers are sometimes subdued by certain medicinal warmths, he will perhaps also allow that fires may be extinguished by fires.

### CHAP. 33 [XXIX.] — NOT EVERY SIN IS PRIDE. HOW PRIDE IS THE COMMENCEMENT OF EVERY SIN.

"But how," asks he, "shall we separate pride itself from sin?" Now, why does he raise such a question, when it is manifest that even pride itself is a sin? "To sin," says he, "is quite as much to be proud, as to be proud is to sin; for only ask what every sin is, and see whether you can find any sin without the designation of pride." Then he thus pursues this opinion, and endeavours to prove it thus: "Every sin," says he, "if I mistake not, is a contempt of God, and every contempt of God is pride. For what is so proud as to despise God? All sin, then, is also pride, even as Scripture says, Pride is the beginning of all sin." [5] Let him seek diligently, and he will find in the law that the sin of pride is quite distinguished from all other sins. For many sins are committed through pride; but yet not all things which are wrongly done are done proudly, — at any rate, not by the ignorant, not by the infirm, and not, generally speaking, by the weeping and sorrowful. And indeed pride, although it be in itself a great sin, is of such sort in itself alone apart from others, that, as I have already remarked, it for the most part follows after and steals with more rapid foot, not so much upon sins as upon things which are actually well done. However, that which he has understood in another sense, is after all most truly said: "Pride is the commencement of all sin;" because it was this which overthrew the devil, from whom arose the origin of sin; and afterwards, when his malice and envy pursued man, who was yet standing in his uprightness, it subverted him in the same way in which he himself fell. For the serpent, in fact, only sought for the door of pride whereby to enter when he said, "Ye shall be as gods." [6] Truly then is it said, "Pride is the commencement of all sin;" [5] and, "The beginning of pride is when a man departeth from God." [7]

### CHAP. 34 [XXX.] — A MAN'S SIN IS HIS OWN, BUT HE NEEDS GRACE FOR HIS CURE.

Well, but what does he mean when he says: "Then again, how can one be subjected to God for the guilt of that sin, which he knows is not his own? For," says he, "his own it is not, if it is necessary. Or, if it is his own, it is voluntary: and if it is voluntary, it can be avoided." We reply: It is unquestionably his own. But the fault by which sin is committed is not yet in every respect healed, and the fact of its becoming permanently fixed in us arises from our not rightly using the healing virtue; and so out of this faulty condition the man who is now grow-

---

[1] Phil. ii. 12, 13.     [2] Ps. xxx. 6.     [3] 1 Cor. vi. 19.
[4] 1 Tim. i. 20.

[5] Ecclus. x. 13.     [6] Gen. iii. 5.     [7] Ecclus. x. 12.

ing strong in depravity commits many sins, either through infirmity or blindness. Prayer must therefore be made for him, that he may be healed, and that he may thenceforward attain to a life of uninterrupted soundness of health; nor must pride be indulged in, as if any man were healed by the self-same power whereby he became corrupted.

CHAP. 35 [XXXI.] — WHY GOD DOES NOT IMMEDIATELY CURE PRIDE ITSELF. THE SECRET AND INSIDIOUS GROWTH OF PRIDE. PREVENTING AND SUBSEQUENT GRACE.

But I would indeed so treat these topics, as to confess myself ignorant of God's deeper counsel, why He does not at once heal the very principle of pride, which lies in wait for man's heart even in deeds rightly done; and for the cure of which pious souls, with tears and strong crying, beseech Him that He would stretch forth His right hand and help their endeavours to overcome it, and somehow tread and crush it under foot. Now when a man has felt glad that he has even by some good work overcome pride, from the very joy he lifts up his head and says: "Behold, I live; why do you triumph? Nay, I live because you triumph." Premature, however, this forwardness of his to triumph over pride may perhaps be, as if it were now vanquished, whereas its last shadow is to be swallowed up, as I suppose, in that noontide which is promised in the scripture which says, "He shall bring forth thy righteousness as the light, and thy judgment as the noonday;"[1] provided that be done which was written in the preceding verse: "Commit thy way unto the Lord; trust also in Him, and He shall bring it to pass,"[2] — not, as some suppose, that they themselves bring it to pass. Now, when he said, "And He shall bring it to pass," he evidently had none other in mind but those who say, We ourselves bring it to pass; that is to say, we ourselves justify our own selves. In this matter, no doubt, we do ourselves, too, work; but we are fellow-workers with Him who does the work, because His mercy anticipates us. He anticipates us, however, that we may be healed; but then He will also follow us, that being healed we may grow healthy and strong. He anticipates us that we may be called; He will follow us that we may be glorified. He anticipates us that we may lead godly lives; He will follow us that we may always live with Him, because without Him we can do nothing.[3] Now the Scriptures refer to both these operations of grace. There is both this: "The God of my mercy shall anticipate me,"[4] and again this: "Thy mercy shall follow me all the days of my life."[5] Let us

therefore unveil to Him our life by confession, not praise it with a vindication. For if it is not His way, but our own, beyond doubt it is not the right one. Let us therefore reveal this by making our confession to Him; for however much we may endeavour to conceal it, it is not hid from Him. It is a good thing to confess unto the Lord.

CHAP. 36 [XXXII.] — PRIDE EVEN IN SUCH THINGS AS ARE DONE ARIGHT MUST BE AVOIDED. FREE WILL IS NOT TAKEN AWAY WHEN GRACE IS PREACHED.

So will He bestow on us whatever pleases Him, that if there be anything displeasing to Him in us, it will also be displeasing to us. "He will," as the Scripture has said, "turn aside our paths from His own way,"[6] and will make that which is His own to be our way; because it is by Himself that the favour is bestowed on such as believe in Him and hope in Him that we will do it. For there is a way of righteousness of which they are ignorant "who have a zeal for God, but not according to knowledge,"[7] and who, wishing to frame a righteousness of their own, "have not submitted themselves to the righteousness of God."[8] "For Christ is the end of the law for righteousness to every one that believeth;"[9] and He has said, "I am the way."[10] Yet God's voice has alarmed those who have already begun to walk in this way, lest they should be lifted up, as if it were by their own energies that they were walking therein. For the same persons to whom the apostle, on account of this danger, says, "Work out your own salvation with fear and trembling, for it is God that worketh in you, both to will and to do of His good pleasure,"[11] are likewise for the selfsame reason admonished in the psalm: "Serve the Lord with fear, and rejoice in Him with trembling. Accept correction, lest at any time the Lord be angry, and ye perish from the righteous way, when His wrath shall be suddenly kindled upon you."[12] He does not say, "Lest at any time the Lord be angry and refuse to show you the righteous way," or, "refuse to lead you into the way of righteousness;" but even after you are walking therein, he was able so to terrify as to say, "Lest ye perish from the righteous way." Now, whence could this arise if not from pride, which (as I have so often said, and must repeat again and again) has to be guarded against even in things which are rightly done, that is, in the very way of righteousness, lest a man, by regarding as his own that which is really God's, lose what is God's and be reduced merely to what is his own? Let us then carry out

---

[1] Ps. xxxvii. 6.　　[2] Ps. xxxvii. 5.　　[3] John xv. 5.
[4] Ps. lix. 10.　　[5] Ps. xxiii. 6.

[6] See Ps. xliv. 18.　　[7] Rom. x. 2.　　[8] Rom. x. 3.
[9] Rom. x. 4　　[10] John xiv. 6.　　[11] Phil. ii. 12.
[12] Ps. ii. 11, 12.

the concluding injunction of this same psalm, "Blessed are all they that trust in Him,"[1] so that He may Himself indeed effect and Himself show His own way in us, to whom it is said, "Show us Thy mercy, O Lord;"[2] and Himself bestow on us the pathway of safety that we may walk therein, to whom the prayer is offered, "And grant us Thy salvation;"[2] and Himself lead us in the self-same way, to whom again it is said, "Guide me, O Lord, in Thy way, and in Thy truth will I walk;"[3] Himself, too, conduct us to those promises whither His way leads, to whom it is said, "Even there shall Thy hand lead me and Thy right hand shall hold me;"[4] Himself pasture therein those who sit down with Abraham, Isaac, and Jacob, of whom it is said, "He shall make them sit down to meat, and will come forth and serve them."[5] Now we do not, when we make mention of these things, take away freedom of will, but we preach the grace of God. For to whom are those gracious gifts of use, but to the man who uses, but humbly uses, his own will, and makes no boast of the power and energy thereof, as if it alone were sufficient for perfecting him in righteousness?

CHAP. 37 [XXXIII.] — BEING WHOLLY WITHOUT SIN DOES NOT PUT MAN ON AN EQUALITY WITH GOD.

But God forbid that we should meet him with such an assertion as he says certain persons advance against him: "That man is placed on an equality with God, if he is described as being without sin;" as if indeed an angel, because he is without sin, is put in such an equality. For my own part, I am of this opinion that the creature will never become equal with God, even when so perfect a holiness shall be accomplished in us, that it shall be quite incapable of receiving any addition. No; all who maintain that our progress is to be so complete that we shall be changed into the substance of God, and that we shall thus become what He is, should look well to it how they build up their opinion; for myself I must confess that I am not persuaded of this.

CHAP. 38 [XXXIV.] — WE MUST NOT LIE, EVEN FOR THE SAKE OF MODERATION. THE PRAISE OF HUMILITY MUST NOT BE PLACED TO THE ACCOUNT OF FALSEHOOD.

I am favourably disposed, indeed, to the view of our author, when he resists those who say to him, "What you assert seems indeed to be reasonable, but it is an arrogant thing to allege that any man can be without sin," with this answer, that if it is at all true, it must not on any account be called an arrogant statement; for with very great truth and acuteness he asks, "On what side must humility be placed? No doubt on the side of falsehood, if you prove arrogance to exist on the side of truth." And so he decides, and rightly decides, that humility should rather be ranged on the side of truth, not of falsehood. Whence it follows that he who said, "If we say that we have no sin, we deceive ourselves, and the truth is not in us,"[6] must without hesitation be held to have spoken the truth, and not be thought to have spoken falsehood for the sake of humility. Therefore he added the words, "And the truth is not in us;" whereas it might perhaps have been enough if he merely said, "We deceive ourselves," if he had not observed that some were capable of supposing that the clause "we deceive ourselves" is here employed on the ground that the man who praises himself is even extolled for a really good action. So that, by the addition of "the truth is not in us," he clearly shows (even as our author most correctly observes) that it is not at all true if we say that we have no sin, lest humility, if placed on the side of falsehood, should lose the reward of truth.

CHAP. 39. — PELAGIUS GLORIFIES GOD AS CREATOR AT THE EXPENSE OF GOD AS SAVIOUR.

Beyond this, however, although he flatters himself that he vindicates the cause of God by defending nature, he forgets that by predicating soundness of the said nature, he rejects the Physician's mercy. He, however, who created him is also his Saviour. We ought not, therefore, so to magnify the Creator as to be compelled to say, nay, rather as to be convicted of saying, that the Saviour is superfluous. Man's nature indeed we may honour with worthy praise, and attribute the praise to the Creator's glory; but at the same time, while we show our gratitude to Him for having created us, let us not be ungrateful to Him for healing us. Our sins which He heals we must undoubtedly attribute not to God's operation, but to the wilfulness of man, and submit them to *His* righteous punishment; as, however, we acknowledge that it was in our power that they should not be committed, so let us confess that it lies in His mercy rather than in our own power that they should be healed. But this mercy and remedial help of the Saviour, according to this writer, consists only in this, that He forgives the transgressions that are past, not that He helps us to avoid such as are to come. Here he is most fatally mistaken; here, however unwittingly — here he hinders us from being watchful, and from praying that "we enter not into temptation," since he

---

[1] Ps. ii. 12.　　[2] Ps. lxxxv. 7.　　[3] Ps. lxxxvi. 11.
[4] Ps. cxxxix. 10.　　[5] Luke xii. 37.

[6] 1 John i. 8.

maintains that it lies entirely in our own control that this should not happen to us.

## CHAP. 40 [XXXV.] — WHY THERE IS A RECORD IN SCRIPTURE OF CERTAIN MEN'S SINS. RECKLESSNESS IN SIN ACCOUNTS IT TO BE SO MUCH LOSS WHENEVER IT FALLS SHORT IN GRATIFYING LUST.

He who has a sound judgment says soundly, "that the examples of certain persons, of whose sinning we read in Scripture, are not recorded for this purpose, that they may encourage despair of not sinning, and seem somehow to afford security in committing sin," — but that we may learn the humility of repentance, or else discover that even in such falls salvation ought not to be despaired of. For there are some who, when they have fallen into sin, perish rather from the recklessness of despair, and not only neglect the remedy of repentance, but become the slaves of lusts and wicked desires, so far as to run all lengths in gratifying these depraved and abandoned dispositions, — as if it were a loss to them if they failed to accomplish what their lust impelled them to, whereas all the while there awaits them a certain condemnation. To oppose this morbid recklessness, which is only too full of danger and ruin, there is great force in the record of those sins into which even just and holy men have before now fallen.

## CHAP. 41. — WHETHER HOLY MEN HAVE DIED WITHOUT SIN.

But there is clearly much acuteness in the question put by our author, "How must we suppose that those holy men quitted this life, — with sin, or without sin?" For if we answer, "With sin," condemnation will be supposed to have been their destiny, which it is shocking to imagine; but if it be said that they departed this life "without sin," then it would be a proof that man had been without sin in his present life, at all events, when death was approaching. But, with all his acuteness, he overlooks the circumstance that even righteous persons not without good reason offer up this prayer: "Forgive us our debts, as we forgive our debtors;"[1] and that the Lord Christ, after explaining the prayer in His teaching, most truly added: "For if ye forgive men their trespasses, your Father will also forgive you your trespasses."[2] Here, indeed, we have the daily incense, so to speak, of the Spirit, which is offered to God on the altar of the heart, which we are bidden "to lift up," — implying that, even if we cannot live here without sin, we may yet die without sin, when in merciful forgiveness the sin is blotted out which is committed in ignorance or infirmity.

## CHAP. 42 [XXXVI.] — THE BLESSED VIRGIN MARY MAY HAVE LIVED WITHOUT SIN. NONE OF THE SAINTS BESIDES HER WITHOUT SIN.

He then enumerates those "who not only lived without sin, but are described as having led holy lives, — Abel, Enoch, Melchizedek, Abraham, Isaac, Jacob, Joshua the son of Nun, Phinehas, Samuel, Nathan, Elijah, Joseph, Elisha, Micaiah, Daniel, Hananiah, Azariah, Mishael, Mordecai, Simeon, Joseph to whom the Virgin Mary was espoused, John." And he adds the names of some women, — "Deborah, Anna the mother of Samuel, Judith, Esther, the other Anna, daughter of Phanuel, Elisabeth, and also the mother of our Lord and Saviour, for of her," he says, "we must needs allow that her piety had no sin in it." We must except the holy Virgin Mary, concerning whom I wish to raise no question when it touches the subject of sins, out of honour to the Lord; for from Him we know what abundance of grace for overcoming sin in every particular was conferred upon her who had the merit to conceive and bear Him who undoubtedly had no sin.[3] Well, then, if, with this exception of the Virgin, we could only assemble together all the forementioned holy men and women, and ask them whether they lived without sin whilst they were in this life, what can we suppose would be their answer? Would it be in the language of our author, or in the words of the Apostle John? I put it to you, whether, on having such a question submitted to them, however excellent might have been their sanctity in this body, they would not have exclaimed with one voice: "If we say we have no sin, we deceive ourselves, and the truth is not in us?"[4] But perhaps this their answer would have been more humble than true! Well, but our author has already determined, and rightly determined, "not to place the praise of humility on the side of falsehood." If, therefore, they spoke the truth in giving such an answer, they would have sin, and since they humbly acknowledged it, the truth would be in them; but if they lied in their answer, they would still have sin, because the truth would not be in them.

## CHAP. 43 [XXXVII.] — WHY SCRIPTURE HAS NOT MENTIONED THE SINS OF ALL.

"But perhaps," says he, "they will ask me: Could not the Scripture have mentioned sins of all of these?" And surely they would say the truth, whoever should put such a question to him; and I do not discover that he has anywhere given a sound reply to them, although I perceive that he was unwilling to be silent.

---

[1] Matt. vi. 12.          [2] Matt. vi. 14.          [3] 1 John iii. 5.          [4] 1 John i. 8.

What he has said, I beg of you to observe: "This," says he, "might be rightly asked of those whom Scripture mentions neither as good nor as bad; but of those whose holiness it commemorates, it would also without doubt have commemorated the sins likewise, if it had perceived that they had sinned in anything." Let him say, then, that their great faith did not attain to righteousness in the case of those who comprised "the multitudes that went before and that followed" the colt on which the Lord rode, when "they shouted and said, Hosanna to the Son of David: Blessed is He that cometh in the name of the Lord," [1] even amidst the malignant men who with murmurs asked why they were doing all this! Let him then boldly tell us, if he can, that there was not a man in all that vast crowd who had any sin at all. Now, if it is most absurd to make such a statement as this, why has not the Scripture mentioned any sins in the persons to whom reference has been made, especially when it has carefully recorded the eminent goodness of their faith?

### CHAP. 44. — PELAGIUS ARGUES THAT ABEL WAS SINLESS.

This, however, even *he* probably observed, and therefore he went on to say: "But, granted that it has sometimes abstained, in a numerous crowd, from narrating the sins of all; still, in the very beginning of the world, when there were only four persons in existence, what reason (asks he) have we to give why it chose not to mention the sins of all? Was it in consideration of the vast multitude, which had not yet come into existence? or because, having mentioned only the sins of those who had transgressed, it was unable to record any of him who had not yet committed sin?" And then he proceeds to add some words, in which he unfolds this idea with a fuller and more explicit illustration. "It is certain," says he, "that in the earliest age Adam and Eve, and Cain and Abel their sons, are mentioned as being the only four persons then in being. Eve sinned, — the Scripture distinctly says so much; Adam also transgressed, as the same Scripture does not fail to inform us; whilst it affords us an equally clear testimony that Cain also sinned: and of all these it not only mentions the sins, but also indicates the character of their sins. Now if Abel had likewise sinned, Scripture would without doubt have said so. But it has not said so, therefore he committed no sin; nay, it even shows him to have been righteous. What we read, therefore, let us believe; and what we do not read, let us deem it wicked to add."

### CHAP. 45 [XXXVIII.] — WHY CAIN HAS BEEN BY SOME THOUGHT TO HAVE HAD CHILDREN BY HIS MOTHER EVE. THE SINS OF RIGHTEOUS MEN. WHO CAN BE BOTH RIGHTEOUS, AND YET NOT WITHOUT SIN.

When he says this, he forgets what he had himself said not long before: "After the human race had multiplied, it was possible that in the crowd the Scripture may have neglected to notice the sins of all men." If indeed he had borne this well in mind, he would have seen that even in one man there was such a crowd and so vast a number of slight sins, that it would have been impossible (or, even if possible, not desirable) to describe them. For only such are recorded as the due bounds allowed, and as would, by few examples, serve for instructing the reader in the many cases where he needed warning. Scripture has indeed omitted to mention concerning the few persons who were then in existence, either how many or who they were, — in other words, how many sons and daughters Adam and Eve begat, and what names they gave them; and from this circumstance some, not considering how many things are quietly passed over in Scripture, have gone so far as to suppose that Cain cohabited with his mother, and by her had the children which are mentioned, thinking that Adam's sons had no sisters, because Scripture failed to mention them in the particular place, although it afterwards, in the way of recapitulation, implied what it had previously omitted, — that "Adam begat sons and daughters," [2] without, however, dropping a syllable to intimate either their number or the time when they were born. In like manner it was unnecessary to state whether Abel, notwithstanding that he is rightly styled "righteous," ever indulged in immoderate laughter, or was ever jocose in moments of relaxation, or ever looked at an object with a covetous eye, or ever plucked fruit to extravagance, or ever suffered indigestion from too much eating, or ever in the midst of his prayers permitted his thoughts to wander and call him away from the purpose of his devotion; as well as how frequently these and many other similar failings stealthily crept over his mind. And are not these failings *sins*, about which the apostle's precept gives us a general admonition that we should avoid and restrain them, when he says: "Let not sin therefore reign in your mortal body, that ye should obey it in the lusts thereof?" [3] To escape from such an obedience, we have to struggle in a constant and daily conflict against unlawful and unseemly inclinations. Only let the eye be directed, or rather abandoned, to an object which it ought to avoid, and let the mischief strengthen and get the mastery, and

[1] Matt. xxi. 9.    [2] Gen. v. 4.    [3] Rom. vi. 12.

adultery is consummated in the body, which is committed in the heart only so much more quickly as thought is more rapid than action and there is no impediment to retard and delay it. They who in a great degree have curbed this sin, that is, this appetite of a corrupt affection, so as not to obey its desires, nor to "yield their members to it as instruments of unrighteousness,"[1] have fairly deserved to be called righteous persons, and this by the help of the grace of God. Since, however, sin often stole over them in very small matters, and when they were off their guard, they were both righteous, and at the same time not sinless. To conclude, if there was in righteous Abel that love of God whereby alone he is truly righteous who is righteous, to enable him, and to lay him under a moral obligation, to advance in holiness, still in whatever degree he fell short therein was of sin. And who indeed can help thus falling short, until he come to that mighty power thereof, in which man's entire infirmity shall be swallowed up?

CHAP. 46 [XXXIX.] — SHALL WE FOLLOW SCRIPTURE, OR ADD TO ITS DECLARATIONS?

It is, to be sure, a grand sentence with which he concluded this passage, when he says: "What we read, therefore, let us believe; and what we do not read, let us deem it wicked to add; and let it suffice to have said this of all cases." On the contrary, I for my part say that we ought not to believe even everything that we read, on the sanction of the apostle's advice: "Read all things; hold fast that which is good."[2] Nor is it wicked to add something which we have not read; for it is in our power to add something which we have *bonâ fide* experienced as witnesses, even if it so happens that we have not read about it. Perhaps he will say in reply: "When I said this, I was treating of the Holy Scriptures." Oh how I wish that he were never willing to add, I will not say anything but what he reads in the Scriptures, but in opposition to what he reads in them; that he would only faithfully and obediently hear that which is written there: "By one man sin entered into the world, and death by sin, and so death passed upon all men; in which all have sinned;"[3] and that he would not weaken the grace of the great Physician, — all by his unwillingness to confess that human nature is corrupted! Oh how I wish that he would, as a Christian, read the sentence, "There is none other name under heaven given among men whereby we must be saved;"[4] and that he would not so uphold the possibility of human nature, as to believe that man can be saved by free will without that Name!

CHAP. 47 [XL.] — FOR WHAT PELAGIUS THOUGHT THAT CHRIST IS NECESSARY TO US.

Perhaps, however, he thinks the name of Christ to be necessary on this account, that by His gospel we may learn how we ought to live; but not that we may be also assisted by His grace, in order withal to lead good lives. Well, even this consideration should lead him at least to confess that there is a miserable darkness in the human mind, which knows how it ought to tame a lion, but knows not how to live. To know this, too, is it enough for us to have free will and natural law? This is that wisdom of word, whereby "the cross of Christ is rendered of none effect."[5] He, however, who said, "I will destroy the wisdom of the wise,"[6] since that cross cannot be made of none effect, in very deed overthrows that wisdom by the foolishness of preaching whereby believers are healed. For if natural capacity, by help of free will, is in itself sufficient both for discovering how one ought to live, and also for leading a holy life, then "Christ died in vain,"[7] and therefore also "the offence of the cross is ceased."[8] Why also may I not myself exclaim? — nay, I will exclaim, and chide them with a Christian's sorrow, — "Christ is become of no effect unto you, whosoever of you are justified by nature; ye are fallen from grace;"[9] for, "being ignorant of God's righteousness, and wishing to establish your own righteousness, you have not submitted yourselves to the righteousness of God."[10] For even as "Christ is the end of the law," so likewise is He the Saviour of man's corrupted nature, "for righteousness to every one that believeth."[11]

CHAP. 48 [XLI.] — HOW THE TERM "ALL" IS TO BE UNDERSTOOD.

His opponents adduced the passage, "All have sinned,"[12] and he met their statement founded on this with the remark that "the apostle was manifestly speaking of the then existing generation, that is, the Jews and the Gentiles;" but surely the passage which I have quoted, "By one man sin entered the world, and death by sin, and so death passed upon all men; in which all have sinned,"[3] embraces in its terms the generations both of old and of modern times, both ourselves and our posterity. He adduces also this passage, whence he would prove that we ought not to understand all without exception, when "all" is used: — "As by the offence of one," he says, "upon all men to condemnation, even so by the righteousness of One, upon all men unto justification of life."[13] "There can be no doubt," he says, "that not all men are sanctified by the righteousness of Christ, but only those who are

---

[1] Rom. vi. 13.  [2] 1 Thess. v. 21.  [3] Rom. v. 12.
[4] Acts iv. 12.

[5] 1 Cor. i. 17.  [6] 1 Cor. i. 19.  [7] Gal. ii. 21.
[8] Gal. v. 11.  [9] Gal. v. 4.  [10] Rom. x. 3.
[11] Rom. x. 4.  [12] Rom. iii. 23.  [13] Rom. v. 18.

willing to obey Him, and have been cleansed in the washing of His baptism." Well, but he does not prove what he wants by this quotation. For as the clause, "By the offence of one, upon all men to condemnation," is so worded that not one is omitted in its sense, so in the correspond-ing clause, "By the righteousness of One, upon all men unto justification of life," no one is omitted in its sense, — not, indeed, because all men have faith and are washed in His baptism, but because no man is justified unless he believes in Christ and is cleansed by His baptism. The term "*all*" is therefore used in a way which shows that no one whatever can be supposed able to be saved by any other means than through Christ Himself. For if in a city there be ap-pointed but one instructor, we are most correct in saying : That man teaches all in that place ; not meaning, indeed, that all who live in the city take lessons of him, but that no one is instructed unless taught by him. In like manner no one is justified unless Christ has justified him.[1]

CHAP. 49 [XLII.] — A MAN CAN BE SINLESS, BUT ONLY BY THE HELP OF GRACE. IN THE SAINTS THIS POSSIBILITY ADVANCES AND KEEPS PACE WITH THE REALIZATION.

"Well, be it so," says he, " I agree ; he testifies to the fact that all were sinners. He says, in-deed, what they have been, not that they might not have been something else. Wherefore," he adds, " if all men could be proved to be sinners, it would not by any means prejudice our own definite position, in insisting not so much on what men are, as on what they are able to be." He is right for once to allow that no man living is justified in God's sight. He contends, how-ever, that this is not the question, but that the point lies in the possibility of a man's not sin-ning, — on which subject it is unnecessary for us to take ground against him ; for, in truth, I do not much care about expressing a definite opin-ion on the question, whether in the present life there ever have been, or now are, or ever can be, any persons who have had, or are having, or are to have, the love of God so perfectly as to admit of no addition to it (for nothing short of this amounts to a most true, full, and perfect right-eousness). For I ought not too sharply to con-tend as to when, or where, or in whom is done that which I confess and maintain can be done by the will of man, aided by the grace of God. Nor do I indeed contend about the actual pos-sibility, forasmuch as the possibility under dispute advances with the realization in the saints, their human will being healed and helped ; whilst "the love of God," as fully as our healed and cleansed nature can possibly receive it, " is shed abroad

in our hearts by the Holy Ghost, which is given to us."[2] In a better way, therefore, is God's cause promoted (and it is to its promotion that our author professes to apply his warm defence of nature) when He is acknowledged as our Saviour no less than as our Creator, than when His succour to us as Saviour is impaired and dwarfed to nothing by the defence of the creature, as if it were sound and its resources entire.

CHAP. 50 [XLIII.] — GOD COMMANDS NO IMPOSSI-BILITIES.

What he says, however, is true enough, "that God is as good as just, and made man such that he was quite able to live without the evil of sin, if only he had been willing." For who does not know that man was made whole and faultless, and endowed with a free will and a free ability to lead a holy life? Our present inquiry, however, is about the man whom " the thieves "[3] left half dead on the road, and who, being disabled and pierced through with heavy wounds, is not so able to mount up to the heights of righteousness as he was able to descend therefrom ; who, more-over, if he is now in " the inn,"[4] is in process of cure. God therefore does not command impos-sibilities ; but in His command He counsels you both to do what you can for yourself, and to ask His aid in what you cannot do. Now, we should see whence comes the possibility, and whence the impossibility. This man says: " That pro-ceeds not from a man's will which he can do by nature." I say : A man is not righteous by his will if he can be by nature. He will, however, be able to accomplish by remedial aid what he is rendered incapable of doing by his flaw.

CHAP. 51 [XLIV.] — STATE OF THE QUESTION BETWEEN THE PELAGIANS AND THE CATHOLICS. HOLY MEN OF OLD SAVED BY THE SELF-SAME FAITH IN CHRIST WHICH WE EXERCISE.

But why need we tarry longer on general statements? Let us go into the core of the question, which we have to discuss with our opponents solely, or almost entirely, on one par-ticular point. For inasmuch as he says that " as far as the present question is concerned, it is not pertinent to inquire whether there have been or now are any men in this life without sin, but whether they had or have the ability to be such persons ; " so, were I even to allow that there have been or are any such, I should not by any means therefore affirm that they had or have the ability, unless justified by the grace of God through our Lord " Jesus Christ and Him cruci-fied."[5] For the same faith which healed the saints of old now heals us, — that is to say,

---

[1] Compare *De Peccatorum Meritis et Remissione*, i. 55.

[2] Rom. v. 5.
[3] Luke x. 30.   Rather, "*robbers ;*" latrones, ληϲταί.
[4] Luke x. 34.                    [5] 1 Cor. ii. 2.

faith "in the one Mediator between God and men, the man Christ Jesus,"[1] — faith in His blood, faith in His cross, faith in His death and resurrection. As we therefore have the same spirit of faith, we also believe, and on that account also speak.

### CHAP. 52. — THE WHOLE DISCUSSION IS ABOUT GRACE.

Let us, however, observe what our author answers, after laying before himself the question wherein he seems indeed so intolerable to Christian hearts. He says: "But you will tell me this is what disturbs a great many, — that you do not maintain that it is by the grace of God that a man is able to be without sin." Certainly this is what causes us disturbance; this is what we object to him. He touches the very point of the case. This is what causes us such utter pain to endure it; this is why we cannot bear to have such points debated by Christians, owing to the love which we feel towards others and towards themselves. Well, let us hear how he clears himself from the objectionable character of the question he has raised. "What blindness of ignorance," he exclaims, "what sluggishness of an uninstructed mind, which supposes that that is maintained and held to be without God's grace which it only hears ought to be attributed to God!" Now, if we knew nothing of what follows this outburst of his, and formed our opinion on simply hearing these words, we might suppose that we had been led to a wrong view of our opponents by the spread of report and by the asseveration of some suitable witnesses among the brethren. For how could it have been more pointedly and truly stated that the possibility of not sinning, to whatever extent it exists or shall exist in man, ought only to be attributed to God? This too is our own affirmation. We may shake hands.

### CHAP. 53 [XLV.] — PELAGIUS DISTINGUISHES BETWEEN A POWER AND ITS USE.

Well, are there other things to listen to? Yes, certainly; both to listen to, and correct and guard against. "Now, when it is said," he says, "that the very ability is not at all of man's will, but of the Author of nature, — that is, God, — how can that possibly be understood to be without the grace of God which is deemed especially to belong to God?" Already we begin to see what he means; but that we may not lie under any mistake, he explains himself with greater breadth and clearness: "That this may become still plainer, we must," says he, "enter on a somewhat fuller discussion of the point. Now we affirm that the possibility of anything

lies not so much in the ability of a man's will as in the necessity of nature." He then proceeds to illustrate his meaning by examples and similes. "Take," says he, "for instance, my ability to speak. That I am able to speak is not my own; but that I do speak is my own, — that is, of my own will. And because the act of my speaking is my own, I have the power of alternative action, — that is to say, both to speak and to refrain from speaking. But because my ability to speak is not my own, that is, is not of my own determination and will, it is of necessity[2] that I am always able to speak; and though I wished not to be able to speak, I am unable, nevertheless, to be unable to speak, unless perhaps I were to deprive myself of that member whereby the function of speaking is to be performed." Many means, indeed, might be mentioned whereby, if he wish it, a man may deprive himself of the possibility of speaking, without removing the organ of speech. If, for instance, anything were to happen to a man to destroy his voice, he would be unable to speak, although the members remained; for a man's voice is of course no member. There may, in short, be an injury done to the member internally, short of the actual loss of it. I am, however, unwilling to press the argument for a word; and it may be replied to me in the contest, Why, even to injure is to lose. But yet we can so contrive matters, by closing and shutting the mouth with bandages, as to be quite incapable of opening it, and to put the opening of it out of our power, although it was quite in our own power to shut it while the strength and healthy exercise of the limbs remained.

### CHAP. 54 [XLVI.] — THERE IS NO INCOMPATIBILITY BETWEEN NECESSITY AND FREE WILL.

Now how does all this apply to our subject? Let us see what he makes out of it. "Whatever," says he, "is fettered by natural necessity is deprived of determination of will and deliberation." Well, now, here lies a question; for it is the height of absurdity for us to say that it does not belong to our will that we wish to be happy, on the ground that it is absolutely impossible for us to be unwilling to be happy, by reason of some indescribable but amiable coercion of our nature; nor dare we maintain that God has not the will but the necessity of righteousness, because He cannot will to sin.

### CHAP. 55 [XLVII.] — THE SAME CONTINUED.

Mark also what follows. "We may perceive," says he, "the same thing to be true of hearing,

---

[1] 1 Tim. ii. 5.

[2] *Necesse est me semper loqui posse.* This obscure sentence seems to point to Pelagius' former statement: *Cujusque rei possibilitatem non tam in arbitrii humani potestate quàm in naturæ necessitate consistere.*

smelling, and seeing, — that to hear, and to smell, and to see is of our own power, while the ability to hear, and to smell, and to see is not of our own power, but lies in a natural necessity." Either I do not understand what he means, or he does not himself. For how is the possibility of seeing not in our own power, if the necessity of not seeing is in our own power because blindness is in our own power, by which we can deprive ourselves, if we will, of this very ability to see? How, moreover, is it in our own power to see whenever we will, when, without any loss whatever to our natural structure of body in the organ of sight, we are unable, even though we wish, to see, — either by the removal of all external lights during the night, or by our being shut up in some dark place? Likewise, if our ability or our inability to hear is not in our own power, but lies in the necessity of nature, whereas our actual hearing or not hearing is of our own will, how comes it that he is inattentive to the fact that there are so many things which we hear against our will, which penetrate our sense even when our ears are stopped, as the creaking of a saw near to us, or the grunt of a pig? Although the said stopping of our ears shows plainly enough that it does not lie within our own power not to hear so long as our ears are open; perhaps, too, such a stopping of our ears as shall deprive us of the entire sense in question proves that even the ability not to hear lies within our own power. As to his remarks, again, concerning our sense of smell, does he not display no little carelessness when he says "that it is not in our own power to be able or to be unable to smell, but that it is in our own power" — that is to say, in our free will — "to smell or not to smell?" For let us suppose some one to place us, with our hands firmly tied, but yet without any injury to our olfactory members, among some bad and noxious smells; in such a case we altogether lose the power, however strong may be our wish, not to smell, because every time we are obliged to draw breath we also inhale the smell which we do not wish.

CHAP. 56 [XLVIII.] — THE ASSISTANCE OF GRACE IN A PERFECT NATURE.

Not only, then, are these similes employed by our author false, but so is the matter which he wishes them to illustrate. He goes on to say: "In like manner, touching the possibility of our not sinning, we must understand that it is of us not to sin, but yet that the ability to avoid sin is not of us." If he were speaking of man's whole and perfect nature, which we do not now possess ( "for we are saved by hope: but hope that is seen is not hope. But if we hope for that we see not, then do we with patience wait

for it " [1]), his language even in that case would not be correct to the effect that to avoid sinning would be of us alone, although to sin would be of us, for even then there must be the help of God, which must shed itself on those who are willing to receive it, just as the light is given to strong and healthy eyes to assist them in their function of sight. Inasmuch, however, as it is about this present life of ours that he raises the question, wherein our corruptible body weighs down the soul, and our earthly tabernacle depresses our sense with all its many thoughts, I am astonished that he can with any heart suppose that, even without the help of our Saviour's healing balm, it is in our own power to avoid sin, and the ability not to sin is of nature, which gives only stronger evidence of its own corruption by the very fact of its failing to see its taint.

CHAP. 57 [XLIX.] — IT DOES NOT DETRACT FROM GOD'S ALMIGHTY POWER, THAT HE IS INCAPABLE OF EITHER SINNING, OR DYING, OR DESTROYING HIMSELF.

"Inasmuch," says he, "as not to sin is ours, we are able to sin and to avoid sin." What, then, if another should say: "Inasmuch as not to wish for unhappiness is ours, we are able both to wish for it and not to wish for it?" And yet we are positively unable to wish for it. For who could possibly wish to be unhappy, even though he wishes for something else from which unhappiness will ensue to him against his will? Then again, inasmuch as, in an infinitely greater degree, it is God's not to sin, shall we therefore venture to say that He is able both to sin and to avoid sin? God forbid that we should ever say that He is able to sin! For He cannot, as foolish persons suppose, therefore fail to be almighty, because He is unable to die, or because He cannot deny Himself. What, therefore, does he mean? by what method of speech does he try to persuade us on a point which he is himself loth to consider? For he advances a step further, and says: "Inasmuch as, however, it is not of us to be able to avoid sin; even if we were to wish not to be able to avoid sin, it is not in our power to be unable to avoid sin." It is an involved sentence, and therefore a very obscure one. It might, however, be more plainly expressed in some such way as this: "Inasmuch as to be able to avoid sin is not of us, then, whether we wish it or do not wish it, we are able to avoid sin!" He does not say, "Whether we wish it or do not wish it, we do not sin," — for we undoubtedly do sin, if we wish; — but yet he asserts that, whether we will or not, we have the capacity of not sinning, — a capacity which

---

[1] Rom. viii. 24, 25.

he declares to be inherent in our nature. Of a man, indeed, who has his legs strong and sound, it may be said admissibly enough, "whether he will or not he has the capacity of walking;" but if his legs be broken, however much he may wish, he has not the capacity. The nature of which our author speaks is corrupted. "Why is dust and ashes proud?"[1] It is corrupted. It implores the Physician's help. "Save me, O Lord,"[2] is its cry; "Heal my soul,"[3] it exclaims. Why does he check such cries so as to hinder future health, by insisting, as it were, on its present capacity?

### CHAP. 58 [L.] — EVEN PIOUS AND GOD-FEARING MEN RESIST GRACE.

Observe also what remark he adds, by which he thinks that his position is confirmed : " No will," says he, " can take away that which is proved to be inseparably implanted in nature." Whence then comes that utterance : "So then ye cannot do the things that ye would?"[4] Whence also this : "For what good I would, that I do not; but what evil I hate, that do I?"[5] Where is that capacity which is proved to be inseparably implanted in nature? See, it is human beings who do not what they will; and it is about not sinning, certainly, that he was treating, — not about not flying, because it was men, not birds, that formed his subject. Behold, it is man who does not the good which he would, but does the evil which he would not : " to will is present with him, but how to perform that which is good is not present."[6] Where is the capacity which is proved to be inseparably implanted in nature? For whomsoever the apostle represents by himself, if he does not speak these things of his own self, he certainly represents a man by himself. By our author, however, it is maintained that our human nature actually possesses an inseparable capacity of not at all sinning. Such a statement, however, even when made by a man who knows not the effect of his words (but this ignorance is hardly attributable to the man who suggests these statements for unwary though God-fearing men), causes the grace of Christ to be "made of none effect,"[7] since it is pretended that human nature is sufficient for its own holiness and justification.

### CHAP. 59 [LI.] — IN WHAT SENSE PELAGIUS ATTRIBUTED TO GOD'S GRACE THE CAPACITY OF NOT SINNING.

In order, however, to escape from the odium wherewith Christians guard their salvation, he parries their question when they ask him, "Why do you affirm that man without the help of God's grace is able to avoid sin?" by saying, "The actual capacity of not sinning lies not so much in the power of will as in the necessity of nature. Whatever is placed in the necessity of nature undoubtedly appertains to the Author of nature, that is, God. How then," says he, "can that be regarded as spoken without the grace of God which is shown to belong in an especial manner to God?" Here the opinion is expressed which all along was kept in the background; there is, in fact, no way of permanently concealing such a doctrine. The reason why he attributes to the grace of God the capacity of not sinning is, that God is the Author of nature, in which, he declares, this capacity of avoiding sin is inseparably implanted. Whenever He wills a thing, no doubt He does it; and what He wills not, that He does not. Now, wherever there is this inseparable capacity, there cannot accrue any infirmity of the will; or rather, there cannot be both a presence of will and a failure in " performance."[6] This, then, being the case, how comes it to pass that " to will is present, but how to perform that which is good " is not present? Now, if the author of the work we are discussing spoke of that nature of man, which was in the beginning created faultless and perfect, in whatever sense his dictum be taken, " that it has an inseparable capacity," — that is, so to say, one which cannot be lost, — then that nature ought not to have been mentioned at all which could be corrupted, and which could require a physician to cure the eyes of the blind, and restore that capacity of seeing which had been lost through blindness. For I suppose a blind man would like to see, but is unable ; but, whenever a man wishes to do a thing and cannot, there is present to him the will, but he has lost the capacity.

### CHAP. 60 [LII.] — PELAGIUS ADMITS " CONTRARY FLESH " IN THE UNBAPTIZED.

See what obstacles he still attempts to break through, if possible, in order to introduce his own opinion. He raises a question for himself in these terms : " But you will tell me that, according to the apostle, the flesh is contrary[4] to us ;" and then answers it in this wise : " How can it be that in the case of any baptized person the flesh is contrary to him, when according to the same apostle he is understood not to be in the flesh? For he says, ' But ye are not in the flesh.' "[8] Very well ; we shall soon see[9] whether it be really true that this says that in the baptized the flesh cannot be contrary to them ; at present, however, as it was impossible for him quite to forget that he was a Christian (although his reminiscence on the point is but slight), he has

---

[1] Ecclus. x. 9.　　　[2] Ps. xii. 1.　　　[3] Ps. xli. 4.
[4] Gal. v. 17.　　　[5] Rom. vii. 15.　　　[6] Rom. vii. 18.
[7] 1 Cor. i. 17. Another reading has *crux Christi* instead of "Christi gratia," thus closely adopting the apostle's words.

[8] Rom. viii. 9.　　　　　　　[9] In the next chapter.

quitted his defence of nature. Where then is that inseparable capacity of his? Are those who are not yet baptized not a part of human nature? Well, now, here by all means, here at this point, he might find his opportunity of awaking out of his sleep; and he still has it if he is careful. "How can it be," he asks, "that in the case of a baptized person the flesh is contrary to him?" Therefore to the unbaptized the flesh can be contrary! Let him tell us how; for even in these there is that nature which has been so stoutly defended by him. However, in these he does certainly allow that nature is corrupted, inasmuch as it was only among the baptized that the wounded traveller left his inn sound and well, or rather remains sound in the inn whither the compassionate Samaritan carried him that he might become cured.[1] Well, now, if he allows that the flesh is contrary even in these, let him tell us what has happened to occasion this, since the flesh and the spirit alike are the work of one and the same Creator, and are therefore undoubtedly both of them good, because He is good, — unless indeed it be that damage which has been inflicted by man's own will. And that this may be repaired in our nature, there is need of that very Saviour from whose creative hand nature itself proceeded. Now, if we acknowledge that this Saviour, and that healing remedy of His by which the Word was made flesh in order to dwell among us, are required by small and great, — by the crying infant and the hoary-headed man alike, — then, in fact, the whole controversy of the point between us is settled.

CHAP. 61 [LIII.] — PAUL ASSERTS THAT THE FLESH IS CONTRARY EVEN IN THE BAPTIZED.

Now let us see whether we anywhere read about the flesh being contrary in the baptized also. And here, I ask, to whom did the apostle say, "The flesh lusteth against the Spirit, and the Spirit against the flesh: and these are contrary the one to the other; so that ye do not the things that ye would?"[2] He wrote this, I apprehend, to the Galatians, to whom he also says, "He therefore that ministereth to you the Spirit, and worketh miracles among you, doeth he it by the works of the law or by the hearing of faith?"[3] It appears, therefore, that it is to Christians that he speaks, to whom, too, God had given His Spirit: therefore, too, to the baptized. Observe, therefore, that even in baptized persons the flesh is found to be contrary; so that they have not that capacity which, our author says, is inseparably implanted in nature. Where then is the ground for his assertion, "How can it be that in the case of a baptized person the flesh is

contrary to him?" in whatever sense he understands the flesh? Because in very deed it is not its nature that is good, but it is the carnal defects of the flesh which are expressly named in the passage before us.[4] Yet observe, even in the baptized, how contrary is the flesh. And in what way contrary? So that, "They do not the things which they would." Take notice that the will is present in a man; but where is that "capacity of nature?" Let us confess that grace is necessary to us; let us cry out, "O wretched man that I am! who shall deliver me from the body of this death?" And let our answer be, "The grace of God, through Jesus Christ our Lord!"[5]

CHAP. 62. — CONCERNING WHAT GRACE OF GOD IS HERE UNDER DISCUSSION. THE UNGODLY MAN, WHEN DYING, IS NOT DELIVERED FROM CONCUPISCENCE.

Now, whereas it is most correctly asked in those words put to him, "Why do you affirm that man without the help of God's grace is able to avoid sin?" yet the inquiry did not concern that grace by which man was created, but only that whereby he is saved through Jesus Christ our Lord. Faithful men say in their prayer, "Lead us not into temptation, but deliver us from evil."[6] But if they already have capacity, why do they pray? Or, what is the evil which they pray to be delivered from, but, above all else, "the body of this death?" And from this nothing but God's grace alone delivers them, through our Lord Jesus Christ. Not of course from the substance of the body, which is good; but from its carnal offences, from which a man is not liberated except by the grace of the Saviour, — not even when he quits the body by the death of the body. If it was this that the apostle meant to declare, why had he previously said, "I see another law in my members, warring against the law of my mind, and bringing me into captivity to the law of sin which is in my members?"[7] Behold what damage the disobedience of the will has inflicted on man's nature! Let him be permitted to pray that he may be healed! Why need he presume so much on the capacity of his nature? It is wounded, hurt, damaged, destroyed. It is a true confession of its weakness, not a false defence of its capacity, that it stands in need of. It requires the grace of God, not that it may be made, but that it may be re-made. And this is the only grace which by our author is proclaimed to be unnecessary; because of this he is silent! If, indeed, he had said nothing at all about God's grace, and had not proposed to himself that question for solution, for the purpose of

---

[1] Luke x. 34.  [2] Gal. v. 17.  [3] Gal. iii. 5.

[4] See the context of Gal. v. 17, in verses 19–21.
[5] Rom. vii. 24, 25.  [6] Matt. vi. 13.  [7] Rom. vii. 23.

removing from himself the odium of this matter,[1] it might have been thought that his view of the subject was consistent with the truth, only that he had refrained from mentioning it, on the ground that not on all occasions need we say all we think. He proposed the question of grace, and answered it in the way that he had in his heart; the question has been defined, — not in the way we wished, but according to the doubt we entertained as to what was his meaning.

<h3>CHAP. 63 [LIV.] — DOES GOD CREATE CONTRARIES?</h3>

He next endeavours, by much quotation from the apostle, about which there is no controversy, to show " that the flesh is often mentioned by him in such a manner as proves him to mean not the substance, but the works of the flesh." What is this to the point? The defects of the flesh are contrary to the will of man; his nature is not accused; but a Physician is wanted for its defects. What signifies his question, " Who made man's spirit?" and his own answer thereto, " God, without a doubt?" Again he asks, " Who created the flesh?" and again answers, " The same God, I suppose." And yet a third question, " Is the God good who created both?" and the third answer, " Nobody doubts it." Once more a question, " Are not both good, since the good Creator made them?" and its answer, " It must be confessed that they are." And then follows his conclusion: " If, therefore, both the spirit is good, and the flesh is good, as made by the good Creator, how can it be that the two good things should be contrary to one another?" I need not say that the whole of this reasoning would be upset if one were to ask him, " Who made heat and cold?" and he were to say in answer, " God, without a doubt." I do not ask the string of questions. Let him determine himself whether these conditions of climate may either be said to be not good, or else whether they do not seem to be contrary to each other. Here he will probably object, " These are not substances, but the qualities of substances." Very true, it is so. But still they are natural qualities, and undoubtedly belong to God's creation; and substances, indeed, are not said to be contrary to each other in themselves, but in their qualities, as water and fire. What if it be so too with flesh and spirit? We do not affirm it to be so; but, in order to show that his argument terminates in a conclusion which does not necessarily follow, we have said so much as this. For it is quite possible for contraries not to be reciprocally opposed to each other, but rather by mutual action to temper health and render it good; just as, in our body, dryness and moisture, cold and heat, — in the tempering of which altogether consists our bodily health. The fact, however, that " the flesh is contrary to the Spirit, so that we cannot do the things that we would," [2] is a defect, not nature. The Physician's grace must be sought, and their controversy must end.

<h3>CHAP. 64. — PELAGIUS' ADMISSION AS REGARDS THE UNBAPTIZED, FATAL.</h3>

Now, as touching these two good substances which the good God created, how, against the reasoning of this man, in the case of unbaptized persons, can they be contrary the one to the other? Will he be sorry to have said this too, which he admitted out of some regard to the Christians' faith? For when he asked, " How, in the case of any person who is already baptized, can it be that his flesh is contrary to him?" he intimated, of course, that in the case of unbaptized persons it is possible for the flesh to be contrary. For why insert the clause, " *who is already baptized*," when without such an addition he might have put his question thus: " How in the case of any person can the flesh be contrary?" and when, in order to prove this, he might have subjoined that argument of his, that as both body and spirit are good (made as they are by the good Creator), they therefore cannot be contrary to each other? Now, suppose unbaptized persons (in whom, at any rate, he confesses that the flesh is contrary) were to ply him with his own arguments, and say to him, Who made man's spirit? he must answer, God. Suppose they asked him again, Who created the flesh? and he answers, The same God, I believe. Suppose their third question to be, Is the God good who created both? and his reply to be, Nobody doubts it. Suppose once more they put to him his yet remaining inquiry, Are not both good, since the good Creator made them? and he confesses it. Then surely they will cut his throat with his own sword, when they force home his conclusion on him, and say: Since therefore the spirit of man is good, and his flesh good, as made by the good Creator, how can it be that the two being good should be contrary to one another? Here, perhaps, he will reply: I beg your pardon, I ought not to have said that the flesh cannot be contrary to the spirit in any baptized person, as if I meant to imply that it is contrary in the unbaptized; but I ought to have made my statement general, to the effect that the flesh in no man's case is contrary. Now see into what a corner he drives himself. See what a man will say, who is unwilling to cry out with the apostle, " Who shall deliver me from the body of this death? The grace of God, through Jesus

---

[1] See above, ch. 59, *sub init.*

[2] Gal. v. 17.

Christ our Lord." [1]  "But why," he asks, "should I so exclaim, who am already baptized in Christ? It is for them to cry out thus who have not yet received so great a benefit, whose words the apostle in a figure transferred to himself, — if indeed even they say so much." Well, this defence of nature does not permit even these to utter this exclamation! For ·in the baptized, there is no nature ; and in the unbaptized, nature is not ! Or if even in the one class it is allowed to be corrupted, so that it is not without reason that men exclaim, " O wretched man that I am ! who shall deliver me from this body of death ? " to the other, too, help is brought in what follows : "The grace of God, through Jesus Christ our Lord ; " then let it at last be granted that human nature stands in need of Christ for its Physician.

CHAP. 65 [LV.] — "THIS BODY OF DEATH," SO CALLED FROM ITS DEFECT, NOT FROM ITS SUBSTANCE.

Now, I ask, when did our nature lose that liberty, which he craves to be given to him when he says : "Who shall liberate me ? " [2]  For even he finds no fault with the substance of the flesh when he expresses his desire to be liberated from the body of this death, since the nature of the body, as well as of the soul, must be attributed to the good God as the author thereof. But what he speaks of undoubtedly concerns the offences of the body. Now from the body the death of the body separates us ; whereas the offences contracted from the body remain, and their just punishment awaits them, as the rich man found in hell.[3]  From these it was that he was unable to liberate himself, who said : "Who shall liberate me from the body of this death ? " [2]  But whensoever it was that he lost this liberty, at least there remains that " inseparable capacity " of nature, — he has the ability from natural resources, — he has the volition from free will. Why does he seek the sacrament of baptism? Is it because of past sins, in order that they may be forgiven, since they cannot be undone ? Well, suppose you acquit and release a man on these terms, he must still utter the old cry ; for he not only wants to be mercifully let off from punishment for past offences, but to be strengthened and fortified against sinning for the time to come. For he " delights in the law of God, after the inward man ; but then he sees another law in his members, warring against the law of his mind." [4]  Observe, he sees that there *is*, not recollects that there *was*. It is a present pressure, not a past memory. And he sees the other law not only "warring," but even " bringing him into captivity to the law of sin, which *is*"

(not which *was*) " in his members." [5]  Hence comes that cry of his : " O wretched man that I am ! who shall liberate me from the body of this death ? " [2]  Let him pray, let him entreat for the help of the mighty Physician. Why gainsay that prayer? Why cry down that entreaty? Why shall the unhappy suitor be hindered from begging for the mercy of Christ, — and that too by Christians? For, it was even they who were accompanying Christ that tried to prevent the blind man, by clamouring him down, from begging for light ; but even amidst the din and throng of the gainsayers He hears the suppliant ; [6]  whence the response : " The grace of God, through Jesus Christ out Lord." [7]

CHAP. 66. — THE WORKS, NOT THE SUBSTANCE, OF THE " FLESH " OPPOSED TO THE " SPIRIT."

Now if we secure even this concession from them, that unbaptized persons may implore the assistance of the Saviour's grace, this is indeed no slight point against that fallacious assertion of the self-sufficiency of nature and of the power of free will. For he is not sufficient to himself who says, " O wretched man that I am ! who shall liberate me ? " Nor can he be said to have full liberty who still asks for liberation. [LVI.] But let us, moreover, see to this point also, whether they who are baptized do the good which they would, without any resistance from the lust of the flesh. That, however, which we have to say on this subject, our author himself mentions, when concluding this topic he says : " As we remarked, the passage in which occur the words, ' The flesh lusteth against the Spirit,' [8] must needs have reference not to the substance, but to the works of the flesh." We too allege that this is spoken not of the substance of the flesh, but of its works, which proceed from carnal concupiscence, — in a word, from sin, concerning which we have this precept : " Not to let it reign in our mortal body, that we should obey it in the lusts thereof." [9]

CHAP. 67 [LVII.] — WHO MAY BE SAID TO BE UNDER THE LAW.

But even our author should observe that it is to persons who have been already baptized that it was said : " The flesh lusteth against the Spirit, and the Spirit against the flesh, so that ye cannot do the things that ye would." [8]  And lest he should make them slothful for the actual conflict, and should seem by this statement to have given them laxity in sinning, he goes on to tell them : " If ye be led of the Spirit, ye are no longer under the law." [10]  For that man is under the law, who, from fear of the punishment which the law threatens, and not from any love for

---

[1] Rom. vii. 24, 25.   [2] Rom. vii. 24.   [3] Luke xvi. 23.
[4] Rom. vii. 22, 23.

[5] Rom. vii. 23.   [6] Mark x. 46–52.   [7] Rom. vii. 25.
[8] Gal. v. 17.   [9] Rom. vi. 12.   [10] Gal. v. 18.

righteousness, obliges himself to abstain from the work of sin, without being as yet free and removed from the desire of sinning. For it is in his very will that he is guilty, whereby he would prefer, if it were possible, that what he dreads should not exist, in order that he might freely do what he secretly desires. Therefore he says, "If ye be led of the Spirit, ye are not under the law," — even the law which inspires fear, but gives not love. For this "love is shed abroad in our hearts," not by the letter of the law, but "by the Holy Ghost, which is given unto us." [1] This is the law of liberty, not of bondage; being the law of love, not of fear; and concerning it the Apostle James says: "Whoso looketh into the perfect law of liberty." [2] Whence he, too, no longer indeed felt terrified by God's law as a slave, but delighted in it in the inward man, although still seeing another law in his members warring against the law of his mind. Accordingly he here says: "If ye be led of the Spirit, ye are not under the law." So far, indeed, as any man is led by the Spirit, he is not under the law; because, so far as he rejoices in the law of God, he lives not in fear of the law, since "fear has torment," [3] not joy and delight.

### CHAP. 68 [LVIII.] — DESPITE THE DEVIL, MAN MAY, BY GOD'S HELP, BE PERFECTED.

If, therefore, we feel rightly on this matter, it is our duty at once to be thankful for what is already healed within us, and to pray for such further healing as shall enable us to enjoy full liberty, in that most absolute state of health which is incapable of addition, the perfect pleasure of God. [4] For we do not deny that human nature can be without sin; nor ought we by any means to refuse to it the ability to become perfect, since we admit its capacity for progress, — by God's grace, however, through our Lord Jesus Christ. By His assistance we aver that it becomes holy and happy, by whom it was created in order to be so. There is accordingly an easy refutation of the objection which our author says is alleged by some against him: "The devil opposes us." This objection we also meet in entirely identical language with that which he uses in reply: "We must resist him, and he will flee. 'Resist the devil,' says the blessed apostle, 'and he will flee from you.' [5] From which it may be observed, what his harming amounts to against those whom he flees; or what power he is to be understood as possessing, when he prevails only against those who do not resist him." Such language is my own also; for it is impossible to employ truer words. There is, however, this difference between us and them, that we, whenever the devil has to be resisted, not only do

not deny, but actually teach, that God's help must be sought; whereas they attribute so much power to will, as to take away prayer from religious duty. Now it is certainly with a view to resisting the devil and his fleeing from us that we say when we pray, "Lead us not into temptation;" [6] to the same end also are we warned by our Captain, exhorting us as soldiers in the words: "Watch ye and pray, lest ye enter into temptation." [7]

### CHAP. 69 [LIX.] — PELAGIUS PUTS NATURE IN THE PLACE OF GRACE.

In opposition, however, to those who ask, "And who would be unwilling to be without sin, if it were put in the power of a man?" he rightly contends, saying "that by this very question they acknowledge that the thing is not impossible; because so much as this, many, if not all men, certainly desire." Well, then, let him only confess the means by which this is possible, and then our controversy is ended. Now the means is "the grace of God through our Lord Jesus Christ;" by which he nowhere has been willing to allow that we are assisted when we pray, for the avoidance of sin. If indeed he secretly allows this, he must forgive us if we suspect otherwise. For he himself works this result, who, though encountering so much obloquy on this subject, wishes to entertain the secret opinion, and yet is unwilling to confess or profess it. It would surely be no great matter were he to speak out, especially since he has undertaken to handle and open this point, as if it had been objected against him on the side of opponents. Why on such occasions did he choose only to defend nature, and assert that man was so created as to have it in his power not to sin if he wished not to sin; and, from the fact that he was so created, definitely say that the power was owing to God's grace which enabled him to avoid sin, if he was unwilling to commit it; and yet refuse to say anything concerning the fact that even nature itself is either, because disordered, healed by God's grace through our Lord Jesus Christ, or else assisted by it, because in itself it is so insufficient?

### CHAP. 70 [LX.] — WHETHER ANY MAN IS WITHOUT SIN IN THIS LIFE.

Now, whether there ever has been, or is, or ever can be, a man living so righteous a life in this world as to have no sin at all, may be an open question among true and pious Christians; [8] but whoever doubts the possibility of this sinless state *after this present life*, is foolish. For my own part, indeed, I am unwilling to dispute the point even as respects this life. For

---

[1] Rom. v. 5.          [2] Jas. i. 25.          [3] 1 John iv. 18.
[4] Ps. xvi. 11.        [5] Jas. iv. 17.

[6] Matt. vi. 13.                    [7] Mark xiv. 38.
[8] See next treatise — its preface, or *Admonitio*.

although that passage seems to me to be incapable of bearing any doubtful sense, wherein it is written, "In thy sight shall no man living be justified"[1] (and so of similar passages), yet I could wish it were possible to show either that such quotations were capable of bearing a better signification, or that a perfect and plenary righteousness, to which it were impossible for any accession to be made, had been realized at some former time in some one whilst passing through this life in the flesh, or was now being realized, or would be hereafter. They, however, are in a great majority, who, while not doubting that to the last day of their life it will be needful to them to resort to the prayer which they can so truthfully utter, "Forgive us our trespasses, as we forgive those who trespass against us,"[2] still trust that in Christ and His promises they possess a true, certain, and unfailing hope. There is, however, no method whereby any persons arrive at absolute perfection, or whereby any man makes the slightest progress to true and godly righteousness, but the assisting grace of our crucified Saviour Christ, and the gift of His Spirit; and whosoever shall deny this cannot rightly, I almost think, be reckoned in the number of any kind of Christians at all.

CHAP. 71 [LXI.] — AUGUSTIN REPLIES AGAINST THE QUOTATIONS WHICH PELAGIUS HAD ADVANCED OUT OF THE CATHOLIC WRITERS. LACTANTIUS.

Accordingly, with respect also to the passages which he has adduced, — not indeed from the canonical Scriptures, but out of certain treatises of catholic writers, — I wish to meet the assertions of such as say that the said quotations make for him. The fact is, these passages are so entirely neutral, that they oppose neither our own opinion nor his. Amongst them he wanted to class something out of my own books, thus accounting me to be a person who seemed worthy of being ranked with them. For this I must not be ungrateful, and I should be sorry — so I say with unaffected friendliness — for him to be in error, since he has conferred this honour upon me. As for his first quotation, indeed, why need I examine it largely, since I do not see here the author's name, either because he has not given it, or because from some casual mistake the copy which you[3] forwarded to me did not contain it? Especially as in writings of such authors I feel myself free to use my own judgment (owing unhesitating assent to nothing but the canonical Scriptures), whilst in fact there is not a passage which he has quoted from the works of this anonymous author[4] that disturbs me. "It be-

hooved," says he, "for the Master and Teacher of virtue to become most like to man, that by conquering sin He might show that man is able to conquer sin." Now, however this passage may be expressed, its author must see to it as to what explanation it is capable of bearing. We, indeed, on our part, could not possibly doubt that in Christ there was no sin to conquer, — born as He was in *the likeness* of sinful flesh, not in sinful flesh itself. Another passage is adduced from the same author to this effect: "And again, that by subduing the desires of the flesh He might teach us that it is not of necessity that one sins, but of set purpose and will."[5] For my own part, I understand these desires of the flesh (if it is not of its unlawful lusts that the writer here speaks) to be such as hunger, thirst, refreshment after fatigue, and the like. For it is through these, however faultless they be in themselves, that some men fall into sin, — a result which was far from our blessed Saviour, even though, as we see from the evidence of the gospel, these affections were natural to Him owing to His likeness to sinful flesh.

CHAP. 72 [LXI.] — HILARY. THE PURE IN HEART BLESSED. THE DOING AND PERFECTING OF RIGHTEOUSNESS.

He quotes the following words from the blessed Hilary: "It is only when we shall be perfect in spirit, and changed in our immortal state, which blessedness has been appointed only for the pure in heart,[6] that we shall see that which is immortal in God."[7] Now I am really not aware what is here said contrary to our own statement, or in what respect this passage is of any use to our opponent, unless it be that it testifies to the possibility of a man's being "pure in heart." But who denies such possibility? Only it must be by the grace of God, through Jesus Christ our Lord, and not merely by our freedom of will. He goes on to quote also this passage: "This Job had so effectually read these Scriptures, that he kept himself from every wicked work, because he worshipped God purely with a mind unmixed with offences: now such worship of God is the proper work of righteousness."[8] It is what Job had done which the writer here spoke of, not what he had brought to perfection in this world, — much less what he had done or perfected without the grace of that Saviour whom he had actually foretold.[9] For that man, indeed, abstains from every wicked work, who does not allow the sin which he has within him to have dominion over him; and who, whenever an unworthy thought stole over him, suffered it not to come to a head in actual deed. It is, how-

[1] Ps. cxliii. 2.    [2] Matt. vi 12.
[3] Timasius and Jacobus, to whom the treatise is addressed. See ch. 1.
[4] Lactantius is the writer from whom Pelagius takes his first quotations here. See his *Instit. Divin.* iv. 24.

[5] Lactantius, *Instit. Divin.* iv. 25
[6] See Matt. v. 8.    [7] Hilary *in loco*.    [8] Hilary's *Fragments*
[9] Job xix. 25.

ever, one thing not to have sin, and another to refuse obedience to its desires. It is one thing to fulfil the command, "Thou shalt not covet;"[1] and another thing, by an endeavour at any rate after abstinence, to do that which is also written, "Thou shalt not go after thy lusts."[2] And yet one is quite aware that he can do nothing of all this without the Saviour's grace. It is to work righteousness, therefore, to fight in an internal struggle with the internal evil of concupiscence in the true worship of God; whilst to perfect it means to have no adversary at all. Now he who has to fight is still in danger, and is sometimes shaken, even if he is not overthrown; whereas he who has no enemy at all rejoices in perfect peace. He, moreover, is in the highest truth said to be without sin in whom no sin has an indwelling, — not he who, abstaining from evil deeds, uses such language as "Now it is no longer I that do it, but the sin that dwelleth in me."[3]

### CHAP. 73. — HE MEETS PELAGIUS WITH ANOTHER PASSAGE FROM HILARY.

Now even Job himself is not silent respecting his own sins; and your friend,[4] of course, is justly of opinion that humility must not by any means "be put on the side of falsehood." Whatever confession, therefore, Job makes, inasmuch as he is a true worshipper of God, he undoubtedly makes it in truth.[5] Hilary, likewise, while expounding that passage of the psalm in which it is written, "Thou hast despised all those who turn aside from Thy commandments,"[6] says: "If God were to despise sinners, He would despise indeed all men, because no man is without sin; but it is those who turn away from Him, whom they call *apostates*, that He despises." You observe his statement: it is not to the effect that no man *was* without sin, as if he spoke of the past; but no man *is* without sin; and on this point, as I have already remarked, I have no contention with him. But if one refuses to submit to the Apostle John, — who does not himself declare, "If we were to say we *have had* no sin," but "If we say we *have* no sin,"[7] — how is he likely to show deference to Bishop Hilary? It is in defence of the grace of Christ that I lift up my voice, without which grace no man is justified, — just as if natural free will were sufficient. Nay, He Himself lifts up His own voice in defence of the same. Let us submit to Him when He says: "Without me ye can do nothing."[8]

### CHAP. 74 [LXIII.] — AMBROSE.

St. Ambrose, however, really opposes those who say that man cannot exist without sin in the present life. For, in order to support his statement, he avails himself of the instance of Zacharias and Elisabeth, because they are mentioned as "having walked in all the commandments and ordinances" of the law "blameless."[9] Well, but does he for all that deny that it was by God's grace that they did this through our Lord Jesus Christ? It was undoubtedly by such faith in Him that holy men lived of old, even before His death. It is He who sends the Holy Ghost that is given to us, through whom that love is shed abroad in our hearts whereby alone whosoever are righteous are righteous. This same Holy Ghost the bishop expressly mentioned when he reminds us that He is to be obtained by prayer (so that the will is not sufficient unless it be aided by Him); thus in his hymn he says:

> "Votisque præstat sedulis,
> Sanctum mereri Spiritum,"[10] —

"To those who sedulously seek He gives to gain the Holy Spirit."

### CHAP. 75. — AUGUSTIN ADDUCES IN REPLY SOME OTHER PASSAGES OF AMBROSE.

I, too, will quote a passage out of this very work of St. Ambrose, from which our opponent has taken the statement which he deemed favourable for citation: "'It seemed good to me,'" he says; "but what he declares seemed good to him cannot have seemed good to him alone. For it is not simply to his human will that it seemed good, but also as it pleased Him, even Christ, who, says he, speaketh in me, who it is that causes that which is good in itself to seem good to ourselves also. For him on whom He has mercy He also calls. He, therefore, who follows Christ, when asked why he wished to be a Christian, can answer: 'It seemed good to me.' In saying this he does not deny that it also pleased God; for from God proceeds the preparation of man's will, inasmuch as it is by God's grace that God is honoured by His saint."[11] See now what your author must learn, if he takes pleasure in the words of Ambrose, how that man's will is prepared by God, and that it is of no importance, or, at any rate, does not much matter, by what means or at what time the preparation is accomplished, provided no doubt is raised as to whether the thing itself be capable of accomplishment without the grace of Christ. Then, again, how important it was that he should observe one line from the words of Ambrose which he quoted! For after that holy man had said, "Inasmuch as the Church has been gathered out of the world, that is, out

---

[1] Ex. xx. 17.　　[2] Ecclus. xviii. 30.　　[3] Rom. vii. 20.
[4] Pelagius, the friend of Timasius and Jacobus.
[5] Job xl. 4, and xlii. 6.　　[6] Ps. cxix. 21, or 118.
[7] 1 John i. 8.　　[8] John xv. 5.

[9] Luke i. 6. See Ambrose *in loco* (Exp. 61, s. 17).
[10] Ambrose's Hymns, 3.　　[11] Ambrose on Luke i. 3.

of sinful men, how can it be unpolluted when composed of such polluted material, except that, in the first place, it be washed of sins by the grace of Christ, and then, in the next place, abstain from sins through its nature of avoiding sin?"—he added the following sentence, which your author has refused to quote for a self-evident reason; for [Ambrose] says: "It was not from the first unpolluted, for that was impossible for human nature: but it is through God's grace and nature that because it no longer sins, it comes to pass that it seems unpolluted."[1] Now who does not understand the reason why your author declined adding these words? It is, of course, so contrived in the discipline of the present life, that the holy Church shall arrive at last at that condition of most immaculate purity which all holy men desire; and that it may in the world to come, and in a state unmixed with anything of evil men, and undisturbed by any law of sin resisting the law of the mind, lead the purest life in a divine eternity. Still he should well observe what Bishop Ambrose says, —and his statement exactly tallies with the Scriptures: "It was not from the first unpolluted, for that condition was impossible for human nature." By his phrase, "from the first," he means indeed from the time of our being born of Adam. Adam no doubt was himself created immaculate; in the case, however, of those who are by nature children of wrath, deriving from him what in him was corrupted, he distinctly averred that it was an impossibility in human nature that they should be immaculate from the first.

CHAP. 76 [LXIV.] — JOHN OF CONSTANTINOPLE.

He quotes also John, bishop of Constantinople, as saying "that sin is not a substance, but a wicked act." Who denies this? "And because it is not natural, therefore the law was given against it, and because it proceeds from the liberty of our will."[2] Who, too, denies this? However, the present question concerns our human nature in its corrupted state; it is a further question also concerning that grace of God whereby our nature is healed by the great Physician, Christ, whose remedy it would not need if it were only whole. And yet your author defends it as capable of not sinning, as if it were sound, or as if its freedom of will were self-sufficient.

CHAP. 77. — XYSTUS.

What Christian, again, is unaware of what he quotes the most blessed Xystus, bishop of Rome and martyr of Christ, as having said, "God has conferred upon men liberty of their own will, in order that by purity and sinlessness of life they may become like unto God?"[3] But the man who appeals to free will ought to listen and believe, and ask Him in whom he believes to give him His assistance not to sin. For when he speaks of "becoming like unto God," it is indeed through God's love that men are to be like unto God, — even the love which is "shed abroad in our hearts," not by any ability of nature or the free will within us, but "by the Holy Ghost which is given unto us."[4] Then, in respect of what the same martyr further says, "A pure mind is a holy temple for God, and a heart clean and without sin is His best altar," who knows not that the clean heart must be brought to this perfection, whilst "the inward man is renewed day by day,"[5] but yet not without the grace of God through Jesus Christ our Lord? Again, when he says, "A man of chastity and without sin has received power from God to be a son of God," he of course meant it as an admonition that on a man's becoming so chaste and sinless (without raising any question as to where and when this perfection was to be obtained by him, — although in fact it is quite an interesting question among godly men, who are notwithstanding agreed as to the possibility of such perfection on the one hand, and on the other hand its impossibility except through "the one Mediator between God and men, the Man Christ Jesus ");[6] — nevertheless, as I began to say, Xystus designed his words to be an admonition that, on any man's attaining such a high character, and thereby being rightly reckoned to be among the sons of God, the attainment must not be thought to have been the work of his own power. This indeed he, through grace, received from God, since he did not have it in a nature which had become corrupted and depraved, — even as we read in the Gospel, "But as many as received Him, to them gave He power to become the sons of God;"[7] which they were not by nature, nor could at all become, unless by receiving Him they also received power through His grace. This is the power which is claimed for itself by the fortitude of that love which is only communicated to us by the Holy Ghost bestowed upon us.

CHAP. 78 [LXV.] — JEROME.

We have next a quotation of some words of the venerable presbyter Jerome, from his exposition of the passage where it is written: "'Blessed are the pure in heart; for they shall see God.'[8] These are they whom no conscious-

---

[1] Ambrose on Luke i. 6.
[2] Compare Chrysostom's Homily on Eph. ii. 3.

[3] This passage, which Pelagius had quoted as from Xystus the Roman bishop and martyr, Augustin subsequently ascertained to have had for its author Sextus, a Pythagorean philosopher. See the passage of the *Retractations*, ii. 42, at the head of this treatise.
[4] Rom. v. 5.      [5] 2 Cor. iv. 16.      [6] 1 Tim. ii. 5.
[7] John i. 12.      [8] Matt. v. 8.

ness of sin reproves," he says, and adds : " The pure man is seen by his purity of heart; the temple of God cannot be defiled." [1]  This perfection is, to be sure, wrought in us by endeavour, by labour, by prayer, by effectual importunity therein that we may be brought to the perfection in which we may be able to look upon God with a pure heart, by His grace through our Lord Jesus Christ. As to his quotation, that the forementioned presbyter said, " God created us with free will; we are drawn by necessity neither to virtue nor to vice; otherwise, where there is necessity there is no crown; " [2] — who would not allow this? Who would not cordially accept it? Who would deny that human nature was so created? The reason, however, why in doing a right action there is no bondage of necessity, is that liberty comes of love.

CHAP. 79 [LXVI.] — A CERTAIN NECESSITY OF SINNING.

But let us revert to the apostle's assertion: " The love of God is shed abroad in our hearts by the Holy Ghost which is given unto us." [3] By whom given if not by Him who " ascended up on high, led captivity captive, and gave gifts unto men?" [4] Forasmuch, however, as there is, owing to the defects that have entered our nature, not to the constitution of our nature, a certain necessary tendency to sin, a man should listen, and in order that the said necessity may cease to exist, learn to say to God, " Bring Thou me out of my necessities; " [5] because in the very offering up of such a prayer there is a struggle against the tempter, who fights against us concerning this very necessity; and thus, by the assistance of grace through our Lord Jesus Christ, both the evil necessity will be removed and full liberty be bestowed.

CHAP. 80 [LXVII.] — AUGUSTIN HIMSELF. TWO METHODS WHEREBY SINS, LIKE DISEASES, ARE GUARDED AGAINST.

Let us now turn to our own case. " Bishop Augustin also," says your author, " in his books on Free Will has these words : ' Whatever the cause itself of volition is, if it is impossible to resist it, submission to it is not sinful; if, however, it may be resisted, let it not be submitted to, and there will be no sin. Does it, perchance, deceive the unwary man? Let him then beware that he be not deceived. Is the deception, however, so potent that it is not possible to guard against it? If such is the case, then there are no sins. For who sins in a case where precaution is quite impossible? Sin, however, is committed; precaution therefore is possible.' " [6]  I acknowledge

it, these are my words; but he, too, should condescend to acknowledge all that was said previously, seeing that the discussion is about the grace of God, which helps us as a medicine through the Mediator; not about the impossibility of righteousness. Whatever, then, may be the cause, it can be resisted. Most certainly it can. Now it is because of this that we pray for help, saying, " Lead us not into temptation," [7] and we should not ask for help if we supposed that resistance were quite impossible. It is possible to guard against sin, but by the help of Him who cannot be deceived. [8]  For this very circumstance has much to do with guarding against sin that we can unfeignedly say, " Forgive us our debts, as we forgive our debtors." [9] Now there are two ways whereby, even in bodily maladies, the evil is guarded against, — to prevent its occurrence, and, if it happen, to secure a speedy cure. To prevent its occurrence, we may find precaution in the prayer, " Lead us not into temptation; " to secure the prompt remedy, we have the resource in the prayer, " Forgive us our debts." Whether then the danger only threaten, or be inherent, it may be guarded against.

CHAP. 81. — AUGUSTIN QUOTES HIMSELF ON FREE WILL.

In order, however, that my meaning on this subject may be clear not merely to him, but also to such persons as have not read those treatises of mine on Free Will, which your author has read, and who have not only not read them, but perchance do read him; I must go on to quote out of my books what he has omitted, but which, if he had perceived and quoted in his book, no controversy would be left between us on this subject. For immediately after those words of mine which he has quoted, I expressly added, and (as fully as I could) worked out, the train of thought which might occur to any one's mind, to the following effect : " And yet some actions are disapproved of, even when they are done in ignorance, and are judged deserving of chastisement, as we read in the inspired authorities." After taking some examples out of these, I went on to speak also of infirmity as follows : " Some actions also deserve disapprobation, that are done from necessity; as when a man wishes to act rightly and cannot. For whence arise those utterances : ' For the good that I would, I do not; but the evil which I would not, that I do' ? " [10]  Then, after quoting some other passages of the Holy Scriptures to the same effect, I say : " But all these are the sayings of persons who are coming out of that condemnation of

[1] Jerome on Matt. v. 8 (*Comm.* Book i. c. 5).
[2] Jerome, *Against Jovinianus*, ii. 3.
[3] Rom. v. 5.    [4] Eph. iv. 8.    [5] Ps. xxv. 17.
[6] Augustin, *De Libero Arbitrio*, iii. 18 (50).

[7] Matt. vi. 13.
[8] Augustin gives a similar reply to the objection in his *Retractations*, i. 9.
[9] Matt. vi. 12.    [10] Rom. vii. 19.

death ; for if this is not man's punishment, but his nature, then those are no sins." Then, again, a little afterwards I add : " It remains, therefore, that this just punishment come of man's condemnation. Nor ought it to be wondered at, that either by ignorance man has not free determination of will to choose what he will rightly do, or that by the resistance of carnal habit (which by force of mortal transmission has, in a certain sense, become engrafted into his nature), though seeing what ought rightly to be done, and wishing to do it, he yet is unable to accomplish it. For this is the most just penalty of sin, that a man should lose what he has been unwilling to make good use of, when he might with ease have done so if he would ; which, however, amounts to this, that the man who knowingly does not do what is right loses the ability to do it when he wishes. For, in truth, to every soul that sins there accrue these two penal consequences — ignorance and difficulty. Out of the ignorance springs the error which disgraces ; out of the difficulty arises the pain which afflicts. But to approve of falsehoods as if they were true, so as to err involuntarily, and to be unable, owing to the resistance and pain of carnal bondage, to refrain from deeds of lust, is not the nature of man as he was created, but the punishment of man as under condemnation. When, however, we speak of a free will to do what is right, we of course mean that liberty in which man was created." Some men at once deduce from this what seems to them a just objection from the transfer and transmission of sins of ignorance and difficulty from the first man to his posterity. My answer to such objectors is this : " I tell them, by way of a brief reply, to be silent, and to cease from murmuring against God. Perhaps their complaint might have been a proper one, if no one from among men had stood forth a vanquisher of error and of lust ; but when there is everywhere present One who calls off from himself, through the creature by so many means, the man who serves the Lord, teaches him when believing, consoles him when hoping, encourages him when loving, helps him when endeavouring, hears him when praying, — it is not reckoned to you as a fault that you are involuntarily ignorant, but that you neglect to search out what you are ignorant of ; nor is it imputed to you in censure that you do not bind up the limbs that are wounded, but that you despise him who wishes to heal them." [1] In such terms did I exhort them, as well as I could, to live righteously ; nor did I make the grace of God of none effect, without which the now obscured and tarnished nature of man can neither be enlightened nor purified. Our whole discussion with them on this subject turns upon this, that we frustrate not the grace of God which is in Jesus Christ our Lord by a perverted assertion of nature. In a passage occurring shortly after the last quoted one, I said in reference to nature : " Of nature itself we speak in one sense, when we properly describe it as that human nature in which man was created faultless after his kind ; and in another sense as that nature in which we are born ignorant and carnally minded, owing to the penalty of condemnation, after the manner of the apostle, ' We ourselves likewise were by nature children of wrath, even as others.' " [2]

## CHAP. 82 [LXVIII.] — HOW TO EXHORT MEN TO FAITH, REPENTANCE, AND ADVANCEMENT.

If, therefore, we wish " to rouse and kindle cold and sluggish souls by Christian exhortations to lead righteous lives," [3] we must first of all exhort them to that faith whereby they may become Christians, and be subjects of His name and authority, without whom they cannot be saved. If, however, they are already Christians but neglect to lead holy lives, they must be chastised with alarms and be aroused by the praises of reward, — in such a manner, indeed, that we must not forget to urge them to godly prayers as well as to virtuous actions, and furthermore to instruct them in such wholesome doctrine that they be induced thereby to return thanks for being able to accomplish any step in that holy life which they have entered upon, without difficulty,[4] and whenever they do experience such " difficulty," that they then wrestle with God in most faithful and persistent prayer and ready works of mercy to obtain from Him facility. But provided they thus progress, I am not overanxious as to the *where* and the *when* of their perfection in fulness of righteousness ; only I solemnly assert, that wheresoever and whensoever they become perfect, it cannot be but by the grace of God through our Lord Jesus Christ. When, indeed, they have attained to the clear knowledge that they have no sin, let them not say they have sin, lest the truth be not in them ; [5] even as the truth is not in those persons who, though they have sin, yet say that they have it not.

## CHAP. 83 [LXIX.] — GOD ENJOINS NO IMPOSSIBILITY, BECAUSE ALL THINGS ARE POSSIBLE AND EASY TO LOVE.

But " the precepts of the law are very good," if we use them lawfully.[6] Indeed, by the very fact (of which we have the firmest conviction)

---

[1] *De Libero Arbitrio*, iii. 19.

[2] Eph. ii. 3.
[3] This passage, and others in this and the following chapters, are marked as quotations, apparently cited from Pelagius by Augustin.
[4] For the " *difficulty*," which is one of the penal consequences of sin, see last chapter, about its middle.
[5] 1 John i. 8.    [6] See 1 Tim. i. 8.

"that the just and good God could not possibly have enjoined impossibilities," we are admonished both what to do in easy paths and what to ask for when they are difficult. Now all things are easy for love to effect, to which (and which alone) "Christ's burden is light," [1] — or rather, it is itself alone the burden which is light. Accordingly it is said, "And His commandments are not grievous;" [2] so that whoever finds them grievous must regard the inspired statement about their "not being grievous" as having been capable of only this meaning, that there may be a state of heart to which they are not burdensome, and he must pray for that disposition which he at present wants, so as to be able to fulfil all that is commanded him. And this is the purport of what is said to Israel in Deuteronomy, if understood in a godly, sacred, and spiritual sense, since the apostle, after quoting the passage, "The word is nigh thee, even in thy mouth and in thy heart" [3] (and, as the verse also has it, *in thine hands*, [4] for in man's heart are his spiritual hands), adds in explanation, "This is the word of faith which we preach." [5] No man, therefore, who "returns to the Lord his God," as he is there commanded, "with all his heart and with all his soul," [6] will find God's commandment "grievous." How, indeed, can it be grievous, when it is the precept of love? Either, therefore, a man has not love, and then it is grievous; or he has love, and then it is not grievous. But he possesses love if he does what is there enjoined on Israel, by returning to the Lord his God with all his heart and with all his soul. "A new commandment," says He, "do I give unto you, that ye love one another;" [7] and "He that loveth his neighbour hath fulfilled the law;" [8] and again, "Love is the fulfilling of the law." [9] In accordance with these sayings is that passage, "Had they trodden good paths, they would have found, indeed, the ways of righteousness easy." [10] How then is it written, "Because of the words of Thy lips, I have kept the paths of difficulty," [11] except it be that both statements are true: These paths are paths of difficulty to fear; but to love they are easy?

CHAP. 84 [LXX.] — THE DEGREES OF LOVE ARE ALSO DEGREES OF HOLINESS.

Inchoate love, therefore, is inchoate holiness; advanced love is advanced holiness; great love is great holiness; "perfect love is perfect holiness," — but this "love is out of a pure heart, and of a good conscience, and of faith unfeigned," [12] "which in this life is then the greatest, when life itself is contemned in comparison with it." [13] I wonder, however, whether it has not a soil in which to grow after it has quitted this mortal life! But in what place and at what time soever it shall reach that state of absolute perfection, which shall admit of no increase, it is certainly not "shed abroad in our hearts" by any energies either of the nature or the volition that are within us, but "by the Holy Ghost which is given unto us," [14] and which both helps our infirmity and co-operates with our strength. For it is itself indeed the grace of God, through our Lord Jesus Christ, to whom, with the Father and the Holy Spirit, appertaineth eternity, and all goodness, for ever and ever. Amen.

---

[1] Matt. xi. 30.    [2] 1 John v. 3.
[3] Deut. xxx. 14, quoted Rom. x. 8.
[4] According to the Septuagint, which adds after ἐν τῇ καρδία σου the words καὶ ἐν ταῖς χερσί σου. This was probably Pelagius' reading. Compare *Quæstion. in Deuteron.* Book v. 54.
[5] Rom. x. 8.    [6] Deut. xxx. 2.

[7] John xiii. 34.    [8] Rom. xiii. 8.    [9] Rom. xiii. 10.
[10] Prov. ii. 20.    [11] Ps. xvii. 4.    [12] 1 Tim. i. 5.
[13] See note at beginning of ch. 82 for the meaning of this mark of quotation.
[14] Rom. v. 5.

A TREATISE CONCERNING MAN'S PERFECTION IN
RIGHTEOUSNESS.

# PREFACE TO THE TREATISE ON MAN'S PERFECTION IN RIGHTEOUSNESS.

AUGUSTIN has made no mention of this treatise in his book of *Retractations*; for the reason, no doubt, that it belonged to the collection of the EPISTLES, for which he designed a separate statement of Retractations. In all the MSS. this work begins with his usual epistolary salutation: "Augustin, to his holy brethren and fellow-bishops Eutropius and Paulus." And yet, by general consent, this epistle has been received as a treatise, not only in those volumes of his works which contain this work, but also in the writings of those ancient authors who quote it. Amongst these, the most renowned and acquainted with Augustin's writings, POSSIDIUS (*In indiculo*, 4) and FULGENTIUS (*Ad Monimum*, i. 3) expressly call this work "*A Treatise on the Perfection of Man's Righteousness*." So far nearly all the MSS. agree, but a few (including the *Codd. Audöenensis* and *Pratellensis*) add these words to the general title: "*In opposition to those who assert that it is possible for a man to become righteous by his own sole strength*." In a MS. belonging to the Church of Rheims there occurs this inscription: "*A Treatise on what are called the definitions of Cœlestius*." Prosper, in his work against the Collator, ch. 43, advises his reader to read, besides some other of Augustin's "*books*," that which he wrote "to the priests Paulus and Eutropius in opposition to the questions of Pelagius and Cœlestius."

From this passage of Prosper, however, in which he mentions, but with no regard to accurate order, some of the short treatises of Augustin against the Pelagians, nobody could rightly show that this work *On the Perfection of Man's Righteousness* was later in time than his work *On Marriage and Concupiscence*, or than the six books against Julianus, which are mentioned previously in the same passage by Prosper. For, indeed, at the conclusion of the present treatise, Augustin hesitates as yet to censure those persons who affirmed that men are living or have lived in this life righteously without any sin at all: their opinion Augustin, in the passage referred to (just as in his treatises *On Nature and Grace*, n, 3, and *On the Spirit and the Letter*, nn. 49, 70), does not yet think it necessary stoutly to resist. Nothing had as yet, therefore, been determined on this point; nor were there yet enacted, in opposition to this opinion, the three well-known canons (6–8) of the Council of Carthage, which was held in the year 418. Afterwards, however, on the authority of these canons, he cautions people against the opinion as a pernicious error, as one may see from many passages in his books *Against the two Epistles of the Pelagians*, especially Book iv. ch. x. (27), where he says: "Let us now consider that third point of theirs, which each individual member of Christ as well as His entire body regards with horror, where they contend that there are in this life, or have been, righteous persons without any sin whatever." Certainly, in the year 414, in an epistle (157) to Hilary, when answering the questions which were then being agitated in Sicily, he expresses himself in the same tone, and almost in the same language, on sinlessness, as that which he employs at the end of this present treatise. "But those persons," says he (in ch. ii. n. 4 of that epistle), "however much one may tolerate them when they affirm that there either are, or have been, men besides the one Saint of saints who have been wholly free from sin; yet when they allege that man's own free will is sufficient for fulfilling the Lord's commandments, even when unassisted by God's grace and the gift of the Holy Spirit for the performance of good works, the idea is altogether worthy of anathema and of perfect detestation." On comparing these words with the conclusion of this treatise before us, nothing will appear more probable than that the work which supplies the refutation of Cœlestius' questions, which were also brought over from Sicily, was written not long after the above-mentioned epistle. This work Possidius, in his index, places immediately after the treatise *On Nature and Grace*, and before the book *On the Proceedings of Pelagius*. Augustin, however, does not mention this work in his epistle (169) which he addressed to Evodius about the end of the year 415; but he intimates in it that he had published an answer to the *Commonitorium* of Orosius, wherein that author stated that "the bishops Eutropius and Paulus had already given information to Augustin about certain formidable heresies." Some suppose that this statement refers to the letter which they despatched to Augustin along with Cœlestius' propositions. However that be, it is not unreasonable to believe that they, not long after Orosius' arrival in Africa (that is, before the midsummer of the year 415), had sent these propositions to him, and that Augustin soon afterwards wrote back to Eutropius and Paulus a refutation of them, his answer to Orosius having been previously given.

Furthermore, Cœlestius, whose name is inscribed in the propositions, "wrote to his parents from his monastery," as Gennadius informs us in his work on Church writers (*De Scriptoribus Ecclesiasticis*), "before he fell in with the teaching of Pelagius, three letters in the shape of short treatises, necessary for all seekers after God."* Afterwards he openly professed the Pelagian heresy, and published a short treatise, in which, besides other topics, he acknowledged in the Church of Carthage that even infants had redemption by being baptized into Christ,—an episcopal decision on the question having been obtained in that city about the commencement of the year 412, as we learn from an epistle to Pope Innocent (amongst the Epistles of Augustin [175, n. 1 and 6]), as well as from the epistle [157, n. 22] which we have referred to above; and from Augustin's work *On the Merits of Sins*, i. 62, and ii. 59; also from his treatise *On Original Sin*, 21; and his work *Against Julianus*, iii. 9. Another work by an anonymous writer, but which was commonly attributed to Cœlestius, divided into chapters, is mentioned in the treatise which follows the present one, *On the Proceedings of Pelagius*; see chapters 29, 30, and 62. There were extant, moreover, in the year 417, several small books or tracts of Cœlestius, which Augustin, in his work *On the Grace of Christ*, 31, 32, and 36, says were produced by Cœlestius himself in some ecclesiastical proceedings at Rome under Zosimus. Augustin, at the commencement of the present work *On the Perfection of Man's Righteousness*, mentions an undoubted work of Cœlestius as having been seen by him, from which he discovered that the definitions or propositions therein examined by Augustin were not unsuited to the tone and temper of Cœlestius. This was very probably the book which Jerome quotes in his Epistle to Ctesiphon, written in the year 413 or 414. These are Jerome's words: "One of his followers [that is, Pelagius'], who was already in fact become the master and the leader of all that army, and 'a vessel of wrath,'[1] in opposition to the apostle, runs on through thickets, not of *syllogisms*, as his admirers are apt to boast, but of *solecisms*, and philosophizes and disputes to the following effect: 'If I do nothing without God's help, and if everything which I shall achieve is owing to His operations solely, then it follows that it is not I who work, but only God's work is to be crowned in me. . In vain, therefore, has He conferred on me the power of will, if I am unable to exercise it fully without His incessant help. That volition, indeed, is destroyed which requires the assistance of another. But it is free will which God has given to me; and *free* it can only remain, if I do whatever I wish. The state of the case then is this: I either use once for all the power which has been bestowed on me, so that free will is preserved; or else, if I require the assistance of another, liberty of decision in me is destroyed.'"

---

[1] Rom. ix. 22.

# CONTENTS OF THE TREATISE "ON MAN'S PERFECTION IN RIGHTEOUSNESS."

# A TREATISE CONCERNING MAN'S PERFECTION IN RIGHTEOUSNESS,

## BY AURELIUS AUGUSTIN, BISHOP OF HIPPO;

## IN ONE BOOK,

### ADDRESSED TO EUTROPIUS AND PAULUS, A.D. 415.

---

A PAPER CONTAINING SUNDRY DEFINITIONS,[1] SAID TO HAVE BEEN DRAWN UP BY CŒLESTIUS, WAS PUT INTO THE HANDS OF AUGUSTIN. IN THIS DOCUMENT, CŒLESTIUS, OR SOME PERSON WHO SHARED IN HIS ERRORS, HAD RECKLESSLY ASSERTED THAT A MAN HAD IT IN HIS POWER TO LIVE HERE WITHOUT SIN. AUGUSTIN FIRST REFUTES THE SEVERAL PROPOSITIONS IN BRIEF ANSWERS, SHOWING THAT THE PERFECT AND PLENARY STATE OF RIGHTEOUSNESS, IN WHICH A MAN EXISTS ABSOLUTELY WITHOUT SIN, IS UNATTAINABLE WITHOUT GRACE BY THE MERE RESOURCES OF OUR CORRUPT NATURE, AND NEVER OCCURS IN THIS PRESENT STATE OF EXISTENCE. HE NEXT PROCEEDS TO CONSIDER THE AUTHORITIES WHICH THE PAPER CONTAINED AS GATHERED OUT OF THE SCRIPTURES; SOME OF THEM TEACHING MAN TO BE "UNSPOTTED" AND "PERFECT;" OTHERS MENTIONING THE COMMANDMENTS OF GOD AS "NOT GRIEVOUS;" WHILE OTHERS AGAIN ARE QUOTED AS OPPOSED TO THE AUTHORITATIVE PASSAGES WHICH THE CATHOLICS WERE ACCUSTOMED TO ADVANCE AGAINST THE PELAGIANS.

---

*Augustin to his holy brethren and fellow-bishops Eutropius and Paulus.[2]*

### CHAP. I.

YOUR love, which in both of you is so great and so holy that it is a delight to obey its commands, has laid me under an obligation to reply to some definitions which are said to be the work of Cœlestius; for so runs the title of the paper which you have given me, "The definitions, so it is said, of Cœlestius." As for this title, I take it that it is not his, but theirs who have brought this work from Sicily, where Cœlestius is said not to be, — although many there[3] make boastful pretension of holding views like his, and, to use the apostle's word, "being themselves deceived, lead others also astray."[4] That these views are, however, his, or those of some associates[5] of his, we, too, can well believe. For the above-mentioned brief definitions, or rather propositions, are by no means at variance with his opinion, such as I have seen it expressed in another work, of which he is the undoubted author. There was therefore good reason, I

---

[1] These *breves definitiones*, which Augustin also calls *ratiocinationes*, are short argumentative statements, which may be designated *breviates*.

[2] [Probably Spanish refugees; they had recently presented to Augustin a memorial against certain heresies. *Oros. ad Aug.* 1. — W.]

[3] In his epistle (157) to Hilary, written a little while before this work, he mentions Cœlestius and the condemnation of his errors in a Council held at Carthage; he expresses also some apprehension of Cœlestius attempting to spread his opinions in *Sicily*: "Whether he be himself there," says Augustin, "or only others who are partners in his errors, there are too many of them; and, unless they be checked, they lead astray others to join their sect; and so great is their increase, that I cannot tell whither they will force their way," etc.

[4] 2 Tim. iii. 13.

[5] *Sociorum* ejus. It has been proposed to read *sectatorum* ejus, — not unsuitably (although not justified by MS. evidence), because Cœlestius "had," to use Jerome's words, "by this time turned out a master with a following, — the leader of a perfect army." — *Jerome's Epistle to Ctesiphon*, written in the year 413 or 414.

think, for the report which those brethren, who brought these tidings to us, heard in Sicily, that Cœlestius taught or wrote such opinions. I should like, if it were possible, so to meet the obligation imposed on me by your brotherly kindness, that I, too, in my own answer should be equally brief. But unless I set forth also the propositions which I answer, who will be able to form a judgment of the value of my answer? Still I will try to the best of my ability, assisted, too, by God's mercy, by your own prayers, so to conduct the discussion as to keep it from running to an unnecessary length.

CHAP. II. (1.) THE FIRST BREVIATE OF CŒLESTIUS.

I. "First of all," says he, "he must be asked who denies man's ability to live without sin, what every sort of sin is,—is it such as can be avoided? or is it unavoidable? If it is unavoidable, then it is not sin; if it can be avoided, then a man can live without the sin which can be avoided. No reason or justice permits us to designate as sin what cannot in any way be avoided." Our answer to this is, that sin can be avoided, if our corrupted nature be healed by God's grace, through our Lord Jesus Christ. For, in so far as it is not sound, in so far does it either through blindness fail to see, or through weakness fail to accomplish, that which it ought to do; "for the flesh lusteth against the spirit, and the spirit against the flesh," [1] so that a man does not do the things which he would.

(2.) THE SECOND BREVIATE.

II. "We must next ask," he says, "whether sin comes from will, or from necessity? If from necessity, it is not sin; if from will, it can be avoided." We answer as before; and in order that we may be healed, we pray to Him to whom it is said in the psalm: "Lead Thou me out of my necessities." [2]

(3.) THE THIRD BREVIATE.

III. "Again we must ask," he says, "what sin is,—natural? or accidental? If natural, it is not sin; if accidental, it is separable; [3] and if it is separable, it can be avoided; and because it can be avoided, man can be without that which can be avoided." The answer to this is, that sin is not natural; but nature (especially in that corrupt state from which we have become by nature "children of wrath" [4]) has too little determination of will to avoid sin, unless assisted and healed by God's grace through Jesus Christ our Lord.

(4.) THE FOURTH BREVIATE.

IV. "We must ask, again," he says, "What is sin,—an act, or a thing? If it is a thing, it must have an author; and if it be said to have an author, then another besides God will seem to be introduced as the author of a thing. But if it is impious to say this, we are driven to confess that every sin is an act, not a thing. If therefore it is an act, for this very reason, because it is an act, it can be avoided." Our reply is, that sin no doubt is called an act, and is such, not a thing. But likewise in the body, lameness for the same reason is an act, not a thing, since it is the foot itself, or the body, or the man who walks lame because of an injured foot, that is the thing; but still the man cannot avoid the lameness, unless his foot be cured. The same change may take place in the inward man, but it is by God's grace, through our Lord Jesus Christ. The defect itself which causes the lameness of the man is neither the foot, nor the body, nor the man, nor indeed the lameness itself; for there is of course no lameness when there is no walking, although there is nevertheless the defect which causes the lameness whenever there is an attempt to walk. Let him therefore ask, what name must be given to this defect,—would he have it called a thing, or an act, or rather a bad property [5] in the thing, by which the deformed act comes into existence? So in the inward man the soul is the thing, theft is an act, and avarice is the defect, that is, the property by which the soul is evil, even when it does nothing in gratification of its avarice,—even when it hears the prohibition, "Thou shalt not covet," [6] and censures itself, and yet remains avaricious. By faith, however, it receives renovation; in other words, it is healed day by day,[7]—yet only by God's grace through our Lord Jesus Christ.

CHAP. III. (5.) THE FIFTH BREVIATE.

V. "We must again," he says, "inquire whether a man ought to be without sin. Beyond doubt he ought. If he ought, he is able; if he is not able, then he ought not. Now if a man ought not to be without sin, it follows that he ought to be with sin,—and then it ceases to be sin at all, if it is determined that it is owed. Or if it is absurd to say this, we are obliged to confess that man ought to be without sin; and it is clear that his obligation is not more than his ability." We frame our answer with the same illustration that we employed in our previous reply. When we see a lame man who has the

---

[1] Gal. v. 17.　　　　　　　[2] Ps. xxv. 17.
[3] [An accident " is a modification or quality which does not essentially belong to a thing, nor form one of its constituent or invariable attributes: as motion in relation to matter, or heat to iron."— FLEMING: *Vocabulary of Philosophy.*— W.]
[4] Eph. ii. 3.

[5] [Cœlestius had in the previous breviate confined sin to either nature or accident: Augustin declares it to be a *property*. By this he apparently means that it is a non-essential attribute, without which man would remain man, but yet not what is called a " separable accident."— W.]
[6] Ex. xx. 17.　　　　　　　[7] 2 Cor. iv. 16.

opportunity of being cured of his lameness, we of course have a right to say : " That man ought not to be lame ; and if he ought, he is able." And yet whenever he wishes he is not immediately able ; but only after he has been cured by the application of the remedy, and the medicine has assisted his will. The same thing takes place in the inward man in relation to sin which is its lameness, by the grace of Him who " came not to call the righteous, but sinners ; "[1] since " the whole need not the physician, but only they that be sick."[2]

### (6.) THE SIXTH BREVIATE.

VI. " Again," he says, " we have to inquire whether man is commanded to be without sin ; for either he is not able, and then he is not commanded ; or else because he is commanded, he is able. For why should that be commanded which cannot at all be done ? " The answer is, that man is most wisely commanded to walk with right steps, on purpose that, when he has discovered his own inability to do even this, he may seek the remedy which is provided for the inward man to cure the lameness of sin, even the grace of God, through our Lord Jesus Christ.

### (7.) THE SEVENTH BREVIATE.

VII. " The next question we shall have to propose," he says, " is, whether God wishes that man be without sin. Beyond doubt God wishes it ; and no doubt he has the ability. For who is so foolhardy as to hesitate to believe that to be possible, which he has no doubt about God's wishing ? " This is the answer. If God wished not that man should be without sin, He would not have sent His Son without sin, to heal men of their sins. This takes place in believers, who are being renewed day by day,[3] until their righteousness becomes perfect, like fully restored health.

### (8.) THE EIGHTH BREVIATE.

VIII. " Again, this question must be asked," he says, " how God wishes man to be, — with sin, or without sin? Beyond doubt, He does not wish him to be with sin. We must reflect how great would be the impious blasphemy for it to be said that man has it in his power to be with sin, which God does not wish ; and for it to be denied that he has it in his power to be without sin, which God wishes : just as if God had created any man for such a result as this, — that he should be able to be what He would not have him, and unable to be what He would have him ; and that he should lead an existence contrary to His will, rather than one which should be in accordance therewith." This has

been in fact already answered ; but I see that it is necessary for me to make here an additional remark, that we are saved by hope. " But hope that is seen is not hope ; for what a man seeth, why doth he yet hope for? But if we hope for that we see not, then do we with patience wait for it."[4] Full righteousness, therefore, will only then be reached, when fulness of health is attained ; and this fulness of health shall be when there is fulness of love, for " love is the fulfilling of the law ; "[5] and then shall come fulness of love, when " we shall see Him even as He is."[6] Nor will any addition to love be possible more, when faith shall have reached the fruition of sight.

### CHAP. IV. — (9.) THE NINTH BREVIATE.

IX. " The next question we shall require to be solved," says he, " is this : By what means is it brought about that man is with sin? — by the necessity of nature, or by the freedom of choice? If it is by the necessity of nature, he is blameless ; if by the freedom of choice, then the question arises, from whom he has received this freedom of choice. No doubt, from God. Well, but that which God bestows is certainly good. This cannot be gainsaid. On what principle, then, is a thing proved to be good, if it is more prone to evil than to good? For it is more prone to evil than to good if by means of it man can be with sin and cannot be without sin." The answer is this : It came by the freedom of choice that man was with sin ; but a penal corruption closely followed thereon, and out of the liberty produced necessity. Hence the cry of faith to God, " Lead Thou me out of my necessities."[7] With these necessities upon us, we are either unable to understand what we want, or else (while having the wish) we are not strong enough to accomplish what we have come to understand. Now it is just liberty itself that is promised to believers by the Liberator. " If the Son," says He, " shall make you free, ye shall be free indeed."[8] For, vanquished by the sin into which it fell by its volition, nature has lost liberty. Hence another scripture says, " For of whom a man is overcome, of the same is he brought in bondage."[9] Since therefore " the whole need not the physician, but only they that be sick ; "[2] so likewise it is not the free that need the Deliverer, but only the enslaved. Hence the cry of joy to Him for deliverance, " Thou hast saved my soul from the straits of necessity."[10] For true liberty is also real health ; and this would never have been lost, if the will had remained good. But because the will has sinned, the hard necessity

---

[1] Matt. ix. 13.    [2] Matt. ix. 12.    [3] 2 Cor. iv. 16.

[4] Rom. viii. 24, 25.    [5] Rom. xiii. 10.    [6] 1 John iii. 2.
[7] Ps. xxv. 17.    [8] John viii. 38.    [9] 2 Pet. ii. 19.
[10] Ps. xxxi. 7.

of having sin has pursued the sinner; until his infirmity be wholly healed, and such freedom be regained, that there must needs be, on the one hand, a permanent will to live happily, and, on the other hand, a voluntary and happy necessity of living virtuously, and never sinning.

#### (10.) THE TENTH BREVIATE.

X. "Since God made man good," he says, "and, besides making him good, further commanded him to do good, how impious it is for us to hold that man is evil, when he was neither made so, nor so commanded; and to deny him the ability of being good, although he was both made so, and commanded to act so!" Our answer here is: Since then it was not man himself, but God, who made man good; so also is it God, and not man himself, who remakes him to be good, while liberating him from the evil which he himself did upon his wishing, believing, and invoking such a deliverance. But all this is effected by the renewal day by day of the inward man,[1] by the grace of God through our Lord Jesus Christ, with a view to the outward man's resurrection at the last day to an eternity not of punishment, but of life.

#### CHAP. V. (11.) THE ELEVENTH BREVIATE.

XI. "The next question which must be put," he says, "is, in how many ways all sin is manifested? In two, if I mistake not: if either those things are done which are forbidden, or those things are not done which are commanded. Now, it is just as certain that all things which are forbidden are able to be avoided, as it is that all things which are commanded are able to be effected. For it is vain either to forbid or to enjoin that which cannot either be guarded against or accomplished. And how shall we deny the possibility of man's being without sin, when we are compelled to admit that he can as well avoid all those things which are forbidden, as do all those which are commanded?" My answer is, that in the Holy Scriptures there are many divine precepts, to mention the whole of which would be too laborious; but the Lord, who on earth consummated and abridged[2] His word, expressly declared that the law and the prophets hung on two commandments,[3] that we might understand that whatever else has been enjoined on us by God ends in these two commandments, and must be referred to them: "Thou shalt love the Lord thy God with all thy heart, and with all thy soul, and with all thy mind;"[4] and "Thou shalt love thy neighbour as thyself."[5] "On these two commandments,"

says He, "hang all the law and the prophets."[3] Whatever, therefore, we are by God's law forbidden, and whatever we are bidden to do, we are forbidden and bidden with the direct object of fulfilling these two commandments. And perhaps the general prohibition is, "Thou shalt not covet;"[6] and the general precept, "Thou shalt love."[7] Accordingly the Apostle Paul, in a certain place, briefly embraced the two, expressing the prohibition in these words, "Be not conformed to this world,"[8] and the command in these, "But be ye transformed by the renewing of your mind."[8] The former falls under the negative precept, not to covet; the latter under the positive one, to love. The one has reference to continence, the other to righteousness. The one enjoins avoidance of evil; the other, pursuit of good. By eschewing covetousness we put off the old man, and by showing love we put on the new. But no man can be continent unless God endow him with the gift;[9] nor is God's love shed abroad in our hearts by our own selves, but by the Holy Ghost that is given to us.[10] This, however, takes place day after day in those who advance by willing, believing, and praying, and who, "forgetting those things which are behind, reach forth unto those things which are before."[11] For the reason why the law inculcates all these precepts is, that when a man has failed in fulfilling them, he may not be swollen with pride, and so exalt himself, but may in very weariness betake himself to grace. Thus the law fulfils its office as "schoolmaster," so terrifying the man as "to lead him to Christ," to give Him his love.[12]

#### CHAP. VI. (12.) THE TWELFTH BREVIATE.

XII. "Again the question arises," he says, "how it is that man is unable to be without sin, — by his will, or by nature? If by nature, it is not sin; if by his will, then will can very easily be changed by will." We answer by reminding him how he ought to reflect on the extreme presumption of saying — not simply that it is possible (for this no doubt is undeniable, when God's grace comes in aid), but — that it is "*very easy*" for will to be changed by will; whereas the apostle says, "The flesh lusteth against the spirit, and the spirit against the flesh: and these are contrary the one to the other; so that ye do not the things that ye would."[13] He does not say, "These are contrary the one to the other, so that ye will not do the things that ye can," but, "so that ye do not the things that ye would."[14] How happens it, then, that the lust of the flesh which of course is culpable and corrupt, and is nothing

---

[1] 2 Cor. iv. 16.
[2] An application of Rom. ix. 28.
[3] Matt. xxii. 40.   [4] Matt. xxii. 37.   [5] Matt. xxii. 39.

[6] Ex. xx 27.   [7] Deut. vi. 5.   [8] Rom. xii. 2.
[9] Wisd. viii. 21.   [10] Rom. v. 5.   [11] Phil. iii. 13.
[12] Gal. iii. 24.   [13] Gal. v. 17.
[14] Ἵνα μὴ ἃ ἂν θέλητε, ταῦτα ποιῆτε.

else than the desire for sin, as to which the same apostle instructs us not to let it "reign in our mortal body;"[1] by which expression he shows us plainly enough that that must have an existence in our mortal body which must not be permitted to hold a dominion in it;—how happens it, I say, that such lust of the flesh has not been changed by that will, which the apostle clearly implied the existence of in his words, "So that ye do not the things that ye *would*," if so be that the will can so easily be changed by will? Not that we, indeed, by this argument throw the blame upon the nature either of the soul or of the body, which God created, and which is wholly good; but we say that it, having been corrupted by its own will, cannot be made whole without the grace of God.

### (13.) THE THIRTEENTH BREVIATE.

XIII. "The next question we have to ask," says he, "is this: If man cannot be without sin, whose fault is it,—man's own, or some one's else? If man's own, in what way is it his fault if he is not that which he is unable to be?" We reply, that it is man's fault that he is not without sin on this account, because it has by man's sole will come to pass that he has come into such a necessity as cannot be overcome by man's sole will.

### (14.) THE FOURTEENTH BREVIATE.

XIV. "Again the question must be asked," he says, "If man's nature is good, as nobody but Marcion or Manichæus will venture to deny, in what way is it good if it is impossible for it to be free from evil? For that all sin is evil who can gainsay?" We answer, that man's nature is both good, and is also able to be free from evil. Therefore do we earnestly pray, "Deliver us from evil."[2] This deliverance, indeed, is not fully wrought, so long as the soul is oppressed by the body, which is hastening to corruption.[3] This process, however, is being effected by grace through faith, so that it may be said by and by, "O death, where is thy struggle? Where is thy sting, O death? The sting of death is sin, and the strength of sin is the law;"[4] because the law by prohibiting sin only increases the desire for it, unless the Holy Ghost spreads abroad that love, which shall then be full and perfect, when we shall see face to face.

### (15.) THE FIFTEENTH BREVIATE.

XV. "And this, moreover, has to be said," he says: "God is certainly righteous; this cannot be denied. But God imputes every sin to man. This too, I suppose, must be allowed, that whatever shall not be imputed as sin is not sin. Now

if there is any sin which is unavoidable, how is God said to be righteous, when He is supposed to impute to any man that which cannot be avoided?" We reply, that long ago was it declared in opposition to the proud, "Blessed is the man to whom the Lord imputeth not sin."[5] Now He does not impute it to those who say to Him in faith, "Forgive us our debts, as we forgive our debtors."[6] And justly does He withhold this imputation, because that is just which He says: "With what measure ye mete, it shall be measured to you again."[7] That, however, is sin in which there is either not the love which ought to be, or where the love is less than it ought to be,[8]—whether it can be avoided by the human will or not; because when it can be avoided, the man's present will does it, but if it cannot be avoided his past will did it; and yet it can be avoided,—not, however, when the proud will is lauded, but when the humble one is assisted.

### CHAP. VII. (16.) THE SIXTEENTH BREVIATE.

XVI. After all these disputations, their author introduces himself in person as arguing with another, and represents himself as under examination, and as being addressed by his examiner: "Show me the man who is without sin." He answers: "I show you one who is able to be without sin." His examiner then says to him: "And who is he?" He answers: "You are the man." "But if," he adds, "you were to say, 'I, at any rate, cannot be without sin,' then you must answer me, 'Whose fault is that?' If you then were to say, 'My own fault,' you must be further asked, 'And how is it your fault, if you cannot be without sin?'" He again represents himself as under examination, and thus accosted: "Are you yourself without sin, who say that a man can be without sin?" And he answers: "Whose fault is it that I am not without sin? But if," continues he, "he had said in reply, 'The fault is your own;' then the answer would be, 'How *my* fault, when I am unable to be without sin?'" Now our answer to all this running argument is, that no controversy ought to have been raised between them about such words as these; because he nowhere ventures to affirm that a man (either any one else, or himself) *is* without sin, but he merely said in reply that he *can be*,—a position which we do not ourselves deny. Only the question arises, when can he, and through whom can he? If at the present time, then by no faithful soul which is enclosed within the body of this death must this prayer be offered, or such words as these be spoken, "Forgive us our debts, as we forgive our

---

[1] Rom. vi. 12.     [2] Matt. vi. 13.     [3] Wisd. ix. 15.
[4] 1 Cor. xv. 35, 36.

[5] Ps. xxxii. 2.     [6] Matt. vi. 12.     [7] Matt. vii. 2.
[8] See above, in his work *De Spiritu et Litterâ*, 64; also *De Naturâ et Gratiâ*, 45.

debtors," [1] since in holy baptism all past debts have been already forgiven. But whoever tries to persuade us that such a prayer is not proper for faithful members of Christ, does in fact acknowledge nothing else than that he is not himself a Christian. If, again, it is through himself that a man is able to live without sin, then did Christ die in vain. But "Christ is not dead in vain." No man, therefore, can be without sin, even if he wish it, unless he be assisted by the grace of God through our Lord Jesus Christ. And that this perfection may be attained, there is even now a training carried on in growing [Christians,] and there will be by all means a completion made, after the conflict with death is spent, and love, which is now cherished by the operation of faith and hope, shall be perfected in the fruition of sight and possession.

CHAP. VIII. (17.) IT IS ONE THING TO DEPART FROM THE BODY, ANOTHER THING TO BE LIBERATED FROM THE BODY OF THIS DEATH.

He next proposes to establish his point by the testimony of Holy Scripture. Let us carefully observe what kind of defence he makes. "There are passages," says he, "which prove that man is commanded to be without sin." Now our answer to this is: Whether such commands are given is not at all the point in question, for the fact is clear enough; but whether the thing which is evidently commanded be itself at all possible of accomplishment in the body of this death, wherein "the flesh lusteth against the spirit, and the spirit against the flesh, so that we cannot do the things that we would." [2] Now from this body of death not every one is liberated who ends the present life, but only he who in this life has received grace, and given proof of not receiving it in vain by spending his days in good works. For it is plainly one thing to depart from the body, which all men are obliged to do in the last day of their present life, and another to be delivered from the body of this death, — which God's grace alone, through our Lord Jesus Christ, imparts to His faithful saints. It is after this life, indeed, that the reward of perfection is bestowed, but only upon those by whom in their present life has been acquired the merit of such a recompense. For no one, after going hence, shall arrive at fulness of righteousness, unless, whilst here, he shall have run his course by hungering and thirsting after it. "Blessed are they which do hunger and thirst after righteousness; for they shall be filled." [3]

(18.) THE RIGHTEOUSNESS OF THIS LIFE COMPREHENDED IN THREE PARTS, — FASTING, ALMSGIVING, AND PRAYER.

As long, then, as we are "absent from the Lord, we walk by faith, not by sight;" [4] whence it is said, "The just shall live by faith." [5] Our righteousness in this pilgrimage is this — that we press forward to that perfect and full righteousness in which there shall be perfect and full love in the sight of His glory; and that now we hold to the rectitude and perfection of our course, by "keeping under our body and bringing it into subjection," [6] by doing our alms cheerfully and heartily, while bestowing kindnesses and forgiving the trespasses which have been committed against us, and by "continuing instant in prayer;" [7] — and doing all this with sound doctrine, whereon are built a right faith, a firm hope, and a pure charity. This is now our righteousness, in which we pass through our course hungering and thirsting after the perfect and full righteousness, in order that we may hereafter be satisfied therewith. Therefore our Lord in the Gospel (after saying, "Take heed that ye do not your righteousness [8] before men, to be seen of them," [9]) in order that we should not measure our course of life by the limit of human glory, declared in his exposition of righteousness itself that there is none except there be these three, — fasting, alms, prayers. Now in *the fasting* He indicates the entire subjugation of the body; in *the alms*, all kindness of will and deed, either by giving or forgiving; and in *prayers* He implies all the rules of a holy desire. So that, although by the subjugation of the body a check is given to that concupiscence, which ought not only to be bridled but to be put altogether out of existence (and which will not be found at all in that state of perfect righteousness, where sin shall be absolutely excluded), — yet it often exerts its immoderate desire even in the use of things which are allowable and right. In that real beneficence in which the just man consults his neighbour's welfare, things are sometimes done which are prejudicial, although it was thought that they would be advantageous. Sometimes, too, through infirmity, when the amount of the kindness and trouble which is expended either falls short of the necessities of the objects, or is of little use under the circumstances, then there steals over us a disappointment which tarnishes that "cheerfulness" which secures to the "giver" the approbation of God. [10] This trail of sadness, however, is the greater or the less, as each man has made more or less progress in his kindly purposes. If, then, these considerations, and such as these, be duly weighed, we are only right when we say in our prayers, "Forgive us our debts, as we also forgive our debtors." [1] But what we say in our prayers we must carry into

---

[1] Matt. vi. 12.    [2] Gal. v. 17.    [3] Matt. v. 6.

[4] 2 Cor. v. 6.    [5] Hab. ii. 4.    [6] 1 Cor. ix. 27.    [7] Rom. xii. 12.
[8] For this reading of δικαιοσύνην instead of ἐλεημοσύνην there is high MS. authority. It is admitted also by Griesbach, Lachmann, Tischendorf, Tregelles, Westcott and Hort, and Alford.
[9] Matt. vi. 1.    [10] 2 Cor. ix. 7.

act, even to loving our very enemies ; or if any one who is still a babe in Christ fails as yet to reach this point, he must at any rate, whenever one who has trespassed against him repents and craves his pardon, exercise forgiveness from the bottom of his heart, if he would have his heavenly Father listen to his prayer.

### (19.) THE COMMANDMENT OF LOVE SHALL BE PERFECTLY FULFILLED IN THE LIFE TO COME.

And in this prayer, unless we choose to be contentious, there is placed before our view a mirror of sufficient brightness in which to behold the life of the righteous, who live by faith, and finish their course, although they are not without sin. Therefore they say, " Forgive us," because they have not yet arrived at the end of their course. Hence the apostle says, " Not as if I had already attained, either were already perfect. . . . Brethren, I count not myself to have apprehended : but this one thing I do, forgetting those things which are behind, and reaching forth unto those things which are before, I press toward the mark, for the prize of the high calling of God in Christ Jesus. Let us therefore, as many as be perfect, be thus minded." [1]   In other words, let us, as many as are running perfectly, be thus resolved, that, being not yet perfected, we pursue our course to perfection along the way by which we have thus far run perfectly, in order that " when that which is perfect is come, then that which is in part may be done away ; " [2] that is, may cease to be but in part any longer, but become whole and complete. For to faith and hope shall succeed at once the very substance itself, no longer to be believed in and hoped for, but to be seen and grasped. Love, however, which is the greatest among the three, is not to be superseded, but increased and fulfilled, — contemplating in full vision what it used to see by faith, and acquiring in actual fruition what it once only embraced in hope. Then in all this plenitude of charity will be fulfilled the commandment, " Thou shalt love the Lord thy God with all thine heart, and with all thy soul, and with all thy mind." [3]   For while there remains any remnant of the lust of the flesh, to be kept in check by the rein of continence, God is by no means loved with all one's soul. For the flesh does not lust without the soul ; although it is the flesh which is said to lust, because the soul lusts carnally. In that perfect state the just man shall live absolutely without any sin, since there will be in his members no law warring against the law of his mind, [4] but wholly will he love God, with all his heart, with all his soul, and

with all his mind, [5] which is the first and chief commandment. For why should not such perfection be enjoined on man, although in this life nobody may attain to it ? For we do not rightly run if we do not know whither we are to run. But how could it be known, unless it were pointed out in precepts ? [6]   Let us therefore " so run that we may obtain." [7]   For all who run rightly will obtain, — not as in the contest of the theatre, where all indeed run, but only one wins the prize. [8]   Let us run, believing, hoping, longing ; let us run, subjugating the body, cheerfully and heartily doing alms, — in giving kindnesses and forgiving injuries, praying that our strength may be helped as we run ; and let us so listen to the commandments which urge us to perfection, as not to neglect running towards the fulness of love.

### CHAP. IX. (20.) WHO MAY BE SAID TO WALK WITHOUT SPOT ; DAMNABLE AND VENIAL SINS.

Having premised these remarks, let us carefully attend to the passages which he whom we are answering has produced, as if we ourselves had quoted them. " In Deuteronomy, ' Thou shalt be perfect before the Lord thy God.' [9] Again, in the same book, ' There shall be not an imperfect man [10] among the sons of Israel.' [11] In like manner the Saviour says in the Gospel, ' Be ye perfect, even as your Father which is in heaven is perfect.' [12]   So the apostle, in his second Epistle to the Corinthians, says : ' Finally, brethren, farewell. Be perfect.' [13]   Again, to the Colossians he writes : ' Warning every man, and teaching every man in all wisdom, that we may present every man perfect in Christ.' [14]   And so to the Philippians : ' Do all things without murmurings and disputings, that ye may be blameless, and harmless, as the immaculate sons of God.' [15]   In like manner to the Ephesians he writes : ' Blessed be the God and father of our Lord Jesus Christ, who hath blessed us with all spiritual blessings in heavenly places in Christ ; according as He hath chosen us in Him before the foundation of the world, that we should be holy and blameless before Him.' [16]   Then again to the Colossians he says in another passage : ' And you, that were sometime alienated, and enemies in your mind by wicked works, yet now hath He reconciled in the body of His flesh through death ; present yourselves holy and unblameable and unreprovable in His sight.' [17]   In the same strain, he says to the Ephesians : ' That He might present to Himself a glorious Church,

---

[1] Phil. iii. 12–15.     [2] 1 Cor. xiii. 10.
[3] *Mente.*   The Septuagint, however, like the Hebrew, has δυναμεως. A. V. " thy might." Comp. Deut. vi. 5 with Matt. xxii. 37.
[4] Rom. vii. 23.

[5] Matt. xxii. 37.
[6] See above in Augustin's *De Spiritu et Littera*, 64.
[7] 1 Cor. ix. 23.     [8] 1 Cor. ix. 24.     [9] Deut. xviii. 13.
[10] Augustin's word is *inconsummatus*. The Septuagint term τελιοκόμενος (which properly signifies *complete, perfect*) comes to mean one *initiated* into the mysteries of idolatrous worship.
[11] Deut. xxiii. 17     [12] Matt. v. 48.     [13] 2 Cor. xiii. 11.
[14] Col. i. 28.     [15] Phil. ii. 14, 15.     [16] Eph. i. 3, 4.
[17] Col. i. 21, 22.

not having spot, or wrinkle, or any such thing; but that it should be holy and without blemish.'[1] So in his first Epistle to the Corinthians he says: 'Be ye sober, and righteous, and sin not.'[2] So again in the Epistle of St. Peter it is written: 'Wherefore gird up the loins of your mind, be sober, and hope to the end, for the grace that is offered to you: . . . as obedient children, not fashioning yourselves according to the former lusts in your ignorance: but as He who hath called you is holy, so be ye holy in all manner of conversation; because it is written,[3] Be ye holy; for I am holy.'[4] Whence blessed David likewise says: 'O Lord, who shall sojourn in Thy tabernacle, or who shall rest on Thy holy mountain? He that walketh without blame, and worketh righteousness.'[5] And in another passage: 'I shall be blameless with Him.'[6] And yet again: 'Blessed are the blameless in the way, who walk in the law of the Lord.'[7] To the same effect it is written in Solomon: 'The Lord loveth holy hearts, and all they that are blameless are acceptable unto Him.'"[8] Now some of these passages exhort men who are running their course that they run perfectly; others refer to the end thereof, that men may reach forward to it as they run. He, however, is not unreasonably said to walk blamelessly, not who has already reached the end of his journey, but who is pressing on towards the end in a blameless manner, free from damnable sins, and at the same time not neglecting to cleanse by almsgiving such sins as are venial. For the way in which we walk, that is, the road by which we reach perfection, is cleansed by clean prayer. That, however, is a clean prayer in which we say in truth, "Forgive us, as we ourselves forgive."[9] So that, as there is nothing censured when blame is not imputed, we may hold on our course to perfection without censure, in a word, blamelessly; and in this perfect state, when we arrive at it at last, we shall find that there is absolutely nothing which requires cleansing by forgiveness.

CHAP. X. (21.) TO WHOM GOD'S COMMANDMENTS ARE GRIEVOUS; AND TO WHOM, NOT. WHY SCRIPTURE SAYS THAT GOD'S COMMANDMENTS ARE NOT GRIEVOUS; A COMMANDMENT IS A PROOF OF THE FREEDOM OF MAN'S WILL; PRAYER IS A PROOF OF GRACE.

He next quotes passages to show that God's commandments are not grievous. But who can be ignorant of the fact that, since the generic commandment is love (for "the end of the commandment is love,"[10] and "love is the fulfilling of the law"[11]), whatever is accomplished by the operation of love, and not of fear, is not grievous? They, however, are oppressed by the commandments of God, who try to fulfil them by fearing. "But perfect love casteth out fear;"[12] and, in respect of the burden of the commandment, it not only takes off the pressure of its heavy weight, but it actually lifts it up as if on wings. In order, however, that this love may be possessed, even as far as it can possibly be possessed in the body of this death, the determination of will avails but little, unless it be helped by God's grace through our Lord Jesus Christ. For as it must again and again be stated, it is "shed abroad in our hearts," not by our own selves, but "by the Holy Ghost which is given unto us."[13] And for no other reason does Holy Scripture insist on the truth that God's commandments are not grievous, than this, that the soul which finds them grievous may understand that it has not yet received those resources which make the Lord's commandments to be such as they are commended to us as being, even gentle and pleasant; and that it may pray with groaning of the will to obtain the gift of facility. For the man who says, "Let my heart be blameless;"[14] and, "Order Thou my steps according to Thy word: and let not any iniquity have dominion over me;"[15] and, "Thy will be done in earth, as it is in heaven;"[16] and, "Lead us not into temptation;"[17] and other prayers of a like purport, which it would be too long to particularize, does in effect offer up a prayer for ability to keep God's commandments. Neither, indeed, on the one hand, would any injunctions be laid upon us to keep them, if our own will had nothing to do in the matter; nor, on the other hand, would there be any room for prayer, if our will were alone sufficient. God's commandments, therefore, are commended to us as being not grievous, in order that he to whom they are grievous may understand that he has not as yet received the gift which removes their grievousness; and that he may not think that he is really performing them, when he so keeps them that they are grievous to him. For it is a cheerful giver whom God loves.[18] Nevertheless, when a man finds God's commandments grievous, let him not be broken down by despair; let him rather oblige himself to seek, to ask, and to knock.

(22.) PASSAGES TO SHOW THAT GOD'S COMMANDMENTS ARE NOT GRIEVOUS.

He afterwards adduces those passages which represent God as recommending His own commandments as not grievous: let us now attend to their testimony. " Because," says he, "God's commandments are not only not impossible, but they are not even grievous. In Deuteronomy:

---

[1] Eph. v. 26, 27.   [2] 1 Cor. xv. 34.   [3] Lev. xix. 2.
[4] 1 Pet. i. 13-16.   [5] Ps. xv. 1, 2.   [6] Ps. xviii. 23.
[7] Ps. cxix. 1.   [8] Prov. xi. 20.   [9] Matt. vi. 12.
[10] 1 Tim. i. 8.   [11] Rom. xiii. 10.

[12] 1 John iv. 18.   [13] Rom. v. 5.   [14] Ps. cxix. 80.
[15] Ps. cxix. 133.   [16] Matt. vi. 10.   [17] Matt. vi. 13.
[18] 2 Cor. ix. 7.

'The Lord thy God will again turn and rejoice over thee for good, as He rejoiced over thy fathers, if ye shall hearken to the voice of the Lord your God, to keep His commandments, and His ordinances, and His judgments, written in the book of this law; if thou turn to the Lord thy God with all thine heart, and with all thy soul. For this command, which I give thee this day, is not grievous, neither is it far from thee: it is not in heaven, that thou shouldest say, Who will ascend into heaven, and obtain it for us, that we may hear and do it? neither is it beyond the sea, that thou shouldest say, Who will cross over the sea, and obtain it for us, that we may hear and do it? The word is nigh thee, in thy mouth, and in thine heart, and in thine hands to do it.'[1] In the Gospel likewise the Lord says: 'Come unto me, all ye that labour and are heavy laden, and I will give you rest. Take my yoke upon you, and learn of me; for I am meek and lowly in heart: and ye shall find rest unto your souls. For my yoke is easy, and my burden is light.'[2] So also in the Epistle of Saint John it is written: 'This is the love of God, that we keep His commandments: and His commandments are not grievous.'"[3] On hearing these testimonies out of the law, and the gospel, and the epistles, let us be built up unto that grace which those persons do not understand, who, "being ignorant of God's righteousness, and wishing to establish their own righteousness, have not submitted themselves unto the righteousness of God."[4] For, if they understand not the passage of Deuteronomy in the sense that the Apostle Paul quoted it, — that "with the heart men believe unto righteousness, and with their mouth make confession unto salvation;"[5] since "they that be whole need not a physician, but they that are sick,"[6] — they certainly ought (by that very passage of the Apostle John which he quoted last to this effect: "This is the love of God, that we keep His commandments; and His commandments are not grievous"[3]) to be admonished that God's commandment is not grievous to the love of God, which is shed abroad in our hearts only by the Holy Ghost, not by the determination of man's will by attributing to which more than they ought, they are ignorant of God's righteousness. This love, however, shall then be made perfect, when all fear of punishment shall be cut off.

CHAP. XI. (23.) PASSAGES OF SCRIPTURE WHICH, WHEN OBJECTED AGAINST HIM BY THE CATHOLICS, CŒLESTIUS ENDEAVOURS TO ELUDE BY OTHER PASSAGES: THE FIRST PASSAGE.

After this he adduced the passages which are usually quoted against them. He does not attempt to explain these passages, but, by quoting what seem to be contrary ones, he has entangled the questions more tightly. "For," says he, "there are passages of Scripture which are in opposition to those who ignorantly suppose that they are able to destroy the liberty of the will, or the possibility of not sinning, by the authority of Scripture. For," he adds, "they are in the habit of quoting against us what holy Job said: 'Who is pure from uncleanness? Not one; even if he be an infant of only one day upon the earth.'"[7] Then he proceeds to give a sort of answer to this passage by help of other quotations; as when Job himself said: "For although I am a righteous and blameless man, I have become a subject for mockery,"[8] — not understanding that a man may be called righteous, who has gone so far towards perfection in righteousness as to be very near it; and this we do not deny to have been in the power of many even in this life, when they walk in it by faith.

(24.) TO BE WITHOUT SIN, AND TO BE WITHOUT BLAME — HOW DIFFERING.

The same thing is affirmed in another passage, which he has quoted immediately afterwards, as spoken by the same Job: "Behold, I am very near my judgment, and I know that I shall be found righteous."[9] Now this is the judgment of which it is said in another scripture: "And He shall bring forth thy righteousness as the light, and thy judgment as the noonday." But he does not say, I am already there; but, "I am very near." If, indeed, the judgment of his which he meant was not that which he would himself exercise, but that whereby he was to be judged at the last day, then in such judgment all will be found righteous who with sincerity pray: "Forgive us our debts, as we forgive our debtors."[10] For it is through this forgiveness that they will be found righteous; on this account that whatever sins they have here incurred, they have blotted out by their deeds of charity. Whence the Lord says: "Give alms; and, behold, all things are clean unto you."[11] For in the end, it shall be said to the righteous, when about to enter into the promised kingdom: "I was an hungered, and ye gave me meat,"[12] and so forth. However, it is one thing to be without sin, which in this life can only be predicated of the Only-begotten, and another thing to be without accusation, which might be said of many just persons even in the present life; for there is a certain measure of a good life, according to which even in this human intercourse there could no just accusation be possibly laid against him. For

---

[1] Deut. xxx. 9–14.  [2] Matt. xi. 28–30.  [3] 1 John v. 3.
[4] Rom. x. 3.  [5] Rom. x. 10.  [6] Matt. ix. 12.
[7] Job xiv. 4, 5.  [8] Job xii. 4.
[9] Job xiii. 18.  [10] Matt. vi. 12.
[11] Luke xi. 41.  [12] Matt. xxv. 35.

who can justly accuse the man who wishes evil to no one, and who faithfully does good to all he can, and never cherishes a wish to avenge himself on any man who does him wrong, so that he can truly say, " As we forgive our debtors?" And yet by the very fact that he truly says, " Forgive, as we also forgive," he plainly admits that he is not without sin.

(25.) Hence the force of the statement: " There was no injustice in my hands, but my prayer was pure."[1] For the purity of his prayer arose from this circumstance, that it was not improper for him to ask forgiveness in prayer, when he really bestowed forgiveness himself.

### (26.) WHY JOB WAS SO GREAT A SUFFERER.

And when he says concerning the Lord, " For many bruises hath He inflicted upon me without a cause,"[2] observe that his words are not, He hath inflicted *none with a cause;* but, " many without a cause." For it was not because of his manifold sins that these many bruises were inflicted on him, but in order to make trial of his patience. For on account of his sins, indeed, without which, as he acknowledges in another passage, he was certainly not, he yet judges that he ought to have suffered less.[3]

### (27.) WHO MAY BE SAID TO KEEP THE WAYS OF THE LORD ; WHAT IT IS TO DECLINE AND DEPART FROM THE WAYS OF THE LORD.

Then again, as for what he says, " For I have kept His ways, and have not turned aside from His commandments, nor will I depart from them ;"[4] he has kept God's ways who does not so turn aside as to forsake them, but makes progress by running his course therein ; although, weak as he is, he sometimes stumbles or falls, onward, however, he still goes, sinning less and less until he reaches the perfect state in which he will sin no more. For in no other way could he make progress, except by keeping His ways. The man, indeed, who declines from these and becomes an apostate at last, is certainly not he who, although he has sin, yet never ceases to persevere in fighting against it until he arrives at the home where there shall remain no more conflict with death. Well now, it is in our present struggle therewith that we are clothed with the righteousness in which we here live by faith, — clothed with it as it were with a breastplate.[5] Judgment also we take on ourselves ; and even when it is against us, we turn it round to our own behalf ; for we become our own accusers and condemn our sins : whence that scripture which says, " The righteous man accuses himself at the beginning of his speech."[6] Hence also he says : " I put on righteousness, and clothed

myself with judgment like a mantle."[7] Our vesture at present no doubt is wont to be armour for war rather than garments of peace, while concupiscence has still to be subdued ; it will be different by and by, when our last enemy death shall be destroyed,[8] and our righteousness shall be full and complete, without an enemy to molest us more.

### (28.) WHEN OUR HEART MAY BE SAID NOT TO REPROACH US ; WHEN GOOD IS TO BE PERFECTED.

Furthermore, concerning these words of Job, " My heart shall not reproach me in all my life,"[9] we remark, that it is in this present life of ours, in which we live by faith, that our heart does not reproach us, if the same faith whereby we believe unto righteousness does not neglect to rebuke our sin. On this principle the apostle says : " The good that I would I do not ; but the evil which I would not, that I do."[10] Now it is a good thing to avoid concupiscence, and this good the just man would, who lives by faith ;[11] and still he does what he hates, because he has concupiscence, although " he goes not after his lusts ;"[12] if he has done this, he has himself at that time really done it, so as to yield to, and acquiesce in, and obey the desire of sin. His heart then reproaches him, because it reproaches himself, and not his sin which dwelleth in him. But whensoever he suffers not sin to reign in his mortal body to obey it in the lusts thereof,[13] and yields not his members as instruments of unrighteousness unto sin,[14] sin no doubt is present in his members, but it does not reign, because its desires are not obeyed. Therefore, while he does that which he would not, — in other words, while he wishes not to lust, but still lusts, — he consents to the law that it is good :[15] for what the law would, that he also wishes ; because it is his desire not to indulge concupiscence, and the law expressly says, " Thou shalt not covet."[16] Now in that he wishes what the law also would have done, he no doubt consents to the law : but still he lusts, because he is not without sin ; it is, however, no longer himself that does the thing, but the sin which dwells within him. Hence it is that " his heart does not reproach him in all his life ;" that is, in his faith, because the just man lives by faith, so that his faith is his very life. He knows, to be sure, that in himself dwells nothing good, — even in his flesh, which is the dwelling-place of sin. By not consenting, however, to it, he lives by faith, wherewith he also calls upon God to help him in his contest against sin. Moreover, there is present to him to will that no sin at all should be in him, but then how to perfect this good is

---

[1] Job xvi. 18.        [2] Job ix. 17.        [3] Job vi. 2, 3.
[4] Job xxiii. 11, 12.    [5] Eph. vi. 14.    [6] Prov. xviii. 17.

[7] Job. xxix. 14.       [8] 1 Cor. xv. 26.      [9] Job xxvii. 6.
[10] Rom. vii. 15.       [11] Hab. ii. 4.        [12] Ecclus. xviii. 30.
[13] Rom. vi. 12.       [14] Rom. vi. 13.        [15] Rom. vii. 16.
[16] Ex. xx. 17.

not present. It is not the mere "doing" of a good thing that is not present to him, but the "perfecting" of it. For in this, that he yields no consent, he does good; he does good again, in this, that he hates his own lust; he does good also, in this, that he does not cease to give alms; and in this, that he forgives the man who sins against him, he does good; and in this, that he asks forgiveness for his own trespasses, — sincerely avowing in his petition that he also forgives those who trespass against himself, and praying that he may not be led into temptation, but be delivered from evil, — he does good. But how to perfect the good is not present to him; it will be, however, in that final state, when the concupiscence which dwells in his members shall exist no more. His heart, therefore, does not reproach him, when it reproaches the sin which dwells in his members; nor can it reproach unbelief in him. Thus "in all his life," — that is, in his faith, — he is neither reproached by his own heart, nor convinced of not being without sin. And Job himself acknowledges this concerning himself, when he says, "Not one of my sins hath escaped Thee; Thou hast sealed up my transgressions in a bag, and marked if I have done iniquity unawares."[1] With regard, then, to the passages which he has adduced from the book of holy Job, we have shown to the best of our ability in what sense they ought to be taken. He, however, has failed to explain the meaning of the words which he has himself quoted from the same Job: "Who then is pure from uncleanness? Not one; even if he be an infant of only one day upon the earth."[2]

CHAP. XII. (29.) THE SECOND PASSAGE. WHO MAY BE SAID TO ABSTAIN FROM EVERY EVIL THING.

"They are in the habit of next quoting," says he, "the passage: 'Every man is a liar.'"[3] But here again he offers no solution of words which are quoted against himself even by himself; all he does is to mention other apparently opposite passages before persons who are unacquainted with the sacred Scriptures, and thus to cast the word of God into conflict. This is what he says: "We tell them in answer, how in the book of Numbers it is said, 'Man is true.'[4] While of holy Job this eulogy is read: 'There was a certain man in the land of Ausis, whose name was Job; that man was true, blameless, righteous, and godly, abstaining from every evil thing.'"[5] I am surprised that he has brought forward this passage, which says that Job "ab-

stained from every evil thing," wishing it to mean "abstained from every sin;" because he has argued already[6] that sin is not a thing, but an act. Let him recollect that, even if it is an act, it may still be called a thing. That man, however, abstains from every evil thing, who either never consents to the sin, which is always with him, or, if sometimes hard pressed by it, is never oppressed by it; just as the wrestling champion, who, although he is sometimes caught in a fierce grapple, does not for all that lose the prowess which constitutes him the better man. We read, indeed, of a man without blame, of one without accusation; but we never read of one without sin, except the Son of man, who is also the only-begotten Son of God.

(30.) "EVERY MAN IS A LIAR," OWING TO HIMSELF ALONE; BUT "EVERY MAN IS TRUE," BY HELP ONLY OF THE GRACE OF GOD.

"Moreover," says he, "in Job himself it is said: 'And he maintained the miracle of a true man.'[7] Again we read in Solomon, touching wisdom: 'Men that are liars cannot remember her, but men of truth shall be found in her.'[8] Again in the Apocalypse: 'And in their mouth was found no guile, for they are without fault.'"[9] To all these statements we reply with a reminder to our opponents, of how a man may be called true, through the grace and truth of God, who is in himself without doubt a liar. Whence it is said: "Every man is a liar."[3] As for the passage also which he has quoted in reference to Wisdom, when it is said, "Men of truth shall be found in her," we must observe that it is undoubtedly not "*in her*," but *in themselves* that men shall be found liars. Just as in another passage: "Ye were sometimes darkness, but now are ye light in the Lord,"[10] — when he said, "Ye were darkness," he did not add, "in the Lord;" but, after saying, "Ye are now light," he expressly added the phrase, "in the Lord," for they could not possibly be "light" in themselves; in order that "he who glorieth may glory in the Lord."[11] The "faultless" ones, indeed, in the Apocalypse, are so called because "no guile was found in their mouth."[9] They did not say they had no sin: if they had said this, they would deceive themselves, and the truth would not be in them;[12] and if the truth were not in them, guile and untruth would be found in their mouth. If, however, to avoid envy, they said they were not without sin, although they were sinless, then this very insincerity would be a lie, and the character given of them would be untrue: "In their mouth was found no guile." Hence indeed "they are without fault;" for as they have

---

[1] Job xiv. 16, 17.    [2] Job xiv. 4, 5.    [3] Ps. cxv. 2.
[4] If this refer to Num. xxiv. 3, 15 (as the editions mark it), the quotation is most inexact. The Septuagint words ὁ ἄνθρωπος ὁ ἀληθινῶς ὁρῶν is not a proposition equal to "*homo verax*," as an antithesis to the proposition "*omnis homo mendax*."
[5] Job i. 1.

[6] See above, ii. (4).    [7] Job xvii. 8.    [8] Ecclus. xv. 8.
[9] Rev. xiv. 5.    [10] Eph. v. 8.    [11] 1 Cor. i. 31.
[12] 1 John i. 8.

forgiven those who have done them wrong, so are they purified by God's forgiveness of themselves. Observe now how we have to the best of our power explained in what sense the quotations he has in his own behalf advanced ought to be understood. But how the passage, "Every man is a liar," is to be interpreted, he on his part has altogether omitted to explain ; nor is an explanation within his power, without a correction of the error which makes him believe that man can be true without the help of God's grace, and merely by virtue of his own free will.

CHAP. XIII. (31.) THE THIRD PASSAGE. IT IS ONE THING TO DEPART, AND ANOTHER THING TO HAVE DEPARTED, FROM ALL SIN. "THERE IS NONE THAT DOETH GOOD," — OF WHOM THIS IS TO BE UNDERSTOOD.

He has likewise propounded another question, as we shall proceed to show, but has failed to solve it ; nay, he has rather rendered it more difficult, by first stating the testimony that had been quoted against him : "There is none that doeth good, no, not one ; "[1] and then resorting to seemingly contrary passages to show that there are persons who do good. This he succeeded, no doubt, in doing. It is, however, one thing for a man not to do good, and another thing not to be without sin, although he at the same time may do many good things. The passages, therefore, which he adduces are not really contrary to the statement that no person is without sin in this life. He does not, for his own part, explain in what sense it is declared that "there is none that doeth good, no, not one." These are his words : "Holy David indeed says, 'Hope thou in the Lord and be doing good.'"[2] But this is a precept, and not an accomplished fact ; and such a precept as is never kept by those of whom it is said, "There is none that doeth good, no, not one." He adds : "Holy Tobit also said, 'Fear not, my son, that we have to endure poverty ; we shall have many blessings if we fear God, and depart from all sin, and do that which is good.'"[3] Most true indeed it is, that man shall have many blessings when he shall have departed from all sin. Then no evil shall betide him ; nor shall he have need of the prayer, "Deliver us from evil."[4] Although even now every man who progresses, advancing ever with an upright purpose, departs from all sin, and becomes further removed from it as he approaches nearer to the fulness and perfection of the righteous state ; because even concupiscence itself, which is sin dwelling in our flesh, never ceases to diminish in those who are making progress, although it still remains in their mortal

members. It is one thing, therefore, to depart from all sin, — a process which is even now in operation, — and another thing to have departed from all sin, which shall happen in the state of future perfection. But still, even he who has departed already from evil, and is continuing to do so, must be allowed to be a doer of good. How then is it said, in the passage which he has quoted and left unsolved, "There is none that doeth good, no, not one," unless that the Psalmist there censures some one nation, amongst whom there was not a man that did good, wishing to remain "children of men," and not sons of God, by whose grace man becomes good, in order to do good? For we must suppose the Psalmist here to mean that "good" which he describes in the context, saying, "God looked down from heaven upon the children of men, to see if there were any that did understand, and seek God."[5] Such good then as this, seeking after God, there was not a man found who pursued it, no, not one ; but this was in that class of men which is predestinated to destruction.[6] It was upon such that God looked down in His foreknowledge, and passed sentence.

CHAP. XIV. (32.) THE FOURTH PASSAGE. IN WHAT SENSE GOD ONLY IS GOOD. WITH GOD TO BE GOOD AND TO BE HIMSELF ARE THE SAME THING.

"They likewise," says he, "quote what the Saviour says : 'Why callest thou me good? There is none good save one, that is, God?'"[7] This statement, however, he makes no attempt whatever to explain ; all he does is to oppose to it sundry other passages which seem to contradict it, which he adduces to show that man, too, is good. Here are his remarks : "We must answer this text with another, in which the same Lord says, 'A good man out of the good treasure of his heart bringeth forth good things.'[8] And again : 'He maketh His sun to rise on the good and on the evil.'[9] Then in another passage it is written, 'For the good things are created from the beginning ; '[10] and yet again, 'They that are good shall dwell in the land.'"[11] Now to all this we must say in answer, that the passages in question must be understood in the same sense as the former one, "There is none good, save one, that is, God." Either because all created things, although God made them very

[5] Ps. xiv. 2.
[6] On this passage Fulgentius remarks (*Ad Monimum*, i. 5): "In no other sense do I suppose that passage of St. Augustin should be taken, in which he affirms that there are certain persons predestinated to destruction, than in regard to their punishment, not their sin : not to the evil which they unrighteously commit, but to the punishment which they shall righteously suffer : not to the sin on account of which they either do not receive, or else lose, the benefit of the first resurrection, but to the retribution which their own personal iniquity evilly incurs, but to the divine justice righteously inflicts."
[7] Luke xviii. 19.        [8] Matt. xii. 35.        [9] Matt. v. 45.
[10] Ecclus. xxxix. 25.        [11] Prov. ii. 21.

[1] Ps. xiv. 3.        [2] Ps. xxxvii. 3.        [3] Tobit iv. 21.
[4] Matt. vi. 13.

good, are yet, when compared with their Creator, not good, being in fact incapable of any comparison with Him. For in a transcendent, and yet very proper sense, He said of Himself, " I AM THAT I AM."[1] The statement therefore before us, " None is good save one, that is, God," is used in some such way as that which is said of John, " He was not that light;"[2] although the Lord calls him "a lamp,"[3] just as He says to His disciples: " Ye are the light of the world: . . . neither do men light a lamp and put it under a bushel."[4] Still, in comparison with that light which is "the true light which lighteth every man that cometh into the world,"[5] he was not light. Or else, because the very sons of God even, when compared with themselves as they shall hereafter become in their eternal perfection, are good in such a way that they still remain also evil. Although I should not have dared to say this of them (for who would be so bold as to call them evil who have God for their Father?) unless the Lord had Himself said: " If ye then, being evil, know how to give good gifts to your children, how much more shall your Father which is in heaven give good things to them that ask Him?"[6] Of course, by applying to them the words, " your Father," He proved that they were already sons of God; and yet at the same time He did not hesitate to say that they were " evil." Your author, however, does not explain to us how they are good, whilst yet " there is none good save one, that is, God." Accordingly the man who asked " what good thing he was to do,"[7] was admonished to seek Him[8] by whose grace he might be good; to whom also *to be good* is nothing else than *to be Himself,* because He is unchangeably good, and cannot be evil at all.

### (33.) THE FIFTH PASSAGE.[9]

" This," says he, " is another text of theirs: ' Who will boast that he has a pure heart?' "[10] And then he answered this with several passages, wishing to show that there can be in man a pure heart. But he omits to inform us how the passage which he reported as quoted against himself must be taken, so as to prevent Holy Scripture seeming to be opposed to itself in this text, and in the passages by which he makes his answer. We for our part indeed tell him, in answer, that the clause, " Who will boast that he has a pure heart?" is a suitable sequel to the preceding sentence, "whenever a righteous king sits upon the throne."[11] For how great so-

ever a man's righteousness may be, he ought to reflect and think, lest there should be found something blameworthy, which has escaped indeed his own notice, when that righteous King shall sit upon His throne, whose cognizance no sins can possibly escape; not even those of which it is said, " Who understandeth his transgressions?"[12] " When, therefore, the righteous King shall sit upon His throne, . . . who will boast that he has a pure heart? or who will boldly say that he is pure from sin?"[13] Except perhaps those who wish to boast of their own righteousness, and not glory in the mercy of the Judge Himself.

### CHAP. XV. (34.) THE OPPOSING PASSAGES.

And yet the passages are true which he goes on to adduce by way of answer, saying: " 'The Saviour in the gospel declares, ' Blessed are the pure in heart; for they shall see God.'[14] David also says, ' Who shall ascend into the hill of the Lord? or who shall stand in His holy place? He that is innocent in his hands, and pure in his heart;'[15] and again in another passage, ' Do good, O Lord, unto those that be good and upright in heart.'[16] So also in Solomon: ' Riches are good unto him that hath no sin on his conscience;'[17] and again in the same book, ' Leave off from sin, and order thine hands aright, and cleanse thy heart from wickedness.'[18] So in the Epistle of John, ' If our heart condemn us not, then have we confidence toward God; and whatsoever we ask, we shall receive of Him.' "[19] For all this is accomplished by the will, by the exercise of faith, hope, and love; by keeping under the body; by doing alms; by forgiving injuries; by earnest prayer; by supplicating for strength to advance in our course; by sincerely saying, " Forgive us, as we also forgive others," and " Lead us not into temptation, but deliver us from evil."[20] By this process, it is certainly brought about that our heart is cleansed, and all our sin taken away; and what the righteous King, when sitting on His throne, shall find concealed in the heart and uncleansed as yet, shall be remitted by His mercy, so that the whole shall be rendered sound and cleansed for seeing God. For " he shall have judgment without mercy, that hath showed no mercy: yet mercy triumpheth against judgment."[21] If it were not so, what hope could any of us have? " When, indeed, the righteous King shall sit upon His throne, who shall boast that he hath a pure heart, or who shall boldly say that he is pure from sin?" Then, however, through His mercy shall the righteous, being by that time fully and perfectly cleansed,

---

[1] Ex. iii 14.    [2] John i. 8.
[3] John v. 35: |" lucernam," not " lux:" as also in the *Dies Iræ* it is said of John, *non lux iste, sed lucernam,*" in allusion to these passages. — W. |
[4] Matt. v. 14, 15.    [5] John i. 9.    [6] Matt. vii. 11.
[7] Matt xix 16.    [8] Luke x. 27, 28.
[9] See also his work *Contra Julianum*, ii. 8.
[10] Prov. xx. 9.    [11] Prov. xx. 8.

[12] Ps. xix. 12.    [13] Prov xx. 8, 9.    [14] Matt. v. 8.
[15] Ps. xxiv. 3, 4.    [16] Ps. cxxv. 4.    [17] Ecclus xiii 24.
[18] Ecclus. xxxviii. 10.    [19] 1 John iii. 21, 22.    [20] Matt. vi. 12, 13.
[21] Jas. ii. 13.

shine forth like the glorious sun in the kingdom of their Father.[1]

### (35.) THE CHURCH WILL BE WITHOUT SPOT AND WRINKLE AFTER THE RESURRECTION.

Then shall the Church realize, fully and perfectly, the condition of "not having spot, or wrinkle, or any such thing,"[2] because then also will it in a real sense be glorious. For inasmuch as he added the epithet "glorious," when he said, "That He might present the Church to Himself, not having spot, or wrinkle, or any such thing," he signified sufficiently when the Church will be without spot, or wrinkle, or anything of this kind, — then of course when it shall be glorious. Because it is not so much when the Church is involved in so many evils, or amidst such offences, and in so great a mixture of very evil men, and amidst the heavy reproaches of the ungodly, that we ought to say that it is glorious, because kings serve it, — a fact which only produces a more perilous and a sorer temptation ; — but then shall it rather be glorious, when that event shall come to pass of which the apostle also speaks in the words, "When Christ, who is your life, shall appear, then shall ye also appear with Him in glory."[3] For since the Lord Himself, in that form of a servant by which He united Himself as Mediator to the Church, was not glorified except by the glory of His resurrection (whence it is said, "The Spirit was not yet given, because Christ was not yet glorified"[4]), how shall His Church be described as *glorious*, before its resurrection? He cleanses it, therefore, now "by the laver of the water in the word,"[5] washing away its past sins, and driving off from it the dominion of wicked angels ; but then by bringing all its healthy powers to perfection, He makes it meet for that glorious state, where it shall shine without a spot or wrinkle. For "whom He did predestinate, them He also called ; and whom He called, them He also justified ; and whom He justified, them He also glorified."[6] It was under this mystery, as I suppose, that that was spoken, " Behold, I cast out devils, and I do cures to-day and to-morrow, and the third day I shall be consummated," or perfected.[7] For He said this in the person of His body, which is His Church, putting *days* for distinct and appointed periods, which He also signified in " the third day " in His resurrection.

### (36.) THE DIFFERENCE BETWEEN THE UPRIGHT IN HEART AND THE CLEAN IN HEART.

I suppose, too, that there is a difference between one who is upright in heart and one who is clean in heart. A man is upright in heart when he " reaches forward to those things which are before, forgetting those things which are behind,"[8] so as to arrive in a right course, that is, with right faith and purpose, at the perfection where he may dwell clean and pure in heart. Thus, in the psalm, the conditions ought to be severally bestowed on each separate character, where it is said, " Who shall ascend into the hill of the Lord? or who shall stand in His holy place? He that is innocent in his hands, and clean in his heart."[9] He shall ascend, innocent in his hands, and stand, clean in his heart, — the one state in present operation, the other in its consummation. And of them should rather be understood that which is written : " Riches are good unto him that hath no sin on his conscience."[10] Then indeed shall accrue the good, or true riches, when all poverty shall have passed away ; in other words, when all infirmity shall have been removed. A man may now indeed " leave off from sin," when in his onward course he departs from it, and is renewed day by day ; and he may " order his hands," and direct them to works of mercy, and " cleanse his heart from all wickedness,"[11] — he may be so merciful that what remains may be forgiven him by free pardon. This indeed is the sound and suitable meaning, without any vain and empty boasting, of that which St. John said : " If our heart condemn us not, then have we confidence toward God. And whatsoever we ask, we shall receive of Him."[12] The warning which he clearly has addressed to us in this passage, is to beware lest our heart should reproach us in our very prayers and petitions ; that is to say, lest, when we happen to resort to this prayer, and say, " Forgive us, even as we ourselves forgive," we should have to feel compunction for not doing what we say, or should even lose boldness to utter what we fail to do, and thereby forfeit the confidence of faithful and earnest prayer.

### CHAP. XVI. (37.) THE SIXTH PASSAGE.

He has also adduced this passage of Scripture, which is very commonly quoted against his party : " For there is not a just man upon earth, that doeth good, and sinneth not."[13] And he makes a pretence of answering it by other passages, — how, " the Lord says concerning holy Job, ' Hast thou considered my servant Job? For there is none like him upon earth, a man who is blameless, true, a worshipper of God, and abstaining from every evil thing.' "[14] On this passage we have already made some remarks.[15] But he has not even attempted to show us how, on the one

---

[1] Matt. xiii. 43.　　　[2] Eph. v. 27.　　　[3] Col. iii. 4.
[4] John vii. 39.　　　[5] Eph. v. 26.　　　[6] Rom. viii. 30.
[7] Luke xiii. 32.

[8] Phil. iii. 13.　　[9] Ps. xxiv. 3, 4.　　[10] Ecclus. xiii. 24.
[11] Ecclus. xxxviii. 10.　　　　　　[12] 1 John iii. 21, 22.
[13] Eccles. vii. 20.　　　　　　　　　[14] Job i. 8.
[15] See above, ch. xii. (29).

hand, Job was absolutely sinless upon earth, — if the words are to bear such a sense ; and, on the other hand, how that can be true which he has admitted to be in the Scripture, "There is not a just man upon earth, that doeth good, and sinneth not." [1]

CHAP. XVII. (38.) THE SEVENTH PASSAGE. WHO MAY BE CALLED IMMACULATE. HOW IT IS THAT IN GOD'S SIGHT NO MAN IS JUSTIFIED.

"They also, says he, "quote the text : 'For in thy sight shall no man living be justified.' " [2] And his affected answer to this passage amounts to nothing else than the showing how texts of Holy Scripture seem to clash with one another, whereas it is our duty rather to demonstrate their agreement. These are his words : "We must confront them with this answer, from the testimony of the evangelist concerning holy Zacharias and Elisabeth, when he says, 'And they were both righteous before God, walking in all the commandments and ordinances of the Lord blameless.' " [3] Now both these righteous persons had, of course, read amongst these very commandments the method of cleansing their own sins. For, according to what is said in the Epistle to the Hebrews of " every high priest taken from among men," [4] Zacharias used no doubt to offer sacrifices even for his own sins. The meaning, however, of the phrase " *blameless*," which is applied to him, we have already, as I suppose, sufficiently explained. [5] "And," he adds, " the blessed apostle says, 'That we should be holy, and without blame before Him.' " [6] This, according to him, is said that we should be so, if those persons are to be understood by " *blameless* " who are altogether without sin. If, however, they are " *blameless* " who are without blame or censure, then it is impossible for us to deny that there have been, and still are, such persons even in this present life ; for it does not follow that a man is without sin because he has not a blot of accusation. Accordingly the apostle, when selecting ministers for ordination, does not say, " If any be *sinless*," for he would be unable to find any such ; but he says, " If any be without accusation," [7] for such, of course, he would be able to find. But our opponent does not tell us how, in accordance with his views, we ought to understand the scripture, " For in Thy sight shall no man living be justified." [2] The meaning of these words is plain enough, receiving as it does additional light from the preceding clause : " Enter not," says the Psalmist, " into judgment with Thy servant, for in Thy sight shall no man living be justified." It is judgment which he fears, therefore he desires that mercy which triumphs over judgment. [8] For the meaning of the prayer, " Enter not into judgment with Thy servant," is this : " Judge me not according to Thyself," who art without sin ; " for in Thy sight shall no man living be justified." This without doubt is understood as spoken of the present life, whilst the predicate " shall not be justified " has reference to that perfect state of righteousness which belongs not to this life.

CHAP. XVIII. (39.) THE EIGHTH PASSAGE. IN WHAT SENSE HE IS SAID NOT TO SIN WHO IS BORN OF GOD. IN WHAT WAY HE WHO SINS SHALL NOT SEE NOR KNOW GOD.

"They also quote," says he, " this passage, " If we say that we have no sin, we deceive ourselves, and the truth is not in us.' " [9] And this very clear testimony he has endeavoured to meet with apparently contradictory texts, saying thus : " The same St. John in this very epistle says, 'This, however, brethren, I say, that ye sin not. Whosoever is born of God doth not commit sin ; for his seed remaineth in him : and he cannot sin.' [10] Also elsewhere : ' Whosoever is born of God sinneth not ; because his being born of God preserveth him, and the evil one toucheth him not.' [11] And again in another passage, when speaking of the Saviour, he says : ' Since He was manifested to take away sins, whosoever abideth in Him sinneth not : whosoever sinneth hath not seen Him, neither known Him.' [12] And yet again : ' Beloved, now are we the sons of God ; and it doth not yet appear what we shall be : but we know that, when He shall appear, we shall be like Him ; for we shall see Him as He is. And every man that hath this hope towards Him purifieth himself, even as He is pure.' " [13] And yet, notwithstanding the truth of all these passages, that also is true which he has adduced, without, however, offering any explanation of it : " If we say that we have no sin, we deceive ourselves, and the truth is not in us." [9] Now it follows from the whole of this, that in so far as we are born of God we abide in Him who appeared to take away sins, that is, in Christ, and sin not, — which is simply that " the inward man is renewed day by day ; " [14] but in so far as we are born of that man " through whom sin entered into the world, and death by sin, and so death passed upon all men," [15] we are not without sin, because we are not as yet free from his infirmity, until, by that renewal which takes place from day to day (for

[1] Eccles. vii. 20.    [2] Ps. cxliii. 2.    [3] Luke i. 6.
[4] Heb. v. 1.    [5] See above, ch. xi. (23).
[6] Eph. i. 4.    [7] Tit. i. 6.

[8] Jas. ii. 13.    [9] 1 John i. 8.    [10] 1 John iii. 9.
[11] 1 John v. 18.    [12] 1 John iii. 5, 6.    [13] 1 John iii. 2, 3.
[14] 2 Cor. iv. 16.    [15] Rom. v. 12.

it is in accordance with this that we were born of God), that infirmity shall be wholly repaired, wherein we were born from the first man, and in which we are not without sin. While the remains of this infirmity abide in our inward man, however much they may be daily lessened in those who are advancing, "we deceive ourselves, and the truth is not in us, if we say that we have no sin." Now, however true it is that "whosoever sinneth hath not seen Him, nor known Him"[1] since with that vision and knowledge, which shall be realized in actual sight, no one can in this life see and know Him; yet with that vision and knowledge which come of faith, there may be many who commit sin, — even apostates themselves, — who still have believed in Him some time or other; so that of none of these could it be said, according to the vision and knowledge which as yet come of faith, that he has neither seen Him nor known Him. But I suppose it ought to be understood that it is the renewal which awaits perfection that sees and knows Him; whereas the infirmity which is destined to waste and ruin neither sees nor knows Him. And it is owing to the remains of this infirmity, of whatever amount, which remain firm in our inward man, that "we deceive ourselves, and have not the truth in us, when we say that we have no sin." Although, then, by the grace of renovation "we are the sons of God," yet by reason of the remains of infirmity within us "it doth not appear what we shall be; only we know that, when He shall appear, we shall be like Him, for we shall see Him as He is." Then there shall be no more sin, because no infirmity shall any longer remain within us or without us. "And every man that hath this hope towards Him purifieth himself, even as He is pure," — purifieth himself, not indeed by himself alone, but by believing in Him, and calling on Him who sanctifieth His saints; which sanctification, when perfected at last (for it is at present only advancing and growing day by day), shall take away from us for ever all the remains of our infirmity.

### CHAP. XIX. (40.) THE NINTH PASSAGE.

"This passage, too," says he, "is quoted by them: 'It is not of him that willeth, nor of him that runneth, but of God that showeth mercy.'"[2] And he observes that the answer to be given to them is derived from the same apostle's words in another passage: "Let him do what he will."[3] And he adds another passage from the Epistle to Philemon, where, speaking of Onesimus, [St. Paul says]: "'Whom I would have retained with me, that in thy stead he might have ministered unto me in the bonds of

the gospel. But without thy mind would I do nothing; that thy benefit should not be as it were of necessity, but willingly.'[4] Likewise, in Deuteronomy: 'Life and death hath He set before thee, and good and evil: . . . choose thou life, that thou mayest live.'[5] So in the book of Solomon: 'God from the beginning made man, and left him in the hand of His counsel; and He added for him commandments and precepts: if thou wilt — to perform acceptable faithfulness for the time to come, they shall save thee. He hath set fire and water before thee: stretch forth thine hand unto whether thou wilt. Before man are good and evil, and life and death; poverty and honour are from the Lord God.'[6] So again in Isaiah we read: 'If ye be willing, and hearken unto me, ye shall eat the good of the land; but if ye be not willing, and hearken not to me, the sword shall devour you: for the mouth of the Lord hath spoken this.'"[7] Now with all their efforts of disguise they here betray their purpose; for they plainly attempt to controvert the grace and mercy of God, which we desire to obtain whenever we offer the prayer, "Thy will be done in earth as it is in heaven;"[8] or again this, "Lead us not into temptation, but deliver us from evil."[9] For indeed why do we present such petitions in earnest supplication, if the result is of him that willeth, and him that runneth, but not of God that showeth mercy? Not that the result is without our will, but that our will does not accomplish the result, unless it receive the divine assistance. Now the wholesomeness of faith is this, that it makes us "seek, that we may find; ask, that we may receive; and knock, that it may be opened to us."[10] Whereas the man who gainsays it, does really shut the door of God's mercy against himself. I am unwilling to say more touching so important a matter, because I do better in committing it to the groans of the faithful, than to words of my own.

### (41.) SPECIMENS OF PELAGIAN EXEGESIS.

But I beg of you to see what kind of objection, after all, he makes, that to him who "willeth and runneth" there is no necessity for God's mercy, which actually anticipates him in order that he may run, — because, forsooth, the apostle says concerning a certain person, "Let him do what he will,"[3] — in the matter, as I suppose, which he goes on to treat, when he says, "He sinneth not, let him marry!"[3] As if indeed it should be regarded as a great matter to be willing to marry, when the subject is a laboured discussion concerning the assistance of God's grace, or that it is of any great advantage

---

[1] 1 John iii. 6.    [2] Rom. ix. 16.    [3] 1 Cor. vii. 36.

[4] Philem. 13, 14.    [5] Deut. xxx. 15, 19.    [6] Ecclus. xv. 14-17.
[7] Isa. i. 19, 20.    [8] Matt. vi. 10.    [9] Matt. vi. 13.
[10] Luke xi. 9.

to will it, unless God's providence, which governs all things, joins together the man and the woman. Or, in the case of the apostle's writing to Philemon, that " his kindness should not be as it were of necessity, but voluntary," — as if any good act could indeed be voluntary otherwise than by God's " working in us both to will and to do of His own good pleasure." [1]   Or, when the Scripture says in Deuteronomy, " Life and death hath He set before man, and good and evil," and admonishes him " to choose life ; " as if, forsooth, this very admonition did not come from God's mercy, or as if there were any advantage in choosing life, unless God inspired love to make such a choice, and gave the possession of it when chosen, concerning which it is said : " For anger is in His indignation, and in His pleasure is life." [2]

Or again, because it is said, " The commandments, if thou wilt, shall save thee," [3] — as if a man ought not to thank God, because he has a will to keep the commandments, since, if he wholly lacked the light of truth, it would not be possible for him to possess such a will.   " Fire and water being set before him, a man stretches forth his hand towards which he pleases ; " [4] and yet higher is He who calls man to his higher vocation than any thought on man's own part, inasmuch as the beginning of correction of the heart lies in faith, even as it is written, " Thou shalt come, and pass on from the beginning of faith." [5]   Every one makes his choice of good, " according as God hath dealt to every man the measure of faith ; " [6] and as the Prince of faith says, " No man can come to me, except the Father which hath sent me draw him." [7]   And that He spake this in reference to the faith which believes in Him, He subsequently explains with sufficient clearness, when He says : " The words that I speak unto you, they are spirit, and they are life ; yet there are some of you that believe not.   For Jesus knew from the beginning who they were that believed not, and who should betray Him.   And He said, Therefore said I unto you, that no man can come unto me, except it were given unto him of my Father." [8]

(42.) GOD'S PROMISES CONDITIONAL.   SAINTS OF THE OLD TESTAMENT WERE SAVED BY THE GRACE OF CHRIST.

He, however, thought he had discovered a great support for his cause in the prophet Isaiah ; because by him God said : " If ye be willing, and hearken unto me, ye shall eat the good of the land ; but if ye be not willing, and hearken not to me, the sword shall devour you : for the mouth of the Lord hath spoken this." [9]   As if

the entire law were not full of conditions of this sort ; or as if its commandments had been given to proud men for any other reason than that " the law was added because of transgression, until the seed should come to whom the promise was made." [10]   " It entered, therefore, that the offence might abound ; but where sin abounded, grace did much more abound." [11]   In other words, That man might receive commandments, trusting as he did in his own resources, and that, failing in these and becoming a transgressor, he might ask for a deliverer and a saviour ; and that the fear of the law might humble him, and bring him, as a schoolmaster, to faith and grace. Thus " their weaknesses being multiplied, they hastened after ; " [12] and in order to heal them, Christ in due season came.   In His grace even righteous men of old believed, and by the same grace were they holpen ; so that with joy did they receive a foreknowledge of Him, and some of them even foretold His coming, — whether they were found among the people of Israel themselves, as Moses, and Joshua the son of Nun, and Samuel, and David, and other such ; or outside that people, as Job ; or previous to that people, as Abraham, and Noah, and all others who are either mentioned or not in Holy Scripture.   " For there is but one God, and one Mediator between God and man, the man Christ Jesus," [13] without whose grace nobody is delivered from condemnation, whether he has derived that condemnation from him in whom all men sinned, or has afterwards aggravated it by his own iniquities.

CHAP. XX. (43.) NO MAN IS ASSISTED UNLESS HE DOES HIMSELF ALSO WORK.   OUR COURSE IS A CONSTANT PROGRESS.

But what is the import of the last statement which he has made : " If any one say, ' May it possibly be that a man sin not even in word ? ' then the answer," says he, " which must be given is, ' Quite possible, if God so will ; and God does so will, therefore it is possible.' "   See how unwilling he was to say, " If God give His help, then it would be possible ; " and yet the Psalmist thus addresses God : " Be Thou my helper, forsake me not ; " [14] where of course help is not sought for procuring bodily advantages and avoiding bodily evils, but for practising and fulfilling righteousness.   Hence it is that we say : " Lead us not into temptation, but deliver us from evil." [15] Now no man is assisted unless he also himself does something ; assisted, however, he is, if he prays, if he believes, if he is " called according to God's purpose ; " [16] for " whom He did foreknow, He also did predestinate to be conformed

[1] Phil. ii. 13.    [2] Ps. xxx. 5.    [3] Ecclus. xv. 15.
[4] Ecclus. xv. 16.    [5] Cant. iv. 8.    [6] Rom. xii. 3.
[7] John vi. 44.    [8] John vi. 62–65.    [9] Isa. i. 19, 20.
[10] Gal. iii. 19.    [11] Rom. v. 20.    [12] Ps. xvi. 4.
[13] 1 Tim. ii. 5.    [14] Ps. xxvii. 9.    [15] Matt. vi. 13.
[16] Rom. viii. 28.

to the image of His Son, that He might be the first-born among many brethren. Moreover, whom He did predestinate, them He also called; and whom He called, them He also justified; and whom He justified, them He also glorified."[1] We run, therefore, whenever we make advance; and our wholeness runs with us in our advance (just as a sore is said to run[2] when the wound is in process of a sound and careful treatment), in order that we may be in every respect perfect, without any infirmity of sin whatever, — a result which God not only wishes, but even causes and helps us to accomplish. And this God's grace does, in co-operation with ourselves, through Jesus Christ our Lord, as well by commandments, sacraments, and examples, as by His Holy Spirit also; through whom there is hiddenly shed abroad in our hearts[3] that love, "which maketh intercession for us with groanings which cannot be uttered,"[4] until wholeness and salvation be perfected in us, and God be manifested to us as He will be seen in His eternal truth.

CHAP. XXI. (44.) CONCLUSION OF THE WORK. IN THE REGENERATE IT IS NOT CONCUPISCENCE, BUT CONSENT, WHICH IS SIN.

Whosoever, then, supposes that any man or any men (except the one Mediator between God and man[5]) have ever lived, or are yet living in this present state, who have not needed, and do not need, forgiveness of sins, he opposes Holy Scripture, wherein it is said by the apostle: "By one man sin entered into the world, and death by sin; and so death passed upon all men, in which all have sinned."[6] And he must needs go on to assert, with an impious contention, that there may possibly be men who are freed and saved from sin without the liberation and salvation of the one Mediator Christ. Whereas He it is who has said: "They that be whole need not a physician, but they that are sick;"[7] "I am not come to call the righteous, but sinners to repentance."[8] He, moreover, who says that any man, after he has received remission of sins, has ever lived in this body, or still is living, so righteously as to have no sin at all, he contradicts the Apostle John, who declares that "If we say we have no sin, we deceive ourselves, and the truth is not in us."[9] Observe, the expression is not *we had*, but "*we have*." If, however, anybody contend that the apostle's statement concerns the sin which dwells in our mortal flesh

according to the defect which was caused by the will of the first man when he sinned, and concerning which the Apostle Paul enjoins us "not" to "obey it in the lusts thereof,"[10] — so that he does not sin who altogether withholds his consent from this same indwelling sin, and so brings it to no evil work, — either in deed, or word, or thought, — although the lusting after it may be excited (which in another sense has received the name of sin, inasmuch as consenting to it would amount to sinning), but excited against our will, — he certainly is drawing subtle distinctions, and should consider what relation all this bears to the Lord's Prayer, wherein we say, "Forgive us our debts."[11] Now, if I judge aright, it would be unnecessary to put up such a prayer as this, if we never in the least degree consented to the lusts of the before-mentioned sin, either in a slip of the tongue, or in a wanton thought; all that it would be needful to say would be, "Lead us not into temptation, but deliver us from evil."[12] Nor could the Apostle James say: "In many things we all offend."[13] For in truth only that man offends whom an evil concupiscence persuades, either by deception or by force, to do or say or think something which he ought to avoid, by directing his appetites or his aversions contrary to the rule of righteousness. Finally, if it be asserted that there either have been, or are in this present life, any persons, with the sole exception of our Great Head, "the Saviour of His body,"[14] who are righteous, without any sin, — and this, either by not consenting to the lusts thereof, or because that must not be accounted as any sin which is such that God does not impute it to them by reason of their godly lives (although the blessedness of being without sin is a different thing from the blessedness of not having one's sin imputed to him),[15] — I do not deem it necessary to contest the point over much. I am quite aware that some hold this opinion,[16] whose views on the subject I have not the courage to censure, although, at the same time, I cannot defend them. But if any man says that we ought not to use the prayer, "Lead us not into temptation" (and he says as much who maintains that God's help is unnecessary to a person for the avoidance of sin, and that human will, after accepting only the law, is sufficient for the purpose), then I do not hesitate at once to affirm that such a man ought to be removed from the public ear, and to be anathematized by every mouth.

---

[1] Rom. viii. 29, 30.　[2] Ps. lxxvii. 2.　[3] Rom. v. 5.
[4] Rom. viii. 26.　[5] 1 Tim. ii. 5.　[6] Rom. v. 12.
[7] Matt. ix. 12.　[8] Matt. ix. 13.　[9] 1 John i. 8.

[10] Rom. vi. 12.　[11] Matt. vi. 12.　[12] Matt. vi. 13.
[13] Jas. iii. 2.　[14] Eph. i. 22, 23, and v. 23.
[15] Ps. xxxii. 2.
[16] See Augustin's treatise, *De Natura et Gratia*, 74, 75.

A WORK ON THE PROCEEDINGS OF PELAGIUS.

# EXTRACT FROM AUGUSTIN'S "RETRACTATIONS,"

## Book II. Chap. 45,

### *ON THE FOLLOWING TREATISE,*

## "DE GESTIS PELAGII."

----

"About the same time, in the East (that is to say, in Palestinian Syria), Pelagius was summoned by certain catholic brethren[1] before a tribunal of bishops, and was heard on his trial by fourteen prelates, in the absence of his accusers, who were unable to be present on the day of the synod. On his condemning the very dogmas which were read from the indictment against him, as assailing the grace of Christ, they pronounced him to be a catholic. But when the Acts of this synod found their way into our hands, I wrote a treatise on them, to prevent the idea gaining ground that, because he had been in a manner acquitted, his opinions also were approved by the bishops; or that the accused could by any chance have escaped condemnation at their hands, unless he had condemned the opinions charged against him. This treatise of mine begins with these words: 'After there came into my hands.'"

----

[1] Their names were Heros and Lazarus.

178

# PREFACE TO THE BOOK ON THE PROCEEDINGS OF PELAGIUS.

IN the year of Christ 415, Pelagius was accused of heresy in Palestine, and brought to trial on one or two occasions. At the first trial, which was held on or about the 30th of July, at a congress of his presbyters, by John, bishop of Jerusalem, no regular record was kept of the proceedings, as we are informed by Augustin in the following work (sec. 39 and 55). The hour and the day of this assembly we may learn from Orosius, a presbyter of Spain, who was present at the congress, and has in his *Apology* committed to writing some of its most memorable acts. We are informed by him that "after a great deal of earnest proceeding on both sides, the bishop John proposed the last resolution, that certain brethren should be sent with a letter to blessed Innocent, Pope of Rome, to the intent that he might decide on all the points which were to follow."

The second trial took place afterwards at Diospolis,[1] a city in Palestine, before fourteen bishops, at which was kept an accurate record of the proceedings. The bishops are severally mentioned by Augustin in his work *against Julianus*, Book i. chs. v. and vii. (19, 32), in the following order: "Eulogius, John, Ammonianus, Porphyry, Eutonius, another Porphyry, Fidus, Zoninus, Zoboennus, Nymphidius, Chromatius, Jovinus, Eleutherius, and Clematius. There can be no doubt that Eulogius, bishop of Cæsarea, was also primate of the province of Palestine, because he is constantly mentioned by Augustin as occupying the first place before the other thirteen bishops, and even before John himself, bishop of Jerusalem.

We find from the epistle of Lucian,[2] *De revelatione corporis Stephani martyris*, that this synod was held at the approach of Christmas. In this epistle he tells us of three visions which God had shown him in the year 415, —the first on December 3d, and the other two on the 10th and 17th of the same month; that he then reported the matter to John, bishop of Jerusalem, who sent him in quest of the martyr's sepulchre. He further informs us that he discovered the sepulchre, and at once returned to John, "who (says he) was attending a synod at Lydda, which is Diospolis." This must have happened about the 21st of the month, since Lucian goes on ₍o say that John came, in the company of two more bishops, Eutonius of Sebaste and Eleutherius of Jericho, and that in their presence the relics of the martyr were removed on the 26th day of the same month of December.

A certain deacon, called Annianus, is supposed to have pleaded the cause of Pelagius at the synod; some learned men finding it easier to interpret of this deacon than of Pelagius what Jerome writes in a letter addressed to Alypius and Augustin (*Epist. Augustinian*. 202, 2): "For every thing which he denies having ever uttered in that miserable synod of Diospolis he professes to hold in this work." Jerome bestowed the epithet of "miserable" on this synod of Diospolis, for no other reason (as we suppose) than because he discovered from its Acts how miserably the synod had been duped by Pelagius. Pope Innocent, after a sight of these Acts, expressly owned (see *Epist. Augustinian*. 183, 4) that "he could not bring himself to refuse either blame or praise of those bishops." Augustin, however, in the following treatise (see chs. 4 and 8), does not hesitate to call them "pious judges," and (in his first book *against Julianus*, i. ch. v. 19) "catholic judges," who, when Pelagius abjured the errors attributed to him, pronounced him a catholic, and acquitted him; indeed, he frequently cites these fourteen bishops as witnesses of the catholic faith in opposition to Julianus.

In his letters addressed to Pope Innocent in the year 416 (see *Epist. Augustinian*. 175, 4, and 177, 2), Augustin intimated that he knew nothing of the Proceedings of the synod except from hearsay; and in a letter to John, bishop of Jerusalem (*Epist*. 179, 4), he earnestly requested him to forward them to him. But the report was in his hands about midsummer in 417, when he wrote his Epistle to Paulinus (*Epist*. 186, 31); so that the date of the following treatise is thus traced to the commencement of the year 417, supposing it to have been published immediately after he had received the Proceedings.

The title given to this work by Augustin, in his book *On Original Sin* (15), stands *De Gestis Palæstinis* [On the Proceedings which took place in Palestine]; by this title Prosper likewise refers to the work (in his book *Adv.*

---

[1] That is, Lydda.   [2] To be found in Migne's *Patrologia Latina*, vol. vii., *Appendix*.

*Collatorem*, 43); but yet we ought to retain the inscription *De Gestis Pelagii*, which is prefixed both to the ancient editions and to the particular *Retractation* in which Augustin reviewed this work. The treatise had this title given to it, no doubt, either because it had been already commonly accepted as a description of these proceedings of Pelagius and his vindication, which led to his boast that he had been acquitted; or else from the fact that an examination had become necessary of those proceedings, which the accused party had himself published in an abridged and garbled form. Hence Possidonius named the treatise by the title, *Contra Gesta Pelagii* [A Protest, or Vindication, against the Proceedings of Pelagius].

Out of this book Photius copied a very accurate account of the Synod of Diospolis and inserted it in his *Bibliotheca* (cod. 54). One may therefore conclude that this work of Augustin's is one of those which Possidonius, in his Life, ch. xi. or xxi., No. 59, mentions as having been "translated into the Greek tongue." The Aurelius to whom the work is dedicated is mentioned by Photius in the passage just cited, and by Prosper before him (in the 43d chapter of the above-quoted *Adversus Collatorem*), as "the bishop of Carthage." If the title-page of old did not give them this information, they could both of them discover it from reading this book, especially ch. 23 [XI.].

# CONTENTS OF THE TREATISE "ON THE PROCEEDINGS OF PELAGIUS."

# A WORK ON THE PROCEEDINGS OF PELAGIUS,[1]

## IN ONE BOOK,

### ADDRESSED TO BISHOP AURELIUS [OF CARTHAGE], BY AURELIUS AUGUSTIN.

#### WRITTEN ABOUT THE COMMENCEMENT OF THE YEAR A.D. 417.

---

THE SEVERAL HEADS OF ERROR WHICH WERE ALLEGED AGAINST PELAGIUS AT THE SYNOD IN PALESTINE, WITH HIS ANSWERS TO EACH CHARGE, ARE MINUTELY DISCUSSED. AUGUSTIN SHOWS THAT, ALTHOUGH PELAGIUS WAS ACQUITTED BY THE SYNOD, THERE STILL CLAVE TO HIM THE SUSPICION OF HERESY; AND THAT THE ACQUITTAL OF THE ACCUSED BY THE SYNOD WAS SO CONTRIVED, THAT THE HERESY ITSELF WITH WHICH HE WAS CHARGED WAS UNHESITATINGLY CONDEMNED.

### CHAP. I. — INTRODUCTION.

AFTER there came into my hands, holy father Aurelius, the ecclesiastical proceedings, by which fourteen bishops of the province of Palestine pronounced Pelagius a catholic, my hesitation, in which I was previously reluctant to make any lengthy or confident statement about the defence which he had made, came to an end. This defence, indeed, I had already read in a paper which he himself forwarded to me. Forasmuch, however, as I received no letter therewith from him, I was afraid that some discrepancy might be detected between my statement and the record of the ecclesiastical proceedings; and that, should Pelagius perhaps deny that he had. sent me any paper (and it would have been difficult for me to prove that he had, when there was only one witness), I should rather seem guilty in the eyes of those who would readily credit his denial, either of an underhanded falsification, or else (to say the least) of a reckless credulity. Now, however, when I am to treat of matters which are shown to have actually transpired, and when, as it appears to me, all doubt is removed whether he really acted in the way described, your holi-

ness, and everybody who reads these pages, will no doubt be able to judge, with greater readiness and certainty, both of his defence and of this my treatment of it.

### CHAP. 2 [I.] — THE FIRST ITEM IN THE ACCUSATION, AND PELAGIUS' ANSWER.

First of all, then, I offer to the Lord my God, who is also my defence and guide, unspeakable thanks, because I was not misled in my views respecting our holy brethren and fellow-bishops who sat as judges in that case. His answers, indeed, they not without reason approved; because they had not to consider how he had in his writings stated the points which were objected against him, but what he had to say about them in his reply at the pending examination. A case of unsoundness in the faith is one thing, one of incautious statement is another thing. Now sundry objections were urged against Pelagius out of a written complaint, which our holy brethren and fellow-bishops in Gaul, Heros and Lazarus, presented, being themselves unable to be present, owing (as we afterwards learned from credible information) to the severe indisposition of one of them. The first of these was, that he writes, in a certain book of his, this: "No man can be

---

[1] More properly called *On the Palestinian Proceedings*.

without sin unless he has acquired a knowledge of the law." After this had been read out, the synod inquired: "Did you, Pelagius, express yourself thus?" Then in answer he said: "I certainly used the words, but not in the sense in which they understand them. I did not say that a man is unable to sin who has acquired a knowledge of the law; but that he is by the knowledge of the law assisted towards not sinning, even as it is written, 'He hath given them a law for help.'"[1] Upon hearing this, the synod declared: "The words which have been spoken by Pelagius are not different from the Church." Assuredly they are not different, as he expressed them in his answer; the statement, however, which was produced from his book has a different meaning. But this the bishops, who were Greek-speaking men, and who heard the words through an interpreter, were not concerned with discussing. All they had to consider at the moment was, what the man who was under examination said was his meaning,—not in what words his opinion was alleged to have been expressed in his book.

CHAP. 3. — DISCUSSION OF PELAGIUS' FIRST ANSWER.

Now to say that "a man is by the knowledge of the law assisted towards not sinning," is a different assertion from saying that "a man cannot be without sin unless he has acquired a knowledge of the law." We see, for example, that corn-floors may be threshed without threshing-sledges,—however much these may assist the operation if we have them; and that boys can find their way to school without the pedagogue, —however valuable for this may be the office of pedagogues; and that many persons recover from sickness without physicians,—although the doctor's skill is clearly of greatest use; and that men sometimes live on other aliments besides bread,—however valuable the use of bread must needs be allowed to be; and many other illustrations may occur to the thoughtful reader, without our prompting. From which examples we are undoubtedly reminded that there are two sorts of aids. Some are indispensable, and without their help the desired result could not be attained. Without a ship, for instance, no man could take a voyage; no man could speak without a voice; without legs no man could walk; without light nobody could see; and so on in numberless instances. Amongst them this also may be reckoned, that without God's grace no man can live rightly. But then, again, there are other helps, which render us assistance in such a way that we might in some other way effect the object to which they are ordinarily auxiliary in their absence. Such are those which I have

already mentioned,—the threshing-sledges for threshing corn, the pedagogue for conducting the child, medical art applied to the recovery of health, and other like instances. We have therefore to inquire to which of these two classes belongs the knowledge of the law,—in other words, to consider in what way it helps us towards the avoidance of sin. If it be in the sense of indispensable aid without which the end cannot be attained; not only was Pelagius' answer before the judges true, but what he wrote in his book was true also. If, however, it be of such a character that it helps indeed if it is present, but even if it be absent, then the result is still possible to be attained by some other means,—his answer to the judges was still true, and not unreasonably did it find favour with the bishops that "man is assisted not to sin by the knowledge of the law;" but what he wrote in his book is not true, that "there is no man without sin except him who has acquired a knowledge of the law,"—a statement which the judges left undiscussed, as they were ignorant of the Latin language, and were content with the confession of the man who was pleading his cause before them, especially as no one was present on the other side who could oblige the interpreter to expose his meaning by an explanation of the words of his book, and to show why it was that the brethren were not groundlessly disturbed. For but very few persons are thoroughly acquainted with the law. The mass of the members of Christ, who are scattered abroad everywhere, being ignorant of the very profound and complicated contents of the law, are commended by the piety of simple faith and unfailing hope in God, and sincere love. Endowed with such gifts, they trust that by the grace of God they may be purged from their sins through our Lord Jesus Christ.

CHAP. 4 [II.] — THE SAME CONTINUED.

If Pelagius, as he possibly might, were to say in reply to this, that that very thing was what he meant by "the knowledge of the law, without which a man is unable to be free from sins," which is communicated by the teaching of faith to converts and to babes in Christ, and in which candidates for baptism are catechetically instructed with a view to their knowing the creed, certainly this is not what is usually meant when any one is said to have a knowledge of the law. This phrase is only applied to such persons as are skilled in the law. But if he persists in describing the knowledge of the law by the words in question, which, however few in number, are great in weight, and are used to designate all who are faithfully baptized according to the prescribed rule of the Churches; and if he maintains that it was of this that he said, "No

---

[1] Isa. viii. 20.

one is without sin, but the man who has acquired the knowledge of the law," — a knowledge which must needs be conveyed to believers before they attain to the actual remission of sins, — even in such case there would crowd around him a countless multitude, not indeed of angry disputants, but of crying baptized infants, who would exclaim, — not, to be sure, in words, but in the very truthfulness of innocence, — "What is it, O what is it that you have written : 'He only can be without sin who has acquired a knowledge of the law?' See here are we, a large flock of lambs, without sin, and yet we have no knowledge of the law." Now surely they with their silent tongue would compel him to silence, or, perhaps, even to confess that he was corrected of his great perverseness ; or else (if you will), that he had already for some time entertained the opinion which he acknowledged before his ecclesiastical examiners, but that he had failed before to express his opinion in words of sufficient care, — that his faith, therefore, should be approved, but this book revised and amended. For, as the Scripture says : "There is that slippeth in his speech, but not in his heart." [1] Now if he would only admit this, or were already saying it, who would not most readily forgive those words which he had committed to writing with too great heedlessness and neglect, especially on his declining to defend the opinion which the said words contain, and affirming that to be his proper view which the truth approves? This we must suppose would have been in the minds of the pious judges themselves, if they could only have duly understood the contents of his Latin book, thoroughly interpreted to them, as they understood his reply to the synod, which was spoken in Greek, and therefore quite intelligible to them, and adjudged it as not alien from the Church. Let us go on to consider the other cases.

CHAP. 5 [III.] — THE SECOND ITEM IN THE ACCUSATION ; AND PELAGIUS' ANSWER.

The synod of bishops then proceeded to say : "Let another section be read." Accordingly there was read the passage in the same book wherein Pelagius had laid down the position that " all men are ruled by their own will." On this being read, Pelagius said in answer : " This I stated in the interest of free will. God is its helper whenever it chooses good ; man, however, when sinning is himself in fault, as under the direction of a free will." Upon hearing this, the bishops exclaimed : " Nor again is this opposed to the doctrine of the Church." For who indeed could condemn or deny the freedom of the will, when God's help is associated with

it? His opinion, therefore, as thus explained in his answer, was, with good reason, deemed satisfactory by the bishops. And yet, after all, the statement made in his book, " All men are ruled by their own will," ought without doubt to have deeply disturbed the brethren, who had discovered what these men are accustomed to dispute against the grace of God. For it is said, " All men are ruled by their own will," as if God rules no man, and the Scripture says in vain, " Save Thy people, and bless Thine inheritance ; rule them, and lift them up for ever." [2] They would not, of course, stay, if they are ruled only by their own will without God, even as sheep which have no shepherd : which, God forbid for us. For, unquestionably to be led is something more compulsory than to be ruled. He who is ruled at the same time does something himself, — indeed, when ruled by God, it is with the express view that he should also act rightly ; whereas the man who is led can hardly be understood to do any thing himself at all. And yet the Saviour's helpful grace is so much better than our own wills and desires, that the apostle does not hesitate to say : " As many as are led by the Spirit of God, they are the sons of God." [3] And our free will can do nothing better for us than to submit itself to be led by Him who can do nothing amiss ; and after doing this, not to doubt that it was helped to do it by Him of whom it is said in the psalm, " He is my God, His mercy shall go before me." [4]

CHAP. 6. — PELAGIUS' ANSWER EXAMINED.

Indeed, in this very book which contains these statements, after laying down the position, " All men are governed by their own will, and every one is submitted to his own desire," Pelagius goes on to adduce the testimony of Scripture, from which it is evident enough that no man ought to trust to himself for direction. For on this very subject the Wisdom of Solomon declares : " I myself also am a mortal man like unto all ; and the offspring of him that was first made of the earth," [5] — with other similar words to the conclusion of the paragraph, where we read : " For all men have one entrance into life, and the like going out therefrom : wherefore I prayed and understanding was given to me ; I called, and the Spirit of Wisdom came into me." [6] Now is it not clearer than light itself, how that this man, on duly considering the wretchedness of human frailty, did not dare to commit himself to his own direction, but prayed, and understanding was given to him, concerning which the apostle says : " But we have the understanding of the Lord ; " [7] and called, and the Spirit of

[1] Ecclus. xix. 16.

[2] Ps. xxviii. 9.　　[3] Rom. viii. 14.　　[4] Ps. lix. 10.
[5] Wisd. vii. 1.　　[6] Wisd. vii. 6, 7.　　[7] 1 Cor. ii. 16.

Wisdom entered into him? Now it is by this Spirit, and not by the strength of their own will, that they who are God's children are governed and led.

### CHAP. 7. — THE SAME CONTINUED.

As for the passage from the psalm, "He loved cursing, and it shall come upon him; and he willed not blessing, so it shall be far removed from him,"[1] which he quoted in the same book of Chapters, as if to prove that "all men are ruled by their own will," who can be ignorant that this is a fault not of nature as God created it, but of human will which departed from God? The fact indeed is, that even if he had not loved cursing, and had willed blessing, he would in this very case, too, deny that his will had received any assistance from God; in his ingratitude and impiety, moreover, he would submit himself to be ruled by himself, until he found out by his penalties that, sunk as he was into ruin, without God to govern him he was utterly unable to direct his own self. In like manner, from the passage which he quoted in the same book under the same head, "He hath set fire and water before thee; stretch forth thy hand unto whether thou wilt; before man are good and evil, life and death, and whichever he liketh shall be given to him,"[2] it is manifest that, if he applies his hand to fire, and if evil and death please him, his human will effects all this; but if, on the contrary, he loves goodness and life, not alone does his will accomplish the happy choice, but it is assisted by divine grace. The eye indeed is sufficient for itself, for not seeing, that is, for darkness; but for seeing, it is in its own light not sufficient for itself unless the assistance of a clear external light is rendered to it. God forbid, however, that they who are "the called according to His purpose, whom He also foreknew, and predestinated to be conformed to the likeness of His Son,"[3] should be given up to their own desire to perish. This is suffered only by "the vessels of wrath,"[4] who are perfected for perdition; in whose very destruction, indeed, God "makes known the riches of His glory on the vessels of His mercy."[5] Now it is on this account that, after saying, "He is my God, His mercy shall go before me,"[6] he immediately adds, "My God will show me vengeance upon my enemies."[6] That therefore happens to them which is mentioned in Scripture, "God gave them up to the lusts of their own heart."[7] This, however, does not happen to the predestinated, who are ruled by the Spirit of God, for not in vain is their cry: "Deliver me not, O Lord, to the sinner, according to my desire."[8]

With regard, indeed, to the evil lusts which assail them, their prayer has ever assumed some such shape as this: "Take away from me the concupiscence of the belly; and let not the desire of lust take hold of me."[9] Upon those whom He governs as His subjects does God bestow this gift; but not upon those who think themselves capable of governing themselves, and who, in the stiff-necked confidence of their own will, disdain to have Him as their ruler.

### CHAP. 8. — THE SAME CONTINUED.

This being the case, how must God's children, who have learned the truth of all this and rejoice at being ruled and led by the Spirit of God, have been affected when they heard or read that Pelagius had declared in writing that "all men are governed by their own will, and that every one is submitted to his own desire?" And yet, when questioned by the bishops, he fully perceived what an evil impression these words of his might produce, and told them in answer that "he had made such an assertion in the interest of free will," — adding at once, "God is its helper whenever it chooses good; whilst man is himself in fault when he sins, as being under the influence of a free will." Although the pious judges approved of this sentiment also, they were unwilling to consider or examine how incautiously he had written, or indeed in what sense he had employed the words found in his book. They thought it was enough that he had made such a confession concerning free will, as to admit that God helped the man who chose the good, whereas the man who sinned was himself to blame, his own will sufficing for him in this direction. According to this, God rules those whom He assists in their choice of the good. So far, then, as they rule anything themselves, they rule it rightly, since they themselves are ruled by Him who is right and good.

### CHAP. 9. — THE THIRD ITEM IN THE ACCUSATION; AND PELAGIUS' ANSWER.

Another statement was read which Pelagius had placed in his book, to this effect: "In the day of judgment no forbearance will be shown to the ungodly and the sinners, but they will be consumed in eternal fires." This induced the brethren to regard the statement as open to the objection, that it seemed so worded as to imply that all sinners whatever were to be punished with an eternal punishment, without excepting even those who hold Christ as their foundation, although "they build thereupon wood, hay, stubble,"[10] concerning whom the apostle writes: "If any man's work shall be burned, he shall suffer loss; but he shall himself be saved, yet

---

1 Ps. cix. 18.     2 Ecclus. xv. 16, 17.     3 Rom. viii. 29.
4 Rom. ix 22.     5 Rom. ix. 23.     6 Ps. lix. 10.
7 Rom. i. 24.     8 Ps. cxl. 8.

9 Ecclus. xxiii. 5, 6.          10 1 Cor. iii. 12.

so as by fire." [1] When, however, Pelagius responded that "he had made his assertion in accordance with the Gospel, in which it is written concerning sinners, 'These shall go away into eternal punishment, but the righteous into life eternal,'" [2] it was impossible for Christian judges to be dissatisfied with a sentence which is written in the Gospel, and was spoken by the Lord; especially as they knew not what there was in the words taken from Pelagius' book which could so disturb the brethren, who were accustomed to hear his discussions and those of his followers. Since also they were absent [3] who presented the indictment against Pelagius to the holy bishop Eulogius, there was no one to urge him that he ought to distinguish, by some exception, between those sinners who are to be saved by fire, and those who are to be punished with everlasting perdition. If, indeed, the judges had come to understand by these means the reason why the objection had been made to his statement, had he then refused to allow the distinction, he would have been justly open to blame.

CHAP. 10. — PELAGIUS' ANSWER EXAMINED. ON ORIGEN'S ERROR CONCERNING THE NON-ETERNITY OF THE PUNISHMENT OF THE DEVIL AND THE DAMNED.

But what Pelagius added, "Who believes differently is an Origenist," was approved by the judges, because in very deed the Church most justly abominates the opinion of Origen, that even they whom the Lord says are to be punished with everlasting punishment, and the devil himself and his angels, after a time, however protracted, will be purged, and released from their penalties, and shall then cleave to the saints who reign with God in the association of blessedness. This additional sentence, therefore, the synod pronounced to be "not opposed to the Church," — not in accordance with Pelagius, but rather in accordance with the Gospel, that such ungodly and sinful men shall be consumed by eternal fires as the Gospel determines to be worthy of such a punishment; and that he is a sharer in Origen's abominable opinion, who affirms that their punishment can possibly ever come to an end, when the Lord has said it is to be eternal. Concerning those sinners, however, of whom the apostle declares that "they shall be saved, yet so as by fire, after their work has been burnt up," [4] inasmuch as no objectionable opinion in reference to them was manifestly charged against Pelagius, the synod determined nothing. Wherefore he who says that the ungodly and sinner, whom the truth consigns to eternal punishment, can ever be liberated there-

from, is not unfitly designated by Pelagius as an "Origenist." But, on the other hand, he who supposes that no sinner whatever deserves mercy in the judgment of God, may be designated by whatever name Pelagius is disposed to give to him, only it must at the same time be quite understood that this error is not received as truth by the Church. "For he shall have judgment without mercy that hath showed no mercy." [5]

CHAP. 11. — THE SAME CONTINUED.

But how this judgment is to be accomplished, it is not easy to understand from Holy Scripture; for there are many modes therein of describing that which is to come to pass only in one mode. In one place the Lord declares that He will "shut the door" against those whom He does not admit into His kingdom; and that, on their clamorously demanding admission, "Open unto us, . . . we have eaten and drunk in Thy presence," and so forth, as the Scripture describes, "He will say unto them in answer, I know you not, . . . all ye workers of iniquity." [6] In another passage He reminds us that He will command "all which would not that He should reign over them to be brought to Him, and be slain in His presence." [7] In another place, again, He tells us that He will come with His angels in His majesty; and before Him shall be gathered all nations, and He shall separate them one from another; some He will set on His right hand, and after enumerating their good works, will award to them eternal life; and others on His left hand, whose barrenness in all good works He will expose, will He condemn to everlasting fire. [8] In two other passages He deals with that wicked and slothful servant, who neglected to trade with His money, [9] and with the man who was found at the feast without the wedding garment, — and He orders them to be bound hand and foot, and to be cast into outer darkness. [10] And in yet another scripture, after admitting the five virgins who were wise, He shuts the door against the other five foolish ones. [11] Now these descriptions, — and there are others which at the instant do not occur to me, — are all intended to represent to us the future judgment, which of course will be held not over one, or over five, but over multitudes. For if it were a solitary case only of the man who was cast into outer darkness for not having on the wedding garment, He would not have gone on at once to give it a plural turn, by saying: "For many are called, but few are chosen;" [12] whereas it is plain that, after the one was cast out and condemned, many still remained behind in the house. However,

---

[1] 1 Cor. iii. 15.    [2] Matt. xxv. 46.
[3] The bishops Heros and Lazarus; see above, 1 [ii.].
[4] 1 Cor. iii. 12, 15.

[5] Jas. ii. 13.    [6] Luke xiii. 25–27.    [7] Luke xix. 27.
[8] Matt. xxv. 33.    [9] Luke xix. 20–24.    [10] Matt. xxii. 11–13.
[11] Matt. xxv. 1–10.    [12] Matt. xxii. 14.

it would occupy us too long to discuss all these questions to the full. This brief remark, however, I may make, without prejudice (as they say in pecuniary affairs) to some better discussion, that by the many descriptions which are scattered throughout the Holy Scriptures there is signified to us but one mode of final judgment, which is inscrutable to us, — with only the variety of deservings preserved in the rewards and punishments. Touching the particular point, indeed, which we have before us at present, it is sufficient to remark that, if Pelagius had actually said that all sinners whatever without exception would be punished in an eternity of punishment by everlasting fire, then whosoever had approved of this judgment would, to begin with, have brought the sentence down on his own head. " For who will boast that he is pure from sins?"[1] Forasmuch, however, as he did not say *all*, nor *certain*, but made an indefinite statement only, — and afterwards, in explanation, declared that his meaning was according to the words of the Gospel, — his opinion was affirmed by the judgment of the bishops to be true; but it does not even now appear what Pelagius really thinks on the subject, and in consequence there is no indecency in inquiring further into the decision of the episcopal judges.

### CHAP. 12 [IV.] — THE FOURTH ITEM IN THE ACCUSATION; AND PELAGIUS' ANSWER.

It was further objected against Pelagius, as if he had written in his book, that " evil does not enter our thoughts." In reply, however, to this charge, he said: " We made no such statement. What we did say was, that the Christian ought to be careful not to have evil thoughts." Of this, as it became them, the bishops approved. For who can doubt that evil ought not to be thought of? And, indeed, if what he said in his book about " evil not being thought " runs in this form, " neither is evil to be thought of," the ordinary meaning of such words is " that evil ought not even to be thought of." Now if any person denies this, what else does he in fact say, than that evil ought to be thought of? And if this were true, it could not be said in praise of love that " it thinketh no evil!"[2] But after all, the phrase about "*not entering into the thoughts*" of righteous and holy men is not quite a commendable one, for this reason, that what enters the mind is commonly called a thought, even when assent to it does not follow. The thought, however, which contracts blame, and is justly forbidden, is never unaccompanied with assent. Possibly those men had an incorrect copy of Pelagius' writings, who thought it proper to object to him that he had used the words : " Evil

does not enter into our thoughts;" that is, that whatever is evil never enters into the thoughts of righteous and holy men. Which is, of course, a very absurd statement. For whenever we censure evil things, we cannot enunciate them in words, unless they have been thought. But, as we said before, that is termed a culpable thought of evil which carries with it assent.

### CHAP. 13 [V.] — THE FIFTH ITEM OF THE ACCUSATION; AND PELAGIUS' ANSWER.

After the judges had accorded their approbation to this answer of Pelagius, another passage which he had written in his book was read aloud: "The kingdom of heaven was promised even in the Old Testament." Upon this, Pelagius remarked in vindication: "This can be proved by the Scriptures: but heretics, in order to disparage the Old Testament, deny this. I, however, simply followed the authority of the Scriptures when I said this; for in the prophet Daniel it is written: 'The saints shall receive the kingdom of the Most High.'"[3] After they had heard this answer, the synod said: "Neither is this opposed to the Church's faith."

### CHAP. 14. — EXAMINATION OF THIS POINT. THE PHRASE "OLD TESTAMENT" USED IN TWO SENSES. THE HEIR OF THE OLD TESTAMENT. IN THE OLD TESTAMENT THERE WERE HEIRS OF THE NEW TESTAMENT.

Was it therefore without reason that our brethren were moved by his words to include this charge among the others against him? Certainly not. The fact is, that the phrase *Old Testament* is constantly employed in two different ways, — in one, following the authority of Holy Scriptures; in the other, following the most common custom of speech. For the Apostle Paul says, in his Epistle to the Galatians: "Tell me, ye that desire to be under the law, do ye not hear the law? For it is written that Abraham had two sons, the one by a bond-maid, the other by a free woman. . . . Which things are an allegory: for these are the two *testaments;* the one which gendereth to bondage, which is Agar. For this is Mount Sinai in Arabia, and is conjoined with the Jerusalem which now is, and is in bondage with her children; whereas the Jerusalem which is above is free, and is the mother of us all."[4] Now, inasmuch as the Old Testament belongs to bondage, whence it is written, "Cast out the bond-woman and her son, for the son of the bond-woman shall not be heir with my son Isaac,"[5] but the kingdom of heaven to liberty; what has the kingdom of heaven to do with the Old Testament? Since, however, as I have already remarked, we are accustomed, in

---

[1] Prov. xx. 9.          [2] 1 Cor. xiii. 5.          [3] Dan. vii. 18.          [4] Gal. iv. 21–26.          [5] Gal. iv. 30.

our ordinary use of words, to designate all those Scriptures of the law and the prophets which were given previous to the Lord's incarnation, and are embraced together by canonical authority, under the name and title of *the Old Testament*, what man who is ever so moderately informed in ecclesiastical lore can be ignorant that the kingdom of heaven could be quite as well promised in those early Scriptures as even the New Testament itself, to which the kingdom of heaven belongs?   At all events, in those ancient Scriptures it is most distinctly written : " Behold, the days come, saith the Lord, that I will consummate a new testament with the house of Israel and with the house of Jacob ; not according to the testament that I made with their fathers, in the day that I took them by the hand, to lead them out of the land of Egypt." [1]   This was done on Mount Sinai.   But then there had not yet risen the prophet Daniel to say : " The saints shall receive the kingdom of the Most High." [2]   For by these words he foretold the merit not of the Old, but of the New Testament.   In the same manner did the same prophets foretell that Christ Himself would come, in whose blood the New Testament was consecrated. Of this Testament also the apostles became the ministers, as the most blessed Paul declares : " He hath made us able ministers of the New Testament ; not in its letter, but in spirit : for the letter killeth, but the spirit giveth life." [3]   In that testament, however, which is properly called the Old, and was given on Mount Sinai, only earthly happiness is expressly promised.   Accordingly that land, into which the nation, after being led through the wilderness, was conducted, is called the land of promise, wherein peace and royal power, and the gaining of victories over enemies, and an abundance of children and of fruits of the ground, and gifts of a similar kind, are the promises of the Old Testament.   And these, indeed, are figures of the spiritual blessings which appertain to the New Testament ; but yet the man who lives under God's law with those earthly blessings for his sanction, is precisely the heir of the Old Testament, for just such rewards are promised and given to him, according to the terms of the Old Testament, as are the objects of his desire according to the condition of the old man.   But whatever blessings are there figuratively set forth as appertaining to the New Testament require the new man to give them effect.   And no doubt the great apostle understood perfectly well what he was saying, when he described the two testaments as capable of the allegorical distinction of the bond-woman and the free, — attributing the children of the flesh to the Old, and to the New

the children of the promise : " They," says he, " which are the children of the flesh, are not the children of God ; but the children of the promise are counted for the seed." [4]   The children of the flesh, then, belong to the earthly Jerusalem, which is in bondage with her children ; whereas the children of the promise belong to the Jerusalem above, the free, the mother of us all, eternal in the heavens. [5]   Whence we can easily see who they are that appertain to the earthly, and who to the heavenly kingdom.   But then the happy persons, who even in that early age were by the grace of God taught to understand the distinction now set forth, were thereby made the children of promise, and were accounted in the secret purpose of God as heirs of the New Testament ; although they continued with perfect fitness to administer the Old Testament to the ancient people of God, because it was divinely appropriated to that people in God's distribution of the times and seasons.

### CHAP. 15. — THE SAME CONTINUED.

How then should there not be a feeling of just disquietude entertained by the children of promise, children of the free Jerusalem, which is eternal in the heavens, when they see that by the words of Pelagius the distinction which has been drawn by Apostolic and catholic authority is abolished, and Agar is supposed to be by some means on a par with Sarah?   He therefore does injury to the scripture of the Old Testament with heretical impiety, who with an impious and sacrilegious face denies that it was inspired by the good, supreme, and very God, — as Marcion does, as Manichæus does, and other pests of similar opinions.   On this account (that I may put into as brief a space as I can what my own views are on the subject), as much injury is done to the New Testament, when it is put on the same level with the Old Testament, as is inflicted on the Old itself when men deny it to be the work of the supreme God of goodness.   Now, when Pelagius in his answer gave as his reason for saying that even in the Old Testament there was a promise of the kingdom of heaven, the testimony of the prophet Daniel, who most plainly foretold that the saints should receive the kingdom of the Most High, it was fairly decided that the statement of Pelagius was not opposed to the catholic faith, although not according to the distinction which shows that the earthly promises of Mount Sinai are the proper characteristics of the Old Testament ; nor indeed was the decision an improper one, considering that mode of speech which designates all the canonical Scriptures which were given to men before the Lord's coming in the flesh by

---

[1] Jer. xxxi. 31, 32.     [2] Dan. vii. 18.     [3] 2 Cor. iii. 6.     [4] Rom. ix. 8.     [5] Gal. iv. 25, 26.

the title of the "Old Testament." The kingdom of the Most High is of course none other than the kingdom of God ; otherwise, anybody might boldly contend that the kingdom of God is one thing, and the kingdom of heaven another.

CHAP. 16 [VI.] — THE SIXTH ITEM OF THE ACCUSATION, AND PELAGIUS' REPLY.

The next objection was to the effect that Pelagius in that same book of his wrote thus : " A man is able, if he likes, to be without sin ; " and that writing to a certain widow he said, flatteringly : " In thee piety may find a dwelling-place, such as she finds nowhere else ; in thee righteousness, though a stranger, can find a home ; truth, which no one any longer recognises, can discover an abode and a friend in thee ; and the law of God, which almost everybody despises, may be honoured by thee alone." And in another sentence he writes to her : " O how happy and blessed art thou, when that righteousness which we must believe to flourish only in heaven has found a shelter on earth only in thy heart !" In another work addressed to her, after reciting the prayer of our Lord and Saviour Jesus Christ, and teaching her in what manner saints ought to pray, he says : " He worthily raises his hands to God, and with a good conscience does he pour out his prayer, who is able to say, ' Thou, O Lord, knowest how holy, and harmless, and pure from all injury and iniquity and violence, are the hands which I stretch out to Thee ; how righteous, and pure, and free from all deceit, are the lips with which I offer to Thee my supplication, that Thou wouldst have mercy upon me.' " To all this Pelagius said in answer : " We asserted that a man could be without sin, and could keep God's commandments if he wished ; for this capacity has been given to him by God. But we never said that any man could be found who at no time whatever, from infancy to old age, had committed sin : but that if any person were converted from his sins, he could by his own labour and God's grace be without sin ; and yet not even thus would he be incapable of change ever afterwards. As for the other statements which they have made against us, they are not to be found in our books, nor have we at any time said such things." Upon hearing this vindication, the synod put this question to him : " You have denied having ever written such words ; are you therefore ready to anathematize those who do hold these opinions ?" Pelagius answered : " I anathematize them as fools, not as heretics, for there is no dogma." The bishops then pronounced their judgment in these words : " Since now Pelagius has with his own mouth anathematized this vague statement as foolish verbiage, justly declaring in his reply, ' That a man is able with God's assist-

ance and grace to be without sin,' let him now proceed to answer the other heads of accusation against him."

CHAP. 17. — EXAMINATION OF THE SIXTH CHARGE AND ANSWERS.

Well, now, had the judges either the power or the right to condemn these unrecognised and vague words, when no person on the other side was present to assert that Pelagius had written the very culpable sentences which were alleged to have been addressed by him to the widow ? In such a matter, it surely could not be enough to produce a manuscript, and to read out of it words as his, if there were not also witnesses forthcoming in case he denied, on the words being read out, that they ever dropped from his pen. But even here the judges did all that lay in their power to do, when they asked Pelagius whether he would anathematize the persons who held such sentiments as he declared he had never himself propounded either in speech or in writing. And when he answered that he did anathematize them as fools, what right had the judges to push the inquiry any further on the matter, in the absence of Pelagius' opponents?

CHAP. 18. — THE SAME CONTINUED.

But perhaps the point requires some consideration, whether he was right in saying that " such as held the opinions in question deserved anathema, not as heretics, but as fools, since it was no dogma." The question, when fairly confronted, is no doubt far from being an unimportant one, — how far a man deserves to be described as a heretic ; on this occasion, however, the judges acted rightly in abstaining from it altogether. If any one, for example, were to allege that eaglets are suspended in the talons of the parent bird, and so exposed to the rays of the sun, and such as wink are flung to the ground as spurious, the light being in some mysterious way the gauge of their genuine nature, he is not to be accounted a heretic, if the story happens to be untrue.[1] And, since it occurs in the writings of the learned and is very commonly received as fact, ought it to be considered a foolish thing to mention it, even though it be not true ? much less ought our credit, which gains for us the name of being trustworthy, to be affected, on the one hand injuriously if the story be believed by us, or beneficially if disbelieved.[2] If, to go a step further in illustration, any one were from this opinion to contend that there existed in birds reasonable souls, from the notion that human souls at intervals passed into them, then indeed we should have to reject from

---

[1] It is told by Pliny, *Hist. Nat.* x. 3 (3), and Lucan, *Pharsalia*, ix. 902, etc.
[2] *Creditum*, however, is read in both clauses ; we should expect *non creditum* in one, as one reading has it. [ ? — W.]

our mind and ears alike an idea like this as the rankest heresy; and even if the story about the eagles were true (as there are many curious facts about bees before our eyes, that are true), we should still have to consider, and demonstrate, the great difference that exists between the condition of creatures like these, which are quite irrational, however surprising in their powers of sensation, and the nature which is common (not to men and beasts, but) to men and angels. There are, to be sure, a great many foolish things said by foolish and ignorant persons, which yet fail to prove them heretics. One might instance the silly talk so commonly heard about the pursuits of other people, from persons who have never learned these pursuits, — equally hasty and untenable whether in the shape of excessive and indiscriminate praise of those they love, or of blame in the case of those they happen to dislike. The same remark might be made concerning the usual current of human conversation: whenever it does touch on a subject which requires dogmatic acuracy of statement, but is thrown out at random or suggested by the passing moment, it is too often pervaded by foolish levity, whether uttered by the mouth or expressed in writing. Many persons, indeed, when gently reminded of their reckless gossip, have afterwards much regretted their conduct; they scarcely recollected what they had never uttered with a fixed purpose, but had poured forth in a sheer volley of casual and unconsidered words. It is, unhappily, almost impossible to be quite clear of such faults. Who is he "that slippeth not in his tongue,"[1] and "offendeth not in word?"[2] It, however, makes all the difference in the world, to what extent, and from what motive, and whether in fact at all, a man when warned of his fault corrects it, or obstinately clings to it so as to make a dogma and settled opinion of that which he had not at first uttered on purpose, but only in levity. Although, then, it turns out eventually that every heretic is a fool, it does not follow that every fool must immediately be named a heretic. The judges were quite right in saying that Pelagius had anathematized the vague folly under consideration by its fitting designation; for even if it were heresy, there could be no doubt of its being foolish prattle. Whatever, therefore, it was, they designated the offence under a general name. But whether the quoted words had been used with any definitely dogmatic purpose, or only in a vague and indeterminate sense, and with an unmeaningness which should be capable of an easy correction, they did not deem it necessary to discuss on the present occasion, since the man who was on his trial before them denied that the words were his at all, in whatever sense they had been employed.

## CHAP. 19. — THE SAME CONTINUED.

Now it so happened that, while we were reading this defence of Pelagius in the small paper which we received at first,[3] there were present certain holy brethren, who said that they had in their possession some hortatory or consolatory works which Pelagius had addressed to a widow lady whose name did not appear, and they advised us to examine whether the words which he had abjured for his own occurred anywhere in these books. They were not themselves aware whether they did or not. The said books were accordingly read through, and the words in question were actually discovered in them. Moreover, they who had produced the copy of the book, affirmed that for now almost four years they had had these books as Pelagius', nor had they once heard a doubt expressed about his authorship. Considering, then, from the integrity of these servants of God, which was very well known to us, how impossible it was for them to use deceit in the matter, the conclusion seemed inevitable, that Pelagius must be supposed by us to have rather been the deceiver at his trial before the bishops; unless we should think it possible that something may have been published, even for so many years, in his name, although not actually composed by him; for our informants did not tell us that they had received the books from Pelagius himself, nor had they ever heard him admit his own authorship. Now, in my own case, certain of our brethren have told me that sundry writings have found their way into Spain under my name. Such persons, indeed, as had read my genuine writings could not recognise those others as mine; although by other persons my authorship of them was quite believed.

## CHAP. 20. — THE SAME CONTINUED. PELAGIUS ACKNOWLEDGES THE DOCTRINE OF GRACE IN DECEPTIVE TERMS.

There can be no doubt that what Pelagius has acknowledged as his own is as yet very obscure. I suppose, however, that it will become apparent in the subsequent details of these proceedings. Now he says: "We have affirmed that a man is able to be without sin, and to keep the commandments of God if he wishes, inasmuch as God has given him this ability. But we have not said that any man can be found, who from infancy to old age has never committed sin; but that if any person were converted from his sins, he could by his own exertion and God's grace

---

[1] See Ecclus. xix. 16.    [2] See Jas. iii. 2.

[3] See below, in chap. 57 [xxxi.].

be without sin; and yet not even thus would he be incapable of change afterwards." Now it is quite uncertain what he means in these words by the grace of God; and the judges, catholic as they were, could not possibly understand by the phrase anything else than the grace which is so very strongly recommended to us in the apostle's teaching. Now this is the grace whereby we hope that we can be delivered from the body of this death through our Lord Jesus Christ,[1] [VII.] and for the obtaining of which we pray that we may not be led into temptation.[2] This grace is not nature, but that which renders assistance to frail and corrupted nature. This grace is not the knowledge of the law, but is that of which the apostle says: "I will not make void the grace of God: for if righteousness come by the law, then Christ is dead in vain."[3] Therefore it is not "the letter that killeth, but the life-giving spirit."[4] For the knowledge of the law, without the grace of the Spirit, produces all kinds of concupiscence in man; for, as the apostle says, "I had not known sin but by the law: I had not known lust, unless the law had said, Thou shalt not covet. But sin, taking occasion by the commandment, wrought in me all manner of concupiscence."[5] By saying this, however, he blames not the law; he rather praises it, for he says afterwards: "The law indeed is holy, and the commandment holy, and just, and good."[6] And he goes on to ask: "Was then that which is good made death unto me? God forbid. But sin, that it might appear sin, wrought death in me by that which is good."[7] And, again, he praises the law by saying: "We know that the law is spiritual; but I am carnal, sold under sin. For that which I do I know not: for what I would, that do I not; but what I hate, that do I. If then I do that which I would not, I consent unto the law that it is good."[8] Observe, then, he knows the law, praises it, and consents to it; for what it commands, that he also wishes; and what it forbids, and condemns, that he also hates: but for all that, what he hates, that he actually does. There is in his mind, therefore, a knowledge of the holy law of God, but still his evil concupiscence is not cured. He has a good will within him, but still what he does is evil. Hence it comes to pass that, amidst the mutual struggles of the two laws within him,— "the law in his members warring against the law of his mind, and making him captive to the law of sin,"[9] — he confesses his misery, and exclaims in such words as these: "O wretched man that I am! who shall deliver me from this body of death? The grace of God, through Jesus Christ our Lord."[1]

### CHAP. 21 [VIII.] — THE SAME CONTINUED.

It is not nature, therefore, which, sold as it is under sin and wounded by the offence, longs for a Redeemer and Saviour; nor is it the knowledge of the law — through which comes the discovery, not the expulsion, of sin — which delivers us from the body of this death; but it is the Lord's good grace through our Lord Jesus Christ.[10]

### CHAP. 21 [IX.] — THE SAME CONTINUED.

This grace is not dying nature, nor the slaying letter, but the vivifying spirit; for already did he possess nature with freedom of will, because he said: "To will is present with me."[11] Nature, however, in a healthy condition and without a flaw, he did not possess, for he said: "I know that in me (that is, in my flesh) dwelleth nothing good."[11] Already had he the knowledge of God's holy law, for he said: "I had not known sin but through the law;"[12] yet for all that, he did not possess strength and power to practise and fulfil righteousness, for he complained: "What I would, that do I not; but what I hate, that do I."[13] And again, "How to accomplish that which is good I find not."[11] Therefore it is not from the liberty of the human will, nor from the precepts of the law, that there comes deliverance from the body of this death; for both of these he had already, — the one in his nature, the other in his learning; but all he wanted was the help of the grace of God, through Jesus Christ our Lord.

### CHAP. 22 [X.] — THE SAME CONTINUED. THE SYNOD SUPPOSED THAT THE GRACE ACKNOWLEDGED BY PELAGIUS WAS THAT WHICH WAS SO THOROUGHLY KNOWN TO THE CHURCH.

This grace, then, which was most completely known in the catholic Church (as the bishops were well aware), they supposed Pelagius made confession of, when they heard him say that "a man, when converted from his sins, is able by his own exertion and the grace of God to be without sin." For my own part, however, I remembered the treatise which had been given to me, that I might refute it, by those servants of God, who had been Pelagius' followers.[14] They, notwithstanding their great affection for him, plainly acknowledged that the passage was his; when, on this question being proposed, because he had already given offence to very many persons from advancing views against the grace of God, he most expressly admitted that "what he meant by God's grace was that, when our nature was created, it received the capacity of not sin-

---

[1] Rom. vii. 24, 25.    [2] Matt. vi. 13.    [3] Gal. ii. 21.
[4] 2 Cor. iii. 6.    [5] Rom. vii. 7, 8.    [6] Rom. vii. 12.
[7] Rom. vii. 13.    [8] Rom. vii. 14-16.    [9] Rom. vii. 23.

[10] Rom. vii. 25.    [11] Rom. vii. 18.    [12] Rom. vii. 7.
[13] Rom. vii. 15.
[14] Timasius and Jacobus, at whose instance Augustin wrote, and to whom he addressed his book De Naturâ et Gratiâ.

ning, because it was created with free will." On account, therefore, of this treatise, I cannot help feeling still anxious, whilst many of the brethren, who are well acquainted with his discussions, share in my anxiety, lest under the ambiguity which notoriously characterizes his words there lies some latent reserve, and lest he should afterwards tell his followers that it was without prejudice to his own doctrine that he made any admissions, — discoursing thus: "I no doubt asserted that a man was able by his own exertion and the grace of God to live without sin; but you know very well what I mean by grace; and you may recollect reading that grace is that in which we are created by God with a free will." Accordingly, while the bishops understood him to mean the grace by which we have by adoption been made new creatures, not that by which we were created (for most plainly does Holy Scripture instruct us in the *former* sense of grace as the true one), ignorant of his being a heretic, they acquitted him as a catholic.[1]  I must say that my suspicion is excited also by this, that in the work which I answered, he most openly said that "righteous Abel never sinned at all."[2]  Now, however, he thus expresses himself: "But we did not say that any man could be found who at no time whatever, from infancy to old age, has committed sin; but that, if any man were converted from his sins, he could by his own labour and God's grace be without sin."[3]  When speaking of righteous Abel, he did not say that after being converted from his sins he became sinless in a new life, but that he never committed sin at all.  If, then, that book be his, it must of course be corrected and amended from his answer. For I should be sorry to say that he was insincere in his more recent statement; lest perhaps he should say that he had forgotten what he had previously written in the book we have quoted. Let us therefore direct our view to what afterwards occurred.  Now, from the sequel of these ecclesiastical proceedings, we can by God's help show that, although Pelagius, as some suppose, cleared himself in his examination, and was at all events acquitted by his judges (who were, however, but human beings after all), that this great heresy,[4] which we should be most unwilling to see making further progress or becoming aggravated in guilt, was undoubtedly itself condemned.

CHAP. 23 [XI.] — THE SEVENTH ITEM OF THE ACCUSATION: THE BREVIATES OF CŒLESTIUS OBJECTED TO PELAGIUS.

Then follow sundry statements charged against Pelagius, which are said to be found among the opinions of his disciple Cœlestius: how that "Adam was created mortal, and would have died whether he had sinned or not sinned; that Adam's sin injured only himself and not the human race; that the law no less than the gospel leads us to the kingdom; that there were sinless men previous to the coming of Christ; that new-born infants are in the same condition as Adam was before the fall; that the whole human race does not, on the one hand, die through Adam's death or transgression, nor, on the other hand, does the whole human race rise again through the resurrection of Christ." These have been so objected to, that they are even said to have been, after a full hearing, condemned at Carthage by your holiness and other bishops associated with you.[5]  I was not present on that occasion, as you will recollect; but afterwards, on my arrival at Carthage, I read over the Acts of the synod, some of which I perfectly well remember, but I do not know whether all the tenets now mentioned occur among them.  But what matters it if some of them were possibly not mentioned, and so not included in the condemnation of the synod when it is quite clear that they deserve condemnation?  Sundry other points of error were next alleged against him, connected with the mention of my own name.[6]  They had been transmitted to me from Sicily, some of our Catholic brethren there being perplexed by questions of this kind; and I drew up a reply to them in a little work addressed to Hilary,[7] who had consulted me respecting them in a letter.  My answer, in my opinion, was a sufficient one.  These are the errors referred to: "That a man is able to be without sin if he wishes.  That infants, even if they die unbaptized, have eternal life.  That rich men, even if they are baptized, unless they renounce all, have, whatever good they may seem to have done, nothing of it reckoned to them; neither can they possess the kingdom of God."

CHAP. 24. — PELAGIUS' ANSWER TO THE CHARGES BROUGHT TOGETHER UNDER THE SEVENTH ITEM.

The following, as the proceedings testify, was Pelagius' own answer to these charges against him: "Concerning a man's being able indeed to be without sin, we have spoken," says he, "already; concerning the fact, however, that before the Lord's coming there were persons without sin, we say now that, previous to Christ's advent, some men lived holy and righteous lives, according to the teaching of the sacred Scriptures.  The rest were not said by me, as even their testimony goes to show, and for them, I

---

[1] The reader may consult the treatise *De Naturâ et Gratiâ*, chs. 53 and 54, on this opinion of Pelagius.
[2] See *De Naturâ et Gratiâ*, xxxvii. (44).
[3] See above, ch. 16 (VI).    [4] Hanc talem hæresim.

[5] Compare Augustin's work *De Peccato Originali*, ch xi (12).
[6] See same treatise as before, and same chapter.
[7] See Augustin's letter to Hilary, in *Epist* 157.

do not feel that I am responsible. But for the satisfaction of the holy synod, I anathematize those who either now hold, or have ever held, these opinions." After hearing this answer of his, the synod said: "With regard to these charges aforesaid, Pelagius has in our presence given us sufficient and proper satisfaction, by anathematizing the opinions which were not his." We see, therefore, and maintain that the most pernicious evils of this heresy have been condemned, not only by Pelagius, but also by the holy bishops who presided over that inquiry: — that "Adam was made mortal;" (and, that the meaning of this statement might be more clearly understood, it was added, "and he would have died whether he had sinned or not sinned;") that his sin injured only himself and not the human race; that the law, no less than the gospel, leads us to the kingdom of heaven; that new born infants are in the same condition that Adam was before the fall; that the entire human race does not, on the one hand, die through Adam's death and transgression, nor, on the other hand, does the whole human race rise again through the resurrection of Christ; that infants, even if they die unbaptized, have eternal life; that rich men, even if baptized, unless they renounce and give up all, have, whatever good they may seem to have done, nothing of it reckoned to them, neither can they possess the kingdom of God;"—all these opinions, at any rate, were clearly condemned in that ecclesiastical court, — Pelagius pronouncing the anathema, and the bishops the interlocutory sentence.

CHAP. 25. — THE PELAGIANS FALSELY PRETENDED THAT THE EASTERN CHURCHES WERE ON THEIR SIDE.

Now, by reason of these questions, and the very contentious assertions of these tenets, which are everywhere accompanied with heated feelings, many weak brethren were disturbed. We have accordingly, in the anxiety of that love which it becomes us to feel towards the Church of Christ through His grace, and out of regard to Marcellinus of blessed memory (who was extremely vexed day by day by these disputers, and who asked my advice by letter), been obliged to write on some of these questions, and especially on the baptism of infants. On this same subject also I afterwards, at your request, and assisted by your prayers, delivered an earnest address, to the best of my ability, in the church of the *Majores*,[1] holding in my hands an epistle of the most glorious martyr Cyprian, and reading therefrom and applying his words on the very matter, in order to remove this dangerous error out of the hearts of sundry persons, who had

been persuaded to take up with the opinions which, as we see, were condemned in these proceedings. These opinions it has been attempted by their promoters to force upon the minds of some of the brethren, by threatenings, as if from the Eastern Churches, that unless they adopted the said opinions, they would be formally condemned by those Churches. Observe, however, that no less than fourteen bishops of the Eastern Church,[2] assembled in synod in the land where the Lord manifested His presence in the days of His flesh, refused to acquit Pelagius unless he condemned these opinions as opposed to the Catholic faith. Since, therefore, he was then acquitted because he anathematized such views, it follows beyond a doubt that the said opinions were condemned. This, indeed, will appear more clearly still, and on still stronger evidence, in the sequel.

CHAP. 26. — THE ACCUSATIONS IN THE SEVENTH ITEM, WHICH PELAGIUS CONFESSED.

Let us now see what were the two points out of all that were alleged which Pelagius was unwilling to anathematize, and admitted to be his own opinions, but to remove their offensive aspect explained in what sense he held them. "That a man," says he, "is able to be without sin has been asserted already." Asserted no doubt, and we remember the assertion quite well; but still it was mitigated, and approved by the judges, in that God's grace was added, concerning which nothing was said in the original draft of his doctrine. Touching the second, however, of these points, we ought to pay careful attention to what he said in answer to the charge against him. "Concerning the fact, indeed," says he, "that before the Lord's coming there were persons without sin, we now again assert that previous to Christ's advent some men lived holy and righteous lives, according to the teaching of the sacred Scriptures." He did not dare to say: "We now again assert that previous to Christ's advent there were persons without sin," although this had been laid to his charge after the very words of Cœlestius. For he perceived how dangerous such a statement was, and into what trouble it would bring him. So he reduced the sentence to these harmless dimensions: "We again assert that before the coming of Christ there were persons who led holy and righteous lives." Of course there were: who would deny it? But to say this is a very different thing from saying that they lived "without sin." Because, indeed, those ancient worthies lived holy and righteous lives, they could for that very reason better confess: "If we say that we have no sin, we deceive ourselves, and the truth is not in

---

[1] " In the *Basilica Majorum*." According to another reading, "the church of *Majorinus*."

[2] Augustin mentions their names in his work *Contra Julianum*, Book i. ch. v. (19).

us."[1]  In the present day, also, many men live holy and righteous lives ; but yet it is no untruth they utter when in their prayer they say : " Forgive us our debts, even as we forgive our debtors."[2]  This avowal was accordingly acceptable to the judges, in the sense in which Pelagius solemnly declared his belief; but certainly not in the sense which Cœlestius, according to the original charge against him, was said to hold. We must now treat in detail of the topics which still remain, to the best of our ability.

### CHAP. 27 [XII.] — THE EIGHTH ITEM IN THE ACCUSATION.

Pelagius was charged with having said : " That the Church here is without spot or wrinkle."  It was on this point that the Donatists also were constantly at conflict with us in our conference. We used, in their case, to lay especial stress on the mixture of bad men with good, like that of the chaff with the wheat ; and we were led to this idea by the similitude of the threshing-floor. We might apply the same illustration in answer to our present opponents, unless indeed they would have the Church consist only of good men, whom they assert to be without any sin whatever, that so the Church might be without spot or wrinkle.  If this be their meaning, then I repeat the same words as I quoted just now ; for how can they be members of the Church, of whom the voice of a truthful humility declares, " If we say that we have no sin, we deceive ourselves, and the truth is not in us? "[1]  or how could the Church offer up that prayer which the Lord taught her to use, " Forgive us our debts,"[2] if in this world the Church is without a spot or blemish?  In short, they must themselves submit to be strictly catechised respecting themselves : do they really allow that they have any sins of their own?  If their answer is in the negative, then they must be plainly told that they are deceiving themselves, and the truth is not in them.  If, however, they shall acknowledge that they do commit sin, what is this but a confession of their own wrinkle and spot? They therefore are not members of the Church ; because the Church is without spot and wrinkle, while they have both spot and wrinkle.

### CHAP. 28. — PELAGIUS' REPLY TO THE EIGHTH ITEM OF ACCUSATION.

But to this objection he replied with a watchful caution such as the catholic judges no doubt approved.  " It has," says he, " been asserted by me, — but in such a sense that the Church is by the laver cleansed from every spot and wrinkle, and in this purity the Lord wishes her to continue."  Whereupon the synod said : " Of

this also we approve."  And who amongst us denies that in baptism the sins of all men are remitted, and that all believers come up spotless and pure from the laver of regeneration?  Or what catholic Christian is there who wishes not, as his Lord also wishes, and as it is meant to be, that the Church should remain always without spot or wrinkle?  For in very deed God is now in His mercy and truth bringing it about, that His holy Church should be conducted to that perfect state in which she is to remain without spot or wrinkle for evermore.  But between the laver, where all past stains and deformities are removed, and the kingdom, where the Church will remain for ever without any spot or wrinkle, there is this present intermediate time of prayer, during which her cry must of necessity be : " Forgive us our debts."  Hence arose the objection against them for saying that " the Church here on earth is without spot or wrinkle ; " from the doubt whether by this opinion they did not boldly prohibit that prayer whereby the Church in her present baptized state entreats day and night for herself the forgiveness of her sins.  On the subject of this intervening period between the remission of sins which takes place in baptism, and the perpetuity of sinlessness which is to be in the kingdom of heaven, no proceedings ensued with Pelagius, and no decision was pronounced by the bishops.  Only he thought that some brief indication ought to be given that he had not expressed himself in the way which the accusation against him seemed to state.  As to his saying, " This has been asserted by me, — but in such a sense," what else did he mean to convey than the idea that he had not in fact expressed himself in the same manner as he was supposed to have done by his accusers?  That, however, which induced the judges to say that they were satisfied with his answer was baptism as the means of being washed from our sins ; and the kingdom of heaven, in which the holy Church, which is now in process of cleansing, shall continue in a sinless state for ever : this is clear from the evidence, so far as I can form an opinion.

### CHAP. 29 [XIII.] — THE NINTH ITEM OF THE ACCUSATION ; AND PELAGIUS' REPLY.

The next objections were urged out of the book of Cœlestius, following the contents of each several chapter, but rather according to the sense than the words.  These indeed he expatiates on rather fully ; they, however, who presented the indictment against Pelagius said that they had been unable at the moment to adduce all the words.  In the first chapter, then, of Cœlestius' book they alleged that the following was written : " That we do more than is commanded us in the law and the gospel."  To this

---

[1] 1 John i. 8.          [2] Matt. vi. 12.

Pelagius replied : " This they have set down as my statement. What we said, however, was in keeping with the apostle's assertion concerning virginity, of which Paul writes : ' I have no commandment of the Lord.' " [1] Upon this the synod said : " This also the Church receives." I have read for myself the meaning which Cœlestius gives to this in his book, — for he does not deny that the book is his. Now he made this statement obviously with the view of persuading us that we possess through the nature of free will so great an ability for avoiding sin, that we are able to do more than is commanded us ; for a perpetual virginity is maintained by very many persons, and this is not commanded ; whereas, in order to avoid sin, it is sufficient to fulfil what is commanded. When the judges, however, accepted Pelagius' answer, they did not take it to convey the idea that those persons keep all the commandments of the law and the gospel who over and above maintain the state of virginity, which is not commanded, — but only this, that virginity, which is not commanded, is something more than conjugal chastity, which is commanded ; so that to observe the one is of course more than to keep the other ; whereas, at the same time, neither can be maintained without the grace of God, inasmuch as the apostle, in speaking of this very subject, says : " But I would that all men were even as I myself. Every man, however, hath his proper gift of God, one after this manner, and another after that." [2] And even the Lord Himself, upon the disciples remarking, " If the case of the man be so with his wife, it is not expedient to marry " (or, as it may be better expressed in Latin, " it is not expedient to take a wife "),[3] said to them : " All men cannot receive this saying, save they to whom it is given." [4] This, therefore, is the doctrine which the bishops of the synod declared to be received by the Church, that the state of virginity, persevered in to the last, which is not commanded, is more than the chastity of married life, which is commanded. In what view Pelagius or Cœlestius regarded this subject, the judges were not aware.

CHAP. 30 [XIV.] — THE TENTH ITEM IN THE ACCUSATION. THE MORE PROMINENT POINTS OF CŒLESTIUS' WORK CONTINUED.

After this we find objected against Pelagius some other points of Cœlestius' teaching, — prominent ones, and undoubtedly worthy of condemnation ; such, indeed, as would certainly have involved Pelagius in condemnation, if he

had not anathematized them in the synod. Under his third head Cœlestius was alleged to have written : " That God's grace and assistance is not given for single actions, but is imparted in the freedom of the will, or in the law and in doctrine." And again : " That God's grace is given in proportion to our deserts ; because, were He to give it to sinful persons, He would seem to be unrighteous." And from these words he inferred that " therefore grace itself has been placed in my will, according as I have been either worthy or unworthy of it. For if we do all things by grace, then whenever we are overcome by sin, it is not *we* who are overcome, but God's grace, which wanted by all means to help us, but was not able." And once more he says : " If, when we conquer sin, it is by the grace of God ; then it is He who is in fault whenever we are conquered by sin, because He was either altogether unable or unwilling to keep us safe." To these charges Pelagius replied : " Whether these are really the opinions of Cœlestius or not, is the concern of those who say that they are. For my own part, indeed, I never entertained such views ; on the contrary, I anathematize every one who does entertain them." Then the synod said : " This holy synod accepts you for your condemnation of these impious words." Now certainly there can be no mistake, in regard to these opinions, either as to the clear way in which Pelagius pronounced on them his anathema, or as to the absolute terms in which the bishops condemned them. Whether Pelagius or Cœlestius, or both of them, or neither of them, or other persons with them or in their name, have ever held or still hold these sentiments, — may be doubtful or obscure ; but nevertheless by this judgment of the bishops it has been declared plainly enough that they have been condemned, and that Pelagius would have been condemned along with them, unless he had himself condemned them too. Now, after this trial, it is certain that whenever we enter on a controversy touching opinions of this kind, we only discuss an already condemned heresy.

CHAP. 31. — REMARKS ON THE TENTH ITEM.

I shall make my next remark with greater satisfaction. In a former section I expressed a fear [5] that, when Pelagius said that " a man was able by the help of God's grace to live without sin," he perhaps meant by the term " grace " the capability possessed by nature as created by God with a free will, as it is understood in that book which I received as his and to which I replied ; [6] and that by these means he was deceiving the

---

[1] 1 Cor. vii. 25.    [2] 1 Cor. vii. 7.
[3] This " better expression," " non expedit *ducere*," Augustin substitutes for the reading " non expedit *nubere*," as applied to a woman's taking a husband. The original, γαμῆσαι [not γαμεῖσθαι], justifies Augustin's preference.
[4] Matt. xix. 10, 11.

[5] See above, (20).
[6] He refers to Pelagius' work which Augustin received from Jacobus and Timasius, and against which he wrote his treatise *De Naturâ et Gratiâ.*

judges, who were ignorant of the circumstances. Now, however, since he anathematizes those persons who hold that "God's grace and assistance is not given for single actions, but is imparted in the freedom of the will, or in the law and in doctrine," it is quite evident that he really means the grace which is preached in the Church of Christ, and is conferred by the ministration of the Holy Ghost for the purpose of helping us in our single actions, whence it is that we pray for needful and suitable grace that we enter not into any temptation. Nor, again, have I any longer a fear that, when he said, "No man can be without sin unless he has acquired a knowledge of the law," and added this explanation of his words, that "he posited in the knowledge of the law, help towards the avoidance of sin," [1] he at all meant the said knowledge to be considered as tantamount to the grace of God; for, observe, he anathematizes such as hold this opinion. See, too, how he refuses to hold our natural free will, or the law and doctrine, as equivalent to that grace of God which helps us through our single actions. What else then is left to him but to understand that grace which the apostle tells us is given by "the supply of the Spirit?" [2] and concerning which the Lord said: "Take no thought how or what ye shall speak; for it shall be given you in that same hour what ye shall speak. For it is not ye that speak, but the Spirit of your Father which speaketh in you." [3] Nor, again, need I be under any apprehension that, when he asserted, "All men are ruled by their own will," and afterwards explained that he had made that statement "in the interest of the freedom of our will, of which God is the helper whenever it makes choice of good," [4] that he perhaps here also held God's helping grace as synonymous with our natural free will and the teaching of the law. For inasmuch as he rightly anathematized the persons who hold that God's grace or assistance is not given for single actions, but lies in the gift of free will, or in the law and doctrine, it follows, of course, that God's grace or assistance is given us for single actions, — free will, or the law and the doctrine, being left out of consideration; and thus through all the single actions of our life, when we act rightly, we are ruled and directed by God; nor is our prayer a useless one, wherein we say: "Order my steps according to Thy word, and let not any iniquity have dominion over me." [5]

CHAP. 32. — THE ELEVENTH ITEM OF THE ACCUSATION.

But what comes afterwards again fills me with anxiety. On its being objected to him, from the fifth chapter of Cœlestius' book, that "they say that every individual has the ability to possess all powers and graces, thus taking away that 'diversity of graces' which the apostle teaches," Pelagius replied: "We have certainly said so much; but yet they have laid against us a malignant and blundering charge. We do not take away the diversity of graces; but we declare that God gives to the person, who has proved himself worthy to receive them, all graces, even as He conferred them on the Apostle Paul." Hereupon the Synod said: "You accordingly do yourself hold the doctrine of the Church touching the gift of the graces, which are collectively possessed by the apostle." Here some one may say, "Why then is he anxious? Do you on your side deny that all the powers and graces were combined in the apostle?" For my own part, indeed, if all those are to be understood which the apostle has himself mentioned together in one passage, — as, I suppose, the bishops understood Pelagius to mean when they approved of his answer, and pronounced it to be in keeping with the sense of the Church, — then I do not doubt that the apostle had them all; for he says: "And God hath set some in the Church, first, apostles; secondarily, prophets; thirdly, teachers; after that miracles; then gifts of healings, helps, governments, diversities of tongues." [6] What then? shall we say that the Apostle Paul did not possess all these gifts himself? Who would be bold enough to assert this? The very fact that he was an apostle showed, of course, that he possessed the grace of the *apostolate*. He possessed also that of *prophecy;* for was not that a prophecy of his in which he says: "In the last times some shall depart from the faith, giving heed to seducing spirits, and doctrines of devils?" [7] He was, moreover, "the *teacher* of the Gentiles in faith and verity." [8] He performed *miracles* also and cures; for he shook off from his hand, unhurt, the biting viper; [9] and the cripple stood upright on his feet at the apostle's word, and his strength was at once restored. [10] It is not clear what he means by *helps*, for the term is of very wide application; but who can say that he was wanting even in this grace, when through his labours such helps were manifestly afforded towards the salvation of mankind? Then as to his possessing the grace of "*government*," what could be more excellent than his administration, when the Lord at that time governed so many churches by his personal agency, and governs them still in our day through his epistles? And in respect of the "*diversities of tongues*," what tongues could have been wanting to him, when he says himself: "I thank my God that I speak with tongues more than you all?" [11]

---

[1] See above, (2).    [2] Phil. i. 19.    [3] Matt. x. 19, 20.
[4] See above, (5).    [5] Ps. cxix. 133.

[6] 1 Cor. xii. 28.    [7] 1 Tim. iv. 1.    [8] 1 Tim. ii 7
[9] Acts xxviii. 5.    [10] Acts xiv. 8, 9.    [11] 1 Cor. xiv 18

It being thus inevitable to suppose that not one of these was wanting to the Apostle Paul, the judges approved of Pelagius' answer, wherein he said "that all graces were conferred upon him." But there are other graces in addition to these which are not mentioned here. For it is not to be supposed, however greatly the Apostle Paul excelled others as a member of Christ's body, that the very Head itself of the entire body did not receive more and ampler graces still, whether in His flesh or His soul as man; for such a created nature did the Word of God assume as His own into the unity of His Person, that He might be our Head, and we His body. And in very deed, if all gifts could be in each member, it would be evident that the similitude, which is used to illustrate this subject, of the several members of our body is inapplicable; for some things are common to the members in general, such as life and health, whilst other things are peculiar to the separate members, since the ear has no perception of colours, nor the eye of voices. Hence it is written: "If the whole body were an eye, where were the hearing? if the whole were hearing, where were the smelling?"[1] Now this of course is not said as if it were impossible for God to impart to the ear the sense of seeing, or to the eye the function of hearing. However, what He does in Christ's body, which is the Church, and what the apostle meant by diversity of graces,[2] as if through the different members, there might be gifts proper even to every one separately, is clearly known. Why, too, and on what ground they who raised the objection were so unwilling to have taken away all difference in graces, why, moreover, the bishops of the synod were able to approve of the answer given by Pelagius in deference to the Apostle Paul, in whom we admit the combination of all those graces which he mentioned in the one particular passage, is by this time clear also.

CHAP. 33. — DISCUSSION OF THE ELEVENTH ITEM CONTINUED.

What, then, is the reason why, as I said just now, I felt anxious on the subject of this head of his doctrine? It is occasioned by what Pelagius says in these words: "That God gives to the man who has proved himself worthy to receive them, all graces, even as He conferred them on the Apostle Paul." Now, I should not have felt any anxiety about this answer of Pelagius, if it were not closely connected with the cause which we are bound to guard with the utmost care — even that God's grace may never be attacked, while we are silent or dissembling in respect of so great an evil. As, therefore, he does not say, that God gives to whom He will, but that "God gives to the man *who has proved himself worthy to receive them,* all these graces," I could not help being suspicious, when I read such words. For the very name of grace, and the thing that is meant by it, is taken away, if it is not bestowed gratuitously, but he only receives it who is worthy of it. Will anybody say that I do the apostle wrong, because I do not admit him to have been worthy of grace? Nay, I should indeed rather do him wrong, and bring on myself a punishment, if I refused to believe what he himself says. Well, now, has he not pointedly so defined *grace* as to show that it is so called because it is bestowed gratuitously? These are his own very words: "And if by grace, then is it no more of works; otherwise grace is no more grace."[3] In accordance with this, he says again: "Now to him that worketh is the reward not reckoned of grace, but of debt."[4] Whosoever, therefore, is worthy, to him it is due; and if it is thus due to him, it ceases to be grace; for grace is given, but a debt is paid. Grace, therefore, is given to those who are unworthy, that a debt may be paid to them when they become worthy. He, however, who has bestowed on the unworthy the gifts which they possessed not before, does Himself take care that they shall have whatever things He means to recompense to them when they become worthy.

CHAP. 34. — THE SAME CONTINUED. ON THE WORKS OF UNBELIEVERS; FAITH IS THE INITIAL PRINCIPLE FROM WHICH GOOD WORKS HAVE THEIR BEGINNING; FAITH IS THE GIFT OF GOD'S GRACE.

He will perhaps say to this: "It was not because of his works, but in consequence of his faith, that I said the apostle was worthy of having all those great graces bestowed upon him. His faith deserved this distinction, but not his works, which were not previously good." Well, then, are we to suppose that faith does not work? Surely faith does work in a very real way, for it "worketh by love."[5] Preach up, however, as much as you like, the works of unbelieving men, we still know how true and invincible is the statement of this same apostle: "Whatsoever is not of faith is sin."[6] The very reason, indeed, why he so often declares that righteousness is imputed to us, not out of our works, but our faith, whereas faith rather works through love, is that no man should think that he arrives at faith itself through the merit of his works; for it is faith which is the beginning whence good works first proceed; since (as has already been stated) whatsoever comes not

---

[1] 1 Cor. xii. 17.
[2] Another reading has *Ecclesiarum,* instead of *gratiarum; q.d.* "difference in churches."

[3] Rom. xi. 6.   [4] Rom. iv. 4.   [5] Gal. v. 6.
[6] Rom. xiv. 23.

from faith is sin. Accordingly, it is said to the Church, in the Song of Songs: "Thou shalt come and pass by from the beginning of faith." [1] Although, therefore, faith procures the grace of producing good works, we certainly do not deserve by any faith that we should have faith itself; but, in its bestowal upon us, in order that we may follow the Lord by its help, "His mercy has prevented us." [2] Was it we ourselves that gave it to us? Did we ourselves make ourselves faithful? I must by all means say here, emphatically: "It is He that hath made us, and not we ourselves." [3] And indeed nothing else than this is pressed upon us in the apostle's teaching, when he says: "For I declare, through the grace that is given unto me, to every man that is among you, not to think of himself more highly than he ought to think; but to think soberly, according as God hath dealt to every man the measure of faith." [4] Whence, too, arises the well-known challenge: "What hast thou that thou didst not receive?" [5] inasmuch as we have received even that which is the spring from which everything we have of good in our actions takes its beginning.

### CHAP. 35. — THE SAME CONTINUED.

"What, then, is the meaning of that which the same apostle says: 'I have fought a good fight, I have finished my course, I have kept the faith: henceforth there is laid up for me a crown of righteousness, which the Lord, the righteous judge, shall give me at that day;' [6] if these are not recompenses paid to the worthy, but gifts bestowed on the unworthy?" He who says this, does not consider that the crown could not have been given to the man who is worthy of it, unless grace had been first bestowed on him whilst unworthy of it. He says indeed: "I have fought a good fight;" [6] but then he also says: "Thanks be to God, who giveth us the victory through Jesus Christ our Lord." [7] He says too: "I have finished my course;" but he says again: "It is not of him that willeth, nor of him that runneth, but of God that showeth mercy." [8] He says, moreover: "I have kept the faith;" but then it is he too who says again: "I know whom I have believed, and am persuaded that He is able to keep my deposit against that day" — that is, "my commendation;" for some copies have not the word *depositum*, but *commendatum*, which yields a plainer sense. [9] Now, what do we commend to God's keeping, except the things which we pray Him to preserve for us, and amongst these our very faith? For what else did the Lord

procure for the Apostle Peter by His prayer for him, [10] of which He said, "I have prayed for thee, Peter, that thy faith fail not," [11] than that God would preserve his faith, that it should not fail by giving way to temptation? Therefore, blessed Paul, thou great preacher of grace, I will say it without fear of any man (for who will be less angry with me for so saying than thyself, who hast told us what to say, and taught us what to teach?) — I will, I repeat, say it, and fear no man for the assertion: Their own crown is recompensed to their merits; but thy merits are the gifts of God!

### CHAP. 36. — THE SAME CONTINUED. THE MONK PELAGIUS. GRACE IS CONFERRED ON THE UN-WORTHY.

His due reward, therefore, is recompensed to the apostle as worthy of it; but still it was grace which bestowed on him the apostleship itself, which was not his due, and of which he was not worthy. Shall I be sorry for having said this? God forbid! For under his own testimony shall I find a ready protection from such reproach; nor will any man charge me with audacity, unless he be himself audacious enough to charge the apostle with mendacity. He frankly says, nay he protests, that he commends the gifts of God within himself, so that he glories not in himself at all, but in the Lord; [12] he not only declares that he possessed no good deserts in himself why he should be made an apostle, but he even mentions his own demerits, in order to manifest and preach the grace of God. "I am not meet," says he, "to be called an apostle;" [13] and what else does this mean than "I am not *worthy*"? — as indeed several Latin copies read the phrase. Now this, to be sure, is the very gist of our question; for undoubtedly in this grace of apostleship all those graces are contained. For it was neither convenient nor right that an apostle should not possess the gift of *prophecy*, nor be a *teacher*, nor be illustrious for *miracles* and *the gifts of healings*, nor furnish needful *helps*, nor provide *governments* over the churches, nor excel in *diversities of tongues*. All these functions the one name of apostleship embraces. Let us, therefore, consult the man himself, nay listen wholly to him. Let us say to him: "Holy Apostle Paul, the monk Pelagius declares that thou wast worthy to receive all the graces of thine apostleship. What dost thou say thyself?" He answers: "I am not worthy to be called an apostle." Shall I then, under pretence of honouring Paul, in a matter concerning Paul, dare to believe Pelagius in preference to Paul? I will

---

[1] Cant. iv. 8.    [2] Ps. lix. 10.    [3] Ps. c. 3.
[4] Rom. xii. 3.    [5] 1 Cor. iv. 7.    [6] 2 Tim. iv. 7.
[7] 1 Cor. xv. 57.    [8] Rom. ix. 16.
[9] 2 Tim. i. 12. St. Paul's phrase, τὴν παραθήκην μου, has been taken in two senses, as (1) what God had entrusted to him; and (2) what the apostle had entrusted to God's keeping. St. Augustin, it will be seen, here takes the latter sense.

[10] There seems to be a corruption in the text here: " *Quid aliud apostolo Petro Dominus commendavit orando.*" Another reading inserts *de* before the word *apostolo.* Our version is rather of the apparent sense than of the words of the passage.
[11] Luke xxii. 32.    [12] 1 Cor. i. 31.    [13] 1 Cor. xv. 9.

not do so; for if I did, I should only prove to be more onerous to myself than honouring to him.[1] Let us hear also why he is not worthy to be called an apostle : "Because," says he, "I persecuted the Church of God."[2] Now, were we to follow up the idea here expressed, who would not judge that he rather deserved from Christ condemnation, instead of an apostolic call? Who could so love the preacher as not to loathe the persecutor? Well, therefore, and truly does he say of himself: "I am not worthy to be called an apostle, because I persecuted the Church of God." As thou wroughtest then such evil, how camest thou to earn such good? Let all men hear his answer: "But by the grace of God, I am what I am." Is there, then, no other way in which grace is commended, than because it is conferred on an unworthy recipient? "And His grace," he adds, "which was bestowed on me was not in vain."[3] He says this as a lesson to others also, to show the freedom of the will, when he says: "We then, as workers together with Him, beseech you also that ye receive not the grace of God in vain."[4] Whence however does he derive his proof, that "His grace bestowed on himself was not in vain," except from the fact which he goes on to mention : "But I laboured more abundantly than they all?"[3] So it seems he did not labour in order to receive grace, but he received grace in order that he might labour. And thus, when unworthy, he gratuitously received grace, whereby he might become worthy to receive the due reward. Not that he ventured to claim even his labour for himself; for, after saying : "I laboured more abundantly than they all," he at once subjoined : "Yet not I, but the grace of God which was with me."[3] O mighty teacher, confessor, and preacher of grace ! What meaneth this : "I laboured more, yet not I?" Where the will exalted itself ever so little, there piety was instantly on the watch, and humility trembled, because weakness recognised itself.

CHAP. 37. — THE SAME CONTINUED. JOHN, BISHOP OF JERUSALEM, AND HIS EXAMINATION.

With great propriety, as the proceedings show, did John, the holy overseer of the Church of Jerusalem, employ the authority of this same passage of the apostle, as he himself told our brethren the bishops who were his assessors at that trial, on their asking him what proceedings had taken place before him previous to the trial.[5] He told them that "on the occasion in question, whilst some were whispering, and remarking on Pelagius' statement, that 'without God's grace

man was able to attain perfection' (that is, as he had previously expressed it, 'man was able to be without sin'), he censured the statement, and reminded them besides, that even the Apostle Paul, after so many labours — not indeed in his own strength, but by the grace of God — said : 'I laboured more abundantly than they all : yet not I, but the grace of God that was with me ;'[3] and again : 'It is not of him that willeth, nor of him that runneth, but of God that showeth mercy ;'[6] and again : 'Except the Lord build the house, they labour but in vain who build it.'[7] And," he added, "we quoted several other like passages out of the Holy Scriptures. When, however, they did not receive the quotations which we made out of the Holy Scriptures, but continued their murmuring noise, Pelagius said : 'This is what I also believe ; let him be anathema, who declares that a man is able, without God's help, to arrive at the perfection of all virtues.'"

CHAP. 38 [XV.] — THE SAME CONTINUED.

Bishop John narrated all this in the hearing of Pelagius ; but he, of course, might respectfully say : "Your holiness is in error ; you do not accurately remember the facts. It was not in reference to the passages of Scripture which you have quoted that I uttered the words : 'This is what I also believe.' Because this is not my opinion of them. I do not understand them to say, that God's grace so co-operates with man, that his abstinence from sin is due, not to 'him that willeth, nor to him that runneth, but to God that showeth mercy.'"[6]

CHAP. 39 [XVI.] — THE SAME CONTINUED. HEROS AND LAZARUS ; OROSIUS.

Now there are some expositions of Paul's Epistle to the Romans which are said to have been written by Pelagius himself,[8]— in which he asserts, that the passage : "Not of him that willeth, nor of him that runneth, but of God that showeth mercy," was "not said in Paul's own person ; but that he therein employed the language of questioning and refutation, as if such a statement ought not to be made." No safe conclusion, therefore, can be drawn, although the bishop John plainly acknowledged the passage in question as conveying the mind of the apostle, and mentioned it for the very purpose of hindering Pelagius from thinking that any man can avoid sin without God's grace, and declared that Pelagius said in answer : "This is what I also believe," and did not, upon hearing all this, repudiate his admission by replying : "This is not my belief." He ought, indeed, either to deny altogether, or unhesitatingly to correct and amend

---

[1] This is a poor imitation of Augustin's playful words: "Me potius *onerabo* quam illum *honorabo.*"
[2] 1 Cor. xv. 9.    [3] 1 Cor. xv. 10.    [4] 2 Cor. vi. 1.
[5] In a conference held at Jerusalem at the end of July in the year 415, as described by Orosius in his *Apology.*

[6] Rom. ix. 16.    [7] Ps. cxxvii. 1.
[8] See the treatise *De Peccatorum Meritis*, iii. 1.

this perverse exposition, in which he would have it, that the apostle must not be regarded as entertaining the sentiment,[1] but rather as refuting it. Now, whatever Bishop John said of our brethren who were absent — whether our brother bishops Heros and Lazarus, or the presbyter Orosius, or any others whose names are not there registered,[2] —I am sure that he did not mean it to operate to their prejudice. For, had they been present, they might possibly (I am far from saying it absolutely) have convicted him of untruth; at any rate they might perhaps have reminded him of something he had forgotten, or something in which he might have been deceived by the Latin interpreter — not, to be sure, for the purpose of misleading him by untruth, but at least, owing to some difficulty occasioned by a foreign language, only imperfectly understood; especially as the question was not treated in the Proceedings,[3] which were drawn up for the useful purpose of preventing deceit on the part of evil men, and of preserving a record to assist the memory of good men. If, however, any man shall be disposed by this mention of our brethren to introduce any question or doubt on the subject, and summon them before the Episcopal judgment, they will not be wanting to themselves, as occasion shall serve. Why need we here pursue the point, when not even the judges themselves, after the narrative of our brother bishop, were inclined to pronounce any definite sentence in consequence of it?

## CHAP. 40 [XVII.] — THE SAME CONTINUED.

Since, then, Pelagius was present when these passages of the Scriptures were discussed, and by his silence acknowledged having said that he entertained the same view of their meaning, how happens it, that, after reconsidering the apostle's testimony, as he had just done, and finding that he said: "I am not meet to be called an apostle, because I persecuted the Church of God; but by the grace of God I am what I am,"[4] he did not perceive that it was improper for him to say, respecting the question of the abundance of the graces which the said apostle received, that he had shown himself "worthy to receive them," when the apostle himself not only confessed, but added a reason to prove, that he was *unworthy* of them — and by this very fact set forth grace *as grace indeed?* If he could not for some reason or other consider or recollect the narrative of his holiness the bishop John, which he had heard some time before, he might surely have respected his own very recent answer at the synod,

and remembered how he anathematized, but a short while before, the opinions which had been alleged against him out of Cœlestius. Now among these it was objected to him that Cœlestius had said: "That the grace of God is bestowed according to our merits." If, then, Pelagius truthfully anathematized this, why does he say that all those graces were conferred on the apostle because he deserved them? Is the phrase "worthy to receive" of different meaning from the expression "to receive according to merit"? Can he by any disputatious subtlety show that a man is worthy who has no merit? But neither Cœlestius, nor any other, all of whose opinions he anathematized, has any intention to allow him to throw clouds over the phrase, and to conceal himself behind them. He presses home the matter, and plainly says: "And this grace has been placed in my will, according as I have been either worthy or unworthy of it." If, then, a statement, wherein it is declared that "God's grace is given in proportion to our deserts, to such as are worthy,"[5] was rightly and truly condemned by Pelagius, how could his heart permit him to think, or his mouth to utter, such a sentence as this: "We say that God gives to the person who has proved himself worthy to receive them, all graces?"[6] Who that carefully considers all this can help feeling some anxiety about his answer or defence?

## CHAP. 41. — AUGUSTIN INDULGENTLY SHOWS THAT THE JUDGES ACTED INCAUTIOUSLY IN THEIR OFFICIAL CONDUCT OF THE CASE OF PELAGIUS.

Why, then (some one will say), did the judges approve of this? I confess that I hardly even now understand why they did. It is, however, not to be wondered at, if some brief word or phrase too easily escaped their attention and ear; or if, because they thought it capable of being somehow interpreted in a correct sense, from seeming to have from the accused himself such clear confessions of truth on the subject, they decided it to be hardly worth while to excite a discussion about a word. The same feeling might have occurred to ourselves also, if we had sat with them at the trial. For if, instead of the term *worthy*, the word *predestinated* had been used, or some such word, my mind would certainly not have entertained any doubt, much less have been disquieted by it; and yet if it were asserted, that he who is justified by the election of grace is called *worthy*, through no antecedent merits of good indeed, but by destination, just as he is called "elect," it would be really difficult to determine whether he might be so designated at all, or at least without some offence to an intelligent view of the subject.

---

[1] Rom. ix. 16.
[2] Avitus, perhaps, Passerius, and Dominus *ex duce*, whose names do not occur in the Acts of the Synod of Diospolis, but are mentioned by Orosius, *Apol.* 3.
[3] Augustin here refers to the Proceedings of the conference at Jerusalem before its bishop John, which sat previous to the Council of Diospolis. See above, 37 (xiv.).
[4] 1 Cor. xv. 9, 10.

[5] See above, 30 (xiv.).   [6] See above, 32.

As for myself, indeed, I might readily pass on from the discussion on this word, were it not that the treatise which called forth my reply, and in which he says that there is no God's grace at all except our own nature gratuitously created [1] with free will, made me suspicious and anxious about the actual meaning of Pelagius — whether he had procured the introduction of the term into the argument without any accurate intention as to its sense, or else as a carefully drawn dogmatic expression. The last remaining statements had such an effect on the judges, that they deemed them worthy of condemnation, without waiting for Pelagius' answer.

CHAP. 42 [XVIII.] — THE TWELFTH ITEM IN THE ACCUSATION. OTHER HEADS OF CŒLESTIUS' DOCTRINE ABJURED BY PELAGIUS.

For it was objected that in the sixth chapter of Cœlestius' work there was laid down this position : " Men cannot be called sons of God, unless they have become entirely free from all sin." It follows from this statement, that not even the Apostle Paul is a child of God, since he said : " Not as though I had already attained, either were already perfect." [2] In the seventh chapter he makes this statement : " Forgetfulness and ignorance have no connection with sin, as they do not happen through the will, but through necessity ; " although David says : " Remember not the sins of my youth, nor my sins of ignorance ; " [3] although too, in the law, sacrifices are offered for ignorance, as if for sin. [4] In his tenth chapter he says : " Our will is free, if it needs the help of God ; inasmuch as every one in the possession of his proper will has either something to do or to abstain from doing." In the twelfth he says : " Our victory comes not from God's help, but from our own free will." And this is a conclusion which he was said to draw in the following terms : " The victory is ours, seeing that we took up arms of our own will ; just as, on the other hand, being conquered is our own, since it was of our own will that we neglected to arm ourselves." And, after quoting the phrase of the Apostle Peter, " partakers of the divine nature," [5] he is said to have made out of it this argument : " Now if our spirit or soul is unable to be without sin, then even God is subject to sin, since this part of Him, that is to say, the soul, is exposed to sin." In his thirteenth chapter he says : " That pardon is not given to penitents according to the grace and mercy of God, but according to their own merits and effort, since through repentance they have been worthy of mercy."

CHAP. 43 [XIX.] — THE ANSWER OF THE MONK PELAGIUS AND HIS PROFESSION OF FAITH.

After all these sentences were read out, the synod said : " What says the monk Pelagius to all these heads of opinion which have been read in his presence ? For this holy synod condemns the whole, as does also God's Holy Catholic Church." Pelagius answered : " I say again, that these opinions, even according to their own testimony, are not mine ; nor for them, as I have already said, ought I to be held responsible. The opinions which I have confessed to be my own, I maintain are sound ; those, however, which I have said are not my own, I reject according to the judgment of this holy synod, pronouncing anathema on every man who opposes and gainsays the doctrines of the Holy Catholic Church. For I believe in the Trinity of the one substance, and I hold all things in accordance with the teaching of the Holy Catholic Church. If indeed any man entertains opinions different from her, let him be anathema."

CHAP. 44 [XX.] — THE ACQUITTAL OF PELAGIUS.

The synod said : " Now since we have received satisfaction on the points which have come before us touching the monk Pelagius, who has been present ; since, too, he gives his consent to the pious doctrines, and even anathematizes everything that is contrary to the Church's faith, we confess him to belong to the communion of the Catholic Church."

CHAP. 45 [XXI.] — PELAGIUS' ACQUITTAL BECOMES SUSPECTED.

If these are the proceedings by which Pelagius' friends rejoice that he was exculpated, we, on our part, — since he certainly took much pains to prove that we were well affected towards him, by going so far as to produce even our private letters to him, and reading them at the trial, — undoubtedly wish and desire his salvation in Christ ; but as regards his exculpation, which is rather believed than clearly shown, we ought not to be in a hurry to exult. When I say this, indeed, I do not charge the judges either with negligence or connivance, or with consciously holding unsound doctrine — which they most certainly would be the very last to entertain. But although by their sentence Pelagius is held by those who are on terms of fullest and closest intimacy with him to have been deservedly acquitted, with the approval and commendation of his judges, he certainly does not appear to me to have been cleared of the charges brought against him. They conducted his trial as of one whom they knew nothing of, especially in the absence of those who had prepared the indictment against him, and were quite unable to ex-

---

[1] We have preferred the reading *gratis creatam* to the obscure *gratiam creaturam.*
[2] Phil. iii. 12.     [3] Ps. xxv. 7.     [4] See Lev. iv.
[5] 2 Pet. i. 4.

amine him with diligence and care ; but, in spite of this inability, they completely destroyed the heresy itself, as even the defenders of his perverseness must allow, if they only follow the judgment through its particulars. As for those persons, however, who well know what Pelagius has been in the habit of teaching, or who have had to oppose his contentious efforts, or those who, to their joy, have escaped from his erroneous doctrine, how can they possibly help suspecting him, when they read the affected confession, wherein he acknowledges past errors, but so expresses himself as if he had never entertained any other opinion than those which he stated in his replies to the satisfaction of the judges?

CHAP. 46 [XXII.]—HOW PELAGIUS BECAME KNOWN TO AUGUSTIN ; CŒLESTIUS CONDEMNED AT CARTHAGE.

Now, that I may especially refer to my own relation to him, I first became acquainted with Pelagius' name, along with great praise of him, at a distance, and when he was living at Rome. Afterwards reports began to reach us, that he disputed against the grace of God. This caused me much pain, for I could not refuse to believe the statements of my informants ; but yet I was desirous of ascertaining information on the matter either from himself or from some treatise of his, that, in case I should have to discuss the question with him, it should be on grounds which he could not disown. On his arrival, however, in Africa, he was in my absence kindly received on our coast of Hippo, where, as I found from our brethren, nothing whatever of this kind was heard from him ; because he left earlier than was expected. On a subsequent occasion, indeed, I caught a glimpse of him, once or twice, to the best of my recollection, when I was very much occupied in preparing for the conference which we were to hold with the heretical Donatists ; but he hastened away across the sea. Meanwhile the doctrines connected with his name were warmly maintained, and passed from mouth to mouth, among his reputed followers— to such an extent that Cœlestius found his way before an ecclesiastical tribunal, and reported opinions well suited to his perverse character. We thought it would be a better way of proceeding against them, if, without mentioning any names of individuals, the errors themselves were met and refuted ; and the men might thus be brought to a right mind by the fear of a condemnation from the Church rather than be punished by the actual condemnation. And so both by books and by popular discussions we ceased not to oppose the evil doctrines in question.

CHAP. 47 [XXIII.]—PELAGIUS' BOOK, WHICH WAS SENT BY TIMASIUS AND JACOBUS TO AUGUSTIN, WAS ANSWERED BY THE LATTER IN HIS WORK "ON NATURE AND GRACE."

But when there was actually placed in my hands, by those faithful servants of God and honourable men, Timasius and Jacobus, the treatise in which Pelagius dealt with the question of God's grace, it became very evident to me — too evident, indeed, to admit of any further doubt — how hostile to salvation by Christ was his poisonous perversion of the truth. He treated the subject in the shape of an objection started, as if by an opponent, in his own terms against himself ; for he was already suffering a good deal of obloquy from his opinions on the question, which he now appeared to solve for himself in no other way than by simply describing the grace of God as nature created with a free will, occasionally combining therewith either the help of the law, or even the remission of sins ; although these additional admissions were not plainly made, but only sparingly suggested by him. And yet, even under these circumstances, I refrained from inserting Pelagius' name in my work, wherein I refuted this book of his ; for I still thought that I should render a prompter assistance to the truth if I continued to preserve a friendly relation to him, and so to spare his personal feelings, while at the same time I showed no mercy, as I was bound not to show it, to the productions of his pen. Hence, I must say, I now feel some annoyance, that in this trial he somewhere said : " I anathematize those who hold these opinions, or have at any time held them." He might have been contented with saying, " *Those who hold these opinions,*" which we should have regarded in the light of a self-censure ; but when he went on to say, " *Or have at any time held them,*" in the first place, how could he dare to condemn so unjustly those harmless persons who no longer hold the errors, which they had learnt either from others, or actually from himself? And, in the second place, who among all those persons that were aware of the fact of his not only having held the opinions in question, but of his having taught them, could help suspecting, and not unreasonably, that he must have acted insincerely in condemning those who now hold those opinions, seeing that he did not hesitate to condemn in the same strain and at the same moment those also who had at any time previously held them, when they would be sure to remember that they had no less a person than himself as their instructor in these errors? There are, for instance, such persons as Timasius and Jacobus, to say nothing of any others. How can he with unblushing face look at them, his dear friends (who have never relinquished their love of him) and his former disciples? These are the persons to whom I addressed the work in which I replied to the statements of his book. I think I ought not to pass over in silence the style and tone which they observed towards me in their correspondence, and I have here added a letter of theirs as a sample.

### CHAP. 48 [XXIV.] — A LETTER WRITTEN BY TIMASIUS AND JACOBUS TO AUGUSTIN ON RECEIVING HIS TREATISE " ON NATURE AND GRACE."

" To his lordship, the truly blessed and deservedly venerable father, Bishop Augustin, Timasius and Jacobus send greeting in the Lord. We have been so greatly refreshed and strengthened by the grace of God, which your word has ministered to us, my lord, our truly blessed and justly venerated father, that we may with the utmost sincerity and propriety say, ' He sent His word and healed them.'[1] We have found, indeed, that your holiness has so thoroughly sifted the contents of his little book as to astonish us with the answers with which even the slightest points of his error have been confronted, whether it be on matters which every Christian ought to rebut, loathe, and avoid, or on those in which he is not with sufficient certainty found to have erred, — although even in these he has, with incredible subtlety, suggested his belief that God's grace should be kept out of sight.[2] There is, however, one consideration which affects us under so great a benefit, — that this most illustrious gift of the grace of God has, however slowly, so fully shone out upon us. If, indeed, it has happened that some are removed from the influence of this clearest light of truth, whose blindness required its illumination, yet even to them, we doubt not, the same grace will find its steady way, however late, by the merciful favour of that God ' who will have all men to be saved and to come unto the knowledge of the truth.'[3] As for ourselves, indeed, thanks to that loving spirit which is in you, we have, in consequence of your instruction, some time since thrown off our subjection to his errors; but we still have even now cause for continued gratitude in the fact that, as we have been informed, the false opinions which we formerly believed are now becoming apparent to others — a way of escape opening out to them in the extremely precious discourse of your holiness." Then, in another hand : " May the mercy of our God keep your blessedness in safety, and mindful of us, for His eternal glory."[4]

### CHAP. 49 [XXV.] — PELAGIUS' BEHAVIOUR CONTRASTED WITH THAT OF THE WRITERS OF THE LETTER.

If now that man,[5] too, were to confess that he had once been implicated in this error as a person possessed, but that he now anathematized all that hold these opinions, whoever should withhold his congratulation from him, now that he was in possession of the way of truth, would surely surrender all the bowels of love. As the case, however, now stands, he has not only not acknowledged his liberation from his pestiential error ; but, as if that were a small thing, he has gone on to anathematize men who have reached that freedom, who love him so well that they would fain desire his own emancipation. Amongst these are those very men who have expressed their good-will towards him in the letter, which they forwarded to me. For he it was whom they had chiefly in view when they said how much they were affected at the fact of my having at last written that work. " If, indeed, it has happened," they say, " that some are removed from the influence of this clearest light of truth, whose blindness required its illumination, yet even to them," they go on to remark, " we doubt not, the self-same grace will find its way, by the merciful favour of God." Any name, or names, even they, too, thought it desirable as yet to suppress, in order that, if friendship still lived on, the error of the friends might the more surely die.

### CHAP. 50. — PELAGIUS HAS NO GOOD REASON TO BE ANNOYED IF HIS NAME BE AT LAST USED IN THE CONTROVERSY, AND HE BE EXPRESSLY REFUTED.

But now if Pelagius thinks of God, if he is not ungrateful for His mercy in having brought him before this tribunal of the bishops, that thus he might be saved from the hardihood of afterwards defending these anathematized opinions, and be at once led to acknowledge them as deserving of abhorrence and rejection, he will be more thankful to us for our book, in which, by mentioning his name, we shall open the wound in order to cure it, than for one in which we were afraid to cause him pain, and, in fact, only produced irritation, — a result which causes us regret. Should he, however, feel angry with us, let him reflect how unfair such anger is ; and, in order to subdue it, let him ask God to give him that grace which, in this trial, he has confessed to be necessary for each one of our actions, that so by His assistance he may gain a real victory. For of what use to him are all those great laudations contained in the letters of the bishops, which he thought fit to be men-

---

[1] Ps. cvii. 20.    [2] Supprimendam.    [3] 1 Tim. ii. 4.
[4] See Augustin's Epist. 168.

[5] Pelagius.

tioned, and even to be read and quoted in his favour, — as if all those persons who heard his strong and, to some extent, earnest exhortations to goodness of life could not have easily discovered how perverse were the opinions which he was entertaining?

### CHAP. 51 [XXVI.] — THE NATURE OF AUGUSTIN'S LETTER TO PELAGIUS.

For my own part, indeed, in my letter which he produced, I not only abstained from all praises of him, but I even exhorted him, with as much earnestness as I could, short of actually mooting the question, to cultivate right views about the grace of God. In my salutation I called him "*lord*" [1] — a title which, in our epistolary style, we usually apply even to some persons who are not Christians, — and this without untruth, inasmuch as we do, in a certain sense, owe to all such persons a *service*, which is yet freedom, to help them in obtaining the salvation which is in Christ. I added the epithet "*most beloved;*" and as I now call him by this term, so shall I continue to do so, even if he be angry with me; because, if I ceased to retain my love towards him, because of his feeling the anger, I should only injure myself rather than him. I, moreover, styled him "*most longed-for,*" because I greatly longed to have a conversation with him in person; for I had already heard that he was endeavouring publicly to oppose grace, whereby we are justified, whenever any mention was made of it. The brief contents of the letter itself indeed show all this; for, after thanking him for the pleasure he gave me by the information of his own health and that of his friends (whose bodily health we are bound of course to wish for, however much we may desire their amendment in other respects), I at once expressed the hope that the Lord would recompense him with such blessings as do not appertain to physical welfare, but which he used to think, and probably still thinks, consist solely in the freedom of the will and his own power, — at the same time, and for this reason, wishing him "eternal life." Then again, remembering the many good and kind wishes he had expressed for me in his letter, which I was answering, I went on to beg of him, too, that he would pray for me, that the Lord would indeed make me such a man as he believed me to be already; that so I might gently remind him, against the opinion he was himself entertaining, that the very righteousness which he had thought worthy to be praised in me was "not of him that willeth, nor of him that runneth, but of God that showeth mercy." [2] This is the sub-

stance of that short letter of mine, and such was my purpose when I dictated it. This is a copy of it:

### CHAP. 52 [XXVII. AND XXVIII.] — THE TEXT OF THE LETTER.

"To my most beloved lord, and most longed-for brother Pelagius, Augustin sends greeting in the Lord. I thank you very much for the pleasure you have kindly afforded me by your letter, and for informing me of your good health. May the Lord requite you with blessings, and may you ever enjoy them, and live with Him for evermore in all eternity, my most beloved lord, and most longed-for brother. For my own part, indeed, although I do not admit your high encomiums of me, which the letter of your Benignity [3] conveys, I yet cannot be insensible of the benevolent view you entertain towards my poor deserts; at the same time requesting you to pray for me, that the Lord would make me such a man as you suppose me to be already." Then, in another hand, it follows: "Be mindful of us; may you be safe, and find favour with the Lord, my most beloved lord, and most longed-for brother."

### CHAP. 53 [XXIX.] — PELAGIUS' USE OF RECOMMENDATIONS.

As to that which I placed in the postscript, — that he might "find favour with the Lord," — I intimated that this lay rather in His grace than in man's sole will; for I did not make it the subject either of exhortation, or of precept, or of instruction, but simply of my wish. But just in the same way as I should, if I had exhorted or enjoined, or even instructed him, simply have shown that all this appertained to free will, without, however, derogating from the grace of God; so in like manner, when I expressed the matter in the way of a wish, I asserted no doubt the grace of God, but at the same time I did not quench the liberty of the will. Wherefore, then, did he produce this letter at the trial? If he had only from the beginning entertained views in accordance with it, very likely he would not have been at all summoned before the bishops by the brethren, who, with all their kindness of disposition, could yet not help being offended with his perverse contentiousness. Now, however, as I have given on my part an account of this letter of mine, so would they, whose epistles he quoted, explain theirs also, if it were necessary; — they would tell us either what they thought, or what they were ignorant of, or with what purpose they wrote to him. Pelagius, therefore, may boast to his heart's content of the friendship of holy men,

---

[1] This term corresponds somewhat to our *Sir;* but Augustin here refers to its more expressive meaning of *Master*, or *Lord*.
[2] Rom. ix. 16.

[3] *Tuæ Benignitatis Epistola* is more than "your kind letter." "*Benignitas*" is a complimentary abstract title addressed to the correspondent.

he may read their letters recounting his praises, he may produce whatever synodal acts he pleases to attest his own acquittal, — there still stands against him the fact, proved by the testimony of competent witnesses, that he has inserted in his books statements which are opposed to that grace of God whereby we are called and justified ; and unless he shall, after true confession, anathematize these statements, and then go on to contradict them both in his writings and discussions, he will certainly seem to all those who have a fuller knowledge of him to have laboured in vain in his attempt to set himself right.

CHAP. 54 [XXX.] — ON THE LETTER OF PELAGIUS, IN WHICH HE BOASTS THAT HIS ERRORS HAD BEEN APPROVED BY FOURTEEN BISHOPS.

For I will not be silent as to the transactions which took place after this trial, and which rather augment the suspicion against him. A certain epistle found its way into our hands, which was ascribed to Pelagius himself, writing to a friend of his, a presbyter, who had kindly admonished him (as appears from the same epistle) not to allow any one to separate himself from the body of the Church on his account. Among the other contents of this document, which it would be both tedious and unnecessary to quote here, Pelagius says : " By the sentence of fourteen bishops our statement was received with approbation, in which we affirmed that ' a man is able to be without sin, and easily to keep the commandments of God, if he wishes.' This sentence," says he, " has filled the mouths of the gainsayers with confusion, and has separated asunder the entire set which was conspiring together for evil." Whether, indeed, this epistle was really written by Pelagius, or was composed by somebody in his name, who can fail to see, after what manner this error claims to have achieved a victory, even in the judicial proceedings where it was refuted and condemned? Now, he has adduced the words we have just quoted according to the form in which they occur in his book of " Chapters," as it is called, not in the shape in which they were objected to him at his trial, and even repeated by him in his answer. For even his accusers, through some unaccountable inaccuracy, left out a word in their indictment, concerning which there is no small controversy. They made him say, that " a man is able to be without sin, if he wishes ; and, if he wishes, to keep the commandments of God." There is nothing said here about this being " *easily* " done. Afterwards, when he gave his answer, he spake thus : " We said, that a man is able to be without sin, and to keep the commandments of God, if he wishes ; " he did not then say, " *easily* keep," but only " keep." So in another place, amongst the statements about which Hilary con-

sulted me, and I gave him my views, it was objected to Pelagius that he had said, " A man is able, if he wishes, to live without sin." To this he himself responded, " That a man is able to be without sin has been said above." Now, on this occasion, we do not find on the part either of those who brought the objection or of him who rebutted it, that the word " *easily* " was used at all. Then, again, in the narrative of the holy Bishop John, which we have partly quoted above,[1] he says, " When they were importunate and exclaimed, ' He is a heretic, because he says, It is true that a man is able, if he only will, to live without sin ; ' and then, when we questioned him on this point, he answered, ' I did not say that man's nature has received the power of being impeccable, — but I said, whosoever is willing, in the pursuit of his own salvation, to labour and struggle to abstain from sinning and to walk in the commandments of God, receives the ability to do so from God.' Then, whilst some were whispering, and remarking on the statement of Pelagius, that ' without God's grace man was able to attain perfection,' I censured the statement, and reminded them, besides, that even the Apostle Paul, after so many labours, — not, indeed, in his own strength, but by the grace of God, — said, ' I laboured more abundantly than they all ; yet not I, but the grace of God that was with me.' "[2] And so on, as I have already mentioned.

CHAP. 55. — PELAGIUS' LETTER DISCUSSED.

What, then, is the meaning of those vaunting words of theirs in this epistle, wherein they boast of having induced the fourteen bishops who sat in that trial to believe not merely that a man has ability but that he has " facility " to abstain from sinning, according to the position laid down in the " Chapters " of this same Pelagius, — when, in the draft of the proceedings, notwithstanding the frequent repetition of the general charge and full consideration bestowed on it, this is nowhere found? How, indeed, can this word fail to contradict the very defence and answer which Pelagius made ; since the Bishop John asserted that Pelagius put in this answer in his presence, that " he wished it to be understood that the man who was willing to labour and agonize for his salvation was able to avoid sin," while Pelagius himself, at this time engaged in a formal inquiry and conducting his defence,[3] said, that " it was by his own labour and the grace of God that a man is able to be without sin?" Now, is a thing *easy* when labour is required to effect it? For I suppose that every man would agree with us in the opinion, that wherever there is labour there

---

[1] In 37 [XIV.].      [2] 1 Cor. xv. 10.
[3] Ch. 16. At the Synod of Diospolis. The proceedings before John, bishop of Jerusalem, were not duly registered. See above, 39.

cannot be facility. And yet a carnal epistle of windiness and inflation flies forth, and, outrunning in speed the tardy record of the proceedings, gets first into men's hands ; so as to assert that fourteen bishops in the East have determined, not only " that a man is able to be without sin, and to keep God's commandments," but "*easily* to keep.*" Nor is God's assistance once named : it is merely said, " If he wishes ; " so that, of course, as nothing is affirmed of the divine grace, for which the earnest fight was made, it remains that the only thing one reads of in this epistle is the unhappy and self-deceiving — because represented as victorious — human pride. As if the Bishop John, indeed, had not expressly declared that he censured this statement, and that, by the help of three inspired texts of Scripture,[1] he had, as if by thunderbolts, struck to the ground the gigantic mountains of such presumption which they had piled up against the still over-towering heights of heavenly grace ; or as if again those other bishops who were John's assessors could have borne with Pelagius, either in mind or even in ear, when he pronounced these words : " We said that a man is able to be without sin and to keep the commandments of God, if he wishes," unless he had gone on at once to say : " For the ability to do this God has given to him " (for they were unaware that he was speaking of nature, and not of that grace which they had learnt from the teaching of the apostle) ; and had afterwards added this qualification : " We never said, however, that any man could be found, who at no time whatever from his infancy to his old age had committed sin, but that if any person were converted from his sins, he could by his own exertion and the grace of God be without sin." Now, by the very fact that in their sentence they used these words, " he has answered correctly, 'that a man can, when he has the assistance and grace of God, be without sin ; '" what else did they fear than that, if he denied this, he would be doing a manifest wrong not to man's ability, but to God's grace ? It has indeed not been defined when a man may become without sin ; it has only been judicially settled, that this result can only be reached by the assisting grace of God ; it has not, I say, been defined whether a man, whilst he is in this flesh which lusts against the Spirit, ever has been, or now is, or ever can be, by his present use of reason and free will, either in the full society of man or in monastic solitude, in such a state as to be beyond the necessity of offering up the prayer, not in behalf of others, but for himself personally : " Forgive us our debts ; "[2] or whether this gift shall be consummated at the time when " we shall be like Him, when we shall see Him as He is,"[3] —

when it shall be said, not by those that are fighting : " I see another law in my members, warring against the law of my mind,"[4] but by those that are triumphing : " O death, where is thy victory? O death, where is thy sting?"[5] Now, this is perhaps hardly a question which ought to be discussed between catholics and heretics, but only among catholics with a view to a peaceful settlement.[6]

## CHAP. 56 [XXXI.] — IS PELAGIUS SINCERE ?

How, then, can it be believed that Pelagius (if indeed this epistle is his) could have been sincere, when he acknowledged the grace of God, which is not nature with its free will, nor the knowledge of the law, nor simply the forgiveness of sins, but a something which is necessary to each of our actions ; or could have sincerely anathematized everybody· who entertained the contrary opinion : — seeing that in his epistle he set forth even the *ease* wherewith a man can avoid sinning (concerning which no question had arisen at this trial) just as if the judges had come to an agreement to receive even this word, and said nothing about the grace of God, by the confession and subsequent addition of which he escaped the penalty of condemnation by the Church?

## CHAP. 57 [XXXII.] — FRAUDULENT PRACTICES PURSUED BY PELAGIUS IN HIS REPORT OF THE PROCEEDINGS IN PALESTINE, IN THE PAPER WHEREIN HE DEFENDED HIMSELF TO AUGUSTIN.

There is yet another point which I must not pass over in silence. In the paper containing his defence which he sent to me by a friend of ours, one Charus, a citizen of Hippo, but a deacon in the Eastern Church, he has made a statement which is different from what is contained in the Proceedings of the Bishops. Now, these Proceedings, as regards their contents, are of a higher and firmer tone, and more straightforward in defending the catholic verity in opposition to this heretical pestilence. For, when I read this paper of his, previous to receiving a copy of the Proceedings, I was not aware that he had made use of those words which he had used at the trial, when he was present for himself ; they are few, and there is not much discrepancy, and they do not occasion me much anxiety. [XXXIII.] But I could not help feeling annoyance that he can appear to have defended sundry sentences of Cœlestius, which, from the Proceedings, it is clear enough that he had anathematized. Now, some of these he disavowed for himself, simply remarking, that " he was not in any way responsible for

[1] See above, 37.     [2] Matt. vi. 12.     [3] 1 John iii. 2.

[4] Rom. vii. 23.          [5] 1 Cor. xv. 55.
[6] This point, however, was definitely settled a year or two afterwards, at a council held in Carthage. (See its Canons 6-8.) See also, above, the Preface to the treatise *On the Perfection of Man's Righteousness.*

them." In his paper, however, he refused to anathematize these same opinions, which are to this effect: "That Adam was created mortal, and that he would have died whether he had sinned or not sinned. That Adam's sin injured only himself, and not the human race. That the law, no less than the gospel, leads us to the kingdom. That new-born infants are in the same condition that Adam was before he fell. That, on the one hand, the entire human race does not die owing to Adam's death and transgression; nor, on the other hand, does the whole human race rise again through the resurrection of Christ. That infants, even if they die unbaptized, have eternal life. That rich men, even if they are baptized, unless they renounce and give up all, have, whatever good they may seem to have done, nothing of it reckoned to them; neither shall they possess the kingdom of heaven." Now, in his paper, the answer which he gives to all this is: "All these statements have not been made by me, even on their own testimony, nor do I hold myself responsible for them." In the Proceedings, however, he expressed himself as follows on these points: "They have not been made by me, as even their testimony shows, and for them I do not feel that I am at all responsible. But yet, for the satisfaction of the holy synod, I anathematize those who either now hold, or have ever held, them." Now, why did he not express himself thus in his paper also? It would not, I suppose, have cost much ink, or writing, or delay; nor have occupied much of the paper itself, if he had done this. Who, however, can help believing that there is a purpose in all this, to pass off this paper in all directions as an abridgment of the Episcopal Proceedings. In consequence of which, men might think that his right still to maintain any of these opinions which he pleased had not been taken away, — on the ground that they had been simply laid to his charge but had not received his approbation, nor yet had been anathematized and condemned by him.

CHAP. 58. — THE SAME CONTINUED.

He has, moreover, in this same paper, huddled together afterwards many of the points which were objected against him out of the "Chapters," of Cœlestius' book; nor has he kept distinct, at the intervals which separate them in the Proceedings, the two answers in which he anathematized these very heads; but has substituted one general reply for them all. This, I should have supposed, had been done for the sake of brevity, had I not perceived that he had a very special object in the arrangement which disturbs us. For thus has he closed this answer: "I say again, that these opinions, even according to their own testimony, are not mine; nor, as I have already

said, am I to be held responsible for them. The opinions which I have confessed to be my own, I maintain are sound and correct; those, however, which I have said are not my own, I reject according to the judgment of the holy Church, pronouncing anathema on every man that opposes and gainsays the doctrines of the holy and catholic Church; and likewise on those who by inventing false opinions have excited odium against us." This last paragraph the Proceedings do not contain; it has, however, no bearing on the matter which causes us anxiety. By all means let them have his anathema who have excited odium against him by their invention of false opinions. But, when first I read, "Those opinions, however, which I have said are not my own, I reject in accordance with the judgment of the holy Church," being ignorant that any judgment had been arrived at on the point by the Church, since there is here nothing said about it, and I had not then read the Proceedings, I really thought that nothing else was meant than that he promised that he would entertain the same view about the "Chapters" as the Church, which had not yet determined the question, might some day decide respecting them; and that he was ready to reject the opinions which the Church had not yet indeed rejected, but might one day have occasion to reject; and that this, too, was the purport of what he further said: "Pronouncing anathema on every man that opposes and gainsays the doctrines of the holy catholic Church." But in fact, as the Proceedings testify, a judgment of the Church had already been pronounced on these subjects by the fourteen bishops; and it was in accordance with this judgment that he professed to reject all these opinions, and to pronounce his anathema against those persons who, by reason of the said opinions, were contravening the judgment which had already, as the Proceedings show, been actually settled. For already had the judges asked: "What says the monk Pelagius to all these heads of opinion which have been read in his presence? For this holy synod condemns them, as does also God's holy catholic Church." Now, they who know nothing of all this, and only read this paper of his, are led to suppose that some one or other of these opinions may lawfully be maintained, as if they had not been determined to be contrary to catholic doctrine, and as if Pelagius had declared himself to be ready to hold the same sentiments concerning them which the Church had not as yet determined, but might have to determine. He has not, therefore, expressed himself in this paper, to which we have so often referred, straightforwardly enough for us to discover the fact, of which we find a voucher in the Proceedings, that all those dogmas by means of which this heresy has been stealing along and growing strong with contentious audacity, have been condemned by fourteen bishops presiding in an ecclesiastical synod! Now, if he was afraid that this fact would become known, as is the case, he has more reason for self-correction than for resentment at the vigilance with which we are watching the controversy to the best of our ability, however late. If, however, it is untrue that he had any such fears, and we are only indulging in a suspicion which is natural to man, let him forgive us; but, at the same time, let him continue to oppose and resist the opinions which were rejected by him with anathemas in the proceedings before the bishops, when he was on his defence; for if he now shows any leniency to them, he would seem not only to have believed these opinions formerly, but to be cherishing them still.

CHAP. 59 [XXXIV.] — ALTHOUGH PELAGIUS WAS ACQUITTED, HIS HERESY WAS CONDEMNED.

Now, with respect to this treatise of mine, which perhaps is not unreasonably lengthy, considering the importance and extent of its subject, I have wished to inscribe it to your Reverence, in order that, if it be not displeasing to your mind, it may become known to such persons as I have thought may stand in need of it under the recommendation of your authority, which carries so much more weight than our own poor industry. Thus it may avail to crush the vain and contentious thoughts of those persons who suppose that, because Pelagius was acquitted, those Eastern bishops who pronounced the judgment approved of those dogmas which are beginning to shed very pernicious influences against the Christian faith, and that grace of God whereby we are called and justified. These the Christian verity never ceases to condemn, as indeed it condemned them even by the authoritative sentence of the fourteen bishops; nor would it, on the occasion in question, have hesitated to condemn Pelagius too, unless he had anathematized the heretical opinions with which he was charged. But now, while we render to this man the respect of brotherly affection (and we have all along expressed with all sincerity our anxiety for him and interest in him), let us observe, with as much brevity as is consistent with accuracy of observation, that, notwithstanding the undoubted fact of his having been acquitted by a human verdict, the heresy itself has ever been held worthy of condemnation by divine judgment, and has actually been condemned by the sentence of these fourteen bishops of the Eastern Church.

CHAP. 60 [XXXV.] — THE SYNOD'S CONDEMNATION OF HIS DOCTRINES.

This is the concluding clause of their judg-ment. The synod said: "Now forasmuch as we have received satisfaction in these inquiries from the monk Pelagius, who has been present, who yields assent to godly doctrines, and rejects and anathematizes those which are contrary to the Church, we confess him still to belong to the communion of the catholic Church." Now, there are two facts concerning the monk Pelagius here contained with entire perspicuity in this brief statement of the holy bishops who judged him: one, that "he yields assent to godly doctrines;" the other, that "he rejects and anathematizes those which are contrary to the Church." On account of these two concessions, Pelagius was pronounced to be "in the communion of the catholic Church." Let us, in pursuit of our inquiry, briefly recapitulate the entire facts, in order to discover what were the words he used which made those two points so clear, as far as men were able at the moment to form a judgment as to what were manifest points. For among the allegations which were made against him, he is said to have rejected and anathematized, as "contrary," all the statements which in his answer he denied were his. Let us, then, summarize the whole case as far as we can.

CHAP. 61. — HISTORY OF THE PELAGIAN HERESY. THE PELAGIAN HERESY WAS RAISED BY SUNDRY PERSONS WHO AFFECTED THE MONASTIC STATE.

Since it was necessary that the Apostle Paul's prediction should be accomplished, — "There must be also heresies among you, that they which are approved may be made manifest among you,"[1] — after the older heresies, there has been just now introduced, not by bishops or presbyters or any rank of the clergy, but by certain would-be monks, a heresy which disputes, under colour of defending free will, against the grace of God which we have through our Lord Jesus Christ; and endeavours to overthrow the foundation of the Christian faith of which it is written, "By one man, death, and by one man the resurrection of the dead; for as in Adam all die, even so in Christ shall all be made alive;"[2] and denies God's help in our actions, by affirming that, "in order to avoid sin and to fulfil righteousness, human nature can be sufficient, seeing that it has been created with free will; and that God's grace lies in the fact that we have been so created as to be able to do this by the will, and in the further fact that God has given to us the assistance of His law and commandments, and also in that He forgives their past sins when men turn to Him;" that "in these things alone is God's grace to be regarded as consisting, not in the help He gives to us for

[1] 1 Cor. xi. 19.   [2] 1 Cor. xv. 21, 22

each of our actions," — "seeing that a man can be without sin, and keep God's commandments easily if he wishes."

CHAP. 62. — THE HISTORY CONTINUED. CŒLESTIUS CONDEMNED AT CARTHAGE BY EPISCOPAL JUDGMENT. PELAGIUS ACQUITTED BY BISHOPS IN PALESTINE, IN CONSEQUENCE OF HIS DECEPTIVE ANSWERS; BUT YET HIS HERESY WAS CONDEMNED BY THEM.

After this heresy had deceived a great many persons, and was disturbing the brethren whom it had failed to deceive, one Cœlestius, who entertained these sentiments, was brought up for trial before the Church of Carthage, and was condemned by a sentence of the bishops.[1] Then, a few years afterwards, Pelagius, who was said to have been this man's instructor, having been accused of holding his heresy, found also his way before an episcopal tribunal.[2] The indictment was prepared against him by the Gallican bishops, Heros and Lazarus, who were, however, not present at the proceedings, and were excused from attendance owing to the illness of one of them. After all the charges were duly recited, and Pelagius had met them by his answers, the fourteen bishops of the province of Palestine pronounced him, in accordance with his answers, free from the perversity of this heresy; while yet without hesitation condemning the heresy itself. They approved indeed of his answer to the objections, that "a man is assisted by a knowledge of the law, towards not sinning; even as it is written, 'He hath given them a law for a help;'"[3] but yet they disapproved of this knowledge of the law being that grace of God concerning which the Scripture says: "Who shall deliver me from the body of this death? The grace of God through Jesus Christ our Lord."[4] Nor did Pelagius say absolutely: "All men are ruled by their own will," as if God did not rule them; for he said, when questioned on this point: "This I stated in the interest of the freedom of our will; God is its helper, whenever it makes choice of good. Man, however, when sinning, is himself in fault, as being under the direction of his free will."[5] They approved, moreover, of his statement, that "in the day of judgment no forbearance will be shown to the ungodly and sinners, but they will be punished in everlasting fires;" because in his defence he said, "that he had made such an assertion in accordance with the gospel, in which it is written concerning sinners, 'These shall go

away into eternal punishment, but the righteous into life eternal.'"[6] But he did not say, *all* sinners are reserved for eternal punishment, for then he would evidently have run counter to the apostle, who distinctly states that some of them will be saved, "yet so as by fire."[7] When also Pelagius said that "the kingdom of heaven was promised even in the Old Testament," they approved of the statement, on the ground that he supported himself by the testimony of the prophet Daniel, who thus wrote: "The saints shall take the kingdom of the Most High."[8] They understood him, in this statement of his, to mean by the term "Old Testament," not simply the Testament which was made on Mount Sinai, but the entire body of the canonical Scriptures which had been given previous to the coming of the Lord. His allegation, however, that "a man is able to be without sin, if he wishes," was not approved by the bishops in the sense which he had evidently meant it to bear in his book[9] — as if this was solely in a man's power by free will (for it was contended that he must have meant no less than this by his saying: "if he wishes"), — but only in the sense which he actually gave to the passage on the present occasion in his answer; in the very sense, indeed, in which the episcopal judges mentioned the subject in their own interlocution with especial brevity and clearness, that a man is able to be without sin with the help and grace of God. But still it was left undetermined when the saints were to attain to this state of perfection, — whether in the body of this death, or when death shall be swallowed up in victory.

CHAP. 63. — THE SAME CONTINUED. THE DOGMAS OF CŒLESTIUS LAID TO THE CHARGE OF PELAGIUS, AS HIS MASTER, AND CONDEMNED.

Of the opinions which Cœlestius has said or written, and which were objected against Pelagius, on the ground that they were the dogmas of his disciple, he acknowledged some as entertained also by himself; but, in his vindication, he said that he held them in a different sense from that which was alleged in the indictment. One of these opinions was thus stated: "Before the advent of Christ some men lived holy and righteous lives."[10] Cœlestius, however, was stated to have said that "they lived *sinless* lives. Again, it was objected that Cœlestius declared "the Church to be without spot and wrinkle."[11] Pelagius, however, said in his reply, "that he had made such an assertion, but as meaning that the Church is by the laver cleansed from every spot and wrinkle, and that in this purity the Lord would have her continue." Respecting that statement

[1] This trial was held at Carthage, before the Bishop Aurelius (to whom Augustin dedicated the present treatise), at the beginning of the year 412, as appears from the letter to Innocentius among Augustin's *Epistles*, 175, Nos. 1 and 6.
[2] This happened in the year 415, in the month of December, at Diospolis.
[3] Isa. viii. 20. See above, 2.
[4] Rom. vii. 24, 25.      [5] See above, 5.

[6] Matt. xxv. 46. See above, 9.      [7] 1 Cor. iii. 15.
[8] Dan. vii. 18. See above, 13.      [9] See above, 16.
[10] See above, 26.      [11] See above, 27.

of Cœlestius : " That we do more than is commanded us in the law and the gospel," Pelagius urged in his own vindication,[1] that " he spoke concerning virginity," of which Paul says : " I have no commandment of the Lord."[2]   Another objection alleged that Cœlestius had maintained that " every individual has the ability to possess all powers and graces," thus annulling that " diversity of gifts " which, the apostle sets forth.[3]   Pelagius, however, answered, that " he did not annul the diversity of gifts, but declared that God gives to the man who has proved himself worthy to receive them, all graces, even as He gave the Apostle Paul."

## CHAP. 64. — HOW THE BISHOPS CLEARED PELAGIUS OF THOSE CHARGES.

These four dogmas, thus connected with the name of Cœlestius, were therefore not approved by the bishops in their judgment, in the sense in which Cœlestius was said to have set them forth, but in the sense which Pelagius gave to them in his reply.   For they saw clearly enough, that it is one thing to be without sin, and another thing to live holily and righteously, as Scripture testifies that some lived even before the coming of Christ. And that although the Church here on earth is not without spot or wrinkle, she is yet both cleansed from every spot and wrinkle by the laver of regeneration, and in this state the Lord would have her continue.   And continue she certainly will, for without doubt she shall reign without spot or wrinkle in an everlasting felicity. And that the perpetual virginity, which is not commanded, is unquestionably more than the purity of wedded life, which is commanded — although virginity is persevered in by many persons, who, notwithstanding, are not without sin. And that all those graces which he enumerates in a certain passage were possessed by the Apostle Paul ; and yet, for all that, either they could quite understand, in regard to his having been worthy to receive them, that the merit was not according to his works, but rather, in some way, according to predestination (for the apostle says himself : " I am not meet to be called an apostle ; ")[4] or else their attention was not arrested by the sense which Pelagius gave to the word, as he himself viewed it.   Such are the points on which the bishops pronounced the agreement of Pelagius with the doctrines of godly truth.

## CHAP. 65. — RECAPITULATION OF WHAT PELAGIUS CONDEMNED.

Let us now, by a like recapitulation, bestow a little more attention on those subjects which the bishops said he rejected and condemned as " contrary ; " for herein especially lies the whole of that heresy.   We will entirely pass over the strange terms of adulation which he is reported to have put into writing in praise of a certain widow ; these he denied having ever inserted in any of his writings, or ever given utterance to, and he anathematized all who held the opinions in question not indeed as heretics, but as fools.[5] The following are the wild thickets of this heresy, which we are sorry to see shooting out buds, nay growing into trees, day by day : — " That[6] Adam was made mortal, and would have died whether he had sinned or not ; that Adam's sin injured only himself, and not the human race ; that the law no less than the gospel leads to the kingdom ; that new-born infants are in the same condition that Adam was before the transgression ; that the whole human race does not, on the one hand, die in consequence of Adam's death and transgression, nor, on the other hand, does the whole human race rise again through the resurrection of Christ ; that infants, even if they die unbaptized, have eternal life ; that rich men, even if baptized, unless they renounce and surrender everything, have, whatever good they may seem to have done, nothing of it reckoned to them, neither can they possess the kingdom of God ; that[7] God's grace and assistance are not given for single actions, but reside in free will, and in the law and teaching ; that the grace of God is bestowed according to our merits, so that grace really lies in the will of man, as he makes himself worthy or unworthy of it ; that men cannot be called children of God, unless they have become entirely free from sin ; that forgetfulness and ignorance do not come under sin, as they do not happen through the will, but of necessity ; that there is no free will, if it needs the help of God, inasmuch as every one has his proper will either to do something, or to abstain from doing it ; that our victory comes not from God's help, but from free will ; that from what Peter says, that ' we are partakers of the divine nature,'[8] it must follow that the soul has the power of being without sin, just in the way that God Himself has."   For this have I read in the eleventh chapter of the book, which bears no title of its author, but is commonly reported to be the work of Cœlestius, — expressed in these words : " Now how can anybody," asks the author, " become *a partaker* of the thing from the condition and power of which he is distinctly declared to be a stranger ? "   Accordingly, the brethren who prepared these objections understood him to have said that man's soul and God are of the same nature, and to have asserted that the soul is part of God ; for thus they understood that he meant that the soul partakes of the

---

[1] See above, 29.    [2] 1 Cor. vii. 25.    [3] See above, 32.
[4] 1 Cor. xv. 9.

[5] See above, 16.    [6] See above, 24.    [7] See above, 30.
[8] 2 Pet. i. 4.

same condition and power as God. Moreover, in the last of the objections laid to his charge there occurs this position : "That pardon is not given to penitents according to the grace and mercy of God, but according to their own merits and effort, since through repentance they have been worthy of mercy." Now all these dogmas, and the arguments which were advanced in support of them, were repudiated and anathematized by Pelagius, and his conduct herein was approved of by the judges, who accordingly pronounced that he had, by his rejection and anathema, condemned the opinions in question as contrary to the faith. Let us therefore rejoice —whatever may be the circumstances of the case, whether Cœlestius laid down these theses or not, or whether Pelagius believed them or not — that the injurious principles of this new heresy were condemned before that ecclesiastical tribunal ; and let us thank God for such a result, and proclaim His praises.

CHAP. 66. — THE HARSH MEASURES OF THE PELAGIANS AGAINST THE HOLY MONKS AND NUNS WHO BELONGED TO JEROME'S CHARGE.

Certain followers of Pelagius are said to have carried their support of his cause after these judicial proceedings to an incredible extent of perverseness and audacity. They are said[1] to have most cruelly beaten and maltreated the servants and handmaidens of the Lord who lived under the care of the holy presbyter Jerome,

---

[1] He here refers to a letter (32) of Pope Innocent to John, Bishop of Jerusalem. It thus commences: "Plunder, slaughter, incendiary fire, every atrocity of the maddest kind have been deplored by the noble and holy virgins Eustochium and Paula, as having been perpetrated, at the devil's instigation, in several places of your diocese," etc. An epistle by the same writer (33) addressed to Jerome, begins with these words: "The apostle testifies that contention never did any good to the Church."

slain his deacon, and burnt his monastic houses ; whilst he himself, by God's mercy, narrowly escaped the violent attacks of these impious assailants in the shelter of a well-defended fortress. However, I think it better becomes me to say nothing of these matters, but to wait and see what measures our brethren the bishops may deem it their duty to adopt concerning such scandalous enormities ; for nobody can suppose that it is possible for them to pass them over without notice. Impious *doctrines* put forth by persons of this character it is no doubt the duty of all catholics, however remote their residence, to oppose and refute, and so to hinder all injury from such opinions wheresoever they may happen to find their way ; but impious *actions* it belongs to the discipline of the episcopal authority on the spot to control, and they must be left for punishment to the bishops of the very place or immediate neighbourhood, to be dealt with as pastoral diligence and godly severity may suggest. We, therefore, who live at so great a distance, are bound to hope that such a stop may there be put to proceedings of this kind, that there may be no necessity elsewhere of further invoking judicial remedies. But what rather befits our personal activity is so to set forth the truth, that the minds of all those who have been severely wounded by the report, so widely spread everywhere, may be healed by the mercy of God following our efforts. With this desire, I must now at last terminate this work, which, should it succeed, as I hope, in commending itself to your mind, will, I trust, with the Lord's blessing, become serviceable to its readers — recommended to them rather by your name than by my own, and through your care and diligence receiving a wider circulation.

# A TREATISE ON THE GRACE OF CHRIST, AND ON ORIGINAL SIN.

# EXTRACT FROM AUGUSTIN'S "RETRACTATIONS,"

## BOOK II. CHAP. 50,

### ON THE FOLLOWING TREATISE,

## "DE GRATIA CHRISTI, ET DE PECCATO ORIGINALI."

---

"AFTER the conviction and condemnation[1] of the Pelagian heresy with its authors by the bishops of the Church of Rome, — first Innocent, and then Zosimus, — with the co-operation of letters of African councils, I wrote two books against them : one *On the Grace of Christ*, and the other *On Original Sin*. The work began with the following words : 'How greatly we rejoice on account of your bodily, and, above all, because of your spiritual welfare.'"

---

[1] From this it follows that we must refer his books *On the Grace of Christ* and *On Original Sin* to the year 418; for it was in this year that the Pelagian heresy was condemned by the pope Zosimus. Somewhat earlier there was held a general council of the bishops of Africa at Carthage, to take measures against the heresy, — the precise date of which council is May 1st of this year 418. Augustin, on account of this council, was detained at Carthage, and his stay in that city was longer than usual, as one may learn from the 94th canon of the council, or from the *Codex Canonum* of the Church of Africa, canon 127, as well as from his epistle (193, sec. 1) to Mercator. And it was in this interval of time, before he started for Mauritania

214

Cæsariensis, that he wrote these two books for Albina, Pinianus, and Melania; accordingly, in his *Retractations*, he places them just previous to the time of his proceedings with Emeritus, which were concluded at Cæsarea on the 20th of September in this very year 418. Julianus, in his work addressed to Turbantius. calumniously attacked a passage in the book *On the Grace of Christ;* the passage is defended by Augustin in his work against Julianus, iv. 8. 47, where he mentions this first book, addressed to *the holy Pinianus*, as he calls him, and gives its title as "Concerning Grace, in opposition to Pelagius." [Albina, with her son-in-law Pinianus, and her daughter Melania, constituted an interesting family of ascetics, which had formerly lived in Africa, but at this time were in Palestine; Pinianus at the head of a monastery, and his wife an inmate of a convent. — W.]

# CONTENTS OF THE TREATISE "ON THE GRACE OF CHRIST, AND ON ORIGINAL SIN."

## BOOK I.

# BOOK II.

# A TREATISE ON THE GRACE OF CHRIST, AND ON ORIGINAL SIN,

*BY AURELIUS AUGUSTIN, BISHOP OF HIPPO;*

In Two Books,

WRITTEN AGAINST PELAGIUS AND CŒLESTIUS IN THE YEAR A.D. 418.

---

## BOOK I.

### *ON THE GRACE OF CHRIST.*

WHEREIN HE SHOWS THAT PELAGIUS IS DISINGENUOUS IN HIS CONFESSION OF GRACE, INASMUCH AS HE PLACES GRACE EITHER IN NATURE AND FREE WILL, OR IN LAW AND TEACHING; AND, MOREOVER, ASSERTS THAT IT IS MERELY THE "POSSIBILITY" (AS HE CALLS IT) OF WILL AND ACTION, AND NOT THE WILL AND ACTION ITSELF, WHICH IS ASSISTED BY DIVINE GRACE; AND THAT THIS ASSISTING GRACE, TOO, IS GIVEN BY GOD ACCORDING TO MEN'S MERITS; WHILST HE FURTHER THINKS THAT THEY ARE SO ASSISTED FOR THE SOLE PURPOSE OF BEING ABLE THE MORE EASILY TO FULFIL THE COMMANDMENTS. AUGUSTIN EXAMINES THOSE PASSAGES OF HIS WRITINGS IN WHICH HE BOASTED THAT HE HAD BESTOWED EXPRESS COMMENDATION ON THE GRACE OF GOD, AND POINTS OUT HOW THEY CAN BE INTERPRETED AS REFERRING TO LAW AND TEACHING, — IN OTHER WORDS, TO THE DIVINE REVELATION AND THE EXAMPLE OF CHRIST WHICH ARE ALIKE INCLUDED IN "THE TEACHING," — OR ELSE TO THE REMISSION OF SINS; NOR DO THEY AFFORD ANY EVIDENCE WHATEVER THAT PELAGIUS REALLY ACKNOWLEDGED CHRISTIAN GRACE, IN THE SENSE OF HELP RENDERED FOR THE PERFORMANCE OF RIGHT ACTION TO NATURAL FACULTY AND INSTRUCTION, BY THE INSPIRATION OF A MOST GLOWING AND LUMINOUS LOVE; AND HE CONCLUDES WITH A REQUEST THAT PELAGIUS WOULD SERIOUSLY LISTEN TO AMBROSE, WHOM HE IS SO VERY FOND OF QUOTING, IN HIS EXCELLENT EULOGY IN COMMENDATION OF THE GRACE OF GOD.

#### CHAP. 1 [I.] — INTRODUCTORY.

How greatly we rejoice on account of your bodily, and, above all, your spiritual welfare, my most sincerely attached brethren and beloved of God, Albina, Pinianus, and Melania,[1] we cannot express in words; we therefore leave all this to your own thoughts and belief, in order that we may now rather speak of the matters on which you consulted us. We have, indeed, had to compose these words to the best of the ability which God has vouchsafed to us, while our messenger was in a hurry to be gone, and amidst many occupations, which are much more absorbing to me at Carthage than in any other place whatever.

---

[1] [See note to the passage from the *Retractations* above; and for full accounts, see Smith and Wace's *Dictionary of Christian Biography*, under these names. — W.]

217

CHAP. 2 [II.] — SUSPICIOUS CHARACTER OF PELA-
GIUS' CONFESSION AS TO THE NECESSITY OF
GRACE FOR EVERY SINGLE ACT OF OURS.

You informed me in your letter, that you had
entreated Pelagius to express in writing his condemnation of all that had been alleged against
him; and that he had said, in the audience of
you all: "I anathematize the man who either
thinks or says that the grace of God, whereby
'Christ Jesus came into the world to save sinners,'[1] is not necessary not only for ever hour
and for every moment, but also for every act of
our lives: and those who endeavour to disannul
it deserve everlasting punishment." Now, whoever hears these words, and is ignorant of the
opinion which he has clearly enough expressed
in his books, — not those, indeed, which he declares to have been stolen from him in an incorrect form, nor those which he repudiates, but
those even which he mentions in his own letter
which he forwarded to Rome, — would certainly
suppose that the views he holds are in strict
accordance with the truth. But whoever notices
what he openly declares in them, cannot fail to
regard these statements with suspicion. Because,
although he makes that grace of God whereby
Christ came into the world to save sinners to
consist simply in the remission of sins, he can
still accommodate his words to this meaning, by
alleging that the necessity of such grace for every
hour and for every moment and for every action
of our life, comes to this, that while we recollect
and keep in mind the forgiveness of our past
sins, we sin no more, aided not by any supply
of power from without, but by the powers of our
own will as it recalls to our mind, in every action
we do, what advantage has been conferred upon
us by the remission of sins. Then, again, whereas
they are accustomed to say that Christ has given
us assistance for avoiding sin, in that He has
left us an example by living righteously and
teaching what is right Himself, they have it in
their power here also to accommodate their
words, by affirming that this is the necessity of
grace to us for every moment and for every
action, namely, that we should in all our conversation regard the example of the Lord's conversation. Your own fidelity, however, enables
you clearly to perceive how such a profession of
opinion as this differs from that true confession
of grace which is now the question before us.
And yet how easily can it be obscured and disguised by their ambiguous statements!

CHAP. 3 [III.] — GRACE ACCORDING TO THE
PELAGIANS.

But why should we wonder at this? For the
same Pelagius, who in the Proceedings of the

episcopal synod unhesitatingly condemned those
who say "that God's grace and assistance are
not given for single acts, but consist in free will,
or in law and teaching,"[2] upon which points we
were apt to think that he had expended all his
subterfuges; and who also condemned such as
affirm that the grace of God is bestowed in proportion to our merits: — is proved, notwithstanding, to hold, in the books which he has published
on the freedom of the will, and which he mentions
in the letter he sent to Rome, no other sentiments
than those which he seemingly condemned. For
that grace and help of God, by which we are
assisted in avoiding sin, he places either in nature and free will, or else in the gift of the law
and teaching; the result of which of course is
this, that whenever God helps a man, He must
be supposed to help him to turn away from evil
and do good, by revealing to him and teaching
him what he ought to do,[3] but not with the
additional assistance of His co-operation and
inspiration of love, that he may accomplish that
which he had discovered it to be his duty to do.

CHAP. 4. — PELAGIUS' SYSTEM OF FACULTIES.

In his system, he posits and distinguishes three
faculties, by which he says God's commandments
are fulfilled, — *capacity*, *volition*, and *action*:[4]
meaning by "capacity," that by which a man is
able to be righteous; by "volition," that by
which he wills to be righteous; by "action,"
that by which he actually is righteous. The first
of these, the capacity, he allows to have been
bestowed on us by the Creator of our nature; it
is not in our power, and we possess it even
against our will. The other two, however, the
volition and the action, he asserts to be our
own; and he assigns them to us so strictly as to
contend that they proceed simply from ourselves.
In short, according to his view, God's grace has
nothing to do with assisting those two faculties
which he will have to be altogether our own, the
volition and the action, but that only which is
not in our own power and comes to us from
God, namely the capacity; as if the faculties
which are our own, that is, the volition and the
action, have such avail for declining evil and
doing good, that they require no divine help,
whereas that faculty which we have of God, that
is to say, the capacity, is so weak, that it is always assisted by the aid of grace.

CHAP. 5 [IV.] — PELAGIUS' OWN ACCOUNT OF
THE FACULTIES, QUOTED.

Lest, however, it should chance to be said
that we either do not correctly understand what

---

[1] 1 Tim. i. 15.

[2] See *De Gestis Pelagii*, c. 30.
[3] We have in these two clauses an explanation of the terms
"law" and "teaching," which Pelagius uses almost technically.
[4] [These three technical terms are, *possibilitas*, *voluntas*, *actio*.
— W.]

he advances, or malevolently pervert to another meaning what he never meant to bear such a sense, I beg of you to consider his own actual words: "We distinguish," says he, "three things, arranging them in a certain graduated order. We put in the first place 'ability;' in the second, 'volition;' and in the third, 'actuality.'"[1] The 'ability' we place in our nature, the 'volition' in our will, and the 'actuality' in the effect. The first, that is, the 'ability,' properly belongs to God, who has bestowed it on His creature; the other two, that is, the 'volition' and the 'actuality,' must be referred to man, because they flow forth from the fountain of the will. For his willing, therefore, and doing a good work, the praise belongs to man; or rather both to man, and to God who has bestowed on him the 'capacity' for his will and work, and who evermore by the help of His grace assists even this capacity. That a man is able to will and effect any good work, comes from God alone. So that this one faculty can exist, even when the other two have no being; but these latter cannot exist without that former one. I am therefore free not to have either a good volition or action; but I am by no means able not to have the capacity of good. This capacity is inherent in me, whether I will or no; nor does nature at any time receive in this point freedom for itself. Now the meaning of all this will be rendered clearer by an example or two. That we are able to see with our eyes is not of us; but it is our own that we make a good or a bad use of our eyes. So again (that I may, by applying a general case in illustration, embrace all), that we are able to do, say, think, any good thing, comes from Him who has endowed us with this 'ability,' and who also assists this 'ability;' but that we really do a good thing, or speak a good word, or think a good thought, proceeds from our own selves, because we are also able to turn all these into evil. Accordingly, — and this is a point which needs frequent repetition, because of your calumniation of us, — whenever we say that a man can live without sin, we also give praise to God by our acknowledgment of the capacity which we have received from Him, who has bestowed such 'ability' upon us; and there is here no occasion for praising the human agent, since it is God's matter alone that is for the moment treated of; for the question is not about 'willing,' or 'effecting,' but simply and solely about that which may possibly be."

## CHAP. 6 [V.] — PELAGIUS AND PAUL OF DIFFERENT OPINIONS.

The whole of this dogma of Pelagius, observe,

is carefully expressed in these words, and none other, in the third book of his treatise in defence of the liberty of the will, in which he has taken care to distinguish with so great subtlety these three things, — the "capacity," the "volition," and the "action," that is, the "ability," the "volition," and the "actuality," — that, whenever we read or hear of his acknowledging the assistance of divine grace in order to our avoidance of evil and accomplishment of good, — whatever he may mean by the said assistance of grace, whether law and the teaching or any other thing, — we are sure of what he says; nor can we run into any mistake by understanding him otherwise than he means. For we cannot help knowing that, according to his belief, it is not our "volition" nor our "action" which is assisted by the divine help, but solely our "capacity" to will and act, which alone of the three, as he affirms, we have of God. As if that faculty were infirm which God Himself placed in our nature; while the other two, which, as he would have it, are our own, are so strong and firm and self-sufficient as to require none of His help! so that He does not help us to will, nor help us to act, but simply helps us to the possibility of willing and acting. The apostle, however, holds the contrary, when he says, "Work out your own salvation with fear and trembling."[2] And that they might be sure that it was not simply in their being able to work (for this they had already received in nature and in teaching), but in their actual working, that they were divinely assisted, the apostle does not say to them, "For it is God that worketh in you to be able," as if they already possessed volition and operation among their own resources, without requiring His assistance in respect of these two; but he says, "For it is God which worketh in you both to will and to perform of His own good pleasure;"[3] or, as the reading runs in other copies, especially the Greek, "both to will and to operate." Consider, now, whether the apostle did not thus long before foresee by the Holy Ghost that there would arise adversaries of the grace of God; and did not therefore declare that God works within us those two very things, even "willing" and "operating," which this man so determined to be our own, as if they were in no wise assisted by the help of divine grace.

## CHAP. 7 [VI.] — PELAGIUS POSITS GOD'S AID ONLY FOR OUR "CAPACITY."

Let not Pelagius, however, in this way deceive incautious and simple persons, or even himself; for after saying, "Man is therefore to be praised for his willing and doing a good work," he added, as if by way of correcting himself, these

---

[1] [The three terms here are, *posse, velle, esse.* — W.]

[2] Phil. ii. 12.      [3] Phil. ii. 13.

words : " Or rather, this praise belongs to man *and to God.*" It was not, however, that he wished to be understood as showing any deference to the sound doctrine, that it is " God which worketh in us both to will and to do," that he thus expressed himself; but it is clear enough, on his own showing, why he added the latter clause, for he immediately subjoins : " Who has bestowed on him the 'capacity' for this very will and work." From his preceding words it is manifest that he places this capacity in our nature. Lest he should seem, however, to have said nothing about grace, he added these words : " And who evermore, by the help of His grace, assists this very capacity," — " *this very capacity,*" observe ; not " *very will,*" or " *very action;* " for if he had said so much as this, he would clearly not be at variance with the teaching of the apostle. But there are his words : " this very capacity ; " meaning that very one of the three faculties which he had placed in our nature. This God " evermore assists by the help of His grace." The result, indeed, is, that " the praise does not belong to man and to God," because man so wills that yet God also inspires his volition with the ardour of love, or that man so works that God nevertheless also co-operates with him, — and without His help, what is man ? But he has associated God in this praise in this wise, that were it not for the nature which God gave us in our creation wherewith we might be able to exercise volition and action, we should neither will nor act.

CHAP. 8. — GRACE, ACCORDING TO THE PELAGIANS, CONSISTS IN THE INTERNAL AND MANIFOLD IL-LUMINATION OF THE MIND.

As to this natural capacity which he, allows, is assisted by the grace of God, it is by no means clear from the passage either what grace he means, or to what extent he supposes our nature to be assisted by it. But, as is the case in other passages in which he expresses himself with more clearness and decision, we may here also perceive that no other grace is intended by him as helping natural capacity than the law and the teaching. [VII.] For in one passage he says : " We are supposed by very ignorant persons to do wrong in this matter to divine grace, because we say that it by no means perfects sanctity in us without our will, — as if God could have imposed any command on His grace, without also supplying the help of His grace to those on whom he imposed His commands, so that men might more easily accomplish through grace what they are required to do by their free will." Then, as if he meant to explain what grace he meant, he immediately went on to add these words : " And this grace we for our part do not,

as you suppose, allow to consist merely in the law, but also in the help of God." Now who can help wishing that he would show us what grace it is that he would have us understand ? Indeed, we have the strongest reason for desiring him to tell us what he means by saying that he does not allow grace merely to consist in the law. Whilst, however, we are in the suspense of our expectation, observe, I pray you, what he has further to tell us : " God helps us," says he, " by His teaching and revelation, whilst He opens the eyes of our heart ; whilst He points out to us the future, that we may not be absorbed in the present ; whilst He discovers to us the snares of the devil ; whilst He enlightens us with the manifold and ineffable gift of heavenly grace." He then concludes his statement with a kind of absolution : " Does the man," he asks, " who says all this appear to you to be a denier of grace ? Does he not acknowledge both man's free will and God's grace ? " But, after all, he has not got beyond his commendation of the law and of teaching ; assiduously inculcating this as the grace that helps us, and so following up the idea with which he had started, when he said, " We, however, allow it to consist in the help of God." God's help, indeed, he supposed must be recommended to us by manifold lures ; by setting forth teaching and revelation, the opening of the eyes of the heart, the demonstration of the future, the discovery of the devil's wiles, and the illumination of our minds by the varied and indescribable gift of heavenly grace, — all this, of course, with a view to our learning the commandments and promises of God. And what else is this than placing God's grace in " the law and the teaching " ?

CHAP. 9 [VIII.] — THE LAW ONE THING, GRACE ANOTHER. THE UTILITY OF THE LAW.

Hence, then, it is clear that he acknowledges that grace whereby God points out and reveals to us what we are bound to do ; but not that whereby He endows and assists us to act, since the knowledge of the law, unless it be accompanied by the assistance of grace, rather avails for producing the transgression of the commandment. " Where there is no law," says the apostle, " there is no transgression ; "[1] and again : " I had not known lust except the law had said, Thou shalt not covet."[2] Therefore so far are the law and grace from being the same thing, that the law is not only unprofitable, but it is absolutely prejudicial, unless grace assists it ; and the utility of the law may be shown by this, that it obliges all whom it proves guilty of transgression to betake themselves to grace for deliverance and help to overcome their evil lusts.

---

[1] Rom. iv. 15.          [2] Rom. vii. 7.

For it rather commands than assists; it discovers disease, but does not heal it; nay, the malady that is not healed is rather aggravated by it, so that the cure of grace is more earnestly and anxiously sought for, inasmuch as "The letter killeth, but the spirit giveth life." [1] "For if there had been a law given which could have given life, verily righteousness should have been by the law." [2] To what extent, however, the law gives assistance, the apostle informs us when he says immediately afterwards: "The Scripture hath concluded all under sin, that the promise by faith of Jesus Christ might be given to them that believe." [3] Wherefore, says the apostle, "the law was our schoolmaster in Christ Jesus." [4] Now this very thing is serviceable to proud men, to be more firmly and manifestly "concluded under sin," so that none may presumptuously endeavour to accomplish their justification by means of free will as if by their own resources; but rather "that every mouth may be stopped, and all the world may become guilty before God. Because by the deeds of the law there shall no flesh be justified in His sight: for by the law is the knowledge of sin. But now the righteousness of God without the law is manifested, being witnessed by the law and the prophets." [5] How then manifested without the law, if witnessed by the law? For this very reason the phrase is not, "manifested without the law," but "the righteousness without the law," because it is "the righteousness of God;" that is, the righteousness which we have not from the law, but from God, — not the righteousness, indeed, which by reason of His commanding it, causes us fear through our knowledge of it; but rather the righteousness which by reason of His bestowing it, is held fast and maintained by us through our loving it, — "so that he that glorieth, let him glory in the Lord." [6]

### CHAP. 10 [IX.] — WHAT PURPOSE THE LAW SUBSERVES.

What object, then, can this man gain by accounting the law and the teaching to be the grace whereby we are helped to work righteousness? For, in order that it may help much, it must help us to feel our need of grace. No man, indeed, is able to fulfil the law through the law. "Love is the fulfilling of the law." [7] And the love of God is not shed abroad in our hearts by the law, but by the Holy Ghost, which is given unto us. [8] Grace, therefore, is pointed at by the law, in order that the law may be fulfilled by grace. Now what does it avail for Pelagius, that he declares the self-same thing under differ-

ent phrases, that he may not be understood to place in law and teaching that grace which, as he avers, assists the "capacity" of our nature? So far, indeed, as I can conjecture, the reason why he fears being so understood is, because he condemned all those who maintain that God's grace and help are not given for a man's single actions, but exist rather in his freedom, or in the law and teaching. And yet he supposes that he escapes detection by the shifts he so constantly employs for disguising what he means by his formula of "law and teaching" under so many various phrases.

### CHAP. 11 [X.] — PELAGIUS' DEFINITION OF HOW GOD HELPS US: "HE PROMISES US FUTURE GLORY."

For in another passage, after asserting at length that it is not by the help of God, but out of our own selves, that a good will is formed within us, he confronted himself with a question out of the apostle's epistle; and he asked this question: "How will this stand consistently with the apostle's words, [9] 'It is God that worketh in you both to will and to perfect'?" Then, in order to obviate this opposing authority, which he plainly saw to be most thoroughly contrasted with his own dogma, he went on at once to add: "He works in us to will what is good, to will what is holy, when He rouses us from our devotion to earthly desires, and from our love of the present only, after the manner of brute animals, by the magnitude of the future glory and the promise of its rewards; when by revealing wisdom to us He stirs up our sluggish will to a longing after God; when (what you are not afraid to deny in another passage) he persuades us to everything which is good." Now what can be plainer, than that by the grace whereby God works within us to will what is good, he means nothing else than the law and the teaching? For in the law and the teaching of the holy Scriptures are promised future glory and its great rewards. To the teaching also appertains the revelation of wisdom, whilst it is its further function to direct our thoughts to everything that is good. And if between teaching and persuading (or rather exhorting) there seems to be a difference, yet even this is provided for in the general term "teaching," which is contained in the several discourses or letters; for the holy Scriptures both teach and exhort, and in the processes of teaching and exhorting there is room likewise for man's operation. We, however, on our side would fain have him sometime confess that grace, by which not only future glory in all its magnitude is promised, but also is believed in and hoped for; by which wisdom is not only re-

---

[1] 2 Cor. iii. 6.    [2] Gal. iii. 21.    [3] Gal. iii. 22.
[4] Gal. iii. 24.    [5] Rom. iii. 19–21.    [6] 1 Cor. i. 31.
[7] Rom. xiii. 10.    [8] Rom. v. 5.

[9] Phil. ii. 13.

vealed, but also loved; by which everything that is good is not only recommended, but pressed upon us until we accept it. For all men do not possess faith,[1] who hear the Lord in the Scriptures promising the kingdom of heaven; nor are all men persuaded, who are counselled to come to Him, who says, "Come unto me, all ye that labour."[2] They, however, who have faith are the same who are also persuaded to come to Him. This He Himself set forth most plainly, when He said, "No man can come to me, except the Father, which hath sent me, draw him."[3] And some verses afterwards, when speaking of such as believe not, He says, "Therefore said I unto you, that no man can come unto me except it were given unto him of my Father."[4] This is the grace which Pelagius ought to acknowledge, if he wishes not only to be called a Christian, but to be one.

CHAP. 12 [XI.] — THE SAME CONTINUED : "HE REVEALS WISDOM."

But what shall I say about the revelation of wisdom? For there is no man who can in the present life very well hope to attain to the great revelations which were given to the Apostle Paul; and of course it is impossible to suppose that anything was accustomed in these revelations to be made known to him but what appertained to wisdom. Yet for all this he says : "Lest I should be exalted above measure through the abundance of the revelations, there was given to me a thorn in the flesh, the messenger of Satan to buffet me. For this thing I besought the Lord thrice, that He would take it away from me. And He said unto me, My grace is sufficient for thee; for my strength is made perfect in weakness."[5] Now, undoubtedly, if there were already in the apostle that perfection of love which admitted of no further addition, and which could be puffed up no more, there could have been no further need of the messenger of Satan to buffet him, and thereby to repress the excessive elation which might arise from abundance of revelations. What means this elation, however, but a being puffed up? And of love it has been indeed most truly said, "Love vaunteth not itself, is not puffed up."[6] This love, therefore, was still in process of constant increase in the great apostle, day by day, as long as his "inward man was renewed day by day,"[7] and would then be perfected, no doubt, when he was got beyond the reach of all further vaunting and elation. But at that time his mind was still in a condition to be inflated by an abundance of revelations before it was perfected in the solid edifice of love; for he had not arrived at the

goal and apprehended the prize, to which he was reaching forward in his course.

CHAP. 13 [XII.] — GRACE CAUSES US TO DO.

To him, therefore, who is reluctant to endure the troublesome process, whereby this vaunting disposition is restrained, before he attains to the ultimate and highest perfection of charity, it is most properly said, "My grace is sufficient for thee; for my strength is made perfect in weakness,"[8] — in weakness, that is, not of the flesh only, as this man supposes, but both of the flesh and of the mind; because the mind, too, was, in comparison of that last stage of complete perfection, weak, and to it also was assigned, in order to check its elation, that messenger of Satan, the thorn in the flesh; although it was very strong, in contrast with the carnal or animal faculties, which as yet understand not the things of the Spirit of God.[9] Inasmuch, then, as strength is made perfect in weakness, whoever does not own himself to be weak, is not in the way to be perfected. This grace, however, by which strength is perfected in weakness, conducts all who are predestinated and called according to the divine purpose[10] to the state of the highest perfection and glory. By such grace is effected, not only that we discover what ought to be done, but also that we do what we have discovered, — not only that we believe what ought to be loved, but also that we love what we have believed.

CHAP. 14 [XIII.] — THE RIGHTEOUSNESS WHICH IS OF GOD, AND THE RIGHTEOUSNESS WHICH IS OF THE LAW.

If this grace is to be called "teaching," let it at any rate be so called in such wise that God may be believed to infuse it, along with an ineffable sweetness, more deeply and more internally, not only by *their* agency who plant and water from without, but likewise by His own too who ministers in secret His own increase, — in such a way, that He not only exhibits truth, but likewise imparts love. For it is thus that God teaches those who have been called according to His purpose, giving them simultaneously both to know what they ought to do, and to do what they know. Accordingly, the apostle thus speaks to the Thessalonians : "As touching love of the brethren, ye need not that I write unto you; for ye yourselves are taught of God to love one another."[11] And then, by way of proving that they had been taught of God, he subjoined : "And indeed ye do it towards all the brethren which are in all Macedonia."[12] As if the surest sign that you have been taught of God, is that you put into practice what you have been taught. Of that character are all who are called accord-

---

[1] 2 Thess. iii. 2.     [2] Matt. xi. 28.     [3] John vi. 44.
[4] John vi. 65.     [5] 2 Cor. xii. 7-9     [6] 1 Cor. xiii. 4.
[7] 2 Cor. iv. 6.

[8] 2 Cor. xii. 9.     [9] 1 Cor. ii. 14     [10] Rom. viii. 28, 30.
[11] 1 Thess. iv. 9.     [12] 1 Thess. iv. 10.

ing to God's purpose, as it is written in the prophets: "They shall be all taught of God." [1] The man, however, who has learned what ought to be done, but does it not, has not as yet been "taught of God" according to grace, but only according to the law, — not according to the spirit, but only according to the letter. Although there are many who appear to do what the law commands, through fear of punishment, not through love of righteousness; and such righteousness as this the apostle calls "his own which is after the law," — a thing as it were commanded, not given. When, indeed, it has been given, it is not called our own righteousness, but God's; because it becomes our own only so that we have it from God. These are the apostle's words: "That I may be found in Him, not having mine own righteousness which is of the law, but that which is through the faith of Christ, the righteousness which is of God by faith." [2] So great, then, is the difference between the law and grace, that although the law is undoubtedly of God, yet the righteousness which is "of the law" is not "of God," but the righteousness which is consummated by grace is "of God." The one is designated "the righteousness of the law," because it is done through fear of the curse of the law; while the other is called "the righteousness of God," because it is bestowed through the beneficence of His grace, so that it is not a terrible but a pleasant commandment, according to the prayer in the psalm: "Good art Thou, O Lord, therefore in Thy goodness teach me Thy righteousness;" [3] that is, that I may not be compelled like a slave to live under the law with fear of punishment; but rather in the freedom of love may be delighted to live with law as my companion. When the freeman keeps a commandment, he does it readily. And whosoever learns his duty in this spirit, does everything that he has learned ought to be done.

### CHAP. 15 [XIV.] — HE WHO HAS BEEN TAUGHT BY GRACE ACTUALLY COMES TO CHRIST.

Now as touching this kind of teaching, the Lord also says: "Every man that hath heard, and hath learned of the Father, cometh unto me." [4] Of the man, therefore, who has not come, it cannot be correctly said: "He has heard and has learned that it is his duty to come to Him, but he is not willing to do what he has learned." It is indeed absolutely improper to apply such a statement to that method of teaching, whereby God teaches by grace. For if, as the Truth says, "Every man that hath learned cometh," it follows, of course, that whoever does not come has not learned. But who can fail to see that a man's coming or not coming is by the determi-

nation of his will? This determination, however, may stand alone, if the man does not come; but if he does come, it cannot be without assistance; and such assistance, that he not only knows what it is he ought to do, but also actually does what he thus knows. And thus, when God teaches, it is not by the letter of the law, but by the grace of the Spirit. Moreover, He so teaches, that whatever a man learns, he not only sees with his perception, but also desires with his choice, and accomplishes in action. By this mode, therefore, of divine instruction, volition itself, and performance itself, are assisted, and not merely the natural "capacity" of willing and performing. For if nothing but this "capacity" of ours were assisted by this grace, the Lord would rather have said, "Every man that hath heard and hath learned of the Father *may possibly* come unto me." This, however, is not what He said; but His words are these: "Every man that hath heard and hath learned of the Father *cometh* unto me." Now *the possibility of coming* Pelagius places in nature, or even — as we found him attempting to say some time ago [5] — in grace (whatever that may mean according to him), — when he says, "whereby this very capacity is assisted;" whereas *the actual coming* lies in the will and act. It does not, however, follow that he who *may* come actually comes, unless he has also willed and acted for the coming. But every one who has learned of the Father not only has the possibility of coming, but *comes;* and in this result are already included the *motion* of the capacity, the *affection* of the will, and the *effect* of the action. [6]

### CHAP. 16 [XV.] — WE NEED DIVINE AID IN THE USE OF OUR POWERS. ILLUSTRATION FROM SIGHT.

Now what is the use of his examples, if they do not really accomplish his own promise of making his meaning clearer to us; [7] not, indeed, that we are bound to admit their sense, but that we may discover more plainly and openly what is his drift and purpose in using them? "That we are able," says he, "to see with our eyes is not of us; but it is of us that we make a good or a bad use of our sight." Well, there is an answer for him in the psalm, in which the psalmist says to God, "Turn Thou away mine eyes, that they behold not iniquity." [8] Now although this was said of the eyes of the mind, it still follows from it, that in respect of our bodily eyes there is either a good use or a bad use that may be made of them: not in the literal sense merely of a good sight when the eyes are sound, and a bad sight when they are bleared, but in the

---

[1] Isa. liv. 13; Jer xxxi. 34; John vi. 45.　　[2] Phil. iii. 9.
[3] Ps cxix. 68.　　[4] John vi. 45.
[5] See above, ch. 7 [vi.]
[6] The technical gradation is here neatly expressed by *profectus*, *affectus*, and *effectus*.
[7] See above, ch. 5 [iv.].　　　　[8] Ps. cxix. 37.

moral sense of a right sight when it is directed towards succouring the helpless, or a bad sight when its object is the indulgence of lust. For although both the pauper who is succoured, and the woman who is lusted after, are seen by these external eyes; it is after all from the inner eyes that either compassion in the one case or lust in the other proceeds. How then is it that the prayer is offered to God, "Turn Thou away mine eyes, that they behold not iniquity"? Or why is that asked for which lies within our own power, if it be true that God does not assist the will?

### CHAP. 17 [XVI.] — DOES PELAGIUS DESIGNEDLY REFRAIN FROM OPENLY SAYING THAT ALL GOOD ACTION IS FROM GOD?

"That we are able to speak," says he, "is of God; but that we make a good or a bad use of speech is of ourselves." He, however, who has made the most excellent use of speech does not teach us so. "For," says He, "it is not ye that speak, but the Spirit of your Father that speaketh in you." [1] "So, again," adds Pelagius, "that I may, by applying a general case in illustration, embrace all, — that we are able to do, say, think any good thing, comes from Him who has endowed us with this ability, and who also assists it." Observe how even here he repeats his former meaning — that of these three, capacity, volition, action, it is only the capacity which receives help. Then, by way of completely stating what he intends to say, he adds: "But that we really do a good thing, or speak a good word, or think a good thought, proceeds from our own selves." He forgot what he had before [2] said by way of correcting, as it were, his own words; for after saying, "Man is to be praised therefore for his willing and doing a good work," he at once goes on to modify his statement thus: "Or rather, this praise belongs both to man, and to God who has given him the capacity of this very will and work." Now what is the reason why he did not remember this admission when giving his examples, so as to say this much at least after quoting them: "That we are able to do, say, think any good thing, comes from Him who has given us this ability, and who also assists it. That, however, we really do a good thing, or speak a good word, or think a good thought, proceeds *both from ourselves and from Him!*" This, however, he has not said. But, if I am not mistaken, I think I see why he was afraid to do so.

### CHAP. 18 [XVII.] — HE DISCOVERS THE REASON OF PELAGIUS' HESITATION SO TO SAY.

For, when wishing to point out why this lies within our own competency, he says: "Because we are able to turn all these actions into evil." This, then, was the reason why he was afraid to admit that such an action proceeds "*both from ourselves and from God*," lest it should be objected to him in reply: "If the fact of our doing, speaking, thinking anything good, is owing both to ourselves and to God, because He has endowed us with this ability, then it follows that our doing, thinking, speaking evil things, is due to ourselves and to God, because He has here also endowed us with ability of indifference; the conclusion from this being — and God forbid that we should admit any such — that just as God is associated with ourselves in the praise of good actions, so must He share with us the blame of evil actions." For that "capacity" with which He has endowed us makes us capable alike of good actions and of evil ones.

### CHAP. 19 [XVIII.] — THE TWO ROOTS OF ACTION, LOVE AND CUPIDITY; AND EACH BRINGS FORTH ITS OWN FRUIT.

Concerning this "capacity," Pelagius thus writes in the first book of his *Defence of Free Will*: "Now," says he, "we have implanted in us by God a capacity for either part.[3] It resembles, as I may say, a fruitful and fecund root which yields and produces diversely according to the will of man, and which is capable, at the planter's own choice, of either shedding a beautiful bloom of virtues, or of bristling with the thorny thickets of vices." Scarcely heeding what he says, he here makes one and the same root productive both of good and evil fruits, in opposition to gospel truth and apostolic teaching. For the Lord declares that "a good tree cannot bring forth evil fruit, neither can a corrupt tree bring forth good fruit;"[4] and when the Apostle Paul says that covetousness is "the root of all evils,"[5] he intimates to us, of course, that love may be regarded as the root of all good things. On the supposition, therefore, that two trees, one good and the other corrupt, represent two human beings, a good one and a bad, what else is the good man except one with a good will, that is, a tree with a good root? And what is the bad man except one with a bad will, that is, a tree with a bad root? The fruits which spring from such roots and trees are deeds, are words, are thoughts, which proceed, when good, from a good will, and when evil, from an evil one.

### CHAP. 20 [XIX.] — HOW A MAN MAKES A GOOD OR A BAD TREE.

Now a man makes a good tree when he receives the grace of God. For it is not by himself that he makes himself good instead of evil; but it is of Him, and through Him, and in Him

---

[1] Matt. x. 20.  [2] See ch. 5.

[3] [The technical phrase is *possibilitas utriusque partis.* — W.]
[4] Matt. vii. 18.  [5] 1 Tim. vi. 10.

who is always good. And in order that he may not only be a good tree, but also bear good fruit, it is necessary for him to be assisted by the self-same grace, without which he can do nothing good. For God Himself co-operates in the production of fruit in good trees, when He both externally waters and tends them by the agency of His servants, and internally by Himself also gives the increase.[1] A man, however, makes a corrupt tree when he makes himself corrupt, when he falls away from Him who is the unchanging good; for such a declension from Him is the origin of an evil will. Now this decline does not initiate some other corrupt nature, but it corrupts that which has been already created good. When this corruption, however, has been healed, no evil remains; for although nature no doubt had received an injury, yet nature was not itself a blemish.[2]

### CHAP. 21 [XX.] — LOVE THE ROOT OF ALL GOOD THINGS; CUPIDITY, OF ALL EVIL ONES.

The "capacity," then, of which we speak is not (as he supposes) the one identical root both of good things and evil. For the love which is the root of good things is quite different from the cupidity which is the root of evil things — as different, indeed, as virtue is from vice. But without doubt this "capacity" is capable of either root: because a man is not only able to possess love, whereby the tree becomes a good one; but he is likewise able to have cupidity, which makes the tree evil. This human cupidity, however, which is a vice, has for its author man, or man's deceiver, but not man's Creator. It is indeed that "lust of the flesh, and the lust of the eyes, and the pride of life, which is not of the Father, but is of the world."[3] And who can be ignorant of the usage of the Scripture, which under the designation of "_the world_" is accustomed to describe those who inhabit the world?

### CHAP. 22 [XXI.] — LOVE IS A GOOD WILL.

That love, however, which is a virtue, comes to us from God, not from ourselves, according to the testimony of Scripture, which says: "Love is of God; and every one that loveth is born of God, and knoweth God: for God is love."[4] It is on the principle of this love that one can best understand the passage, "Whosoever is born of God doth not commit sin;"[5] as well as the sentence, "And he cannot sin."[6] Because the love according to which we are born of God "doth not behave itself unseemly," and "thinketh no evil."[7] Therefore, whenever a man sins, it is not according to love: but it is according to cupidity that he commits sin; and following such a disposition, he is not born of God. Because, as it has been already stated, "the capacity" of which we speak is capable of either root. When, therefore, the Scripture says, "Love is of God," or still more pointedly, "God is love;" when the Apostle John so very emphatically exclaims, "Behold what manner of love the Father hath bestowed upon us, that we should be called, and be, the sons of God!"[8] with what face can this writer, on hearing that "God is love," persist in maintaining his opinion, that we have of God one only of those three,[9] namely, "the capacity;" whereas it is of ourselves that we have "the good will" and "the good action?" As if, indeed, this good will were a different thing from that love which the Scripture so loudly proclaims to have come to us from God, and to have been given to us by the Father, that we might become His children.

### CHAP. 23 [XXII.] — PELAGIUS' DOUBLE DEALING CONCERNING THE GROUND OF THE CONFERRENCE OF GRACE.

Perhaps, however, our own antecedent merits caused this gift to be bestowed upon us; as this writer has already suggested in reference to God's grace, in that work which he addressed to a holy virgin,[10] whom he mentions in the letter sent by him to Rome. For, after adducing the testimony of the Apostle James, in which he says, "Submit yourselves unto God; but resist the devil, and he will flee from you,"[11] he goes on to say: "He shows us how we ought to resist the devil, if we submit ourselves indeed to God and by doing His will merit His divine grace, and by the help of the Holy Ghost more easily withstand the evil spirit." Judge, then, how sincere was his condemnation in the Palestine Synod of those persons who say that God's grace is conferred on us according to our merits! Have we any doubt as to his still holding this opinion, and most openly proclaiming it? Well, how could that confession of his before the bishops have been true and real? Had he already written the book in which he most explicitly alleges that grace is bestowed on us according to our deserts — the very position which he without any reservation condemned at that Synod in the East? Let him frankly acknowledge that he once held the opinion, but that he holds it no longer; so should we most frankly rejoice in his improvement. As it is, however, when, besides other objections, this one was laid to his charge which we are now discussing, he said in reply: "Whether these are the opinions of Cœlestius or not, is the concern of those who affirm that

---

[1] 1 Cor. iii. 7.
[2] [Here the phraseology contrasts _vitium naturæ_, with _vitium natura_. — W.]
[3] 1 John ii. 16.　　[4] 1 John iv. 7, 8.　　[5] 1 John iii. 9.
[6] Same verse.　　[7] 1 Cor. xiii. 5.

[8] 1 John iii. 1.　　　　　　[9] See above, ch. 4.
[10] _Epistola ad Demetriadem_, c. 25.　　[11] Jas. iv. 7.

they are. For my own part, indeed, I never entertained such views; on the contrary, I anathematize every one who does entertain them."[1] But how could he "never have entertained such views," when he had already composed this work? Or how does he still "anathematize everybody who entertains these views," if he afterwards composed this work?

CHAP. 24. — PELAGIUS PLACES FREE WILL AT THE BASIS OF ALL TURNING TO GOD FOR GRACE.

But perhaps he may meet us with this rejoinder, that in the sentence before us he spoke of our "meriting the divine grace by doing the will of God," in the sense that grace is added to those who believe and lead godly lives, whereby they may boldly withstand the tempter; whereas their very first reception of grace was, that they might do the will of God. Lest, then, he make such a rejoinder, consider some other words of his on this subject: "The man," says he, "who hastens to the Lord, and desires to be directed by Him, that is, who makes his own will depend upon God's, who moreover cleaves so closely to the Lord as to become (as the apostle says) 'one spirit' with Him,[2] does all this by nothing else than by his freedom of will." Observe how great a result he has here stated to be accomplished only by our freedom of will; and how, in fact, he supposes us to cleave to God without the help of God: for such is the force of his words, "by nothing else than by his own freedom of will." So that, after we have cleaved to the Lord without His help, we even then, because of such adhesion of our own, deserve to be assisted. [XXIII.] For he goes on to say: "Whosoever makes a right use of this" (that is, rightly uses his freedom of will), "does so entirely surrender himself to God, and does so completely mortify his own will, that he is able to say with the apostle, 'Nevertheless it is already not I that live, but Christ liveth in me;'[3] and 'He placeth his heart in the hand of God, so that He turneth it whithersoever He willeth.'"[4] Great indeed is the help of the grace of God, so that He turns our heart in whatever direction He pleases. But according to this writer's foolish opinion, however great the help may be, we deserve it all at the moment when, without any assistance beyond the liberty of our will, we hasten to the Lord, desire His guidance and direction, suspend our own will entirely on His, and by close adherence to Him become one spirit with Him. Now all these vast courses of goodness, forsooth, we (according to him) accomplish, simply by the freedom of our own free will; and by reason of such antecedent merits we so secure His grace, that He turns our heart

which way soever He pleases. Well, now, how is *that* grace which is not gratuitously conferred? How can it be grace, if it is given in payment of a debt? How can that be true which the apostle says, "It is not of yourselves, but it is the gift of God; not of works, lest any man should boast;"[5] and again, "If it is of grace, then is it no more of works, otherwise grace is no more grace:"[6] how, I repeat, can this be true, if such meritorious works precede as to procure for us the bestowal of grace? Surely, under the circumstances, there can be no gratuitous gift, but only the recompense of a due reward. Is it the case, then, that in order to find their way to the help of God, men run to God without God's help? And in order that we may receive God's help while cleaving to Him, do we without His help cleave to God? What greater gift, or even what similar gift, could grace itself bestow upon any man, if he has already without grace been able to make himself one spirit with the Lord by no other power than that of his own free will?

CHAP. 25 [XXIV.] — GOD BY HIS WONDERFUL POWER WORKS IN OUR HEARTS GOOD DISPOSITIONS OF OUR WILL.

Now I want him to tell us whether that king of Assyria,[7] whose holy wife Esther "abhorred his bed,"[8] whilst sitting upon the throne of his kingdom, and clothed in all his glorious apparel, adorned all over with gold and precious stones, and dreadful in his majesty, when he raised his face, which was inflamed with anger, in the midst of his splendour, and beheld her, with the glare of a wild bull in the fierceness of his indignation; and the queen was afraid, and her colour changed as she fainted, and she bowed herself upon the head of the maid that went before her;[9] — I want him to tell us whether this king had yet "hastened to the Lord, and had desired to be directed by Him, and had subordinated his own will to His, and had, by cleaving fast to God, become one spirit with Him, simply by the force of his own free will." Had he surrendered himself wholly to God, and entirely mortified his own will, and placed his heart in the hand of God? I suppose that anybody who should think this of the king, in the state he was then in, would be not foolish only, but even mad. And yet God converted him, and turned his indignation into gentleness. Who, however, can fail to see how much greater a task it is to change and turn wrath completely into gentleness, than to bend the heart to something, when it is not

---

[1] See the *De Gestis Pelagii*, ch. 30 [xiv.].
[2] 1 Cor. vi. 17.  [3] Gal. ii. 20.  [4] Prov. xxi. 1.

[5] Eph. ii. 8, 9.  [6] Rom. xi. 6.
[7] The reading "*Assyrius*" is replaced in some editions by the more suitable word "*Assuerus*."
[8] This "*exsecrabatur cubile*" seems to refer to Esther's words in her prayer, βδελυσσομαι κοιτην απεριτμητων, "I abhor the couch of the uncircumcised" (Esth. iv., Septuagint).
[9] Esth v. 1.

preoccupied with either affection, but is indifferently poised between the two? Let them therefore read and understand, observe and acknowledge, that it is not by law and teaching uttering their lessons from without, but by a secret, wonderful, and ineffable power operating within, that God works in men's hearts not only revelations of the truth, but also good dispositions of the will.

CHAP. 26 [XXV.] — THE PELAGIAN GRACE OF "CAPACITY" EXPLODED. THE SCRIPTURE TEACHES THE NEED OF GOD'S HELP IN DOING, SPEAKING, AND THINKING, ALIKE.

Let Pelagius, therefore, cease at last to deceive both himself and others by his disputations against the grace of God. It is not on account of only one of these three [1] — that is to say, of the "capacity" of a good will and work — that the grace of God towards us ought to be proclaimed; but also on account of the good "will" and "work" themselves. This "capacity," indeed, according to his definition, avails for both directions; and yet our sins must not also be attributed to God in consequence, as our good actions, according to his view, are attributed to Him owing to the same capacity. It is not only, therefore, on this account that the help of God's grace is maintained, because it assists our natural capacity. He must cease to say, "That we are able to do, say, think any good, is from Him who has given us this ability, and who also assists this ability; whereas that we really do a good thing, or speak a good word, or think a good thought, proceeds from our own selves." He must, I repeat, cease to say this. For God has not only given us the ability and aids it, but He further works in us "to will and to do." [2] It is not because we do not will, or do not do, that we will and do nothing good, but because we are without His help. How can he say, "That we are able to do good is of God, but that we actually do it is of ourselves," when the apostle tells us that he "prays to God" in behalf of those to whom he was writing, "that they should do no evil, but that they should do that which is good?" [3] His words are not, "We pray that ye be able to do nothing evil;" but, "that ye do no evil." Neither does he say, "that ye be able to do good;" but, "that ye do good." Forasmuch as it is written, "As many as are led by the Spirit of God, they are the sons of God," [4] it follows that, in order that they may do that which is good, they must be led by Him who is good. How can Pelagius say, "That we are able to make a good use of speech comes from God; but that we do actually make this good

use of speech proceeds from ourselves," when the Lord declares, "It is the Spirit of your Father which speaketh in you"? [5] He does not say, "It is not you who have given to yourselves the power of speaking well;" but His words are, "It is not ye that speak." [5] Nor does He say, "It is the Spirit of your Father which giveth, or hath given, you the power to speak well;" but He says, "which speaketh in you." He does not allude to the motion [6] of "the capacity," but He asserts the effect of the co-operation. How can this arrogant asserter of free will say, "That we are able to think a good thought comes from God, but that we actually think a good thought proceeds from ourselves"? He has his answer from the humble preacher of grace, who says, "Not that we are sufficient of ourselves to think anything as of ourselves, but our sufficiency is of God." [7] Observe he does not say, "to be able to think anything;" but, "to think anything."

CHAP. 27 [XXVI.] — WHAT TRUE GRACE IS, AND WHEREFORE GIVEN. MERITS DO NOT PRECEDE GRACE.

Now even Pelagius should frankly confess that this grace is plainly set forth in the inspired Scriptures; nor should he with shameless effrontery hide the fact that he has too long opposed it, but admit it with salutary regret; so that the holy Church may cease to be harassed by his stubborn persistence, and rather rejoice in his sincere conversion. Let him distinguish between knowledge and love, as they ought to be distinguished; because "knowledge puffeth up, but love edifieth." [8] And then knowledge no longer puffeth up when love builds up. And inasmuch as each is the gift of God (although one is less, and the other greater), he must not extol our righteousness above the praise which is due to Him who justifies us, in such a way as to assign to the lesser of these two gifts the help of divine grace, and to claim the greater one for the human will. And should he consent that we receive love from the grace of God, he must not suppose that any merits of our own preceded our reception of the gift. For what merits could we possibly have had at the time when we loved not God? In order, indeed, that we might receive that love whereby we might love, we were loved while as yet we had no love ourselves. This the Apostle John most expressly declares: "Not that we loved God," says he, "but that He loved us;" [9] and again, "We love Him, because He first loved us." [10] Most excellently and truly spoken! For we could not have wherewithal to love Him, unless we received it from Him in His first loving us.

[1] See above, ch. 4.　　[2] Phil. ii. 13.　　[3] See 2 Cor. xiii. 7.
[4] Rom. viii. 14.

[5] Matt. x. 20.　　[6] See ch. 15 at the end.　　[7] 2 Cor. iii. 5.
[8] 1 Cor. viii. 1.　　[9] 1 John iv. 10.　　[10] 1 John iv. 19.

And what good could we possibly do if we possessed no love? Or how could we help doing good if we have love? For although God's commandment appears sometimes to be kept by those who do not love Him, but only fear Him; yet where there is no love, no good work is imputed, nor is there any good work, rightly so called; because "whatsoever is not of faith is sin,"[1] and "faith worketh by love."[2] Hence also that grace of God, whereby "His love is shed abroad in our hearts through the Holy Ghost, which is given unto us,"[3] must be so confessed by the man who would make a true confession, as to show his undoubting belief that nothing whatever in the way of goodness pertaining to godliness and real holiness can be accomplished without it. Not after the fashion of him who clearly enough shows us what he thinks of it when he says, that "grace is bestowed in order that what God commands may be the more easily fulfilled;" which of course means, that even without grace God's commandments may, although less easily, yet actually, be accomplished.

CHAP. 28 [XXVII.] — PELAGIUS TEACHES THAT SATAN MAY BE RESISTED WITHOUT THE HELP OF THE GRACE OF GOD.

In the book which he addressed to a certain holy virgin, there is a passage which I have already mentioned,[4] wherein he plainly indicates what he holds on this subject; for he speaks of our "deserving the grace of God, and by the help of the Holy Ghost *more easily* resisting the evil spirit." Now why did he insert the phrase "more easily"? Was not the sense already complete: "And by the help of the Holy Ghost resisting the evil spirit"? But who can fail to perceive what an injury he has done by this insertion? He wants it, of course, to be supposed, that so great are the powers of our nature, which he is in such a hurry to exalt, that even without the assistance of the Holy Ghost the evil spirit can be resisted — less easily it may be, but still in a certain measure.

CHAP. 29 [XXVIII.] — WHEN HE SPEAKS OF GOD'S HELP, HE MEANS IT ONLY TO HELP US DO WHAT WITHOUT IT WE STILL COULD DO.

Again, in the first book of his *Defence of the Freedom of the Will*, he says: "But while we have within us a free will so strong and so stedfast against sinning, which our Maker has implanted in human nature generally, still, by His unspeakable goodness, we are further defended by His own daily help." What need is there of such help, if free will is so strong and so stedfast against sinning? But here, as before, he would have it understood that the purpose of the alleged assistance is, that that may be more easily accomplished by grace which he nevertheless supposes may be effected, less easily, no doubt, but yet actually, without grace.

CHAP. 30 [XXIX.] — WHAT PELAGIUS THINKS IS NEEDFUL FOR EASE OF PERFORMANCE IS REALLY NECESSARY FOR THE PERFORMANCE.

In like manner, in another passage of the same book, he says: "In order that men may more easily accomplish by grace that which they are commanded to do by free will." Now, expunge the phrase "*more easily*," and you leave not only a full, but also a sound sense, if it be regarded as meaning simply this: "That men may accomplish through grace what they are commanded to do by free will." The addition of the words "more easily," however, tacitly suggests the possibility of accomplishing good works even without the grace of God. But such a meaning is disallowed by Him who says, "Without me ye can do nothing."[5]

CHAP. 31 [XXX.] — PELAGIUS AND CŒLESTIUS NOWHERE REALLY ACKNOWLEDGE GRACE.

Let him amend all this, that if human infirmity has erred in subjects so profound, he may not add to the error diabolical deception and wilfulness, either by denying what he has really believed, or by maintaining what he has rashly believed, after he has once discovered, on recollecting the light of truth, that he ought never to have so believed. As for that grace, indeed, by which we are justified, — in other words, whereby "the love of God is shed abroad in our hearts by the Holy Ghost, which is given unto us,"[3] — I have nowhere, in those writings of Pelagius and Cœlestius which I have had the opportunity of reading, found them acknowledging it as it ought to be acknowledged. In no passage at all have I observed them recognising "the children of the promise," concerning whom the apostle thus speaks: "They which are children of the flesh, these are not the children of God; but the children of the promise are counted for the seed."[6] For that which God promises we do not ourselves bring about by our own choice or natural power, but He Himself effects it by grace.

CHAP. 32. — WHY THE PELAGIANS DEEMED PRAYERS TO BE NECESSARY. THE LETTER WHICH PELAGIUS DESPATCHED TO POPE INNOCENT WITH AN EXPOSITION OF HIS BELIEF.

Now I will say nothing at present about the works of Cœlestius, or those tracts of his which

---

[1] Rom. xiv. 23.          [2] Gal. v. 6.          [3] Rom. v. 5.
[4] Quoted above, ch. 23 [xxii.], from the *Epistola ad Demetriadem*.

[5] John xv. 5.          [6] Rom. ix. 8.

he produced in those ecclesiastical proceedings,[1] copies of the whole of which we have taken care to send to you, along with another letter which we deemed it necessary to add. If you carefully examine all these documents, you will observe that he does not posit the grace of God, which helps us whether to avoid evil or to do good, beyond the natural choice of the will, but only in the law and teaching. Thus he even asserts that their very prayers are necessary for the purpose of showing men what to desire and love. All these documents, however, I may omit further notice of at present; for Pelagius himself has lately forwarded to Rome both a letter and an exposition of his belief, addressing it to Pope Innocent, of blessed memory, of whose death he was ignorant. Now in this letter he says that "there are certain subjects about which some men are trying to vilify him. One of these is, that he refuses to infants the sacrament of baptism, and promises the kingdom of heaven to some, independently of Christ's redemption. Another of them is, that he so speaks of man's ability to avoid sin as to exclude God's help, and so strongly confides in free will that he repudiates the help of divine grace." Now, as touching the perverted opinion he holds about the baptism of infants (although he allows that it ought to be administered to them), in opposition to the Christian faith and catholic truth, this is not the place for us to enter on an accurate discussion, for we must now complete our treatise on the assistance of grace, which is the subject we undertook. Let us see what answer he makes out of this very letter to the objection which he has proposed concerning this matter. Omitting his invidious complaints about his opponents, we approach the subject before us; and find him expressing himself as follows.

### CHAP. 33 [XXXI.] — PELAGIUS PROFESSES NOTHING ON THE SUBJECT OF GRACE WHICH MAY NOT BE UNDERSTOOD OF THE LAW AND TEACHING.

"See," he says, "how this epistle will clear me before your Blessedness; for in it we clearly and simply declare, that we possess a free will which is unimpaired for sinning and for not sinning;[2] and this free will is in all good works *always* assisted by divine help." Now you perceive, by the understanding which the Lord has given you, that these words of his are inadequate to solve the question. For it is still open to us

to inquire what the help is by which he would say that the free will is assisted; lest perchance he should, as is usual with him, maintain that law and teaching are meant. If, indeed, you were to ask him why he used the word "*always*," he might answer: Because it is written, "And in His law will he meditate day and night."[3] Then, after interposing a statement about the condition of man, and his natural capacity for sinning and not sinning, he added the following words: "Now this power of free will we declare to reside generally in all alike — in Christians, in Jews, and in Gentiles. In all men free will exists equally by nature, but in Christians alone is it assisted by grace." We again ask: "By what grace?" And again he might answer: "By the law and the Christian teaching."

### CHAP. 34. — PELAGIUS SAYS THAT GRACE IS GIVEN ACCORDING TO MEN'S MERITS. THE BEGINNING, HOWEVER, OF MERIT IS FAITH; AND THIS IS A GRATUITOUS GIFT, NOT A RECOMPENSE FOR OUR MERITS.

Then, again, whatever it is which he means by "grace," he says is given even to Christians according to their merits, although (as I have already mentioned above[4]), when he was in Palestine, in his very remarkable vindication of himself, he condemned those who hold this opinion. Now these are his words: "In the one," says he, "the good of their created[5] condition is naked and defenceless;" meaning in those who are not Christians. Then adding the rest: "In these, however, who belong to Christ, there is defence afforded by Christ's help." You see it is still uncertain what the help is, according to the remark we have already made on the same subject. He goes on, however, to say of those who are not Christians: "Those deserve judgment and condemnation, because, although they possess free will whereby they could come to have faith and deserve God's grace, they make a bad use of the freedom which has been granted to them. But these deserve to be rewarded, who by the right use of free will merit the Lord's grace, and keep His commandments." Now it is clear that he says grace is bestowed according to merit, whatever and of what kind soever the grace is which he means, but which he does not plainly declare. For when he speaks of those persons as deserving reward who make a good use of their free will, and as therefore meriting the Lord's grace, he asserts in fact that a debt is paid to them. What, then, becomes of the apostle's saying, "Being justified freely by His grace"?[6] And what of his other statement too, "By grace are ye saved"?[7] — where, that he might prevent

---

[1] Augustin again mentions a short treatise by Cœlestius produced by him at ·Rome in some proceedings of the church there, below, in ch. 36 (xxxiii.), and also in his work *De Peccato Originali*, chs. 2 and 5 (ii., v.), etc. Those acts of the Roman church were drawn up (as Augustin testifies in his *Contra duas Epistolas Pelagianorum*, ii. 3, "when Cœlestius was present to answer charges laid against him ") in the time of Pope Zosimus, A.D. 417.

[2] [Ad peccandum et ad non peccandum integrum liberum arbitrium. — W.]

[3] Ps. i. 2.　　[4] In ch. 23 [xxii.].　　[5] Conditionis bonum.

[6] Rom. iii. 24.　　[7] Eph. i. 8.

men's supposing that it is by works, he expressly added, "*by faith.*"[1]   And yet further, lest it should be imagined that faith itself is to be attributed to men independently of the grace of God, the apostle says : "And that not of yourselves ; for it is the gift of God."[1]   It follows, therefore, that we receive, without any merit of our own, that from which everything which, according to them, we obtain because of our merit, has its beginning — that is, faith itself. If, however, they insist on denying that this is freely given to us, what is the meaning of the apostle's words : "According as God hath dealt to every man the measure of faith"?[2]   But if it is contended that faith is so bestowed as to be a recompense for merit, not a free gift, what then becomes of another saying of the apostle : "Unto you it is given in the behalf of Christ, not only to believe in Him, but also to suffer for His sake"?[3]   Each is by the apostle's testimony made a gift, — both that he believes in Christ, and that each suffers for His sake.   These men however, attribute faith to free will in such a way as to make it appear that grace is rendered to faith not as a gratuitous gift, but as a debt — thus ceasing to be grace any longer, because that is not grace which is not gratuitous.

CHAP. 35 [XXXII.] — PELAGIUS BELIEVES THAT INFANTS HAVE NO SIN TO BE REMITTED IN BAPTISM.

But Pelagius would have the reader pass from this letter to the book which states his belief. This he has made mention of to yourselves, and in it he has discoursed a good deal on points about which no question was raised as to his views.   Let us, however, look simply at the subjects about which our own controversy with them is concerned.   Having, then, terminated a discussion which he had conducted to his heart's content, — from the Unity of the Trinity to the resurrection of the flesh, on which nobody was questioning him, — he goes on to say : "We hold likewise one baptism, which we aver ought to be administered to infants in the same sacramental formula as it is to adults."   Well, now, you have yourselves affirmed that you heard him admit at least as much as this in your presence.   What, however, is the use of his saying that the sacrament of baptism is administered to children "in the same words as it is to adults," when our inquiry concerns the thing, not merely the words?   It is a more important matter, that (as you write) with his own mouth he replied to your own question, that "infants receive baptism for the remission of sins."   For he did not say here, too, "in words of remission of sins," but he acknowledged that they are

baptized for the remission itself ; and yet for all this, if you were to ask him what the sin is which he supposes to be remitted to them, he would contend that they had none whatever.

CHAP. 36 [XXXIII.] — CŒLESTIUS OPENLY DECLARES INFANTS TO HAVE NO ORIGINAL SIN.

Who would believe that, under so clear a confession, there is concealed a contrary meaning, if Cœlestius had not exposed it?   He who in that book of his, which he quoted at Rome in the ecclesiastical proceedings there,[4] distinctly acknowledged that "infants too are baptized for the remission of sins," also denied "that they have any original sin."   But let us now observe what Pelagius thought, not about the baptism of infants, but rather about the assistance of divine grace, in this exposition of his belief which he forwarded to Rome.   "We confess," says he, "free will in such a sense that we declare ourselves to be always in need of the help of God."   Well, now, we ask again, what the help is which he says we require ; and again we find ambiguity, since he may possibly answer that he meant the law and the teaching of Christ, whereby that natural "capacity" is assisted.   We, however, on our side require them to acknowledge a grace like that which the apostle describes, when he says : "For God hath not given us the spirit of fear ; but of power, and of love, and of a sound mind ;"[5] although it does not follow by any means that the man who has the gift of knowledge, whereby he has discovered what he ought to do, has also the grace of love so as to do it.

CHAP. 37 [XXXIV.] — PELAGIUS NOWHERE ADMITS THE NEED OF DIVINE HELP FOR WILL AND ACTION.

I also have read those books or writings of his which he mentions in the letter which he sent to Pope Innocent, of blessed memory, with the exception of a brief epistle which he says he sent to the holy Bishop Constantius ; but I have nowhere been able to find in them that he acknowledges such a grace as helps not only that "natural capacity of willing and acting" (which according to him we possess, even when we neither will a good thing nor do it), but also the will and the action itself, by the ministration of the Holy Ghost.

CHAP. 38 [XXXV.] — A DEFINITION OF THE GRACE OF CHRIST BY PELAGIUS.

"Let them read," says he, "the epistle which we wrote about twelve years ago to that holy man Bishop Paulinus : its subject throughout in some three hundred lines is the confession of

[1] Eph. i. 8.          [2] Rom. xii. 3.          [3] Phil. i. 29.

[4] See above, ch. 32 [xxx.] ; compare *De Pecc. Orig.* chs. 5, 6.
[5] 2 Tim. i. 7.

God's grace and assistance alone, and our own inability to do any good thing at all without God." Well, I have read this epistle also, and found him dwelling throughout it on scarcely any other topic than the faculty and capacity of nature, whilst he makes God's grace consist almost entirely· in this. Christ's grace, indeed, he treats with great brevity, simply mentioning its name, so that his only aim seems to have been to avoid the scandal of ignoring it altogether. It is, however, absolutely uncertain whether he means Christ's grace to consist in the remission of sins, or even in the teaching of Christ, including also the example of His life (a meaning which he asserts in several passages of his treatises) ; or whether he believes it to be a help towards good living, in addition to nature and teaching, through the inspiring influence of a burning and shining love.

### CHAP. 39 [XXXVI.] — A LETTER OF PELAGIUS UNKNOWN TO AUGUSTIN.

" Let them also read," says he, " my epistle to the holy Bishop Constantius, wherein I have — briefly no doubt, but yet plainly — conjoined the grace and help of God with man's free will." This epistle, as I have already stated,[1] I have not read ; but if it is not unlike the other writings which he mentions, and with which I am acquainted, even this work does nothing for the subject of our present inquiry.

### CHAP. 40 [XXXVII.] — THE HELP OF GRACE PLACED BY PELAGIUS IN THE MERE REVELATION OF TEACHING.

" Let them read, moreover," says he, " what I wrote,[2] when I was in the East, to Christ's holy virgin Demetrias, and they will find that we so commend the nature of man as always to add the help of God's grace." Well, I read this letter too ; and it had almost persuaded me that he did acknowledge therein the grace about which our discussion is concerned, although he did certainly seem in many passages of this work to contradict himself. But when there also came to my hands those other treatises which he afterwards wrote for more extensive circulation, I discovered in what sense he must have intended to speak of grace, — concealing what he believed under an ambiguous generality, but employing the term " grace " in order to break the force of obloquy, and to avoid giving offence. For at the very commencement of this work (where he says : " Let us apply ourselves with all earnestness to the task which we have set before us, nor let us have any misgiving because of our own humble ability ; for we believe that we are assisted by the mother's

faith and her daughter's merit "[3]) he appeared to me at first to acknowledge the grace which helps us to individual action ; nor did I notice at once the fact that he might possibly have made this grace consist simply in the revelation of teaching.

### CHAP. 41. — RESTORATION OF NATURE UNDERSTOOD BY PELAGIUS AS FORGIVENESS OF SINS.

In this same work he says in another passage : " Now, if even without God men show of what character they have been made by God, see what Christians have it in their power to do, whose nature has been through Christ restored to a better condition, and who are, moreover, assisted by the help of divine grace." [4]  By this restoration of nature to a better state he would have us understand the remission of sins. This he has shown with sufficient clearness in another passage of this epistle, where he says : " Even those who have become in a certain sense obdurate through their long practice of sinning, can be restored through repentance." [5]  But he may even here too make the assistance of divine grace consist in the revelation of teaching.

### CHAP. 42 [XXXVIII.] — GRACE PLACED BY PELAGIUS IN THE REMISSION OF SINS AND THE EXAMPLE OF CHRIST.

Likewise in another place in this epistle of his he says : " Now, if even before the law, as we have already remarked, and long previous to the coming of our Lord and Saviour, some men are related to have lived righteous and holy lives ; how much more worthy of belief is it that we are capable of doing this since the illumination of His coming, who have been restored by the grace of Christ, and born again into a better man? How much better than they, who lived before the law, ought we to be, who have been reconciled and cleansed by His blood, and by His example encouraged to the perfection of righteousness ! " [6]  Observe how even here, although in different language, he has made the assistance of grace to consist in the remission of sins and the example of Christ. He then completes the passage by adding these words : " Better than they were even who lived under the law ; according to the apostle, who says, ' Sin shall not have dominion over you : for ye are not under the law, but under grace.' [7] Now, inasmuch as we have," says he, " said enough, as I suppose, on this point, let us describe a perfect virgin, who shall testify the good at once of nature and of grace by the holiness of her conduct, evermore warmed with the virtues of both." [8]  Now you ought to notice that

---

[1] See above, ch. 37 [xxxiv.].    [2] See above, ch. 23.

[3] Epistle to Demetrias, ch. 1.    [4] Epistle to Demetrias, ch. 3.
[5] Epistle to Demetrias, ch. 17.    [6] Epistle to Demetrias, ch. 8.
[7] Rom. vi. 14.    [8] Epistle to Demetrias, ch. 9.

in these words also he wished to conclude what he was saying in such a way that we might understand the good of nature to be that which we received when we were created; but the good of grace to be that which we receive when we regard and follow the example of Christ, — as if sin were not permitted to those who were or are under the law, on this account, because they either had not Christ's example, or else do not believe in Him.

CHAP. 43 [XXXIX.] — THE FORGIVENESS OF SINS AND EXAMPLE OF CHRIST HELD BY PELAGIUS ENOUGH TO SAVE THE MOST HARDENED SINNER.

That this, indeed, is his meaning, other words also of his show us, — not contained in this work, but in the third book of his *Defence of Free Will,* wherein he holds a discussion with an opponent, who had insisted on the apostle's words when he says, " For what I would, that do I not ; "[1] and again, " I see another law in my members, warring against the law of my mind."[2] To this he replied in these words : " Now that which you wish us to understand of the apostle himself, all Church writers[3] assert that he spoke in the person of the sinner, and of one who was still under the law, — such a man as was, by reason of a very long custom of vice, held bound, as it were, by a certain necessity of sinning, and who, although he desired good with his will, in practice indeed was hurried headlong into evil. In the person, however, of one man," he continues, " the apostle designates the people who still sinned under the ancient law. This nation he declares was to be delivered from this evil of custom through Christ, who first of all remits all sins in baptism to those who believe in Him, and then urges them by an imitation of Himself to perfect holiness, and by the example of His own virtues overcomes the evil custom of their sins." Observe in what way he supposes them to be assisted who sin under the law : they are to be delivered by being justified through Christ's grace, as if the law alone were insufficient for them, without some reinforcement from Christ, owing to their long habit of sinning ; not the inspiration of love by His Holy Spirit, but the contemplation and copy of His example in the inculcation of virtue by the gospel. Now here, at any rate, there was the very greatest call on him to say plainly what grace he meant, seeing that the apostle closed the very passage which formed the ground of discussion with these telling words : " O wretched man that I am, who shall deliver me from the body of this death? The grace of God, through Jesus Christ our Lord."[4] Now, when he places this grace, not in the aid of His power, but in His example for imitation, what further hope must we entertain of him, since everywhere the word " grace " is mentioned by him under an ambiguous generality?

CHAP. 44 [XL.] — PELAGIUS ONCE MORE GUARDS HIMSELF AGAINST THE NECESSITY OF GRACE.

Then, again, in the work addressed to the holy virgin,[5] of which we have spoken already, there is this passage : " Let us submit ourselves to God, and by doing His will let us merit the divine grace ; and let us the more easily, by the help of the Holy Ghost, resist the evil spirit." Now, in these words of his, it is plain enough that he regards us as assisted by the grace of the Holy Ghost, not because we are unable to resist the tempter without Him by the sheer capacity of our nature, but in order that we may resist *more easily.* With respect, however, to the quantity and quality, whatever these might be, of this assistance, we may well believe that he made them consist of the additional knowledge which the Spirit reveals to us through teaching, and which we either cannot, or scarcely can, possess by nature. Such are the particulars which I have been able to discover in the book which he addressed to the virgin of Christ, and wherein he seems to confess grace. Of what purport and kind these are, you of course perceive.

CHAP. 45 [XLI.] — TO WHAT PURPOSE PELAGIUS THOUGHT PRAYERS OUGHT TO BE OFFERED.

" Let them also read," says he, " my recent little treatise which we were obliged to publish a short while ago in defence of free will, and let them acknowledge how unfair is their determination to disparage us for a denial of grace, when we throughout almost the whole work acknowledge fully and sincerely both free will and grace." There are four books in this treatise, all of which I read, marking such passages as required consideration, and which I proposed to discuss : these I examined as well as I was able, before we came to that epistle of his which was sent to Rome. But even in these four books, that which he seems to regard as the grace which helps us to turn aside from evil and to do good, he describes in such a manner as to keep to his old ambiguity of language, and thus have it in his power so to explain to his followers, that they may suppose the assistance which is rendered by grace, for the purpose of helping our natural capacity, consists of nothing else than the law and the teaching. Thus our

---

[1] Rom. vii. 15.    [2] Rom. vii. 23.
[3] By his *ecclesiastici viri* he refers, of course, to ecclesiastical writers who had commented on St. Paul's doctrine. See also Augustin's *Contra duas Epistt. Pelag.* i. 14 [viii.]; *Contra Julianum,* ii. 5 [iii.], 8 [iv.], 13 [v.], 30 [viii.]; and *De Predestinatione Sanctorum,* 4 [iv.].

[4] Rom. vii. 25.
[5] The nun Demetrias. See above, chs. 23, 28.

very prayers (as, indeed, he most plainly affirms in his writings) are of no other use, in his opinion, than to procure for us the explanation of the teaching by a divine revelation, not to procure help for the mind of man to perfect by love and action what it has learned should be done. The fact is, he does not in the least relinquish that very manifest dogma of his system in which he sets forth those three things, capacity, volition, action; maintaining that only the first of these, the capacity, is favoured with the constant assistance of divine help, but supposing that the volition and the action stand in no need of God's assistance. Moreover, the very help which he says assists our natural capacity, he places in the law and teaching. This teaching, he allows, is revealed or explained to us by the Holy Ghost, on which account it is that he concedes the necessity of prayer. But still this assistance of law and teaching he supposes to have existed even in the days of the prophets; whereas the help of grace, which is properly so called, he will have to lie simply in the example of Christ. But this example, you can plainly see, pertains after all to "teaching,"—even that which is preached to us as the gospel. The general result, then, is the pointing out, as it were, of a road to us by which we are bound to walk, by the powers of our free will, and needing no assistance from any one else, may suffice to ourselves not to faint or fail on the way. And even as to the discovery of the road itself, he contends that nature alone is competent for it; only the discovery will be *more* easily effected if grace renders assistance.

### CHAP. 46 [XLII.] — PELAGIUS PROFESSES TO RESPECT THE CATHOLIC AUTHORS.

Such are the particulars which, to the best of my ability, I have succeeded in obtaining from the writings of Pelagius, whenever he makes mention of grace. You perceive, however, that men who entertain such opinions as we have reviewed are "ignorant of God's righteousness, and desire to establish their own,"[1] and are far off from "the righteousness which we have of God"[2] and not of ourselves; and this they ought to have discovered and recognised in the very holy canonical Scriptures. Forasmuch, however, as they read these Scriptures in a sense of their own, they of course fail to observe even the most obvious truths therein. Would that they would but turn their attention in no careless mood to what might be learned concerning the help of God's grace in the writings, at all events, of catholic authors; for they freely allow that the Scriptures were correctly understood by these, and that they would not pass them by

in neglect, out of an overweening fondness for their own opinions. For note how this very man Pelagius, in that very treatise of his so recently put forth, and which he formally mentions in his self-defence (that is to say, in the third book of his *Defence of Free Will*), praises St. Ambrose.

### CHAP. 47 [XLIII.] — AMBROSE MOST HIGHLY PRAISED BY PELAGIUS.

"The blessed Bishop Ambrose," says he, "in whose writings the Roman faith shines forth with especial brightness, and whom the Latins have always regarded as the very flower and glory of their authors, and who has never found a foe bold enough to censure his faith or the purity of his understanding of the Scriptures." Observe the sort as well as the amount of the praises which he bestows; nevertheless, however holy and learned he is, he is not to be compared to the authority of the canonical Scripture. The reason of this high commendation of Ambrose lies in the circumstance, that Pelagius sees proper to quote a certain passage from his writings to prove that man is able to live without sin.[3] This, however, is not the question before us. We are at present discussing that assistance of grace which helps us towards avoiding sin, and leading holy lives.

### CHAP. 48 [XLIV]. — AMBROSE IS NOT IN AGREEMENT WITH PELAGIUS.

I wish, indeed, that he would listen to the venerable bishop when, in the second book of his *Exposition of the Gospel according to Luke*,[4] he expressly teaches us that the Lord co-operates also with our wills. "You see, therefore," says he, "because the power of the Lord co-operates everywhere with human efforts, that no man is able to build without the Lord, no man to watch without the Lord, no man to undertake anything without the Lord. Whence the apostle thus enjoins: 'Whether ye eat, or whether ye drink, do all to the glory of God.'"[5] You observe how the holy Ambrose takes away from men even their familiar expressions,—such as, "We undertake, but God accomplishes,"—when he says here that "no man is able to undertake anything without the Lord." To the same effect he says, in the sixth book of the same work,[6] treating of the two debtors of a certain creditor: "According to men's opinions, he perhaps is the greater offender who owed most. The case, however, is altered by the Lord's mercy, so that he loves the most who owes the most, if he yet obtains grace." See how the catholic doctor most plainly declares that the very love which prompts every

---

[1] Rom. x. 3.      [2] Phil. iii. 9.

[3] See *On Nature and Grace*, above, ch. 74.
[4] Book ii. c. 84, on Luke iii. 22. Compare *Against Two Letters of the Pelagians*, below, iv. ch. 30.
[5] 1 Cor. x. 31.      [6] Book vi. c. 25, on Luke vii. 41.

man to an ampler love appertains to the kindly gift of grace.

CHAP. 49 [XLV.] — AMBROSE TEACHES WITH WHAT EYE CHRIST TURNED AND LOOKED UPON PETER.

That repentance, indeed, itself, which beyond all doubt is an action of the will, is wrought into action by the mercy and help of the Lord, is asserted by the blessed Ambrose in the following passage in the ninth book of the same work:[1] "Good," says he, "are the tears which wash away sin. They upon whom the Lord at last turns and looks, bewail. Peter denied Him first, and did not weep, because the Lord had not turned and looked upon him. He denied Him a second time, and still wept not, because the Lord had not even yet turned and looked upon him. The third time also he denied Him, Jesus turned and looked, and then he wept most bitterly." Let these persons read the Gospel; let them consider how that the Lord Jesus was at that moment within, having a hearing before the chief of the priests; whilst the Apostle Peter was outside,[2] and down in the hall,[3] sitting at one time with the servants at the fire,[4] at another time standing,[5] as the most accurate and consistent narrative of the evangelists shows. It cannot therefore be said that it was with His bodily eyes that the Lord turned and looked upon him by a visible and apparent admonition. That, then, which is described in the words, "The Lord turned and looked upon Peter,"[6] was effected internally; it was wrought in the mind, wrought in the will. In mercy the Lord silently and secretly approached, touched the heart, recalled the memory of the past, with His own internal grace visited Peter, stirred and brought out into external tears the feelings of his inner man. Behold in what manner God is present with His help to our wills and actions; behold how "He worketh in us both to will and to do."

CHAP. 50. — AMBROSE TEACHES THAT ALL MEN NEED GOD'S HELP.

In the same book the same St. Ambrose says again:[7] "Now if Peter fell, who said, 'Though all men shall be offended, yet will I never be offended,' who else shall rightly presume concerning himself? David, indeed, because he had said, 'In my prosperity I said, I shall never be moved,' confesses how injurious his confidence had proved to himself: 'Thou didst turn away Thy face,' he says, 'and I was troubled.'"[8] Pelagius ought to listen to the teaching of so eminent a man, and should follow his faith, since he has commended his teaching and faith. Let him listen humbly; let him follow with fidelity; let him indulge no longer in obstinate presumption, lest he perish. Why does Pelagius choose to be sunk in that sea whence Peter was rescued by the Rock?[9]

CHAP. 51 [XLVI.] — AMBROSE TEACHES THAT IT IS GOD THAT DOES FOR MAN WHAT PELAGIUS ATTRIBUTES TO FREE WILL.

Let him lend an ear also to the same godly bishop, who says, in the sixth book of this same book:[10] "The reason why they would not receive Him is mentioned by the evangelist himself in these words, 'Because His face was as though He would go to Jerusalem.'[11] But His disciples had a strong wish that He should be received into the Samaritan town. God, however, calls whomsoever He deigns, and whom He wills He makes religious." What wise insight of the man of God, drawn from the very fountain of God's grace! "God," says he, "calls whomsoever He deigns, and whom He wills He makes religious." See whether this is not the prophet's own declaration: "I will have mercy on whom I will have mercy, and will show pity on whom I will be pitiful;"[12] and the apostle's deduction therefrom: "So then," says he, "it is not of him that willeth, nor of him that runneth, but of God that showeth mercy."[13] Now, when even his model man of our own times says, that "whomsoever God deigns He calls, and whom He wills He makes religious," will any one be bold enough to contend that that man is not yet religious "who hastens to the Lord, and desires to be directed by Him, and makes his own will depend upon God's; who, moreover, cleaves so closely to the Lord, that he becomes (as the apostle says) 'one spirit' with Him?"[14] Great, however, as is this entire work of a "religious man," Pelagius maintains that "it is effected only by the freedom of the will." But his own blessed Ambrose, whom he so highly commends in word, is against him, saying, "The Lord God calls whomsoever He deigns, and whom He wills He makes religious." It is God, then, who makes religious whomsoever He pleases, in order that he may "hasten to the Lord, and desire to be directed by Him, and make his own will depend upon God's, and cleave so closely to the Lord as to become (as the apostle says) 'one spirit' with Him;" and all this none but a religious man does. Who, then, ever does so much, unless he be made by God to do it?

---

[1] "In the *ninth* book of the same work," says St. Augustin. The reference, however, is to book x. of the editions, c. 89, on Luke xxii. 61.
[2] Matt. xxvi. 69, 71.    [3] Mark xiv. 66.    [4] Luke xxii. 55.
[5] John xviii. 16.    [6] Luke xxii. 61.    [7] Book x. c. 89.
[8] Ps. xxx. 7.

[9] It is impossible to preserve the paronomasia of the original, which plays on the meaning of the names *Pelagius* (*pelago*, sea) and *Petrus* (*petra*, rock).
[10] It is the *seventh* book in the editions, c. 27, on Luke ix. 53.
[11] Luke ix. 53.    [12] Ex. xxxiii. 19.    [13] Rom. ix. 16.
[14] 1 Cor. vi. 17. These are the words of Pelagius, which have been already quoted above, in ch. 24.

CHAP. 52 [XLVII.] — IF PELAGIUS AGREES WITH AMBROSE, AUGUSTIN HAS NO CONTROVERSY WITH HIM.

Inasmuch, however, as the discussion about free will and God's grace has such difficulty in its distinctions, that when free will is maintained, God's grace is apparently denied; whilst when God's grace is asserted, free will is supposed to be done away with, — Pelagius can so involve himself in the shades of this obscurity as to profess agreement with all that we have quoted from St. Ambrose, and declare that such is, and always has been, his opinion also; and endeavour so to explain each, that men may suppose his opinion, to be in fair accord with Ambrose's. So far, therefore, as concerns the questions of God's help and grace, you are requested to observe the three things which he has distinguished so very plainly, under the terms "ability," "will," and "actuality," that is, "capacity," "volition," and "action." [1] If, then, he has come round to an agreement with us, then not the "capacity" alone in man, even if he neither wills nor performs the good, but the volition and the action also, — in other words, our willing well and doing well, — things which have no existence in man, except when he has a good will and acts rightly: — if, I repeat, he thus consents to hold with us, that even the volition and the action are assisted by God, and so assisted that we can neither will nor do any good thing without such help; if, too, he believes that this is that very grace of God through our Lord Jesus Christ which makes us righteous through His righteousness, and not our own, so that our true righteousness is that which we have of Him, — then, so far as I can judge, there will remain no further controversy between us concerning the assistance we have from the grace of God.

CHAP. 53 [XLVIII.] — IN WHAT SENSE SOME MEN MAY BE SAID TO LIVE WITHOUT SIN IN THE PRESENT LIFE.

But in reference to the particular point in which he quoted the holy Ambrose with so much approbation, — because he found in that author's writings, from the praises he accorded to Zacharias and Elisabeth, the opinion that a man might possibly in this life be without sin; [2] although this cannot be denied if God wills it, with whom all things are possible, yet he ought to consider more carefully *in what sense* this was said. Now, so far as I can see, this statement was made in accordance with a certain standard of conduct, which is among men held to be worthy of approval and praise, and which no human being could justly call in question for the purpose of laying accusation or censure.

Such a standard Zacharias and his wife Elisabeth are said to have maintained in the sight of God, for no other reason than that they, by walking therein, never deceived people by any dissimulation; but as they in their sincerity appeared to men, so were they known in the sight of God. [3] The statement, however, was not made with any reference to that perfect state of righteousness in which we shall one day live truly and absolutely in a condition of spotless purity. The Apostle Paul, indeed, has told us that he was "blameless, as touching the righteousness which is of the law;" [4] and it was in respect of the same law that Zacharias also lived a blameless life. This righteousness, however, the apostle counted as "dung" and "loss," in comparison with the righteousness which is the object of our hope, [5] and which we ought to "hunger and thirst after," [6] in order that hereafter we may be satisfied with the vision thereof, enjoying it now by faith, so long as "the just do live by faith." [7]

CHAP. 54 [XLIX.] — AMBROSE TEACHES THAT NO ONE IS SINLESS IN THIS WORLD.

Lastly, let him give good heed to his venerable bishop, when he is expounding the Prophet Isaiah, [8] and says that "no man in this world can be without sin." Now nobody can pretend to say that by the phrase "*in this world*" he simply meant, in the love of this world. For he was speaking of the apostle, who said, "Our conversation is in heaven;" [9] and while unfolding the sense of these words, the eminent bishop expressed himself thus: "Now the apostle says that many men, even while living in the present world, are perfect with themselves, who could not possibly be deemed perfect, if one looks at true perfection. For he says himself: 'We now see through a glass, darkly; but then face to face: now I know in part; but then shall I know, even as also I am known.' [10] Thus, there are those who are spotless in this world, there are those who will be spotless in the kingdom of God; although, of course, if you sift the thing minutely, no one could be spotless, because no one is without sin." That passage, then, of the holy Ambrose, which Pelagius applies in support of his own opinion, was either written in a qualified sense, probable, indeed, but not expressed with minute accuracy; or if the holy and lowly-minded author did think that Zacharias and Elisabeth lived according to the highest and abso-

---

[1] See above, ch. 4.  [2] Ambrose on St. Luke, Book i. c. 17.

[3] Luke i. 6; compare *De Perfect. Just.* ch. 38.
[4] Phil. iii. 6.  [5] Phil. iii. 8.  [6] Matt. v. 6.
[7] Rom. i. 17.
[8] This work of Ambrose is no longer extant. It is again quoted by Augustin in his work, *De Peccato Originali*, c. 47 [xli.]; in his *De Nuptiis et Concupisc.* i. 40 [xxxv.]; in his *Contra Julianum*, i. 11 [iv.], ii. 24 [viii.]; and in his *Contra duas Epist. Pelagianorum*, c. 30 [xi.]. Ambrose himself mentions this work of his in his *Exposition of Luke*, Book ii. c. 56, on Luke ii. 19.
[9] Phil. iii. 20.  [10] 1 Cor. xiii. 13.

lutely perfect righteousness, which was incapable of increase or addition, he certainly corrected his opinion on a minuter examination of it.

CHAP. 55 [L.] — AMBROSE WITNESSES THAT PER-FECT PURITY IS IMPOSSIBLE TO HUMAN NATURE.

He ought, moreover, carefully to note that, in the very same context from which he quoted that passage of Ambrose's, which seemed so satisfactory for his purpose, he also said this: "To be spotless from the beginning is an im-possibility to human nature."[1]   In this sentence the venerable Ambrose does undoubtedly predi-cate feebleness and infirmity of that natural "capacity," which Pelagius refuses faithfully to regard as corrupted by sin, and therefore boast-fully extols.   Beyond question, this runs counter to this man's will and inclination, although it does not contravene the truthful confession of the apostle, wherein he says: "We too were once by nature the children of wrath, even as others."[2]   For through the sin of the first man, which came from his free will, our nature became corrupted and ruined; and nothing but God's grace alone, through Him who is the Mediator between God and men, and our Al-mighty Physician, succours it.   Now, since we have already prolonged this work too far in treat-ing of the assistance of the divine grace towards our justification, by which God co-operates in all things for good with those who love Him,[3] and whom He first loved[4] — giving to them that He might receive from them: we must commence another treatise, as the Lord shall enable us, on the subject of sin also, which by one man has entered into the world, along with death, and so has passed upon all men,[5] setting forth as much as shall seem needful and suffi-cient, in opposition to those persons who have broken out into violent and open error, contrary to the truth here stated.

---

[1] See Augustin, above, *De Naturâ et Gratiâ,* c. 75 [lxiii.].

[2] Eph. ii. 3.     [3] Rom. viii. 28.     [4] 1 John iv. 19.
[5] Rom. v. 12.

# BOOK II.

## *ON ORIGINAL SIN.*

WHEREIN AUGUSTIN SHOWS THAT PELAGIUS REALLY DIFFERS IN NO RESPECT, ON
THE QUESTION OF ORIGINAL SIN AND THE BAPTISM OF INFANTS, FROM HIS FOL-
LOWER CŒLESTIUS, WHO, REFUSING TO ACKNOWLEDGE ORIGINAL SIN AND EVEN
DARING TO DENY THE DOCTRINE IN PUBLIC, WAS CONDEMNED IN TRIALS BEFORE
THE BISHOPS — FIRST AT CARTHAGE, AND AFTERWARDS AT ROME; FOR THIS
QUESTION IS NOT, AS THESE HERETICS WOULD HAVE IT, ONE WHEREIN PERSONS
MIGHT ERR WITHOUT DANGER TO THE FAITH. THEIR HERESY, INDEED, AIMED
AT NOTHING ELSE THAN THE VERY FOUNDATIONS OF CHRISTIAN BELIEF. HE
AFTERWARDS REFUTES ALL SUCH AS MAINTAINED THAT THE BLESSING OF
MATRIMONY IS DISPARAGED BY THE DOCTRINE OF ORIGINAL DEPRAVITY, AND
AN INJURY DONE TO GOD HIMSELF, THE CREATOR OF MAN WHO IS BORN BY
MEANS OF MATRIMONY.

CHAP. 1 [I.] — CAUTION NEEDED IN ATTENDING TO PELAGIUS' DELIVERANCES ON INFANT BAPTISM.

NEXT I beg of you,[1] carefully to observe with what caution you ought to lend an ear, on the question of the baptism of infants, to men of this character, who dare not openly deny the laver of regeneration and the forgiveness of sins to this early age, for fear that Christian ears would not bear to listen to them; and who yet persist in holding and urging their opinion, that the carnal generation is not held guilty of man's first sin, although they seem to allow infants to be baptized for the remission of sins. You have, indeed, yourselves informed me in your letter, that you heard Pelagius say in your presence, reading out of that book of his which he declared that he had also sent to Rome, that they maintain that "infants ought to be baptized with the same formula of sacramental words as adults."[2] Who, after that statement, would suppose that one ought to raise any question at all on this subject? Or if he did, to whom would he not seem to indulge a very calumnious disposition — previous to the perusal of their plain assertions, in which they deny that infants inherit original sin, and contend that all persons are born free from all corruption?

CHAP. 2 [II.] — CŒLESTIUS, ON HIS TRIAL AT CARTHAGE, REFUSES TO CONDEMN HIS ERROR; THE WRITTEN STATEMENT WHICH HE GAVE TO ZOSIMUS.

Cœlestius, indeed, maintained this erroneous doctrine with less restraint. To such an extent did he push his freedom as actually to refuse, when on trial before the bishops at Carthage,[3] to condemn those who say, "That Adam's sin injured only Adam himself, and not the human race; and that infants at their birth are in the same state that Adam was in before his transgression."[4] In the written statement, too, which he presented to the most blessed Pope Zosimus at Rome, he declared with especial plainness, "that original sin binds no single infant." Concerning the ecclesiastical proceedings at Carthage we copy the following account of his words.

CHAP. 3 [III.] — PART OF THE PROCEEDINGS OF THE COUNCIL OF CARTHAGE AGAINST CŒLESTIUS.

"The bishop Aurelius said: 'Let what follows be recited.' It was accordingly recited, 'That the sin of Adam was injurious to him alone, and not to the human race.' Then, after the recital, Cœlestius said: 'I said that I was in doubt about the transmission of sin,[5] but so as to yield assent

---

[1] For the persons addressed, see above, in Book i. c. 1, of *On the Grace of Christ.*
[2] See above, *On the Grace of Christ,* ch. 35.

[3] See *Concerning the Proceedings of Pelagius,* ch. 23.
[4] Pelagius, at Diospolis, condemned this position of Cœlestius. Hence the comparative restraint of Pelagius, and the greater freedom in holding the error which is here attributed to Cœlestius.
[5] *De traduce peccati,* the technical phrase to express the conveyance by birth of original sin.

to any man whom God has gifted with the grace of knowledge; for I have heard different opinions from those who have been even appointed presbyters in the Catholic Church.' The deacon Paulinus[1] said: 'Tell us their names.' Cœlestius answered: 'The holy presbyter Rufinus,[2] who lived at Rome with the holy Pammachius. I have heard him declare that there is no transmission of sin.' The deacon Paulinus then asked: 'Is there any one else?' Cœlestius replied: 'I have heard more say the same.' The deacon Paulinus rejoined: 'Tell us their names.' Cœlestius said: 'Is not one priest enough for you?'" Then afterwards in another place we read: "The bishop Aurelius said: 'Let the rest of the accusation be read.' It then was recited 'That infants at their birth are in the same state that Adam was before the transgression;' and they read to the very end of the brief accusation which had been previously put in. [IV.] The bishop Aurelius inquired: 'Have you, Cœlestius, taught at any time, as the deacon Paulinus has stated, that infants are at their birth in the same state that Adam was before his transgression?' Cœlestius answered: 'Let him explain what he meant when he said, "*before the transgression*."' The deacon Paulinus then said: 'Do you on your side deny that you ever taught this doctrine? It must be one of two things: he must either say that he never so taught, or else he must now condemn the opinion.' Cœlestius rejoined: 'I have already said, Let him explain the words he mentioned, "*before the transgression*."' The deacon Paulinus then said: 'You must deny ever having taught this.' The bishop Aurelius said: 'I ask, What conclusion I have on my part to draw from this man's obstinacy; my affirmation is, that although Adam, as created in Paradise, is said to have been made immortal at first, he afterwards became corruptible through transgressing the commandment. Do you say this, brother Paulinus?' 'I do, my lord,' answered the deacon Paulinus. Then the bishop Aurelius said: 'As regards the condition of infants before baptism at the present day, the

deacon Paulinus wishes to be informed whether it is such as Adam's was before the transgression; and whether it derives the guilt of transgression from the same origin of sin from which it is born?' The deacon Paulinus asked: 'Let him deny whether he taught this, or not.' Cœlestius answered: 'As touching the transmission of sin, I have already asserted, that I have heard many persons of acknowledged position in the catholic Church deny it altogether; and on the other hand, others affirm it: it may be fairly deemed a matter for inquiry, but not a heresy. I have always maintained that infants require baptism, and ought to be baptized. What else does he want?'"

## CHAP. 4. — CŒLESTIUS CONCEDES BAPTISM FOR INFANTS, WITHOUT AFFIRMING ORIGINAL SIN.

You, of course, see that Cœlestius here conceded baptism for infants only in such a manner as to be unwilling to confess that the sin of the first man, which is washed away in the laver of regeneration, passes over to them, although at the same time he did not venture to deny this; and on account of this doubt he refused to condemn those who maintain "That Adam's sin injured only himself, and not the human race;" and "that infants at their birth are in the same condition wherein Adam was before the transgression."

## CHAP. 5 [V.] — CŒLESTIUS' BOOK WHICH WAS PRODUCED IN THE PROCEEDINGS AT ROME.

But in the book which he published at Rome, and produced in the proceedings before the church there, he so speaks on this question as to show that he really believes what he had professed to be in doubt about. For these are his words:[3] "That infants, however, ought to be baptized for the remission of sins, according to the rule of the Church universal, and according to the meaning of the Gospel, we confess. For the Lord has determined that the kingdom of heaven should only be conferred on baptized persons;[4] and since the resources of nature do not possess it, it must necessarily be conferred by the gift of grace." Now if he had not said anything elsewhere on this subject, who would not have supposed that he acknowledged the remission of original sin even in infants at their baptism, by saying that they ought to be baptized for the remission of sins? Hence the point of what you have stated in your letter, that Pelagius' answer to you was on this wise, "That infants are baptized with the same words of sacramental formula as adults," and that you were rejoiced to hear the very thing which you were desirous of hearing,

---

[1] This Paulinus, according to Mercator (*Commonit. super nomine Cœlestii*), was the deacon of Ambrose, Bishop of Milan, and the author of his biography, which he wrote at the instance of Augustin. According to his own showing, he lived in Africa, and wrote the *Life of Ambrose* when John was pretorian prefect, *i.e.* either in the year 412, or 413, or 422. The trial mentioned in the text took place about the commencement of the year 412, according to Augustin's letter to Pope Innocent (See above, in the letter, 175, 1. 6). See above, in the treatise *On the Proceedings of Pelagius*, 23.

[2] Mercator (*Commonit. adv. Hæres. Pelagii*) informs us that a certain Syrian called Rufinus introduced the discussion against original sin and its transmission into Rome in the pontificate of Anastasius. According to some, this was the Rufinus of Aquileia, whom Jerome (*in Epist. ad Ctesiphont.*) notices as the precursor of Pelagius in his error about the sinless nature of man; according, however, to others, it is the other Rufinus, mentioned by Jerome in his 66th Epistle, who is possibly the same as he who rejects the transmission of original sin in a treatise *On Faith*, which J. Sismondi published as the work of Rufinus, a presbyter of the province of Palestine. It is, at any rate, hardly possible to suppose that the Aquileian Rufinus either went to Rome, or lodged there with Pammachius, in the time of Pope Anastasius.

[3] See above, *On the Grace of Christ*, ch. 36.  [4] John iii. 5.

and yet that you preferred holding a consultation with us concerning his words.

### CHAP. 6 [VI.] — CŒLESTIUS THE DISCIPLE IS IN THIS WORK BOLDER THAN HIS MASTER.

Carefully observe, then, what Cœlestius has advanced so very openly, and you will discover what amount of concealment Pelagius has practised upon you. Cœlestius goes on to say as follows: "That infants, however, must be baptized for the remission of sins, was not admitted by us with the view of our seeming to affirm sin by transmission. This is very alien from the catholic meaning, because sin is not born with a man, — it is subsequently committed by the man : for it is shown to be a fault, not of nature, but of the will. It is fitting, therefore, to confess this, lest we should seem to make different kinds of baptism ; it is, moreover, necessary to lay down this preliminary safeguard, lest by the occasion of this mystery evil should, to the disparagement of the Creator, be said to be conveyed to man by nature, before that it has been committed by man." Now Pelagius was either afraid or ashamed to avow this to be his own opinion before you ; although his disciple experienced neither a qualm nor a blush in openly professing it to be his, without any obscure subterfuges, in presence of the Apostolic See.

### CHAP. 7. — POPE ZOSIMUS KINDLY EXCUSES HIM.

The bishop, however, who presides over this See, upon seeing him hurrying headlong in so great presumption like a madman, chose in his great compassion, with a view to the man's repentance, if it might be, rather to bind him tightly by eliciting from him answers to questions proposed by himself, than by the stroke of a severe condemnation to drive him over the precipice, down which he seemed to be even now ready to fall. I say advisedly, "down which he seemed to be ready to fall," rather than "over which he had actually fallen," because he had already in this same book of his forecast the subject with an intended reference to questions of this sort in the following words : "If it should so happen that any error of ignorance has stolen over us human beings, let it be corrected by your decisive sentence."

### CHAP. 8 [VII.] — CŒLESTIUS CONDEMNED BY ZOSIMUS.

The venerable Pope Zosimus, keeping in view this deprecatory preamble, dealt with the man, puffed up as he was with the blasts of false doctrine, so as that he should condemn all the objectionable points which had been alleged against him by the deacon Paulinus, and that he should yield his assent to the rescript of the Apostolic See which had been issued by his pred-

ecessor of sacred memory. The accused man, however, refused to condemn the objections raised by the deacon, yet he did not dare to hold out against the letter of the blessed Pope Innocent ; indeed, he went so far as to " promise that he would condemn all the points which the Apostolic See condemned." Thus the man was treated with gentle remedies, as a delirious patient who required rest ; but, at the same time, he was not regarded as being yet ready to be released from the restraints of excommunication. The interval of two months being granted him, until communications could be received from Africa, a place for recovery was conceded to him, under the mild restorative of the sentence which had been pronounced. For in truth, if he would have laid aside his vain obstinacy, and be now willing to carry out what he had undertaken, and would carefully read the very letter to which he had replied by promising submission, he would yet come to a better mind. But after the rescripts were duly issued from the council of the African bishops, there were very good reasons why the sentence should be carried out against him, in strictest accordance with equity. What these reasons were you may read for yourselves, for we have sent you all the particulars.

### CHAP. 9 [VIII.] — PELAGIUS DECEIVED THE COUNCIL IN PALESTINE, BUT WAS UNABLE TO DECEIVE THE CHURCH AT ROME.

Wherefore Pelagius, too, if he will only reflect candidly on his own position and writings, has no reason for saying that he ought not to have been banned with such a sentence. For although he deceived the council in Palestine, seemingly clearing himself before it, he entirely failed in imposing on the church at Rome (where, as you well know, he is by no means a stranger), although he went so far as to make the attempt, if he might somehow succeed. But, as I have just said, he entirely failed. For the most blessed Pope Zosimus recollected what his predecessor, who had set him so worthy an example, had thought of these very proceedings. Nor did he omit to observe what opinion was entertained about this man by the trusty Romans, whose faith deserved to be spoken of in the Lord,[1] and whose consistent zeal in defence of catholic truth against this heresy he saw prevailing amongst them with warmth, and at the same time most perfect harmony. The man had lived among them for a long while, and his opinions could not escape their notice ; moreover, they had so completely found out his disciple Cœlestius, as to be able at once to adduce the most trustworthy and irrefragable evidence

---

[1] Rom. i. 8.

on this subject. Now what was the solemn judgment which the holy Pope Innocent formed respecting the proceedings in the Synod of Palestine, by which Pelagius boasts of having been acquitted, you may indeed read in the letter which he addressed to me. It is duly mentioned also in the answer which was forwarded by the African Synod to the venerable Pope Zosimus, and which, along with the other instructions, we have despatched to your loving selves.[1] But it seems to me, at the same time, that I ought not to omit producing the particulars in the present work.

CHAP. 10 [IX.] — THE JUDGMENT OF INNOCENT RESPECTING THE PROCEEDINGS IN PALESTINE.

Five bishops, then, of whom I was one, wrote him a letter,[2] wherein we mentioned the proceedings in Palestine, of which the report had already reached us. We informed him that in the East, where this man lived, there had taken place certain ecclesiastical proceedings, in which he was thought to have been acquitted on all the charges. To this communication from us Innocent replied in a letter which contains the following among other words: "There are," says he, "sundry positions, as stated in these very Proceedings, which, when they were objected against him, he partly suppressed by avoiding them, and partly confused in absolute obscurity, by wresting the sense of many words; whilst there are other allegations which he cleared off, — not, indeed, in the honest way which he might seem at the time to use, but rather by methods of sophistry, meeting some of the objections with a flat denial, and tampering with others by a fallacious interpretation. Would, however, that he would even now adopt what is the far more desirable course of turning from his own error back to the true ways of catholic faith; that he would also, duly considering God's daily grace, and acknowledging the help thereof, be willing and desirous to appear, amidst the approbation of all men, to be truly corrected by the method of open conviction, — not, indeed, by judicial process, but by a hearty conversion to the catholic faith. We are therefore unable either to approve of or to blame their proceedings at that trial; for we cannot tell whether the proceedings were true, or even, if true, whether they do not really show that the man escaped by subterfuge, rather than that he cleared himself by entire truth."[3] You see clearly from these words, how that the most blessed Pope Innocent without doubt speaks of this man as of one who was by no means unknown to him.

You see what opinion he entertained about his acquittal. You see, moreover, what his successor the holy Pope Zosimus was bound to recollect, — as in truth he did, — so as to confirm without hesitation the judgment of his predecessor in this case.

CHAP. 11 [X.] — HOW THAT PELAGIUS DECEIVED THE SYNOD OF PALESTINE.

Now I pray you carefully to observe by what evidence Pelagius is shown to have deceived his judges in Palestine, not to mention other points, on this very question of the baptism of infants, lest we should seem to any one to have used calumny and suspicion, rather than to have ascertained the certain fact, when we alleged that Pelagius concealed the opinion which Cœlestius expressed with greater frankness, while at the same time he actually entertained the same views. Now, from what has been stated above, it has been clearly seen that Cœlestius refused to condemn the assertion that "Adam's sin injured only himself, and not the human race, and that infants at their birth are in the same state that Adam was before the transgression," because he saw that, if he condemned these propositions, he would affirm that there was in infants a transmission of sin from Adam. When, however, it was objected to Pelagius that he was of one mind with Cœlestius on this point, he condemned the words without hesitation. I am quite aware that you have read all this before. Since, however, we are not writing this account for you alone, we proceed to transcribe the very words of the synodal acts, lest the reader should be unwilling either to turn to the record for himself, or if he does not possess it, take the trouble to procure a copy. Here, then, are the words: —

CHAP. 12 [XI.] — A PORTION OF THE PROCEEDINGS OF THE SYNOD OF PALESTINE IN THE CAUSE OF PELAGIUS.

"The synod said:[4] Now, forasmuch as Pelagius has pronounced his anathema on this uncertain utterance of folly, rightly replying that a man by God's help and grace is able to live ἀναμάρτητος, that is to say, without sin, let him give us his answer on other articles also. Another particular in the teaching of Cœlestius, disciple of Pelagius, selected from the heads which were mentioned and heard at Carthage before the holy Aurelius bishop of Carthage, and other bishops, was to this effect: 'That Adam was made mortal, and that he would have died, whether he sinned or did not sin; that Adam's sin injured himself alone, and not the human race; that the law no less than the gospel leads us to the kingdom; that before the coming of

---

[1] Albina, Pinianus, and Melania. Literally, they are here addressed as "your Love."
[2] *Epistle* 177, in the collection of Augustin's letters.
[3] Innocent's letter occurs amongst *the epistles of Augustin,* letter 183. 3, 4.

[4] Compare *On the Proceedings of Pelagius*, chs. 16, 23.

Christ there were persons without sin; that new-born infants are in the same condition that Adam was before the transgression; that, on the one hand, the entire human race does not die on account of Adam's death and transgression, nor, on the other hand, does the whole human race rise again through the resurrection of Christ; that the holy bishop Augustin wrote a book in answer to his followers in Sicily, on articles which were subjoined, and in this book, which was addressed to Hilary, are contained the following statements: That a man is able to be without sin if he wishes; that infants, even if they are unbaptized, have eternal life; that rich men, even if they are baptized, unless they renounce and give up all, have, whatever good they may seem to have done, nothing of it reckoned unto them, neither can they possess the kingdom of heaven.' Pelagius then said: As regards man's ability to be without sin, my opinion has been already spoken. With respect, however, to the allegation that there were even before the Lord's coming persons who lived without sin, we also on our part say, that before the coming of Christ there certainly were persons who passed their lives in holiness and righteousness, according to the accounts which have been handed down to us in the Holy Scriptures. As for the other points, indeed, even on their own showing, they are not of a character which obliges me to be answerable for them; but yet, for the satisfaction of the sacred Synod, I anathematize those who either now hold or have ever held these opinions."

CHAP. 13 [XII.] — CŒLESTIUS THE BOLDER HERE-TIC; PELAGIUS THE MORE SUBTLE.

You see, indeed, not to mention other points, how that Pelagius pronounced his anathema against those who hold that "Adam's sin injured only himself, and not the human race; and that infants are at their birth in the same condition in which Adam was before the transgression." Now what else could the bishops who sat in judgment on him have possibly understood him to mean by this, but that the sin of Adam is transmitted to infants? It was to avoid making such an admission that Cœlestius refused to con-demn this statement, which this man on the contrary anathematized. If, therefore, I shall show that he did not really entertain any other opinion concerning infants than that they are born without any contagion of a single sin, what difference will there remain on this question be-tween him and Cœlestius, except this, that the one is more open, the other more reserved; the one more pertinacious, the other more menda-cious; or, at any rate, that the one is more candid, the other more astute? For, the one before the church of Carthage refused to con-

demn what he afterwards in the church at Rome publicly confessed to be a tenet of his own; at the same time professing himself "ready to sub-mit to correction if an error had stolen over him, considering that he was but human;" whereas the other both condemned this dogma as being contrary to the truth lest he should himself be condemned by his catholic judges, and yet kept it in reserve for subsequent defence, so that either his condemnation was a lie, or his interpretation a trick.

CHAP. 14 [XIII.] — HE SHOWS THAT, EVEN AFTER THE SYNOD OF PALESTINE, PELAGIUS HELD THE SAME OPINIONS AS CŒLESTIUS ON THE SUBJECT OF ORIGINAL SIN.

I see, however, that it may be most justly de-manded of me, that I do not defer my promised demonstration, that he actually entertains the same views as Cœlestius. In the first book of his more recent work, written in defence of free will (which work he mentions in the letter he despatched to Rome), he says: "Everything good, and everything evil, on account of which we are either laudable or blameworthy, is not born with us but done by us: for we are born not fully developed, but with a capacity for either conduct; and we are procreated as without virtue, so also without vice; and previous to the action of our own proper will, that alone is in man which God has formed." Now you perceive that in these words of Pelagius, the dogma of both these men is contained, that infants are born without the contagion of any sin from Adam. It is therefore not astonishing that Cœlestius refused to condemn such as say that Adam's sin injured only himself, and not the human race; and that infants are at their birth in the same state in which Adam was before the transgression. But it is very much to be wondered at, that Pelagius had the effrontery to anathematize these opinions. For if, as he alleges, "evil is not born with us, and we are procreated without fault, and the only thing in man previous to the action of his own will is what God has formed," then of course the sin of Adam did only injure himself, inasmuch as it did not pass on to his offspring. For there is not any sin which is not an evil; or a sin that is not a fault; or else sin was created by God. But he says: "Evil is not born with us, and we are procreated without fault; and the only thing in men at their birth is what God has formed." Now, since by this language he supposes it to be most true, that, according to the well-known sentence of his: "Adam's sin was injurious to himself alone, and not to the human race," why did Pelagius condemn this, if it were not for the purpose of deceiving his catholic judges? By parity of reasoning, it may also be argued: "If evil is not born with us, and if we are procreated without fault, and if the only thing found in man at the time of his birth is what God has formed," it follows beyond a doubt that "infants at their birth are in the same condition that Adam was before the transgression," in whom no evil or fault was inherent, and in whom that alone existed which God had formed. And yet Pelagius pronounced anathema on all those persons "who hold now, or have at any time held, that new-born babes are placed by their birth in the same state that Adam was in before the transgression," —in other words, are without any evil, without any fault, having that only which God had formed. Now, why again did Pelagius condemn this tenet also, if it were not for the purpose of deceiving the catholic Synod, and saving himself from the condemnation of an heretical innovator?

CHAP. 15 [XIV.] — PELAGIUS BY HIS MENDACITY AND DECEPTION STOLE HIS ACQUITTAL FROM THE SYNOD IN PALESTINE.

For my own part, however, I, as you are quite aware, and as I also stated in the book which I addressed to our venerable and aged Aurelius on the proceedings in Palestine, really felt glad that Pelagius in that answer of his had exhausted the whole of this question.[1] To me, indeed, he seemed most plainly to have acknowledged that there is original sin in infants, by the anathema which he pronounced against those persons who supposed that by the sin of Adam only himself, and not the human race, was injured, and who entertained the opinion that infants are in the same state in which the first man was before the transgression. When, however, I had read his four books (from the first of which I copied the words which I have just now quoted), and discovered that he was still cherishing thoughts which were opposed to the catholic faith touching infants, I felt all the greater surprise at a mendacity which he so unblushingly maintained in a synod of the Church, and on so great a question. For if he had already written these books, how did he profess to anathematize those who had ever entertained the opinions alluded to? If he purposed, however, afterwards to publish such a work, how could he anathematize those who at the time were holding the opinions? Unless, to be sure, by some ridiculous subterfuge he meant to say that the objects of his anathema were such persons as had in some previous time held, or were then holding, these opinions; but that in respect of the future — that is, as regarded those persons who were about to take up with such views — he felt that it would be impossible for him to prejudge either himself or other people, and that therefore he was guilty

of no lie when he was afterwards detected in the maintenance of similar errors. This plea, however, he does not advance, not only because it is a ridiculous one, but because it cannot possibly be true; because in these very books of his he both argues against the transmission of sin from Adam to infants, and glories in the proceedings of the Synod in Palestine, where he was supposed to have sincerely anathematized such as hold the opinions in dispute, and where he, in fact, stole his acquittal by practising deceit.

CHAP. 16 [XV.] — PELAGIUS' FRAUDULENT AND CRAFTY EXCUSES.

For what is the significance to the matter with which we now have to do of his answers to his followers, when he tells them that "the reason why he condemned the points which were objected against him, is because he himself maintains that that primal sin was injurious not only to the first man, but to the whole human race, not by transmission, but by example;" in other words, not because those who have been propagated from him have derived any fault from him, but because all who afterwards have sinned, have imitated him who committed the first sin? Or when he says that "the reason why infants are not in the same state in which Adam was before the transgression, is because they are not yet able to receive the commandment, whereas he was able; and because they do not yet make use of that choice of a rational will which he certainly made use of, since otherwise no commandment would have been given to him"? How does such an exposition as this of the points alleged against him justify him in thinking that he rightly condemned the propositions, "Adam's sin injured only himself, and not the whole race of man;" and "infants at their birth are in the self-same state in which Adam was before he sinned;" and that by the said condemnation he is not guilty of deceit in holding such opinions as are found in his subsequent writings, how that "infants are born without any evil or fault, and that there is nothing in them but what God has formed," — no wound, in short, inflicted by an enemy?

CHAP. 17. — HOW PELAGIUS DECEIVED HIS JUDGES.

Now, is it by making such statements as these, meeting objections which are urged in one sense with explanations which are meant in another, that he designs to prove to us that he did not deceive those who sat in judgment on him? Then he utterly fails in his purpose. In proportion to the craftiness of his explanations, was the stealthiness with which he deceived them. For, just because they were catholic bishops, when they heard the man pouring out anathemas upon those who maintained that "Adam's sin was

---

[1] See *On the Proceedings of Pelagius*, ch. 24.

injurious to none but himself, and not to the human race," they understood him to assert nothing but what the catholic Church has been accustomed to declare, on the ground of which it truly baptizes infants for the remission of sins — not, indeed, sins which they have committed by imitation owing to the example of the first sinner, but sins which they have contracted by their very birth, owing to the corruption of their origin. When, again, they heard him anathematizing those who assert that "infants at their birth are in the same state in which Adam was before the transgression," they supposed him to refer to none others than those persons who "think that infants have derived no sin from Adam, and that they are accordingly in that state that he was in before his sin." For, of course, no other objection would be brought against him than that on which the question turned. When, therefore, he so explains the objection as to say that infants are not in the same state that Adam was in before he sinned, simply because they have not yet arrived at the same firmness of mind or body, not because of any propagated fault that has passed on to them, he must be answered thus: "When the objections were laid against you for condemnation, the catholic bishops did not understand them in this sense; therefore, when you condemned them, they believed that you were a catholic. That, accordingly, which they supposed you to maintain, deserved to be released from censure; but that which you really maintained was worthy of condemnation. It was not you, then, that were acquitted, who held tenets which ought to be condemned; but that opinion was freed from censure which you ought to have held and maintained. You could only be supposed to be acquitted by having been believed to entertain opinions worthy to be praised; for your judges could not suppose that you were concealing opinions which merited condemnation. Rightly have you been adjudged an accomplice of Cœlestius, in whose opinions you prove yourself to be a sharer. And though you kept your books shut during your trial, you published them to the world after it was over."

CHAP. 18 [XVII.] — THE CONDEMNATION OF PELAGIUS.

This being the case, you of course feel that episcopal councils, and the Apostolic See, and the whole Roman Church, and the Roman Empire itself,[1] which by God's gracious favour has become Christian, has been most righteously moved against the authors of this wicked error, until they repent and escape from the snares of the devil. For who can tell whether God may not give them repentance to discover, and acknowledge, and even proclaim His truth,[2] and to condemn their own damnable error? But whatever may be the bent of their own will, we cannot doubt that the merciful kindness of the Lord has sought the good of many persons who followed them, for no other reason than because they saw them associated in communion with the catholic Church.

CHAP. 19. — PELAGIUS' ATTEMPT TO DECEIVE THE APOSTOLIC SEE; HE INVERTS THE BEARINGS OF THE CONTROVERSY.

But I would have you carefully observe the way in which Pelagius endeavoured by deception to overreach even the judgment of the bishop of the Apostolic See on this very question of the baptism of infants. He sent a letter to Rome to Pope Innocent of blessed memory; and when it found him not in the flesh, it was handed to the holy Pope Zosimus, and by him directed to us. In this letter he complains of being "defamed by certain persons for refusing the sacrament of baptism to infants, and promising the kingdom of heaven irrespective of Christ's redemption." The objections, however, are not urged against them in the manner he has stated. For they neither deny the sacrament of baptism to infants, nor do they promise the kingdom of heaven to any irrespective of the redemption of Christ. As regards, therefore, his complaint of being defamed by sundry persons, he has set it forth in such terms as to be able to give a ready answer to the alleged charge against him, without injury to his own dogma. [XVIII.] The real objection against them is, that they refuse to confess that unbaptized infants are liable to the condemnation of the first man, and that original sin has been transmitted to them and requires to be purged by regeneration; their contention being that infants must be baptized solely for being admitted into the kingdom of heaven, as if they could only have eternal death apart from the kingdom of heaven, who cannot have eternal life without partaking of the Lord's body and blood. This, I would have you know, is the real objection to them respecting the baptism of infants; and not as he has represented it, for the purpose of enabling himself to save his own dogmas while answering what is actually a proposition of his own, under colour of meeting an objection.

---

[1] Possidius, in his *Life of Augustin*, ch. 18, says: "Even the most pious Emperor Honorius, upon hearing that the weighty sentence of the catholic Church of God had been pronounced against them, in pursuance of the same, determined that they should be regarded as heretics, under condemnation by his own laws." These enactments are printed by the Benedictine editors in the second part of their Appendix.

[2] 2 Tim. ii. 25, 26.

CHAP. 20. — PELAGIUS PROVIDES A REFUGE FOR HIS FALSEHOOD IN AMBIGUOUS SUBTERFUGES.

And then observe how he makes his answer, how he provides in the obscure mazes of his double sense retreats for his false doctrine, quenching the truth in his dark mist of error; so that even we, on our first perusal of his words, almost rejoiced at their propriety and correctness. But the fuller discussions in his books, in which he is generally forced, in spite of all his efforts at concealment, to explain his meaning, have made even his better statements suspicious to us, lest on a closer inspection of them we should detect them to be ambiguous. For, after saying that "he had never heard even an impious heretic say this" (namely, what he set forth as the objection) "about infants," he goes on to ask: "Who indeed is so unacquainted with Gospel lessons, as not only to attempt to make such an affirmation, but even to be able to lightly say it or even let it enter his thought? And then who is so impious as to wish to exclude infants from the kingdom of heaven, by forbidding them to be baptized and to be born again in Christ?"

CHAP. 21 [XIX.] — PELAGIUS AVOIDS THE QUESTION AS TO WHY BAPTISM IS NECESSARY FOR INFANTS.

Now it is to no purpose that he says all this. He does not clear himself thereby. Not even they have ever denied the impossibility of infants entering the kingdom of heaven without baptism. But this is not the question; what we are discussing concerns the obliteration [1] of original sin in infants. Let him clear himself on this point, since he refuses to acknowledge that there is anything in infants which the laver of regeneration has to cleanse. On this account we ought carefully to consider what he has afterwards to say. After adducing, then, the passage of the Gospel which declares that "whosoever is not born again of water and the Spirit cannot enter into the kingdom of heaven" [2] (on which matter, as we have said, they raise no question), he goes on at once to ask: "Who indeed is so impious as to have the heart to refuse the common redemption of the human race to an infant of any age whatever?" But this is ambiguous language; for what redemption does he mean? Is it from evil to good? or from good to better? Now even Cœlestius, at Carthage, [3] allowed a redemption for infants in his book; although, at the same time, he would not admit the transmission of sin to them from Adam.

CHAP. 22 [XX.] — ANOTHER INSTANCE OF PELAGIUS' AMBIGUITY.

Then, again, observe what he subjoins to the last remark: "Can any one," says he, "forbid a second birth to an eternal and certain life, to him who has been born to this present uncertain life?" In other words: "Who is so impious as to forbid his being born again to the life which is sure and eternal, who has been born to this life of uncertainty?" When we first read these words, we supposed that by the phrase "uncertain life" he meant to designate this present temporal life; although it appeared to us that he ought rather to have called it "mortal" than "uncertain," because it is brought to a close by certain death. But for all this, we thought that he had only shown a preference for calling this mortal life an *uncertain* one, because of the general view which men take that there is undoubtedly not a moment in our lives when we are free from this uncertainty. And so it happened that our anxiety about him was allayed to some extent by the following consideration, which rose almost to a proof, notwithstanding the fact of his unwillingness openly to confess that infants incur eternal death who depart this life without the sacrament of baptism. We argued: "If, as he seems to admit, eternal life can only accrue to them who have been baptized, it follows of course that they who die unbaptized incur everlasting death. This destiny, however, cannot by any means justly befall those who never in this life committed any sins of their own, unless on account of original sin."

CHAP. 23 [XXI.] — WHAT HE MEANS BY OUR BIRTH TO AN "UNCERTAIN" LIFE.

Certain brethren, however, afterwards failed not to remind us that Pelagius possibly expressed himself in this way, because on this question he is represented as having his answer ready for all inquirers, to this effect: "As for infants who die unbaptized, I know indeed whither they go not; yet whither they go, I know not;" that is, I know they do not go into the kingdom of heaven. But as to whither they go, he was (and for the matter of that, *still is* [4]) in the habit of saying that he knew not, because he dared not say that those went to eternal death, who he was persuaded had never committed sin in this life, and whom he would not admit to have inherited original sin. Consequently those very words of his which were forwarded to Rome to secure his absolute acquittal, are so steeped in ambiguity that they afford a shelter for their doctrine, out of which may sally forth an heretical sense to entrap the unwary straggler; for when no one

---

[1] Purgatione.     [2] John iii. 5.
[3] See above, in the preface to the treatise *On the Perfection of a Righteous Man*, towards the end.

[4] *Dicebat, aut dicit.* These two latter words are not superfluous, as some have thought; they intimate that Pelagius still clave to his error.

is at hand who can give the answer, any solitary man may find himself weak.

## CHAP. 24. — PELAGIUS' LONG RESIDENCE AT ROME.

The truth indeed is, that in the book of his faith which he sent to Rome with this very letter[1] to the before-mentioned Pope Innocent, to whom also he had written the letter, he only the more evidently exposed himself by his efforts at concealment. He says:[2] "We hold one baptism, which we say ought to be administered in the same sacramental words in the case of infants as in the case of adults." He did not, however, say, "in the same sacrament" (although if he had so said, there would still have been ambiguity), but "in the same sacramental words," — as if remission of sins in infants were declared by the sound of the words, and not wrought by the effect of the acts. For the time, indeed, he seemed to say what was agreeable with the catholic faith; but he had it not in his power permanently to deceive that see. Subsequent to the rescript of the African Council, into which province this pestilent doctrine had stealthily made its way — without, however, spreading widely or sinking deeply — other opinions also of this man were by the industry of some faithful brethren discovered and brought to light at Rome, where he had dwelt for a very long while, and had already engaged in sundry discourses and controversies. In order to procure the condemnation of these opinions, Pope Zosimus, as you may read, annexed them to his letter, which he wrote for publication throughout the catholic world. Among these statements, Pelagius, pretending to expound the Apostle Paul's Epistle to the Romans, argues in these words: "If Adam's sin injured those who have not sinned, then also Christ's righteousness profits those who do not believe." He says other things, too, of the same purport; but they have all been refuted and answered by me with the Lord's help in the books which I wrote, *On the Baptism of Infants*.[3] But he had not the courage to make those objectionable statements in his own person in the fore-mentioned so-called exposition. This particular one, however, having been enunciated in a place where he was so well known, his words and their meaning could not be disguised. In those books, from the first of which I have already before quoted,[4] he treats this point without any suppression of his views. With all the energy of which he is capable, he most plainly asserts that human nature in infants cannot in any wise be supposed to be corrupted by propagation; and by claiming salvation for them as their due, he does despite to the Saviour.

## CHAP. 25 [XXII.] — THE CONDEMNATION OF PELAGIUS AND CŒLESTIUS.

These things, then, being as I have stated them, it is now evident that there has arisen a deadly heresy, which, with the Lord's help, the Church by this time guards against more directly — now that those two men, Pelagius and Cœlestius, have been either offered repentance, or on their refusal been wholly condemned. They are reported, or perhaps actually proved, to be the authors of this perversion; at all events, if not the authors (as having learnt it from others), they are yet its boasted abettors and teachers, through whose agency the heresy has advanced and grown to a wider extent. This boast, too, is made even in their own statements and writings, and in unmistakeable signs of reality, as well as in the fame which arises and grows out of all these circumstances. What, therefore, remains to be done? Must not every catholic, with all the energies wherewith the Lord endows him, confute this pestilential doctrine, and oppose it with all vigilance; so that whenever we contend for the truth, compelled to answer, but not fond of the contest, the untaught may be instructed, and that thus the Church may be benefited by that which the enemy devised for her destruction; in accordance with that word of the apostle's, "There must be heresies, that they which are approved may be made manifest among you"?[5]

## CHAP. 26 [XXIII.] — THE PELAGIANS MAINTAIN THAT RAISING QUESTIONS ABOUT ORIGINAL SIN DOES NOT ENDANGER THE FAITH.

Therefore, after the full discussion with which we have been able to rebut in writing this error of theirs, which is so inimical to the grace of God bestowed on small and great through our Lord Jesus Christ, it is now our duty to examine and explode that assertion of theirs, which in their desire to avoid the odious imputation of heresy they astutely advance, to the effect that "calling this subject into question produces no danger to the faith," — in order that they may appear, forsooth, if they are convicted of having deviated from it, to have erred not criminally, but only, as it were, courteously.[6] This, accordingly, is the language which Cœlestius used in the ecclesiastical process at Carthage:[7] "As touching the transmission of sin," he said, "I have already said that I have heard many persons of acknowledged position in the catholic Church deny it, and on the other hand many affirm it; it may fairly, indeed, be deemed a matter for inquiry, but not a heresy. I have always maintained that

---

[1] See above, ch. 19.
[2] See above, ch. 1, and *On the Grace of Christ*, ch. 35.
[3] See especially Book iii. chs. 2, 5, 6 [III.].　　[4] In ch. 14 [XIII.].

[5] 1 Cor. xi. 19.
[6] This is far from a clear translation of the terse original: *Non criminaliter, sed quasi civiliter errasse videantur.*
[7] See above, ch. 3 [IV.]

infants require baptism, and ought to be baptized. What else does he want?" He said this, as if he wanted to intimate that only then could he be deemed chargeable with heresy, if he were to assert that they ought not to be baptized. As the case stood, however, inasmuch as he acknowledged that they ought to be baptized, he thought that he had not erred [criminally], and therefore ought not to be adjudged a heretic, even though he maintained the reason of their baptism to be other than the truth holds, or the faith claims as its own. On the same principle, in the book which he sent to Rome, he first explained his belief, so far as it suited his pleasure, from the Trinity of the One Godhead down to the kind of resurrection of the dead that is to be; on all which points, however, no one had ever questioned him, or been questioned by him. And when his discourse reached the question which was under consideration, he said : " If, indeed, any questions have arisen beyond the compass of the faith, on which there might be perhaps dissension on the part of a great many persons, in no case have I pretended to pronounce a decision on any dogma, as if I possessed a definitive authority in the matter myself; but whatever I have derived from the fountain of the prophets and the apostles, I have presented for approbation to the judgment of your apostolic office; so that if any error has crept in among us, human as we are, through our ignorance, it may be corrected by your sentence." [1] You of course clearly see that in this action of his he used all this deprecatory preamble in order that, if he had been discovered to have erred at all, he might seem to have erred not on a matter of faith, but on questionable points outside the faith; wherein, however necessary it may be to correct the error, it is not corrected as a heresy; wherein also the person who undergoes the correction is declared indeed to be in error, but for all that is not adjudged a heretic.

CHAP. 27 [XXIII.] — ON QUESTIONS OUTSIDE THE FAITH — WHAT THEY ARE, AND INSTANCES OF THE SAME.

But he is greatly mistaken in this opinion. The questions which he supposes to be outside the faith are of a very different character from those in which, without any detriment to the faith whereby we are Christians, there exists either an ignorance of the real fact, and a consequent suspension of any fixed opinion, or else a conjectural view of the case, which, owing to the infirmity of human thought, issues in conceptions at variance with truth : as when a question arises about the description and locality of that Paradise where God placed man whom He formed out of the ground, without any disturbance, however, of the Christian belief that there undoubtedly is such a Paradise; or as when it is asked where Elijah is at the present moment, and where Enoch — whether in this Paradise or in some other place, although we doubt not of their existing still in the same bodies in which they were born; or as when one inquires whether it was in the body or out of the body that the apostle was caught up to the third heaven, — an inquiry, however, which betokens great lack of modesty on the part of those who would fain know what he who is the subject of the mystery itself expressly declares his ignorance of,[2] without impairing his own belief of the fact; or as when the question is started, how many are those heavens, to the "third" of which he tells us that he was caught up; or whether the elements of this visible world are four or more; what it is which causes those eclipses of the sun or the moon which astronomers are in the habit of foretelling for certain appointed seasons; why, again, men of ancient times lived to the age which Holy Scripture assigns to them; and whether the period of their puberty, when they begat their first son, was postponed to an older age, proportioned to their longer life; or where Methuselah could possibly have lived, since he was not in the Ark, inasmuch as (according to the chronological notes of most copies of the Scripture, both Greek and Latin) he is found to have survived the deluge; or whether we must follow the order of the fewer copies — and they happen to be extremely few — which so arrange the years as to show that he died before the deluge. Now who does not feel, amidst the various and innumerable questions of this sort, which relate either to God's most hidden operations or to most obscure passages of the Scriptures, and which it is difficult to embrace and define in any certain way, that ignorance may on many points be compatible with sound Christian faith, and that occasionally erroneous opinion may be entertained without any room for the imputation of heretical doctrine?

CHAP. 28 [XXIV.] — THE HERESY OF PELAGIUS AND CŒLESTIUS AIMS AT THE VERY FOUNDATIONS OF OUR FAITH.

This is, however, in the matter of the two men by one of whom we are sold under sin,[3] by the other redeemed from sins — by the one have been precipitated into death, by the other are liberated unto life; the former of whom has ruined us in himself, by doing his own will instead of His who created him; the latter has saved us in Himself, by not doing His own will,

---

[1] See above, ch. 6.  [2] 2 Cor. xii. 2.  [3] Rom. vii. 14.

but the will of Him who sent Him : [1] and it is in what concerns these two men that the Christian faith properly consists. For " there is one God, and one Mediator between God and men, the man Christ Jesus ; " [2] since " there is none other name under heaven given to men, whereby we must be saved ; " [3] and " in Him hath God defined unto all men their faith, in that He hath raised Him from the dead." [4] Now without this faith, that is to say, without a belief in the one Mediator between God and men, the man Christ Jesus ; without faith, I say, in His resurrection, by which God has given assurance to all men, and which no man could of course truly believe, were it not for His incarnation and death ; without faith, therefore, in the incarnation and death and resurrection of Christ, the Christian verity unhesitatingly declares that the ancient saints could not possibly have been cleansed from sin, so as to have become holy, and justified by the grace of God. And this is true both of the saints who are mentioned in Holy Scripture, and of those also who are not indeed mentioned therein, but must yet be supposed to have existed, — either before the deluge, or in the interval between that event and the giving of the law, or in the period of the law itself, — not merely among the children of Israel, as the prophets, but even outside that nation, as for instance Job. For it was by the self-same faith in the one Mediator that the hearts of these, too, were cleansed, and there also was " shed abroad in them the love of God by the Holy Ghost," [5] " who bloweth where He listeth," [6] not following men's merits, but even producing these very merits Himself. For the grace of God will in no wise exist unless it be wholly free.

CHAP. 29. — THE RIGHTEOUS MEN WHO LIVED IN THE TIME OF THE LAW WERE FOR ALL THAT NOT UNDER THE LAW, BUT UNDER GRACE. THE GRACE OF THE NEW TESTAMENT HIDDEN UNDER THE OLD.

Death indeed reigned from Adam until Moses,[7] because it was not possible even for the law given through Moses to overcome it : it was not given, in fact, as something able to give life ; [8] but as something that ought to show those that were dead and for whom grace was needed to give them life, that they were not only prostrated under the propagation and domination of sin, but also convicted by the additional guilt of breaking the law itself : not in order that any one might perish who in the mercy of God understood this even in that early age ; but that, destined though he was to punishment, owing to the dominion of death, and manifested, too, as

guilty through his own violation of the law, he might seek God's help, and so where sin abounded, grace might much more abound,[9] even the grace which alone delivers from the body of this death.[10] [xxv.] Yet, notwithstanding this, although not even the law which Moses gave was able to liberate any man from the dominion of death, there were even then, too, at the time of the law, men of God who were not living under the terror and conviction and punishment of the law, but under delight and healing and liberation of grace. Some there were who said, " I was shapen in iniquity, and in sin did my mother conceive me ; " [11] and, " There is no rest in my bones, by reason of my sins ; " [12] and, " Create in me a clean heart, O God ; and renew a right spirit in my inward parts ; " [13] and, " Stablish me with Thy directing Spirit ; " [14] and, " Take not Thy Holy Spirit from me." [15] There were some, again, who said : " I believed, therefore have I spoken." [16] For they too were cleansed with the self-same faith with which we ourselves are. Whence the apostle also says : " We having the same spirit of faith, according as it is written, I believe, and therefore have I spoken ; we also believe, and therefore speak." [17] Out of very faith was it said, " Behold, a virgin shall conceive and bear a son, and they shall call His name Emmanuel," [18] " which is, being interpreted, God with us." [19] Out of very faith too was it said concerning Him : " As a bridegroom He cometh out of His chamber ; as a giant did He exult to run His course. His going forth is from the extremity of heaven, and His circuit runs to the other end of heaven ; and no one is hidden from His heat." [20] Out of very faith, again, was it said to Him : " Thy throne, O God, is for ever and ever ; a sceptre of righteousness is the sceptre of Thy kingdom. Thou hast loved righteousness, and hated iniquity ; therefore God, Thy God, hath anointed Thee with the oil of gladness above Thy fellows." [21] By the self-same Spirit of faith were all these things foreseen by them as to happen, whereby they are believed by us as having happened. They, indeed, who were able in faithful love to foretell these things to us were not themselves partakers of them. The Apostle Peter says, " Why tempt ye God to put a yoke upon the neck of the disciples, which neither our fathers nor we were able to bear? But we believe that through the grace of the Lord Jesus Christ we shall be saved, even as they." [22] Now on what principle does he make this statement, if it be not because even they were saved through the grace of the Lord Jesus

[1] John iv. 34, v. 30.  [2] 1 Tim. ii. 5.  [3] Acts iv. 12.
[4] Acts xvii. 31.  [5] Rom. v. 5.  [6] John iii. 8.
[7] Rom. v. 14.  [8] Gal. iii. 21.

[9] Rom. v. 20.  [10] Rom. vii. 24, 25.  [11] Ps. li. 5.
[12] Ps. xxxviii. 3.  [13] Ps. li. 10.  [14] Ps. li. 12.
[15] Ps. li. 11.  [16] Ps. cxvi. 10.  [17] 2 Cor. iv. 13.
[18] Isa. vii. 14.  [19] Matt. i. 23.  [20] Ps. xix. 5, 6.
[21] Ps. xlv. 6, 7.  [22] Acts xv. 10, 11.

Christ, and not the law of Moses, from which comes not the cure, but only the knowledge of sin?[1] Now, however, the righteousness of God without the law is manifested, being witnessed by the law and the prophets.[2] If, therefore, it is now manifested, it even then existed, but it was hidden. This concealment was symbolized by the veil of the temple. When Christ was dying, this veil was rent asunder,[3] to signify the full revelation of Him. Even of old, therefore, there existed amongst the people of God this grace of the one Mediator between God and men, the man Christ Jesus; but like the rain in the fleece which God sets apart for His inheritance,[4] not of debt, but of His own will, it was latently present, but is now patently visible amongst all nations as its "floor," the fleece being dry, — in other words, the Jewish people having become reprobate.[5]

CHAP. 30 [XXVI.] — PELAGIUS AND CŒLESTIUS DENY THAT THE ANCIENT SAINTS WERE SAVED BY CHRIST.

We must not therefore divide the times, as Pelagius and his disciples do, who say that men first lived righteously by nature, then under the law, thirdly under grace, — by nature meaning all the long time from Adam before the giving of the law. "For then," say they, "the Creator was known by the guidance of reason; and the rule of living rightly was carried written in the hearts of men, not in the law of the letter, but of nature. But men's manners became corrupt; and then," they say, "when nature now tarnished began to be insufficient, the law was added to it, whereby as by a moon the original lustre was restored to nature after its blush was impaired. But after the habit of sinning had too much prevailed among men, and the law was unequal to the task of curing it, Christ came; and the Physician Himself, through His own self, and not through His disciples, brought relief to the malady at its most desperate development."

CHAP. 31. — CHRIST'S INCARNATION WAS OF AVAIL TO THE FATHERS, EVEN THOUGH IT HAD NOT YET HAPPENED.

By disputation of this sort, they attempt to exclude the ancient saints from the grace of the Mediator, as if the man Christ Jesus were not the Mediator between God and *those men;* on the ground that, not having yet taken flesh of the Virgin's womb, He was not yet man at the time when those righteous men lived. If this, however, were true, in vain would the apostle say: "By man came death, by man came also the resurrection of the dead; for as in Adam all die, even so in Christ shall all be made alive."[6]

For inasmuch as those ancient saints, according to the vain conceits of these men, found their nature self-sufficient, and required not the man Christ to be their Mediator to reconcile them to God, so neither shall they be made alive in Him, to whose body they are shown not to belong as members, according to the statement that it was on man's account that He became man. If, however, as the Truth says through His apostles, even as all die in Adam, even so shall all be made alive in Christ; forasmuch as the resurrection of the dead comes through the one man, even as death comes through the other man; what Christian man can be bold enough to doubt that even those righteous men who pleased God in the more remote periods of the human race are destined to attain to the resurrection of eternal life, and not eternal death, because they shall be made alive in Christ? that they are made alive in Christ, because they belong to the body of Christ? that they belong to the body of Christ, because Christ is the head even to them?[7] and that Christ is the head even to them, because there is but one Mediator between God and men, the man Christ Jesus? But this He could not have been to them, unless through His grace they had believed in His resurrection. And how could they have done this, if they had been ignorant that He was to come in the flesh, and if they had not by this faith lived justly and piously? Now, if the incarnation of Christ could be of no concern to them, on the ground that it had not yet come about, it must follow that Christ's judgment can be of no concern to us, because it has not yet taken place. But if we shall stand at the right hand of Christ through our faith in His judgment, which has not yet transpired, but is to come to pass, it follows that those ancient saints are members of Christ through their faith in His resurrection, which had not in their day happened, but which was one day to come to pass.

CHAP. 32 [XXVII.] — HE SHOWS BY THE EXAMPLE OF ABRAHAM THAT THE ANCIENT SAINTS BELIEVED IN THE INCARNATION OF CHRIST.

For it must not be supposed that those saints of old only profited by Christ's divinity, which was ever existent, and not also by the revelation of His humanity, which had not yet come to pass. What the Lord Jesus says, "Abraham desired to see my day, and he saw it, and was glad,"[8] meaning by the phrase *his day* to understand *his time*, affords of course a clear testimony that Abraham was fully imbued with belief in His incarnation. It is in respect of this that He has a "time;" for His divinity exceeds all time, for it was by IT that all times were created. If, however, any one supposes that the phrase in question must be understood of that eternal

---

[1] Rom. iii. 20.    [2] Rom. iii. 21.    [3] Matt. xxvii. 51.
[4] Ps. lxviii. 9.    [5] Judg. vi. 36-40.    [6] 1 Cor. xv. 21, 22.    [7] 1 Cor. xi. 3.    [8] John viii. 56.

"day" which is limited by no morrow, and preceded by no yesterday, — in a word, of the very eternity in which He is co-eternal with the Father, — how would Abraham really desire this, unless he was aware that there was to be a future mortality belonging to Him whose eternity he wished for? Or, perhaps, some one would confine the meaning of the phrase so far as to say, that nothing else is meant in the Lord's saying, "He desired to see my day," than "He desired to see me," who am the never-ending Day, or the unfailing Light, as when we mention the life of the Son, concerning which it is said in the Gospel: "So hath He given to the Son to have life in Himself."[1] Here the life is nothing less than Himself. So we understand the Son Himself to be the life, when He said, "I am the way, the truth, and the life;"[2] of whom also it was said, "He is the true God, and eternal life."[3] Supposing, then, that Abraham desired to see this equal divinity of the Son's with the Father, without any precognition of His coming in the flesh — as certain philosophers sought Him, who knew nothing of His flesh — can that other act of Abraham, when he orders his servant to place his hand under his thigh, and to swear by the God of heaven,[4] be rightly understood by any one otherwise than as showing that Abraham well knew that the flesh in which the God of heaven was to come was the offspring of that very thigh?[5]

CHAP. 33 [XVIII.] — HOW CHRIST IS OUR MEDIATOR.

Of this flesh and blood Melchizedek also, when he blessed Abram himself,[6] gave the testimony which is very well known to Christian believers, so that long afterwards it was said to Christ in the Psalms: "Thou art a Priest for ever, after the order of Melchizedek."[7] This was not then an accomplished fact, but was still future; yet that faith of the fathers, which is the self-same faith as our own, used to chant it. Now, to all who find death in Adam, Christ is of this avail, that He is the Mediator for life. He is, however, not a Mediator, because He is equal with the Father; for in this respect He is Himself as far distant from us as the Father; and how can there be any medium where the distance is the very same? Therefore the apostle does not say, "There is one Mediator between God and men, even Jesus Christ;" but his words are, "The MAN Christ Jesus."[8] He is the Mediator, then, in that He is man, — inferior to the Father, by so much as He is nearer to ourselves, and superior to us, by so much as He is nearer to the Father. This is more openly expressed thus: "He is inferior to the Father, because in the form of a servant;"[9] superior to us, because without spot of sin.

CHAP. 34 [XXIX.] — NO MAN EVER SAVED SAVE BY CHRIST.

Now, whoever maintains that human nature at any period required not the second Adam for its physician, because it was not corrupted in the first Adam, is convicted as an enemy to the grace of God; not in a question where doubt or error might be compatible with soundness of belief, but in that very rule of faith which makes us Christians. How happens it, then, that the human nature, which first existed, is praised by these men as being so far less tainted with evil manners? How is it that they overlook the fact that men were even then sunk in so many intolerable sins, that, with the exception of one man of God and his wife, and three sons and their wives, the whole world was in God's just judgment destroyed by the flood, even as the little land of Sodom was afterwards with fire?[10] From the moment, then, when "by one man sin entered into the world, and death by sin, and so death passed upon all men, in whom all sinned,"[11] the entire mass of our nature was ruined beyond doubt, and fell into the possession of its destroyer. And from him no one — no, not one — has been delivered, or is being delivered, or ever will be delivered, except by the grace of the Redeemer.

CHAP. 35 [XXX.] — WHY THE CIRCUMCISION OF INFANTS WAS ENJOINED UNDER PAIN OF SO GREAT A PUNISHMENT.

The Scripture does not inform us whether before Abraham's time righteous men or their children were marked by any bodily or visible sign.[12] Abraham himself, indeed, received the sign of circumcision, a seal of the righteousness of faith.[13] And he received it with this accompanying injunction: All the male infants of his household were from that very time to be circumcised, while fresh from their mother's womb, on the eighth day from their birth;[14] so that even they who were not yet able with the heart to believe unto righteousness, should nevertheless receive the seal of the righteousness of faith.

---

[1] John. v. 26.     [2] John xiv. 6.     [3] 1 John v. 20.
[4] Gen. xxiv. 2, 3.
[5] The word "thigh," יָרֵךְ, occurs in the phrase, "to come out from the thigh of any one," in the sense of *being begotten by any one*, or *descended from him*, in several passages: see Gen. xlvi. 26; Ex. i. 5; Judg. viii. 30. In the last of these passages, the A. V. phrase, "of his body begotten," is יֹצְאֵי יְרֵכוֹ, *the offspring of his thigh*. Abraham was the first to use this form of adjuration; after him his grandson Jacob, Gen. xlvii. 29. The comment of Augustin in the text, which he repeats elsewhere (see his *Sermon* 75), occurs also in other Fathers, *e.g.* Jerome, Theodoret, Ambrose (*De Abrahamo,* i. cap. ult.), Prosper (*Prædicat.* i. 7), and Gregory the Great, who says: "He orders him to put his hand under his thigh, since through that member would descend the flesh of Him who was Abraham's son according to the flesh, and his Lord owing to His divinity."
[6] Gen. xiv. 18-20.                      [7] Ps. cx. 4.

[8] 1 Tim. ii. 5.       [9] Phil. ii. 7.        [10] See Gen. vii. and xix.
[11] Rom. v. 12.       [12] Sacramento.       [13] Rom. iv. 11.
[14] Gen. xvii. 10.

And this command was imposed with so fearful a sanction, that God said: "That soul shall be cut off from his people, whose flesh of his foreskin is not circumcised on the eighth day."[1] If inquiry be made into the justice of so terrible a penalty, will not the entire argument of these men about free will, and the laudable soundness and purity of nature, however cleverly maintained, fall to pieces, struck down and fractured to atoms? For, pray tell me, what evil has an infant committed of his own will, that, for the negligence of another in not circumcising him, he himself must be condemned, and with so severe a condemnation, that that soul must be cut off from his people? It was not of any temporal death that this fear was inflicted, since of righteous persons, when they died, it used rather to be said, "And he was gathered unto his people;"[2] or, "He was gathered to his fathers:"[3] for no attempt to separate a man from his people is long formidable to him, when his own people is itself the people of God.

### CHAP. 36 [XXXI.] — THE PLATONISTS' OPINION ABOUT THE EXISTENCE OF THE SOUL PREVIOUS TO THE BODY REJECTED.

What, then, is the purport of so severe a condemnation, when no wilful sin has been committed? For it is not as certain Platonists have thought, because every such infant is thus requited in his soul for what it did of its own wilfulness previous to the present life, as having possessed previous to its present bodily state a free choice of living either well or ill; since the Apostle Paul says most plainly, that before they were born they did neither good nor evil.[4] On what account, therefore, is an infant rightly punished with such ruin, if it be not because he belongs to the mass of perdition, and is properly regarded as born of Adam, condemned under the bond of the ancient debt unless he has been released from the bond, not according to debt, but according to grace? And what grace but God's, through our Lord Jesus Christ? Now there was a forecast of His coming undoubtedly contained not only in other sacred institutions[5] of the ancient Jews, but also in their circumcision of the foreskin. For the eighth day, in the recurrence of weeks, became the Lord's day, on which the Lord arose from the dead; and Christ was the rock[6] whence was formed the stony blade for the circumcision;[7] and the flesh of the foreskin was the body of sin.

### CHAP. 37 [XXXII.] — IN WHAT SENSE CHRIST IS CALLED "SIN."

There was a change of the sacramental ordinances made after the coming of Him whose advent they prefigured; but there was no change in the Mediator's help, who, even previous to His coming in the flesh, all along delivered the ancient members of His body by their faith in His incarnation; and in respect of ourselves too, though we were dead in sins and in the uncircumcision of our flesh, we are quickened together in Christ, in whom we are circumcised with the circumcision not made with the hand,[8] but such as was prefigured by the old manual circumcision, that the body of sin might be done away[9] which was born with us from Adam. The propagation of a condemned origin condemns us, unless we are cleansed by the likeness of sinful flesh, in which He was sent without sin, who nevertheless concerning sin condemned sin, having been made sin for us.[10] Accordingly the apostle says: "We beseech you in Christ's stead, be ye reconciled unto God. For He hath made Him to be sin for us, who knew no sin; that we might be made the righteousness of God in Him."[11] God, therefore, to whom we are reconciled, has made Him to be sin for us, — that is to say, a sacrifice by which our sins may be remitted; for by sins are designated the sacrifices for sins. And indeed He was sacrificed for our sins, the only one among men who had no sins, even as in those early times one was sought for among the flocks to prefigure the Faultless One who was to come to heal our offences. On whatever day, therefore, an infant may be baptized after his birth, he is as if circumcised on the eighth day; inasmuch as he is circumcised in Him who rose again the third day indeed after He was crucified, but the eighth according to the weeks. He is circumcised for the putting off of the body of sin; in other words, that grace of spiritual regeneration may do away with the debt which the contagion of carnal generation contracted. "For no one is pure from uncleanness" (what uncleanness, pray, but that of sin?), "not even the infant, whose life is but that of a single day upon the earth."[12]

### CHAP. 38 [XXXIII.] — ORIGINAL SIN DOES NOT RENDER MARRIAGE EVIL.

But they argue thus, saying: "Is not, then, marriage an evil, and the man that is produced by marriage not God's work?" As if the good of the married life were that disease of concupiscence with which they who know not God love their wives — a course which the apostle forbids;[13] and not rather that conjugal chastity, by which carnal lust is reduced to the good purposes of the appointed procreation of children. Or as if, forsooth, a man could possibly be anything

---

1 Gen. xvii. 14.    2 Gen. xxv. 17.    3 1 Macc. ii. 69.    8 Col. ii. 11, 13.    9 Rom. vi. 6.
4 Rom. ix. 11.    5 Sacramenta.    6 1 Cor. x. 4.    10 Rom. viii. 3 and Gal. iii. 13.    11 2 Cor. v. 20, 21.
7 Ex. iv. 25.    12 Job xiv. 4, 5.    13 1 Thess. iv. 5.

but God's work, not only when born in wedlock, but even if he be produced in fornication or adultery. In the present inquiry, however, when the question is not for what a Creator is necessary, but for what a Saviour, we have not to consider what good there is in the procreation of nature, but what evil there is in sin, whereby our nature has been certainly corrupted. No doubt the two are generated simultaneously — both nature and nature's corruption; one of which is good, the other evil. The one comes to us from the bounty of the Creator, the other is contracted from the condemnation of our origin; the one has its cause in the good-will of the Supreme God, the other in the depraved will of the first man; the one exhibits God as the maker of the creature, the other exhibits God as the punisher of disobedience: in short, the very same Christ was the *maker* of man for the creation of the one, and was *made*[1] man for the healing of the other.

CHAP. 39 [XXXIV.] — THREE THINGS GOOD AND LAUDABLE IN MATRIMONY.

Marriage, therefore, is a good in all the things which are proper to the married state. And these are three: it is the ordained means of procreation, it is the guarantee[2] of chastity, it is the bond of union.[3] In respect of its ordination for generation the Scripture says, "I will therefore that the younger women marry, bear children, guide the house;"[4] as regards its guaranteeing chastity, it is said of it, "The wife hath not power of her own body, but the husband; and likewise also the husband hath not power of his own body, but the wife;"[5] and considered as the bond of union: "What God hath joined together, let not man put asunder."[6] Touching these points, we do not forget that we have treated at sufficient length, with whatever ability the Lord has given us, in other works of ours, which are not unknown to you.[7] In relation to them all the Scripture has this general praise: "Marriage is honourable in all, and the bed undefiled."[8] For, inasmuch as the wedded state is good, insomuch does it produce a very large amount of good in respect of the evil of concupiscence; for it is not lust, but reason, which makes a good use of concupiscence. Now lust lies in that law of the "disobedient" members which the apostle notes as "warring against the law of the mind;"[9] whereas reason lies in that law of the wedded state which makes good use of concupiscence. If, however, it were impossible for any good to arise out of evil, God

could not create man out of the embraces of adultery. As, therefore, the damnable evil of adultery, whenever man is born in it, is not chargeable on God, who certainly amidst man's evil work actually produces a good work; so, likewise, all which causes shame in that rebellion of the members which brought the accusing blush on those who after their sin covered these members with the fig-tree leaves,[10] is not laid to the charge of marriage, by virtue of which the conjugal embrace is not only allowable, but is even useful and honourable; but it is imputable to the sin of that disobedience which was followed by the penalty of man's finding his own members emulating against himself that very disobedience which he had practised against God. Then, abashed at their action, since they moved no more at the bidding of his rational will, but at their own arbitrary choice as it were, instigated by lust, he devised the covering which should conceal such of them as he judged to be worthy of shame. For man, as the handiwork of God, deserved not confusion of face; nor were the members which it seemed fit to the Creator to form and appoint by any means designed to bring the blush to the creature. Accordingly, that simple nudity was displeasing neither to God nor to man: there was nothing to be ashamed of, because nothing at first accrued which deserved punishment.

CHAP. 40 [XXXV.] — MARRIAGE EXISTED BEFORE SIN WAS COMMITTED. HOW GOD'S BLESSING OPERATED IN OUR FIRST PARENTS.

There was, however, undoubtedly marriage, even when sin had no prior existence; and for no other reason was it that woman, and not a second man, was created as a help for the man. Moreover, those words of God, "Be fruitful and multiply,"[11] are not prophetic of sins to be condemned, but a benediction upon the fertility of marriage. For by these ineffable words of His, I mean by the divine methods which are inherent in the truth of His wisdom by which all things were made, God endowed the primeval pair with their seminal power. Suppose, however, that nature had not been dishonoured by sin, God forbid that we should think that marriages in Paradise must have been such, that in them the procreative members would be excited by the mere ardour of lust, and not by the command of the will for producing offspring, — as the foot is for walking, the hand for labour, and the tongue for speech. Nor, as now happens, would the chastity of virginity be corrupted to the conception of offspring by the force of a turbid heat, but it would rather be submissive to the power of the gentlest love; and thus there

---

[1] This translation is intended to preserve, however faintly, Augustin's antithesis, *factor est hominis* and *factus est homo*.
[2] Fides.          [3] Connubii sacramentum.          [4] 1 Tim. v. 14.
[5] 1 Cor. vii. 4.          [6] Matt. xix. 6.
[7] *De Bono Conjugali*, 3 sqq.          [8] Heb. xiii. 4.
[9] Rom. vii. 23.

[10] Gen. iii. 7.          [11] Gen. i. 28.

would be no pain, no blood-effusion of the concumbent virgin, as there would also be no groan of the parturient mother. This, however, men refuse to believe, because it has not been verified in the actual condition of our mortal state. Nature, having been vitiated by sin, has never experienced an instance of that primeval purity. But we speak to faithful men, who have learnt to believe the inspired Scriptures, even though no examples are adduced of actual reality. For how could I now possibly *prove* that a man was made of the dust, without any parents, and a wife formed for him out of his own side?[1] And yet faith takes on trust what the eye no longer discovers.

CHAP. 41 [XXXVI.] — LUST AND TRAVAIL COME FROM SIN. WHENCE OUR MEMBERS BECAME A CAUSE OF SHAME.

Granted, therefore, that we have no means of showing both that the nuptial acts of that primeval marriage were quietly discharged, undisturbed by lustful passion, and that the motion of the organs of generation, like that of any other members of the body, was not instigated by the ardour of lust, but directed by the choice of the will (which would have continued such with marriage had not the disgrace of sin intervened); still, from all that is stated in the sacred Scriptures on divine authority, we have reasonable grounds for believing that such was the original condition of wedded life. Although, it is true, I am not told that the nuptial embrace was unattended with prurient desire; as also I do not find it on record that parturition was unaccompanied with groans and pain, or that actual birth led not to future death; yet, at the same time, if I follow the verity of the Holy Scriptures, the travail of the mother and the death of the human offspring would never have supervened if sin had not preceded. Nor would that have happened which abashed the man and woman when they covered their loins; because in the same sacred records it is expressly written that the sin was first committed, and then immediately followed this hiding of their shame.[2] For unless some indelicacy of motion had announced to their eyes — which were of course not closed, though not open to this point, that is, not attentive — that those particular members should be corrected, they would not have perceived anything on their own persons, which God had entirely made worthy of all praise, that called for either shame or concealment. If, indeed, the sin had not first occurred which they had dared to commit in their disobedience, there would not have followed the disgrace which their shame would fain conceal.

CHAP. 42 [XXXVII.] — THE EVIL OF LUST OUGHT NOT TO BE ASCRIBED TO MARRIAGE. THE THREE GOOD RESULTS OF THE NUPTIAL ORDINANCE: OFFSPRING, CHASTITY, AND THE SACRAMENTAL UNION.

It is then manifest that that must not be laid to the account of marriage, even in the absence of which, marriage would still have existed. The good of marriage is not taken away by the evil, although the evil is by marriage turned to a good use. Such, however, is the present condition of mortal men, that the connubial intercourse and lust are at the same time in action; and on this account it happens, that as the lust is blamed, so also the nuptial commerce, however lawful and honourable, is thought to be reprehensible by those persons who either are unwilling or unable to draw the distinction between them. They are, moreover, inattentive to that good of the nuptial state which is the glory of matrimony; I mean offspring, chastity, and the pledge.[3] The evil, however, at which even marriage blushes for shame is not the fault of marriage, but of the lust of the flesh. Yet because without this evil it is impossible to effect the good purpose of marriage, even the procreation of children, whenever this process is approached, secrecy is sought, witnesses removed, and even the presence of the very children which happen to be born of the process is avoided as soon as they reach the age of observation. Thus it comes to pass that marriage is permitted to effect all that is lawful in its state, only it must not forget to conceal all that is improper. Hence it follows that infants, although incapable of sinning, are yet not born without the contagion of sin, — not, indeed, because of what is lawful, but on account of that which is unseemly: for from what is lawful nature is born; from what is unseemly, sin. Of the nature so born, God is the Author, who created man, and who united male and female under the nuptial law; but of the sin the author is the subtlety of the devil who deceives, and the will of the man who consents.

CHAP. 43 [XXXVIII.] — HUMAN OFFSPRING, EVEN PREVIOUS TO BIRTH, UNDER CONDEMNATION AT THE VERY ROOT. USES OF MATRIMONY UNDERTAKEN FOR MERE PLEASURE NOT WITHOUT VENIAL FAULT.

Where God did nothing else than by a just sentence to condemn the man who wilfully sins, together with his stock; there also, as a matter of course, whatsoever was even not yet born is justly condemned in its sinful root. In this condemned stock carnal generation holds every man; and from it nothing but spiritual regeneration liberates him. In the case, therefore, of regenerate par-

---

[1] Gen. ii. 7, 22.    [2] Gen. iii. 7.    [3] Sacramentum; see above, ch. 39.

ents, if they continue in the same state of grace, it will undoubtedly work no injurious consequence, by reason of the remission of sins which has been bestowed upon them, unless they make a perverse use of it, — not alone all kinds of lawless corruptions, but even in the marriage state itself, whenever husband and wife toil at procreation, not from the desire of natural propagation of their species, but are mere slaves to the gratification of their lust out of very wantonness. As for the permission which the apostle gives to husbands and wives, "not to defraud one another, except with consent for a time, that they may have leisure for prayer," [1] he concedes it by way of indulgent allowance, and not as a command ; but this very form of the concession evidently implies some degree of fault. The connubial embrace, however, which marriage-contracts point to as intended for the procreation of children, considered in itself simply, and without any reference to fornication, is good and right ; because, although it is by reason of this body of death (which is unrenewed as yet by the resurrection) impracticable without a certain amount of bestial motion, which puts human nature to the blush, yet the embrace is not after all a sin in itself, when reason applies the concupiscence to a good end, and is not overmastered to evil.

CHAP. 44 [XXXIX.] — EVEN THE CHILDREN OF THE REGENERATE BORN IN SIN. THE EFFECT OF BAPTISM.

This concupiscence of the flesh would be prejudicial,* just in so far as it is present in us,* if the remission of sins were not so beneficial * that while it is present in men, both as born and as born again, it may in the former be prejudicial as well as present, but in the latter present simply but never prejudicial. In the unregenerate it is prejudicial to such an extent indeed, that, unless they are born again, no advantage can accrue to them from being born of regenerate parents. The fault of our nature remains in our offspring so deeply impressed as to make it guilty, even when the guilt of the self-same fault has been washed away in the parent by the remission of sins — until every defect which ends in sin by the consent of the human will is consumed and done away in the last regeneration. This will be identical with that renovation of the very flesh itself which is promised in its future resurrection, when we shall not only commit no sins, but be even free from those corrupt desires which lead us to sin by yielding consent to them. To this blessed consummation advances are even now made by us, through the grace of that holy laver which we have put within our reach. The same regeneration which now renews our spirit, so that all our past sins are remitted, will by and by also operate, as might be expected, to the renewal to eternal life of that very flesh, by the resurrection of which to an incorruptible state the incentives of all sins will be purged out of our nature. But this salvation is as yet only accomplished in hope : it is not realized in fact ; it is not in present possession, but it is looked forward to with patience. [XL.] And thus there is a whole and perfect cleansing, in the self-same baptismal laver, not only of all the sins remitted now in our baptism, which make us guilty owing to the consent we yield to wrong desires, and to the sinful acts in which they issue ; but of these said wrong desires also, which, if not consented to by us, would contract no guilt of sin, and which, though not in this present life removed, will yet have no existence in the life beyond.

CHAP. 45. — MAN'S DELIVERANCE SUITED TO THE CHARACTER OF HIS CAPTIVITY.

The guilt, therefore, of that corruption of which we are speaking will remain in the carnal offspring of the regenerate, until in them also it be washed away in the laver of regeneration. A regenerate man does not regenerate, but generates, sons according to the flesh ; and thus he transmits to his posterity, not the condition of the regenerated, but only of the generated. Therefore, be a man guilty of unbelief, or a perfect believer, he does not in either case beget faithful children, but sinners ; in the same way that the seeds, not only of a wild olive, but also of a cultivated one, produce not cultivated olives, but wild ones. So, likewise, his first birth holds a man in that bondage from which nothing but his second birth delivers him. The devil holds him, Christ liberates him : Eve's deceiver holds him, Mary's Son frees him : he holds him, who approached the man through the woman ; He frees him, who was born of a woman that never approached a man : he holds him, who injected into the woman the cause of lust ; He liberates him, who without any lust was conceived in the woman. The former was able to hold all men in his grasp through one ; nor does any deliver them out of his power but One, whom he was unable to grasp. The very sacraments indeed of the Church, which she [2] administers with due ceremony, according to the authority of very ancient tradition (so that these men, notwithstanding their opinion that the sacraments are imitatively rather than really used in the case of infants, still do not venture

---

[1] 1 Cor. vii. 5.
* The three phrases here marked with asterisks have a more clearly expressed relation in the original: *obesset, inesset, prodesset.*

[2] That is, *the Church*, according to one reading — *concelebrat ;* but another reading, *concelebrant*, understands " the Pelagians " to be the subject of the proposition.

to reject them with open disapproval), — the very sacraments, I say, of the holy Church show plainly enough that infants, even when fresh from the womb, are delivered from the bondage of the devil through the grace of Christ. For, to say nothing of the fact that they are baptized for the remission of sins by no fallacious, but by a true and faithful mystery, there is previously wrought on them the exorcism and the exsufflation of the hostile power, which they profess to renounce by the mouth of those who bring them to baptism. Now, by all these consecrated and evident signs of hidden realities, they are shown to pass from their worst oppressor to their most excellent Redeemer, who, by taking on Himself our infirmity in our behalf, has bound the strong man, that He may spoil his goods;[1] seeing that the weakness of God is stronger, not only than men, but also than angels. While, therefore, God delivers small as well as great, He shows in both instances that the apostle spoke under the direction of the Truth. For it is not merely adults, but little babes too, whom He rescues from the power of darkness, in order to transfer them to the kingdom of God's dear Son.[2]

### CHAP. 46. — DIFFICULTY OF BELIEVING ORIGINAL SIN. MAN'S VICE IS A BEAST'S NATURE.

No one should feel surprise, and ask : " Why does God's goodness create anything for the devil's malignity to take possession of?" The truth is, God's gift is bestowed on the seminal elements of His creature with the same bounty wherewith " He maketh His sun to rise on the evil and on the good, and sendeth rain on the just and on the unjust." [3] It is with so large a bounty that God has blessed the very seeds, and by blessing has constituted them. Nor has this blessing been eliminated out of our excellent nature by a fault which puts us under condemnation. Owing, indeed, to God's justice, who punishes, this fatal flaw has so far prevailed, that men are born with the fault of original sin ; but yet its influence has not extended so far as to stop the birth of men. Just so does it happen in persons of adult age : whatever sins they commit, do not eliminate his manhood from man ; nay, God's work continues still good, however evil be the deeds of the impious. For although " man being placed in honour abideth not ; and being without understanding, is compared with the beasts, and is like them," [4] yet the resemblance is not so absolute that he becomes a beast. There is a comparison, no doubt, between the two ; but it is not by reason of nature, but through vice — not vice in the beast, but in nature. For so excellent is a man in comparison with a beast, that man's vice is beast's na-

ture ; still man's nature is never on this account changed into beast's nature. God, therefore, condemns man because of the fault wherewithal his nature is disgraced, and not because of his nature, which is not destroyed in consequence of its fault. Heaven forbid that we should think beasts are obnoxious to the sentence of condemnation ! It is only proper that they should be free from our misery, inasmuch as they cannot partake of our blessedness. What, then, is there surprising or unjust in man's being subjected to an impure spirit — not on account of nature, but on account of that impurity of his which he has contracted in the stain of his birth, and which proceeds, not from the divine work, but from the will of man ; — since also the impure spirit itself is a good thing considered as spirit, but evil in that it is impure ? For the one is of God, and is His work, while the other emanates from man's own will. The stronger nature, therefore, that is, the angelic one, keeps the lower, or human, nature in subjection, by reason of the association of vice with the latter. Accordingly the Mediator, who was stronger than the angels, became weak for man's sake.[5] So that the pride of the Destroyer is destroyed by the humility of the Redeemer ; and he who makes his boast over the sons of men of his angelic strength, is vanquished by the Son of God in the human weakness which He assumed.

### CHAP. 47 [XLI.] — SENTENCES FROM AMBROSE IN FAVOUR OF ORIGINAL SIN.

And now that we are about to bring this book to a conclusion, we think it proper to do on this subject of *Original Sin* what we did before in our treatise *On Grace*,[6] — adduce in evidence against the injurious talk of these persons that servant of God, the Archbishop Ambrose, whose faith is proclaimed by Pelagius to be the most perfect among the writers of the Latin Church ; for *grace* is more especially honoured in doing away with *original sin*. In the work which the saintly Ambrose wrote, *Concerning the Resurrection*, he says : " I fell in Adam, in Adam was I expelled from Paradise, in Adam I died ; and He does not recall me unless He has found me in Adam, — so as that, as I am obnoxious to the guilt of sin in him, and subject to death, I may be also justified in Christ." [7] Then, again, writing against the Novatians, he says : " We men are all of us born in sin ; our very origin is in sin ; as you may read when David says, ' Behold, I was shapen in iniquity, and in sin did my mother conceive me.' [8] Hence it is that Paul's flesh is ' a body of death ; ' [9] even as he says himself, ' Who shall deliver me from the body of this death?' Christ's flesh, however, has con-

---

[1] Matt. xii. 29.     [2] Col. i. 13.     [3] Matt. v. 45.
[4] Ps. xlix. 12.
[5] 2 Cor. viii. 9.
[6] See above, *De Gratiâ Christi*, 49-51 (xlv., xlvi.).
[7] Ambrose's *De Exc. Sal.* ii. 6.     [8] Ps. li. 5.     [9] Rom. vii 24.

demned sin, which He experienced not by being born, and which by dying He crucified, that in our flesh there might be justification through grace, where previously there was impurity through sin."[1]  The same holy man also, in his *Exposition of Isaiah*, speaking of Christ, says : "Therefore as man He was tried in all things, and in the likeness of men He endured all things ; but as born of the Spirit, He was free from sin. For every man is a liar, and no one but God alone is without sin. It is therefore an observed and settled fact, that no man born of a man and a woman, that is, by means of their bodily union, is seen to be free from sin. Whosoever, indeed, is free from sin, is free also from a conception and birth of this kind."[2]  Moreover, when expounding the Gospel according to Luke, he says : "It was no cohabitation with a husband which opened the secrets of the Virgin's womb ; rather was it the Holy Ghost which infused immaculate seed into her unviolated womb. For the Lord Jesus alone of those who are born of woman is holy, inasmuch as He experienced not the contact of earthly corruption, by reason of the novelty of His immaculate birth ; nay, He repelled it by His heavenly majesty."[3]

CHAP. 48. — PELAGIUS RIGHTLY CONDEMNED AND REALLY OPPOSED BY AMBROSE.

These words, however, of the man of God are contradicted by Pelagius, notwithstanding all his commendation of his author, when he himself declares that "we are procreated, as without virtue, so without vice."[4]  What remains, then, but that Pelagius should condemn and renounce this error of his ; or else be sorry that he has quoted Ambrose in the way he has? Inasmuch, however, as the blessed Ambrose, catholic bishop as he is, has expressed himself in the above-quoted passages in accordance with the catholic faith, it follows that Pelagius, along with his disciple Cœlestius, was justly condemned by the authority of the catholic Church for having turned aside from the true way of faith, since he repented not for having bestowed commendation on Ambrose, and for having at the same time entertained opinions in opposition to him. I know full well with what insatiable avidity you[5] read whatever is written for edification and in confirmation of the faith ; but yet, notwithstanding its utility as contributing to such an end, I must at last bring this treatise to a conclusion.

---

[1] Ambrose's *De Pœnitentia*, i. 2, 3.
[2] Quoted from a work by St. Ambrose, *On Isaiah*, not now extant.
[3] See Book ii. 56 of this *Commentary on St. Luke*, ch. ii.

[4] See above, ch. 14 (xiii.).
[5] The three friends to whom these two books are addressed were pious members of the same family; Pinianus was the husband, Melania his wife, and Albina her mother.

ON MARRIAGE AND CONCUPISCENCE.

# EXTRACT FROM AUGUSTIN'S "RETRACTATIONS,"

## BOOK II. CHAP. 53,

### ON THE FOLLOWING TREATISE,

## "DE NUPTIIS ET CONCUPISCENTIA."

---

"I ADDRESSED two books to the Illustrious Count Valerius, upon hearing that the Pelagians had brought sundry vague charges against us, — how, for instance, we condemned marriage by maintaining Original Sin. These books are entitled, *On Marriage and Concupiscence*. We maintain that marriage is good; and that it must not be supposed that the concupiscence of the flesh, or "the law in our members which wars against the law of our mind,"[1] is a fault of marriage. Conjugal chastity makes a good use of the evil of concupiscence in the procreation of children. My treatise contained two books. The first of them found its way into the hands of Julianus the Pelagian, who wrote four books in opposition to it. Out of these, somebody extracted sundry passages, and sent them to Count Valerius; he handed them to us, and after I had received them I wrote a second book in answer to these extracts. The first book of this work of mine opens with these words: "Our new heretics, most beloved son Valerius," while the second begins thus: "Amid the cares of your duty as a soldier."

---

[1] Rom. vii. 23.

# ADVERTISEMENT TO THE READER ON THE FOLLOWING TREATISE.

---

On revising these two Books, which he addressed to the Count Valerius, Augustin placed them immediately after his reply to the discourse of the Arians, which was affixed to the *Proceedings with Emeritus*.[1] Now these proceedings are stated to have taken place on the 20th of September, in the year of our Lord 418.[2] There can be no doubt, then, that these subjoined books — or, at any rate, the former of them — were written either at the close of the year 418, or in the beginning of the year 419. For, concerning this first book, Augustin says himself: "This book of mine, however, which he [Julianus] says he answered in four books, I wrote after the condemnation of Pelagius and Cœlestius. This," he adds, "I have deemed it right to mention, because he declares that my words had been used by the enemies of the truth to bring it into odium. Let no one, therefore, suppose that it was owing to this book of mine that condemnation had been passed on the new heretics who are enemies of the grace of Christ."[3] From these words one may see at once that this first book was published about the same time as the condemnation of the Pelagians in the year 418.

Soon after its publication it began to be assailed by the Pelagians, who observed that its perusal was producing in the minds of the catholics much odium against their heresy. One of them, Julianus,[4] influenced with a warm desire of furthering the heretical movement, attacked the first book of Augustin's treatise in four books of his own. Out of these, sundry extracts were culled by some interested person, and forwarded to Count Valerius. Valerius despatched them from Ravenna to Rome, to Alypius,[5] in order that he, on returning to Africa, might hand them to Augustin for the purpose of an early refutation, together with a letter in which Valerius thanked Augustin for the previous work which he also mentioned. Augustin saw at once that these extracts had been taken out of the work of Julianus; and, although he preferred reserving his answer to the selections till he had received the entire work from which they were culled, he still thought that he was bound to avoid all delay in satisfying the Count Valerius. Without loss of time, therefore, he drew up in answer his second book, with the same title as before, *On Marriage and Concupiscence*, which, as we think, must be assigned to the year 420, since the holy doctor wrote it immediately after the expression of thanks for the first book; for it is clearly improbable that Valerius should have waited two years or more to make the acknowledgment of his gratitude.

Moreover, the Valerius whom Augustin dignifies with the title of *Illustrious* as well as *Count*, was much employed in public life — not, to be sure, in the forum, but in the field; and from this circumstance we find it difficult to accede to the opinion that supposes him to have been the same person with the Valerius who was Count of the Private Estate in the year 425, Consul in 432, and lastly Master of the Offices under Theodosius the younger in the year 434. These appointments, indeed, had no connection with military service, nor had the prefects of Theodosius anything in common with those of Honorius.

---

[1] The Donatist bishop.

[2] [This work gives an account of the meeting of the catholic bishops at Cæsarea on Sept. 20, 418, at which Emeritus was present by invitation. Cf. Smith and Wace, *Dict. of Christ. Biog.* ii. 107. — W.]

[3] *Against Two Epistles of the Pelagians*, ch. 9.

[4] Bishop of Eclanum in Italy. See below at beginning of Book ii.

[5] The great friend of Augustin.

# A LETTER[1] ADDRESSED TO THE COUNT VALERIUS,

## *ON AUGUSTIN'S FORWARDING TO HIM WHAT HE CALLS HIS FIRST BOOK "ON MARRIAGE AND CONCUPISCENCE."*

---

TO THE ILLUSTRIOUS AND DESERVEDLY EMINENT LORD AND HIS MOST DEARLY BELOVED SON IN THE LOVE OF CHRIST, VALERIUS, AUGUSTIN SENDS GREETING IN THE LORD.

1. WHILE I was chafing at the long disappointment of receiving no acknowledgments from your Highness of the many letters which I had written to you, I all at once received three letters from your Grace, — one by the hand of my fellow bishop Vindemialis, which was not meant for me only, and two, soon afterwards, through my brother presbyter Firmus. This holy man, who is bound to me, as you may have ascertained from his own lips, by the ties of a most intimate love, had much conversation with me about your excellence, and gave me undoubted proofs of his complete knowledge of your character "in the bowels of Christ;"[2] by these means he had sight, not only of the letters of which the fore-mentioned bishop and he himself had been the bearers, but also of those which we expressed our disappointment at not having received. Now his information respecting you was all the more pleasant to us, inasmuch as he gave me to understand, what it was out of your power to do, that you would not, even at my earnest request for an answer, become the extoller of your own praises, contrary to the permission of Holy Scripture.[3] But I ought myself to hesitate to write to you in this strain, lest I should incur the suspicion of flattering you, my illustrious and deservedly eminent lord and dearly beloved son in the love of Christ.

2. Now, as to your praises in Christ, or rather Christ's praises in you, see what delight and joy it was to me to hear of them from him, who could neither deceive me because of his fidelity to me, nor be ignorant of them by reason of his friendship with you. But other testimony, which though inferior in amount and certainty has still reached my ear from divers quarters, assures me how sound and catholic is your faith; how devout your hope of the future; how great your love to God and the brethren; how humble your mind amid the highest honours, as you do not trust in uncertain riches, but in the living God, and art rich in good works;[4] how your house is a rest and comfort of the saints, and a terror to evil-doers; how great is your care that no man lay snares for Christ's members (either among His old enemies or those of more recent days), although he use Christ's name as a cloak for his wiles; and at the same time, though you give no quarter to the error of these enemies, how provident you are to secure their salvation. This and the like, we frequently hear, as I have already said, even from others; but at the present moment we have, by means of the above-mentioned brother, received a fuller and more trustworthy knowledge.

3. Touching, however, the subject of conjugal purity, that we might be able to bestow our commendation and love upon you for it, could we possibly listen to the information of any one but some bosom friend of your own, who had no mere superficial acquaintance with you, but knew your innermost life? Concerning, therefore, this excellent gift of God to you, I am delighted to converse with you with more frankness and at greater length. I am quite sure that I shall not prove burdensome to you, even if I send you a prolix treatise, the perusal of which will only ensure a longer converse between us. For this have I discovered, that amidst your manifold and weighty cares you pursue your reading with ease and pleasure; and that you take great delight in any little performances of ours, even if they are addressed to other persons, whenever they have chanced to fall into your hands. Whatever, therefore, is addressed to *yourself*, in which I can speak to you as it were personally, you will deign both to notice with greater attention, and to receive with a higher pleasure. From the perusal, then, of this letter, turn to the book which I send with it. It will in its very commencement, in a more convenient manner, intimate to your Reverence the reason, both why it has been written, and why it has been submitted specially to your consideration.

---

[1] This is the 200th in the collection of Augustin's *Letters.*

[2] Phil. i. 8.　　　　　　　　　[3] Prov. xxvii. 2.　　　　　　　　　[4] 1 Tim. vi. 17.

# CONTENTS OF THE TREATISE "ON MARRIAGE AND CONCUPISCENCE."

## BOOK I.

# BOOK II.

# ON MARRIAGE AND CONCUPISCENCE.

In Two Books,

## ADDRESSED TO THE COUNT VALERIUS

*BY AURELIUS AUGUSTIN, BISHOP OF HIPPO;*

WRITTEN IN 419 AND 420.

---

# BOOK I.[1]

WHEREIN HE EXPOUNDS THE PECULIAR AND NATURAL BLESSINGS OF MARRIAGE. HE SHOWS THAT AMONG THESE BLESSINGS MUST NOT BE RECKONED FLESHLY CONCUPISCENCE; INSOMUCH AS THIS IS WHOLLY EVIL, SUCH AS DOES NOT PROCEED FROM THE VERY NATURE OF MARRIAGE, BUT IS AN ACCIDENT THEREOF ARISING FROM ORIGINAL SIN. THIS EVIL, NOTWITHSTANDING, IS RIGHTLY EMPLOYED BY MARRIAGE FOR THE PROCREATION OF CHILDREN. BUT, AS THE RESULT OF THIS CONCUPISCENCE, IT COMES TO PASS THAT, EVEN FROM THE LAWFUL MARRIAGE OF THE CHILDREN OF GOD, MEN ARE NOT BORN CHILDREN OF GOD, BUT OF THE WORLD, AND ARE BOUND WITH THE CHAIN OF SIN, ALTHOUGH THEIR PARENTS HAVE BEEN LIBERATED THEREFROM BY GRACE; AND ARE LED CAPTIVE BY THE DEVIL, IF THEY BE NOT IN LIKE MANNER RESCUED BY THE SELF-SAME GRACE OF CHRIST. HE EXPLAINS HOW IT IS THAT CONCUPISCENCE REMAINS IN THE BAPTIZED IN ACT THOUGH NOT IN GUILT. HE TEACHES, THAT BY THE SANCTITY OF BAPTISM, NOT MERELY THIS ORIGINAL GUILT, BUT ALL OTHER SINS OF MEN WHATEVER, ARE TAKEN AWAY. HE LASTLY QUOTES THE AUTHORITY OF AMBROSE TO SHOW THAT THE EVIL OF CONCUPISCENCE MUST BE DISTINGUISHED FROM THE GOOD OF MARRIAGE.

CHAP. I. — CONCERNING THE ARGUMENT OF THIS TREATISE.

OUR new heretics, my dearest sòn Valerius, who maintain that infants born in the flesh have no need of that medicine of Christ whereby sins are healed, are constantly affirming, in their excessive hatred of us, that we condemn marriage and that divine procedure by which God creates human beings by means of men and women, inasmuch as we assert that they who are born of such a union contract that original sin of which the apostle says, "By one man sin entered into the world, and death by sin; and so death passed upon all men, for in him all sinned;"[2] and because we do not deny, that of whatever kind of parents they are born, they are still under the devil's dominion, unless they be born again in Christ, and by His grace be removed from the power of darkness and translated into His kingdom,[3] who willed not to be born from the same union of the two sexes. Because, then, we affirm this doctrine, which is contained in the oldest and unvarying rule of the catholic faith, these propounders of the novel and perverse dogma, who assert that there is no sin in infants to be washed away in the laver of regen-

[1] Written about the beginning of the year A.D. 419.

[2] In quo omnes peccaverunt, Rom. v. 5.

[3] Col. i. 15.

eration,[1] in their unbelief or ignorance calumniate us, as if we condemned marriage, and as if we asserted to be the devil's work what is God's own work — the human being which is born of marriage. Nor do they reflect that the good of marriage is no more impeachable on account of the original evil which is derived therefrom, than the evil of adultery and fornication is excusable on account of the natural good which is born of them. For as sin is the work of the devil, from whencesoever contracted by infants ; so man is the work of God, from whencesoever born. Our purpose, therefore, in this book, so far as the Lord vouchsafes us in His help, is to distinguish between the evil of carnal concupiscence from which man who is born therefrom contracts original sin, and the good of marriage. For there would have been none of this shame-producing concupiscence, which is impudently praised by impudent men, if man had not previously sinned ; while as to marriage, it would still have existed, even if no man had sinned, since the procreation of children in the body that belonged to that life would have been effected without that malady which in " the body of this death "[2] cannot be separated from the process of procreation.

### CHAP. 2 [II.] — WHY THIS TREATISE WAS ADDRESSED TO VALERIUS.

Now there are three very special reasons, which I will briefly indicate, why I wished to write to you particularly on this subject. One is, because by the gift of Christ you are a strict observer of conjugal chastity. Another is, because by your great care and diligence you have effectually withstood those profane novelties which we are resisting in our present discussion. The third is, because of my learning that something which they had committed to writing had found its way into your hands ; and although in your robust faith you could despise such an attempt, it is still a good thing for us also to know how to bring aid to our faith by defending it. For the Apostle Peter instructs us to be " ready always to give an answer to every one that asketh us a reason of the faith and hope that is in us ; "[3] and the Apostle Paul says, " Let your speech be alway with grace, seasoned with salt, that ye may know how ye ought to answer every man."[4] These are the motives which chiefly impel me to hold such converse with you in this volume, as the Lord shall enable me. I have never liked, indeed, to intrude the perusal of any of my humble labours on any eminent person, who is like yourself conspicuous to all from the elevation of his office, without his own request, — especially when he is not blessed with the enjoyment of a dignified retirement, but is still occupied in the public duties of a soldier's profession ; this has always seemed to me to savour more of impertinence than of respectful esteem. If, then, I have incurred censure of this kind, while acting on the reasons which I have now mentioned, I crave the favour of your forgiveness, and a kindly regard to the following arguments.

### CHAP. 3 [III.] — CONJUGAL CHASTITY THE GIFT OF GOD.

That chastity in the married state is God's gift, is shown by the most blessed Paul, when, speaking on this very subject, he says : " But I would that all men were even as I myself : but every man hath his proper gift of God, one after this manner, and another after that."[5] Observe, he tells us that this gift is from God ; and although he classes it below that continence in which he would have all men to be like himself, he still describes it as a gift of God. Whence we understand that, when these precepts are given to us in order that we should do them, nothing else is stated than that there ought to be within us our own will also for receiving and having them. When, therefore, these are shown to be gifts of God, it is meant that they must be sought from Him if they are not already possessed ; and if they are possessed, thanks must be given to Him for the possession ; moreover, that our own wills have but small avail for seeking, obtaining, and holding fast these gifts, unless they be assisted by God's grace.

### CHAP. 4. — A DIFFICULTY AS REGARDS THE CHASTITY OF UNBELIEVERS. NONE BUT A BELIEVER IS TRULY A CHASTE MAN.[6]

What, then, have we to say when conjugal chastity is discovered even in some unbelievers ? Must it be said that they sin, in that they make a bad use of a gift of God, in not restoring it to the worship of Him from whom they received it ? Or must these endowments, perchance, be not regarded as gifts of God at all, when they are not believers who exercise them ; according to the apostle's sentiment, when he says, " Whatsoever is not of faith is sin ? "[7] But who would dare to say that a gift of God is sin ? For the soul and the body, and all the natural endowments which are implanted in the soul and the body, even in the persons of sinful men, are still gifts of God ; for it is God who made them, and not they themselves. When it is said, " Whatsoever is not of faith is sin," only those

---

[1] Titus iii. 5.          [2] Rom. vii. 24.
[3] 1 Pet. iii. 15. [The reading " faith and hope " stands in certain Latin Biblical MSS. Also, e.g., Codices Harleianus and Toletanus. Traces of a similar reading are not unknown also in Greek (Origen, Basil) and Syriac (Peshitto) sources. — W.]
[4] Col. iv. 6.

[5] 1 Cor. vii. 7.
[6] See Augustin's work *Against Julianus*, iv. 3.
[7] Rom. xiv. 23.

things are meant which men themselves do. When men, therefore, do without faith those things which seem to appertain to conjugal chastity, they do them either to please men, whether themselves or others, or to avoid incurring such troubles as are incidental to human nature in those things which they corruptly desire, or to pay service to devils. Sins are not really restrained, but some sins are overpowered by other sins. God forbid, then, that a man be truly called chaste who observes connubial fidelity to his wife from any other motive than devotion to the true God.

### CHAP. 5 [IV.] — THE NATURAL GOOD OF MARRIAGE. ALL SOCIETY NATURALLY REPUDIATES A FRAUDULENT COMPANION. WHAT IS TRUE CONJUGAL PURITY? NO TRUE VIRGINITY AND CHASTITY, EXCEPT IN DEVOTION TO TRUE FAITH.

The union, then, of male and female for the purpose of procreation is the natural good of marriage. But he makes a bad use of this good who uses it bestially, so that his intention is on the gratification of lust, instead of the desire of offspring. Nevertheless, in sundry animals unendowed with reason, as, for instance, in most birds, there is both preserved a certain kind of confederation of pairs, and a social combination of skill in nest-building; and their mutual division of the periods for cherishing their eggs and their alternation in the labor of feeding their young, give them the appearance of so acting, when they mate, as to be intent rather on securing the continuance of their kind than on gratifying lust. Of these two, the one is the likeness of man in a brute; the other, the likeness of the brute in man. With respect, however, to what I ascribed to the nature of marriage, that the male and the female are united together as associates for procreation, and consequently do not defraud each other (forasmuch as every associated state has a natural abhorrence of a fraudulent companion), although even men without faith possess this palpable blessing of nature, yet, since they use it not in faith, they only turn it to evil and sin. In like manner, therefore, the marriage of believers converts to the use of righteousness that carnal concupiscence by which "the flesh lusteth against the Spirit."[1] For they entertain the firm purpose of generating offspring to be regenerated — that the children who are born of them as "children of the world" may be born again and become "sons of God." Wherefore all parents who do not beget children with this intention, this will, this purpose, of transferring them from being members of the first man into being members of Christ, but boast as unbelieving parents over unbelieving

children, — however circumspect they be in their cohabitation, studiously limiting it to the begetting of children, — really have no conjugal chastity in themselves. For inasmuch as chastity is a virtue, having unchastity as its contrary vice, and as all the virtues (even those whose operation is by means of the body) have their seat in the soul, how can the body be in any true sense said to be chaste, when the soul itself is committing fornication against the true God? Now such fornication the holy psalmist censures when he says: "For, lo, they that are far from Thee shall perish: Thou hast destroyed all them that go a whoring from Thee."[2] There is, then, no true chastity, whether conjugal, or vidual, or virginal, except that which devotes itself to true faith. For though consecrated virginity is rightly preferred to marriage, yet what Christian in his sober mind would not prefer catholic Christian women who have been even more than once married, to not only vestals, but also to heretical virgins? So great is the avail of faith, of which the apostle says, "Whatsoever is not of faith is sin;"[3] and of which it is written in the Epistle to the Hebrews, "Without faith it is impossible to please God."[4]

### CHAP. 6 [V.] — THE CENSURING OF LUST IS NOT A CONDEMNATION OF MARRIAGE; WHENCE COMES SHAME IN THE HUMAN BODY. ADAM AND EVE WERE NOT CREATED BLIND; MEANING OF THEIR "EYES BEING OPENED."

Now, this being the real state of the question, they undoubtedly err who suppose that, when fleshly lust is censured, marriage is condemned; as if the malady of concupiscence was the outcome of marriage and not of sin. Were not those first spouses, whose nuptials God blessed with the words, "Be fruitful and multiply,"[5] naked, and yet not ashamed? Why, then, did shame arise out of their members after sin, except because an indecent motion arose from them, which, if men had not sinned, would certainly never have existed in marriage? Or was it, forsooth, as some hold (who give little heed to what they read), that human beings were, like dogs, at first created blind; and — absurder still — obtained sight, not as dogs do, by growing, but by sinning? Far be it from us to entertain such an opinion. But they gather that opinion of theirs from reading: "She took of the fruit thereof, and did eat; and gave also unto her husband with her, and he did eat: and the eyes of them both were opened, and they knew that they were naked."[6] This accounts for the opinion of unintelligent persons, that the eyes of the first man and woman were previously closed, because Holy Scripture testifies that they were

---

[1] Gal. v. 17

[2] Ps. lxxiii. 27.    [3] Rom. xiv. 23.    [4] Heb. xi. 6.
[5] Gen. i. 28.    [6] Gen. iii. 6, 7.

then opened. Well, then, were Hagar's eyes, the handmaid of Sarah, previously shut, when, with her thirsty and sobbing child, she opened her eyes [1] and saw the well? Or did those two disciples, after the Lord's resurrection, walk in the way with Him with their eyes shut, since the evangelist says of them that "in the breaking of bread their eyes were opened, and they knew Him"? [2] What, therefore, is written concerning the first man and woman, that "the eyes of them both were opened," [3] we ought to understand as that they gave attention to perceiving and recognising the new state which had befallen their body. Now that their eyes were opened, their body appeared to them naked, and they knew it. If this were not the meaning, how, when the beasts of the field and the fowls of the air were brought unto him, [4] could Adam have given them names if his eyes were shut? He could not have done this without distinguishing them; and he could not distinguish them without seeing them. How, too, could the woman herself have been beheld so clearly by him when he said, "This is now bone of my bone, and flesh of my flesh"? [5] If, indeed, any one shall be so determined on cavilling as to insist that Adam might have acquired a discernment of these objects, not by sight but by touch, what explanation will he have to give of the passage wherein we are told how the woman "saw that the tree," from which she was about to pluck the forbidden fruit, "was pleasant for the eyes to behold"? [6] No; "they were both naked, and were not ashamed," [7] not because they had no eyesight, but because they perceived no reason to be ashamed in their members, which had all along been seen by them. For it is not said: They were both naked, *and knew it not;* but "they were not ashamed." Because, indeed, nothing had previously happened which was not lawful, so nothing had ensued which could cause them shame.

## CHAP. 7 [VI.] — MAN'S DISOBEDIENCE JUSTLY REQUITED IN THE REBELLION OF HIS OWN FLESH; THE BLUSH OF SHAME FOR THE DISOBEDIENT MEMBERS OF THE BODY.

When the first man transgressed the law of God, he began to have another law in his members which was repugnant to the law of his mind, and he felt the evil of his own disobedience when he experienced in the disobedience of his flesh a most righteous retribution recoiling on himself. Such, then, was "the opening of his eyes" which the serpent had promised him in his temptation [8] — the knowledge, in fact, of something which he had better been ignorant of. Then, indeed, did man perceive within himself what he had done;

then did he distinguish evil from good, — not by avoiding it, but by enduring it. For it certainly was not just that obedience should be rendered by his servant, that is, his body, to him, who had not obeyed his own Lord. Well, then, how significant is the fact that the eyes, and lips, and tongue, and hands, and feet, and the bending of back, and neck, and sides, are all placed within our power — to be applied to such operations as are suitable to them, when we have a body free from impediments and in a sound state of health; but when it must come to man's great function of the procreation of children, the members which were expressly created for this purpose will not obey the direction of the will, but lust has to be waited for to set these members in motion, as if it had legal right over them, and sometimes it refuses to act when the mind wills, while often it acts against its will! Must not this bring the blush of shame over the freedom of the human will, that by its contempt of God, its own Commander, it has lost all proper command for itself over its own members? Now, wherein could be found a more fitting demonstration of the just depravation of human nature by reason of its disobedience, than in the disobedience of those parts whence nature herself derives subsistence by succession? For it is by an especial propriety that those parts of the body are designated as *natural.* This, then, was the reason why the first human pair, on experiencing in the flesh that motion which was indecent because disobedient, and on feeling the shame of their nakedness, covered these offending members with fig-leaves; [3] in order that, at the very least, by the will of the ashamed offenders, a veil might be thrown over that which was put into motion without the will of those who wished it: and since shame arose from what indecently pleased, decency might be attained by concealment.

## CHAP. 8 [VII.] — THE EVIL OF LUST DOES NOT TAKE AWAY THE GOOD OF MARRIAGE.

Forasmuch, then, as the good of marriage could not be lost by the addition of this evil, some imprudent persons suppose that this is not an added evil, but something which appertains to the original good. A distinction, however, occurs not only to subtle reason, but even to the most ordinary natural judgment, which was both apparent in the case of the first man and woman, and also holds good still in the case of married persons to-day. What they afterward effected in propagation, — that is the good of marriage; but what they first veiled through shame, — that is the evil of concupiscence, which everywhere shuns sight, and in its shame seeks privacy. Since, therefore, marriage effects some good even out of that evil, it has whereof to glory;

---

[1] Gen. xxi. 17-19.　　[2] Luke xxiv. 31.　　[3] Gen. iii. 7.
[4] Gen. ii. 19.　　[5] Gen. ii. 23.　　[6] Gen. iii. 6.
[7] Gen. ii. 25.　　[8] Gen. iii. 5.

but since the good cannot be effected without the evil, it has reason for feeling shame. The case may be illustrated by the example of a lame man. Suppose him to attain to some good object by limping after it, then, on the one hand, the attainment itself is not evil because of the evil of the man's lameness; nor, on the other hand, is the lameness good because of the goodness of the attainment. So, on the same principle, we ought not to condemn marriage because of the evil of lust; nor must we praise lust because of the good of marriage.

CHAP. 9 [VIII.] — THIS DISEASE OF CONCUPISCENCE IN MARRIAGE IS NOT TO BE A MATTER OF WILL, BUT OF NECESSITY; WHAT OUGHT TO BE THE WILL OF BELIEVERS IN THE USE OF MATRIMONY; WHO IS TO BE REGARDED AS USING, AND NOT SUCCUMBING TO, THE EVIL OF CONCUPISCENCE; HOW THE HOLY FATHERS OF THE OLD TESTAMENT FORMERLY USED WIVES.

This disease of concupiscence is what the apostle refers to, when, speaking to married believers, he says: "This is the will of God, even your sanctification, that ye should abstain from fornication: that every one of you should know how to possess his vessel in sanctification and honour; not in the disease of desire, even as the Gentiles which know not God."[1] The married believer, therefore, must not only not use another man's vessel, which is what they do who lust after others' wives; but he must know that even his own vessel is not to be possessed in the disease of carnal concupiscence. And this counsel is not to be understood as if the apostle prohibited conjugal — that is to say, lawful and honourable — cohabitation; but so as that that cohabitation (which would have no adjunct of unwholesome lust, were it not that man's perfect freedom of choice had become by preceding sin so disabled that it has this fatal adjunct) should not be a matter of will, but of necessity, without which, nevertheless, it would be impossible to attain to the fruition of the will itself in the procreation of children. And this wish is not in the marriages of believers determined by the purpose of having such children born as shall pass through life in this present world, but such as shall be born again in Christ, and remain in Him for evermore. Now if this result should come about, the reward of a full felicity will spring from marriage; but if such result be not realized, there will yet ensue to the married pair the peace of their good will. Whosoever possesses his vessel (that is, his wife) with this intention of heart, certainly does not possess her in the "disease of desire," as the Gentiles which know not God, but in sanctification and

honour, as believers who hope in God. A man turns to use the evil of concupiscence, and is not overcome by it, when he bridles and restrains its rage, as it works in inordinate and indecorous motions; and never relaxes his hold upon it except when intent on offspring, and then controls and applies it to the carnal generation of children to be spiritually regenerated, not to the subjection of the spirit to the flesh in a sordid servitude. That the holy fathers of olden times after Abraham, and before him, to whom God gave His testimony that "they pleased Him,"[2] thus used their wives, no one who is a Christian ought to doubt, since it was permitted to certain individuals amongst them to have a plurality of wives, where the reason was for the multiplication of their offspring, not the desire of varying gratification.

CHAP. 10 [IX.] — WHY IT WAS SOMETIMES PERMITTED THAT A MAN SHOULD HAVE SEVERAL WIVES, YET NO WOMAN WAS EVER ALLOWED TO HAVE MORE THAN ONE HUSBAND. NATURE PREFERS SINGLENESS IN HER DOMINATIONS.

Now, if to the God of our fathers, who is likewise our God, such a plurality of wives had not been displeasing for the purpose that lust might have a fuller range of indulgence; then, on such a supposition, the holy women also ought each to have rendered service to several husbands. But if any woman had so acted, what feeling but that of a disgraceful concupiscence could impel her to have more husbands, seeing that by such licence she could not have more children? That the good purpose of marriage, however, is better promoted by one husband with one wife, than by a husband with several wives, is shown plainly enough by the very first union of a married pair, which was made by the Divine Being Himself, with the intention of marriages taking their beginning therefrom, and of its affording to them a more honourable precedent. In the advance, however, of the human race, it came to pass that to certain good men were united a plurality of good wives, — many to each; and from this it would seem that moderation sought rather unity on one side for dignity, while nature permitted plurality on the other side for fecundity. For on natural principles it is more feasible for one to have dominion over many, than for many to have dominion over one. Nor can it be doubted, that it is more consonant with the order of nature that men should bear rule over women, than women over men. It is with this principle in view that the apostle says, "The head of the woman is the man;"[3] and, "Wives, submit yourselves unto your own husbands."[4] So also

---

[1] 1 Thess. iv. 3-5.

[2] See Heb. xi. 4-6.  [3] 1 Cor. xi. 3.  [4] Col. iii. 18.

the Apostle Peter writes : " Even as Sara obeyed Abraham, calling him lord." [1] Now, although the fact of the matter is, that while nature loves singleness in her dominations, but we may see plurality existing more readily in the subordinate portion of our race ; yet for all that, it was at no time lawful for one man to have a plurality of wives, except for the purpose of a greater number of children springing from him. Wherefore, if one woman cohabits with several men, inasmuch as no increase of offspring accrues to her therefrom, but only a more frequent gratification of lust, she cannot possibly be a wife, but only a harlot.

CHAP. 11 [X.] — THE SACRAMENT OF MARRIAGE ; MARRIAGE INDISSOLUBLE ; THE WORLD'S LAW ABOUT DIVORCE DIFFERENT FROM THE GOSPEL'S.

It is certainly not fecundity only, the fruit of which consists of offspring, nor chastity only, whose bond is fidelity, but also a certain sacramental bond [2] in marriage which is recommended to believers in wedlock. Accordingly it is enjoined by the apostle : " Husbands, love your wives, even as Christ also loved the Church." [3] Of this bond the substance [4] undoubtedly is this, that the man and the woman who are joined together in matrimony should remain inseparable as long as they live ; and that it should be unlawful for one consort to be parted from the other, except for the cause of fornication. [5] For this is preserved in the case of Christ and the Church ; so that, as a living one with a living one, there is no divorce, no separation for ever. And so complete is the observance of this bond in the city of our God, in His holy mountain [6] — that is to say, in the Church of Christ — by all married believers, who are undoubtedly members of Christ, that, although women marry, and men take wives, for the purpose of procreating children, it is never permitted one to put away even an unfruitful wife for the sake of having another to bear children. And whosoever does this is held to be guilty of adultery by the law of the gospel ; though not by this world's rule, which allows a divorce between the parties, without even the allegation of guilt, and the contraction of other nuptial engagements, — a concession which, the Lord tells us, even the holy Moses extended to the people of Israel, because of the hardness of their hearts. [7] The same condemnation applies to the woman, if she is married to another man. So enduring, indeed, are the rights of marriage between those who have contracted them, as long as they both live, that even they are looked on as man and wife still, who have separated from one another, rather than they between whom a new connection has been formed. For by this new connection they would not be guilty of adultery, if the previous matrimonial relation did not still continue. If the husband die, with whom a true marriage was made, a true marriage is now possible by a connection which would before have been adultery. Thus between the conjugal pair, as long as they live, the nuptial bond has a permanent obligation, and can be cancelled neither by separation nor by union with another. But this permanence avails, in such cases, only for injury from the sin, not for a bond of the covenant. In like manner the soul of an apostate, which renounces as it were its marriage union with Christ, does not, even though it has cast its faith away, lose the sacrament of its faith, which it received in the laver of regeneration. It would undoubtedly be given back to him if he were to return, although he lost it on his departure from Christ. He retains, however, the sacrament after his apostasy, to the aggravation of his punishment, not for meriting the reward.

CHAP. 12 [XI.] — MARRIAGE DOES NOT CANCEL A MUTUAL VOW OF CONTINENCE ; THERE WAS TRUE WEDLOCK BETWEEN MARY AND JOSEPH ; IN WHAT WAY JOSEPH WAS THE FATHER OF CHRIST.

But God forbid that the nuptial bond should be regarded as broken between those who have by mutual consent agreed to observe a perpetual abstinence from the use of carnal concupiscence. Nay, it will be only a firmer one, whereby they have exchanged pledges together, which will have to be kept by an especial endearment and concord, — not by the voluptuous links of bodies, but by the voluntary affections of souls. For it was not deceitfully that the angel said to Joseph : " Fear not to take unto thee Mary thy wife." [8] She is called his wife because of her first troth of betrothal, although he had had no carnal knowledge of her, nor was destined to have. The designation of wife was neither destroyed nor made untrue, where there never had been, nor was meant to be, any carnal connection. That virgin wife was rather a holier and more wonderful joy to her husband because of her very pregnancy without man, with disparity as to the child that was born, without disparity in the faith they cherished. And because of this conjugal fidelity they are both deservedly called " parents " [9] of Christ (not only she as His mother, but he as His father, as being her husband), both having been such in mind and purpose, though not in the flesh. But while the one was His father in purpose only, and the other His mother in the flesh also, they were both of them, for all that, only the parents of His humility, not of His sublimity ; of His weakness, not of His divinity.

---

[1] 1 Pet. iii. 6.
[2] Quoddam sacramentum. See above, On Original Sin, ch. 39 [xxxiv.].
[3] Eph. v. 25.  [4] Res sacramenti.  [5] Matt. v. 32.
[6] Ps. xlviii. 2.  [7] Matt. xix. 8.
[8] Matt. i. 20.  [9] Luke ii. 41.

For the Gospel does not lie, in which one reads, "Both His father and His mother marvelled at those things which were spoken about Him;"[1] and in another passage, "Now His parents went to Jerusalem every year;"[2] and again a little afterwards, "His mother said unto Him, Son, why hast Thou thus dealt with us? Behold, Thy father and I have sought Thee sorrowing."[3] In order, however, that He might show them that He had a Father besides them, who begat Him without a mother, He said to them in answer: "How is it that ye sought me? Wist ye not that I must be about my Father's business?"[4] Furthermore, lest He should be thought to have repudiated them as His parents by what He had just said, the evangelist at once added: "And they understood not the saying which He spake unto them; and He went down with them, and came to Nazareth, and was subject unto them."[5] Subject to whom but His parents? And who was the subject but Jesus Christ, "who, being in the form of God, thought it not robbery to be equal with God"?[6] And wherefore subject to them, who were far beneath the form of God, except that "He emptied Himself, and took upon Him the form of a servant,"[7] — the form in which His parents lived? Now, since she bore Him without his engendering, they could not surely have both been His parents, of that form of a servant, if they had not been conjugally united, though without carnal connection. Accordingly the genealogical series (although both parents of Christ are mentioned together in the succession)[8] had to be extended, as it is in fact,[9] down rather to Joseph's name, that no wrong might be done, in the case of this marriage, to the male, and indeed the stronger sex, while at the same time there was nothing detrimental to truth, since Joseph, no less than Mary, was of the seed of David,[10] of whom it was foretold that Christ should come.

CHAP. 13. — IN THE MARRIAGE OF MARY AND JOSEPH THERE WERE ALL THE BLESSINGS OF THE WEDDED STATE; ALL THAT IS BORN OF CONCUBINAGE IS SINFUL FLESH.

The entire good, therefore, of the nuptial institution was effected in the case of these parents of Christ: there was offspring, there was faithfulness, there was the bond.[11] As offspring, we recognise the Lord Jesus Himself; the fidelity, in that there was no adultery; the bond,[11] because there was no divorce. [XII.] Only there was no nuptial cohabitation; because He who was to be without sin, and was sent not in sinful flesh, but

in *the likeness* of sinful flesh,[12] could not possibly have been made in sinful flesh itself without that shameful lust of the flesh which comes from sin, and without which He willed to be born, in order that He might teach us, that every one who is born of sexual intercourse is in fact sinful flesh, since that alone which was not born of such intercourse was not sinful flesh. Nevertheless conjugal intercourse is not in itself sin, when it is had with the intention of producing children; because the mind's good-will leads the ensuing bodily pleasure, instead of following its lead; and the human choice is not distracted by the yoke of sin pressing upon it, inasmuch as the blow of the sin is rightly brought back to the purposes of procreation. This blow has a certain prurient activity which plays the king in the foul indulgences of adultery, and fornication, and lasciviousness, and uncleanness; whilst in the indispensable duties of the marriage state, it exhibits the docility of the slave. In the one case it is condemned as the shameless effrontery of so violent a master; in the other, it gets modest praise as the honest service of so submissive an attendant. This lust, then, is not in itself the good of the nuptial institution; but it is obscenity in sinful men, a necessity in procreant parents, the fire of lascivious indulgences, the shame of nuptial pleasures. Wherefore, then, may not persons remain man and wife when they cease by mutual consent from cohabitation; seeing that Joseph and Mary continued such, though they never even began to cohabit?

CHAP. 14 [XIII.] — BEFORE CHRIST IT WAS A TIME FOR MARRYING; SINCE CHRIST IT HAS BEEN A TIME FOR CONTINENCE.

Now this propagation of children which among the ancient saints was a most bounden duty for the purpose of begetting and preserving a people for God, amongst whom the prophecy of Christ's coming must needs have had precedence over everything, now has no longer the same necessity. For from among all nations the way is open for an abundant offspring to receive spiritual regeneration, from whatever quarter they derive their natural birth. So that we may acknowledge that the scripture which says there is "a time to embrace, and a time to refrain from embracing,"[13] is to be distributed in its clauses to the periods before Christ and since. The former was the time to embrace, the latter to refrain from embracing.

CHAP. 15. — THE TEACHING OF THE APOSTLE ON THIS SUBJECT.

Accordingly the apostle also, speaking apparently with this passage in view, declares: "But this I say, brethren, the time is short: it re-

---

[1] Luke ii. 33. So the Vulgate as well as the best Greek texts, instead of the "And Joseph and His mother marvelled," etc., of the common text.
[2] Luke ii. 41.        [3] Luke ii. 48.        [4] Luke ii. 49.
[5] Luke ii. 50, 51.    [6] Phil. ii. 6.        [7] Phil. ii. 7.
[8] Matt. i. 16.        [9] Compare Luke iii. 23 with Matt. i. 16.
[10] Luke i. 27.        [11] Sacramentum.
[12] Rom. viii. 3.                              [13] Eccles. iii. 5.

maineth, that both they that have wives be as though they had them not; and they that weep, as though they wept not; and they that rejoice, as though they rejoiced not; and they that buy, as though they possessed not; and they that use this world, as though they used it not: for the fashion of this world passeth away. But I would have you without solicitude."[1] This entire passage (that I may express my view on this subject in the shape of a brief exposition of the apostle's words) I think must be understood as follows: "This I say, brethren, the time is short." No longer is God's people to be propagated by carnal generation; but, henceforth, it is to be gathered out by spiritual regeneration. "It remaineth, therefore, that they that have wives" be not subject to carnal concupiscence; "and they that weep," under the sadness of present evil, should rejoice in the hope of future blessing; "and they that rejoice," over any temporary advantage, should fear the eternal judgment; "and they that buy," should so hold their possessions as not to cleave to them by overmuch love; "and they that use this world" should reflect that it is passing away, and does not remain. "For the fashion of this world passeth away: but," he says, "I would have you to be without solicitude," — in other words: I would have you lift up your heart, that it may dwell among those things which do not pass away. He then goes on to say: "He that is unmarried careth for the things that belong to the Lord, how he may please the Lord: but he that is married careth for the things that are of the world, how he may please his wife."[2] And thus to some extent he explains what he had already said: "Let them that have wives be as though they had none." For they who have wives in such a way as to care for the things of the Lord, how they may please the Lord, without having any care for the things of the world in order to please their wives, are, in fact, just as if they had no wives. And this is effected with greater ease when the wives, too, are of such a disposition, because they please their husbands not merely because they are rich, because they are high in rank, noble in race, and amiable in natural temper, but because they are believers, because they are religious, because they are chaste, because they are good men.

CHAP. 16 [XIV.] — A CERTAIN DEGREE OF INTEMPERANCE IS TO BE TOLERATED IN THE CASE OF MARRIED PERSONS; THE USE OF MATRIMONY FOR THE MERE PLEASURE OF LUST IS NOT WITHOUT SIN, BUT BECAUSE OF THE NUPTIAL RELATION THE SIN IS VENIAL.

But in the married, as these things are desirable and praiseworthy, so the others are to be

tolerated, that no lapse occur into damnable sins; that is, into fornications and adulteries. To escape this evil, even such embraces of husband and wife as have not procreation for their object, but serve an overbearing concupiscence, are permitted, so far as to be within range of forgiveness, though not prescribed by way of commandment:[3] and the married pair are enjoined not to defraud one the other, lest Satan should tempt them by reason of their incontinence.[4] For thus says the Scripture: "Let the husband render unto the wife her due:[5] and likewise also the wife unto the husband. The wife hath not power of her own body, but the husband: and likewise also the husband hath not power of his own body, but the wife. Defraud ye not one the other; except it be with consent for a time, that ye may have leisure for prayer;[6] and then come together again, that Satan tempt you not for your incontinency. But I speak this by permission,[7] and not of commandment."[8] Now in a case where permission[7] must be given, it cannot by any means be contended that there is not some amount of sin. Since, however, the cohabitation for the purpose of procreating children, which must be admitted to be the proper end of marriage, is not sinful, what is it which the apostle allows to be permissible,[7] but that married persons, when they have not the gift of continence, may require one from the other the due of the flesh — and that not from a wish for procreation, but for the pleasure of concupiscence? This gratification incurs not the imputation of guilt on account of marriage, but receives permission[7] on account of marriage. This, therefore, must be reckoned among the praises of matrimony; that, on its own account, it makes pardonable that which does not essentially appertain to itself. For the nuptial embrace, which subserves the demands of concupiscence, is so effected as not to impede the child-bearing, which is the end and aim of marriage.

CHAP. 17 [XV.] — WHAT IS SINLESS IN THE USE OF MATRIMONY? WHAT IS ATTENDED WITH VENIAL SIN, AND WHAT WITH MORTAL?

It is, however, one thing for married persons to have intercourse only for the wish to beget children, which is not sinful: it is another thing for them to desire carnal pleasure in cohabitation, but with the spouse only, which involves venial sin. For although propagation of offspring is not the motive of the intercourse, there

---

[1] 1 Cor. vii. 29–31.  [2] 1 Cor. iii. 32, 33.

[3] 1 Cor. vii. 6.  [4] 1 Cor. vii. 5.
[5] So also the best MSS. of the original.
[6] So again, after the best witnesses in the original.
[7] [The Latin word for "permission" is *venia*, which also means "indulgence," "forbearance," "forgiveness;" and so the sins that may be forgiven are called "*venial* sins," i.e. "pardonable," and in this sense "permissible," sins. Augustin's argument here turns on this word. — W.]
[8] 1 Cor. vii. 3–6.

is still no attempt to prevent such propagation, either by wrong desire or evil appliance. They who resort to these, although called by the name of spouses, are really not such; they retain no vestige of true matrimony, but pretend the honourable designation as a cloak for criminal conduct. Having also proceeded so far, they are betrayed into exposing their children, which are born against their will. They hate to nourish and retain those whom they were afraid they would beget. This infliction of cruelty on their offspring so reluctantly begotten, unmasks the sin which they had practised in darkness, and drags it clearly into the light of day. The open cruelty reproves the concealed sin. Sometimes, indeed, this lustful cruelty, or, if you please, cruel lust, resorts to such extravagant methods as to use poisonous drugs to secure barrenness; or else, if unsuccessful in this, to destroy the conceived seed by some means previous to birth, preferring that its offspring should rather perish than receive vitality; or if it was advancing to life within the womb, should be slain before it was born. Well, if both parties alike are so flagitious, they are not husband and wife; and if such were their character from the beginning, they have not come together by wedlock but by debauchery. But if the two are not alike in such sin, I boldly declare either that the woman is, so to say, the husband's harlot; or the man, the wife's adulterer.

CHAP. 18 [XVI.] — CONTINENCE BETTER THAN MARRIAGE; BUT MARRIAGE BETTER THAN FORNICATION.

Forasmuch, then, as marriage cannot be such as that of the primitive men might have been, if sin had not preceded; it may yet be like that of the holy fathers of the olden time, in such wise that the carnal concupiscence which causes shame (which did not exist in paradise previous to the fall, and after that event was not allowed to remain there), although necessarily forming a part of the body of this death, is not subservient to it, but only submits its function, when forced thereto, for the sole purpose of assisting in the procreation of children; otherwise, since the present time (as we have already [1] said) is the period for abstaining from the nuptial embrace, and therefore makes no necessary demand on the exercise of the said function, seeing that all nations now contribute so abundantly to the production of an offspring which shall receive spiritual birth, there is the greater room for the blessing of an excellent continence. "He that is able to receive it, let him receive it." [2] He, however, who cannot receive it, "even if he marry, sinneth not;" [3] and if a

woman have not the gift of continence, let her also marry. [4] "It is good, indeed, for a man not to touch a woman." [5] But since "all men cannot receive this saying, save they to whom it is given," [6] it remains that "to avoid fornication, every man ought to have his own wife, and every woman her own husband." [7] And thus the weakness of incontinence is hindered from falling into the ruin of profligacy by the honourable estate of matrimony. Now that which the apostle says of women, "I will therefore that the younger women marry," [8] is also applicable to males: I will that the younger men take wives; that so it may appertain to both sexes alike "to bear children, to be" fathers and "mothers of families, to give none occasion to the adversary to speak reproachfully." [8]

CHAP. 19 [XVII.] — BLESSINGS OF MATRIMONY.

In matrimony, however, let these nuptial blessings be the objects of our love — offspring, fidelity, the sacramental bond.[9] Offspring, not that it be born only, but born again; for it is born to punishment unless it be born again to life. Fidelity, not such as even unbelievers observe one towards the other, in their ardent love of the flesh. For what husband, however impious himself, likes an adulterous wife? Or what wife, however impious she be, likes an adulterous husband? This is indeed a natural good in marriage, though a carnal one. But a member of Christ ought to be afraid of adultery, not on account of himself, but of his spouse; and ought to hope to receive from Christ the reward of that fidelity which he shows to his spouse. The sacramental bond, again, which is lost neither by divorce nor by adultery, should be guarded by husband and wife with concord and chastity. For it alone is that which even an unfruitful marriage retains by the law of piety, now that all that hope of fruitfulness is lost for the purpose of which the couple married. Let these nuptial blessings be praised in marriage by him who wishes to extol the nuptial institution. Carnal concupiscence, however, must not be ascribed to marriage: it is only to be tolerated in marriage. It is not a good which comes out of the essence of marriage, but an evil which is the accident of original sin.

CHAP. 20 [XVIII.] — WHY CHILDREN OF WRATH ARE BORN OF HOLY MATRIMONY.

This is the reason, indeed, why of even the just and lawful marriages of the children of God are born, not children of God, but children of the world; because also those who generate, if they are already regenerate, beget children not as chil-

---

[1] See above, ch. 14 [XIII.].　　[2] Matt xix. 12.　[3] 1 Cor. vii. 28.　　　　[4] 1 Cor. vii. 9.　　[5] 1 Cor. vii. 1.　　[6] Matt. xix. 9.　[7] 1 Cor. vii. 2.　[8] 1 Tim. v. 14.　[9] See above, ch. 11, and On Original Sin, ch. 39.

dren of God, but as still children of the world. "The children of this world," says our Lord, beget and are begotten."[1] From the fact, therefore, that we are still children of this world, our outer man is in a state of corruption; and on this account our offspring are born as children of the present world; nor do they become sons of God, except they be regenerated.[2] Yet inasmuch as we are children of God, our inner man is renewed from day to day.[3] And yet even our outer man has been sanctified through the laver of regeneration, and has received the hope of future incorruption, on which account it is justly designated as "the temple of God." "Your bodies," says the apostle, "are the temples of the Holy Ghost, which is in you, and which ye have of God; and ye are not your own, for ye are bought with a great price: therefore glorify and carry God in your body."[4] The whole of this statement is made in reference to our present sanctification, but especially in consequence of that hope of which he says in another passage, "We ourselves also, which have the first-fruits of the Spirit, even we ourselves groan within ourselves, waiting for the adoption, to wit, the redemption of our body."[5] If, then, the redemption of our body is expected, as the apostle declares, it follows, that being an expectation, it is as yet a matter of hope, and not of actual possession. Accordingly the apostle adds: "For we are saved by hope: but hope that is seen is not hope: for what a man seeth, why doth he yet hope for? But if we hope for that we see not, then do we with patience wait for it."[6] Not, therefore, by that which we are waiting for, but by that which we are now enduring, are the children of our flesh born. God forbid that a man who possesses faith should, when he hears the apostle bid men "love their wives,"[7] love that carnal concupiscence in his wife which he ought not to love even in himself; as he may know, if he listens to the words of another apostle: "Love not the world, neither the things that are in the world. If any man love the world, the love of the Father is not in him. For all that is in the world, the lust of the flesh, and the lust of the eyes, and the pride of life, is not of the Father, but is of the world. And the world passeth away, and the lust thereof: but he that doeth the will of God abideth for ever, even as also God abideth for ever."[8]

CHAP. 21 [XIX.] — THUS SINNERS ARE BORN OF RIGHTEOUS PARENTS, EVEN AS WILD OLIVES SPRING FROM THE OLIVE.

That, therefore, which is born of the lust of the flesh is really born of the world, and not of God; but it is born of God, when it is born again of water and of the Spirit. The guilt of this concupiscence, regeneration alone remits, even as natural generation contracts it. What, then, is generated must be regenerated, in order that likewise since it cannot be otherwise, what has been contracted may be remitted. It is, no doubt, very wonderful that what has been remitted in the parent should still be contracted in the offspring; but nevertheless such is the case. That this mysterious verity, which unbelievers neither see nor believe, might get some palpable evidence in its support, God in His providence has secured in the example of certain trees. For why should we not suppose that for this very purpose the wild olive springs from the olive? Is it not indeed credible that, in a thing which has been created for the use of mankind, the Creator provided and appointed what should afford an instructive example, applicable to the human race? It is a wonderful thing, then, how those who have been themselves delivered by grace from the bondage of sin, should still beget those who are tied and bound by the self-same chain, and who require the same process of loosening? Yes; and we admit the wonderful fact. But that the embryo of wild olive trees should latently exist in the germs of true olives, who would deem credible, if it were not proved true by experiment and observation? In the same manner, therefore, as a wild olive grows out of the seed of the wild olive, and from the seed of the true olive springs also nothing but a wild olive, notwithstanding the very great difference there is between the wild olive and the olive; so what is born in the flesh, either of a sinner or of a just man, is in both instances a sinner, notwithstanding the vast distinction which exists between the sinner and the righteous man. He that is begotten is no sinner as yet in act, and is still new from his birth; but in guilt he is old. Human from the Creator, he is a captive of the destroyer, and needs a redeemer. The difficulty, however, is how a state of captivity can possibly befall the offspring, when the parents have been themselves previously redeemed from it. Now it is no easy matter to unravel this intricate point, or to explain it in a set discourse; therefore unbelievers refuse to accept it as true; just as if in that other point about the wild olive and the olive, which we gave in illustration, any reason could be easily found, or explanation clearly given, why the self-same shoot should sprout out of so dissimilar a stock. The truth,

---

[1] Luke xx. 34. Augustin quotes an interpolation current in the Latin Bibles of his day, and found also in certain Greek (D. Origen) and Syriac (Curetonian version) witnesses.
[2] See De Peccatorum Meritis et Remissione, ii. 11 [IX.].
[3] 2 Cor. iv. 16.
[4] 1 Cor. vi. 19, 20. Note the odd interpolation "and carry," which was a common Latin reading.
[5] Rom. viii. 23.        [6] Rom. viii. 24, 25.        [7] Col. iii. 19.
[8] 1 John ii. 15–17. The last clause, though not in Jerome's Vulgate, was yet read by some of the Latin Fathers — by Cyprian and Lucifer, for instance, and something like it also by one of the Egyptian versions.

however, of this can be discovered by any one who is willing to make the experiment. Let it then serve for a good example for suggesting belief of what admits not of ocular demonstration.

CHAP. 22 [XX.] — EVEN INFANTS, WHEN UNBAPTIZED, ARE IN THE POWER OF THE DEVIL; EXORCISM IN THE CASE OF INFANTS, AND RENUNCIATION OF THE DEVIL.

Now the Christian faith unfalteringly declares, what our new heretics have begun to deny, both that they who are cleansed in the laver of regeneration are redeemed from the power of the devil, and that those who have not yet been redeemed by such regeneration are still captive in the power of the devil, even if they be infant children of the redeemed, unless they be themselves redeemed by the self-same grace of Christ. For we cannot doubt that that blessing of God applies to every stage of human life, which the apostle describes when he says concerning Him : " Who hath delivered us from the power of darkness, and hath translated us into the kingdom of His dear Son."¹ From this power of darkness, therefore, of which the devil is the prince, — in other words, from the power of the devil and his angels, — infants are delivered when they are baptized ; and whosoever denies this, is convicted by the truth of the Church's very sacraments, which no heretical novelty in the Church of Christ is permitted to destroy or change, so long as the Divine Head rules and helps the entire body which He owns — small as well as great. It is true, then, and in no way false, that the devil's power is exorcised in infants, and that they renounce him by the hearts and mouths of those who bring them to baptism, being unable. to do so by their own ; in order that they may be delivered from the power of darkness, and be translated into the kingdom of their Lord. What is that, therefore, within them which keeps them in the power of the devil until they are delivered from it by Christ's sacrament of baptism? What is it, I ask, but sin? Nothing else, indeed, has the devil found which enables him to put under his own control that nature of man which the good Creator made good. But infants have committed no sin of their own since they have been alive. Only original sin, therefore, remains, whereby they are made captive under the devil's power, until they are redeemed therefrom by the laver of regeneration and the blood of Christ, and pass into their Redeemer's kingdom, — the power of their enthraller being frustrated, and power being given them to become " sons of God " instead of children of this world.²

¹ Col. i. 13.          ² John i. 12.

CHAP. 23 [XXI.] — SIN HAS NOT ARISEN OUT OF THE GOODNESS OF MARRIAGE ; THE SACRAMENT OF MATRIMONY A GREAT ONE IN THE CASE OF CHRIST AND THE CHURCH — A VERY SMALL ONE IN THE CASE OF A MAN AND HIS WIFE.

If now we interrogate, so to speak, those goods of marriage to which we have often referred,³ and inquire how it is that sin could possibly have been propagated from them to infants, we shall get this answer from the first of them — the work of procreation of offspring : " My happiness would in paradise have been greater if sin had not been committed. For to me belongs that blessing of almighty God : ' Be fruitful, and multiply.' ⁴ For accomplishing this good work, divers members were created suited to each sex ; these members were, of course, in existence before sin, but they were not objects of shame." This will be the answer of the second good — the fidelity of chastity : " If sin had not been committed, what in paradise could have been more secure than myself, when there was no lust of my own to spur me, none of another to tempt me ? " And then this will be the answer of the sacramental bond of marriage, — the third good : " Of me was that word spoken in paradise before the entrance of sin : ' A man shall leave his father and his mother, and shall cleave unto his wife ; and they two shall become one flesh.' " ⁵ This the apostle applies to the case of Christ and of the Church, and calls it then " a great sacrament." ⁶ What, then, in Christ and in the Church is great, in the instances of each married pair it is but very small, but even then it is the sacrament of an inseparable union. What now is there in these three blessings of marriage out of which the bond of sin could pass over to posterity? Absolutely nothing. And in these blessings it is certain that the goodness of matrimony, is entirely comprised ; and even now good wedlock consists of these same blessings.

CHAP. 24. — LUST AND SHAME COME FROM SIN ; THE LAW OF SIN ; THE SHAMELESSNESS OF THE CYNICS.

But if, in like manner, the question be asked of the concupiscence of the flesh, how it is that acts now bring shame which once were free from shame, will not her answer be, that she only began to have existence in men's members after sin ? [XXII.] And, therefore, that the apostle designated her influence as " the law of sin," ⁷ inasmuch as she subjugated man to herself when he was unwilling to remain subject to

³ See above, chs. 11, 19, and *On Original Sin*, ch. 39.
⁴ Gen. i. 29.          ⁵ Gen. ii. 24.
⁶ Eph. v. 32. [In the original Greek, " a great mystery ; " *i.e.*, " a great revelation." — W.]
⁷ Rom. vii. 23.

his God; and that it was she who made the first married pair ashamed at that moment when they covered their loins; even as all are still ashamed, and seek out secret retreats for cohabitation, and dare not have even the children, whom they have themselves thus begotten, to be witnesses of what they do. It was against this modesty of natural shame that the Cynic philosophers, in the error of their astonishing shamelessness, struggled so hard: they thought that the intercourse indeed of husband and wife, since it was lawful and honourable, should therefore be done in public. Such barefaced obscenity deserved to receive the name of dogs; and so they went by the title of " Cynics." [1]

## CHAP. 25 [XXIII.] — CONCUPISCENCE IN THE REGENERATE WITHOUT CONSENT IS NOT SIN; IN WHAT SENSE CONCUPISCENCE IS CALLED SIN.

Now this concupiscence, this law of sin which dwells in our members, to which the law of righteousness forbids allegiance, saying in the words of the apostle, " Let not sin, therefore, reign in your mortal body, that ye should obey it in the lusts thereof; neither yield ye your members as instruments of unrighteousness unto sin: " [2] — this concupiscence, I say, which is cleansed only by the sacrament of regeneration, does undoubtedly, by means of natural birth, pass on the bond of sin to a man's posterity, unless they are themselves loosed from it by regeneration. In the case, however, of the regenerate, concupiscence is not itself sin any longer, whenever they do not consent to it for illicit works, and when the members are not applied by the presiding mind to perpetrate such deeds. So that, if what is enjoined in one passage, " Thou shalt not covet," [3] is not kept, that at any rate is observed which is commanded in another place, " Thou shalt not go after thy concupiscences." [4] Inasmuch, however, as by a certain manner of speech it is called sin, since it arose from sin, and, when it has the upper hand, produces sin, the guilt of it prevails in the natural man; but this guilt, by Christ's grace through the remission of all sins, is not suffered to prevail in the regenerate man, if he does not yield obedience to it whenever it urges him to the commission of evil. As arising from sin, it is, I say, called sin, although in the regenerate it is not actually sin; and it has this designation applied to it, just as speech which the tongue produces is itself called " tongue;" and just as the word " hand" is used in the sense of writing, which the hand produces. In the same way concupiscence is called sin, as producing sin when it conquers the will: so to cold

and frost the epithet " sluggish " is given; not as arising from, but as productive of, sluggishness; benumbing us, in fact.

## CHAP. 26. — WHATEVER IS BORN THROUGH CONCUPISCENCE IS NOT UNDESERVEDLY IN SUBJECTION TO THE DEVIL BY REASON OF SIN; THE DEVIL DESERVES HEAVIER PUNISHMENT THAN MEN.

This wound which the devil has inflicted on the human race compels everything which has its birth in consequence of it to be under the devil's power, as if he were rightly plucking fruit off his own tree. Not as if man's nature, which is only of God, came from him, but sin alone, which is not of God. For it is not on its own account that man's nature is under condemnation, because it is the work of God, and therefore laudable; but on account of that condemnable corruption by which it has been vitiated. Now it is by reason of this condemnation that it is in subjection to the devil, who is also in the same damnable state. For the devil is himself an unclean spirit: good, indeed, so far as he is a spirit, but evil as being unclean; for by nature he is a spirit, by the corruption thereof an unclean one. Of these two, the one is of God, the other of himself. His hold over men, therefore, whether of an advanced age or in infancy, is not because they are human, but because they are polluted. He, then, who feels surprise that God's creature is a subject of the devil, should cease from such feeling. For one creature of God is in subjection to another creature of God, the less to the greater, a human being to an angelic one; and this is not owing to nature, but to a corruption of nature: polluted is the sovereign, polluted also the subject. All this is the fruit of that ancient stock of pollution which he has planted in man; himself being destined to suffer a heavier punishment at the last judgment, as being the more polluted; but at the same time even they who will have to bear a less heavy burden in that condemnation are subjects of him as the prince and author of sin, for there will be no other cause of condemnation than sin.

## CHAP. 27 [XXIV.] — THROUGH LUST ORIGINAL SIN IS TRANSMITTED; VENIAL SINS IN MARRIED PERSONS; CONCUPISCENCE OF THE FLESH, THE DAUGHTER AND MOTHER OF SIN.

Wherefore the devil holds infants guilty who are born, not of the good by which marriage is good, but of the evil of concupiscence, which, indeed, marriage uses aright, but at which even marriage has occasion to feel shame. Marriage is itself " honourable in all " [5] the goods which properly appertain to it; but even when it has

---

[1] Cynici, i.e. Κυνικοί, " dog-like."     [2] Rom. vi 12, 13.
[3] Ex. xx. 17; " non concupisces " in the Latin; hence the play on the word.
[4] Ecclus. xviii. 30.

[5] Heb. xiii. 4.

its " bed undefiled " (not only by fornication and adultery, which are damnable disgraces, but also by any of those excesses of cohabitation such as do not arise from any prevailing desire of children, but from an overbearing lust of pleasure, which are venial sins in man and wife), yet, whenever it comes to the actual process of generation, the very embrace which is lawful and honourable cannot be effected without the ardour of lust, so as to be able to accomplish that which appertains to the use of reason and not of lust. Now, this ardour, whether following or preceding the will, does somehow, by a power of its own, move the members which cannot be moved simply by the will, and in this manner it shows itself not to be the servant of a will which commands it, but rather to be the punishment of a will which disobeys it. It shows, moreover, that it must be excited, not by a free choice, but by a certain seductive stimulus, and that on this very account it produces shame. This is the carnal concupiscence, which, while it is no longer accounted sin in the regenerate, yet in no case happens to nature except from sin. It is the daughter of sin, as it were ; and whenever it yields assent to the commission of shameful deeds, it becomes also the mother of many sins. Now from this concupiscence whatever comes into being by natural birth is bound by original sin, unless, indeed, it be born again in Him whom the Virgin conceived without this concupiscence. Wherefore, when He vouchsafed to be born in the flesh, He alone was born without sin.

CHAP. 28 [XXV.]—CONCUPISCENCE REMAINS AFTER BAPTISM, JUST AS LANGUOR DOES AFTER RECOVERY FROM DISEASE ; CONCUPISCENCE IS DIMINISHED IN PERSONS OF ADVANCING YEARS, AND INCREASED IN THE INCONTINENT.

If the question arises, how this concupiscence of the flesh remains in the regenerate, in whose case has been effected a remission of all sins whatever ; seeing that human semination takes place by its means, even when the carnal offspring of even a baptized parent is born : or, at all events, if it may be in the case of a baptized parent concupiscence and not be sin, why should this same concupiscence be sin in the offspring? — the answer to be given is this : Carnal concupiscence is remitted, indeed, in baptism ; not so that it is put out of existence, but so that it is not to be imputed for sin. Although its guilt is now taken away, it still remains until our entire infirmity be healed by the advancing renewal of our inner man, day by day, when at last our outward man shall be clothed with incorruption.[1] It does not remain, however, substantially, as a body, or

a spirit ; but it is nothing more than a certain affection of an evil quality, such as languor, for instance. There is not, to be sure, anything remaining which may be remitted whenever, as the Scripture says, " the Lord forgiveth all our iniquities." [2] But until that happens which immediately follows in the same passage, " Who healeth all thine infirmities, who redeemeth thy life from corruption," [3] there remains this concupiscence of the flesh in the body of this death. Now we are admonished not to obey its sinful desires to do evil : " Let not sin reign in your mortal body." [4] Still this concupiscence is daily lessened in persons of continence and increasing years, and most of all when old age makes a near approach. The man, however, who yields to it a wicked service, receives such great energies that, even when all his members are now failing through age, and those especial parts of his body are unable to be applied to their proper function, he does not ever cease to revel in a still increasing rage of disgraceful and shameless desire.

CHAP. 29 [XXVI.]—HOW CONCUPISCENCE REMAINS IN THE BAPTIZED IN ACT, WHEN IT HAS PASSED AWAY AS TO ITS GUILT.

In the case, then, of those persons who are born again in Christ, when they receive an entire remission of all their sins, it is of course necessary that the guilt also of the still indwelling concupiscence should be remitted, in order that (as I said) it should not be imputed to them for sin. For even as in the case of those sins which cannot be themselves permanent, since they pass away as soon as they are committed, the guilt yet is permanent, and (if not remitted) will remain for evermore ; so, when the concupiscence is remitted, the guilt of it also is taken away. For not to have sin means this, not to be deemed guilty of sin. If a man have (for example) committed adultery, though he do not repeat the sin, he is held to be guilty of adultery until the indulgence in guilt be itself remitted. He has the sin, therefore, remaining, although the particular act of his sin no longer exists, since it has passed away along with the time when it was committed. For if to desist from sinning were the same thing as not to have sins, it would be sufficient if Scripture were content to give us the simple warning, " My son, hast thou sinned? Do so no more." [5] This, however, does not suffice, for it goes on to say, " Ask forgiveness for thy former sins." [5] Sins remain, therefore, if they are not forgiven. But how do they remain if they are passed away? Only thus, they have passed away in their *act*, but they are permanent in their *guilt*. Contrari-

---

[1] 1 Cor. xv. 53.

[2] Ps. ciii. 3.　　[3] Ps. ciii. 4.　　[4] Rom. vi. 12.
[5] Ecclus. xxi. 1.

wise, then, may it happen that a thing may remain in act, but pass away in guilt.

CHAP. 30 [XXVII.] — THE EVIL DESIRES OF CONCUPISCENCE; WE OUGHT TO WISH THAT THEY MAY NOT BE.

For the concupiscence of the flesh is in some sort active, even when it does not exhibit either an assent of the heart, where its seat of empire is, or those members whereby, as its weapons, it fulfils what it is bent on. But what in this action does it effect, unless it be its evil and shameful desires? For if these were good and lawful, the apostle would not forbid obedience to them, saying, " Let not sin therefore reign in your mortal body, that ye should obey the lusts thereof." [1] He does not say, that ye should have the lusts thereof, but " that ye should obey the lusts thereof;" in order that (as these desires are greater or less in different individuals, according as each shall have progressed in the renewal of the inner man) we may maintain the fight of holiness and chastity, for the purpose of withholding obedience to these lusts. Nevertheless, our wish ought to be nothing less than the non-existence of these very desires, even if the accomplishment of such a wish be not possible in the body of this death. This is the reason why the same apostle, in another passage, addressing us as if in his own person, gives us this instruction : " For what I would," says he, " that do I not; but what I hate, that do I." [2] In a word, " I covet." [3] For he was unwilling to do this, that he might be perfect on every side. " If, then, I do that which I would not," he goes on to say, " I consent unto the law that it is good." [4] Because the law, too, wills not that which I also would not. For it wills not that I should have concupiscence, for it says, " Thou shalt not covet ; " [3] and I am no less unwilling to cherish so evil a desire. In this, therefore, there is complete accord between the will of the law and my own will. But because he was unwilling to covet,[3] and yet did covet,[3] and for all that did not by any means obey this concupiscence so as to yield assent to it, he immediately adds these words : " Now, then, it is no more I that do it, but sin that dwelleth in me." [5]

CHAP. 31 [XXVIII.] — WHO IS THE MAN THAT CAN SAY, " IT IS NO MORE I THAT DO IT " ?

A man, however, is much deceived if, while consenting to the lust of his flesh, and then both resolving in his mind to do its desires and setting about it, he supposes that he has still a right to say, " It is not I that do it," even if he hates and loathes himself for assenting to evil desires. The two things are simultaneous in his case : he hates the thing himself because he knows that it is evil ; and yet he does it, because he is bent on doing it. Now if, in addition to all this, he proceeds to do what the Scripture forbids him, when it says, " Neither yield ye your members as instruments of unrighteousness unto sin," [6] and completes with a bodily act what he was bent on doing in his mind ; and says, " It is not I that do the thing, but sin that dwelleth in me," [5] because he feels displeased with himself for resolving on and accomplishing the deed, — he so greatly errs as not to know his own self. For, whereas he is altogether himself, his mind determining and his body executing his own purpose, he yet supposes that he is himself no longer ! [XXIX.] That man, therefore, alone speaks the truth when he says, " It is no more I that do it, but sin that dwelleth in me," who only feels the concupiscence, and neither resolves on doing it with the consent of his heart, nor accomplishes it with the ministry of his body.

CHAP. 32. — WHEN GOOD WILL BE PERFECTLY DONE.

The apostle then adds these words : " For I know that in me (that is, in my flesh) dwelleth no good thing : for to will is present with me ; but how to perfect that which is good I find not." [7] Now this is said, because a good thing is not then perfected, when there is an absence of evil desires, as evil is perfected when evil desires are obeyed. But when they are present, but are not obeyed, neither evil is performed, since obedience is not yielded to them ; nor good, because of their inoperative presence. There is rather an intermediate condition of things : good is effected in some degree, because the evil concupiscence has gained no assent to itself ; and in some degree there is a remnant of evil, because the concupiscence is present. This accounts for the apostle's precise words. He does not say, To *do* good is not present to him, but " how to perfect it." For the truth is, one *does* a good deal of good when he does what the Scripture enjoins, " Go not after thy lusts ; " [8] yet he falls short of perfection, in that he fails to keep the great commandment, " Thou shalt not covet." [9] The law said, " Thou shalt not covet," in order that, when we find ourselves lying in this diseased state, we might seek the medicine of Grace, and by that commandment know both in what direction our endeavours should aim as we advance in our present mortal condition, and to what a height it is possible to reach in the future immortality. For unless perfection could somewhere be attained, this commandment would never have been given to us.

---

[1] Rom. vi. 12.    [2] Rom. vii. 15.
[3] " *Concupisco*" in the Latin, and hence used in this discussion.
[4] Rom. vii. 16.    [5] Rom. vii. 17.
[6] Rom. vi. 13.    [7] Rom. vii. 18.    [8] Ecclus. xviii. 30.
[9] Ex. xx. 7.

CHAP. 33 [XXX.] — TRUE FREEDOM COMES WITH WILLING DELIGHT IN GOD'S LAW.

The apostle then repeats his former statement, the more fully to recommend its purport: " For the good," says he, " that I would, I do not: but the evil which I would not, that I do. Now, if I do that I would not, it is no more I that do it, but sin that dwelleth in me." Then follows this : " I find then the law, when I would act, to be good to me ; for evil is present with me." [1] In other words, I find that the law is a good to me, when I wish to do what the law would have me do ; inasmuch as it is not with the law itself (which says, " Thou shalt not covet ") that evil is present ; no, it is with myself that the evil is present, which I would not do, because I have the concupiscence even in my willingness. " For," he adds, " I delight in the law of God after the inward man ; but I see another law in my members warring against the law of my mind, and bringing me into captivity to the law of sin which is in my members." [2] This delight with the law of God [3] after the inward man, comes to us from the mighty grace of God ; for thereby is our inward man renewed day by day,[4] because it is thereby that progress is made by us with perseverance. In it there is not the fear that has torment, but the love that cheers and gratifies. We are truly free there, where we have no unwilling joy.

CHAP. 34. — HOW CONCUPISCENCE MADE A CAPTIVE OF THE APOSTLE ; WHAT THE LAW OF SIN WAS TO THE APOSTLE.

Then, indeed, this statement, " I see another law in my members warring against the law of my mind," refers to that very concupiscence which we are now speaking of — the law of sin in our sinful flesh. But when he said, " And bringing me into captivity to the law of sin," that is, to its own self, " which is in my members," he either meant " bringing me into captivity," in the sense of *endeavouring to make* me captive, that is, urging me to approve and accomplish evil desire ; or rather (and this opens no controversy), in the sense of leading me captive according to the flesh, and, if this is not possessed by the carnal concupiscence which he calls the law of sin, no unlawful desire — such as our mind ought not to obey — would, of course, be there to excite and disturb. The fact, however, that the apostle does not say, Bringing *my flesh* into captivity, but " Bringing *me* into captivity," leads us to look out for

some other meaning for the phrase, and to understand the term " bringing me into captivity " as if he had said, endeavouring to make me captive. But why, after all, might he not say, " Bringing me into captivity," and at the same time mean us to understand his flesh? Was it not spoken by one concerning Jesus, when His flesh was not found in the sepulchre : " They have taken away my Lord, and I know not where they have laid Him " ? [5] Was Mary's then an improper question, because she said, " My Lord," and not " My Lord's body " or " flesh "?

CHAP. 35 [XXXI.] — THE FLESH, CARNAL AFFECTION.

But we have in the apostle's own language, a little before, a sufficiently clear proof that he might have meant his flesh when he said, " Bringing *me* into captivity." For after declaring, " I know that *in me* dwelleth no good thing," he at once added an explanatory sentence to this effect, " That is, *in my flesh*." [6] It is then the flesh, in which there dwells nothing good, that is brought into captivity to the law of sin. Now he designates that as the flesh wherein lies a certain morbid carnal affection, not the mere conformation of our bodily fabric whose members are not to be used as weapons for sin — that is, for that very concupiscence which holds this flesh of ours captive. So far, indeed, as concerns this actual bodily substance and nature of ours, it is already God's temple in all faithful men, whether living in marriage or in continence. If, however, absolutely nothing of our flesh were in captivity, not even to the devil, because there has accrued to it the remission of sin, that sin be not imputed to it (and this is properly designated the law of sin) ; yet if under this law of sin, that is, under its own concupiscence, our flesh were not to some degree held captive, how could that be true which the apostle states, when he speaks of our " waiting for the adoption, to wit, the redemption of our body " ? [7] In so far, then, as there is now this waiting for the redemption of our body, there is also in some degree still existing something in us which is a captive to the law of sin. Accordingly he exclaims, " O wretched man that I am ! who shall deliver me from the body of this death? The grace of God, through Jesus Christ our Lord." [8] What are we to understand by such language, but that our body, which is undergoing corruption, weighs heavily on our soul? When, therefore, this very body of ours shall be restored to us in an incorrupt state, there shall be a full liberation from the body of this death ; but there will be no such deliverance for them who shall rise again to condemnation. To the body of this death then is

---

[1] Rom. vii. 19–21. The punctuation of the passage in Latin differs from that ordinarily used with us, and hence this sense results.
[2] Rom. vii. 22, 23.
[3] This sharing of joy with the law of God: " *Ista condelectatio legi Dei.*"
[4] 2 Cor. iv. 16.

[5] John xx. 2.    [6] Rom. vii. 18.    [7] Rom. viii. 23.
[8] Rom. vii. 24.

understood to be owing the circumstance that there is in our members another law which wars against the law of the mind, so long as the flesh lusts against the spirit — without, however, sub-jugating the mind, inasmuch as on its side, too, the spirit has a concupiscence contrary to the flesh.[1] Thus, although the actual law of sin partly holds the flesh in captivity (whence comes its resistance to the law of the mind), still it has not an absolute empire in our body, notwith-standing its mortal state, since it refuses obedi-ence to its desires.[2] For in the case of hostile armies between whom there is an earnest con-flict, even the side which is inferior in the fight usually holds a something which it has captured ; and although in some such way there is some-what in our flesh which is kept under the law of sin, yet it has before it the hope of redemption : and then there will remain not a particle of this corrupt concupiscence ; but our flesh, healed of that diseased plague, and wholly clad in immor-tality, shall live for evermore in eternal blessed-ness.

CHAP. 36. — EVEN NOW WHILE WE STILL HAVE CONCUPISCENCE WE MAY BE SAFE IN CHRIST.

But the apostle pursues the subject, and says, " So then with the mind I myself serve the law of God, but with the flesh the law of sin ; "[3] which must be thus understood : " With my mind I serve the law of God," by refusing my consent to the law of sin ; " with my flesh, how-ever," I serve " the law of sin," by having the desires of sin, from which I am not yet entirely freed, although I yield them no assent. Then let us observe carefully what he has said after all the above : " There is therefore now no con-demnation to them which are in Christ Jesus."[4] Even *now*, says he, when the law in my mem-bers keeps up its warfare against the law of my mind, and retains in captivity somewhat in the body of this death, there is no condemnation to them which are in Christ Jesus. And listen why : " For the law of the spirit of life in Christ Jesus," says he, " hath made me free from the law of sin and death."[5] How made me free, except by abolishing its sentence of guilt by the remission of all my sins ; so that, though it still remains, only daily lessening more and more, it is nevertheless not imputed to me as sin?

CHAP. 37 [XXXII.] — THE LAW OF SIN WITH ITS GUILT IN UNBAPTIZED INFANTS. BY ADAM'S SIN THE HUMAN RACE HAS BECOME A " WILD OLIVE TREE."

Until, then, this remission of sins takes place in the offspring, they have within them the law of sin in such manner, that it is really imputed

to them as sin ; in other words, with that law there is attaching to them its sentence of guilt, which holds them debtors to eternal condemna-tion. For what a parent transmits to his carnal offspring is the condition of his own carnal birth, not that of his spiritual new birth. For, that he was born in the flesh, although no hindrance after the remission of his guilt to his fruit, still remains hidden, as it were, in the seed of the olive, even though, because of the remission of his sins, it in no respect injures the oil — that is, in plain language, his life which he lives, " righteous by faith,"[6] after Christ, whose very name comes from the oil, that is, from the anointing.[7] That, however, which in the case of a regenerate parent, as in the seed of the pure olive, is covered without any guilt, which has been re-mitted, is still no doubt retained in the case of his offspring, which is yet unregenerate, as in the wild olive, with all its guilt, until here also it be remitted by the self-same grace. When Adam sinned, he was changed from that pure olive, which had no such corrupt seed whence should spring the bitter issue of the wild olive, into a wild olive tree ; and, inasmuch as his sin was so great, that by it his nature became com-mensurately changed for the worse, he converted the entire race of man into a wild olive stock. The effect of this change we see illustrated, as has been said above, in the instance of these very trees. Whenever God's grace converts a sapling into a good olive, so that the fault of the first birth (that original sin which had been derived and contracted from the concupiscence of the flesh) is remitted, covered, and not im-puted, there is still inherent in that nature from which is born a wild olive, unless it, too, by the same grace, is by the second birth changed into a good olive.

CHAP. 38 [XXXIII.] — TO BAPTISM MUST BE RE-FERRED ALL REMISSION OF SINS, AND THE COM-PLETE HEALING OF THE RESURRECTION. DAILY CLEANSING.

Blessed, therefore, is the olive tree " whose iniquities are forgiven, and whose sins are covered ; " blessed is it " to which the Lord hath not imputed sin."[8] But this, which has received the remission, the covering, and the acquittal, even up to the complete change into an eternal immortality, still retains a secret force which furnishes seed for a wild and bitter olive tree, unless the same tillage of God prunes it also, by remission, covering, and acquittal. There will, however, be left no corruption at all in even carnal seed, when the same regeneration, which

---

[1] Gal. v. 17.        [2] Rom. vi. 12.        [3] Rom. vii. 25.
[4] Rom. viii. 1.      [5] Rom. viii. 2.

[6] Rom. i. 17.
[7] An allusion, of course, to the meaning of the word " Christ," from *Chrisma*, and meaning " the Anointed One."
[8] Ps. xxxiii. 1, 2.

is now effected through the sacred laver, purges and heals all man's evil to the very end. By its means the very same flesh, through which the carnal mind was formed, shall become spiritual, — no longer having that carnal lust which resists the law of the mind, no longer emitting carnal seed. For in this sense must be understood that which the apostle whom we have so often quoted says elsewhere: "Christ loved the Church, and gave Himself for it; that He might sanctify and cleanse it by the washing of water by the word; that He might present it to Himself a glorious Church, not having spot, or wrinkle, or any such thing."[1] It must, I say, be understood as implying, that by this laver of regeneration and word of sanctification all the evils of regenerate men of whatever kind are cleansed and healed, — not the sins only which are all now remitted in baptism, but those also which after baptism are committed by human ignorance and frailty; not, indeed, that baptism is to be repeated as often as sin is repeated, but that by its one only ministration it comes to pass that pardon is secured to the faithful of all their sins both before and after their regeneration. For of what use would repentance be, either before baptism, if baptism did not follow; or after it, if it did not precede? Nay, in the Lord's Prayer itself, which is our daily cleansing, of what avail or advantage would it be for that petition to be uttered, "Forgive us our debts,"[2] unless it be by such as have been baptized? And in like manner, how great soever be the liberality and kindness of a man's alms, what, I ask, would they profit him towards the remission of his sins if he had not been baptized? In short, on whom but on the baptized shall be bestowed the very felicities of the kingdom of heaven; where the Church shall have no spot, or wrinkle, or any such thing; where there shall be nothing blameworthy, nothing unreal; where there shall be not only no guilt for sin, but no concupiscence to excite it?

CHAP. 39 [XXXIV.] — BY THE HOLINESS OF BAPTISM, NOT SINS ONLY, BUT ALL EVILS WHATSOEVER, HAVE TO BE REMOVED. THE CHURCH IS NOT YET FREE FROM ALL STAIN.

And thus not only all the sins, but all the ills of men of what kind soever, are in course of removal by the holiness of that Christian laver whereby Christ cleanses His Church, that He may present it to Himself, not in this world, but in that which is to come, as not having spot, or wrinkle, or any such thing. Now there are some who maintain that such is the Church even now, and yet they are in it. Well then, since they confess that they have some sins themselves, if they say the truth in this (and, of course, they do, as they are not free from sins), then the Church has "a spot" in them; whilst if they tell an untruth in their confession (as speaking from a double heart), then the Church has in them "a wrinkle." If, however, they assert that it is themselves, and not the Church, which has all this, they then as good as acknowledge that they are not its members, nor belong to its body, so that they are even condemned by their own confession.

CHAP. 40 [XXXV.] — REFUTATION OF THE PELAGIANS BY THE AUTHORITY OF ST. AMBROSE, WHOM THEY QUOTE TO SHOW THAT THE DESIRE OF THE FLESH IS A NATURAL GOOD.

In respect, however, to this concupiscence of the flesh, we have striven in this lengthy discussion to distinguish it accurately from the goods of marriage. This we have done on account of our modern heretics, who cavil whenever concupiscence is censured, as if it involved a censure of marriage. Their object is to praise concupiscence as a natural good, that so they may defend their own baneful dogma, which asserts that those who are born by its means do not contract original sin. Now the blessed Ambrose, bishop of Milan, by whose priestly office I received the washing of regeneration, briefly spoke on this matter, when, expounding the prophet Isaiah, he gathered from him the nativity of Christ in the flesh: "Thus," says the bishop, "He was both tempted in all points as a man,[3] and in the likeness of man He bare all things; but inasmuch as He was born of the Spirit, He kept Himself from sin. For every man is a liar; and there is none without sin but God alone. It has, therefore, been ever firmly maintained, that it is clear that no man from husband and wife, that is to say, by means of that conjunction of their persons, is free from sin. He who is free from sin is also free from conception of this kind." Well now, what is it which St. Ambrose has here condemned in the true doctrine of this deliverance? — is it the goodness of marriage, or not rather the worthless opinion of these heretics, although they had not then come upon the stage? I have thought it worth while to adduce this testimony, because Pelagius mentions Ambrose with such commendation as to say: "The blessed Bishop Ambrose, in whose writings more than anywhere else the Roman faith is clearly stated, has flourished like a beautiful flower among the Latin writers. His fidelity and extremely pure perception of the sense of Scripture no opponent even has ever ventured to impugn."[4] I hope he may regret having entertained opinions opposed to Ambrose, but

---

[1] Eph. v. 25.        [2] Matt. vi. 12.        [3] Heb. iv. 15.        [4] Pro libero arbitrio, lib. 3.

not that he has bestowed this praise on that holy man.

Here, then, you have my book, which, owing to its tedious length and difficult subject, it has been as troublesome for me to compose as for you to read, in those little snatches of time in which you have been able (or at least, as I suppose, have been able) to find yourself at leisure. Although it has been indeed drawn up with considerable labour amidst my ecclesiastical duties, as God has vouchsafed to give me His help, I should hardly have intruded it on your notice, with all your public cares, if I had not been informed by a godly man, who has an intimate knowledge of you, that you take such pleasure in reading as to lie awake by the hour, night after night, spending the precious time in your favourite pursuit.

# PRELIMINARY NOTES ON THE SECOND BOOK.

## (1) FROM THE PREFACE OF AUGUSTIN'S "UNFINISHED WORK AGAINST JULIANUS."

I WROTE a treatise, under the title *On Marriage and Concupiscence,* and addressed it to the Count VALERIUS, on learning that he had been informed of the Pelagians that they charge us with condemning marriage. Now in that treatise I showed the distinction, as critically and accurately as I was able, between the good of marriage and the evil of carnal concupiscence, — an evil which is well used by conjugal chastity. On receiving my treatise, the illustrious man whom I have named sent me in a short paper[1] a few sentences culled from a work of Julianus,[2] a Pelagian heretic. In this work he has thought fit to extend to four books his answer to the before-mentioned treatise of mine, which is limited to one book only, *On Marriage and Concupiscence.* I do not know to whom we were indebted for the said extracts: he confined his selection, evidently on purpose, to the first book of Julianus' work. At the request of Valerius, I lost no time in drawing up my answer to the extracts. And thus it happened that I have written a second book also under the same title; and in reply to this, Julianus has drawn up eight books, in the excess of his loquacious powers.

## (2) FROM AUGUSTIN'S EPISTLE TO CLAUDIUS [CCVII.].

"Whoever has perused this second book of mine, addressed (as the first was) to the Count Valerius, and drawn up (as, indeed, both were) for his use, will have discovered that there are some points in which I have not answered Julianus, but that I meant my work rather for him who made the extracts from that writer's books, and who did not arrange them in the order in which he found them. He deemed some considerable alteration necessary in his arrangement, very probably with the view of appropriating by this method as his own the thoughts which evidently were another person's."

---

[1] In chartula.

[2] [This able and learned man was much the most formidable of the Pelagian writers. Besides this book, Augustin wrote three large works against him, the treatise *Against Two Letters of the Pelagians,* and the two treatises *Against Julian,* the last of which is usually called *The Unfinished Work* from the circumstance that Augustin left it incomplete at his death. Julian was a son of a dear friend of Augustin, and was himself much loved by him. He became a "lector" in 404, and was ordained bishop by Innocent I. about 417. Under Zosimus' vacillating policy he took strong ground on the Pelagian side, and, refusing to sign Zosimus' *Tractoria,* was exiled with his seventeen fellow-recusants, and passed his long life in vain endeavours to obtain recognition for the Pelagian party. His writings included two letters to Zosimus, a *Confession of Faith,* the two letters answered in *Against Two Letters of the Pelagians* (though he seems to have repudiated the former of these), and two large books against Augustin, the first of which was his four books against the first book of the present treatise, against extracts from which the second book was written, whilst Augustin's *Against Julian,* in six books, traverses the whole work. To this second book Julian replied in a rejoinder addressed to Florus, and consisting of eight books. Augustin's *Unfinished Work* is a reply to this. Julian's character was as noble as his energy was great and his pen acute. He stands out among his fellow-Pelagians as the sufferer for conscience' sake. A full account of his works may be read in the Benedictine Preface to Augustin's *Unfinished Work,* with which may be compared the article on him in Smith and Wace's *Dictionary of Christian Biography.* — W.]

# BOOK II.[1]

AUGUSTIN, IN THIS LATTER BOOK, REFUTES SUNDRY SENTENCES WHICH HAD BEEN CULLED BY SOME UNKNOWN AUTHOR FROM THE FIRST OF FOUR BOOKS THAT JULIANUS HAD PUBLISHED IN OPPOSITION TO THE FORMER BOOK OF HIS TREATISE "ON MARRIAGE AND CONCUPISCENCE;" WHICH SENTENCES HAD BEEN FORWARDED TO HIM AT THE INSTANCE OF THE COUNT VALERIUS. HE VINDICATES THE CATHOLIC DOCTRINE OF ORIGINAL SIN FROM HIS OPPONENT'S CAVILS AND SUBTLETIES, AND PARTICULARLY SHOWS HOW DIVERSE IT IS FROM THE INFAMOUS HERESY OF THE MANICHEANS.

CHAP. 1 [I.] — INTRODUCTORY STATEMENT.

I CANNOT tell you, dearly loved and honoured son Valerius, how great is the pleasure which my heart receives when I hear of your warm and earnest interest in the testimony of the word of God against the heretics; and this, too, amidst your military duties and the cares which devolve on you in the eminent position you so justly occupy, and the pressing functions, moreover, of your political life. After reading the letter of your Eminence, in which you acknowledge the book which I dedicated to you, I was roused to write this also; for you request me to attend to the statement, which my brother and fellow-bishop Alypius is commissioned to make to me, about the discussion which is being raised by the heretics over sundry passages of my book. Not only have I received this information from the narrative of my said brother, but I have also read the extracts which he produced, and which you had yourself forwarded to Rome, after his departure from Ravenna. On discovering the boastful language of our adversaries, as I could easily do in these extracts, I determined, with the help of the Lord, to reply to their taunts with all the truthfulness and scriptural authority that I could command.

CHAP. 2 [II.] — IN THIS AND THE FOUR NEXT CHAPTERS HE ADDUCES THE GARBLED EXTRACTS HE HAS TO CONSIDER.

The paper which I now answer starts with this title: "*Headings out of a book written by Augustin, in reply to which I have culled a few passages out of books.*" I perceive from this that the person who forwarded these written papers to your Excellency wanted to make his extracts out of the books he does not name,

with a view, so far as I can judge, to getting a quicker answer, in order that he might not delay your urgency. Now, after considering what books they were which he meant, I suppose that it must have been those which Julianus mentioned in the Epistle he sent to Rome,[2] a copy of which found its way to me at the same time. For he there says: "They go so far as to allege that marriage, now in dispute, was not instituted by God, — a declaration which may be read in a work of Augustin's, to which I have lately replied in a treatise of four books." These are the books, as I believe, from which the extracts were taken. It would, then, have been perhaps the better course if I had set myself deliberately to disprove and refute that entire work of his,[3] which he spread out into four volumes. But I was most unwilling to delay my answer, even as you yourself lost no time in forwarding to me the written statements which I was requested to reply to.

CHAP. 3. — THE SAME CONTINUED.

The words which he has quoted and endeavoured to refute out of my book, which I sent to you, and with which you are very well acquainted, are the following: "They are constantly affirming, in their excessive hatred of us, that we condemn marriage and that divine procedure by which God creates human beings by means of men and women, inasmuch as we maintain that they who are born of such a union contract original sin, and do not deny that, of whatever parents they are born, they are still under the devil's dominion unless they be born again in

---

[1] Written A.D. 420.

[2] See Augustin's *Unfinished Work against Julian*, i. 18.
[3] This Augustin afterwards did by the publication of six books against Julianus, on receiving his entire work. Augustin tells us (*Unfinished Work*, i. 19) that he had long endeavoured to procure a copy of Julianus' books for the purpose of refuting them, and only succeeded in getting them after some difficulty and delay.

Christ." [1]  Now, in quoting these words of mine, he took care to omit the testimony of the apostle, which I adduced by the weighty significance of which he felt himself too hard pressed. For, after saying that men at their birth contract original sin, I at once introduced the apostle's words: "By one man sin entered into the world, and death by sin; and so death passed upon all men, for in him all men sinned." [2]  Well, as I have already mentioned, he omitted this passage of the apostle, and then closed up the other remarks of mine which have been now quoted. For he knew too well how acceptable to the hearts and consciences of all faithful catholics are these words of the apostle, which I had adopted, but which he omitted, — words which are so direct and so clear, that these new-fangled heretics use every effort in their dark and tortuous glosses to obscure and deprave their force.

### CHAP. 4. — THE SAME CONTINUED.

But he has added other words of mine, where I have said: "Nor do they reflect that the good of marriage is no more impeachable by reason of the original evil which is derived therefrom, than the evil of adultery and fornication can be excused by reason of the natural good which is born of them. For as sin is the work of the devil, whether derived from this source or from that; so is man, whether born of this or that, the work of God." Here, too, he has left out some words, in which he was afraid of catholic ears. For to come to the words here quoted, it had previously been said by us: "Because, then, we affirm this doctrine, which is contained in the oldest and unvarying rule of the catholic faith, these propounders of novel and perverse dogmas, who deny that there is in infants any sin to be washed away in the laver of regeneration, in their unbelief or ignorance calumniate us as if we condemned marriage, and as if we asserted to be the devil's work what is God's own work, to wit, the human being which is born of marriage." [3]  All this passage he has passed over, and merely quoted the words which follow it, as given above. Now, in the omitted words he was afraid of the clause which suits all hearts in the catholic Church and appeals to the very faith which has been firmly established and transmitted from ancient times with unfaltering voice and excites their hostility most strongly against us. The clause is this: "They deny that there is in infants any sin to be washed away in the laver of regeneration." For all persons run to church with their infants for no other reason in the world than that the original sin which is contracted in them by their first and natural birth may be cleansed by the regeneration of their second birth.

### CHAP. 5. — THE SAME CONTINUED.

He then returns [4] to our words, which were quoted before: "We maintain that they who are born of such a union contract original sin; and we do not deny that, of whatever parents they are born, they are still under the devil's dominion unless they be born again in Christ." Why he should again refer to these words of ours I cannot tell; he had already cited them a little before. He then proceeds to quote what we said of Christ: "Who willed not to be born from the same union of the two sexes." But here again he quietly ignored the words which I placed just previous to these words; my entire sentence being this: "That by His grace they may be removed from the power of darkness, and translated into the kingdom of Him who willed not to be born from the same union of the two sexes." Observe, I pray you, what my words were which he shunned, in the temper of one who is thoroughly opposed to that grace of God which comes through our "Lord Jesus Christ." He knows well enough that it is the height of improbity and impiety to exclude infants from their interest in the apostle's words, where he said of God the Father: "Who hath delivered us from the power of darkness, and hath translated us into the kingdom of His dear son." [5]  This, no doubt, is the reason why he preferred to omit rather than quote these words.

### CHAP. 6. — THE SAME CONTINUED.

He has next adduced that passage of ours, wherein we said: "For there would have been none of this shame-producing concupiscence, which is impudently praised by impudent men, if man had not previously sinned; while as to marriage, it would still have existed, even if no man had sinned: for the procreation of children would have been effected without this disease." Up to this point he cited my words; but he shrank from adding what comes next — "in the body of that chaste life, although without it this cannot be done in 'the body of this death.'" He would not complete my sentence, but mutilated it somewhat, because he dreaded the apostle's exclamation, of which my words gave him a reminder: "O wretched man that I am! who shall deliver me from the body of this death? The grace of God, through Jesus Christ our Lord." [6]  For the body of this death existed not in paradise before sin; therefore did we say, "In the body of that chaste life," which was the life of paradise, "the procreation of children could have been effected without the disease, without

---

[1] See above, Book i. ch. 1 of this treatise.
[2] Rom. v. 12.    [3] Book i. of this treatise, ch. 1.

[4] See *The Unfinished Work*, i. 64.    [5] Col. i. 13.
[6] Rom. vii. 24.

which now in the body of this death it cannot be done." The apostle, however, before arriving at that mention of man's misery and God's grace which we have just quoted, had first said : " I see another law in my members warring against the law of my mind, and bringing me into captivity to the law of sin which is in my members." Then it is that he exclaimed, " O wretched man that I am ! who shall deliver me from the body of this death ? The grace of God, through Jesus Christ our Lord." In the body of this death, therefore, such as it was in paradise before sin, there certainly was not " another law in our members warring against the law of our mind " — which now, even when we are unwilling, and withhold consent, and use not our members to fulfil that which it desires, still dwells in these members, and harasses our resisting and repugnant mind. And this conflict in itself, although not involving condemnation, because it does not consummate sin, is nevertheless " wretched," inasmuch as it has no peace. I think, then, that I have shown you clearly enough that this man had a special object as well as method in quoting my words : he adduced them for refutation in such manner as in some instances to interrupt the context of my sentences by removing what stood between them, and in other instances to curtail them by withdrawing their concluding words ; and his reason for doing all this I think I have sufficiently explained.

CHAP. 7 [III.] — AUGUSTIN ADDUCES A PASSAGE SELECTED FROM THE PREFACE OF JULIANUS. (SEE " THE UNFINISHED WORK," i. 73.)

Let us now look at those words of ours which he adduced just as it suited him, and to which he would oppose his own. For they are followed by his words ; moreover, as the person insinuated who sent you the paper of extracts, he copied something out of a preface, which was no doubt the preface of the books from which he selected a few passages. The paragraph thus copied stands as follows : " The teachers of our day, most holy brother,[1] who are the instigators of the disgraceful faction which is now overheated with its zeal, are determined on compassing the injury and discredit of the men with whose sacred fervour they are set on fire, by nothing less than the ruin of the whole Church ; little thinking how much honour they have conferred on those whose renown they have shown to be only capable of being destroyed along with the catholic religion. For, if one should say, either that there is free will in man, or that God is the Creator of those that are born,[2] he is at once set down as a Cœles-

tian and a Pelagian. To avoid being called heretics, they turn Manicheans ; and so, whilst shirking a pretended infamy, they incur a real reproach : just like the animals, which in hunting they surround with dyed feathers, in order to scare and drive them into their nets ;[3] the poor brutes are not gifted with reason, and so they are thrust all together by a vain panic into a real destruction."[4]

CHAP. 8. — AUGUSTIN REFUTES THE PASSAGE ADDUCED ABOVE.

Well, now, whoever you are that have said all this, what you say is by no means true ; by no means, I repeat ; you are much deceived, or you aim at deceiving others. We do not deny free will ; but, even as the Truth declares, " if the Son shall make you free, then shall ye be free indeed."[5] It is yourselves who invidiously deny this Liberator, since you ascribe a vain liberty to yourselves in your captivity. Captives you are ; for " of whom a man is overcome," as the Scripture says, " of the same is he brought in bondage ; "[6] and no one except by the grace of the great Liberator is loosed from the chain of this bondage, from which no man living is free. For " by one man sin entered into the world, and death by sin ; and so death passed upon all men, for in him all have sinned."[7] Thus, then, God is the Creator of those that are born in such wise that all pass from the one into condemnation, who have not the One Liberator by regeneration. For He is described as " the Potter, forming out of the same lump one vessel unto honour in His mercy, and another unto dishonour[8] in judgment." And so runs the Church's canticle " mercy and judgment."[9] You are therefore only misleading yourself and others when you say, " If one should affirm, either that there is free will in man, or that God is the Creator of those that are born, he is at once set down as a Cœlestian and a Pelagian ; "[10] for the catholic faith says these things. If, however, any one says that there is a free will in man for worshipping God aright, without His assistance ; and whosoever says that God is the Creator of those that are born, in such wise as to deny that infants have any need of one to redeem them from the power of the devil : that is the man who is set down as a disciple of Cœlestius and Pelagius. Therefore that men have within them a free will, and that God is the Creator of those that are born, are propositions which we both allow. You are not Cœlestians and Pelagians for merely saying this. But what you do really say is this, that any man whatever has freedom enough of will

---

[1] He calls Florus " most holy father " elsewhere (see *The Unfinished Work*, iv. 5). This man, to whom Julianus dedicated his work, is called a *colleague* or fellow-bishop of Julianus by Augustin (*The Unfinished Work*, iii. 187).
[2] *Conditor nascentium, i.e.* the Maker of all men's births.

[3] For a description of this curious mode of capture, see Dr. Smith's *Greek and Roman Antiquities*, s. v. RETE.
[4] See *The Unfinished Work*, i. 3.　　[5] John viii 36.
[6] 2 Pet. ii. 19.　　[7] Rom. v. 12.　　[8] Rom. ix. 21.
[9] Ps. ci. 1.　　[10] See *The Unfinished Work*, iii. 101.

for doing good without God's help, and that infants undergo no such change as being "delivered from the power of darkness and translated into the kingdom of God;"[1] and because you say so, you are Cœlestians and Pelagians. Why, then, do you hide under the covering of a common dogma for deceit, concealing your own especial delinquency which has gained for you a party-name; and why, to terrify the ignorant with a shocking term, do you say of us, "To avoid being called heretics, they turn Manicheans?"

CHAP. 9.—THE CATHOLICS MAINTAIN THE DOCTRINE OF ORIGINAL SIN, AND THUS ARE FAR FROM BEING MANICHEANS.

Listen, then, for a little while, and observe what is involved in this question. Catholics say that human nature was created good by the good God as Creator; but that, having been corrupted by sin, it needs the physician Christ. The Manicheans affirm, that human nature was not created by God good, and corrupted by sin; but that man was formed by the prince of eternal darkness of a mixture of two natures which had ever existed—one good and the other evil. The Pelagians and Cœlestians say that human nature was created good by the good God; but that it is still so sound and healthy in infants at their birth, that they have no need at that age of Christ's medicine. Recognise, then, your name in your dogma; and cease from intruding upon the catholics, who refute you, a name and a dogma which belong to others. For truth rejects both parties—the Manicheans and yourselves. To the Manicheans it says: "Have ye not read that He which made man at the beginning, made them male and female; and said, For this cause shall a man leave father and mother, and shall cleave to his wife; and they twain shall be one flesh? Wherefore they are no more twain, but one flesh. What, therefore, God hath joined together, let not man put asunder."[2] Now Christ shows, in this passage, that God is both the Creator of man, and the uniter in marriage of husband and wife; whereas the Manicheans deny both these propositions. To you, however, He says: "The Son of man is come to seek and to save that which is lost."[3] But you, admirable Christians as you are, answer Christ: "If you came to seek and to save that which was lost, then you did not come for infants; for they were not lost, but are born in a state of salvation: go to older men; we give you a rule from your own words: 'They that be whole need not a physician, but they that are sick.'"[4] Now, as it happens, the Manichean, who says that man has evil mixed in his nature, must wish his good soul

at any rate to be saved by Christ; whereas you contend that there is in infants nothing to be saved by Christ, since they are already safe.[5] And thus the Manichean besets human nature with his detestable censure, and you with your cruel praise. For whosoever shall believe your laudation, will never bring their babes to the Saviour. Entertaining such impious views as these, of what use is it that you fearlessly face that which is enacted for you[6] in order to induce salutary fear and to treat you as a human being, and not as that poor animal of yours which was surrounded with the coloured feathers to be driven into the hunting toils? Need was that you should hold the truth, and, on account of zeal for it, have no fear; but, as things are, you evade fear in such wise that, if you feared, you would rather run away from the net of the malignant one than run into it. The reason why your catholic mother alarms you is, because she fears for both you and others from you; and if by the help of her sons who possess any authority in the State she acts with a view to make you afraid, she does so, not from cruelty, but from love. You, however, are a very brave man; and you deem it the coward's part to be afraid of men. Well then, fear God; and do not try with such obstinacy to subvert the ancient foundations of the catholic faith. Although I could even wish that that spirited temper of yours would entertain some little fear of human authority, at least in the present case. I could wish, I say, that it would rather tremble through cowardice than perish through audacity.

CHAP. 10 [IV.]—IN WHAT MANNER THE ADVERSARY'S CAVILS MUST BE REFUTED.

Let us now look at the rest of what he has joined together in his selections. But what should be my course of proceeding? Ought I to set forth every passage of his for the purpose of answering it, or, omitting everything which the catholic faith contains, as not in dispute between us, only handle and confute those statements in which he strays away from the beaten path of truth, and endeavours to graft on catholic stems the poisonous shoots of his Pelagian heresy? This is, no doubt, the easier course. But I suppose I must not lose sight of a possible contingency, that any one, after reading my book, without perusing all that has been alleged by him, may think that I was unwilling to bring forward the passages on which his allegations depend, and by which are shown to be truly deduced the statements which I am controverting as false. I

---

[1] Col. i. 13.　　[2] Matt. xix. 4–6.　　[3] Luke xix. 10.
[4] Matt. ix. 12.

[5] The words "in body" are added here in the text of the Benedictine edition, though it is found in almost none of the MSS., because it is found in the passage as quoted in the *Unfinished Work*, iii. 138.
[6] This clause alludes to the Imperial edicts which Honorius issued, enacting penalties against the Pelagian heretics.

should be glad, therefore, if the reader will without exception kindly observe and consider the two classes of contributions which occur in this little work of ours — that is to say, all that he has alleged, and the answers which on my side I give him.

### CHAP. 11. — THE DEVIL THE AUTHOR, NOT OF NATURE, BUT ONLY OF SIN.

Now, the man who forwarded to your Love the paper in question has introduced the contents thereof with this title : " In opposition to those persons who condemn matrimony, and ascribe its fruits to the devil." This, then, is not in opposition to us, who neither condemn matrimony, which we even commend in its order with a just commendation, nor ascribe its fruits to the devil. For the fruits of matrimony are men which are orderly engendered from it, and not the sins which accompany their birth. Human beings are not under the devil's dominion because they are human beings, in which respect they are the fruits of matrimony ; but because they are sinful, in which resides the transmission of their sins. For the devil is the author of sin, not of nature.

### CHAP. 12. — EVE'S NAME MEANS LIFE, AND IS A GREAT SACRAMENT OF THE CHURCH.

Now, observe the rest of the passage in which he thinks he finds, to our prejudice, what is consonant with the above-quoted title. " God," says he, " who had framed Adam out of the dust of the ground, formed Eve out of his rib,[1] and said, She shall be called Life, because she is the mother of all who live." Well now, it is not so written. But what matters that to us? For it constantly happens that our memory fails in verbal accuracy, while the sense is still maintained. Nor was it God, but her husband, who gave Eve her name, which should signify *Life;* for thus it is written : "And Adam called his wife's name Life, because she is the mother of all living."[2] But very likely he might have understood the Scripture as testifying that God gave Eve this name through Adam, as His prophet. For in that she was called Life, and the mother of all living, there lies a great sacrament of the Church, of which it would detain us long to speak, and which is unnecessary to our present undertaking. The very same thing which the apostle says, " This is a great sacrament : but I speak concerning Christ and the Church," was also spoken by Adam when he said, " For this cause shall a man leave his father and his mother, and shall cleave unto his wife ; and they twain shall be one flesh."[3] The Lord Jesus, however, in the Gospel mentions God as having said this of Eve ; and the reason, no doubt, is, that God declared through the man

what the man, in fact, uttered as a prophecy. Now, observe what follows in the paper of extracts : " By that primitive name," says he, " He showed for what labour the woman had been provided ; and He said accordingly, 'Be fruitful, and multiply, and replenish the earth.' "[4] Now, who amongst ourselves denies that the woman was provided for the work of child-bearing by the Lord God, the beneficent Creator of all good? See further what he goes on to say : " God, therefore, who created them male and female,[5] furnished them with members suitable for procreation, and ordained that bodies should be produced from bodies ; and yet is security for their capacity for effecting the work, executing all that exists with that power which He used in creation."[6] Well, even this we acknowledge to be catholic doctrine, as we also do with regard to the passage which he immediately subjoins : " If, then, offspring comes only through sex, and sex only through the body, and the body through God, who can hesitate to allow that fecundity is rightly attributed to God?"

### CHAP. 13. — THE PELAGIAN ARGUMENT TO SHOW THAT THE DEVIL HAS NO RIGHTS IN THE FRUITS OF MARRIAGE.

After these true and catholic statements, which are, moreover, really contained in the Holy Scriptures, although they are not adduced by him in a catholic spirit, with the earnestness of a catholic mind, he loses no time in introducing to us the heresy of Pelagius and Cœlestius, for which purpose he wrote, indeed, his previous remarks. Mark carefully the following words : ' You now who say, ' We do not deny that they, are still, of whatever parents born, under the devil's power, unless they be born again in Christ,' show us what the devil can recognise as his own in the sexes, by reason of which he can (to use your phrase) rightly claim as his property the fruit which they produce. Is it the *difference* of the sexes? But this is inherent in the bodies which God made. Is it their *union?* But this union is justified in the privilege of the primeval blessing no less than institution. For it is the voice of God that says, ' A man shall leave his father and his mother, and shall cleave to his wife ; and they two shall be one flesh.'[7] It is again the voice of God which says, ' Be fruitful, and multiply, and replenish the earth.'[4] Or is it, perchance, their *fertility?* But this is the very reason why matrimony was instituted."

---

[1] Gen. ii. 22, 23.          [2] Gen. iii. 20, margin.
[3] Compare Eph. v. 32 with Gen. ii. 24.

[4] Gen. i. 28.          [5] Gen. i. 27.
[6] For once a difficulty occurs (for which, however, St. Augustin is not responsible) in the construction of the original. The obscure passage is here translated in accordance with a suggestion in some of the editions. It stands in the original thus : " Quorum tamen efficientiæ potentiâ operationis intervenit omne quod est eâ administrans virtute quâ condidit." Some editors suggest " *potentia* (nominative) *Dei operationis intervenit ;*" but there is no MS. authority for the *Dei.*
[7] Gen. ii. 24.

CHAP. 14 [V.] — CONCUPISCENCE ALONE, IN MARRIAGE, IS NOT OF GOD.

You see the terms of his question to us: what the devil can find in the sexes to call his own, by reason of which they should be in his power, who are born of parents of whatsoever kind, unless they be born again in Christ; he asks us, moreover, whether it is the difference in the sexes which we ascribe to the devil, or their union, or their very fruitfulness. We answer, then, nothing of these qualities, inasmuch as the difference of sex belongs to "the vessels" of the parents; while the union of the two pertains to the procreation of children; and their fruitfulness to the blessing pronounced on the marriage institution. But all these things are of God; yet amongst them he was unwilling to name that "lust of the flesh, which is not of the Father, but is of the world;"[1] and "of this world" the devil is said to be "the prince."[2] Now, the devil found no carnal concupiscence in the Lord, because the Lord did not come as a man to men by its means. Accordingly, He says Himself: "The prince of this world cometh, and findeth nothing in me"[2] — nothing, that is, of sin; neither that which is derived from birth, nor that which is added during life. Among all the natural goods of procreation which he mentioned, he was, I repeat, unwilling to name this particular fact of concupiscence, over which even marriage blushes, which glories in all these before-mentioned goods. For why is the especial work of parents withdrawn and hidden even from the eyes of their children, except that it is impossible for them to be occupied in laudable procreation without shameful lust? Because of this it was that even they were ashamed who first covered their nakedness.[3] These portions of their person were not suggestive of shame before, but deserved to be commended and praised as the work of God. They put on their covering when they felt their shame, and they felt their shame when, after their own disobedience to their Maker, they felt their members disobedient to themselves. Our quoter of extracts likewise felt ashamed of this concupiscence. For he mentioned the difference of the sexes; he mentioned also their union, and he mentioned their fertility; but this last concomitant of lust he blushed to mention. And no wonder if mere talkers are ashamed of that which we see parents themselves, so interested in their function, blush to think of.

CHAP. 15. — MAN, BY BIRTH, IS PLACED UNDER THE DOMINION OF THE DEVIL THROUGH SIN; WE WERE ALL ONE IN ADAM WHEN HE SINNED.

He then proceeds to ask: "Why, then, are they in the devil's power whom God created?" And he finds an answer to his own question apparently from a phrase of mine. "Because of sin," says he, "not because of nature." Then framing his answer in reference to mine, he says: "But as there cannot be offspring without the sexes, so there cannot be sin without the will." Yes, indeed, such is the truth. For even as "by one man sin entered into the world, and death by sin; so also has death passed through to all men, for in him all have sinned."[4] By the evil will of that one man all sinned in him, since all were that one man, from whom, therefore, they individually derived original sin. "For you allege," says he, "that the reason why they are in the devil's power is because they are born of the union of the two sexes." I plainly aver that it is by reason of transgression that they are in the devil's power, and that their participation, moreover, of this transgression is due to the circumstance that they are born of the said union of the sexes, which cannot even accomplish its own honourable function without the incident of shameful lust. This has also, in fact, been said by Ambrose, of most blessed memory, bishop of the church in Milan, when he gives as the reason why Christ's birth in the flesh was free from all sinful fault, that His conception was not the result of a union of the two sexes; whereas there is not one among human beings conceived in such union who is without sin. These are his precise words: "On that account, and being man, He was tried by every sort of temptation, and in the likeness of man He bore them all; inasmuch, however, as He was born of the Spirit, He abstained from all sin. For every man is a liar, and none is without sin, but God only. It has accordingly," adds he, "been constantly observed, that clearly no one who is born of a man and a woman, that is to say, through the union of their bodies, is free from sin; for whoever is free from sin is free also from conception of this kind."[5] Well now, will you dare, ye disciples of Pelagius and Cœlestius, to call this man a Manichean? as the heretic Jovinian did, when the holy bishop maintained the permanent virginity of the blessed Mary even after child-bearing, in opposition to this man's impiety. If, however, you do not dare to call him a Manichean, why do you call us Manicheans when we defend the catholic faith in the self-same cause and with the selfsame opinions? But if you will taunt that most faithful man with having entertained Manichean error in this matter, there is no help for it, you must enjoy your taunts as best you may, and so fill up Jovinian's measure more fully; as for ourselves, we can patiently endure along with

---

[1] 1 John ii. 16.    [2] John xiv. 30.    [3] Gen. iii. 7.

[4] Rom. v. 12.
[5] Ambrose *On Isaiah;* see also his *Epistle* (81) *to Siricius.*

such a man of God your taunts and jibes. And yet your heresiarch Pelagius commends Ambrose's faith and extreme purity in the knowledge of the Scriptures so greatly, as to declare that not even an enemy could venture to find fault with him. Observe, then, to what length you have gone, and refrain from following any further in the audacious steps of Jovinian. And yet that man, although by his excessive commendation of marriage he put it on a par with holy virginity, never denied the necessity of Christ to save those who are born of marriage even fresh from their mother's womb, and to redeem them from the power of the devil. This, however, you deny; and because we oppose you in defence of those who cannot yet speak for themselves, and in defence of the very foundations of the catholic faith, you taunt us with being Manicheans. But let us now see what comes next.

### CHAP. 16 [VI.] — IT IS NOT OF US, BUT OUR SINS, THAT THE DEVIL IS THE AUTHOR.

He puts to us, then, another question, saying, " Whom, then, do you confess to be the author of infants? The true God?" I answer: [1] " Yes; the true God." He then remarks, " But He did not make evil;" and again asks, " Whether we confess the devil to be the creator of infants?" Then again he answers, " But *he* did not create human nature." He then closes the subject, as it were, with this inference : " Since union is evil, and the condition of our bodies is degraded, therefore you ascribe our bodies to an evil creator." My answer to this is, I do not ascribe to an evil creator our bodies, but our sins ; by reason of which it came to pass that, whereas in our bodies, that is to say, in what God has made, all was honourable and well-pleasing, there yet accrued in the intercourse of male and female what caused shame, so that their union was not such as might have been in the body of that unimpaired life, but such as we see with a blush in the body of this death. " But God," says he, " has divided in sex what He would unite in operation. So that from Him comes the union of bodies, from whom first came the creation of bodies." We have already furnished an answer to this statement, when we said that these bodies are of God. But as regards the disobedience of the members of these bodies, this comes through the lust of the flesh, which " is not of the Father." [2] He goes on to say, that " it is impossible for evil fruits to spring from so many good things, such as bodies, sexes, and their unions ; or that human beings should be made by God for the purpose of their being,

by lawful right, as you maintain, held in possession by the devil." Now it has been already affirmed, that they are not thus held because they are men, which designation belongs to their nature, of which the devil is not the author ; but because they are sinners, which designation is the result of that fault of nature of which the devil is the author.

### CHAP. 17 [VII.] — THE PELAGIANS ARE NOT ASHAMED TO EULOGIZE CONCUPISCENCE, ALTHOUGH THEY ARE ASHAMED TO MENTION ITS NAME.

But among so many names of good things, such as bodies, sexes, unions, he never once mentions the lust or concupiscence of the flesh. He is silent, because he is ashamed ; and yet with a strange shamelessness of shame (if the expression may be used), he is not ashamed to praise what he is ashamed to mention. Now just observe how he prefers to point to his object by circumlocution rather than by direct mention of it. " After that the man," says he, " by natural appetite knew his wife." See again, he refused to say, He knew his wife by carnal concupiscence ; but he used the phrase, " by natural appetite," by which it is open to us to understand that holy and honourable will which wills the procreation of children, and not that lust, of which even he is so much ashamed, forsooth, that he prefers to use ambiguous language to us, to expressing his mind in unmistakeable words. " Now what is the meaning of his phrase — " by natural appetite "? Is not both the wish to be saved and the wish to beget, nourish, and educate children, natural appetite? and is it not likewise of reason, and not of lust? Since, however, we can ascertain his intention, we are pretty sure that he meant by these words to indicate the lust of the organs of generation. Do not the words in question appear to you to be the fig-leaves, under cover of which is hidden nothing else but that which he feels ashamed of? For just as they of old sewed the leaves together [3] as a girdle of concealment, so has this man woven a web of circumlocution to hide his meaning. Let him weave out his statement : " But when the man knew his wife by natural appetite, the divine Scripture says, Eve conceived, and bare a son, and called his name Cain. But what," he adds, " does Adam say? Let us hear : I have obtained a man from God. So that it is evident that he was God's work, and the divine Scripture testifies to his having been received from God." [4] Well, who can entertain a doubt on this point? Who can deny this statement, especially if he be a catholic Christian? A man is God's work ; but carnal concupiscence (without which, if sin had not preceded, man would

---

[1] This is the Benedictine reading; but another reading has " he answers," which seems to suit the context. See the following: " again *he* answers."
[2] 1 John ii. 16.
[3] Gen. iii. 7.      [4] Gen. iv. 1.

have been begotten by means of the organs of generation, not less obedient than the other members to a quiet and normal will) is not of the Father, but is of the world.[1]

### CHAP. 18. — THE SAME CONTINUED.

But now, I pray you, look a little more attentively, and observe how he contrives to find a name wherewith to cover again what he blushes to unfold. "For," says he, "Adam begot him by the power of his members, not by diversity of merits." Now I confess I do not understand what he meant by the latter clause, *not by diversity of merits;* but when he said, "by the power of his members," I believe he wished to express what he is ashamed to say openly and clearly. He preferred to use the phrase, "by the power of his members," rather than say, "by the lust of the flesh." Plainly — even if the thought did not occur to him — he intimated a something which has an evident application to the subject. For what is more powerful than a man's members, when they are not in due submission to a man's will? Even if they be restrained by temperance or continence, their use and control are not in any man's power. Adam, then, begat his sons by what our author calls "the power of his members," over which, before he begat them, he blushed, after his sin. If, however, he had never sinned, he would not have begotten them by the *power,* but in the *obedience,* of his members. For he would himself have had the *power* to rule them as subjects to his will, if he, too, by the same will had only submitted himself as a subject to a more powerful One.

### CHAP. 19 [VIII.] — THE PELAGIANS MISUNDERSTAND "SEED" IN SCRIPTURE.

He goes on to say: "After a while the divine Scripture says again, 'Adam knew Eve his wife; and she bare a son, and he called his name Seth: saying, The Lord hath raised me up another seed instead of Abel, whom Cain slew.'" He then adds: "The Divinity is said to have raised up the seed itself; as a proof that the sexual union was His appointment." This person did not understand what the Scripture records; for he supposed that the reason why it is said, The Lord hath raised me up another seed instead of Abel, was none other than that God might be supposed to have excited in him a desire for sexual intercourse, by means whereof seed might be raised for being poured into the woman's womb. He was perfectly unaware that what the Scripture has said is not "Has raised me up seed" in the sense he uses, but only as meaning "Has given me a son." Indeed, Adam did not use the words in question after his sexual

intercourse, when he emitted his seed, but after his wife's confinement, in which he received his son by the gift of God. For what gratification is there (except perhaps for lascivious persons, and those who, as the apostle says with prohibition, "possess their vessel in the lust of concupiscence"[2]) in the mere shedding of seed as the ultimate pleasure of sexual union, unless it is followed by the true and proper fruit of marriage — conception and birth?

### CHAP. 20. — ORIGINAL SIN IS DERIVED FROM THE FAULTY CONDITION OF HUMAN SEED.

This, however, I would not say, as implying at all that we must look for some other creator than the supreme and true God, of either human seed or of man himself who comes from the seed; but as meaning, that the seed would have issued from the human being by the quiet and normal obedience of his members to his will's command, if sin had not preceded. The question now before us does not concern the nature of human seed, but its corruption. Now the *nature* has God for its author; it is from its corruption that original sin is derived. If, indeed, the seed had itself no corruption, what means that passage in the Book of Wisdom, "Not being ignorant that they were a naughty generation, and that their malice was inbred, and that their cogitation would never be changed; for their seed was accursed from the beginning"?[3] Now whatever may be the particular application of these words, they are spoken of mankind. How, then, is the malice of every man inbred, and his seed cursed from the beginning, unless it be in respect of the fact, that "by one man sin entered into the world, and death by sin; and so death passed upon all men, for in him all have sinned"?[4] But where is the man whose "evil cogitation can never be changed," unless because it cannot be effected by himself, but only by divine grace; without the assistance of which, what are human beings, but that which the Apostle Peter says of them, when he describes them as "natural brute beasts made to be taken and destroyed"?[5] Accordingly, the Apostle Paul, in a certain passage, having both conditions in view, — even the wrath of God with which we are born, and the grace whereby we are delivered, — says: "Among whom also we all had our conversation in times past in the lusts of our flesh, fulfilling the desires of the flesh and of the mind; and were by nature the children of wrath, even as others. But God, who is rich in mercy, for His great love wherewith He loved us, even when we were dead in sins, hath quickened us together with Christ; by whose grace we are saved."[6] What, then, is

---

[1] 1 John ii. 16.

[2] 1 Thess. iv. 5.　　[3] Wisd. xii. 10, 11.　　[4] Rom. v. 12.
[5] 2 Pet. ii. 12.　　[6] Eph. ii. 3-5.

man's "natural malice," and "the seed cursed from the beginning;" and what are "the natural brute beasts made to be taken and destroyed," and what the "by nature children of wrath"? Was this the condition of the nature which was formed in Adam? God forbid! Inasmuch as his pure nature, however, was corrupted in him, it has run on in this condition by natural descent through all, and still is running; so that there is no deliverance for it from this ruin, except by the grace of God through our Lord Jesus Christ.

CHAP. 21 [IX.] — IT IS THE GOOD GOD THAT GIVES FRUITFULNESS, AND THE DEVIL THAT CORRUPTS THE FRUIT.

What, therefore, is this man's meaning, in the next passage, wherein he says concerning Noah and his sons, that "they were blessed, even as Adam and Eve were; for God said unto them, 'Be fruitful, and multiply, and have dominion over the earth'"?[1] To these words of the Almighty he added some of his own, saying: "Now that pleasure, which you would have seem diabolical, was resorted to in the case of the above-mentioned married pairs; and it continued to exist, both in the goodness of its institution and in the blessing attached to it. For there can be no doubt that the following words were addressed to Noah and his sons in reference to their bodily connection with their wives, which had become by this time unalterably fixed by use: 'Be fruitful, and multiply, and replenish the earth.'" It is unnecessary for us to employ many words in repeating our former argument. The point here in question is the corruption in our nature, whereby its goodness has been depraved, of which corruption the devil is the author. That goodness of nature, as it is in itself, the author of which is God, is not the question we have to consider. Now God has never withdrawn from corrupted and depraved nature His own mercy and goodness, so as to deprive man of fruitfulness, vivacity, and health, as well as the very substance of his mind and body, his senses also and reason, as well as food, and nourishment, and growth. He, moreover, "maketh His sun to arise on the evil and on the good, and sendeth rain on the just and on the unjust;"[2] and all that is good in human nature is from the good God, even in the case of those men who will not be delivered from evil.

CHAP. 22. — SHALL WE BE ASHAMED OF WHAT WE DO, OR OF WHAT GOD DOES?

It is, however, of *pleasure* that this man spoke in his passage, because pleasure can be even honourable: of carnal concupiscence, or lust,

which produces shame, he made no mention. In some subsequent words, however, he uncovered his susceptibility of shame; and he was unable to dissemble what nature herself has prescribed so forcibly. "There is also," says he, "that statement: 'Therefore shall a man leave his father and his mother, and shall cleave unto his wife; and they twain shall be one flesh.'" Then after these words of God, he goes on to offer some of his own, saying: "That he might express faith in works, the prophet approached very near to a perilling of modesty." What a confession! How clear and extorted from him by the force of truth! The prophet, it would seem, to express faith in works, almost imperilled modesty, when he said, "They twain shall become one flesh;" wishing it to be understood of the sexual union of the male and the female! Let the cause be alleged, why the prophet, in expressing the works of God, should approach so near an imperilling of modesty? Is it then the case that the works of man ought not to produce shame, but must be gloried in at all events, and that the works of God must produce shame? Is it, that in setting forth and expressing the works of God the prophet's love or labour receives no honour, but his modesty is imperilled? What, then, was it possible for God to do, which it would be a shame for His prophet to describe? And, what is a weightier question still, could a man be ashamed of any work which not man, but God, has made in man? whereas workmen in all cases strive, with all the labour and diligence in their power, to avoid shame in the works of their own hands. The truth, however, is, that we are ashamed of that very thing which made those primitive human beings ashamed, when they covered their loins. That is the penalty of sin; that is the plague and mark of sin; that is the temptation and very fuel of sin; that is the law in our members warring against the law of our mind; that is the rebellion against our own selves, proceeding from our very selves, which by a most righteous retribution is rendered us by our disobedient members. It is this which makes us ashamed, and justly ashamed. If it were not so, what could be more ungrateful, more irreligious in us, if in our members we were to suffer confusion of face, not for our own fault or penalty, but because of the works of God?

CHAP. 23 [X.] — THE PELAGIANS AFFIRM THAT GOD IN THE CASE OF ABRAHAM AND SARAH AROUSED CONCUPISCENCE AS A GIFT FROM HEAVEN.

He has much also to say, though to no purpose, concerning Abraham and Sarah, how they received a son according to the promise; and at last he mentions the word *concupiscence*. But

---

[1] Gen. ix. 1.         [2] Matt. v. 45.

he does not add the usual phrase, "of the flesh," because this is the very thing which causes the shame. Whereas, on account of concupiscence there is sometimes a call for boasting, inasmuch as there is a concupiscence of the spirit against the flesh,[1] and a concupiscence of wisdom.[2] Accordingly, he says: " Now you have certainly defined as naturally evil this concupiscence which is indispensable for fecundity; whence comes it, therefore, that it is aroused in aged men by the gift of Heaven? Make it clear then, if you can, that that belongs to the devil's work, which you see is conferred by God as a gift." He says this, just as if concupiscence of the flesh had been previously wanting in them, and as if God had bestowed it upon them. No doubt it was inherent in this body of death; that fecundity, however, was wanting of which God is the author; and this was actually given whensoever God willed to confer the gift. Be it, however, far from us to affirm, what he thought we meant to say, that Isaac was begotten without the heat of sexual union.

CHAP. 24 [XI.] — WHAT COVENANT OF GOD THE NEW-BORN BABE BREAKS. WHAT WAS THE VALUE OF CIRCUMCISION.

But let him inform us how it was that his[3] soul would be cut off from his people if he had not been circumcised on the eighth day. How could he have so sinned, how so offended God, as to be punished for the neglect of others towards him with so severe a sentence, had there been no original sin in the case? For thus ran the commandment of God concerning the circumcision of infants: "The uncircumcised man-child, whose flesh of his foreskin is not circumcised on the eighth day, his soul shall be cut off from his people; because he hath broken my covenant."[4] Let him tell us, if he can, how that child broke God's covenant, — an innocent babe, so far as he was personally concerned, of eight days' age; and yet there is by no means any falsehood uttered here by God or Holy Scripture. The fact is, the covenant of God which he then broke was not this which commanded circumcision, but that which forbade the tree; when "by one man sin entered into the world, and death by sin; and so death passed upon all men, for in him all have sinned."[5] And in his case the expiation of this was signified by the circumcision of the eighth day, that is, by the sacrament of the Mediator who was to be incarnate. For it was through this same faith in Christ, who was to come in the flesh, and was to die for us, and on the third day (which coming after the seventh or Sabbath day, was to be the eighth) to rise again, that even holy men were saved of old. For " He was delivered for our offences, and raised again for our justification."[6] Ever since circumcision was instituted amongst the people of God, which was at that time the sign of the righteousness of faith, it availed also to signify the cleansing even in infants of the original and primitive sin, just as baptism in like manner from the time of its institution began to be of avail for the renewal of man. Not that there was no justification by faith before circumcision; for even when he was still in uncircumcision, Abraham was himself justified by faith, being the father of those nations which should also imitate his faith.[7] In former times, however, the sacramental mystery of justification by faith lay concealed in every mode. Still it was the self-same faith in the Mediator which saved the saints of old, both small and great — not the old covenant, "which gendereth to bondage;"[8] not the law, which was not so given as to be able to give life;[9] but the grace of God through Jesus Christ our Lord.[10] For as we believe that Christ has come in the flesh, so they believed that He was to come; as, again, we believe that He has died, so they believed that He would die; and as we believe that He has risen from the dead, so they believed that He would rise again; whilst both we and they believe alike, that He will hereafter come to judge the quick and the dead. Let not this man, then, throw any hindrance in the way of its salvation upon human nature, by setting up a bad defence of its merits; because we are all born under sin, and are delivered therefrom by the only One who was born without sin.

CHAP. 25 [XII.] — AUGUSTIN NOT THE DEVISER OF ORIGINAL SIN.

" This sexual connection of bodies," he says, " together with the ardour, with the pleasure, with the emission of seed, was made by God, and is praiseworthy on its own account, and is therefore to be approved; it, moreover, became sometimes even a great gift to pious men." He distinctly and severally repeated the phrases, "with ardour," " with pleasure," " with emission of seed." He did not, however, venture to say, " with lust." Why is this, if it be not that he is ashamed to name what he does not blush to praise? A gift, indeed, for pious men is the prosperous propagation of children; but not that shame-producing excitement of the members, which our nature would not feel were it in a sound state, although corrupted nature now experiences it. On this account, indeed, it is that he who is born of it requires to be born again, in order that he may be a member of Christ; and that

---

[1] Gal. v. 17.
[2] Wisd. vi. 21. The word in the Latin Bible in both cases is " concupiscentia."
[3] i.e., Isaac's.    [4] Gen. xvii. 14.    [5] Rom. v. 12.

[6] Rom. iv. 25.    [7] Rom. iv. 10, 11.    [8] Gal. iv. 24.
[9] Gal. iii. 21.    [10] Rom. vii. 25.

he of whom he is born, even though he be already born again, wants to be freed from that which exists in this body of death by reason of the law of sin. Now since this is the case, how is it he goes on to say, "You must, therefore, of necessity confess that the original sin which you had devised is done away with"? It was not I who devised the original sin, which the catholic faith holds from ancient times; but you, who deny it, are undoubtedly an innovating heretic. In the judgment of God, all are in the devil's power, born in sin, unless they are regenerated in Christ.

### CHAP. 26 [XIII.] — THE CHILD IN NO SENSE FORMED BY CONCUPISCENCE.

But as he was speaking of Abraham and Sarah, he goes on to say: "If, indeed, you were to affirm that the natural use was strong in them, and there was no offspring, my answer will be: Whom the Creator promised, the Creator also gave; the child which is born is not the work of cohabitation, but of God. He, indeed, who made the first man of the dust, fashions all men out of seed. As, therefore, the dust of the earth, which was taken as the material, was not the author of man; so likewise that power of sexual pleasure which forms and commingles the seminal elements does not complete the entire process of man's making, but rather presents to God, out of the treasures of nature, material with which He vouchsafes to make the human being." Now the whole of this statement of his, except where he says, that the seminal elements are formed and commingled by sexual pleasure, would be correctly expressed by him were he only earnest in making it to defend the catholic sense. To us, however, who are fully aware what he strives to make out of it, he speaks indeed correctly in a perverse manner. The exceptional statement to the general truth, which I do not deny belongs to this passage, is untrue for this reason, because the pleasure in question of carnal concupiscence does not form the seminal elements. These are already in the body, and are formed by the same true God who created the body itself. They do not receive their existence from the libidinous pleasure, but are excited and emitted in company with it. Whether, indeed, such pleasure accompanies the commingling of the seminal elements of the two sexes in the womb, is a question which perhaps women may be able to determine from their inmost feelings; but it is improper for us to push an idle curiosity so far. That concupiscence, however, which we have to be ashamed of, and the shame of which has given to our secret members their shameful designation, *pudenda*, had no existence in the body during its life in paradise before the entrance of sin; but

it began to exist "in the body of this death" after sin, the rebellion of the members retaliating man's own disobedience. Without this concupiscence it was quite possible to effect the function of the wedded pair in the procreation of children: just as many a laborious work is accomplished by the compliant operation of our other limbs, without any lascivious heat; for they are simply moved by the direction of the will, not excited by the ardour of concupiscence.

### CHAP. 27. — THE PELAGIANS ARGUE THAT GOD SOMETIMES CLOSES THE WOMB IN ANGER, AND OPENS IT WHEN APPEASED.

Carefully consider the rest of his remarks: "This likewise," says he, "is confirmed by the apostle's authority. For when the blessed Paul spoke of the resurrection of the dead, he said, 'Thou fool, that which thou sowest is not quickened.'[1] And afterwards, 'But God giveth it a body as it pleaseth Him, and to every seed its own body.' If, therefore, God," says he, "has assigned to human seed, as to every thing else, its own proper body, which no wise or pious man will deny, how will you prove that any person is born guilty? Do, I beg of you, reflect with what a noose this assertion of natural sin is choked. But come," he says, "deal more gently with yourself, I pray you. Believe me, God made even you: it must, however, be confessed, that a serious error has infected you. For what profaner opinion can be broached than that either God did not make man, or else that He made him for the devil; or, at any rate, that the devil framed God's image, that is, man, — which clearly is a statement not more absurd than impious? Is then," says he, "God so poor in resources, so lacking in all sense of propriety, as not to have had aught which He could confer on holy men as their reward, except what the devil, after making them his dupes, might infuse into them for their vitiation?[2] Would you like to know, however, that even in the case of those who are no saints, God can be proved to have bestowed this power of procreation of children? When Abraham, struck with fear among a foreign nation, said that Sarah, his wife, was his sister, it is said that Abimelech, the king of the country, abducted her for a night's enjoyment of her. But God, who had the holy woman's honour in His keeping, appeared to Abimelech in his sleep, and restrained the royal audacity; threatening him with death if he went to the length of violating the wife. Then Abimelech said: 'Wilt thou, O Lord, slay an innocent and righteous nation? Did they not tell me that they were brother and sister? Therefore Abime-

---

[1] 1 Cor. xv. 36.
[2] The translation adopts the conjecture of the Benedictine editors: *in vitium*, instead of *in vitio* or *initio*, as the MSS. read.

lech arose early in the morning, and took a thousand pieces of silver, and sheep, and oxen, and men-servants, and women-servants, and gave them to Abraham, and sent away his wife untouched. But Abraham prayed unto God for Abimelech; and God healed Abimelech, and his wife, and his maid-servants.'"[1] Now why he narrated all this at so great a length, you may find in these few words which he added: "God," he says, "at the prayer of Abraham, restored their potency of generation, which had been taken away from the wombs of even the meanest servants; because God had closed up every womb in the house of Abimelech.[2] Consider now," says he, "whether that ought to be called a natural evil which sometimes God when angry takes away, and when appeased restores. He," says he, "makes the children both of the pious and of the ungodly, inasmuch as the circumstance of their being parents appertains to that nature which rejoices in God as its Author, whilst the fact of their impiety belongs to the depravity of their desires, and this comes to every person whatever as the consequence of free will."

CHAP. 28 [XIV.] — AUGUSTIN'S ANSWER TO THIS ARGUMENT. ITS DEALING WITH SCRIPTURE.

Now to this lengthy statement of his we have to say in answer, that, in the passages which he has quoted from the sacred writings, there is nothing said about that shameful lust, which we say did not exist in the body of our first parents in their blessedness, when they were naked and were not ashamed.[3] The first passage from the apostle was spoken of the seeds of corn, which first die in order to be quickened. For some reason or other, he was unwilling to complete the verse for his quotation. All he adduces from it is: "Thou fool, that which thou sowest is not quickened;" but the apostle adds, "except it die."[4] This writer, however, so far as I can judge, wished this passage, which treats only of corn seeds, to be understood of human seed, by such as read it without either understanding the Holy Scriptures or recollecting them. Indeed, he not merely curtailed this particular sentence, by omitting the clause, "except it die," but he omitted the following words, in which the apostle explained of what seeds he was speaking; for the apostle adds: "And that which thou sowest, thou sowest not that body which shall be, but the bare grain, it may chance of wheat, or of some other grain."[5] This he omitted, and closed up his context with what the apostle then writes: "But God giveth it a body as it hath pleased Him, and to every seed its own body;" just as if the apostle spoke of

man in cohabitation when he said, "Thou fool, that which thou sowest is not quickened," with a view to our understanding of human seed, that it is quickened by God, not by man in cohabitation begetting children. For he had previously said: "Sexual pleasure does not complete the entire process of man's making, but rather presents to God, out of the treasures of nature, material with which He vouchsafes to make the human being."[6] He then added the quotation, as if the apostle affirmed as follows: Thou fool, that which thou sowest *is* not quickened, — quickened, that is, by thyself; but God forms the human being out of thy seed. As if the apostle had not said the intermediate words, which this writer chose to pass over; and as if the apostle's aim was to speak of human seed thus: "Thou fool, that which thou sowest is not quickened; but God giveth to the seed a body such as pleaseth Him, and to every seed its own body." Indeed, after the apostle's words, he introduces remarks of his own to this effect: "If, therefore, God has assigned to human seed, as to everything else, its own proper body, which no wise or pious man will deny;" quite as if the apostle in the passage in question spoke of human seed.

CHAP. 29. — THE SAME CONTINUED. AUGUSTIN ALSO ASSERTS THAT GOD FORMS MAN AT BIRTH.

Though I have given special attention to the point, I have failed to discover what assistance he could obtain from this deceitful use of Scripture, except that he wanted to produce the apostle as a witness, and by him to prove, what we also assert, that God forms man of human seed. And inasmuch as no passage directly occurred to him, he deceitfully manipulated this particular one; fearing no doubt that, if the apostle should chance to seem to have spoken of corn seeds, and not of human, in this passage, we should have suggested to us at once by such procedure of his, how to refute him: not indeed as the pure-minded advocate of a chastened will, but as the impudent proclaimer of a profligate voluptuousness. But from the very seeds, forsooth, which the farmers sow in their fields he can be refuted. For why can we not suppose that God could have granted to man in his happy state in paradise, the same course with regard to his own seed which we see granted to the seeds of corn, in such wise that the former might be sown without any shameful lust, the members of generation simply obeying the inclination of the will; just as the latter is sown without any shameful lust, the hands of the husbandman merely moving in obedience to his will? There being, indeed, this difference, that

---

[1] See Gen. xx. 2, 4, 5, 8, 14, 17.    [2] Gen. xx. 18.
[3] Gen. ii. 25.    [4] 1 Cor. xv. 36.    [5] 1 Cor. xv. 37.    [6] Above, ch. 26 [XIII.].

the desire of begetting children in the parent is a nobler one than that which characterizes the farmer, of filling his barns. Then, again, why might not the almighty Creator, with His incontaminable ubiquity, and his power of creating from human seed just what it pleased Him, have operated in women, with respect to what He even now makes, in the self-same manner as He operates in the ground with corn seeds according to His will, making blessed mothers conceive without lustful passion, and bring forth children without parturient pains, inasmuch as there was not (in that state of happiness, and in the body which was not as yet the body of this death, but rather of that life) in woman when receiving seed anything to produce shame, as there was nothing when giving birth to offspring to cause pain? Whoever refuses to believe this, or is unwilling to have it supposed that, while men previous to any sin lived in that happy state of paradise, such a condition as that which we have sketched could not have been permitted in God's will and kindness, must be regarded as the lover of shameful pleasure, rather than the encomiast of desirable fecundity.

### CHAP. 30 [XV.] — THE CASE OF ABIMELECH AND HIS HOUSE EXAMINED.

Then, again, as to the passage which he has adduced from the inspired history concerning Abimelech, and God's choosing to close up every womb in his household that the women should not bear children, and afterwards opening them that they might become fruitful, what is all this to the point? What has it to do with that shameful concupiscence which is now the question in dispute? Did God, then, deprive those women of this feeling, and give it to them again just when He liked? The punishment, however, was that they were unable to bear children, and the blessing that they were able to bear them, after the manner of this corruptible flesh. For God would not confer such a blessing upon this body of death, as only that body of life in paradise could have had before sin entered; that is, the process of conceiving without the prurience of lust, and of bearing children without excruciating pain. But why should we not suppose, since, indeed, Scripture says that every womb was closed, that this took place with something of pain, so that the women were unable to bear cohabitation, and that God inflicted this pain in His wrath, and removed it in His mercy? For if lust was to be taken away as an impediment to begetting offspring, it ought to have been taken away from the men, not from the women. For a woman might perform her share in cohabitation by her will, even if the lust ceased by which she is stimulated, provided it were not absent from the

man for exciting him; unless, perhaps (as Scripture informs us that even Abimelech himself was healed), he would tell us that virile concupiscence was restored to him. If, however, it were true that he had lost this, what necessity was there that he should be warned by God to hold no connection with Abraham's wife? The truth is, Abimelech is said to have been healed, because his household was cured of the affliction which smote it.

### CHAP. 31 [XVI.] — WHY GOD PROCEEDS TO CREATE HUMAN BEINGS, WHO HE KNOWS WILL BE BORN IN SIN.

Let us now look at those three clauses of his, than which three, he says, nothing more profane could possibly be uttered: "Either God did not make man, or else He made him for the devil; or, at any rate, the devil framed God's image, that is, man." Now, the first and the last of these sentences, even he himself must allow, if he be not reckless and perverse, were never uttered by us. The dispute is confined to that which he puts second between the other two. In respect of this, he is so far mistaken as to suppose that we had said that God made man for the devil; as if, in the case of human beings whom God creates of human parents, His care and purpose and provision were, that by means of His workmanship the devil should have as slaves those whom he is unable to make for himself. God forbid that any sort of pious belief, however childish, should ever entertain such a sentiment as this! Of His own goodness God has made man — the first without sin, all others under sin — for the purposes of His own profound thoughts. For just as He knew full well what to do with reference to the malice of the devil himself, and what He does is just and good, however unjust and evil he is, about whom He takes His measures; and just as He was not unwilling to create him because He foresaw that he would be evil; so in regard to the entire human race, though not a man of it is born without the taint of sin, He who is supremely good Himself is always working out good, making some men, as it were, "vessels of mercy," whom grace distinguishes from those who are "vessels of wrath;" whilst He makes others, as it were, "vessels of wrath," that He may make known the riches of His glory towards the vessels of mercy.[1] Let, then, this objector go and contest the point against the apostle, whose words I use; nay, against the very Potter, whom the apostle forbids us answering again, in the well-known words: "Who art thou, O man, that repliest against God! Shall the thing formed say to him that formed it, Why hast

---

[1] Rom. ix. 23.

thou made me thus? Hath not the potter power over the clay, of the same lump to make one vessel unto honour, and another unto dishonour?"[1] Well now, will this man contend that the vessels of wrath are not under the dominion of the devil? or else, because they are under this dominion, are they made by another creator than He who makes the vessels of mercy? Or does He make them of other material, and not out of the self-same lump? Here, then, he may object, and say: "Therefore God makes these vessels for the devil." As if God knew not how to make such a use of even these for the furtherance of His own good and righteous works, as He makes of the very devil himself.

### CHAP. 32 [XVII.] — GOD NOT THE AUTHOR OF THE EVIL IN THOSE WHOM HE CREATES.

Then, does God feed the children of perdition, the goats on His left hand,[2] for the devil, and nourish and clothe them for the devil, "because He maketh His sun to rise on the evil and the good, and sendeth rain upon the just and the unjust"?[3] He creates, then, the evil, just in the same way as He feeds and nourishes the evil; because what He bestows on them by creating them appertains to the goodness of nature; and the growth which He gives them by food and nourishment, He bestows on them, of course, as a kindly help, not to their evil character, but to that same good nature which He in His goodness created. For in as far as they are human beings — this is a good of that nature whose author and maker is God; but in as far as they are born with sin and so destined to perdition unless they are born again, they belong to the seed which was cursed from the beginning,[4] by the fault of the primitive disobedience. This fault, however, is turned to good account by the Maker of even the vessels of wrath, that He may make known the riches of His glory on the vessels of mercy:[5] and that no one may attribute to any merits of his own, pertaining as he does to the self-same mass, his deliverance through grace; but "he that glorieth, let him glory in the Lord."[6]

### CHAP. 33 [XVIII.] — THOUGH GOD MAKES US, WE PERISH UNLESS HE RE-MAKES US IN CHRIST.

From this most true and firmly-established principle of the apostolic and catholic faith the writer before us departs in company with the Pelagians. He will not have it that men are born under the dominion of the devil, lest infants be carried to Christ to be delivered from the power of darkness, and to be trans-lated into His kingdom.[7] Thus he becomes the accuser of the Church which is spread over the world; into this Church everywhere infants, when to be baptized, are first exorcised, for no other reason than that the prince of this world may be cast out[8] of them. For by him must they be necessarily possessed, as vessels of wrath, since they are born of Adam, unless they be born again in Christ, and transferred through grace as vessels of mercy into His kingdom. In his attack, however, upon this most firmly-established truth, he would avoid the appearance of an assault upon the entire Church of Christ. Accordingly, he limits his appeal to me alone, and in the tone of reproof and admonition he says: "But God made even you, though it must be confessed that a serious error has infected you." Well now, I thankfully acknowledge that God did make even me; and still I must have perished with the vessels of wrath, if He had only made me of Adam, and had not re-made me in Christ. Possessed, however, as this man is with the heresy of Pelagius, he does not believe this: if, indeed, he persists in so great an error to the very end, then not he, but catholics, will be able to see the character and extent of the error which has not simply infected, but absolutely destroyed[9] him.

### CHAP. 34 [XIX.] — THE PELAGIANS ARGUE THAT COHABITATION RIGHTLY USED IS A GOOD, AND WHAT IS BORN FROM IT IS GOOD.

I request your attention now to the following words. He says, "That children, however, who are conceived in wedlock are by nature good, we may learn from the apostle's words, when he speaks of men who, leaving the natural use of the woman, burned in their lust, men with men working together that which is disgraceful.[10] Here," says he, "the apostle shows the use of the woman to be both natural, and, in its way, laudable; the abuse consisting in the exercise of one's own will in opposition to the decent use of the institution. Deservedly then," says he, "in those who make a right use thereof, concupiscence is commended in its kind and mode; whilst the excess of it, in which abandoned persons indulge, is punished. Indeed, at the very time when God punished the abuse in Sodom with His judgment of fire, He invigorated the generative powers of Abraham and Sarah, which had become impotent through old age.[11] If, therefore," he goes on to say, "you think that fault must be found with the strength of the generative organs, because the Sodomites were steeped in sin thereby, you will have also to censure such created things as bread and

---

[1] Rom. ix. 20, 21.  [2] Matt. xxv. 33.  [3] Matt. v. 45.
[4] Wisd. xii. 11.  [5] Rom. ix. 33.  [6] 2 Cor. x. 17.

[7] Col. i. 13.  [8] John xii. 31.
[9] There is a climax in *infecerit* and *interfecerit*.
[10] Rom. i. 27.  [11] Gen. xxi. 1, 2, and xix. 24.

wine, since Holy Scripture informs us that they sinned also in the abuse of these gifts. For the Lord, by the mouth of His prophet Ezekiel, says : ' These, moreover, were the sins of thy sister Sodom ; in their pride, she and her children overflowed in fulness of bread and abundance of wine ; and they helped not the hand of the poor and needy.' [1] Choose, therefore," says he, " which alternative you would rather have : either impute to the work of God the sexual connection of human bodies, or account such created things as bread and wine to be equally evil. But if you should prefer this latter conclusion, you prove yourself to be a Manichean. The truth, however, is this : he who observes moderation in natural concupiscence uses a good thing well; but he who does not observe moderation, abuses a good thing. What means your statement, then," [2] he asks, " when you say that ' the good of marriage is no more impeachable on account of the original sin which is derived herefrom, than the evil of adultery and fornication can be excused because of the natural good which is born of them '? In these words," says he, " you conceded what you had denied, and what you had conceded you nullified ; and you aim at nothing so much as to be unintelligible. Show me any bodily marriage without sexual connection. Else impose some one name on this operation, and designate the conjugal union as either a good or an evil. You answer, no doubt, that you have already defined marriages to be good. Well then, if marriage is good, — if the human being is the good fruit of marriage ; if this fruit, being God's work, cannot be evil, born as it is by good agency out of good, — where is the original evil which has been set aside by so many prior admissions ? "

CHAP. 35 [XX.] — HE ANSWERS THE ARGUMENTS OF JULIANUS. WHAT IS THE NATURAL USE OF THE WOMAN ? WHAT IS THE UNNATURAL USE ?

My answer to this challenge is, that not only the children of wedlock, but also those of adultery, are a good work in so far as they are the work of God, by whom they are created : but as concerns original sin, they are all born under condemnation of the first Adam ; not only those who are born in adultery, but likewise such as are born in wedlock, unless they be regenerated in the second Adam, which is Christ. As to what the apostle says of the wicked, that " leaving the natural use of the woman, the men burned in their lust one toward another : men with men working that which is unseemly ; " [3] he did not speak of the conjugal use, but the " natural use," wishing us to understand how it

comes to pass that by means of the members created for the purpose the two sexes can combine for generation. Thus it follows, that even when a man unites with a harlot to use these members, the use is a natural one. It is not, however, commendable, but rather culpable. But as regards any part of the body which is not meant for generative purposes, should a man use even his own wife in it, it is against nature and flagitious. Indeed, the same apostle had previously [4] said concerning women : " Even their women did change the natural use into that which is against nature ; " and then concerning men he added, that they worked that which is unseemly by leaving the natural use of the woman. Therefore, by the phrase in question, " the natural use," it is not meant to praise conjugal connection ; but thereby are denoted those flagitious deeds which are more unclean and criminal than even men's use of women, which, even if unlawful, is nevertheless natural.

CHAP. 36 [XXI.] — GOD MADE NATURE GOOD : THE SAVIOUR RESTORES IT WHEN CORRUPTED.

Now we do not reprehend bread and wine because some men are luxurious and drunkards, any more than we disapprove of gold because of the greedy and avaricious. Wherefore on the same principle we do not censure the honourable connection between husband and wife, because of the shame-causing lust of bodies. For the former would have been quite possible before any antecedent commission of sin, and by it the united pair would not have been made to blush ; whereas the latter arose after the perpetration of sin, and they were obliged to hide it, from very shame. [5] Accordingly, in all united pairs ever since, however well and lawfully they have used this evil, there has been a permanent necessity of avoiding the sight of man in any work of this kind, and thus acknowledging what caused inevitable shame, though a good thing would certainly cause no man to be ashamed. In this way we have two distinct facts insensibly introduced to our notice : the good of that laudable union of the sexes for the purpose of generating children ; and the evil of that shameful lust, in consequence of which the offspring must be regenerated in order to escape condemnation. The man, therefore, who, though with the lust which causes shame, joins in lawful cohabitation, turns an evil to good account ; whereas he who joins in an unlawful cohabitation uses an evil badly ; for that is more correctly called evil than good, at which both bad and good alike blush. We do better to believe him who has said, " I know that in me, that is, in my flesh, dwelleth no good thing," [6] rather than him who calls that

[1] Ezek. xvi. 49.
[2] See first chapter of the first book of this treatise.
[3] Rom. i. 27.

[4] Rom. ix. 26.    [5] Gen. iii. 7.    [6] Rom. vii. 18.

good, by which he is so conformed that he admits it to be evil; but if he feels no shame, he adds the worse evil of impudence. Rightly then did we declare that "the good of marriage is no more impeachable because of the original sin which is derived therefrom, than the evil of adultery and fornication can be excused, because of the natural good which is born of them : " since the human nature which is born, whether of wedlock or of adultery, is the work of God. Now if this nature were an evil, it ought not to have been born; if it had not evil, it would not have to be regenerated ; and (that I may combine the two cases in one and the same predicate) if human nature were an evil thing, it would not have to be saved; if it had not in it any evil, it would not have to be saved. He, therefore, who contends that nature is not good, says that the Maker of the creature is not good; whilst he who will have it, that nature has no evil in it, deprives it in its corrupted condition of a merciful Saviour. From this, then, it follows, that in the birth of human beings neither fornication is to be excused on account of the good which is formed out of it by the good Creator, nor is marriage to be impeached by reason of the evil which has to be healed in it by the merciful Saviour.

CHAP. 37 [XXII.] — IF THERE IS NO MARRIAGE WITHOUT COHABITATION, SO THERE IS NO COHABITATION WITHOUT SHAME.

"Show me," he says, "any bodily marriage without sexual connection." I do not show him any bodily marriage without sexual connection; but then, neither does he show me any case of sexual connection which is without shame. In paradise, however, if sin had not preceded, there would not have been, indeed, generation without union of the sexes, but this union would certainly have been without shame; for in the sexual union there would have been a quiet acquiescence of the members, not a lust of the flesh productive of shame. Matrimony, therefore, is a good, in which the human being is born after orderly conception; the fruit, too, of matrimony is good, as being the very human being which is thus born; sin, however, is an evil with which every man is born. Now it was God who made and still makes man; but "by one man sin entered into the world, and death by sin ; and so death passed upon all men, for in him all sinned." [1]

CHAP. 38 [XXIII.] — JOVINIAN USED FORMERLY TO CALL CATHOLICS MANICHEANS ; THE ARIANS ALSO USED TO CALL CATHOLICS SABELLIANS.

" By your new mode of controversy," says he,

"you both profess to be a catholic and patronize Manichæus, inasmuch as you designate matrimony both as a great good and a great evil." Now he is utterly ignorant of what he says, or pretends to be ignorant. Or else he does not understand what we say, or does not wish it to be understood. But if he does not understand, he is impeded by the pre-occupation of error ; or if he does not wish our meaning to be understood, then obstinacy is the fault with which he defends his error. Jovinian, too, who endeavoured a few years ago to found a new heresy, used to declare that the catholics patronized the Manicheans, because in opposition to him they preferred holy virginity to marriage. But this man is sure to reply, that he does not agree with Jovinian in his indifference about marriage and virginity. I do not myself say that this is their opinion ; still these new heretics must allow, by the fact of Jovinian's playing off the Manicheans upon the catholics, that the expedient is not a novel one. We then declare that marriage is a good, not an evil. But just as the Arians charge us with being Sabellians, although we do not say that the Father, and the Son, and the Holy Ghost are one and the same, as the Sabellians hold ; but affirm that the Father, and the Son, and the Holy Ghost have one and the same nature, as the catholics believe : so do the Pelagians cast the Manicheans in our teeth, although we do not declare marriage to be an evil, as the Manicheans pretend, but affirm that evil accrued to the first man and woman, that is to say, to the first married pair, and from them passed on to all men, as the catholics hold. As, however, the Arians, while avoiding the Sabellians, fall into worse company, because they have had the audacity to divide not the Persons of the Trinity, but the natures ; so the Pelagians, in their efforts to escape from the pestilent error of the Manicheans, by taking the opposite extreme, are convicted of entertaining worse sentiments than the Manicheans themselves touching the fruit of matrimony, inasmuch as they believe that infants stand in no need of Christ as their Physician.

CHAP. 39 [XXIV.] — MAN BORN OF WHATEVER PARENTAGE IS SINFUL AND CAPABLE OF REDEMPTION.

He then says : "You conclude that a human being, if born of fornication; is not guilty ; and if born in wedlock, is not innocent. Your assertion, therefore, amounts to this, that natural good may possibly subsist from adulterous connections, while original sin is actually derived from marriage." Well now, he here attempts, but in vain before an intelligent reader, to give a wrong turn to words which are correct enough. Far be it from us to say, that a human being, if born in fornication, is not guilty. But we ·do

---

[1] Rom. v. 12.

affirm, that a human being, whether he be born in wedlock or in fornication, is in some respect good, because of the Author of nature, God; we add, however, that he derives some evil by reason of original sin. Our statement, therefore, "that natural good can subsist even from adulterous parentage, but that original sin is derived even from marriage," does not amount to what he endeavours to make of it, that one born in adultery is not guilty, nor innocent when born in wedlock; but that one who is generated in either condition is guilty, because of original sin; and that the offspring of either state may be freed by regeneration, because of the good of nature.

### CHAP. 40 [XXV.] — AUGUSTIN DECLINES THE DILEMMA OFFERED HIM.

"One of these propositions," says he, "is true, the other false." My reply is as brief as the allegation: Both are really true, neither is false. "It is true," he goes on to say, "that the sin of adultery cannot be excused by reason of the man who is born of it; inasmuch as the sin which adulterers commit, pertains to corruption of the will; but the offspring which they produce tends to the praise of fecundity. If one were to sow wheat which had been stolen, the crop which springs up is none the worse. Of course," says he, "I blame the thief, but I praise the corn. So I pronounce him innocent who is born of the generous fruitfulness of the seed; even as the apostle puts it: 'God giveth it a body, as it pleases Him; and to every seed its own body;'[1] but, at the same time, I condemn the flagitious man who has committed his adulterous sin in his perverse use of the divine appointment."

### CHAP. 41 [XXVI.] — THE PELAGIANS ARGUE THAT ORIGINAL SIN CANNOT COME THROUGH MARRIAGE IF MARRIAGE IS GOOD.

After this he proceeds with the following words: "Certainly if evil is contracted from marriage, it may be blamed, nay, cannot be excused; and you place under the devil's power its work and fruit, because everything which is the cause of evil is itself without good. The human being, however, who is born of wedlock owes his origin not to the reproaches of wedlock, but to its seminal elements: the cause of these, however, lies in the condition of bodies; and whosoever makes a bad use of these bodies, deals a blow at the good desert thereof, not at their nature. It is therefore clear," argues he, "that the good is not the cause of the evil. If, therefore," he continues, "original evil is derived even from marriage, the cause of the evil is the compact of marriage; and that must needs be

evil by which and from which the evil fruit has made its appearance; even as the Lord says in the Gospel: 'A tree is known by its fruits.'[2] How then," he asks, "do you think yourself worthy of attention, when you say that marriage is good, and yet declare that nothing but evil proceeds from it? It is evident, then, that marriages are guilty, since original sin is deduced from them; and they are indefensible, too, unless their fruit be proved innocent. But they are defended, and pronounced good; therefore their fruit is proved to be innocent."

### CHAP. 42. — THE PELAGIANS TRY TO GET RID OF ORIGINAL SIN BY THEIR PRAISE OF GOD'S WORKS; MARRIAGE, IN ITS NATURE AND BY ITS INSTITUTION, IS NOT THE CAUSE OF SIN.

I have an answer ready for all this; but before I give it, I wish the reader carefully to notice, that the result of the opinions of these persons is, that no Saviour is necessary for infants, whom they deem to be entirely without any sins to be saved from. This vast perversion of the truth, so hostile to God's great grace, which is given through our Lord Jesus Christ, who "came to seek and to save what was lost,"[3] tries to insinuate its way into the hearts of the unintelligent by eulogizing the works of God; that is, by its eulogy of human nature, of human seed, of marriage, of sexual intercourse, of the fruits of matrimony — which are all of them good things. I will not say that he adds the praise of lust; because he too is ashamed even to name it, so that it is something else, and not *it*, which he seems to praise. By this method of his, not distinguishing between the evils which have accrued to nature and the goodness of nature's very self, he does not, indeed, show it to be sound (because that is untrue), but he does not permit its diseased condition to be healed. And, therefore, that first proposition of ours, to the effect that the good thing, even the human being, which is born of adultery, does not excuse the sin of adulterous connection, he allows to be true; and this point, which occasions no question to arise between us, he even defends and strengthens (as he well may) by his similitude of the thief who sows the seed which he stole, and out of which there arises a really good harvest. Our other proposition, however, that "the good of marriage cannot be blamed for the original sin which is derived from it," he will not admit to be true; if, indeed, he assented to it, he would not be a Pelagian heretic, but a catholic Christian. "Certainly," says he, "if evil arises from marriage, it may be blamed, nay, cannot be excused; and you place its work and fruit under the devil's power, because everything which is

---

[1] 1 Cor. xv. 38.          [2] Matt. vii. 16.          [3] Luke xix. 10.

the cause of evil is itself without good." And in addition to this, he contrived other arguments to show that good could not possibly be the cause of evil; and from this he drew the inference, that marriage, which is a good, is not the cause of evil; and that consequently from it no man could be born in a sinful state, and having need of a Saviour: just as if we said that marriage is the cause of sin, though it is true that the human being which is born in wedlock is not born without sin. Marriage was instituted not for the purpose of sinning, but of producing children. Accordingly the Lord's blessing on the married state ran thus: "Be fruitful, and multiply, and replenish the earth."[1] The sin, however, which is derived to children from marriage does not belong to marriage, but to the evil which accrues to the human agents, from whose union marriage comes into being. The truth is, both the evil of shameful lust can exist without marriage, and marriage might have been without it. It appertains, however, to the condition of the body (not of that life, but) of this death, that marriage cannot exist without it, though it may exist without marriage. Of course, that lust of the flesh which causes shame has existence out of the married state, whenever it urges men to the commission of adultery, chambering and uncleanness, so utterly hostile to the purity of marriage; or again, when it does not commit any of these things, because the human agent gives no permission or assent to their commission, but still rises and is set in motion and creates disturbance, and (especially in dreams) effects the likeness of its own veritable work, and reaches the end of its own emotion. Well, now, this is an evil which is not even in the married state actually an evil of marriage; but it has this apparatus all ready in the body of this death, even against its own will, which is indispensable no doubt for the accomplishment of that which it does will. The evil in question, therefore, does not accrue to marriage from its own institution, which was blessed; but entirely from the circumstance that sin entered into the world by one man, and death by sin; and so death passed upon all men, for in him all sinned.[2]

CHAP. 43. — THE GOOD TREE IN THE GOSPEL THAT CANNOT BRING FORTH EVIL FRUIT, DOES NOT MEAN MARRIAGE.

What, then, does he mean by saying, "A tree is known by its fruits," on the ground of our reading that the Lord spake thus in the Gospel? Was, then, the Lord speaking of this question in these words, and not rather of men's two wills, the good and the evil, calling one of these the

good tree, and the other the corrupt tree, inasmuch as good works spring out of a good will, and evil ones out of an evil will — the converse being impossible, good works out of an evil will, and evil ones out of a good will? If, however, we were to suppose marriage to be the good tree, according to the Gospel simile which he has mentioned, then, of course, we must on the other hand assume fornication to be the corrupt tree. Wherefore, if a human being is said to be the fruit of marriage, in the sense of the good fruit of a good tree, then undoubtedly a human being could never have been born in fornication. "For a corrupt tree bringeth not forth good fruit."[3] Once more, if he were to say that not adultery must be supposed to occupy the place of the tree, but rather human nature, of which man is born, then in this way not even marriage can stand for the tree, but only the human nature of which man is born. His simile, therefore, taken from the Gospel avails him nothing in elucidating this question, because marriage is not the cause of the sin which is transmitted in the natural birth, and atoned for in the new birth; but the voluntary transgression of the first man is the cause of original sin. "You repeat," says he, "your allegation, 'Just as sin, from whatever source it is derived to infants, is the work of the devil, so, man, howsoever he be born, is the work of God.'" Yes, I said this, and most truly too; and if this man were not a Pelagian, but a catholic, he too would have nothing else to avow in the catholic faith.

CHAP. 44 [XXVII.] — THE PELAGIANS ARGUE THAT IF SIN COMES BY BIRTH, ALL MARRIED PEOPLE DESERVE CONDEMNATION.

What, then, is his object when he inquires of us, "By what means sin may be found in an infant, through the will, or through marriage, or through its parents"? He speaks, indeed, in such a way as if he had an answer to all these questions, and as if by clearing all of sin together he would have nothing remain in the infant whence sin could be found. I beg your attention to his very words: "Through what," says he, "is sin found in an infant? Through the will? But there has never been one in him? Through marriage? But this appertains to the parents' work, of whom you had previously declared that in this action they had not sinned; though it appears from your subsequent words that you did not make this concession truly. Marriage, therefore," he says, "must be condemned, since it furnished the cause of the evil. Yet marriage only indicates the work of personal agents. The parents, therefore, who by their coming together afforded occasion for the sin, are properly de-

---

[1] Gen. i. 28.          [2] Rom. v. 12.          [3] Matt. vii. 18.

serving of the condemnation. It does not then admit of doubt," says he, " any longer, if we are to follow your opinion, that married persons are handed over to eternal punishment, it being by their means brought about that the devil has come to exercise dominion over men. And what becomes of what you just before had said, that man was the work of God? Because if through their birth it happens that evil is in men, and through the evil that the devil has power over men, so in fact you declare the devil to be the author of men, from whom comes their origin at birth. If, however, you believe that man is made by God, and that husband and wife are innocent, see how impossible is your standpoint, that original sin is derived from them."

CHAP. 45. — ANSWER TO THIS ARGUMENT : THE APOSTLE SAYS WE ALL SINNED IN ONE.

Now, there is an answer for him to all these questions given by the apostle, who censures neither the infant's will, which is not yet matured in him for sinning, nor marriage, which, as such, has not only its institution, but its blessing also, from God ; nor parents, so far as they are parents, who are united together properly and lawfully for the procreation of children ; but he says, " By one man sin entered into the world, and death by sin ; and so death passed upon all men, tor in him all have sinned." [1] Now, if these persons would only receive this statement with catholic hearts and ears, they would not have rebellious feelings against the grace and faith of Christ, nor would they vainly endeavour to convert to their own particular and heretical sense these very clear and manifest words of the apostle, when they assert that the purport of the passage is to this effect : that Adam was the first to sin, and that any one who wished afterwards to commit sin found an example for sinning in him ; so that sin, you must know, did not pass from this one upon all men by birth, but by the imitation of this one. Whereas it is certain that if the apostle meant this imitation to be here understood, he would have said that sin had entered into the world and passed upon all men, not by one man, but rather by the devil. For of the devil it is written : " They that are on his side do imitate him." [2] He used the phrase " by one man," from whom the generation of men, of course, had its beginning, in order to show us that original sin had passed upon all men by generation.

CHAP. 46. — THE REIGN OF DEATH, WHAT IT IS ; THE FIGURE OF THE FUTURE ADAM ; HOW ALL MEN ARE JUSTIFIED THROUGH CHRIST.

But what else is meant even by the apostle's subsequent words? For after he had said the above, he added, " For until the law sin was in the world," [3] as much as to say that not even the law was able to take away sin. " But sin," adds he, " was not imputed when there was no law." [3] It existed then, but was not imputed, for it was not set forth so that it might be imputed. It is on the same principle, indeed, that he says in another passage : " By the law is the knowledge of sin." [4] " Nevertheless," says he, " death reigned from Adam to Moses ; " [5] that is, as he had already expressed it, " until the law." Not that there was no sin after Moses, but because even the law, which was given by Moses, was unable to deprive death of its power, which, of course, reigns only by sin. Its reign, too, is such as to plunge mortal man even into that second death which is to endure for evermore. " Death reigned," but over whom? " Even over them that had not sinned after the similitude of Adam's transgression, who is the figure of Him that was to come." [5] Of whom that was to come, if not Christ? And in what sort a figure, except in the way of contrariety? which he elsewhere briefly expresses : " As in Adam all die, even so in Christ shall all be made alive." [6] The one condition was in one, even as the other condition was in the other ; this is the figure. But this figure is not conformable in every respect ; accordingly the apostle, following up the same idea, added, " But not as the offence, so also is the free gift. For if through the offence of one many be dead ; much more the grace of God, and the gift by grace, which is by one man, Jesus Christ, hath abounded unto many." [7] But why " hath it much more abounded," except it be that all who are delivered through Christ suffer temporal death on Adam's account, but have everlasting life in store for the sake of Christ Himself? " And not as it was by one that sinned," says he, " so is the gift : for the judgment was from one to condemnation, but the free gift is from many offences unto justification." [7] " By one " what, but offence? since it is added, " the free gift is from many offences." Let these objectors tell us how it can be " by one offence unto condemnation," unless it be that even the one original sin which has passed over unto all men is sufficient for condemnation? Whereas the free gift delivers from many offences to justification, because it not only cancels the one offence, which is derived from the primal sin, but all others also which are added in every individual man by the motion of his own will. " For if by one man's offence death reigned by one, much more they which receive abundance of grace and righteousness shall reign in life by One, Jesus Christ. Therefore, by the offence of

---

[1] Rom. v. 12.        [2] Wisd. ii. 24.

[3] Rom. v. 13.    [4] Rom. iii. 20.    [5] Rom. v. 14.
[6] 1 Cor. xv. 22.    [7] Rom. v. 15.

one upon all men to condemnation; so by the righteousness of one upon all men unto justification of life."[1] Let them after this persist in their vain imaginations, and maintain that one man did not hand on sin by propagation, but only set the example of committing it. How is it, then, that by one's offence judgment comes on all men to condemnation, and not rather by each man's own numerous sins, unless it be that even if there were but that one sin, it is sufficient, without the addition of any more, to lead to condemnation,—as, indeed, it does lead all who die in infancy who are born of Adam, without being born again in Christ? Why, then, does he, when he refuses to hear the apostle, ask us for an answer to his question, "By what means may sin be discovered in an infant,—through the will, or through marriage, or through its parents?" Let him listen in silence, and hear by what means sin may be discovered in an infant. "By the offence of one," says the apostle, "upon all men to condemnation." He said, moreover, all to condemnation through Adam, and all to justification through Christ: not, of course, that Christ removes to life all those who die in Adam; but he said "all" and "all," because, as without Adam no one goes to death, so without Christ no man to life. Just as we say of a teacher of letters, when he is alone in a town: This man teaches all their learning; not because all the inhabitants take lessons, but because no man who learns at all is taught by any but him. Indeed, the apostle afterwards designates as *many* those whom he had previously described as *all*, meaning the self-same persons by the two different terms. "For," says he, "as by one man's disobedience many were made sinners, so by the obedience of one shall many be made righteous."[2]

CHAP. 47.—THE SCRIPTURES REPEATEDLY TEACH US THAT ALL SIN IN ONE.

Still let him ply his question: "By what means may sin be discovered in an infant?" He may find an answer in the inspired pages: "By one man sin entered into the world, and death by sin; and so death passed upon all men, for in him all sinned." "Through the offence of one many are dead." "The judgment was from one to condemnation." "By one man's offence death reigned by one." "By the offence of one, judgment came upon all men to condemnation." "By one man's disobedience many were made sinners."[3] Behold, then, "by what means sin may be discovered in an infant." Let him now believe in original sin; let him permit infants to come to Christ, that they may be saved. [xxviii.] What means this passage of his: "He sins not

who is born; he sins not who begat him; He sins not who created him. Amidst these intrenchments of innocence, therefore, what are the breaches through which you pretend that sin entered?" Why does he search for a hidden chink when he has an open door? "By one man," says the apostle; "through the offence of one," says the apostle; "By one man's disobedience," says the apostle. What does he want more? What does he require plainer? What does he expect to be more impressively repeated?

CHAP. 48.—ORIGINAL SIN AROSE FROM ADAM'S DEPRAVED WILL. WHENCE THE CORRUPT WILL SPRANG.

"If," says he, "sin comes from the will, it is an evil will that causes sin; if it comes from nature, then nature is evil." I at once answer, Sin does come from the will. Perhaps he wants to know, whether original sin also? I answer, most certainly original sin also. Because it, too, was engendered from the will of the first man; so that it both existed in him, and passed on to all. As for what he next proposes, "If it comes from nature, then nature is evil," I request him to answer, if he can, to this effect: As it is manifest that all evil works spring from a corrupt will, like the fruits of a corrupt tree; so let him say whence arose the corrupt will itself—the corrupt tree which yields the corrupt fruits. If from an angel, what was the angel, but the good work of God? If from man, what was even he, but the good work of God? Nay, inasmuch as the corrupt will arose in the angel from an angel, and in man from man, what were both these, previous to the evil arising within them, but the good work of God, with a good and laudable nature? Behold, then, evil arises out of good; nor was there any other source, indeed, whence it could arise, but out of good. I call that will bad which no evil has preceded; no evil works, of course, since they only proceed from an evil will, as from a corrupt tree. Nevertheless, that the evil will arose out of good, could not be, because that good was made by the good God, but because it was created out of nothing—not out of God. What, therefore, becomes of his argument, "If nature is the work of God, it will never do for the work of the devil to permeate the work of God"? Did not the work of the devil, I ask, arise in a work of God, when it first arose in that angel who became the devil? Well, then, if evil, which was absolutely nowhere previously, could arise in a work of God, why could not evil, which had by this time found an existence somewhere, pervade the work of God; especially when the apostle uses the very expression in the passage, "And so death passed

[1] Rom. v. 17, 18.        [2] Rom. v. 19.        [3] Rom. v. 12-19.

upon all men"?[1]　Can it be that men are not the work of God?　Sin, therefore, has passed upon all men — in other words, the devil's work has penetrated the work of God; or putting the same meaning in another shape, The work done by a work of God has pervaded God's work. And this is the reason why God alone has an unchangeable and almighty goodness: even before any evil came into existence He made all things good; and out of all the evils which have arisen in the good things which He has made, He works through all for good.

CHAP. 49 [XXIX.] — IN INFANTS NATURE IS OF GOD, AND THE CORRUPTION OF NATURE OF THE DEVIL.

"In a single man rightly is the intention blamed and the origin praised; because there must be two things to admit of contraries: in an infant, however, there is but one thing, nature only; because will has no existence in his case.　Now this one thing," says he, "is ascribable either to God or to the devil.　If nature," he goes on to observe, "is of God, there cannot be original evil in it.　If of the devil, there will be nothing on the ground of which man may be vindicated for the work of God.　So that he is completely a Manichean who maintains original sin."　Let him hear rather what is true in opposition to all this.　In a single man the will is to be blamed, and his nature to be praised; because there should be two things for the application of contraries.　Still, even in an infant, it is not the case that there is but one thing only, that is, the nature in which man was created by the good God; for he has also that corruption, which has passed upon all men by one, as the apostle wisely says, and not as the folly of Pelagius, or Cœlestius, or any of their disciples would represent the matter.　Of these two things, then, which we have said exist in an infant, one is ascribed to God, the other to the devil.　From the fact, however, that (owing to one of the two, even the corruption) both are subjected to the power of the devil, there really ensues no incongruity; because this happens not from the power of the devil himself, but of God.　In fact, corruption is subjected to corruption, nature to nature, because the two are even in the devil; so that whenever those who are beloved and elect are "delivered from the power of darkness"[2] to which they are justly exposed, it is clear enough how great a gift is bestowed on the justified and good by the good God, who brings good even out of evil.

CHAP. 50. — THE RISE AND ORIGIN OF EVIL.　THE EXORCISM AND EXSUFFLATION OF INFANTS, A PRIMITIVE CHRISTIAN RITE.

As to the passage, which he seemed to him-self to indite in a pious vein, as it were, "If nature is of God, there cannot be original sin in it," would not another person seem even to him to give a still more pious turn to it, thus: "If nature is of God, there cannot arise *any* sin in it?"　And yet this is not true.　The Manicheans, indeed, meant to assert this, and they endeavoured to steep in all sorts of evil the very nature of God itself, and not His creature, made out of nothing.　For evil arose in nothing else than what was good — not, however, the supreme and unchangeable good which is God's nature, but that which was made out of nothing by the wisdom of God.　This, then, is the reason why man is claimed for a divine work; for he would not be man unless he were made by the operation of God.　But evil would not exist in infants, if evil had not been committed by the wilfulness of the first man, and original sin derived from a nature thus corrupted.　It is not true, then, as he puts it, "He is completely a Manichean who maintains original sin;" but rather, he is completely a Pelagian who does not believe in original sin.　For it is not simply from the time when the pestilent opinions of Manichæus began to grow that in the Church of God infants about to be baptized were for the first time exorcised with exsufflation, — which ceremonial was intended to show that they were not removed into the kingdom of Christ without first being delivered from the power of darkness;[2] nor is it in the books of Manichæus that we read how "the Son of man come to seek and to save that which was lost,"[3] or how "by one man sin entered into the world,"[1] with those other similar passages which we have quoted above; or how God "visits the sins of the fathers upon the children;"[4] or how it is written in the Psalm, "I was shapen in iniquity, and in sin did my mother conceive me;"[5] or again, how "man was made like unto vanity: his days pass away like a shadow;"[6] or again, "behold, Thou hast made my days old, and my existence as nothing before Thee; nay, every man living is altogether vanity;"[7] or how the apostle says, "every creature was made subject to vanity;"[8] or how it is written in the book of Ecclesiastes, "vanity of vanities; all is vanity: what profit hath a man of all his labour which he taketh under the sun?"[9] and in the book of Ecclesiasticus, "a heavy yoke is upon the sons of Adam from the day that they go out of their mother's womb to the day that they return to the mother of all things;"[10] or how again the apostle writes, "in Adam all die;"[11] or how holy Job says, when speaking about his own sins, "for man that is born of a woman is short-lived and full of wrath: as

---

[1] Rom. v. 12.　　　　　[2] Col. i. 13.

[3] Luke xix. 10.　　　[4] Ex. xx. 5.　　　[5] Ps. li. 5.
[6] Ps. cxliv. 4.　　　[7] Ps. xxxix. 5.　　　[8] Rom. viii. 20.
[9] Eccles. i. 2, 3.　　[10] Ecclus. xl. 1.　　[11] 1 Cor. xv. 22.

the flower of grass, so does he fall; and he departs like a shadow, nor shall he stay. Hast Thou not taken account even of him, and caused him to enter into judgment in Thy sight? For who shall be pure from uncleanness? Not even one, even if his life should be but of one day upon the earth."[1] Now when he speaks of *uncleanness* here, the mere perusal of the passage is enough to show that he meant *sin* to be understood. It is plain from the words, of what he is speaking. The same phrase and sense occur in the prophet Zechariah, in the place where "the filthy garments" are removed from off the high priest, and it is said to him, "I have taken away thy sins."[2] Well now, I rather think that all these passages, and others of like import, which point to the fact that man is born in sin and under the curse, are not to be read among the dark recesses of the Manicheans, but in the sunshine of catholic truth.

CHAP. 51. — TO CALL THOSE THAT TEACH ORIGINAL SIN MANICHEANS IS TO ACCUSE AMBROSE, CYPRIAN, AND THE WHOLE CHURCH.

What, moreover, shall I say of those commentators on the divine Scriptures who have flourished in the catholic Church? They have never tried to pervert these testimonies to an alien sense, because they were firmly established in our most ancient and solid faith, and were never moved aside by the novelty of error. Were I to wish to collect these together, and to make use of their testimony, the task would both be too long, and I should probably seem to have bestowed less preference than I ought on canonical authorities,[3] from which one must never deviate. I will merely mention the most blessed Ambrose, to whom (as I have already observed[4]) Pelagius accorded so signal a testimony of his integrity in the faith. This Ambrose, however, maintained that there was nothing else in infants, which required the healing grace of Christ, than original sin.[5] But in respect of Cyprian, with his all-glorious crown,[6] will any one say of him, that he either was, or ever could by any possibility have been, a Manichean, when he suffered before the pestilent heresy had made its appearance in the Roman world? And yet, in his book on the baptism of infants, he so vigorously maintains original sin as to declare, that even before the eighth day, if necessary, the infant ought to be baptized, lest his soul should be lost; and he wished it to be understood, that the infant could the more readily attain to the indulgence of baptism, inasmuch as it is not so much his own sins, but the sins of another, which are remitted to him. Well, then,

let this writer dare to call these Manicheans; let him, moreover, under this scandalous imputation asperse that most ancient tradition of the Church, whereby infants are, as I have said, exorcised with exsufflation, for the purpose of being translated into the kingdom of Christ, after they are delivered from the power of darkness — that is to say, of the devil and his angels. As for ourselves, indeed, we are more ready to be associated with these men, and with the Church of Christ, so firmly rooted in this ancient faith, in suffering any amount of curse and contumely, than with the Pelagians, to be covered with the flattery of public praise.

CHAP. 52 [XXX.] — SIN WAS THE ORIGIN OF ALL SHAMEFUL CONCUPISCENCE.

"Do you," he asks, "repeat your affirmation, 'There would be no concupiscence if man had not first sinned; marriage, however, would have existed, even if no one had sinned'?" I never said, "There would be no concupiscence," because there is a concupiscence of the spirit, which craves wisdom.[7] My words were, "There would be no *shameful* concupiscence."[8] Let my words be re-perused, even those which he has cited, that it may be clearly seen how dishonestly they are handled by him. However, let him call it by any name he likes. What I said would not have existed unless man had previously sinned, was that which made them ashamed in paradise when they covered their loins, and which every one will allow would not have been felt, had not the sin of disobedience first occurred. Now he who wishes to understand what they felt, ought to consider what it was they covered. For of the fig-leaves they made themselves "aprons," not clothes; and these aprons or kilts are called περιζώματα in Greek. Now all know well enough what it is which these *peri-zomata* cover, which some Latin writers explain by the word *campestria*. Who is ignorant of what persons wore this kilt, and what parts of the body such a dress concealed; even the same which the Roman youths used to cover when they practised naked in the *campus*, from which circumstance the name *campester* was given to the apron.[9]

CHAP. 53 [XXXI.] — CONCUPISCENCE NEED NOT HAVE BEEN NECESSARY FOR FRUITFULNESS.

He says: "Therefore that marriage which might have been without concupiscence, without bodily motion, without necessity for sexual organs — to use your own statement — is pronounced by you to be laudable; whereas such marriages as are now enacted are, according to

---

[1] Job xiv. 1–5.    [2] Zech. iii. 4.    [3] *i.e.*, Scripture.
[4] See Book i. of this treatise, last chapter.
[5] Ambrose *On Isaiah:* cited in the same Book, i. ch. 35.
[6] *i.e.*, of martyrdom.

[7] Wisd. vi. 21.    [8] See above, Book i. ch. 1.
[9] See *On the City of God*, Book xi. ch. 17.

your decision, the invention of the devil. Those, therefore, whose institution was possible in your dreams, you deliberately assert to be good, while those which Holy Scripture intends, when it says, 'Therefore shall a man leave his father and his mother, and shall cleave unto his wife, and they shall be one flesh,'[1] you pronounce to be diabolical evils, worthy, in short, to be called a pest, not matrimony." It is not to be wondered at, that these Pelagian opponents of mine try to twist my words to any meaning they wish them to bear, when it has been their custom to do the same thing with the Holy Scriptures, and not simply in obscure passages, but where their testimony is clear and plain: a custom, indeed, which is followed by all other heretics. Now who could make such an assertion, as that it was possible for marriages to be "without bodily motion, without necessity for sexual organs"? For God made the sexes; because, as it is written, "He created them male and female."[2] But how could it possibly happen, that they who were to be united together, and by the very union were to beget children, were not to move their bodies, when, of course, there can be no bodily contact of one person with another if bodily motion be not resorted to? The question before us, then, is not about the motion of bodies, without which there could not be sexual intercourse; but about the shameful motion of the organs of generation, which certainly could be absent, and yet the fructifying connection be still not wanting, if the organs of generation were not obedient to lust, but simply to the will, like the other members of the body. Is it not even now the case, in "the body of this death," that a command is given to the foot, the arm, the finger, the lip, or the tongue, and they are instantly set in motion at this intimation of our will? And (to take a still more wonderful case) even the liquid contained in the urinary vessels obeys the command to flow from us, at our pleasure, and when we are not pressed with its overflow; while the vessels, also, which contain the liquid, discharge without difficulty, if they are in a healthy state, the office assigned them by our will of propelling, pressing out, and ejecting their contents. With how much greater ease and quietness, then, if the generative organs of our body were compliant, would natural motion ensue, and human conception be effected; except in the instance of those persons who violate natural order, and by a righteous retribution are punished with the intractability of these members and organs! This punishment is felt by the chaste and pure, who, without doubt, would rather beget children by mere natural desire than by voluptuous pruriency; while un-

chaste persons, who are impelled by this diseased passion, and bestow their love upon harlots as well as wives, are excited by a still heavier mental remorse in consequence of this carnal chastisement.

CHAP. 54 [XXXII.] — HOW MARRIAGE IS NOW DIFFERENT SINCE THE EXISTENCE OF SIN.

God forbid that we should say, what this man pretends we say, "Such marriages as are now enacted are the invention of the devil." Why, they are absolutely the same marriages as God made at the very first. For this blessing of His, which He appointed for the procreation of mankind, He has not taken away even from men under condemnation, any more than He has deprived them of their senses and bodily limbs, which are no doubt His gifts, although they are condemned to die by an already incurred retribution. This, I say, is the marriage whereof it was said (only excepting the great sacrament of Christ and the Church, which the institution prefigured): "For this cause shall a man leave his father and his mother, and shall cleave unto his wife; and they twain shall be one flesh."[1] For this, no doubt, was said before sin; and if no one had sinned, it might have been done without shameful lust. And now, although it is not done without that, in the body of this death, there is that nevertheless which does not cease to be done so that a man may cleave to his wife, and they twain be one flesh. When, therefore, it is alleged that marriage is now one thing, but might have been another had no one sinned, this is not predicated of its nature, but of a certain quality which has undergone a change for the worse. Just as a man is said to be different, though he is actually the same individual, when he has changed his manner of life either for the better or the worse; for as a righteous man is one thing, and as a sinful man another, though the man himself be really the same individual. In like manner, marriage without shameful lust is one thing, and marriage with shameful lust is another. When, however, a woman is lawfully united to her husband in accordance with the true constitution of wedlock, and fidelity to what is due to the flesh is kept free from the sin of adultery, and so children are lawfully begotten, it is actually the very same marriage which God instituted at first, although by his primeval inducement to sin, the devil inflicted a heavy wound, not, indeed, on marriage itself, but on man and woman by whom marriage is made, by his prevailing on them to disobey God, — a sin which is requited in the course of the divine judgment by the reciprocal disobedience of man's own members. United in this matrimonial state, although they were ashamed of their nakedness, still they were not by any means able altogether to lose the blessedness of marriage which God appointed.

CHAP. 55 [XXXIII.] — LUST IS A DISEASE; THE WORD "PASSION" IN THE ECCLESIASTICAL SENSE.

He then passes on from those who are united in marriage to those who are born of it. It is in relation to these that we have to encounter the most laborious discussions with the new heretics in connection with our subject. Impelled by some hidden instinct from God, he makes avowals which go far to untie the whole knot. For in his desire to raise greater odium against us, because we had said that infants are born in sin even of lawful wedlock, he makes the following observation: "You assert that they, indeed, who have not been ever born might possibly have been good; those, however, who have peopled the world, and for whom Christ died, you decide to be the work of the devil, born in a disordered state, and guilty from the beginning. Therefore," he continues, "I have shown that you are doing nothing else than denying that God is the Creator of the men who actually exist." I beg to say, that I declare none but God to be the Creator of all men, however true it be that all are born in sin, and must perish unless born again. It was, indeed, the sinful corruption which had been sown in them by the devil's persuasion that became the means of their being born in sin; not the created nature of which men are composed. Shameful lust, however, could not excite our members, except at our own will, if it were not a disease. Nor would even the lawful and honourable cohabiting of husband and wife raise a blush, with avoidance of any eye and desire of secrecy, if there were not a diseased condition about it. Moreover, the apostle would not prohibit the possession of wives in this disease, did not disease exist in it. The phrase in the Greek text, ἐν πάθει ἐπιθυμίας, is by some rendered in Latin, *in morbo desiderii* vel *concupiscentiæ*, in the disease of desire or of concupiscence; by others, however, *in passione concupiscentiæ*, in the passion of concupiscence; or however it is found otherwise in different copies: at any rate, the Latin equivalent *passio* (passion), especially in the ecclesiastical use, is usually understood as a term of censure.

CHAP. 56. — THE PELAGIANS ALLOW THAT CHRIST DIED EVEN FOR INFANTS; JULIANUS SLAYS HIMSELF WITH HIS OWN SWORD.

But whatever opinion he may entertain about the shame-causing concupiscence of the flesh, I must request your attention to what he has said respecting infants (and it is in their behalf that we labour), as to their being supposed to need a

Saviour, if they are not to die without salvation. I repeat his words once more: "You assert," says he to me, "that they, indeed, who have not been ever born might possibly have been good; those, however, who have peopled the world, *and for whom Christ died*, you decide to be the work of the devil, born in a disordered state, and guilty from the very beginning." Would that he only solved the entire controversy as he unties the knot of this question! For will he pretend to say that he merely spoke of adults in this passage? Why, the subject in hand is about infants, about human beings at their birth; and it is about these that he raises odium against us, because they are defined by us as guilty from the very first, because we declare them to be guilty, since Christ died for them. And why did Christ die for them if they are not guilty? It is entirely from them, yes, from them, we shall find the reason, wherefore he thought odium should be raised against me. He asks: "How are infants guilty, for whom Christ died?" We answer: Nay, how are infants not guilty, since Christ died for them? This dispute wants a judge to determine it. Let Christ be the Judge, and let Him tell us what is the object which has profited by His death? "This is my blood," He says, "which shall be shed[1] for many for the remission of sins."[2] Let the apostle, too, be His assessor in the judgment; since even in the apostle it is Christ Himself that speaks. Speaking of God the Father, he exclaims: "He who spared not His own Son, but delivered Him up for us all!"[3] I suppose that he describes Christ as so delivered up for us all, that infants in this matter are not separated from ourselves. But what need is there to dwell on this point, out of which even he no longer raises a contest? For the truth is, he not only confesses that Christ died even for infants, but he also reproves us out of this admission, because we say that these same infants are guilty for whom Christ died. Now, then, let the apostle, who says that Christ was delivered up for us all, also tell us why Christ was delivered up for us. "He was delivered," says he, "for our offences, and rose again for our justification."[4] If, therefore, as even this man both confesses and professes, both admits and objects, infants, too, are included amongst those for whom Christ was delivered up; and if it was for our sins that Christ was delivered up, even infants, of course, must have original sins, for whom Christ was delivered up; He must have something in them to heal, who (as Himself affirms) is not needed as a Physician by the whole, but by the sick;[5] He must have a reason for saving them, seeing that He came into the world, as the Apostle Paul says,

---

[1] Effundetur.　　　[2] Matt. xxvi. 28.　　　[3] Rom. viii. 32.
[4] Rom. iv. 25.　　　[5] Matt. ix. 12.

"to save sinners;"[1] He must have something in them to remit, who testifies that He shed His blood "for the remission of sins;"[2] He must have good reason for seeking them out, who "came," as He says, "to seek and to save that which was lost;"[3] the Son of man must find in them something to destroy, who came for the express purpose, as the Apostle John says, "that He might destroy the works of the devil."[4] Now to this salvation of infants He must be an enemy, who asserts their innocence, in such a way as to deny them the medicine which is required by the hurt and wounded.

### CHAP. 57 [XXXIV.] — THE GREAT SIN OF THE FIRST MAN.

Now observe what follows, as he goes on to say: "If, before sin, God created a source from which men should be born, but the devil a source from which parents were disturbed, then beyond a doubt holiness must be ascribed to those that are born, and guilt to those that produce. Since, however, this would be a most manifest condemnation of marriage; remove, I pray you, this view from the midst of the churches, and really believe that all things were made by Jesus Christ, and that without Him nothing was made."[5] He so speaks here, as if he would make us say, that there is a something in man's substance which was created by the devil. The devil persuaded evil as a sin; he did not create it as a nature. No doubt he persuaded nature, for man is nature; and therefore by his persuasion he corrupted it. He who wounds a limb does not, of course, create it, but he injures it.[6] Those wounds, indeed, which are inflicted on the body produce lameness in a limb, or difficulty of motion; but they do not affect the virtue whereby a man becomes righteous: that wound, however, which has the name of sin, wounds the very life, which was being righteously lived. This wound was at that fatal moment of the fall inflicted by the devil to a vastly wider and deeper extent than are the sins which are known amongst men. Whence it came to pass, that our nature having then and there been deteriorated by that great sin of the first man, not only was made a sinner, but also generates sinners; and yet the very weakness, under which the virtue of a holy life has drooped and died, is not really nature, but corruption; precisely as a bad state of health is not a bodily substance or nature, but disorder; very often, indeed, if not always, the ailing character of parents is in a certain way implanted, and reappears in the bodies of their children.

### CHAP. 58. — ADAM'S SIN IS DERIVED FROM HIM TO EVERY ONE WHO IS BORN EVEN OF REGENERATE PARENTS; THE EXAMPLE OF THE OLIVE TREE AND THE WILD OLIVE.

But this sin, which changed man for the worse in paradise, because it is far greater than we can form any judgment of, is contracted by every one at his birth, and is remitted only in the regenerate; and this derangement is such as to be derived even from parents who have been regenerated, and in whom the sin is remitted and covered, to the condemnation of the children born of them, unless these, who were bound by their first and carnal birth, are absolved by their second and spiritual birth. Of this wonderful fact the Creator has produced a wonderful example in the cases of the olive and the wild olive trees, in which, from the seed not only of the wild olive, but even of the good olive, nothing but a wild olive springs. Wherefore, although even in persons whose natural birth is followed by regeneration through grace, there exists this carnal concupiscence which contends against the law of the mind, yet, seeing that it is remitted in the remission of sins, it is no longer accounted to them as sin, nor is it in any degree hurtful, unless consent is yielded to its motions for unlawful deeds. Their offspring, however, being begotten not of spiritual concupiscence, but of carnal, like a wild olive of our race from the good olive, derives guilt from them by natural birth to such a degree that it cannot be liberated from that pest except by being born again. How is it, then, that this man affirms that we ascribe holiness to those who are born, and guilt to their parents? when the truth rather shows that even if there has been holiness in the parents, original sin is inherent in their children, which is abolished in them only if they are born again.

### CHAP. 59 [XXXV.] — THE PELAGIANS CAN HARDLY VENTURE TO PLACE CONCUPISCENCE IN PARADISE BEFORE THE COMMISSION OF SIN.

This being the case, let him think what he pleases about this concupiscence of the flesh and about the lust which lords it over the unchaste, has to be mastered by the chaste, and yet is to be blushed at both by the chaste and the unchaste; for I see plainly he is much pleased with it. Let him not hesitate to praise what he is ashamed to name; let him call it (as he has in fact called it) the vigour of the members, and let him not be afraid of the horror of chaste ears; let him designate it the power of the members, and let him not care about the impudence. Let him say, if his blushes permit him, that if no one had sinned, this vigour must have flourished like a flower in paradise; nor would there have been any need to cover that which would

---

[1] 1 Tim. i. 15.    [2] Matt. xxvi. 28.    [3] Luke xix. 10.
[4] 1 John iii. 8.    [5] John i. 3.
[6] Vexat. Another reading has *vitiat*, "corrupts."

have been so moved that no one should have felt ashamed; rather, with a wife provided, it would have been ever exercised and never repressed, lest so great a pleasure should ever be denied to so vast a happiness. Far be it from being thought that such blessedness could in such a spot fail to have what it wished, or ever experience in mind or body what it disliked. And so, should the motion of lust precede men's will, then the will would immediately follow it. The wife, who ought certainly never to be absent in this happy state of things, would be urged on by it, whether about to conceive or already pregnant; and, either a child would be begotten, or a natural and laudable pleasure would be gratified, — for perish all seed rather than disappoint the appetite of so good a concupiscence. Only be sure that the united pair do not apply themselves to that use of each other which is contrary to nature, then (with so modest a reservation) let them use, as often as they would have delight, their organs of generation, created for the purpose. But what if this very use, which is contrary to nature, should peradventure give them delight; what if the aforesaid laudable lust should hanker even after such delight; I wonder whether they should pursue it because it was sweet, or loathe it because it was base? If they should pursue it to gratification, what becomes of all thought about honour? If they should loathe it, where is the peaceful composure of so good a happiness? But at this point perchance his blushes will awake, and he will say that so great is the tranquillity of this happy state, and so entire the orderliness which may have existed in this state of things, that carnal concupiscence never preceded these persons' will: only whenever they themselves wished, would it then arise; and only then would they entertain the wish, when there was need for begetting children; and the result would be, that no seed would ever be emitted to no purpose, nor would any embrace ever ensue which would not be followed by conception and birth; the flesh would obey the will, and concupiscence would vie with it in subserviency. Well, if he says all this of the imagined happy state, he must at least be pretty sure that what he describes does not now exist among men. And even if he will not concede that lust is a corrupt condition, let him at least allow that through the disobedience of the man and woman in the happy state the very concupiscence of their flesh was corrupted, so that what would once be excited obediently and orderly is now moved disobediently and inordinately, and that to such a degree that it is not obedient to the will of even chaste-minded husbands and wives, so that it is excited when it is not wanted; and whenever it is necessary, it never, indeed, follows their will, but sometimes too hurriedly, at other times too tardily, exerts its own movements. Such, then, is the rebellion of this concupiscence which the primitive pair received for their own disobedience, and transfused by natural descent to us. It certainly was not at their bidding, but in utter disorder, that it was excited, when they covered their members, which at first were worthy to be gloried in, but had then become a ground of shame.

CHAP. 60. — LET NOT THE PELAGIANS INDULGE THEMSELVES IN A CRUEL DEFENCE OF INFANTS.

As I said, however, let him entertain what views he likes of this lust; let him proclaim it as he pleases, praise it as much as he chooses (and he pleases *much*, as several of his extracts show), that the Pelagians may gratify themselves, if not with its uses, at all events with its praises, as many of them as fail to enjoy the limitation of continence enjoined in wedlock. Only let him spare the infants, so as not to praise their condition uselessly, and defend them cruelly. Let him not declare them to be safe; let him suffer them to come, not, indeed, to Pelagius for eulogy, but to Christ for salvation. For, that this book may be now brought to a termination, since the dissertation of this man is ended, which was written on the short paper you sent me, I will close with his last words: "Really believe that all things were made by Jesus Christ, and that without Him nothing was made."[1] Let him grant that Jesus is Jesus even to infants; and as he confesses that all things were made by Him, in that He is God the Word, so let him acknowledge that infants, too, are saved by Him in that He is Jesus; let him, I say, do this if he would be a catholic Christian. For thus it is written in the Gospel: "And they shall call His name Jesus; for He shall save His people from their sins"[2] — Jesus, because Jesus is in Latin *Salvator*, "Saviour." He shall, indeed, save His people; and amongst His people surely there are infants. "From their sins" shall He save them; in infants, too, therefore, are there original sins, on account of which He can be Jesus, that is, Saviour, even unto them.

---

[1] John i. 3.                    [2] Matt. i. 21.

# A TREATISE ON THE SOUL AND ITS ORIGIN.

# EXTRACT FROM AUGUSTIN'S "RETRACTATIONS,"

## BOOK II. CHAP. 56,

### ON THE FOLLOWING TREATISE,

## "DE ANIMA ET EJUS ORIGINE."

---

"AT that time one Vincentius discovered in the possession of a certain presbyter cal'ed Peter, in Mauritania Cæsariensis, a little work of mine, in a particular passage of which, touching the origin of souls in individual men, I had confessed that I knew not whether they are propagated from the primeval soul of the first man, and from that by parental descent, or whether they are severally assigned to each person without propagation, as the first was to Adam ; but that I was, at the same time, quite sure that the soul was not body, but spirit. In opposition to these opinions of mine, he addressed to this Peter two books, which were sent to me from Cæsarea by the monk Renatus. Having read these books, I replied in four others, — one addressed to the monk Renatus, another to the presbyter Peter, and two more to Victor himself. That to Peter, however, though it has all the lengthiness of a book, is yet only a letter, which I did not like to be kept separate from the other three works. In all of them, while discussing many points which were unavoidable, I defended my hesitancy on the point of the origin of the souls which are given to individual men ; and I pointed out this man's many errors and presumptuous pravity. At the same time, I treated the young man as gently as I could, — not as one who ought to be denounced all out of hand, but as one who ought to be still instructed ; and I accepted the account of his conduct which he wrote back to me. In this work of mine, the book addressed to Renatus begins with these words : "Your sincerity towards us ;" while that which was written to Peter begins thus : "To his Lordship, my dearly beloved brother and co-presbyter Peter." Of the last two books, which are addressed to Vincentius Victor, the former one thus opens : "As to that which I have thought it my duty to write to you."

# ADVERTISEMENT TO THE READER OF THIS TREATISE.

THE occasion of these four books was furnished by a young man named Vincentius Victor, a native of Mauritania Cæsariensis, a convert to the catholic Church from the Rogatian faction (which split off from the Donatist schism, and inhabited that part of Mauritania which lay around Cartenna). This Victor, they say, had previously so high an opinion of the Vincentius who succeeded Rogatus as the head of the before-mentioned faction, that he adopted his name as his own.[1] Happening to meet with a certain work of Augustin's, in which the writer acknowledged himself to be incapable of saying whether all souls were propagated from Adam's soul simply, or whether every man severally had his soul given to him by God, even as Adam himself had, without propagation, although he declared, for all that, his conviction that the soul was in its nature spirit, not body, Victor was equally offended with both statements: he wondered that so great a man as Augustin did not unhesitatingly teach what one ought to hold concerning the origin of the soul, especially as he thought its propagation probable; and also that he did state with so great assurance the nature of the soul to be incorporeal. He accordingly published two books written to one Peter, a presbyter of Spain, against Augustin on this subject, containing some conceits of the Pelagian heretics, and other things even worse than these.[2]

A monk called Renatus happened then to be at Cæsarea. It appears that this man had shown to Augustin, who was staying at the same place in the autumn of the year 418, a letter of the Bishop Optatus consulting him about the origin of the soul.[3] This monk, of the order of laymen, but perfectly orthodox in the faith, induced by the circumstance, carefully copied the books of Victor, and forwarded them from Cæsarea to Hippo the next summer; Augustin, however, only received them at the end of autumn of the year 419, as is supposed. As soon as the holy doctor read them, he without delay wrote the first of the four following books to the good monk, and then the second, in the shape of a letter, to the presbyter Peter, and the two last books to Victor himself, but after a considerable interval, as it appears from the following words of the fourth chapter of the second book: "If, indeed, the Lord will that I should write to the young man, as I desire to do." In the *Retractations* this little work of Augustin is placed immediately after the treatises of the year 419, *i.e.* in the fifth place after *the Proceedings with Emeritus*, which were completed in the month of September in the year 418. It belongs, therefore, to the termination of the year 419 or to the commencement of the year 420, having been written after "the condemnation of the Pelagians by the authority of catholic Councils and of the Apostolic See,"[4] but "very soon after,"[5] as that happy event had happened in the year of Christ 418.

In BOOK I., written to Renatus, he points out his own opinion about the nature of the soul, and his hesitation as to its origin, which had been unjustly blamed by Victor. He reproves the man's juvenile forwardness, shows him he had fallen into grave and unheard-of errors while venturing to take upon himself the solution of a question which exceeded his abilities, and points out that he adduced only doubtful passages of Scripture, and such as were not applicable to the subject, in his endeavour to prove that souls are not propagated, but that entirely new ones are breathed by God into every man at his separate birth.

In BOOK II., he advises Peter not to incur the imputation of having approved of the books which had been addressed to him by Victor *On the Origin of the Soul* by any use he might make of them, nor to take as catholic doctrines that person's rash utterances contrary to the Christian faith. Victor's various and very serious errors he points out and briefly confutes; and he concludes with advising Peter himself to try to persuade Victor to correct his errors.

In BOOK III., which was written to Victor himself, he points out the corrections which Victor ought to make in his books if he wished to be deemed a catholic; those opinions also and paradoxes of his, which had been already refuted in the preceding books to Renatus and Peter, the author briefly censures in this third book, and classifies under eleven heads of error.

In BOOK IV., addressed to the same Victor, he first shows that his hesitation on the subject of the origin of souls was undeservedly blamed, and that he was wrongly compared with cattle, because he had refrained from any bold conclusions on the subject. Then again, with regard to his own unhesitating statement, that the soul was spirit, not body, he points out how rashly Victor disapproved of this assertion, especially when he was vainly expending his efforts to prove that the soul was corporeal in its own nature, and that the spirit in man was distinct from the soul itself.

---

[1] See below, Book iii. c. 2.    [2] See below, ii. 13, 15.    [3] See Augustin's letter 190, ch. 1.    [4] See Book ii. 17.    [5] See Book i. 34.

# CONTENTS OF THE TREATISE "ON THE SOUL AND ITS ORIGIN."

---

## BOOK I.

## BOOK II.

# BOOK III.

# BOOK IV.

# A TREATISE ON THE SOUL AND ITS ORIGIN,

## BY AURELIUS AUGUSTIN, BISHOP OF HIPPO;

## IN FOUR BOOKS,

### WRITTEN TOWARDS THE END OF 419.

---

## BOOK I.[1]

### ADDRESSED TO RENATUS, THE MONK.

ON RECEIVING FROM RENATUS THE TWO BOOKS OF VINCENTIUS VICTOR, WHO DIS-APPROVED OF AUGUSTIN'S OPINION TOUCHING THE NATURE OF THE SOUL, AND OF HIS HESITATION IN RESPECT OF ITS ORIGIN, AUGUSTIN POINTS OUT HOW THE YOUNG OBJECTOR, IN HIS SELF-CONCEIT IN AIMING TO DECIDE ON SO ABSTRUSE A SUBJECT, HAD FALLEN INTO INSUFFERABLE MISTAKES. HE THEN PROCEEDS TO SHOW THAT THOSE PASSAGES OF SCRIPTURE BY WHICH VICTOR THOUGHT HE COULD PROVE THAT HUMAN SOULS ARE NOT DERIVED BY PROPAGATION, BUT ARE BREATHED BY GOD AFRESH INTO EACH MAN AT BIRTH, ARE AMBIGUOUS, AND INADEQUATE FOR THE CONFIRMATION OF THIS OPINION OF HIS.

CHAP. 1 [I.] — RENATUS HAD DONE HIM A KIND-NESS BY SENDING HIM THE BOOKS WHICH HAD BEEN ADDRESSED TO HIM.

YOUR sincerity towards us, dearest brother Renatus, and your brotherly kindness, and the affection of mutual love between us, we already had clear proof of; but now you have afforded us a still clearer proof, by sending me two books, written by a person whom I knew, indeed, nothing of, — though he was not on that account to be despised, — called Vincentius Victor (for in such form did I find his name placed at the head of his work) : this you did in the summer of last year; but owing to my absence from home, it was the end of autumn before they found their way to me. How, indeed, would you be likely with your very great affection for me to fail either in means or inclination to bring under my notice any writings of the kind, by whomsoever com-posed, if they fell into your hands, even if they were addressed to some one else? How much less likely, when my own name was mentioned and read — and that in a context of gainsaying some words of mine, which I had published in certain little treatises? Now you have done all this in the way you were sure to act as my very sincere and beloved friend.

CHAP. 2 [II.] — HE RECEIVES WITH A KINDLY AND PATIENT FEELING THE BOOKS OF A YOUNG AND INEXPERIENCED MAN WHO WROTE AGAINST HIM IN A TONE OF ARROGANCE. VINCENTIUS VICTOR CONVERTED FROM THE SECT OF THE ROGATIANS.

I am somewhat pained, however, at being thus far less understood by your Holiness than I should like to be; forasmuch as you supposed that I should so receive your communication, as if you did me an injury, by making known to me what another had done. You may see, indeed, how far this feeling is from my mind, in that I have no complaint to make of having suffered

[1] Written about the end of 419.

any wrong even from him. For, when he entertained views different from my own, was he bound to preserve silence? It ought, no doubt, to be even pleasant to me, that he broke silence in such a way as to put it in our power to read what he had to say. He ought, I certainly think, to have written simply to me, rather than to another concerning me; but as he was unknown to me, he did not venture to intrude personally on me in refuting my words. He thought there was no necessity for applying to me in a matter on which he seemed to himself least of all liable to be doubted,[1] but to be holding a perfectly well-known and certain opinion. He, moreover, acted in obedience to a friend of his, by whom he tells us he was compelled to write. And if he expressed any sentiment during the controversy which was contumelious to me, I would prefer supposing that he did this, not with any wish to treat me with incivility, but from the necessity of thinking differently from me. For in all cases where a person's *animus* towards one is indeterminate and unknown, I think it better to suppose the existence of the kindlier motive, than to find fault with an undiscovered one. Perhaps, too, he acted from love to me, as knowing that what he had written might possibly reach me; being at the same time unwilling that I should be in error on such points as he especially thinks himself to be free from error regarding. I ought, therefore, to be grateful for his kindness, although I feel obliged to disapprove of his opinion. Accordingly, as regards the points on which he does not entertain right views, he appears to me to deserve gentle correction rather than severe disapproval; more especially because, if I am rightly informed, he has lately become a catholic — a matter in which he is to be congratulated. For he has freed himself from the schism and errors of the Donatists (or rather the Rogatists) in which he was previously implicated; and if he understands the catholic verity as he ought, we may really rejoice at his conversion.

CHAP. 3 [III.] — THE ELOQUENCE OF VINCENTIUS, ITS DANGERS AND ITS TOLERABLENESS.

For he has an eloquence by which he is able to explain what he thinks. He must, therefore, be dealt with accordingly; and we must hope that he may entertain right sentiments, and that he may not turn useless things into objects of desire; that he may not seem to have propounded as true whatever he may have expressed with eloquence. But in his very outspokenness he may have much to correct, and to prune of redundant verbiage. And this characteristic

[1] [The Edinburgh translator conjectures *minime dubitandam* here: "on which he seemed to himself to be holding no doubtful, but a perfectly well-known and certain opinion." — W.]

of his has actually given offence to you, who are a person of gravity, as your own writings indicate. This fault, however, is either easily corrected, or, if it be resorted to with fondness by light minds, and borne with by serious ones, it is not attended with any injury to their faith. For we have already amongst us men who are frothy in speech, but sound in the faith. We need not then despair that this quality even in him (it might be endurable, however, even if it proved permanent) may be tempered and cleansed — in fact, may be either extended or recalled to an entire and solid criterion; especially as he is said to be young, so that diligence may supply to him whatever defect his inexperience may possess, and ripeness of age may digest what crude loquacity finds indigestible. The troublesome, dangerous, and pernicious thing is, when folly is set off by the commendation which is accorded to eloquence, and when a poisonous draught is drunk out of a precious goblet.

CHAP. 4 [IV.] — THE ERRORS CONTAINED IN THE BOOKS OF VINCENTIUS VICTOR. HE SAYS THAT THE SOUL COMES FROM GOD, BUT WAS NOT MADE EITHER OUT OF NOTHING OR OUT OF ANY CREATED THING.

I will now proceed to point out what things are chiefly to be avoided in his contentious statement. He says that the soul was made, indeed, by God, but that it is not a portion of God or of the nature of God, — which is an entirely true statement. When, however, he refuses to allow that it is made out of nothing, and mentions no other created thing out of which it was made; and makes God its author, in such a sense that He must be supposed to have made it, neither out of any non-existing things, that is, out of nothing, nor out of anything which exists other than God, but out of His very self: he is little aware that in the revolution of his thoughts he has come back to the position which he thinks he has avoided, even that the soul is nothing else than the nature of God; and consequently that there is an actual something made out of the nature of God by the self-same God, for the making of which the material of which He makes it is His own very self who makes it; and that thus God's nature is changeable, and by being changed for the worse the very nature of God Himself incurs condemnation at the hands of the self-same God! How far all this is from being fit for your intelligent faith to suppose, how alien it is from the heart of a catholic, and how much to be avoided, you can readily see. For the soul is either so made out of the breath, or God's breath is so made into it, that it was not created out of Himself, but by Himself out of nothing. It is not, indeed, like the case of a human being, when he breathes: he cannot form a breath out of nothing, but he restores to the air the breath which he inhaled out of it. We may in some such manner suppose that certain airs surrounded the Divine Being, and that He inhaled a particle of it by breathing, and exhaled it again by respiration, when He breathed into man's face, and so formed for him a soul. If this were the process, it could not have been out of His very self, but out of the circumambient airy matter, that what He breathed forth must have arisen. Far be it, however, from us to say, that the Almighty could not have made the breath of life out of nothing, by which man might become a living soul; and to crowd ourselves into such straits, as that we must either think that something already existed other than Himself, out of which He formed breath, or else suppose that He formed out of Himself that which we see was made subject to change. Now, whatever is out of Himself, must necessarily be of the self-same nature as Himself, and therefore immutable: but the soul (as all allow) is mutable. Therefore it is not out of Him, because it is not immutable, as He is. If, however, it was not made of anything else, it was undoubtedly made out of nothing — but by Himself.

CHAP. 5 [V.] — ANOTHER OF VICTOR'S ERRORS, THAT THE SOUL IS CORPOREAL.

But as regards his contention, "that the soul is not spirit, but body," what else can he mean to make out, than that we are composed, not of soul and body, but of two or even three bodies? For inasmuch as he says that we consist of spirit, soul and body, and asserts that all the three are bodies; it follows, that he supposes us to be made up of three bodies. How absurd this conclusion is, I think ought rather to be demonstrated to him than to you. But this is not an intolerable error on the part of a person who has not yet discovered that there is in existence a something, which, though it be not corporeal, yet may wear somewhat of the similitude of a body.

CHAP. 6 [VI.] — ANOTHER ERROR OUT OF HIS SECOND BOOK, TO THE EFFECT, THAT THE SOUL DESERVED TO BE POLLUTED BY THE BODY.

But he is plainly past endurance in what he says in his second book, when he endeavours to solve a very difficult question on original sin, how it belongs to body and soul, if the soul is not derived by parental descent but is breathed afresh by God into a man. Striving to explain this troublesome and profound point, he thus expresses his view: "Through the flesh the soul fitly recovers its primitive condition, which it seemed to have gradually lost through the flesh,

in order that it may begin to be regenerated by the very flesh by which it had deserved to be polluted." You observe how this person, having been so bold as to undertake what exceeds his powers, has fallen down such a precipice as to say, that the soul deserved to be defiled by the body; although he could in no wise declare whence it drew on itself this desert, before it put on flesh. For if it first had from the flesh its desert of sin, let him tell us (if he can) whence (previous to sin) it derived its desert to be contaminated by the flesh. For this desert, which projected it into sinful flesh to be polluted by it, it of course had either from itself, or, which is much more offensive to our mind, from God. It certainly could not, previous to its being invested with the flesh, have received from that flesh that ill desert by reason of which it was projected into the flesh, in order to be defiled by it. Now, if it had the ill desert from its own self, how did it get it, seeing that it did no sin previous to its assumption of flesh? But if it be alleged that it had the ill desert from God, then, I ask, who could listen to such blasphemy? Who could endure it? Who could permit it to be alleged with impunity? For the question which arises here, remember, is not, what was the ill desert which adjudged the soul to be condemned after it became incarnate? but what was its ill desert prior to the flesh, which condemned it to the investiture of the flesh, that it might be thereby polluted? Let him explain this to us, if he can, seeing that he has dared to say that the soul deserved to be defiled by the flesh.

CHAP. 7 [VII.] — VICTOR ENTANGLES HIMSELF IN AN EXCEEDINGLY DIFFICULT QUESTION. GOD'S FOREKNOWLEDGE IS NO CAUSE OF SIN.

In another passage, also, on proposing for explanation the very same question in which he had entangled himself, he says, speaking in the person of certain objectors: "Why, they ask, did God inflict upon the soul so unjust a punishment as to be willing to relegate it into a body, when, by reason of its association with the flesh, that begins to be sinful which could not have been sinful?" Now, amidst the reefy sea of such a question, it was surely his duty to beware of shipwreck; nor to commit himself to dangers which he could not hope to escape by passing over them, and where his only chance of safety lay in putting back again — in a word, by repentance. He tries to free himself by means of the foreknowledge of God, but to no purpose. For God's foreknowledge only marks beforehand those sinners whom He purposes to heal. For if He liberates from sin those souls which He Himself involved in sin when innocent and pure, He then heals a wound which Himself inflicted on us, not which He found in us. May God, however, forbid it, and may it be altogether far from us to say, that when God cleanses the souls of infants by the laver of regeneration, He then corrects evils which He Himself made for them, when He commingled them, which had no sin before, with sinful flesh, that they might be contaminated by its original sin. As regards, however, the souls which this calumniator alleges to have deserved pollution by the flesh, he is quite unable to tell us how it is they deserved so vast an evil, previous to their connection with the flesh.

### CHAP. 8 [VIII.] — VICTOR'S ERRONEOUS OPINION, THAT THE SOUL DESERVED TO BECOME SINFUL.

Vainly supposing, then, that he was able to solve this question from the foreknowledge of God, he keeps floundering on, and says: "If the soul deserved to be sinful which could not have been sinful, yet neither did it remain in sin, because, as prefigured in Christ, it was not bound to be in sin, even as it was unable to be." Now what can he mean when he says, "which could not have been sinful," or "was unable to be in sin," except, as I suppose, this, if it did not come into the flesh? For, of course, it could not have been sinful through original sin, or have been at all involved in original sin, except through the flesh, if it is not derived from the parent. We see it, then, liberated from sin through grace, but we do not see how it deserved to be involved in sin. What, then, is the meaning of these words of his, "If the soul deserved to be sinful, yet neither did it remain in sin"? For if I were to ask him, why it did not remain in sin, he would very properly answer, Because the grace of Christ delivered it therefrom. Since, then, he tells us how it came to pass that an infant's soul was liberated from its sinfulness, let him further tell us how it happened that it deserved to be sinful.

### CHAP. 9. — VICTOR UTTERLY UNABLE TO EXPLAIN HOW THE SINLESS SOUL DESERVED TO BE MADE SINFUL.

But what does he mean by that, which in his introduction he says has befallen him? For previous to proposing that question of his, and as introducing it, he affirms: "There are other opprobrious expressions underlying the querulous murmurings of those who rail at us; and, shaken about as in a hurricane, we are again and again dashed amongst enormous rocks." Now, if I were to express myself about him in this style, he would probably be angry. The words are his; and after premising them, he propounded his question, by way of showing us

the very rocks against which he struck and was wrecked. For to such lengths was he carried, and against such frightful reefs was he borne, drifted, and struck, that his escape was a perfect impossibility without a retreat — a correction, in short, of what he had said; since he was unable to show by what desert the soul was made sinful; though he was not afraid to say, that previous to any sin of its own it had deserved to become sinful. Now, who deserves, without committing any sin, so immense a punishment as to be conceived in the sin of another, before leaving his mother's womb, and then to be no longer free from sin? But from this punishment the free grace of God delivers the souls of such infants as are regenerated in Christ, with no previous merits of their own — "otherwise grace is no grace." [1] With regard, then, to this person, who is so vastly intelligent, and who in the great depth of his wisdom is displeased at our hesitation, which, if not well informed, is at all events circumspect, let him tell us, if he can, what the merit was which brought the soul into such a punishment, from which grace delivers it without any merit. Let him speak, and, if he can, defend his assertion with some show of reason. I would not, indeed, require so much of him, if he had not himself declared that the soul deserved to become sinful. Let him tell us what the desert was — whether good desert or evil? If good, how could well-deserving lead to evil? If evil, whence could arise any ill desert previous to the commission of any sin? I have also to remark, that if there be a good desert, then the liberation of the soul would not be of free grace, but it would be due to the previous merit, and thus "grace would be no more grace." If there be, however, an evil desert, then I ask what it is. Is it true that the soul has come into the flesh; and that it would not have so come unless He in whom there is no sin had Himself sent it? Never, therefore, except by floundering worse and worse, will he contrive to set up this view of his, in which he predicates of the soul that it deserved to be sinful. In the case of those infants, too, in whose baptism original sin is washed away, he found something to say after a fashion, — to the effect, that being involved in the sin of another could not possibly have been detrimental to them, predestinated as they were to eternal life in the foreknowledge of God. This might admit of a tolerably good sense, if he had not entangled himself in that formula of his, in which he asserts that the soul deserved to be sinful: from this difficulty he can only extricate himself by revoking his words, with regret at having expressed them.

---

[1] Rom. xi. 6.

CHAP. 10 [IX.] — ANOTHER ERROR OF VICTOR'S, THAT INFANTS DYING UNBAPTIZED MAY ATTAIN TO THE KINGDOM OF HEAVEN. ANOTHER, THAT THE SACRIFICE OF THE BODY OF CHRIST MUST BE OFFERED FOR INFANTS WHO DIE BEFORE THEY ARE BAPTIZED.

But when he wished to answer with respect, however, to those infants who are prevented by death from being first baptized in Christ, he was so bold as to promise them not only paradise, but also the kingdom of heaven, — finding no way else of avoiding the necessity of saying that God condemns to eternal death innocent souls, which, without any previous desert of sin, He introduces into sinful flesh. He saw, however, to some extent what evil he was giving utterance to, in implying that without any grace of Christ the souls of infants are redeemed to everlasting life and the kingdom of heaven, and that in their case original sin may be cancelled without Christ's baptism, in which is effected the forgiveness of sins : observing all this, and into what a depth he had plunged in his sea of shipwreck, he says, " I am of opinion that for them, indeed, constant oblations and sacrifices must be continually offered up by holy priests." You may here behold another danger, out of which he will never escape except by regret and a recall of his words. For who can offer up the body of Christ for any except for those who are members of Christ? Moreover, from the time when He said, " Except a man be born of water and of the Spirit, he cannot enter into the kingdom of heaven ; " [1] and again, " He that loseth his life for my sake shall find it ; " [2] no one becomes a member of Christ except it be either by baptism in Christ, or death for Christ.[3]

CHAP. 11. — MARTYRDOM FOR CHRIST SUPPLIES THE PLACE OF BAPTISM. THE FAITH OF THE THIEF WHO WAS CRUCIFIED ALONG WITH CHRIST TAKEN AS MARTYRDOM AND HENCE FOR BAPTISM.

Accordingly, the thief, who was no follower of the Lord previous to the cross, but His confessor upon the cross, from whose case a presumption is sometimes taken, or attempted, against the sacrament of baptism, is reckoned by St. Cyprian [4] among the martyrs who are baptized in their own blood, as happens to many unbaptized persons in times of hot persecution. For to the fact that he confessed the crucified Lord so much weight is attributed and so much availing value assigned by Him who knows how to weigh and value such evidence, as if he had been crucified for the Lord. Then, indeed, his faith

on the cross flourished when that of the disciples failed, and that without recovery if it had not bloomed again by the resurrection of Him before the terror of whose death it had drooped. They despaired of Him when dying, — he hoped when joined with Him in dying ; they fled from the author of life, — he prayed to his companion in punishment ; they grieved as for the death of a man, — he believed that after death He was to be a king ; they forsook the sponsor of their salvation, — he honoured the companion of His cross. There was discovered in him the full measure of a martyr, who then believed in Christ when they fell away who were destined to be martyrs. All this, indeed, was manifest to the eyes of the Lord, who at once bestowed so great felicity on one who, though not baptized, was yet washed clean in the blood, as it were, of martyrdom. But even of ourselves, who cannot reflect with how much faith, how much hope, how much charity he might have undergone death for Christ when living, who begged life of Him when dying? Besides all this, there is the circumstance, which is not incredibly reported, that the thief who then believed as he hung by the side of the crucified Lord was sprinkled, as in a most sacred baptism, with the water which issued from the wound of the Saviour's side. I say nothing of the fact that nobody can prove, since none of us knows that he had not been baptized previous to his condemnation. However, let every man take this in the sense he may prefer ; only let no rule about baptism affecting the Saviour's own precept be taken from this example of the thief ; and let no one promise for the case of unbaptized infants, between damnation and the kingdom of heaven, some middle place of rest and happiness, such as he pleases and where he pleases. For this is what the heresy of Pelagius promised them : he neither fears damnation for infants, whom he does not regard as having any original sin, nor does he give them the hope of the kingdom of heaven, since they do not approach to the sacrament of baptism. As for this man, however, although he acknowledges that infants are involved in original sin, he yet boldly promises them, even without baptism, the kingdom of heaven. This even the Pelagians had not the boldness to do, though asserting infants to be absolutely without sin. See, then, what a network of presumptuous opinion he entangles, unless he regret having committed such views to writing.

CHAP. 12 [X.] — DINOCRATES, BROTHER OF THE MARTYR ST. PERPETUA, IS SAID TO HAVE BEEN DELIVERED FROM THE STATE OF CONDEMNATION BY THE PRAYERS OF THE SAINT.

Concerning Dinocrates, however, the brother

---

[1] John iii. 5.      [2] Matt. x. 39.
[3] [Augustin here confesses the validity of the " baptism of blood," that is, martyrdom, which may take the place of baptism. See the next chapter, and also Book ii. 17. — W.]
[4] Cyprian's *Letter to Jubianus.* See likewise Augustin's work *Against the Donatists,* iv. 29; also *On Leviticus,* question 84; also his *Retractations,* ii. 18, 55.

of St. Perpetua, there is no record in the canonical Scripture; nor does the saint herself, or whoever it was that wrote the account, say that the boy, who had died at the age of seven years, died without baptism; in his behalf she is believed to have had, when her martyrdom was imminent, her prayers effectually heard that he should be removed from the penalties of the lost to rest. Now, boys at that time of life are able both to lie, and, saying the truth, both to confess and deny. Therefore, when they are baptized they say the Creed, and answer in their behalf to such questions as are proposed to them in examination. Who can tell, then, whether that boy, after baptism, in a time of persecution was estranged from Christ to idolatry by an impious father, and on that account incurred mortal condemnation, from which he was only delivered for Christ's sake, given to the prayers of his sister when she was at the point of death?

CHAP. 13 [XI.] — THE SACRIFICE OF THE BODY AND BLOOD OF CHRIST WILL NOT AVAIL FOR UNBAPTIZED PERSONS, AND CAN NOT BE OFFERED FOR THE MAJORITY OF THOSE WHO DIE UNBAPTIZED.

But even if it be conceded to this man (what cannot by any means be allowed with safety to the catholic faith and the rule of the Church), that the sacrifice of the body and blood of Christ may be offered for unbaptized persons of every age, as if they were to be helped by this kind of piety on the part of their friends to reaching the kingdom of heaven: what will he have to say to our objections respecting the thousands of infants who are born of impious parents and never fall, by any mercy of God or man, into the hands of pious friends, and who depart from that wretched life of theirs at their most tender age without the washing of regeneration? Let him tell us, if he only can, how it is that those souls deserved to be made sinful to such a degree as, certainly never afterwards to be delivered from sin. For if I ask him why they deserve to be condemned if they are not baptized, he will rightly answer me: On account of original sin. If I then inquire whence they derived original sin, he will answer, From sinful flesh, of course. If I go on to ask why they deserved to be condemned to a sinful flesh, seeing they had done no evil before they came in the flesh, and to be so condemned to undergo the contagion of the sin of another, that neither baptism shall regenerate them, born as they are in sin, nor sacrifices expiate them in their pollution: let him find something to reply to this! For in such circumstances and of such parents have these infants been born, or are still being born, that it is not possible for them to be reached with such help. Here, at any rate, all argument is lacking. Our question is not, why souls have deserved to be condemned subsequently to their consorting with sinful flesh? But we ask, how it is that souls have deserved to be condemned to undergo at all this association with sinful flesh, seeing that they have no sin previous to this association. There is no room for him to say: "It was no detriment to them that they shared for a season the contagion of another's sin, since in the prescience of God redemption had been provided for them." For we are now speaking of those to whom no redemption brings help, since they depart from the body before they are baptized. Nor is there any propriety in his saying: "The souls which baptism does not cleanse, the many sacrifices which are offered up for them will cleanse. God foreknew this, and willed that they should for a little while be implicated in the sins of another without incurring eternal damnation, and with the hope of eternal happiness." For we are now speaking of those whose birth among impious persons and of impious parents could by no possibility find such defences and helps. And even if these could be applied, they would, it is certain, be unable to benefit any who are unbaptized; just as the sacrifices which he has mentioned out of the book of the Maccabees could be of no use for the sinful dead for whom they were offered, inasmuch as they had not been circumcised.[1]

CHAP. 14. — VICTOR'S DILEMMA: HE MUST EITHER SAY ALL INFANTS ARE SAVED, OR ELSE GOD SLAYS THE INNOCENT.

Let him, then, find an answer, if he can, when the question is asked of him, why it was that the soul, without any sin whatever, either original or personal, deserved so to be condemned to undergo the original sin of another as to be unable to be delivered from it; let him see which he will choose of two alternatives: Either to say that even the souls of dying infants who depart hence without the washing of regeneration, and for whom no sacrifice of the Lord's body is offered, are absolved from the bond of original sin — although the apostle teaches that "from one all go into condemnation,"[2] — all, that is, of course, to whom grace does not find its way to help, in order that by One all might escape into redemption. Or else to say that souls which have no sin, either their own or original, and are in every respect innocent, simple, and pure, are punished with eternal damnation by the righteous God when He inserts them Himself into sinful flesh without any deliverance therefrom.

---

[1] 2 Macc. xii. 43.          [2] Rom. v. 16.

CHAP. 15 [XII.] — GOD DOES NOT JUDGE ANY ONE FOR WHAT HE MIGHT HAVE DONE IF HIS LIFE HAD BEEN PROLONGED, BUT SIMPLY FOR THE DEEDS HE ACTUALLY COMMITS.

For my own part, indeed, I affirm that neither of the alternative cases ought to be admitted, nor that third opinion which would have it that souls sinned in some other state previous to the flesh, and so deserved to be condemned to the flesh; for the apostle has most distinctly stated that "the children being not yet born, had done neither good nor evil."[1] So it is evident that infants can have contracted none but original sin to require remission of sins. Nor, again, that fourth position, that the souls of infants who will die without baptism are by the righteous God banished and condemned to sinful flesh, since He foreknew that they would lead evil lives if they grew old enough for the use of free will. But this not even he has been daring enough to affirm, though embarrassed in such perplexities. On the contrary, he has declared, briefly indeed, yet manifestly, against this vain opinion in these words: "God would have been unrighteous if He had willed to judge any man yet unborn, who had done nothing whatever of his own free will." This was his answer when treating a question in opposition to those persons who ask why God made man, when in His foreknowledge He knew that he would not be good? He would be judging a man before he was born if He had been unwilling to create him because He knew beforehand that he would not turn out good. And there can be no doubt about it, even as this person himself thought, that the proper course would be for the Almighty to judge a man for his works when accomplished, not for such as might be foreseen, nor such as might be permitted to be done some time or other. For if the sins which a man would have committed if he were alive are condemned in him when dead, even when they have not been committed, no benefit is conferred on him when he is taken away that no wickedness might change his mind; inasmuch as judgment will be given upon him according to the wickedness which might have developed in him, not according to the uprightness which was actually found in him. Nor will any man possibly be safe who dies after baptism, because even after baptism men may, I will not say sin in some way or other, but actually go so far as to commit apostasy. What then? Suppose a man who has been taken away after baptism should, if he had lived, have become an apostate, are we to think that no benefit was conferred even upon him in that he was removed and was saved from the misery of his mind being changed by wickedness? And

are we to imagine that he will have to be judged, by reason of God's foreknowledge, as an apostate, and not as a faithful member of Christ? How much better, to be sure, would it have been — if sins are punished not as they have been committed or contemplated by the human agent, but foreknown and to happen in the cognizance of the Almighty — if the first pair had been cast forth from paradise previous to their fall, and so sin have been prevented in so holy and blessed a place! What, too, is to be said about the entire nullification of foreknowledge itself, when what is foreknown is not to happen? How, indeed, can that be rightly called the prescience of something to be, which in fact will not come to pass? And how are sins punished which are none, that is to say, which are not committed before the assumption of flesh, since life itself is not yet begun; nor after the assumption, since death has prevented?

CHAP. 16 [XIII.] — DIFFICULTY IN THE OPINION WHICH MAINTAINS THAT SOULS ARE NOT BY PROPAGATION.

This means, then, of settling the point whereby the soul was sent into the flesh until what time it should be delivered from the flesh, — seeing that the soul of an infant, which has not grown old enough for the will to become free, is the case supposed, — makes no discovery of the reason why condemnation should overtake it without the reception of baptism, except the reason of original sin. Owing to this sin, we do not deny that the soul is righteously condemned, because for sin God's righteous law has appointed punishment. But then we ask, why the soul has been made to undergo this sinful state, if it is not derived from that one primeval soul which sinned in the first father of the human race. Wherefore, if God does not condemn the innocent, — if He does not make guilty those whom He sees to be innocent, — and if nothing liberates souls from either original sins or personal ones but Christ's baptism in Christ's Church, — and if sins, before they are committed, and much more when they have never been committed, cannot be condemned by any righteous law: then this writer cannot adduce any of these four cases; he must, if he can, explain, in respect to the souls of infants, which, as they quit life without baptism, are sent into condemnation, by what desert of theirs it is that they, without having ever sinned, are consigned to a sinful flesh, there to find the sin which is to secure their just condemnation. Moreover, if he shrinks from these four cases which sound doctrine condemns, — that is to say, if he has not the courage to maintain that souls, when they are even without sin, are made sinful by God, or that they are freed from the original sin that is in them without

[1] Rom. ix. 11.

Christ's sacrament, or that they committed sin in some other state before they were sent into the flesh, or that sins which they never committed are condemned in them, — if, I say, he has not the courage to tell us these things because they really do not deserve to be mentioned, but should affirm that infants do not inherit original sin, and have no reason why they should be condemned should they depart hence without receiving the sacrament of regeneration, he will without doubt, to his own condemnation, run into the damnable heresy of Pelagius. To avoid this, how much better is it for him to share my hesitation about the soul's origin, without daring to affirm that which he cannot comprehend by human reason nor defend by divine authority! So shall he not be obliged to utter foolishness, whilst he is afraid to confess his ignorance.

CHAP. 17 [XIV.] — HE SHOWS THAT THE PASSAGES OF SCRIPTURE ADDUCED BY VICTOR DO NOT PROVE THAT SOULS ARE MADE BY GOD IN SUCH A WAY AS NOT TO BE DERIVED BY PROPAGATION : FIRST PASSAGE.

Here, perhaps, he may say that his opinion is backed by divine authority, since he supposes that he proves by passages of the Holy Scriptures that souls are not made by God by way of propagation, but that they are by distinct acts of creation breathed afresh into each individual. Let him prove this if he can, and I will allow that I have learnt from him what I was trying to find out with great earnestness. But he must go in quest of other defences, which, perhaps, he will not find, for he has not proved his point by the passages which he has thus far advanced. For all he has applied to the subject are to some extent undoubtedly suitable, but they afford only doubtful demonstration to the point which he raises respecting the soul's origin. For it is certain that God has given to man breath and spirit, as the prophet testifies : "Thus saith the Lord, who made the heaven, and founded the earth, and all that is therein ; who giveth breath to the people upon it, and spirit to them that walk over it." [1]   This passage he wishes to be taken in his own sense, which he is defending ; so that the words, " who giveth breath to the people," may be understood as implying that He creates souls for people not by propagation, but by insufflation of new souls in every case. Let him, then, boldly maintain at this rate that He does not give us flesh, on the ground that our flesh derives its original from our parents. In the instance, too, which the apostle adduces, " God giveth it a body as it hath pleased Him," [2] let him deny, if he dares, that corn springs from corn, and grass from grass, from the seed, each

after its kind. And if he dares not deny this, how does he know in what sense it is said, " He giveth breath to the people " ? — whether by derivation from parents, or by fresh breathing into each individual?

CHAP. 18. — BY "BREATH" IS SIGNIFIED SOMETIMES THE HOLY SPIRIT.

How, again, does he know whether the repetition of the idea in the sentence, " who giveth breath to the people upon it, and spirit to them that walk over it," may not be understood of only one thing under two expressions, and may not mean, not the life or spirit whereby human nature lives, but the Holy Spirit? For if by the " breath " the Holy Ghost could not be signified, the Lord would not, when He " breathed upon " His disciples after His resurrection, have said, " Receive ye the Holy Ghost." [3]   Nor would it have been thus written in the Acts of the Apostles, " Suddenly there came a sound from heaven, as if a mighty breath were borne in upon them ; and there appeared unto them cloven tongues, like as of fire, and it sat upon each of them, and they were all filled with the Holy Ghost." [4]   Suppose, now, that it was this which the prophet foretold in the words, " who giveth breath unto the people upon it ; " and then, as an exposition of what he had designated " breath," he went on to say, " and spirit to them that walk over it." Surely this prediction was most manifestly fulfilled when they were all filled with the Holy Ghost. If, however, the term " people " is not yet applicable to the one hundred and twenty persons who were then assembled together in one place, at all events, when the number of believers amounted to four or five thousand, who when they were baptized received the Holy Ghost, [5] can any doubt that the recipients of the Holy Ghost were then " the people," even " the men walking in the earth " ? For that spirit which is given to man as appertaining to his nature, whether it be given by propagation or be inbreathed as something new to individuals (and I do not determine which of these two modes ought to be affirmed, at least until one of the two can be clearly ascertained beyond a doubt), is not given to men when they " walk over the earth," but whilst they are still shut up in their mother's womb. " He gave breath, therefore, to the people upon the earth, and spirit to them that walk over it," when many became believers together, and were together filled with the Holy Ghost. And He gives Him to His people, although not to all at the same time, but to every one in His own time, until, by departing from this life, and by coming into it, the entire number of His people

---

be fulfilled. In this passage of Holy Scripture, therefore, *breath* is not one thing, and *spirit* another thing; but there is a repetition of one and the same idea. Just as "He that sitteth in the heavens" is not one, and "the Lord" is not another; nor, again, is it one thing "to laugh," and another thing "to hold in derision;" but there is only a repetition of the same meaning in the passage where we read, "He that sitteth in the heavens shall laugh: the Lord shall have them in derision."[1] So, in precisely the same manner, in the passage, "I will give Thee the heathen for Thine inheritance, and the uttermost parts of the earth for Thy possession,"[2] it is certainly not meant that "inheritance" is one thing, and "possession" another thing; nor that "the heathen" means one thing, and "the uttermost parts of the earth" another; there is only a repetition of the self-same thing. He will, indeed, discover innumerable expressions of this sort in the sacred writings, if he will only attentively consider what he reads.[3]

### CHAP. 19. — THE MEANING OF "BREATH" IN SCRIPTURE.

The term, however, that is used in the Greek version, πνοή, is variously rendered in Latin: sometimes by *flatus*, breath; sometimes by *spiritus*, spirit; sometimes by *inspiratio*, inspiration. This term occurs in the Greek editions of the passage which we are now reviewing, "Who giveth breath to the people upon it," the word for *breath* being πνοή.[4] The same word is used in the narrative where man was endued with life: "And God breathed upon his face the breath of life."[5] Again, in the psalm the same term occurs: "Let every thing that hath spirit praise the Lord."[6] It is the same word also in the Book of Job: "The inspiration of the Almighty is that which teaches."[7] The translator refused the word *flatus*, breath, for *adspiratio*, inspiration, although he had before him the very term πνοή, which occurs in the text of the prophet which we are considering. We can hardly doubt, I think, that in this passage of Job the Holy Ghost is signified. The question discussed was concerning wisdom, whence it comes to men: "It cometh not from number of years; but the Spirit is in mortals, and the inspiration of the Almighty is that which teaches."[8] By this repetition of terms

it may be quite understood that he did not speak of man's own spirit in the clause, "The Spirit is in mortals." He wanted to show whence men have wisdom, — that it is not from their own selves; so by using a duplicate expression he explains his idea; "The inspiration of the Almighty is that which teaches." Similarly, in another passage of the same book, he says, "The understanding of my lips shall meditate purity. The divine Spirit is that which formed me, and the breath of the Almighty is that which teacheth me."[9] Here, likewise, what he calls *adspiratio*, or "inspiration," is in Greek πνοή, the same word which is translated *flatus*, "breath," in the passage quoted from the prophet. Therefore, although it is rash to deny that the passage, "Who giveth breath to the people upon it, and spirit to them that walk over it," has reference to the soul or spirit of man, — although the Holy Ghost may with greater credibility be understood as referred to in the passage: yet I ask on what ground anybody can boldly determine that the prophet meant in these words to intimate that the soul or spirit whereby our nature possesses vitality [is not given to us by God through the process of propagation?][10] Of course if the prophet had very plainly said, "Who giveth soul to the people upon earth," it still would remain to be asked whether God Himself gives it from an origin in the preceding generation, just as He gives the body out of such prior material, and that not only to men or cattle, but also to the seed of corn, or to any other body whatever, just as it pleases Him; or whether He bestows it by inbreathing as a new gift to each individual, as the first man received it from Him?

### CHAP. 20. — OTHER WAYS OF TAKING THE PASSAGE.

There are also some persons who understand the prophet's words, "He gave breath to the people upon it," that is to say, upon the earth, as if the word "breath," *flatus*, were simply equivalent to "soul," *anima;* while they construe the next clause, "and spirit to them that walk over it," as referring to the Holy Ghost; and they suppose that the same order is observed by the prophet that is mentioned by the apostle: "That was not first which is spiritual, but that which is natural; and afterward that which is spiritual."[11] Now from this view of the prophet's words an elegant interpretation may, no doubt,

[1] Ps. ii. 4.                    [2] Ps. ii. 8.
[3] [It is the *parallelism* of Hebrew poetry to which Augustin here appeals: and that soundly, although the interpretation of "spirit" in the passage in hand, which is suggested in the chapter, is untenable. — W.]
[4] The passage stands in the LXX.: Καὶ διδοὺς πνοὴν τῷ λαῷ τῷ ἐπ' αὐτῆς.
[5] The LXX. text of Gen. ii. 7 is, Καὶ ἐνεφύσησεν εἰς τὸ πρόσω πον αὐτοῦ πνοὴν ζωῆς.
[6] Ps. cl. 6: Πᾶσα πνοὴ αἰνεσάτω τὸν Κύριον.
[7] According to the LXX., Πνοὴ δὲ παντοκράτορός ἐστιν ἡ διδάσκουσα.
[8] Job xxxii. 7, 8.

[9] Job xxx. 3, 4, according to the LXX., of which the text is, Σύνεσις δὲ χειλέων μου καθαρὰ νοήσει. Πνεῦμα θεῖον τὸ ποιῆσαν με, πνοὴ δὲ παντοκράτορός ἐστιν ἡ διδάσκουσα.
[10] The words here given in brackets are suggested by the Benedictine editor. [The Latin as it stands may be translated simply: "that the prophet meant to signify in these words the soul or spirit whereby our nature lives?" and is not this better than the conjecture? — W.]
[11] 1 Cor. xv. 46.

be formed consistent with the apostle's sense. The phrase, "to them that walk over it," is in the Latin, "*calcantibus eam;*" and as the literal meaning of these words is "treading upon it," we may understand the idea of contempt of it to be implied. For they who receive the Holy Ghost despise earthly things in their love of heavenly things. None of these opinions, however, is contrary to the faith, whether one regards the two terms, *breath* and *spirit,* to pertain to human nature, or both of them to the Holy Ghost, or one of them, *breath,* to the soul, and the other, *spirit,* to the Holy Ghost. If, however, the soul and spirit of the human being be the meaning here, since undoubtedly it ought to be, as the gift of God to him, then we must further inquire, in what way does God bestow this gift? Is it by propagation, as He gives us our bodily limbs by this process? Or is it bestowed on each person severally by God's inbreathing, not by propagation, but as always a fresh creation? These questions are not ambiguous, as this man would make them; but we wish that they be defended by the most certain warrant of the divine Scriptures.

CHAP. 21. — THE SECOND PASSAGE QUOTED BY VICTOR.

On the same principle we treat the passage in which God says: "For my Spirit shall go forth from me; and I have created every breath." [1] Here the former clause, "My Spirit shall go forth from me," must be taken as referring to the Holy Ghost, of whom the Saviour similarly says, "He proceedeth from the Father." [2] But the other clause, "I have created every breath," is undeniably spoken of each individual soul. Well; but God also creates the entire body of man; and, as nobody doubts, He makes the human body by the process of propagation: it is therefore, of course, still open to inquiry concerning the soul (since it is evidently God's work), whether He creates it as He does the body, by propagation, or by inbreathing, as He made the first soul.

CHAP. 22. — VICTOR'S THIRD QUOTATION.

He proceeds to favour us with a third passage, in which it is written: "Who forms the spirit of man within him." [3] As if any one denied this! No; all our question is as to the *mode* of the formation. Now let us take the eye of the body, and ask, who but God forms it? I suppose that He forms it not externally, but in itself, and yet, most certainly, by propagation. Since, then, He also forms "the human spirit in him," the question still remains, whether it be derived by a fresh insufflation in every instance, or by propagation.

CHAP. 23. — HIS FOURTH QUOTATION.

We have read all about the mother of the Maccabean youths, who was really more fruitful in virtues when her children suffered than of children when they were born; how she exhorted them to constancy, speaking in this wise: "I cannot tell, my sons, how ye came into my womb. For it was not I who gave you spirit and soul, nor was it I that formed the members of every one of you; but it was God, who also made the world, and all things that are therein; who, moreover, formed the generation of men; and searches the action [4] of all; and who will Himself of His great mercy restore to you your spirit and soul." [5] All this we know; but how it supports this man's assertion we do not see. For what Christian would deny that God gives to men soul and spirit? But similarly, I suppose that he cannot deny that God gives to men their tongue, and ear, and hand, and foot, and all their bodily sensations, and the form and nature of all their limbs. For how is he going to deny all these to be the gifts of God, unless he forgets that he is a Christian? As, however, it is evident that these were made by Him, and bestowed on man by propagation; so also the question must arise, by what means man's spirit and soul are formed by Him; by what efficiency given to man — from the parents, or from nothing, or (as this man asserts, in a sense which we must by all means guard against) from some existing nature of the divine breath, not created out of nothing, but out of His own self?

CHAP. 24 [XV.] — WHETHER OR NO THE SOUL IS DERIVED BY NATURAL DESCENT (EX TRADUCE), HIS CITED PASSAGES FAIL TO SHOW.

Forasmuch, then, as the passages of Scripture which he mentions by no means show what he endeavours to enforce (since, indeed, they express nothing at all on the immediate question before us), what can be the meaning of these words of his: "We firmly maintain that the soul comes from the breath of God, not from natural generation, because it is given from God"? As if, forsooth, the body could be given from another, than from Him by whom it is created, "Of whom are all things, through whom are all things, in whom are all things;" [6] not that they are of His nature, but of His workmanship. "Nor is it from nothing," says he, "because it comes forth from God." Whether this be so, is (we must say) not the question to be here entertained. At the same time, we do not hesitate to

_____

[1] Isa. lvii. 16. In the Septuagint it is, Πνεῦμα γὰρ παρ' ἐμοῦ ἐξελεύσεται, καὶ πνοὴν πᾶσαν ἐγὼ ἐποίησα.
[2] John xv. 26.
[3] Zech. xii. 1, which in the Septuagint is, Κύριος . . . πλάσσων πνεῦμα ἀνθρώπου ἐν αὐτῷ.

[4] *Actum;* another reading is *ortum,* more in accordance with the Greek γένεσιν, the meaning of which would be: "Searches the *origin* of all things."
[5] 2 Macc. vii. 22, 23.        [6] Rom. xi. 36.

affirm, that the proposition which he advances, that the soul comes to man neither out of descent nor out of nothing, is certainly not true : this, I say, we affirm to be without doubt not true. For it is one of two things : if the soul is not derived by natural descent from the parent, it comes out of nothing. To pretend that it is derived from God in such wise as to be a portion of His nature, is simply sacrilegious blasphemy. But we solicit and seek up to the present time some plain passages of Scripture bearing on the point, whether the soul does not come by parental descent ; but we do not want such passages as he has adduced, which yield no illustration of the question now before us.

CHAP. 25. — JUST AS THE MOTHER KNOWS NOT WHENCE COMES HER CHILD WITHIN HER, SO WE KNOW NOT WHENCE COMES THE SOUL.

How I wish that, on so profound a question, so long as he is ignorant what he should say, he would imitate the mother of the Maccabean youths ! Although she knew very well that she had conceived children of her husband, and that they had been created for her by the Creator of all, both in body and in soul and spirit, yet she says, " I cannot tell, my sons, how ye came into my womb." Well now, I only wish this man would tell us that which she was ignorant of ! She, of course, knew (on the points I have mentioned) how they came into her womb as to their bodily substance, because she could not possibly doubt that she had conceived them by her husband. She furthermore confessed — because this, too, she was, of course, well aware of — that it was God who gave them their soul and spirit, and that it was He also who formed for them their features and their limbs. What was it, then, that she was so ignorant of ? Was it not probably (what we likewise are equally unable to determine) whether the soul and spirit, which God no doubt bestowed upon them, was derived to them from their parents, or breathed into them separately as it had been into the first man ? But whether it was this, or some other particular respecting the constitution of human nature, of which she was ignorant, she frankly confessed her ignorance ; and did not venture to defend at random what she knew nothing about. Nor would this man say to her, what he has not been ashamed to say to us : " Man being in honour doth not understand ; he is compared to the senseless cattle, and is like unto them." [1] Behold how that woman said of her sons, " I cannot tell how ye came into my womb," and yet she is not compared to the senseless brutes. " I cannot tell," she said ; then, as if they would inquire of her why she was ignorant, she went on

to say, " For it was not I who gave you spirit and soul." He, therefore, who gave them that gift, knows whence He made what He gave, whether He communicated it by propagation, or breathed it as a fresh creation, — a point which (this man says) I for my part know nothing of. " Nor was it I that formed the features and members of every one of you." He, however, who formed them, knows whether He formed them with the soul, or gave the soul to them after they had been formed. She had no idea of the manner, this or that, in which her sons came into her womb ; only one thing was she sure of, that He who gave her all she had would restore to her what He gave. But this man would choose out what that woman was ignorant of, on so profound and abstruse a fact of our nature ; only he would not judge her, if in error ; nor compare her, if ignorant, to the senseless cattle. Whatever the point was about which she was ignorant, it certainly pertained to man's nature ; and yet anybody would be blameless for such ignorance. Wherefore, I too, on my side, say concerning my soul, I have no certain knowledge how it came into my body ; for it was not I who gave it to myself. He who gave it to me knows whether He imparted it to me from my father, or created it afresh for me, as He did for the first man. But even I shall know, when He Himself shall teach me, in His own good time. Now, however, I do not know ; nor am I ashamed, like him, to confess my ignorance of what I know not.

CHAP. 26 [XVI.] — THE FIFTH PASSAGE OF SCRIPTURE QUOTED BY VICTOR.

" Learn," says he, " for, behold the apostle teaches you." Yes, indeed, I will learn, if the apostle teaches ; since it is God alone who teaches by the apostle. But, pray, what is it which the apostle teaches ? " Behold," he adds, " how, when speaking to the men of Athens, he strongly set forth this truth, saying : ' Seeing He giveth to all life and spirit.' " Well, who thinks of denying this ? " But understand," he says, " what it is the apostle states : *He giveth;* not, *He hath given.* He refers us to continuous and indefinite time, and does not proclaim past and completed time. Now that which he gives without cessation, He is always giving ; just as He who gives is Himself ever existent." I have quoted his words precisely as I found them in the second of the books which you sent me. First, I beg you to notice to what lengths he has gone, while endeavouring to affirm what he knows nothing about. For he has dared to say, that God, without any cessation, and not merely in the present time, but for ever and ever, gives souls to persons when they are born. " He is

___
[1] Ps. xlviii. 12.

always giving," says he, "just as He who gives is Himself ever existent." Far be it from me to say that I do not understand what the apostle said, for it is plain enough. But what this man says, he even ought himself to know, is contrary to the Christian faith; and he should be on his guard against going any further in such assertions. For, of course, when the dead shall rise again, there will be no more persons to be born; therefore God will bestow no longer any souls at any birth; but those which He is now giving to men along with their bodies He will judge. So that He is not always giving, although He is ever existent, who at present is giving. Nor, indeed, is that at all derivable from the apostle's expression, *who giveth* (not *hath given*), which this writer wishes to deduce, namely, that God does not give men souls by propagation. For souls are still given by Him, even if it be by propagation; even as bodily endowments, such as limbs, and sensations, and shape, and, in fact, the whole substance, are given by God Himself to human beings, although it be by propagation that He gives them. Nor again, because the Lord says,[1] "If God so clothes the grass of the field, which to-day is, and to-morrow is cast into the oven" (not using the preterite time, *hath clothed*, as when He first formed the material; but employing the present form, *clothes*, which, indeed, He still is doing), shall we on that account say, that the lilies are not produced from the original source of their own kind. What, therefore, if the soul and spirit of a human being in like manner is given by God Himself, whenever it is given; and given, too, by propagation from its own kind? Now this is a position which I neither maintain nor refute. Nevertheless, if it must be defended or confuted, I certainly recommend its being done by clear, and not doubtful proofs. Nor do I deserve to be compared with senseless cattle because I avow myself to be as yet incapable of determining the question, but rather with cautious persons, because I do not recklessly teach what I know nothing about. But I am not disposed on my own part to return railing for railing and compare this man with brutes; but I warn him as a son to acknowledge that he is really ignorant of that which he knows nothing about; nor to attempt to teach that which he has not yet learnt, lest he should deserve to be compared with those persons whom the apostle mentions as "desiring to be teachers of the law, understanding neither what they say nor whereof they affirm."[2]

CHAP. 27 [XVII.] — AUGUSTIN DID NOT VENTURE TO DEFINE ANYTHING ABOUT THE PROPAGATION OF THE SOUL.

For whence comes it that he is so careless about the Scriptures, which he talks of, as not to notice that when he reads of human beings being from God, it is not merely, as he contends, in respect of their soul and spirit, but also as regards their body? For the apostle's statement, "We are His offspring,"[3] this man supposes must not be referred to the body, but only to the soul and spirit. If, indeed, our human bodies are not of God, then that is false which the Scripture says: "For of Him are all things, through Him are all things, and in Him are all things."[4] Again, with reference to the same apostle's statement, "For as the woman is of the man, so also is the man by the woman,"[5] let him explain to us what propagation he would choose to be meant in the process, — that of the soul, or of the body, or of both? But he will not allow that souls come by propagation: it remains, therefore, that, according to him and all who deny the propagation of souls, the apostle signified the masculine and feminine body only, when he said, "As the woman is of the man, so also is the man by the woman;" the woman having been made out of the man, in order that the man might afterwards, by the process of birth, come out of the woman. If, therefore, the apostle, when he said this, did not intend the soul and spirit also to be understood, but only the bodies of the two sexes, why does he immediately add, "But all things are of God,"[5] unless it be that bodies also are of God? For so runs his entire statement: "As the woman is of the man, so also is the man by the woman; but all things are of God." Let, then, our disputant determine of what this is said. If of men's bodies, then, of course, even bodies are of God. How comes it to pass, therefore, that whenever this person reads in Scripture the phrase, "*of God*," when man is in question, he will have the words understood, not in reference to men's bodies, but only as concerning their souls and spirits? But if the expression, "All things are of God," was spoken both of the body of the two sexes, and of their soul and spirit, it follows that in all things the woman is of the man, for the woman comes from the man, and the man is by the woman: but all things of God. What "all things" are meant, except those he was speaking of, namely, the man of whom came the woman, and the woman who was of the man, and also the man who came by the woman? For that man came not by woman, out of whom came the woman; but only he who afterwards was born of man by woman, just as men are now born. Hence it follows that if the apostle, when he said the words we have quoted from him, spoke of men's bodies, undoubtedly the bodies of persons of both sexes are of God. Furthermore, if he insists that nothing in man comes

---

[1] Matt. vi. 30.　　[2] 2 Tim. i. 7.　　[3] Acts xvii. 28.　　[4] Rom. xi. 36.　　[5] 1 Cor. xi. 12.

from God except their souls and spirits, then, of course, the woman is of the man even as regards her soul and spirit; so that nothing is left to those who dispute against the propagation of souls. But if he is for dividing the subject in such a manner as to say that the woman is of the man as regards her body, but is of God in respect of her soul and spirit, how, then, will that be true which the apostle says, "All things of God," if the woman's body is of the man in such a sense that it is not of God? Wherefore, allowing that the apostle is more likely to speak the truth than that this person must be preferred as an authority to the apostle, the woman is of the man, whether in regard to her body only, or in reference to the entire whole of which human nature consists (but we assert nothing on these points as an absolute certainty, but are still inquiring after their truth); and the man is through the woman, whether it be that his whole nature as man is derived to him from his father, and is born in him through the woman, or the flesh alone; about which points the question is still undecided. "All things, however, are of God," and about this there is no question; and in this phrase are included the body, soul, and spirit, both of the man and the woman. For even if they were not born or derived from God, or emanated from Him as portions of His nature, yet they are of God, inasmuch as whatever is created, formed, and made by Him, has from Him the reality of its existence.

CHAP. 28. — A NATURAL FIGURE OF SPEECH MUST NOT BE LITERALLY PRESSED.

He goes on to remark: "But the apostle, by saying, 'And He Himself giveth life and spirit to all,' and then by adding the words, 'And hath made the whole race of men of one blood,'[1] has referred this soul and spirit to the Creator in respect of their origin, and the body to propagation." Now, certainly any one who does not wish to deny at random the propagation of souls, before ascertaining clearly whether the opinion is correct or not, has ground for understanding, from the apostle's words, that he meant the expression, *of one blood*, to be equivalent to *of one man*, by the figure of speech which understands the whole from its part. Well, then, if it be allowable for this man to take the whole from a part in the passage, "And man became a living soul,"[2] as if the spirit also was understood to be implied, about which the Scripture there said nothing, why is it not allowable to others to attribute an equally comprehensive sense to the expression, *of one blood*, so that the soul and spirit may be considered as included in it, on the ground that the human being who is signi-fied by the term "*blood*" consists not of body alone, but also of soul and spirit? For just as the controversialist who maintains the propagation of souls, ought not, on the one hand, to press this man too hard, because the Scripture says concerning the first man, "In whom all have sinned"[3] (for the expression is not, In whom the flesh of all has sinned, but "all," that is, "all men," seeing that man is not flesh only); — as, I repeat, he ought not to be too hard pressed himself, because it happens to be written "all men," in such a way that they might be understood simply in respect of the flesh; so, on the other hand, he ought not to bear too hard on those who hold the propagation of souls, on the ground of the phrase, "The whole race of men of one blood," as if this passage proved that flesh alone was transmitted by propagation. For if it is true, as they[4] assert, that soul does not descend from soul, but flesh only from flesh, then the expression, "*of one blood*," does not signify the entire human being, on the principle of a part for the whole, but merely the flesh of one person alone; while that other expression, "In whom all have sinned," must be so understood as to indicate merely the flesh of all men, which has been handed on from the first man, the Scripture signifying a part by the whole. If, on the other hand, it is true that the entire human being is propagated of each man, himself also entire, consisting of body, soul, and spirit, then the passage, "In whom all have sinned," must be taken in its proper literal sense; and the other phrase, "*of one blood*," is used metaphorically, the whole being signified by a part, that is to say, the whole man who consists of soul and flesh; or rather (as this person is fond of putting it) of soul, and spirit, and flesh. For both modes of expression the Holy Scriptures are in the habit of employing, putting both a part for the whole and the whole for a part. A part, for instance, implies the whole, in the place where it is said, "Unto Thee shall all flesh come;"[5] the whole man being understood by the term *flesh*. And the whole sometimes implies a part, as when it is said that Christ was buried, whereas it was only His flesh that was buried. Now as regards the statement which is made in the apostle's testimony, to the effect that "He giveth life and spirit to all," I suppose that nobody, after the foregoing discussion, will be moved by it. No doubt "He giveth;" the fact is not in dispute; our question is, How does He give it? By fresh inbreathing in every instance, or by propagation? For with perfect propriety is He said to give the substance of the flesh to the

---

[1] Acts xvii. 25.    [2] Gen. ii. 7.

[3] Rom. v. 12.
[4] Another reading has "he asserts," *i.e.* Augustin's opponent, Victor.
[5] Ps. lxv. 2.

human being, though at the same time it is not denied that He gives it by means of propagation.

## CHAP. 29 [XVIII.] — THE SIXTH PASSAGE OF SCRIPTURE QUOTED BY VICTOR.

Let us now look at the quotation from Genesis, where the woman was created out of the side of the man, and was brought to him, and he said: "This is now bone of my bones, and flesh of my flesh." Our opponent thinks that "Adam ought to have said, 'Soul of my soul, or spirit of my spirit,' if this, too, had been derived from him." But, in fact, they who maintain the opinion of the propagation of souls feel that they possess a more impregnable defence of their position in the fact that in the Scripture narrative which informs us that God took a rib out of the man's side and formed it into a woman, it is not added that He breathed into her face the breath of life; for this reason, as they say, because she had already been ensouled[1] from the man. If, indeed, she had not, they say, the sacred Scripture would certainly not have kept us in ignorance of the circumstance. With regard to the fact that Adam says, "This is now bone of my bone, and flesh of my flesh,"[2] without adding, Spirit or soul, from my spirit or soul, they may answer, just as it has been already shown, that the expression, "my flesh and bone," may be understood as indicating the whole by a part, only that the portion that was taken out of man was not dead, but ensouled;[1] for no good ground for denying that the Almighty was able to do all this is furnished by the circumstance that not a human being could be found capable of cutting off a part of a man's flesh along with the soul. Adam went on, however, to say, "She shall be called woman, because she was taken out of man."[2] Now, why does he not rather say (and thus confirm the opinion of our opponents), "Since her flesh was taken out of man"? As the case stands, indeed, they who hold the opposite view may well contend, from the fact that it is written, not woman's flesh, but the woman herself was taken out of man, that she must be considered in her entire nature endued with soul and spirit. For although the soul is undistinguished by sex, yet when women are mentioned it is not necessary to regard them apart from the soul. On no other principle would they be thus admonished with respect to self-adornment. "Not with braided hair, or gold, or pearls, or costly array; but which (says the apostle) becometh women professing godliness with a good conversation."[3] Now, "godliness," of course, is an inner principle in the soul or spirit; and yet they are called women, although the ornamentation concerns that internal portion of their nature which has no sex.

## CHAP. 30 — THE DANGER OF ARGUING FROM SILENCE.

Now, while the disputants are thus contending with one another in alternate argument, I so judge between them that they must not rely on uncertain evidence; nor make bold assertions on points of which they are ignorant. For if the Scripture had said, "God breathed into the woman's face the breath of life, and she became a living soul," it would not have followed even then that the human soul is not derived by propagation from parents, except the same statement were likewise made concerning their son. For it might have been that whilst an unensouled[4] member taken from the body might require to be ensouled,[4] yet that the soul of the son might be derived from the father, transfused by propagation through the mother. There is, however, an absolute silence on the point; it is entirely concealed from our view. Nothing is denied, but at the same time nothing is affirmed. And thus, if in any place the Scripture is possibly not quite silent, the point requires to be supported by clearer proofs. Whence it follows, that neither they who maintain the propagation of souls receive any assistance from the circumstance that God did not breathe into the woman's face; nor ought they, who deny this doctrine on the ground that Adam did not say, "This is soul of my soul," to persuade themselves to believe what they know nothing of. For just as it has been possible for the Scripture to be silent on the point of the woman's having received her soul, like the man, by the inbreathing of God, without the question before us being solved, but, on the contrary, remaining open; so has it been possible for the same question to remain open and unsolved, notwithstanding the silence of Scripture, as to whether or not Adam said, This is soul of my soul. And hence, if the soul of the first woman comes from the man, a part signifies the whole in his exclamation, "This is now bone of my bones, and flesh of my flesh;" inasmuch as not her flesh alone, but the entire woman, was taken out of man. If, however, it is not from the man, but came by God's inbreathing into her, as at first into the man, then the whole signifies a part in the passage, "She was taken out of the man;" since on the supposition it was not her whole self, but her flesh that was taken.

## CHAP. 31. — THE ARGUMENT OF THE APOLLINARIANS TO PROVE THAT CHRIST WAS WITHOUT THE HUMAN SOUL OF THIS SAME SORT.

Although, then, this question remains unsolved

---

[1] "Animata," possessing the "anima," or soul.
[2] Gen. ii. 23.　　　[3] 1 Tim. ii. 9, 10.

[4] Animari," or endued with the "anima," or soul.

by these passages of Scripture, which are certainly indecisive so far as pertains to the point before us, yet I am quite sure of this, that those persons who think that the soul of the first woman did not come from her husband's soul, on the ground of its being only said, "Flesh of my flesh," and not, "Soul of my soul," do, in fact, argue in precisely the same manner as the Apollinarians argue, and all such gainsayers, in opposition to the Lord's human soul, which they deny for no other reason than because they read in the Scripture, "The Word was made flesh."[1] For if, say they, there was a soul in Him also, it ought to have been said, "The Word was made man." But the reason why the great truth is stated in the terms in question really is, that under the designation *flesh*, Holy Scripture is accustomed to describe the entire human being, as in the passage, "And all flesh shall see the salvation of God."[2] For flesh alone without the soul cannot see anything. Besides, many other passages of the Holy Scriptures go to make it manifest, without any ambiguity, that in the man Christ there is not only flesh, but a human — that is, a reasonable — soul also. Whence they, who maintain the propagation of souls, might also understand that a part is put for the whole in the passage, "Bone of my bone, and flesh of my flesh," in such wise that the soul, too, be understood as implied in the words, in the same manner as we believe that the Word became flesh, not without the soul. All that is wanted is, that they should support their opinion of the propagation of souls on passages which are unambiguous; just as other passages of Scripture show us that Christ possesses a human soul. On precisely the same principle we advise the other side also, who do away with the opinion of the propagation of souls, that they should produce certain proofs for their assertion that souls are created by God in every fresh case by insufflation, and that they should then maintain the position that the saying, "This is bone of my bone, and flesh of my flesh," was not spoken figuratively as a part for the whole, including the soul in its signification, but in a bare literal sense of the flesh alone.

### CHAP. 32 [XIX.] — THE SELF-CONTRADICTION OF VICTOR AS TO THE ORIGIN OF THE SOUL.

Under these circumstances, I find that this treatise of mine must now be closed. It contains, in fact, all that seemed to me chiefly necessary to the subject under discussion. They who peruse its contents will know how to be on their guard against agreeing with the person whose two books you sent me, so as not to believe with

him, that souls are produced by the breath of God in such wise as not to be made out of nothing. The man, indeed, who supposes this, however much he may in words deny the conclusion, does in reality affirm that souls have the substance of God, and are His offspring, not by endowment, but by nature. For from whomsoever a man derives the origin of his nature, from him, in all sober earnestness, it must needs be admitted, that he also derives the kind of his nature. But this author is, after all, self-contradictory : at one time he says that "souls are the offspring of God, — not, indeed, by nature, but by endowment ;" and at another time he says, that "they are not made out of nothing, but derive their origin from God." Thus he does not hesitate to refer them to the nature of God, a position which he had previously denied.

### CHAP. 33. — AUGUSTIN HAS NO OBJECTION TO THE OPINION ABOUT THE PROPAGATION OF SOULS BEING REFUTED, AND THAT ABOUT THEIR INSUFFLATION BEING MAINTAINED.

As for the opinion, that new souls are created by inbreathing without being propagated, we certainly do not in the least object to its maintenance, — only let it be by persons who have succeeded in discovering some new evidence, either in the canonical Scriptures, in the shape of unambiguous testimony towards the solution of a most knotty question, or else in their own reasonings, such as shall not be opposed to catholic truth, but not by such persons as this man has shown himself to be. Unable to find anything worth saying, and at the same time unwilling to suspend his disputatious propensity, without measuring his strength at all, in order to avoid saying nothing, he boldly affirmed that "the soul deserved to be polluted by the flesh," and that "the soul deserved to become sinful ;" though previous to its incarnation he was unable to discover any merit in it, whether good or evil. Moreover, that "in infants departing from the body without baptism original sin may be remitted, and that the sacrifice of Christ's body must be offered for them," who have not been incorporated into Christ through His sacraments in His Church, and that "they, quitting this present life without the laver of regeneration, not only can go to rest, but can even attain to the kingdom of heaven." He has propounded a good many other absurdities, which it would be evidently tedious to collect together, and to consider in this treatise. If the doctrine of the propagation of souls is false, may its refutation not be the work of such disputants ; and may the defence of the rival principle of the insufflation of new souls in every creative act, proceed from better hands.

---

[1] John i. 14.　　　[2] Luke iii. 6, and Isa. xl. 5.

CHAP. 34. — THE MISTAKES WHICH MUST BE AVOIDED BY THOSE WHO SAY THAT MEN'S SOULS ARE NOT DERIVED FROM THEIR PARENTS, BUT ARE AFRESH INBREATHED BY GOD IN EVERY INSTANCE.

All, therefore, who wish to maintain that new souls are rightly said to be breathed into persons at their birth, and not derived from their parents, must by all means be cautious on each of the four points which I have already mentioned. That is to say, do not let them affirm that souls become sinful by another's original sin; do not let them affirm that infants who died unbaptized can possibly reach eternal life and the kingdom of heaven by the remission of original sin in any other way whatever; do not let them affirm that souls had sinned in some other place previous to their incarnation, and that on this account they were forcibly introduced into sinful flesh; nor let them affirm that the sins which were not actually found in them were, because they were foreknown, deservedly punished, although they were never permitted to reach that life where they could be committed. Provided that they affirm none of these points, because each of them is simply false and impious, they may, if they can, produce any conclusive testimonies of the Holy Scriptures on this question; and they may maintain their own opinion, not only without any prohibition from me, but even with my approbation and best thanks. If, however, they fail to discover any very decided authority on the point in the divine oracles, and are obliged to propound any one of the four opinions by reason of their failure, let them restrain their imagination, lest they should be driven in their difficulty to enunciate the now damnable and very recently condemned heresy of Pelagius, to the effect that the souls of infants have not original sin. It is, indeed, better for a man to confess his ignorance of what he knows nothing about, than either to run into heresy which has been already condemned, or to found some new heresy, while recklessly daring to defend over and over again opinions which only display his ignorance. This man has made some other absurb mistakes, indeed many, in which he has wandered out of the beaten track of truth, without going, however, to dangerous

lengths; and I would like, if the Lord be willing, to write even to himself something on the subject of his books; and probably I shall point them all out to him, or a good many of them if I should be unable to notice all.

CHAP. 35 [XX.] — CONCLUSION.

As for this present treatise, which I have thought it proper to address to no other person in preference to yourself, who have taken a kindly and true interest both in our common faith and my character, as a true catholic and a good friend, you will give it to be read or copied by any persons you may be able to find interested in the subject, or may deem worthy to be trusted. In it I have thought proper to repress and confute the presumption of this young man, in such a way, however, as to show that I love him, wishing him to be amended rather than condemned, and to make such progress in the great house which is the catholic Church, whither the divine compassion has conducted him, that he may be therein "a vessel unto honour, sanctified, and meet for the Master's use, and prepared unto every good work," [1] both by holy living and sound teaching. But I have this further to say: if it behoves me to bestow my love upon him, as I sincerely do, how much more ought I to love you, my brother, whose affection towards me and whose catholic faith I have found by the best of proofs to be cautious and sober! The result of your loyalty has been, that you have, with a brother's real love and duty, taken care to have the books, which displeased you, and wherein you found my name treated in a way which ran counter to your liking, copied out and forwarded to me. Now, I am so far from feeling offended at this charitable act of yours, because you did it, that I think I should have had a right, on the true claims of friendship, to have been angry with you if you had not done it. I therefore give you my most earnest thanks. Moreover, I have afforded a still plainer indication of the spirit in which I have accepted your service, by instantly composing this treatise for your consideration, as soon as I had read those books of his.

---

[1] 2 Tim. ii. 21.

# BOOK II.

## *IN THE SHAPE OF A LETTER ADDRESSED TO THE PRESBYTER PETER.*

HE ADVISES PETER NOT TO INCUR THE IMPUTATION OF HAVING APPROVED OF THE
BOOKS WHICH HAD BEEN ADDRESSED TO HIM BY VICTOR ON THE ORIGIN OF THE
SOUL, BY ANY USE HE MIGHT MAKE OF THEM, NOR TO TAKE AS CATHOLIC DOC-
TRINES THAT PERSON'S RASH UTTERANCES CONTRARY TO THE CHRISTIAN FAITH.
VICTOR'S VARIOUS ERRORS, AND THOSE, TOO, OF A VERY SERIOUS CHARACTER, HE
POINTS OUT AND BRIEFLY CONFUTES; AND HE CONCLUDES WITH ADVISING PETER
HIMSELF TO TRY TO PERSUADE VICTOR TO AMEND HIS ERRORS.

To his Lordship, my dearly beloved brother and fellow-presbyter Peter, Augustin, bishop, sendeth greeting in the Lord.

### CHAP. 1 [I.] — DEPRAVED ELOQUENCE AN INJURIOUS ACCOMPLISHMENT.

There have reached me the two books of Vincentius Victor, which he addressed in writing to your Holiness; they have been forwarded to me by our brother Renatus, a layman indeed, but a person who has a prudent and religious care about the faith both of himself and of all he loves. On reading these books, I saw that their author was a man of great resources in speech, of which he had enough, and more than enough; but that on the subjects of which he wished to teach, he was as yet insufficiently instructed. If, however, by the gracious gift of the Lord this qualification were also conferred upon him, he would be serviceable to many. For he possesses in no slight degree the faculty of explaining and beautifying what he thinks; all that is wanted is, that he should first take care to think rightly. Depraved eloquence is a hurtful accomplishment; for to persons of inadequate information it always carries the appearance of truth in its readiness of speech. I know not, indeed, how you received his books; but if I am correctly informed, you are said, after reading them, to have been so greatly overjoyed, that you (though an elderly man and a presbyter) kissed the face of this youthful layman, and thanked him for having taught you what you had been previously ignorant of. Now, in this conduct of yours I do not disapprove of your humility; indeed, I rather commend it; for it was not the man whom you praised, but the truth itself which deigned to speak to you through him: only I wish you were able to point out to

me what was the truth which you received through him. I should, therefore, be glad if you would show me, in your answer to this letter, what it was he taught you. Be it far from me to be ashamed to learn from a presbyter, since you did not blush to be instructed by a layman, in proclaiming and imitating your humble conduct, if the lessons were only true in which you received instruction.

### CHAP. 2 [II.] — HE ASKS WHAT THE GREAT KNOWLEDGE IS THAT VICTOR IMPARTS.

Therefore, brother greatly beloved, I desire to know what you learned of him, in order that, if I have already possessed the knowledge, I may participate in your joy; but if I happen to be ignorant, I may be instructed by you. Did you not then understand that there are two somethings, soul and spirit, according as it is said in Scripture, "Thou wilt separate my soul from my spirit"?[1] And that both of them pertain to man's nature, so that the whole man consists of spirit, and soul, and body? Sometimes, however, these two are combined together under the designation of *soul;* for instance, in the passage, "And man became a living soul."[2] Now, in this place the *spirit* is implied. Similarly in sundry passages the two are described under the name of spirit, as when it is written, "And He bowed His head and gave up the spirit;"[3] in which passage it is the soul that must also be understood. And that the two are of one and the same substance? I suppose that you already knew all this. But if you did not, then you may as well know that you have not acquired any great knowledge, the ignorance of which would be attended with much danger.

---

[1] Job vii. 14. Ἀπαλλάξεις ἀπὸ πνεύματός μου τὴν ψυχήν μου, Sept.  [2] Gen. ii. 7.  [3] John xix. 30.

And if there must be any more subtle discussion on such points, it would be better to carry on the controversy with himself, whose wordy qualities we have already discovered. The questions we might consider are : whether, when mention is made of the soul, the spirit is also implied in the term in such a way that the two comprise the soul, the spirit being, as it were, some part of it, — whether, in fact (as this person seemed to think), under the designation *soul*, the whole is so designated from only a part ; or else, whether the two together make up the spirit, that which is properly called soul being a part thereof ; whether again, in fact, the whole is not called from only a part, when the term *spirit* is used in such a wide sense as to comprehend the soul also, as this man supposes. These, however, are but subtle distinctions, and ignorance about them certainly is not attended with any great danger.

## CHAP. 3. — THE DIFFERENCE BETWEEN THE SENSES OF THE BODY AND SOUL.

Again, I wonder whether this man taught you the difference between the bodily senses and the sensibilities of the soul ; and whether you, who were a person of considerable age and position before you took lessons of this man, used to consider to be one and the same that faculty by which white and black are distinguished, which sparrows even see as well as ourselves, and that by which justice and injustice are discriminated, which Tobit also perceived even after he lost the sight of his eyes.[1] If you held the identity, then, of course, when you heard or read the words, " Lighten my eyes, that I sleep not in death,"[2] you merely thought of the eyes of the body. Or if this were an obscure point, at all events when you recalled the words of the apostle, " The eyes of your heart being enlightened,"[3] you must have supposed that we possessed a heart somewhere between our forehead and cheeks. Well, I am very far from thinking this of you, so that this instructor of yours could not have given you such a lesson.

## CHAP. 4. — TO BELIEVE THE SOUL IS A PART OF GOD IS BLASPHEMY.

And if you happened to suppose, before receiving the instruction from this teacher, which you are rejoicing to have received, that the human soul is a portion of God's nature, then you were ignorant how false and terribly dangerous this opinion was. And if you only were taught by this person that the soul is not a portion of God, then I bid you thank God as earnestly as you can that you were not taken away out of the body before learning so important a lesson.

For you would have quitted life a great heretic and a terrible blasphemer. However, I never could have believed this of you, that a man who is both a catholic and a presbyter of no contemptible position like yourself, could by any means have thought that the soul's nature is a portion of God. I therefore cannot help expressing to your beloved self my fears that this man has by some means or other taught you that which is decidedly opposed to the faith which you were holding.

## CHAP. 5 [III.] — IN WHAT SENSE CREATED BEINGS ARE OUT OF GOD.

Now, just because I do not suppose that you, a member of the catholic Church, ever believed the human soul to be a portion of God, or that the soul's nature is in any degree identical with God's, I have some apprehension lest you may have been induced to fall in with this man's opinion, that " God did not make the soul from nothing, but that the soul is so far out of Him as to have emanated from Him." For he has put out such a statement as this, with his other opinions, which have led him out of the usual track on this subject to a huge precipice. Now, if he has taught you this, I do not want you to teach it to me ; nay, I should wish you to unlearn what you have been taught. For it is not enough to avoid believing and saying that the soul is a part of God. We do not even say that the Son or the Holy Ghost is a part of God, although we affirm that the Father, the Son, and the Holy Spirit are all of one and the same nature. It is not, then, enough for us to avoid saying that the soul is a part of God, but it is of indispensable importance that we should say that the soul and God are not of one and the self-same nature. This person is therefore right in declaring that " souls are God's offspring, not by nature, but by gift ; " and then, of course, not the souls of all men, but of the faithful. But afterwards he returned to the statement from which he had shrunk, and affirmed that God and the soul are of the same nature — not, indeed, in so many words, but plainly and manifestly to such a purport. For when he says that the soul is out of God, in such a manner that God created it not out of any other nature, nor out of nothing, but out of His own self, what would he have us believe but the very thing which he denies, in other words, even that the soul is of the self-same nature as God Himself is ? For every nature is either God, who has no author ; or out of God, as having Him for its Author. But the nature which has for its author God, out of whom it comes, is either not made, or made. Now, that nature which is not made and yet is out of Him, is either begotten by Him or proceeds from Him. That which is begotten is His only Son,

---

[1] Tobit iv. 5, 6 ; compare ii. 10.  [2] Ps. xiii. 3.  [3] Eph. i. 18.

that which proceedeth is the Holy Ghost, and this Trinity is of one and the self-same nature. For these three are one, and each one is God, and all three together are one God, unchangeable, eternal, without any beginning or ending of time. That nature, on the other hand, which is made is called " creature ; " God is its Creator, even the blessed Trinity. The creature, therefore, is said to be out *of God* in such wise as not to be made out of His nature. It is predicated as out *of Him*, inasmuch as it has in Him the author of its being, not so as to have been born of Him, or to have proceeded from Him, but as having been created, moulded, and formed by Him, in some cases, out of no other substance, — that is, absolutely out of nothing, as, for instance, the heaven and the earth, or rather the whole material of the universe coeval in its creation with the world — but, in some cases, out of another nature already created and in existence, as, for instance, man out of the dust, woman out of the man, and man out of his parents. Still, every creature is out of God, — but out of God as its creator either out of nothing, or out of something previously existing, not, however, as its begetter or its producer from His own very self.

CHAP. 6. — SHALL GOD'S NATURE BE MUTABLE, SINFUL, IMPIOUS, EVEN ETERNALLY DAMNED.

All this, however, I am saying to a catholic : advising with him rather than teaching him. For I do not suppose that these things are new to you ; or that they have been long heard of by you, but not believed. This epistle of mine, you will, I am sure, so read as to recognise in its statement your own faith also, which is by the gracious gift of the Lord the common property of us all in the catholic Church. Since, then (as I was saying), I am now speaking to a catholic, whence I pray you tell me, do you suppose that the soul, I will not say your soul or my own soul, but the soul of the first man, was given to him? If you admit that it came from nothing, made, however, and inbreathed into him by God, then your belief tallies with my own. If, on the contrary, you suppose that it came out of some other created thing, which served as the material, as it were, for the divine Artificer to make the soul out of, just as the dust was the material of which Adam was formed, or the rib whence Eve was made, or the waters whence the fishes and the fowls were created, or the ground out of which the terrestrial animals were formed : then this opinion is not catholic, nor is it true. But further, if you think, which may God forbid, that the divine Creator made, or is still making, human souls neither out of nothing, nor out of some other created thing, but out of His own self, that is, out of His own nature, then you have learnt this of your new instructor ;

but I cannot congratulate you, or flatter you, on the discovery. You have wandered along with him very far from the catholic faith. Better would it be, though it would be untrue, yet it would be better, I say, and more tolerable, that you should believe the soul to have been made out of some other created substance which God had already formed, than out of God's own uncreated substance, so that what is mutable, and sinful, and impious, and if persistent to the end in the impiety will have to suffer eternal damnation, should not with horrible blasphemy be referred to the nature of God ! Away, brother, I beseech you, away with this, I will not call it faith, but execrably impious error. May God avert from you, a man of gravity and a presbyter, the misery of being seduced by a youthful layman ; and, while supposing that your opinion is the catholic faith, of being lost from the number of the faithful. For I must not deal with you as I might with him ; nor does this tremendous error, when yours, deserve the same indulgence as being that of this young man, although you may have derived it from him. *He* has but just now found his way to the catholic fold to get healing and safety ;[1] *you* have a rank among the very shepherds of that fold. But we would not that a sheep which comes to the Lord's flock for shelter from error, should be healed of his sores in such a way, as first to infect and destroy the shepherd by his contagious presence.

CHAP. 7. — TO THINK THE SOUL CORPOREAL AN ERROR.

But if you say to me, He has not taught me this ; nor have I by any means given my assent to this erroneous opinion of his, however much I was enchanted by the sweetness of his eloquent and elegant discourse ; then I earnestly thank God. Still I cannot help asking, why, even with kisses, as the report goes, you expressed your gratitude to him for having taught you what you were ignorant of, previous to hearing his discussion. Now if it be a false report which makes you to have done and said so much, then I beg you to be kind enough to give me this assurance, that the idle rumour may be stopped by your own written authority. If, however, it is true that you bestowed your thanks with such humility upon this man, I should rejoice, indeed, if he has not taught you to believe the opinion which I have already pointed out as a detestable one, and to be carefully avoided as such. Nor shall I find fault [IV.] if your humble thanks to your instructor were further earned by your having acquired from discussions with him some other true and

---

[1] See below in ch. 14 [X.].

useful knowledge. But may I ask you what it is? Is it that the soul is not spirit, but body? Well, I really do not think ignorance on such a point is any great injury to Christian learning; and if you indulge in more subtle disputes about the different kinds of bodily substance, I think the information you obtain is more difficult than serviceable. If, however, the Lord will that I should write to this young man himself, as I desire to do, then perhaps your loving self[1] will know to what extent you are not indebted to him for your instruction; although you rejoice in what you have learnt from him. And now I request you not to feel annoyance in writing me an answer; so that what is clearly useful and pertinent to our indispensable faith may not by any chance turn out to be something different.

CHAP. 8. — THE THIRST OF THE RICH MAN IN HELL DOES NOT PROVE THE SOUL TO BE CORPOREAL.

Now with regard to the point, which with perfect propriety and great soundness of view he believes, that souls after quitting the body are judged, before they come to that final judgment to which they must submit when their bodies are restored to them, and are either tormented or glorified in the very same flesh wherein they once lived here on earth; is it, let me ask you, the case that you were really ignorant of this? Who ever had his mind so obstinately set against the gospel as not to hear these truths, and after hearing to believe them, in the parable of the poor man who was carried away after death to Abraham's bosom, and of the rich man who is set forth as suffering torment in hell?[2] But has this man taught you how it was that the soul apart from the body could crave from the beggar's finger a drop of water;[3] when he himself confessed, that the soul did not require bodily aliment except for the purpose of protecting the perishing body which encloses it from dissolution? These are his words: "Is it," asks he, "because the soul craves meat and drink, that we suppose material food passes into it?" Then shortly afterwards he says: "From this circumstance it is understood and proved, that the sustenance of meat and drink is not wanted for the soul, but for the body: for which clothing also, in addition to food, is provided in like manner; so that the supplying of food seems to be necessary to that nature, which is also fitted for wearing clothes." This opinion of his he expounds clearly enough; but he adds some illustrative similes, and says: "Now what do we suppose the occupier of a house does on an inspection of his dwelling? If he observe the tenement has a shaky roof, or a nodding wall, or a weak foundation, does he not fetch girders and build up buttresses, in order that he may succeed in propping up by his care and diligence the fabric which threatened to fall, so that in the dangerous plight of the residence the peril which evidently overhung the occupier might be warded off? From this simile," says he, "see how the soul craves for its flesh, from which it undoubtedly conceives the craving itself." Such are the very lucid and adequate words in which this young person has explained his ideas: he asserts that it is not the soul, but the body, which requires food; out of a careful regard, no doubt, of the former for the latter, as one that occupies a dwelling-house, and by a prudent repair prevents the downfall with which the fleshly tenement was threatened. Well, now, let him go on to explain to you what probable ruin this particular soul of the rich man was so eager to prevent by propping up, seeing that it no longer possessed a mortal body, and yet suffered thirst, and begged for the drop of water from the poor man's finger. Here is a good knotty question for this astute instructor of elderly men to exercise himself on; let him inquire, and find a solution if he can: for what purpose did that soul in hell beg the aliment of ever so small a drop of water, when it had no ruinous tenement to support?

CHAP. 9 [V.] — HOW COULD THE INCORPOREAL GOD BREATHE OUT OF HIMSELF A CORPOREAL SUBSTANCE?

In that he believes God to be truly incorporeal, I congratulate him that herein, at all events, he has kept himself uninfluenced by the ravings of Tertullian. For *he* insisted, that as the soul is corporeal, so likewise is God.[4] It is therefore specially surprising that our author, who differs from Tertullian in this point, yet labours to persuade us that the incorporeal God does not make the soul out of nothing, but exhales it as a corporeal breath out of Himself. What a wonderful learning that must be to which every age erects its attentive ears, and which contrives to gain for its disciples men of advanced years, and even presbyters! Let this eminent man read what he has written, read it in public; let him invite to hear the reading well-known persons and unknown ones, learned and unlearned. Old men, assemble with your younger instructors; learn what you used to know nothing about; hear now what you had never heard before. Behold, according to the teaching of this scribe, God creates a breath, not out of something else which exists in some way or other, and not out of that which absolutely has

[4] See Tertullian's treatise *On the Soul* in *The Ante-Nicene Christian Fathers*, vol. iii. p. 181 sq. See also Augustin, *On Heresies*, 86, and *Epistles*, No. 190.

no existence; but out of that which He is Himself, perfectly incorporeal, He breathes a body: so that He actually changes His own incorporeal nature into a body, before it undergoes the change into the body of sin. Does he say, that He does not change something out of His own nature, when He creates breath? Then, of course, He does not make that breath out of Himself: for He is not Himself one thing, and His nature another thing. What is this insane man thinking of? But if he says that God creates breath out of His own nature in such a way as to remain absolutely entire Himself, this is not the question. The question is, whether that which comes not of some previously created substance, nor from nothing, but from Him, is not what He is, that is, of the same nature and essence? Now He remains absolutely entire after the generation of His Son; but because He begat Him of His own nature, He did not beget a something which was different from that which He is Himself. For, putting to one side the circumstance that the Word took on Himself a human nature and became flesh, the Word who is the Son of God is another but not another thing: that is, He is another person but not a different nature. And whence does this come to pass, except from the fact that He is not created out of something else, or out of nothing, but was begotten out of Himself; not that He might be better than He was, but that He might be altogether even what *He* is of whom He is begotten; that is, of one and the same nature, equal, co-eternal, in every way like, equally unchangeable, equally invisible, equally incorporeal, equally God; in a word, that He might be altogether what the Father is, except that He actually is Himself the Son, and not the Father? But if He remains Himself the same God entire and unimpaired, but yet creates something different from Himself, and worse than Himself, not out of nothing, nor out of some other creature, but out of His very self; and that something emanates as a body out of the incorporeal God; then God forbid that a catholic should imbibe such an opinion, for it does not flow from the divine fountain, but it is a mere fiction of the human mind.

CHAP. 10 [VI.] — CHILDREN MAY BE FOUND OF LIKE OR OF UNLIKE DISPOSITIONS WITH THEIR PARENTS.

Then, again, how ineptly he labours to free the soul, which he supposes to be corporeal, from the passions of the body, raising questions about the soul's infancy; about the soul's emotions, when paralysed and oppressed; about the amputation of bodily limbs, without cutting or dividing the soul. But in dealing with such points as these, my duty is to treat rather with him than with you; it is for him to labour to assign a reason for all he says. In this way we shall not seem to wish to be too importunate with an elderly man's gravity on the subject of a young man's work. As to the similarity of disposition to the parents which is discovered in their children, he does not dispute its coming from the soul's seed. Accordingly, this is the opinion also of those persons who do away with the soul's propagation; but the opposite party who entertain this theory do not place on this the weight of their assertion. For they observe also that children are unlike their parents in disposition; and the reason of this, as they suppose, is, that one and the same person very often has various dispositions himself, unlike each other, — not, of course, that he has received another soul, but that his life has undergone a change for the better or for the worse. So they say that there is no impossibility in a soul's not possessing the same disposition which he had by whom it was propagated, seeing that the selfsame soul may have different dispositions at different times. If, therefore, you think that you have learnt this of him, that the soul does not come to us by natural transmission at birth, — I only wish that you had discovered from him the truth of the case, — I would with the greatest pleasure resign myself to your hands to learn the whole truth. But really to learn is one thing, and to seem to yourself to have learned is another thing. If, then, you suppose that you have learned what you still are ignorant of, you have evidently not learnt, but given a random credence to a pleasant hearsay. Falsity has stolen over you in the suavity.[1] Now I do not say this from feeling as yet any certainty as to the proposition being false, which asserts that souls are created afresh by God's inbreathing rather than derived from the parents at birth; for I think that this is a point which still requires proof from those who find themselves able to teach it. No; my reason for saying it is, that this person has discussed the whole subject in such a way as not only not to solve the point still in dispute, but even to indulge in statements which leave no doubt as to their falsity. In his desire to prove things of doubtful import, he has boldly stated things which undoubtedly merit reprobation.

CHAP. 11 [VII.] — VICTOR IMPLIES THAT THE SOUL HAD A "STATE" AND "MERIT" BEFORE INCARNATION.

Would you hesitate yourself to reprobate what he has said concerning the soul? "You will not have it," he says, "that the soul contracts from the sinful flesh the health, to which holy

---

[1] This play of words too inadequately represents Augustin's *Subrepsit tibi falsiloquium per suaviloquium.*

state you can see it in due course pass by means of the flesh, so as to amend its state through that by which it had lost its merit? Or is it because baptism washes the body that what is believed to be conferred by baptism does not pass on to the soul or spirit? It is only right, therefore, that the soul should, by means of the flesh, repair that old condition which it had seemed to have gradually lost through the flesh, in order that it may begin a regenerate state by means of that whereby it had deserved to be polluted." [1] Now, do observe how grave an error this teacher has fallen into! He says that " the soul repairs its condition by means of the flesh through which it had lost its merit." The soul, then, must have possessed some state and some good merit previous to the flesh, which he would have that it recovers through the flesh, when the flesh is cleansed in the laver of regeneration. Therefore, previous to the flesh, the soul had lived somewhere in a good state and merit, which state and merit it lost when it came into the flesh. His words are, " that the soul repairs by means of the flesh that primitive condition which it had seemed to have gradually lost through the flesh." The soul, then, possessed before the flesh, an ancient condition (for his term *"primitive"* describes the antiquity of the state) ; and what could that ancient condition have possibly been, but a blessed and laudable state? Now, he avers that this happiness is recovered through the sacrament of baptism, although he will not admit that the soul derives its origin through propagation from that soul which was once manifestly happy in paradise. How is it, then, that in another passage he says that " he constantly affirms of the soul that it exists not by propagation, nor comes out of nothing, nor exists by its own self, nor previous to the body"? You see how in this place he insists that souls do exist prior to the body somewhere or other, and that in so happy a state that the same happiness is restored to them by means of baptism. But, as if forgetful of his own views, he goes on to speak of its " beginning a regenerate state by means of that," meaning the flesh, "whereby it had deserved to be polluted." In a previous statement he had indicated some good desert which had been lost by means of the flesh ; now, however, he speaks of some evil desert, by means of which it had happened that the soul had to come, or be sent, into the flesh ; for his words are, " By which it had deserved to be polluted ; " and if it deserved to be polluted, its merits could not, of course, have been good. Pray let him tell us what sin it had committed previous to its pollution by the flesh, in consequence of which it

merited such pollution by the flesh. Let him, if he can, explain to us a matter which is utterly beyond his power, because it is certainly far above his reach to discover what to tell us on this subject which shall be true.

CHAP. 12 [VIII.] — HOW DID THE SOUL DESERVE TO BE INCARNATED?

He also says some time afterwards : " The soul therefore, if it deserved to be sinful, although it could not have been sinful, yet did not remain in sin ; because, as it was prefigured in Christ, it was bound not to be in a sinful state, even as it was unable to be." [2] Now, my brother, do you, I ask, really think thus? At any rate, have you formed such an opinion, after having read and duly considered his words, and after having reflected upon what extorted from you praise during his reading, and the expression of your gratitude after he had ended? I pray you, tell me what this means : " Although the soul deserved to be sinful, which could not have been sinful." What mean his phrases, *deserved* and *could not?* For it could not possibly have deserved its alleged fate, unless it had been sinful ; nor would it have been, unless it could have been, sinful, — so as, by committing sin previous to any evil desert, it might make for itself a position whence it might, under God's desertion, advance to the commission of other sins. When he said, "which could not have been sinful," did he mean, which would not have been able to be sinful, unless it came in the flesh? But how did it deserve a mission at all into a state where it could be sinful, when it could not possibly have become capable of sinning anywhere else, unless it entered that particular state? Let him, then, tell us how it so deserved. For if it deserved to become capable of sinning, it must certainly have already committed some sin, in consequence of which it deserved to be sinful again. These points, however, may perhaps appear to be obscure, or may be tauntingly said to be of such a character, but they are really most plain and clear. The truth is, he ought not to have said that " the soul deserved to become sinful through the flesh," when he will never be able to discover any desert of the soul, either good or bad, previous to its being in the flesh.

CHAP. 13 [IX.] — VICTOR TEACHES THAT GOD THWARTS HIS OWN PREDESTINATION.

Let us now go on to plainer matters. For while he was confined within these great straits, as to how souls can be held bound by the chain of original sin, when they derive not their origin from the soul which first sinned, but the Creator breathes them afresh at every birth into sinful

---

[1] See below, Book iii. 9.

[2] See above, Book i. 8, and below, Book iii. 11.

flesh, — pure from all contagion and propagation of sin : — in order that he might avoid the objection being brought against his argument, that thus God makes them guilty by such insufflation, he first of all had recourse to the theory drawn from God's prescience, that " He had provided redemption for them." Infants are by the sacrament of this redemption baptized, so that the original sin which they contracted from the flesh is washed away, as if God were remedying His own acts for having made these souls polluted. But afterwards, when he comes to speak of those who receive no such assistance, but expire before they are baptized, he says : " In this place I do not offer myself as an authority, but I present you with an example by way of conjecture. We say, then, that some such method as this must be had recourse to in the case of infants, who, being predestinated for baptism, are yet, by the failing of this life, hurried away before they are born again in Christ. We read," adds he, " it written of such, Speedily was he taken away, lest that wickedness should alter his understanding, or deceit beguile his soul. Therefore He hasted to take him away from among the wicked, for his soul pleased the Lord ; and, being made perfect in a short time, he fulfilled a long time." [1] Now who would disdain having such a teacher as this ? Is it the case, then, with infants, whom people usually wish to have baptized, even hurriedly, before they die, that, if they should be detained ever so short a time in this life, that they might be baptized, and then at once die, wickedness would alter their understanding, and deceit beguile their soul ; and to prevent this happening to them, a hasty death came to their rescue, so that they were suddenly taken away before they were baptized ? By their very baptism, then, they were changed for the worse, and beguiled by deceit, if it was after baptism that they were snatched away. O excellent teaching, worthy to be admired and closely followed ! But he presumed greatly on the prudence of all you who were present at his reading, and especially on yours, to whom he addressed this treatise and handed it after the reading, in supposing that you would believe that the scripture he quoted was intended for the case of unbaptized infants, although it was written of the immature ages of all those saints whom foolish men deem to be hardly dealt with, whenever they are suddenly removed from the present life and are not permitted to attain to the years which people covet for themselves as a great gift of God. What, however, is the meaning of these words of his : " Infants predestinated for baptism, who are yet, by the failing of this life, hurried away before they are born again in Christ," as if some

power of fortune, or fate, or anything else you please, did not permit God to fulfil what He had fore-ordained ? And how is it that He hurries them Himself away, when they have pleased Him ? Then, does He really predestinate them to be baptized, and then Himself hinder the accomplishment of the very thing which He has predestinated ?

CHAP. 14 [X.] — VICTOR SENDS THOSE INFANTS WHO DIE UNBAPTIZED TO PARADISE AND THE HEAVENLY MANSIONS, BUT NOT TO THE KINGDOM OF HEAVEN.

But I beg you mark how bold he is, who is displeased with hesitancy, which prefers to be cautious rather than overknowing in a question so profound as this : " I would be bold to say " — such are his words — " that they can attain to the forgiveness of their original sins, yet not so as to be admitted into the kingdom of heaven. Just as in the case of the thief on the cross, who confessed but was not baptized, the Lord did not give him the kingdom of heaven, but paradise ; [2] the words remaining accordingly in full force, ' Except a man be born again of water and of the Holy Ghost, he shall not enter into the kingdom of heaven.' [3] This is especially true, inasmuch as the Lord acknowledges that in His Father's house are many mansions, [4] by which are indicated the many different merits of those who dwell in them ; so that in these abodes the unbaptized is brought to forgiveness, and the baptized to the reward which by grace has been prepared for him." You observe how the man keeps paradise and the mansions of the Father's house distinct from the kingdom of heaven, so that even unbaptized persons may have an abundant provision in places of eternal happiness. Nor does he see, when he says all this, that he is so unwilling to distinguish the future abode of a baptized infant from the kingdom of heaven as to have no fear in keeping distinct therefrom the very house of God the Father, or the several parts thereof. For the Lord Jesus did not say : In all the created universe, or in any portion of that universe, but, " In my Father's house, are many mansions." But in what way shall an unbaptized person live in the house of God the Father, when he cannot possibly have God for his Father, except he be born again ? He should not be so ungrateful to God, who has vouchsafed to deliver him from the sect of the Donatists or Rogatists, as to aim at dividing the house of God the Father, and to put one portion of it outside the kingdom of heaven, where the unbaptized may be able to dwell. And on what terms does he himself presume that he is to enter into the kingdom of heaven, when from that kingdom he

---

[1] Wisd. iv. 11, 14, 13.        [2] Luke xxiii. 43.        [3] John iii. 5.        [4] John xiv. 2.

excludes the house of the King Himself, in what part soever He pleases? From the case, however, of the thief who, when crucified at the Lord's side, put his hope in the Lord who was crucified with him, and from the case of Dinocrates, the brother of St. Perpetua, he argues that even to the unbaptized may be given the remission of sins and an abode with the blessed; as if any one unbelief in whom would be a sin, had shown him that the thief and Dinocrates had not been baptized. Concerning these cases, however, I have more fully explained my views in the book which I wrote to our brother Renatus.[1] This your loving self will be able to ascertain if you will condescend to read the book; for I am sure our brother will not find it in his heart to refuse you, if you ask him the loan of it.

CHAP. 15 [XI.] — VICTOR "DECIDES" THAT OBLATIONS SHOULD BE OFFERED UP FOR THOSE WHO DIE UNBAPTIZED.

Still he chafes with indecision, and is well-nigh suffocated in the terrible straits of his theory; for very likely he descries with a more sensitive eye than you, the amount of evil which he enunciates, to the effect that original sin in infants is effaced without Christ's sacrament of baptism. It is, indeed, for the purpose of finding an escape to some extent, and tardily, in the Church's sacraments that he says: "In their behalf I most certainly decide that constant oblations and incessant sacrifices must be offered up on the part of the holy priests." Well, then, you may take him if you like for your arbiter, if it were not enough to have him as your instructor. Let him decide that you must offer up the sacrifice of Christ's body even for those who have not been incorporated into Christ. Now this is quite a novel idea, and foreign to the Church's discipline and the rule of truth: and yet, when daring to propound it in his books, he does not modestly say, I rather think; he does not say, I suppose; he does not say, I am of opinion; nor does he say, I at least would suggest, or mention; — but he says, I give it as my decision; so that, should we be (as might be likely) offended by the novelty or the perverseness of his opinion, we might be overawed by the authority of his judicial determination. It is your own concern, my brother, how to be able to bear him as your instructor in these views. Catholic priests, however, of right feeling (and among them you ought to take your place) could never keep quiet — God forbid it — and hear this man pronounce his decisions, when they would wish him rather to recover his senses, and be sorry both for having entertained such opinions, and for having

gone so far as to commit them to writing, and chastise himself with the most wholesome discipline of repentance. "Now it is," says he, "on this example of the Maccabees who fell in battle that I ground the necessity of doing this When they offered stealthily some interdicted sacrifices, and after they had fallen in the battle, we find," says he, "that this remedial measure was at once resorted to by the priests, — sacrifices were offered up to liberate their souls, which had been bound by the guilt of their forbidden conduct."[2] But he says all this, as if (according to his reading of the story) those atoning sacrifices were offered up for uncircumcised persons, as he has decided that these sacrifices of ours must be offered up for unbaptized persons. For circumcision was the sacrament of that period, which prefigured the baptism of our day.

CHAP. 16 [XII.] — VICTOR PROMISES TO THE UNBAPTIZED PARADISE AFTER THEIR DEATH, AND THE KINGDOM OF HEAVEN AFTER THEIR RESURRECTION, ALTHOUGH HE ADMITS THAT THIS OPPOSES CHRIST'S STATEMENT.

But your friend, in comparison with what he has shown himself to be further on, thus far makes mistakes which one may somewhat tolerate. He apparently felt some disposition to relent; not, to be sure, at what he ought to have misgivings about, namely, for having ventured to assert that original sin is relaxed even in the case of the unbaptized, and that remission is given to them of all their sins, so that they are admitted into paradise, that is, to a place of great happiness, and possess a claim to the happy mansions in our Father's house; but he seems to have entertained some regret at having conceded to them abodes of lesser blessedness outside the kingdom of heaven. Accordingly he goes on to say, "Or if any one is perhaps reluctant to believe that paradise is bestowed as a temporary and provisional gift on the soul of the thief or of Dinocrates (for there remains for them still, in the resurrection, the reward of the kingdom of heaven), although that principal passage stands in the way,[3] — 'Except a man be born again of water and of the Spirit, he shall not enter into the kingdom of God,'[4] — he may yet hold my assent as ungrudgingly given to this point; only let him magnify[5] both the aim and the effect of the divine compassion and foreknowledge." These words have I copied, as I read them in his second book. Well, now, could any one have shown on this erroneous

[1] See Book i. of the present treatise, chs. 11 [IX.] and 12 [X.].

[2] This is a loose reference to the narrative in 2 Macc. xii. 39-45.
[3] *Sententia illa principalis,* in which *principalis* may mean either "principal," "chief," or "belonging to the Prince."
[4] John iii. 5.
[5] Or perhaps, "as simply amplifying both the effect and the purpose of," etc., etc.

point greater boldness, recklessness, or presumption? He actually quotes and calls attention to the Lord's weighty sentence, encloses it in a statement of his own, and then says, " Although the opinion is opposed to the ' principal passage,' ' Except a man be born again of water and of the Spirit, he shall not enter into the kingdom of God; ' " he dares then to lift his haughty head in censure against the Prince's judgment: " He may yet hold my assent as ungrudgingly given to this point; " and he explains his point to be, that the souls of unbaptized persons have a claim to paradise as a temporary gift; and in this class he mentions the dying thief and Dinocrates, as if he were prescribing, or rather prejudging, their destination; moreover, in the resurrection, he will have them transferred to a better provision, even making them receive the reward of the kingdom of heaven. " Although," says he, " this is opposed to the sentence of the Prince." Now, do you, my brother, I pray you, seriously consider this question: What sentence of the Prince shall that man deserve to have passed upon him, who imposes on any person an assent of his own which runs counter to the authority of the Prince Himself?

CHAP. 17. — DISOBEDIENT COMPASSION AND COMPASSIONATE DISOBEDIENCE REPROBATED. MARTYRDOM IN LIEU OF BAPTISM.

The new-fangled Pelagian heretics have been most justly condemned by the authority of catholic councils and of the Apostolic See, on the ground of their having dared to give to unbaptized infants a place of rest and salvation, even apart from the kingdom of heaven. This they would not have dared to do, if they did not deny their having original sin, and the need of its remission by the sacrament of baptism. This man, however, professes the catholic belief on this point, admitting that infants are tied in the bonds of original sin, and yet he releases them from these bonds without the laver of regeneration, and after death, in his compassion, he admits them into paradise; while, with a still ampler compassion, he introduces them after the resurrection even to the kingdom of heaven. Such compassion did Saul see fit to assume when he spared the king whom God commanded to be slain; [1] deservedly, however, was his disobedient compassion, or (if you prefer it) his compassionate disobedience, reprobated and condemned, that man may be on his guard against extending mercy to his fellow-man, in opposition to the sentence of Him by whom man was made. Truth, by the mouth of Itself incarnate, proclaims as if in a voice of thunder: " Except

a man be born again of water and of the Spirit, he cannot enter into the kingdom of God." [2] And in order to except martyrs from this sentence, to whose lot it has fallen to be slain for the name of Christ before being washed in the baptism of Christ, He says in another passage, " He that loseth his life for my sake shall find it." [3] And so far from promising the abolition of original sin to any one who has not been regenerated in the laver of Christian faith, the apostle exclaims, " By the offence of one, judgment came upon all men to condemnation." [4] And as a counterbalance against this condemnation, the Lord exhibits the help of His salvation alone, saying, " He that believeth, and is baptized, shall be saved; but he that believeth not shall be damned." [5] Now the mystery of this believing in the case of infants is completely effected by the response of the sureties by whom they are taken to baptism; and unless this be effected, they all pass by the offence of one into condemnation. And yet, in opposition to such clear declarations uttered by the Truth, forth marches before all men a vanity which is more foolish than pitiful, and says: Not only do infants not pass into condemnation, though no laver of Christian faith absolves them from the chain of original sin, but they even after death have an intermediate enjoyment of the felicities of paradise, and after the resurrection they shall possess even the happiness of the kingdom of heaven. Now, would this man dare to say all this in opposition to the firmly-established catholic faith, if he had not presumptuously undertaken to solve a question which transcends his powers touching the origin of the soul?

CHAP. 18 [XIII.] — VICTOR'S DILEMMA AND FALL.

For he is hemmed in within terrible straits by those who make the natural inquiry: " Why has God visited on the soul so unjust a punishment as to have willed to relegate it into a body of sin, since by its consorting with the flesh that began to be sinful, which else could not have been sinful? " For, of course, they say: " The soul could not have been sinful, if God had not commingled it in the participation of sinful flesh." Well, this opponent of mine was unable to discover the justice of God's doing this, especially in consequence of the eternal damnation of infants who die without the remission of original sin by baptism; and his inability was equally great in finding out why the good and righteous God both bound the souls of infants, who He foresaw would derive no advantage from the sacrament of Christian grace, with the chain of original sin, by sending them into the body which they derive from Adam, — the souls them-

---

[1] 1 Sam. xv. 9.

[2] John iii. 5.      [3] Matt. x. 39.      [4] Rom. v. 18.
[5] Mark xvi. 16.

selves being free from all taint of propagation, —and by this means also made them amenable to eternal damnation. No less was he unwilling to admit that these very souls likewise derived their sinful origin from that one primeval soul. And so he preferred escaping by a miserable shipwreck of faith, rather than to furl his sails and steady his oars, in the voyage of his controversy, and by such prudent counsel check the fatal rashness of his course. Worthless in his youthful eye was our aged caution; just as if this most troublesome and perilous question of his was more in need of a torrent of eloquence than the counsel of prudence. And this was foreseen even by himself, but to no purpose; for, as if to set forth the points which were objected to him by his opponents, he says: "After them other reproachful censures are added to the querulous murmurings of those who rail against us; and, as if tossed about in a whirlwind, we are dashed repeatedly among huge rocks." After saying this, he propounded for himself the very dangerous question, which we have already treated, wherein he has wrecked the catholic faith, unless by a real repentance he shall have repaired the faith which he had shattered. That whirlwind and those rocks I have myself avoided, unwilling to entrust my frail barque to their dangers; and when writing on this subject I have expressed myself in such a way as rather to explain the grounds of my hesitancy, than to exhibit the rashness of presumption.[1] This little work of mine excited his derision, when he met with it at your house, and in utter recklessness he flung himself upon the reef: he showed more spirit than wisdom in his conduct. To what lengths, however, that over-confidence of his led him, I suppose that you can now yourself perceive. But I give heartier thanks to God, since you even before this descried it. For all the while he was refusing to check his headlong career, when the issue of his course was still in doubt, he alighted on his miserable enterprise, and maintained that God, in the case of infants who died without Christian regeneration, conferred upon them paradise at once, and ultimately the kingdom of heaven.

CHAP. 19 [XIV.] — VICTOR RELIES ON AMBIGUOUS SCRIPTURES.

The passages of Scripture, indeed, which he has adduced in the attempt to prove from them that God did not derive human souls by propagation from the primitive soul, but as in that first instance that He formed them by breathing them into each individual, are so uncertain and ambiguous, that they can with the utmost facility

be taken in a different sense from that which he would assign to them. This point I have already demonstrated[2] with sufficient clearness, I think, in the book which I addressed to that friend of ours, of whom I have made mention above. The passages which he has used for his proofs, inform us that God gives, or makes, or fashions men's souls; but whence He gives them, or of what He makes or fashions them, they tell us nothing: they leave untouched the question, whether it be by propagation from the first soul, or by insufflation, like the first soul. This writer, however, simply because he reads that God "giveth" souls,[3] "hath made" souls, "formeth" souls, supposes that these phrases amount to a denial of the propagation of souls; whereas, by the testimony of the same scripture, God *gives* men their bodies, or *makes* them, or *fashions* and *forms* them; although no one doubts that the said bodies are given, made, and formed by Him by seminal propagation.

CHAP. 20. — VICTOR QUOTES SCRIPTURES FOR THEIR SILENCE, AND NEGLECTS THE BIBLICAL USAGE.

As for the passage which affirms that "God hath made of one blood all nations of men,"[4] and that in which Adam says, "This is now bone of my bones, and flesh of my flesh,"[5] inasmuch as it is not said in the one, "*of one soul*," and in the other, "*soul of my soul*," he supposes that it is denied that children's souls come from their parents, or the first woman's from her husband; just as if, forsooth, had the sentence run in the way suggested, "*of one soul*," instead of "of one blood," anything else than the whole human being could be understood, without any denial of the propagation of the body. So likewise, if it had been said, "*soul of my soul*," the flesh would not be denied, of course, which evidently had been taken out of the man. Constantly does Holy Scripture indicate the whole by a part, and a part by the whole. For certainly, if in the passage which this man has quoted as his proof it had been said that the human race had been made, not "of one blood," but "of one man," it could not have prejudiced the opinion of those who deny the propagation of souls, although man is not soul alone, nor only flesh, but both. For they would have their answer ready to this effect, that the Scripture here might have meant to indicate a part by the whole, that is to say, the flesh only by the entire human being. In like manner, they who maintain the propagation of souls contend that in the passage where it is said, "of one blood," the human being is implied by the term "blood," on the principle of the whole being expressed by a part. For just as the one party seems to be assisted by the expres-

[1] See Augustin's treatises, *On Free Will*, iii. 21; *On the Merits of Sins*, ii. (last chapter); *Letter* (166) *to Jerome*, and (190) *to Optatus*.

[2] See above in Book i. 17 [XIV.] and following chapters.
[3] Isa. xlii. 5.     [4] Acts xvii. 26.     [5] Gen. ii. 23.

sion, "of one blood," instead of the phrase, "of one man," so the other side evidently gets countenance from the statement being so plainly written, "By one man sin entered into the world, and death by sin ; and so death passed upon all men, for in him all sinned,"[1] instead of its being said, "in whom the flesh of all sinned." Similarly, as one party seems to receive assistance from the fact that Scripture says, "This is now bone of my bones, and flesh of my flesh," on the ground that a part covers the whole ; so, again, the other side derives some advantage from what is written in the immediate sequel of the passage, "She shall be called woman, because she was taken out of her husband." For, according to their contention, the latter clause should have run, "Because her flesh was taken out of her husband," if it was not true that the entire woman, soul and all, but only her flesh, was taken out of man. The fact, however, of the whole matter is simply this, that after hearing both sides, anybody whose judgment is free from party prejudice sees at once that loose quotation is unavailing in this controversy ; for against one party, which maintains the opinion of the propagation of souls, those passages must not be adduced which mention only a part, inasmuch as the Scripture might mean by the part to imply the whole in all such passages ; as, for instance, when we read, "The Word was made flesh,"[2] we of course understand not the flesh only, but the entire human being ; nor against the other party, who deny this doctrine of the soul's propagation, is it of any avail to quote those passages which do not mention a part of the human being, but the whole ; because in these the Scripture might possibly mean to imply a part by the whole ; as we confess that Christ was buried, whereas it was only His flesh that was laid in the sepulchre. We therefore say, that on such grounds there is no ground on the one hand for rashly constructing, nor on the other hand for, with equal rashness, demolishing the theory of propagation ; but we add this advice, that other passages be duly looked out, such as admit of no ambiguity.[3]

CHAP. 21 [XV.] — VICTOR'S PERPLEXITY AND FAILURE.

For these reasons I fail thus far to discover what this instructor has taught you, and what grounds you have for the gratitude you have lavished upon him. For the question remains just as it was, which inquires about the origin of souls, whether God gives, forms, and makes them for men by propagating them from that one soul which He breathed into the first man, or whether it is by His own inbreathing that He does this

in every case, as He did for the first man. For that God *does* form, and make, and bestow souls on men, the Christian faith does not hesitate to aver. Now, when this person endeavoured to solve the question without gauging his own resources, by denying the propagation of souls, and asserting that the Creator inbreathed them into men pure from all contagion of sin, — not out of nothing, but out of Himself, — He dishonoured the very nature of God by opprobriously attributing mutability to it, an imputation which was necessarily untenable. Then, desirous of avoiding all implication which might lead to God's being deemed unrighteous, if He ties with the bond of original sin souls which are pure of all actual sin, although not redeemed by Christian regeneration, he has given utterance to words and sentiments which I only wish he had not taught you. For he has accorded to unbaptized infants such happiness and salvation as even the Pelagian heresy could not have ventured on doing. And yet for all this, when the question touches the many thousands of infants who are born of the ungodly, and die among the ungodly, — I do not mean those whom charitable persons are unable to assist by baptism, however desirous of doing so, but those of whose baptism nobody either has been able or shall be able to think, and for whom no one has offered or is likely to offer the sacrifice which, as this instructor of yours thought, ought to be offered even for those who have not been baptized,[4] — he has discovered no means of solving it. If he were questioned concerning them, what their souls deserved that God should involve them in sinful flesh to incur eternal damnation, never to be washed in the laver of baptism, nor atoned for by the sacrifice of Christ's body and blood, he will then either feel himself at an utter loss, and so will regard our hesitation with a real, though tardy favour ; or else will determine that Christ's body must be offered for all those infants which all the world over die without Christian baptism (their names having been never heard of, since they are unknown in the Church of Christ), although not incorporated into the body of Christ.

CHAP. 22 [XVI.] — PETER'S RESPONSIBILITY IN THE CASE OF VICTOR.

Far be it from you, my brother, that such views should be pleasant to you, or that you should either feel pleasure in having acquired them, or presume ever to teach them. Otherwise, even he would be a far better man than yourself. Because at the commencement of his first book he has prefixed the following modest

---

[1] Rom. v. 12.  [2] John i. 14.
[3] Compare on this chapter Book i. 29.

[4] [The editions give the manifestly false reading *nobis* for *non*, yielding the sense: "even for ourselves who have been baptized." — W.]

and humble preface : " Though I desire to comply with your request, I am only affording a clear proof of my presumption." And a little further on he says,[1] " Inasmuch as I am, indeed, by no means confident of being able to prove what I may have advanced ; and moreover I should always be anxious not to insist on any opinion of my own, if it is found to be an improbable one ; and it would be my hearty desire, in case my own judgment is condemned, earnestly to follow better and truer views. For as it shows evidence of the best intention, and a laudable purpose, to permit yourself to be easily led to truer views of a subject ; so it betokens an obstinate and depraved mind to refuse to turn quickly aside into the pathway of reason." Now, as he said all this sincerely, and still feels as he spoke, he no doubt entertains a very hopeful feeling about a right issue. In similar strain he concludes his second book : " You must not think," says he, " that there is any chance of its ever recoiling invidiously against you, that I constitute you the judge of my words. And lest by chance the sharp eye of some inquisitive reader may have opportunity of turning up and encountering any possible vestiges of elemental error which may be left behind on my illegal sheets, I beg you to tear up page after page with unsparing hand, if need be ; and after expending on me your critical censure, punish me further, by smearing out the very ink which has given form to my worthless words ; so that, having your full opportunity, you may prevent all ridicule, on the score either of the favourable opinion you so strongly entertain of me, or of the inaccuracies which lurk in my writings."

CHAP. 23 [XVII.] — WHO THEY ARE THAT ARE NOT INJURED BY READING INJURIOUS BOOKS.

Forasmuch, then, as he has both commenced and terminated his books with such safeguards, and has placed on your shoulders the religious burden of their correction and emendation, I only trust that he may find in you all that he has asked you for, that you may " correct him righteously in mercy, and reprove him ; whilst the oil of the sinner which anoints his head "[2] is absent from your hands and eyes, — even the indecent compliance of the flatterer, and the deceitful leniency of the sycophant. If, however, you decline to apply correction when you see anything to amend, you offend against love ; but if he does not appear to you to require correction, because you think him to be right in his opinions, then you are wise against truth. He, therefore, is a better man (since he is only too

ready to be corrected, if a true censurer be at hand) than yourself, if either knowing him to be in error you despise him with derision, or ignorant of his wandering course you at the same time closely follow his error. Everything, therefore, which you find in the books that he has addressed and forwarded to you, I beg you to consider with sobriety and vigilance ; and you will perhaps make fuller discoveries than I have myself of statements which deserve to be censured. And as for such of their contents as are worthy of praise and approbation, — whatever good you have learnt therein, and by his instruction, which perhaps you were really ignorant of before, tell us plainly what it is, that all may know that it was for this particular benefit that you expressed your obligations to him, and not for the manifold statements in his books which call for their disapproval, — all, I mean, who, like yourself, heard him read his writings, or who afterwards read the same for themselves : lest in his ornate style they may drink poison, as out of a choice goblet, at your instance, though not after your own example, because they know not precisely what it is you have drunk yourself, and what you have left untasted, and because, from your high character, they suppose that whatever is drunk out of this fountain would be for their health. For what else are hearing, and reading, and copiously depositing things in the memory, than several processes of drinking ? The Lord, however, foretold concerning His faithful followers, that even " if they should drink any deadly thing, it should not hurt them." [3] And thus it happens that they who read with judgment, and bestow their approbation on whatever is commendable according to the rule of faith, and disapprove of things which ought to be reprobated, even if they commit to their memory statements which are declared to be worthy of disapproval, they receive no harm from the poisonous and depraved nature of the sentences. To myself, through the Lord's mercy, it can never become a matter of the least regret, that, actuated by our previous love, I have given your reverend and religious self advice and warning on these points, in whatever way you may receive the admonition for which I have regarded you as possessing the first claim upon me. Abundant thanks, indeed, shall I give unto Him in whose mercy it is most salutary to put one's trust, if this letter of mine shall either find or else make your faith both free from the depraved and erroneous opinions which I have been able herein to point out from this man's books, and sound in catholic integrity.

---

[1] See below in Book iii. 20 (XIV.).        [2] Ps. cxli. 5.        [3] Mark xvi. 18.

# BOOK III.

## *ADDRESSED TO VINCENTIUS VICTOR.*

AUGUSTIN POINTS OUT TO VINCENTIUS VICTOR THE CORRECTIONS WHICH HE OUGHT
TO MAKE IN HIS BOOKS CONCERNING THE ORIGIN OF THE SOUL, IF HE WISHES TO
BE A CATHOLIC. THOSE OPINIONS ALSO WHICH HAD BEEN ALREADY REFUTED IN
THE PRECEDING BOOKS ADDRESSED TO RENATUS AND PETER, AUGUSTIN BRIEFLY
CENSURES IN THIS THIRD BOOK, WHICH IS WRITTEN TO VICTOR HIMSELF : MORE-
OVER, HE CLASSIFIES THEM UNDER ELEVEN HEADS OF ERROR.

CHAP. 1 [I.] — AUGUSTIN'S PURPOSE IN WRITING.

As to that which I have thought it my duty to
write to you, my much-loved son Victor, I would
have you to entertain this above all other
thoughts in your mind, if I seemed to despise
you, that it was certainly not my intention to do
so. At the same time I must beg of you not
to abuse our condescension in such a way as to
suppose that you possess my approval merely
because you have not my contempt. For it is
not to follow, but to correct you, that I give you
my love ; and since I by no means despair of
the possibility of your amendment, I do not
want you to be surprised at my inability to despise the man who has my love. Now, since it
was my bounden duty to love you before you
had united with us, in order that you might
become a catholic ; how much more ought I
now to love you since your union with us, to
prevent your becoming a new heretic, and that
you may become so firm a catholic that no
heretic may be able to withstand you ! So far
as appears from the mental endowments which
God has largely bestowed upon you, you would
be undoubtedly a wise man if you only did not
believe that you were one already, and begged
of Him who maketh men wise, with a pious,
humble, and earnest prayer, that you might become one, and preferred not to be led astray
with error rather than to be honoured with the
flattery of those who go astray.

CHAP. 2 [II.] — WHY VICTOR ASSUMED THE NAME
OF VINCENTIUS. THE NAMES OF EVIL MEN
OUGHT NEVER TO BE ASSUMED BY OTHER PER-
SONS.

The first thing which caused me some anxiety
about you was the title which appeared in your
books with your name ; for on inquiring of those
who knew you, and were probably your associates in opinion, who Vincentius Victor was,
I found that you had been a Donatist, or rather
a Rogatist, but had lately come into communion
with the catholic Church. Now, while I was
rejoicing, as one naturally does at the recovery
of those whom he sees rescued from that system
of error, — and in your case my joy was all the
greater because I saw that your ability, which so
much delighted me in your writings, had not
remained behind with the enemies of truth, —
additional information was given me by your
friends which caused me sorrow amid my joy,
to the effect that you wished to have the name
Vincentius prefixed to your own name, inasmuch
as you still held in affectionate regard the successor of Rogatus, who bore this name, as a
great and holy man, and that for this reason you
wished his name to become your surname.
Some persons also told me that you had, moreover, boasted about his having appeared in some
sort of a vision to you, and assisted you in composing those books the subject of which I have
discussed with you in this small work of mine,
and to such an extent as to dictate to you himself the precise topics and arguments which you
were to write about. Now, if all this be true, I
no longer wonder at your having been able to
make those statements which, if you will only
lend a patient ear to my admonition, and with
the attention of a catholic duly consider and
weigh those books, you will undoubtedly come
to regret having ever advanced. For he who,
according to the apostle's portrait, "transforms
himself into an angel of light,"[1] has transformed
himself before you into a shape which you
believe to have been, or still to be, an angel of
light. In this way, indeed, he is less able to

---

[1] 2 Cor. xi. 14.

deceive catholics when his transformations are not into angels of light, but into heretics; now, however, that you are a catholic, I should be sorry for you to be beguiled by him. He will certainly feel torture at your having learnt the truth, and so much the more in proportion to the pleasure he formerly experienced in having persuaded you to believe error. With a view, however, to your refraining from loving a dead person, when the love can neither be service-able to yourself nor profitable to him, I advise you to consider for a moment this one point — that he is not, of course, a just and holy man, since you withdrew yourself from the snares of the Donatists or Rogatists on the score of their heresy; but if you do think him to be just and holy, you ruin yourself by holding communion with catholics. You are, indeed, only feigning yourself a catholic if you are in mind the same as he was on whom you bestow your love; and you are aware how terribly the Scripture has spoken on this subject: "The Holy Spirit of discipline will flee from the man who feigns."[1] If, however, you are sincere in communicating with us, and do not merely pretend to be a catholic, how is it that you still love a dead man to such a degree as to be willing even now to boast of the name of one in whose errors you no longer permit yourself to be held? We really do not like your having such a surname, as if you were the monument of a dead heretic. Nor do we like your book to have such a title as we should say was a false one if we read it on his tomb. For we are sure Vincentius is not *Victor*, the conqueror, but *Victus*, the conquered; — may it be, however, with fruitful effect, even as we wish you to be conquered by the truth! And yet your thought was an astute and skilful one, when you designated the books, which you wish us to suppose were dictated to you by his inspiration, by the name of Vincentius Victor; as much as to intimate that it was rather he than you who wished to be designated by the victo-rious appellation, as having been himself the conqueror of error, by revealing to you what were to be the contents of your written treatise. But of what avail is all this to you, my son? Be, I pray you, a true catholic, not a feigned one, lest the Holy Spirit should flee from you, and that Vincentius be unable to profit you at all, into whom the most malignant spirit of error has transformed himself for the purpose of de-ceiving you; for it is from that one that all these evil opinions have proceeded, notwithstanding the artful fraud which has persuaded you to the contrary. If this admonition shall only induce you to correct these errors with the humility of a God-fearing man and the peaceful submission

of a catholic, they will be regarded as the mis-takes of an over-zealous young man, who is eager rather to amend them than to persevere in them. But if he shall have by his influence prevailed on you to contend for these opinions with obstinate perseverance, which God forbid, it will in such a case be necessary to condemn them and their author as heretical, as is re-quired by the pastoral and remedial nature of the Church's charge, to check the dire contagion before it quietly spreads through the heedless masses, while wholesome correction is neglected, under the name but without the reality of love.

CHAP. 3 [III.] — HE ENUMERATES THE ERRORS WHICH HE DESIRES TO HAVE AMENDED IN THE BOOKS OF VINCENTIUS VICTOR. THE FIRST ERROR.

If you ask me what the particular errors are, you may read what I have written to our breth-ren, that servant of God Renatus, and the pres-byter Peter, to the latter of whom you yourself thought it necessary to write the very works of which we are now treating, "in obedience," as you allege, "to his own wish and request." Now, they will, I doubt not, lend you my trea-tises for your perusal if you should like it, and even press them upon your attention without being asked. But be that as it may, I will not miss this present opportunity of informing you what amendments I desire to have made in these writings of yours, as well as in your belief. The first is, that you will have it that "The soul was not so made by God that He made it out of nothing, but out of His own very self."[2] Here you do not reflect what the necessary conclusion is, that the soul must be of the nature of God; and you know very well, of course, how impious such an opinion is. Now, to avoid such impiety as this, you ought so to say that God is the Author of the soul as that it was made by Him, but not of Him. For whatever is of Him (as, for instance, His only-begotten Son) is of the self-same nature as Himself. But, that the soul might not be of the same nature as its Creator, it was made by Him, but not of Him. Or, then, tell me whence it is, or else confess that it is of nothing. What do you mean by that expression of yours, "That it is a certain particle of an exhalation from the nature of God"? Do you mean to say, then, that the exhalation[3] itself from the nature of God, to which the particle in question belongs, is not of the same nature as God is Himself? If this be your meaning, then God made out of nothing that exhalation of which you will have the soul to be a particle. Or, if not out of nothing, pray tell me of what God made it? If He made it out of Himself,

---

[1] Wisd. i. 5.

[2] See above, Book i. 4 and Book ii. 5.    [3] Halitus (breath).

it follows that He is Himself (what should never be affirmed) the material of which His own work is formed. But you go on to say: "When, however, He made the exhalation or breath out of Himself, He remained at the same time whole and entire;" just as if the light of a candle did not also remain entire when another candle is lighted from it, and yet be of the same nature, and not another.

CHAP. 4 [IV.] — VICTOR'S SIMILE TO SHOW THAT GOD CAN CREATE BY BREATHING WITHOUT IMPARTATION OF HIS SUBSTANCE.

"But," you say, "when we inflate a bag, no portion of our nature or quality is poured into the bag, while the very breath, by the current of which the filled bag is extended, is emitted from us without the least diminution of ourselves." Now, you enlarge and dwell upon these words of yours, and inculcate the simile as necessary for our understanding how it is that God, without any injury to His own nature, makes the soul out of His own self, and how, when it is thus made out of Himself, it is not what Himself is. For you ask: "Is this inflation of the bag a portion of our own soul? Or do we create human beings when we inflate bags? Or do we suffer any injury in anything at all when we impart our breath by inflation on diverse things? But we suffer no injury when we transfer breath from ourselves to anything, nor do we ever remember experiencing any damage to ourselves from inflating a bag, the full quality and entire quantity of our breath remaining in us notwithstanding the process." Now, however elegant and applicable this simile seems to you, I beg you to consider how greatly it misleads you. For you affirm that the incorporeal God breathes out a corporeal soul, — not made out of nothing, but out of Himself, — whereas the breath which we ourselves emit is corporeal, although of a more subtle nature than our bodies; nor do we exhale it out of our soul, but out of the air through internal functions in our bodily structure. Our lungs, like a pair of bellows, are moved by the soul (at the command of which also the other members of the body are moved), for the purpose of inhaling and exhaling the atmospheric air. For, besides the aliments, solid or fluid, which constitute our meat and drink, God has surrounded us with this third aliment of the atmosphere which we breathe; and that with so good effect, that we can live for some time without meat and drink, but we could not possibly subsist for a moment without this third aliment, which the air, surrounding us on all sides, supplies us with as we breathe and respire. And as our meat and drink have to be not only introduced into the body, but also to be expelled by passages formed for the purpose, to prevent in-

jury accruing either way (from either not entering or not quitting the body); so this third airy aliment (not being permitted to remain within us, and thus not becoming corrupt by delay, but being expelled as soon as it is introduced) has been furnished, not with different, but with the self-same channels both for its entrance and for its exit, even the mouth, or the nostrils, or both together.

CHAP. 5. — EXAMINATION OF VICTOR'S SIMILE: DOES MAN GIVE OUT NOTHING BY BREATHING?

Prove now yourself what I say, for your own satisfaction in your own case; emit breath by exhalation, and see whether you can continue long without catching back your breath; then again catch it back by inhalation, and see what discomfort you experience unless you again emit it. Now, when we inflate a bag, as you prescribe, we do, in fact, the same thing which we do to maintain life, except that in the case of the artificial experiment our inhalation is somewhat stronger, in order that we may emit a stronger breath, so as to fill and distend the bag by compressing the air we blow into it, rather in the manner of a hard puff than of the gentle process of ordinary breathing and respiration. On what ground, then, do you say, "We suffer no injury whenever we transfer breath from ourselves to any object, nor do we ever remember experiencing any damage to ourselves from inflating a bag, the full quality and entire quantity of our own breath remaining in us notwithstanding the process"? It is very plain, my son, if ever you have inflated a bag, that you did not carefully observe your own performance. For you do not perceive what you lose by the act of inflation by reason of the immediate recovery of your breath. But you can learn all this with the greatest ease if you would simply prefer doing so to stiffly maintaining your own statements for no other reason than because you have made them — not inflating the bag, but inflated yourself to the full, and inflating your hearers (whom you should rather edify and instruct by veritable facts) with the empty prattle of your turgid discourse. In the present case I do not send you to any other teacher than your own self. Breathe, then, a good breath into the bag; shut your mouth instantly, hold tight your nostrils, and in this way discover the truth of what I say to you. For when you begin to suffer the intolerable inconvenience which accompanies the experiment, what is it you wish to recover by opening your mouth and releasing your nostrils? Surely there would be nothing to recover, if your supposition be a correct one, that you have lost nothing whenever you breathe. Observe what a plight you would be in, if by inhalation you did not regain what you had parted with by your breathing outwards. See, too, what loss and injury the insufflation would produce, were it not for the repair and reaction caused by respiration. For unless the breath which you expend in filling the bag should all return by the re-opened channel to discharge its function of nourishing yourself, what, I wonder, would be left remaining to you, — I will not say to inflate another bag, but to supply your very means of living?

CHAP. 6. — THE SIMILE REFORMED IN ACCORDANCE WITH TRUTH.

Well, now, you ought to have thought of all this when you were writing, and not to have brought God before our eyes in that favourite simile of yours, of inflated and inflateable bags, breathing forth souls out of some other nature which was already in existence, just as we ourselves make our breath from the air which surrounds us; or certainly you should not, in a manner which is really as diverse from your similitude as it is abundant in impiety, have represented God as either producing some changeable thing without injury, indeed, to Himself, but yet out of His own substance; or what is worse, creating it in such wise as to be Himself the material of His own work. If, however, we are to employ a similitude drawn from our breathing which shall suitably illustrate this subject, the following one is more credible: Just as we, whenever we breathe, make a breath, not out of our own nature, but, because we are not omnipotent, out of that air that surrounds us, which we inhale and discharge whenever we breathe and respire; and the said breath is neither living nor sentient, although we are ourselves living and sentient; so God can — not, indeed, out of His own nature, but (as being so omnipotent as to be able to create whatever He wills) even out of that which has no existence at all, that is to say, out of nothing — make a breath that is living and sentient, but evidently mutable, though He be Himself immutable.

CHAP. 7 [V.] — VICTOR APPARENTLY GIVES THE CREATIVE BREATH TO MAN ALSO.

But what is the meaning of that, which you have thought proper to add to this simile, with regard to the example of the blessed Elisha because he raised the dead by breathing into his face?[1] Now, do you really suppose that Elisha's breath was made the soul of the child? I could not believe that even you could stray so far away from the truth. If, now, that soul which was taken from the living child so as to cause his death, was itself afterwards restored to him so as to cause his restoration to life: where, I ask, is the pertinence of your remark when you say " that no diminution accrued to Elisha," as if it

could be imagined that anything had been transferred from the prophet to the child to cause his revival? But if you meant no more than that the prophet breathed and remained entire, where was the necessity for your saying that of Elisha, when raising the dead child, which you might with no less propriety say of any one whatever when emitting a breath, and reviving no one? Then, again, you spoke unadvisedly (though God forbid that you should believe the breath of Elisha to have become the soul of the resuscitated child!) when you intimated your meaning to be a desire to keep separate what was first done by God from this that was done by the prophet, in that the One breathed but once, and the other thrice. These are your words: " Elisha breathed into the face of the deceased child of the Shunammite, after the manner of the original creation. And when by the prophet's breathing a divine force inspired the dead limbs, reanimated to their original vigour, no diminution accrued to Elisha, through whose breathing the dead body recovered its revived soul and spirit. Only there is this difference, the Lord breathed but once into man's face and he lived, while Elisha breathed three times into the face of the dead and he lived again." Thus your words sound as if the number of the breathings alone made all the difference, why we should not believe that the prophet actually did what God did. This statement, then, requires to be entirely revised. There was so complete a difference between that work of God and this of Elisha, that the former breathed the breath of life whereby man became a living soul, and the latter breathed a breath which was not itself sentient nor endued with life, but was figurative for the sake of some signification. The prophet did not really cause the child to live again by giving him life, but he procured God's doing that by giving him love.[2] As to what you allege, that he breathed three times, either your memory, as often happens, or a faulty reading of the text, must have misled you. Why need I enlarge? You ought not to be seeking for examples and arguments to establish your point, but rather to amend and change your opinion. I beg of you neither to believe, nor to say, nor to teach " that God made the human soul not out of nothing, but out of His own substance," if you wish to be a catholic.

CHAP. 8 [VI.] — VICTOR'S SECOND ERROR. (SEE ABOVE IN BOOK I. 26 [XVI.].)

Do not, I pray you, believe, say, or teach that " Thus is God ever giving souls through infinite time, just as He who gives is Himself ever

---

[1] 2 Kings iv. 34.

[2] In the original we have here another instance of Augustin's frequent play on words, Non *animando*, ·ed *amando:* " not by ensouling but by loving him," or " not by enlivening but by loving him.''

existent," if you wish to be a catholic. For a time will come when God will not give souls, although He will not therefore Himself cease to exist. Your phrase, "is ever giving," might be understood "to give without cessation," so long as men are born and get offspring, even as it is said of certain men that they are "ever learning, and never coming to the knowledge of the truth." [1] For this term "ever" is not in this passage taken to mean "never ceasing to learn," inasmuch as they do cease to learn when they have ceased to exist in this body, or have begun to suffer the fiery pains of hell. You, however, did not allow your word to be understood in this sense when you said "is ever giving," since you thought that it must be applied to infinite time. And even this was a small matter; for, as if you had been asked to explain your phrase, "ever giving," more explicitly, you went on to say, "just as He is Himself ever existent who gives." This assertion the sound and catholic faith utterly condemns. For be it far from us to believe that God is ever giving souls, just as He is Himself, who gives them, ever existent. He is Himself ever existent in such a sense as never to cease to exist; souls, however, He will not be ever giving; but He will beyond doubt cease to give them when the age of generation ceases, and children are no longer born to whom they are to be given.

#### CHAP. 9 [VII.] — HIS THIRD ERROR. (SEE ABOVE IN BOOK II. 11 [VII.].)

Again, do not, I pray you, believe, say, or teach that "the soul deservedly lost something by the flesh, although it was of good merit previous to the flesh," if you wish to be a catholic. For the apostle declares that "children who are not yet born, have done neither good nor evil." [2] How, therefore, could their soul, previous to its participation of flesh, have had anything like good desert, if it had not done any good thing? Will you by any chance venture to assert that it had, previous to the flesh, lived a good life, when you cannot actually prove to us that it even existed at all? How, then, can you say: "You will not allow that the soul contracts health from the sinful flesh; and to this holy state, then, you can see it in due course pass, with the view of amending its condition, through that very flesh by which it had lost merit"? Perhaps you are not aware that these opinions, which attribute to the human soul a good state and a good merit previous to the flesh, have been already condemned by the catholic Church, not only in the case of some ancient heretics, whom I do not here mention, but also more recently in the instance of the Priscillianists.

#### CHAP. 10. — HIS FOURTH ERROR. (SEE ABOVE IN BOOK I. 6 [VI.] AND BOOK II. 11 [VII.].)

Neither believe, nor say, nor teach that "the soul, by means of the flesh, repairs its ancient condition, and is born again by the very means through which it had deserved to be polluted," if you wish to be a catholic. I might, indeed, dwell upon the strange discrepancy with your own self which you have exhibited in the next sentence, wherein you said that "the soul through the flesh deservedly recovers its primitive condition, which it had seemed to have gradually lost through the flesh, in order that it may begin to be regenerated by the very flesh through which it had deserved to be polluted." Here you — the very man who had just before said that the soul repairs its condition through the flesh, by reason of which it had lost its desert (where nothing but *good desert* can be meant, which you will have to be recovered in the flesh, by baptism, of course) — said in another turn of your thought, that through the flesh the soul had deserved to be polluted (in which statement it is no longer the good desert, but *an evil one*, which must be meant). What flagrant inconsistency! but I will pass it over, and content myself with observing, that it is absolutely uncatholic to believe that the soul, previous to its incarnate state, deserved either good or evil.

#### CHAP. 11 [VIII.] — HIS FIFTH ERROR. (SEE ABOVE IN BOOK I. 8 [VIII.] AND BOOK II. 12 [VIII.].)

Neither believe, nor say, nor teach, if you wish to be a catholic, that "the soul deserved to be sinful before any sin." It is, to be sure, an extremely bad desert to have deserved to be sinful. And, of course, it could not possibly have incurred so bad a desert previous to any sin, especially prior to its coming into the flesh, when it could have possessed no merit either way, either evil or good. How, then, can you say: "If, therefore, the. soul, which could not be sinful, deserved to be sinful, it yet did not remain in sin, because as it was prefigured in Christ it was bound not to be in a sinful state, even as it was unable to be"? Now, just for a little consider what it is you say, and desist from repeating such a statement. How did the soul deserve, and how was it unable, to be sinful? How, I pray you tell me, did that deserve to be sinful which never lived sinfully? How, I ask again, was that made sinful which was not able to be sinful? Or else, if you mean your phrase, "*was unable*," to imply inability apart from the flesh, how in that case did the soul deserve to be sinful, and by reason of what desert was it sent into the flesh, when previous to its union

---

[1] 2 Tim. iii. 7.          [2] Rom. ix. 11.

with the flesh it was not able to be sinful, so as to deserve any evil at all?

CHAP. 12 [IX.] — HIS SIXTH ERROR. (SEE ABOVE IN BOOK I. 10-12 [IX., X.], AND IN BOOK II. 13, 14 [IX., X.].)

If you wish to be a catholic, refrain from believing, or saying, or teaching that "infants which are forestalled by death before they are baptized may yet attain to forgiveness of their original sins." For the examples by which you are misled — that of the thief who confessed the Lord upon the cross, or that of Dinocrates the brother of St. Perpetua — contribute no help to you in defence of this erroneous opinion. As for the thief, although in God's judgment he might be reckoned among those who are purified by the confession of martyrdom, yet you cannot tell whether he was not baptized. For, to say nothing of the opinion that he might have been sprinkled with the water which gushed at the same time with the blood out of the Lord's side,[1] as he hung on the cross next to Him, and thus have been washed with a baptism of the most sacred kind, what if he had been baptized in prison, as in after times some under persecution were enabled privately to obtain? or what if he had been baptized previous to his imprisonment? If, indeed, he had been, the remission of his sins which he would have received in that case from God would not have protected him from the sentence of public law, so far as appertained to the death of the body. What if, being already baptized, he had committed the crime and incurred the punishment of robbery and lawlessness, but yet received, by virtue of repentance added to his baptism, forgiveness of the sins which, though baptized, he had committed? For beyond doubt his faith and piety appeared to the Lord clearly in his heart, as they do to us in his words. If, indeed, we were to conclude that all those who have quitted life without a record of their baptism died unbaptized, we should calumniate the very apostles themselves; for we are ignorant when they were, any of them, baptized, except the Apostle Paul.[2] If, however, we could regard as an evidence that they were really baptized the circumstance of the Lord's saying to St. Peter, "He that is washed needeth not save to wash his feet,"[3] what are we to think of the others, of whom we do not read even so much as this, — Barnabas, Timothy, Titus, Silas, Philemon, the very evangelists Mark and Luke, and innumerable others, about whose baptism God forbid that we should entertain any doubt, although we read no record of it? As for Dinocrates, he was a child of seven years of age; and as children who are baptized so old as that

can now recite the creed and answer for themselves in the usual examination, I know not why he may not be supposed after his baptism to have been recalled by his unbelieving father to the sacrilege and profanity of heathen worship, and for this reason to have been condemned to the pains from which he was liberated at his sister's intercession. For in the account of him you have never read, either that he was never a Christian, or died a catechumen. But for the matter of that, the account itself that we have of him does not occur in that canon of Holy Scripture whence in all questions of this kind our proofs ought always to be drawn.

CHAP. 13 [X.] — HIS SEVENTH ERROR. (SEE ABOVE IN BOOK II. 13 [IX.].)

If you wish to be a catholic, do not venture to believe, to say, or to teach that "they whom the Lord has predestinated for baptism can be snatched away from his predestination, or die before that has been accomplished in them which the Almighty has predestined." There is in such a dogma more power than I can tell assigned to chances in opposition to the power of God, by the occurrence of which casualties that which He has predestinated is not permitted to come to pass. It is hardly necessary to spend time or earnest words in cautioning the man who takes up with this error against the absolute vortex of confusion into which it will absorb him, when I shall sufficiently meet the case if I briefly warn the prudent man who is ready to receive correction against the threatening mischief. Now these are your words: "We say that some such method as this must be had recourse to in the case of infants who, being predestinated for baptism, are yet, by the failing of this life, hurried away before they are born again in Christ." Is it then really true that any who have been predestinated to baptism are forestalled before they come to it by the failing of this life? And could God predestinate anything which He either in His foreknowledge saw would not come to pass, or in ignorance knew not that it could not come to pass, either to the frustration of His purpose or the discredit of His foreknowledge? You see how many weighty remarks might be made on this subject; but I am restrained by the fact of having treated on it a little while ago, so that I content myself with this brief and passing admonition.

CHAP. 14. — HIS EIGHTH ERROR. (SEE ABOVE IN BOOK II. 13 [IX.].)

Refuse, if you wish to be a catholic, to believe, or to say, or to teach that "it is of infants, who are forestalled by death before they are born again in Christ, that the Scripture says, 'Speedily was he taken away, lest that wickedness should

---

[1] John xix. 34.    [2] Acts ix. 18.    [3] John xiii. 10.

alter his understanding, or deceit beguile his soul. Therefore God hastened to take him away from among the wicked; for his soul pleased the Lord; and being made perfect in a short time, he fulfilled long seasons.'" [1] For this passage has nothing to do with those to whom you apply it, but rather belongs to those who, after they have been baptized and have progressed in pious living, are not permitted to tarry long on earth, — having been made perfect, not with years, but with the grace of heavenly wisdom. This error, however, of yours, by which you think that this scripture was spoken of infants who die unbaptized, does an intolerable wrong to the holy laver itself, if an infant, who could have been " hurried away" after baptism, has been " hurried away" before this, for this reason: — " lest wickedness should alter his understanding, or deceit beguile his soul." As if this " wickedness," and this " deceit which beguiles the soul," and changes it for the worse, if it be not before taken away, is to be believed to be in baptism itself! In a word, since his soul had pleased God, He hastened to remove him out of the midst of iniquity; and he tarried not for ever so little while, in order to fulfil in him what He had predestinated; but preferred to act in opposition to His predestined purpose, and actually hastened lest what had pleased Him so well in the unbaptized child should be exterminated by his baptism! As if the dying infant would perish in that, whither we ought to run with him in our arms in order to save him from perdition. Who, therefore, in respect of these words of the Book of Wisdom, could believe, or say, or write, or quote them as having been written concerning infants who die without baptism, if he only reflected upon them with proper consideration?

CHAP. 15 [XI.] — HIS NINTH ERROR. (SEE ABOVE IN BOOK II. 14 [X.].)

If you wish to be a catholic, I pray you, neither believe, nor say, nor teach that " there are some mansions outside the kingdom of God which the Lord said were in His Father's house." For He does not affirm, as you have adduced his testimony, " There are with my Father (*apud Patrem meum*) many mansions;" although, if He had even expressed Himself so, the mansions could hardly be supposed to have any other situation than *in the house* of His Father; but He plainly says, " In my Father's house are many mansions." [2] Now, who would be so reckless as to separate some parts of God's house from the kingdom of God; so that, whilst the kings of the earth are found reigning, not in their house only, nor only in their own country, but far and wide, even in regions across the sea, the King who made the heaven and the earth is not described as reigning even over all His own house?

CHAP. 16. — GOD RULES EVERYWHERE: AND YET THE " KINGDOM OF HEAVEN " MAY NOT BE EVERYWHERE.

You may, however, not improbably contend that all things, it is true, belong to the kingdom of God, because He reigns in heaven, reigns on earth, in the depths beneath, in paradise, in hell (for where does He not reign, since His power is everywhere supreme?); but that the kingdom of heaven is one thing, into which none are permitted to enter, according to the Lord's own true and settled sentence, unless they are washed in the laver of regeneration, while quite another thing is the kingdom over the earth, or over any other parts of creation, in which there may be some mansions of God's house; but these, although appertaining to the kingdom of God, belong not to that kingdom of heaven where God's kingdom exists with an especial excellence and blessedness; and that it hence happens that, while no parts and mansions of God's house can be rudely separated from the kingdom of God, yet not all the mansions are prepared in the kingdom of heaven; and still, even in the abodes which are not situated in the kingdom of heaven, those may live happily, to whom, if they are even unbaptized, God has willed to assign such habitations. They are no doubt in the kingdom of God, although (as not having been baptized) they cannot possibly be in the kingdom of heaven.

CHAP. 17. — WHERE THE KINGDOM OF GOD MAY BE UNDERSTOOD TO BE.

Now, they who say this, do no doubt seem to themselves to say a good deal, because theirs is only a slight and careless view of Scripture; nor do they understand in what sense we use the phrase, " kingdom of God," when we say of it in our prayers, " Thy kingdom come;" [3] for that is called the kingdom of God, in which His whole family shall reign with Him in happiness and for ever. Now, in respect of the power which He possesses over all things, he is of course even now reigning. What, therefore, do we intend when we pray that His kingdom may come unless that we may deserve to reign with Him? But even they will be under His power who shall have to suffer the pains of eternal fire. Well, then, do we mean to predicate of these unhappy beings that they too will be in the kingdom of God? Surely it is one thing to be honoured with the gifts and privileges of the kingdom of God, and another thing to be restrained and punished by the laws of the same.

---

[1] Wisd. iv. 11.          [2] John xiv. 2.          [3] Matt. vi. 10.

However, that you may have a very manifest proof that on the one hand the kingdom of heaven must not be parcelled out to the baptized, and other portions of the kingdom of God be given to the unbaptized, as you seem to have determined, I beg of you to hear the Lord's own words ; He does not say, "Except a man be born again of water and of the Spirit, he cannot enter into the kingdom of heaven;" but His words are, " he cannot enter into the kingdom of God." His discourse with Nicodemus on the subject before us runs thus : " Verily, verily, I say unto thee, Except a man be born again, he cannot see the kingdom of God." Observe, He does not here say, *the kingdom of heaven*, but *the kingdom of God*. And then, on Nicodemus asking Him in reply, " How can a man be born when he is old? can he enter the second time into his mother's womb and be born?" the Lord, in explanation, repeats His former statement more plainly and openly : " Verily, verily, I say unto you, Except a man be born again of water and of the Spirit, he cannot enter into the kingdom of God." Observe again, He uses the same phrase, *the kingdom of God*, not *the kingdom of heaven*.[1] It is worthy of remark, that while He varies two expressions in explaining them the second time (for after saying, " Except a man be born *again*," He interprets that by the fuller expression, " Except a man be born *of water and the Spirit;* " and in like manner He explains, " he cannot *see*," by the completer phrase, " he cannot *enter into*"), He yet makes no variation here ; He said " the kingdom of God " the first time, and He afterwards repeated the same phrase exactly. It is not now necessary to raise and discuss the question, whether the kingdom of God and the kingdom of heaven must be understood as involving different senses, or whether only one thing is described under two designations. It is enough to find that no one can enter into the kingdom of God, except he be washed in the laver of regeneration. I suppose you perceive by this time how wide of the truth it is to separate from the kingdom of God any mansions that are placed in the house of God. And as to the idea which you have entertained that there will be found dwelling among the various mansions, which the Lord has told us abound in His Father's house, some who have not been born again of water and the Spirit, I advise you, if you will permit me, not to defer amending it, in order that you may hold the catholic faith.

CHAP. 18 [XII.] — HIS TENTH ERROR. (SEE ABOVE IN BOOK I. 13 [XI.] AND BOOK II. 15 [XI.].

Again, if you wish to be a catholic, I pray you, neither believe, nor say, nor teach that " the sacrifice of Christians ought to be offered in behalf of those who have departed out of the body without having been baptized." Because you fail to show that the sacrifice of the Jews, which you have quoted out of the books of the Maccabees,[2] was offered in behalf of any who had departed this life without circumcision. In this novel opinion of yours, which you have advanced against the authority and teaching of the whole Church, you have used a very arrogant mode of expression. You say, " In behalf of these, I most certainly decide that constant oblations and incessant sacrifices must be offered up on the part of the holy priests." Here you show, as a layman, no submission to God's priests for instruction ; nor do you associate yourself with them (the least you could do) for inquiry ; but you put yourself before them by your proud assumption of judgment. Away, my son, with all this pretension ; men walk not so arrogantly in the Way, which the Humble Christ taught that He Himself is.[3] No man enters through His narrow gate with so proud a disposition as this.

CHAP. 19 [XIII.] — HIS ELEVENTH ERROR. (SEE ABOVE IN BOOK I. 15 [XII.] AND BOOK II. 16.)

Once more, if you desire to be a catholic, do not believe, or say, or teach that " some of those persons who have departed this life without Christ's baptism, do not in the meantime go into the kingdom of heaven, but into paradise ; yet afterwards in the resurrection of the dead they attain also to the blessedness of the kingdom of heaven." Even the Pelagian heresy was not daring enough to grant them this, although it holds that infants do not contract original sin. You, however, as a catholic, confess that they are born in sin ; and yet by some unaccountable perverseness in the novel opinion you put forth, you assert that they are absolved from that sin with which they were born, and admitted into the kingdom of heaven without the baptism which saves. Nor do you seem to be aware how much below Pelagius himself you are in your views on this point. For he, being alarmed by that sentence of the Lord which does not permit unbaptized persons to enter into the kingdom of heaven, does not venture to send infants thither, although he believes them to be free from all sin ; whereas you have so little regard for what is written, " Except a man be born again of water and of the Spirit, he cannot enter into the kingdom of God,"[4] that (to say nothing of the error which induces you recklessly to sever paradise from the kingdom of God) you do not hesitate to promise to certain persons, whom you, as a catholic, believe to be born un-

---

[1] John iii. 3-6.

[2] 2 Macc. xii. 43.　　[3] John xiv. 6.　　[4] John iii. 5.

der guilt, both absolution from this guilt and the kingdom of heaven, even when they die without baptism. As if you could possibly be a true catholic because you build up the doctrine of original sin against Pelagius, if you show yourself a new heretic against the Lord, by pulling down His statement respecting baptism. For our own part, beloved brother, we do not desire thus to gain victories over heretics : vanquishing one error by another, and, what is still worse, a less one by a greater. You say, "Should any one perhaps be reluctant to allow that paradise was temporarily bestowed in the meantime on the souls of the dying thief and of Dinocrates, while there still remains to them the reversion of the kingdom of heaven at the resurrection, seeing that the principal passage stands in the way of the opinion, 'Except a man be born again of water and the Holy Spirit, he cannot enter into the kingdom of heaven,' he may still hold my ungrudging assent on this point ; only let him do full honour to both the effect and the aim [1] of the divine mercy and foreknowledge." These are your own words, and in them you express your agreement with the man who says that paradise is conferred on certain unbaptized for a time, in such a sense that at the resurrection there is in store for them the reward of the kingdom of heaven, in opposition to "that principal passage" which has determined that none shall enter into that kingdom who has not been born again of water and the Holy Ghost. Pelagius was afraid to oppose himself to this " principal passage " of the Gospel, and he did not believe that any (whom he still did not suppose to be sinners) would enter into the kingdom of heaven unbaptized. You, on the contrary, acknowledge that infants have original sin, and yet you absolve them from it without the laver of regeneration, and send them for a temporary residence in paradise, and subsequently permit them to enter even into the kingdom of heaven.

CHAP. 20 [XIV.] — AUGUSTIN CALLS ON VICTOR TO CORRECT HIS ERRORS. (SEE ABOVE IN BOOK II. 22 [XVI.].)

Now these errors, and such as these, with whatever others you may perhaps be able to discover in your books on a more attentive and leisurely perusal, I beg of you to correct, if you possess a catholic mind ; in other words, if you spoke in perfect sincerity when you said, that you were not over-confident in yourself that what statements you had made were all capable of proof ; and that your constant aim was not to maintain even your own opinion, if it were shown to be improbable ; and that it gave you much pleasure, if your own judgment were condemned, to adopt and pursue better and truer

sentiments. Well now, my dear brother, show that you said this in no fallacious sense ; so that the catholic Church may rejoice in your capacity and character, as possessing not only genius, but prudence withal, and piety, and moderation, rather than that the madness of heresy should be kindled by your contentious persistence in these errors. Now you have an opportunity of showing also how sincerely you expressed your feelings in the passage which immediately follows the satisfactory statement which I have just now mentioned of yours. "For," you say, "as it is the mark of every highest aim and laudable purpose to transfer one's self readily to truer views ; so it shows a depraved and obstinate judgment to refuse to return promptly to the pathway of reason." Well, then, show yourself to be influenced by this high aim and laudable purpose, and transfer your mind readily to truer views ; and do not display a depraved and obstinate judgment by refusing to return promptly to the pathway of reason. For if your words were uttered in frank sincerity, if they were not mere sound of the lips, if you really felt them in your heart, then you cannot but abhor all delay in accomplishing the great good of correcting yourself. It was not, indeed, much for you to allow, that it showed a depraved and obstinate judgment to refuse to return to the pathway of reason, unless you had added "promptly." By adding this, you showed us how execrable is his conduct who never accomplishes the reform ; inasmuch as even he who effects it but tardily appears to you to deserve so severe a censure, as to be fairly described as displaying a depraved and obstinate mind. Listen, therefore, to your own admonition, and turn to good account mainly and largely the fruitful resources of your eloquence ; that so you may promptly return to the pathway of reason, more promptly, indeed, than when you declined therefrom, at an unstable period of your age, when you were fortified with too little prudence and less learning.

CHAP. 21. — AUGUSTIN COMPLIMENTS VICTOR'S TALENTS AND DILIGENCE.

It would take me too long a time to handle and discuss fully all the points which I wish to be amended in your books, or rather in your own self, and to give you even a brief reason for the correction of each particular. And yet you must not because of them despise yourself, so as to suppose that your ability and powers of speech are to be thought lightly of. I have discovered in you no small recollection of the sacred Scriptures ; but your erudition is less than was proportioned to your talent, and the labour you bestowed on them. My desire, therefore, is that you should not, on the one hand, grow vain by attributing too much to yourself ; nor, on the

---

[1] Et effectum et affectum.

other hand, become cold and indifferent by prostration or despair. I only wish that I could read your writings in company with yourself, and point out the necessary emendations in conversation rather than by writing. This is a matter which could be more easily accomplished by oral communication between ourselves than in letters. If the entire subject were to be treated in writing, it would require many volumes. Those chief errors, however, which I have wished to sum up comprehensively in a definite number, I at once call your attention to, in order that you may not postpone the correction of them, but banish them entirely from your preaching and belief; so that the great faculty which you possess of disputation, may, by God's grace, be employed by you usefully for edification, not for injuring and destroying sound and wholesome doctrine.

## CHAP. 22 [XV.] — A SUMMARY RECAPITULATION OF THE ERRORS OF VICTOR.

What these particular errors are, I have, to the best of my ability, already explained. But I will run over them again with a brief recapitulation. One is, "That God did not make the soul out of nothing, but out of His own self." A *second* is, that "just as God who gives is Himself ever existent, so is He ever giving souls through infinite time." The *third* is, that "the soul lost some merit by the flesh, which it had had previous to the flesh." The *fourth* is, that "the soul by means of the flesh recovers its ancient condition, and is born again through the very same flesh by which it had deserved to be polluted." The *fifth* is, that "the soul deserved to be sinful, previous to any sin." The *sixth* is, that "infants which are forestalled by death before they are baptized, may yet attain to forgiveness of their original sins." The *seventh* is, that "they whom the Lord has predestinated to be baptized may be taken away from his predestination, or die before that has been accomplished in them which the Almighty has predestined." The *eighth* is, that "it is of infants who are forestalled by death, before they are born again in Christ, that the Scripture says, 'Speedily was he taken away, lest wickedness should alter his understanding,'" with the remainder of the passage to the same effect in the Book of Wisdom. The *ninth* is, that "there are outside the kingdom of God some of those mansions which the Lord said were in His Father's house." The *tenth* is, that "the sacrifice of Christians ought to be offered in behalf of those who have departed out of the body without being baptized." The *eleventh* is, that "some of those persons who have departed this life without the baptism of Christ do not in the meanwhile go into the kingdom, but into paradise; afterwards, however, in the resurrection of the dead, they attain even to the blessedness of the kingdom of heaven."

## CHAP. 23. — OBSTINACY MAKES THE HERETIC.

Well, now, as for these eleven propositions, they are extremely and manifestly perverse and opposed to the catholic faith; so that you should no longer hesitate to root them out and cast them away from your mind, from your words, and from your pen, if you are desirous that we should rejoice not only at your having come over to our catholic altars, but at your being really and truly a catholic. For if these dogmas of yours are severally maintained with pertinacity, they may possibly engender as many heresies as they number opinions. Wherefore consider, I pray you, how dreadful it is that they should be all concentrated in one person, when they would, if held severally by various persons, be every one of them damnable in each holder. If, however, you would in your own person cease to fight contentiously in their defence, nay, would turn your arms against them by faithful words and writings, you would acquire more praise as the censurer of your own self than if you directed any amount of right criticism against any other person; and your amendment of your own errors would bring you more admiration than if you had never entertained them. May the Lord be present to your heart and mind, and by His Spirit pour into your soul such readiness in humility, such light of truth, such sweetness of love, and such peaceful piety, that you may prefer being a conqueror of your own spirit in the truth, than of any one else who gainsays it with his errors. But I do not by any means wish you to think, that by holding these opinions you have departed from the catholic faith, although they are unquestionably opposed to the catholic faith; if so be you are able, in the presence of that God whose eye infallibly searches every man's heart, to look back on your own words as being truly and sincerely expressed, when you said that you were not over-confident in yourself as to the opinions you had broached, that they were all capable of proof; and that your constant aim was not to persist in your own sentiments, if they were shown to be improbable; inasmuch as it was a real pleasure to you, when any judgment of yours was condemned, to adopt and pursue better and truer thoughts. Now such a temper as this, even in relation to what may have been said in an uncatholic form through ignorance, is itself catholic by the very purpose and readiness of amendment which it premeditates. With this remark, however, I must now end this volume, where the reader may rest a while, ready to renew his attention to what is to follow, when I begin my next book.

# BOOK IV.

## *ADDRESSED TO VINCENTIUS VICTOR.*

HE FIRST SHOWS, THAT HIS HESITATION ON THE SUBJECT OF THE ORIGIN OF SOULS WAS UNDESERVEDLY BLAMED, AND THAT HE WAS WRONGLY COMPARED WITH CATTLE, BECAUSE HE HAD REFRAINED FROM ANY RASH CONCLUSIONS ON THE SUBJECT. THEN, AGAIN, WITH REGARD TO HIS OWN UNHESITATING STATEMENT, THAT THE SOUL WAS SPIRIT, NOT BODY, HE POINTS OUT HOW RASHLY VICTOR DISAPPROVED OF THIS ASSERTION, ESPECIALLY WHEN HE WAS VAINLY EXPENDING HIS EFFORTS TO PROVE THAT THE SOUL WAS CORPOREAL IN ITS OWN NATURE, AND THAT THE SPIRIT IN MAN WAS DISTINCT FROM THE SOUL ITSELF.

CHAP. 1 [I.] — THE PERSONAL CHARACTER OF THIS BOOK.

I MUST now, in the sequel of my treatise, request you to hear what I desire to say to you concerning myself — as I best can ; or rather as He shall enable me in whose hand are both ourselves and our words. For you blamed me on two several occasions, even going so far as to mention my name. In the beginning of your book you spoke of yourself as being perfectly conscious of your own want of skill, and as being destitute of the support of learning ; and, when you mentioned me, bestowed on me the complimentary phrases of " most learned " and " most skilful." But yet, all the while, on those subjects in which you seemed to yourself to be perfectly acquainted with what I either confess my ignorance of, or presume with no unbecoming liberty to have some knowledge of, you — young as you are, and a layman too — did not hesitate to censure me, an old man and a bishop, and a person withal whom in your own judgment you had pronounced most learned and most skilful. Well, for my own part, I know nothing about my great learning and skill ; nay, I am very certain that I possess no such eminent qualities ; moreover, I have no doubt that it is quite within the scope of possibility, that it may fall to the lot of even an unskilful and unlearned man occasionally to know what a learned and skilful person is ignorant of ; and in this I plainly commend you, that you have preferred to merely personal regard a love of truth, — for if you have not understood the truth, yet at any rate you have thought it such. This you have done no doubt with temerity, because you thought you knew what you were really ignorant of ; and without restraint, because, having no respect of persons, you chose to publish abroad whatever was in your mind. You ought therefore to understand how much greater our care should be to recall the Lord's sheep from their errors ; since it is evidently wrong for even the sheep to conceal from the shepherds whatever faults they have discovered in them. O that you censured me in such things as are indeed worthy of just blame ! For I must not deny that both in my conduct and in my writings there are many points which may be censured by a sound judge without temerity. Now, if you would select any of these for your censure, I might be able by them to show you how I should like you to behave in those particulars which you judiciously and fairly condemned ; moreover, I should have (as an elder to a younger, and as one in authority to him who has to obey) an opportunity of setting you an example under correction which should not be more humble on my part than wholesome to both of us. With respect, however, to the points on which you have actually censured me, they are not such as humility obliges me to correct, but such as truth compels me partly to acknowledge and partly to defend.

CHAP. 2 [II.] — THE POINTS WHICH VICTOR THOUGHT BLAMEWORTHY IN AUGUSTIN.

And they are these : The first, that I did not venture to make a definite statement touching the origin of those souls which have been given, or are being given, to human beings, since the first man — because I confess my ignorance of the subject ; the second, because I said I was sure the soul was spirit, not body. Under this second point, however, you have included two grounds of censure : one, because I refused to believe the soul to be corporeal ; the other, because I affirmed it to be spirit. For to you the soul appears both to be body and not to be spirit. I must therefore request your attention to my own defence against your censure, and ask you to embrace the opportunity which my self-defence affords you of learning what points there are in yourself also which require your amendment. Recall, then, the words of your book in which you first mentioned my name. " I know," you say, " many men of very great reputation who when consulted have kept silence, or admitted nothing clearly, but have withdrawn from their discussions everything definite when they commence their exposition. Of such character are the contents of sundry writings which I have read at your house by a very learned man and renowned bishop, called Augustin. The truth is, I suppose, they have with an overweening modesty and diffidence investigated the mysteries of this subject, and have consumed within themselves the judgment of their own treatises, and have professed themselves incapable of determining anything on this point. But, I assure you, it appears to me excessively absurd and unreasonable that a man should be a stranger to himself ; or that a person who is supposed to have acquired the knowledge of all things, should regard himself as unknown to his very self. For what difference is there between a man and a brute beast, if he knows not how to discuss and determine his own quality and nature? so that there may justly be applied to him the statement of Scripture : ' Man, although he was in honour, understood not ; he is like the cattle, and is compared with them.' [1] For when the good and gracious God created everything with reason and wisdom, and produced man as a rational animal, capable of understanding, endowed with reason, and lively with sensation, — because by His prudent arrangement He assigns their place to all creatures which do not participate in the faculty of reason, — what more incongruous idea could be suggested, than that God had withheld from him the simple knowledge of himself? The wisdom of this world, indeed, is ever aiming with much effort to attain to the knowledge of truth ; its researches, no doubt, fall short of the aim, from its inability to know through what agency it is permitted that truth should be ascertained ; but yet there are some things on the nature of the soul, near (I might even say, akin) to the truth which it has attempted to discern. Under these circumstances, how unbecoming and even shameful a thing it is, that any man of religious principle should either have no intelli-

gent views on this very subject, or prohibit himself from acquiring any ! "

CHAP. 3. — HOW MUCH DO WE KNOW OF THE NATURE OF THE BODY?

Well, now, this extremely lucid and eloquent castigation which you have inflicted on our ignorance lays you so strictly under the necessity of knowing every possible thing which appertains to the nature of man, that, should you unhappily be ignorant of any particular, you must (and remember it is not I, but you, that have made the necessity) be compared with " the cattle." For although you appear to aim your censure at us more especially, when you quote the passage, " Man, although he was in honour, understood not," inasmuch as we (unlike yourself) hold an honourable place in the Church ; yet even you occupy too honourable a rank in nature, not to be preferred above the cattle, with which according to your own judgment you will have to be compared, if you should happen to be ignorant on any of the points which manifestly appertain to your nature. For you have not merely aspersed with your censure those who are affected with the same ignorance as I am myself labouring under, that is to say, concerning the origin of the human soul (although I am not indeed absolutely ignorant even on this point, for I know that God breathed into the face of the first man, and that " man then became a living soul," [2] — a truth, however, which I could never have known by myself, unless I had read of it in the Scripture) ; but you asked in so many words, " What difference is there between a man and a brute beast, if he knows not how to discuss and determine his own quality and nature? " And you seem to have entertained your opinion so distinctly, as to have thought that a man ought to be able to discuss and determine the facts of his own entire quality and nature so clearly, that nothing concerning himself should escape his observation. Now, if this is really the truth of the matter, I must now compare you to " the cattle," if you cannot tell me the precise number of the hairs of your head. But if, however far we may advance in this life, you allow us to be ignorant of sundry facts appertaining to our nature, I then want to know how far your concession extends, lest, perchance, it may include the very point we are now raising, that we do not by any means know the origin of our soul ; although we know, — a thing which belongs to faith, — beyond all doubt, that the soul is a gift to man from God, and that it still is not of the same nature as God Himself. Do you, moreover, think that each person's ignorance of his own nature must be exactly on the same level as

---

[1] Ps. xlix. 12.

[2] Gen. ii. 7.

your ignorance of it? Must everybody's knowledge, too, of the subject be equal to what you have been able to attain to? So that if he is so unfortunate as to possess a slightly larger amount of ignorance than yourself, you must compare him with cattle; and on the same principle, if any one shall be ever so little wiser than yourself on this subject, he will have the pleasure of comparing you with equal justice to the aforesaid cattle. I must therefore request you to tell me, to what extent you permit us to be ignorant of our nature so as to save our distance from the formidable cattle; and I beg you besides duly to reflect, whether he is not further removed from cattle who knows his ignorance of any part of the subject, than he is who thinks he knows what in fact he knows not. The entire nature of man is certainly spirit, soul, and body; therefore, whoever would alienate the body from man's nature, is unwise. Those medical men, however, who are called anatomists have investigated with careful scrutiny, by dissecting processes, even living men, so far as men have been able to retain any life in the hands of the examiners; their researches have penetrated limbs, veins, nerves, bones, marrow, the internal vitals; and all to discover the nature of the body. But none of these men have ever thought of comparing us with the cattle, because of our ignorance of their subject. But perhaps you will say that it is those who are ignorant of the nature of the soul, not of the body, who are to be compared with the brute beasts. Then you ought not to have expressed yourself at starting in the way you have done. Your words are not, " For what difference is there between a man and cattle, if he is ignorant of the nature and quality of the soul;" but you say, " if he knows not how to discuss and determine his own nature and quality." Of course our quality and our nature must be taken account of together with the body, but at the same time the investigation of the several elements of which we are composed is conducted in each case separately. For my own part, indeed, if I wished to display how far it was in my power to treat scientifically and intelligently the entire field of man's nature, I should have to fill many volumes; not to mention how many topics there are which I must confess my ignorance of.

### CHAP. 4 [III.] — IS THE QUESTION OF BREATH ONE THAT CONCERNS THE SOUL, OR BODY, OR WHAT?

But to what, in your judgment, does that which we discussed in our former book concerning the breath of man belong? — to the nature of the soul, seeing that it is the soul which effects it in man; or to that of the body, since the body is moved by the soul to effect it; or to that of this air, by whose alternation of action it is discovered to effect it; or rather to all three, that is to say, to the soul as that which moves the body, and to the body which by its motion receives and emits the breath, and also to the circumambient air which raises by its entrance, and by its departure depresses? And yet you were evidently ignorant of all this, learned and eloquent though you are, when you supposed, and said, and wrote, and read in the presence of the crowd assembled to hear your opinion, that it was out of our own nature that we inflated a bag, and yet had no diminution of our nature at all by the operation; although you might most easily ascertain how we accomplish the process, not by any tedious examination of the pages either of human or of inspired writings, but by a simple investigation of your own physical action, whenever you liked. This, then, being the case, how can I trust you to teach me concerning the origin of souls, — a subject which I confess myself to be ignorant of, — you who are actually ignorant of what you are doing unintermittingly with your nose and mouth, and of why you are doing it? May the Lord bring it to pass that you may be advised by me, and accept rather than resist so manifest a truth, and one so ready to your hand. May you also not interrogate your lungs about the bag inflation in such a temper as to prefer inflating them in opposition to me, rather than acquiesce in their tuition, when they answer your inquiry with entire truth, — not by speech and altercation, but by breath and respiration. Then I could bear with you patiently while you correct and reproach me for my ignorance of the origin of souls; nay, I could even warmly thank you, if, besides inflicting on me rebuke, you would convince me with truth. For if you could teach me the truth I am ignorant of, it would be my duty to bear with all patience any blows you might deal against me, not in word only, but even with hand.

### CHAP. 5 [IV.] — GOD ALONE CAN TEACH WHENCE SOULS COME.

Now with respect to the question between us, I confess to your loving self [1] I greatly desire to know one of two things if I can, — either concerning the origin of souls, of which I am ignorant, or whether this knowledge is within our reach so long as we are in the present life. For what if our controversy touches the very points of which it is enjoined to us, " Seek not out the things that are too high for thee, neither search the things that are above thy strength; but whatever things the Lord hath commanded and taught thee, think thereupon for evermore." [2] This, then, is what I desire to know, either from

---

[1] Dilectioni tuæ.　　　[2] Ecclus. iii. 21, 22.

God Himself, who knows what He creates, or even from some competently learned man who knows what he is saying, not from a person who is ignorant of the breath he heaves. It is not everybody who recollects his own infancy; and do you suppose that a man is able, without divine instruction, to know whence he began to exist in his mother's womb, — especially if the knowledge of human nature has so completely eluded him as to leave him ignorant, not only of what is within him, but of that also which is added to his nature from without? Will you, my dearest brother, be able to teach me, or any one else, whence human beings at their birth are ensouled,[1] when you still know not how it is that their life is so sustained by food, that they are certain to die if the aliment is withdrawn for a while? Or will you be able to teach me, or any one else, whence men obtain their souls, when you are still actually ignorant whence bags, when inflated, get the filling? My only wish, as you are ignorant whence souls have their origin, is, that I may on my side know whether such knowledge is attainable by me in this present life. If this be one of the things which are too high for us, and which we are forbidden to seek out or search into, then we have good grounds for fearing lest we should sin, not by our ignorance of it, but our quest after it. For we ought not to suppose that a subject, to fall under the category of the things which are too high for us, must appertain to the nature of God, and not to our own.

CHAP. 6 [V.] — QUESTIONS ABOUT THE NATURE OF THE BODY ARE SUFFICIENTLY MYSTERIOUS, AND YET NOT HIGHER THAN THOSE OF THE SOUL.

What do you say to the statement, that amongst the works of God there are some which it is more difficult to know than even God Himself, — so far, indeed, as He can be an object of knowledge to us at all? For we have learnt that God is a Trinity; but to this very day we do not know how many kinds of animals, not even of land animals which were able to enter Noah's ark,[2] He has created — unless by some happy chance you have ascertained this fact. Again, in the Book of Wisdom it is written, " For if they were able to prevail so much, that they could know and estimate the world; how is it that they did not more easily find out the Lord thereof? "[3] Is it because the subject before us is *within* us that it is therefore not too high for us? For it must be granted that the nature of our soul is a more internal thing than our body. As if the soul has been no better able to explore the body itself externally by the eyes of that body than internally by its own means. For what is there

in the inward parts of the body where the soul does not exist? But yet, even with regard to these several inner and vital portions of our frame, the soul has examined and searched them out by the bodily eyes; and all that it has succeeded in learning of them it has acquired by means of the eyes of the body; and, without doubt, all the material substance was there, even when the soul knew not of it. Since also our inward parts are incapable of living without the soul, it follows that the soul has been more able to give them life than to know them. Well, then, is the soul's body a higher object for its knowledge than the soul's own self? And therefore if it wishes to inquire and consider when human seed is converted into blood, when into solid flesh; when the bones begin to harden, and when to fill with marrow; how many kinds of veins and nerves there are; by what channels and circuits the former serve for irrigation and the latter for ligature to the entire body; whether the skin is to be reckoned among the nerves, and the teeth among the bones, — for they show some difference, inasmuch as they have no marrow; and in what respect the nails differ from both, being similar to them in hardness, while they possess a quality in common with the hair, in being capable of growing and being cut; what, again, is the use of those veins wherein air, instead of blood, circulates, which they call *the arteries*[4] — if, I repeat, the soul desired to come to know these and similar points respecting the nature of its body, ought it then to be said to a man, " Seek not out the things that are too high for thee, neither search the things that are above thy strength?" But, if the inquiry be made into the soul's own origin, of which subject it knows nothing, the matter then, forsooth, is not too high or beyond one's strength to be capable of apprehension? And you deem it an absurd thing, and incompatible with reason, for the soul not to know whether it is inbreathed by God, or whether it is derived from the parents, although it does not remember this event as soon as it is past, and reckons it among the things which it has forgotten beyond recall, — like infancy, and all other stages of life which followed close upon birth, though doubtless, when they happened, they were not unaccompanied with sensation. But yet you do not deem it absurd or unreasonable that it should be ignorant of the body which is subject to it, and should know nothing whatever about incidents pertaining to it which are not in the category of things that are past, but of present facts,

---

[4] These vessels which carry the blood from the heart were formerly supposed, from being found empty after death, to contain only air; and hence, indeed, their name, — for " the artery " was originally the windpipe. Comp. Cicero (*De Nat. Deor.* ii. 55, 138) : " Sanguis per *venas* in omne corpus diffunditur, et spiritus per *arterias;* " i.e. Blood is diffused throughout the body by the *veins,* and air by the *arteries.*

---

[1] Animentur = " are furnished with their *animæ*."
[2] Gen. vii. 8, 9.        [3] Wisd. xiii. 9.

— as to whether it sets the veins in motion in order to produce life in the body, but the nerves in order to operate by the limbs of the body; and if so, why it does not move the nerves except at its especial will, whereas it affects the pulsations of the veins without intermission, even without willing; from what part of the body that which they call the ἡγεμονικόν (the authoritative part of the soul, the reason) exercises its universal rule, whether from the heart, or from the brain, or by a distribution, the motions from the heart and the sensations from the brain, — or from the brain, both the sensations and voluntary motions, but from the heart, the involuntary pulsations of the veins; and once more, if it does both of these from the brain, how is it that it has the sensations, even without willing, while it does not move the limbs except it wills? Inasmuch, then, as only the soul itself does all this in the body, how is it that it knows not what it does? or whence its power to do it? And it is no disgrace to it to be so ignorant. Then do you suppose it to be a discredit if it knows not whence or how it was itself made, since it certainly did not make itself? Well, then, none know how or whence the soul effects all its action in the body; do you not therefore think that it, too, appertains to those things which are said to be "too high for us, and above our strength"?

CHAP. 7 [VI.] — WE OFTEN NEED MORE TEACHING AS TO WHAT IS MOST INTIMATELY OURS THAN AS TO WHAT IS FURTHER FROM US.

But I have to put to you a far wider question arising out of our subject. Why should only a very few know why all men do what they do? Perhaps you will tell me, Because they have learnt the art of anatomy or experiment, which are both comprised in the physician's education, which few obtain, while others have refused to acquire the information, although they might, of course, if they had liked. Here, then, I say nothing of the point why many try to acquire this information, but cannot, because they are hindered by a slow intellect (which, however, is a very strange fact) from learning of others what is done by their own selves and in their own selves. But this is a very important question which I now ask, Why I should have no need of art to know that there is a sun in the heavens, and a moon, and other stars; but must have the aid of art to know, on moving my finger, whence the act begins, — from the heart, or the brain, or from both, or from neither: why I do not require a teacher to know what is so much higher than me; but must yet wait for some one else to learn whence that is done by me which is done within me? For although we are said to think in our heart, and although

we know what our thoughts are, without the knowledge of any other person, yet we know not in what part of the body we have the heart itself, where we do our thinking, unless we are taught it by some other person, who yet is ignorant of what we think. I am not unaware that when we hear that we should love God with our whole heart, this is not said of that portion of our flesh which lies under our ribs, but of that power that originates our thoughts. And this is properly designated by this name, because, as motion does not cease in the heart whence the pulsation of the veins radiates in every direction, so in the process of thought we do not rest in the act itself and abstain from further pondering. But although every sensation is imparted even to the body by the soul, how is it that we can count our external limbs, even in the dark and with closed eyes, by the bodily sense which is called "touch," but we know nothing of our internal functions in the very central region of the soul itself, where that power is present which imparts life and animation to all else, — a mystery this which, I apprehend, no medical men of any kind, whether empirics, or anatomists, or dogmatists, or methodists,[1] or any man living, have any knowledge of?

CHAP. 8. — WE HAVE NO MEMORY OF OUR CREATION.

And whosoever shall have attempted to fathom such knowledge may not improperly have addressed to him the words we have before quoted, "Seek not out the things that are too high for thee, neither search the things that are above thy strength." Now it is not a question of mere altitude, such as is beyond our stature, but it is an elevation which our intelligence cannot reach, and a strength which our mental power cannot cope with. And yet it is neither the heaven of heavens, nor the measure of the stars, nor the scope of sea and land, nor the nethermost hell; it is our own selves that we are incapable of comprehending; it is our own selves, who, in our too great height and strength, transcend the humble limits of our own knowledge; it is our own selves, whom we are incapable of embracing, although we are certainly not beside ourselves. But we are not to be compared with cattle simply because we do not perfectly discover what we ourselves are: and yet you think that we deserve the humiliating comparison, if we have forgotten what we were, even though we knew it once. My soul is not now being derived from my parents, is not now receiving insufflation from God. Whichever of these two processes He used, He used when He created

---

[1] [The names of these various medical schools may be found explained in the article "Medicine" in the ninth edition of the *Encyclopædia Britannica*, vol. xv. See especially p. 802. — W.]

me; He is not at this moment using it of me, or within me. It is past and gone, — not a present thing, nor a recent one to me. I do not even know whether I was aware of it and then forgot it; or whether I was unable, even at the time when it was done, to feel and to know it.

CHAP. 9 [VII.] — OUR IGNORANCE OF OURSELVES ILLUSTRATED BY THE REMARKABLE MEMORY OF ONE SIMPLICIUS.

Observe now, while we are, while we live, while we know that we live, while we are certain that we possess memory, understanding, and will; who boast of ourselves as having a great knowledge of our own nature; — observe, I say, how entirely ignorant we are of what avail to us is our memory, or our understanding, or our will. A certain man who from his youth has been a friend of mine, named Simplicius, is a person of accurate and astonishing memory. I once asked him to tell me what were the last lines but one of all the books of Virgil; he immediately answered my question without the least hesitation, and with perfect accuracy. I then asked him to repeat the preceding lines; he did so. And I really believe that he could have repeated Virgil line after line backward. For wherever I wished, I made trial whether he could do it, and he did it. Similarly in prose, from any of Cicero's orations, which he had learnt by heart, he would perform a similar feat at our request, by reciting backwards as far as we wished. Upon our expressing astonishment, he called God to witness that he had no idea of this ability of his previous to that trial. So far, therefore, as memory is concerned, his mind only then learnt its own power; and such discovery would at no time be possible except by trial and experiment. Moreover, he was of course the very same man before he tried his powers; how was it, then, that he was ignorant of himself?

CHAP. 10. — THE FIDELITY OF MEMORY; THE UNSEARCHABLE TREASURE OF MEMORY; THE POWERS OF A MAN'S UNDERSTANDING SUFFICIENTLY UNDERSTOOD BY NONE.

We often assume that we shall retain a thing in our memory; and so thinking, we do not write it down. But afterwards, when we wish to recall it, it refuses to come to mind; and we are then sorry that we thought it would return to memory, or that we did not secure it in writing so as to prevent its escape; and lo, on a sudden, without our seeking it, it occurs to us. Then does it follow that we were not ourselves when we thought this? And that we cease to be the same thing that we were, when we are no longer able to think it? Now how does it happen that I know not how we are abstracted from, and

denied to, ourselves; and similarly am ignorant how we are restored and returned to ourselves? As if we are other persons, and elsewhere, when we seek, but fail to find, what we deposited in our memory; and are ourselves incapable of returning to ourselves, as if we were situated somewhere else; but afterwards return again, on finding ourselves out. For where do we make our quest, except in our own selves? And what is it we search for, except our own selves? As if we were not actually at home in our persons, but had gone somewhither. Do you not observe, even with alarm, so deep a mystery? And what is all this but our own nature — not what it has been, but such as it now is? And observe how much more we seek than we comprehend. I have often believed that I could understand a question which had been submitted to me, if I were to bestow thought upon it. Well, I have bestowed the thought, but have not been able to solve the question; and many a time I have not so believed, and yet have been able to determine the point. The powers, then, of my own understanding have not been really known to me; nor, I apprehend, have they been to you either.

CHAP. 11. — THE APOSTLE PETER TOLD NO LIE, WHEN HE SAID HE WAS READY TO LAY DOWN HIS LIFE FOR THE LORD, BUT ONLY WAS IGNORANT OF HIS WILL.

But perhaps you despise me for confessing all this, and will in consequence compare me with "cattle." For myself, however, I will not cease to advise you, or (if you refuse to listen to me) at all events to warn you, to acknowledge rather this common infirmity, in which virtue is perfected; lest, by assuming unknown things to be known, you fail to attain to the truth. For I suppose that there is something which even you wish to understand, but are unable; which you would never seek to understand, unless you hoped some day to succeed in your research. Thus you also are ignorant of the powers of your own understanding, who profess to know all about your own nature, and decline to follow me in my confession of ignorance. Well, there is also the will; what am I to say about that, where certainly free choice is ostentatiously claimed by us? The blessed Apostle Peter, indeed, was willing to lay down his life for the Lord. He was no doubt sincere in his willingness; nor was he treacherous to the Lord when he made the promise. But his will was entirely ignorant of its own powers. Therefore the great apostle, who had discovered his Master to be the Son of God, was unknown to himself. Thus we are quite aware respecting ourselves that we will a thing, or "nill" it; but although our will is a good one, we are ignorant, my dear son, unless we deceive ourselves, of its strength, of its resources, of what temptations it may yield to, or of what it may resist.

## CHAP. 12 [VIII.] — THE APOSTLE PAUL COULD KNOW THE THIRD HEAVEN AND PARADISE, BUT NOT WHETHER HE WAS IN THE BODY OR NOT.

See therefore how many facts of our nature, not of the past but of the present time, and not pertaining to the body only, but also to our inner man, we know nothing about, without deserving to be compared with the brute beasts. And yet this is the opprobrious comparison which you have thought me worthy of, because I have not complete knowledge of the past origin of my soul — although I am not wholly ignorant of it, inasmuch as I know that it was given me by God, and yet that it is not out of God. But when can I enumerate all the particulars relating to the nature of our spirit and our soul of which we are ignorant? Whereas we ought rather to utter that exclamation before God, which the Psalmist uttered: "The knowledge of Thee is too wonderful for me; it is very difficult, I cannot attain to it." [1] Now why did he add the words *for me*, except because he conjectured how incomprehensible was the knowledge of God for himself, inasmuch as he was unable to comprehend even his own self? The apostle was caught up into the third heaven, and heard unspeakable words, which it is not lawful for a man to utter; and whether this had happened to him in the body or out of the body, he declares himself unable to say; [2] but yet he has no fear of encountering from you comparison with the cattle. His spirit knew that it was in the third heaven, in paradise; but knew not whether it was in the body. The third heaven, of course, and paradise were not the Apostle Paul himself; but his body and soul and spirit were himself. Behold, then, the curious fact: he knew the great things — lofty and divine — which were not himself; but that which appertained to his own nature he was ignorant of. Who in the vast knowledge of such occult things can help being astonished at his great ignorance of his own existence? Who, in short, would believe it possible, if one who errs not had not told us, that "we know not what we should pray for as we ought"? [3] Where, then, ought our bent and purpose mainly to be — to "reach forth to those things which are before"? And yet you compare me to cattle, if among the things which are behind I have forgotten anything concerning my own origin — although you hear the same apostle say: "Forgetting those things which are behind, and reaching forth unto those things which are before, I press toward the mark, for the prize of the high calling of God in Christ Jesus." [4]

## CHAP. 13 [IX.] — IN WHAT SENSE THE HOLY GHOST IS SAID TO MAKE INTERCESSION FOR US.

Do you perhaps also think me ridiculous and like the irrational beasts, because I said, "We know not what we should pray for as we ought"? Perhaps this is not quite so intolerable. For since, in the dictates of a sound and righteous judgment, we prefer our future to our past; and since our prayer must have reference not to what we have been, but what we shall be, it is of course much more injurious not to know what we should pray for, than to be ignorant of the manner of our origin. But recollect whose words I repeated, or read them again for yourself, and reflect whence they come; and do not pelt me with your reproaches, lest the stone you throw should alight on a head you would not wish. For it is the great teacher of the Gentiles, the Apostle Paul himself, who said, "For we know not what we should pray for as we ought." [3] And he not only taught this lesson by word, but also illustrated it by his example. For, contrary to his own advantage and the promotion of his own salvation, he once in his ignorance prayed that "the thorn in the flesh might depart from him," which he said had been given to him "lest he should be exalted above measure by the abundance of the revelations which were given him." [5] But the Lord loved him, and so did not do what he had requested Him to do. Nevertheless, when the apostle said, "We know not what we should pray for as we ought," he immediately added, "But the Spirit Himself maketh intercession for us with groanings which cannot be uttered. And He that searcheth the hearts knoweth what is the mind of the Spirit, because He maketh intercession for the saints according to the will of God" [6] — that is to say, He makes the saints offer intercessions. He, of course, is that Spirit "whom God hath sent into our hearts, crying, Abba, Father;" [7] and "by whom we cry, Abba, Father;" [8] for both expressions are used by the apostle — both that we have received *the Spirit who cries, Abba, Father;* and also that it is through Him that *we cry, Abba, Father.* His object is to explain by these varied statements in what sense he used the word "*crying:*" he meant *causing to cry;* so that it is we who cry at His instance and impulse. Let Him therefore teach me this too, whenever He pleases, if He knows it to be expedient for me, that I should know whence I derive my origin as regards my soul. But let me be taught by that Spirit who searches the deep things of God; not by a

---

[1] Ps. cxxxix. 6.       [2] 2 Cor. xii. 4.       [3] Rom. viii. 26.

[4] Phil. iii. 13, 14.       [5] 2 Cor. xii. 7, 8.       [6] Rom. viii. 26, 27.
[7] Gal. iv. 6.       [8] Rom. viii. 15.

man who knows nothing of the breath which inflates a bag. However, be it far from me to compare you with brutes because of this piece of ignorance; because it arose not from incurable inability, but from sheer inadvertence.

CHAP. 14 [X.] — IT IS MORE EXCELLENT TO KNOW THAT THE FLESH WILL RISE AGAIN AND LIVE FOR EVERMORE, THAN TO LEARN WHATEVER SCIENTIFIC MEN HAVE BEEN ABLE TO TEACH US CONCERNING ITS NATURE.

But although the questions which arise touching the origin of souls are "higher," no doubt, than that which treats of the source whence the breath comes which we inhale and exhale, you yet believe that those things are "higher" which you have learnt out of the Holy Scriptures, from which we derive what we learn by faith; and such as are not traceable by any human minds. Of course it is far more excellent to know that the flesh will rise again and will live for evermore, than any thing that scientific men have been able to discover in it by careful examination, which the soul perceives by no outward sense, although its presence quickens all the things of which it is ignorant. It is also far better to know that the soul, which has been born again and renewed in Christ, will be blessed for ever, than to discover all that we are ignorant of touching its memory, understanding, and will. Now these subjects, which I have designated as more excellent and as better, we could by no means find out, unless we believed them on the testimony of the inspired Scriptures. These Scriptures you perhaps think you so thoroughly believe, that you do not hesitate to draw out of them a definite theory about the origin of souls. Well, then, first of all, if it be as you suppose, you ought never to have attributed to human nature itself what man knows by discussion and inquiry about his own nature and quality, but to God's gift. Now you asked: "Wherein does a man differ from the cattle, if he is ignorant of this?" But why need we read any thing, in order to know this, if we ought already to know it by the very fact that we are different from cattle? For just as you do not read anything to me for the purpose of teaching me that I am alive (my own nature making it impossible that I should be ignorant of this fact), so if it is an attribute of nature to know this other matter, why do you produce passages of Scripture for me to believe concerning this subject? Is it then only those persons who read them that differ from the cattle? Are we not so created as to be different from brute animals, even before we can acquire the art of reading? Pray, tell me how it is that you put in so high a claim for our nature, that by the very circumstance of its differing from cattle it already knows how to discuss and in-

quire into the origin of souls; while at the same time you make it so inexpert in this knowledge, as to be unable by human endowment to know this without it believe the divine testimonies.

CHAP. 15 [XI.] — WE MUST NOT BE WISE ABOVE WHAT IS WRITTEN.

But then, again, you are mistaken in this matter; for the passages of Scripture which you chose to produce for the solution of this question of yours, do not prove the point. For it is another thing which they prove, without which we cannot really lead a pious life, namely, that we have in God the giver, creator, and fashioner of our souls. But how He does this for them, whether by inbreathing them as new, or by deriving them from the parents, they do not tell us — except in the instance of that one soul which He gave to the first man. Read attentively what I have written to that servant of God, our brother Renatus;[1] for inasmuch as I have pointed it all out to him there, it is not necessary for me to repeat my proofs here. But you would like me to follow your example in definiteness of theory, and so thrust myself into such difficulties as you have surrounded yourself with. Involved in these, you have spoken many stout words against the catholic faith; if, however, you would faithfully and humbly bethink yourself and consider, you would assuredly see how greatly it would have profited you, if you had only known how to be natural and consistent in your ignorance; and how this advantage is still open to you, if you were even now able to maintain such propriety. Now, since understanding so pleases you in man's nature (for, truly enough, if our nature were without it, we should not be different from brute beasts, so far as our souls are concerned), understand, I beg of you, what it is that you do not understand, lest you should understand nothing: and do not despise any man who, in order that he may truly understand, understands that he does not understand that which he does not understand.[2] With regard, however, to the passage in the inspired psalm, "Man, being in honour, understandeth not; he is compared to the senseless cattle, and is like unto them;"[3] read and understand these words, that you may rather with a humble spirit guard against the opprobrium yourself, than arrogantly throw it out against another person. The passage applies to those who regard only that as a life worth living which they live in the flesh — having no hope after death — just like "cattle;" it has no reference to those who never deny their

---

[1] See above, Book i. 17 [XIV.], and following.
[2] This repetition of one word for rhetorical effect is characteristic of our author (as, before him, it was of the Apostle Paul): "*Intellige quid non intelligas, ne totum non intelligas . . . qui ut veraciter intelligat, quod non intelligit hoc se non intelligere intelligit.*"
[3] Ps. xlix. 12, 13.

knowledge of what they actually know, and always acknowledge their ignorance of what they really do not know ; who, in point of fact, are aware of their weakness, rather than confident of their strength.

CHAP. 16. — IGNORANCE IS BETTER THAN ERROR. PREDESTINATION TO ETERNAL LIFE, AND PRE-DESTINATION TO ETERNAL DEATH.

Do not, my son, let senile timidity displease your youthful confidence. For my own part, indeed, if I proved unequal, either under the teaching of God or of some spiritual instructor, to the task of understanding the subject of our present inquiry on the origin of souls, I am more prepared to vindicate God's righteous will, that we should remain in ignorance on this point, as on many others, than to say in my rashness what either is so obscure that I can neither bring it home to the intelligence of other people, nor understand it myself ; or certainly even to help the cause of the heretics who endeavour to persuade us that the souls of infants are entirely free from guilt, on the ground, forsooth, that such guilt would only recoil on God as its Author, for having compelled innocent souls (for the help of which He knew beforehand no laver of regeneration was prepared) to become sinful, by assigning them to sinful flesh without any provision for that grace of baptism which should prevent their incurring eternal damnation. For the fact undoubtedly is, that numberless souls of infants pass out of the body before they are baptized. God forbid that I should cast about for any futile effort to dilute this stern fact, and say what you have yourself said : " That the soul deserved to be polluted by the flesh, and to become sinful, though it previously had no sin, by reason of which it could be rightly said to have incurred this desert." And again : "That even without baptism original sins may be remitted." And once more : " That even the kingdom of heaven is at last bestowed on those who have not been baptized." Now, if I were not afraid to utter these and similar poisonous allegations against the faith, I should probably not be afraid to propound some definite theory on this subject. How much better, then, is it, that I should not separately dispute and affirm about the soul, what I am ignorant of ; but simply hold what I see the apostle has most plainly taught us : That owing to one man all pass into condemnation who are born of Adam [1] unless they are born again in Christ, even as He has appointed them to be regenerated, before they die in the body, whom He predestinated to everlasting life, as the most merciful bestower of grace ; whilst to those whom He has predestinated to eternal death, He is

also the most righteous awarder of punishment, not only on account of the sins which they add in the indulgence of their own will, but also because of their original sin, even if, as in the case of infants, they add nothing thereto. Now this is my definite view on that question, so that the hidden things of God may keep their secret, without impairing my own faith.

CHAP. 17 [XII.] — A TWOFOLD QUESTION TO BE TREATED CONCERNING THE SOUL ; IS IT " BODY " ? AND IS IT " SPIRIT " ? WHAT BODY IS.

And now, as far as the Lord vouchsafes to enable me, I must reply also to that allegation of yours, in which, speaking of the soul, you again mention my name, and say, " We do not, as the very able and learned bishop Augustin professes, allow it to be incorporeal and also a spirit." We have therefore, first, to discuss the question, whether the soul is to be deemed incorporeal, as I have said ; or corporeal, as you hold. Then, secondly, whether in our Scriptures it is called a spirit — although not the whole but its own separate part is also properly called spirit.[2] Well, I should, to begin with, like to know how you define body. For if that is not " body " which does not consist of limbs of flesh, then the earth cannot be a body, nor the sky, nor a stone, nor water, nor the stars, nor anything of the kind. If, however, a " body " is whatever consists of parts, whether greater or less, which occupy greater or smaller local spaces, then all the things which I have just mentioned are bodies ; the air is a body ; the visible light is a body ; and so are all the things which the apostle has in view, when he says, " There are celestial bodies, and bodies terrestrial." [3]

CHAP. 18. — THE FIRST QUESTION, WHETHER THE SOUL IS CORPOREAL ; BREATH AND WIND, NOTHING ELSE THAN AIR IN MOTION.

Now whether the soul is such a substance, is an extremely nice and subtle question. You, indeed, with a promptitude for which I very greatly congratulate you, affirm that God is not a body. But then, again, you give me some anxiety when you say, " If the soul lacks body, so as to be (as some persons are pleased to suppose) of hollow emptiness, of airy and futile substance." Now, from these words you seem to believe, that everything which lacks body is of an empty substance. Well, if this is the case, how do you dare to say that God lacks body, without fearing the consequence that He is of an empty substance ? If, however, God has not

---

[1] See Rom. v. 18.

[2] [The author seems here to have such texts as 1 Thess. v. 23 in mind (see below, chs. 19 and 36), and to mean that sometimes the whole inner man is called " spirit," and sometimes " spirit " is distinguished from " soul." — W.]

[3] 1 Cor. xv. 40.

a body, as you have just allowed; and if it be profane to say that He is of an empty substance; then not everything which lacks body is an empty substance. And therefore a person who contends that the soul is incorporeal does not necessarily mean, that it is of an empty and futile substance; for he allows that God, who is not an empty being, is at the same time incorporeal. But observe what great difference there is between my actual assertion, and what you suppose me to say. I do not say that the soul is an airy substance; if I did, I should admit that it is a body. For air is a body; as all who understand what they say declare, whenever they speak concerning bodily substances. But you, because I called the soul incorporeal, supposed me not only to predicate mere emptiness of it, but, as the result of such predication, to say that it is "an airy substance;" whereas I must have said both that it has not corporeity, which air has, and that what is filled with air could not be empty. And your own bag similes failed to remind you of this. For when the bags are inflated, what is it but air that is pressed into them? And they are so far from being empty, that by reason of their distension they become even ponderous. But perhaps the breath seems to you to be a different thing from air; although your very breath is nothing else than air in motion; and what this is, can be seen from the shaking of a fan. With respect to any hollow vessels, which you may suppose to be empty, you may ascertain with certainty that they are really full, by lowering them straight into the water, with the mouth downwards. You see no water can get in, by reason of the air with which they are filled. If, however, they are lowered either in the opposite way, with mouth upward, or aslant, they then fill, as the water enters at the same opening where the air passes out and escapes. This could be, of course, more easily proved by performing the experiment, than by a description in writing. This, however, is not the time or place for longer delay on the subject; for whatever may be your perception of the nature of the air, as to whether it has corporeity or not, you certainly ought not to suppose me to have said that the soul is an aerial thing, but absolutely incorporeal. And this even you acknowledge God to be, whom you do not dare to describe as an empty substance, while you cannot but admit that He has an essence which is unchangeable and almighty. Now, why should we fear that the soul is an empty void, if it be incorporeal, when we confess that God is incorporeal, and at the same time deny Him to be an empty void? Thus it was within the competency of an Incorporeal Being to create an incorporeal soul, even as the living God made living man; although, as the unchangeable and

the almighty, He communicated not these attributes to the changeable and far inferior creature.

CHAP. 19 [XIII.]— WHETHER THE SOUL IS A SPIRIT.

But again, why you would have the soul to be a body, and refuse to deem it a spirit, I cannot see. For if it is not a spirit, on the ground that the apostle named it with distinction from the spirit, when he said, "I pray God your whole spirit, and soul, and body be preserved,"[1] the same is a good reason why it is not a body, inasmuch as he named the body, too, as distinct from it. If you affirm that the soul is a body, although they are both distinctly named; you should allow it to be a spirit, although these are also distinctly named. Indeed, the soul has a much greater claim to be regarded by you as a spirit than a body; because you acknowledge the spirit and the soul to be of one substance, but deny the soul and the body to be of one substance. On what principle, then, is the soul a body, when its nature is different from that of a body; and not a spirit, although its nature and a spirit's is one and the same? Why, according to your argument, must you not confess that even the spirit is a body? For otherwise, if the spirit is not a body, and the soul is a body, the soul and the spirit are not of one and the same substance. You, however, allow them both (although believing them to be two separate things) to have one substance. Therefore, if the soul is a body, the spirit is a body also; for under no other condition can they be regarded as being of one and the same nature. On your own principles, therefore, the statement of the apostle, who mentions, "Your spirit, and soul, and body," must imply three bodies; yet the body, which has likewise the name of flesh, is of a different nature. And of these three bodies, as you would call them, of which one is of a different, and the other two of one and the same substance, the entire human being is composed — one thing and one existence. Now, although you assert this, yet you will not allow that the two which are of one and the same substance, that is, the soul and the spirit, should have the one designation of spirit; whilst the two things which are not of one and the same substance ought, as you suppose, to have the one name of body.

CHAP. 20 [XIV.] — THE BODY DOES NOT RECEIVE GOD'S IMAGE.

But I pass by all this, lest the discussion between us should degenerate into one of names rather than things. Let us, then, see whether the inner man be the soul, or the spirit, or both. I observe, however, that you have expressed

---

[1] 1 Thess. v. 23.

your opinion on the point in writing, calling the inner man the soul; for of this you spoke when you said: "And as the substance congealed, which was incapable of comprehension, it would produce another body within the body rounded and amassed by the force and twirl of its own nature, and thus an inner man would begin to appear, who, being moulded in a corporeal sheath, would in its lineaments be shaped after the likeness of its outer man." And from this you draw the following inference: "God's breath, therefore, made the soul; yea, that breath from God was made the soul, an image, substantial, corporeal according to its own nature, like its own body, and conformed to its image." After this you proceed to speak of the spirit, and say: "This soul which had its origin from the breath of God could not exist without an innermost sense and intellect of its own; and such is the spirit." As I, then, understand your statement, you mean the inner man to be the soul, and the inmost one to be the spirit; as if the latter were inferior to the soul, as this is to the body. Whence it comes to pass, that just as the body receives another body pervading its own inner cavity, which (as you suppose) is the soul; so in its turn must the soul be regarded as having its interior emptiness also, where it could receive the third body, even the spirit; and thus the whole man consists of three, the outer, the inner, and the inmost. Now, do you not yet perceive what great absurdities follow in your wake, when you attempt the asseveration that the soul is corporeal? Tell me, I pray you, which of the two is it that is to be renewed in the knowledge of God, after the image of Him that created him?[1] The inner, or the inmost? For my own part, indeed, I do not see that the apostle, besides the inner and the outer man, knows anything of another man inside the inner one, that is, of an inmost man. But you must decide which it is you would have to be renewed after the image of God. How is he to receive this, who has already got the image of the outer man? For if the inner man has run throughout the limbs of the outward one, and *congealed* (for this is the term you have used; as if a molten shape were formed out of soft clay, which was thickened out of the dust), how, if this same figure which has been impressed upon it, or rather *expressed* out of a body, is to retain its place, could it be refashioned after the image of God? Is it to have two images — God's from above, that of the body from below — as is said in the case of money, "Heads and Tails"?[2] Will you perhaps say, that the soul received the

bodily image, and that the spirit takes God's image, as if the former were contiguous to the body, and the latter to God; and that, therefore, it is really the inmost man which is refashioned after the image of God, and not the inner man? Well, but this pretence is useless. For if the inmost man is as entirely diffused through all the members of the soul, as the inner man of the soul is through the limbs of the body; even it has now, through the soul, received the image of the body, as the soul moulded the same; and thus it results that it has no means whereby to receive God's image, while the afore-mentioned image of the body remains impressed upon it; except as in the case of the money which I have just quoted, where there is one form on the upper surface, and another on the lower one. These are the absurd lengths to which you are driven, whether you will or no, when you apply to the consideration of the soul the material ideas of bodily substances. But, as even you yourself with perfect propriety confess, God is not a body. How, then, could a body receive His image? "I beseech you, brother, that you be not conformed to this world, but be transformed by the renewing of your mind;"[3] and cherish not "the carnal mind, which is death."[4]

CHAP. 21 [XV.] — RECOGNITION AND FORM BELONG TO SOULS AS WELL AS BODIES.

But you say: "If the soul is incorporeal, what was it that the rich man saw in hell? He certainly recognised Lazarus; he did [not[5]] know Abraham. Whence arose to him the knowledge of Abraham, who had died so long before?" By using these words, I suppose that you do not think a man can be recognised and known without his bodily form. To know yourself, therefore, I imagine that you often stand before your looking-glass, lest by forgetting your features you should be unable to recognise yourself. But let me ask you, what man does anybody know more than himself; and whose face can he see less than his own? But who could possibly know God, whom even you do not doubt to be incorporeal, if knowledge could not (as you suppose) accrue without bodily shape; that is, if bodies alone can be recognised? What Christian, however, when discussing subjects of such magnitude and difficulty, can give such little heed to the inspired word as to say, "If the soul be incorporeal, it must of necessity lack form"? Have you forgotten that in that word you have read of "a form of doctrine"?[6] Have you forgotten, too, that it is written con-

---

[1] Col. iii. 10.
[2] *Caput et Navia*, literally "head and ship," the piece of money having a head of Janus on one side, and a ship on the other. See the matter illustrated in Macrobius, *Saturnalia*, i. 7, Aur. Vict. *Orig.* 3.

[3] Rom. xii. 1, 2.　　[4] Rom. viii. 6.
[5] Luke xvi. 19-31. Non noverat Abraham. But some MSS. omit *non*; rightly, one would think. The meaning then is: "He recognised Abraham."
[6] Rom. vi. 17.

cerning Christ Jesus, previous to His clothing Himself with humanity, that He was "in the form of God"?[1] How, then, can you say, "If the soul is incorporeal, it must of necessity lack form;" when you hear of "the form of God," whom you acknowledge to be incorporeal; and so express yourself, as if form could not possibly exist except in bodies?

## CHAP. 22.—NAMES DO NOT IMPLY CORPOREITY.

You also say, that "names cease to be given, when form is not distinguished; and that, where there is no designation of persons, there is no giving of names." Your aim is to prove that Abraham's soul was corporeal, inasmuch as he could be addressed as "Father Abraham." Now, we have already said, that there is form even where there is no body. If, however, you think that where there are not bodies there is no assigning of names, I must beg of you to count the names which occur in this passage of Scripture, "But the fruit of the Spirit is love, joy, peace, long-suffering, gentleness, goodness, faith, meekness, temperance,"[2] and tell me whether you do not recognise the very things of which these are the names; or whether you recognise them so as to descry some outlines of bodies. Come, tell me, to mention only love, for instance, what are its members, its figure, its colour? For if you are not yourself empty-headed, these appurtenances cannot possibly be regarded by you as an empty thing. Then you go on to say: "The look and form must, of course, be corporeal of him whose help is implored." Well, let men hear what you say; and let no one implore God's help, because no one can possibly see anything corporeal in Him.

## CHAP. 23 [XVI.]—FIGURATIVE SPEECH MUST NOT BE TAKEN LITERALLY.

"In short," you say, "members are in this parable ascribed to the soul, as if it were really a body." You will have it, that "by the eye the whole head is understood," because it is said, that "he lifted up his eyes." Again you say, that "by tongues are meant jaws, and by finger the hand," because it is said, "Send Lazarus, that he may dip the tip of his finger in water, and cool my tongue."[3] And yet to save yourself from the inconsistency of ascribing corporeal qualities to God, you say that "by these terms must be understood incorporeal functions and powers;" because with the greatest propriety you insist on it, that God is not corporeal. What is the reason, therefore, that the names of these limbs do not argue corporeity in God, although they do in the case of the soul? Is it that these terms must be understood literally when spoken

of the creature, and only metaphorically and figuratively when predicated of the Creator? Then you will have to give us wings of literal bodily substance, since it is not the Creator, but only a human creature, who said, "If I should take my wings like a dove."[4] Moreover, if the rich man of the parable had a bodily tongue, on the ground of his exclaiming, "Let him cool my tongue," it would look very much as if our tongue, even while we are in the flesh, itself possessed material hands, because it is written, "Death and life are in the *hands* of the tongue."[5] I suppose it is even to yourself self-evident, that sin is neither a creature nor a bodily substance; why, then, has it a face? For do you not hear the psalmist say, "There is no peace in my bones, in the *face* of my sins"?[6]

## CHAP. 24.—ABRAHAM'S BOSOM—WHAT IT MEANS.

As to your supposing that "the Abraham's bosom referred to is corporeal," and your further assertion, that "by it is meant his whole body," I fear that you must be regarded (even in such a subject) as trying to joke and raise a laugh, instead of acting gravely and seriously. For you could not else be so foolish as to think that the material bosom of one person could receive so many souls; nay, to use your own words, "bear the bodies of as many meritorious men as the angels carry thither, as they did Lazarus." Unless it happen to be your opinion, that his soul alone deserved to find its way to the said bosom. If you are not, then, in fun, and do not wish to make childish mistakes, you must understand by "Abraham's bosom" that remote and separate abode of rest and peace in which Abraham now is; and that what was said to Abraham[7] did not merely refer to him personally, but had reference to his appointment as the father of many nations,[8] to whom he was presented for imitation as the first and principal example of faith; even as God willed Himself to be called "the God of Abraham, the God of Isaac, and the God of Jacob," although He is the God of an innumerable company.

## CHAP. 25 [XVII.]—THE DISEMBODIED SOUL MAY THINK OF ITSELF UNDER A BODILY FORM.

You must not, however, suppose that I say all this as if denying it to be possible that the soul of a dead man, like a person asleep, may think either good or evil thoughts in the similitude of his body. For, in dreams, when we suffer anything harsh and troublesome, we are, of course,

---

[1] Phil. ii. 6.    [2] Gal. v. 22, 23.    [3] Luke xvi. 24.

[4] Augustin's reading of Ps. cxxxix. 9.
[5] In *manibus* linguæ = the Hebrew phrase בְּיַד־לָשׁוֹן, Prov. xviii. 21.
[6] Ps. xxxviii. 3, מִפְּנֵי חַטָּאתִי.    [7] In Luke xvi. 24.
[8] Gen. xvii. 5.

still ourselves; and if the distress do not pass away when we awake, we experience very great suffering. But to suppose that they are veritable bodies in which we are hurried, or flit, about hither and thither in dreams, is the idea of a person who has thought only carelessly on such subjects; for it is in fact mainly by these imaginary sights that the soul is proved to be non-corporeal; unless you choose to call even the objects which we see so often in our dreams, besides ourselves, bodies, such as the sky, the earth, the sea, the sun, the moon, the stars, and rivers, mountains, trees, or animals. Whoever takes these phantoms to be bodies, is incredibly foolish; although they are certainly very like bodies. Of this character also are those phenomena which are demonstrably of divine significance, whether seen in dreams or in a trance. Who can possibly trace out or describe their origin, or the material of which they consist? It is, beyond question, spiritual, not corporeal. Now things of this kind, which look like bodies, but are not really corporeal, are formed in the thoughts of persons when they are awake, and are held in the depths of their memories, and then out of these secret recesses, by some wonderful and ineffable process, they come out to view in the operation of our memory, and present themselves as if palpably before our eyes. If, therefore, the soul were a material body, it could not possibly contain so many things and such large forms of bodily substances in its scope of thought, and in the spaces of its memory; for, according to your own definition, "it does not exceed this external body in its own corporeal substance." Possessing, therefore, no magnitude of its own, what capacity has it to hold the images of vast bodies, spaces, and regions? What wonder is it, then, if it actually itself appears to itself in the likeness of its own body, even when it appears without a body? For it never appears to itself in dreams with its own body; and yet in the very similitude of its own body it runs hither and thither through known and unknown places, and beholds many sad and joyous sights. I suppose, however, that you really would not, yourself, be so bold as to maintain that there is true corporeity in that form of limb and body which the soul seems to itself to possess in dreams. For at that rate that will be a real mountain which it appears to ascend; and that a material house which it seems to enter; and that a veritable tree, with real wood and bulk, beneath which it apparently reclines; and that actual water which it imagines itself to drink. All the things with which it is conversant, as if they were corporeal, would be undoubted bodies, if the soul were itself corporeal, as it ranges about amongst them all in the likeness of a body.

Some notice must be taken of sundry accounts of martyrs' visions, because you have thought proper to derive some of your evidence therefrom. St. Perpetua, for instance, seemed to herself in dreams to be wrestling with an Egyptian, after being changed into a man. Now, who can doubt that it was her soul in that apparent bodily form, not her body, which, of course, remained in her own sex as a woman, and lay on the bed with her senses steeped in sleep, whilst her soul was struggling in the similitude of a man's body? What have you to say to this? Was that male likeness a veritable body, or was it no body at all, although possessing the appearance of a body? Choose your alternative. If it was a body, why did it not maintain its sexual integrity? For in that woman's flesh were found no virile functions of generation, whence by any such process as that which you call *congelation* could be moulded this similitude of a man's body. We will conclude then, if you please, that, as her body was still alive while she slept, notwithstanding the wrestling of her soul, she remained in her own natural sex, enclosed, of course, in all her proper limbs which belong to her in her living state, and was still in possession of that bodily shape and the lineaments of which she had been originally formed. She had not resigned, as she would by death, her joints and limbs; nor had she withdrawn from the transposing power, which arises from the operation of the power of death, any of her members which had already received their fixed form. Whence, then, did her soul get that virile body in which she seemed to wrestle with her adversary? If, however, this [male likeness] was not a body, although such a semblance of one as admitted the sensation in it of a real struggle or a real joy, do you not by this time see, as far as may be, that there can be in the soul a certain resemblance of a bodily substance, while the soul is not itself a body?

## CHAP. 27. — IS THE SOUL WOUNDED WHEN THE BODY IS WOUNDED?

What, then, if some such thing is exhibited among the departed; and souls recognise themselves among them, not, indeed, by bodies, but by the semblances of bodies? Now, when we suffer pain, if only in our dreams, although it is only the similitude of bodily limbs which is in action, and not the bodily limbs themselves, still the pain is not merely in semblance, but in reality; as is also the case in the instance of joyous sensations. Inasmuch, however, as St. Perpetua was not yet dead, you probably are unwilling to lay down a precise rule for yourself from that circumstance (although it bears strongly on the question), as to what nature you will suppose these semblances of bodies to partake of, which we have in our dreams. If you allow them to be like bodies, but not bodies actually, then the entire question would be settled. But her brother Dinocrates was dead; she saw him with the wound which he received while alive, and which caused his death. Where is the ground for the earnest contention to which you devoted your efforts, when you laboured to show, that when a limb is cut off, the soul must not be supposed as suffering a like amount of loss by amputation? Observe, the wound was inflicted on the soul of Dinocrates, expelling it by its force from his body, when it was inhabiting that body. How, then, can your opinion be correct, that "when the limbs of the body are cut off, the soul withdraws itself from the stroke, and after condensation retires to other parts, so that no portion of it is amputated with the wound inflicted on the body," even if the person be asleep and unconscious when the loss of limb is suffered? So great is the vigilance which you have ascribed to the soul, that even should the stroke fall on any part of the flesh without its knowledge, when it is absorbed in the visions of dreams, it would instantly, and by a providential instinct, withdraw itself, and so render it impossible for any blow, or injury, or mutilation to be inflicted upon it. However, you may, as much as you will, ransack your ingenuity for an answer to the natural question, how the soul withdraws the portions of its own existence, and retreats within itself, so that, whenever a limb of the body is cut off or broken, it does not suffer any amputation or fracture in itself; but I cannot help asking you to look at the case of Dinocrates, and to explain to me why his soul did not withdraw from that part of his body which received the mortal wound, and so escape from suffering in itself what was plainly enough seen in his face, even after his body was dead? Is it, perchance, your good pleasure that we should suppose the phenomena in question to be rather the semblances of bodies than the reality; so that as that which is really no wound seems to be a wound, so that which is no body at all wears the appearance of corporeity? If, indeed, the soul can be wounded by those who wound the body, should we not have good reason to fear that it can be killed also by those who kill the body? This, however, is a fate which the Lord Himself most plainly declares it to be impossible to happen.[1] And the soul of Dinocrates could not at any rate have died of the blow which killed his body: its wound, too,

was only an apparent one; for not being corporeal, it was not really wounded, as the body had been; possessing the likeness of the body, it shared also the resemblance of its wound. Still it may be further said, that in its unreal body the soul felt a real misery, which was signified by the shadow of the body's wound. It was from this real misery that he earned deliverance by the prayers of his holy sister.

CHAP. 28. — IS THE SOUL DEFORMED BY THE BODY'S IMPERFECTIONS?

Now, again, what means it that you say, "The soul acquires form from the body, and grows and extends with the increase of the body," without keeping in view what a monstrosity the soul of either a young man or an old man would become if his arm had been amputated when he was an infant? "The hand of the soul," you say, "contracts itself, so that it is not amputated with the hand of the body, and by condensation it shrinks into other parts of the body." At this rate the aforesaid arm of the soul will be kept, wherever it holds its ground, as short as it was at first when it received the form of the body, because it has lost the form by the growth of which it might itself have increased at an equal degree of expansion. Thus the soul of the young man or the old man who lost his hand in his infancy advances with two hands, indeed (because the one which shrank back escaped the amputation of the bodily limb), but one of these was the hand of an adult, young or old, according to the hypothesis, while the other was only an infant's hand, just as it was when the amputation happened. Such souls, believe me, are not made in the mould and form of the body, but they are fictitiously framed under the deformed stamp of error. It seems to me impossible for you to be rescued from this error, unless with God's help you fully and calmly examine the visions of those who dream, and from these convince yourself that some forms are not real bodies, but only the semblances of bodies. Now, although even those objects which we suppose to be like bodies are of the same class,[2] yet so far as the dead are concerned, we can form an after guess about them from persons who are asleep. For it is not in vain that Holy Scripture describes as "asleep" those who are dead,[3] were it only because in a certain sense "sleep is akin to death."[4]

CHAP. 29 [XIX.] — DOES THE SOUL TAKE THE BODY'S CLOTHES ALSO AWAY WITH IT?

If, indeed, the soul were body, and the form

---

[1] Matt. x. 28.

[2] That is (in opposition to the really "dead," afterwards mentioned), such as are seen by living persons in visions.

[3] 1 Thess. iv. 13.

[4] Virgil. Æneid, vi. 279, "Consanguineus Lethi sopor" (Death's own brother, Sleep).

were also a corporeal figure in which it sees itself in dreams, on the ground that it received its expression from the body in which it is enclosed : not a human being, if he lost a limb, would in dreams see himself bereft of the amputated member, although actually deprived of it. On the contrary, he would always appear to himself entire and unmutilated, from the circumstance that no part has been cut away from the soul itself. But since persons sometimes see themselves whole and sometimes mutilated in limb, when this happens to be their actual plight, what else does this fact show than that the soul, both in respect of other things seen by it in dreams and in reference to the body, bears about, hither and thither, not their reality, but only their resemblance ? The soul's joy, however, or sadness, its pleasure or pain, are severally real emotions, whether experienced in actual or in apparent bodies. Have you not yourself said (and with perfect truth) : " Aliments and vestments are not wanted by the soul, but only by the body " ? Why, then, did the rich man in hell crave for the drop of water ?[1] Why did holy Samuel appear after his death (as you have yourself noticed) clothed in his usual garments ?[2] Did the one wish to repair the ruins of the soul, as of the flesh, by the aliment of water ? Did the other quit life with his clothes on him ? Now in the former case there was a real suffering, which tormented the soul ; but not a real body, such as required food. While the latter might have seemed to be clothed, not as being a veritable body, but a soul only, having the semblance of a body with a dress. For although the soul extends and contracts itself to suit the members of the body, it does not similarly adapt itself to the clothes, so as to fit its form to them.

## CHAP. 30. — IS CORPOREITY NECESSARY FOR RECOGNITION ?

But who is able to trace out what capacity of recognition even souls which are not good possess after death when relieved of the corruptible bodies, so as to be able by an inner sense to observe and recognise either souls that are evil like themselves, or even good ones, either in states which are actually not corporeal, but the semblances of bodies ; or else in good or evil affections of the mind, in which there occur no lineaments whatever of bodily members ? Whence arises the fact that the rich man in the parable, though in torments, recognised " Father Abraham," whose face and figure he had never seen, but the semblance of whose body his soul, though incorporeal, was able to comprehend ?[3] But who could rightly say that he had known any man, except in so far as he

has had means of knowing his life and disposition, which have, of course, neither material substance nor colours ? It is in this way that we know ourselves more certainly than any others, because our own consciousness and disposition are all before us. This we plainly perceive, and yet we see therein no similitude of a bodily substance. But we do not perceive this inner quality of our nature in another man, even if he be present before our eyes ; though in his absence we recollect his features, and recognise them, and think of them. Our own features, however, we cannot in the same manner recollect, and recognise, and think of ; and yet with most perfect truth we say that we are ourselves better known to ourselves than he is, so manifest is it where lies the stronger and truer knowledge of man.

## CHAP. 31　[XX.] — MODES OF KNOWLEDGE IN THE SOUL DISTINGUISHED.

Forasmuch, then, as there is one function in the soul, by which we perceive real bodies, which we do by the five bodily senses ; another, which enables us to discern apart from these non-corporeal likenesses of bodies (and by this we can have a view of ourselves also, as not otherwise than like to bodies) ; and a third, by which we gain a still surer and stronger insight into objects fitted for its faculty, which are neither corporeal nor are like bodily substances, — such as faith, hope, charity, — things which have neither complexion, nor passion, nor any such thing : on which of these functions ought we to dwell more intently, and to some degree more familiarly, and where be renewed in the knowledge of God after the image of Him who created us ? Is it not on and in that which I have now put in the third place ? And here we shall certainly experience neither sexual difference nor the semblance thereof.

## CHAP. 32. — INCONSISTENCY OF GIVING THE SOUL ALL THE PARTS OF SEX AND YET NO SEX.

For that form of the soul, whether masculine or feminine, which has the distinction of members characteristic of man and woman, being no semblance merely of body, but actual body, is either a male or a female, whether you will or no, precisely as it appears to be a man or a woman. But if your opinion be correct, and the soul is a body, even a living body, then it both possesses swelling and pendent breasts, and lacks a beard, it has a womb, and all the generative organs of a woman, yet is not a woman after all. Will not mine, then, be a statement more consistent with truth : the soul, indeed, has an eye and has a tongue, has a finger, and all other members which resemble those of the body, and yet the whole is the semblance

---

of a body, not a body really? My statement is open to a general test; everybody can prove it in himself, when he brings home to his mind the image of absent friends; he can prove it with certainty when he recalls the figures both of himself and other persons, which have occurred to him in his dreams. On your part, however, no example can throughout nature be produced of such a monstrosity as you have imagined, where there is a woman's real and living body, but not a woman's sex.

CHAP. 33. — THE PHENIX AFTER DEATH COMING TO LIFE AGAIN.

Now, what you say about the phenix has nothing whatever to do with the subject before us. For the phenix symbolizes the resurrection of the body; it does not do away with the sex of souls; if indeed, as is thought, he is born afresh after his death. I suppose, however, that you thought your discourse would not be sufficiently plausible unless you declaimed a good deal about the phenix, after the fashion of young people. Now do you find in the body of your bird male organs of generation and not a male bird; or female ones, and not a female? But, I beg of you, reflect on what it is you say, — what theory you are trying to construct, and to recommend for our acceptance. You say that the soul, spread through all the limbs of the body, grew stiff by congelation, and received the entire shape of the whole body from the crown of the head to the soles of the feet, and from the inmost marrow to the skin's outward surface. At this rate it must have received, in the case of a female body, all the inner appurtenances of a woman's body, and yet not be a woman! Why, pray, are all the members feminine in a true living body, and yet the whole no woman? And why all be male, and the result not a man? Who can be so presumptuous as to believe, and profess, and teach all this? Is it that souls never generate? Then, of course, mules and she-mules are not male and female. Is it that souls without bodies of flesh would be unable to cohabit? Well, but this deprivation is shared by castrated men; and yet, although both the process and the motion be taken from them, their sex is not removed — some slender remnant of their male members being still left to them. Nobody ever said that a eunuch is not a male. What now becomes of your opinion, that the souls even of eunuchs have the generative organs unimpaired, and that these organs will remain entire, on your principle, in their souls, even when they are clean removed from their bodily structure? For you say, the soul knows how to withdraw itself when that part of the flesh begins to be cut off, so that the form which has been removed when amputated is not lost; but although spread over it by condensation, it retires by an extremely rapid movement, and so buries itself within as to be kept quite safe; yet that cannot, forsooth, be a male in the other world which carries with it thither the whole appendage of male organs of generation, and which, if it had not even other signs in the body, was a male by reason of those organs alone. These opinions, my son, have no truth in them; if you will not allow that there is sex in the soul, there cannot be a body either.

CHAP. 34 [XXI.] — PROPHETIC VISIONS.

Not every semblance of a body is itself a body. Fall asleep and you will see this; but when you awake again, carefully discern what it is you have seen. For in your dreams you will appear to yourself as if endued with a body; but it really is not your body, but your soul; nor is it a real body, but the semblance of a body. Your body will be lying on the bed, but the soul walking; the tongue of your body will be silent, but that of your soul in the dream will talk; your eyes will be shut, but your soul will be awake; and, of course, the limbs of your body stretched out in your bed will be alive, not dead. Consequently that congealed form, as you regard it, of your soul is not yet extracted, as it were, out of its sheath; and yet in it is seen the whole and perfect semblance of your fleshly frame. Belonging to this class of similitudes of corporeity, which are not real bodies, though they seem to be such, are all those appearances which you read of in the Holy Scriptures in the visions even of the prophets, without, however, understanding them; by which are also signified the things which come to pass in all time — present, past, and future. You make mistakes about these, not because they are in themselves deceptive, but because you do not accept them as they ought to be taken. For in the same apocalyptic vision where "the souls of the martyrs" are seen,[1] there is also beheld "a lamb as it were slain, having seven horns:"[2] there are also horses and other animals figuratively described with all consistency;[3] and lastly, there were the stars falling, and the earth rolled up like a book;[4] nor does the world, in spite of all, then actually collapse. If therefore we understand all these things wisely, although we say they are true apparitions, yet we do not call them real bodies.

CHAP. 35. — DO ANGELS APPEAR TO MEN IN REAL BODIES?

It would, however, require too lengthy a discourse to enter very carefully on a discussion

---

[1] Rev. vi. 9.  [2] Rev. v. 6.  [3] Rev. vi. and ix.
[4] Rev. vi. 13, 14.

concerning this kind of corporeal semblances; whether angels even, either good ones or evil ones, appear in this manner,[1] whenever they appear in the likeness of human beings or of any bodies whatever; or whether they possess real bodies, and show themselves in this veritable state of corporeity; or, again, whether by persons when dreaming, indeed, or in a trance they are perceived in these forms — not in bodies, but in the likeness of bodies — while to persons when awake they present real bodies which can be seen, and, if necessary, actually touched. Such questions as these, however, I do not deem it at all requisite to investigate and fully treat in this book. By this time enough has been advanced respecting the soul's incorporeity. If you would rather persist in your opinion that it is corporeal, you must first of all define what "*body*" means; lest, peradventure, it may turn out that we are agreed about the thing itself, but labouring to no purpose about its name. The absurd conclusions, however, to which you would be reduced if you thought of such a body in the soul, as are those substances which are called "bodies" by all learned men, — I mean such as occupy portions of space, smaller ones for their smaller parts, and larger ones for their larger, — by means of the different relations of length and breadth and thickness, I venture to think you are by this time able intelligently to observe.

CHAP. 36 [XXII.] — HE PASSES ON TO THE SECOND QUESTION ABOUT THE SOUL, WHETHER IT IS CALLED SPIRIT.

It now remains for me to show how it is that while the designation *spirit* is rightly predicated of a part of the soul, not the whole of it, — even as the apostle says, "Your whole spirit, and soul, and body;"[2] or, according to the much more expressive statement in the Book of Job, "Thou wilt separate my soul from my spirit,"[3] — yet the whole soul is also called by this name; although this question seems to be much more a question of names than of things. For since it is certainly a fact that there is a something in the soul which is properly called "spirit," while (this being left out of question) it is also designated with equal propriety "soul," our present contention is not about the things themselves;[4] mainly because I on my side certainly admit, and you on your part say the same, that that is properly called spirit by which we reason and understand, and yet that these things are dis-

tinguishingly designated, as the apostle says "your whole spirit, and soul, and body." This spirit, however, the same apostle appears also to describe as *mind;* as when he says, "So then with the mind I serve the law of God, but with the flesh the law of sin."[5] Now the meaning of this is precisely what he expresses in another passage thus: "For the flesh lusteth against the spirit, and the spirit against the flesh."[6] What he designates *mind* in the former place, he must be understood to call *spirit* in the latter passage. Not as you interpret the statement, "The whole mind is meant, which consists of soul and spirit," — a view which I know not where you obtained. By our "mind," indeed, we usually understand nothing but our rational and intellectual faculty; and thus, when the apostle says, "Be ye renewed in the spirit of your mind,"[7] what else does he mean than, Be ye renewed in your mind? "The spirit of the mind" is, accordingly, nothing else than the mind, just as "the body of the flesh" is nothing but the flesh; thus it is written, "In putting off the body of the flesh,"[8] where the apostle calls the flesh "the body of the flesh." He designates it, indeed, in another point of view as the spirit of man, which he quite distinguishes from the mind: "If," says he, "I pray with the tongue, my spirit prayeth, but my mind is unfruitful."[9] We are not now, however, speaking of that spirit which is distinct from the mind; and this involves a question relating to itself which is really a difficult one. For in many ways and in divers senses the Holy Scriptures make mention of the *spirit;* but with respect to that we are now speaking of, by which we exercise reason, intelligence, and wisdom, we are both agreed that it is called (and indeed rightly called) "spirit," in such a sense as not to include the entire soul, but a part of it. If, however, you contend that the soul is not the spirit, on the ground that the understanding is distinctly called "spirit," you may as well deny that the whole seed of Jacob is called Israel, since, apart from Judah, the same appellation was distinctly and separately borne by the ten tribes which were then organized in Samaria. But why need we linger any longer here on this subject?

CHAP. 37 [XXIII.] — WIDE AND NARROW SENSE OF THE WORD "SPIRIT."

But now, with a view to our easier elucidation, I beg you to observe that what is the soul is also designated spirit in the scripture which narrates an incident in our Lord's death, thus, "He bowed His head and gave up the spirit."[10] Now, when you hear or read these words, you wish to understand them as if the whole were signified

---

[1] That is, as true apparitions indeed, but *not* as real bodies.
[2] 1 Thess. v. 23.    [3] Job vii. 15.
[4] [Compare *On the City of God*, xiv. 2, 6, and *On the Trinity*, x. 11, 18. Augustin denied the *trichotomy* of the Greek Fathers before Apollinaris, and held that the soul and spirit constituted a single substantial unity, and this one spiritual essence was "soul" (*anima*) so far as it was the informing and vivifying principle of the body, and "spirit" (*spiritus*) so far as it was the power of rational thought. — W.]

[5] Rom. vii. 25.    [6] Gal. v. 17.    [7] Eph. iv. 23.
[8] Col. ii. 11.    [9] 1 Cor. xiv. 14.    [10] John xix. 30.

by a part, and not because that which is the soul may also be called spirit. But I shall, for the purpose of being able the more readily to prove what I say, actually summon yourself with all promptitude and convenience as my witness. For you have defined spirit in such terms that cattle appear not to have a spirit, but a soul. Irrational animals are so called, because they have not the power of intelligence and reason. Accordingly, when you admonished man himself to know his own nature, you spoke as follows: "Now, inasmuch as the good God has made nothing without a purpose, He has produced man himself as a rational animal, capable of intelligence, endowed with reason, and enlivened by sensibility, so as to be able to distribute in a wise arrangement all things that are void of reason." In these words of yours you have plainly asserted what is certainly most true, that man is endowed with reason and capable of intelligence, which, of course, animals void of reason are not. And you have, in accordance with this view, quoted a passage of Scripture, and, adopting its language, have compared men of no understanding to the cattle, which, of course, have not intellect.[1] A statement the like to which occurs in another passage of Scripture: "Be ye not as the horse or as the mule, which have no understanding."[2] This being the case, I want you also to observe in what terms you have defined and described the spirit when trying to distinguish it from the soul: "This soul," you say, "which has its origin from the breath of God, could not have possibly been without an inner sense and intellect of its own; and this is the spirit." A little afterwards you add: "And although the soul animates the body, yet inasmuch as it possesses sense, and wisdom, and vigour, there must needs be a spirit." And then somewhat further on you say: "The soul is one thing, and the spirit — which is the soul's wisdom and sense — is another." In these words you plainly enough indicate what you take the spirit of man to mean; that it is even our rational faculty, whereby the soul exercises sense and intelligence, — not, indeed, the sensation which is felt by the bodily senses, but the operation of that innermost sense from which arises the term sentiment. Owing to this it is, no doubt, that we are placed above brute animals, since these are unendowed with reason. These animals therefore have not spirit, — that is to say, intellect and a sense of reason and wisdom, — but only soul. For it is of these that it was spoken, "Let the waters bring forth the creeping creatures that have a living soul;"[3] and again, "Let the earth bring forth the living soul."[4] In order, indeed, that you may have the fullest and

clearest assurance that what is the soul is in the usage of the Holy Scriptures also called spirit, the soul of a brute animal has the designation of spirit. And of course cattle have not that spirit which you, my beloved brother, have defined as being distinct from the soul. It is therefore quite evident that the soul of a brute animal could be rightly called "spirit" in a general sense of the term; as we read in the Book of Ecclesiastes, "Who knoweth the spirit of the sons of men, whether it goeth upward; and the spirit of the beast, whether it goeth downward into the earth?"[5] In like manner, touching the devastation of the deluge, Scripture testifies, "All flesh died that moved upon the earth, both of fowl, and of cattle, and of beast, and of every creeping thing that creepeth upon the earth, and every man: and all things which have the spirit of life."[6] Here, if we remove all the windings of doubtful disputation, we understand the term spirit to be synonymous with soul in its general sense. Of so wide a signification is this term, that even God is called "a spirit;"[7] and a stormy blast of the air, although it has material substance, is called by the psalmist the "spirit" of a tempest.[8] For all these reasons, therefore, you will no longer deny that what is the soul is called also spirit; I have, I think, adduced enough from the pages of Holy Scripture to secure your assent in passages where the soul of the very brute beast, which has no understanding, is designated spirit. If, then, you take and wisely consider what has been advanced in our discussion about the incorporeity of the soul, there is no further reason why you should take offence at my having said that I was sure the soul was not body, but spirit, — both because it is proved to be not corporeal, and because in its general sense it is denominated spirit.

CHAP. 38 [XXIV.] — VICTOR'S CHIEF ERRORS AGAIN POINTED OUT.

Wherefore if you take these books, which I have with a sincere and affectionate interest written in answer to your opinions, and read them with a reciprocal love for me; if you attend to what you have yourself declared in the beginning of your first book, and "are anxious not to insist on any opinion of your own, if it be found an improbable one,"[9] then I beseech you to beware especially of those eleven errors which I warned you of in the preceding book of this treatise.[10] Do not say, that "the soul is of God in such a sense that He created it not out of no, nor out of another, but out of His own nature;" or that, "as God who gives is Himself ever ex-

---

[1] Ps. xlix. 12.    [2] Ps. xxxii. 9.    [3] Gen. i. 20.
[4] Gen. i. 24.

[5] Eccles. iii. 21.    [6] Gen. vii. 21, 22.    [7] John iv. 24.
[8] He seems to refer to Ps. lv. 8.
[9] See above in Book ii. 22 [XVI.].
[10] See Book iii., next to last chapter.

istent, so is He ever giving souls through infinite time ;" or that "the soul lost some merit through the flesh, which it had previous to the flesh ;" or that "the soul by means of the flesh repairs its ancient condition, and is born again through the very same flesh, by which it had deserved to be polluted ;" or that "the soul deserved to be sinful even prior to sin ;" or that "infants who die without the regeneration of baptism, may yet attain to forgiveness of their original sins ;" or that "they whom the Lord has predestinated to be baptized can be taken away from His predestination, or die before that has been accomplished in them which the Almighty had predetermined ;" or that "it is of those who expire before they are baptized that the Scripture says, 'Speedily was he taken away, lest wickedness should alter his understanding,' " — with the remainder of the passage to the same effect ; or that "there are some mansions outside the kingdom of God, belonging to the 'many,' which the Lord said were in His Father's house ;" or that "the sacrifice of the body and blood of Christ ought to be offered in behalf of those who have departed out of the body without being baptized ;" or that "any of those persons who die without Christ's baptism, are received for a while into paradise, and afterwards attain even to the blessedness of the kingdom of heaven." Above all things, beware of these opinions, my son, and, as you wish to be the vanquisher of error, do not rejoice in the surname of "Vincentius." And when you are ignorant on any subject, do not think that you know it ; but in order to get real knowledge, learn how to be ignorant. For we commit a sin by affecting to be ignorant of nothing among "the secret things of God ;" by constructing random theories about unknown things, and taking them for known ; and by producing and defending errors as if they were truth. As for my own ignorance on the question whether the souls of men are created afresh at every birth, or are transmitted by the parents (an ignorance which is, however, modified by my belief, which it would be impious to falter in, that they are certainly made by the Divine Creator, though not of His own substance), I think that your loving self will by this time be persuaded that it either ought not to be censured at all, or, if it ought, that it should be done by a man who is capable by his learning of removing it altogether ;

and so also with respect to my other opinions, that while souls have in them the incorporeal semblances of bodies, they are not themselves bodies ; and that, without impairing the natural distinction between soul and spirit, the soul is in a general sense actually designated spirit. If, indeed, I have unfortunately failed to persuade you, I must leave it rather to my readers to determine whether what I have advanced ought not to have convinced you.

## CHAP. 39. — CONCLUDING ADMONITION.

If, as may possibly be the case, you desire to know whether there are many other points which appear to me to require emendation in your books, it cannot be troublesome for you to come to me, — not, indeed, as a scholar to his master, but as a person in his prime to one full of years, and as a strong man to a weak one. And although you ought not to have published your books, still there is a greater and a truer glory in a man's being censured, when he confesses with his own lips the justice of his correction, than in being lauded out of the mouth of any defender of error. Now, while I should be unwilling to believe that all those who listened to your reading of the afore-mentioned books, and lavished their praises on you, had either previously held for themselves the opinions which sound doctrine disapproves of, or were induced by you to entertain them, I still cannot help thinking that they had the keenness of their mind blunted by the impetuous and constant flow of your elocution, and so were unable to bestow adequate attention on the contents of your discourse ; or else, that when they were in any case capable of understanding what you said, it was less for any very clear statement of the truth that they praised you than for the affluence of your language, and the facility and resources of your mental powers. For praise, and fame, and kindly regard are very commonly bestowed on a young man's eloquence in anticipation of the future, though as yet it lacks the mellowed perfection and fidelity of a fully-informed instructor. In order, then, that you may attain to true wisdom yourself, and that what you say may be able not only to delight, but even edify other people, it behoves you, after removing from your mind the dangerous applause of others, to keep conscientious watch over your own words.

# A TREATISE AGAINST TWO LETTERS OF THE PELAGIANS.

# EXTRACT FROM AUGUSTIN'S "RETRACTATIONS,"

## Book II. Chap. 61,

### *ON THE FOLLOWING TREATISE,*

## "CONTRA DUAS EPISTOLAS PELAGIANORUM."

---

THEN follow four books which I wrote to Boniface, bishop of the Roman Church, in opposition to two letters of the Pelagians, because when they came into his hands he had sent them to me, finding in them a calumnious mention of my name. This work commences on this wise : " I had indeed known you by the praise of your renowned fame."

# CONTENTS OF THE TREATISE "AGAINST TWO LETTERS OF THE PELAGIANS."

---

## BOOK I.

## BOOK II.

# BOOK III.

# BOOK IV.

# A TREATISE AGAINST TWO LETTERS OF THE PELAGIANS,[1]

## BY AURELIUS AUGUSTIN, BISHOP OF HIPPO

### IN FOUR BOOKS,

WRITTEN TO BONIFACE, BISHOP OF THE ROMAN CHURCH, IN OPPOSITION TO TWO LETTERS OF THE PELAGIANS, A.D. 420, OR A LITTLE LATER.

---

## BOOK I.

AUGUSTIN REPLIES TO A LETTER SENT BY JULIAN, AS IT WAS SAID, TO ROME; AND FIRST OF ALL VINDICATES THE CATHOLIC DOCTRINE FROM HIS CALUMNIES; THEN DISCOVERS AND CONFUTES THE HERETICAL SENSE OF THE PELAGIANS HIDDEN IN THAT PROFESSION OF FAITH WHICH THE AUTHOR OF THE LETTER OPPOSED TO THE CATHOLICS.

### CHAP. I. — INTRODUCTION: ADDRESS TO BONIFACE.

I HAD indeed known you by the praise of your renowned fame; and by very numerous and veracious messengers I had learned how full you were of the grace of God, most blessed and venerable Pope Boniface! But after my brother Alypius saw you even in bodily presence; and, having been received by you with all kindness and sincerity, held, at the bidding of affection, conversations with you; and living with you, and, although only for a short time, united with you in earnest affection, poured out to your mind both himself and me; and brought you back to me in his mind: — the more assured was your friendship, the greater became in me the conviction of your holiness. For you, who mind not high things, however loftily you are placed, did not disdain to be a friend of the lowly and to return the love bestowed upon you. For what else is friendship which has its name from no other source than love,[2] and is nowhere faithful but in Christ, in whom alone it can be eternal and happy? Whence, also, having received a greater assurance by means of that brother, through whom I have learned to know you more familiarly, I have ventured to write something to your blessedness concerning those things which at this juncture are claiming by a later stimulus the episcopal care, as far as we are able, to vigilance on behalf of the Lord's flock.

### CHAP. 2. — WHY HERETICAL WRITINGS MUST BE ANSWERED.

For the new heretics, enemies of the grace of God which is given by Jesus Christ our Lord to small and great, although they are already shown more openly to need to be avoided by a manifest disapprobation, still do not cease by their writings to try the hearts of the less cautious and less learned. And these must certainly be answered, lest they should confirm themselves or their friends in that wicked error; even if we were not afraid that they might deceive some one of the catholics by their plausible discourse. But since they do not cease to growl at the entrances

---

[1] [When Augustin's friend Alypius brought to Africa the extracts from Julian's reply to Augustin's first book *On Marriage and Concupiscence*, which were sent by Count Valerius, and which occasioned the writing of his second book on the same subject (see above, pp. 259 and 281), he also brought two letters sent by Pope Boniface; the one ascribed to Julian, and the other to eighteen bishops including Julian, which attacked the catholic faith, and Augustin personally. It was in answer to these that this treatise was written. — W.]

[2] The Latin words being *amicitia* (friendship) and *amor* (love).

to the Lord's fold, and from every side to tear open approaches with a view to tear in pieces the sheep redeemed at such a price ; and since the pastoral watch-tower is common to all of us who discharge the office of the episcopate (although you are prominent therein on a loftier height), I do what I can in respect of my small portion of the charge, as the Lord condescends by the aid of your prayers to grant me power, to oppose to their pestilent and crafty writings, healing and defensive writings, so that the madness with which they are raging may either itself be cured, or may be prevented from hurting others.

CHAP. 3. — WHY HE ADDRESSES HIS BOOK TO BONIFACE.

But these words which I am answering to their two letters, — the one, to wit, which Julian is said to have sent to Rome, that by its means, as I believe, he might find or make as many allies as he could ; and the other, which eighteen so-called bishops, sharers in his error, dared to write to Thessalonica, not to any and every body, but to the bishop of that place itself, with a view of tempting him by their craftiness and bringing him over, if it could be done, to their views ; — these words which, as I said, I am writing in answer to those two letters of theirs in respect of that argument, I have determined to address especially to your sanctity, not so much for your learning as for your examination, and, if perchance anything should displease you, for your correction. For my brother intimated to me that you yourself condescended to give those letters to him, which could not come into your hands except by the most watchful diligence of my brethren, your sons. And I thank your most sincere kindness to me that you have been unwilling that those letters of the enemies of God's grace should be hidden from me, seeing that in them you have found my name calumniously as well as openly expressed. But I hope from my Lord God that not without the reward which is in heaven do those tear me with their scurrilous teeth to whom I oppose myself on behalf of the little ones, that they may not be left for destruction to the deceitful flatterer Pelagius, but may be presented for deliverance to the truthful Saviour Christ.

CHAP. 4 [II.] — THE CALUMNY OF JULIAN, — THAT THE CATHOLICS TEACH THAT FREE WILL IS TAKEN AWAY BY ADAM'S SIN.

Let us now, therefore, reply to Julian's letter. "Those Manicheans say," says he, " with whom now we do not communicate, — that is, the whole of them with whom we differ, — that by the sin of the first man, that is, of Adam, free will perished : and that no one has now the power of living well, but that all are constrained into sin by the necessity of their flesh." He calls the catholics Manicheans, after the manner of that Jovinian who a few years ago, as a new heretic, destroyed the virginity of the blessed Mary, and placed the marriage of the faithful on the same level with her sacred virginity. And he did not object this to the catholics on any other ground than that he wished them to seem to be either accusers or condemners of marriage.

CHAP. 5. — FREE CHOICE DID NOT PERISH WITH ADAM'S SIN. WHAT FREEDOM DID PERISH.

But in defending free will they hasten to confide rather in it for doing righteousness than in God's aid, and to glory every one in himself, and not in the Lord.[1] But who of us will say that by the sin of the first man free will perished from the human race ? Through sin freedom indeed perished, but it was that freedom which was in Paradise, to have a full righteousness with immortality ; and it is on this account that human nature needs divine grace, since the Lord says, " If the Son shall make you free, then shall ye be free indeed "[2] — free of course to live well and righteously. For free will in the sinner up to this extent did not perish, — that by it all sin, especially they who sin with delight and with love of sin ; what they are pleased to do gives them pleasure. Whence also the apostle says, "When ye were the servants of sin, ye were free from righteousness."[3] Behold, they are shown to have been by no means able to serve sin except by another freedom. They are not, then, free from righteousness except by the choice of the will, but they do not become free from sin save by the grace of the Saviour. For which reason the admirable Teacher also distinguished these very words : "For when ye were the servants," says he, " of sin, ye were free from righteousness. What fruit had ye, then, in those things whereof ye are now ashamed? for the end of those things is death. But now being freed from sin and become servants to God, ye have your fruit unto holiness, and the end eternal life."[3] He called them " free " from righteousness, not " freed ;" but from sin not " free," lest they should attribute this to themselves, but most watchfully he preferred to say " freed," referring this to that declaration of the Lord, " If the Son shall make you free, then shall ye be free indeed."[4] Since, then, the sons of men do not live well unless they are made the sons of God, why is it that this writer wishes to give the power of good living to free will, when this power is not given save by God's grace through Jesus Christ our Lord, as the gospel says : " And as many as re-

---

[1] 1 Cor. i. 31.	[2] John viii. 36.	[3] Rom. vi. 20.
[4] John viii. 36 ff.

ceived Him, to them gave He power to become the sons of God "?[1]

## CHAP. 6 [III.] — GRACE IS NOT GIVEN ACCORDING TO MERITS.

But lest perchance they say that they are aided to this, — that they may "have power to become the sons of God," but that they may deserve to receive this power they have first "received Him" by free will with no assistance of grace (because this is the purpose of their endeavour to destroy grace, that they may contend that it is given according to our deservings) ; lest perchance, then, they so divide that evangelical statement as to refer merit to that portion of it wherein it is said, "But as many as received Him," and then say that in that which follows, "He gave them power to become the sons of God," grace is not given freely, but is repaid to this merit ; if it is asked of them what is the meaning of "received Him," will they say anything else than "believed on Him"? And in order, therefore, that they may know that this also pertains to grace, let them read what the apostle says : "And that ye be in nothing terrified by your adversaries, which indeed is to them a cause of perdition, but of your salvation, and that of God ; for unto you it is given in the behalf of Christ not only to believe on Him, but also to suffer for His sake."[2]  Certainly he said that both were given. Let them read what he said also: "Peace be to the brethren, and love, with faith from God the Father and the Lord Jesus Christ."[3]  Let them also read what the Lord Himself says : "No man can come to me, except the Father who hath sent me shall draw him."[4]  Where, lest any one should suppose that anything else is said in the words "come to me" than "believe in me," a little after, when He was speaking of His body and blood, and many were offended at His discourse, He says, "The words which I have spoken unto you are spirit and life ; but there are some of you which believe not."[5]  Then the Evangelist added, "For Jesus knew from the beginning who they were that believed, and who should betray Him. And He said, Therefore I said unto you that no man can come unto me except it were given him of my Father."[6]  He repeated, to wit, the saying in which He had said, "No man can come unto me, except the Father who hath sent me shall draw him." And He declared that He said this for the sake of believers and unbelievers, explaining what He had said, "except the Father who hath sent me shall draw him," by repeating the very same thing in other words in that which He said, "except it were given him of my Father." Because he is drawn

to Christ to whom it is given to believe on Christ. Therefore the power is given that they who believe on Him should become the sons of God, since this very thing is given, that they believe on Him. And unless this power be given from God, out of free will there can be none ; because it will not be free for good if the deliverer have not made it free ; but in evil he has a free will in whom a deceiver, either secret or manifest, has grafted the love of wickedness, or he himself has persuaded himself of it.

## CHAP. 7. — HE CONCLUDES THAT HE DOES NOT DEPRIVE THE WICKED OF FREE WILL.

It is not, therefore, true, as some affirm that we say, and as that correspondent of yours ventures moreover to write, that "all are forced into sin," as if they were unwilling, "by the necessity of their flesh ;" but if they are already of the age to use the choice of their own mind, they are both retained in sin by their own will, and by their own will are hurried along from sin to sin. For even he who persuades and deceives does not act in them, except that they may commit sin by their will, either by ignorance of the truth or by delight in iniquity, or by both evils, — as well of blindness as of weakness. But this will, which is free in evil things because it takes pleasure in evil, is not free in good things, for the reason that it has not been made free. Nor can a man will any good thing unless he is aided by Him who cannot will evil, — that is, by the grace of God through Jesus Christ our Lord. For "everything which is not of faith is sin."[7] And thus the good will which withdraws itself from sin is faithful, because the just lives by faith.[8] And it pertains to faith to believe on Christ. And no man can believe on Christ — that is, come to Him — unless it be given to him.[9] No man, therefore, can have a righteous will, unless, with no foregoing merits, he has received the true, that is, the gratuitous grace from above.

## CHAP. 8 [IV.] — THE PELAGIANS DEMOLISH FREE WILL.

These proud and haughty people will not have this ; and yet they do not maintain free will by purifying it, but demolish it by exaggerating it. For they are angry with us who say these things, for no other reason than that they disdain to glory in the Lord. Yet Pelagius feared the episcopal judgment of Palestine ; and when it was objected to him that he said that the grace of God is given according to our merits, he denied that he said so, and condemned those who said this with an anathema.[10]  And yet nothing else is found to be defended in the books which he afterwards wrote, thinking that he had made a

---

[1] John i. 12.       [2] Phil. i. 28, 29.       [3] Eph. vi. 23.
[4] John vi. 44.      [5] John vi. 64.          [6] John vi. 64 ff.
[7] Rom. xiv. 23.     [8] Hab. ii. 4.          [9] Rom. i. 17.
[10] *On the Proceedings of Pelagius*, 30.

fraud upon the men who were his judges, by lying or by hiding his meaning, I know not how, in ambiguous words.[1]

CHAP. 9 [V.] — ANOTHER CALUMNY OF JULIAN, — THAT "IT IS SAID THAT MARRIAGE IS NOT APPOINTED BY GOD."

But now let us see what follows. "They say also," he says, "that those marriages which are now celebrated were not appointed by God, and this is to be read in Augustin's book,[2] against which I replied in four books. And the words of this Augustin our enemies have taken up by way of hostility to the truth." To these most calumnious words I see that a brief answer must be made, because he repeats them afterwards when he wishes to insinuate what such men as they would say, as if against my words. On that point, with God's assistance, I must contend with him as far as the matter shall seem to demand. Now, therefore, I reply that marriage was ordained by God both then, when it was said, "Therefore shall a man leave his father and his mother, and shall cleave unto his wife, and they shall be two in one flesh,"[3] and now, wherefore it is written, "A woman is joined to a man by the Lord."[4] For nothing else is even now done than that a man cleave to his wife, and they become two in one flesh. Because concerning that very marriage which is now contracted, the Lord was consulted by the Jews whether it was lawful for any cause to put away a wife. And to the testimony of the law on the occasion mentioned, He added, "What, therefore, God hath joined together, let not man put asunder."[5] The Apostle Paul also applied this witness of the law when he admonished husbands that their wives should be loved by them.[6] Away, then, with the notion that in my book that man should read anything opposed to these divine testimonies! But either by not understanding, or rather by calumniating, he seeks to twist what he reads into another meaning. But I wrote my book, against which he mentions that he replied in four books, after the condemnation of Pelagius and Cœlestius. And this, I have thought, must be said, because that man avers that my words had been taken up by his enemies in hostility to the truth, lest any one should think that these new heretics were condemned as enemies of the grace of Christ on account of this book of mine. But in that book is found the defence rather than the censure of marriage.

CHAP. 10. — THE THIRD CALUMNY, — THE ASSERTION THAT CONJUGAL INTERCOURSE IS CONDEMNED.

"They say also," says he, "that sexual impulse and the intercourse of married people were devised by the devil, and that therefore those who are born innocent are guilty, and that it is the work of the devil, not of God, that they are born of this diabolical intercourse. And this, without any ambiguity, is Manicheism." Nay, as I say that marriage was appointed by God for the sake of the ordinance of the begetting of children, so I say that the propagation of children to be begotten could not have taken place without sexual impulse, and without intercourse of husband and wife, even in Paradise, if children were begotten there. But whether such impulse and intercourse would have existed, as is now the case with shameful lust, if no one had sinned, here is the question concerning which I shall argue hereafter, if God will.

CHAP. 11 [VI.] — THE PURPOSE OF THE PELAGIANS IN PRAISING THE INNOCENCE OF CONJUGAL INTERCOURSE.

Yet what it is they wish, what they purpose, to what result they are striving to bring the matter, the words that are added by that writer declare, when he asserts that I say, "that therefore they who are born innocent are guilty, and that it is the work of the devil, not of God, that they are born of this diabolical intercourse." Since, therefore, I neither say that this intercourse of husband and wife is diabolical, especially in the case of believers, which is effected for the sake of generating children who are afterwards to be regenerated ; nor that any men are made by the devil, but, in so far as they are men, by God ; and nevertheless that even of believing husband and wife are born guilty persons (as if a wild olive were produced from an olive),[7] on account of original sin, and on this account are under the devil unless they are born again in Christ, because the devil is the author of the fault, not of the nature : what, on the other hand, are they labouring to bring about who say that infants inherit no original sin, and therefore are not under the devil, except that that grace of God in infants may be made of no effect, by which He has plucked us out, as the apostle says, from the power of darkness, and has translated us into the kingdom of the Son of His love?[8] [VII.] When, indeed, they deny that infants are in the power of darkness even before the help of the Lord the deliverer, they are in such wise praising in them the Creator's work as to destroy the mercy of the Redeemer. And because I confess this both in grown-up people and in infants, he says that this is without any ambiguity Manicheism, although it is the most ancient catholic dogma by which the new heretical dogma of these men is overturned.

[1] On the Grace of Christ, 3, 34.
[2] On Marriage and Concupiscence, Book i.　　　[3] Gen. ii. 24.
[4] Prov. xix. 24.　　　[5] Matt. xix. 3, 6.　　　[6] Eph. v. 25.
[7] On Marriage and Concupiscence, i. 37.　　　[8] 1 Cor. i. 13.

CHAP. 12. — THE FOURTH CALUMNY, — THAT THE SAINTS OF THE OLD TESTAMENT ARE SAID TO BE NOT FREE FROM SINS.

"They say," says he, "that the saints in the Old Testament were not without sins, — that is, that they were not free from crimes even by amendment, but they were seized by death in their guilt." Nay, I say that either before the law, or in the time of the Old Testament, they were freed from sins, — not by their own power, because "cursed is every one that hath put his hope in man," [1] and without any doubt those are under this curse whom also the sacred Psalm notifies, "who trust in their own strength;" [2] nor by the old covenant which gendereth to bondage,[3] although it was divinely given by the grace of a sure dispensation; nor by that law itself, holy and just and good as it was, where it is written, "Thou shalt not covet," [4] since it was not given as being able to give life, but it was added for the sake of transgression until the seed should come to whom the promise was made; but I say that they were freed by the blood of the Redeemer Himself, who is the one Mediator of God and man, the man Christ Jesus.[5] But those enemies of the grace of God, which is given to small and great through Jesus Christ our Lord, say that the men of God of old were of a perfect righteousness, lest they should be supposed to have needed the incarnation, the passion, and resurrection of Christ, by belief in whom they were saved.

CHAP. 13 [VIII.] — THE FIFTH CALUMNY, — THAT IT IS SAID THAT PAUL AND THE REST OF THE APOSTLES WERE POLLUTED BY LUST.

He says, "They say that even the Apostle Paul, even all the apostles, were always polluted by immoderate lust." What man, however profane he may be, would dare to say this? But doubtless this man thus misrepresents because they contend that what the apostle said, "I know that in me, that is, in my flesh, dwelleth no good thing, for to will is present with me, but how to perform that which is good I find not," [6] and other such things, he said not of himself, but that he introduced the person of somebody else, I know not who, who was suffering these things. Wherefore that passage in his epistle must be carefully considered and investigated, that their error may not lurk in any obscurity of his. Although, therefore, the apostle is here arguing broadly, and with great and lasting conflict maintaining grace against those who were boasting in the law, yet we do come upon a few matters which pertain to the matter in hand. On which subject he says: "Because by the law there shall no flesh be justified in His sight.

For by the law is the knowledge of sin. But now the righteousness of God without the law is manifested, being witnessed by the law and the prophets, even the righteousness of God by the faith of Jesus Christ unto all them that believe. For there is no difference. For all have sinned and come short of the glory of God, being justified freely by His grace through the redemption that is in Christ Jesus." [7] And again: "Where is boasting? It is excluded. By what law? Of works? No; but by the law of faith. Therefore we conclude that a man is justified by faith without the works of the law." [8] And again: "For the promise that he should be the heir of the world was not to Abraham or to his seed through the law, but by the righteousness of faith. For if they which are of the law be heirs, faith is made void, and the promise made of none effect. Because the law worketh wrath, for where no law is, there is no transgression." [9] And in another place: "Moreover, the law entered that the offence might abound. But where sin abounded grace did much more abound." [10] In still another place: "For sin shall not have dominion over you, for ye are not under law, but under grace." [11] And again in another place: "Know ye not, brethren (for I speak to them that know the law), that the law hath dominion over a man so long as he liveth? For the woman which is under a husband is joined to her husband by the law so long as he liveth; but if her husband be dead, she is freed from the law of her husband." [12] And a little after: "Therefore, my brethren, ye also are become dead to the law by the body of Christ, that ye should belong to another, who has risen from the dead that we should bring forth fruit unto God. For when we were in the flesh the passions of sins which are by the law did work in our members to bring forth fruit unto death, but now we are delivered from the law of death in which we were held, so that we may serve in newness of spirit, and not in the oldness of the letter." [13] With these and such like testimonies that teacher of the Gentiles showed with sufficient evidence that the law could not take away sin, but rather increased it, and that grace takes it away; since the law knew how to command, to which command weakness gives way, while grace knows to assist, whereby love is infused.[14] And lest any one, on account of these testimonies, should reproach the law, and contend that it is evil, the apostle, seeing what might occur to those who ill understand it, himself proposed to himself the same question. "What shall we say, then?" said he. "Is the law sin? Far from it. But I did not know sin except by the law." [15] He had

---

[1] Jer. xvii. 5.  [2] Ps. xlix. 6.  [3] Gal. iv. 24.
[4] Ex. xx. 7.  [5] 1 Tim. ii. 5.  [6] Rom. vii. 18.

[7] Rom. iii. 20.  [8] Rom. iii. 27.  [9] Rom. iv. 13, etc.
[10] Rom. v. 20.  [11] Rom. vi. 14.  [12] Rom. vii. 1, 2.
[13] Rom. vii. 4 ff.  [14] On the Spirit and the Letter, 6.
[15] Rom. vii. 7.

already said before, " For by the law is the knowledge of sin." It is not, therefore, the taking away, but the knowledge of sin.

CHAP. 14. — THAT THE APOSTLE IS SPEAKING IN HIS OWN PERSON AND THAT OF OTHERS WHO ARE UNDER GRACE, NOT STILL UNDER LAW.

And from this point he now begins — and it was on account of this that I undertook the consideration of these things — to introduce his own person, and to speak as if about himself; where the Pelagians will not have it that the apostle himself is to be understood, but say that he has transfigured another person into himself, — that is, a man placed still under the law, not yet freed by grace. And here, indeed, they ought at least to concede that " in the law no one is justified," as the same apostle says elsewhere; but that the law avails for the knowledge of sin, and for the transgression of the law itself, so that sin, being known and increased, grace may be sought for through faith. But they do not fear that those things should be understood concerning the apostle which he might also say concerning his past, but they fear those things which follow. For here he says: " I had not known lust if the law had not said, Thou shalt not covet. But the occasion being taken, sin wrought in me by the commandment all manner of lust. For without the law sin was dead. But I was alive without the law once, but when the commandment came, sin revived, and I died, and the commandment which was for life was found for me to be death. For sin, taking occasion by the commandment, deceived me, and by it slew me. Therefore the law indeed is holy, and the commandment holy, just, and good. Was, then, that which is good made death unto me? By no means. But sin, that it might appear sin, worked death to me by that which is good, that the sinner or the sin might become by the commandment excessive."[1] All these things, as I have said, the apostle can seem to have commemorated from his past life: so that from what he says, " For I was alive without the law once," he may have wished his first age from infancy to be understood, before the years of reason; but in that he added, " But when the commandment came, sin revived, but I died," he would fain show himself able to receive the commandment, but not to do[2] it, and therefore a transgressor of the law.

CHAP. 15 [IX.] — HE SINS IN WILL WHO IS ONLY DETERRED FROM SINNING BY FEAR.

Nor let us be disturbed by what he wrote to the Philippians: " Touching the righteousness which is in the law, one who is without blame."[3] For he could be within in evil affections a transgressor of the law, and yet fulfil the open works of the law, either by the fear of men or of God Himself; but by terror of punishment, not by love and delight in righteousness. For it is one thing to do good with the will of doing good, and another thing to be so inclined by the will to do evil, that one would actually do it if it could be allowed without punishment. For thus assuredly he is sinning within in his will itself, who abstains from sin not by will but by fear. And knowing himself to have been such in these his internal affections, before the grace of God which is through Jesus Christ our Lord, the apostle elsewhere confesses this very plainly. For writing to the Ephesians, he says: " And you, though ye were dead in your trespasses and sins, wherein sometime ye walked according to the course of this world, according to the prince of the power of the air, of that spirit that now worketh in the children of disobedience, in whom also we all at one time had our conversation in the lusts of our flesh, doing the will of our flesh and our affections, and were by nature the children of wrath, even as others also: but God, who is rich in mercy, for His great love wherewith He loved us even when we were dead in sins, quickened us together with Christ, by whose grace we are saved."[4] Again to Titus he says: " For we ourselves also were sometime foolish and unbelieving, erring, serving various lusts and pleasures, living in malice and envy, hateful, and holding one another in hatred."[5] Such was Saul when he says that he was, touching the righteousness which is in the law, without reproach. For that he had not pressed on in the law, and changed his character so as to be without reproach after this hateful life, he plainly shows in what follows, when he says that he was not changed from these evils except by the grace of the Saviour. For adding also this very thing, here as well as to the Ephesians, he says: " But when the kindness and love of God our Saviour shone forth, not by works of righteousness which we have done, but according to His mercy He saved us, by the washing of regeneration, and of the renewal of the Holy Spirit, whom He shed on us most abundantly, through Jesus Christ our Saviour, that being justified by His grace we should be made heirs according to the hope of eternal life."[6]

CHAP. 16. — HOW SIN DIED, AND HOW IT REVIVED.

And what he says in that passage of the Epistle to the Romans, " Sin, that it might appear sin, wrought death to me by that which is good," [1] agrees with the former passages where he said, " But I had not known sin but by the law, for I had not known lust unless the law had said, Thou shalt not covet." [2]  And previously, " By the law is the knowledge of sin," for he said this also here, " that it might appear sin ; " that we might not understand what he had said, " For without law sin was dead," except in the sense as if it were not, " it lies hidden, it does not appear, is completely ignored, as if it were buried in I know not what darkness of ignorance."  And in that he says, " And I was alive once without the law," what does he say except, I seemed to myself to live ?  And with respect to what he added, " But when the commandment came, sin revived," what else is it but sin shone forth, became apparent ?  Nor yet does he say lived, but revived.  For it had lived formerly in Paradise, where it sufficiently appeared, admitted in opposition to the command given ; but when it is inherited by children coming into the world, it lies concealed, as if it were dead, until its evil, resisting righteousness, is felt by its prohibition, when one thing is commanded and approved, another thing delights and rules : then, in some measure sin revives in the knowledge of the man that is born, although it had lived already for some time in the knowledge of the man as at first made.

### CHAP. 17 [X.] — " THE LAW IS SPIRITUAL, BUT I AM CARNAL," TO BE UNDERSTOOD OF PAUL.

But it is not so clear how what follows can be understood concerning Paul.  " For we know," says he, " that the law is spiritual, but I am carnal." [3]  He does not say, " I was," but, " I am."  Was, then, the apostle, when he wrote this, carnal ? or does he say this with respect to his body ?  For he was still in the body of this death, not yet made what he speaks of elsewhere : " It is sown a natural body, it shall be raised a spiritual body." [4]  For then, of the whole of himself, that is, of both parts of which he consists, he shall be a spiritual man, when even the body shall be spiritual.  For it is not absurd that in that life even the flesh should be spiritual, if in this life in those who still mind earthly things even the spirit itself may be carnal.  Thus, then, he said, " But I am carnal," because the apostle had not yet a spiritual body, as he might say, " But I am mortal," which assuredly he could not be understood to have said except in respect of his body, which had not yet been clothed with immortality.  Moreover, in reference to what he added, " sold under sin," [3] lest any one think that he was not yet redeemed by

the blood of Christ, this also may be understood in respect of that which he says : " And we ourselves, having the first-fruits of the Spirit, even we ourselves groan within ourselves, waiting for the adoption, to wit, the redemption of our body." [5]  For if in this respect he says that he was sold under sin, that as yet his body has not been redeemed from corruption ; or that he was sold once in the first transgression of the commandment so as to have a corruptible body which drags down the soul ; [6] what hinders the apostle here from being understood to say about himself that which he says in such wise that it may be understood also of himself, even if in his person he wishes not himself alone, but all, to be received who had known themselves as struggling, without consent, in spiritual delight with the affection of the flesh ?

### CHAP. 18. — HOW THE APOSTLE SAID THAT HE DID THE EVIL THAT HE WOULD NOT.

Or by chance do we fear what follows, " For that which I do I know not, for what I will I do not, but what I hate that I do," [7] lest perhaps from these words some one should suspect that the apostle is consenting to the evil works of the concupiscence of the flesh ?  But we must consider what he adds : " But if I do that which I will not, I consent to the law that it is good."  For he says that he rather consents to the law than to the concupiscence of the flesh.  For this he calls by the name of sin.  Therefore he said that he acted and laboured not with the desire of consenting and fulfilling, but from the impulse of lusting itself.  Hence, then, he says, " I consent to the law that it is good."  I consent because I do not will what it does not will.  Afterwards he says, " Now, then, it is no more I that do it, but sin which dwelleth in me." [8]  What does he mean by " now then," but, now at length, under the grace which has delivered the delight of my will from the consent of lust ?  For, " it is not I that do it," cannot be better understood than that he does not consent to set forth his members as instruments of unrighteousness unto sin.  For if he lusts and consents and acts, how can he be said not to do the thing himself, even although he may grieve that he does it, and deeply groan at being overcome ?

### CHAP. 19. — WHAT IT IS TO ACCOMPLISH WHAT IS GOOD.

And now does not what follows most plainly show whence he spoke ?  " For I know that in me, that is, in my flesh, dwelleth no good thing " ? [9]  For if he had not explained what he said by the addition of " that is, in my flesh," it might, perchance, be otherwise understood,

[1] Rom. vii. 13.  [2] Rom. vii. 7.  [3] Rom. vii. 14.
[4] 1 Cor. xv. 44.  [The Latin word for "natural" is *animale*, i.e., "animated," "living," derived from the word *anima*, " soul," or " animated and animating principle."  Compare the note on ch. 36 of *On the Soul and its Origin*, above. — W.]

[5] Rom. viii. 23.  [6] Wisd. ix. 15.  [7] Rom. vii. 15.
[8] Rom. vii. 17.  [9] Rom. vii. 18.

when he said, "in me." And therefore he repeats and urges the same thing in another form: "For to will is present with me, but to perform that which is good is not."[1] For this is to perform that which is good, that a man should not even lust. For the good is incomplete when one lusts, even although a man does not consent to the evil of lust. "For the good that I would," says he, "I do not; but the evil that I would not, that I do. Now, if I do that I would not, it is no more I that do it, but sin that dwelleth in me."[2] This he repeated impressively, and as it were to stir up the most slothful from slumber: "I find then that the law," said he, "is for me wishing to do good, since evil is present with me."[3] The law, then, is for one who would do good, but evil is present from lust, though he does not consent to this who says, "It is no longer I that do it."

### CHAP. 20. — IN ME, THAT IS, IN MY FLESH.

And he declares both more plainly in what follows: "For I delight in the law of God after the inward man; but I see another law in my members, warring against the law of my mind, and bringing me into captivity to the law of sin which is in my members."[4] But in that he said, "bringing me into captivity," he can feel emotion without consenting to it. Whence, because of those three things, two, to wit, of which we have already argued, in that he says, "But I am carnal," and "Sold under sin," and this third, "Bringing me into captivity in the law of sin, which is in my members," the apostle seems to be describing a man who is still living under the law, and is not yet under grace. But as I have expounded the former two sayings in respect of the still corruptible flesh, so also this latter may be understood as if he had said, "bringing me into captivity," in the flesh, not in the mind; in emotion, not in consent; and therefore "bringing me into captivity," because even in the flesh there is not an alien nature, but our own. As, therefore, he himself expounded what he had said, "For I know that in me, that is, in my flesh, dwelleth no good thing," so also now out of the exposition of that we ought to learn the meaning of this passage, as if he had said, "Bringing *me* into captivity," that is, "my flesh," "to the law of sin, which is in my members."

### CHAP. 21. — NO CONDEMNATION IN CHRIST JESUS.

Then he adds the reason why he said all these things: "O wretched man that I am! who shall deliver me from the body of this death? The grace of God, through Jesus Christ our Lord!" And thence he concludes: "Therefore I myself with the mind serve the law of God, but with the flesh the law of sin."[5] To wit, with the flesh, the law of sin, by lusting; but with the mind, the law of God, by not consenting to that lust. "For there is now no condemnation to those who are in Christ Jesus."[6] For he is not condemned who does not consent to the evil of the lust of the flesh. "For the law of the Spirit of life in Christ Jesus has made thee free from the law of sin and death," so that, to wit, the lust of the flesh may not appropriate to itself thy consent. And what follows more and more demonstrates the same meaning. But moderation must be used.

### CHAP. 22. — WHY THE PASSAGE REFERRED TO MUST BE UNDERSTOOD OF A MAN ESTABLISHED UNDER GRACE.

And it had once appeared to me also that the apostle was in this argument of his describing a man under the law.[7] But afterwards I was constrained to give up the idea by those words where he says, "Now, then, it is no more I that do it." For to this belongs what he says subsequently also: "There is, therefore, now no condemnation to them that are in Christ Jesus." And because I do not see how a man under the law should say, "I delight in the law of God after the inward man;" since this very delight in good, by which, moreover, he does not consent to evil, not from fear of penalty, but from love of righteousness (for this is meant by "delighting"), can only be attributed to grace.

### CHAP. 23 [XI.] — WHAT IT IS TO BE DELIVERED FROM THE BODY OF THIS DEATH.

For when he says also, "Who shall deliver me from the body of this death?"[8] who can deny that when the apostle said this he was still in the body of this death? And certainly the wicked are not delivered from this, to whom the same bodies are returned for eternal torment. Therefore, to be delivered from the body of this death is to be healed of all the weakness of fleshly lust, and to receive the body, not for penalty, but for glory. With this passage also those words are sufficiently in harmony: "Ourselves also, which have the firstfruits of the Spirit, even we ourselves groan within ourselves, waiting for the adoption, the redemption, of our body." For surely we groan with that groaning wherein we say, "O wretched man that I am! who shall deliver me from the body of this death?" That also where he says, "For what I do, I know not;" what else is it than: "I will not, I do not approve, I do not consent, I do not do"? Otherwise it is con-

---

[1] Rom. vii. 18.     [2] Rom. vii. 20.     [3] Rom. vii. 21.
[4] Rom. vii. 21, 22.

[5] Rom. vii. 24, 25.     [6] Rom. viii. 1.
[7] See Augustin's *Exposition of Certain Propositions in the Epistle to the Romans*, 44, 45; also his *Commentary on Galatians*, v. 17; also his letter to *Simplicianus*, book i. 7, 9.
[8] Rom. vii. 24.

trary to what he said above, " By the law is the knowledge of sin," and, " I had not known sin but by the law," and, " Sin, that it might appear sin, worked death in me by that which is good." For how did he know sin, of which he was ignorant, by the law? How does sin which is not known appear? Therefore it is said, " I know not," for " I do not," because I myself commit it with no consent of mine ; in the same way in which the Lord will say to the wicked, " I know you not," [1] although, beyond a doubt, nothing can be hid from Him ; and as it is said, " Him who had not known sin," [2] which means who had not done sin, for He had not known what He condemned.

### CHAP. 24. — HE CONCLUDES THAT THE APOSTLE SPOKE IN HIS OWN PERSON, AND THAT OF THOSE WHO ARE UNDER GRACE.

On the careful consideration of these things, and things of the same kind in the context of that apostolical Scripture, the apostle is rightly understood to have signified not, indeed, himself alone in his own person, but others also established under grace, and with him not yet established in that perfect peace in which death shall be swallowed up in victory.[3] And concerning this he afterwards says, " But if Christ be in you, the body is dead because of sin, but the spirit is life because of righteousness. If, then, the Spirit of Him that raised up Jesus from the dead dwelleth in you, He that raised up Jesus from the dead shall also quicken your mortal bodies by His Spirit that dwelleth in you." [4] Therefore, after our mortal bodies have been quickened, not only will there be no consent to sinning, but even the lust of the flesh itself, to which there is no consent, will not remain. And not to have this resistance to the spirit in the mortal flesh, was possible only to that man who came not by the flesh to men. And that the apostles, because they were men, and carried about in the mortality of this life a body which is corrupted and weighs down the soul,[5] were, therefore, " always polluted with excessive lust," as that man injuriously affirms, be it far from me to say. But I do say that although they were free from consent to depraved lusts, they nevertheless groaned concerning the concupiscence of the flesh, which they bridled by restraint with such humility and piety, that they desired rather not to have it than to subdue it.

### CHAP. 25 [XII.] — THE SIXTH CALUMNY, — THAT AUGUSTIN ASSERTS THAT EVEN CHRIST WAS NOT FREE FROM SINS.

In like manner as to what he added, that I say,[6] " that Christ even was not free from sins, but that, from the necessity of the flesh, He spoke falsely, and was stained with other faults," he should see from whom he heard these things, or in whose letters he read them ; for that, indeed, he perchance did not understand them, and turned them by the deceitfulness of malice into calumnious meanings.

### CHAP. 26 [XIII.] — THE SEVENTH CALUMNY, — THAT AUGUSTIN ASSERTS THAT IN BAPTISM ALL SINS ARE NOT REMITTED.

" They also say," says he, " that baptism does not give complete remission of sins, nor take away crimes, but that it shaves them off, so that the roots of all sins are retained in the evil flesh." Who but an unbeliever can affirm this against the Pelagians? I say, therefore, that baptism gives remission of all sins, and takes away guilt, and does not shave them off ; and " that the roots of all sins are " not " retained in the evil flesh, as if of shaved hair on the head, whence the sins may grow to be cut down again." For it was I that found out that similitude, too, for them to use for the purposes of their calumny, as if I thought and said this.

### CHAP. 27. — IN WHAT SENSE LUST IS CALLED SIN IN THE REGENERATE.

But concerning that concupiscence of the flesh of which they speak, I believe that they are deceived, or that they deceive ; for with this even he that is baptized must struggle with a pious mind, however carefully he presses forward, and is led by the Spirit of God. But although this is called sin, it is certainly so called not because it is sin, but because it is made by sin, as a writing is said to be some one's " hand " because the hand has written it. But they are sins which are unlawfully done, spoken, thought, according to the lust of the flesh, or to ignorance — things which, once done, keep their doers guilty if they are not forgiven. And this very concupiscence of the flesh is in such wise put away in baptism, that although it is inherited by all that are born, it in no respect hurts those that are born anew. And yet from these, if they carnally beget children, it is again derived ; and again it will be hurtful to those that are born, unless by the same form it is remitted to them as born again, and remains in them in no way hindering the future life, because its guilt, derived by generation, has been put away by regeneration ; and thus it is now no more sin, but is called so, whether because it became what it is by sin, or because it is stirred by the delight of sinning, although by the conquest of the delight of righteousness consent is not given to it. Nor is it on account of this, the guilt of which has already been taken away in the laver of regeneration, that the baptized say in their prayer, "Forgive us our debts, as we also forgive our debtors;"[1] but on account of sins which are committed, whether in consentings to it, when what is right is overcome by that which pleases, or when by ignorance evil is accepted as if it were good. And they are committed, whether by acting, or by speaking, or — and this is the easiest and the quickest — by thinking. From all which things what believer ever will boast that he has his heart pure? or who will boast that he is pure from sin?[2] Certainly that which follows in the prayer is said on account of concupiscence: "Lead us not into temptation, but deliver us from evil." "For every one," as it is written, "is tempted when he is drawn away of his own concupiscence, and enticed; then, when concupiscence hath conceived, it bringeth forth sin."[3]

CHAP. 28 [XIV.] — MANY WITHOUT CRIME, NONE WITHOUT SIN.

All these products of concupiscence, and the old guilt of concupiscence itself, are put away by the washing of baptism. And whatever that concupiscence now brings forth, if they are not those products which are called not only sins, but even crimes, are purified by that method of daily prayer when we say, "Forgive us our debts, as we forgive," and by the sincerity of alms-giving. For no one is so foolish as to say that that precept of our Lord does not refer to baptized people: "Forgive and it shall be forgiven you, give and it shall be given you."[4] But none could rightly be ordained a minister in the Church if the apostle had said, "If any is without sin," where he says, "If any is without crime;"[5] or if he had said, "Having no sin," where he says, "Having no crime."[6] Because many baptized believers are without crime, but I should say that no one in this life is without sin, — however much the Pelagians are inflated, and burst asunder in madness against me because I say this: not because there remains anything of sin which is not remitted in baptism; but because by us who remain in the weakness of this life such sins do not cease daily to be committed, as are daily remitted to those who pray in faith and work in mercy. This is the soundness of the catholic faith, which the Holy Spirit everywhere sows, — not the vanity and presumption of spirit of heretical pravity.

CHAP. 29 [XV.] — JULIAN OPPOSES THE FAITH OF HIS FRIENDS TO THE OPINIONS OF CATHOLIC BELIEVERS. FIRST OF ALL, OF FREE WILL.

Now therefore let us see, for the rest, in what way — after thinking that he might calumniously object against me what I believe, and feign what I do not believe — he himself professes his own faith or that of the Pelagians. "In opposition to these things," he says, "we daily argue, and we are unwilling to yield our consent to transgressors, because we say that free will is in all by nature, and could not perish by the sin of Adam; which assertion is confirmed by the authority of all Scriptures." If in any degree it is necessary to say this, you should not say it against the grace of God, — you should not give your consent to transgressors, but you should correct your opinion. But about this, as much as I could, and as far as it seemed to be sufficient, I have argued above.

CHAP. 30. — SECONDLY, OF MARRIAGE.

"We say," says he, "that that marriage which is now celebrated throughout the earth was ordained by God, and that married people are not guilty, but that fornicators and adulterers are to be condemned." This is true and catholic doctrine; but what you want to gather from this, to wit, that from the intercourse of male and female those who are born derive no sin to be put away by the laver of regeneration, — this is false and heretical.

CHAP. 31. — THIRDLY, OF CONJUGAL INTERCOURSE.

"We say," says he, "that the sexual impulse — that is, that the virility itself, without which there can be no intercourse — is ordained by God." To this I reply that the sexual impulse, and, to make use of his word, virility, without which there can be no intercourse, was so appointed by God that there was in it nothing to be ashamed of. For it was not fit that His creature should blush at the work of his Creator; but by a just punishment the disobedience of the members was the retribution to the disobedience of the first man, for which disobedience they blushed when they covered with fig-leaves those shameful parts which previously were not shameful.

CHAP. 32 [XVI.] — THE APRONS WHICH ADAM AND EVE WORE.

For they did not use for themselves tunics to cover their whole bodies after their sin, but aprons,[7] which some of the less careful of our translators have translated as "coverings." And this indeed is true; but "covering" is a general name, by which may be understood every kind of clothing and veil. And ambiguity ought to be avoided, so that, as the Greek called them περιζώματα, by which only the shameful parts of the body are covered, so also the Latin should either use the Greek word itself, because now

---

[1] Matt. vi. 12.    [2] Prov. xx. 9.    [3] Jas. i. 14.
[4] Luke vi. 37, 38.    [5] Tit. i. 6.    [6] 1 Tim. iii. 10.    [7] Gen. iii. 7.

custom has come to use it instead of the Latin, or, as some do, use the word aprons,[1] or, as others have better named them, wrestling aprons.[2] Because this name is taken from that ancient Roman custom whereby the youth covered their shameful parts when they were exercised naked in the field; whence even at this day they are called *campestrati*,[3] since they cover those members with the girdle. Although, if those members by which sin was committed were to be covered after the sin, men ought not indeed to have been clothed in tunics, but to have covered their hand and mouth, because they sinned by taking and eating. What, then, is the meaning, when the prohibited food was taken, and the transgression of the precept had been committed, of the look turned towards those members? What unknown novelty is felt there, and compels itself to be noticed? And this is signified by the opening of the eyes. For their eyes were not closed, either when Adam gave names to the cattle and birds, or when Eve saw the trees to be beautiful and good; but they were made open — that is, attentive — to consider; as it is written of Agar, the handmaid of Sarah, that she opened her eyes and saw a well,[4] although she certainly had not had them closed before. As, therefore, they were so suddenly ashamed of their nakedness, which they were daily in the habit of looking upon and were not confused, that they could now no longer bear those members naked, but immediately took care to cover them; did not they — he in the open, she in the hidden impulse — perceive those members to be disobedient to the choice of their will, which certainly they ought to have ruled like the rest by their voluntary command? And this they deservedly suffered, because they themselves also were not obedient to their Lord. Therefore they blushed that they in such wise had not manifested service to their Creator, that they should deserve to lose dominion over those members by which children were to be procreated.

### CHAP. 33. — THE SHAME OF NAKEDNESS.

This kind of shame — this necessity of blushing — is certainly born with every man, and in some measure is commanded by the very laws of nature; so that, in this matter, even virtuous married people are ashamed. Nor can any one go to such an extreme of evil and disgrace, as, because he knows God to be the author of nature and the ordainer of marriage, to have intercourse even with his wife in any one's sight, or not to blush at those impulses and seek secrecy, where

he can shun the sight not only of strangers, but even of all his own relatives. Therefore let human nature be permitted to acknowledge the evil that happens to it by its own fault, lest it should be compelled either not to blush at its own impulses, which is most shameless, or else to blush at the work of its Creator, which is most ungrateful. Of this evil, nevertheless, virtuous marriage makes good use for the sake of the benefit of the begetting of children. But to consent to lust for the sake of carnal pleasure alone is sin, although it may be conceded to married people with permission.

### CHAP. 34 [XVII.] — WHETHER THERE COULD BE SENSUAL APPETITE IN PARADISE BEFORE THE FALL.

But, while maintaining, ye Pelagians, the honourableness and fruitfulness of marriage, determine, if nobody had sinned, what you would wish to consider the life of those people in Paradise, and choose one of these four things. For beyond a doubt, either as often as ever they pleased they would have had intercourse; or they would bridle lust when intercourse was not necessary; or lust would arise at the summons of will, just at the time when chaste prudence would have perceived beforehand that intercourse was necessary; or, with no lust existing at all, as every other member served for its own work, so for its own work the organs of generation also would obey the commands of those that willed, without any difficulty. Of these four suppositions, choose which you please; but I think you will reject the two former, in which lust is either obeyed or resisted. For the first one would not be in accordance with so great a virtue, and the second not in harmony with so great a happiness. For be the idea far from us, that the glory of so great a blessedness as that should either be most basely enslaved by always following a preceding lust, or, by resisting it, should not enjoy the most abounding peace. Away, I say, with the thought that that mind should either be gratified by consenting to satisfy the concupiscence of the flesh, arising not opportunely for the sake of procreation, but with unregulated excitement, or that that quiet should find it necessary to restrain it by refusing.

### CHAP. 35. — DESIRE IN PARADISE WAS EITHER NONE AT ALL, OR IT WAS OBEDIENT TO THE IMPULSE OF THE WILL.

But whichever you choose of the two other alternatives, there is no necessity for striving against you with any disputation. For even if you should refuse to elect the fourth, in which there is the highest tranquillity of all the obedient members without any lust, since already the urgency of your arguments has made you hostile

---

[1] *Succinctoria.*
[2] *Campestria*, which, as Augustin explains, is derived from "*campester*," and that from "*campus*." See *On the City of God*, xiv. 17.
[3] *i.e.* "campestre-clad."      [4] Gen. xxi. 19.

to it ; that will doubtless please you which I have put in the third place, that that carnal concupiscence, whose impulse attains to the final pleasure which much delights you, should never arise in Paradise except at the bidding of the will when it would be necessary for procreation. If it is agreeable to you to arrange this in Paradise, and if, by means of such a concupiscence of the flesh which should neither anticipate, nor impede, nor exceed the bidding of the will, it appears to you that children could have been begotten, I have no objection. For, as far as I am concerned in this matter, it is enough for me that such a concupiscence of the flesh is not now among men, as you concede there might have been in that place of happiness. For what it now is, the sense of all men certainly confesses, although with modesty ; because it both solicits with excessive and importunate uneasiness the chaste, even when they are unwilling and are checking it by moderation, and frequently withdraws itself from the willing and inflicts itself on the unwilling ; so that, by its disobedience, it testifies that it is nothing else than the punishment of that first disobedience. Whence, reasonably, both then the first men when they covered their nakedness, and now whoever considers himself to be a man, every no less modest than immodest person is confounded at it — far be it from us to say by the work of God, but — by the penalty of the first and ancient sin. You, however, not for the sake of religious reasoning, but for excited contention, — not on behalf of human modesty, but for your own madness, that even the concupiscence of the flesh itself should not be thought to be currupted, and original sin to be derived from it, — are endeavouring by your argument to recall it absolutely, such as it now is, into Paradise ; and to contend that that concupiscence could have been there which would either always be followed by a disgraceful consent, or would sometimes be restrained by a pitiable refusal. I, however, do not greatly care what it delights you to think of it. Still, whatever of men is born by its means, if he is not born again, without doubt he is damned ; and he must be under the dominion of the devil, if he is not delivered thence by Christ.

CHAP. 36 [XVIII.] — JULIAN'S FOURTH OBJECTION, THAT MAN IS GOD'S WORK, AND IS NOT CONSTRAINED TO EVIL OR GOOD BY HIS POWER.

"We maintain," says he, " that men are the work of God, and that no one is forced unwillingly by His power either into evil or good, but that man does either good or ill of his own will ; but that in a good work he is always assisted by God's grace, while in evil he is incited by the suggestions of the devil." To this I answer, that men, in so far as they are men, are the work

of God ; but in so far as they are sinners, they are under the devil, unless they are plucked from thence by Him who became the Mediator between God and man, for no other reason than because He could not be a sinner from men. And that no one is forced by God's power unwillingly either into evil or good, but that when God forsakes a man, he deservedly goes to evil, and that when God assists, without deserving he is converted to good. For a man is not good if he is unwilling, but by the grace of God he is even assisted to the point of being willing ; because it is not vainly written, " For it is God that worketh in you, both to will and to do for His good pleasure," [1] and, " The will is prepared by God." [2]

CHAP. 37 [XIX.] — THE BEGINNING OF A GOOD WILL IS THE GIFT OF GRACE.

But you think that a man is so aided by the grace of God in a good work, that in stirring up his will to that very good work you believe that grace does nothing ; for this your own words sufficiently declare. For why have you not said that a man is incited by God's grace to a good work, as you have said that he is incited to evil by the suggestions of the devil, but have said that in a good work he is always aided by God's grace? — as if by his own will, and without any grace of God, he undertook a good work, and were then divinely assisted in the work itself, for the sake, that is to say, of the merits of his good will ; so that grace is rendered as due, — not given as not due, — and thus grace is made no more grace. [3] But this is what, in the Palestinian judgment, Pelagius with a deceitful heart condemned, — that the grace of God, namely, is given according to our merits. Tell me, I beseech you, what good, Paul, while he was as yet Saul, willed, and not rather great evils, when breathing out slaughter he went, in horrible darkness of mind and madness, to lay waste the Christians? [4] For what merits of a good will did God convert him by a marvellous and sudden calling from those evils to good things? What shall I say, when he himself cries, " Not by works of righteousness that we have done, but according to His mercy He saved us"? [5] What is that which I have already mentioned [6] as having been said by the Lord, " No one can come to me," — which is understood as "believe on me," — unless it were given him of my Father" ? [7] Whether is this given to him who is already willing to believe, for the sake of the merits of a good will? or rather is the will itself, as in the case of Saul, stirred up from above, that he may believe, even although he is so averse from the

---

[1] Phil. ii. 13.  [2] Prov. viii. 35.  [3] Rom. xi. 6.
[4] Acts ix. 1.  [5] Tit. iii. 5.  [6] See above, ch. 6.
[7] John vi. 66.

faith as even to persecute the believers? For how has the Lord commanded us to pray for those who persecute us? Do we pray thus that the grace of God may be recompensed them for the sake of their good will, and not rather that the evil will itself may be changed into a good one? Just as we believe that at that time the saints whom he was persecuting did not pray for Saul in vain, that his will might be converted to the faith which he was destroying. And indeed that his conversion was effected from above, appeared even by a manifest miracle. But how many enemies of Christ are at the present day suddenly drawn by God's secret grace to Christ! And if I had not set down this word from the gospel, what things would that man have said in this behalf concerning me, since even now he is stirring, not against me, but against Him who cries, "No man can come to me, except the Father who hath sent me draw him"![1] For He does not say, "except He lead him," so that we can thus in any way understand that his will precedes. For who is "drawn," if he was already willing? And yet no man comes unless he is willing. Therefore he is drawn in wondrous ways to will, by Him who knows how to work within the very hearts of men. Not that men who are unwilling should believe, which cannot be, but that they should be made willing from being unwilling.

CHAP. 38 [XX.]—THE POWER OF GOD'S GRACE IS PROVED.

That this is true we do not surmise by human conjecture, but we discern by the most evident authority of the divine Scriptures. It is read in the books of the Chronicles: "Also in Judah, the hand of God was made to give them one heart, to do the commandment of the king and of the princes in the word of the Lord."[2] Also by Ezekiel the prophet the Lord says, "I will give them another heart, and a new spirit will I give them; and I will take away their stony heart out of their flesh, and I will give them an heart of flesh, that they may walk in my commandments and observe my judgments and do them."[3] And what is that which Esther the queen prays when she says, "Give me eloquent speech in my mouth, and enlighten my words in the sight of the lion, and turn his heart to hatred of him that fighteth against us"?[4] How does she say such things as these in her prayer to God, if God does not work His will in men's hearts? But perchance the woman was foolish in praying thus. Let us see, then, whether the desire of the petitioner was vainly sent on in advance, and whether the result did not follow as of one who heard. Lo, she goes in to the king. We need not say much. And because she did not approach him in her own order, under the compulsion of her great necessity, "he looked upon her," as it is written, "like a bull in the impulse of his indignation. And the queen feared, and her colour was changed through faintness, and she bowed herself upon the head of her maid, who went before her. And God changed him, and converted his indignation into mildness."[5] Now what need is there to relate what follows, where the divine Scripture testifies that God fulfilled what she had asked for by working in the heart of the king nothing other than the will by which he commanded, and it was done as the queen had asked of him? And now God had heard her that it should be done, who changed the heart of the king by a most secret and efficacious power before he had heard the address of the woman beseeching him, and moulded it from indignation to mildness,—that is, from the will to hurt, to the will to favour,—according to that word of the apostle, "God worketh in you to will also." Did the men of God who wrote these things—nay, did the Spirit of God Himself, under whose guidance such things were written by them—assail the free will of man? Away with the notion! But He has commended both the most righteous judgment and the most merciful aid of the Omnipotent in all cases. For it is enough for man to know that there is no unrighteousness with God. But how He dispenses those benefits, making some deservedly vessels of wrath, others graciously vessels of mercy,—who has known the mind of the Lord, or who has been His counsellor? If, then, we attain to the honour of grace, let us not be ungrateful by attributing to ourselves what we have received. "For what have we which we have not received?"[6]

CHAP. 39 [XXI.] — JULIAN'S FIFTH OBJECTION CONCERNING THE SAINTS OF THE OLD TESTAMENT.

"We say," says he, "that the saints of the Old Testament, their righteousness being perfected here, passed to eternal life,—that is, that by the love of virtue they departed from all sins; because those whom we read of as having committed any sin, we nevertheless know to have amended themselves." Of whatever virtue you may declare that the ancient righteous men were possessed, nothing saved them but the belief in the Mediator who shed His blood for the remission of their sins. For their own word is, "I believed, and therefore I spoke."[7] Whence the Apostle Paul also says, "And we having the same Spirit of faith, according as it is written, I believed,

---

[1] John vi. 44.
[2] 2 Chron. xxx. 12.
[3] Ezek. xxxvi. 26, 27.
[4] Esther xiv. 13.
[5] Esther xv. 5 ff.
[6] 1 Cor. iv. 7.
[7] Ps. cxvi. 10.

and therefore have I spoken; we also believe, and therefore speak."[1] What is "the same Spirit," but that Spirit whom these righteous men also had who said such things? The Apostle Peter also says, "Why do ye wish to put a yoke upon the heathen, which neither we nor our fathers have been able to bear? But, by the grace of the Lord Jesus Christ, we believe that we shall be saved, even as they."[2] You who are enemies to this grace do not wish this, that the ancients should be believed to have been saved by the same grace of Jesus Christ; but you distribute the times according to Pelagius,[3] in whose books this is read, and you say that before the law men were saved by nature, then by the law, lastly by Christ, as if to men of the two former times, that is to say, before the law and under the law, the blood of Christ had not been necessary; making void what is said: "For there is one God and one Mediator between God and men, the man Christ Jesus."[4]

CHAP. 40 [XXII.] — THE SIXTH OBJECTION, CONCERNING THE NECESSITY OF GRACE FOR ALL, AND CONCERNING THE BAPTISM OF INFANTS.

They say, "We confess that the grace of Christ is necessary to all, both to grown-up people and to infants; and we anathematize those who say that a child born of two baptized people ought not to be baptized." I know in what sense you say such things as these — not according to the Apostle Paul, but according to the heretic Pelagius; — to wit, that baptism is necessary for infants, not for the sake of the remission of sins, but only for the sake of the kingdom of heaven; for you give them outside the kingdom of heaven a place of salvation and life eternal, even if they have not been baptized. Nor do you regard what is written, "Whosoever believeth and is baptized shall be saved; but he who believeth not shall be condemned."[5] For which reason, in the Church of the Saviour, infants believe by means of other people, even as they have derived those sins which are remitted them in baptism from other people. Nor do you think thus, that they cannot have life who have been without the body and blood of Christ, although He said Himself, "Unless ye eat my flesh and drink my blood, ye shall have no life in you."[6] Or if you are forced by the words of the gospel to confess that infants departing from the body cannot have either life or salvation unless they have been baptized, ask why those who are not baptized are compelled to undergo the judgment of the second death, by the judgment of Him who condemns nobody undeservingly, and you will find what you do not want, — original sin!

CHAP. 41 [XXIII.] — THE SEVENTH OBJECTION, OF THE EFFECT OF BAPTISM.

"We condemn," says he, "those who affirm that baptism does not do away all sins, because we know that full cleansing is conferred by these mysteries." We also say this; but you do not say that infants are also by those same mysteries freed from the bonds of their first birth and of their hateful descent. On which account it behoves you, like other heretics also, to be separated from the Church of Christ, which holds this of old time.

CHAP. 42 [XXIV.] — HE REBUTS THE CONCLUSION OF JULIAN'S LETTER.

But now the manner in which he concludes the letter by saying, "Let no one therefore seduce you, nor let the wicked deny that they think these things. But if they speak the truth, either let a hearing be given, or let those very bishops who now disagree with me condemn what I have above said that they hold with the Manicheans, as we condemn those things which they declare concerning us, and a full agreement shall be made; but if they will not, know ye that they are Manicheans, and abstain from their company;" — this is rather to be despised than rebuked. For which of us hesitates to pronounce an anathema against the Manicheans, who say that from the good God neither proceed men, nor was ordained marriage, nor was given the law, which was ministered to the Hebrew people by Moses! But against the Pelagians also, not without reason, we pronounce an anathema, for that they are so hostile to God's grace, which comes through Jesus Christ our Lord, as to say that it is given not freely, but according to our merits, and thus grace is no more grace;[7] and place so much in free will by which man is plunged into the abyss, as to say that by making good use of it man deserves grace, — although no man can make good use of it except by grace, which is not repaid according to debt, but is given freely by God's mercy. And they so contend that infants are already saved, that they dare deny that they are to be saved by the Saviour. And holding and disseminating these execrable dogmas, they still over and above constantly demand a hearing, when, as condemned, they ought to repent.

---

[1] 2 Cor. iv. 13.          [2] Acts xv. 10, 11.
[3] See above, *On Original Sin*, 30.   [4] 1 Tim. ii. 5.
[5] Mark xvi. 16.         [6] John vi. 34.

[7] Rom. xi. 6.

# BOOK II.

HE UNDERTAKES TO EXAMINE THE SECOND LETTER OF THE PELAGIANS, FILLED, LIKE THE FIRST, WITH CALUMNIES AGAINST THE CATHOLICS — A LETTER THAT WAS SENT BY THEM TO THESSALONICA IN THE NAME OF EIGHTEEN BISHOPS; AND, FIRST OF ALL, HE SHOWS, BY THE COMPARISON OF THE HERETICAL WRITINGS WITH ONE ANOTHER, THAT THE CATHOLICS ARE BY NO MEANS FALLING INTO THE ERRORS OF THE MANICHEANS IN DETESTING THE DOGMAS OF THE PELAGIANS. HE REPELS THE CALUMNY OF PREVARICATION INCURRED BY THE ROMAN CLERGY IN THE LATTER CONDEMNATION OF PELAGIUS AND CŒLESTIUS BY ZOSIMUS, SHOWING THAT THE PELAGIAN DOGMAS WERE NEVER APPROVED AT ROME, ALTHOUGH FOR SOME TIME, BY THE CLEMENCY OF ZOSIMUS, CŒLESTIUS WAS MERCIFULLY DEALT WITH, WITH A VIEW TO LEADING HIM TO THE CORRECTION OF HIS ERRORS. HE SHOWS THAT, UNDER THE NAME OF GRACE, CATHOLICS NEITHER ASSERT A DOCTRINE OF FATE, NOR ATTRIBUTE RESPECT OF PERSONS TO GOD; ALTHOUGH THEY TRULY SAY THAT GOD'S GRACE IS NOT GIVEN ACCORDING TO HUMAN MERITS, AND THAT THE FIRST DESIRE OF GOOD IS INSPIRED BY GOD; SO THAT A MAN DOES NOT AT ALL MAKE A BEGINNING OF A CHANGE FROM BAD TO GOOD, UNLESS THE UNBOUGHT AND GRATUITOUS MERCY OF GOD EFFECTS THAT BEGINNING IN HIM.

## CHAP. I. — INTRODUCTION; THE PELAGIANS IMPEACH CATHOLICS AS MANICHEANS.

LET me now consider a second letter, not of Julian's alone, but common to him with several bishops, which they sent to Thessalonica; and let me answer it, with God's help, as I best can. And lest this work of mine become longer than the necessity of the subject itself requires, what need is there to refute those things which do not contain the insidious poison of their doctrine, but seem only to plead for the acquiescence of the Eastern bishops for their assistance, or, on behalf of the catholic faith, against the profanity, as they say, of the Manicheans; with no other view except, a horrible heresy being presented to them, whose adversaries they profess themselves to be, to lie hid as the enemies of grace in praise of nature? For who at any time has stirred any question of these matters against them? or what catholic is displeased because they condemn those whom the apostle foretold as departing from the faith, having their conscience seared, forbidding to marry, abstaining from meats that they think unclean, not thinking that all things were created by God?[1] Who at any time constrained them to deny that every creature of God is good, and there is no substance which the supreme God has not made, except God Himself, who was not made by any? It is not such things as these, which it is plain are catholic truths, that are rebuked and condemned in them; because not alone the catholic faith holds in detestation the Manichean impiety as exceedingly foolish and mischievous, but also all heretics who are not Manicheans. Whence even these Pelagians do well to utter an anathema against the Manicheans, and to speak against their errors. But they do two evil things, for which they themselves must also be anathematized — one, that they impeach catholics under the name of Manicheans, the other, that they themselves also are introducing the heresy of a new error. For they are not therefore sound in the faith because they are not labouring under the disease of the Manicheans. The kind of pestilence is not always one and the same — as in the bodies, so also in the minds. As, therefore, the physician of the body would not have pronounced a man free from peril of death whom he might have declared free from dropsy, if he had seen him to be sick of some other mortal disease; so truth is not acknowledged in their case because they are not Manicheans, if they are raving in some other kind of perversity. Wherefore what we anathematize with them is one thing, what we anathematize in them is another. For we hold in abhorrence with them what is rightly offensive to them also; just as, nevertheless, we hold in

---

[1] 1 Tim. iv. ff.

abhorrence in them that for which they themselves are rightly offensive.

CHAP. 2 [II.] — THE HERESIES OF THE MANICHEANS AND PELAGIANS ARE MUTUALLY OPPOSED, AND ARE ALIKE REPROBATED BY THE CATHOLIC CHURCH.

The Manicheans say that the good God is not the Creator of all natures; the Pelagians say that God is not the Purifier, the Saviour, the Deliverer of all ages among men. The catholic Church condemns both; as well maintaining God's creation against the Manicheans, that no nature may be denied to be framed by Him, as maintaining against the Pelagians that in all ages human nature must be sought after as ruined. The Manicheans rebuke the concupiscence of the flesh, not as if it were an accidental vice, but as if it were a nature bad from eternity; the Pelagians approve it as if it were no vice, but even a natural good. The catholic faith condemns both, saying to the Manicheans, "It is not nature, but it is vice;" saying to the Pelagians, "It is not of the Father, but it is of the world;" in order that both may allow it as an evil sickness to be cured — the former by ceasing to believe it, as it were, incurable, the latter by ceasing to proclaim it as laudable. The Manicheans deny that to a good man the beginning of evil came from free will; the Pelagians say that even a bad man has free will sufficiently to perform the good commandment. The catholic Church condemns both, saying to the former, "God made man upright,"[1] and saying to the latter, "If the Son shall make you free, ye shall be free indeed."[2] The Manicheans say that the soul, as a particle of God, has sin by the commixture of an evil nature; the Pelagians say that the soul is upright, not indeed a particle, but a creature of God, and has not even in this corruptible life any sin. The catholic Church condemns both, saying to the Manicheans, "Either make the tree good and its fruit good, or make the tree evil and its fruit evil,"[3] which would not be said to man who cannot make his own nature, unless because sin is not nature, but vice; and saying to the Pelagians, "If we say that we have no sin we deceive ourselves, and the truth is not in us."[4] In these diseases, opposed as they are to one another, the Manicheans and the Pelagians are at issue, with dissimilar will but with similar vanity, separated by different opinions, but close together by a perverse mind.

CHAP. 3. — HOW FAR THE MANICHEANS AND PELAGIANS ARE JOINED IN ERROR; HOW FAR THEY ARE SEPARATED.

Still, indeed, they alike oppose the grace of Christ, they alike make His baptism of no account, they alike dishonour His flesh; but, moreover, they do these things in different ways and for different reasons. For the Manicheans assert that divine assistance is given to the merits of a good nature, but the Pelagians, to the merits of a good will. The former say, God owes this to the labours of His members; the latter say, God owes this to the virtues of His servants. In both cases, therefore, the reward is not imputed according to grace, but according to debt. The Manicheans contend, with a profane heart, that the washing of regeneration — that is, the water itself — is superfluous, and is of no advantage. But the Pelagians assert that what is said in holy baptism for the putting away of sins is of no avail to infants, as they have no sin; and thus in the baptism of infants, as far as pertains to the remission of sins, the Manicheans destroy the visible element, but the Pelagians destroy even the invisible sacrament. The Manicheans dishonour Christ's flesh by blaspheming the birth from the Virgin; but the Pelagians by making the flesh of those to be redeemed equal to the flesh of the Redeemer. Since Christ was born, not of course in sinful flesh, but in the likeness of sinful flesh, while the flesh of the rest of mankind is born sinful. The Manicheans, therefore, who absolutely abominate all flesh, take away the manifest truth from the flesh of Christ; but the Pelagians, who maintain that no flesh is born sinful, take away from Christ's flesh its special and proper dignity.

CHAP. 4. — THE TWO CONTRARY ERRORS.

Let the Pelagians, then, cease to object to the catholics that which they are not, but let them rather hasten to amend what they themselves are; and let them not wish to be considered deserving of approval because they are opposed to the hateful error of the Manicheans, but let them acknowledge themselves to be deservedly hateful because they do not put away their own error. For two errors may be opposed to one another, although both are to be reprobated because both are alike opposed to the truth. For if the Pelagians are to be loved because they hate the Manicheans, the Manicheans should also be loved because they hate the Pelagians. But be it far from our catholic mother to choose some to love on the ground that they hate others, when by the warning and help of the Lord she ought to avoid both, and should desire to heal both.

CHAP. 5 [III.] — THE CALUMNY OF THE PELAGIANS AGAINST THE CLERGY OF THE ROMAN CHURCH.

Moreover, they accuse the Roman clergy, writing, "That, driven by the fear of a command, they have not blushed to be guilty of the

---

[1] Eccles. vii. 30.     [2] John viii. 36.     [3] Matt. xii. 33.
[4] 1 John i. 8.

crime of prevarication; so that, contrary to their previous judgment, wherein by their proceedings they had assented to the catholic dogma, they subsequently pronounced that the nature of men is evil." Nay, but the Pelagians had conceived, with a false hope, that the new and execrable dogma of Pelagius or Cœlestius could be made acceptable to the catholic intelligences of certain Romans, when those crafty spirits — however perverted by a wicked error, yet not contemptible, since they appeared rather to be deserving of considerate correction than of easy condemnation — were treated with somewhat more of lenity than the stricter discipline of the Church required. For while so many and such important ecclesiastical documents were passing and repassing between the Apostolical See and the African bishops,[1] — and, moreover, when the proceedings in this matter in that see were completed, with Cœlestius present and making answer, — what sort of a letter, what decree, is found of Pope Zosimus, of venerable memory, wherein he prescribed that it must be believed that man is born without any taint of original sin? Absolutely he never said this — never wrote it at all. But since Cœlestius had written this in his pamphlet, among those matters, merely, on which he confessed that he was still in doubt and desired to be instructed, the desire of amendment in a man of so acute an intellect, who, if he could be put right, would assuredly be of advantage to many, and not the falsehood of the doctrine, was approved. And therefore his pamphlet was called catholic, because this also is the part of a catholic disposition, — if by chance in any matters a man thinks differently from what the truth demands, not with the greatest accuracy to define those matters, but, if detected and demonstrated, to reject them. For it was not to heretics, but to catholics, that the apostle was speaking when he said, " Let us, therefore, as many as are perfect, be thus minded; and if in anything ye be otherwise minded, God shall reveal even this unto you." [2] This was thought to have been the case in him when he replied that he consented to the letters of Pope Innocent of blessed memory, in which all doubt about this matter was removed. And in order that this might be made fuller and more manifest in him, matters were delayed until letters should come from Africa, in which province his craftiness had in some sort become more evidently known. And afterwards these letters came to Rome containing this, that it was not sufficient for men of more sluggish and anxious minds that he confessed his general consent to the letters of Bishop Innocent, but that he ought openly to anathematize the mischievous statements which he had made in his pamphlet; lest if he did not do so, many people of better intelligence should rather believe that in his pamphlet those poisons of the faith had been approved by the catholic see, because it had been affirmed by that see that that pamphlet was catholic, than that they had been amended because of his answer that he consented to the letters of Pope Innocent. Then, therefore, when his presence was demanded, in order that by certain and clear answers either the craft of the man or his correction might plainly appear and remain doubtful to no one, he withdrew himself and refused the examination. Neither would the delay which had already been made for the advantage of others have taken place, if it could not be of advantage to the pertinacity and madness of those who were excessively perverse. But if, which be far from the case, it had so been judged in the Roman Church concerning Cœlestius or Pelagius, that those dogmas of theirs, which in themselves and with themselves Pope Innocent had condemned, should be pronounced worthy of approval and maintenance, the mark of prevarication would rather have to be branded on the Roman clergy for this. But now, when the first letters of the most blessed Pope Innocent, in reply to the letters of the African bishops,[3] would have equally condemned this error which these men are endeavouring to commend to us; and his successor, the holy Pope Zosimus, would never have said, never have written, that this dogma which these men think concerning infants is to be held; nay, would even have bound Cœlestius by a repeated sentence, when he endeavoured to clear himself, to a consent to the above-mentioned letters of the Apostolic See; — assuredly, whatever in the meanwhile was done more leniently concerning Cœlestius, provided the stability of the most ancient and robust faith were maintained, was the most merciful persuasion of correction, not the most pernicious approval of wickedness; and that afterwards, by the same priesthood, Cœlestius and Pelagius were condemned by repeated authority, was the proof of a severity, for a little while intermitted, at length of necessity to be carried out, not a denial of a previously-known truth or a new acknowledgment of truth.

## CHAP. 6 [IV.] — WHAT WAS DONE IN THE CASE OF CŒLESTIUS AND ZOSIMUS.

But what need is there for us to delay longer in speaking of this matter, when there are extant here and there proceedings and writings drawn up, where all those things just as they were

---

[1] See *On Original Sin*, 9, 5, 8.      [2] Phil. iii. 15.      [3] See Augustin's *Letters*, 181, 182, 183.

transacted may be either learnt or recalled? For who does not see in what degree Cœlestius was bound by the interrogations of your holy predecessor and by the answers of Cœlestius, whereby he professed that he consented to the letters of Pope Innocent, and fastened by a most wholesome chain, so as not to dare any further to maintain that the original sin of infants is not put away in baptism? Because these are the words of the venerable Bishop Innocent concerning this matter to the Carthaginian Council: "For once," he said, "he bore free will; but, using his advantage inconsiderately, and falling into the depths of apostasy, he was overwhelmed, and found no way whereby he could rise from thence; and, deceived for ever by his liberty, he would have lain under the oppression of this ruin, if the advent of Christ had not subsequently for his grace delivered him, and, by the purification of a new regeneration, purged all past sin by the washing of His baptism." [1] What could be more clear or more manifest than that judgment of the Apostolical See? To this Cœlestius professed that he assented, when it was said to him by your holy predecessor, "Do you condemn all those things that are bandied about under your name?" and he himself replied, "I condemn them in accordance with the judgment of your predecessor Innocent, of blessed memory." But among other things which had been uttered under his name, the deacon Paulinus had objected to Cœlestius that he said "that the sin of Adam was prejudicial to himself alone, and not to the human race, and that infants newly born were in the same condition in which Adam was before his sin." [2] Accordingly, if he would condemn the views objected to by Paulinus with a truthful heart and tongue, according to the judgment of the blessed Pope Innocent, what could remain to him afterwards whence he could contend that there was no sin in infants resulting from the past transgression of the first man, which would be purged in holy baptism by the purification of the new regeneration? But he showed that he had answered deceitfully by the final event, when he withdrew himself from the examination, lest he should be compelled, according to the African rescripts, absolutely to mention and anathematize the very words themselves concerning this question which he wrote in his tractate.

CHAP. 7. — HE SUGGESTS A DILEMMA TO CŒLESTIUS.

What was that which the same pope replied to the bishops of Numidia concerning this very cause, because he had received letters from both Councils, as well from the Council of Carthage as from the Council of Mileve — does he not speak most plainly concerning infants? For these are his words: [3] "For what your Fraternity [4] asserts that they preach, that infants can be endowed with the rewards of eternal life even without the grace of baptism, is excessively silly; for unless they shall eat the flesh of the Son of man, and drink His blood, they shall not have life in themselves. [5] And they who maintain this as being theirs without regeneration, appear to me to wish to destroy baptism itself, since they proclaim that these have that which we believe is not to be conferred on them without baptism." What does the ungrateful man say to this, when the Apostolic See had already spared him on his profession, as if he were corrected by its most benignant lenity? What does he say to this? Will infants after the end of their life, even if while they live they are not baptized in Christ, be in eternal life, or will they not? If he should say, "They will," how then did he answer that he had condemned what had been uttered under his name "according to the judgment of Innocent, of blessed memory"? Lo, Pope Innocent, of blessed memory, says that infants have not life without Christ's baptism, and without partaking of Christ's body and blood. If he should say, "They will not," how then, if they do not receive eternal life, are they certainly by consequence condemned in eternal death if they derive no original sin?

CHAP. 8. — THE CATHOLIC FAITH CONCERNING INFANTS.

What do they say to these things who dare also to write their mischievous impieties, and dare to send them to the Eastern bishops? Cœlestius is held to have given consent to the letters of the venerable Innocent; the letters themselves of the prelate mentioned are read, and he writes that infants who are not baptized cannot have life. And who will deny that, as a consequence, they have death, if they have not life? Whence, then, in infants, is so wretched a penalty as that, if there is no original fault? How, then, are the Roman clergy charged with prevarication by those forsakers of the faith and opponents of grace under Bishop Zosimus, as if they had had any other view in the subsequent condemnation of Cœlestius and Pelagius than that which they had in a former one under Innocent? Because, certainly, since by the letters of the venerable Innocent concerning the abode of infants in eternal death unless they were baptized in Christ, the antiquity of the catholic faith shone forth, assuredly he would rather be a prevaricator from the Roman Church who should

---

[1] Augustin's *Letters*, 181, 7.    [2] See *On Original Sin*, 3.

[3] See Augustin's *Letters*, 182, 5.
[4] An address like "your Honour," "your Love," etc.
[5] John vi. 54.

deviate from that judgment; and since with God's blessing this did not happen, but that judgment itself was constantly maintained in the repeated condemnation of Cœlestius and Pelagius, let them understand that they themselves are in the position wherein they accuse others of being, and let them hereafter be healed of their prevarication from the faith. Because the catholic faith does not say that the nature of man is bad in as far as he was made man at first by the Creator; nor now is what God creates in that nature when He makes men from men, his evil; but what he derives from that sin of the first man.

CHAP. 9 [V.] — HE REPLIES TO THE CALUMNIES OF THE PELAGIANS.

And now we must look to those things which they objected to us in their letters, and briefly mentioned. And to these this is my answer. We do not say that by the sin of Adam free will perished out of the nature of men; but that it avails for sinning in men subjected to the devil; while it is not of avail for good and pious living, unless the will itself of man should be made free by God's grace, and assisted to every good movement of action, of speech, of thought. We say that no one but the Lord God is the maker of those who are born, and that marriage was ordained not by the devil, but by God Himself; yet that all are born under sin on account of the fault of propagation, and that, therefore, all are under the devil until they are born again in Christ. Nor are we maintaining fate under the name of grace, because we say that the grace of God is preceded by no merits of man. If, however, it is agreeable to any to call the will of the Almighty God by the name of fate, while we indeed shun profane novelties of words, we have no use for contending about words.

CHAP. 10. — WHY THE PELAGIANS FALSELY ACCUSE CATHOLICS OF MAINTAINING FATE UNDER THE NAME OF GRACE.

But, as I was somewhat more attentively considering for what reason they should think it well to object this to us, that we assert fate under the name of grace, I first of all looked into those words of theirs which follow. For thus they have thought that this was to be objected to us: "Under the name," say they, "of grace, they so assert fate as to say that unless God inspired unwilling and resisting man with the desire of good, and that good imperfect, he would neither be able to decline from evil nor to lay hold of good." Then a little after, where they mention what they maintain, I gave heed to what was said by them about this matter. "We confess," say they, "that baptism is necessary for all ages, and that grace, moreover, assists the good pur-

pose of everybody; but yet that it does not infuse the love of virtue into a reluctant one, because there is no acceptance of persons with God."[1] From these words of theirs, I perceived that for this reason they either think, or wish it to be thought, that we assert fate under the name of grace, because we say that God's grace is not given in respect of our merits, but according to His own most merciful will, in that He said, "I will be gracious to whom I will be gracious, and will show mercy on whom I will show mercy."[2] Where, by way of consequence, it is added, "Therefore it is not of him that willeth, nor of him that runneth, but of God that showeth mercy."[3] Here any one might be equally foolish in thinking or saying that the apostle is an assertor of fate. But here these people sufficiently lay themselves open; for when they malign us by saying that we maintain fate under the name of grace, because we say that God's grace is not given on account of our merits, beyond a doubt they confess that they themselves say that it is given on account of our merits; thus their blindness could not conceal and dissimulate that they believe and think thus, although, when this view was objected to him, Pelagius, in the episcopal judgment of Palestine, with crafty fear condemned it. For it was objected to him from the words of his own disciple Cœlestius, indeed, that he himself also was in the habit of saying that God's grace is given on account of our merits. And he in abhorrence, or in pretended abhorrence, of this, did not delay, with his lips at least, to anathematize it;[4] but, as his later writings indicate, and the assertion of those followers of his makes evident, he kept it in his deceitful heart, until afterwards his boldness might put forth in letters[5] what the cunning of a denier had then hidden for fear. And still the Pelagian bishops do not dread, and at least are not ashamed, to send their letters to the catholic Eastern bishops, in which they charge us with being assertors of fate because we do not say that even grace is given according to our merits; although Pelagius, fearing the Eastern bishops, did not dare to say this, and so was compelled to condemn it.

CHAP. 11 [VI.] — THE ACCUSATION OF FATE IS THROWN BACK UPON THE ADVERSARIES.

But is it true, O children of pride, enemies of God's grace, new Pelagian heretics, that whoever says that all man's good deservings are preceded by God's grace, and that God's grace is not given to merits, lest it should not be grace if it is not given freely but be repaid as due to those who deserve it, seems to you to assert fate?

---

[1] Rom. ii. 11; Col. iii. 25.   [2] Ex. xxxiii. 19; Rom. ix. 15.
[3] Rom. ix. 16.
[4] See *On the Proceedings of Pelagius*, 30.
[5] See *On the Proceedings of Pelagius*, 34.

Do not you yourselves also say, whatever be your purpose, that baptism is necessary for all ages? Have you not written in this very letter of yours that opinion concerning baptism, and that concerning grace, side by side? Why did not baptism, which is given to infants, by that very juxtaposition admonish you what you ought to think concerning grace? For these are your words: "We confess that baptism is necessary for all ages, and that grace, moreover, assists the good purpose of everybody; but yet that it does not infuse the love of virtue into a reluctant one, because there is no acceptance of persons with God." In all these words of yours, I for the meanwhile say nothing of what you have said concerning grace. But give a reason concerning baptism, why you should say that it is necessary for all ages; say why it is necessary for infants. Assuredly because it confers some good upon them; and that same something is neither small nor moderate, but of great account. For although you deny that they contract the original sin which is remitted in baptism, yet you do not deny that in that laver of regeneration they are adopted from the sons of men unto the sons of God; nay, you even preach this. Tell us, then, how the infants, whoever they are, that are baptized in Christ and have departed from the body, received so lofty a gift as this, and with what preceding merits. If you should say that they have deserved this by the piety of their parents, it will be replied to you, Why is this benefit sometimes denied to the children of pious people and given to the children of the wicked? For sometimes the offspring born from religious people, in tender age, and thus fresh from the womb, is forestalled by death before it can be washed in the laver of regeneration, and the infant born of Christ's foes is baptized in Christ by the mercy of Christians, — the baptized mother bewails her own little one not baptized, and the chaste virgin gathers in to be baptized a foreign offspring, exposed by an unchaste mother. Here, certainly, the merits of parents are wanting, and even by your own confession the merits of the infants themselves are wanting also. For we know that you do not believe this of the human soul, that it has lived somewhere before it inhabited this earthly body, and has done something either of good or of evil for which it might deserve such difference in the flesh. What cause, then, has procured baptism for this infant, and has denied it to that? Do they have fate because they do not have merit? or is there in these things acceptance of persons with God? For you have said both, — first fate, afterwards acceptance of persons, — that, since both must be refuted, there may remain the merit which you wish to introduce against grace. Answer, then, concerning the merits of infants, why some should depart from their bodies baptized, others not baptized, and by the merits of their parents neither possess nor fail of so excellent a gift that they should become sons of God from sons of men, by no deserving of their parents, by no deservings of their own. You are silent, forsooth, and you find yourselves rather in the same position which you object to us. For if when there is no merit you say that consequently there is fate, and on this account wish the merit of man to be understood in the grace of God, lest you should be compelled to confess fate; see, you rather assert a fate in the baptism of infants, since you avow that in them there is no merit. But if, in the case of infants to be baptized, you deny that any merit at all precedes, and yet do not concede that there is a fate, why do you cry out, — when we say that the grace of God is therefore given freely, lest it should not be grace, and is not repaid as if it were due to preceding merits, — that we are assertors of fate? — not perceiving that in the justification of the wicked, as there are no merits because it is God's grace, so that it is not fate because it is God's grace, and so that it is not acceptance of persons because it is God's grace.

CHAP. 12. — WHAT IS MEANT UNDER THE NAME OF FATE.

Because they who affirm fate contend that not only actions and events, but, moreover, our very wills themselves depend on the position of the stars at the time in which one is conceived or born; which positions they call "constellations." But the grace of God stands above not only all stars and all heavens, but, moreover, all angels. In a word, the assertors of fate attribute both men's good and evil doings and fortunes to fate; but God in the ill fortunes of men follows up their merits with due retribution, while good fortunes He bestows by undeserved grace with a merciful will; doing both the one and the other not according to a temporal conjunction of stars, but according to the eternal and high counsel of His severity and goodness. We see, then, that neither belongs to fate. Here, if you answer that this very benevolence of God, by which He follows not merits, but bestows undeserved benefits with gratuitous bounty, should rather be called "fate," when the apostle calls this "grace," saying, "By grace are ye saved through faith; and that not of yourselves, but it is the gift of God; not of works, lest perchance any one should be lifted up,"[1] — do you not consider, do you not perceive that it is not by us that fate is asserted under the name of grace, but it is rather by you that divine grace is called by the name of fate?

[1] Eph. ii. 8.

## CHAP. 13 [VII.] — HE REPELS THE CALUMNY CONCERNING THE ACCEPTANCE OF PERSONS.

And, moreover, we rightly call it "acceptance of persons" where he who judges, neglecting the merit of the cause concerning which he is judging, favours the one against the other, because he finds something in his person which is worthy of honour or of pity. But if any one have two debtors, and he choose to remit the debt to the one, to require it of the other, he gives to whom he will and defrauds nobody; nor is this to be called "acceptance of persons," since there is no injustice. The acceptance of persons may seem otherwise to those who are of small understanding, where the lord of the vineyard gave to those labourers who had done work therein for one hour as much as to those who had borne the burden and heat of the day, making them equal in wages in the labour of whom there had been such a difference. But what did he reply to those who murmured against the goodman of the house concerning this, as it were, acceptance of persons? "Friend," said he, "I do thee no wrong. Hast not thou agreed with me for a denarius? Take what thine is, and go; but I choose to give to this last as to thee. Is it not lawful to me to do what I will? Is thine eye evil because I am good?" [1] Here, forsooth, is the entire justice: "I choose this. To thee," he says, "I have repaid; on him I have bestowed; nor have I taken anything away from thee to bestow it on him; nor have I either diminished or denied what I owed to you." "May I not do what I will? Is thine eye evil because I am good?" As, therefore. here there is no acceptance of persons, because one is honoured freely in such wise as that another is not defrauded of what is due to him : so also when, according to the purpose of God, one is called, another is not called, a gratuitous benefit is bestowed on the one that is called, of which benefit the calling itself is the beginning, — an evil is repaid to him that is not called, because all are guilty, from the fact that by one man sin entered into the world. And in that parable of the labourers, indeed, where they received one denarius who laboured for one hour, as well as those who laboured twelve times as long, — though assuredly these latter, according to human reasonings, however vain, ought in proportion to the amount of their labour to have received twelve denarii, — both were put on an equality in respect of benefit, not some delivered and others condemned ; because even those who laboured more had it from the goodman of the house himself, both that they were so called as to come, and that they were so fed as to have no want. But where it is said, "Therefore, on whom He will He has mercy, and whom He will He hardeneth," [2] who "maketh one vessel to honour and another to dishonour," [3] it is given indeed without deserving, and freely, because he is of the same mass to whom it is not given; but evil is deservedly and of debt repaid, since in the mass of perdition evil is not repaid to the evil unjustly. And to him to whom it is repaid it is evil, because it is his punishment ; while to Him by whom it is repaid it is good, because it is His right to do it. Nor is there any acceptance of persons in the case of two debtors equally guilty, if to the one is remitted and from the other is claimed that which is equally owed by both.

## CHAP. 14. — HE ILLUSTRATES HIS ARGUMENT BY AN EXAMPLE.

But that what I am saying may be made clear by the exhibition of an example, let us suppose certain twins, born of a certain harlot, and exposed that they might be taken up by others. One of them has expired without baptism ; the other is baptized. What can we say was in this case the "fate" or the "fortune," which are here absolutely nothing? What "acceptance of persons," when with God there is none, even if there could be any such thing in these cases, seeing that they certainly had nothing for which the one could be preferred to the other, and no merits of their own, — whether good, for which the one might deserve to be baptized ; or evil, for which the other might deserve to die without baptism? Were there any merits in their parents, when the father was a fornicator, the mother a harlot? But of whatever kind those merits were, there were certainly not any that were different in those who died in such different conditions, but all were common to both. If, then, neither fate, since no stars made them to differ ; nor fortune, since no fortuitous accidents produce these things ; nor the diversity of persons nor of merits have done this ; what remains, so far as it refers to the baptized child, save the grace of God, which is given freely to vessels made unto honour ; but, as it refers to the unbaptized child, the wrath of God, which is repaid to the vessels made for dishonour in respect of the deservings of the lump itself? But in that one which is baptized we constrain you to confess the grace of God, and convince you that no merit of its own preceded ; but as to that one which died without baptism, why that sacrament should have been wanting to it, which even you confess to be needful for all ages, and what in that manner may have been punished in him, it is for you to see who will not have it that there is any original sin.

---

[1] Matt. xx. 9 ff.      [2] Rom. ix. 18.      [3] Rom. ix. 21.

CHAP. 15. — THE APOSTLE MEETS THE QUESTION
BY LEAVING IT UNSOLVED.

Since in the case of those two twins we have
without a doubt one and the same case, the difficulty of the question why the one died in one
way, and the other in another, is solved by the
apostle as it were by not solving it ; for, when
he had proposed something of the same kind
about two twins, seeing that it was said (not
of works, since they had not as yet done anything either of good or of evil, but of Him that
calleth), " The elder shall serve the younger," [1]
and, " Jacob have I loved, and Esau have I
hated ; " [1] and he had prolonged the horror of
this deep thing even to the point of saying,
" Therefore hath He mercy on whom He will,
and whom He will He hardeneth : " [2] he perceived at once what the trouble was, and opposed
to himself the words of a gainsayer which he
was to check by apostolical authority. For he
says, " You say, then, unto me, " Why doth He
yet find fault ? For who has resisted His will ? "
And to him who says this he answered, " O
man, who art thou that repliest against God ?
Doth the thing formed say to him that formed
it, Why hast thou made me thus ? Hath not
the potter power of the clay of the same lump
to make one vessel unto honour and another
unto dishonour ? " [3]   Then, following on, he
opened up this great and hidden secret as far as
he judged it fit that it should be disclosed to
men, saying, " But if God, willing to show His
wrath and to demonstrate His power, endured
in much patience the vessels of wrath fitted for
destruction, even that He might make known
the riches of His glory on the vessels of mercy
which He has prepared for glory." [4]   This is not
only the assistance, but, moreover, the proof of
God's grace — the assistance, namely, in the
vessels of mercy, but the proof in the vessels of
wrath ; for in these He shows His anger and
makes known His power, because His goodness
is so mighty that He even uses the evil well ; and
in those He makes known the riches of His
glory on the vessels of mercy, because what the
justice of a punisher requires from the vessels of
wrath, the grace of the Deliverer remits to the
vessels of mercy.   Nor would the kindness
which is bestowed on some freely appear, unless
to others equally guilty and from the same mass
God showed what was really due to both, and
condemned them with a righteous judgment.
" For who maketh thee to differ ? " [5] says the
same apostle to a man as it were boasting concerning himself and his own benefits.   " For
who maketh thee to differ " from the vessels of
wrath ; of course, from the mass of perdition
which has sent all by one into damnation?

" Who maketh thee to differ ? "   And as if he
had answered, " My faith maketh me to differ,
— my purpose, my merit," — he says, " For
what hast thou which thou hast not received ?
But if thou hast received it, why dost thou boast
as if thou receivedst it not ? " — that is, as if that
by which thou art made to differ were of thine
own.   Therefore He maketh thee to differ who
bestows that whence thou art made to differ, by
removing the penalty that is due, by conferring
the grace which is not due.   He maketh to
differ, who, when the darkness was upon the face
of the abyss, said, " Let there be light ; and there
was light, and divided " — that is, made to differ
— " between the light and the darkness." [6]   For
when there was only darkness, He did not find
what He should make to differ ; but by making
the light, He made to differ ; so that it may be
said to the justified wicked, " For ye were sometime darkness, but now are ye light in the
Lord." [7]   And thus he who glories must glory
not in himself, but in the Lord.   He makes to
differ who — of those who are not yet born, and
who have not yet done any good or evil, that
His purpose, according to the election, might
stand not of works, but of Himself that calleth
— said, The elder shall serve the younger, and
commending that very purpose afterwards by
the mouth of the prophet, said, " Jacob have I
loved, but Esau have I hated." [8]   Because he
said " the election," and in this God does not
find made by another what He may choose, but
Himself makes what He may find ; just as it is
written of the remnant of Israel : " There is
made a remnant by the election of grace ; but
if by grace, then it is no more of works, otherwise grace is no more grace." [9]   On which
account you are certainly foolish who, when the
Truth declares, " Not of works, but of Him that
calleth, it was said," say that Jacob was loved
on account of future works which God foreknew
that he would do, and thus contradict the apostle
when he says, " Not of works ; " as if he could
not have said, " Not of present, but of future
works."   But he says, " Not of works," that He
might commend grace ; " but if of grace, now
is it no more of works, otherwise grace is no
more grace."   For grace, not due, but free,
precedes, that by it good works may be done ;
but if good works should precede, grace should
be repaid, as it were, to works, and thus grace
should be no more grace.

CHAP. 16. — THE PELAGIANS ARE REFUTED BY THE
CASE OF THE TWIN INFANTS DYING, THE ONE
AFTER, AND THE OTHER WITHOUT, THE GRACE
OF BAPTISM.

But that every lurking-place of your darkness

---

[1] Rom. ix. 11.        [2] Rom. ix. 18.        [3] Rom. ix. 19.
[4] Rom. ix. 22, 23.    [5] 1 Cor. iv. 7.
[6] Gen. i. 2.        [7] Eph. v. 8.        [8] Mal. i. 2.
[9] Rom. xi. 5.

may be taken away from you, I have proposed to you the case of such twins as were not assisted by the merits of their parents, and both died in the very beginning of infancy, the one baptized, the other without baptism; lest you should say that God foreknew their future works, as you say of Jacob and Esau, in opposition to the apostle. For how did He foreknow that those things should be, which, in those infants who were to die in infancy, He rather foreknew as not to be, since His foreknowledge cannot be deceived? Or what does it profit those who are taken away from this life that wickedness may not change their understanding, nor deceit beguile their soul, if even the sin which has not been done, said, or thought, is thus punished as if it had been committed? Because, if it is most absurd, silly, and senseless, that certain men should have to be condemned for those sins, the guilt of which they could neither derive from their parents, as you say, nor could incur themselves, either by committing them, or even by conceiving of them, there comes back to you that unbaptized twin brother of the baptized one, and silently asks you for what reason he was made to differ from his brother in respect of happiness, —why he was punished with that infelicity, so that, while his brother was adopted into a child of God, he himself should not receive that sacrament which, as you confess, is necessary for every age, if, even as there is not a fortune or a fate, or an acceptance of persons with God, so there is no gift of grace without merits, and no original sin. To this dumb child you absolutely submit your tongue and voice; to this witness who says nothing, — you have nothing at all to say!

CHAP. 17 [VIII.] — EVEN THE DESIRE OF AN IMPERFECT GOOD IS A GIFT OF GRACE, OTHERWISE GRACE WOULD BE GIVEN ACCORDING TO MERITS.

Let us now see, as we can, the nature of this thing which they will have to precede in man, in order that he may be regarded as worthy of the assistance of grace, and to the merit of which in him grace is not given as if unearned, but is rendered as due; and thus grace is no more grace. Let us see, however, what this is. "Under the name," say they, "of grace, they so assert fate as to say that unless God should have inspired the desire for good, and that, imperfect good, into unwilling and resisting man, he would neither be able to decline from evil nor to grasp after good." I have already shown what empty things they speak about fate and grace. Now the question which I ought to consider is this, whether God inspires the desire of good into unwilling and resisting man, that he may be no longer unwilling, no longer resisting, but con-

senting to the good and willing the good. For those men will have it that the desire of good in man begins from man himself; that the merit of this beginning is, moreover, attended with the grace of completion — if, at least, they will allow so much as even this. For Pelagius says that what is good is "more easily" fulfilled if grace assists.[1] By which addition — that is, by adding "more easily" — he certainly signifies that he is of the opinion that, even if the aid of grace should be wanting, yet good might be accomplished, although with greater difficulty, by free will. But let me prescribe to my present opponents what they should think in this matter, without speaking of the author of this heresy himself. Let us allow them, with their free will, to be free even from Pelagius himself, and rather give heed to their words which they have written in this letter to which I am replying.

CHAP. 18. — THE DESIRE OF GOOD IS GOD'S GIFT.

For they have thought that it was to be objected to us that we say "that God inspires into unwilling and resisting man the desire," not of any very great good, but "even of imperfect good." Possibly, then, they themselves are keeping open, in some sense at least, a place for grace, as thinking that man may have the desire of good without grace, but only of imperfect good; while of perfect, he could not easily have the desire with grace, but except with it they could not have it at all. Truly, even in this way, too, they are saying that God's grace is given according to our merits, which Pelagius, in the ecclesiastical meeting in the East, condemned, in the fear of being condemned. For if without God's grace the desire of good begins with ourselves, merit itself will have begun — to which, as if of debt, comes the assistance of grace; and thus God's grace will not be bestowed freely, but will be given according to our merit. But that he might furnish a reply to the future Pelagius, the Lord does not say, "Without me it is with difficulty that you can do anything," but He says, "Without me ye can do nothing."[2] And, that He might also furnish an answer to these future heretics, in that very same evangelical saying He does not say, "Without me you can *perfect* nothing," but "*do*" nothing. For if He had said "perfect," they might say that God's aid is necessary not for beginning good, which is of ourselves, but for perfecting it. But let them hear also the apostle. For when the Lord says, "Without me ye can do nothing," in this one word He comprehends both the beginning and the ending. The apostle, indeed, as if he were an expounder of the Lord's saying, distinguished both very clearly when he says, "Because

---

[1] See above, *On the Grace of Christ*, ch. 8.
[2] John xv. 5.

He who hath begun a good work in you will perfect it even to the day of Christ Jesus." [1] But in the Holy Scriptures, in the writings of the same apostle, we find more about that of which we are speaking. For we are now speaking of the desire of good, and if they will have this to begin of ourselves and to be perfected by God, let them see what they can answer to the apostle when he says, "Not that we are sufficient to think anything as of ourselves, but our sufficiency is of God." [2] "To think anything," he says, — he certainly means, "to think anything good;" but is it less to think than to desire. Because we think all that we desire, but we do not desire all that we think; because sometimes also we think what we do not desire. Since, then, it is a smaller thing to think than to desire, — for a man may think good which he does not yet desire, and by advancing may afterwards desire what before without desire he thought of, — how are we not sufficient as of ourselves to that which is less, that is, to the thinking of something good, but our sufficiency is of God; while to that which is greater, — that is, to the desire of some good thing — without the divine help, we are sufficient of free will? For what the apostle says here is not, "Not that we are sufficient as of ourselves to think that which is perfect;" but he says, "to think anything," to which "nothing" is the contrary. And this is the meaning of what the Lord says, "Without me ye can do nothing."

CHAP. 19 [IX.] — HE INTERPRETS THE SCRIPTURES WHICH THE PELAGIANS MAKE ILL USE OF.

But assuredly, as to what is written, "The preparation of the heart is man's part, and the answer of the tongue is from the Lord," [3] they are misled by an imperfect understanding, so as to think that to prepare the heart — that is, to begin good — pertains to man without the aid of God's grace. Be it far from the children of promise thus to understand it! As if, when they heard the Lord saying, "Without me ye can do nothing," [4] they would convict Him by saying, "Behold, without Thee we can prepare the heart;" or when they heard from Paul the apostle, "Not that we are sufficient to think anything as of ourselves, but our sufficiency is of God," [2] as if they would also convict him, saying, "Behold, we are sufficient of ourselves to prepare our heart, and thus also to think some good thing; for who can without good thought prepare his heart for good?" Be it far from any thus to understand the passage, except the proud maintainers of free will and forsakers of the catholic faith! Therefore, since it is written, "It is man's part to prepare the heart, and the answer of the tongue is from the Lord," it is that man pre-

pares his heart, not, however, without the aid of God, who so touches the heart that man prepares the heart. But in the answer of the tongue — that is, in that which the divine tongue answers to the prepared heart — man has no part; but the whole is from the Lord God.

CHAP. 20. — GOD'S AGENCY IS NEEDFUL EVEN IN MAN'S DOINGS.

For as it is said, "It is man's part to prepare his heart, and the answer of the tongue is from the Lord;" so also is it said, "Open thy mouth, and I will fill it." [5] For although, save by His assistance without whom we can do nothing, we cannot open our mouth, yet we open it by His aid and by our own agency, while the Lord fills it without our agency. For what is to prepare the heart and to open the mouth, but to prepare the will? And yet in the same scriptures is read, "The will is prepared by the Lord," [6] and, "Thou shalt open my lips, and my mouth shall show forth Thy praise." [7] So God admonishes us to prepare our will in what we read, "It is man's part to prepare his heart;" and yet, that man may do this, God helps him, because the will is prepared by the Lord. And, "Open thy mouth." This He so says by way of command, as that nobody can do this unless it is done by His aid, to whom it is said, "Thou shalt open my lips." Are any of these men so foolish as to contend that the mouth is one thing, the lips another; and to say with marvellous triviality that man opens his own mouth, and God opens man's lips? And yet God restrains them from even that absurdity where He says to Moses His servant, "I will open thy mouth, and I will instruct thee what thou oughtest to speak." [8] In that clause, therefore, where He says, "Open thy mouth and I will fill it," it seems, as it were, that one of them pertains to man, the other to God. But in this, where it is said, "I will open thy mouth and will instruct thee," both belong to God. Why is this, except that in one of these cases He co-operates with man as the agent, in the other He does it alone?

CHAP. 21. — MAN DOES NO GOOD THING WHICH GOD DOES NOT CAUSE HIM TO DO.

Wherefore God does many good things in man which man does not do; but man does none which God does not cause man to do. Accordingly, there would be no desire of good in man from the Lord if it were not a good; but if it is a good, we have it not save from Him who is supremely and incommunicably good. For what is the desire for good but love, of which John the apostle speaks without any ambiguity, and

---

[1] Phil. i. 6.    [2] 2 Cor. iii. 5.    [3] Prov. xvi. 1.
[4] John xv. 5.

[5] Ps. lxxxi. 10.    [6] Prov. viii.    [7] Ps. li. 15.
[8] Ex. iv. 12.

says, "Love is of God"?¹ Nor is its beginning of ourselves, and its perfection of God; but if love is of God, we have the whole of it from God. May God by all means turn away this folly of making ourselves first in His gifts, Himself last, — because "His mercy shall prevent me."² And it is He to whom is faithfully and truthfully sung, "For Thou hast prevented him with the blessings of sweetness."³ And what is here more fitly understood than that very desire of good of which we are speaking? For good begins then to be longed for when it has begun to grow sweet. But when good is done by the fear of penalty, not by the love of righteousness, good is not yet well done. Nor is that done in the heart which seems to be done in the act, when a man would rather not do it if he could evade it with impunity. Therefore the "blessing of sweetness" is God's grace, by which is caused in us that what He prescribes to us delights us, and we desire it, — that is, we love it; in which if God does not precede us, not only is it not perfected, but it is not even begun, from us. For, if without Him we are able to do nothing actually, we are able neither to begin nor to perfect, — because to begin, it is said, "His mercy shall prevent me;"² to finish, it is said, "His mercy shall follow me."⁴

CHAP. 22 [X.] — ACCORDING TO WHOSE PURPOSE THE ELECT ARE CALLED.

Why, then, is it that, in what follows, where they mention what they themselves think, they say they confess "That grace also assists the good purpose of every one, but that yet it does not infuse the desire of virtue into a reluctant heart"? Because they so say this as if man of himself, without God's assistance, has a good purpose and a desire of virtue; and this precedent merit is worthy of being assisted by the subsequent grace of God. For they think, perchance, that the apostle thus said, "For we know that He worketh all things for good to them that love God, to them who are called according to the purpose,"⁵ so as to wish the purpose of man to be understood, which purpose, as a good merit, the mercy of the God that calleth might follow; being ignorant that it is said, "Who are called according to the purpose," so that there may be understood the purpose of God, not man, whereby those whom He foreknew and predestinated as conformed to the image of His Son, He elected before the foundation of the world. For not all the called are called according to purpose, since "many are called, few are chosen."⁶ They, therefore, are called according to the purpose, who were elected before the foundation of the

world. Of this purpose of God, that also was said which I have already mentioned concerning the twins Esau and Jacob, "That according to the election the purpose of God might remain, not of works, but of Him that calleth; it was said, that the elder shall serve the younger."⁷ This purpose of God is also mentioned in that place where, writing to Timothy, he says, "Labour with the gospel according to the power of God, who saves us and calls us with this holy calling; not according to our works, but according to His purpose and grace, which was given to us in Christ Jesus before the eternal ages, but is now made manifest by the coming of our Saviour Jesus Christ."⁸ This, then, is the purpose of God, whereof it is said, "He worketh together all things for good for those who are called according to the purpose." But subsequent grace indeed assists man's good purpose, but the purpose would not itself exist if grace did not precede. The desire of man, also, which is called good, although in beginning to exist it is aided by grace, yet does not begin without grace, but is inspired by Him of whom the apostle says, "But thanks be to God, who has given the same desire for you in the heart of Titus."⁹ If God gives desire that every one may have it for others, who else will give it that a man may have it for himself?

CHAP. 23. — NOTHING IS COMMANDED TO MAN WHICH IS NOT GIVEN BY GOD.

Since these things are so, I see that nothing is commanded to man by the Lord in the Holy Scriptures, for the sake of trying his free will, which is not found either to begin by His goodness, or to be asked in order to demonstrate the aid of grace; nor does man at all begin to be changed by the beginning of faith from evil to good, unless the unbought and gratuitous mercy of God effects this in him. Of which one recalling his thought, as we read in the Psalms, says, "Shall God forget to be gracious? or will He restrain His mercies in His anger? And I said, Now have I begun; this change is of the right hand of the Most High."¹⁰ When, therefore, he had said, "Now have I begun," he does not say, "This change is of my will," but "of the right hand of the Most High." So, therefore, let God's grace be thought of, that from the beginning of his good changing, even to the end of his completion, he who glorieth may glory in the Lord; because, as no one can perfect good without the Lord, so no one can begin it without the Lord. But let this be the end of this book, that the attention of the reader may be refreshed and strengthened for what follows.

---

¹ 1 John iv. 7.  ² Ps. lix. 10.  ³ Ps. xxi. 3.
⁴ Ps. xxiii. 6.  ⁵ Rom. viii. 28.  ⁶ Matt. xx. 16.
⁷ Rom. ix. 11.  ⁸ 2 Tim. i. 8.  ⁹ 2 Cor. viii. 16.
¹⁰ Ps. lxxvii. 9, 10.

# BOOK III.

AUGUSTIN GOES ON TO REFUTE OTHER MATTERS WHICH ARE CALUMNIOUSLY OBJECTED BY THE PELAGIANS IN THE SAME LETTER SENT TO THESSALONICA ; AND EXPOUNDS, IN OPPOSITION TO THEIR HERESY, WHAT THOSE WHO ARE TRULY CATHOLIC SAY CONCERNING THE UTILITY OF THE LAW ; WHAT THEY TEACH OF THE EFFECT AND VIRTUE OF BAPTISM ; WHAT OF THE DISCREPANCY BETWEEN THE TWO TESTAMENTS, THE OLD AND THE NEW ; WHAT CONCERNING THE RIGHTEOUSNESS AND PERFECTION OF THE PROPHETS AND APOSTLES ; WHAT OF THE APPELLATION OF SIN IN CHRIST, WHEN HE IS SAID IN THE LIKENESS OF SINFUL FLESH CONCERNING SIN TO HAVE CONDEMNED SIN, OR TO HAVE BECOME SIN ; AND FINALLY, WHAT THEY PROFESS CONCERNING THE FULFILMENT OF THE COMMANDMENTS IN THE FUTURE LIFE.

## CHAP. I [I.] — STATEMENT.

THERE still follow things which they calumniously object to us ; they do not yet begin to work out those things which they themselves think. But lest the prolixity of these writings should be an offence, I have divided those matters which they object into two Books, — the former of which being completed, which is the Second Book of this entire work, I am here commencing the other, and joining it as the Third to the First and Second.

## CHAP. 2 [II.] — THE MISREPRESENTATION OF THE PELAGIANS CONCERNING THE USE OF THE OLD LAW.

They declare " that we say that the law of the Old Testament was given not for the end that it might justify the obedient, but rather that it might become the cause of greater sin." Certainly, they do not understand what we say concerning the law ; because we say what the apostle says, whom they do not understand. For who can say that they are not justified who are obedient to the law, when, unless they were justified, they could not be obedient? But we say, that by the law is effected that what God wills to be done is heard, but that by grace is effected that the law is obeyed. " For not the hearers of the law," says the apostle, " are just before God, but the doers of the law shall be justified." [1] Therefore the law makes hearers of righteousness, grace makes doers. " For what was impossible to the law," says the same apostle, " in that it was weak through the flesh, God sent His Son in the likeness of sinful flesh, and for sin condemned

sin in the flesh : that the righteousness of the law might be fulfilled in us who walk not according to the flesh, but according to the Spirit." [2] This is what we say ; — let them pray that they may one day understand it, and not dispute so as never to understand it. For it is impossible that the law should be fulfilled by the flesh, — that is, by carnal presumption, in which the proud, who are ignorant of the righteousness of God, — that is, which is of God to man, that he may be righteous, — and desirous of establishing their own righteousness, — as if by their own will, unassisted from above, the law could be fulfilled, — are not subjected to the righteousness of God. [3] Therefore the righteousness of the law is fulfilled in them who walk not according to the flesh — that is, according to man, ignorant of the righteousness of God and desirous of establishing his own — but walk according to the Spirit. But who walks according to the Spirit, except whosoever is led by the Spirit of God? " For as many as are led by the Spirit of God, these are the sons of God." [4] Therefore " the letter killeth, but the Spirit maketh alive." [5] And the letter is not evil because it killeth ; but it convicts the wicked of transgression. " For the law is holy, and the commandment holy and just and good. Was, then," says he, " that which is good made death unto me? By no means ; but sin, that it might appear sin, worked death in me by that which is good, that it might become above measure a sinner or a sin by the commandment." [6] This is what is the meaning of " the letter killeth." " For the sting of death is sin, but the

---

[1] Rom. ii. 13.

[2] Rom. viii. 3, 4.    [3] Rom. x. 3.    [4] Rom. viii. 14.
[5] 2 Cor. iii. 6.    [6] Rom. vii. 12, 13.

strength of sin is the law;"[1] because by the prohibition it increases the desires of sin, and thence slays a man unless grace by coming to his assistance makes him alive.[2]

CHAP. 3. — SCRIPTURAL CONFIRMATION OF THE CATHOLIC DOCTRINE.

This is what we say; this is that about which they object to us that we say "that the law was so given as to be a cause of greater sin." They do not hear the apostle saying, "For the law worketh wrath; for where no law is, there is no transgression;"[3] and, "The law was added for the sake of transgression until the seed should come to whom the promise was made;"[4] and, "If there had been a law given which could have given life, righteousness should altogether have been by the law; but the Scripture hath concluded all under sin, that the promise by faith of Jesus Christ might be given to them that believe."[5] Hence it is that the Old Testament, from the Mount Sinai, where the law was given, gendereth to bondage, which is Agar. "Now we," says he, "are not children of the bondmaid but of the freewoman."[6] Therefore they are not children of the freewoman who have accepted the law of the letter, whereby they can be shown to be not only sinners, but moreover transgressors; but they who have received the Spirit of grace, whereby the law itself, holy and just and good, may be fulfilled. This is what we say: let them attend and not contend; let them seek enlightenment and not bring false accusations.

CHAP. 4 [III.] — MISREPRESENTATION CONCERNING THE EFFECT OF BAPTISM.

"They assert," say they, "that baptism, moreover, does not make men new — that is, does not give complete remission of sins; but they contend that they are partly made children of God and partly remain children of the world, that is, of the devil." They deceive; they lay traps; they shuffle; we do not say this. For we say that all men who are children of the devil are also children of the world; but not that all children of the world are also children of the devil. Far be it from us to say that the holy fathers Abraham, Isaac, and Jacob, and others of this kind, were children of the devil when they were begetting in marriage, and those believers who until now and still hereafter continue to beget. And yet we cannot contradict the Lord when He says, "The children of this world marry and give in marriage."[7] Some, therefore, are children of this world, and yet are not children of the devil. For although the devil is the author and source of all sins, yet it is not every

sin that makes children of the devil; for the children of God also sin, since if they say they have no sins they deceive themselves, and the truth is not in them.[8] But they sin in virtue of that condition by which they are still children of this world; but by that grace wherewith they are the children of God they certainly sin not, because every one that is born of God sinneth not.[9] But unbelief makes children of the devil; and unbelief is specially called sin, as if it were the only one, if it is not expressed what is the nature of the sin. As when the "apostle" is spoken of, if it be not expressed what apostle, none is understood but Paul; because he is better known by his many epistles, and he laboured more than they all. For which reason, in what the Lord said of the Holy Spirit, "He shall convict the world of sin,"[10] He meant unbelief to be understood; for He said this when He was explaining, "Of sin because they believed not on me,"[11] and when He says, "If I had not come and spoken to them, they should not have sin."[12] For He meant not that before they had no sin, but He wished to indicate that very want of faith by which they did not believe Him even when He was present to them and speaking to them; since they belonged to him of whom the apostle says, "According to the prince of the power of the air, who now worketh in the children of unbelief."[13] Therefore they in whom there is not faith are the children of the devil, because they have not in the inner man any reason why there should be forgiven them whatever is committed either by human infirmity, or by ignorance, or by any evil will whatever. But those are the children of God who certainly, if they should "say that they have no sin, deceive themselves, and the truth is not in them, but immediately" (as it continues) "when they confess their sins" (which the children of the devil do not do, or do not do according to the faith which is peculiar to the children of God), "He is faithful and just to forgive them their sins, and to cleanse them from all unrighteousness."[8] And in order that what we say may be more fully understood, let Jesus Himself be heard, who certainly was speaking to the children of God when He said: "And if ye, being evil, know how to give good gifts to your children, how much more shall your Father which is in heaven give good things to them that ask Him."[14] For if these were not the children of God, He would not say to them, "Your Father which is in heaven." And yet He says that they are evil, and that they know how to give good gifts to their children. Are they, then, evil in that they are the children of God? Away with the thought! But they are thence evil be-

---

[1] 1 Cor. xv. 56.  [2] See *On the Spirit and the Letter*, 6.
[3] Rom. iv. 15.  [4] Gal. iii. 19.  [5] Gal. iii. 21, 23.
[6] Gal. iv. 24, 31.  [7] Luke xx. 34.

[8] 1 John i. 8.  [9] 1 John iii. 9.  [10] John xvi. 8.
[11] John xvi. 9.  [12] John xv. 22.  [13] Eph. ii. 2.
[14] Matt. vii. 11.

cause they are still the children of this world, although now made children of God by the pledge of the Holy Spirit.

CHAP. 5. — BAPTISM PUTS AWAY ALL SINS, BUT IT DOES NOT AT ONCE HEAL ALL INFIRMITIES.

Baptism, therefore, washes away indeed all sins — absolutely all sins, whether of deeds or words or thoughts, whether original or added, whether such as are committed in ignorance or allowed in knowledge ; but it does not take away the weakness which the regenerate man resists when he fights the good fight, but to which he consents when as man he is overtaken in any fault ; on account of the former, rejoicing with thanksgiving, but on account of the latter, groaning in the utterance of prayers. On account of the former, saying, "What shall I render to the Lord for all that He has given me?"[1] On account of the latter, saying, "Forgive us our debts."[2] On account of the former, saying, "I will love Thee, O Lord, my strength."[3] On account of the latter, saying, "Have mercy on me, O Lord ; for I am weak."[4] On account of the former, saying, "Mine eyes are ever towards the Lord ; for He shall pluck my feet out of the net."[5] On account of the latter, saying, "Mine eye is troubled with wrath."[6] And there are innumerable passages with which the divine writings are filled, which alternately, either in exultation over God's benefits or in lamentation over our own evils, are uttered by children of God by faith as long as they are still children of this world in respect of the weakness of this life ; whom, nevertheless, God distinguishes from the children of the devil, not only by the laver of regeneration, but moreover by the righteousness of that faith which worketh by love, because the just lives by faith. But this weakness with which we contend, with alternating failure and progress, even to the death of the body, and which is of great importance as to what it can overcome in us, shall be consumed by another regeneration, of which the Lord says, "In the regeneration when the Son of man shall sit on the throne of His glory, ye also shall sit upon twelve thrones,"[7] etc. Certainly in this passage He without doubt calls the last resurrection the regeneration, which Paul the Apostle also calls both the adoption and the redemption, where he says, "But even we ourselves, which have the first-fruits of the Spirit, ourselves also groan within ourselves, waiting for the adoption, the redemption, of our body."[8] Have we not been regenerated, adopted, and redeemed by the holy washing? And yet there remains a regeneration, an adoption, a redemption, which we ought now patiently to be

waiting for as to come in the end, that we may then be in no degree any longer children of this world. Whosoever, then, takes away from baptism that which we only receive by its means, corrupts the faith ; but whosoever attributes to it now that which we shall receive by its means indeed, but yet hereafter, cuts off hope. For if any one should ask of me whether we have been saved by baptism, I shall not be able to deny it, since the apostle says, "He saved us by the washing of regeneration and renewing of the Holy Ghost."[9] But if he should ask whether by the same washing He has already absolutely in every way saved us, I shall answer : It is not so. Because the same apostle also says, "For we are saved by hope ; but hope that is seen is not hope : for what a man seeth, why doth he yet hope for? But if we hope for that we see not, we with patience wait for it."[10] Therefore the salvation of man is effected in baptism, because whatever sin he has derived from his parents is remitted, or whatever, moreover, he himself has sinned on his own account before baptism ; but his salvation will hereafter be such that he cannot sin at all.

CHAP. 6 [IV.] — THE CALUMNY CONCERNING THE OLD TESTAMENT AND THE RIGHTEOUS MEN OF OLD.

Now if these things are so, out of these things are rebutted those which they subsequently object to us. For what catholic would say that which they charge us with saying, "that the Holy Spirit was not the assister of virtue in the old testament," unless when we so understand "the old testament" in the manner in which the apostle spoke of it as "gendering from Mount Sinai into bondage"? But because in it was prefigured the new testament, the men of God who at that time understood this according to the ordering of the times, were indeed the stewards and bearers of the old testament, but are shown to be the heirs of the new. Shall we deny that he belongs to the new testament who says, "Create in me a clean heart, O God ; and renew a right spirit within me"?[11] or he who says, "He hath set my feet upon a rock, and directed my goings ; and he hath put a new song in my mouth, even a hymn to our God"?[12] or that father of the faithful before the old testament which is from Mount Sinai, of whom the apostle says, "Brethren, I speak after the manner of men ; yet even a man's testament, when it is confirmed, no man disannulleth or addeth thereto. To Abraham and to his seed were the promises made. He saith not, And to seeds, as of many, but as of one ; and to thy seed, which is Christ. And this I say," said he, "that the testament

---

[1] Ps. cxvi. 12.    [2] Matt. vi. 12.    [3] Ps. cxviii. 1.
[4] Ps. vi. 2.    [5] Ps. xxv. 15.    [6] Ps. xxxi. 9.
[7] Matt. xix. 28.    [8] Rom. viii. 23.

[9] Tit. iii. 5.    [10] Rom. viii. 24, 25.    [11] Ps. li. 10.
[12] Ps. xl. 2, 3.

confirmed by God, the law which was made four hundred and thirty years after, does not weaken, so as to make the promise of none effect. For if the inheritance be of the law, it is no more of promise : but God gave it to Abraham by promise." [1]

## CHAP. 7. — THE NEW TESTAMENT IS MORE ANCIENT THAN THE OLD ; BUT IT WAS SUBSEQUENTLY REVEALED.

Here, certainly, if we ask whether this testament, which, he says, being confirmed by God was not weakened by the law, which was made four hundred and thirty years after, is to be understood as the new or the old one, who can hesitate to answer " the new, but hidden in the prophetic shadows until the time should come wherein it should be revealed in Christ "? For if we should say the old, what will that be which genders from Mount Sinai ·to bondage? For there was made the law four hundred and thirty years after, by which law he asserts that this testament of the promise of Abraham could not be weakened ; and he will have this which was made by Abraham to pertain rather to us, whom he will have to be children of the freewoman, not of the bondwoman, heirs by the promise, not by the law, when he says, " For if the inheritance be by the law, it is no more of promise : but God gave it to Abraham by promise." [2] So that, because the law was made four hundred and thirty years after, it might enter that the offence might abound ; [3] since by sin the pride of man presuming on his own righteousness is convinced of transgression, and where sin abounded grace much more abounded,[3] by the faith of the now humble man failing in the law and taking refuge in God's mercy. Therefore, when he had said, " For if the inheritance be of the law, it is no longer of promise : but God gave it to Abraham by promise," [2] as if it might be said to him, " Why then was the law made afterwards ? " he added and said, " What then is the law ? " [4] To which interrogation he immediately replied, " It was added because of transgression, until the seed should come to which the promise was made." [4] This he says again, thus : " For if they who are of the law be heirs, faith is made void, and the promise is made of none effect : because the law worketh wrath : for where there is no law, there is no transgression." [5] What he says in the former testimony : " For if the inheritance be of the law, it is no more of promise : but God gave it to Abraham by promise," this he says in the latter : " For if they who are of the law be heirs, faith is made void ; and the promise is made of none effect ; " sufficiently showing that to our faith

(which certainly is of the new testament) belongs what God gave to Abraham by promise. And what he says in the former testimony, " What then is the law ? " and answered, " It was added for the sake of transgression," this he instantly added in the latter testimony, " For the law worketh wrath : for where there is no law, there is no transgression."

## CHAP. 8. — ALL RIGHTEOUS MEN BEFORE AND AFTER ABRAHAM ARE CHILDREN OF THE PROMISE AND OF GRACE.

Whether, then, Abraham, or righteous men before him or after him, even to Moses himself, by whom was given the testament gendering to bondage from Mount Sinai, or the rest of the prophets after him, and the holy men of God till John the Baptist, they are all children of the promise and of grace according to Isaac the son of the freewoman, — not of the law, but of the promise, heirs of God and joint-heirs with Christ. Far be it from us to deny that righteous Noah and the righteous men of the earlier times, and whoever from that time till the time of Abraham could be righteous, either manifestly or hiddenly, belong to the Jerusalem which is above, who is our mother, although they are found to be earlier in time than Sarah, who bore the prophecy and figure of the free mother herself. How much more evidently, then, after Abraham, to whom that promise was declared, that he should be called the father of many nations, must all, whoever have pleased God, be esteemed the children of the promise ! For from Abraham, and the righteous men who followed him, the generation is not found more true, but the prophecy more plain.

## CHAP. 9. — WHO ARE THE CHILDREN OF THE OLD COVENANT.

But those belong to the old testament, " which gendereth from Mount Sinai to bondage," which is Agar, who, when they have received a law which is holy and just and good, think that the letter can suffice them for life ; and do not seek the divine mercy, so as they may become doers of the law, but, being ignorant of the righteousness of God, and wishing to establish their own righteousness, are not subject to the righteousness of God. Of this kind was that multitude which murmured against God in the wilderness, and made an idol ; and that multitude which even in the very land of promise committed fornication after strange gods. But this multitude, even in the old testament itself, was strongly rebuked. They, moreover, whoever they were at that time who followed after those earthly promises alone which God promises there, and who were ignorant of that which those promises signify under the new testament, and

---

[1] Gal. iii. 15 ff.     [2] Gal. iii. 18.     [3] Rom. v. 20.
[4] Gal. iii. 19.     [5] Rom. iv. 14.

who kept God's commandments with the desire of gaining and with the fear of losing those promises, — certainly did not observe them, but only seemed to themselves to observe. For there was no faith in them that worked by love, but earthly cupidity and carnal fear. But he who thus fulfils the commandments beyond a doubt fulfils them unwillingly, and then does not do them in his heart; for he would rather not do them at all, if in respect of those things which he desires and fears he might be allowed to neglect them with impunity. And thus, in the will itself within him, he is guilty; and it is here that God, who gives the command, looks. Such were the children of the earthly Jerusalem, concerning which the apostle says, "For she is in bondage with her children," [1] and belongs to the old testament "which gendereth to bondage from Mount Sinai, which is Agar." Of that same kind were they who crucified the Lord, and continued in the same unbelief. Thence there are still their children in the great multitude of the Jews, although now the new testament as it was prophesied is made plain and confirmed by the blood of Christ; and the gospel is made known from the river where He was baptized and began His teachings, even to the ends of the earth. And these Jews, according to the prophecies which they read, are dispersed everywhere over all the earth, that even from their writings may not be wanting a testimony to Christian truth.

CHAP. 10. — THE OLD LAW ALSO GIVEN BY GOD.

And it is for this reason that God made the old testament, because it pleased God to veil the heavenly promises in earthly promises, as if established in reward, until the fulness of time; and to give to a people which longed for earthly blessings, and therefore had a hard heart, a law, which, although spiritual, was yet written on tables of stone. Because, with the exception of the sacraments of the old books, which were only enjoined for the sake of their significance (although in them also, since they are to be spiritually understood, the law is rightly called spiritual), the other matters certainly which pertain to piety and to good living must not be referred by any interpretation to some significancy, [2] but are to be done absolutely as they are spoken. Assuredly no one will doubt that that law of God was necessary not alone for that people at that time, but also is now necessary for us for the right ordering of our life. For if Christ took away from us that very heavy yoke of many observances, so that we are not circumcised according to the flesh, we do not immolate victims of the cattle, we do not rest even from necessary works on the Sabbath, retaining the seventh in the revolution of the days, and other things of this kind; but keep them as spiritually understood, and, the symbolizing shadows being removed, are watchful in the light of those things which are signified by them; shall we therefore say, that when it is written that whoever finds another man's property of any kind that has been lost, should return it to him who has lost it, [3] it does not pertain to us? and many other like things whereby people learn to live piously and uprightly? and especially the Decalogue itself, which is contained in those two tables of stone, apart from the carnal observance of the Sabbath, which signifies spiritual sanctification and rest? For who can say that Christians ought not to be observant to serve the one God with religious obedience, not to worship an idol, not to take the name of the Lord in vain, to honour one's parents, not to commit adulteries, murders, thefts, false witness, not to covet another man's wife, or anything at all that belongs to another man? Who is so impious as to say that he does not keep those precepts of the law because he is a Christian, and is established not under the law, but under grace?

CHAP. 11. — DISTINCTION BETWEEN THE CHILDREN OF THE OLD AND OF THE NEW TESTAMENTS.

But there is plainly this great difference, that they who are established under the law, whom the letter killeth, do these things either with the desire of gaining, or with the fear of losing earthly happiness; and that thus they do not truly do them, since fleshly desire, by which sin is rather bartered or increased, is not healed by desire of another kind. These pertain to the old testament, which genders to bondage; because carnal fear and desire make them servants, gospel faith and hope and love do not make them children. But they who are placed under grace, whom the Spirit quickens, do these things of faith which worketh by love in the hope of good things, not carnal but spiritual, not earthly but heavenly, not temporal but eternal; especially believing on the Mediator, by whom they do not doubt but that a Spirit of grace is ministered to them, so that they may do these things well, and that they may be pardoned when they sin. These pertain to the new testament, are the children of promise, and are regenerated by God the Father and a free mother. Of this kind were all the righteous men of old, and Moses himself, the minister of the old testament, the heir of the new, — because of the faith whereby we live, of one and the same they lived, believing the incarnation, passion, and resurrection of Christ

---

[1] Gal. iv. 25.
[2] [i.e., they must not be treated *allegorically*, as if their *literal* sense was not important, and they were given only to teach something symbolically or typically. — W.]

[3] Lev. vi. 3.

as future, which we believe as already accomplished, — even until John the Baptist himself, as it were a certain limit of the old dispensation, who, signifying that the Mediator Himself would come, not with any shadow of the future or allegorical intimation, or with any prophetical announcement, but pointing Him out with his finger, said : " Behold the Lamb of God ; behold Him who taketh away the sin of the world." [1] As if saying, Whom many righteous men have desired to see, on whom, as about to come, they have believed from the beginning of the human race itself, concerning whom the promises were spoken to Abraham, of whom Moses wrote, of whom the law and the prophets are witnesses : " Behold the Lamb of God, who taketh away the sin of the world." From this John and afterwards, all those things concerning Christ began to become past or present, which by all the righteous men of the previous time were believed, hoped for, desired, as future. Therefore the faith is the same as well in those who, although not yet in name, were in fact previously Christians, as in those who not only are so but are also called so ; and in both there is the same grace by the Holy Spirit. Whence says the apostle : " We having the same Spirit of faith, according as it is written, I believed, therefore have I spoken ; we also believe, and therefore speak." [2]

CHAP. 12. — THE OLD TESTAMENT IS PROPERLY ONE THING — THE OLD INSTRUMENT ANOTHER.

Therefore, by a custom of speech already prevailing, in one way the law and all the prophets who prophesied until John are called the " Old Testament ; " although this is more definitely called the " Old Instrument " rather than the " Old Testament ; " but this name is used in another way by the apostolical authority, whether expressly or impliedly. For the apostle is express when he says, " Until this day, as long as Moses is read, remaineth the same veil in the reading of the old testament ; because it is not revealed, because it is made of no effect in Christ." [3] For thus certainly the old testament referred to the ministry of Moses. Moreover, he says, " That we should serve in the newness of the Spirit, and not in the oldness of the letter," [4] signifying that same testament under the name of the letter. In another place also, " Who also hath made us able ministers of the new testament ; not of the letter, but of the Spirit : for the letter killeth, but the Spirit maketh alive." [5] And here, by the mention of the new, he certainly meant the former to be understood as the old. But much more evidently, although he did not say either old or new, he distinguished

the two testaments and the two sons of Abraham, the one of the bondwoman, the other of the free, as I have above mentioned. For what can be more express than his saying, " Tell me, ye that desire to be under the law, have ye not heard the law ? For it is written, that Abraham had two sons, the one by a bondmaid, the other by a freewoman. But he who was of the bondwoman was born after the flesh ; but he of the freewoman was by promise. Which things are in allegory ; for these are the two testaments ; the one in the Mount Sinai, gendering to bondage, which is Agar. For Sinai is a mountain in Arabia, which is associated with Jerusalem which now is, for it is in bondage with her children. But Jerusalem that is above is free, which is our mother ? " [6] What is more clear, what more certain, what more remote from all obscurity and ambiguity to the children of the promise ? And a little after, " Now we, brethren, as Isaac was, are the children of promise." [7] Also a little after, " But we, brethren, are not children of the bondwoman, but of the free," [8] with the liberty with which Christ has made us free. Let us, therefore, choose whether to call the righteous men of old the children of the bondwoman or of the free. Be it far from us to say, of the bondwoman ; therefore if of the free, they pertain to the new testament in the Holy Spirit, whom, as making alive, the apostle opposes to the killing letter. For on what ground do they not belong to the grace of the new testament, from whose words and looks we convict and rebut such most frantic and ungrateful enemies of the same grace as these ?

CHAP. 13. — WHY ONE OF THE COVENANTS IS CALLED OLD, THE OTHER NEW.

But some one will say, " In what way is that called the old which was given by Moses four hundred and thirty years after ; and that called the new which was given so many years before to Abraham ? " Let him who on this subject is disturbed, not litigiously but earnestly, first understand that when from its earlier time one is called " old," and from its posterior time the other " new," it is the revelation of them that is considered in their names, not their institution. Because the old testament was revealed through Moses, by whom the holy and just and good law was given, whereby should be brought about not the doing away but the knowledge of sin, — by which the proud might be convicted who were desirous of establishing their own righteousness, as if they had no need of divine help, and being made guilty of the letter, might flee to the Spirit of grace, not to be justified by their own righteousness, but by that of God — that

---

[1] John i. 29.    [2] 2 Cor. iv. 13.    [3] 2 Cor. iii. 14.
[4] Rom. vii. 6.    [5] 2 Cor. iii. 6.

[6] Gal. iv. 21 ff.    [7] Gal. iv. 28.    [8] Gal. iv. 31.

is, by the righteousness which was given to them of God. For as the same apostle says, " By the law is the knowledge of sin. But now the righteousness of God without the law is manifested, being witnessed by the law and by the prophets." [1] Because the law, by the very fact that in it no man is justified, affords a witness to the righteousness of God. For that in the law no man is justified before God is manifest, because " the just by faith lives." [2] Thus, therefore, although the law does not justify the wicked when he is convicted of transgression, it sends to the God who justifieth, and thus affords a testimony to the righteousness of God. Moreover, the prophets offer testimony to God's righteousness by fore-announcing Christ, " who is made unto us wisdom from God, and righteousness, and sanctification, and redemption: that, as it is written, he that glorieth, let him glory in the Lord." [3] But that law was kept hidden from the beginning, when nature itself convicted wicked men, who did to others what they would not have done to themselves. But the revelation of the new testament in Christ was made when He was manifested in the flesh, wherein appeared the righteousness of God — that is, the righteousness which is to men from God. For hence he says, " But now the righteousness of God without the law is manifested." [4] This is the reason why the former is called the old testament, because it was revealed in the earlier time; and the latter the new, because it was revealed in the later time. In a word, it is because the old testament pertains to the old man, from which it is necessary that a man should make a beginning; but the new to the new man, by which a man ought to pass from his old state. Thus, in the former are earthly promises, in the latter heavenly promises; because this pertained to God's mercy, that no one should think that even earthly felicity of any kind whatever could be conferred on anybody, save from the Lord, who is the Creator of all things. But if God is worshipped for the sake of that earthly happiness, the worship is that of a slave, belonging to the children of the bondmaid; but if for the sake of God Himself, so that in the life eternal God may be all things in all, it is a free service belonging to the children of the freewoman, who is our mother eternal in the heavens — who first seemed, as it were, barren, when she had not any children manifest; but now we see what was prophesied concerning her: " Rejoice, thou barren, that bearest not; break forth and cry, thou that travailest not: for there are many children of the desolate more than of her who has an husband," [5] — that is, more than of that Jerusalem,

who in a certain manner is married in the bond of the law, and is in bondage with her children. In the time, then, of the old testament, we say that the Holy Spirit, in those who even then were the children of promise according to Isaac, was not only an assistant, which these men think is sufficient for their opinion, but also a bestower of virtue; and this they deny, attributing it rather to their free will, in contradiction to those fathers who knew how to cry unto God with truthful piety, " I will love Thee, O Lord, my strength." [6]

CHAP. 14 [V.] — CALUMNY CONCERNING THE RIGHTEOUSNESS OF THE PROPHETS AND APOSTLES.

They say, moreover, " that all the apostles or prophets are not defined as entirely holy by us, but that we say that they were less wicked in comparison with those that were worse; and that this is the righteousness to which God affords His testimony, so that, as the prophet says that Sodom was justified in comparison with the Jews, so also we say that the saints exercised some goodness in comparison with criminal men." Be it far from us to say such things; but either they are not able to understand, or they are unwilling to observe, or, for the sake of misrepresentation, they pretend that they do not know what we say. Let them hear, therefore, either themselves, or rather those whom, as inexperienced and unlearned persons, they are striving to deceive. Our faith — that is, the catholic faith — distinguishes the righteous from the unrighteous not by the law of works, but by that of faith, because the just by faith lives. By which distinction it results that the man who leads his life without murder, without theft, without false-witness, without coveting other men's goods, giving due honour to his parents, chaste even to continence from all carnal intercourse whatever, even conjugal, most liberal in almsgiving, most patient of injuries; who not only does not deprive another of his goods, but does not even ask again for what has been taken away from himself; or who has even sold all his own property and appropriated it to the poor, and possesses nothing which belongs to him as his own; — with such a character as this, laudable as it seems to be, if he has not a true and catholic faith in God, must yet depart from this life to condemnation. But another, who has good works from a right faith which worketh by love, maintains his continency in the honesty of wedlock, although he does not, like the other, well refrain altogether, but pays and repays the debt of carnal connection, and has intercourse not only for the sake of offspring, but also for the sake of pleasure, although only with his

[1] Rom. iii. 20, 21.  [2] Gal. iii. 11.  [3] 1 Cor. i. 30, 31.
[4] Rom. iii. 21.  [5] Isa. liv. 1.

[6] Ps. xviii. 1.

wife, which the apostle allows to those that are married as pardonable;—does not receive injuries with so much patience, but is raised into anger with the desire of vengeance, although, in order that he may say, "As we also forgive our debtors," forgives when he is asked;—possesses personal property, giving thence indeed some alms, but not as the former so liberally;—does not take away what belongs to another, but, although by ecclesiastical, not by civil judgment, yet contends for his own: certainly this man, who seems so inferior in morals to the former, on account of the right faith which he has in God, by which he lives, and according to which in all his wrong-doings he accuses himself, and in all his good works praises God, giving to himself the shame, to God the glory, and receiving from Him both forgiveness of sins and love of right deeds,—shall be delivered for this life, and depart to be received into the company of those who shall reign with Christ. Wherefore, if not on account of faith? Which, although without works it saves no man (for it is not a reprobate faith, since it worketh by love), yet by it even sins are loosed, because the just by faith liveth; but without it, even those things which seem good works are turned into sins: "For everything which is not of faith is sin."[1] And it is brought about, on account of this great difference, that although with no possibility of doubt a persevering integrity of virginity is preferable to conjugal chastity, yet a woman even twice married, if she be a catholic, is preferred to a professed virgin that is a heretic; nor is she in such wise preferred because this one is better in God's kingdom, but because the other is not there at all. Now the former, indeed, whom we have described as being of better morals, if a true faith be his, surpasses the second one, although both will be in heaven; yet if the faith be wanting to him, he is so surpassed by him that he himself is not there at all.

## CHAP. 15.— THE PERFECTION OF APOSTLES AND PROPHETS.

Since, then, all righteous men, both the more ancient and the apostles, lived from a right faith which is in Christ Jesus our Lord; and had with their faith morals so holy, that although they might not be of such perfect virtue in this life as that which should be after this life, yet whatever of sin might creep in from human infirmity might be constantly done away by the piety of their faith itself: it results from this that, in comparison with the wicked whom God will condemn, it must be said that these were "righteous," since by their pious faith they were so

far removed into the opposite of those wicked men that the apostle cries out, "What part hath he that believeth with an infidel?"[2] But it is plain that the Pelagians, these modern heretics, seem to themselves to be religious lovers and praisers of the saints, since they do not dare to say that they were of an imperfect virtue; although that elected vessel confesses this, who, considering in what state he still was, and that the body which is corrupted drags down the soul, says, "Not that I have already attained or am yet perfect; brethren, I count not myself to have apprehended."[3] And yet a little after, he who had denied himself to be perfect says, "Let us therefore, as many as be perfect, be thus minded,"[4] in order that he might show that, according to the measure of this life, there is a certain perfection, and that to that perfection this also is to be attributed, even although any one may know that he is not yet perfect. For what is more perfect, or what was more excellent, than the holy priests among the ancient people? And yet God prescribed to them to offer sacrifice first of all for their own sins. And what is more holy among the new people than the apostles? And yet the Lord prescribed to them to say in their prayer, "Forgive us our debts." For all the pious, therefore, who lie under this burden of a corruptible flesh, and groan in the infirmity of this life of theirs, there is one hope: "We have an advocate with the Father, Jesus Christ the righteous: and He is the propitiation for our sins."[5]

## CHAP. 16 [VI.] — MISREPRESENTATION CONCERNING SIN IN CHRIST.

They have not a righteous advocate, who are (even if that were the only difference) distinguished absolutely and widely from the righteous. Be it far from us to say, as they themselves slanderously affirm, that this just Advocate "spoke falsely by the necessity of the flesh;" but we say that He, in the likeness of sinful flesh, in respect of sin, condemned sin. And they, perchance not understanding this, and being blinded by the desire of misrepresentation, and ignorant of the number of ways in which the name of sin is accustomed to be used in the Holy Scriptures, declare that we affirm sin of Christ. Therefore we assert that Christ both had no sin,—neither in soul nor in the body; and that, by taking upon Him flesh in the likeness of sinful flesh, in respect of sin He condemned sin. And this assertion, somewhat obscurely made by the apostle, is explained in two ways,—either that the likenesses of things are accustomed to be called by the names of those things to which they are like, so that the

---

[1] Rom. xiv. 23.

[2] 2 Cor. vi. 14.     [3] Phil. iii. 12, 13.     [4] Phil. iii. 15.
[5] 1 John ii. 1.

apostle may be understood to have intended to call this likeness of sinful flesh by the name of " sin ; " or else that the sacrifices for sins were under the law called " sins," all which things were figures of the flesh of Christ, which is the true and only sacrifice for sins, — not only for those which are all washed away in baptism, but also for those which afterwards creep in from the weakness of this life, on account of which the universal Church daily cries in prayer to God, " Forgive us our debts," and they are forgiven us by means of that singular sacrifice for sins which the apostle, speaking according to the law, did not hesitate to call " sin." Whence, moreover, is that much plainer passage of his, which is not uncertain by any twofold ambiguity, " We beseech you in Christ's stead to be reconciled to God. He made Him to be sin for us, who had not known sin ; that we might be the righteousness of God in Him." [1] For the passage which I have above mentioned, " In respect of sin, He condemned sin," because it was not said, " In respect of *his* sin," may be understood by any one, as if He said that He condemned sin in respect of the sin of the Jews ; because in respect of their sin who crucified Him, it happened that He shed His blood for the remission of sins. But this passage, where God is said to have made Christ Himself " sin," who had not known sin, does not seem to me to be more fittingly understood than that Christ was made a sacrifice for sins, and on this account was called " sin."

CHAP. 17 [VII.] — THEIR CALUMNY ABOUT THE FULFILMENT OF PRECEPTS IN THE LIFE TO COME.

But who can bear their objecting to us, " that we say that after the resurrection such is to be our progress, that there men can begin to fulfil the commands of God, which they would not here ; " since we say that there will be no sin at all, no struggle with any desire of sin ; as if they themselves would dare to deny this? That wisdom also and the knowledge of God, is then perfected in us, and that in the Lord there is such rejoicing that it is a full and a true security, who will deny, unless he is so averse from the truth that on this very account he cannot attain unto it? But these things will not be in precepts, but in reward of those precepts which should here be observed ; the neglect of which precepts, indeed, does not lead thither to the reward. But here the grace of God gives the desire of keeping His commandments ; and if anything in these commandments is less perfectly observed, He forgives it on account of what we say in prayer, as well " Thy will be done," as " Forgive us our debts." Here, then,

it is prescribed that we sin not ; there, the reward is that we cannot sin. Here, the precept is that we obey not the desires of sin ; there, the reward that we have no desires of sin. Here, the precept is, " Understand, ye senseless among the people ; and ye fools, be at some time wise ; " [2] there, the reward is full wisdom and perfect knowledge. " For we see now through a glass in an enigma," says the apostle, " but then face to face : now I know in part ; but then I shall know even as also I am known." [3] Here, the precept is, " Exult unto the Lord, our helper," [4] and, " Rejoice, ye righteous, in the Lord ; " [5] there, the reward is to rejoice with a perfect and unspeakable joy. Lastly, in the precept it is written, " Blessed are they which hunger and thirst after righteousness ; " but in the reward, " Because they shall be filled." [6] Whence, I ask, shall they be filled, except with what they hunger and thirst after? Who, then, is so abhorrent, not only from the divine perception, but also from the human perception, as to say that in man there can be such righteousness while he is hungering and thirsting for it, as there will be when he shall be filled with it? But when we are hungering and thirsting after righteousness, if the faith of Christ is watchful in us, what is it to be believed that we are hungering and thirsting for, save Christ? " For He is made unto us wisdom from God, and righteousness, and sanctification, and redemption ; that, as it is written, He that glorieth, let him glory in the Lord." [7] And because we only believe on Him not seeing Him, therefore we thirst and hunger after righteousness. For as long as we are in the body, we wander from the Lord ; for we walk by faith, not by appearance. But when we shall see Him, and attain certainly to the appearance, we shall rejoice with joy unspeakable ; and then we shall be filled with righteousness, since now we say to Him with pious longing, " I shall be satisfied when Thy glory shall be manifested." [8]

CHAP. 18. — PERFECTION OF RIGHTEOUSNESS AND FULL SECURITY WAS NOT EVEN IN PAUL IN THIS LIFE.

But how impudent I do not say, but how insane, is the pride which, not yet being equal to the angels of God, thinks itself already able to have a righteousness equal to the angels of God ; and does not consider so great and holy a man, who assuredly hungered and thirsted after that very perfection of righteousness, when he was unwilling to be lifted up by the greatness of his revelations ; and yet that he might not be lifted up, he was not left to his own choice and will,

---

[1] 2 Cor. v. 20, 21.

[2] Ps. cxiv. 8.  
[5] Ps. xxxiii. 1.  
[8] Ps. xvii. 15.

[3] 1 Cor. xiii. 12.  
[6] Matt. v. 6.

[4] Ps. lxxxi. 1.  
[7] 1 Cor. i. 30, 31.

but received " the thorn in the flesh, a messenger of Satan, to buffet him ; on which account he besought the Lord thrice that it might depart from him, and the Lord said unto him, My grace is sufficient for thee, for strength is made perfect in weakness." [1]    What strength, save that to which it belongs not to be lifted up? And who doubts that this belongs to righteousness?    The angels of God, then, are endowed with this perfection of righteousness, since they always behold the face of the Father, and thus of the entire Trinity, because they see through the Son, in the Holy Spirit.    But nothing is more sublime than that revelation, nor yet does any of the angels in that contemplation of rejoicing ones find a messenger of Satan needful that he may be buffeted by him, lest so great a magnitude of revelation should lift him up.    The apostle Paul certainly had not yet that perfection of virtue, nor yet was he equal to the angels of God ; but there was in Him the weakness of lifting himself up, which also had to be checked by the angel of Satan, lest he should be lifted up by the magnitude of his revelations. Although, then, the first lifting up cast down Satan,[2] yet that greatest Physician, who well knew how to make use of even evil things, applied from the angel of Satan, against the mischief of elation, a wholesome, although a painful, medicament, just as an antidote used to be made even of serpents against the poisons of serpents.    What, then, is the meaning of " My grace is sufficient for thee," except that you may not by giving way succumb to the buffet of the messenger of Satan?    And what is " Strength is made perfect in weakness," except that in that place of weakness hitherto, there may be the perfection of virtue, so that in the very presence of infirmity, lifting-up may be repressed?    Which infirmity assuredly shall be healed by future immortality.    For how is that soundness to be called perfect where medicine is still needful, even from the buffet of an angel of Satan?

CHAP. 19. — IN WHAT SENSE THE RIGHTEOUSNESS OF MAN IN THIS LIFE IS SAID TO BE PERFECT.

From this it results that the virtue which is now in the righteous man is named perfect up to this point, that to its perfection belong both the true knowledge and humble confession of even imperfection itself.    For, in respect to this infirmity, that little righteousness of man's is perfect according to its measure, when it understands even what it lacks.    And therefore the apostle calls himself both perfect and imperfect,[3]

— imperfect, to wit, in the thought of how much is wanting to him for the righteousness for the fulness of which he is still hungering and thirsting ; but perfect in that he does not blush to confess his own imperfection, and goes forward in good that he may attain.    As we can say that the wayfarer is perfect whose approach is well forwarded, although his intention is not carried out unless his arrival be actually effected. Therefore, when he had said, " According to the righteousness which is in the law, I am one who has been without blame," he immediately added, " What things were gain to me, those I counted but loss for Christ's sake.    Yea, doubtless, and I count all things to be loss for the sake of the eminent knowledge of Christ Jesus our Lord : for whose sake I have believed all things not only to be losses, but I have thought them to be even as dung, that I might gain Christ and be found in Him, not having my own righteousness, which is of the law, but that which is by the faith of Christ, the righteousness which is of God in faith." [4]    See ! the apostle does not, of course, say falsely, that " according to the righteousness which is of the law he was without blame ; " and yet those things which were gain to him, he casts away for Christ's sake, and thinks them losses, injuries, dung.    And not only these things, but all other things which he mentioned previously ; not on account of any kind of knowledge, but, as he himself says, " the eminent knowledge of Christ Jesus our Lord," which, beyond a doubt, he had as yet in faith, but not yet in sight.    For then the knowledge of Christ will be eminent, when He shall be so revealed that what is believed is seen.    Whence, in another place, he thus says, " For ye have died, and your life is hidden with Christ in God.    When Christ, your life, shall appear, then shall ye also appear with Him in glory." [5]    Hence, also, the Lord Himself says, " He who loveth me shall be loved of my Father, and I will love him, and will manifest myself to him." [6]    Hence John the Evangelist says, " Beloved, now are we the sons of God, and it has not yet appeared what we shall be : but we know, that when He shall appear, we shall be like Him ; for we shall see Him as He is." [7] Then shall the knowledge of Christ be eminent. For now it is, as it were, hidden away in faith ; but it does not yet appear eminent in sight.

CHAP. 20. — WHY THE RIGHTEOUSNESS WHICH IS OF THE LAW IS VALUED SLIGHTLY BY PAUL.

Therefore the blessed Paul casts away those past attainments of his righteousness, as " losses " and " dung," that " he may win Christ and be found in Him, not having his own righteousness, which is of the law."    Wherefore his own, if it

[1] 2 Cor. xii. 7.
[2] [The reference is to the sin of pride, by which Satan himself fell from the estate of holiness in which he was created. — W.]
[3] Phil. iii. 12, 15.

[4] Phil. iii. 6, etc.    [5] Col. iii. 3, etc.    [6] John xiv. 21.
[7] 1 John iii. 2.

is of the law? For that law is the law of God. Who has denied this, save Marcion and Manicheus, and such like pests? Since, then, that is the law of God, he says it is " his own " righteousness "which is of the law ; " and this righteousness of his own he would not have, but cast it forth as " dung." Why so, except because it is this which I have above demonstrated,[1] that those are under the law who, being ignorant of the righteousness of God, and going about to establish their own, are not subject to the righteousness of God?[2] For they think that, by the strength of their own will, they will fulfil the commands of the law ; and wrapped up in their pride, they are not converted to assisting grace. Thus the letter killeth[3] them either openly, as being guilty to themselves, by not doing what the law commands ; or by thinking that they do it, although they do it not with spiritual love, which is of God. Thus they remain either plainly wicked or deceitfully righteous, — manifestly cut off in open unrighteousness, or foolishly elated in fallacious righteousness. And by this means — marvellous indeed, but yet true — the righteousness of the law is not fulfilled by the righteousness which is in the law, or by the law, but by that which is in the Spirit of grace. Because the righteousness of the law is fulfilled in those, as it is written, who walk not according to the flesh, but according to the Spirit. But, according to the righteousness which is in the law, the apostle says that he was blameless in the flesh, not in the Spirit ; and he says that the righteousness which is of the law was his, not God's. It must be understood, therefore, that the righteousness of the law is not fulfilled according to the righteousness which is in the law or of the law, that is, according to the righteousness of man, but according to the righteousness which is in the Spirit of grace, therefore according to the righteousness of God, that is, which man has from God. Which may be thus more clearly and briefly stated : That the righteousness of the law is not fulfilled when the law commands, and man as it were of his own strength obeys ; but when the Spirit aids, and man's free will, but freed by the grace of God, performs. Therefore the righteousness of the law is to command what is pleasing to God, to forbid what is displeasing ; but the righteousness in the law is to obey the letter, and beyond it to seek for no assistance of God for holy living. For when he had said, " Not having my own righteousness, which is of the law, but that which is by the faith of Christ," he added, " Which is from God." That, therefore, is itself the righteousness of God, being ignorant of which the proud go about to establish their own ; for it is not called the righteousness of God because by it God is righteous, but because man has it from God.

## CHAP. 21. — THAT RIGHTEOUSNESS IS NEVER PERFECTED IN THIS LIFE.

Now, according to this righteousness of God, that is, which we have from God, faith now worketh by love. But it worketh that, in what way man can attain to Him on whom now, not seeing, he believes ; and when he shall see Him, then that which was in faith through a glass enigmatically, shall at length be in sight face to face ; and then shall be perfected even love itself. Because it is said with excessive folly, that God is loved as much before He is seen, as He will be loved when He is seen. Further, if in this life, as no religious person doubts, the more we love God, so much the more righteous we certainly are, who can doubt that pious and true righteousness will then be perfected when the love of God shall be perfect? Then the law, therefore, shall be fulfilled ; so that nothing at all is wanting to it, of which law, according to the apostle, the fulfilling is Love. And thus, when he had said, " Not having my own righteousness, which is of the law, but that which is by the faith of Jesus Christ, which is the righteousness from God in faith," he then added, " That I may know Him, and the power of His resurrection, and the fellowship of His sufferings."[4] All these things were not yet full and perfect in the apostle ; but, as if he were placed on the way, he was running towards their fulness and perfection. For how had he already perfectly known Christ, who says in another place, " Now I know in part ; but then I shall know even as I am known " ?[5] And how had he already perfectly known the power of His resurrection, to whom it remained to know it yet more fully by experience at the time of the resurrection of the flesh? And how had he perfectly known already the fellowship of His suffering, if he had not yet experienced for him the suffering of death? Finally, he adds and says, " If in any manner I may attain unto the resurrection of the dead."[6] And then he says, " Not that I have already received or am already perfected." What, then, does he confess that he has not yet received, and in what is he not yet perfected, except that righteousness which is of God, which he desired, not willing to have his own righteousness, which is of the law? For hence he was speaking, and such was the reason for his saying these things in resistance to the enemies of the grace of God, for the bestowal of which Christ was crucified ; and of the race of whom are also these.

---

[1] See above, ch. 6.    [2] Rom. x. 3.    [3] 2 Cor. iii. 6.    [4] Phil. iii. 9, 10.    [5] 1 Cor. xiii. 12.    [6] Phil. iii. 11, 12.

## CHAP. 22. — NATURE OF HUMAN RIGHTEOUSNESS AND PERFECTION.

For from the place in which he undertook to say these things, he thus began, "Beware of dogs, beware of evil workers, beware of the concision. For we are the circumcision, who serve God in the Spirit," — or, as some codices have it, "who serve God the Spirit," or "the Spirit of God," — "and glory in Christ Jesus, and have no confidence in the flesh."[1] Here it is manifest that he is speaking against the Jews, who, observing the law carnally, and going about to establish their own righteousness, were slain by the letter, and not made alive by the Spirit, and gloried in themselves while the apostles and all the children of the promise were glorying in Christ. Then he added, "Although I may have confidence in the flesh. If any one else thinks that he has confidence in the flesh, I more."[2] And enumerating all things which have glory according to the flesh, he ended at that point where he says, "According to the righteousness which is in the law, blameless." And when he had said that he regarded all these things as altogether loss and disadvantage and dung that he might gain Christ, he added the passage which I am treating, "And be found in Him, not having my own righteousness, but that which is by the faith of Christ, which is from God." He confessed that he had not yet received the perfection of this righteousness, which will not be except in that excellent knowledge of Christ, on account of which he said that all things were loss to him; and he confessed, therefore, that he was not yet perfect. "But I follow on," said he, "if I may apprehend that in which I also am apprehended of Christ Jesus."[3] "I may apprehend that in which I also am apprehended," is much the same as, "I may know, even as I also am known." "Brethren," says he, "I count not myself to have apprehended: but one thing, forgetting those things which are behind, and reaching forward to those which are before, I follow on according to the purpose for the reward of the supreme calling of God in Christ Jesus."[4] The order of the words is, "But one thing I follow." Of which one thing the Lord also is well understood to have admonished Martha, where he says, "Martha, Martha, thou art careful and troubled about many things: but one thing is needful."[5] The apostle, wishing to apprehend this as if set in the way, said that he followed on to the reward of the high calling of God in Christ Jesus. For who can delay when he would apprehend that which he declares that he is following, that he shall then have a righteousness equal to the righteousness

of the holy angels, none of whom, of course, does any messenger of Satan buffet lest he should be lifted up with the greatness of his revelations? Then, admonishing those who might think themselves already perfect with the fulness of that righteousness, he says, "Let as many of us, therefore, as are perfect, be thus minded."[6] As if he should say, If, according to the capacity of mortal man for the little measure of this life, we are perfect, let us understand that it also belongs to that perfection that we perceive that we are not yet perfected in that angelical righteousness which we shall have in the manifestation of Christ. "And if in anything," he said, "ye be otherwise minded, God shall also reveal even this unto you."[6] How, save to those that are walking and advancing in the way of the faith, until that wandering be finished and they come to the actual vision? Whence following on, he added, "Nevertheless, whereunto we have already attained, let us walk therein."[6] Then he concludes that they should be bewared of, concerning whom this passage treated at its beginning. "Brethren, be imitators of me, and mark them which so walk as ye have our example. For many walk, of whom I have spoken often, and now tell you even weeping, whose end is destruction,"[7] and the rest. These are the very ones of whom, in the beginning, he had said, "Beware of dogs, beware of evil workers," and what follows. Therefore all are enemies of the cross of Christ who, going about to establish their own righteousness, which is of the law, — that is, where only the letter commands, and the Spirit does not fulfil, — are not subject to the law of God. For if they who are of the law be heirs, faith is made an empty thing. "If righteousness is by the law, then Christ has died in vain: then is the offence of the cross done away." And thus those are enemies of the cross of Christ who say that righteousness is by the law, to which it belongs to command, not to assist. But the grace of God through Jesus Christ the Lord in the Holy Spirit helpeth our infirmity.

## CHAP. 23. — THERE IS NO TRUE RIGHTEOUSNESS WITHOUT THE FAITH OF THE GRACE OF CHRIST.

Wherefore he who lives according to the righteousness which is in the law, without the faith of the grace of Christ, as the apostle declares that he lived blameless, must be accounted to have no true righteousness; not because the law is not true and holy, but because to wish to obey the letter which commands, without the Spirit of God which quickens, as if of the strength of free will, is not true righteousness. But the righteousness according to which the

---

[1] Phil. iii. 2, 3.　　[2] Phil. iii. 4.　　[3] Phil. iii. 12.
[4] Phil. iii. 13, 14.　　[5] Luke x. 41.

[6] Phil. iii. 15.　　[7] Phil. iii. 16.

righteous man lives by faith, since man has it from God by the Spirit of grace, is true righteousness. And although this is not undeservedly said to be perfect in some righteous men, according to the capacity of this life, yet it is but little to that great righteousness which the equality of the angels receives. And he who had not yet possessed this, on the one hand, in respect of that which was already in him, said that he was perfect; and in respect of that which was still wanting to him, said that he was imperfect. But manifestly that lower degree of righteousness makes merit, that higher kind becomes reward. Whence he who does not strive after the former does not attain unto the latter. Wherefore, after the resurrection of man, to deny that there will be a fulness of righteousness, and to think that the righteousness in the body of that life will be such as it can be in the body of this death, is singular folly. But it is most true that men do not there begin to fulfil those commands of God which here they have been unwilling to obey. For there will be the fulness of the most perfect righteousness, yet not of men striving after what is commanded, and making gradual endeavours after that fulness; but in the twinkling of an eye, even as shall be that resurrection of the dead itself, because that greatness of perfect righteousness will be given as a reward to those who here have obeyed the commandments, and will not itself be commanded to them as a thing to be accomplished. But I should in such wise say they have done the commandments, that we might remember that to these very commandments belongs the prayer in which the holy children of promise daily say with truth, "Thy will be done,"[1] and "Forgive us our debts."[2]

CHAP. 24 [VIII.] — THERE ARE THREE PRINCIPAL HEADS IN THE PELAGIAN HERESY.

When, then, the Pelagians are pressed with these and such like testimonies and words of truth, not to deny original sin; not to say that the grace of God whereby we are justified is not given freely, but according to our merits; nor to say that in mortal man, however holy and well doing, there is so great righteousness that even after the washing of regeneration, until he finishes this life of his, forgiveness of sins is not necessary to him, — therefore when they are pressed not to make these three assertions, and by their means alienate men who believe them from the grace of the Saviour, and persuade the lifted-up unto pride to go headlong unto the judgment of the devil: they introduce the clouds of other questions in which their impiety — in the sight of men more simple

minded, whether that they are more slow or less instructed in the sacred writings — may be concealed. These are the misty questions of the praise of the creature, of the praise of marriage, of the praise of the law, of the praise of free will, of the praise of the saints; as if any one of our people were in the habit of disparaging those things, and not rather of announcing all things with due praises to the honour of the Creator and Saviour. But even the creature does not desire in such wise to be praised as to be unwilling to be healed. And the more marriage is to be praised, the less is to be attributed to it the shameful concupiscence of the flesh, which is not of the Father, but of the world; and which assuredly marriage found and did not make in men; because, moreover, it is actually in very many without marriage, and if nobody had sinned marriage itself might be without it. And the law, holy and just and good, is neither grace itself, nor is anything rightly done by it without grace; because the law is not given that it may give life, but it was added because of transgression, that it might conclude all persons convicted under sin, and that the promise by faith of Jesus Christ might be given to them that believe.[3] And the free will taken captive does not avail, except for sin; but for righteousness, unless divinely set free and aided, it does not avail. And thus, also, all the saints, whether from that ancient Abel to John the Baptist, or from the apostles themselves up to this time, and henceforth even to the end of the world, are to be praised in the Lord, not in themselves. Because the voice, even of those earlier ones, is, "In the Lord shall my soul be praised."[4] And the voice of the later ones is, "By the grace of God I am what I am."[5] And to all belongs, "That he that glorieth may glory in the Lord." And it is the common confession of all, "If we say that we have no sin, we deceive ourselves, and the truth is not in us."[6]

CHAP. 25 [IX.] — HE SHOWS THAT THE OPINION OF THE CATHOLICS IS THE MEAN BETWEEN THAT OF THE MANICHEANS AND PELAGIANS, AND REFUTES BOTH.

But since, in these five particulars which I have set forth, in which they seek lurking-places, and from which they weave misrepresentations, they are forsaken and convicted by the divine writings, they have thought to deter those whom they could by the hateful name of Manicheans, lest in opposition to their most perverse teachings their ears should be conformed to the truth; because doubtless the Manicheans blasphemously condemn the three former of those five dogmas, saying that neither the human creature, nor

---

[1] Matt. vi. 10.          [2] Matt. vi. 12.
[3] Gal. iii. 22.          [4] Ps. xxxiv. 2.          [5] 1 Cor. xv. 10.
[6] 1 John i. 8.

marriage, nor the law was ordained by the supreme and true God. But they do not receive what the truth says, that sin took its origin from free will, and that all evil, whether of angel or man, comes from it; because they prefer to believe, in their turning aside from God, that the nature of evil was always evil, and co-eternal with God. They, moreover, attack the holy patriarchs and prophets with as many execrations as they can. This is the way in which the modern heretics think, that by objecting the name of Manicheans, they evade the force of truth. But they do not evade it; because it follows them up, and overturns at once Manicheans and Pelagians. For in that when a man is born there is something good, so far as he is a man, he condemns the Manichean, and praises the Creator; but in so far as he derives original sin, he condemns the Pelagian, and holds a Saviour necessary. For even because that nature is said to be *healable*, it repels both teachings; because it would not, on the one hand, have need of medicine if it were sound, which is opposed to the Pelagian, nor could it be healed at all if the evil in it were eternal and immutable, which is opposed to the Manichean. Moreover, in that to marriage, which we praise as ordained of God, we do not say that the concupiscence of the flesh is to be attributed, this is both contrary to the Pelagians, who make this concupiscence itself a matter of praise, and contrary to the Manicheans, who attribute it to a foreign and evil nature, when it really is an evil accidental to our nature, not to be separated by the disjunction from God, but to be healed by the mercy of God. Moreover, in that we say that the law, holy and just and good, was given not for the justification of the wicked, but for the conviction of the proud, for the sake of transgressions, — this, is, on the one hand, opposed to the Manicheans, in that according to the apostle the law is praised; and on the other opposed to the Pelagians, in that, in accordance with the apostle, no one is justified by the law; and therefore, for the sake of making alive those whom the letter has killed, that is, whom the law, enjoining good, makes guilty by transgressions, the Spirit of grace freely brings aid. Also in that we say that the will is free in evil, but for doing good it must be made free by God's grace, this is opposed to the Pela-

gians; but in that we say it originated from that which previously was not evil, this is opposed to the Manicheans. Again, that we honour the holy patriarchs and prophets with praises due to them in God, is in opposition to the Manicheans; but that we say that even to them, however righteous and pleasing to God they might have been, the propitiation of the Lord was necessary, this is in opposition to the Pelagians. The catholic faith, therefore, finds them both, as it does also other heretics, in opposition to it, and convicts both by the authority of the divine testimonies and by the light of truth.

CHAP. 26 [x.] — THE PELAGIANS STILL STRIVE AFTER A HIDING-PLACE, BY INTRODUCING THE NEEDLESS QUESTION OF THE ORIGIN OF THE SOUL.

The Pelagians, indeed, add to the clouds which envelop their lurking-places the unnecessary question concerning the origin of the soul, for the purpose of erecting a hiding-place by disturbing manifest things by the obscurity of other matters. For they say "that we guard the continuous propagation of souls with the continuous propagation of sin." And where and when they have read this, either in the addresses or in the writings of those who maintain the catholic faith against this, I do not know; because, although I find something written by catholics on the subject, yet the defence of the truth had not yet been undertaken against those men, neither was there any anxiety to answer them. But this I say, that according to the Holy Scriptures original sin is so manifest, and that this is put away in infants by the laver of regeneration is confirmed by such antiquity and authority of the catholic faith, notorious by such a clear concurrent testimony of the Church, that what is argued by the inquiry or affirmation of anybody concerning the origin of the soul, if it is contrary to this, cannot be true. Wherefore, whoever builds up, either concerning the soul or any other obscure matter, any edifice whence he may destroy this, which is true, best founded, and best known, whether he is a son or an enemy of the Church, must either be corrected or avoided. But let this be the end of this Book, that the things which follow may have another beginning.

# BOOK IV.

AFTER HAVING SET ASIDE IN THE FORMER BOOKS THE CALUMNIES HURLED AGAINST
THE CATHOLICS, AUGUSTIN HERE PROCEEDS TO OPEN UP THE SNARES WHICH LIE
HIDDEN IN THE REMAINING PART OF THE SECOND EPISTLE OF THE PELAGIANS,
IN THE FIVE HEADS OF THEIR DOCTRINE — IN THE PRAISE, TO WIT, OF THE
CREATURE, THE PRAISE OF MARRIAGE, THE PRAISE OF THE LAW, THE PRAISE
OF FREE WILL, AND THE PRAISE OF THE SAINTS; IN CONNECTION WITH WHICH
HEADS THE PELAGIANS MALIGNANTLY BOAST THAT THEY ARE AT ISSUE NOT
MORE WITH THE MANICHEANS THAN WITH THE CATHOLICS. HENCE THESE FIVE
POINTS MAY BRING US BACK TO THIS, THAT THEY PUT FORWARD THEIR THREE-
FOLD ERROR — NAMELY, THE TWO FIRST, THE DENIAL OF ORIGINAL SIN; THE
TWO FOLLOWING, THE ASSERTION THAT GRACE IS GIVEN ACCORDING TO MERITS;
THE FIFTH, THEIR STATEMENT THAT THE SAINTS HAD NOT SINNED IN THIS LIFE.
AUGUSTIN SHOWS THAT BOTH HERESIES, THAT OF THE MANICHEANS AND THAT OF THE
PELAGIANS, ARE OPPOSED AND EQUALLY ODIOUS TO THE CATHOLIC FAITH, WHERE-
BY WE PROFESS, FIRST, THAT THE NATURE CREATED BY A GOOD GOD WAS GOOD,
BUT THAT, NEVERTHELESS, IT IS IN NEED OF A SAVIOUR BECAUSE OF ORIGINAL
SIN, WHICH PASSED INTO ALL MEN FROM THE TRANSGRESSION OF THE FIRST
MAN: THEN SECONDLY, THAT MARRIAGE IS GOOD, TRULY INSTITUTED BY GOD,
BUT THAT THAT CONCUPISCENCE IS EVIL WHICH WAS ASSOCIATED WITH MARRIAGE
BY SIN: ALSO THIRDLY THAT THE LAW OF GOD IS GOOD, BUT IN SUCH WISE AS
ONLY TO MANIFEST SIN, NOT TO TAKE IT AWAY: THAT FOURTHLY FREE WILL IS
ASSUREDLY INHERENT IN THE NATURE OF MAN, BUT THAT NOW, HOWEVER, IT
IS SO ENSLAVED THAT IT DOES NOT AVAIL TO THE DOING OF RIGHTEOUSNESS,
UNLESS WHEN IT SHALL HAVE BEEN MADE FREE BY GRACE: BUT THAT FIFTHLY
THE SAINTS, WHETHER OF THE OLD OR NEW TESTAMENT, WERE INDEED ENDUED
WITH A RIGHTEOUSNESS, WHICH WAS TRUE BUT NOT PERFECT, NOR SO FULL THAT
THEY SHOULD BE FREE FROM ALL SIN. IN CONCLUSION, HE BRINGS FORWARD
THE TESTIMONIES OF CYPRIAN AND AMBROSE ON BEHALF OF THE CATHOLIC FAITH,
SOME CONCERNING ORIGINAL SIN, OTHERS ABOUT THE ASSISTANCE OF GRACE,
AND THE LAST CONCERNING THE IMPERFECTION OF PRESENT RIGHTEOUSNESS.

## CHAP. 1 [I.] — THE SUBTERFUGES OF THE PELA-GIANS ARE FIVE.

AFTER the matters which I have considered, and to which I have answered, they repeat the same things as those contained in the letter which I have refuted, but in a different manner. For before, they put them forward as objecting to us things which we think as it were falsely; but afterwards, as explaining what they themselves think, they have presented the same things from the opposite side, adding two certain points which they had not mentioned — that is, "that they say that baptism is necessary for all ages," and "that by Adam death passed upon us, not sins," which things must also themselves be considered in their own place. Hence, because in the former Book which I have just finished I said that they alleged hindrances of five matters in which lurk their dogmas hostile to God's grace and to the catholic faith, — the praise, to wit, of the creature, the praise of marriage, the praise of the law, the praise of free will, the praise of the saints, — I think it is more convenient to make a general discrimination of all that they maintain, the contrary of which they object to us, and to show which of those things pertain to any of those five, that so my answer may be by that very distinction clearer and briefer.

## CHAP. 2 [II.] — THE PRAISE OF THE CREATURE.

They accomplish the praise of the creature, inasmuch as it pertains to the human race of which the question now is, in these statements: "That God is the Maker of all those that are born, and that the sons of men are God's work; and that all sin descends not from nature, but from the will." With this praise of the creature they connect, "that they say that baptism is necessary for every age, so that," namely, "the creature itself may be adopted among the children of God; not because it derives anything from its parents which must be purified in the laver of regeneration." To this praise they add also, "that they say that Christ the Lord was sprinkled with no stain of sin as far as pertains to His infancy;" because they assert that His flesh was most pure from all contagion of sin, not by His own excellence and singular grace, but by His fellowship with the nature which is shared by all infants. It also belongs to this that they introduce the question "of the origin of the soul," thus endeavouring to make all the souls of infants equal to the soul of Christ, maintaining that they likewise are sprinkled with no stain of sin. On this account, also, they say, "that nothing of evil passed from Adam upon the rest of humanity except death, which," they say, "is not always an evil, since to the martyrs, for instance, it is for the sake of rewards; and it is not the dissolution of the bodies, which in every kind of men shall be raised up, that can make death to be called either good or evil, but the diversity of merits which arises from human liberty." These things they write in this letter concerning the praise of the creature.

They praise marriage truly according to the Scriptures, "because the Lord saith in the gospel, He who made men from the beginning made them male and female, and said, Increase and multiply, and replenish the earth." Although this is not written in that passage of the gospel, yet it is written in the law. They add, moreover, "What therefore God hath joined together, let not man put asunder."[1] And these we acknowledge to be gospel words.

In the praise of the law they say, "that the old law was, according to the apostle, holy and just and good; that on those who keep its commandments, and live righteously by faith, such as the prophets and patriarchs, and all the saints, life eternal could be conferred."

In the praise of free will they say, "that free will has not perished, since the Lord says by the prophets, 'If ye be willing and will hear me, ye shall eat the good things of the land: if ye are unwilling, and will not hear, the sword shall devour you.'[2] And thus, also, it is that grace assists the good purpose of any person, but yet does not infuse a desire of virtue into the reluctant heart, because there is no acceptance of persons with God."

In the praise of the saints they conceal themselves, saying "that baptism perfectly renews men, inasmuch as the apostle is a witness who testifies that, by the washing of water, the Church is made out of the heathen holy and spotless;[3] that the Holy Spirit also assisted pious souls in ancient times, even as the prophet says to God, 'Thy good Spirit shall lead me into the right way;'[4] that all the prophets, moreover, and apostles or saints, as well of the New as of the Old Testament, to whom God gives witness, were righteous, not in comparison with the wicked, but by the rule of virtue; and that in future time there is a reward as well of good works as of evil. But that no one can then perform the commandment which here he may have contemned, because the apostle said, 'We must be manifested before the judgment-seat of Christ, that every one may receive the things belonging to the body, according to what he has done, whether good or evil.'"[5]

In all these points, whatever they say of the praise of the creature and of marriage, they endeavour to bring us back to this, — that there is no original sin; whatever of the praise of law and of free will, to this, that grace does not assist without merit, and that thus grace is no more grace; whatever of the praise of the saints, to this, that mortal life in the saints appears not to have sin, and that it is not necessary for them to pray God for the remitting of their debts.

CHAP. 3 [III.] — THE CATHOLICS PRAISE NATURE, MARRIAGE, LAW, FREE WILL, AND THE SAINTS, IN SUCH WISE AS TO CONDEMN AS WELL PELAGIANS AS MANICHEANS.

Let every one who, with a catholic mind, shudders at these impious and damnable doctrines, in this tripartite division, shun the lurking-places and snares of this fivefold error, and be so careful between one and another as in such wise to decline from the Manicheans as not to incline to the Pelagians; and again, so to separate himself from the Pelagians as not to associate himself with the Manicheans; or, if he should already be taken hold of in one or the other bondage, that he should not so pluck himself out of the hands of either as to rush into those of the other. Because they seem to be contrary to one another; since the Manicheans manifest themselves by vituperating these five points, and the Pelagians conceal themselves by praising them. Wherefore he condemns and shuns both, whoever he may be, who according to the rule of the catholic faith so glorifies the Creator in men, that are born of the good creature of flesh and soul (for this the Manichean

---

[1] Matt. xix. 4.    [2] Isa. i. 19.    [3] Eph. v. 26.    [4] Ps. cxliii. 10.    [5] 2 Cor. v. 10.

will not have), as that he yet confesses that on account of the corruption which has passed over into them by the sin of the first man, even infants need a Saviour (for this the Pelagian will not have). He who so distinguishes the evil of shameful concupiscence from the blessing of marriage, as neither, like the Manicheans, to reproach the source of our birth, nor, like the Pelagians, to praise the source of our disorder. He who so maintains the law to have been given holy and just and good through Moses by a holy and just and good God (which Manicheus, in opposition to the apostle, denies), as to say that it both shows forth sin and yet does not take it away, and commands righteousness which yet it does not give (which, again, in opposition to the apostle, Pelagius denies). He who so asserts free will as to say that the evil of both angel and man began, not from I know not what nature always evil, which is no nature, but from the will itself, which overturns Manichean heresy, and nevertheless that even thus the captive will cannot breathe into a wholesome liberty save by God's grace, which overturns the Pelagian heresy. He who so praises in God the holy men of God, not only after Christ manifested in the flesh and subsequently, but even those of the former times, whom the Manicheans dare to blaspheme, as yet to believe their own confessions concerning themselves, more than the lies of the Pelagians. For the word of the saints is, " If we should say that we have no sin, we deceive ourselves, and the truth is not in us." [1]

CHAP. 4 [IV.] — PELAGIANS AND MANICHEANS ON THE PRAISE OF THE CREATURE.

These things being so, what advantage is it to new heretics, enemies of the cross of Christ and opposers of divine grace, that they seem sound from the error of the Manicheans, if they are dying by another pestilence of their own? What advantage is it to them, that in the praise of the creature they say " that the good God is the maker of those that are born, by whom all things were made, and that the children of men are His work," whom the Manicheans say are the work of the prince of darkness ; when between them both, or among them both, God's creation, which is in infants, is perishing? For both of them refuse to have it delivered by Christ's flesh and blood, — the one, because they destroy that very flesh and blood, as if He did not take upon Him these at all in man or of man ; and the other, because they assert that there is no evil in infants from which they should be delivered by the sacrament of this flesh and blood. Between them lies the human creature in infants,

with a good origination, with a corrupted propagation, confessing for its goods a most excellent Creator, seeking for its evils a most merciful Redeemer, having the Manicheans as disparagers of its benefits, having the Pelagians as deniers of its evils, and both as persecutors. And although in infancy there is no power to speak, yet with its silent look and its hidden weakness it addresses the impious vanity of both, saying to the one, " Believe that I am created by Him who creates good things ; " and saying to the other, " Suffer me to be healed by Him who created me." The Manicheans say, " There is nothing of this infant save the good soul to be delivered ; the rest," which belongs not to the good God, but to the prince of darkness, " is to be rejected." The Pelagians say, " Certainly there is nothing of this infant to be delivered, because we have shown the whole to be safe." Both lie ; but now the accuser of the flesh alone is more bearable than the praiser, who is convicted of cruelty against the whole. But neither does the Manichean help the human soul by blaspheming God, the Author of the entire man ; nor does the Pelagian permit the divine grace to come to the help of human infancy by denying original sin. Therefore it is by the catholic faith that God has mercy, seeing that by condemning both mischievous doctrines it comes to the help of the infant for salvation. It says to the Manicheans, " Hear the apostle crying, ' Know ye not that your body is the temple of the Holy Ghost in you ? ' [2] and believe that the good God is the Creator of bodies, because the temple of the Holy Ghost cannot be the work of the prince of darkness." It says to the Pelagians, " The infant that you look upon ' was conceived in iniquity, and in sin its mother nourished it in the womb.' [3] Why, as if in defending it as free from all mischief, do you not permit it to be delivered by mercy? No one is pure from uncleanness, not even the infant whose life is of one day upon the earth. [4] Allow the wretched creatures to receive remission of sins, through Him who alone neither as small nor great could have any sin."

CHAP. 5. — WHAT IS THE SPECIAL ADVANTAGE IN THE PELAGIAN OPINIONS?

What advantage, then, is it to them that they say " that all sin descends not from nature, but from the will," and resist by the truth of this judgment the Manicheans, who say that evil nature is the cause of sin ; when by being unwilling to admit original sin although itself also descends from the will of the first man, they make infants to depart in guilt from the body? What advantage is it to them " that they confess

---

[1] 1 John i. 8.                [2] 1 Cor. vi. 19.    [3] Ps. li. 5.    [4] Job xiv. 4, 5. See LXX.

that baptism is necessary for all ages," while the Manicheans say that it is superfluous for every age, while they say that in infants it is false so far as it pertains to the forgiveness of sins? What advantage is it to them that they maintain "the flesh of Christ" (which the Manicheans contend was either no flesh at all, or a feigned flesh) to have been not only the true flesh, but also "that the soul itself was stained by no spot of sin," when other infants are by them so put on the same level with His infancy, with not unequal purity, as that both that flesh does not appear to keep its own holiness in comparison with these, and these obtain no salvation from that?

### CHAP. 6. — NOT DEATH ALONE, BUT SIN ALSO, HAS PASSED INTO US BY MEANS OF ADAM.

In that particular, indeed, wherein they say "that death passed to us by Adam, not sins," they have not the Manicheans as their adversaries: since they, too, deny that original sin from the first man, at first of pure and upright body and spirit, and afterwards depraved by free will, subsequently passed and passes as sin into all with death; but they say that the flesh was evil from the beginning, and was created by an evil spirit and along with an evil spirit; but that a good soul — a portion, to wit, of God — for the deserts of its defilement by food and drink, in which it was before bound up, came into man, and thus by means of copulation was bound in the chain of the flesh. And thus the Manicheans agree with the Pelagians that it was not the guilt of the first man that passed into the human race — neither by the flesh, which they say was never good; nor by the soul, which they assert comes into the flesh of man with the merits of its own defilements, with which it was polluted before the flesh. But how do the Pelagians say "that only death passed upon us by Adam's means"? For if we die because he died, but he died because he sinned, they say that the punishment passed without the guilt, and that innocent infants are punished with an unjust penalty by deriving death without the deserts of death. This, the catholic faith has known of the one and only mediator between God and man, the man Christ Jesus, who condescended to undergo death — that is, the penalty of sin — without sin, for us. As He alone became the Son of man, in order that we might become through Him sons of God, so He alone, on our behalf, undertook punishment without ill deservings, that we through Him might obtain grace without good deservings. Because as to us nothing good was due, so to Him nothing bad was due. Therefore, commending His love to them to whom He was about to give undeserved life, He was willing to suffer for them an unde-

served death. This special prerogative of the Mediator the Pelagians endeavour to make void, so that this should no longer be special in the Lord, if Adam in such wise suffered a death due to him on account of his guilt, as that infants, drawing from him no guilt, should suffer undeserved death. For although very much good is conferred on the good by means of death, whence some have fitly argued even "of the benefit of death;" yet from this what can be declared except the mercy of God, since the punishment of sin is converted into beneficent uses?

### CHAP. 7. — WHAT IS THE MEANING OF "IN WHOM ALL HAVE SINNED"?

But these speak thus who wish to wrest men from the apostle's words into their own thought. For where the apostle says, "By one man sin entered into the world, and death by sin, and so passed upon all men,"[1] they will have it there understood not that "sin" passed over, but "death." What, then, is the meaning of what follows, "Wherein all have sinned"? For either the apostle says that in that "one man" all have sinned of whom he had said, "By one man sin entered into the world," or else in that "sin," or certainly in "death." For it need not disturb us that he said not "in which" [using the feminine form of the pronoun], but "in whom" [using the masculine] all have sinned; since "death" in the Greek language is of the masculine gender. Let them, then, choose which they will, — for either in that "man" all have sinned, and it is so said because when he sinned all were in him; or in that "sin" all have sinned, because that was the doing of all in general which all those who were born would have to derive; or it remains for them to say that in that "death" all sinned. But in what way this can be understood, I do not clearly see. For all die in the sin; they do not sin in the death; for when sin precedes, death follows — not when death precedes, sin follows. Because sin is the sting of death — that is, the sting by whose stroke death occurs, not the sting with which death strikes.[2] Just as poison, if it is drunk, is called the cup of death, because by that cup death is caused, not because the cup is caused by the death, or is given by death. But if "sin" cannot be understood by those words of the apostle as being that "wherein all have sinned," because in Greek, from which the Epistle is translated, "sin" is expressed in the feminine gender, it remains that all men are understood to have sinned in that first "man," because all men were in him when he sinned; and from him sin is derived by birth, and is not remitted save by being born again.

---

[1] Rom. v. 12.

[2] [This is a distinction as to the *kind* of genitive involved in the phrase "sting of death." Augustin says "of death" is genitive of *the object*, not of *the author* or *subject*. — W.]

For thus also the sainted Hilary understood what is written, "wherein all have sinned;" for he says, "wherein," that is, in Adam, "all have sinned." [1] Then he adds, "It is manifest that all have sinned in Adam, as it were in the mass; for he himself was corrupted by sin, and all whom he begot were born under sin." When he wrote this, Hilary, without any ambiguity, indicated how we should understand the words, "wherein all have sinned."

### CHAP. 8. — DEATH PASSED UPON ALL BY SIN.

But on account of what does the same apostle say that we are reconciled to God by Christ, except on account of what we had become enemies? And what is this but sin? Whence also the prophet says, "Your sins separate between you and God." [2] On account of this separation, therefore, the Mediator was sent, that He might take away the sin of the world, by which we were separated as enemies, and that we, being reconciled, might be made from enemies children. About this, certainly, the apostle was speaking; hence it happened that he interposed what he says, "That sin entered by one man." For these are his former words. He says, "But God commendeth His love towards us in that, while we were yet sinners, Christ died for us. Much more, then, being now justified in His blood, we shall be saved from wrath through Him. For if, when we were enemies, we were reconciled to God by the death of His Son, much more, being reconciled, we shall be saved in His life. And not only so, but glorying also in God through Jesus Christ our Lord, by whom also we have now received reconciliation." Then he subjoins, "Therefore, as by one man sin entered into this world, and death by sin, and so passed upon all men, for in him all have sinned." [3] Why do the Pelagians evade this matter? If reconciliation through Christ is necessary to all men, on all men has passed sin by which we have become enemies, in order that we should have need of reconciliation. This reconciliation is in the laver of regeneration and in the flesh and blood of Christ, without which not even infants can have life in themselves. For as there was one man for death on account of sin, so there is one man for life on account of righteousness; because "as in Adam all die, so also in Christ shall all be made alive;" [4] and "as by the sin of one upon all men to condemnation, so also by the righteousness of one upon all men unto justification of life." [5] Who is there that has turned a deaf ear to these apostolical words with such hardness of wicked impiety, as, having heard them, to contend that death passed upon us through Adam

without sin, unless, indeed, they are opposers of the grace of God and enemies of the cross of Christ? — whose end is destruction if they continue in this obstinacy. But let it suffice to have said thus much for the sake of that serpentine subtlety of theirs, by which they wish to corrupt simple minds, and to turn them away from the simplicity of the faith, as if by the praise of the creature.

### CHAP. 9 [V.] — OF THE PRAISE OF MARRIAGE.

But further, concerning the praise of marriage, [6] what advantage is it to them that, in opposition to the Manicheans, who assign marriage not to the true and good God, but to the prince of darkness, these men resist the words of true piety, and say, "That the Lord speaks in the gospel, saying, Who from the beginning made them male and female, and said, Increase and multiply and replenish the earth. What therefore God hath joined together, let not man put asunder"? [7] What does this profit them, by means of the truth to seduce to a falsehood? For they say this in order that infants may be thought to be born free from all fault, and thus that there is no need of their being reconciled to God through Christ, since they have no original sin, on account of which reconciliation is necessary to all by means of one who came into the world without sin, just as the enmities of all were caused by means of one through whom sin entered into the world. And this is believed by catholics for the sake of the salvation of the nature of men, without detracting from the praise of marriage; because the praise of marriage is a righteous intercourse of the sexes, not a wicked defence of vices. And thus, when, by their praise of marriage, these persons wish to draw over men from the Manicheans to themselves, they desire merely to change their disease, not to heal it.

### CHAP. 10. — OF THE PRAISE OF THE LAW.

Once more, in the praise of the law, what advantage is it to them that, in opposition to the Manicheans, they say the truth when they wish to bring men from that view to this which they hold falsely against the catholics? For they say, "We confess that even the old law, according to the apostle, is holy and just and good, and that this could confer eternal life on those that kept its commandments, and lived righteously by faith, like the prophets and patriarchs, and all the saints." By which words, very craftily expressed, they praise the law in opposition to grace; for certainly that law, although just and holy and good, could not confer eternal life on all those men of God, but the

[1] Commentaries by Hilary the Deacon, printed among the *Works* of Ambrose, vol. iv. (*Patrol Lat.* xvii.).
[2] Isa. lix. 2.    [3] Rom. v. 8 ff.    [4] 1 Cor. xv. 22.
[5] Rom. v. 18.     [6] See *On Original Sin*, ch. 38.    [7] Matt. xix. 4, etc.

faith which is in Christ. For this faith worketh by love, not according to the letter which killeth, but according to the Spirit which maketh alive, to which grace of God the law, as it were a schoolmaster, leads by deterring from transgression, that so that might be conferred upon man which it could not itself confer. For to those words of theirs in which they say "that the law was able to confer eternal life on the prophets and patriarchs, and all saints who kept its commandments," the apostle replies, " If righteousness be by the law, then has Christ died in vain." [1] " If the inheritance be by the law, then is it no more of promise." [2] " If they which are of the law be heirs, faith is made void, and the promise is made of none effect." [3] " But that no man is justified by the law in the sight of God, is evident: for, The just by faith liveth." [4] " But the law is not of faith: but, The man that doeth them shall live in them." [5] Which testimony, quoted by the apostle from the law, is understood in respect of temporal life, in respect of the fear of losing which, men were in the habit of doing the works of the law, not of faith ; because the transgressors of the law were commanded by the same law to be put to death by the people. Or, if it must be understood more highly, that " He who doeth these things shall live in them " was written in reference to eternal life ; the power of the law is so expressed that the weakness of man in himself, itself failing to do what the law commands, might seek help from the grace of God rather of faith, seeing that by His mercy even faith itself is bestowed. Because faith is thus possessed, according as God has given to every one the measure of faith.[6] For if men have it not of themselves, but men receive the Spirit of power and of love and of continence, whence that very same teacher of the Gentiles says, " For we have not received the spirit of fear, but of power, and of love, and of continence," [7] — assuredly also the Spirit of faith is received, of which he says, " Having also the same Spirit of faith." [8] Truly, then, says the law, " He who doeth these things shall live in them." But in order to do these things, and live in them, there is necessary not law which ordains this, but faith which obtains this. Which faith, however, that it may deserve to receive these things, is itself given freely.

### CHAP. 11.—THE PELAGIANS UNDERSTAND THAT THE LAW ITSELF IS GOD'S GRACE.

But those enemies of grace never endeavour to lay more secret snares for more vehement opposition to that same grace than when they praise the law, which, without doubt, is worthy to be praised.[9] Because, by their different modes of speaking, and by variety of words in all their arguments, they wish the law to be understood as " grace " — that, to wit, we may have from the Lord God the help of knowledge, whereby we may know those things which have to be done, — not the inspiration of love, that, when known, we may do them with a holy love, which is properly grace. For the knowledge of the law without love puffeth up, does not edify, according to the same apostle, who most openly says, " Knowledge puffeth up, but love edifieth." [10] Which saying is like to that in which it is said, " The letter killeth, the spirit maketh alive." [11] For " Knowledge puffeth up," corresponds to " The letter killeth : " and, " Love edifieth," to " The spirit maketh alive ; " because " the love of God is shed abroad in our hearts by the Holy Spirit who is given unto us." [12] Therefore the knowledge of the law makes a proud transgressor ; but, by the gift of charity, he delights to be a doer of the law. We do not then make void the law through faith, but we establish the law,[13] which by terrifying leads to faith. Thus certainly the law worketh wrath, that the mercy of God may bestow grace on the sinner, frightened and turned to the fulfilment of the righteousness of the law through Jesus Christ our Lord, who is that wisdom of God of which it is written, " She carries law and mercy on her tongue," [14] — law whereby she frightens, mercy by which she may help, — law by His servant, mercy by Himself, — the law, as it were, in the staff which Elisha [15] sent to raise up the son of the widow, and it failed to raise him up, " For if a law had been given which could have given life, righteousness would altogether have been by the law," [16] but mercy, as it were, in Elisha himself, who, wearing the figure of Christ, by giving life to the dead was joined in the signification of the great sacrament, as it were, of the New Testament.

### CHAP. 12 [VI.]—OF THE PRAISE OF FREE WILL.

Moreover, that, in opposition to the Manicheans, they praise free will, making use of the prophetic testimony, " If ye shall be willing and will hear me, ye shall eat what is good in the land ; but if ye shall be unwilling and will not hear me, the sword shall consume you : " [17] what advantage is this to them, when, indeed, it is not so much against the Manicheans that they are maintaining, as against the catholics that they are extolling, free will? For they wish what is said, " If ye be willing and will hear me," to be so understood, as if in the preceding will

---

[1] Gal. ii. 21.   [2] Gal. iii. 18.   [3] Rom. iv. 14.
[4] Gal iii. 11.   [5] Gal. iii. 12.   [6] Rom. xii. 3.
[7] 2 Tim. i. 7.   [8] 2 Cor. iv. 13.

[9] See *On the Grace of Christ*, ch. 8, and following.
[10] 1 Cor. viii. 1.   [11] 2 Cor. iii. 6.   [12] Rom. v. 5.
[13] Rom. iii. 31.   [14] Prov. iii. 16.   [15] 2 Kings iv. 29 sq.
[16] Gal. iii. 21.   [17] Isa. i. 19, 20.

itself were the merit of the grace that follows; and thus grace were no more grace, seeing that it is not free when it is rendered as a debt. But if they should so understand what is written, "If ye be willing," as to confess that He prepares even that good will itself of whom it is written, "The will is prepared by the Lord,"[1] they would use this testimony as catholics, and not only would overcome the ancient heresy of the Manicheans, but would not found the new one of the Pelagians.

## CHAP. 13. — GOD'S PURPOSES ARE EFFECTS OF GRACE.

What does it profit them, that in the praise of that same free will "they say that grace assists the good purpose of every one"?[2] This would be received without scruple as being said in a catholic spirit, if they did not attribute merit to the good purpose, to which merit now a wage is paid of debt, not according to grace, but would understand and confess that even that very good purpose, which the grace which follows assists, could not have been in the man if grace had not preceded it. For how is there a good purpose in a man without the mercy of God first, since it is that very good will which is prepared by the Lord?[1] But when they had said this, "that grace also assists every one's good purpose," and presently added, "yet does not infuse the love of virtue into a resisting heart," it might be fitly understood, if it were not said by those whose meaning is known. For, for the resisting heart a hearing for the divine call is first procured by the grace of God itself, and then in that heart, now no more resisting, the desire of virtue is kindled. Nevertheless, in all things which any one does according to God, His mercy precedes him. And this they will not have, because they choose to be not catholics, but Pelagians. For it much delights a proud impiety, that even that which a man is forced to confess to be given by the Lord should seem to be not bestowed on himself, but repaid; so that, to wit, the children of perdition, not of the promise, may be thought themselves to have made themselves good, and God to have repaid to those who are now good, having been made so by themselves, the reward due for that their work.

## CHAP. 14. — THE TESTIMONIES OF SCRIPTURE IN FAVOUR OF GRACE.

For that very pride has so stopped the ears of their heart that they do not hear, "For what hast thou that thou hast not received?"[3] They do not hear, "Without me ye can do nothing;"[4] they do not hear, "Love is of God;"[5] they do not hear, "God hath dealt the measure of faith;"[6] they do not hear, "The Spirit breatheth where it will,"[7] and, "They who are led by the Spirit of God, they are the sons of God;"[8] they do not hear, "No one can come unto me, unless it were given him of my Father;"[9] they do not hear what Esdras writes, "Blessed is the Lord of our fathers, who hath put into the heart of the king to glorify His house which is in Jerusalem;"[10] they do not hear what the Lord says by Jeremiah, "And I will put my fear into their heart, that they depart not from me; and I will visit them to make them good;"[11] and especially that word by Ezekiel the prophet, where God fully shows that He is induced by no good deservings of men to make them good, that is, obedient to His commands, but rather that He repays to them good for evil, by doing this for His own sake, and not for theirs. For He says, "These things saith the Lord God: I do not this for your sakes, O house of Israel, but for mine own holy name's sake, which has been profaned among the nations, whither ye have gone in there; and I will sanctify my great name, which has been profaned among the nations, and which ye have profaned in the midst of them; and the nations shall know that I am the Lord, saith Adonai the Lord, when I shall be sanctified among you before their eyes. And I will take you from among the nations, and gather you together out of all lands, and will bring you into your own land. And I will sprinkle upon you clean water, and ye shall be cleansed from all your filthiness, and I will cleanse you. And I will give unto you a new heart, and a new spirit will I put within you: and the stony heart shall be taken away out of your flesh, and I will give you a heart of flesh. And I will put my Spirit within you, and will cause you to walk in my righteousness, and to observe my judgments, and do them."[12] And after a few words, by the same prophet He says, "Not for your sakes do I do this, saith the Lord God; it shall be known unto you: be ye confounded and blush for your ways, O house of Israel. These things saith the Lord God: In the day in which I shall cleanse you from all your iniquities, and shall ordain cities, and the wilderness shall be built, and the desolated land shall be tilled, whereas it was desolated before the eyes of every passer by. And they shall say, This land that was desolated has become as a garden of pleasure; and the wasted and desolated and ruined cities have settled down fortified. And whatever nations have been left round about you shall know that I the Lord have built the ruined places, I have planted the desolated places: I the Lord have spoken, and have done it. Thus saith the Lord: I will yet

---

[1] Prov. viii. 35.      [2] See above, Book ii. ch. 11.
[3] 1 Cor. iv. 7.      [4] John xv. 5.      [5] 1 John iv. 7.

[6] Rom. xii. 3.      [7] John iii. 8.      [8] Rom. viii. 14.
[9] John vi. 65.      [10] 1 Esdras viii. 25.      [11] Jer. xxxii. 40, 41.
[12] Ezek. xxxvi. 22 ff.

for this inquire of the house of Israel, that I may do it for them; I will multiply them men like sheep, as holy sheep, as the sheep of Jerusalem in the days of her feast; so shall be those desolated cities full of men as sheep: and they shall know that I am the Lord." [1]

## CHAP. 15. — FROM SUCH SCRIPTURES GRACE IS PROVED TO BE GRATUITOUS AND EFFECTUAL.

What remained to the carrion skin whence it might be puffed up, and could disdain when it glories to glory in the Lord? [2] What remained to it, when whatsoever it shall have said that it has done in such a way that after that preceding merit of man had originated from man, God should subsequently do that of which the man is deserving, — it shall be answered, it shall be exclaimed against, it shall be contradicted, "I do it; but for my own holy name's sake; not for your sakes, do I do it, saith the Lord God"? [3] Nothing so overturns the Pelagians when they say that the grace of God is given in respect of our merits. Which, indeed, Pelagius himself condemned, [4] and if not by correcting it, yet by being afraid of the Eastern judges. Nothing so overturns the presumption of men who say, "We do it, that we may deserve those things with which God may do it." It is not Pelagius that answers you, but the Lord Himself, "I do it, and not for your sakes, but for my own holy name's sake." [3] For what good can ye do out of a heart which is not good? But that you may have a good heart, He says, "I will give you a new heart, and I will put a new Spirit within you." Can you say, We will first walk in His righteousness, and will observe His judgment, and will do so that we may be worthy, such as He should give His grace to? But what good would ye evil men do, and how should you do those good things, unless you were yourselves good? But who causes that men should be good save Him who said, "And I will visit them to make them good"? and who said "I will put my Spirit within you, and will cause you to walk in my righteousness, and to observe my judgments, and do them"? Are ye thus not yet awake? Do ye not yet hear, "I will cause you to walk, I will make you to observe," lastly, "I will make you to do"? What! are you still puffing yourselves up? We indeed walk, it is true; we observe; we do; but He makes us to walk, to observe, to do. This is the grace of God making us good; this is His mercy preventing us. What do waste and desolated and dug-up places deserve, which yet shall be built and tilled and fortified? Are these things for the merits of their wasteness, their desolation, their uprooting? Far from it. For such things

as these are evil deservings, while those gifts are good. Therefore good things are given for evil ones — gratuitous, therefore; not of debt, and therefore grace. "I," saith the Lord: "I, the Lord." Does not such a word as that restrain you, O human pride, when you say, I do such things as to deserve from the Lord to be built and planted? Do you not hear, "I do it not on your account; I the Lord have built up the destroyed cities, and I have planted the desolated lands; I the Lord have spoken, and I have done it, yet not for your sakes, but for my own holy name's sake"? Who multiplies men as sheep, as holy sheep, as the sheep of Jerusalem? Who causes those desolated cities to be full of men as sheep, save He who goes on, and says, "And they shall know that I am the Lord"? But with what men as sheep does He fill the cities as He promised? those which He finds, or those which He makes? Let us interrogate the Psalm; lo, it answers; let us hear: "O come, let us worship and fall down before Him: and let us weep before the Lord who made us; because He is our God, and we are the people of His pasture, and the sheep of His hand." [5] He therefore makes the sheep, with which He may fill the desolated cities. What wonder, when, indeed, to that single sheep, that is, the Church whose members are all the human sheep, it is said, "Because I am the Lord who make thee"? What do you pretend to me of free will, which will not be free to do righteousness, unless you should be a sheep? He then who makes men His sheep, He frees the wills of men for the obedience of piety.

## CHAP. 16. — WHY GOD MAKES OF SOME SHEEP, OTHERS NOT.

But wherefore does God make these men sheep, and those not, since with Him there is no acceptance of persons? This is the very question which the blessed apostle thus answers to those who propose it with more curiosity than propriety, "O man, who art thou that repliest against God? Does the thing formed say to him that formed it, Wherefore hast thou made me thus?" [6] This is the very question which belongs to that depth desiring to look into which the same apostle was in a certain measure terrified, and exclaimed, "Oh the depth of the riches of the wisdom and the knowledge of God! how unsearchable are His judgments, and His ways past finding out! For who has known the mind of the Lord? or who has been His counsellor? Or who has first given to Him, that it should be recompensed to Him again? Because of Him, and through Him, and in Him, are all things: to Him be glory for ages of ages." [7] Let them

---

[1] Ezek. xxxvi. 32 ff.   [2] 1 Cor. i. 31.   [3] Ezek. xxxvi. 22
[4] *On the Proceedings of Pelagius*, 30.

[5] Ps. xcv. 6, 7.   [6] Rom. ix. 20.   [7] Rom. xi. 33 ff.

not, then, dare to pry into that unsearchable question who defend merit before grace, and therefore even against grace, and wish first to give unto God, that it may be given to them again, — first, of course, to give something of free will, that grace may be given them again as a reward; and let them wisely understand or faithfully believe that even what they think that they have first given, they have received from Him, from whom are all things, by whom are all things, in whom are all things. But why this man should receive, and that should not receive, when neither of them deserves to receive, and whichever of them receives, receives undeservingly, — let them measure their own strength, and not search into things too strong for them. Let it suffice them to know that there is no unrighteousness with God. For when the apostle could find no merits for which Jacob should take precedence of his twin-brother with God, he said, " What, then, shall we say? Is there unrighteousness with God? Away with the thought! For He says to Moses, I will have mercy on whom I will have mercy, and I will show compassion on whom I will show compassion. Therefore it is not of him that willeth, nor of him that runneth, but of God that showeth mercy." [1] Let, therefore, His free compassion be grateful to us, even although this profound question be still unsolved; which, nevertheless, is so far solved as the same apostle solves it, saying, " But if God, willing to show His wrath, and to demonstrate His power, endured in much patience the vessels of wrath which are fitted to destruction; and that He might make known the riches of His glory on the vessels of mercy, which He has prepared for glory." [2] Certainly wrath is not repaid unless it is due, lest there be unrighteousness with God; but mercy, even when it is bestowed, and not due, is not unrighteousness with God. And hence, let the vessels of mercy understand how freely mercy is afforded to them, because to the vessels of wrath with whom they have common cause and measure of perdition, is repaid wrath, righteous and due. This is now enough in opposition to those who, by freedom of will, desire to destroy the liberality of grace.

CHAP. 17 [VII.] — OF THE PRAISE OF THE SAINTS.

In that, indeed, in the praise of the saints, they will not drive us with the zeal of that publican [3] to hunger and thirst after righteousness, but with the vanity of the Pharisees, as it were, to overflow with sufficiency and fulness; what does it profit them that — in opposition to the Manicheans, who do away with baptism — they say " that men are perfectly renewed by baptism," and apply the apostle's testimony for this, —

" who testifies that, by the washing of water, the Church is made holy and spotless from the Gentiles," [4] — when, with a proud and perverse meaning, they put forth their arguments in opposition to the prayers of the Church itself. For they say this in order that the Church may be believed after holy baptism — in which is accomplished the forgiveness of all sins — to have no further sin; when, in opposition to them, from the rising of the sun even to its setting, in all its members it cries to God, " Forgive us our debts." [5] But if they are interrogated regarding themselves in this matter, they find not what to answer. For if they should say that they have no sin, John answers them, that they deceive themselves, and the truth is not in them. [6] But if they confess their sins, since they wish themselves to be members of Christ's body, how will that body, that is, the Church, be even in this time perfectly, as they think, without spot or wrinkle, if its members without falsehood confess themselves to have sins? Wherefore in baptism all sins are forgiven, and, by that very washing of water in the word, the Church is set forth in Christ without spot or wrinkle; [7] and unless it were baptized, it would fruitlessly say, " Forgive us our debts," until it be brought to glory, when there is in it absolutely no spot or wrinkle. [8]

CHAP. 18. — THE OPINION OF THE SAINTS THEMSELVES ABOUT THEMSELVES.

It is to be confessed that " the Holy Spirit, even in the old times," not only " aided good dispositions," which even they allow, but that it even made them good, which they will not have. " That all, also, of the prophets and apostles or saints, both evangelical and ancient, to whom God gives His witness, were righteous, not in comparison with the wicked, but by the rule of virtue," is not doubtful. And this is opposed to the Manicheans, who blaspheme the patriarchs and prophets; but what is opposed to the Pelagians is, that all of these, when interrogated concerning themselves while they lived in the body, with one most accordant voice would answer, " If we should say that we have no sin, we deceive ourselves, and the truth is not in us." [6] " But in the future time," it is not to be denied " that there will be a reward as well of good works as of evil, and that no one will be commanded to do the commandments there which here he has contemned," but that a sufficiency of perfect righteousness where sin cannot be, a righteousness which is here hungered and thirsted after by the saints, is here hoped for in precept, is there received as a reward, on the entreaty of alms and

---

[1] Rom. ix. 14 ff.    [2] Rom. ix. 22, 23.    [3] Luke xviii. 10-14.

[4] Eph. v. 26.      [5] Matt. vi. 12.      [6] 1 John i. 8.
[7] Eph. v. 27.
[8] See On the Perfection of Man's Righteousness, 35, and On the Proceedings of Pelagius, 27.

prayers ; so that what here may have been wanting in fulfilment of the commandments may become unpunished for the forgiveness of sin.[1]

### CHAP. 19. — THE CRAFT OF THE PELAGIANS.

And if these things be so, let the Pelagians cease by their most insidious praises of these five things — that is, the praise of the creature, the praise of marriage, the praise of the law, the praise of free will, the praise of the saints — from feigning that they desire to pluck men, as it were, from the little snares of the Manicheans, in order that they may entangle them in their own nets — that is, that they may deny original sin ; may begrudge to infants the aid of Christ the physician ; may say that the grace of God is given according to our merits, and thus that grace is no more grace ; and may say that the saints in this life had not sin, and thus make the prayer of none effect which He gave to the saints who had no sin, and by which all sin is pardoned to the saints that pray unto Him. To these three evil doctrines, they by their deceitful praise of these five good things seduce careless and unlearned men. Concerning all which things, I think I have sufficiently censured their most cruel and wicked and proud vanity.

### CHAP. 20 [VIII.] — THE TESTIMONIES OF THE ANCIENTS AGAINST THE PELAGIANS.

But since they say "that their enemies have taken up our words for hatred of the truth," and complained that "throughout nearly the whole of the West a dogma not less foolish than impious is taken up, and from simple bishops sitting in their places without a Synodal congregation a subscription is extorted to confirm this dogma," — although the Church of Christ, both Western and Eastern, shuddered at the profane novelties of their words, — I think it belongs to my care not only to avail myself of the sacred canonical Scriptures as witnesses against them, which I have already sufficiently done, but, moreover, to bring forward some proofs from the writings of the holy men who before us have treated upon those Scriptures with the most widespread reputation and great glory. Not that I would put the authority of any controversialist on a level with the canonical books, as if there were nothing which is better or more truly thought by one catholic than by another who likewise is a catholic ; but that those may be admonished who think that these men say anything as it used to be said, before their empty talk on these subjects, by catholic teachers following the divine oracles, and may know that the true and anciently established catholic faith is by us defended against the receding presumption and mischief of the Pelagian heretics.

### CHAP. 21. — PELAGIUS, IN IMITATION OF CYPRIAN, WROTE A BOOK OF TESTIMONIES.

Even that heresiarch of these men, Pelagius himself, mentions with the honour that is certainly due to him, the most blessed Cyprian, most glorious with even the crown of martyrdom, not only in the African and the Western, but also in the Eastern Churches, well known by the report of fame, and by the diffusion far and wide of his writings, — when, writing a book of testimonies,[2] he asserts that he is imitating him, saying that " he was doing to Romanus what Cyprian had done to Quirinus." Let us, then, see what Cyprian thought concerning original sin, which entered by one man into the world. In the epistle on " Works and Alms "[3] he thus speaks " When the Lord at His advent had cured these wounds which Adam had introduced, and had healed the old poisons of the serpent, He gave a law to the sound man, and bade him sin no more, lest a worse thing should happen to him if he sinned. We had been limited and shut up into a narrow space by the commandment of innocence ; nor would the infirmity and weakness of human frailty have any resource unless the divine mercy coming once more in aid should open some way of securing salvation by pointing out works of justice and mercy, so that by almsgiving we may wash away whatever foulness we subsequently contract." By this testimony this witness refutes two falsehoods of theirs, — the one, wherein they say that the human race draws no sin from Adam which needs cure and healing through Christ ; the other, in which they say that the saints have no sin after baptism. Again, in the same epistle[4] he says, " Let each one place before his eyes the devil with his servants, — that is, with the people of perdition and death, — as springing forth into the midst and provoking the people of Christ, — Himself being present and judging, — with the trial of comparison in these words : ' I, on behalf of those whom thou seest with me, neither received buffets, nor bore scourgings, nor endured the cross, nor shed my blood, nor redeemed my family at the price of my suffering and blood ; but neither do I promise them a celestial kingdom, nor do I recall them to Paradise, having again restored to them immortality.' " Let the Pelagians answer and say when we could have been in the immortality of Paradise, and how we could have been expelled thence so as to be recalled thither by the grace of Christ. And, although they may

---

[1] See above, Book iii. 17.

[2] That is, his *Capitula*. See *On the Proceedings of Pelagius*, 6.
[3] Work cited, ch. 1; see *The Ante-Nicene Fathers*, vol. v. p 476.
[4] Work cited, ch. 22; in *The Ante-Nicene Fathers*, vol. v. p. 482.

be unable to find what they can answer in this case on behalf of their own perversity, let them observe in what manner Cyprian understood what the apostle says, "In whom all have sinned." And let not the Pelagian heretics, freed from the old Manichean heretics, dare to suggest any calumny against a catholic, lest they should be convicted of doing so wicked a wrong even to the ancient martyr Cyprian.

CHAP. 22. — FURTHER REFERENCES TO CYPRIAN.

For he says also this in the epistle whose title is inscribed, "On the Mortality:"[1] "The kingdom of God, beloved brethren, is beginning to be at hand; the reward of life, and the rejoicing of eternal salvation and perpetual gladness, and the possession formerly lost of Paradise, are now coming with the passing away of the world." This again, in the same epistle, he says: "Let us greet the day which assigns each of us to his own home, which snatches us hence and sets us free from the snares of the world, and restores us to Paradise and the kingdom." Moreover, he says in the epistle concerning Patience: "Let the judgment of God be pondered, which, even in the beginning of the world and of the human race, Adam, forgetful of the commandment and a transgressor of the law that had been given, received. Then we shall know how patient in this life we ought to be, who are born in such a state that we labour here with afflictions and contests. Because, says He, 'thou hast hearkened to the voice of thy wife, and hast eaten of the tree of which alone I had charged thee that thou shouldest not eat, cursed shall be the ground in all thy works: in sorrow and in groaning shalt thou eat of it all the days of thy life. Thorns and thistles shall it give forth to thee, and thou shalt eat the food of the field. In the sweat of thy face thou shalt eat thy bread, till thou return unto the ground from which thou wast taken: for earth thou art, and unto earth shalt thou go.' We are all tied and bound with the chain of this sentence until, death being destroyed, we depart from this world."[2] And, moreover, in the same epistle he says: "For, since in that first transgression of the commandment strength of body departed with immortality, and weakness came on with death, and strength cannot be received unless when immortality also has been received, it behoves us in this bodily frailty and weakness always to struggle and fight; and this struggle and encounter cannot be sustained but by the strength of patience."[3]

CHAP. 23. — FURTHER REFERENCES TO CYPRIAN.

And in the epistle which he wrote with sixty-six of his joint-bishops to Bishop Fidus, when he was consulted by him in respect of the law of circumcision, whether an infant might be baptized before the eighth day, this matter is treated in such a way as if by a divine forethought the catholic Church would already confute the Pelagian heretics who would appear so long afterwards. For he who had consulted had no doubt on the subject whether children on birth inherited original sin, which they might wash away by being born again. For be it far from the Christian faith to have at any time doubted on this matter. But he was in doubt whether the washing of regeneration, by which he made no question but that original sin was put away, ought to be given before the eighth day. To which consultation the most blessed Cyprian in reply said: "But as regards the case of infants, which you say ought not to be baptized within the second or third day after their birth, and that the law of the ancient circumcision should be regarded, so that you think that one who is born should not be baptized and sanctified within the eighth day, we all thought very differently in our council. For to the course which you thought was to be taken no one agreed, but we all rather judged that the grace of a merciful God was not to be denied to any one born of men; for, as the Lord says in His gospel, 'the Son of man is not come to destroy men's lives, but to save them.'[4] As far as we can, we must strive that, if possible, no soul be lost."[5] And a little afterwards he says: "Nor ought any of us to shudder at what God hath condescended to make. For although the infant is still fresh from its birth, yet it is not such that any one should shudder at kissing it in giving grace and in making peace, since in the kiss of an infant every one of us ought for his very religion's sake to consider the still recent hands of God themselves, which in some sort we are kissing in the man just formed and newly born, when we are embracing that which God has made."[6] A little after, also, he says: "But if anything could hinder men from obtaining grace, their more heinous sins might rather hinder those who are mature and grown up and older. But again, if even to the greatest sinners, and to those who have before sinned much against God, when they have subsequently believed, remission of sins is granted, and nobody is hindered from baptism and from grace; how much rather ought we to shrink from hindering an infant, who, being lately born, has not sinned, except that, being born after the flesh according to Adam, he has contracted the contagion of the ancient death at his earliest birth; who approaches more easily on this very account to

---

[1] Chs. 2, 18: *The Ante-Nicene Fathers*, v. pp. 469, 473.
[2] Ch. 11: *The Ante-Nicene Fathers*, v. 487.
[3] Ch. 9; *The Ante-Nicene Fathers*, v. 486.

[4] Luke ix. 56.
[5] Cyprian's *Letters*, No. 64, chs. 2, 4, 5: see *The Ante-Nicene Fathers*, vol. v. p. 353 (Ep. 58).
[6] *Ibid.* as cited.

the reception of the forgiveness of sins, in that to him are remitted not his own sins, but the sins of another!"[1]

## CHAP. 24.—THE DILEMMA PROPOSED TO THE PELAGIANS.

What will be said to such things as these, by those who are not only the forsakers, but also the persecutors of God's grace? What will they say to such things as these? On what ground is the "possession of Paradise" restored to us? How are we restored to Paradise if we have never been there? Or how have we been there, except because we were there in Adam? And how do we belong to that "judgment" which was spoken against the transgressor, if we do not inherit injury from the transgressor? Finally, he thinks that infants are to be baptized, even before the eighth day; lest "by the contagion of the ancient death, contracted in the first birth," the souls of the infants should perish. How do they perish if they who are born even of believing men are not held by the devil until they are born again in Christ, and plucked out from the power of darkness, and transferred into His kingdom? And who says that the souls of those who are born will perish unless they are born again? No other than he who so praises the Creator and the creature, the workman and the work, as to restrain and correct the horror of human feeling with which men refuse to kiss infants fresh from the womb, by interposing the veneration of the Creator Himself, saying that in the kiss of infants of that age the recent hands of God were to be considered! Did he, then, in confessing original sin, condemn either nature or marriage? Did he, because he applied to the infant born guilty from Adam, the cleansing of regeneration, therefore deny God as the Creator of those that were born? Because, in his dread that souls of any age whatever should perish, he, with his council of colleagues, decided that even before the eighth day they were to be delivered by the sacrament of baptism, did he therefore accuse marriage, when, indeed, in the case of an infant, — whether born of marriage or of adultery, yet because it was born a man, — he declared that the recent hands of God were worthy even of the kiss of peace? If, then, the holy bishop and most glorious martyr Cyprian could think that original sin in infants must be healed by the medicine of Christ, without denying the praise of the creature, without denying the praise of marriage, why does a novel pestilence, although it does not dare to call such an one as him a Manichean, think that another person's fault is to be objected against catholics who maintain these things, in order to conceal its own? So the most lauded commentator on the divine declarations, before even the slightest taint of the Manichean plague had touched our lands, without any reproach of the divine work and of marriage, confesses original sin, — not saying that Christ was stained with any spot of sin, nor yet comparing with Him the flesh of sin in others that were born, to whom by means of the likeness of sinful flesh He might afford the aid of cleansing; neither is he deterred by the obscure question of the origin of souls, from confessing that those who are made free by the grace of Christ return into Paradise. Does he say that the condition of death passed upon men from Adam without the contagion of sin? For it is not on account of avoiding the death of the body, but on account of the sin which entered by one man into the world,[2] that he says that help is to be afforded by baptism to infants, however fresh they may be from the womb.

## CHAP. 25 [IX.]—CYPRIAN'S TESTIMONIES CONCERNING GOD'S GRACE.

But now it plainly appears in what way Cyprian proclaims the grace of God against such as these, when he is arguing about the Lord's Prayer. For he says: "We say, 'May Thy name be made holy,'[3] not that we wish for God that He may be made holy by our prayers, but that we beseech of Him that His name may be made holy in us. But by whom is God made holy, since He Himself makes holy? But, because He says, 'Be ye holy, because I also am holy,' we ask and entreat this, that we who were made holy in baptism may continue in that which we have begun to be."[4] And in another place in the same epistle he says: "We add also, and say, 'Thy will be done in heaven, and in earth,' not in order that God may do what He wills, but that we may be able to do what God wills. For who resists God that He may not do what He wills? But, since we are hindered by the devil from obeying God with our thought and deed in all things, we pray and ask that God's will may be done in us. And that it may be done in us, we have need of God's will, that is, of His help and protection; since no one is strong in his own strength, but he is safe by the indulgence and mercy of God."[5] In another place also: "Moreover, we ask that the will of God may be done both in heaven and in earth, each of which things pertains to the fulfilment of our safety and salvation. For since we possess the body from the earth, and the spirit from heaven, we are ourselves earth and heaven; and

---

[1] Cyprian, as cited.

[2] Rom. v. 12.     [3] *i.e.* "Hallowed be Thy name."
[4] Cyprian, *On the Lord's Prayer*, ch. 9 (XII.), see *The Ante-Nicene Fathers*, v. p. 450.
[5] *Ibid.* ch. 13 (XVI.); see *The Ante-Nicene Fathers*, v. 451.

in both, that is, both in body and in spirit, we pray that God's will be done. For between the flesh and the spirit there is a struggle, and there is a daily strife as they disagree one with the other; so that we cannot do the very things that we would, in that the spirit seeks heavenly and divine things, while the flesh lusts after earthly and temporal things. And, therefore, we ask that, by the help and assistance of God, agreement may be made between these two natures; so that while the will of God is done both in the spirit and in the flesh, the soul which is new-born by Him may be preserved. And this the Apostle Paul openly and manifestly declares by his words. 'The flesh,' says he, 'lusteth against the spirit, and the spirit against the flesh; for these are contrary the one to the other, so that ye cannot do the things that ye would.' "[1] And a little after he says: " And it may be thus understood, most beloved brethren, that since the Lord commands and teaches us even to love our enemies, and to pray even for those who persecute us, we should ask even for those who are still earth, and have not yet begun to be heavenly, that even in respect of these God's will may be done, which Christ accomplished in preserving and renewing humanity."[2] And again, in another place he says: " But we ask that this bread should be given to us daily, that we who are in Christ, and daily receive the Eucharist for the food of salvation, may not, by the interposition of some more heinous sin, — by being prevented, as those abstaining and not communicating, from partaking of the heavenly bread, — be separated from Christ's body."[3] And a little afterwards, in the same treatise he says: " But when we ask that we may not come into temptation, we are reminded of our infirmity and weakness, while we so ask as that no one should insolently vaunt himself; that none should proudly and arrogantly assume anything to himself; that none should take to himself the glory either of confession or of suffering as his own, when the Lord Himself teaching humility said, 'Watch and pray, that ye come not into temptation: the spirit indeed is willing, but the flesh is weak;'[4] so that while a humble and submissive confession comes first, and all is attributed to God, whatever is sought for suppliantly, with fear and honour of God, may be granted by His own loving-kindness."[5] Moreover, in his treatise addressed to Quirinus, in respect to which work Pelagius wishes himself to appear as his imitator, he says in the Third Book " that we must boast in nothing, since

nothing is our own."[6] And subjoining the divine testimonies to this proposition, he added among others that apostolic word with which especially the mouths of such as these must be closed: " For what hast thou, which thou hast not received? But if thou hast received it, why boastest thou as if thou hadst not received it?" Also in the epistle concerning Patience he says: " For we have this virtue in common with God. From Him patience begins; from Him its glory and its dignity take their rise. The origin and greatness of patience proceed from God as its Author."[7]

CHAP. 26. — FURTHER APPEALS TO CYPRIAN'S TEACHING.

Does that holy and so memorable instructor of the Churches in the word of truth, deny that there is free will in men, because he attributes to God the whole of your righteous living? Does he reproach God's law, because he intimates that man is not justified by it, seeing that he declares that what that law commands must be obtained from the Lord God by prayers? Does he assert fate under the name of grace, by saying that we must boast in nothing, since nothing is our own? Does he, like these, believe that the Holy Spirit is in such wise the aider of virtue, as if that very virtue which it assists springs from ourselves, when, asserting that nothing is our own, he mentions in this respect that the apostle said, " For what hast thou that thou hast not received?" and says that the most excellent virtue, that is, patience, does not begin from us, and afterwards receive aid by the Spirit of God, but from Him Himself takes its source, from Him takes its origin? Finally, he confesses that neither good purpose, nor desire of virtue, nor good dispositions, begin to be in men without God's grace, when he says that " we must boast in nothing, since nothing is our own." What is so established in free will as what the law says, that we must not worship an idol, must not commit adultery, must do no murder? Nay, these crimes, and such like, are of such a kind that, if any one should commit them, he is removed from the communion of the body of Christ. And yet, if the blessed Cyprian thought that our own will was sufficient for not committing these crimes, he would not in such wise understand what we say in the Lord's Prayer, " Give us this day our daily bread," as that he should assert that we ask " that we may not by the interposition of some heinous sin — by being prevented as abstaining, and not communicating, from partaking of the heavenly bread — be separated from Christ's body." Let these new heretics answer

[1] Cyprian, On the Lord's Prayer, ch. 11 (XIV.); see The Ante-Nicene Fathers, v. 451.
[2] Ibid. ch. 15 (XVII.); vol. v. 452.
[3] Ibid. ch. 18 (XX.), p. 452.
[4] Matt. xxvi. 41, or Mark xiv. 38.
[5] Cyprian, work cited, ch. 19 (XXVI.); see The Ante-Nicene Fathers, v. 454.

[6] Cyprian's Testimonies, iii. 4; vol. v. p. 528.
[7] Cyprian, On Patience; The Ante-Nicene Fathers, vol. v. p. 484.

of a surety what good merit precedes, in men who are enemies of the name of Christ? For not only have they no good merit, but they have, moreover, the very worst merit. And yet, Cyprian even thus understands what we say in the prayer, "Thy will be done in heaven, and in earth:" that we pray also for those very persons who in this respect are called *earth*. We pray, therefore, not only for the unwilling, but also for the objecting and resisting. What, then, do we ask, but that from unwilling they may be made willing; from objecting, consenting; from resisting, loving? And by whom, but by Him of whom it is written, "The will is prepared by God"?[1] Let them, then, who disdain, if they do not do any evil and if they do any good, to glory, not in themselves, but in the Lord, learn to be catholics.

CHAP. 27 [X.] — CYPRIAN'S TESTIMONIES CONCERNING THE IMPERFECTION OF OUR OWN RIGHTEOUSNESS.

Let us, then, see that third point, which in these men is not less shocking to every member of Christ and to His whole body, — that they contend that there are in this life, or that there have been, righteous men having absolutely no sin.[2] In which presumption they most manifestly contradict the Lord's Prayer, wherein, with truthful heart and with daily words, all the members of Christ cry aloud, "Forgive us our debts." Let us see, then, what Cyprian, most glorious in the Lord, thought of this, — what he not only said for the instruction of the Churches, not, of course, of the Manicheans, but of the catholics, but also committed to letters and to memory. In the epistle on "Works and Alms," he says: "Let us then acknowledge, beloved brethren, the wholesome gift of the divine mercy, and let us who cannot be without some wound of conscience heal our wounds by the spiritual remedies for the cleansing and purging of our sins. Nor let any one so flatter himself with the notion of a pure and immaculate heart, as, in dependence on his own innocence, to think that the medicine needs not to be applied to his wounds; since it is written, 'Who shall boast that he hath a clean heart, or who shall boast that he is pure from sins?'[3] And again, in his epistle, John lays it down and says, 'If we say that we have no sin, we deceive ourselves, and the truth is not in us.'[4] But if no one can be without sin, and whoever should say that he is without fault is either proud or foolish, how needful, how kind is the divine mercy, which, knowing that there are still found some wounds in those that have been healed, has given even after their healing wholesome

remedies for the curing and healing of their wounds anew!"[5] Again, in the same treatise he says: "And since there cannot fail daily to be sins committed in the sight of God, there failed not daily sacrifices wherewith the sins might be cleansed away."[6] Also, in the treatise on the Mortality, he says: "Our warfare is with avarice, with immodesty, with anger, with ambition; our trying and toilsome wrestling ·with carnal vices, with the enticements of the world. The mind of man besieged, and on every hand invested with the onsets of the devil, scarcely meets the repeated attacks, scarcely resists them. If avarice is prostrated, lust springs up. If lust is overcome, ambition takes its place. If ambition is despised, anger exasperates, pride puffs up, wine-bibbing entices; envy breaks concord; jealousy cuts friendship; you are constrained to curse, which the divine law forbids; you are compelled to swear, which is not lawful. So many persecutions the soul suffers daily, with so many risks is the heart wearied; and yet it delights to abide here long among the devil's weapons, although it should rather be our craving and wish to hasten to Christ by the aid of a quicker death."[7] Again, in the same treatise he says: "The blessed Apostle Paul in his epistle lays it down, saying, 'To me to live is Christ, and to die is gain;'[8] counting the greatest gain no longer to be held by the snares of this world, no longer to be liable to the sins and vices of the flesh."[9] Moreover, on the Lord's Prayer, explaining what it is we ask when we say, "Hallowed be thy name," he says, among other matters: "For we have need of daily sanctification, that we, who daily fall away, may wash out our sins by continual sanctification."[10] Again, in the same treatise, when he would explain our saying, "Forgive us our debts," he says: "And how necessarily, how providently and salutarily, are we admonished that we are sinners, since we are compelled to entreat for our sins; and while pardon is asked for from God, the soul recalls its own consciousness of guilt. Lest any one should flatter himself as being innocent, and by exalting himself should more deeply perish, he is instructed and taught that he sins daily, in that he is bidden to entreat daily for his sins. Thus, moreover, John also in his epistle warns us, and says: 'If we say that we have no sin, we deceive ourselves, and the truth is not in us. But if we confess our sins, He is faithful and just to forgive us our sins.'"[11] Rightly, also, he proposed in his letter to Quirinus his own most absolute judgment on this subject, to which he subjoined the

---

[1] Prov. viii. 36.
[2] This assertion of the Pelagians was condemned in an African Council in 418.
[3] Prov. xx. 9.          [4] 1 John i. 8.

[5] Cyprian, work cited, ch. 2; *The Ante-Nicene Fathers*, vol. v. p. 476.
[6] *Ibid.*, p. 480.          [7] *Ibid.* work cited, chs. 3, 4, p. 470.
[8] Phil. i 21.               [9] Cyprian, *ibid.*
[10] Cyprian, work cited, ch. 9, p. 450.
[11] Cyprian, *ibid.* ch. 16 (XXII.), p. 453.

divine testimonies, "That no one is without filth and without sin."[1] There also he set down those testimonies by which original sin is confirmed, which these men endeavour to twist into I know not what new and evil meanings, whether what the holy Job says, "No one is pure from filth, not one even if his life be of one day upon the earth,"[2] or what is read in the Psalm, "Behold, I was conceived in iniquity; and in sins hath my mother nourished me in the womb."[3] To which testimonies, on account of those also who are already holy in mature age, since even they are not without filth and sin, he added also that word of the most blessed John, which he often mentions in many other places besides, "If we say that we have no sin, we deceive ourselves;"[4] and other passages of the same sentiment, which are asserted by all catholics, by way of opposing those "who deceive themselves, and the truth is not in them."

CHAP. 28.—CYPRIAN'S ORTHODOXY UNDOUBTED.

Let the Pelagians say, if they dare, that this man of God was perverted by the error of the Manicheans, in so praising the saints as yet to confess that no one in this life had attained to such a perfection of righteousness as to have no sin at all, confirming his judgment by the clear truth and divine authority of the canonical testimonies. For does he deny that in baptism all sins are forgiven, because he confesses that there remain frailty and infirmity, whence he says that we sin after baptism and even to the end of this life, having unceasing conflict with the vices of the flesh? Or did he not remember what the apostle said about the Church without spot, that he prescribed that no one ought so to flatter himself in respect of a pure and spotless heart as to trust in his own innocence, and think that no medicine needed to be applied to his wounds? I think that these new heretics may concede to this catholic man that he knew "that the Holy Spirit even in the old times aided good dispositions;" nay, even, what they themselves will not allow, that they could not have possessed good dispositions except through the Holy Spirit. I think that Cyprian knew that all the prophets and apostles or saints of any kind soever who pleased the Lord at any time were righteous —"not in comparison with the wicked," as they falsely assert that we say, "but by the rule of virtue," as they boast that they say; although Cyprian says, nevertheless, no one can be without sin, and whoever should assert that he is blameless is either proud or a fool. Nor is it with reference to anything else that he understands the Scripture, "Who shall boast that he has a pure heart? or who shall boast that he is pure from sins?"[5] I think that Cyprian would not have needed to be taught by such as these, what he very well knew, "that, in the time to come, there would be a reward of good works and a punishment of evil works, but that no one could then perform the commands which here he might have despised;" and yet he does not understand and assert the Apostle Paul, who was assuredly not a contemner of the divine commands, to have said, "To me to live is Christ, and to die is gain,"[6] on any other account, except that he reckoned it the greatest gain after this life no longer to be held in worldly entanglements, no longer to be obnoxious to the sins and vices of the flesh. Therefore the most blessed Cyprian felt, and in the truth of the divine Scriptures saw, that even the life of the apostles themselves, however good, holy, and righteous, suffered some involvements of worldly entanglements, was obnoxious to some sins and vices of the flesh; and that they desired death that they might be free from those evils, and that they might attain to that perfect righteousness which would not suffer such things, and which would no more have to be achieved in the way of command merely, but to be received in the way of reward. For not even when that shall have come for which we pray when we say, "Thy kingdom come," will there be in that kingdom of God no righteousness; since the apostle says, "The kingdom of God is not meat and drink, but righteousness, and peace, and joy in the Holy Ghost."[7] Certainly these three things are commanded among other divine precepts. Here righteousness is prescribed to us when it is said, "Do righteousness;"[8] peace is prescribed when it is said, "Have peace among yourselves;"[9] joy is prescribed when it is said, "Rejoice in the Lord always."[10] Let, then, the Pelagians deny that these things shall be in the kingdom of God, where we shall live without end; or let them be so mad, if it appears good, as to contend that righteousness, peace, and joy, will be such there as they are here to the righteous. But if they both shall be, and yet shall not be the same, assuredly here, in respect of the commandment of them, the doing is to be cared for, —there the perfection is to be hoped for in the way of reward; when, not being withheld by any earthly entanglements, and being liable to no sins and vices of the flesh (on account of which the apostle, as Cyprian received this testimony, said that to die would be to him gain), we may perfectly love God, the contemplation of whom will be face to face; we may also perfectly love our neighbour, since, when the thoughts of the heart are made manifest, no suspicion of any evil can disturb any one concerning any one.

---

[1] Cyprian, *Testimonies*, iii. 54: *The Ante-Nicene Fathers*, v. p 529    [2] Job xiv 4, 5.    [3] Ps li 5    [4] 1 John i. 8.    [5] Prov. xx. 9.    [6] Phil. ii. 21.    [7] Rom. xiv. 17.    [8] Isa. lvi. 1.    [9] Mark ix. 49.    [10] Phil. iv. 4.

CHAP. 29 [XI.] — THE TESTIMONIES OF AMBROSE AGAINST THE PELAGIANS, AND FIRST OF ALL CONCERNING ORIGINAL SIN.

But now also to the most glorious martyr Cyprian, let me add, for the sake of more amply confuting these men, the most blessed Ambrose; because even Pelagius praised him so much as to say that in his writings could be found nothing to be blamed even by his enemies.[1] Since, then, the Pelagians say that there is no original sin with which infants are born, and object to the catholics the guilt of the Manichean heresy, who withstand them on behalf of the most ancient faith of the Church, let this catholic man of God, Ambrose, praised even by Pelagius himself in the truth of the faith, answer them concerning this matter. When he was expounding the prophet Isaiah, he says: "Christ was, therefore, without spot, because He was not stained even in the usual condition itself of birth."[2] And in another place in the same work, speaking of the Apostle Peter, he says: "He offered himself, which he thought before to be sin, asking for himself that not only his feet but his head also should be washed, because he had directly understood that by the washing of the feet, for those who fell in the first man, the filth of the obnoxious succession was abolished."[2] Also in the same work he says: "It was preserved, therefore, that of a man and woman, that is, by that mingling of bodies, no one could be seen to be free from sin; but He who is free from sin is free also from this kind of conception." Also writing against the Novatians he says: "All of us men are born under sin. And our very origin is in corruption, as you have it read in the words of David,[3] 'For lo, I was conceived in iniquities; and in sins hath my mother brought me forth.'"[4] Also in the apology of the prophet David, he says: "Before we are born we are spotted with contagion, and before the use of light we receive the mischief of that origin. We are conceived in iniquity."[5] Also speaking of the Lord, he says: "It was certainly fitting that He who was not to have the sin of a bodily fall, should feel no natural contagion of generation. Rightly, therefore, David with weeping deplored in himself these defilements of nature, and the fact that the stain had begun in man before his life."[6] Again, in the Ark of Noah he says: "Therefore by one Lord Jesus the coming salvation is declared to the nations; for He only could be righteous, although every generation should go astray, nor for any other reason than that, being born of a virgin, He was not at all bound by the ordinance of a guilty generation. 'Behold,' he says, 'I was conceived in iniquities; and in sins has my mother brought me forth;'[7] he who was esteemed righteous beyond others so speaks. Whom, then, should I now call righteous unless Him who is free from those chains, whom the bonds of our common nature do not hold fast?"[8] Behold, this holy man, most approved, even by the witness of Pelagius, in the catholic faith, condemned the Pelagians who deny original sin with such evidence as this; and yet he does not with the Manicheans deny either God to be the Creator of those who are born, or condemn marriage, which God ordained and blessed.

CHAP. 30. — THE TESTIMONIES OF AMBROSE CONCERNING GOD'S GRACE.

The Pelagians say that merit begins from man by free will, to which God repays the subsequent aid of grace. Let the venerable Ambrose here also refute them, when he says, in his exposition of the prophet Isaiah, "that human care without divine help is powerless for healing, and needs a divine helper." Also, in the treatise which is inscribed, "On the Avoidance of the World,"[9] he says: "Our discourse is frequent on the avoidance of this world; and I wish that our disposition were as cautious and careful as our discourse is easy. But what is worse, the enticement of earthly lusts frequently creeps in, and the flowing forth of vanities takes hold of the mind, so that the very thing that you desire to avoid you think upon, and turn over in your mind; and this it is difficult for a man to beware of, but to get rid of it is impossible. Finally, that that is rather a matter to be wished than to be accomplished the prophet testifies when he says, 'Incline my heart unto thy testimonies, and not to avarice.'[10] For our heart and our thoughts are not in our power, seeing that they are suddenly forced forth and confuse the mind and the soul, and draw them in other directions from those which you have proposed for them; — they recall to things of time, they suggest worldly things, they obtrude voluptuous thoughts, they inweave seducing thoughts, and, in the very season in which we are proposing to lift up our mind, vain thoughts are intruded upon us, and we are cast down for the most part to things of earth; and who is so happy as always to rise upwards in his heart? And how can this be done without the divine help? Absolutely in no manner. Finally, of old Scripture says the same thing, 'Blessed is the man whose help is of Thee, O Lord; in his heart is going up.'"[11] What can be said more openly and more sufficiently? But lest the Pelagians perchance should answer that, in that very point in which divine help is

---

[1] See *On the Grace of Christ*, ch. 47.
[2] This work is not extant.
[3] Ps. li. 5.
[4] *On Penitence*, Book i. ch. 13.
[5] *Apology of the Prophet David*, ch. 56.
[6] *Ibid.* ch. 57.
[7] Ps. li. 5.
[8] *On Noah and the Ark*, ch. 7 (?).
[9] Work cited, ch. 1.
[10] Ps. cxix. 36.
[11] Ps. lxxxiv. 5 [LXX.].

asked for, man's merit precedes, saying that that very thing is merit, that by his prayer he is desiring that divine grace should come to his assistance, let them give heed to what the same holy man says in his exposition of Isaiah. He says : "And to pray God is a spiritual grace ; for no man says that Jesus is the Lord, except in the Holy Spirit." [1] Whence also, expounding the Gospel according to Luke, [2] he says : "You see certainly that everywhere the power of the Lord co-operates with human desires, so that no man can build without the Lord, no man can undertake anything without the Lord." Because such a man as Ambrose says this, and commends God's grace, as it is fitting for a son of promise to do, with grateful piety, does he therefore destroy free will? Or does he mean grace to be understood as the Pelagians in their different discourses will have to appear nothing but law —so that, for instance, God may be believed to help us not to do what we may know, but to know what we may do? If they think that such a man of God as this is of this mind, let them hear what he has said about the law itself. In the book "On the Avoidance of the World," he says : "The law could stop the mouth of all men ; it could not convert their mind." [3] In another place also, in the same treatise, he says : "The law condemns the deed ; it does not take away its wickedness." [4] Let them see that this faithful and catholic man agrees with the apostle who says, "Now we know that what things soever the law says, it says to those who are under the law : that every mouth may be stopped, and all the world may become guilty before God. Because by the law no flesh shall be justified in His sight." [5] For from that apostolic opinion Ambrose took and wrote these things.

CHAP. 31. — THE TESTIMONIES OF AMBROSE ON THE IMPERFECTION OF PRESENT RIGHTEOUSNESS.

But now, since the Pelagians say that there either are or have been righteous men in this life who have lived without any sin, to such an extent that the future life which is to be hoped for as a reward cannot be more advanced or more perfect, let Ambrose here also answer them and refute them. For, expounding Isaiah the Prophet in reference to what is written, "I have begotten and brought up children, and they have despised me," [6] he undertook to dispute concerning the generations which are of God, and in that argument he quoted the testimony of John when he says, "He that is born of God sinneth not." [7] And, treating the same very difficult question, he says : "Since in this world there is none who is free from sin ; since John himself says, 'If we say that we have not

sinned, we make Him a liar.' [8] But if 'they that are born of God sin not,' and if these words refer to those of them who are in the world, it is necessary that we should regard them as those numberless people who have obtained God's grace by the regeneration of the laver. But yet, when the prophet says, 'All things are waiting upon Thee, that Thou mayest give them meat in season. That Thou givest them they gather for themselves ; when Thou openest Thine hand, all things shall be filled with goodness. But when Thou turnest away Thy face, they shall be troubled : Thou shalt take away their breath, and they shall fail, and shall be turned into their dust. Thou shalt send forth Thy Spirit, and they shall be created : and Thou shalt renew the face of the earth,' [9] such things as these cannot seem to have been said of any time whatever but of that future time, in which there shall be a new earth and a new heaven. Therefore they shall be disturbed that they may take their beginning. 'And when Thou openest Thy hand all things shall be filled with goodness,' which is not easily characteristic of this age. For concerning this age what does Scripture say? 'There is none that doeth good, no, not one.' [10] If, therefore, there are different generations, — and here the very entrance into this life is the receiver of sins to such an extent that even he who begot should be despised ; while another generation does not receive sins ; — let us consider whether by any means there may not be a regeneration for us after the course of this life, — of which regeneration it is said, ' In the regeneration when the Son of man shall sit in the throne of His glory.' [11] For as that is called the regeneration of washing whereby we are renewed from the filth of sins washed away, so that seems to be called a regeneration by which we are purified from every stain of bodily materiality, and are regenerated in the pure sense of the soul to life eternal ; so that every quality of regeneration may be purer than of that washing, so that no suspicion of sins can fall either on a man's doings, or even on his very thoughts themselves." Moreover, in another place in the same work he says : "We see it to be impossible that any person created in a body can be absolutely spotless, since even Paul says that he is imperfect. For thus he has it : ' Not that I have already received, or am already perfect ; ' [12] and yet after a little he says, ' As many of us, therefore, as are perfect.' [13] Unless, perchance, there is one perfection in this world, another after this is completed, of which he says to the Corinthians, ' When that which is perfect is come ; ' [14] and elsewhere, ' Till we all

[1] 1 Cor. xii. 13.　　[2] *Commentary on Luke*, lib. ii. ch. 3, p. 84.　　[3] Ch. 15.　　[4] Ch. 29.　　[5] Rom. iii. 19, 20.　　[6] Isa. i. 2.　　[7] 1 John iii. 9.

[8] 1 John i. 10.　　[9] Ps. civ. 27, etc.　　[10] Ps. xiv. 1.　　[11] Matt. xix. 28.　　[12] Phil. iii. 12.　　[13] Phil. iii. 15.　　[14] 1 Cor. xiii. 10.

come into the unity of the faith, and the knowledge of the Son of God, into the perfect man, to the measure of the age of the fulness of Christ.'[1]  As, then, the apostle says that many are placed in this world who are perfect along with him, but who, if you have regard to true perfection, could not be perfect, since he says, 'We see now through a mirror, enigmatically; but then face to face : now I know in part; but then I shall know even as also I am known:'[2] so also there both are those who are 'spotless' in this world, and will be those who are 'spotless' in the kindom of God, although certainly, if you consider it accurately, no person can be spotless, because no person is without sin." Also in the same he says : "We see that, while we live in this life, we ought to purify ourselves and to seek God ; and to begin from the purification of our soul, and as it were to establish the foundations of virtue, so that we may deserve to attain the perfection of our purgation after this life."  And again, in the same he says : "But laden and groaning, who does not say, 'O wretched man that I am ! who shall deliver me from the body of this death?'[3]  So with the same teacher we give all varieties of interpretation.  For if he is unhappy who recognises himself as involved in the evils of the body, certainly everybody is unhappy ; for I should not call that man happy who, being confused with any darkness of his mind, does not know his own condition.  That, moreover, has not absurdly come to be understood ; for if a man who knows himself is unhappy, assuredly all are wretched, because every one either recognises his weakness by wisdom, or by folly is ignorant of it."  Moreover, in the treatise "On the Benefit of Death," he says :[4] "Let death work in us, in order that that may work life also, a good life after death, — that is, a good life after victory, a good life after the contest is finished ; so that now no longer the law of the flesh may know how to resist the law of the mind, that no longer we may have any contention with the body of death."  Again, in the same treatise he says : "Therefore, because the righteous have this reward, that they see the face of God, and that light which lightens every man, let us henceforth put on the desire of this kind of reward, that our soul may draw near to God, our prayer may draw near to Him, our desire may cleave to Him, that we be not separated from Him. And placed here as we are, let us by meditating, by reading, by seeking, be united with God.  Let us know Him as we can.  For we know Him in part here ; because here all things are imperfect, there all are perfect ; here we are infants, there we shall be strong men.  'We

see,' says he, 'now through a mirror in an enigma, but then face to face.'  Then, His face being revealed, we shall be allowed to look upon the glory of God, which now our souls, involved in the compacted dregs of this body, and shadowed by some stains and filth of this flesh, cannot clearly see.  'For who,' He says, 'shall see my face and live?' and rightly.  For if our eyes cannot bear the rays of the sun, — and if any one should gaze too long on the region of the sun he is said to be blinded, — if a creature cannot look upon a creature without deceit and offence, how can he without his own peril look upon the glittering face of the eternal Creator, covered as he is with the clothing of this body?  For who is justified in God's sight, when even the infant of one day cannot be pure from sin, and no one can boast of his integrity and pureness of heart?"

CHAP. 32 [XII.] — THE PELAGIAN'S HERESY AROSE LONG AFTER AMBROSE.

It would be too long if I were to seek to mention everything which the holy Ambrose said and wrote against this heresy of the Pelagians, which was to arise so long afterwards ; not indeed with a view to answer them, but with a view to declare the catholic faith, and to build up men in it.  Moreover, I neither could nor ought to mention all those things which Cyprian, most glorious in the Lord, wrote in his letters, whereby it is shown how this which we hold is the true and truly Christian and catholic faith, as it was delivered of old by the Holy Scriptures, and so retained and kept by our fathers and even to this time, in which these heretics have attempted to destroy it, and as it will hereafter by God's good will be retained and kept.  For that these things and things of this kind were thus delivered to Cyprian, and by Cyprian, is testified by the testimonies produced from his letters ; and that thus they were maintained up to our times is shown by these things which Ambrose wrote about these matters before these heretics had begun to rage, and catholic ears had shuddered at their profane novelties which are everywhere ; and that thus, moreover, they shall be maintained hereafter, was declared with sufficient vigour partly by the condemnation of such opinions as these, partly by their correction.  For whatever they may dare to mutter against the sound faith of Cyprian and Ambrose, I do not think that they will break out into such a madness as to dare to call those noted and memorable men of God, Manicheans.

CHAP. 33. — OPPOSITION OF THE MANICHEAN AND CATHOLIC DOGMAS.

What is it, then, which in their raging blindness of mind they are now spreading about,[5]

---

[1] Eph. iv. 13.   [2] 1 Cor. xiii. 12.   [3] Rom. vii. 24.
[4] Work cited, chs. 9, 49.

[5] See above, ch. 20.

" that almost throughout the entire West a dogma not less foolish than impious is taken up ; " when by the mercy of God and by His merciful governance of His Church, the catholic faith has been so watchful that the dogma, "not less foolish than wicked," as of the Manicheans, so also of these heretics, should not be taken up? So holy and learned catholic men, such as are attested to be so by the report of the whole Church, praise both God's creation, and marriage as ordained by Him, and the law given by Him by means of the holy Moses, and the free will implanted into man's nature, and the holy patriarchs and prophets, with due and fitting proclamation ; all which five things the Manicheans condemn, partly by denying, and partly also by abominating. Whence it appears that these catholic doctors were far removed from the notions of the Manicheans, and yet they assert original sin ; they assert God's grace above free will, as antecedent to all merit, so as truly to afford a gratuitous divine assistance ; they assert that the saints lived righteously in this flesh, in such wise that the help of prayer was necessary to them, by which their daily sins might be forgiven ; and that a perfected righteousness which could not have sin would be in another life the reward of those who should live righteously here.

CHAP. 34. — THE CALLING TOGETHER OF A SYNOD NOT ALWAYS NECESSARY TO THE CONDEMNATION OF HERESIES.

What is it, then, that they say, that "subscription was extorted from simple bishops sitting in their places without any Synodal congregation "? Was subscription extorted against such heretics as these from the most blessed and excellent men in the faith, Cyprian and Ambrose, before such heretics as these were in existence ? — seeing that they overthrow their impious dogmas with such clearness that we can scarcely find anything more manifest to say against them. Or, indeed, was there any need of the congregation of a Synod to condemn this open pest, as if no heresy could at any time be condemned except by a Synodal congregation? — when, on the contrary, very few heresies can be found for the sake of condemning which any such necessity has arisen ; and those have been many and incomparably more which have deserved to be accused and condemned in the place where they arose, and thence could be known and avoided over the rest of the lands. But the pride of such as these, which lifts itself up so much against God as not to be willing to glory in Him but rather in free will, is understood as grasping also at this glory, that a Synod of the East and West should be gathered together on their account. In fact, they endeavour, forsooth, to disturb the catholic world, because, the Lord being against them, they are unable to pervert it ; when rather they ought to have been trodden out wherever those wolves might have appeared, by watchfulness and pastoral diligence, after a competent and sufficient judgment made concerning them ; whether with a view of their being healed and changed, or with a view of their being shunned by the safety and soundness of others, by the help of the Shepherd of the sheep, who seeks the lost sheep also among the little ones, who makes the sheep holy and righteous freely ; who both providently instructs them, although sanctified and justified, yet in their frailty and infirmity to pray for a daily remission for their daily sins, without which no one lives in this world, even although he may live well ; and mercifully listens to their prayers.

# A TREATISE ON GRACE AND FREE WILL.

# EXTRACT FROM AUGUSTIN'S "RETRACTATIONS,"

## BOOK II. CHAP. 66,

### ON THE FOLLOWING TREATISE,

## "DE GRATIA ET LIBERO ARBITRIO."

---

THERE are some persons who suppose that the freedom of the will is denied whenever God's grace is maintained, and who on their side defend their liberty of will so peremptorily as to deny the grace of God. This grace, as they assert, is bestowed according to our own merits. It is in consequence of their opinions that I wrote the book entitled *On Grace and Free Will.* This work I addressed to the monks of Adrumetum,[1] in whose monastry first arose the controversy on that subject, and that in such a manner that some of them were obliged to consult me thereon. The work begins with these words: "With reference to those persons who so preach the liberty of the human will."

---

[1] Adrumetum, a maritime city of Africa, was the metropolis of the Province of Byzacium, as Procopius informs us, *De Aedificiis*.

*Justiniani* VI. It was in a monastery here that the monks resided for whose instruction Augustin composed the two following treatises, — the former entitled *De Gratiâ et Libero Arbitrio,* and the latter *De Correptione et Gratiâ,* in the year of Christ 426 or 427. In our opinion, no later date can be well assigned to these writings, inasmuch as they are mentioned in *The Retractations,* which was published about the year 427; nor can they be placed earlier in date, because they are in that work mentioned the very last.

# TWO LETTERS WRITTEN BY AUGUSTIN TO VALENTINUS AND THE MONKS OF ADRUMETUM,

## AND FORWARDED[1] WITH THE FOLLOWING TREATISE.

---

## LETTER I.

### [*The 214th of Augustin's Epistles.*]

TO MY VERY DEAR LORD AND MOST HONOURED BROTHER AMONG THE MEMBERS OF CHRIST, VALENTINUS, AND TO THE BRETHREN THAT ARE WITH YOU, AUGUSTIN SENDS GREETING IN THE LORD.

1. Two young men, Cresconius and Felix, have found their way to us, and, introducing themselves as belonging to your brotherhood, have told us that your monastery was disturbed with no small commotion, because certain amongst you preach grace in such a manner as to deny that the will of man is free; and maintain — a more serious matter — that in the day of judgment God will not render to every man according to his works.[2] At the same time, they have pointed out to us, that many of you do not entertain this opinion, but allow that free will is assisted by the grace of God, so as that we may think and do aright; so that, when the Lord shall come to render unto every man according to his works,[2] He shall find those works of ours good which God has prepared in order that we may walk in them.[3] They who think this think rightly.

2. "I beseech you therefore, brethren," even as the apostle besought the Corinthians, "by the name of our Lord Jesus Christ, that ye all speak the same thing, and that there be no divisions among you." For, in the first place, the Lord Jesus, as it is written in the Gospel of the Apostle John, "came not to condemn the world, but that the world by Himself might be saved."[4] Then, afterwards, as the Apostle Paul writes, "God shall judge the world[5] when He shall come," as the whole Church confesses in the Creed, "to judge the quick and the dead." Now, I would ask, if there is no grace of God, how does He save the world? and if there is no free will, how does He judge the world? That book of mine, therefore, or epistle, which the above-mentioned brethren have brought with them to you, I wish you to understand in accordance with this faith, so that you may neither deny God's grace, nor uphold free will in such wise as to separate the latter from the grace of God, as if without this we could by any means either think or do anything according to God, — which is quite beyond our power. On this account, indeed, it is, that the Lord when speaking of the fruits of righteousness said, "Without me ye can do nothing."[6]

3. From this you may understand why I wrote the letter which has been referred to,[7] to Sixtus, presbyter of the Church at Rome, against the new Pelagian heretics, who say that the grace of God is bestowed according to our own merits, so that he who glories has to glory not in the Lord, but in himself, — that is to say, in man, not in the Lord. This, however, the apostle forbids in these words: "Let no man glory in man;"[8] while in another passage he says, "He that glorieth let him glory in the Lord."[9] But these heretics, under the idea that they are justified by their own selves, just as if God did not bestow on them this gift, but they themselves obtained it by themselves, glory of course in themselves, and not in the Lord. Now, the apostle says to such, "Who maketh thee to differ from another?"[10] and this he does on the ground that out of the mass of perdition which arose from Adam, none but God distinguishes a man to make him a vessel to honour, and not to dishonour.[11] Lest, however, the carnal man in his foolish pride should, on hearing the question, "Who maketh thee to differ

---

[1] See the Second Letter, ch. 2.  [2] See Matt. xvi. 17, and Rom. ii. 6.  [3] Eph. ii. 10.  [4] John iii. 17.  [5] Rom. iii. 6.
[6] John xv. 5.  [7] *Ep.* 194.  [8] 1 Cor. iii. 21.  [9] 1 Cor. i. 31, and 2 Cor. x. 17.
[10] 1 Cor. iv. 7.  [11] Rom. ix. 21.

from another?" either in thought or in word answer and say: My faith, or my prayer, or my righteousness makes me to differ from other men, the apostle at once adds these words to the question, and so meets all such notions, saying, " What hast thou that thou didst not receive? now, if thou didst receive it, why dost thou glory, as if thou didst not receive it?"[1] Now, they boast as if they did not receive their gifts by grace, who think that they are justified of their own selves, and who, on this account, glory in themselves, and not in the Lord.

4. Therefore I have in this letter, which has reached you, shown by passages of Holy Scripture, which you can examine for yourselves, that our good works and pious prayers and right faith could not possibly have been in us unless we had received them all from Him, concerning whom the Apostle James says, " Every good gift and every perfect gift is from above, and cometh down from the Father of lights."[2] And so no man can say that it is by the merit of his own works, or by the merit of his own prayers, or by the merit of his own faith, that God's grace has been conferred upon him; nor suppose that the doctrine is true which those heretics hold, that the grace of God is given us in proportion to our own merit. This is altogether a most erroneous opinion; not, indeed, because there is no desert, good in pious persons, or evil in impious ones (for how else shall God judge the world?),[3] but because a man is converted by that mercy and grace of God, of which the Psalmist says, " As for my God, His mercy shall prevent me;"[4] so that the unrighteous man is justified, that is, becomes just instead of impious, and begins to possess that good desert which God will crown when the world shall be judged.

5. There were many things which I wanted to send you, by the perusal whereof you would have been able to gain a more exact and full knowledge of all that has been done by the bishops in their councils against these Pelagian heretics. But the brethren were in haste who came to us from your company. By them we have sent you this letter; which is, however, not an answer to any communication, because, in truth, they brought us no epistle from your beloved selves. Yet we had no hesitation in receiving them; for their simple manners proved to us clearly enough that there could have been nothing unreal or deceptive in their visit to us. They were, however, in much haste, as wishing to spend Easter at home with you; and my earnest prayer is, that so sacred a day may, by the Lord's help, bring peace to you, and not dissension.

6. You will, indeed, take the better course (as I earnestly request you), if you will not refuse to send to me the very person by whom they say they have been disturbed. For either he does not understand my book, or else, perhaps, he is himself misunderstood, when he endeavours to solve and explain a question which is a very difficult one, and intelligible to few. For it is none other than the question of God's grace which has caused persons of no understanding to think that the Apostle Paul prescribes it to us as a rule, " Let us do evil that good may come."[5] It is in reference to these that the Apostle Peter writes in his second Epistle: " Wherefore, beloved, seeing that ye look for such things, be diligent, that ye may be found of Him in peace, without spot and blameless and account that the long-suffering of our Lord is salvation; even as our beloved brother Paul also, according to the wisdom given unto him, hath written unto you; as also in all his epistles, speaking in them of these things: in which are some things hard to be understood, which they that are unlearned and unstable wrest, as they do also the other Scriptures, unto their own destruction."[6]

7. Take good heed, then, to these fearful words of the great apostle; and when you feel that you do not understand, put your faith in the meanwhile in the inspired word of God, and believe both that man's will is free, and that there is also God's grace, without whose help man's free will can neither be turned towards God, nor make any progress in God. And what you piously believe, that pray that you may have a wise understanding of. And, indeed, it is for this very purpose, — that is, that we may have a wise understanding, that there is a free will. For unless we understood and were wise with a free will, it would not be enjoined to us in the words of Scripture, " Understand now, ye simple among the people; and ye fools, at length be wise."[7] The very precept and injunction which calls on us to be intelligent and wise, requires also our obedience; and we could exercise no obedience without free will. But if it were in our power to obey this precept to be understanding and wise by free will, without the help of God's grace, it would be unnecessary to say to God, " Give me understanding, that I may learn Thy commandments;"[8] nor would it have been written in the gospel, " Then opened He their understanding, that they might understand the Scriptures;"[9] nor should the Apostle James address us in such words as, " If any of you lack wisdom, let him ask of God, who giveth to all men liberally, and upbraideth not; and it shall be given him."[10] But the Lord is able to grant, both to you and to us, that we may rejoice over very speedy tidings of your peace and pious unanimity. I send you greeting, not in my own name only, but of the brethren also who are with me; and I ask you to pray for us with one accord and with all earnestness. The Lord be with you.

---

[1] 1 Cor. iv. 7.   [2] Jas. i. 17.   [3] Rom. iii. 6.   [4] Ps. lix. 10.   [5] Rom. iii. 8.
[6] 2 Pet. iii. 14–16.   [7] Ps. xciv. 8.   [8] Ps. cxix. 73.   [9] Luke xxiv. 45.   [10] Jas. i. 5.

# LETTER II.

### [*The 215th of Augustin's Epistles.*]

TO MY VERY DEAR LORD AND MOST HONOURED BROTHER AMONG THE MEMBERS OF CHRIST, VALENTINUS, AND TO THE BRETHREN THAT ARE WITH YOU, AUGUSTIN SENDS GREETING IN THE LORD.

1. THAT Cresconius and Felix, and another Felix, the servants of God, who came to us from your brother-hood, have spent Easter with us is known to your Love.[1] We have detained them somewhile longer in order that they might return to you better instructed against the new Pelagian heretics, into whose error every one falls who supposes that it is according to any human merits that the grace of God is given to us, which alone delivers a man through Jesus Christ our Lord. But he, too, is no less in error who thinks that, when the Lord shall come to judgment, a man is not judged according to his works who has been able to use throughout his life free choice of will. For only infants, who have not yet done any works of their own, either good or bad, will be condemned on account of original sin alone, when they have not been delivered by the Saviour's grace in the laver of regeneration. As for all others who, in the use of their free will, have added to original sin, sins of their own commission, but who have not been delivered by God's grace from the power of darkness and removed into the kingdom of Christ, they will receive judgment according to the deserts not of their original sin only, but also of the acts of their own will. The good, indeed, shall receive their reward according to the merits of their own good-will, but then they received this very good-will through the grace of God; and thus is accomplished that sentence of Scripture, "Indignation and wrath, tribulation and anguish, upon every soul of man that doeth evil, of the Jew first, and also of the Gentile: but glory, honour, and peace to every man that worketh good; to the Jew first, and also to the Gentile."[2]

2. Touching the very difficult question of will and grace, I have felt no need of treating it further in this letter, having given them another letter also when they were about to return in greater haste. I have written a book likewise for you,[3] and if you, by the Lord's help, read it, and have a lively understanding of it, I think that no further dissension on this subject will arise among you. They take with them other documents besides, which, as we supposed, ought to be sent to you, in order that from these you may ascertain what means the catholic Church has adopted for repelling, in God's mercy, the poison of the Pelagian heresy. For the letters to Pope Innocent, Bishop of Rome, from the Council of the province of Carthage, and from the Council of Numidia, and one written with exceeding care by five bishops, and what he wrote back to these three; our letter also to Pope Zosimus about the African Council, and his answer addressed to all bishops throughout the world; and a brief constitution, which we drew up against the error itself at a later plenary Council of all Africa; and the above-mentioned book of mine, which I have just written for you, — all these we have both read over with them, while they were with us, and have now despatched by their hands to you.[4]

3. Furthermore, we have read to them the work of the most blessed martyr Cyprian on the Lord's Prayer, and have pointed out to them how He taught that all things pertaining to our morals, which constitute right living, must be sought from our Father which is in heaven, lest, by presuming on free will, we fall from divine grace. From the same treatise we have also shown them how the same glorious martyr has taught us that it behoves us to pray even for our enemies who have not yet believed in Christ, that they may believe; which would of course be all in vain unless the Church believed that even the evil and unbelieving wills of men might, by the grace of God, be converted to good. This book of St. Cyprian, however, we have not sent you, because they told us that you possessed it among yourselves already. My letter, also, which had been sent to Sixtus, presbyter of the Church at Rome,[5] and which they brought with them to us, we read over with them, and pointed out how that it had been written in opposition to those who say that God's grace is bestowed according to our merits, — that is to say, in opposition to the same Pelagians.

4. As far, then, as lay in our power, we have used our influence with them, as both your brethren and our own, with a view to their persevering in the soundness of the catholic faith, which neither denies free will whether for an evil or a good life, nor attributes to it so much power that it can avail anything without God's grace, whether that it may be changed from evil to good, or that it may persevere in the pursuit of good, or that it may attain to eternal good when there is no further fear of failure. To yourselves, too, my most dearly beloved, I also, in this letter, give the same exhortation which the apostle addresses to us all, "not to think

---

[1] The phrase of Christian salutation, *vestra caritas* which may be rendered "your loving or beloved selves;" it is a parallel phrase with the more familiar one to modern ears, "Your Honour."

[2] Rom. ii. 8, 9.   [3] The following treatise is here referred to, — *On Grace and Free Will.*

[4] See *Epp.* 175-177, and 181-183.   [5] *Ep.* 194.

of yourselves more highly than you ought to think; but to think soberly, according as God hath dealt to every man the measure of faith."[1]

5. Mark well the counsel which the Holy Ghost gives us by Solomon: "Make straight paths for thy feet, and order thy ways aright. Turn not aside to the right hand nor to the left, but turn away thy foot from the evil way; for the Lord knoweth the ways on the right hand, but those on the left are perverse. He will make thy ways straight, and will direct thy steps in peace."[2] Now consider, my brethren, that in these words of Holy Scripture, if there were no free will, it would not be said, "Make straight paths for thy feet, and order thy ways; turn not aside to the right hand, nor to the left." Nor yet, were this possible for us to achieve without the grace of God, would it be afterwards added, "He will make thy ways straight, and will direct thy steps in peace."

6. Decline, therefore, neither to the right hand nor to the left, although the paths on the right hand are praised, and those on the left hand are blamed. This is why he added, "Turn away thy foot from the evil way," —that is, from the left-hand path. This he makes manifest in the following words, saying, "For the Lord knoweth the ways on the right hand; but those on the left are perverse." In those ways we ought surely to walk which the Lord knows; and it is of these that we read in the Psalm, "The Lord knoweth the way of the righteous, but the way of the ungodly shall perish;"[3] for this way, which is on the left hand, the Lord does not know. As He will also say at last to such as are placed on His left hand at the day of judgment: "I know you not."[4] Now what is that which He knows not, who knows all things, both good and evil, in man? But what is the meaning of the words, "I know you not," unless it be that you are now such as I never made you? Precisely as that passage runs, which is spoken of the Lord Jesus Christ, that "He knew no sin."[5] How knew it not, except that He had never made it? And, therefore, how is to be understood the passage, "The ways which are on the right hand the Lord knoweth," except in the sense that He made those ways Himself, — even "the paths of the righteous," which no doubt are "those good works that God," as the apostle tells us, "hath before ordained that we should walk in them"?[6] Whereas the left-hand ways — those perverse paths of the unrighteous — He truly knows nothing of, because He never made them for man, but man made them for himself. Wherefore He says, "The perverse ways of the wicked I utterly abhor; they are on the left hand."

7. But the reply is made: Why did He say, "Turn not aside to the right hand, nor to the left," when he clearly ought rather to have said, Keep to the right hand, and turn not off to the left, if the right-hand paths are good? Why, do we think, except this, that the paths on the right hand are so good that it is not good to turn off from them, even to the right? For that man, indeed, is to be understood as declining to the right who chooses to attribute to himself, and not to God, even those good works which appertain to right-hand ways. Hence it was that after saying, "For the Lord knoweth the ways on the right hand, but those on the left hand are perverse," as if the objection were raised to Him, Wherefore, then, do you not wish us to turn aside to the right? He immediately added as follows: "He will Himself make thy paths straight, and will direct thy ways in peace." Understand, therefore, the precept, "Make straight paths for thy feet, and order thy ways aright," in such a sense as to know that whenever you do all this, it is the Lord God who enables you to do it. Then you will not turn off to the right, although you are walking in right-hand paths, not trusting in your own strength; and He will Himself be your strength, who will make straight paths for your feet, and will direct your ways in peace.

8. Wherefore, most dearly beloved, whosoever says, My will suffices for me to perform good works, declines to the right. But, on the other hand, they who think that a good way of life should be forsaken, when they hear God's grace so preached as to lead to the supposition and belief that it of itself makes men's wills from evil to good, and it even of itself keeps them what it has made them; and who, as the result of this opinion, go on to say, "Let us do evil that good may come,"[7] —these persons decline to the left. This is the reason why he said to you, "Turn not aside to the right hand, nor to the left;" in other words, do not uphold free will in such wise as to attribute good works to it without the grace of God, nor so defend and maintain grace as if, by reason of it, you may love evil works in security and safety, —which may God's grace itself avert from you! Now it was the words of such as these which the apostle had in view when he said, "What shall we say, then? Shall we continue in sin that grace may abound?"[8] And to this cavil of erring men, who know nothing about the grace of God, he returned such an answer as he ought in these words: "God forbid. How shall we, that are dead to sin, live any longer therein?" Nothing could have been said more succinctly, and yet to the point. For what more useful gift does the grace of God confer upon us, in this present evil world, than our dying unto sin? Hence he shows himself ungrateful to grace itself who chooses to live in sin by reason of that whereby we die unto sin. May God, however, who is rich in mercy, grant you both to think soundly and wisely, and to continue perseveringly and progressively to the end in every good determination and purpose. For yourselves, for us, for all who love you, and for those who hate you, pray that this gift may be attained, — pray earnestly and vigilantly in brotherly peace. Live unto God. If I deserve any favour at your hands, let brother Florus come to me.

---

[1] Rom. xii. 3.  [2] Prov. iv. 26, 27.  [3] Ps. i. 6.  [4] Matt. vii. 23.  [5] 2 Cor. v. 21.
[6] Eph. ii. 10.  [7] Rom. iii. 8.  [8] Rom. vi. 1, 2.

# CONTENTS OF THE TREATISE "ON GRACE AND FREE WILL."

# A TREATISE ON GRACE AND FREE WILL,

### *BY AURELIUS AUGUSTIN, BISHOP OF HIPPO;*

## ADDRESSED TO VALENTINUS AND THE MONKS OF ADRUMETUM, AND COMPLETED IN ONE BOOK.

### WRITTEN IN A.D. 426 OR A.D. 427.

---

IN THIS TREATISE AUGUSTIN TEACHES US TO BEWARE OF MAINTAINING GRACE BY DENYING FREE WILL, OR FREE WILL BY DENYING GRACE; FOR THAT IT IS EVIDENT FROM THE TESTIMONY OF SCRIPTURE THAT THERE IS IN MAN A FREE CHOICE OF WILL; AND THERE ARE ALSO IN THE SAME SCRIPTURES INSPIRED PROOFS GIVEN OF THAT VERY GRACE OF GOD WITHOUT WHICH WE CAN DO NOTHING GOOD. AFTERWARDS, IN OPPOSITION TO THE PELAGIANS, HE PROVES THAT GRACE IS NOT BESTOWED ACCORDING TO OUR MERITS. HE EXPLAINS HOW ETERNAL LIFE, WHICH IS RENDERED TO GOOD WORKS, IS REALLY OF GRACE. HE THEN GOES ON TO SHOW THAT THE GRACE WHICH IS GIVEN TO US THROUGH OUR LORD JESUS CHRIST IS NEITHER THE KNOWLEDGE OF THE LAW, NOR NATURE, NOR SIMPLY REMISSION OF SINS; BUT THAT IT IS GRACE THAT MAKES US FULFIL THE LAW, AND CAUSES NATURE TO BE LIBERATED FROM THE DOMINION OF SIN. HE DEMOLISHES THAT VAIN SUBTERFUGE OF THE PELAGIANS, TO THE EFFECT THAT "GRACE, ALTHOUGH IT IS NOT BESTOWED ACCORDING TO THE MERITS OF GOOD WORKS, IS YET GIVEN ACCORDING TO THE MERITS OF THE ANTECEDENT GOOD-WILL OF THE MAN WHO BELIEVES AND PRAYS." HE INCIDENTALLY TOUCHES THE QUESTION, WHY GOD COMMANDS WHAT HE MEANS HIMSELF TO GIVE, AND WHETHER HE IMPOSES ON US ANY COMMANDS WHICH WE ARE UNABLE TO PERFORM. HE CLEARLY SHOWS THAT THE LOVE WHICH IS INDISPENSABLE FOR FULFILLING THE COMMANDMENTS IS ONLY WITHIN US FROM GOD HIMSELF. HE POINTS OUT THAT GOD WORKS IN MEN'S HEARTS TO INCLINE THEIR WILLS WHITHERSOEVER HE WILLETH, EITHER TO GOOD WORKS ACCORDING TO HIS MERCY, OR TO EVIL ONES IN RETURN FOR THEIR DESERVING; HIS JUDGMENT, INDEED, BEING SOMETIMES MANIFEST, SOMETIMES HIDDEN, BUT ALWAYS RIGHTEOUS. LASTLY, HE TEACHES US THAT A CLEAR EXAMPLE OF THE GRATUITOUSNESS OF GRACE, NOT GIVEN IN RETURN FOR OUR DESERTS, IS SUPPLIED TO US IN THE CASE OF THOSE INFANTS WHICH ARE SAVED, WHILE OTHERS PERISH THOUGH THEIR CASE IS IDENTICAL WITH THAT OF THE REST.

CHAP. I [I.] — THE OCCASION AND ARGUMENT OF THIS WORK.

WITH reference to those persons who so preach and defend man's free will, as boldly to deny, and endeavour to do away with, the grace of God which calls us to Him, and delivers us from our evil deserts, and by which we obtain the good deserts which lead to everlasting life: we have already said a good deal in discussion, and committed it to writing, so far as the Lord has vouchsafed to enable us. But since there are some persons who so defend God's grace as to deny man's free will, or who suppose that free will is denied when grace is defended, I have determined to write somewhat on this point to your Love,[1] my brother Valentinus, and the rest of you, who are serving God together under the impulse of a mutual love. For it has been told me concerning you, brethren, by some members of your brotherhood who have visited us, and are the bearers of this communication of ours to you, that there are dissensions among you on this subject. This, then, being the case, dearly beloved, that you be not disturbed by the obscurity of this question, I counsel you first to thank God for such things as you understand; but as for all which is beyond the reach of your mind, pray for understanding from the Lord, observing, at the same time, peace and love among yourselves; and until He Himself lead you to perceive what at present is beyond your comprehension, walk firmly on the ground of which you are sure. This is the advice of the Apostle Paul, who, after saying that he was not yet perfect,[2] a little later adds, " Let us, therefore, as many as are perfect, be thus minded,"[3] — meaning perfect to a certain extent, but not having attained to a perfection sufficient for us; and then immediately adds, " And if, in any thing, ye be otherwise minded, God shall reveal even this unto you. Nevertheless, whereunto we have already attained, let us walk by the same rule."[4] For by walking in what we have attained, we shall be able to advance to what we have not yet attained, — God revealing it to us if in anything we are otherwise minded, — provided we do not give up what He has already revealed.

CHAP. 2 [II.].— HE PROVES THE EXISTENCE OF FREE WILL IN MAN FROM THE PRECEPTS ADDRESSED TO HIM BY GOD.

Now He has revealed to us, through His Holy Scriptures, that there is in a man a free choice of will. But how He has revealed this I do not recount in human language, but in divine. There is, to begin with, the fact that God's precepts themselves would be of no use to a man unless he had free choice of will, so that by performing them he might obtain the promised rewards. For they are given that no one might be able to plead the excuse of ignorance, as the Lord says concerning the Jews in the gospel: " If I had not come and spoken unto them, they would not have sin; but now they have no excuse for their sin."[5] Of what sin does He speak but of that great one which He foreknew, while speaking thus, that they would make their own — that is, the death they were going to inflict upon Him? For they did not have " no sin " before Christ came to them in the flesh.

The apostle also says : " The wrath of God is revealed from heaven against all ungodliness and unrighteousness of men who hold back the truth in unrighteousness; because that which may be known of God is manifest in them; for God hath showed it unto them. For the invisible things of Him are from the creation of the world clearly seen — being understood by the things that are made — even His eternal power and Godhead, so that they are inexcusable."[6] In what sense does he pronounce them to be " inexcusable," except with reference to such excuse as human pride is apt to allege in such words as, " If I had only known, I would have done it; did I not fail to do it because I was ignorant of it?" or, " I would do it if I knew how; but I do not know, therefore I do not do it"? All such excuse is removed from them when the precept is given them, or the knowledge is made manifest to them how to avoid sin.

CHAP. 3. — SINNERS ARE CONVICTED WHEN ATTEMPTING TO EXCUSE THEMSELVES BY BLAMING GOD, BECAUSE THEY HAVE FREE WILL.

There are, however, persons who attempt to find excuse for themselves even from God. The Apostle James says to such : " Let no man say when he is tempted, I am tempted of God; for God cannot be tempted with evil, neither tempteth He any man. But every man is tempted when he is drawn away of his own lust, and enticed. Then, when lust hath conceived, it bringeth forth sin : and sin, when it is finished, bringeth forth death."[7] Solomon, too, in his book of Proverbs, has this answer for such as wish to find an excuse for themselves from God Himself: " The folly of a man spoils his ways; but he blames God in his heart."[8] And in the book of Ecclesiasticus we read : " Say not thou, It is through the Lord that I fell away; for thou oughtest not to do the things that He hateth : nor do thou say, He hath caused me to err; for He hath no need of the sinful man. The Lord hateth all abomination, and they that fear God love it not. He Himself made man from the beginning, and left him in the hand of His counsel. If thou be willing, thou shalt keep His commandments, and perform true fidelity. He hath set fire and water before thee : stretch forth thine hand unto whether thou wilt. Before man is life and death, and whichsoever pleaseth him shall be given to him."[9] Observe how very plainly is set before our view the free choice of the human will.

CHAP. 4. — THE DIVINE COMMANDS WHICH ARE MOST SUITED TO THE WILL ITSELF ILLUSTRATE ITS FREEDOM.

What is the import of the fact that in so many

---

[1] A form of address, like "your Honour."    [2] Phil. iii. 12.
[3] Phil iii. 15.    [4] Phil. iii. 16.    [5] John xv. 22.
[6] Rom. i. 18-20.    [7] Jas. i. 13-15.    [8] Prov. xix. 3.
[9] Ecclus. xv. 11-17.

passages God requires all His commandments to be kept and fulfilled? How does He make this requisition, if there is no free will? What means "the happy man," of whom the Psalmist says that "his will has been the law of the Lord"?[1] Does he not clearly enough show that a man by his own will takes his stand in the law of God? Then again, there are so many commandments which in some way are expressly adapted to the human will; for instance, there is, "Be not overcome of evil,"[2] and others of similar import, such as, "Be not like a horse or a mule, which have no understanding;"[3] and, "Reject not the counsels of thy mother;"[4] and, "Be not wise in thine own conceit;"[5] and, "Despise not the chastening of the Lord;"[6] and, "Forget not my law;"[7] and, "Forbear not to do good to the poor;"[8] and, "Devise not evil against thy friend;"[9] and, "Give no heed to a worthless woman;"[10] and, "He is not inclined to understand how to do good;"[11] and, "They refused to attend to my counsel;"[12] with numberless other passages of the inspired Scriptures of the Old Testament. And what do they all show us but the free choice of the human will? So, again, in the evangelical and apostolic books of the New Testament what other lesson is taught us? As when it is said, "Lay not up for yourselves treasures upon earth;"[13] and, "Fear not them which kill the body;"[14] and, "If any man will come after me, let him deny himself;"[15] and again, "Peace on earth to men of good will."[16] So also that the Apostle Paul says: "Let him do what he willeth; he sinneth not if he marry. Nevertheless, he that standeth stedfast in his heart, having no necessity, but hath power over his own will, and hath so decreed in his heart that he will keep his virgin, doeth well."[17] And so again, "If I do this willingly, I have a reward;"[18] while in another passage he says, "Be ye sober and righteous, and sin not;"[19] and again, "As ye have a readiness to will, so also let there be a prompt performance;"[20] then he remarks to Timothy about the younger widows, "When they have begun to wax wanton against Christ, they choose to marry." So in another passage, "All that will to live godly in Christ Jesus shall suffer persecution;"[21] while to Timothy himself he says, "Neglect not the gift that is in thee."[22] Then to Philemon he addresses this explanation: "That thy benefit should not be as it were of necessity, but of thine own will."[23] Servants also he advises to obey their masters "with a good will."[24] In strict accordance with

this, James says: "Do not err, my beloved brethren . . . and have not the faith of our Lord Jesus Christ with respect to persons;"[25] and, "Do not speak evil one of another."[26] So also John in his Epistle writes, "Do not love the world,"[27] and other things of the same import. Now wherever it is said, "Do not do this," and "Do not do that," and wherever there is any requirement in the divine admonitions for the work of the will to do anything, or to refrain from doing anything, there is at once a sufficient proof of free will. No man, therefore, when he sins, can in his heart blame God for it, but every man must impute the fault to himself. Nor does it detract at all from a man's own will when he performs any act in accordance with God. Indeed, a work is then to be pronounced a good one when a person does it willingly; then, too, may the reward of a good work be hoped for from Him concerning whom it is written, "He shall reward every man according to his works."[28]

CHAP. 5. — HE SHOWS THAT IGNORANCE AFFORDS NO SUCH EXCUSE AS SHALL FREE THE OFFENDER FROM PUNISHMENT; BUT THAT TO SIN WITH KNOWLEDGE IS A GRAVER THING THAN TO SIN IN IGNORANCE.

The excuse such as men are in the habit of alleging from ignorance is taken away from those persons who know God's commandments. But neither will those be without punishment who know not the law of God. "For as many as have sinned without law shall also perish without law; and as many as have sinned in the law shall be judged by the law."[29] Now the apostle does not appear to me to have said this as if he meant that they would have to suffer something worse who in their sins are ignorant of the law than they who know it. [III.] It is seemingly worse, no doubt, "to perish" than "to be judged;" but inasmuch as he was speaking of the Gentiles and of the Jews when he used these words, because the former were without the law, but the latter had received the law, who can venture to say that the Jews who sin in the law will not perish, since they refused to believe in Christ, when it was of them that the apostle said, "They shall be judged by the law"? For without faith in Christ no man can be delivered; and therefore they will be so judged that they perish. If, indeed, the condition of those who are ignorant of the law of God is worse than the condition of those who know it, how can that be true which the Lord says in the gospel: "The servant who knows not his lord's will, and commits things worthy of stripes, shall be beaten with few stripes; whereas the servant who knows his lord's will, and commits things worthy of

---

1 Ps. i. 2.
2 Rom. xii. 1.
3 Ps. xxxii. 9.
4 Prov. i. 8.
5 Prov. iii. 7.
6 Prov. iii. 11.
7 Prov. iii. 1.
8 Prov. iii. 27.
9 Prov. iii. 29.
10 Prov. v. 2.
11 Ps. xxxvi. 3.
12 Prov. i. 30.
13 Matt. vi. 19.
14 Matt. x. 28.
15 Matt. xvi. 24.
16 Luke ii. 14.
17 1 Cor. vii. 36, 37.
18 1 Cor. ix. 17.
19 1 Cor. xv. 34.
20 2 Cor. viii. 11.
21 2 Tim. iii. 12.
22 1 Tim. iv. 14.
23 Philemon 14.
24 Eph. vi. 7.

25 Jas. i. 16, and ii. 1.
26 Jas. iv. 11.
27 1 John ii. 15.
28 Matt. xvi. 27.
29 Rom. ii. 12.

stripes, shall be beaten with many stripes"?[1] Observe how clearly He here shows that it is a graver matter for a man to sin with knowledge than in ignorance. And yet we must not on this account betake ourselves for refuge to the shades of ignorance, with the view of finding our excuse therein. It is one thing to be ignorant, and another thing to be unwilling to know. For the will is at fault in the case of the man of whom it is said, "He is not inclined to understand, so as to do good."[2] But even the ignorance, which is not theirs who refuse to know, but theirs who are, as it were, simply ignorant, does not so far excuse any one as to exempt him from the punishment of eternal fire, though his failure to believe has been the result of his not having at all heard what he should believe; but probably only so far as to mitigate his punishment. For it was not said without reason: "Pour out Thy wrath upon the heathen that have not known Thee;"[3] nor again according to what the apostle says: "When He shall come from heaven in a flame of fire to take vengeance on them that know not God."[4] But yet in order that we may have that knowledge that will prevent our saying, each one of us, "I did not know," "I did not hear," "I did not understand;" the human will is summoned, in such words as these: "Wish not to be as the horse or as the mule, which have no understanding;"[5] although it may show itself even worse, of which it is written, "A stubborn servant will not be reproved by words; for even if he understand, yet he will not obey."[6] But when a man says, "I cannot do what I am commanded, because I am mastered by my concupiscence," he has no longer any excuse to plead from ignorance, nor reason to blame God in his heart, but he recognises and laments his own evil in himself; and still to such an one the apostle says: "Be not overcome by evil, but overcome evil with good;"[7] and of course the very fact that the injunction, "Consent not to be overcome," is addressed to him, undoubtedly summons the determination of his will. For to consent and to refuse are functions proper to will.

CHAP. 6 [IV.] — GOD'S GRACE TO BE MAINTAINED AGAINST THE PELAGIANS; THE PELAGIAN HERESY NOT AN OLD ONE.

It is, however, to be feared lest all these and similar testimonies of Holy Scripture (and undoubtedly there are a great many of them), in the maintenance of free will, be understood in such a way as to leave no room for God's assistance and grace in leading a godly life and a good conversation, to which the eternal reward is due; and lest poor wretched man, when he leads a good life and performs good works (or rather thinks that he leads a good life and performs good works), should dare to glory in himself and not in the Lord, and to put his hope of righteous living in himself alone; so as to be followed by the prophet Jeremiah's malediction when he says, "Cursed is the man who has hope in man, and maketh strong the flesh of his arm, and whose heart departeth from the Lord."[8] Understand, my brethren, I pray you, this passage of the prophet. Because the prophet did not say, "Cursed is the man who has hope in his own self," it might seem to some that the passage, "Cursed is the man who has hope in man," was spoken to prevent man having hope in any other man but himself. In order, therefore, to show that his admonition to man was not to have hope in himself, after saying, "Cursed is the man who has hope in man," he immediately added, "And maketh strong the flesh of his arm." He used the word "arm" to designate *power in operation.* By the term "*flesh,*" however, must be understood *human frailty.* And therefore he makes strong the flesh of his arm who supposes that a power which is frail and weak (that is, human) is sufficient for him to perform good works, and therefore puts not his hope in God for help. This is the reason why he subjoined the further clause, "And whose heart departeth from the Lord." Of this character is the Pelagian heresy, which is not an ancient one, but has only lately come into existence. Against this system of error there was first a good deal of discussion; then, as the ultimate resource, it was referred to sundry episcopal councils, the proceedings of which, not, indeed, in every instance, but in some, I have despatched to you for your perusal. In order, then, to our performance of good works, let us not have hope in man, making strong the flesh of our arm; nor let our heart ever depart from the Lord, but let it say to him, "Be Thou my helper; forsake me not, nor despise me, O God of my salvation."[9]

CHAP. 7. — GRACE IS NECESSARY ALONG WITH FREE WILL TO LEAD A GOOD LIFE.

Therefore, my dearly beloved, as we have now proved by our former testimonies from Holy Scripture that there is in man a free determination of will for living rightly and acting rightly; so now let us see what are the divine testimonies concerning the grace of God, without which we are not able to do any good thing. And first of all, I will say something about the very profession which you make in your brotherhood. Now your society, in which you are leading lives of continence, could not hold together unless you de-

---

[1] Luke xii. 47, 48.  [2] Ps. xxxvi. 3.  [3] Ps. lxix. 6.
[4] 2 Thess. i. 7, 8.  [5] Ps. xxxii. 9.  [6] Prov. xxix. 19.
[7] Rom. xii. 21.

[8] Jer. xvii. 5.  [9] Ps. xxvii. 9.

spised conjugal pleasure. Well, the Lord was one day conversing on this very topic, when His disciples remarked to Him, " If such be the case of a man with his wife, it is not good to marry." He then answered them, "All men cannot receive this saying, save they to whom it is given." [1] And was it not to Timothy's free will that the apostle appealed, when he exhorted him in these words : " Keep thyself continent " ? [2] He also explained the power of the will in this matter when He said, " Having no necessity, but possessing power over his own will, to keep his virgin." [3] And yet " all men do not receive this saying, except those to whom the power is given." Now they to whom this is not given either are unwilling or do not fulfil what they will ; whereas they to whom it is given so will as to accomplish what they will. In order, therefore, that this saying, which is not received by all men, may yet be received by some, there are both the gift of God and free will.

## CHAP. 8. — CONJUGAL CHASTITY IS ITSELF THE GIFT OF GOD.

It is concerning conjugal chastity itself that the apostle treats, when he says, " Let him do what he will, he sinneth not if he marry ; " [4] and yet this too is God's gift, for the Scripture says, " It is by the Lord that the woman is joined to her husband." Accordingly the teacher of the Gentiles, in one of his discourses, commends both conjugal chastity, whereby adulteries are prevented, and the still more perfect continence which foregoes all cohabitation, and shows how both one and the other are severally the gift of God. Writing to the Corinthians, he admonished married persons not to defraud each other ; and then, after his admonition to these, he added : " But I could wish that all men were even as I am myself," [5] — meaning, of course, that he abstained from all cohabitation ; and then proceeded to say : " But every man hath his own gift of God, one after this manner, and another after that." [5] Now, do the many precepts which are written in the law of God, forbidding all fornication and adultery, indicate anything else than free will ? Surely such precepts would not be given unless a man had a will of his own, wherewith to obey the divine commandments. And yet it is God's gift which is indispensable for the observance of the precepts of chastity. Accordingly, it is said in the Book of Wisdom : " When I knew that no one could be continent, except God gives it, then this became a point of wisdom to know whose gift it was." [6] " Every man," however, " is tempted when he is drawn away of his own lust, and enticed " [7] not to observe and

keep these holy precepts of chastity. If he should say in respect of these commandments, " I wish to keep them, but am mastered by my concupiscence," then the Scripture responds to his free will, as I have already said : " Be not overcome of evil, but overcome evil with good." [8] In order, however, that this victory may be gained, grace renders its help ; and were not this help given, then the law would be nothing but the strength of sin. For concupiscence is increased and receives greater energies from the prohibition of the law, unless the spirit of grace helps. This explains the statement of the great Teacher of the Gentiles, when he says, " The sting of death is sin, and the strength of sin is the law." [9] See, then, I pray you, whence originates this confession of weakness, when a man says, " I desire to keep what the law commands, but am overcome by the strength of my concupiscence." And when his will is addressed, and it is said, " Be not overcome of evil," of what avail is anything but the succour of God's grace to the accomplishment of the precept ? This the apostle himself afterwards stated ; for after saying, " The strength of sin is the law," he immediately subjoined, " But thanks be to God, who giveth us the victory, through our Lord Jesus Christ." [10] It follows, then, that the victory in which sin is vanquished is nothing else than the gift of God, who in this contest helps free will.

## CHAP. 9. — ENTERING INTO TEMPTATION. PRAYER IS A PROOF OF GRACE.

Wherefore, our Heavenly Master also says : " Watch and pray, that ye enter not into temptation." [11] Let every man, therefore, when fighting against his own concupiscence, pray that he enter not into temptation ; that is, that he be not drawn aside and enticed by it. But he does not enter into temptation if he conquers his evil concupiscence by good will. And yet the determination of the human will is insufficient, unless the Lord grant it victory in answer to prayer that it enter not into temptation. What, indeed, affords clearer evidence of the grace of God than the acceptance of prayer in any petition ? If our Saviour had only said, " Watch that ye enter not into temptation," He would appear to have done nothing further than admonish man's will ; but since He added the words, " and pray," He showed that God helps us not to enter into temptation. It is to the free will of man that the words are addressed : " My son, remove not thyself from the chastening of the Lord." [12] And the Lord said : " I have prayed for thee, Peter, that thy faith fail not." [13] So that a man is assisted by grace, in order that his will may not be uselessly commanded.

[1] Matt. xix. 10.　[2] 1 Tim. v. 22.　[3] 1 Cor. vii. 37.
[4] 1 Cor. vii. 36.　[5] 1 Cor. vii. 7.　[6] Wisd. viii. 21.
[7] Jas. i. 14.

[8] Rom. xii. 21.　[9] 1 Cor. xv. 56.　[10] 1 Cor. xv. 57.
[11] Matt. xxvi. 41.　[12] Prov. iii. 11.　[13] Luke xxii. 32.

CHAP. 10 [V.] — FREE WILL AND GOD'S GRACE ARE SIMULTANEOUSLY COMMENDED.

When God says, "Turn ye unto me, and I will turn unto you,"[1] one of these clauses — that which invites our return to God — evidently belongs to our will ; while the other, which promises His return to us, belongs to His grace. Here, possibly, the Pelagians think they have a justification for their opinion which they so prominently advance, that God's grace is given according to our merits. In the East, indeed, that is to say, in the province of Palestine, in which is the city of Jerusalem, Pelagius, when examined in person by the bishop,[2] did not venture to affirm this. For it happened that among the objections which were brought up against him, this in particular was objected, that he maintained that the grace of God was given according to our merits, — an opinion which was so diverse from catholic doctrine, and so hostile to the grace of Christ, that unless he had anathematized it, as laid to his charge, he himself must have been anathematized on its account. He pronounced, indeed, the required anathema upon the dogma, but how insincerely his later books plainly show ; for in them he maintains absolutely no other opinion than that the grace of God is given according to our merits. Such passages do they collect out of the Scriptures, — like the one which I just now quoted, "Turn ye unto me, and I will turn unto you," — as if it were owing to the merit of our turning to God that His grace were given us, wherein He Himself even turns unto us. Now the persons who hold this opinion fail to observe that, unless our turning to God were itself God's gift, it would not be said to Him in prayer, "Turn us again, O God of hosts ;"[3] and, "Thou, O God, wilt turn and quicken us ;"[4] and again, "Turn us, O God of our salvation,"[5] — with other passages of similar import, too numerous to mention here. For, with respect to our coming unto Christ, what else does it mean than our being turned to Him by believing? And yet He says : "No man can come unto me, except it were given unto him of my Father."[6]

CHAP. 11. — OTHER PASSAGES OF SCRIPTURE WHICH THE PELAGIANS ABUSE.

Then, again, there is the Scripture contained in the second book of the Chronicles : "The Lord is with you when ye are with Him : and if ye shall seek Him ye shall find Him ; but if ye forsake Him, He also will forsake you."[7] This passage, no doubt, clearly manifests the choice of the will. But they who maintain that God's grace is given according to our merits, receive these testimonies of Scripture in such a manner as to believe that our merit lies in the circumstance of our "being with God," while His grace is given according to this merit, so that He too may be with us. In like manner, that our merit lies in the fact of "our seeking God," and then His grace is given according to this merit, in order that we may find Him." Again, there is a passage in the first book of the same Chronicles which declares the choice of the will : "And thou, Solomon, my son, know thou the God of thy father, and serve Him with a perfect heart and with a willing mind, for the Lord searcheth all hearts, and understandeth all the imaginations of the thoughts ; if thou seek Him, He will be found of thee ; but if thou forsake Him, He will cast thee off for ever."[8] But these people find some room for human merit in the clause, "If thou seek Him," and then the grace is thought to be given according to this merit in what is said in the ensuing words, "He will be found of thee." And so they labour with all their might to show that God's grace is given according to our merits, — in other words, that grace is not grace. For, as the apostle most expressly says, to them who receive reward according to merit "the recompense is not reckoned of grace but of debt."[9]

CHAP. 12. — HE PROVES OUT OF ST. PAUL THAT GRACE IS NOT GIVEN ACCORDING TO MEN'S MERITS.

Now there was, no doubt, a decided merit in the Apostle Paul, but it was an *evil* one, while he persecuted the Church, and he says of it : "I am not meet to be called an apostle, because I persecuted the Church of God."[10] And it was while he had this evil merit that a good one was rendered to him instead of the evil ; and, therefore, he went on at once to say, "But by the grace of God I am what I am."[11] Then, in order to exhibit also his free will, he added in the next clasue, "And His grace within me was not in vain, but I have laboured more abundantly than they all." This free will of man he appeals to in the case of others also, as when he says to them, "We beseech you that ye receive not the grace of God in vain."[12] Now, how could he so enjoin them, if they received God's grace in such a manner as to lose their own will? Nevertheless, lest the will itself should be deemed capable of doing any good thing without the grace of God, after saying, "His grace within me was not in vain, but I have laboured more abundantly than they all," he immediately added the qualifying clause, "Yet not I, but the grace of God which was with me."[11] In other words, Not I alone, but the grace of God with me.

---

[1] Zech. i. 3.
[2] See *On the Proceedings of Pelagius*, above, ch. xiv. (30–37).
[3] Ps. lxxx 7.    [4] Ps lxxxv. 6.    [5] Ps. lxxxv. 4.
[6] John vi. 65.    [7] 2 Chron. xv. 2.

[8] 1 Chron. xxviii. 9.    [9] Rom. iv. 4.    [10] 1 Cor. xv. 9.
[11] 1 Cor. xv. 10.    [12] 2 Cor. vi. 1.

And again, lest they should say they deserved so great a gift by their works, he immediately added, "Not of works, lest any man should boast."[1] Not that he denied good works, or emptied them of their value, when he says that God renders to every man according to his works;[2] but because works proceed from faith, and not faith from works. Therefore it is from Him that we have works of righteousness, from whom comes also faith itself, concerning which it is written, "The just shall live by faith."[3]

### CHAP. 18. — FAITH WITHOUT GOOD WORKS IS NOT SUFFICIENT FOR SALVATION.

Unintelligent persons, however, with regard to the apostle's statement: "We conclude that a man is justified by faith without the works of the law,"[4] have thought him to mean that faith suffices to a man, even if he lead a bad life, and has no good works. Impossible is it that such a character should be deemed "a vessel of election" by the apostle, who, after declaring that "in Christ Jesus neither circumcision availeth anything, nor uncircumcision,"[5] adds at once, "but faith which worketh by love." It is such faith which severs God's faithful from unclean demons, — for even these "believe and tremble,"[6] as the Apostle James says; but they do not do well. Therefore they possess not the faith by which the just man lives, — the faith which works by love in such wise, that God recompenses it according to its works with eternal life. But inasmuch as we have even our good works from God, from whom likewise comes our faith and our love, therefore the selfsame great teacher of the Gentiles has designated "eternal life" itself as His gracious "gift."[7]

### CHAP. 19 [VIII.] — HOW IS ETERNAL LIFE BOTH A REWARD FOR SERVICE AND A FREE GIFT OF GRACE?

And hence there arises no small question, which must be solved by the Lord's gift. If eternal life is rendered to good works, as the Scripture most openly declares: "Then He shall reward every man according to his works:"[8] how can eternal life be a matter of grace, seeing that grace is not rendered to works, but is given gratuitously, as the apostle himself tells us: "To him that worketh is the reward not reckoned of grace, but of debt;"[9] and again: "There is a remnant saved according to the election of grace;" with these words immediately subjoined: "And if of grace, then is it no more of works; otherwise grace is no more grace"?[10] How, then, is eternal life by grace, when it is received from works? Does the apostle perchance not say that eternal life is a grace? Nay, he has so called it, with a clearness which none can possibly gainsay. It requires no acute intellect, but only an attentive reader, to discover this. For after saying, "The wages of sin is death," he at once added, "The grace of God is eternal life through Jesus Christ our Lord."[7]

### CHAP. 20. — THE QUESTION ANSWERED. JUSTIFICATION IS GRACE SIMPLY AND ENTIRELY. ETERNAL LIFE IS REWARD AND GRACE.

This question, then, seems to me to be by no means capable of solution, unless we understand that even those good works of ours, which are recompensed with eternal life, belong to the grace of God, because of what is said by the Lord Jesus: "Without me ye can do nothing."[11] And the apostle himself, after saying, "By grace are ye saved through faith; and that not of yourselves, it is the gift of God: not of works, lest any man should boast;"[12] saw, of course, the possibility that men would think from this statement that good works are not necessary to those who believe, but that faith alone suffices for them; and again, the possibility of men's boasting of their good works, as if they were of themselves capable of performing them. To meet, therefore, these opinions on both sides, he immediately added, "For we are His workmanship, created in Christ Jesus unto good works, which God hath before ordained that we should walk in them."[13] What is the purport of his saying, "Not of works, lest any man should boast," while commending the grace of God? And then why does he afterwards, when giving a reason for using such words, say, "For we are His workmanship, created in Christ Jesus unto good works"? Why, therefore, does it run, "Not of works, lest any man should boast"? Now, hear and understand. "Not of works" is spoken of the works which you suppose have their origin in yourself alone; but you have to think of works for which God has moulded (that is, has formed and created) you. For of these he says, "We are His workmanship, created in Christ Jesus unto good works." Now he does not here speak of that creation which made us human beings, but of that in reference to which one said who was already in full manhood, "Create in me a clean heart, O God;"[14] concerning which also the apostle says, "Therefore, if any man be in Christ, he is a new creature: old things are passed away; behold, all things are become new. And all things are of God."[15] We are framed, therefore, that is, formed and created, "in the good works which" we have not ourselves prepared, but "God hath before ordained that we should walk in them."

---

[1] Eph. ii. 9.    [2] Rom. ii. 6.    [3] Habak. ii. 4.
[4] Rom. iii. 28.    [5] Gal. v. 6.    [6] Jas. ii. 19.
[7] Rom. vi. 23.    [8] Matt. xvi. 27.    [9] Rom. iv. 4.
[10] Rom. xi. 5, 6.

[11] John xv. 5.    [12] Eph. ii. 8, 9.    [13] Eph. ii. 10.
[14] Ps. li. 12    [15] 2 Cor. v. 17, 18.

It follows, then, dearly beloved, beyond all doubt, that as your good life is nothing else than God's grace, so also the eternal life which is the recompense of a good life is the grace of God; moreover it is given gratuitously, even as that is given gratuitously to which it is given. But that to which it is given is solely and simply grace; this therefore is also that which is given to it, because it is its reward; — grace is for grace, as if remuneration for righteousness; in order that it may be true, because it is true, that God "shall reward every man according to his works."[1]

#### CHAP. 21 [IX.] — ETERNAL LIFE IS "GRACE FOR GRACE."

Perhaps you ask whether we ever read in the Sacred Scriptures of "*grace for grace.*" Well, you possess the Gospel according to John, which is perfectly clear in its very great light. Here John the Baptist says of Christ: "Of His fulness have we all received, even *grace for grace.*"[2] So that out of His fulness we have received, according to our humble measure, our particles of ability as it were for leading good lives — "according as God hath dealt to every man his measure of faith;"[3] because "every man hath his proper gift of God; one after this manner, and another after that."[4] And this is grace. But, over and above this, we shall also receive "grace for grace," when we shall have awarded to us eternal life, of which the apostle said: "The grace of God is eternal life through Jesus Christ our Lord,"[5] having just said that "the wages of sin is death." Deservedly did he call it "*wages,*" because everlasting death is awarded as its proper due to diabolical service. Now, when it was in his power to say, and rightly to say: "But the wages of righteousness is eternal life," he yet preferred to say: "The grace of God is eternal life;" in order that we may hence understand that God does not, for any merits of our own, but from His own divine compassion, prolong our existence to everlasting life. Even as the Psalmist says to his soul, "Who crowneth thee with mercy and compassion."[6] Well, now, is not a crown given as the reward of good deeds? It is, however, only because He works good works in good men, of whom it is said, "It is God which worketh in you both to will and to do of His good pleasure,"[7] that the Psalm has it, as just now quoted: "He crowneth thee with mercy and compassion," since it is through His mercy that we perform the good deeds to which the crown is awarded. It is not, however, to be for a moment supposed, because he said, "It is God that worketh in you both to will and to do of his own good pleasure," that free will is taken away. If this, indeed, had been his meaning, he would not have said just before, "Work out your own salvation with fear and trembling."[8] For when the command is given "to work," their free will is addressed; and when it is added, "with fear and trembling," they are warned against boasting of their good deeds as if they were their own, by attributing to themselves the performance of anything good. It is pretty much as if the apostle had this question put to him: "Why did you use the phrase, 'with fear and trembling'?" And as if he answered the inquiry of his examiners by telling them, "For it is God which worketh in you." Because if you fear and tremble, you do not boast of your good works — as if they were your own, since it is God who works within you.

#### CHAP. 22 [X.] — WHO IS THE TRANSGRESSOR OF THE LAW? THE OLDNESS OF ITS LETTER. THE NEWNESS OF ITS SPIRIT.

Therefore, brethren, you ought by free will not do evil but do good; this, indeed, is the lesson taught us in the law of God, in the Holy Scriptures — both Old and New. Let us, however, read, and by the Lord's help understand, what the apostle tells us: "Because by the deeds of the law there shall no flesh be justified in His sight; for by the law is the knowledge of sin."[9] Observe, he says "*the knowledge,*" not "the destruction," of sin. But when a man knows sin, and grace does not help him to avoid what he knows, undoubtedly the law works wrath. And this the apostle explicitly says in another passage. His words are: "The law worketh wrath."[10] The reason of this statement lies in the fact that God's wrath is greater in the case of the transgressor who by the law knows sin, and yet commits it; such a man is thus a transgressor of the law, even as the apostle says in another sentence, "For where no law is, there is no transgression."[10] It is in accordance with this principle that he elsewhere says, "That we may serve in newness of spirit, and not in the oldness of the letter;"[11] wishing *the law* to be here understood by "the oldness of the letter," and what else by "newness of spirit" than *grace?* Then, that it might not be thought that he had brought any accusation, or suggested any blame, against the law, he immediately takes himself to task with this inquiry: "What shall we say, then? Is the law sin? God forbid." He then adds the statement: "Nay, I had not known sin but by the law;"[12] which is of the same import as the passage above quoted: "By the law

---

[1] Matt. xvi. 27; Ps. lxii. 12; Rev. xxii. 12.    [2] John i. 16.
[3] Rom. xii. 3.         [4] 1 Cor. vii. 7.         [5] Rom. vi. 23.
[6] Ps. ciii. 4.         [7] Phil. ii. 13.

[8] Phil. ii. 12.      [9] Rom. iii. 20.      [10] Rom. iv. 15.
[11] Rom. vii. 6.      [12] Rom. vii. 6, 7.

is the knowledge of sin."[1] Then: "For I had not known lust," he says, "except the law had said, 'Thou shalt not covet.'[2] But sin, taking occasion by the commandment, wrought in me all manner of concupiscence. For without the law sin was dead. For I was alive without the law once; but when the commandment came, sin revived, and I died. And the commandment, which was ordained to life, I found to be unto death. For sin, taking occasion by the commandment, deceived me, and by it slew me. Wherefore the law is holy; and the commandment holy, just, and good. Was, then, that which is good made death unto me? God forbid. But sin, that it might appear sin, worked death in me by that which is good, — in order that the sinner, or[3] the sin, might by the commandment become beyond measure."[4] And to the Galatians he writes: "Knowing that a man is not justified by the works of the law, except through faith in Jesus Christ, even we have believed in Jesus Christ, that we might be justified by the faith of Christ, and not by the works of the law; for by the works of the law shall no flesh be justified."[5]

CHAP. 23 [XI.] — THE PELAGIANS MAINTAIN THAT THE LAW IS THE GRACE OF GOD WHICH HELPS US NOT TO SIN.

Why, therefore, do those very vain and perverse Pelagians say that the law is the grace of God by which we are helped not to sin? Do they not, by making such an allegation, unhappily and beyond all doubt contradict the great apostle? He, indeed, says, that by the law sin received strength against man; and that man, by the commandment, although it be holy, and just, and good, nevertheless dies, and that death works in him through that which is good, from which death there is no deliverance unless the Spirit quickens him, whom the letter had killed, — as he says in another passage, "The letter killeth, but the Spirit giveth life."[6] And yet these obstinate persons, blind to God's light, and deaf to His voice, maintain that the letter which kills gives life, and thus gainsay the quickening Spirit. "Therefore, brethren" (that I may warn you with better effect in the words of the apostle himself), "we are debtors not to the flesh, to live after the flesh; for if ye live after the flesh ye shall die; but if ye through the Spirit do mortify the deeds of the body, ye shall live."[7] I have said this to deter your free will from evil, and to exhort it to good by apostolic words; but yet you must not therefore

glory in man, — that is to say, in your own selves, — and not in the Lord, when you live not after the flesh, but through the Spirit mortify the deeds of the flesh. For in order that they to whom the apostle addressed this language might not exalt themselves, thinking that they were themselves able of their own spirit to do such good works as these, and not by the Spirit of God, after saying to them, "If ye through the Spirit do mortify the deeds of the flesh, ye shall live," he at once added, "For as many as are led by the Spirit of God, they are the sons of God."[8] When, therefore, you by the Spirit mortify the deeds of the flesh, that you may have life, glorify Him, praise Him, give thanks to Him by whose Spirit you are so led as to be able to do such things as show you to be the children of God; "for as many as are led by the Spirit of God, they are the sons of God."

CHAP. 24 [XII.] — WHO MAY BE SAID TO WISH TO ESTABLISH THEIR OWN RIGHTEOUSNESS. "GOD'S RIGHTEOUSNESS," SO CALLED, WHICH MAN HAS FROM GOD.

As many, therefore, as are led by their own spirit, trusting in their own virtue, with the addition merely of the law's assistance, without the help of grace, are not the sons of God. Such are they of whom the same apostle speaks as "being ignorant of God's righteousness, and wishing to establish their own righteousness, who have not submitted themselves to the righteousness of God."[9] He said this of the Jews, who in their self-assumption rejected grace, and therefore did not believe in Christ. Their own righteousness, indeed, he says, they wish to establish; and this righteousness is of the law, — not that the law was established by themselves, but that they had constituted their righteousness in the law which is of God, when they supposed themselves able to fulfil that law by their own strength, ignorant of God's righteousness, — not indeed that by which God is Himself righteous, but that which man has from God. And that you may know that he designated as *theirs* the righteousness which is of the law, and as *God's* that which man receives from God, hear what he says in another passage, when speaking of Christ: "For whose sake I counted all things not only as loss, but I deemed them to be dung, that I might win Christ, and be found in Him — not having my own righteousness, which is of the law, but that which is through the faith of Christ, which is of God."[10] Now what does he mean by "not having my own righteousness, which is of the law," when the law is really not his at all, but God's, — except this, that he called it his own righteousness, although it was of the law, because he

---

[1] Rom. iii. 20.    [2] Ex. xx. 17.
[3] *Ut fiat supra modum peccator, aut peccatum*, etc. [This odd reading probably arose from mistaking the Greek article ἡ for the disjunctive particle ἤ. It occurs frequently in Augustin. — W.]
[4] Rom. vii. 7-13.    [5] Gal. ii. 16.    [6] 2 Cor. iii. 6.
[7] Rom. viii. 12-13.

[8] Rom. viii. 14.    [9] Rom. x. 3.    [10] Phil. iii. 8, 9.

thought he could fulfil the law by his own will, without the aid of grace which is through faith in Christ? Wherefore, after saying, " Not having my own righteousness, which is of the law," he immediately subjoined, " But that which is through the faith of Christ, which is of God." This is what they were ignorant of, of whom he says, " Being ignorant of God's righteousness," — that is, the righteousness which is of God (for it is given not by the letter, which kills, but by the life-giving Spirit), " and wishing to establish their own righteousness," which he expressly described as the righteousness of the law, when he said, " Not having my own righteousness, which is of the law ; " they were not subject to the righteousness of God, — in other words, they submitted not themselves to the grace of God. For they were under the law, not under grace, and therefore sin had dominion over them, from which a man is not freed by the law, but by grace. On which account he elsewhere says, " For sin shall not have dominion over you ; because ye are not under the law, but under grace." [1] Not that the law is evil ; but because they are under its power, whom it makes guilty by imposing commandments, not by aiding. It is by grace that any one is a doer of the law ; and without this grace, he who is placed under the law will be only a hearer of the law. To such persons he addresses these words : " Ye who are justified by the law are fallen from grace." [2]

CHAP. 25 [XIII.] — AS THE LAW IS NOT, SO NEITHER IS OUR NATURE ITSELF THAT GRACE BY WHICH WE ARE CHRISTIANS.

Now who can be so insensible to the words of the apostle, who so foolishly, nay, so insanely ignorant of the purport of his statement, as to venture to affirm that the law is grace, when he who knew very well what he was saying emphatically declares, " Ye who are justified by the law are fallen from grace " ? Well, but if the law is not grace, seeing that in order that the law itself may be kept, it is not the law, but only grace which can give help, will not nature at any rate be grace? For this, too, the Pelagians have been bold enough to aver, that grace is the nature in which we were created, so as to possess a rational mind, by which we are enabled to understand, — formed as we are in the image of God, so as to have dominion over the fish of the sea, and over the fowl of the air, and over every living thing that creepeth upon the earth. This, however, is not the grace which the apostle commends to us through the faith of Jesus Christ. For it is certain that we possess this nature in common with ungodly men and unbelievers ; whereas the grace which comes through

the faith of Jesus Christ belongs only to them to whom the faith itself appertains. " For all men have not faith." [3] Now, as the apostle, with perfect truth, says to those who by wishing to be justified by the law have fallen from grace, " If righteousness come by the law, then Christ is dead in vain ; " [4] so likewise, to those who think that the grace which he commends and faith in Christ receives, is nature, the same language is with the same degree of truth applicable : if righteousness come from nature, then Christ is dead in vain. But the law was in existence up to that time, and it did not justify ; and nature existed too, but it did not justify. It was not, then, in vain that Christ died, in order that the law might be fulfilled through Him who said, " I am come not to destroy the law, but to fulfil it ; " [5] and that our nature, which was lost through Adam, might through Him be recovered, who said that " He was come to seek and to save that which was lost ; " [6] in whose coming the old fathers likewise who loved God believed.

CHAP. 26. — THE PELAGIANS CONTEND THAT THE GRACE, WHICH IS NEITHER THE LAW NOR NATURE, AVAILS ONLY TO THE REMISSION OF PAST SINS, BUT NOT TO THE AVOIDANCE OF FUTURE ONES.

They also maintain that God's grace, which is given through the faith of Jesus Christ, and which is neither the law nor nature, avails only for the remission of sins that have been committed, and not for the shunning of future ones, or the subjugation of those which are now assailing us. Now if all this were true, surely after offering the petition of the Lord's Prayer, " Forgive us our debts, as we forgive our debtors," we could hardly go on and say, " And lead us not into temptation." [7] The former petition we present that our sins may be forgiven ; the latter, that they may be avoided or subdued, — a favour which we should by no means beg of our Father who is in heaven if we were able to accomplish it by the virtue of our human will. Now I strongly advise and earnestly require your Love [8] to read attentively the book of the blessed Cyprian which he wrote *On the Lord's Prayer*. As far as the Lord shall assist you, understand it, and commit it to memory. In this work you will see how he so appeals to the free will of those whom he edifies in his treatise, as to show them, that whatever they have to fulfil in the law, they must ask for in the prayer. But this, of course, would be utterly empty if the human will were sufficient for the performance without the help of God.

[3] 2 Thess. iii. 2.    [4] Gal. ii. 21.    [5] Matt. v. 17.
[6] Matt. xviii. 11; Luke xix. 10.    [7] Matt. vi. 12, 13
[8] *Caritatem vestram*, a phrase of the same sort as our common address, " your Honour."

CHAP. 27 [XIV.] — GRACE EFFECTS THE FULFIL-
MENT OF THE LAW, THE DELIVERANCE OF NA-
TURE, AND THE SUPPRESSION OF SIN'S DOMINION.

It has, however, been shown to demonstration, that instead of really maintaining free will, they have only inflated a theory of it, which, having no stability, has fallen to the ground. Neither the knowledge of God's law, nor nature, nor the mere remission of sins is that grace which is given to us through our Lord Jesus Christ; but it is this very grace which accomplishes the fulfilment of the law, and the liberation of nature, and the removal of the dominion of sin. Being, therefore, convicted on these points, they resort to another expedient, and endeavour to show in some way or other that the grace of God is given us according to our merits. For they say: "Granted that it is not given to us according to the merits of good works, inasmuch as it is through it that we do any good thing, still it is given to us according to the merits of a good will; for," say they, "the good will of him who prays precedes his prayer, even as the will of the believer preceded his faith, so that according to these merits the grace of God who hears, follows."

CHAP. 28. — FAITH IS THE GIFT OF GOD.

I have already discussed[1] the point concerning faith, that is, concerning the will of him who believes, even so far as to show that it appertains to grace, — so that the apostle did not tell us, "I have obtained mercy because I was faithful;" but he said, "I have obtained mercy in order to be faithful."[2] And there are many other passages of similar import, — among them that in which he bids us "think soberly, according as God hath dealt out to every man the proportion of faith;"[3] and that which I have already quoted: "By grace are ye saved through faith; and that not of yourselves; it is the gift of God;"[4] and again another in the same Epistle to the Ephesians: "Peace be to the brethren, and love with faith, from God the Father, and the Lord Jesus Christ;"[5] and to the same effect that passage in which he says, "For unto you it is given in the behalf of Christ not only to believe on Him, but also to suffer for His sake."[6] Both alike are therefore due to the grace of God, — the faith of those who believe, and the patience of those who suffer, because the apostle spoke of both as *given*. Then, again, there is the passage, especially noticeable, in which he says, "We, having the same spirit of faith,"[7] for his phrase is not "*the knowledge of faith*," but "*the spirit of faith;*" and he expressed himself thus in order that we might understand how that

faith is given to us, even when it is not sought, so that other blessings may be granted to it at its request. For "how," says he, "shall they call upon Him in whom they have not believed?"[8] The spirit of grace, therefore, causes us to have faith, in order that through faith we may, on praying for it, obtain the ability to do what we are commanded. On this account the apostle himself constantly puts faith before the law; since we are not able to do what the law commands unless we obtain the strength to do it by the prayer of faith.

CHAP. 29. — GOD IS ABLE TO CONVERT OPPOSING WILLS, AND TO TAKE AWAY FROM THE HEART ITS HARDNESS.

Now if faith is simply of free will, and is not given by God, why do we pray for those who will not believe, that they may believe? This it would be absolutely useless to do, unless we believe, with perfect propriety, that Almighty God is able to turn to belief wills that are perverse and opposed to faith. Man's free will is addressed when it is said, "To-day, if ye will hear His voice, harden not your hearts."[9] But if God were not able to remove from the human heart even its obstinacy and hardness, He would not say, through the prophet, "I will take from them their heart of stone, and will give them a heart of flesh."[10] That all this was foretold in reference to the New Testament is shown clearly enough by the apostle when he says, "Ye are our epistle, . . . written not with ink, but with the Spirit of the living God; not in tables of stone, but in fleshly tables of the heart."[11] We must not, of course, suppose that such a phrase as this is used as if those might live in a fleshly[12] way who ought to live spiritually; but inasmuch as a stone has no feeling, with which man's hard heart is compared, what was there left Him to compare man's intelligent heart with but the flesh, which possesses feeling? For this is what is said by the prophet Ezekiel: "I will give them another heart, and I will put a new spirit within you; and I will take the stony heart out of their flesh, and will give them a heart of flesh; that they may walk in my statutes, and keep mine ordinances, and do them: and they shall be my people, and I will be their God, saith the Lord."[13] Now can we possibly, without extreme absurdity, maintain that there previously existed in any man the good merit of a good will, to entitle him to the removal of his stony heart, when all the while this very heart of stone signifies nothing else than a will of the hardest kind and such as is absolutely inflexible against God? For

---

[1] See above, ch. vii. (16, 17, 18).    [2] 1 Cor. vii. 25.
[3] Rom. xii. 3.    [4] Eph. ii. 8.    [5] Eph. vi. 23.
[6] Phil. i. 29.    [7] 2 Cor. iv. 13.

[8] Rom. x. 14.    [9] Ps. xcv. 7, 8.    [10] Ezek. xi. 19.
[11] 2 Cor. iii. 2, 3.
[12] [That is, "*carnally*," the Latin phrase in 2 Cor. iii. 3 being capable alike of the literal and metaphorical sense of "fleshly."—W.]
[13] Ezek. xi. 19, 20.

where a good will precedes, there is, of course, no longer a heart of stone.

## CHAP. 30. — THE GRACE BY WHICH THE STONY HEART IS REMOVED IS NOT PRECEDED BY GOOD DESERTS, BUT BY EVIL ONES.

In another passage, also, by the same prophet, God, in the clearest language, shows us that it is not owing to any good merits on the part of men, but for His own name's sake, that He does these things. This is His language: "This I do, O house of Israel,[1] but for mine holy name's sake, which ye have profaned among the heathen, whither ye went. And I will sanctify my great name, which was profaned among the heathen, which ye have profaned in the midst of them; and the heathen shall know that I am the Lord, saith the Lord God, when I shall be sanctified in you before their eyes. For I will take you from among the heathen, and gather you out of all countries, and will bring you into your own land. Then will I sprinkle you with clean water, and ye shall be clean: from all your own filthiness, and from all your idols will I cleanse you. A new heart also will I give you, and a new spirit will I put within you; and the stony heart shall be taken away out of your flesh, and I will give you a heart of flesh. And I will put my Spirit within you, and will cause you to walk in my statutes, and ye shall keep my judgments, and do them."[2] Now who is so blind as not to see, and who so stone-like as not to feel, that this grace is not given according to the merits of a good will, when the Lord declares and testifies, "It is I, O house of Israel, who do this, but for my holy name's sake"? Now why did He say "It is I that do it, but for my holy name's sake," were it not that they should not think that it was owing to their own good merits that these things were happening, as the Pelagians hesitate not unblushingly to say? But there were not only no good merits of theirs, but the Lord shows that evil ones actually preceded; for He says, "But for my holy name's sake, *which ye have profaned among the heathen.*" Who can fail to observe how dreadful is the evil of profaning the Lord's own holy name? And yet, for the sake of this very name of mine, says He, which ye have profaned, I, even I, will make you good, but not for your own sakes; and, as He adds, "I will sanctify my great name, which was profaned among the heathen, which ye have profaned in the midst of them." He says that He sanctifies His name, which He had already declared to be holy. Therefore, this is just what we pray for in the Lord's Prayer — "Hallowed be Thy name."[3] We ask for the hallowing among men of that which is in itself undoubtedly always holy. Then it follows, "And the heathen shall know that I am the Lord, saith the Lord God, when I shall be sanctified in you." Although, then, He is Himself always holy, He is, nevertheless, sanctified in those on whom He bestows His grace, by taking from them that stony heart by which they profaned the name of the Lord.

## CHAP. 31 [XV.] — FREE WILL HAS ITS FUNCTION IN THE HEART'S CONVERSION; BUT GRACE TOO HAS ITS.

Lest, however, it should be thought that men themselves in this matter do nothing by free will, it is said in the Psalm, "Harden not your hearts;"[4] and in Ezekiel himself, "Cast away from you all your transgressions, which ye have impiously committed against me; and make you a new heart and a new spirit; and keep all my commandments. For why will ye die, O house of Israel, saith the Lord? for I have no pleasure in the death of him that dieth, saith the Lord God: and turn ye, and live."[5] We should remember that it is He who says, "Turn ye and live," to whom it is said in prayer, "Turn us again, O God."[6] We should remember that He says, "Cast away from you all your transgressions," when it is even He who justifies the ungodly. We should remember that He says, "Make you a new heart and a new spirit," who also promises, "I will give you a new heart, and a new spirit will I put within you."[7] How is it, then, that He who says, "Make you," also says, "I will give you"? Why does He command, if He is to give? Why does He give if man is to make, except it be that He gives what He commands when He helps him to obey when He commands? There is, however, always within us a free will, — but it is not always good; for it is either free from righteousness when it serves sin, — and then it is evil, — or else it is free from sin when it serves righteousness, — and then it is good. But the grace of God is always good; and by it it comes to pass that a man is of a good will, though he was before of an evil one. By it also it comes to pass that the very good will, which has now begun to be, is enlarged, and made so great that it is able to fulfil the divine commandments which it shall wish, when it shall once firmly and perfectly wish. This is the purport of what the Scripture says: "If thou wilt, thou shalt keep the commandments;"[8] so that the man who wills but is not able knows that he does not yet fully will, and prays that he may

---

[1] In several editions and MSS. there is inserted here the phrase "*not for your sakes.*"
[2] Ezek. xxxvi. 22-27.

[3] Matt. vi. 9. [The word-play is significant in the Latin: "He says that he sanctifies (*sanctificare*) His name which He had already declared to be Holy (*sanctum*). This is, therefore, what we pray for in the Lord's Prayer when we say, "Hallowed (*sanctificatur*) be thy name," etc. — W.]
[4] Ps. xcv. 8.     [5] Ezek. xviii. 31, 32.     [6] Ps. lxxx. 3.
[7] Ezek. xxxvi 26.     [8] Ecclus. xv. 15.

have so great a will that it may suffice for keeping the commandments. And thus, indeed, he receives assistance to perform what he is commanded. Then is the will of use when we have ability; just as ability is also then of use when we have the will. For what does it profit us if we will what we are unable to do, or else do not will what we are able to do?

CHAP. 32 [XVI.] — IN WHAT SENSE IT IS RIGHTLY SAID THAT, IF WE LIKE, WE MAY KEEP GOD'S COMMANDMENTS.

The Pelagians think that they know something great when they assert that "God would not command what He knew could not be done by man." Who can be ignorant of this? But God commands some things which we cannot do, in order that we may know what we ought to ask of Him. For this is faith itself, which obtains by prayer what the law commands. He, indeed, who said, "If thou wilt, thou shalt keep the commandments," did in the same book of Ecclesiasticus afterwards say, "Who shall give a watch before my mouth, and a seal of wisdom upon my lips, that I fall not suddenly thereby, and that my tongue destroy me not."[1] Now he had certainly heard and received these commandments: "Keep thy tongue from evil, and thy lips from speaking guile."[2] Forasmuch, then, as what he said is true: "If thou wilt, thou shalt keep the commandments," why does he want a watch to be given before his mouth, like him who says in the Psalm, "Set a watch, O Lord, before my mouth"?[3] Why is he not satisfied with God's commandment and his own will; since, if he has the will, he shall keep the commandments? How many of God's commandments are directed against pride! He is quite aware of them; if he will, he may keep them. Why, therefore, does he shortly afterwards say, "O God, Father and God of my life, give me not a proud look"?[4] The law had long ago said to him, "Thou shalt not covet;"[5] let him then only will, and do what he is bidden, because, if he has the will, he shall keep the commandments. Why, therefore, does he afterwards say, "Turn away from me concupiscence"?[6] Against luxury, too, how many commandments has God enjoined! Let a man observe them; because, if he will, he may keep the commandments. But what means that cry to God, "Let not the greediness of the belly nor lust of the flesh take hold on me!"?[7] Now, if we were to put this question to him personally, he would very rightly answer us and say, From that prayer of mine, in which I offer this particular petition to God, you may understand in what sense I said, "If thou wilt, thou mayest keep the commandments." For it is certain that we keep the commandments if we will; but because the will is prepared by the Lord, we must ask of Him for such a force of will as suffices to make us act by the willing. It is certain that it is we that *will* when we will, but it is He who makes us will what is good, of whom it is said (as he has just now expressed it), "The will is prepared by the Lord."[8] Of the same Lord it is said, "The steps of a man are ordered by the Lord, and his way doth He will."[9] Of the same Lord again it is said, "It is God who worketh in you, even to will!"[10] It is certain that it is we that act when we act; but it is He who makes us act, by applying efficacious powers to our will, who has said, "I will make you to walk in my statutes, and to observe my judgments, and to do them."[11] When he says, "I will make you . . . to do them," what else does He say in fact than, "I will take away from you your heart of stone,"[12] from which used to arise your inability to act, "and I will give you a heart of flesh,"[13] in order that you may act? And what does this promise amount to but this: I will remove your hard heart, out of which you did not act, and I will give you an obedient heart, out of which you shall act? It is He who causes us to act, to whom the human suppliant says, "Set a watch, O Lord, before my mouth."[3] That is to say: Make or enable me, O Lord, to set a watch before my mouth, — a benefit which he had already obtained from God who thus described its influence: "I set a watch upon my mouth."[14]

CHAP. 33 [XVII.] — A GOOD WILL MAY BE SMALL AND WEAK; AN AMPLE WILL, GREAT LOVE. OPERATING AND CO-OPERATING GRACE.

He, therefore, who wishes to do God's commandment, but is unable, already possesses a good will, but as yet a small and weak one; he will, however, become able when he shall have acquired a great and robust will. When the martyrs did the great commandments which they obeyed, they acted by a great will, — that is, with great love. Of this love the Lord Himself thus speaks: "Greater love hath no man than this, that a man lay down his life for his friends."[15] In accordance with this, the apostle also says, "He that loveth his neighbour hath fulfilled the law. For this: Thou shalt not commit adultery, Thou shalt not kill, Thou shalt not steal, Thou shalt not covet; and if there be any other commandment, it is briefly comprehended in this saying, namely, Thou shalt love thy neighbour as thyself.[16] Love worketh no ill to his neighbour: therefore love is the fulfilling of the

---

[1] Ecclus. xxii. 27.      [2] Ps. xxxiv. 13.      [3] Ps. cxli. 3.
[4] Ecclus. xxiii. 4.      [5] Ex. xx. 17.       [6] Ecclus. xxiii. 5.
[7] Ecclus. xxiii. 6.

[8] Prov. viii. 35.      [9] Ps. xxxvii. 23.      [10] Phil. ii. 13.
[11] Ezek. xxxvi. 27.      [12] Ezek. xi. 19, and xxxvi. 26.
[13] Ezek. xxxvi. 26.      [14] Ps. xxxix. 1.      [15] John xv. 13.
[16] Lev. xix. 18.

law."[1]  This love the Apostle Peter did not yet possess, when he for fear thrice denied the Lord.[2] "There is no fear in love," says the Evangelist John in his first Epistle, " but perfect love casteth out fear."[3]  But yet, however small and imperfect his love was, it was not wholly wanting when he said to the Lord, " I will lay down my life for Thy sake ; "[4] for he supposed himself able to effect what he felt himself willing to do. And who was it that had begun to give him his love, however small, but He who prepares the will, and perfects by His co-operation what He initiates by His operation?  Forasmuch as in beginning He works in us that we may have the will, and in perfecting works with us when we have the will.[5]  On which account the apostle says, " I am confident of this very thing, that He which hath begun a good work in you will perform it until the day of Jesus Christ."[6]  He operates, therefore, without us, in order that we may will ; but when we will, and so will that we may act, He co-operates with us.  We can, however, ourselves do nothing to effect good works of piety without Him either working that we may will, or co-working when we will.  Now, concerning His working that we may will, it is said : " It is God which worketh in you, even to will."[7] While of His co-working with us, when we will and act by willing, the apostle says, " We know that in all things there is co-working for good to them that love God."[8]  What does this phrase, " all things," mean, but the terrible and cruel sufferings which affect our condition?  That burden, indeed, of Christ, which is heavy for our infirmity, becomes light to love.  For to such did the Lord say that His burden was light,[9] as Peter was when he suffered for Christ, not as he was when he denied Him.

CHAP. 34. — THE APOSTLE'S EULOGY OF LOVE. CORRECTION TO BE ADMINISTERED WITH LOVE.

This charity, that is, this will glowing with intensest love, the apostle eulogizes with these words : " Who shall separate us from the love of Christ?  shall tribulation, or distress, or persecution, or famine, or nakedness, or peril, or the sword?  (As it is written, For Thy sake we are killed all the day long ; we are accounted as sheep for the slaughter.)  Nay, in all these things we are more than conquerors, through Him that loved us.  For I am persuaded, that neither death, nor life, nor angels, nor principalities, nor things present, nor things to come, nor height, nor depth, nor any other creature, shall be able to separate us from the love of God,

which is in Christ Jesus our Lord."[10]  And in another passage he says, " And yet I show unto you a more excellent way.  Though I speak with the tongues of men and of angels, and have not love, I am become as sounding brass, or a tinkling cymbal.  And though I have the gift of prophecy, and understand all mysteries, and all knowledge ; and though I have all faith, so that I could remove mountains, and have not love, I am nothing.  And though I bestow all my goods to feed the poor, and though I give my body to be burned, and have not love, it profiteth me nothing.  Love suffereth long, and is kind ; love envieth not ; love vaunteth not itself, is not puffed up, doth not behave itself unseemly, seeketh not her own, is not easily provoked, thinketh no evil ; rejoiceth not in iniquity, but rejoiceth in the truth ; beareth all things, believeth all things, hopeth all things, endureth all things.  Love never faileth."[11]  And a little afterwards he says, " And now abideth faith, hope, love, these three ; but the greatest of these is love.  Follow after love."[12]  He also says to the Galatians, " For, brethren, ye have been called unto liberty ; only use not liberty for an occasion to the flesh, but by love serve one another.  For all the law is fulfilled in one word, even in this, Thou shalt love thy neighbour as thyself."[13]  This is the same in effect as what he writes to the Romans : " He that loveth another hath fulfilled the law."[14] In like manner he says to the Colossians, " And above all these things, put on love, which is the bond of perfectness."[15]  And to Timothy he writes, " Now the end of the commandment is love ; " and he goes on to describe the quality of this grace, saying, " Out of a pure heart, and of a good conscience, and of faith unfeigned."[16] Moreover, when he says to the Corinthians, " Let all your things be done with love,"[17] he shows plainly enough that even those chastisements which are deemed sharp and bitter by those who are corrected thereby, are to be administered with love.  Accordingly, in another passage, after saying, " Warn them that are unruly, comfort the feeble-minded, support the weak, be patient toward all men," he immediately added, " See that none render evil for evil unto any man."[18] Therefore, even when the unruly are corrected, it is not rendering evil for evil, but contrariwise, good.  However, what but love worketh all these things?

CHAP. 35. — COMMENDATIONS OF LOVE.

The Apostle Peter, likewise, says, " And, above all things, have fervent love among yourselves : for love shall cover the multitude of sins."[19]  The Apostle James also says, " If ye

---

[1] Rom. xiii. 8-10.　　[2] Matt. xxvi. 69-75.　　[3] 1 John iv. 18.
[4] John xiii. 37.
[5] Compare Art. X. of the Church of England.
[6] Phil. i. 6.　　　　　　　　　　　　[7] Phil. ii. 13.
[8] Rom. viii. 28.  The Latin indefinite passive *co-operatur* invited this turn in the usage of the passage.
[9] Matt. xi. 30.

[10] Rom. viii. 35-39.　　　　[11] 1 Cor. xii. 31, xiii. 8.
[12] 1 Cor. xiii. 13, and xiv. 1.　　[13] Gal. v. 13, 14, and Lev. xix. 18.
[14] Rom. xiii. 8.　　[15] Col. iii. 14.　　[16] 1 Tim. i. 5.
[17] 1 Cor. xvi. 14.　　[18] 1 Thess. v. 14, 15.　　[19] 1 Pet. iv. 8.

fulfil the royal law, according to the Scripture, Thou shalt love thy neighbour as thyself, ye do well." [1] So also the Apostle John says, "He that loveth his brother abideth in the right; " [2] again, in another passage, "Whosoever doeth not righteousness is not of God, neither he that loveth not his brother; for this is the message which we have heard from the beginning, that we should love one another." [3] Then he says again, "This is His commandment, that we should believe on the name of His Son Jesus Christ, and love one another." [4] Once more: "And this commandment have we from Him, that he who loveth God love his brother also." [5] Then shortly afterwards he adds, "By this we know that we love the children of God, when we love God, and keep His commandments; for this is the love of God, that we keep His commandments: and His commandments are not grievous." [6] While, in his second Epistle, it is written, "Not as though I wrote a new commandment unto thee, but that which we had from the beginning, that we love one another." [7]

CHAP. 36. — LOVE COMMENDED BY OUR LORD HIMSELF.

Moreover, the Lord Jesus Himself teaches us that the whole law and the prophets hang upon the two precepts of love to God and love to our neighbour. Concerning these two commandments the following is written in the Gospel according to St. Mark : "And one of the scribes came, and having heard them reasoning together, and perceiving that He had answered them well, asked Him : Which is the first commandment of all? And Jesus answered him : The first of all the commandments is, Hear, O Israel ! the Lord our God is one Lord ; and thou shalt love the Lord thy God with all thine heart, and with all thy soul, and with all thy mind, and with all thy strength.[8] This is the first commandment. And the second is like unto it : Thou shalt love thy neighbour as thyself.[9] There is none other commandment greater than these." [10] Also, in the Gospel according to St. John, He says, "A new commandment I give unto you, that ye love one another; as I have loved you, that ye also love one another. By this shall all men know that ye are my disciples, if ye have love to one another." [11]

CHAP. 37 [XVIII.] — THE LOVE WHICH FULFILS THE COMMANDMENTS IS NOT OF OURSELVES, BUT OF GOD.

All these commandments, however, respecting love or charity [12] (which are so great, and such

that whatever action a man may think he does well is by no means well done if done without love) would be given to men in vain if they had not free choice of will. But forasmuch as these precepts are given in the law, both old and new (although in the new came the grace which was promised in the old, but the law without grace is the letter which killeth, but in grace the Spirit which giveth life), from what source is there in men the love of God and of one's neighbour but from God Himself? For indeed, if it be not of God but of men, the Pelagians have gained the victory; but if it come from God, then we have vanquished the Pelagians. Let, then, the Apostle John sit in judgment between us; and let him say to us, "Beloved, let us love one another." [13] Now, when they begin to extol themselves on these words of John, and to ask why this precept is addressed to us at all if we have not of our own selves to love one another, the same apostle proceeds at once, to their confusion, to add, "For love is of God." [13] It is not of ourselves, therefore, but it is of God. Wherefore, then, is it said, "Let us love one another, for love is of God," unless it be as a precept to our free will, admonishing it to seek the gift of God? Now, this would be indeed a thoroughly fruitless admonition if the will did not previously receive some donation of love, which might seek to be enlarged so as to fulfil whatever command was laid upon it. When it is said, "Let us love one another," it is law; when it is said, "For love is of God," it is grace. For God's "wisdom carries law and mercy upon her tongue." [14] Accordingly, it is written in the Psalm, "For He who gave the law will give blessings." [15]

CHAP. 38. — WE WOULD NOT LOVE GOD UNLESS HE FIRST LOVED US. THE APOSTLES CHOSE CHRIST BECAUSE THEY WERE CHOSEN; THEY WERE NOT CHOSEN BECAUSE THEY CHOSE CHRIST.

Let no one, then, deceive you, my brethren, for we should not love God unless He first loved us. John again gives us the plainest proof of this when he says, "We love Him because He first loved us." [16] Grace makes us lovers of the law; but the law itself, without grace, makes us nothing but breakers of the law. And nothing else than this is shown us by the words of our Lord when He says to His disciples, "Ye have not chosen me, but I have chosen you." [17] For if we first loved Him, in order that by this merit He might love us, then we first chose Him that we might deserve to be chosen by Him. He, however, who is the Truth says otherwise, and flatly contradicts this vain conceit of men. "You have not chosen me,"

---

[1] Jas. ii. 8.  [2] 1 John ii. 10.  [3] 1 John iii. 10, 11.
[4] 1 John iii. 23.  [5] 1 John iv. 21.  [6] 1 John v. 2, 3.
[7] 2 John ver. 5.  [8] Deut. vi. 4, 5.  [9] Lev. xix. 18.
[10] Mark xii. 28–31.  [11] John xiii. 34, 35.
[12] ["Love or charity," the disjunctive being intended to *identify*, not *distinguish*, the two. The word *amor* is distinguishable from the pair (*dilectio* and *charitas*) here used, though even this must not be pressed too far. See Augustin's *City of God*, xiv. 7. — W.]

[13] 1 John iv. 7.  [14] Prov. iii. 16.  [15] Ps. lxxxiv. 6.
[16] 1 John iv. 19.  [17] John xv. 16.

He says. If, therefore, you have not chosen me, undoubtedly you have not loved me (for how could they choose one whom they did not love?). "But I," says He, "have chosen you." And then could they possibly help choosing Him afterwards, and preferring Him to all the blessings of this world? But it was because they had been chosen, that they chose Him; not because they chose Him that they were chosen. There could be no merit in men's choice of Christ, if it were not that God's grace was prevenient in His choosing them. Whence the Apostle Paul pronounces in the Thessalonians this benediction: "The Lord make you to increase and abound in love one toward another, and toward all men." [1] This benediction to love one another He gave us, who had also given us a law that we should love each other. Then, in another passage addressed to the same church, seeing that there now existed in some of its members the disposition which he had wished them to cultivate, he says, "We are bound to thank God always for you, brethren, as it is meet, because that your faith groweth exceedingly, and the charity of every one of you all toward each other aboundeth." [2] This he said lest they should make a boast of the great good which they were enjoying from God, as if they had it of their own mere selves. Because, then, your faith has so great a growth (this is the purport of his words), and the love of every one of you all toward each other so greatly abounds, we ought to thank God concerning you, but not to praise you, as if you possessed these gifts of yourselves.

### CHAP. 39. — THE SPIRIT OF FEAR A GREAT GIFT OF GOD.

The apostle also says to Timothy, "For God hath not given to us the spirit of fear, but of power, and of love, and of a sound mind." [3] Now in respect of this passage of the apostle, we must be on our guard against supposing that we have not received the spirit of the fear of God, which is undoubtedly a great gift of God, and concerning which the prophet Isaiah says, "The Spirit of the Lord shall rest upon thee, the spirit of wisdom and understanding, the spirit of counsel and might, the spirit of knowledge and piety, the spirit of the fear of the Lord." [4] It is not the fear with which Peter denied Christ that we have received the spirit of, but that fear concerning which Christ Himself says, "Fear Him who hath power to destroy both soul and body in hell; yea, I say unto you, Fear Him." [5] This, indeed, He said, lest we should deny Him from the same fear which shook Peter; for such cowardice he plainly wished to be removed from us when He, in the preceding passage, said, "Be not afraid of them that kill the body, and after that have no more that they can do." [6] It is not of this fear that we have received the spirit, but of power, and of love, and of a sound mind. And of this spirit the same Apostle Paul discourses to the Romans: "We glory in tribulations, knowing that tribulation worketh patience; and patience, experience; and experience, hope; and hope maketh not ashamed; because the love of God is shed abroad in our hearts by the Holy Ghost, which is given unto us." [7] Not by ourselves, therefore, but by the Holy Ghost which is given to us, does it come to pass that, through that very love, which he shows us to be the gift of God, tribulation does not do away with patience, but rather produces it. Again, he says to the Ephesians, "Peace be to the brethren, and love with faith." [8] Great blessings these! Let him tell us, however, whence they come. "From God the Father," says he immediately afterwards, "and the Lord Jesus Christ." [9] These great blessings, therefore, are nothing else than God's gifts to us.

### CHAP. 40 [XIX.] — THE IGNORANCE OF THE PELAGIANS IN MAINTAINING THAT THE KNOWLEDGE OF THE LAW COMES FROM GOD, BUT THAT LOVE COMES FROM OURSELVES.

It is no wonder that light shineth in darkness, and the darkness comprehendeth it not.[9] In John's Epistle the Light declares, "Behold what manner of love the Father hath bestowed upon us, that we should be called the sons of God." [10] And in the Pelagian writings the darkness says, "Love comes to us of our own selves." Now, if they only possessed the true, that is, Christian love, they would also know whence they obtained possession of it; even as the apostle knew when he said, "But we have received not the spirit of the world, but the Spirit which is of God, that we might know the things that are freely given to us of God." [11] John says, "God is love." [12] And thus the Pelagians affirm that they actually have God Himself, not from God, but from their own selves! and although they allow that we have the knowledge of the law from God, they will yet have it that love is from our very selves. Nor do they listen to the apostle when he says, "Knowledge puffeth up, but love edifieth." [13] Now what can be more absurd, nay, what more insane and more alien from the very sacredness of love itself, than to maintain that from God proceeds the knowledge which, apart from love, puffs us up, while the love which prevents the possibility of this infla-

---

[1] 1 Thess. iii. 12.    [2] 2 Thess. i. 3.    [3] 2 Tim. i. 7.
[4] Isa. xi. 2.    [5] Luke xii. 5.

[6] Luke xii. 4.    [7] Rom. v. 3, 4, 5.    [8] Eph. vi. 23.
[9] John i. 5.    [10] 1 John iii. 1.    [11] 1 Cor. ii. 12.
[12] 1 John iv. 16.    [13] 1 Cor. viii. 1.

tion of knowledge springs from ourselves? And again, when the apostle speaks of "the love of Christ as surpassing knowledge," [1] what can be more insane than to suppose that the knowledge which must be subordinated to love comes from God, while the love which surpasses knowledge comes from man? The true faith, however, and sound doctrine declare that both graces are from God; the Scripture says, "From His face cometh knowledge and understanding;" [2] and another Scripture says, "Love is of God." [3] We read of "the Spirit of wisdom and understanding." [4] Also of "the Spirit of power, and of love, and of a sound mind." [5] But love is a greater gift than knowledge; for whenever a man has the gift of knowledge, love is necessary by the side of it, that he be not puffed up. For "love envieth not, vaunteth not itself, is not puffed up." [6]

CHAP. 41 [XX.] — THE WILLS OF MEN ARE SO MUCH IN THE POWER OF GOD, THAT HE CAN TURN THEM WHITHERSOEVER IT PLEASES HIM.

I think I have now discussed the point fully enough in opposition to those who vehemently oppose the grace of God, by which, however, the human will is not taken away, but changed from bad to good, and assisted when it is good. I think, too, that I have so discussed the subject that it is not so much I myself as the inspired Scripture which has spoken to you, in the clearest testimonies of truth; and if this divine record be looked into carefully, it shows us that not only men's good wills, which God Himself converts from bad ones, and, when converted by Him, directs to good actions and to eternal life, but also those which follow the world are so entirely at the disposal of God, that He turns them whithersoever He wills, and whensoever He wills, — to bestow kindness on some, and to heap punishment on others, as He Himself judges right by a counsel most secret to Himself, indeed, but beyond all doubt most righteous. For we find that some sins are even the punishment of other sins, as are those "vessels of wrath" which the apostle describes as "fitted to destruction;" [7] as is also that hardening of Pharaoh, the purpose of which is said to be to set forth in him the power of God; [8] as, again, is the flight of the Israelites from the face of the enemy before the city of Ai, for fear arose in their heart so that they fled, and this was done that their sin might be punished in the way it was right that it should be; by reason of which the Lord said to Joshua the son of Nun, "The children of Israel shall not be able to stand before the face of their enemies." [9] What is the

meaning of, "They shall not be able to stand"? Now, why did they not stand by free will, but, with a will perplexed by fear, took to flight, were it not that God has the lordship even over men's wills, and when He is angry turns to fear whomsoever He pleases? Was it not of their own will that the enemies of the children of Israel fought against the people of God, as led by Joshua, the son of Nun? And yet the Scripture says, "It was of the Lord to harden their hearts, that they should come against Israel in battle, that they might be exterminated." [10] And was it not likewise of his own will that the wicked son of Gera cursed King David? And yet what says David, full of true, and deep, and pious wisdom? What did he say to him who wanted to smite the reviler? "What," said he, "have I to do with you, ye sons of Zeruiah? Let him alone and let him curse, because the Lord hath said unto him, Curse David. Who, then, shall say, Wherefore hast thou done so?" [11] And then the inspired Scripture, as if it would confirm the king's profound utterance by repeating it once more, tells us: "And David said to Abishai, and to all his servants, Behold, my son, which came forth from my bowels, seeketh my life: how much more may this Benjamite do it! Let him alone, and let him curse; for the Lord hath bidden him. It may be that the Lord will look on my humiliation, and will requite me good for his cursing this day." [12] Now what prudent reader will fail to understand in what way the Lord bade this profane man to curse David? It was not by a command that He bade him, in which case his obedience would be praiseworthy; but He inclined the man's will, which had become debased by his own perverseness, to commit this sin, by His own just and secret judgment. Therefore it is said, "The Lord said unto him." Now if this person had obeyed a command of God, he would have deserved to be praised rather than punished, as we know he was afterwards punished for this sin. Nor is the reason an obscure one why the Lord told him after this manner to curse David. "It may be," said the humbled king, "that the Lord will look on my humiliation, and will requite me good for his cursing this day." See, then, what proof we have here that God uses the hearts of even wicked men for the praise and assistance of the good. Thus did He make use of Judas when betraying Christ; thus did He make use of the Jews when they crucified Christ. And how vast the blessings which from these instances He has bestowed upon the nations that should believe in Him! He also uses our worst enemy, the devil himself, but in the best way, to exercise and try the faith and piety of good men, — not

---

[1] Eph. iii. 19.  [2] Prov. ii. 6.  [3] 1 John iv. 7.  [4] Isa. xi 2.  [5] 2 Tim. i. 7  [6] 1 Cor. xiii. 4.  [7] Rom. ix. 22  [8] See Ex. vii. 3, and x. 1.  [9] See Josh vii. 4, 12.

[10] Josh. xi. 20.  [11] 2 Sam. xvi. 9, 10.  [12] 2 Sam. xvi. 11, 12.

for Himself indeed, who knows all things before they come to pass, but for our sakes, for whom it was necessary that such a discipline should be gone through with us. Did not Absalom choose by his own will the counsel which was detrimental to him? And yet the reason of his doing so was that the Lord had heard his father's prayer that it might be so. Wherefore the Scripture says that "the Lord appointed to defeat the good counsel of Ahithophel, to the intent that the Lord might bring all evils upon Absalom."[1] It called Ahithophel's counsel "*good*," because it was for the moment of advantage to his purpose. It was in favour of the son against his father, against whom he had rebelled; and it might have crushed him, had not the Lord defeated the counsel which Ahithophel had given, by acting on the heart of Absalom so that he rejected this counsel, and chose another which was not expedient for him.

CHAP. 42 [XXI.] — GOD DOES WHATSOEVER HE WILLS IN THE HEARTS OF EVEN WICKED MEN.

Who can help trembling at those judgments of God by which He does in the hearts of even wicked men whatsoever He wills, at the same time rendering to them according to their deeds? Rehoboam, the son of Solomon, rejected the salutary counsel of the old men, not to deal harshly with the people, and preferred listening to the words of the young men of his own age, by returning a rough answer to those to whom he should have spoken gently. Now whence arose such conduct, except from his own will? Upon this, however, the ten tribes of Israel revolted from him, and chose for themselves another king, even Jeroboam, that the will of God in His anger might be accomplished which He had predicted would come to pass.[2] For what says the Scripture? "The king hearkened not unto the people; for the turning was from the Lord, that He might perform His saying, which the Lord spake to Ahijah the Shilonite concerning Jeroboam the son of Nebat."[3] All this, indeed, was done by the will of man, although the turning was from the Lord. Read the books of the Chronicles, and you will find the following passage in the second book: "Moreover, the Lord stirred up against Jehoram the spirit of the Philistines, and of the Arabians, that were neighbours to the Ethiopians; and they came up to the land of Judah, and ravaged it, and carried away all the substance which was found in the king's house."[4] Here it is shown that God stirs up enemies to devastate the countries which He adjudges deserving of such chastisement. Still, did these Philistines and Arabians invade the land of Judah to waste it with no will

of their own? Or were their movements so directed by their own will that the Scripture lies which tells us that "the Lord stirred up their spirit" to do all this? Both statements to be sure are true, because they both came by their own will, and yet the Lord stirred up their spirit; and this may also with equal truth be stated the other way: The Lord both stirred up their spirit, and yet they came of their own will. For the Almighty sets in motion even in the innermost hearts of men the movement of their will, so that He does through their agency whatsoever He wishes to perform through them, — even He who knows not how to will anything in unrighteousness. What, again, is the purport of that which the man of God said to King Amaziah: "Let not the army of Israel go with thee; for the Lord is not with Israel, even with all the children of Ephraim: for if thou shalt think to obtain with these, the Lord shall put thee to flight before thine enemies: for God hath power either to strengthen or to put to flight"?[5] Now, how does the power of God help some in war by giving them confidence, and put others to flight by injecting fear into them, except it be that He who has made all things according to His own will, in heaven and on earth,[6] also works in the hearts of men? We read also what Joash, king of Israel, said when he sent a message to Amaziah, king of Judah, who wanted to fight with him. After certain other words, he added, "Now tarry at home; why dost thou challenge me to thine hurt, that thou shouldest fall, even thou, and Judah with thee?"[7] Then the Scripture has added this sequel: "But Amaziah would not hear; for it came of God, that he might be delivered into their hands, because they sought after the gods of Edom."[8] Behold, now, how God, wishing to punish the sin of idolatry, wrought this in this man's heart, with whom He was indeed justly angry, not to listen to sound advice, but to despise it, and go to the battle, in which he with his army was routed. God says by the prophet Ezekiel, "If the prophet be deceived when he hath spoken a thing, I the Lord have deceived that prophet: I will stretch out my hand upon him, and will destroy him from the midst of my people Israel."[9] Then there is the book of Esther, who was a woman of the people of Israel, and in the land of their captivity became the wife of the foreign King Ahasuerus. In this book it is written, that, being driven by necessity to interpose in behalf of her people, whom the king had ordered to be slain in every part of his dominions, she prayed to the Lord. So strongly was she urged by the necessity of the case, that she even ventured into the royal presence with-

[1] 2 Sam. xvii. 14.　　[2] 1 Kings xii. 8-14.　　[3] 1 Kings xii. 15.
[4] 2 Chron. xxi. 16. 17.

[5] 2 Chron. xxv. 7, 8.　　[6] Ps. cxxxv. 6.　　[7] 2 Kings xiv. 10.
[8] 2 Chron. xxv. 20.　　[9] Ezek. xiv. 9.

out the king's command, and contrary to her own custom. Now observe what the Scripture says : " He looked at her like a bull in the vehemence of his indignation ; and the queen was afraid, and her colour changed as she fainted ; and she bowed herself upon the head of her delicate maiden which went before' her. But God turned the king, and transformed his indignation into gentleness." [1] The Scripture says in the Proverbs of Solomon, " Even as the rush of water, so is the heart of a king in God's hand ; He will turn it in whatever way He shall choose." [2]   Again, in the 104th Psalm, in reference to the Egyptians, one reads what God did to them : " And He turned their heart to hate His people, to deal subtilly with His servants." [3] Observe, likewise, what is written in the letters of the apostles. In the Epistle of Paul, the Apostle, to the Romans occur these words : " Wherefore God gave them up to uncleanness, through the lusts of their own hearts ; " [4] and a little afterwards : " For this cause God gave them up unto vile affections ; " [5] again, in the next passage : " And even as they did not like to retain God in their knowledge, God gave them over to a reprobate mind, to do those things which are not convenient." [6]   So also in his second Epistle to the Thessalonians, the apostle says of sundry persons, " Inasmuch as they received not the love of the truth, that they might be saved ; therefore also God shall send them strong delusion, that they should believe a lie ; that they all might be judged who believed not the truth, but had pleasure in unrighteousness." [7]

CHAP. 43. — GOD OPERATES ON MEN'S HEARTS TO INCLINE THEIR WILLS WHITHERSOEVER HE PLEASES.

From these statements of the inspired word, and from similar passages which it would take too long to quote in full, it is, I think, sufficiently clear that God works in the hearts of men to incline their wills whithersoever He wills, whether to good deeds according to His mercy, or to evil after their own deserts ; His own judgment being sometimes manifest, sometimes secret, but always righteous. This ought to be the fixed and immoveable conviction of your heart, that there is no unrighteousness with God. Therefore, whenever you read in the Scriptures of Truth, that men are led aside, or that their hearts are blunted and hardened by God, never doubt that some ill deserts of their own have first occurred, so that they justly suffer these things. Thus you will not run counter to that proverb of Solomon : " The foolishness of a

man perverteth his ways, yet he blameth God in his heart." [8]   Grace, however, is not bestowed according to men's deserts ; otherwise grace would be no longer grace. [9]   For grace is so designated because it is given gratuitously. [10]   Now if God is able, either through the agency of angels (whether good ones or evil), or in any other way whatever, to operate in the hearts even of the wicked, in return for their deserts, — whose wickedness was not made by Him, but was either derived originally from Adam, or increased by their own will, — what is there to wonder at if, through the Holy Spirit, He works good in the hearts of the elect, who has wrought it that their hearts become good instead of evil ?

CHAP. 44 [XXII.] — GRATUITOUS GRACE EXEMPLIFIED IN INFANTS.

Men, however, may suppose that there are certain good deserts which they think are precedent to justification through God's grace ; all the while failing to see, when they express such an opinion, that they do nothing else than deny grace. But, as I have already remarked, let them suppose what they like respecting the case of adults, in the case of infants, at any rate, the Pelagians find no means of answering the difficulty. For these in receiving grace have no will, from the influence of which they can pretend to any precedent merit. We see, moreover, how they cry and struggle when they are baptized, and feel the divine sacraments. Such conduct would, of course, be charged against them as a great impiety, if they already had free will in use ; and notwithstanding this, grace cleaves to them even in their resisting struggles. But most certainly there is no prevenient merit, otherwise the grace would be no longer grace. Sometimes, too, this grace is bestowed upon the children of unbelievers, when they happen by some means or other to fall, by reason of God's secret providence, into the hands of pious persons ; but, on the other hand, the children of believers fail to obtain grace, some hindrance occurring to prevent the approach of help to rescue them in their danger. These things, no doubt, happen through the secret providence of God, whose judgments are unsearchable, and His ways past finding out. These are the words of the apostle ; and you should observe what he had previously said, to lead him to add such a remark. He was discoursing about the Jews and Gentiles, when he wrote to the Romans — themselves Gentiles — to this effect : " For as ye, in times past, have not believed God, yet have now obtained mercy through their unbelief ; even so have these also now not believed,

---

[1] Esther v. (according to the *Sept*.).     [2] Prov. xxi. 1.
[3] Ps. cv. 25.       [4] Rom. i. 24.      [5] Rom. i. 26.
[6] Rom i. 28.       [7] 2 Thess. ii. 10–12.

[8] Prov. xix. 3.       [9] Rom. xi. 6.       [10] Latin, *gratis*.

that through your mercy they also may obtain mercy; for God hath concluded them all in unbelief, that He might have mercy upon all." [1] Now, after he had thought upon what he said, full of wonder at the certain truth of his own assertion, indeed, but astonished at its great depth, how God concluded all in unbelief that He might have mercy upon all, — as if doing evil that good might come, — he at once exclaimed, and said, "O the depth of the riches both of the wisdom and knowledge of God! how unsearchable are His judgments, and His ways past finding out!" [2] Perverse men, who do not reflect upon these unsearchable judgments and untraceable ways, indeed, but are ever prone to censure, being unable to understand, have supposed the apostle to say, and censoriously gloried over him for saying, "Let us do evil, that good may come!" God forbid that the apostle should say so! But men, without understanding, have thought that this was in fact said, when they heard these words of the apostle: "Moreover, the law entered, that the offence might abound; but where sin abounded, grace did much more abound." [3] But grace, indeed, effects this purpose — that good works should now be wrought by those who previously did evil; not that they should persevere in evil courses and suppose that they are recompensed with good. Their language, therefore, ought not to be: "Let us do evil, that good may come;" but: "We have done evil, and good has come; let us henceforth do good, that in the future world we may receive good for good, who in the present life are receiving good for evil." Wherefore it is written in the Psalm, "I will sing of mercy and judgment unto Thee, O Lord." [4] When the Son of man, therefore, first came into the world, it was not to judge the world, but that the world through Him might be saved. [5] And this dispensation was for mercy; by and by, however, He will come for judgment — to judge the quick and the dead. And yet even in this present time salvation itself does not eventuate without judgment — although it be a hidden one; therefore He says, "For judgment I am come into this world, that they which see not may see, and that they which see may be made blind." [6]

CHAP. 45 [XXIII.] — THE REASON WHY ONE PERSON IS ASSISTED BY GRACE, AND ANOTHER IS NOT HELPED, MUST BE REFERRED TO THE SECRET JUDGMENTS OF GOD.

You must refer the matter, then, to the hidden determinations of God, when you see, in one and the same condition, such as all infants unquestionably have, — who derive their hereditary

evil from Adam, — that one is assisted so as to be baptized, and another is not assisted, so that he dies in his very bondage; and again, that one baptized person is left and forsaken in his present life, who God foreknew would be ungodly, while another baptized person is taken away from this life, "lest that wickedness should alter his understanding;" [7] and be sure that you do not in such cases ascribe unrighteousness or unwisdom to God, in whom is the very fountain of righteousness and wisdom, but, as I have exhorted you from the commencement of this treatise, "whereto you have already attained, walk therein," [8] and "even this shall God reveal unto you," [9] — if not in this life, yet certainly in the next, "for there is nothing covered that shall not be revealed." [10] When, therefore, you hear the Lord say, "I the Lord have deceived that prophet," [11] and likewise what the apostle says: "He hath mercy on whom He will have mercy, and whom He will He hardeneth," [12] believe that, in the case of him whom He permits to be deceived and hardened, his evil deeds have deserved the judgment; whilst in the case of him to whom He shows mercy, you should loyally and unhesitatingly recognise the grace of the God who "rendereth not evil for evil; but contrariwise blessing." [13] Nor should you take away from Pharaoh free will, because in several passages God says, "I have hardened Pharaoh;" or, "I have hardened or I will harden Pharaoh's heart;" [14] for it does not by any means follow that Pharaoh did not, on this account, harden his own heart. For this, too, is said of him, after the removal of the fly-plague from the Egyptians, in these words of the Scripture: "And Pharaoh hardened his heart at this time also; neither would he let the people go." [15] Thus it was that both God hardened him by His just judgment, and Pharaoh by his own free will. Be ye then well assured that your labour will never be in vain, if, setting before you a good purpose, you persevere in it to the last. For God, who fails to render, according to their deeds, only to those whom He liberates, will then "recompense every man according to his works." [16] God will, therefore, certainly recompense both evil for evil, because He is just; and good for evil, because He is good; and good for good, because He is good and just; only, evil for good He will never recompense, because He is not unjust. He will, therefore, recompense evil for evil — punishment for unrighteousness; and He will recompense good for evil — grace for unrighteousness; and He will recompense good for good — grace for grace.

---

[1] Rom. xi. 30–32.      [2] Rom. xi. 33.      [3] Rom. v. 20.
[4] Ps. ci. 1.            [5] John iii. 17.      [6] John ix. 39.

[7] Wisd. iv. 11.        [8] Phil. iii. 16.      [9] Phil. iii. 15.
[10] Matt. x. 26.        [11] Ezek. xiv. 9.      [12] Rom. ix. 18.
[13] 1 Pet. iii. 9.       [14] See Ex. iv. 21, vii. 3, xiv. 4.
[15] Ex. viii. 32.        [16] Matt. xvi 27.

CHAP. 46 [XXIV.] — UNDERSTANDING AND WISDOM MUST BE SOUGHT FROM GOD.

Peruse attentively this treatise, and if you understand it, give God the praise; but where you fail to understand it, pray for understanding, for God will give you understanding. Remember what the Scriptures say: "If any of you lack wisdom, let him ask of God, who giveth to all men liberally, and upbraideth not; and it shall be given to him."[1] Wisdom itself cometh down from above, as the Apostle James himself tells us.[2] There is, however, another wisdom, which you must repel from you, and pray against its remaining in you; this the same apostle expressed his detestation of when he said, "But if ye have bitter envying and strife in your hearts, . . . this is not the wisdom which descendeth from above, but is earthly, sensual, devilish. For wherever there is envying and strife, there is also confusion, and every evil work. But the wisdom which is from above is first pure, then peaceable, gentle, and easy to be entreated, full of mercy and good works, without partiality, and without hypocrisy."[3] What blessing, then, will that man not have who has prayed for this wisdom and obtained it of the Lord? And from this you may understand what grace is; because if this wisdom were of ourselves, it would not be from above; nor would it be an object to be asked for of the God who created us. Brethren, pray ye for us also, that we may live "soberly, righteously, and godly in this present world; looking for that blessed hope, and the glorious appearing of our Lord and Saviour Jesus Christ,"[4] to whom belong the honour, and the glory, and the kingdom, with the Father and the Holy Ghost, for ever and ever. Amen.

---

[1] Jas. i. 5.　　　[2] Jas. i. 17, and iii. 17.　　　[3] Jas. iii. 14-17.　　　[4] Titus ii. 12.

# A TREATISE ON REBUKE AND GRACE.

# EXTRACT FROM AUGUSTIN'S "RETRACTATIONS,"

## BOOK II. CHAP. 67,

### *ON THE FOLLOWING TREATISE,*

## "DE CORREPTIONE ET GRATIA."

---

I WROTE again to the same persons [1] another treatise, which I entitled *On Rebuke and Grace,* because I had been told that some one there had said that no man ought to be rebuked for not doing God's commandments, but that prayer only should be made on his behalf, that he may do them. This book begins on this wise, "I have read your letters, dearly beloved brother Valentine."

[1] Valentine, to wit, and the monks with him who inhabited the convent at Adrumetum. See above, at the beginning of the preceding treatise. *On Grace and Free Will.*

# CONTENTS OF THE TREATISE "ON REBUKE AND GRACE."

# TREATISE ON REBUKE AND GRACE.

*BY AURELIUS AUGUSTIN, BISHOP OF HIPPO;*

### In One Book,

## ADDRESSED TO VALENTINE, AND WITH HIM TO THE MONKS OF ADRUMETUM.

A.D. 426 OR 427.

---

IN THE BEGINNING THE WRITER SETS FORTH WHAT IS THE CATHOLIC FAITH CONCERNING LAW, CONCERNING FREE WILL, AND CONCERNING GRACE. HE TEACHES THAT THE GRACE OF GOD BY JESUS CHRIST IS THAT BY WHICH ALONE MEN ARE DELIVERED FROM EVIL, AND WITHOUT WHICH THEY DO ABSOLUTELY NO GOOD; AND THIS NOT ONLY BY THE FACT THAT IT POINTS OUT WHAT IS TO BE DONE, BUT THAT IT ALSO SUPPLIES THE MEANS OF DOING IT WITH LOVE, SINCE GOD BESTOWS ON MEN THE INSPIRATION OF A GOOD WILL AND DEED. HE TEACHES THAT THE REBUKE OF EVIL MEN WHO HAVE NOT RECEIVED THIS GRACE IS NEITHER UNJUST — SINCE THEY ARE EVIL BY THEIR OWN WILL — NOR USELESS, ALTHOUGH IT MUST BE CONFESSED THAT IT IS ONLY BY GOD'S AGENCY THAT IT CAN AVAIL. THAT PERSEVERANCE IN GOOD IS TRULY A GREAT GIFT OF GOD, BUT THAT STILL THE REBUKE OF ONE WHO HAS NOT PERSEVERED MUST NOT ON THAT ACCOUNT BE NEGLECTED; AND THAT IF A MAN WHO HAS NOT RECEIVED THIS GIFT SHOULD RELAPSE OF HIS OWN WILL INTO SIN, HE IS NOT ONLY DESERVING OF REBUKE, BUT IF HE SHOULD CONTINUE IN EVIL UNTIL HIS DEATH, HE IS MOREOVER WORTHY OF ETERNAL DAMNATION. THAT IT IS INSCRUTABLE WHY ONE SHOULD RECEIVE THIS GIFT AND ANOTHER SHOULD NOT RECEIVE IT. THAT OF THOSE WHO ARE PREDESTINATED NONE CAN PERISH. AND THAT THE PERSEVERANCE, WHICH ALL DO NOT RECEIVE WHO ARE HERE CALLED CHILDREN OF GOD, IS CONSTANTLY GIVEN TO ALL THOSE WHO ARE TRULY CHILDREN BY GOD'S FOREKNOWLEDGE AND PREDESTINATION. HE ANSWERS THE QUESTION WHICH SUGGESTS ITSELF CONCERNING ADAM — IN WHAT WAY HE SINNED BY NOT PERSEVERING, SINCE HE DID NOT RECEIVE PERSEVERANCE. HE SHOWS THAT SUCH ASSISTANCE WAS AT THE FIRST GIVEN TO HIM, AS THAT WITHOUT IT HE COULD NOT CONTINUE IF HE WOULD, NOT AS THAT WITH IT IT MUST RESULT THAT HE WOULD. BUT THAT NOW THROUGH CHRIST IS GIVEN US NOT ONLY SUCH HELP AS THAT WITHOUT IT WE CANNOT CONTINUE EVEN IF WE WILL, BUT MOREOVER SUCH AND SO GREAT AS THAT BY IT WE WILL. HE PROVES THAT THE NUMBER OF THE PREDESTINATED, TO WHOM A GIFT OF THIS KIND IS APPROPRIATED, IS CERTAIN, AND CAN NEITHER BE INCREASED NOR

DIMINISHED.   AND SINCE IT IS UNKNOWN WHO BELONGS TO THAT NUMBER, AND
WHO DOES NOT, THAT MEDICINAL REBUKE MUST BE APPLIED TO ALL WHO SIN,
LEST THEY SHOULD EITHER THEMSELVES PERISH, OR BE THE RUIN OF OTHERS.
FINALLY, HE CONCLUDES THAT NEITHER IS REBUKE PROHIBITED BY GRACE, NOR
IS GRACE DENIED BY REBUKE.

### CHAP. 1 [I.] — INTRODUCTORY.

I HAVE read your letter — Valentine, my dearly
beloved brother, and you who are associated
with him in the service of God — which your
Love sent by brother Florus and those who came
to us with him ; and I gave God thanks that I
have known your peace in the Lord and agreement in the truth and ardour in love, by your discourse delivered to us.   But that an enemy has
striven among you to the subversion of some,
has, by the mercy of God and His marvellous
goodness in turning his arts to the advantage [1] of
His servants, rather availed to this result, that
while none of you were cast down for the worse,
some were built up for the better.   There is
therefore no need to reconsider again and again
all that I have already transmitted to you, sufficiently argued out in a lengthy treatise ; [2] for
your replies indicate how you have received this.
Nevertheless, do not in any wise suppose that,
when once read, it can have become sufficiently
well known to you.   Therefore if you desire to
have it exceedingly productive, do not count it
a grievance by re-perusal to make it thoroughly
familiar ; so that you may most accurately [3] know
what and what kind of questions they are, for
the solution and satisfaction of which there arises
an authority not human but divine, from which
we ought not to depart if we desire to attain to
the point whither we are tending.

### CHAP. 2. — THE CATHOLIC FAITH CONCERNING LAW, GRACE, AND FREE WILL.

Now the Lord Himself not only shows us
what evil we should shun, and what good we
should do, which is all that the letter of the
law is able to effect ; but He moreover helps us
that we may shun evil and do good, [4] which none
can do without the Spirit of grace ; and if this
be wanting, the law comes in merely to make us
guilty and to slay us.   It is on this account that
the apostle says, " The letter killeth, but the
Spirit giveth life." [5]   He, then, who lawfully
uses the law learns therein evil and good, and,
not trusting in his own strength, flees to grace,
by the help of which he may shun evil and do
good.   But who is there who flees to grace except when " the steps of a man are ordered by
the Lord, and He shall determine his way " ? [6]
And thus also to desire the help of grace is the

beginning of grace ; of which, says he, " And I
said, Now I have begun ; this is the change of
the right hand of the Most High." [7]   It is to be
confessed, therefore, that we have free choice to
do both evil and good ; but in doing evil every
one is free from righteousness and a servant of
sin, while in doing good no one can be free, unless he have been made free by Him who said,
" If the Son shall make you free, then you shall
be free indeed." [8]   Neither is it thus, that when
any one has been made free from the dominion
of sin, he no longer needs the help of his Deliverer ; but rather thus, that hearing from Him,
" Without me ye can do nothing," [9] he himself
also says to Him, " Be thou my helper ! Forsake
me not." [10]   I rejoice that I have found in our
brother Florus also this faith, which without
doubt is the true and prophetical and apostolical
and catholic faith ; whence those are the rather
to be corrected — whom indeed I now think to
have been corrected by the favour of God — who
did not understand him.

### CHAP. 3 [II.] — WHAT THE GRACE OF GOD THROUGH JESUS CHRIST IS.

For the grace of God through Jesus Christ
our Lord must be apprehended, — as that by
which alone men are delivered from evil, and
without which they do absolutely no good thing,
whether in thought, or will and affection, or in
action ; not only in order that they may know,
by the manifestation of that grace, what should
be done, but moreover in order that, by its enabling, they may do with love what they know.
Certainly the apostle asked for this inspiration
of good will and work on behalf of those to
whom he said, " Now we pray to God that ye
do no evil, not that we should appear approved,
but that ye should do that which is good." [11]
Who can hear this and not awake and confess
that we have it from the Lord God that we turn
aside from evil and do good ? — since the apostle
indeed says not, We admonish, we teach, we
exhort, we rebuke ; but he says, " We pray to
God that ye do no evil, but that ye should do
that which is good." [11]   And yet he was also in
the habit of speaking to them, and doing all
those things which I have mentioned, — he admonished, he taught, he exhorted, he rebuked.
But he knew that all these things which he was
doing in the way of planting and watering

---

[1] Or according to some MSS., " progress "
[2] Treatise on *Grace and Free Will*, see above.
[3] Or, " most clearly."          [4] Ps. xxxvii. 27.
[5] 2 Cor. iii. 6.          [6] Ps. xxxvii. 23.

[7] Ps. lxxvi. 10.          [8] John viii. 36.          [9] John xv. 5.
[10] Ps. xxvii. 9.          [11] 2 Cor. xiii. 7.

openly [1] were of no avail unless He who giveth the increase in secret should give heed to his prayer on their behalf. Because, as the same teacher of the Gentiles says, " Neither is he that planteth anything, neither he that watereth, but God that giveth the increase." [2]

## CHAP. 4. — THE CHILDREN OF GOD ARE LED BY THE SPIRIT OF GOD.

Let those, therefore, not deceive themselves who ask, " Wherefore is it preached and prescribed to us that we should turn away from evil and do good, if it is not we that do this, but ' God who worketh in us to will and to do it ' ? " [3] But let them rather understand that if they are the children of God, they are led by the Spirit of God [4] to do that which should be done; and when they have done it, let them give thanks to Him by whom they act. For they are acted upon that they may act, not that they may themselves do nothing; and in addition to this, it is shown them what they ought to do, so that when they have done it as it ought to be done — that is, with the love and the delight of righteousness — they may rejoice in having received " the sweetness which the Lord has given, that their [5] land should yield her increase." [6] But when they do not act, whether by not doing at all or by not doing from love, let them pray that what as yet they have not, they may receive. For what shall they have which they shall not receive? or what have they which they have not received? [7]

## CHAP. 5 [III.] — REBUKE MUST NOT BE NEGLECTED.

" Then," say they, " let those who are over us only prescribe to us what we ought to do, and pray for us that we may do it; but let them not rebuke and censure us if we should not do it." Certainly let all be done, since the teachers of the churches, the apostles, were in the habit of doing all, — as well prescribing what things should be done, as rebuking if they were not done, and praying that they might be done. The apostle prescribes, saying, " Let all your things be done with love." [8] He rebukes, saying, " Now therefore there is utterly a fault among you, because ye have judgments among yourselves. For why do ye not rather suffer wrong? Why are ye not rather defrauded? Nay, ye do wrong and defraud; and that, your brethren. Know ye not that the unrighteous shall not possess the kingdom of God?" [9] Let us hear him also praying: " And the Lord," says he, " multiply you, and make you to abound in love one towards another

and towards all men." [10] He prescribes, that love should be maintained; he rebukes, because love is not maintained; he prays, that love may abound. O man! learn by his precept what you ought to have; learn by his rebuke that it is by your own fault that you have it not; learn by his prayer whence you may receive what you desire to have.

## CHAP. 6 [IV.] — OBJECTIONS TO THE USE OF REBUKE.

" How," says he, [11] " is it my fault that I have not what I have not received from Him, when unless it is given by Him, there is no other at all whence such and so great a gift can be had?" Suffer me a little, my brethren, not as against you whose heart is right with God, but as against those who mind earthly things, or as against those human modes of thinking themselves, to contend for the truth of the heavenly and divine grace. For they who say this are such as in their wicked works are unwilling to be rebuked by those who proclaim this grace. " Prescribe to me what I shall do, and if I should do it, give thanks to God for me who has given me to do it; but if I do it not, I must not be rebuked, but He must be besought to give what He has not given; that is, that very believing love of God and of my neighbour by which His precepts are [12] observed. Pray, then, for me that I may receive this, and may by its means do freely and with good will that which He commands. But I should be justly rebuked if by my own fault I had it not; that is, if I myself could give it to myself, or could receive it, and did not do so, or if He should give it and I should be unwilling to receive it. But since even the will itself is prepared [13] by the Lord, why dost thou rebuke me because thou seeest me unwilling to do His precepts, and dost not rather ask Him Himself to work in me the will also?"

## CHAP. 7 [V.] — THE NECESSITY AND ADVANTAGE OF REBUKE.

To this we answer: Whoever you are that do not the commandments of God that are already known to you, and do not wish to be rebuked, you must be rebuked even for that very reason that you do not wish to be rebuked. For you do not wish that your faults should be pointed out to you; you do not wish that they should be touched, and that such a useful pain should be caused you that you may seek the Physician; you do not desire to be shown to yourself, that, when you see yourself to be deformed, you may wish for the Reformer, and

---

[1] *In aperto.*  
[4] Rom. viii. 14.  
[6] Ps. lxxxv. 12.  
[9] 1 Cor. vi. *7 et seq.*  

[2] 1 Cor. iii. 7.  
[5] Some MSS. have " his land."  
[7] 1 Cor. iv 7.  

[3] Phil. ii. 13.  
[8] 1 Cor. xvi. 14.  

[10] 1 Thess. iii. 12.       [11] *i.e.* the objecting Pelagian.  
[12] So the MSS.; the older editors read *fiant*, that is, " *may be* observed."  
[13] Prov. xvi. 1.

may supplicate Him that you may not continue in that repulsiveness. For it is your fault that you are evil ; and it is a greater fault to be unwilling to be rebuked because you are evil, as if faults should either be praised, or regarded with indifference so as neither to be praised nor blamed, or as if, indeed, the dread, or the shame, or the mortification of the rebuked man were of no avail, or were of any other avail in healthfully stimulating, except to cause that He who is good may be besought, and so out of evil men who are rebuked may make good men who may be praised. For what he who will not be rebuked desires to be done for him, when he says, " Pray for me rather," — he must be rebuked for that very reason that he may himself also do for himself ; because that mortification with which he is dissatisfied with himself when he feels the sting of rebuke, stirs him up to a desire for more earnest prayer,[1] that, by God's mercy, he may be aided by the increase of love, and cease to do things which are shameful and mortifying, and do things praiseworthy and gladdening. This is the benefit of rebuke that is wholesomely applied, sometimes with greater, sometimes with less severity, in accordance with the diversity of sins ; and it is then wholesome when the supreme Physician looks. For it is of no profit unless when it makes a man repent of his sin. And who gives this but He who looked upon the Apostle Peter when he denied,[2] and made him weep? Whence also the Apostle Paul, after he said that they were to be rebuked with moderation who thought otherwise, immediately added, " Lest perchance God give them repentance, to the acknowledging of the truth, and they recover themselves out of the snares of the devil."[3]

CHAP. 8. — FURTHER REPLIES TO THOSE WHO OBJECT TO REBUKE.

But wherefore do they, who are unwilling to be rebuked, say, " Only prescribe to me, and pray for me that I may do what you prescribe?" Why do they not rather, in accordance with their own evil inclination, reject these things also, and say, " I wish you neither to prescribe to me, nor to pray for me"? For what man is shown to have prayed for Peter, that God should give him the repentance wherewith he bewailed the denial of his Lord? What man instructed Paul in the divine precepts which pertain to the Christian faith? When, therefore, he was heard preaching the gospel, and saying, " For I certify you, brethren, that the gospel which was preached of me is not after man. For I neither received it from man, nor did I learn it, but by the revelation of Jesus Christ,"[4] — would it be replied to him : " Why are you troubling us to receive

and to learn from you that which you have not received nor learnt from man? He who gave to you is able also to give to us in like manner as to you." Moreover, if they dare not say this, but suffer the gospel to be preached to them by man, although it cannot be given to man by man, let them concede also that they ought to be rebuked by those who are set over them, by whom Christian grace is preached ; although it is not denied that God is able, even when no man rebukes, to correct whom He will, and to lead him on to the wholesome mortification of repentance by the most hidden and mighty power of His medicine. And as we are not to cease from prayer on behalf of those whom we desire to be corrected, — even although without any man's prayer on behalf of Peter, the Lord looked upon him and caused him to bewail his sin, — so we must not neglect rebuke, although God can make those whom He will to be corrected, even when not rebuked. But a man then profits by rebuke when He pities and aids who makes those whom He will to profit even without rebuke. But wherefore these are called to be reformed in one way, those in another way, and others in still another way, after different and innumerable manners, be it far from us to assert that it is the business of the clay to judge, but of the potter.

CHAP. 9 [VI.] — WHY THEY MAY JUSTLY BE REBUKED WHO DO NOT OBEY GOD, ALTHOUGH THEY HAVE NOT YET RECEIVED THE GRACE OF OBEDIENCE.

" The apostle says," say they, " ' For who maketh thee to differ? And what hast thou that thou hast not received? Now also if thou hast received it, why dost thou glory as if thou hadst not received it?'[5] Why, then, are we rebuked, censured, reproved, accused? What do we do, we who have not received?" They who say this wish to appear without blame in respect of their not obeying God, because assuredly obedience itself is His gift ; and that gift must of necessity be in him in whom dwells love, which without doubt is of God,[6] and the Father gives it to His children. " This," say they, " we have not received. Why, then, are we rebuked, as if we were able to give it to ourselves, and of our own choice would not give it?" And they do not observe that, if they are not yet regenerated, the first reason why, when they are reproached because they are disobedient to God, they ought to be dissatisfied with themselves is, that God made man upright from the beginning of the human creation,[7] and there is no unrighteousness with God.[8] And thus the first depravity, whereby God is not obeyed, is of man,

[1] Or, "more earnest desire for prayer."     [2] Luke xxii. 61.
[3] 2 Tim ii. 25                               [4] Gal. i. 11.
[5] 2 Cor. iv. 7.     [6] 1 John iv. 7.     [7] Eccles. vii. 30.
[8] Rom. ix. 14.

because, falling by his own evil will from the rectitude in which God at first made him, he became depraved. Is, then, that depravity not to be rebuked in a man because it is not peculiar to him who is rebuked, but is common to all? Nay, let that also be rebuked in individuals, which is common to all. For the circumstance that none is altogether free from it is no reason why it should not attach to each man. Those original sins, indeed, are said to be the sins of others, because individuals derived them from their parents; but they are not unreasonably said to be our own also, because in that one, as the apostle says, all have sinned.[1] Let, then, the damnable source be rebuked, that from the mortification of rebuke may spring the will of regeneration, — if, indeed, he who is rebuked is a child of promise, — in order that, by the noise of the rebuke sounding and lashing from without, God may by His hidden inspiration work in him from within to will also. If, however, being already regenerate and justified, he relapses of his own will into an evil life, assuredly he cannot say, "I have not received," because of his own free choice to evil he has lost the grace of God, that he had received. And if, stung with compunction by rebuke, he wholesomely bewails, and returns to similar good works, or even better, certainly here most manifestly appears the advantage of rebuke. But yet for rebuke by the agency of man to avail, whether it be of love or not, depends only upon God.

### CHAP. 10. — ALL PERSEVERANCE IS GOD'S GIFT.

Is such an one as is unwilling to be rebuked still able to say, "What have I done, — I who have not received?" when it appears plainly that he has received, and by his own fault has lost that which he has received? "I am able," says he, "I am altogether able, — when you reprove me for having of my own will relapsed from a good life into a bad one, — still to say, What have I done, — I who have not received? For I have received faith, which worketh by love, but I have not received perseverance therein to the end. Will any one dare to say that this perseverance is not the gift of God, and that so great a possession as this is ours in such wise that if any one have it the apostle could not say to him, 'For what hast thou which thou hast not received?'[2] since he has this in such a manner as that he has not received it?" To this, indeed, we are not able to deny, that perseverance in good, progressing even to the end, is also a great gift of God; and that it exists not save it come from Him of whom it is written, "Every best gift and every perfect gift is from above, coming down from the Father of lights."[3] But the re-

buke of him who has not persevered must not on that account be neglected, "lest God perchance give unto him repentance, and he recover from the snares of the devil;"[4] since to the usefulness of rebuke the apostle has subjoined this decision, saying, as I have above mentioned, "Rebuking with moderation those that think differently, lest at any time God give them repentance."[4] For if we should say that such a perseverance, so laudable and so blessed, is man's in such wise as that he has it not from God, we first of all make void that which the Lord says to Peter: "I have prayed for thee that thy faith fail not."[5] For what did He ask for him, but perseverance to the end? And assuredly, if a man could have this from man, it should not have been asked from God. Then when the apostle says, "Now we pray to God that ye do no evil,"[6] beyond a doubt he prays to God on their behalf for perseverance. For certainly he does not "do no evil" who forsakes good, and, not persevering in good, turns to the evil, from which he ought to turn aside.[7] In that place, moreover, where he says, "I thank my God in every remembrance of you, always in every prayer of mine for you all making request with joy for your fellowship[8] in the gospel from the first day until now, being confident of this very thing, that He who has begun a good work in you will perform it until the day of Jesus Christ,"[9] — what else does he promise to them from the mercy of God than perseverance in good to the end? And again where he says, "Epaphras saluteth you, who is one of you, a servant of Christ Jesus, always striving for you in prayer, that you may stand perfect and fulfilled in all the will of God,"[10] — what is "that you may stand," but "that you may persevere"? Whence it was said of the devil, "He stood not in the truth;"[11] because he was there, but he did not continue. For assuredly those were already standing in the faith. And when we pray that he who stands may stand, we do not pray for anything else than that he may persevere. Jude the apostle, again, when he says, "Now unto Him that is able to keep you without offence, and to establish you before the presence of His glory, immaculate in joy,"[12] does he not most manifestly show that perseverance in good unto the end is God's gift? For what but a good perseverance does He give who preserves without offence that He may place before the presence of His glory immaculate in joy? What

---

[1] Rom. iii. 23.          [2] 1 Cor. iv. 7.          [3] Jas. i. 17.

[4] 2 Tim ii. 25.          [5] Luke xxii. 32.          [6] 2 Cor. xiii. 7.
[7] [The editors have without reason inserted a "not" before "ought" in this sentence, yielding the sense: "who forsakes good, even that from which he ought not to turn away;" Erasmus changes the place of "and," reading: "who forsakes good from which he ought not to turn aside, and is inclined to evil." The MS. text is entirely satisfactory." — W.]
[8] Many MSS. read "communication."          [9] Phil. i. 3, et seq.
[10] Col. iv. 12.          [11] John viii. 24.          [12] Jude 24.

is it, moreover, that we read in the Acts of the Apostles: "And when the Gentiles heard, they rejoiced and received the word of the Lord; and as many as were ordained to eternal life believed"?[1] Who could be ordained to eternal life save by the gift of perseverance? And when we read, "He that shall persevere unto the end shall be saved;"[2] with what salvation but eternal? And when, in the Lord's Prayer, we say to God the Father, "Hallowed be Thy name,"[3] what do we ask but that His name may be hallowed in us? And as this is already accomplished by means of the laver of regeneration, why is it daily asked by believers, except that we may persevere in that which is already done in us? For the blessed Cyprian also understands this in this manner, inasmuch as, in his exposition of the same prayer, he says: "We say, 'Hallowed be Thy name,' not that we wish for God that He may be hallowed by our prayers, but that we ask of God that His name may be hallowed in us. But by whom is God hallowed, since He Himself hallows? Well, because He said, 'Be ye holy, since I also am holy;'[4] we ask and entreat that we who have been hallowed in baptism may persevere in that which we have begun to be."[5] Behold the most glorious martyr is of this opinion, that what in these words Christ's faithful people are daily asking is, that they may persevere in that which they have begun to be. And no one need doubt, but that whosoever prays from the Lord that he may persevere in good, confesses thereby that such perseverance is His gift.

CHAP. II [VII.] — THEY WHO HAVE NOT RECEIVED THE GIFT OF PERSEVERANCE, AND HAVE RELAPSED INTO MORTAL SIN AND HAVE DIED THEREIN, MUST RIGHTEOUSLY BE CONDEMNED.

If, then, these things be so, we still rebuke those, and reasonably rebuke them, who, although they were living well, have not persevered therein; because they have of their own will been changed from a good to an evil life, and on that account are worthy of rebuke; and if rebuke should be of no avail to them, and they should persevere in their ruined life until death, they are also worthy of divine condemnation for ever. Neither shall they excuse themselves, saying, — as now they say, "Wherefore are we rebuked?" — so then, "Wherefore are we condemned, since indeed, that we might return from good to evil, we did not receive that perseverance by which we should abide in good?" They shall by no means deliver themselves by this excuse from righteous condemnation. For if, according to the word of

truth, no one is delivered from the condemnation which was incurred through Adam except through the faith of Jesus Christ, and yet from this condemnation they shall not deliver themselves who shall be able to say that they have not heard the gospel of Christ, on the ground that "faith cometh by hearing,"[6] how much less shall they deliver themselves who shall say, "We have not received perseverance!" For the excuse of those who say, "We have not received hearing," seems more equitable than that of those who say, "We have not received perseverance;" since it may be said, O man, in that which thou hadst heard and kept, in *that* thou mightest persevere if thou wouldest; but in no wise can it be said, That which thou hadst not heard thou mightest believe if thou wouldest.

CHAP. I2. — THEY WHO HAVE NOT RECEIVED PERSEVERANCE ARE NOT DISTINGUISHED FROM THE MASS OF THOSE THAT ARE LOST.

And, consequently, both those who have not heard the gospel, and those who, having heard it and been changed by it for the better, have not received perseverance, and those who, having heard the gospel, have refused to come to Christ, that is, to believe on Him, since He Himself says, "No man cometh unto me, except it were given him of my Father,"[7] and those who by their tender age were unable to believe, but might be absolved from original sin by the sole laver of regeneration, and yet have not received this laver, and have perished in death: are not made to differ from that lump which it is plain is condemned, as all go from one into condemnation. Some are made to differ, however, not by their own merits, but by the grace of the Mediator; that is to say, they are justified freely in the blood of the second Adam. Therefore, when we hear, "For who maketh thee to differ? and what hast thou that thou hast not received? Now, if thou hast received it, why dost thou glory as if thou hadst not received it?"[8] we ought to understand that from that mass of perdition which originated through the first Adam, no one can be made to differ except he who has this gift, which whosoever has, has received by the grace of the Saviour. And this apostolical testimony is so great, that the blessed Cyprian writing to Quirinus put it in the place of a title, when he says, "That we must boast in nothing, since nothing is our own."[9]

CHAP. I3. — ELECTION IS OF GRACE, NOT OF MERIT.

Whosoever, then, are made to differ from that original condemnation by such bounty of divine

---

[1] Acts xiii 48.  [2] Matt. x. 22.  [3] Matt. vi. 9.
[4] Nearly all MSS : "even as I am holy."
[5] Cyprian, *Treatise on the Lord's Prayer*, ch. 12; see *The Ante-Nicene Fathers*, vol. v. p. 450.

[6] Rom. x. 17.  [7] John vi. 65.  [8] 1 Cor. iv. 7.
[9] Cyprian, *Testimonies*, Book iii. ch. 4; see *The Ante-Nicene Fathers*, vol. v. pp. 528 and 533.

grace, there is no doubt but that for such it is provided that they should hear the gospel, and when they hear they believe, and in the faith which worketh by love they persevere unto the end; and if, perchance, they deviate from the way, when they are rebuked they are amended; and some of them, although they may not be rebuked by men, return into the path which they had left; and some who have received grace in any age whatever are withdrawn from the perils of this life by swiftness of death. For He worketh all these things in them who made them vessels of mercy, who also elected them in His Son before the foundation of the world by the election of grace: "And if by grace, then is it no more of works, otherwise grace is no more grace." [1] For they were not so called as not to be elected, in respect of which it is said, "For many are called but few are elected; " [2] but because they were called according to the purpose, they are of a certainty also elected by the election, as it is said, of grace, not of any precedent merits of theirs, because to them grace is all merit.

CHAP. 14. — NONE OF THE ELECT AND PREDESTINATED CAN PERISH.

Of such says the apostle, "We know that to those that love God He worketh together all things for good, to them who are called according to His purpose; because those whom He before foreknew, He also did predestinate to be conformed to the image of His Son, that He might be the first-born among many brethren. Moreover, whom He did predestinate, them He also called; and whom He called, them He also justified; and whom He justified, them He also glorified." [3] Of these no one perishes, because all are elected. And they are elected because they were called according to the purpose — the purpose, however, not their own, but God's; of which He elsewhere says, "That the purpose of God according to election might stand, not of works, but of Him that calleth, it was said unto her that the elder shall serve the younger." [4] And in another place he says, "Not according to our works, but according to His own purpose and grace." [5] When, therefore, we hear, "Moreover, whom He did predestinate, them He also called," [6] we ought to acknowledge that they were called according to His purpose; since He thence began, saying, "He worketh together all things for good to those who are called according to His purpose," and then added, "Because those whom He before foreknew, He also did predestinate, to be conformed to the image of His Son, that He might be the first-born

among many brethren." And to these promises He added, "Moreover, whom He did predestinate, them He also called." He wishes these, therefore, to be understood whom He called according to His purpose, lest any among them should be thought to be called and not elected, on account of that sentence of the Lord's: "Many the called but few are elected." [2] For whoever are elected are without doubt also called; but not whosoever are called are as a consequence elected. Those, then, are elected, as has often been said, who are called according to the purpose, who also are predestinated and foreknown. If any one of these perishes, God is mistaken; but none of them perishes, because God is not mistaken. If any one of these perish, God is overcome by human sin; but none of them perishes, because God is overcome by nothing. Moreover, they are elected to reign with Christ, not as Judas was elected, to a work for which he was fitted. Because he was chosen by Him who well knew how to make use even of wicked men, so that even by his damnable deed that venerable work, for the sake of which He Himself had come, might be accomplished. When, therefore, we hear, "Have not I chosen you twelve, and one of you is a devil?" [7] we ought to understand that the rest were elected by mercy, but he by judgment; those to obtain His kingdom, he to shed His blood!

CHAP. 15. — PERSEVERANCE IS GIVEN TO THE END.

Rightly follows the word to the kingdom of the elect: "If God be for us, who can be against us? He that spared not His own Son, but delivered Him up for us all, how has He not also with Him given us all things? Who shall lay anything to the charge of God's elect? God who justifieth? Who condemneth? Christ who died? yea, rather who rose again also, who is at the right hand of God, who also soliciteth on our behalf?" [8] And of how stedfast a perseverance even to the end they have received the gift, let them follow on to say: "Who shall separate us from the love of Christ? shall tribulation, or distress, or persecution, or famine, or nakedness, or peril, or sword? As it is written, Because for thy sake we are killed all the day long, we are accounted as sheep for the slaughter. But in all these things we are more than conquerors, through Him that hath loved us. For I am certain, that neither death, nor life, nor angel, nor principality, nor things present, nor things to come, nor power, nor height, nor depth, nor any other creature, shall be able to separate us from the love of God which is in Christ Jesus our Lord." [9]

---

[1] Rom. xi. 6.    [2] Matt. xx. 16.    [3] Rom. viii. 28 ff.
[4] Rom. ix. 11.    [5] 2 Tim. i. 9.    [6] Rom. viii. 29.

[7] John vi. 70.    [8] Rom. viii. 31 ff    [9] Rom. viii. 35 ff.

CHAP. 16. — WHOSOEVER DO NOT PERSEVERE ARE NOT DISTINGUISHED FROM THE MASS OF PERDITION BY PREDESTINATION.

Such as these were they who were signified to Timothy, where, when it had been said that Hymenæus and Philetus had subverted the faith of some, it is presently added, "Nevertheless the foundation of God standeth sure, having this seal, The Lord has known them that are His."[1] The faith of these, which worketh by love, either actually does not fail at all, or, if there are any whose faith fails, it is restored before their life is ended, and the iniquity which had intervened is done away, and perseverance even to the end is allotted to them. But they who are not to persevere, and who shall so fall away from Christian faith and conduct that the end of this life shall find them in that case, beyond all doubt are not to be reckoned in the number of these, even in that season wherein they are living well and piously. For they are not made to differ from that mass of perdition by the foreknowledge and predestination of God, and therefore are not called according to God's purpose, and thus are not elected; but are called among those of whom it was said, " Many are called," not among those of whom it was said, " But few are elected." And yet who can deny that they are elect, since they believe and are baptized, and live according to God? Manifestly, they are called elect by those who are ignorant of what they shall be, but not by Him who knew that they would not have the perseverance which leads the elect forward into the blessed life, and knows that they so stand, as that He has foreknown that they will fall.

CHAP. 17 [VIII.] — WHY PERSEVERANCE SHOULD BE GIVEN TO ONE AND NOT ANOTHER IS INSCRUTABLE.

Here, if I am asked why God should not have given them perseverance to whom He gave that love by which they might live Christianly, I answer that I do not know. For I do not speak arrogantly, but with acknowledgment of my small measure, when I hear the apostle saying, "O man, who art thou that repliest against God?"[2] and, " O the depth of the riches of the wisdom and knowledge of God! how unsearchable are His judgments, and His ways untraceable!"[3] So far, therefore, as He condescends to manifest His judgments to us, let us give thanks; but so far as He thinks fit to conceal them, let us not murmur against His counsel, but believe that this also is the most wholesome for us. But whoever you are that are hostile to His grace, and thus ask, what do you yourself say? it is well that you do not deny yourself to be a Christian and boast of being a catholic. If, therefore, you confess that to persevere to the end in good is God's gift, I think that equally with me you are ignorant why one man should receive this gift and another should not receive it; and in this case we are both unable to penetrate the unsearchable judgments of God. Or if you say that it pertains to man's free will — which you defend, not in accordance with God's grace, but in opposition to it — that any one should persevere in good, or should not persevere, and it is not by the gift of God if he persevere, but by the performance of human will, why will you strive against the words of Him who says, " I have prayed for thee, Peter, that thy faith fail not"?[4] Will you dare to say that even when Christ prayed that Peter's faith might not fail, it would still have failed if Peter had willed it to fail; that is, if he had been unwilling that it should continue even to the end? As if Peter could in any measure will otherwise than Christ had asked for him that he might will. For who does not know that Peter's faith would then have perished if that will by which he was faithful should fail, and that it would have continued if that same will should abide? But because " the will is prepared by the Lord,"[5] therefore Christ's petition on his behalf could not be a vain petition. When, then, He prayed that his faith should not fail, what was it that he asked for, but that in his faith he should have a most free, strong, invincible, persevering will! Behold to what an extent the freedom of the will is defended in accordance with the grace of God, not in opposition to it; because the human will does not attain grace by freedom, but rather attains freedom by grace, and a delightful constancy, and an insuperable fortitude that it may persevere.

CHAP. 18. — SOME INSTANCES OF GOD'S AMAZING JUDGMENTS.

It is, indeed, to be wondered at, and greatly to be wondered at, that to some of His own children — whom He has regenerated in Christ — to whom He has given faith, hope, and love, God does not give perseverance also, when to children of another He forgives such wickedness, and, by the bestowal of His grace, makes them His own children. Who would not wonder at this? Who would not be exceedingly astonished at this? But, moreover, it is not less marvellous, and still true, and so manifest that not even the enemies of God's grace can find any means of denying it, that some children of His friends, that is, of regenerated and good believers, departing this life as infants without baptism, — although He certainly might provide the grace

---

[1] 2 Tim. ii. 19.　　[2] Rom. ix. 20.　　[3] Rom. xi. 33.　　[4] Luke xxii. 32.　　[5] Prov. viii. 35.

of this laver if He willed, since in His power are all things, — He alienates from His kingdom into which He introduces their parents; and some children of His enemies He causes to come into the hands of Christians, and by means of this laver introduces into the kingdom, from which their parents are aliens; although, as well to the former infants there is no evil deserving, as to the latter there is no good, of their own proper will. Certainly, in this case the judgments of God, because they are righteous and deep, may neither be blamed nor penetrated. Among these also is that concerning perseverance, of which we are now discoursing. Of both, therefore, we may exclaim, "O the depth of the riches of the wisdom and knowledge of God! how unsearchable are His judgments!"[1]

CHAP. 19. — GOD'S WAYS PAST FINDING OUT.

Nor let us wonder that we cannot trace His unsearchable ways. For, to say nothing of innumerable other things which are given by the Lord God to some men, and to others are not given, since with Him is no respect of persons; such things as are not conferred on the merits of will, as bodily swiftness, strength, good health, and beauty of body, marvellous intellects and mental natures capable of many arts, or such as fall to man's lot from without, such as are wealth, nobility, honours, and other things of this kind, which it is in the power of God alone that a man should have; not to dwell even on the baptism of infants (which none of those objectors can say does not pertain, as might be said of those other matters, to the kingdom of God), why it is given to this infant and not given to that, since both of them are equally in God's power, and without that sacrament none can enter into the kingdom of God; — to be silent, then, on these matters, or to leave them on one side, let men consider those very special cases of which we are treating. For we are discoursing of such as have not perseverance in goodness, but die in the decline of their good will from good to evil. Let the objectors answer, if they can, why, when these were living faithfully and piously, God did not then snatch them from the perils of this life, "lest wickedness should change their understanding, and lest deceit should beguile their souls"?[2] Had He not this in His power, or was He ignorant of their future sinfulness? Assuredly, nothing of this kind is said, except most perversely and insanely. Why, then, did He not do this? Let them reply who mock at us when in such matters we exclaim, "How inscrutable are His judgments, and His ways past finding out!"[1] For either God giveth this to whom He will, or certainly that Scripture is wrong which says concerning the immature death of the righteous man, "He was taken away lest wickedness should change his understanding, or lest deceit should beguile his soul."[2] Why, then, does God give this so great benefit to some, and not give it to others, seeing that in Him is no unrighteousness[3] nor acceptance of persons,[4] and that it is in His power how long every one may remain in this life, which is called a trial upon earth?[5] As, then, they are constrained to confess that it is God's gift for a man to end this life of his before it can be changed from good to evil, but they do not know why it is given to some and not given to others, so let them confess with us that perseverance in good is God's gift, according to the Scriptures, from which I have already set down many testimonies; and let them condescend with us to be ignorant, without a murmur against God, why it is given to some and not given to others.

CHAP. 20 [IX.] — SOME ARE CHILDREN OF GOD ACCORDING TO GRACE TEMPORALLY RECEIVED, SOME ACCORDING TO GOD'S ETERNAL FOREKNOWLEDGE.

Nor let it disturb us that to some of His children God does not give this perseverance. Be this far from being so, however, if these were of those who are predestinated and called according to His purpose, — who are truly the children of the promise. For the former, while they live piously, are called children of God; but because they will live wickedly, and die in that impiety, the foreknowledge of God does not call them God's children. For they are children of God whom as yet we have not, and God has already, of whom the Evangelist John says, "that Jesus should die for that nation, and not for that nation only, but that also He should gather together in one the children of God which were scattered abroad;"[6] and this certainly they were to become by believing, through the preaching of the gospel. And yet before this had happened they had already been enrolled as sons of God with unchangeable stedfastness in the memorial of their Father. And, again, there are some who are called by us children of God on account of grace received even in temporal things, yet are not so called by God; of whom the same John says, "They went out from us, but they were not of us, because if they had been of us they would, no doubt, have continued with us."[7] He does not say, "They went out from us, but because they did not abide with us they are no longer now of us;" but he says, "They went out from us, but they were not of us," — that is to say, even when they appeared among us, they were not of us. And as if it were said to him, Whence

[1] Rom. xi 33       [2] Wisd. iv. 11.

[3] Rom. ix. 14.    [4] Rom ii. 11.    [5] Job vii. 1.
[6] John xi. 51, 52.   [7] 1 John ii. 19.

do you prove this? he says, "Because if they had been of us, they would assuredly have continued with us." [1] It is the word of God's children; John is the speaker, who was ordained to a chief place among the children of God. When, therefore, God's children say of those who had not perseverance, "They went out from us, but they were not of us," and add, "Because if they had been of us, they would assuredly have continued with us," what else do they say than that they were not children, even when they were in the profession and name of children? Not because they simulated righteousness, but because they did not continue in it. For he does not say, "For if they had been of us, they would assuredly have maintained a real and not a feigned righteousness with us;" but he says, "If they had been of us, they would assuredly have continued with us." Beyond a doubt, he wished them to continue in goodness. Therefore they were in goodness; but because they did not abide in it, — that is, they did not persevere unto the end, — he says, They were not of us, even when they were with us, — that is, they were not of the number of children, even when they were in the faith of children; because they who are truly children are foreknown and predestinated as conformed to the image of His Son, and are called according to His purpose, so as to be elected. For the son of promise does not perish, but the son of perdition.[2]

CHAP. 21. — WHO MAY BE UNDERSTOOD AS GIVEN TO CHRIST.

Those, then, were of the multitude of the called, but they were not of the fewness of the elected. It is not, therefore, to His predestinated children that God has not given perseverance, for they would have it if they were in that number of children; and what would they have which they had not received, according to the apostolical and true judgment?[3] And thus such children would be given to Christ the Son just as He Himself says to the Father, "That all that Thou hast given me may not perish, but have eternal life." [4] Those, therefore, are understood to be given to Christ who are ordained to eternal life. These are they who are predestinated and called according to the purpose, of whom not one perishes. And therefore none of them ends this life when he has changed from good to evil, because he is so ordained, and for that purpose given to Christ, that he may not perish, but may have eternal life. And again, those whom we call His enemies, or the infant children of His enemies, whomever of them He will so regenerate that they may end this life in that faith which worketh by love, are already, and before this is done,

in that predestination His children, and are given to Christ His Son, that they may not perish, but have everlasting life.

CHAP. 22. — TRUE CHILDREN OF GOD ARE TRUE DISCIPLES OF CHRIST.

Finally, the Saviour Himself says, "If ye continue in my word, ye are indeed my disciples." [5] Is Judas, then, to be reckoned among them, since he did not continue in His word? Are they to be reckoned among them of whom the gospel speaks in such wise, where, when the Lord had commanded His flesh to be eaten and His blood to be drunk, the Evangelist says, "These things said He in the synagogue as He taught in Capernaum. Many, therefore, of His disciples, when they had heard this, said, This is a hard saying; who can hear it? But Jesus, knowing in Himself that His disciples were murmuring at it, said to them, Doth this offend you? What and if ye shall see the Son of man ascending where He was before? It is the Spirit that quickeneth, but the flesh profiteth nothing. The words that I have spoken unto you are spirit and life. But there are some of you who believe not. For Jesus knew from the beginning who were the believing ones, and who should betray Him; and He said, Therefore said I unto you, that no man cometh unto me except it were given of my Father. From this time many of His disciples went away back from Him, and no longer walked with Him." [6] Are not these even in the words of the gospel called disciples? And yet they were not truly disciples, because they did not continue in His word, according to what He says: "If ye continue in my word, then are ye indeed my disciples." [5] Because, therefore, they possessed not perseverance, as not being truly disciples of Christ, so they were not truly children of God even when they appeared to be so, and were so called. We, then, call men elected, and Christ's disciples, and God's children, because they are to be so called whom, being regenerated, we see to live piously; but they are then truly what they are called if they shall abide in that on account of which they are so called. But if they have not perseverance, — that is, if they continue not in that which they have begun to be, — they are not truly called what they are called and are not; for they are not this in the sight of Him to whom it is known what they are going to be, — that is to say, from good men, bad men.

CHAP. 23. — THOSE WHO ARE CALLED ACCORDING TO THE PURPOSE ALONE ARE PREDESTINATED.

For this reason the apostle, when he had said, "We know that to those who love God He work-

---

[1] Rom. viii 29    [2] John xvii. 12.    [3] 1 Cor. iv. 7.
[4] Matt. xx. 16.

[5] John viii. 31.    [6] John vi. 59 ff.

eth all things together for good," — knowing that some love God, and do not continue in that good way unto the end, — immediately added, " to them who are the called according to His purpose." [1]   For these in their love for God continue even to the end ; and they who for a season wander from the way return, that they may continue unto the end what they had begun to be in good. Showing, however, what it is to be called according to His purpose, he presently added what I have already quoted above, " Because whom He did before foreknow, He also predestinated to be conformed to the image of His Son, that He might be the first-born among many brethren. Moreover, whom He did predestinate, them He also called," to wit, according to His purpose ; " and whom He called, them He also justified ; and whom He justified, them He also glorified." [2]   All those things are already done : He foreknew, He predestinated, He called, He justified ; because both all are already foreknown and predestinated, and many are already called and justified ; but that which he placed at the end, " them He also glorified " (if, indeed, that glory is here to be understood of which the same apostle says, " When Christ your life shall appear, then shall ye also appear with Him in glory " [3]), this is not yet accomplished. Although, also, those two things — that is, He called, and He justified — have not been effected in all of whom they are said, — for still, even until the end of the world, there remain many to be called and justified, — nevertheless, He used verbs of the past tense, even concerning things future, as if God had already arranged from eternity that they should come to pass. For this reason, also, the prophet Isaiah says concerning Him, " Who has made the things that shall be." [4]   Whosoever, therefore, in God's most providential ordering, are foreknown, predestinated, called, justified, glorified, — I say not, even although not yet born again, but even although not yet born at all, are already children of God, and absolutely cannot perish. These truly come to Christ, because they come in such wise as He Himself says, " All that the Father giveth me shall come to me, and him that cometh to me I will not cast out; " [5] and a little after He says, " This is the will of the Father who hath sent me, that of all that He hath given me I shall lose nothing." [6]  From Him, therefore, is given also perseverance in good even to the end ; for it is not given save to those who shall not perish, since they who do not persevere shall perish.

CHAP. 24. — EVEN THE SINS OF THE ELECT ARE TURNED BY GOD TO THEIR ADVANTAGE.

To such as love Him, God co-worketh with all things for good ; so absolutely all things, that even if any of them go astray, and break out of the way, even this itself He makes to avail them for good, so that they return more lowly and more instructed. For they learn that in the right way [7] itself they ought to rejoice with trembling ; not with arrogation to themselves of confidence of abiding as if by their own strength ; not with saying, in their abundance, " We shall not be moved for ever." [8]   For which reason it is said to them, " Serve the Lord in fear, and rejoice unto Him with trembling, lest at any time the Lord should be angry, and ye perish from the right way." [9]   For He does not say, " And ye come not into the right way ; " but He says, " Lest ye perish from the right way." And what does this show, but that those who are already walking in the right way are reminded to serve God in fear ; that is, " not to be high-minded, but to fear " ? [10] which signifies, that they should not be haughty, but humble. Whence also He says in another place, " not minding high things, but consenting with the lowly ; " [11] let them rejoice in God, but with trembling ; glorying in none, since nothing is ours, so that he who glorieth may glory in the Lord, lest they perish from the right way in which they have already begun to walk, while they are ascribing to themselves their very presence in it. These words also the apostle made use of when he says, " Work out your own salvation with fear and trembling." [12]  And setting forth why with fear and trembling, he says, " For it is God that worketh in you, both to will and to do for His good pleasure." [13]   For he had not this fear and trembling who said in his abundance, " I shall not be moved for ever." [8]  But because he was a child of the promise, not of perdition, he experienced in God's desertion for a little while what he himself was : " Lord," said he, " in Thy favour Thou gavest strength to my honour ; Thou turnedst away Thy face from me, and I became troubled." [14]   Behold how much better instructed, and for this reason also more humble, he held on his way, at length seeing and confessing that by His will God had endowed his honour with strength ; and this he had attributed to himself and presumed to be from himself, in such abundance as God had afforded it, and not from Him who had given it, and so had said, " I shall not be moved for ever !" Therefore he became troubled so that he found himself, and being lowly minded learnt not only of eternal life, but, moreover, of a pious conversation and perseverance in this life, as that in which hope should be maintained. This might moreover be the word of the Apostle Peter, because he also had said in his abundance, " I will

---

[1] Rom. viii. 28.      [2] Rom. viii. 29.      [3] Col. iii. 4.
[4] Isa. xlv 11.        [5] John vi. 37.       [6] John vi. 39.
[7] Or, " life."       [8] Ps. xxx. 6.        [9] Ps. ii. 11.
[10] Rom. xi. 20.      [11] Rom. xii. 16.     [12] Phil. ii. 12, 13.
[13] Phil. ii. 13.     [14] Ps. xxx. 7.

lay down my life for Thy sake ; " [1] attributing to himself, in his eagerness, what was afterwards to be bestowed on him by his Lord. But the Lord turned away His face from him, and he became troubled, so that in his fear of dying for Him he thrice denied Him. But the Lord again turned His face to him, and washed away his sin with his tears. For what else is, " He turned and looked upon him," [2] but, He restored to him the face which, for a little while, He had turned away from him? Therefore he had become troubled ; but because he learned not to be confident concerning himself, even this was of excellent profit to him, by His agency who co-works for good with all things to those who love Him ; because he had been called according to the purpose, so that no one could pluck him out of the hand of Christ, to whom he had been given.

CHAP. 25. — THEREFORE REBUKE IS TO BE USED.

Let no one therefore say that a man must not be rebuked when he deviates from the right way, but that his return and perseverance must only be asked for from the Lord for him. Let no considerate and believing man say this. For if such an one is called according to the purpose, beyond all doubt God is co-working for good to him even in the fact of his being rebuked. But since he who rebukes is ignorant whether he is so called, let him do with love what he knows ought to be done ; for he knows that such an one ought to be rebuked. God will show either mercy or judgment ; mercy, indeed, if he who is rebuked is " made to differ " by the bestowal of grace from the mass of perdition, and is not found among the vessels of wrath which are completed for destruction, but among the vessels of mercy which God has prepared for glory ; [3] but judgment, if among the former he is condemned, and is not predestinated among the latter.

CHAP. 26 [X.] — WHETHER ADAM RECEIVED THE GIFT OF PERSEVERANCE.

Here arises another question, not reasonably to be slighted, but to be approached and solved in the help of the Lord in whose hand are both we and our discourses. [4] For I am asked, in respect of this gift of God which is to persevere in good to the end, what I think of the first man himself, who assuredly was made upright without any fault. And I do not say : If he had not perseverance, how was he without fault, seeing that he was in want of so needful a gift of God ? For to this interrogatory the answer is easy, that he had not perseverance, because he did not persevere in that goodness in which

he was without sin ; for he began to have sin from the point at which he fell ; and if he began, certainly he was without sin before he had begun. For it is one thing not to have sin, and it is another not to abide in that goodness in which there is no sin. Because in that very fact, that he is not said never to have been without sin, but he is said not to have continued without sin, beyond all doubt it is demonstrated that he was without sin, seeing that he is blamed for not having continued in that goodness. But it should rather be asked and discussed with greater pains in what way we can answer those who say, " If in that uprightness in which he was made without sin he had perseverance, beyond all doubt he persevered in it ; and if he persevered, he certainly did not sin, and did not forsake that his uprightness. But that he did sin, and was a forsaker of goodness, the Truth declares. Therefore he had not perseverance in that goodness ; and if he had it not, he certainly received it not. For how should he have both received perseverance, and not have persevered ? Further, if he had it not because he did not receive it, what sin did he commit by not persevering, if he did not receive perseverance ? For it cannot be said that he did not receive it, for the reason that he was not separated by the bestowal of grace from the mass of perdition. Because that mass of perdition did not as yet exist in the human race before he had sinned from whom the corrupted source was derived."

CHAP. 27. — THE ANSWER.

Wherefore we most wholesomely confess what we most correctly believe, that the God and Lord of all things, who in His strength created all things good, and foreknew that evil things would arise out of good, and knew that it pertained to His most omnipotent goodness even to do good out of evil things rather than not to allow evil things to be at all, so ordained the life of angels and men that in it He might first of all show what their free will was capable of, and then what the kindness of His grace and the judgment of His righteousness was capable of. Finally, certain angels, of whom the chief is he who is called the devil, became by free will outcasts from the Lord God. Yet although they fled from His goodness, wherein they had been blessed, they could not flee from His judgment, by which they were made most wretched. Others, however, by the same free will stood fast in the truth, and merited the knowledge of that most certain truth that they should never fall. [5] For if from the Holy Scriptures we have been able to attain the knowledge that none of

[1] John xiii. 37.    [2] Luke xxii. 61.    [3] Rom. ix. 22, 23.
[4] Wisd. vii. 16.

[5] " Eamque [*scil.* veritatem] de suo casu nunquam futuro certissimam scire."

the holy angels shall fall evermore, how much more have they themselves attained this knowledge by the truth more sublimely revealed to them! Because to us is promised a blessed life without end, and equality with the angels,[1] from which promise we are certified that when after judgment we shall have come to that life, we shall not fall from it; but if the angels are ignorant of this truth concerning themselves, we shall not be their equals, but more blessed than they. But the Truth has promised us equality with them. It is certain, then, that they have known this by sight, which we have known by faith, to wit, that there shall be now no more any fall of any holy angel. But the devil and his angels, although they were blessed before they fell, and did not know that they should fall unto misery, — there was still something which might be added to their blessedness, if by free will they had stood in the truth, until they should receive that fulness of the highest blessing as the reward of that continuance; that is, that by the great abundance of the love of God, given by the Holy Spirit, they should absolutely not be able to fall any more, and that they should know this with complete certainty concerning themselves. They had not this plenitude of blessedness; but since they were ignorant of their future misery, they enjoyed a blessedness which was less, indeed, but still without any defect. For if they had known their future fall and eternal punishment, they certainly could not have been blessed; since the fear of so great an evil as this would compel them even then to be miserable.

## CHAP. 28. — THE FIRST MAN HIMSELF ALSO MIGHT HAVE STOOD BY HIS FREE WILL.

Thus also He made man with free will; and although ignorant of his future fall, yet therefore happy, because he thought it was in his own power both not to die and not to become miserable. And if he had willed by his own free will to continue in this state of uprightness and freedom from sin, assuredly without any experience of death and of unhappiness he would have received by the merit of that continuance the fulness of blessing with which the holy angels also are blessed; that is, the impossibility of falling any more, and the knowledge of this with absolute certainty. For even he himself could not be blessed although in Paradise, nay, he would not be there, where it would not become him to be miserable, if the foreknowledge of his fall had made him wretched with the dread of such a disaster. But because he forsook God of his free will, he experienced the just judgment of God, that with his whole race, which being as

yet all placed in him had sinned with him, he should be condemned. For as many of this race as are delivered by God's grace are certainly delivered from the condemnation in which they are already held bound. Whence, even if none should be delivered, no one could justly blame the judgment of God. That, therefore, in comparison of those that perish *few*, but in their absolute number *many*, are delivered, is effected by grace,[2] is effected freely:[2] thanks must be given, because it is effected, so that no one may be lifted up as of his own deservings, but that every mouth may be stopped,[3] and he that glorieth may glory in the Lord.[4]

## CHAP. 29 [XI.] — DISTINCTION BETWEEN THE GRACE GIVEN BEFORE AND AFTER THE FALL.

What then? Did not Adam have the grace of God? Yes, truly, he had it largely, but of a different kind. He was placed in the midst of benefits which he had received from the goodness of his Creator; for he had not procured those benefits by his own deservings; in which benefits he suffered absolutely no evil. But saints in this life, to whom pertains this grace of deliverance, are in the midst of evils out of which they cry to God, "Deliver us from evil."[5] He in those benefits needed not the death of Christ: these, the blood of that Lamb absolves from guilt, as well inherited as their own. He had no need of that assistance which they implore when they say, "I see another law in my members warring against the law of my mind, and making me captive in the law of sin which is in my members. O wretched man that I am! who shall deliver me from the body of this death? The grace of God through Jesus Christ our Lord."[6] Because in them the flesh lusteth against the spirit, and the spirit against the flesh, and as they labour and are imperilled in such a contest, they ask that by the grace of Christ the strength to fight and to conquer may be given them. He, however, tempted and disturbed in no such conflict concerning himself against himself, in that position of blessedness enjoyed his peace with himself.

## CHAP. 30. — THE INCARNATION OF THE WORD.

Hence, although these do not now require a grace more joyous for the present, they nevertheless need a more powerful grace; and what grace is more powerful than the only-begotten Son of God, equal to the Father and co-eternal, made man for them, and, without any sin of His own, either original or actual, crucified by men who were sinners? And although He rose again on the third day, never to die any more, He yet bore death for men and gave life to the dead, so

---

[1] Matt. xxii. 30.

[2] *Gratiâ — gratis.*    [3] Rom. iii. 19.    [4] Jer. ix. 24.
[5] Matt. vi. 13.    [6] Rom. vii. 23.

that redeemed by His blood, having received so great and such a pledge, they could say, " If God be for us, who is against us? He who spared not His own Son, but delivered Him up for us all, how has He not with Him also given to us all things?"[1]   God therefore took upon Him our nature — that is, the rational soul and flesh of the man Christ — by an undertaking singularly marvellous, or marvellously singular; so that with no preceding merits of His own righteousness He might in such wise be the Son of God from the beginning, in which He had begun to be man, that He, and the Word which is without beginning, might be one person.   For there is no one blinded by such ignorance of this matter and the Faith as to dare to say that, although born of the Holy Spirit and the Virgin Mary the Son of man, yet of His own free will by righteous living and by doing good works, without sin, He deserved to be the Son of God; in opposition to the gospel, which says, " The Word was made flesh."[2]   For where was this made flesh except in the Virginal womb, whence was the beginning of the man Christ?   And, moreover, when the Virgin asked how that should come to pass which was told her by the angel, the angel answered, " The Holy Ghost shall come over on to thee, and the power of the Highest shall overshadow thee, therefore that holy thing that shall be born of thee shall be called the Son of God."[3]   " Therefore," he said; not because of works, of which certainly of a yet unborn infant there are none; but " therefore," because " the Holy Ghost shall come over on to thee, and the power of the Highest shall overshadow thee, that holy thing which shall be born of thee shall be called the Son of God."   That nativity, absolutely gratuitous, conjoined, in the unity of the person, man to God, flesh to the Word!   Good works followed that nativity; good works did not merit it.   For it was in no wise to be feared that the human nature taken up by God the Word in that ineffable manner into a unity of person, would sin by free choice of will, since that taking up itself was such that the nature of man so taken up by God would admit into itself no movement of an evil will.   Through this Mediator God makes known that He makes those whom He redeemed by His blood from evil, everlastingly good; and Him He in such wise assumed that He never would be evil, and, not being made out of evil, would always be good.[4]

CHAP. 31. — THE FIRST MAN HAD RECEIVED THE GRACE NECESSARY FOR HIS PERSEVERANCE, BUT ITS EXERCISE WAS LEFT IN HIS FREE CHOICE.

The first man had not that grace by which he should never will to be evil; but assuredly he had that in which if he willed to abide he would never be evil, and without which, moreover, he could not by free will be good, but which, nevertheless, by free will he could forsake.   God, therefore, did not will even him to be without His grace, which He left in his free will; because free will is sufficient for evil, but is too little[5] for good, unless it is aided by Omnipotent Good.   And if that man had not forsaken that assistance of his free will, he would always have been good; but he forsook it, and he was forsaken.   Because such was the nature of the aid, that he could forsake it when he would, and that he could continue in it if he would; but not such that it could be brought about that he would.   This first is the grace which was given to the first Adam; but more powerful than this is that in the second Adam.   For the first is that whereby it is effected that a man may have righteousness if he will; the second, therefore, can do more than this, since by it it is even effected that he will, and will so much, and love with such ardour, that by the will of the Spirit he overcomes the will of the flesh, that lusteth in opposition to it.[6]   Nor was that, indeed, a small grace by which was demonstrated even the power of free will, because man was so assisted that without this assistance he could not continue in good, but could forsake this assistance if he would.   But this latter grace is by so much the greater, that it is too little for a man by its means to regain his lost freedom; it is too little, finally, not to be able without it either to apprehend the good or to continue in good if he will, unless he is also *made to will*.

CHAP. 32. — THE GIFTS OF GRACE CONFERRED ON ADAM IN CREATION.

At that time, therefore, God had given to man a good will,[7] because in that will He had made him, since He had made him upright.   He had given help without which he could not continue therein if he would; but that he should will, He left in his free will.   He could therefore continue if he would, because the help was not wanting whereby he could, and without which he could not, perseveringly hold fast the good which he would.   But that he willed not to continue is absolutely the fault of him whose merit it would have been if he had willed to continue; as the holy angels did, who, while others fell by free will, themselves by the same free will stood, and deserved to receive the due reward of this continuance — to wit, such a fulness of blessing that by it they might have the fullest certainty of always abiding in it.   If, however, this help

---

[1] Rom. viii. 31, 32.        [2] John i. 14.        [3] Luke i. 35.
[4] Some editions have, instead of " and not being made," etc.,
" lest being made of evil he should not always be good."

[5] Some MSS. read, " of no avail."
[6] There are other readings of this passage, but coming to the same substantial result.
[7] Some MSS. read, " a free will."

had been wanting, either to angel or to man when they were first made, since their nature was not made such that without the divine help it could abide if it would, they certainly would not have fallen by their own fault, because the help would have been wanting without which they could not continue. At the present time, however, to those to whom such assistance is wanting, it is the penalty of sin; but to those to whom it is given, it is given of grace, not of debt; and by so much the more is given through Jesus Christ our Lord to those to whom it has pleased God to give it, that not only we have that help without which we cannot continue even if we will, but, moreover, we have so great and such a help as to *will*. Because by this grace of God there is caused in us, in the reception of good and in the persevering hold of it, not only to be able to do what we will, but even to will to do what we are able. But this was not the case in the first man; for the one of these things was in him, but the other was not. For he did not need grace to receive good, because he had not yet lost it; but he needed the aid of grace to continue in it, and without this aid he could not do this at all; and he had received the ability if he would, but he had not the will for what he could; for if he had possessed it, he would have persevered. For he could persevere if he would; but that he would not was the result of free will, which at that time was in such wise free that he was capable of willing well and ill. For what shall be more free than free will, when it shall not be able to serve sin? and this should be to man also as it was made to the holy angels, the reward of deserving. But now that good deserving has been lost by sin, in those who are delivered that has become the gift of grace which would have been the reward of deserving.

CHAP. 33 [XII.] — WHAT IS THE DIFFERENCE BE-
TWEEN THE ABILITY NOT TO SIN, TO DIE, AND
FORSAKE GOOD, AND THE INABILITY TO SIN, TO
DIE, AND TO FORSAKE GOOD?

On which account we must consider with diligence and attention in what respect those pairs differ from one another, — to be able not to sin, and not to be able to sin; to be able not to die, and not to be able to die; to be able not to forsake good, and not to be able to forsake good. For the first man was able not to sin, was able not to die, was able not to forsake good. Are we to say that he who had such a free will could not sin? Or that he to whom it was said, " If thou shalt sin thou shalt die by death," could not die? Or that he could not forsake good, when he would forsake this by sinning, and so die? Therefore the first liberty of the will was *to be able not to sin*, the last will be much greater, *not to be able to sin*; the first

immortality was to be able not to die, the last will be much greater, not to be able to die; the first was the power of perseverance, to be able not to forsake good — the last will be the felicity of perseverance, not to be able to forsake good. But because the last blessings will be preferable and better, were those first ones, therefore, either no blessings at all, or trifling ones?

CHAP. 34. — THE AID WITHOUT WHICH A THING
DOES NOT COME TO PASS, AND THE AID WITH
WHICH A THING COMES TO PASS.

Moreover, the aids themselves are to be distinguished. The aid without which a thing does not come to pass is one thing, and the aid by which a thing comes to pass is another. For without food we cannot live; and yet although food should be at hand, it would not cause a man to live who should will to die. Therefore the aid of food is that without which it does not come to pass that we live, not that by which it comes to pass that we live. But, indeed, when the blessedness which a man has not is given him, he becomes at once blessed. For the aid is not only that without which that does not happen, but also with which that does happen for the sake of which it is given. Wherefore this is an assistance both by which it comes to pass, and without which it does not come to pass; because, on the one hand, if blessedness should be given to a man, he becomes at once blessed; and, on the other, if it should never be given he will never be so. But food does not of necessity cause a man to live, and yet without it he cannot live. Therefore to the first man, who, in that good in which he had been made upright, had received the ability not to sin, the ability not to die, the ability not to forsake that good itself, was given the aid of perseverance, — not that by which it should be brought about that he should persevere, but that without which he could not of free will persevere. But now to the saints predestinated to the kingdom of God by God's grace, the aid of perseverance that is given is not such as the former, but such that to them perseverance itself is bestowed; not only so that without that gift they cannot persevere, but, moreover, so that by means of this gift they cannot help persevering. For not only did He say, " Without me ye can do nothing," [1] but He also said, " Ye have not chosen me, but I have chosen you, and ordained you that ye should go and bring forth fruit, and that your fruit should remain." [2] By which words He showed that He had given them not only righteousness, but perseverance therein. For when Christ thus ordained them that they should go and bring forth fruit, and that their

---

[1] John xv. 5.                    [2] John xv. 16.

fruit should remain, who would dare to say, It shall not remain? Who would dare to say, Perchance it will not remain? "For the gifts and calling of God are without repentance;"[1] but the calling is of those who are called according to the purpose. When Christ intercedes, therefore, on behalf of these, that their faith should not fail, doubtless it will not fail unto the end. And thus it shall persevere even unto the end; nor shall the end of this life find it anything but continuing.

## CHAP. 35. — THERE IS A GREATER FREEDOM NOW IN THE SAINTS THAN THERE WAS BEFORE IN ADAM.

Certainly a greater liberty is necessary in the face of so many and so great temptations, which had no existence in Paradise, — a liberty fortified and confirmed by the gift of perseverance, so that this world, with all its loves, its fears, its errors, may be overcome: the martyrdoms of the saints have taught this. In fine, he [Adam], not only with nobody to make him afraid, but, moreover, in spite of the authority of God's fear, using free will, did not stand in such a state of happiness, in such a facility[2] of [not] sinning. But these [the saints], I say, not under the fear of the world, but in spite of the rage of the world lest they should stand, stood firm in the faith; while he could see the good things present which he was going to forsake, they could not see the good things future which they were going to receive. Whence is this, save by the gift of Him from whom they obtained mercy to be faithful; from whom they received the spirit, not of fear, whereby they would yield to the persecutors, but of power, and of love, and of continence, in which they could overcome all threatenings, all seductions, all torments? To him, therefore, without any sin, was given the free will with which he was created; and he made it to serve sin. But although the will of these had been the servant of sin, it was delivered by Him who said, "If the Son shall make you free, then shall ye be free indeed."[3] And by that grace they receive so great a freedom, that although as long as they live here they are fighting against sinful lusts, and some sins creep upon them unawares, on account of which they daily say, "Forgive us our debts,"[4] yet they do not any more obey the sin which is unto death, of which the Apostle John says, "There is a sin unto death: I do not say that he shall pray for it."[5] Concerning which sin (since it is not expressed) many and different notions may be entertained. I, however, say, that that sin is to forsake even unto death the faith which worketh by love. This sin they no longer serve who are not in the first condition, as Adam, free; but are freed by the grace of God through the second Adam, and by that deliverance have that free will which enables them to serve God, not that by which they may be made captive by the devil. From being made free from sin they have become the servants of righteousness,[6] in which they will stand till the end, by the gift to them of perseverance from Him who foreknew them, and predestinated them, and called them according to His purpose, and justified them, and glorified them, since He has even already formed those things that are to come which He promised concerning them. And when He promised, "Abraham believed Him, and it was counted unto him for righteousness."[7] For "he gave glory to God, most fully believing," as it is written, "that what He has promised He is able also to perform."[7]

## CHAP. 36. — GOD NOT ONLY FOREKNOWS THAT MEN WILL BE GOOD, BUT HIMSELF MAKES THEM SO.

It is He Himself, therefore, that makes those men good, to do good works. For He did not promise them to Abraham because He foreknew that of themselves they would be good. For if this were the case, what He promised was not His, but theirs. But it was not thus that Abraham believed, but "he was not weak in faith, giving glory to God;" and "most fully believing that what He has promised He is able also to perform."[8] He does not say, "What He foreknew, He is able to promise;" nor "What He foretold, He is able to manifest;" nor "What He promised, He is able to foreknow:" but "What He promised, He is able also to do." It is He, therefore, who makes them to persevere in good, who makes them good. But they who fall and perish have never been in the number of the predestinated. Although, then, the apostle might be speaking of all persons regenerated and living piously when he said, "Who art thou that judgest another man's servant? To his own master he standeth or falleth;" yet he at once had regard to the predestinated, and said, "But he shall stand;" and that they might not arrogate this to themselves, he says, "For God is able to make him stand."[9] It is He Himself, therefore, that gives perseverance, who is able to establish those who stand, so that they may stand fast with the greatest perseverance; or to restore those who have fallen, for "the Lord setteth up those who are broken down."[10]

---

[1] Rom. xi. 29.
[2] The original is, *in tanti peccandi facilitate.* Of course, *non* must be inserted, but the translator ventures to conjecture *facultate* instead of *facilitate.*
[3] John viii. 36.   [4] Matt. vi. 12.   [5] 1 John v. 16.

[6] Rom. vi. 18.   [7] Rom. iv. 3, and 20, 21.
[8] Rom. iv. 19.   [9] Rom. xiv. 4, etc.   [10] Ps. cxlv. 8.

CHAP. 37. — TO A SOUND WILL IS COMMITTED THE POWER OF PERSEVERING OR OF NOT PERSEVERING.

As, therefore, the first man did not receive this gift of God, — that is, perseverance in good, — but it was left in his choice to persevere or not to persevere, his will had such strength, — inasmuch as it had been created without any sin, and there was nothing in the way of concupiscence of himself that withstood it, — that the choice of persevering could worthily be entrusted to such goodness and to such facility in living well. But God at the same time foreknew what he would do in unrighteousness; foreknew, however, but did not compel him to this; but at the same time He knew what He Himself would do in righteousness concerning him. But now, since that great freedom has been lost by the desert of sin, our weakness has remained to be aided by still greater gifts. For it pleased God, in order most effectually to quench the pride of human presumption, "that no flesh should glory in His presence" — that is, "no man."[1] But whence should flesh not glory in His presence, save concerning its merits? Which, indeed, it might have had, but lost; and lost by that very means whereby it might have had them, that is, by its free will; on account of which there remains nothing to those who are to be delivered, save the grace of the Deliverer. Thus, therefore, no flesh glories in His presence. For the unrighteous do not glory, since they have no ground of glory; nor the righteous, because they have a ground from Him, and have no glory of theirs, but Himself, to whom they say, "My glory, and the lifter up of my head."[2] And thus it is that what is written pertains to every man, "that no flesh should glory in His presence." To the righteous, however, pertains that Scripture: "He that glorieth, let him glory in the Lord."[3] For this the apostle most manifestly showed, when, after saying "that no flesh should glory in His presence," lest the saints should suppose that they had been left without any glory, he presently added, "But of Him are ye in Christ Jesus, who of God is made unto us wisdom, and righteousness, and sanctification, and redemption: that, according as it is written, He that glorieth, let him glory in the Lord."[4] Hence it is that in this abode of miseries, where trial is the life of man upon the earth, "strength is made perfect in weakness."[5] What strength, save "that he that glorieth should glory in the Lord"?

CHAP. 38. — WHAT IS THE NATURE OF THE GIFT OF PERSEVERANCE THAT IS NOW GIVEN TO THE SAINTS.

And thus God willed that His saints should not — even concerning perseverance in goodness itself — glory in their own strength, but in Himself, who not only gives them aid such as He gave to the first man, without which they cannot persevere if they will, but causes in them also the will; that since they will not persevere unless they both can and will, both the capability and the will to persevere should be bestowed on them by the liberality of divine grace. Because by the Holy Spirit their will is so much enkindled that they therefore can, because they so will; and they therefore so will, because God works in them to will. For if in so much weakness of this life (in which weakness, however, for the sake of checking pride, strength behoved to be perfected) their own will should be left to themselves, that they might, if they willed, continue in the help of God, without which they could not persevere, and God should not work in them to will, in the midst of so many and so great weaknesses their will itself would give way, and they would not be able to persevere, for the reason that failing from infirmity they would not will, or in the weakness of will they would not so will that they would be able. Therefore aid is brought to the infirmity of human will, so that it might be unchangeably and invincibly[6] influenced by divine grace; and thus, although weak, it still might not fail, nor be overcome by any adversity. Thus it happens that man's will, weak and incapable, in good as yet small, may persevere by God's strength; while the will of the first man, strong and healthful, having the power of free choice, did not persevere in a greater good; because although God's help was not wanting, without which it could not persevere if it would, yet it was not such a help as that by which God would work in man to will. Certainly to the strongest He yielded and permitted to do what He willed; to those that were weak He has reserved that by His own gift they should most invincibly will what is good, and most invincibly refuse to forsake this. Therefore when Christ says, "I have prayed for thee that thy faith fail not,"[7] we may understand that it was said to him who is built upon the rock. And thus the man of God, not only because he has obtained mercy to be faithful, but also because faith itself does not fail, if he glories, must glory in the Lord.

CHAP. 39 [XIII.] — THE NUMBER OF THE PREDESTINATED IS CERTAIN AND DEFINED.

I speak thus of those who are predestinated to the kingdom of God, whose number is so certain that one can neither be added to them nor taken from them; not of those who, when He had

---

[1] 1 Cor. i. 29.    [2] Ps. iii. 3.    [3] 1 Cor. i. 31.
[4] 1 Cor. i. 30.    [5] 2 Cor. xii. 9.

[6] "*Insuperabiliter*," the reading of the best MSS. Some editions read "*inseparabiliter*," in a dogmatic interest.
[7] Luke xxii. 32.

announced and spoken, were multiplied beyond number. For they may be said to be called but not chosen, because they are not called according to the purpose. But that the number of the elect is certain, and neither to be increased nor diminished, — although it is signified by John the Baptist when he says, "Bring forth, therefore, fruits meet for repentance: and think not to say within yourselves, We have Abraham to our father: for God is able of these stones to raise up children to Abraham,"[1] to show that they were in such wise to be cut off if they did not produce fruit, that the number which was promised to Abraham would not be wanting, — is yet more plainly declared in the Apocalypse: "Hold fast that which thou hast, lest another take thy crown."[2] For if *another* would not receive unless *one* should have lost, the number is fixed.

CHAP. 40. — NO ONE IS CERTAIN AND SECURE OF HIS OWN PREDESTINATION AND SALVATION.

But, moreover, that such things as these are so spoken to saints who will persevere, as if it were reckoned uncertain whether they will persevere, is a reason that they ought not otherwise to hear these things, since it is well for them "not to be high-minded, but to fear."[3] For who of the multitude of believers can presume, so long as he is living in this mortal state, that he is in the number of the predestinated? Because it is necessary that in this condition that should be kept hidden; since here we have to beware so much of pride, that even so great an apostle was buffeted by a messenger of Satan, lest he should be lifted up.[4] Hence it was said to the apostles, "If ye abide in me;"[5] and this He said who knew for a certainty that they would abide; and through the prophet, "If ye shall be willing, and will hear me,"[6] although He knew in whom He would work to will also. And many similar things are said. For on account of the usefulness of this secrecy, lest, perchance, any one should be lifted up, but that all, even although they are running well, should fear, in that it is not known who may attain, — on account of the usefulness of this secrecy, it must be believed that some of the children of perdition, who have not received the gift of perseverance to the end, begin to live in the faith which worketh by love, and live for some time faithfully and righteously, and afterwards fall away, and are not taken away from this life before this happens to them. If this had happened to none of these, men would have that very wholesome fear, by which the sin of presumption is kept down, only so long as until they should attain to the grace of Christ by which to live piously, and afterwards

would for time to come be secure that they would never fall away from Him. And such presumption in this condition of trials is not fitting, where there is so great weakness, that security may engender pride. Finally, this also shall be the case; but it shall be at that time, in men also as it already is in the angels, when there cannot be any pride. Therefore the number of the saints, by God's grace predestinated to God's kingdom, with the gift of perseverance to the end bestowed on them, shall be guided thither in its completeness, and there shall be at length without end preserved in its fullest completeness, most blessed, the mercy of their Saviour still cleaving to them, whether in their conversion, in their conflict, or in their crown!

CHAP. 41. — EVEN IN JUDGMENT GOD'S MERCY WILL BE NECESSARY TO US.

For the Holy Scripture testifies that God's mercy is then also necessary for them, when the Saint says to his soul concerning the Lord its God, "Who crowneth thee in mercy and compassion."[7] The Apostle James also says: "He shall have judgment without mercy who hath showed no mercy;"[8] where he sets forth that even in that judgment in which the righteous are crowned and the unrighteous are condemned, some will be judged with mercy, others without mercy. On which account also the mother of the Maccabees says to her son, "That in that mercy I may receive thee with thy brethren."[9] "For when a righteous king," as it is written, "shall sit on the throne, no evil thing shall oppose itself to him. Who will boast that he has a pure heart? or who will boast that he is pure from sin?"[10] And thus God's mercy is even then necessary, by which he is made "blessed to whom the Lord has not imputed sin."[11] But at that time even mercy itself shall be allotted in righteous judgment in accordance with the merits of good works. For when it is said, "Judgment without mercy to him that hath showed no mercy," it is plainly shown that in those in whom are found the good works of mercy, judgment shall be executed with mercy; and thus even that mercy itself shall be returned to the merits of good works. It is not so now; when not only no good works, but many bad works precede, His mercy anticipates a man so that he is delivered from evils, — as well from evils which he has done, as from those which he would have done if he were not controlled by the grace of God; and from those, too, which he would have suffered for ever if he were not plucked from the power of darkness, and transferred into the kingdom of the Son of God's love.[12] Nevertheless, since even that life eternal

---

[1] Matt. iii. 8, 9.　　[2] Rev. iii. 11.　　[3] Rom. xi. 20.
[4] 2 Cor. xii. 7.　　[5] John xv. 7.　　[6] Isa. i. 19.
[7] Ps. ciii. 4.　　[8] Jas. ii. 13.　　[9] 2 Macc. vii. 29.
[10] Prov. xx. 8.　　[11] Ps. xxxii. 2.　　[12] Col. i. 13.

itself, which, it is certain, is given as due to good works, is called by so great an apostle the grace of God, although grace is not rendered to works, but is given freely, it must be confessed without any doubt, that eternal life is called grace for the reason that it is rendered to those merits which grace has conferred upon man. Because that saying is rightly understood which in the gospel is read, " grace for grace," [1] — that is, for those merits which grace has conferred.

#### CHAP. 42. — THE REPROBATE ARE TO BE PUNISHED FOR MERITS OF A DIFFERENT KIND.

But those who do not belong to this number of the predestinated, whom — whether that they have not yet any free choice of their will, or with a choice of will truly free, because freed by grace itself — the grace of God brings to His kingdom, — those, then, who do not belong to that most certain and blessed number, are most righteously judged according to their deservings. For either they lie under the sin which they have inherited by original generation, and depart hence with that inherited debt which is not put away by regeneration, or by their free will have added other sins besides ; their will, I say, *free*, but not *freed*, — free from righteousness, but enslaved to sin, by which they are tossed about by divers mischievous lusts, some more evil, some less, but all evil ; and they must be adjudged to diverse punishments, according to that very diversity. Or they receive the grace of God, but they are only for a season, and do not persevere ; they forsake and are forsaken. For by their free will, as they have not received the gift of perseverance, they are sent away by the righteous and hidden judgment of God.

#### CHAP. 43 [XIV.] — REBUKE AND GRACE DO NOT SET ASIDE ONE ANOTHER.

Let men then suffer themselves to be rebuked when they sin, and not conclude against grace from the rebuke itself, nor from grace against rebuke ; because both the righteous penalty of sin is due, and righteous rebuke belongs to it, if it is medicinally applied, even although the salvation of the ailing man is uncertain ; so that if he who is rebuked belongs to the number of the predestinated, rebuke may be to him a wholesome medicine ; and if he does not belong to that number, rebuke may be to him a penal infliction. Under that very uncertainty, therefore, it must of love be applied, although its result is unknown ; and prayer must be made on his behalf to whom it is applied, that he may be healed. But when men either come or return into the way of righteousness by means of rebuke, who is it that worketh salvation in their

hearts but that God who giveth the increase, whoever plants and waters, and whoever labours on the fields or shrubs, — that God whom no man's will resists when He wills to give salvation ? For so to will or not to will is in the power of Him who willeth or willeth not, as not to hinder the divine will nor overcome the divine power. For even concerning those who do what He wills not, He Himself does what He will.

#### CHAP. 44. — IN WHAT WAY GOD WILLS ALL MEN TO BE SAVED.

And what is written, that " He wills all men' to be saved," [2] while yet all men are not saved, may be understood in many ways, some of which I have mentioned in other writings [3] of mine ; but here I will say one thing : " He wills all men to be saved," is so said that all the predestinated may be understood by it, because every kind of men is among them. Just as it was said to the Pharisees, " Ye tithe every herb ; " [4] where the expression is only to be understood of every herb that they had, for they did not tithe every herb which was found throughout the whole earth. According to the same manner of speaking, it was said, " Even as I also please all men in all things." [5] For did he who said this please also the multitude of his persecutors ? But he pleased every kind of men that assembled in the Church of Christ, whether they were already established therein, or were to be introduced into it.

#### CHAP. 45. — SCRIPTURAL INSTANCES WHEREIN IT IS PROVED THAT GOD HAS MEN'S WILLS MORE IN HIS POWER THAN THEY THEMSELVES HAVE.

It is not, then, to be doubted that men's wills cannot, so as to prevent His doing what he wills, withstand the will of God, " who hath done all things whatsoever He pleased in heaven and in earth," [6] and who also " has done those things that are to come ; " [7] since He does even concerning the wills themselves of men what He will, when He will. Unless, perchance (to mention some things among many), when God willed to give the kingdom to Saul, it was so in the power of the Israelites, as it certainly was placed in their will, either to subject themselves or not to the man in question, that they could even prevail to withstand God. God, however, did not do this, save by the will of the men themselves, because he beyond doubt had the most omnipotent power of inclining men's hearts whither it pleased Him. For thus it is written : " And Samuel sent the people away, and every one went away unto his own place. And Saul went away to his house in Gibeah : and there went away

[1] John i. 16.

[2] 1 Tim. ii. 4.
[3] *Enchirid,* c. 103; *City of God,* xxii. 1, 2. *Against Julian,* iv. 8.
[4] Luke xi. 42.　　[5] 1 Cor. x. 33.　　[6] Ps. cxxxv. 6.
[7] Isa. xlv 11.

with Saul mighty men, whose hearts the Lord touched. And pestilent children said, Who shall save us ? This man ? And they despised him, and brought him no presents." ¹ Will any one say that any of those whose hearts the Lord touched to go with Saul would not have gone with him, or that any of those pestilent fellows, whose hearts He did not touch to do this, would have gone? Of David also, whom the Lord ordained to the kingdom in a more prosperous succession, we read thus : " And David continued to increase, and was magnified, and the Lord was with him." ² This having been premised, it is said a little afterwards, " And the Spirit clothed Amasai, chief of the thirty, and he said, We are thine, O David, and we will be with thee, O son of Jesse : Peace, peace be unto thee, and peace be to thy helpers ; because the Lord has helped thee." ³ Could he withstand the will of God, and not rather do the will of Him who wrought in his heart by His Spirit, with which he was clothed, to will, speak, and do thus? Moreover, a little afterwards the same Scripture says, " All these warlike men, setting the battle in array, came with a peaceful heart to Hebron to establish David over all Israel." ⁴ By their own will, certainly, they appointed David king. Who cannot see this? Who can deny it? For they did not do it under constraint or without good-will, since they did it with a peaceful heart. And yet He wrought this in them who worketh what He will in the hearts of men. For which reason the Scripture premised, " And David continued to increase, and was magnified, and the Lord Omnipotent was with him." And thus the Lord Omnipotent, who was with him, induced these men to appoint him king. And how did He induce them? Did He constrain thereto by any bodily fetters? He wrought within ; He held their hearts ; He stirred their hearts, and drew them by their own wills, which He Himself wrought in them. If, then, when God wills to set up kings in the earth, He has the wills of men more in His power than they themselves have, who else causes rebuke to be wholesome and correction to result in the heart of him that is rebuked, that he may be established in the kingdom of heaven?

CHAP. 46 [XV.] — REBUKE MUST BE VARIED ACCORDING TO THE VARIETY OF FAULTS. THERE IS NO PUNISHMENT IN THE CHURCH GREATER THAN EXCOMMUNICATION.

Therefore, let brethren who are subject be rebuked by those who are set over them, with rebukes that spring from love, varied according to the diversity of faults, whether smaller or greater. Because that very penalty that is called condemnation,⁵ which episcopal judgment inflicts, than which there is no greater punishment in the Church, may, if God will, result and be of advantage for most wholesome rebuke. For we know not what may happen on the coming day ; nor must any one be despaired of before the end of this life ; nor can God be contradicted, that He may not look down and give repentance, and receive the sacrifice of a troubled spirit and a contrite heart, and absolve from the guilt of condemnation, however just, and so Himself not condemn the condemned person. Yet the necessity of the pastoral office requires, in order that the terrible contagion may not creep through the many, that the diseased sheep should be separated from the sound ones ; perchance, by that very separation, to be healed by Him to whom nothing is impossible. For as we know not who belongs to the number of the predestinated, we ought in such wise to be influenced by the affection of love as to will all men to be saved. For this is the case when we endeavour to lead every individual to that point where they may meet with those agencies by which we may prevail, to the accomplishment of the result, that being justified by faith they may have peace with God,⁶ — which peace, moreover, the apostle announced when he said, " Therefore, we discharge an embassage for Christ, as though God were exhorting by us, we pray you in Christ's stead to be reconciled to God." ⁷ For what is " to be reconciled " to Him but to have peace with Him ? For the sake of which peace, moreover, the Lord Jesus Christ Himself said to His disciples, " Into whatsoever house ye enter first, say, Peace be to this house ; and if the son of peace be there, your peace shall rest upon it ; but if not, it shall return to you again." ⁸ When they preach the gospel of this peace of whom it is predicted, " How beautiful are the feet of those that publish peace, that announce good things ! " ⁹ to us, indeed, every one then begins to be a son of peace who obeys and believes this gospel, and who, being justified by faith, has begun to have peace towards God ; but, according to God's predestination, he was already a son of peace. For it was not said, Upon whomsoever your peace shall rest, he shall become a son of peace ; but Christ says, " If the son of peace be there, your peace shall rest upon that house." Already, therefore, and before the announcement of that peace to him, the son of peace was there, as he had been known and foreknown, by — not the evangelist, but — God. For we need not fear lest we should lose it, if in our ignorance he to whom we preach is not a son of peace, for it will return to us again — that is, that preaching will profit us, and not him ; but if the peace

¹ 1 Sam. x. 25 ff.  ² 1 Chron. xi. 9.  ³ 1 Chron xii. 18.
⁴ 1 Chron. xii. 38.  ⁵ Query, *Excommunication ?*  ⁶ Rom. v. 1.
⁷ 2 Cor. v. 20.  ⁸ Luke x. 5, 6.  ⁹ Isa. lii. 7.

proclaimed shall rest upon him, it will profit both us and him.

### CHAP. 47. — ANOTHER INTERPRETATION OF THE APOSTOLIC PASSAGE, "WHO WILL HAVE ALL MEN TO BE SAVED."

That, therefore, in our ignorance of who shall be saved, God commands us to will that all to whom we preach this peace may be saved, and Himself works this in us by diffusing that love in our hearts by the Holy Spirit who is given to us, — may also thus be understood, that God wills all men to be saved, because He makes us to will this ; just as "He sent the Spirit of His Son, crying, Abba, Father ; "[1] that is, making us to cry, Abba, Father. Because, concerning that same Spirit, He says in another place, "We have received the Spirit of adoption, in whom we cry, Abba, Father ! "[2] We therefore cry, but He is said to cry who makes us to cry. If, then, Scripture rightly said that the Spirit was crying by whom we are made to cry, it rightly also says that God wills, when by Him we are made to will. And thus, because by rebuke we ought to do nothing save to avoid departure from that peace which is towards God, or to induce return to it of him who had departed, let us do in hope what we do. If he whom we rebuke is a son of peace, our peace shall rest upon him ; but if not, it shall return to us again.

### CHAP. 48. — THE PURPOSE OF REBUKE.

Although, therefore, even while the faith of some is subverted, the foundation of God standeth sure, since the Lord knoweth them that are His, still, we ought not on that account to be indolent and negligent in rebuking those who should be rebuked. For not for nothing was it said, "Evil communications corrupt good manners ; "[3] and, "The weak brother shall perish in thy knowledge, on account of whom Christ died."[4] Let us not, in opposition to these precepts, and to a wholesome fear, pretend to argue, saying, "Well, let evil communications corrupt good manners, and let the weak brother perish. What is that to us? The foundation of God standeth sure, and no one perishes but the son of perdition." [XVI.] Be it far from us to babble in this wise, and think that we ought to be secure in this negligence. For it is true that no one perishes except the son of perdition, but God says

by the mouth of the prophet Ezekiel :[5] "He shall surely die in his sin, but his blood will I require at the hand of the watchman."

### CHAP. 49. — CONCLUSION.

Hence, as far as concerns us, who are not able to distinguish those who are predestinated from those who are not, we ought on this very account to will all men to be saved. Severe rebuke should be medicinally applied to all by us that they perish not themselves, or that they may not be the means of destroying others. It belongs to God, however, to make that rebuke useful to them whom He Himself has foreknown and predestinated to be conformed to the image of His Son. For, if at any time we abstain from rebuking, for fear lest by rebuke a man should perish, why do we not also rebuke, for fear lest a man should rather perish by our withholding it? For we have no greater bowels of love than the blessed apostle who says, "Rebuke those that are unruly ; comfort the feeble-minded ; support the weak ; be patient towards all men. See that none render to any man evil for evil."[6] Where it is to be understood that evil is then rather rendered for evil when one who ought to be rebuked is not rebuked, but by a wicked dissimulation is neglected. He says, moreover, "Them that sin rebuke before all, that others also may fear ; "[7] which must be received concerning those sins which are not concealed, lest he be thought to have spoken in opposition to the word of the Lord. For He says, "If thy brother shall sin against thee, rebuke him between thee and him."[8] Notwithstanding, He Himself carries out the severity of rebuke to the extent of saying, "If he will not hear the Church, let him be unto thee as a heathen man and a publican."[9] And who has more loved the weak than He who became weak for us all, and of that very weakness was crucified for us all? And since these things are so, grace neither restrains rebuke, nor does rebuke restrain grace ; and on this account righteousness is so to be prescribed that we may ask in faithful prayer, that, by God's grace, what is prescribed may be done ; and both of these things are in such wise to be done that righteous rebuke may not be neglected. But let all these things be done with love, since love both does not sin, and does cover the multitude of sins.

---

[1] Gal. iv. 6.     [2] Rom. viii. 15.     [3] 1 Cor. xv. 33.
[4] 1 Cor. viii. 11.

[5] Ezek. iii. 18.     [6] 1 Thess. v. 14.     [7] 1 Tim. v. 20.
[8] Matt. xviii. 15.     [9] Matt. xviii. 17.

# A TREATISE ON THE PREDESTINATION OF THE SAINTS.

# CONTENTS OF THE TREATISE "ON THE PREDESTINATION OF THE SAINTS."

# A TREATISE ON THE PREDESTINATION OF THE SAINTS,

*BY AURELIUS AUGUSTIN, BISHOP OF HIPPO.*

## THE FIRST BOOK.[1]

### ADDRESSED TO PROSPER AND HILARY.[2]

#### AD. 428 OR 429.

---

WHEREIN THE TRUTH OF PREDESTINATION AND GRACE IS DEFENDED AGAINST THE SEMI-PELAGIANS, — THOSE PEOPLE, TO WIT, WHO BY NO MEANS WITHDRAW ALTOGETHER FROM THE PELAGIAN HERESY, IN THAT THEY CONTEND THAT THE BEGINNING OF SALVATION AND OF FAITH IS OF OURSELVES; SO THAT IN VIRTUE, AS IT WERE, OF THIS PRECEDENT MERIT, THE OTHER GOOD GIFTS OF GOD ARE ATTAINED. AUGUSTIN SHOWS THAT NOT ONLY THE INCREASE, BUT THE VERY BEGINNING ALSO OF FAITH, IS IN GOD'S GIFT. ON THIS MATTER HE DOES NOT DISAVOW THAT HE ONCE THOUGHT DIFFERENTLY, AND THAT IN SOME SMALL WORKS, WRITTEN BEFORE HIS EPISCOPATE, HE WAS IN ERROR, AS IN THAT EXPOSITION, WHICH THEY OBJECT TO HIM, OF PROPOSITIONS FROM THE EPISTLE TO THE ROMANS. BUT HE POINTS OUT THAT HE WAS SUBSEQUENTLY CONVINCED CHIEFLY BY THIS TESTIMONY, "BUT WHAT HAST THOU THAT THOU HAST NOT RECEIVED?" WHICH HE PROVES IS TO BE TAKEN AS A TESTIMONY CONCERNING FAITH ITSELF ALSO. HE SAYS THAT FAITH IS TO BE COUNTED AMONG OTHER WORKS, WHICH THE APOSTLE DENIES TO ANTICIPATE GOD'S GRACE WHEN HE SAYS, "NOT OF WORKS." HE DECLARES THAT THE HARDNESS OF THE HEART IS TAKEN AWAY BY GRACE, AND THAT ALL COME TO CHRIST WHO ARE TAUGHT TO COME BY THE FATHER; BUT THAT THOSE WHOM HE TEACHES, HE TEACHES IN MERCY, WHILE THOSE WHOM HE TEACHES NOT, IN JUDGMENT HE TEACHES NOT. THAT THE PASSAGE FROM HIS HUNDRED AND SECOND EPISTLE, QUESTION 2, "CONCERNING THE TIME OF THE CHRISTIAN RELIGION," WHICH IS ALLEGED BY THE SEMI-PELAGIANS, MAY RIGHTLY BE EXPLAINED WITHOUT DETRIMENT TO THE DOCTRINE OF GRACE AND PREDESTINATION. HE TEACHES WHAT IS THE DIFFERENCE BETWEEN GRACE AND PREDESTINATION. FURTHER, HE SAYS THAT GOD IN HIS PREDESTINATION FOREKNEW WHAT HE HAD PURPOSED TO DO. HE MARVELS GREATLY THAT THE ADVERSARIES OF PREDESTINATION, WHO ARE SAID TO BE UNWILLING TO BE DEPENDENT ON THE UNCERTAINTY OF GOD'S WILL, PREFER RATHER TO TRUST THEMSELVES TO THEIR OWN WEAKNESS THAN TO

---

[1] This Treatise is the first portion of a work, of which the following, *On the Gift of Perseverance*, is the second.

[2] [These two books that follow, viz., *On the Predestination of the Saints* and *On the Gift of Perseverance*, were called out by two long letters, one from Prosper and the other from Hilary, acquainting Augustin with the Semi-Pelagian outbreak in Southern Gaul, and earnestly beseeching his aid in meeting it. These letters are Nos. 225 and 226 in the collection of Augustin's letters. Prosper was just beginning his great career as champion of Augustinianism in Southern Gaul. Hilary was also a layman, and may perhaps be identified with the Hilary who much earlier wrote to Augustin about the Pelagians of Sicily (see Letter 156), and to whom the long Letter 157 was written. — W.]

THE STRENGTH OF GOD'S PROMISE. HE CLEARLY POINTS OUT THAT THEY ABUSE THIS AUTHORITY, "IF THOU BELIEVEST, THOU SHALT BE SAVED." THAT THE TRUTH OF GRACE AND PERSEVERANCE SHINES FORTH IN THE CASE OF INFANTS THAT ARE SAVED, WHO ARE DISTINGUISHED BY NO MERITS OF THEIR OWN FROM OTHERS WHO PERISH. FOR THAT THERE IS NO DIFFERENCE BETWEEN THEM ARISING FROM THE FOREKNOWLEDGE OF MERITS WHICH THEY WOULD HAVE HAD IF THEY HAD LIVED LONGER. THAT THAT TESTIMONY IS WRONGFULLY REJECTED BY THE ADVERSARIES AS BEING UNCANONICAL, WHICH HE ADDUCED FOR THE PURPOSE OF THIS DISCUSSION, "HE WAS TAKEN AWAY LEST WICKEDNESS," ETC. THAT THE MOST ILLUSTRIOUS INSTANCE OF PREDESTINATION AND GRACE IS THE SAVIOUR HIMSELF, IN WHOM A MAN OBTAINED THE PRIVILEGE OF BEING THE SAVIOUR AND THE ONLY-BEGOTTEN SON OF GOD, THROUGH BEING ASSUMED INTO ONENESS OF PERSON BY THE WORD CO-ETERNAL WITH THE FATHER, ON ACCOUNT OF NO PRECEDENT MERITS, EITHER OF WORKS OR OF FAITH. THAT THE PRE-DESTINATED ARE CALLED BY SOME CERTAIN CALLING PECULIAR TO THE ELECT, AND THAT THEY HAVE BEEN ELECTED BEFORE THE FOUNDATION OF THE WORLD; NOT BECAUSE THEY WERE FOREKNOWN AS MEN WHO WOULD BELIEVE AND WOULD BE HOLY, BUT IN ORDER THAT BY MEANS OF THAT VERY ELECTION OF GRACE THEY MIGHT BE SUCH, ETC.

## CHAP. I [I.] — INTRODUCTION.

WE know that in the Epistle to the Philippians the apostle said, "To write the same things to you to me indeed is not grievous, but for you it is safe;"[1] yet the same apostle, writing to the Galatians, when he saw that he had done enough among them of what he regarded as being needful for them, by the ministry of his preaching, said, "For the rest let no man cause me labour,"[2] or as it is read in many codices, "Let no one be troublesome to me." But although I confess that it causes me trouble that the divine word in which the grace of God is preached (which is absolutely no grace if it is given according to our merits), great and manifest as it is, is not yielded to, nevertheless my dearest sons, Prosper and Hilary, your zeal and brotherly affection — which makes you so reluctant to see any of the brethren in error, as to wish that, after so many books and letters of mine on this subject, I should write again from here — I love more than I can tell, although I do not dare to say that I love it as much as I ought. Wherefore, behold, I write to you again. And although not with you, yet through you I am still doing what I thought I had done sufficiently.

## CHAP. 2. — TO WHAT EXTENT THE MASSILIANS[3] WITHDRAW FROM THE PELAGIANS.

For on consideration of your letters, I seem to see that those brethren on whose behalf you exhibit a pious care that they may not hold the poetical opinion in which it is affirmed, "Every one is a hope for himself,"[4] and so fall under that condemnation which is, not poetically, but prophetically, declared, "Cursed is every man that hath hope in man,"[5] must be treated in that way wherein the apostle dealt with those to whom he said, "And if in anything ye be otherwise minded, God shall reveal even this unto you."[6] For as yet they are in darkness on the question concerning the predestination of the saints, but they have that whence, "if in anything they are otherwise minded, God will reveal even this unto them," if they are walking in that to which they have attained. For which reason the apostle, when he had said, "If ye are in anything otherwise minded, God shall reveal even this unto you," says, "Nevertheless, where-unto we have attained, let us walk in the same."[7] And those brethren of ours, on whose behalf your pious love is solicitous, have attained with Christ's Church to the belief that the human race is born obnoxious to the sin of the first man, and that none can be delivered from that evil save by the righteousness of the Second Man. Moreover, they have attained to the confession that men's wills are anticipated by God's grace; and to the agreement that no one can suffice to himself either for beginning or for completing any good work. These things, therefore, unto which they have attained, being held fast, abundantly distinguish them from the error of the Pelagians. Further, if they walk in them, and beseech Him who giveth understanding, if in anything concerning predestination they are otherwise minded, He will reveal even this unto them. Yet let us also spend upon them the influence of our love, and the ministry of our

---

[1] Phil. iii. 1.      [2] Gal. vi. 17.
[3] [The party which Augustin is here opposing had its chief centre in Marseilles, and hence is called "Massilians." Prosper in his letter called them *reliquiæ Pelagianorum*, i.e., "the remnants of the Pelagians." They are now most commonly called "Semi-Pelagians." — W.]

[4] Virg. *Æneid*, xi. 309.    [5] Jer. xvii. 5.    [6] Phil. iii. 15.
[7] Phil. iii. 16.

discourse, according to His gift, whom we have asked that in these letters we might say what should be suitable [1] and profitable to them. For whence do we know whether by this our service, wherein we are serving them in the free love of Christ, our God may not perchance will to effect that purpose?

### CHAP. 3 [II.] — EVEN THE BEGINNING OF FAITH IS OF GOD'S GIFT.

Therefore I ought first to show that the faith by which we are Christians is the gift of God, if I can do that more thoroughly than I have already done in so many and so large volumes. But I see that I must now reply to those who say that the divine testimonies which I have adduced concerning this matter are of avail for this purpose, to assure us that we have faith itself of ourselves, but that its increase is of God; as if faith were not given to us by Him, but were only increased in us by Him, on the ground of the merit of its having begun from us. Thus there is here no departure from that opinion which Pelagius himself was constrained to condemn in the judgment of the bishops of Palestine, as is testified in the same Proceedings, "That the grace of God is given according to our merits," [2] if it is not of God's grace that we begin to believe, but rather that on account of this beginning an addition is made to us of a more full and perfect belief; and so we first give the beginning of our faith to God, that His supplement may also be given to us again, and whatever else we faithfully ask.

### CHAP. 4. — CONTINUATION OF THE PRECEDING.

But why do we not, in opposition to this, rather hear the words, "Who hath first given to Him and it shall be recompensed to him again? since of Him, and through Him, and in Him, are all things"? [3] And from whom, then, is that very beginning of our faith if not from Him? For this is not excepted when other things are spoken of as of Him; but "of Him, and through Him, and in Him, are *all* things." But who can say that he who has already begun to believe deserves nothing from Him in whom he has believed? Whence it results that, to him who already deserves, other things are said to be added by a divine retribution, and thus that God's grace is given according to our merits. And this assertion when put before him, Pelagius himself condemned, that he might not be condemned. Whoever, then, wishes on every side to avoid this condemnable opinion, let him understand that what the apostle says is said with entire truthfulness, "Unto you it is given in the behalf of Christ not only to believe on

Him, but also to suffer for His sake." [4] He shows that both are the gifts of God, because he said that both were given. And he does not say, "to believe on Him more fully and perfectly," but, "to believe on Him." Neither does he say that he himself had obtained mercy to be more faithful, but "to be faithful," [5] because he knew that he had not first given the beginning of his faith to God, and had its increase given back to him again by Him; but that he had been made faithful by God, who also had made him an apostle. For the beginnings of his faith are recorded, and they are very well known by being read in the church on an occasion calculated to distinguish them: [6] how, being turned away from the faith which he was destroying, and being vehemently opposed to it, he was suddenly by a more powerful grace converted to it, by the conversion of Him, to whom as One who would do this very thing it was said by the prophet, "Thou wilt turn and quicken us;" [7] so that not only from one who refused to believe he was made a willing believer, but, moreover, from being a persecutor, he suffered persecution in defence of that faith which he persecuted. Because it was given him by Christ "not only to believe on Him, but also to suffer for His sake."

### CHAP. 5. — TO BELIEVE IS TO THINK WITH ASSENT.

And, therefore, commending that grace which is not given according to any merits, but is the cause of all good merits, he says, "Not that we are sufficient to think anything as of ourselves, but our sufficiency is of God." [8] Let them give attention to this, and well weigh these words, who think that the beginning of faith is of ourselves, and the supplement of faith is of God. For who cannot see that thinking is prior to believing? For no one believes anything unless he has first thought that it is to be believed. For however suddenly, however rapidly, some thoughts fly before the will to believe, and this presently follows in such wise as to attend them, as it were, in closest conjunction, it is yet necessary that everything which is believed should be believed after thought has preceded; although even belief itself is nothing else than to think with assent. For it is not every one who thinks that believes, since many think in order that they may not believe; but everybody who believes, thinks, — both thinks in believing, and believes in thinking. Therefore in what pertains to religion and piety (of which the apostle was speaking), if we are not capable of thinking anything as of ourselves, but our sufficiency is

---

[1] Some MSS. read *aperta, scil.* "plain."
[2] *On the Proceedings of Pelagius*, ch. 30.   [3] Rom. xi. 35.
[4] Phil. i. 29.   [5] 1 Cor. vii. 25.
[6] The Acts of the Apostles were read during Easter.
[7] Ps. lxxxv. 6.   [8] 2 Cor. iii. 5.

of God, we are certainly not capable of believing anything as of ourselves, since we cannot do this without thinking ; but our sufficiency, by which we begin to believe, is of God. Wherefore, as no one is sufficient for himself, for the beginning or the completion of any good work whatever, — and this those brethren of yours, as what you have written intimates, already agree to be true, whence, as well in the beginning as in the carrying out of every good work, our sufficiency is of God, — so no one is sufficient for himself, either to begin or to perfect faith ; but our sufficiency is of God. Because if faith is not a matter of thought, it is of no account ; and we are not sufficient to think anything as of ourselves, but our sufficiency is of God.

## CHAP. 6. — PRESUMPTION AND ARROGANCE TO BE AVOIDED.

Care must be taken, brethren, beloved of God, that a man do not lift himself up in opposition to God, when he says that he does what God has promised. Was not the faith of the nations promised to Abraham, "and he, giving glory to God, most fully believed that what He promised He is able also to perform"?[1] He therefore makes the faith of the nations, who is able to do what He has promised. Further, if God works our faith, acting in a wonderful manner in our hearts so that we believe, is there any reason to fear that He cannot do the whole ; and does man on that account arrogate to himself its first elements, that he may merit to receive its last from God? Consider if in such a way any other result be gained than that the grace of God is given in some way or other, according to our merits, and so grace is no more grace. For on this principle it is rendered as debt, it is not given gratuitously ; for it is due to the believer that his faith itself should be increased by the Lord, and that the increased faith should be the wages of the faith begun ; nor is it observed when this is said, that this wage is assigned to believers, not of grace, but of debt. And I do not at all see why the whole should not be attributed to man, — as he who could originate for himself what he had not previously, can himself increase what he had originated, — except that it is impossible to withstand the most manifest divine testimony, by which faith, whence piety takes its beginning, is shown also to be the gift of God : such as is that testimony that " God hath dealt to every man the measure of faith ; "[2] and that one, " Peace be to the brethren, and love with faith, from God the Father, and the Lord Jesus Christ,"[3] and other similar passages. Man, therefore, unwilling to resist such clear testimonies as these, and yet desiring himself to

have the merit of believing, compounds as it were with God to claim a portion of faith for himself, and to leave a portion for Him ; and, what is still more arrogant, he takes the first portion for himself, and gives the subsequent to Him ; and so in that which he says belongs to both, he makes himself the first, and God the second !

## CHAP. 7 [III.] — AUGUSTIN CONFESSES THAT HE HAD FORMERLY BEEN IN ERROR CONCERNING THE GRACE OF GOD.

It was not thus that that pious and humble teacher thought — I speak of the most blessed Cyprian — when he said "that we must boast in nothing, since nothing is our own."[4] And in order to show this, he appealed to the apostle as a witness, where he said, " For what hast thou that thou hast not received? And if thou hast received it, why boastest thou as if thou hadst not received it?"[5] And it was chiefly by this testimony that I myself also was convinced when I was in a similar error, thinking that faith whereby we believe on God is not God's gift, but that it is in us from ourselves, and that by it we obtain the gifts of God, whereby we may live temperately and righteously and piously in this world. For I did not think that faith was preceded by God's grace, so that by its means would be given to us what we might profitably ask, except that we could not believe if the proclamation of the truth did not precede ; but that we should consent when the gospel was preached to us I thought was our own doing, and came to us from ourselves. And this my error is sufficiently indicated in some small works of mine written before my episcopate. Among these is that which you have mentioned in your letters,[6] wherein is an exposition of certain propositions from the Epistle to the Romans. Eventually, when I was retracting all my small works, and was committing that retractation to writing, — of which task I had already completed two books before I had taken up your more lengthy letters, — when in the first volume I had reached the retractation of this book, I then spoke thus : — " Also discussing, I say, ' what God could have chosen in him who was as yet unborn, whom He said that the elder should serve ; and what in the same elder, equally as yet unborn, He could have rejected ; concerning whom, on this account, the prophetic testimony is recorded, although declared long subsequently, " Jacob have I loved, and Esau have I hated,"'[7] I carried out my reasoning to the point of saying : ' God did not therefore choose the works of any one in foreknowledge of what He Himself would

---

[1] Rom. iv. 20.        [2] Rom. xii. 3.        [3] Eph. vi. 23.

[4] Cyprian, *Testimonies to Quirinus*, Book iii. ch. 4; *The Ante-Nicene Fathers*, vol. v, p. 528.
[5] 1 Cor. iv. 7.
[6] Hilary's Letter, No. 226 in the collection of Augustin's *Letters*.
[7] Mal. i. 2, 3. Cf. Rom. ix. 13.

give them, but he chose the faith, in the foreknowledge that He would choose that very person whom He foreknew would believe on Him,—to whom He would give the Holy Spirit, so that by doing good works he might obtain eternal life also.' I had not yet very carefully sought, nor had I as yet found, what is the nature of the election of grace, of which the apostle says, 'A remnant are saved according to the election of grace.'[1] Which assuredly is not grace if any merits precede it; lest what is now given, not according to grace, but according to debt, be rather paid to merits than freely given. And what I next subjoined: 'For the same apostle says, "The same God which worketh all in all;"[2] but it was never said, God believeth all in all;' and then added, 'Therefore what we believe is our own, but what good thing we do is of Him who giveth the Holy Spirit to them that believe:' I certainly could not have said, had I already known that faith itself also is found among those gifts of God which are given by the same Spirit. Both, therefore, are ours on account of the choice of the will, and yet both are given by the spirit of faith and love. For faith is not alone, but, as it is written, 'Love with faith, from God the Father, and our Lord Jesus Christ.'[3] And what I said a little after,—' For it is ours to believe and to will, but it is His to give to those who believe and will, the power of doing good works through the Holy Spirit, by whom love is shed abroad in our hearts,'—is true indeed; but by the same rule both are also God's, because God prepares the will; and both are ours too, because they are only brought about with our good wills. And thus what I subsequently said also: 'Because we are not able to will unless we are called; and when, after our calling, we would will, our willing is not sufficient, nor our running, unless God gives strength to us that run, and leads us whither He calls us;' and thereupon added: 'It is plain, therefore, that it is not of him that willeth, nor of him that runneth, but of God that showeth mercy, that we do good works,'—this is absolutely most true. But I discovered little concerning the calling itself, which is according to God's purpose; for not such is the calling of all that are called, but only of the elect. Therefore what I said a little afterwards: 'For as in those whom God elects it is not works but faith that begins the merit so as to do good works by the gift of God, so in those whom He condemns, unbelief and impiety begin the merit of punishment, so that even by way of punishment itself they do evil works,'—I spoke most truly. But that even the merit itself of faith was God's gift, I neither thought of inquiring into,

nor did I say. And in another place I say: 'For whom He has mercy upon, He makes to do good works, and whom He hardeneth He leaves to do evil works; but that mercy is bestowed upon the preceding merit of faith, and that hardening is applied to preceding iniquity.' And this indeed is true; but it should further have been asked, whether even the merit of faith does not come from God's mercy,—that is, whether that mercy is manifested in man only because he is a believer, or whether it is also manifested that he may be a believer? For we read in the apostle's words: 'I obtained mercy to be a believer.'[4] He does not say, 'Because I was a believer.' Therefore, although it is given to the believer, yet it has been given also that he may be a believer. Therefore, also, in another place in the same book I most truly said: 'Because, if it is of God's mercy, and not of works, that we are even called that we may believe, and it is granted to us who believe to do good works, that mercy must not be grudged to the heathen;'—although I there discoursed less carefully about that calling which is given according to God's purpose."[5]

CHAP. 8 [IV.]—WHAT AUGUSTIN WROTE TO SIMPLICIANUS, THE SUCCESSOR OF AMBROSE, BISHOP OF MILAN.

You see plainly what was at that time my opinion concerning faith and works, although I was labouring in commending God's grace; and in this opinion I see that those brethren of ours now are, because they have not been as careful to make progress with me in my writings as they were in reading them. For if they had been so careful, they would have found that question solved in accordance with the truth of the divine Scriptures in the first book of the two which I wrote in the very beginning of my episcopate to Simplicianus, of blessed memory, Bishop of the Church of Milan, and successor to St. Ambrose. Unless, perchance, they may not have known these books; in which case, take care that they do know them. Of this first of those two books, I first spoke in the second book of the *Retractations*; and what I said is as follows: "Of the books, I say, on which, as a bishop, I have laboured, the first two are addressed to Simplicianus, president of the Church of Milan, who succeeded the most blessed Ambrose,—concerning divers questions, two of which I gathered into the first book from the Epistle of Paul the Apostle to the Romans. The former of them is about what is written: 'What shall we say, then? Is the law sin? By no means;'[6] as far as the passage where he says, 'Who shall deliver me from the body of this death? The

---

[1] Rom. xi. 5.    [2] 1 Cor. xii. 6.    [3] Eph. vi. 23.
[4] 1 Cor. vii. 25.    [5] *Retractations*, Book i. ch. 23, Nos. 3, 4.
[6] Rom. vii. 7.

grace of God through Jesus Christ our Lord.'[1] And therein I have expounded those words of the apostle: 'The law is spiritual; but I am carnal,'[2] and others in which the flesh is declared to be in conflict against the Spirit, in such a way as if a man were there described as still under law, and not yet established under grace. For, long afterwards, I perceived that those words might even be (and probably were) the utterance of a spiritual man. The latter question in this book is gathered from that passage where the apostle says, 'And not only this, but when Rebecca also had conceived by one act of intercourse, even by our father Isaac,'[3] as far as that place where he says, 'Except the Lord of Sabaoth had left us a seed, we should be as Sodoma, and should have been like unto Gomorrah.'[4] In the solution of this question I laboured indeed on behalf of the free choice of the human will, but God's grace overcame, and I could only reach that point where the apostle is perceived to have said with the most evident truth, 'For who maketh thee to differ? and what hast thou that thou hast not received? Now, if thou hast received it, why dost thou glory as if thou receivedst it not?'[5] And this the martyr Cyprian was also desirous of setting forth when he compressed the whole of it in that title: 'That we must boast in nothing, since nothing is our own.'"[6] This is why I previously said that it was chiefly by this apostolic testimony that I myself had been convinced, when I thought otherwise concerning this matter; and this God revealed to me as I sought to solve this question when I was writing, as I said, to the Bishop Simplicianus. This testimony, therefore, of the apostle, when for the sake of repressing man's conceit he said, "For what hast thou which thou hast not received?"[5] does not allow any believer to say, I have faith which I received not. All the arrogance of this answer is absolutely repressed by these apostolic words. Moreover, it cannot even be said, "Although I have not a perfected faith, yet I have its beginning, whereby I first of all believed in Christ." Because here also is answered: "But what hast thou that thou hast not received? Now, if thou hast received it, why dost thou glory as if thou receivedst it not?"

CHAP. 9 [V.] — THE PURPOSE OF THE APOSTLE IN THESE WORDS.

The notion, however, which they entertain, "that these words, 'What hast thou that thou hast not received?' cannot be said of this faith, because it has remained in the same nature,

although corrupted, which at first was endowed with health and perfection,"[7] is perceived to have no force for the purpose that they desire, if it be considered why the apostle said these words. For he was concerned that no one should glory in man, because dissensions had sprung up among the Corinthian Christians, so that every one was saying, "I, indeed, am of Paul, and another, I am of Apollos, and another, I am of Cephas;"[8] and thence he went on to say: "God hath chosen the foolish things of the world to confound the wise; and God hath chosen the weak things of the world to confound the strong things; and God hath chosen the ignoble things of the world, and contemptible things, and those things which are not, to make of no account things which are; that no flesh should glory before God."[9] Here the intention of the apostle is of a certainty sufficiently plain against the pride of man, that no one should glory in man; and thus, no one should glory in himself. Finally, when he had said "that no flesh should glory before God," in order to show in what man ought to glory, he immediately added, "But it is of Him that ye are in Christ Jesus, who is made unto us wisdom from God, and righteousness, and sanctification, and redemption: that according as it is written, He that glorieth, let him glory in the Lord."[10] Thence that intention of his progressed, till afterwards rebuking them he says, "For ye are yet carnal; for whereas there are among you envying and contention, are ye not carnal, and walk according to man? For while one saith I am of Paul, and another, I am of Apollos, are ye not men? What, then, is Apollos, and what Paul? Ministers by whom ye believed; and to every one as the Lord has given. I have planted, and Apollos watered; but God gave the increase. Therefore, neither is he that planteth anything, nor he that watereth, but God that giveth the increase."[11] Do you not see that the sole purpose of the apostle is that man may be humbled, and God alone exalted? Since in all those things, indeed, which are planted and watered, he says that not even are the planter and the waterer anything, but God who giveth the increase: and the very fact, also, that one plants and another waters he attributes not to themselves, but to God, when he says, "To every one as the Lord hath given; I have planted, Apollos watered." Hence, therefore, persisting in the same intention he comes to the point of saying, "Therefore let no man glory in man,"[12] for he had already said, "He that glorieth, let him glory in the Lord." After these and some other matters which are associated

---

[1] Rom. vii. 24.     [2] Rom. vii. 14.     [3] Rom. ix. 10.
[4] Rom. ix 29.     [5] 1 Cor. iv. 7.
[6] Cypr. *Test.* Book iii. ch. 4; see *The Ante-Nicene Fathers,* p 528. Augustin's *Retractations,* II. i. 1.

[7] See Epistle of Hilary (Augustin's *Epistles,* 226).
[8] 1 Cor. i. 12.     [9] 1 Cor. i. 27.     [10] 1 Cor. i. 30.
[11] 1 Cor. iii. 3 ff.     [12] 1 Cor. iii. 21.

therewith, that same intention of his is carried on in the words: "And these things, brethren, I have in a figure transferred to myself and to Apollos for your sakes, that ye might learn in us that no one of you should be puffed up for one against another above that which is written. For who maketh thee to differ? And what hast thou which thou hast not received? Now, if thou hast received it, why dost thou glory as if thou receivedst it not?"[1]

CHAP. 10. — IT IS GOD'S GRACE WHICH SPECIALLY DISTINGUISHES ONE MAN FROM ANOTHER.

In this the apostle's most evident intention, in which he speaks against human pride, so that none should glory in man but in God, it is too absurd, as I think, to suppose God's natural gifts, whether man's entire and perfected nature itself, as it was bestowed on him in his first state, or the remains, whatever they may be, of his degraded nature. For is it by such gifts as these, which are common to all men, that men are distinguished from men? But here he first said, "For who maketh thee to differ?" and then added, "And what hast thou that thou hast not received?" Because a man, puffed up against another, might say, "My faith makes me to differ," or "My righteousness," or anything else of the kind. In reply to such notions, the good teacher says, "But what hast thou that thou hast not received?" And from whom but from Him who maketh thee to differ from another, on whom He bestowed not what He bestowed on thee? "Now if," says he, "thou hast received it, why dost thou glory as if thou receivedst it not?" Is he concerned, I ask, about anything else save that he who glorieth should glory in the Lord? But nothing is so opposed to this feeling as for any one to glory concerning his own merits in such a way as if he himself had made them for himself, and not the grace of God, — a grace, however, which makes the good to differ from the wicked, and is not common to the good and the wicked. Let the grace, therefore, whereby we are living and reasonable creatures, and are distinguished from cattle, be attributed to nature; let that grace also by which, among men themselves, the handsome are made to differ from the ill-formed, or the intelligent from the stupid, or anything of that kind, be ascribed to nature. But he whom the apostle was rebuking did not puff himself up as contrasted with cattle, nor as contrasted with any other man, in respect of any natural endowment which might be found even in the worst of men. But he ascribed to himself, and not to God, some good gift which pertained to a holy life, and was puffed up therewith when he

deserved to hear the rebuke, "Who hath made thee to differ? and what hast thou that thou receivedst not?" For though the capacity to have faith is of nature, is it also of nature to have it? "For all men have not faith,"[2] although all men have the capacity to have faith. But the apostle does not say, "And what hast thou capacity to have, the capacity to have which thou receivedst not?" but he says, "And what hast thou which thou receivedst not?" Accordingly, the capacity to have faith,[3] as the capacity to have love, belongs to men's nature; but to have faith, even as to have love, belongs to the grace of believers. That nature, therefore, in which is given to us the capacity of having faith, does not distinguish man from man, but faith itself makes the believer to differ from the unbeliever. And thus, when it is said, "For who maketh thee to differ? and what hast thou that thou receivedst not?" if any one dare to say, "I have faith of myself, I did not, therefore, receive it," he directly contradicts this most manifest truth, — not because it is not in the choice of man's will to believe or not to believe, but because in the elect the will is prepared by the Lord. Thus, moreover, the passage, "For who maketh thee to differ? and what hast thou that thou receivedst not?" refers to that very faith which is in the will of man.

CHAP. 11 [VI.] — THAT SOME MEN ARE ELECTED IS OF GOD'S MERCY.

"Many hear the word of truth; but some believe, while others contradict. Therefore, the former will to believe; the latter do not will." Who does not know this? Who can deny this? But since in some the will is prepared by the Lord, in others it is not prepared, we must assuredly be able to distinguish what comes from God's mercy, and what from His judgment. "What Israel sought for," says the apostle, "he hath not obtained, but the election hath obtained it; and the rest were blinded, as it is written, God gave to them the spirit of compunction, — eyes that they should not see, and ears that they should not hear, even to this day. And David said, Let their table be made a snare, a retribution, and a stumblingblock to them; let their eyes be darkened, that they may not see; and bow down their back always."[4] Here is mercy and judgment, — mercy towards the election which has obtained the righteousness of God, but judgment to the rest which have been blinded. And yet the former, because they

---

[1] 1 Cor. iv. 6.

[2] 2 Thess. iii. 2.
[3] Thence says Bernard, in his treatise *On Grace and Free Will*, ch. i.: "God is the author of salvation. Free will is only capable of it." Comp. *On the Calling of the Gentiles*, Book ii. ch. 2, and Fulgentius, *On the Incarnation and Grace of our Lord Jesus Christ*, chs. 22, 23, and 24.
[4] Rom. xi. 7.

willed,[1] believed; the latter, because they did not will believed not. Therefore mercy and judgment were manifested in the very wills themselves. Certainly such an election is of grace, not at all of merits. For he had before said, "So, therefore, even at this present time, the remnant has been saved by the election of grace. And if by grace, now it is no more of works; otherwise grace is no more grace."[2] Therefore the election obtained what it obtained gratuitously; there preceded none of those things which they might first give, and it should be given to them again. He saved them for nothing. But to the rest who were blinded, as is there plainly declared, it was done in recompense. "All the paths of the Lord are mercy and truth."[3] But His ways are unsearchable. Therefore the mercy by which He freely delivers, and the truth by which He righteously judges, are equally unsearchable.

CHAP. 12 [VII.] — WHY THE APOSTLE SAID THAT WE ARE JUSTIFIED BY FAITH AND NOT BY WORKS.

But perhaps it may be said: "The apostle distinguishes faith from works; he says, indeed, that grace is not of works, but he does not say that it is not of faith." This, indeed, is true. But Jesus says that faith itself also is the work of God, and commands us to work it. For the Jews said to Him, "What shall we do that we may work the work of God? Jesus answered, and said unto them, This is the work of God, that ye believe on Him whom He hath sent."[4] The apostle, therefore, distinguishes faith from works, just as Judah is distinguished from Israel in the two kingdoms of the Hebrews, although Judah is Israel itself. And he says that a man is justified by faith and not by works, because faith itself is first given, from which may be obtained other things which are specially characterized as works, in which a man may live righteously. For he himself also says, "By grace ye are saved through faith; and this not of yourselves; but it is the gift of God,"[5] — that is to say, "And in saying, 'through faith,' even faith itself is not of yourselves, but is God's gift." "Not of works," he says, "lest any man should be lifted up." For it is often said, "He deserved to believe, because he was a good man even before he believed." Which may be said of Cornelius,[6] since his alms were accepted and his prayers heard before he had believed on Christ; and yet without some faith he neither gave alms nor prayed. For how did he call on Him on whom he had not believed? But if he could have been saved without the faith of Christ, the Apostle Peter would not have been sent as an architect to build him up; although, "Except the Lord build the house, they labour in vain who build it."[7] And we are told, Faith is of ourselves; other things which pertain to works of righteousness are of the Lord; as if faith did not belong to the building, — as if, I say, the foundation did not belong to the building. But if this primarily and especially belongs to it, he labours in vain who seeks to build up the faith by preaching, unless the Lord in His mercy builds it up from within. Whatever, therefore, of good works Cornelius performed, as well before he believed in Christ as when he believed and after he had believed, are all to be ascribed to God, lest, perchance any man be lifted up.

CHAP. 13 [VIII.] — THE EFFECT OF DIVINE GRACE.

Accordingly, our only Master and Lord Himself, when He had said what I have above mentioned, — "This is the work of God, that ye believe on Him whom He hath sent," — says a little afterwards in that same discourse of His, " I said unto you that ye also have seen me and have not believed. All that the Father giveth me shall come to me."[8] What is the meaning of "shall come to me," but, "shall believe in me"? But it is the Father's gift that this may be the case. Moreover, a little after He says, "Murmur not among yourselves. No one can come to me, except the Father which hath sent me draw him; and I will raise him up at the last day. It is written in the prophets, And they shall be all teachable[9] of God. Every man that hath heard of the Father, and hath learned, cometh unto me."[10] What is the meaning of, "Every man that hath heard from the Father, and hath learned, cometh unto me," except that there is none who hears from the Father, and learns, who cometh not to me? For if every one who has heard from the Father, and has learned, comes, certainly every one who does not come has not heard from the Father; for if he had heard and learned, he would come. For no one has heard and learned, and has not come; but every one, as the Truth declares, who has heard from the Father, and has learned, comes. Far removed from the senses of the flesh is this teaching in which the Father is heard, and teaches to come to the Son. Engaged herein is also the Son Himself, because He is His Word by which He thus teaches; and He does not do this through the ear of the flesh, but of the heart. Herein engaged, also, at the same time, is the Spirit of the Father and of the Son; and He, too, teaches, and does not teach separately, since we have learned that the workings of the Trinity are inseparable. And

---

[1] According to the Vatican MSS. is read, "The former who willed," and below, "The latter who willed not."
[2] Rom. xi. 5.　　[3] Ps. xxv. 10.　　[4] John vi. 28.
[5] Eph. ii 8.　　[6] Acts x.
[7] Ps. cxxvii. 1.　　[8] John vi. 36
[9] Or, "docile towards God."　　[10] John vi. 43 ff.

that is certainly the same Holy Spirit of whom the apostle says, " We, however, having the same Spirit of faith." [1]   But this is especially attributed to the Father, for the reason that of Him is begotten the Only Begotten, and from Him proceeds the Holy Spirit, of which it would be tedious to argue more elaborately ; and I think that my work in fifteen books on the Trinity which God is, has already reached you. Very far removed, I say, from the senses of the flesh is this instruction wherein God is heard and teaches. We see that many come to the Son because we see that many believe on Christ, but when and how they have heard this from the Father, and have learned, we see not. It is true that that grace is exceedingly secret, but who doubts that it is grace? This grace, therefore, which is hiddenly bestowed in human hearts by the Divine gift, is rejected by no hard heart, because it is given for the sake of first taking away the hardness of the heart. When, therefore, the Father is heard within, and teaches, so that a man comes to the Son, He takes away the heart of stone and gives a heart of flesh, as in the declaration of the prophet He has promised. Because He thus makes them children and vessels of mercy which He has prepared for glory.

CHAP. 14. — WHY THE FATHER DOES NOT TEACH ALL THAT THEY MAY COME TO CHRIST.

Why, then, does He not teach all that they may come to Christ, except because all whom He teaches, He teaches in mercy, while those whom He teaches not, in judgment He teaches not? Since, " On whom He will He has mercy, and whom He will He hardeneth." [2]   But He has mercy when He gives good things. He hardens when He recompenses what is deserved. Or if, as some would prefer to distinguish them, those words also are his to whom the apostle says, " Thou sayest then unto me," so that he may be regarded as having said, " Therefore hath He mercy on whom He will, and whom He will He hardeneth," as well as those which follow, — to wit, " What is it that is still complained of ? for who resists His will ?" does the apostle answer, " O man, what thou hast said is false ? " No ; but he says, " O man, who art thou that repliest against God ? Doth the thing formed say to him that formed it, Why hast thou made me thus ? Hath not the potter power over the clay of the same lump ? " [3] and what follows, which you very well know. And yet in a certain sense the Father teaches all men to come to His Son. For it was not in vain that it was written in the prophets, " And they shall all be teachable of God." [4]   And when He

too had premised this testimony, He added, " Every man, therefore, who has heard of the Father, and has learned, cometh to me." As, therefore, we speak justly when we say concerning any teacher of literature who is alone in a city, He teaches literature here to everybody, — not that all men learn, but that there is none who learns literature there who does not learn from him, — so we justly say, God teaches all men to come to Christ, not because all come, but because none comes in any other way. And why He does not teach all men the apostle explained, as far as he judged that it was to be explained, because, " willing to show His wrath, and to exhibit His power, He endured with much patience the vessels of wrath which were perfected for destruction ; and that He might make known the riches of His glory on the vessels of mercy which He has prepared for glory." [5] Hence it is that the " word of the cross is foolishness to them that perish ; but unto them that are saved it is the power of God." [6]   God teaches all such to come to Christ, for He wills all such to be saved, and to come to the knowledge of the truth. And if He had willed to teach even those to whom the word of the cross is foolishness to come to Christ, beyond all doubt these also would have come. For He neither deceives nor is deceived when He says, " Every one that hath heard of the Father, and hath learned, cometh to me." Away, then, with the thought that any one cometh not, who has heard of the Father and has learned.

CHAP. 15. — IT IS BELIEVERS THAT ARE TAUGHT OF GOD.

" Why," say they, " does He not teach all men ? " If we should say that they whom He does not teach are unwilling to learn, we shall be met with the answer : And what becomes of what is said to Him, " O God, Thou wilt turn us again, and quicken us " ? [7]   Or if God does not make men willing who were not willing, on what principle does the Church pray, according to the Lord's commandment, for her persecutors ? For thus also the blessed Cyprian [8] would have it to be understood that we say, " Thy will be done, as in heaven so in earth," — that is, as in those who have already believed, and who are, as it were, *heaven*, so also in those who do not believe, and on this account are still *the earth*. What, then, do we pray for on behalf of those who are unwilling to believe, except that God would work in them to will also? Certainly the apostle says, " Brethren, my heart's good will, indeed, and my prayer to God for them, is for their salvation." [9]   He prays for those who do not believe, — for what, except

---

[1] 2 Cor. iv. 13.     [2] Rom. ix. 18.     [3] Rom. ix. 18, ff.
[4] John vi. 45.

[5] Rom. ix. 22.     [6] 1 Cor. i. 18.     [7] Ps. lxxx. 7.
[8] Cypr. *Treatise on the Lord's Prayer.*     [9] Rom. x. 1.

that they may believe? For in no other way do they obtain salvation. If, then, the faith of the petitioners precede the grace of God, does the faith of them on whose behalf prayer is made that they may believe precede the grace of God?—since this is the very thing that is besought for them, that on them that believe not—that is, who have not faith—faith itself may be bestowed? When, therefore, the gospel is preached, some believe, some believe not; but they who believe at the voice of the preacher from without, hear of the Father from within, and learn; while they who do not believe, hear outwardly, but inwardly do not hear nor learn; —that is to say, to the former it is given to believe; to the latter it is not given. Because "no man," says He, "cometh to me, except the Father which sent me draw him."[1] And this is more plainly said afterwards. For after a little time, when He was speaking of eating his flesh and drinking His blood, and some even of His disciples said, "This is a hard saying, who can hear it? Jesus, knowing in Himself that His disciples murmured at this, said unto them, Doth this offend you?"[2] And a little after He said, "The words that I have spoken unto you are spirit and life; but there are some among you which believe not."[3] And immediately the evangelist says, "For Jesus knew from the beginning who were the believers, and who should betray Him; and He said, Therefore said I unto you, that no man can come unto me except it were given him of my Father." Therefore, to be drawn to Christ by the Father, and to hear and learn of the Father in order to come to Christ, is nothing else than to receive from the Father the gift by which to believe in Christ. For it was not the hearers of the gospel that were distinguished from those who did not hear, but the believers from those who did not believe, by Him who said, "No man cometh to me except it were given him of my Father."

CHAP. 16.—WHY THE GIFT OF FAITH IS NOT GIVEN TO ALL.

Faith, then, as well in its beginning as in its completion, is God's gift; and let no one have any doubt whatever, unless he desires to resist the plainest sacred writings, that this gift is given to some, while to some it is not given. But why it is not given to all ought not to disturb the believer, who believes that from one all have gone into a condemnation, which undoubtedly is most righteous; so that even if none were delivered therefrom, there would be no just cause for finding fault with God. Whence it is plain that it is a great grace for many to be delivered, and to acknowledge in those that are not delivered

what would be due to themselves; so that he that glorieth may glory not in his own merits, which he sees to be equalled in those that are condemned, but in the Lord. But why He delivers one rather than another,—"His judgments are unsearchable, and His ways past finding out."[4] For it is better in this case for us to hear or to say, "O man, who art thou that repliest against God?"[5] than to dare to speak as if we could know what He has chosen to be kept secret. Since, moreover, He could not will anything unrighteous.

CHAP. 17 [IX.]—HIS ARGUMENT IN HIS LETTER AGAINST PORPHYRY, AS TO WHY THE GOSPEL CAME SO LATE INTO THE WORLD.

But that which you remember my saying in a certain small treatise of mine against Porphyry, under the title of *The Time of the Christian Religion*, I so said for the sake of escaping this more careful and elaborate argument about grace; although its meaning, which could be unfolded elsewhere or by others, was not wholly omitted, although I had been unwilling in that place to explain it. For, among other matters, I spoke thus in answer to the question proposed, why it was after so long a time that Christ came: "Accordingly, I say, since they do not object to Christ that all do not follow His teaching (for even they themselves feel that this could not be objected at all with any justice, either to the wisdom of the philosophers or even to the deity of their own gods), what will they reply, if—leaving out of the question that depth of God's wisdom and knowledge where perchance some other divine plan is far more secretly hidden, without prejudging also other causes, which cannot be traced out by the wise—we say to them only this, for the sake of brevity in the arguing of this question, that Christ willed to appear to men, and that His doctrine should be preached among them, at that time when He knew, and at that place where He knew, that there were some who would believe on Him. For at those times, and in those places, at which His gospel was not preached, He foreknew that all would be in His preaching such as, not indeed all, but many were in His bodily presence, who would not believe on Him, even when the dead were raised by Him; such as we see many now, who, although the declarations of the prophets concerning Him are fulfilled by such manifestations, are still unwilling to believe, and prefer to resist by human astuteness, rather than yield to divine authority so clear and perspicuous, and so lofty, and sublimely made known, so long as the human understanding is small and weak in its approach to divine truth. What wonder is it, then, if

---

[1] John vi. 44.    [2] John vi. 60 ff.    [3] John vi. 63 ff.    [4] Rom. xi. 33.    [5] Rom. ix. 20.

Christ knew the world in former ages to be so full of unbelievers, that He should reasonably refuse to appear, or to be preached to them, who, as He foreknew, would believe neither His words nor His miracles? For it is not incredible that all at that time were such as from His coming even to the present time we marvel that so many have been and are. And yet from the beginning of the human race, sometimes more hiddenly, sometimes more evidently, even as to Divine Providence the times seemed to be fitting, there has neither been a failure of prophecy, nor were there wanting those who believed on Him; as well from Adam to Moses, as in the people of Israel itself, which by a certain special mystery was a prophetic people; and in other nations before He had come in the flesh. For as some are mentioned in the sacred Hebrew books, as early as the time of Abraham, — neither of his fleshly race nor of the people of Israel, nor of the foreign society among the people of Israel, — who were, nevertheless, sharers in their sacrament, why may we not believe that there were others elsewhere among other people, here and there, although we do not read any mention of them in the same authorities? Thus the salvation of this religion, by which only true one true salvation is truly promised, never failed him who was worthy of it; and whoever it failed was not worthy of it. And from the very beginning of the propagation of man, even to the end, the gospel is preached, to some for a reward, to some for judgment; and thus also those to whom the faith was not announced at all were foreknown as those who would not believe; and those to whom it was announced, although they were not such as would believe, are set forth as an example for the former; while those to whom it is announced who should believe, are prepared for the kingdom of heaven, and the company of the holy angels."[1]

CHAP. 18. — THE PRECEDING ARGUMENT APPLIED TO THE PRESENT TIME.

Do you not see that my desire was, without any prejudgment of the hidden counsel of God, and of other reasons, to say what might seem sufficient about Christ's foreknowledge, to convince the unbelief of the pagans who had brought forward this question? For what is more true than that Christ foreknew who should believe on Him, and at what times and places they should believe? But whether by the preaching of Christ to themselves by themselves they were to have faith, or whether they would receive it by God's gift, — that is, whether God only foreknew them, or also predestinated them, I did not at that time think it necessary to inquire or to discuss.

Therefore what I said, "that Christ willed to appear to men at that time, and that His doctrine should be preached among them when He knew, and where He knew, that there were those who would believe on Him," may also thus be said, "That Christ willed to appear to men at that time, and that His gospel should be preached among those, whom He knew, and where He knew, that there were those who had been elected in Himself before the foundation of the world." But since, if it were so said, it would make the reader desirous of asking about those things which now by the warning of Pelagian errors must of necessity be discussed with greater copiousness and care, it seemed to me that what at that time was sufficient should be briefly said, leaving to one side, as I said, the depth of the wisdom and knowledge of God, and without prejudging other reasons, concerning which I thought that we might more fittingly argue, not then, but at some other time.

CHAP. 19 [X.] — IN WHAT RESPECTS PREDESTINATION AND GRACE DIFFER.

Moreover, that which I said, "That the salvation of this religion has never been lacking to him who was worthy of it, and that he to whom it was lacking was not worthy," — if it be discussed and it be asked whence any man can be worthy, there are not wanting those who say — by human will. But we say, by divine grace or predestination. Further, between grace and predestination there is only this difference, that predestination is the preparation for grace, while grace is the donation itself. When, therefore, the apostle says, "Not of works, lest any man should boast. For we are His workmanship, created in Christ Jesus in good works,"[2] it is grace; but what follows — "which God hath prepared that we should walk in them" — is predestination, which cannot exist without foreknowledge, although foreknowledge may exist without predestination; because God foreknew by predestination those things which He was about to do, whence it was said, "He made those things that shall be."[3] Moreover, He is able to foreknow even those things which He does not Himself do, — as all sins whatever. Because, although there are some which are in such wise sins as that they are also the penalties of sins, whence it is said, "God gave them over to a reprobate mind, to do those things which are not convenient,"[4] it is not in such a case the sin that is God's, but the judgment. Therefore God's predestination of good is, as I have said, the preparation of grace; which grace is the effect of that predestination. Therefore when God promised to Abraham in his seed the faith of the nations,

---

[1] Augustin's *Epistles*, 102, chs. 14, 15.

[2] Eph. ii. 9, 10.  [3] Isa. xlv. 11.  [4] Rom. i. 28.

saying, "I have established thee a father of many nations," [1] whence the apostle says, "Therefore it is of faith, that the promise, according to grace, might be established to all the seed," [2] He promised not from the power of our will, but from His own predestination. For He promised what He Himself would do, not what men would do. Because, although men do those good things which pertain to God's worship, He Himself makes them to do what He has commanded; it is not they that cause Him to do what He has promised. Otherwise the fulfilment of God's promises would not be in the power of God, but in that of men; and thus what was promised by God to Abraham would be given to Abraham by men themselves. Abraham, however, did not believe thus, but "he believed, giving glory to God, that what He promised He is able also to do." [3] He does not say, "to foretell"—he does not say, "to foreknow;" for He can foretell and foreknow the doings of strangers also; but he says, "He is able also to do;" and thus he is speaking not of the doings of others, but of His own.

### CHAP. 20.—DID GOD PROMISE THE GOOD WORKS OF THE NATIONS, AND NOT THEIR FAITH, TO ABRAHAM?

Did God, perchance, promise to Abraham in his seed the good works of the nations, so as to promise that which He Himself does, but did not promise the faith of the Gentiles, which men do for themselves; but so as to promise what He Himself does, did He foreknow that men would effect that faith? The apostle, indeed, does not speak thus, because God promised children to Abraham, who should follow the footsteps of his faith, as he very plainly says. But if He promised the works, and not the faith of the Gentiles, certainly since they are not good works unless they are of faith (for "the righteous lives of faith," [4] and, "Whatsoever is not of faith is sin," [5] and, "Without faith it is impossible to please" [6] ), it is nevertheless in man's power that God should fulfil what He has promised. For unless man should do what without the gift of God pertains to man, he will not cause God to give,—that is, unless man have faith of himself. God does not fulfil what He has promised, that works of righteousness should be given by God. And thus that God should be able to fulfil His promises is not in God's power, but in man's. And if truth and piety do not forbid our believing this, let us believe with Abraham, that what He has promised He is able also to perform. But He promised children to Abraham; and this men cannot be unless they have faith, therefore He gives faith also.

Certainly, when the apostle says, "Therefore it is of faith that the promise may be sure according to grace," [2] I marvel that men would rather entrust themselves to their own weakness, than to the strength of God's promise. But sayest thou, God's will concerning myself is to me uncertain? What then? Is thine own will concerning thyself certain to thee? and dost thou not fear,—"Let him that thinketh he standeth take heed lest he fall"? [7] Since, then, both are uncertain, why does not man commit his faith, hope, and love to the stronger will, rather than to the weaker?

### CHAP. 22.—GOD'S PROMISE IS SURE.

"But," say they, "when it is said, 'If thou believest, thou shalt be saved,' one of these things is required; the other is offered. What is required is in man's power; what is offered is in God's." [8] Why are not both in God's, as well what He commands as what He offers? For He is asked to give what He commands. Believers ask that their faith may be increased; they ask on behalf of those who do not believe, that faith may be given to them; therefore both in its increase and in its beginnings, faith is the gift of God. But it is said thus: "If thou believest, thou shalt be saved," in the same way that it is said, "If by the Spirit ye shall mortify the deeds of the flesh, ye shall live." [9] For in this case also, of these two things one is required, the other is offered. It is said, "If by the Spirit ye shall mortify the deeds of the flesh, ye shall live." Therefore, that we mortify the deeds of the flesh is required, but that we may live is offered. Is it, then, fitting for us to say, that to mortify the deeds of the flesh is not a gift of God, and not to confess it to be a gift of God, because we hear it required of us, with the offer of life as a reward if we shall do it? Away with this being approved by the partakers and champions of grace! This is the condemnable error of the Pelagians, whose mouths the apostle immediately stopped when he added, "For as many as are led by the Spirit of God, they are the sons of God;" [10] lest we should believe that we mortify the deeds of the flesh, not by God's Spirit, but by our own. And of this Spirit of God, moreover, he was speaking in that place where he says, "But all these worketh that one and the self-same Spirit, dividing unto every man what is his own, as He will;" [11] and among all these things, as you know, he also

---

[1] Gen. xvii. 5.   [2] Rom. iv. 16.   [3] Rom. iv. 21.
[4] Hab. ii. 4.   [5] Rom. xiv. 23.   [6] Heb. xi. 6.
[7] 1 Cor. x. 12.
[8] See Hilary's Letter in Augustin's *Letters*, 226, ch. 2.
[9] Rom. viii. 13.   [10] Rom. viii. 14.   [11] 1 Cor. xii. 11.

named faith. As, therefore, although it is the gift of God to mortify the deeds of the flesh, yet it is required of us, and life is set before us as a reward; so also faith is the gift of God, although when it is said, " If thou believest, thou shalt be saved," faith is required of us, and salvation is proposed to us as a reward. For these things are both commanded us, and are shown to be God's gifts, in order that we may understand both that we do them, and that God makes us to do them, as He most plainly says by the prophet Ezekiel. For what is plainer than when He says, " I will cause you to do " ?[1] Give heed to that passage of Scripture, and you will see that God promises that He will make them to do those things which He commands to be done. He truly is not silent as to the merits but as to the evil deeds, of those to whom He shows that He is returning good for evil, by the very fact that He causeth them thenceforth to have good works, in causing them to do the divine commands.

CHAP. 23 [XII.] — REMARKABLE ILLUSTRATIONS OF GRACE AND PREDESTINATION IN INFANTS, AND IN CHRIST.

But all this reasoning, whereby we maintain that the grace of God through Jesus Christ our Lord is truly grace, that is, is not given according to our merits, although it is most manifestly asserted by the witness of the divine declarations, yet, among those who think that they are withheld from all zeal for piety unless they can attribute to themselves something, which they first give that it may be recompensed to them again, involves somewhat of a difficulty in respect of the condition of grown-up people, who are already exercising the choice of will. But when we come to the case of infants, and to the Mediator between God and man Himself, the man Christ Jesus, there is wanting all assertion of human merits that precede the grace of God, because the former are not distinguished from others by any preceding good merits that they should belong to the Deliverer of men; any more than He Himself, being Himself a man, was made the Deliverer of men by virtue of any precedent human merits.

CHAP. 24. — THAT NO ONE IS JUDGED ACCORDING TO WHAT HE WOULD HAVE DONE IF HE HAD LIVED LONGER.

For who can hear that infants, baptized in the condition of mere infancy, are said to depart from this life by reason of their future merits, and that others not baptized are said to die in the same age because their future merits are foreknown, — but as evil; so that God rewards or condemns in them not their good or evil life, but no life at all?[2] The apostle, indeed, fixed a limit which man's incautious suspicion, to speak gently, ought not to transgress, for he says, " We shall all stand before the judgment-seat of Christ; that every one may receive according to the things which he has done by means of the body, whether it be good or evil."[3] " Has done," he said; and he did not add, " or would have done." But I know not whence this thought should have entered the minds of such men, that infants' future merits (which shall not be) should be punished or honoured. But why is it said that a man is to be judged according to those things which he has done by means of the body, when many things are done by the mind alone, and not by the body, nor by any member of the body; and for the most part things of such importance, that a most righteous punishment would be due to such thoughts, such as, — to say nothing of others, — that " The fool hath said in his heart there is no God " ?[4] What, then, is the meaning of, " According to those things that he hath done by means of the body," except according to those things which he has done during that time in which he was in the body, so that we may understand " by means of the body " as meaning " throughout the season of bodily life " ? But after the body, no one will be in the body except at the last resurrection, — not for the purpose of establishing any claims of merit, but for the sake of receiving recompenses for good merits, and enduring punishments for evil merits. But in this intermediate period between the putting off and the taking again of the body, the souls are either tormented or they are in repose, according to those things which they have done during the period of the bodily life. And to this period of the bodily life moreover pertains, what the Pelagians deny, but Christ's Church confesses, original sin; and according to whether this is by God's grace loosed, or by God's judgment not loosed, when infants die, they pass, on the one hand, by the merit of regeneration from evil to good, or on the other, by the merit of their origin from evil to evil. The catholic faith acknowledges this, and even some heretics, without any contradiction, agree to this. But in the height of wonder and astonishment I am unable to discover whence men, whose intelligence your letters show to be by no means contemptible, could entertain the opinion that any one should be judged not according to the merits that he had as long as he was in the body, but according to the merits which he would have had if he had lived longer in the body; and I should not dare to believe that there were such men, if I could venture to disbelieve you.

---

[1] Ezek. xxxvi. 27.

[2] See Prosper's Letter in Augustin's *Letters*, 225, ch. 5.
[3] 2 Cor. v. 10.                    [4] Ps. xiv. 1.

But I hope that God will interpose, so that when they are admonished they may at once perceive, that if those sins which, as is said, would have been, can rightly be punished by God's judgment in those who are not baptized, they may also be rightly remitted by God's grace in those who are baptized. For whoever says that future sins can only be punished by God's judgment, but cannot be pardoned by God's mercy, ought to consider how great a wrong he is doing to God and His grace ; as if future sin could be foreknown, and could not be foregone.[1] And if this is absurd, it is the greater reason that help should be afforded to those who would be sinners if they lived longer, when they die in early life, by means of that laver wherein sins are washed away.

CHAP. 25 [XIII.] — POSSIBLY THE BAPTIZED INFANTS WOULD HAVE REPENTED IF THEY HAD LIVED, AND THE UNBAPTIZED NOT.

But if, perchance, they say that sins are re-remitted to penitents, and that those who die in infancy are not baptized because they are fore-known as not such as would repent if they should live, while God has foreknown that those who are baptized and die in infancy would have re-pented if they had lived, let them observe and see that if it be so it is not in this case original sins which are punished in infants that die with-out baptism, but what would have been the sins of each one had he lived ; and also in baptized infants, that it is not original sins that are washed away, but their own future sins if they should live, since they could not sin except in more mature age ; but that some were foreseen as such as would repent, and others as such as would not repent, therefore some were baptized, and others departed from this life without baptism. If the Pelagians should dare to say this, by their denial of original sin they would thus be relieved of the necessity of seeking, on behalf of infants out-side of the kingdom of God, for some place of I know not what happiness of their own ; especially since they are convinced that they cannot have eternal life because they have not eaten the flesh nor drunk the blood of Christ ; and because in them who have no sin at all, baptism, which is given for the remission of sins, is falsified. For they would go on to say that there is no original sin, but that those who as infants are released are either baptized or not baptized according to their future merits if they should live, and that according to their future merits they either re-ceive or do not receive the body and blood of Christ, without which they absolutely cannot have life ; and are baptized for the true remission of sins although they derived no sins from Adam, because the sins are remitted unto them concern-ing which God foreknew that they would repent. Thus with the greatest ease they would plead and would win their cause, in which they deny that there is any original sin, and contend that the grace of God is only given according to our merits. But that the future merits of men, which merits will never come into existence, are beyond all doubt no merits at all, it is certainly most easy to see : for this reason even the Pelagians were not able to say this ; and much rather these ought not to say it. For it cannot be said with what pain I find that they who with us on catholic authority condemn the error of those heretics, have not seen this, which the Pelagians themselves have seen to be most false and absurd.

CHAP. 26 [XIV.] — REFERENCE TO CYPRIAN'S TREATISE " ON THE MORTALITY."

Cyprian wrote a work *On the Mortality,*[2] known with approval to many and almost all who love ecclesiastical literature, wherein he says that death is not only not disadvantageous to believers, but that it is even found to be advan-tageous, because it withdraws men from the risks of sinning, and establishes them in a security of not sinning. But wherein is the advantage of this, if even future sins which have not been com-mitted are punished ? Yet he argues most co-piously and well that the risks of sinning are not wanting in this life, and that they do not con-tinue after this life is done ; where also he ad-duces that testimony from the book of Wisdom : " He was taken away, lest wickedness should alter his understanding."[3] And this was also adduced by me, though you said that those brethren of yours had rejected it on the ground of its not having been brought forward from a canonical book ; as if, even setting aside the attestation of this book, the thing itself were not clear which I wished to be taught therefrom. For what Christian would dare to deny that the righteous man, if he should be prematurely laid hold of by death, will be in repose ? Let who will, say this, and what man of sound faith will think that he can withstand it ? Moreover, if he should say that the righteous man, if he should depart from his righteousness in which he has long lived, and should die in that impiety after having lived in it, I say not a year, but one day, will go hence into the punishment due to the wicked, his righteousness having no power in the future to avail him, — will any believer contradict this evident truth ? Further, if we are asked whether, if he had died then at the time that he was right-eous, he would have incurred punishment or repose, shall we hesitate to answer, repose ? This is the whole reason why it is said,    who-

---

[1] *Prænosci possit, nec possit ignosci.*

[2] Cyprian, Works in *The Ante-Nicene Fathers,* vol. v. p. 469.
[3] Wisd. iv. 11.

ever says it, — "He was taken away, lest wickedness should alter his understanding." For it was said in reference to the risks of this life, not with reference to the foreknowledge of God, who foreknew that which was to be, not that which was not to be — that is, that He would bestow on him an untimely death in order that he might be withdrawn from the uncertainty of temptations; not that he would sin, since he was not to remain in temptation. Because, concerning this life, we read in the book of Job, "Is not the life of man upon earth a temptation?"[1] But why it should be granted to some to be taken away from the perils of this life while they are righteous, while others who are righteous until they fall from righteousness are kept in the same risks in a more lengthened life, — who has known the mind of the Lord? And yet it is permitted to be understood from this, that even those righteous people who maintain good and pious characters, even to the maturity of old age and to the last day of this life, must not glory in their own merits, but in the Lord, since He who took away the righteous man from the shortness of life, lest wickedness should alter his understanding, Himself guards the righteous man in any length of life, that wickedness may not alter his understanding. But why He should have kept the righteous man here to fall, when He might have withdrawn him before, — His judgments, although absolutely righteous, are yet unsearchable.

CHAP. 27. — THE BOOK OF WISDOM OBTAINS IN THE CHURCH THE AUTHORITY OF CANONICAL SCRIPTURE.

And since these things are so, the judgment of the book of Wisdom ought not to be repudiated, since for so long a course of years that book has deserved to be read in the Church of Christ, from the station of the readers of the Church of Christ, and to be heard by all Christians, from bishops downwards, even to the lowest lay believers, penitents, and catechumens, with the veneration paid to divine authority. For assuredly, if, from those who have been before me in commenting on the divine Scriptures, I should bring forward a defence of this judgment, which we are now called upon to defend more carefully and copiously than usual against the new error of the Pelagians, — that is, that God's grace is not given according to our merits, and that it is given freely to whom it is given, because it is neither of him that willeth, nor of him that runneth, but of God that showeth mercy; but that by righteous judgment it is not given to whom it is not given, because there is no unrighteousness with God; — if, therefore, I

should put forth a defence of this opinion from catholic commentators on the divine oracles who have preceded us, assuredly these brethren for whose sake I am now discoursing would acquiesce, for this you have intimated in your letters. What need is there, then, for us to look into the writings of those who, before this heresy sprang up, had no necessity to be conversant in a question so difficult of solution as this, which beyond a doubt they would have done if they had been compelled to answer such things? Whence it arose that they touched upon what they thought of God's grace briefly in some passages of their writings, and cursorily; but on those matters which they argued against the enemies of the Church, and in exhortations to every virtue by which to serve the living and true God for the purpose of attaining eternal life and true happiness, they dwelt at length. But the grace of God, what it could do, shows itself artlessly by its frequent mention in prayers; for what God commands to be done would not be asked for from God, unless it could be given by Him that it should be done.

CHAP. 28. — CYPRIAN'S TREATISE "ON THE MORTALITY."

But if any wish to be instructed in the opinions of those who have handled the subject, it behoves them to prefer to all commentators the book of Wisdom, where it is read, "He was taken away, that wickedness should not alter his understanding;" because illustrious commentators, even in the times nearest to the apostles, preferred it to themselves, seeing that when they made use of it for a testimony, they believed that they were making use of nothing but a divine testimony; and certainly it appears that the most blessed Cyprian, in order to commend the advantage of an earlier death, contended that those who end this life, wherein sin is possible, are taken away from the risks of sins. In the same treatise, among other things, he says, "Why, when you are about to be with Christ, and are secure of the divine promise, do you not embrace being called to Christ, and rejoice that you are free from the devil?"[2] And in another place he says, "Boys escape the peril of their unstable age."[2] And again, in another place, he says, "Why do we not hasten and run, that we may see our country, that we may hail our relatives? A great number of those who are dear to us are expecting us there, — a dense and abundant crowd of parents, brethren, sons, are longing for us; already secure of their own safety, but still anxious about our salvation."[2] By these and such like sentiments, that teacher sufficiently and plainly testifies, in the clearest

---

[1] Job vii. 1.

[2] Cyprian, *On the Mortality*, as above.

light of the catholic faith, that perils of sin and trials are to be feared even until the putting off of this body, but that afterwards no one shall suffer any such things. And even if he did not testify thus, when could any manner of Christian be in doubt on this matter? How, then, should it not have been of advantage to a man who has lapsed, and who finishes his life wretchedly in that same state of lapse, and passes into the punishment due to such as he, — how, I say, should it not have been of the greatest and highest advantage to such an one to be snatched by death from this sphere of temptations before his fall?

## CHAP. 29. — GOD'S DEALING DOES NOT DEPEND UPON ANY CONTINGENT MERITS OF MEN.

And thus, unless we indulge in reckless disputation, the entire question is concluded concerning him who is taken away lest wickedness should alter his understanding. And the book of Wisdom, which for such a series of years has deserved to be read in Christ's Church, and in which this is read, ought not to suffer injustice because it withstands those who are mistaken on behalf of men's merits, so as to come in opposition to the most manifest grace of God : and this grace chiefly appears in infants, and while some of these baptized, and some not baptized, come to the end of this life, they sufficiently point to God's mercy and His judgment, — His mercy, indeed, gratuitous, His judgment, of debt. For if men should be judged according to the merits of their life, which merits they have been prevented by death from actually having, but would have had if they had lived, it would be of no advantage to him who is taken away lest wickedness should alter his understanding ; it would be of no advantage to those who die in a state of lapse if they should die before. And this no Christian will venture to say. Wherefore our brethren, who with us on behalf of the catholic faith assail the pest of the Pelagian error, ought not to such an extent to favour the Pelagian opinion, wherein they conceive that God's grace is given according to our merits, as to endeavour (which they cannot dare) to invalidate a true sentiment, plainly and from ancient times Christian, — " He was taken away, lest wickedness should alter his understanding ; " and to build up that which we should think, I do not say, no one would believe, but no one would dream, — to wit, that any deceased person would be judged according to those things which he would have done if he had lived for a more lengthened period. Surely thus what we say manifests itself clearly to be incontestable, — that the grace of God is not given according to our merits ; so that ingenious men who contradict this truth are constrained to say things which must be rejected from the ears and from the thoughts of all men.

## CHAP. 30 [XV.] — THE MOST ILLUSTRIOUS INSTANCE OF PREDESTINATION IS CHRIST JESUS.

Moreover, the most illustrious Light of predestination and grace is the Saviour Himself, — the Mediator Himself between God and men, the man Christ Jesus. And, pray, by what preceding merits of its own, whether of works or of faith, did the human nature which is in Him procure for itself that it should be this? Let this have an answer, I beg. That man, whence did He deserve this, — to be assumed by the Word co-eternal with the Father into unity of person, and be the only-begotten Son of God? Was it because any kind of goodness in Him preceded? What did He do before? What did He believe? What did He ask, that He should attain to this unspeakable excellence? Was it not by the act and the assumption of the Word that that man, from the time He began to be, began to be the only Son of God? Did not that woman, full of grace, conceive the only Son of God? Was He not born the only Son of God, of the Holy Spirit and the Virgin Mary, — not of the lust of the flesh, but by God's peculiar gift? Was it to be feared that as age matured this man, He would sin of free will? Or was the will in Him not free on that account? and was it not so much the more free in proportion to the greater impossibility of His becoming the servant of sin? Certainly, in Him human nature — that is to say, our nature — specially received all those specially admirable gifts, and any others that may most truly be said to be peculiar to Him, by virtue of no preceding merits of its own. Let a man here answer to God if he dare, and say, Why was it not I also? And if he should hear, " O man, who art thou that repliest against God?" [1] let him not at this point restrain himself, but increase his impudence and say, " How is it that I hear, Who art thou, O man? since I am what I hear, — that is, a man, and He of whom I speak is but the same? Why should not I also be what He is? For it is by grace that He is such and so great ; why is grace different when nature is common? Assuredly, there is no respect of persons with God." I say, not what Christian man, but what madman will say this?

## CHAP. 31. — CHRIST PREDESTINATED TO BE THE SON OF GOD.

Therefore in Him who is our Head let there appear to be the very fountain of grace, whence, according to the measure of every man, He diffuses Himself through all His members. It is by that grace that every man from the beginning of his faith becomes a Christian, by which grace that one man from His beginning became

---

[1] Rom. ix. 10.

Christ. Of the same Spirit also the former is born again of which the latter was born. By the same Spirit is effected in us the remission of sins, by which Spirit it was effected that He should have no sin. God certainly foreknew that He would do these things. This, therefore, is that same predestination of the saints which most especially shone forth in the Saint of saints; and who is there of those who rightly understand the declarations of the truth that can deny this predestination? For we have learned that the Lord of glory Himself was predestinated in so far as the man was made the Son of God. The teacher of the Gentiles exclaims, in the beginning of his epistles, " Paul, a servant of Jesus Christ, called to be an apostle, separated unto the gospel of God (which He had promised afore by His prophets in the Holy Scriptures) concerning His Son, which was made of the seed of David according to the flesh, who was predestinated the Son of God in power, according to the Spirit of sanctification by the resurrection of the dead." [1] Therefore Jesus was predestinated, so that He who was to be the Son of David according to the flesh should yet be in power the Son of God, according to the Spirit of sanctification, because He was born of the Holy Spirit and of the Virgin Mary. This is that ineffably accomplished sole taking up of man by God the Word, so that He might truly and properly be called at the same time the Son of God and the Son of man, — Son of man on account of the man taken up, and the Son of God on account of the God only-begotten who took Him up, so that a Trinity and not a Quaternity might be believed in. Such a transporting of human nature was predestinated, so great, so lofty, and so sublime that there was no exalting it more highly, — just as on our behalf that divinity had no possibility of more humbly putting itself off, than by the assumption of man's nature with the weakness of the flesh, even to the death of the cross. As, therefore, that one man was predestinated to be our Head, so we being many are predestinated to be His members. Here let human merits which have perished through Adam keep silence, and let that grace of God reign which reigns through Jesus Christ our Lord, the only Son of God, the one Lord. Let whoever can find in our Head the merits which preceded that peculiar generation, seek in us His members for those merits which preceded our manifold regeneration. For that generation was not recompensed to Christ, but given; that He should be born, namely, of the Spirit and the Virgin, separate from all entanglement of sin. Thus also our being born again of water and the Spirit is not recompensed to us

for any merit, but freely given; and if faith has brought us to the laver of regeneration, we ought not therefore to suppose that we have first given anything, so that the regeneration of salvation should be recompensed to us again; because He made us to believe in Christ, who made for us a Christ on whom we believe. He makes in men the beginning and the completion of the faith in Jesus who made the man Jesus the beginner and finisher of faith; [2] for thus, as you know, He is called in the epistle which is addressed to the Hebrews.

CHAP. 32 [XVI.] — THE TWOFOLD CALLING.

God indeed calls many predestinated children of His, to make them members of His only predestinated Son, — not with that calling with which they were called who would not come to the marriage, since with that calling were called also the Jews, to whom Christ crucified is an offence, and the Gentiles, to whom Christ crucified is foolishness; but with that calling He calls the predestinated which the apostle distinguished when he said that he preached Christ, the wisdom of God and the power of God, to them that were called, Jews as well as Greeks. For thus he says, " But unto them which are called," [3] in order to show that there were some who were not called; knowing that there is a certain sure calling of those who are called according to God's purpose, whom He has foreknown and predestinated before to be conformed to the image of His Son. And it was this calling he meant when he said, " Not of works, but of Him that calleth; it was said unto her, That the elder shall serve the younger." [4] Did he say, " Not of works, but of him that believeth "? Rather, he actually took this away from man, that he might give the whole to God. Therefore he said, " But of Him that calleth," — not with any sort of calling whatever, but with that calling wherewith a man is made a believer.

CHAP. 33. — IT IS IN THE POWER OF EVIL MEN TO SIN; BUT TO DO THIS OR THAT BY MEANS OF THAT WICKEDNESS IS IN GOD'S POWER ALONE.

Moreover, it was this that he had in view when he said, " The gifts and calling of God are without repentance." [5] And in that saying also consider for a little what was its purport. For when he had said, " For I would not, brethren, that ye should be ignorant of this mystery, that ye may not be wise in yourselves, that blindness in part is happened to Israel, until the fulness of the Gentiles be come in, and so all Israel should be saved; as it is written, There shall come out of Sion one who shall deliver, and turn away impiety from Jacob: and this is the

---

[1] Rom. i. 1 ff.
[2] Heb. xii. 2.     [3] 1 Cor. i. 24.     [4] Rom. ix. 12.
[5] Rom. xi. 29.

covenant to them from me, when I shall take away their sins;"[1] he immediately added, what is to be very carefully understood, "As concerning the gospel, indeed, they are enemies for your sakes: but as concerning the election, they are beloved for their fathers' sakes."[2] What is the meaning of, "as concerning the gospel, indeed, they are enemies for your sakes," but that their enmity wherewith they put Christ to death was, without doubt, as we see, an advantage to the gospel? And he shows that this came about by God's ordering, who knew how to make a good use even of evil things; not that the vessels of wrath might be of advantage to Him, but that by His own good use of them they might be of advantage to the vessels of mercy. For what could be said more plainly than what is actually said, "As concerning the gospel, indeed, they are enemies for your sakes"? It is, therefore, in the power of the wicked to sin; but that in sinning they should do this or that by that wickedness is not in their power, but in God's, who divides the darkness and regulates it; so that hence even what they do contrary to God's will is not fulfilled except it be God's will. We read in the Acts of the Apostles that when the apostles had been sent away by the Jews, and had come to their own friends, and shown them what great things the priests and elders said to them, they all with one consent lifted up their voices to the Lord, and said, "Lord, thou art God, which hast made heaven, and earth, and the sea, and all things that are therein; who, by the mouth of our father David, thy holy servant, hast said, Why did the heathen rage, and the peoples imagine vain things? The kings of the earth stood up, and the princes were gathered together against the Lord, and against His Christ. For in truth, there have assembled together in this city against Thy holy child Jesus, whom Thou hast anointed, Herod and Pilate, and the people of Israel, to do whatever Thy hand and counsel predestinated to be done."[3] See what is said: "As concerning the gospel, indeed, they are enemies for your sakes." Because God's hand and counsel predestinated such things to be done by the hostile Jews as were necessary for the gospel, for our sakes. But what is it that follows? "But as concerning the election, they are beloved for their fathers' sakes." For are those enemies who perished in their enmity, and those of the same people who still perish in their opposition to Christ,—are those chosen and beloved? Away with the thought! Who is so utterly foolish as to say this? But both expressions, although contrary to one another—that is, "enemies" and "beloved"—are appropri-

ate, though not to the same men, yet to the same Jewish people, and to the same carnal seed of Israel, of whom some belonged to the falling away, and some to the blessing of Israel himself. For the apostle previously explained this meaning more clearly when he said, "That which Israel wrought for, he hath not obtained; but the election hath obtained it, and the rest were blinded."[4] Yet in both cases it was the very same Israel. Where, therefore, we hear, "Israel hath not obtained," or, "The rest were blinded," there are to be understood the enemies for our sakes; but where we hear, "that the election hath obtained it," there are to be understood the beloved for their fathers' sakes, to which fathers those things were assuredly promised; because "the promises were made to Abraham and his seed,"[5] whence also in that olive-tree is grafted the wild olive-tree of the Gentiles. Now subsequently we certainly ought to fall in with the election, of which he says that it is according to grace, not according to debt, because "there was made a remnant by the election of grace."[6] This election obtained it, the rest being blinded. As concerning this election, the Israelites were beloved for the sake of their fathers. For they were not called with that calling of which it is said, "Many are called," but with that whereby the chosen are called. Whence also after he had said, "But as concerning the election, they are beloved for the fathers' sakes," he went on to add those words whence this discussion arose: "For the gifts and calling of God are without repentance,"—that is, they are firmly established without change. Those who belong to this calling are all teachable by God; nor can any of them say, "I believed in order to being thus called," because the mercy of God anticipated him, because he was so called in order that he might believe. For all who are teachable of God come to the Son because they have heard and learned from the Father through the Son, who most clearly says, "Every one who has heard of the Father, and has learned, cometh unto me."[7] But of such as these none perishes, because "of all that the Father hath given Him, He will lose none."[8] Whoever, therefore, is of these does not perish at all; nor was any who perishes ever of these. For which reason it is said, "They went out from among us, but they were not of us; for if they had been of us, they would certainly have continued with us."[9]

CHAP. 34 [XVII.]—THE SPECIAL CALLING OF THE ELECT IS NOT BECAUSE THEY HAVE BELIEVED, BUT IN ORDER THAT THEY MAY BELIEVE.

Let us, then, understand the calling whereby

---

[1] Rom. xi. 25 ff.    [2] Rom xi. 28.    [3] Acts iv. 24 ff.

[4] Rom. xi. 7.    [5] Gal. iii. 16.    [6] Rom. xi. 5.
[7] John vi. 45.    [8] John vi. 39.    [9] John ii. 19.

they become elected, — not those who are elected because they have believed, but who are elected that they may believe. For the Lord Himself also sufficiently explains this calling when He says, "Ye have not chosen me, but I have chosen you." [1] For if they had been elected because they had believed, they themselves would certainly have first chosen Him by believing in Him, so that they should deserve to be elected. But He takes away this supposition altogether when He says, "Ye have not chosen me, but I have chosen you." And yet they themselves, beyond a doubt, chose Him when they believed on Him. Whence it is not for any other reason that He says, "Ye have not chosen me, but I have chosen you," than because they did not choose Him that He should choose them, but He chose them that they might choose Him; because His mercy preceded them according to grace, not according to debt. Therefore He chose them out of the world while He was wearing flesh, but as those who were already chosen in Himself before the foundation of the world. This is the changeless truth concerning predestination and grace. For what is it that the apostle says, "As He hath chosen us in Himself before the foundation of the world"? [2] And assuredly, if this were said because God foreknew that they would believe, not because He Himself would make them believers, the Son is speaking against such a foreknowledge as that when He says, "Ye have not chosen me, but I have chosen you;" when God should rather have foreknown this very thing, that they themselves would have chosen Him, so that they might deserve to be chosen by Him. Therefore they were elected before the foundation of the world with that predestination in which God foreknew what He Himself would do; but they were elected out of the world with that calling whereby God fulfilled that which He predestinated. For whom He predestinated, them He also called, with that calling, to wit, which is according to the purpose. Not others, therefore, but those whom He predestinated, them He also called; nor others, but those whom He so called, them He also justified; nor others, but those whom He predestinated, called, and justified, them He also glorified; assuredly to that end which has no end. Therefore God elected believers; but He chose them that they might be so, not because they were already so. The Apostle James says: "Has not God chosen the poor in this world, rich in faith, and heirs of the kingdom which God hath promised to them that love Him?" [3] By choosing them, therefore; He makes them rich in faith, as He makes them heirs of the kingdom; because He

is rightly said to choose that in them, in order to make which in them He chose them. I ask, who can hear the Lord saying, "Ye have not chosen me, but I have chosen you," and can dare to say that men believe in order to be elected, when they are rather elected to believe; lest against the judgment of truth they be found to have first chosen Christ to whom Christ says, "Ye have not chosen me, but I have chosen you"? [4]

CHAP. 35 [XVIII.] — ELECTION IS FOR THE PURPOSE OF HOLINESS.

Who can hear the apostle saying, "Blessed be the God and Father of our Lord Jesus Christ, who hath blessed us in all spiritual blessing in the heavens in Christ; as He has chosen us in Him before the foundation of the world, that we should be holy and without spot in His sight; in love predestinating us to the adoption of children by Jesus Christ to Himself according to the good pleasure of His will, wherein He hath shown us favour in His beloved Son; in whom we have redemption through His blood, the remission of sins according to the riches of His grace, which hath abounded to us in all wisdom and prudence; that He might show to us the mystery of His will according to His good pleasure, which He hath purposed in Himself, in the dispensation of the fulness of times, to restore all things in Christ, which are in heaven, and in the earth, in Him: in whom also we have obtained a share, being predestinated according to the purpose; who worketh all things according to the counsel of His will, that we should be to the praise of his glory;" [5] — who, I say, can hear these words with attention and intelligence, and can venture to have any doubt concerning a truth so clear as this which we are defending? God chose Christ's members in Him before the foundation of the world; and how should He choose those who as yet did not exist, except by predestinating them? Therefore He chose us by predestinating us. Would he choose the unholy and the unclean? Now if the question be proposed, whether He would choose such, or rather the holy and unstained, who can ask which of these he may answer, and not give his opinion at once in favour of the holy and pure?

CHAP. 36. — GOD CHOSE THE RIGHTEOUS; NOT THOSE WHOM HE FORESAW AS BEING OF THEMSELVES, BUT THOSE WHOM HE PREDESTINATED FOR THE PURPOSE OF MAKING SO.

"Therefore," says the Pelagian, "He foreknew who would be holy and immaculate by the choice of free will, and on that account elected them

---

before the foundation of the world in that same foreknowledge of His in which He foreknew that they would be such. Therefore He elected them," says he, "before they existed, predestinating them to be children whom He foreknew to be holy and immaculate. Certainly He did not make them so; nor did He foresee that He would make them so, but that they would be so." Let us, then, look into the words of the apostle and see whether He chose us before the foundation of the world because we were going to be holy and immaculate, or in order that we might be so. "Blessed," says he, "be the God and Father of our Lord Jesus Christ, who hath blessed us in all spiritual blessing in the heavens in Christ; even as He hath chosen us in Himself before the foundation of the world, that we should be holy and unspotted."[1] Not, then, because we were to be so, but that we might be so. Assuredly it is certain, — assuredly it is manifest. Certainly we were to be such for the reason that He has chosen us, predestinating us to be such by His grace. Therefore "He blessed us with spiritual blessing in the heavens in Christ Jesus, even as He chose us in Him before the foundation of the world, that we should be holy and immaculate in His sight, predestinating us in love to the adoption of children through Jesus Christ to Himself." Attend to what he then adds: "According to the good pleasure," he says, "of His will;" in order that we might not in so great a benefit of grace glory concerning the good pleasure of our will. "In which," says he, "He hath shown us favour in His beloved Son," — in which, certainly, His own will, He hath shown us favour. Thus, it is said, He hath shown us grace by grace, even as it is said, He has made us righteous by righteousness. "In whom," he says, "we have redemption through His blood, the forgiveness of sins, according to the riches is His grace, which has abounded to us in all wus dom and prudence; that He might show to of the mystery of His will, according to His good pleasure." In this mystery of His will, He placed the riches of His grace, according to His good pleasure, not according to ours, which could not possibly be good unless He Himself, according to His own good pleasure, should aid it to become so. But when he had said, "According to His good pleasure," he added, "which He purposed in Him," that is, in His beloved Son, "in the dispensation of the fulness of times to restore all things in Christ, which are in heaven, and which are in earth, in Him: in whom also we too have obtained a lot, being predestinated according to His purpose who worketh all things according to the counsel of

His will; that we should be to the praise of His glory."

CHAP. 37. — WE WERE ELECTED AND PREDESTINATED, NOT BECAUSE WE WERE GOING TO BE HOLY, BUT IN ORDER THAT WE MIGHT BE SO.

It would be too tedious to argue about the several points. But you see without doubt, you see with what evidence of apostolic declaration this grace is defended, in opposition to which human merits are set up, as if man should first give something for it to be recompensed to him again. Therefore God chose us in Christ before the foundation of the world, predestinating us to the adoption of children, not because we were going to be of ourselves holy and immaculate, but He chose and predestinated us that we might be so. Moreover, He did this according to the good pleasure of His will, so that nobody might glory concerning his own will, but about God's will towards himself. He did this according to the riches of His grace, according to His good-will, which He purposed in His beloved Son, in whom we have obtained a share, being predestinated according to the purpose, not ours, but His, who worketh all things to such an extent as that He worketh in us to will also. Moreover, He worketh according to the counsel of His will, that we may be to the praise of His glory.[2] For this reason it is that we cry that no one should glory in man, and, thus, not in himself; but whoever glorieth let him glory in the Lord, that he may be for the praise of His glory. Because He Himself worketh according to His purpose that we may be to the praise of His glory, and, of course, holy and immaculate, for which purpose He called us, predestinating us before the foundation of the world. Out of this, His purpose, is that special calling of the elect for whom He co-worketh with all things for good, because they are called according to His purpose, and "the gifts and calling of God are without repentance."[3]

CHAP. 38 [XIX.] — WHAT IS THE VIEW OF THE PELAGIANS, AND WHAT OF THE SEMI-PELAGIANS, CONCERNING PREDESTINATION.

But these brethren of ours, about whom and on whose behalf we are now discoursing, say, perhaps, that the Pelagians are refuted by this apostolical testimony in which it is said that we ate chosen in Christ and predestinated before the foundation of the world, in order that we should be holy and immaculate in His sight in love. For they think that "having received God's commands we are of ourselves by the choice of our free will made holy and immaculate in His sight in love; and since God foresaw

---

[1] Eph. i. 3.  [2] Phil. ii. 13.  [3] Rom. xi. 29.

that this would be the case," they say, " He therefore chose and predestinated us in Christ before the foundation of the world." Although the apostle says that it was not because He foreknew that we should be such, but in order that we might be such by the same election of His grace, by which He showed us favour in His beloved Son. When, therefore, He predestinated us, He foreknew His own work by which He makes us holy and immaculate. Whence the Pelagian error is rightly refuted by this testimony. " But we say," say they, " that God did not foreknow anything as ours except that faith by which we begin to believe, and that He chose and predestinated us before the foundation of the world, in order that we might be holy and immaculate by His grace and by His work." But let them also hear in this testimony the words where he says, " We have obtained a lot, being predestinated according to His purpose who worketh all things." [1] He, therefore, worketh the beginning of our belief who worketh all things ; because faith itself does not precede that calling of which it is said : " For the gifts and calling of God are without repentance ; " [2] and of which it is said : " Not of works, but of Him that calleth " [3] (although He might have said, " of Him that believeth ") ; and the election which the Lord signified when He said : " Ye have not chosen me, but I have chosen you." [4] For He chose us, not because we believed, but that we might believe, lest we should be said first to have chosen Him, and so His word be false (which be it far from us to think possible), " Ye have not chosen me, but I have chosen you." Neither are we called because we believed, but that we may believe ; and by that calling which is without repentance it is effected and carried through that we should believe. But all the many things which we have said concerning this matter need not be repeated.

CHAP. 39. — THE BEGINNING OF FAITH IS GOD'S GIFT.

Finally, also, in what follows this testimony, the apostle gives thanks to God on behalf of those who have believed ; — not, certainly, because the gospel has been declared to them, but because they have believed. For he says, " In whom also after ye had heard the word of truth, the gospel of your salvation ; in whom also, after that ye believed, ye were sealed with the Holy Spirit of promise, which is the pledge of our inheritance, to the redemption of the purchased possession unto the praise of His glory. Wherefore I also, after I had heard of your faith in Christ Jesus and with reference to all the saints, cease not to give thanks for you." [5]

Their faith was new and recent on the preaching of the gospel to them, which faith when he hears of, the apostle gives thanks to God on their behalf. If he were to give thanks to man for that which he might either think or know that man had not given, it would be called a flattery or a mockery, rather than a giving of thanks. " Do not err, for God is not mocked ; " [6] for His gift is also the beginning of faith, unless the apostolic giving of thanks be rightly judged to be either mistaken or fallacious. What then ? Does that not appear as the beginning of the faith of the Thessalonians, for which, nevertheless, the same apostle gives thanks to God when he says, " For this cause also we thank God without ceasing, because when ye had received from us the word of the hearing of God, ye received it not as the word of men, but as it is in truth the word of God, which effectually worketh in you and which ye believed " ? [7] What is that for which he here gives thanks to God ? Assuredly it is a vain and idle thing if He to whom he gives thanks did not Himself do the thing. But, since this is not a vain and idle thing, certainly God, to whom he gave thanks concerning this work, Himself did it ; that when they had received the word of the hearing of God, they received it not as the word of men, but as it is in truth the word of God. God, therefore, worketh in the hearts of men with that calling according to His purpose, of which we have spoken a great deal, that they should not hear the gospel in vain, but when they heard it, should be converted and believe, receiving it not as the word of men, but as it is in truth the word of God.

CHAP. 40 [XX.] — APOSTOLIC TESTIMONY TO THE BEGINNING OF FAITH BEING GOD'S GIFT.

Moreover, we are admonished that the beginning of men's faith is God's gift, since the apostle signifies this when, in the Epistle to the Colossians, he says, " Continue in prayer, and watch in the same in giving of thanks. Withal praying also for us that God would open unto us the door of His word, to speak the mystery of Christ, for which also I am in bonds, that I may so make it manifest as I ought to speak." [8] How is the door of His word opened, except when the sense of the hearer is opened so that he may believe, and, having made a beginning of faith, may admit those things which are declared and reasoned, for the purpose of building up wholesome doctrine, lest, by a heart closed through unbelief, he reject and repel those things which are spoken ? Whence, also, he says to the Corinthians : " But I will tarry at Ephesus until Pentecost. For a great and evident door is

---

[1] Eph. i. 11.    [2] Rom. xi. 29.    [3] Rom. ix. 12.
[4] John xv. 16.    [5] Eph. i. 13 ff.

[6] Gal. vi. 7.    [7] 1 Thess. ii. 13.    [8] Col. iv. 2 ff.

opened unto me, and there are many adversaries."[1] What else can be understood here, save that, when the gospel had been first of all preached there by him, many had believed, and there had appeared many adversaries of the same faith, in accordance with that saying of the Lord, "No one cometh unto me, unless it were given him of my Father;"[2] and, "To you it is given to know the mysteries of the kingdom of heaven, but to them it is not given"?[3] Therefore, there is an open door in those to whom it is given, but there are many adversaries among those to whom it is not given.

## CHAP. 41. — FURTHER APOSTOLIC TESTIMONIES.

And again, the same apostle says to the same people, in his second Epistle: "When I had come to Troas for the gospel of Christ, and a door had been opened unto me in the Lord, I had no rest in my spirit, because I found not Titus, my brother: but, making my farewell to them, I went away into Macedonia."[4] To whom did he bid farewell but to those who had believed, — to wit, in whose hearts the door was opened for his preaching of the gospel? But attend to what he adds, saying, " Now thanks be unto God, who always causes us to triumph in Christ, and maketh manifest the savour of His knowledge by us in every place: because we are unto God a sweet savour of Christ in them who are saved, and in them who perish: to some, indeed, we are the savour of death unto death, but to some the savour of life unto life."[5] See concerning what this most zealous soldier and invincible defender of grace gives thanks. See concerning what he gives thanks, — that the apostles are a sweet savour of Christ unto God, both in those who are saved by His grace, and in those who perish by His judgment. But in order that those who little understand these things may be less enraged, he himself gives a warning when he adds the words: " And who is sufficient for these things?"[6] But let us return to the opening of the door by which the apostle signified the beginning of faith in his hearers. For what is the meaning of, " Withal praying also for us that God would open unto us a door of the word,"[7] unless it is a most manifest demonstration that even the very beginning of faith is the gift of God? For it would not be sought for from Him in prayer, unless it were believed to be given by Him. This gift of heavenly grace had descended to that seller of purple[8] for whom, as Scripture says in the Acts of the Apostles, "The Lord opened her heart, and she gave heed unto the things which were said by Paul;" for she was so called that she might

believe. Because God does what He will in the hearts of men, either by assistance or by judgment; so that, even through their means, may be fulfilled what His hand and counsel have predestinated to be done.

## CHAP. 42. — OLD TESTAMENT TESTIMONIES.

Therefore also it is in vain that objectors have alleged, that what we have proved by Scripture testimony from the books of Kings and Chronicles is not pertinent to the subject of which we are discoursing:[9] such, for instance, as that when God wills that to be done which ought only to be done by the willing men, their hearts are inclined to will this, — inclined, that is to say, by His power, who, in a marvellous and ineffable manner, worketh in us also to will. What else is this than to say nothing, and yet to contradict? Unless, perchance, they have given some reason to you for the view that they have taken, which reason you have preferred to say nothing about in your letters. But what that reason can be I do not know. Whether, possibly, since we have shown that God has so acted on the hearts of men, and has induced the wills of those whom He pleased to this point, that Saul or David should be established as king, — do they not think that these instances are appropriate to this subject, because to reign in this world temporally is not the same thing as to reign eternally with God? And so do they suppose that God inclines the wills of those whom He pleases to the attainment of earthly kingdoms, but does not incline them to the attainment of a heavenly kingdom? But I think that it was in reference to the kingdom of heaven, and not to an earthly kingdom, that it was said, " Incline my heart unto Thy testimonies;"[10] or, " The steps of a man are ordered by the Lord, and He will will His way;"[11] or, " The will is prepared by the Lord;"[12] or, " Let our Lord be with us as with our fathers; let Him not forsake us, nor turn Himself away from us; let Him incline our hearts unto Him, that we may walk in all His ways;"[13] or, " I will give them a heart to know me, and ears that hear;"[14] or, " I will give them another heart, and a new spirit will I give them."[15] Let them also hear this, " I will give my Spirit within you, and I will cause you to walk in my righteousnesses; and ye shall observe my judgments, and do them."[16] Let them hear, " Man's goings are directed by the Lord, and how can a man understand His ways?"[17] Let them hear, " Every man seemeth right to himself, but the Lord directeth the hearts."[18] Let them hear, " As many as were ordained to eternal life be-

---

[1] 1 Cor. xvi. 8.　　[2] John vi. 66.　　[3] Luke viii. 10.
[4] 2 Cor. ii. 12, 13.　[5] 2 Cor. ii. 14 ff.　[6] 2 Cor. ii. 16.
[7] Col. iv. 3.　　　[8] Acts xvi. 14.

[9] Hilary's Letter in Augustin's *Letters*, 226, sec. 7.
[10] Ps. cxix. 36.　　　　　　　[11] Ps. xxxvii. 23.
[12] Prov. viii. [see LXX.].　　　　[13] 1 Kings viii. 57.
[14] Baruch ii. 31.　　　　　　　[15] Ezek. xi. 19.
[16] Ezek. xxxvi. 27.　　[17] Prov. xx. 24.　　[18] Prov. xxi. 2.

lieved." [1] Let them hear these passages, and whatever others of the kind I have not mentioned in which God is declared to prepare and to convert men's wills, even for the kingdom of heaven and for eternal life. And consider what sort of a thing it is to believe that God worketh men's wills for the foundation of earthly kingdoms, but that men work their own wills for the attainment of the kingdom of heaven.

### CHAP. 43 [XXI.] — CONCLUSION.

I have said a great deal, and, perchance, I could long ago have persuaded you what I wished, and am still speaking this to such intelligent minds as if they were obtuse, to whom even what is too much is not enough. But let them pardon me, for a new question has compelled me to this. Because, although in my former little treatises I had proved by sufficiently appropriate proofs that faith also was the gift of God, there was found this ground of contradiction, viz., that those testimonies were good for this purpose, to show that the increase of faith

was God's gift, but that the beginning of faith, whereby a man first of all believes in Christ, is of the man himself, and is not the gift of God, — but that God requires this, so that when it has preceded, other gifts may follow, as it were on the ground of this merit, and these are the gifts of God ; and that none of them is given freely, although in them God's grace is declared, which is not grace except as being gratuitous. And you see how absurd all this is. Wherefore I determined, as far as I could, to set forth that this very beginning also is God's gift. And if I have done this at a greater length than perhaps those on whose account I did it might wish, I am prepared to be reproached for it by them, so long as they nevertheless confess that, although at greater length than they wished, although with the disgust and weariness of those that understand, I have done what I have done : that is, I have taught that even the beginning of faith, as continence, patience, righteousness, piety, and the rest, concerning which there is no dispute with them, is God's gift. Let this, therefore, be the end of this treatise, lest too great length in this one may give offence.

---

[1] Acts xiii. 48.

# A TREATISE ON THE GIFT OF PERSEVERANCE.

# CONTENTS OF THE TREATISE "ON THE GIFT OF PERSEVERANCE."

---

# A TREATISE ON THE GIFT OF PERSEVERANCE.[1]

## BY AURELIUS AUGUSTIN, BISHOP OF HIPPO.

## BEING THE SECOND BOOK

## OF THE TREATISE "ON THE PREDESTINATION OF THE SAINTS."

### ADDRESSED TO PROSPER AND HILARY.

### A.D. 428 OR 429.

IN THE FIRST PART OF THE BOOK HE PROVES THAT THE PERSEVERANCE BY WHICH A MAN PERSEVERES IN CHRIST TO THE END IS GOD'S GIFT; FOR THAT IT IS A MOCKERY TO ASK OF GOD THAT WHICH IS NOT BELIEVED TO BE GIVEN BY GOD. MOREOVER, THAT IN THE LORD'S PRAYER SCARCELY ANYTHING IS ASKED FOR BUT PERSEVERANCE, ACCORDING TO THE EXPOSITION OF THE MARTYR CYPRIAN, BY WHICH EXPOSITION THE ENEMIES TO THIS GRACE WERE CONVICTED BEFORE THEY WERE BORN. HE TEACHES THAT THE GRACE OF PERSEVERANCE IS NOT GIVEN ACCORDING TO THE MERITS OF THE RECEIVERS, BUT TO SOME IT IS GIVEN BY GOD'S MERCY; TO OTHERS IT IS NOT GIVEN, BY HIS RIGHTEOUS JUDGMENT. THAT IT IS INSCRUTABLE WHY, OF ADULTS, ONE RATHER THAN ANOTHER SHOULD BE CALLED; JUST AS, MOREOVER, OF TWO INFANTS IT IS INSCRUTABLE WHY THE ONE SHOULD BE TAKEN, THE OTHER LEFT. BUT THAT IT IS STILL MORE INSCRUTABLE WHY, OF TWO PIOUS PERSONS, TO ONE IT SHOULD BE GIVEN TO PERSEVERE, TO THE OTHER IT SHOULD NOT BE GIVEN; BUT THAT THIS IS MOST CERTAIN, THAT THE FORMER IS OF THE PREDESTINATED, THE LATTER IS NOT. HE OBSERVES THAT THE MYSTERY OF PREDESTINATION IS SET FORTH IN OUR LORD'S WORDS CONCERNING THE PEOPLE OF TYRE AND SIDON, WHO WOULD HAVE REPENTED IF THE SAME MIRACLES HAD BEEN DONE AMONG THEM WHICH HAD BEEN DONE IN CHORAZIN. HE SHOWS THAT THE CASE OF INFANTS IS OF FORCE TO CONFIRM THE TRUTH OF PREDESTINATION AND GRACE IN OLDER PEOPLE; AND HE ANSWERS THE PASSAGE OF HIS THIRD BOOK ON FREE WILL, UNSOUNDLY ALLEGED ON THIS POINT BY HIS ADVERSARIES. SUBSEQUENTLY, IN THE SECOND PART OF THIS WORK, HE REBUTS WHAT THEY SAY, — TO WIT, THAT THE DEFINITION OF PREDESTINATION IS OPPOSED TO THE USEFULNESS OF EXHORTATION AND REBUKE. HE ASSERTS, ON THE OTHER HAND, THAT IT IS ADVANTAGEOUS TO PREACH PREDESTINATION, SO THAT MAN MAY NOT GLORY IN HIMSELF, BUT IN THE LORD. AS TO THE OBJECTIONS, HOW-

---

[1] [In some editions and in many mss. the title is, *On the Benefit of Perseverance*, and the book is so cited by Remigius, Florus (or Bede), Hincmar, and others. Probably neither title is authentic. Prosper speaks of it to Hilary as if it simply bore the name of the second book of the *Predestination of the Saints*. " In the books," he writes, " of Bishop Augustin, of blessed memory, which bear the title, *On the Predestination of the Saints*." — W.]

EVER, WHICH THEY MAKE AGAINST PREDESTINATION, HE SHOWS THAT THE SAME OBJECTIONS MAY BE TWISTED IN NO UNLIKE MANNER EITHER AGAINST GOD'S FORE-KNOWLEDGE OR AGAINST THAT GRACE WHICH THEY ALL AGREE TO BE NECESSARY FOR OTHER GOOD THINGS (WITH THE EXCEPTION OF THE BEGINNING OF FAITH AND THE COMPLETION OF PERSEVERANCE). FOR THAT THE PREDESTINATION OF THE SAINTS IS NOTHING ELSE THAN GOD'S FOREKNOWLEDGE AND PREPARATION FOR HIS BENEFITS, BY WHICH WHOEVER ARE DELIVERED ARE MOST CERTAINLY DELIVERED. BUT HE BIDS THAT PREDESTINATION SHOULD BE PREACHED IN A HARMONIOUS MANNER, AND NOT IN SUCH A WAY AS TO SEEM TO AN UNSKILFUL MULTITUDE AS IF IT WERE DISPROVED BY ITS VERY PREACHING. LASTLY, HE COMMENDS TO US JESUS CHRIST, AS PLACED BEFORE OUR EYES, AS THE MOST EMINENT INSTANCE OF PREDESTINATION.

CHAP. I [I.] — OF THE NATURE OF THE PERSE-VERANCE HERE DISCOURSED OF.

I HAVE now to consider the subject of perseverance with greater care; for in the former book also I said some things on this subject when I was discussing the beginning of faith. I assert, therefore, that the perseverance by which we persevere in Christ even to the end is the gift of God; and I call that the end by which is finished that life wherein alone there is peril of falling. Therefore it is uncertain whether any one has received this gift so long as he is still alive. For if he fall before he dies, he is, of course, said not to have persevered; and most truly is it said. How, then, should he be said to have received or to have had perseverance who has not persevered? For if any one have continence, and fall away from that virtue and become incontinent, — or, in like manner, if he have righteousness, if patience, if even faith, and fall away, he is rightly said to have had these virtues and to have them no longer; for he was continent, or he was righteous, or he was patient, or he was believing, as long as he was so; but when he ceased to be so, he no longer is what he was. But how should he who has not persevered have ever been persevering, since it is only by persevering that any one shows himself persevering, — and this he has not done? But lest any one should object to this, and say, If from the time at which any one became a believer he has lived — for the sake of argument — ten years, and in the midst of them has fallen from the faith, has he not persevered for five years? I am not contending about words. If it be thought that this also should be called perseverance, as it were for so long as it lasts, assuredly he is not to be said to have had in any degree that perseverance of which we are now discoursing, by which one perseveres in Christ even to the end. And the believer of one year, or of a period as much shorter as may be conceived of, if he has lived faithfully until he died, has rather had this perseverance than the believer of many years' standing, if a

little time before his death he has fallen away from the stedfastness of his faith.

CHAP. 2 [II.] — FAITH IS THE BEGINNING OF A CHRISTIAN MAN. MARTYRDOM FOR CHRIST'S SAKE IS HIS BEST ENDING.

This matter being settled, let us see whether this perseverance, of which it was said, "He that persevereth unto the end, the same shall be saved,"[1] is a gift of God. And if it be not, how is that saying of the apostle true: "Unto you it is given in the behalf of Christ, not only to believe on Him, but also to suffer for His sake"?[2] Of these things, certainly, one has respect to the beginning, the other to the end. Yet each is the gift of God, because both are said to be given; as, also, I have already said above. For what is more truly the beginning for a Christian than to believe in Christ? What end is better than to suffer for Christ? But so far as pertains to believing in Christ, whatever kind of contradiction has been discovered, that not the beginning but the increase of faith should be called God's gift, — to this opinion, by God's gift, I have answered enough, and more than enough. But what reason can be given why perseverance to the end should not be given in Christ to him to whom it is given to suffer for Christ, or, to speak more distinctly, to whom it is given to die for Christ? For the Apostle Peter, showing that this is the gift of God, says, "It is better, if the will of God be so, to suffer for well-doing than for evil-doing."[3] When he says, "If the will of God be so," he shows that this is divinely given, and yet not to all saints, to suffer for Christ's sake. For certainly those whom the will of God does not will to attain to the experience and the glory of suffering, do not fail to attain to the kingdom of God if they persevere in Christ to the end. But who can say that this perseverance is not given to those who die in Christ from any weakness of body, or by any kind of accident, although a far more difficult perseverance is given to those by whom even

---

[1] Matt. x. 22.    [2] Phil. ii. 29.    [3] 1 Pet. iii. 17.

death itself is undergone for Christ's sake? Because perseverance is much more difficult when the persecutor is engaged in preventing a man's perseverance; and therefore he is sustained in his perseverance unto death. Hence it is more difficult to have the former perseverance, — easier to have the latter; but to Him to whom nothing is difficult it is easy to give both. For God has promised this, saying, "I will put my fear in their hearts, that they may not depart from me."[1] And what else is this than, "Such and so great shall be my fear that I will put into their hearts that they will perseveringly cleave to me"?

### CHAP. 3. — GOD IS BESOUGHT FOR IT, BECAUSE IT IS HIS GIFT.

But why is that perseverance asked for from God if it is not given by God? Is that, too, a mocking petition, when that is asked from Him which it is known that He does not give, but, though He gives it not, is in man's power; just as that giving of thanks is a mockery, if thanks are given to God for that which He did not give nor do? But what I have said there,[2] I say also here again: "Be not deceived," says the apostle, "God is not mocked."[3] O man, God is a witness not only of your words, but also of your thoughts. If you ask anything in truth and faith, of one who is so rich, believe that you receive from Him from whom you ask, what you ask. Abstain from honouring Him with your lips and extolling yourself over Him in your heart, by believing that you have from yourself what you are pretending to beseech from Him. Is not this perseverance, perchance, asked for from Him? He who says this is not to be rebuked by any arguments, but must be overwhelmed[4] with the prayers of the saints. Is there any of these who does not ask for himself from God that he may persevere in Him, when in that very prayer which is called the Lord's — because the Lord taught it — when it is prayed by the saints, scarcely anything else is understood to be prayed for but perseverance?

### CHAP. 4. — THREE LEADING POINTS OF THE PELAGIAN DOCTRINE.

Read with a little more attention its exposition in the treatise of the blessed martyr Cyprian, which he wrote concerning this matter, the title of which is, *On the Lord's Prayer;* and see how many years ago, and what sort of an antidote was prepared against those poisons which the Pelagians were one day to use. For there are three points, as you know, which the catholic Church chiefly maintains against them. One of

these is, that the grace of God is not given according to our merits; because even every one of the merits of the righteous is God's gift, and is conferred by God's grace. The second is, that no one lives in this corruptible body, however righteous he may be, without sins of some kind. The third is, that man is born obnoxious to the first man's sin, and bound by the chain of condemnation, unless the guilt which is contracted by generation be loosed by regeneration. Of these three points, that which I have placed last is the only one that is not treated of in the above-named book of the glorious martyr; but of the two others the discourse there is of such perspicuity, that the above-named heretics, modern enemies of the grace of Christ, are found to have been convicted long before they were born. Among these merits of the saints, then, which are no merits unless they are the gifts of God, he says that perseverance also is God's gift, in these words: "We say, 'Hallowed be Thy name;' not that we ask for God that He may be hallowed by our prayers, but that we beseech of Him that His name may be hallowed in us. But by whom is God sanctified, since He Himself sanctifies? Well, because He says, Be ye holy because I also am holy, we ask and entreat that we, who were sanctified in baptism, may persevere in that which we have begun to be."[5] And a little after, still arguing about that self-same matter, and teaching that we entreat perseverance from the Lord, which we could in no wise rightly and truly do unless it were His gift, he says: "We pray that this sanctification may abide in us; and because our Lord and Judge warns the man that was healed and quickened by Him to sin no more, lest a worse thing happen unto him, we make this supplication in our constant prayers; we ask this, day and night, that the sanctification and quickening which is received from the grace of God may be preserved by His protection."[6] That teacher, therefore, understands that we are asking from Him for perseverance in sanctification, that is, that we should persevere in sanctification, when we who are sanctified say, "Hallowed be Thy name." For what else is it to ask for what we have already received, than that it be given to us also not to cease from its possession? As, therefore, the saint, when he asks God that he may be holy, is certainly asking that he may continue to be holy, so certainly the chaste person also, when he asks that he may be chaste, the continent that he may be continent, the righteous that he may be righteous, the pious that he may be pious, and the like, — which things, against the Pelagians, we maintain to be God's gifts, — are asking, without doubt,

---

[1] Jer. xxxii. 40.
[2] *On the Predestination of the Saints,* above, ch. 39.
[3] Gal. vi. 6.    [4] Some editions read "recalled."

[5] Cyprian, *On the Lord's Prayer;* see *The Ante-Nicene Fathers,* vol. v. p. 450.
[6] Cyprian, *On the Lord's Prayer,* as above.

that they may persevere in those good things which they have acknowledged that they have received. And if they receive this, assuredly they also receive perseverance itself, the great gift of God, whereby His other gifts are preserved.

CHAP. 5. — THE SECOND PETITION IN THE LORD'S PRAYER.

What, when we say, "Thy kingdom come," do we ask else, but that that should also come to us which we do not doubt will come to all saints? And therefore here also, what do they who are already holy pray for, save that they may persevere in that holiness which has been given them? For no otherwise will the kingdom of God come to them; which it is certain will come not to others, but to those who persevere to the end.

CHAP. 6 [III.] — THE THIRD PETITION. HOW HEAVEN AND EARTH ARE UNDERSTOOD IN THE LORD'S PRAYER.

The third petition is, "Thy will be done in heaven and in earth;" or, as it is read in many codices, and is more frequently made use of by petitioners, "As in heaven, so also in earth," which many people understand, "As the holy angels, so also may we do thy will." That teacher and martyr will have heaven and earth, however, to be understood as spirit and flesh, and says that we pray that we may do the will of God with the full concord of both. He saw in these words also another meaning, congruous to the soundest faith, of which meaning I have already spoken above, — to wit, that for unbelievers, who are as yet *earth*, bearing in their first birth only the earthly man, believers are understood to pray, who, being clothed with the heavenly man, are not unreasonably called by the name of *heaven;* where he plainly shows that the beginning of faith also is God's gift, since the holy Church prays not only for believers, that faith may be increased or may continue in them, but, moreover, for unbelievers, that they may begin to have what they have not had at all, and against which, besides, they were indulging hostile feelings. Now, however, I am arguing not concerning the beginning of faith, of which I have already spoken much in the former book, but of that perseverance which must be had even to the end, — which assuredly even the saints, who do the will of God, seek when they say in prayer, "Thy will be done." For, since it is already done in them, why do they still ask that it may be done, except that they may persevere in that which they have begun to be? Nevertheless, it may here be said that the saints do not ask that the will of God may be done in heaven, but that it may be done in earth as in

heaven, — that is to say, that earth may imitate heaven, that is, that man may imitate the angel, or that an unbeliever may imitate a believer; and thus that the saints are asking that that may be which is not yet, not that that which is may continue. For, by whatever holiness men may be distinguished, they are not yet equal to the angels of God; not yet, therefore, is the will of God done in them as it is in heaven. And if this be so, in that portion indeed in which we ask that men from unbelievers may become believers, it is not perseverance, but beginning, that seems to be asked for; but in that in which we ask that men may be made equal to the angels of God in doing God's will, — where the saints pray for this, they are found to be praying for perseverance; since no one attains to that highest blessedness which is in the kingdom, unless he shall persevere unto the end in that holiness which he has received on earth.

CHAP. 7 [IV.] — THE FOURTH PETITION.

The fourth petition is, "Give us this day our daily bread," [1] where the blessed Cyprian shows how here also perseverance is understood to be asked for. Because he says, among other things, "And we ask that this bread should be given to us daily, that we who are in Christ, and daily receive the Eucharist for the food of salvation, may not by the interposition of some heinous sin be separated from Christ's body by being withheld from communicating and prevented from partaking of the heavenly bread." [2] These words of the holy man of God indicate that the saints ask for perseverance directly from God, when with this intention they say, "Give us this day our daily bread," that they may not be separated from Christ's body, but may continue in that holiness in which they allow no crime by which they may deserve to be separated from it.

CHAP. 8 [V.] — THE FIFTH PETITION. IT IS AN ERROR OF THE PELAGIANS THAT THE RIGHTEOUS ARE FREE FROM SIN.

In the fifth sentence of the prayer we say, "Forgive us our debts, as we also forgive our debtors," [3] in which petition alone perseverance is not found to be asked for. For the sins which we ask to be forgiven us are past, but perseverance, which saves us for eternity, is indeed necessary for the time of this life; but not for the time which is past, but for that which remains even to its end. Yet it is worth the labour to consider for a little, how even already in this petition the heretics who were to arise long after were transfixed by the tongue of Cyprian, as if by the most invincible dart of truth. For the Pelagians dare to say even this: that the right-

[1] Matt. vi. 11.   [2] Cyprian, *On the Lord's Prayer*, as above.
[3] Matt. vi. 12.

eous man in this life has no sin at all, and that in such men there is even at the present time a Church not having spot or wrinkle or any such thing,[1] which is the one and only bride of Christ; as if she were not His bride who throughout the whole earth says what she has learnt from Him, "Forgive us our debts." But observe how the most glorious Cyprian destroys these. For when he was expounding that very clause of the Lord's Prayer, he says among other things: "And how necessarily, how providently, and salutarily are we admonished that we are sinners, since we are compelled to entreat for our sins; and while pardon is asked for from God, the soul recalls its own consciousness. Lest any one should flatter himself that he is innocent, and by exalting himself should more deeply perish, he is instructed and taught that he sins daily, in that he is bidden daily to entreat for his sins. Thus, moreover, John also in his Epistle warns[2] us, and says,[3] 'If we say that we have no sin, we deceive ourselves, and the truth is not in us.'"[4] And the rest, which it would be long to insert in this place.

### CHAP. 9. — WHEN PERSEVERANCE IS GRANTED TO A PERSON, HE CANNOT BUT PERSEVERE.

Now, moreover, when the saints say, "Lead us not into temptation, but deliver us from evil,"[5] what do they pray for but that they may persevere in holiness? For, assuredly, when that gift of God is granted to them, — which is sufficiently plainly shown to be God's gift, since it is asked of Him, — that gift of God, then, being granted to them that they may not be led into temptation, none of the saints fails to keep his perseverance in holiness even to the end. For there is not any one who ceases to persevere in the Christian purpose unless he is first of all led into temptation. If, therefore, it be granted to him according to his prayer that he may not be led, certainly by the gift of God he persists in that sanctification which by the gift of God he has received.

### CHAP. 10 [VI.] — THE GIFT OF PERSEVERANCE CAN BE OBTAINED BY PRAYER.

But you write that "these brethren will not have this perseverance so preached as that it cannot be obtained by prayer or lost by obstinacy."[6] In this they are little careful in considering what they say. For we are speaking of that perseverance whereby one perseveres unto the end, and if this is given, one does persevere unto the end; but if one does not persevere unto the end, it is not given, which I have already sufficiently discussed above. Let not men say, then, that perseverance is given to any one to

the end, except when the end itself has come, and he to whom it has been given has been found to have persevered unto the end. Certainly, we say that one whom we have known to be chaste is chaste, whether he should continue or not in the same chastity; and if he should have any other divine endowment which may be kept and lost, we say that he has it as long as he has it; and if he should lose it, we say that he had it. But since no one has perseverance to the end except he who does persevere to the end, many people may have it, but none can lose it. For it is not to be feared that perchance when a man has persevered unto the end, some evil will may arise in him, so that he does not persevere unto the end. This gift of God, therefore, may be obtained by prayer, but when it has been given, it cannot be lost by contumacy. For when any one has persevered unto the end, he neither can lose this gift, nor others which he could lose before the end. How, then, can that be lost, whereby it is brought about that even that which could be lost is not lost?

### CHAP. 11. — EFFECT OF PRAYER FOR PERSEVERANCE.

But, lest perchance it be said that perseverance even to the end is not indeed lost when it has once been given, — that is, when a man has persevered unto the end, — but that it is lost, in some sense, when a man by contumacy so acts that he is not able to attain to it; just as we say that a man who has not persevered unto the end has lost eternal life or the kingdom of God, not because he had already received and actually had it, but because he would have received and had it if he had persevered; — let us lay aside controversies of words, and say that some things even which are not possessed, but are hoped to be possessed, may be lost. Let any one who dares, tell me whether God cannot give what He has commanded to be asked from Him. Certainly he who affirms this, I say not is a fool, but he is mad. But God commanded that His saints should say to Him in prayer, "Lead us not into temptation." Whoever, therefore, is heard when he asks this, is not led into the temptation of contumacy, whereby he could or would be worthy to lose perseverance in holiness.

### CHAP. 12. — OF HIS OWN WILL A MAN FORSAKES GOD, SO THAT HE IS DESERVEDLY FORSAKEN OF HIM.

But, on the other hand, "of his own will a man forsakes God, so as to be deservedly forsaken by God." Who would deny this? But it is for that reason we ask not to be led into temptation, so that this may not happen. And if we are heard, certainly it does not happen, because God does not allow it to happen. For

1 Eph. v. 27.
2 "Potens" or "ponens" are different readings.
3 1 John i 8        4 Cyprian, as above.        5 Matt. vi. 13.
6 Hilary's Letter in Augustin's *Letters*, 226, ch. 3.

nothing comes to pass except what either He Himself does, or Himself allows to be done. Therefore He is powerful both to turn wills from evil to good, and to convert those that are inclined to fall, or to direct them into a way pleasing to Himself. For to Him it is not said in vain, "O God, Thou shalt turn again and quicken us;"[1] it is not vainly said, "Give not my foot to be moved;"[2] it is not vainly said, "Give me not over, O Lord, from my desire to the sinner;"[3] finally, not to mention many passages, since probably more may occur to you, it is not vainly said, "Lead us not into temptation."[4] For whoever is not led into temptation, certainly is not led into the temptation of his own evil will; and he who is not led into the temptation of his own evil will, is absolutely led into no temptation. For "every one is tempted," as it is written, "when he is drawn away of his own lust, and enticed;"[5] "but God tempteth no man,"[6] — that is to say, with a hurtful temptation. For temptation is moreover beneficial by which we are not deceived or overwhelmed, but proved, according to that which is said, "Prove me, O Lord, and try me."[7] Therefore, with that hurtful temptation which the apostle signifies when he says, "Lest by some means the tempter have tempted you, and our labour be in vain,"[8] "God tempteth no man," as I have said, — that is, He brings or leads no one into temptation. For to be tempted and not to be led into temptation is not evil, — nay, it is even good; for this it is to be proved. When, therefore, we say to God, "Lead us not into temptation," what do we say but, "Permit us not to be led"? Whence some pray in this manner, and it is read in many codices, and the most blessed Cyprian thus uses it: "Do not suffer us to be led into temptation." In the Greek gospel, however, I have never found it otherwise than, "Lead us not into temptation." We live, therefore, more securely if we give up the whole to God, and do not entrust ourselves partly to Him and partly to ourselves, as that venerable martyr saw. For when he would expound the same clause of the prayer, he says among other things, "But when we ask that we may not come into temptation, we are reminded of our infirmity and weakness while we thus ask, lest any should insolently vaunt himself, — lest any should proudly and arrogantly assume anything to himself, — lest any should take to himself the glory either of confession or suffering as his own; since the Lord Himself, teaching humility, said, 'Watch and pray, that ye enter not into temptation; the Spirit indeed is willing, but the flesh is weak.' So that when a humble and submissive confession comes first

and all is attributed to God, whatever is sought for suppliantly, with the fear of God, may be granted by His own loving-kindness."[9]

CHAP. 13 [VII.] — TEMPTATION THE CONDITION OF MAN.

If, then, there were no other proofs, this Lord's Prayer alone would be sufficient for us on behalf of the grace which I am defending; because it leaves us nothing wherein we may, as it were, glory as in our own, since it shows that our not departing from God is not given except by God, when it shows that it must be asked for from God. For he who is not led into temptation does not depart from God. This is absolutely not in the strength of free will, such as it now is; but it had been in man before he fell. And yet how much this freedom of will availed in the excellence of that primal state appeared in the angels; who, when the devil and his angels fell, stood in the truth, and deserved to attain to that perpetual security of not falling, in which we are most certain that they are now established. But, after the fall of man, God willed it to pertain only to His grace that man should approach to Him; nor did He will it to pertain to aught but His grace that man should not depart from Him.

CHAP. 14. — IT IS GOD'S GRACE BOTH THAT MAN COMES TO HIM, AND THAT MAN DOES NOT DEPART FROM HIM.

This grace He placed "in Him in whom we have obtained a lot, being predestinated according to the purpose of Him who worketh all things."[10] And thus as He worketh that we come to Him, so He worketh that we do not depart. Wherefore it was said to Him by the mouth of the prophet, "Let Thy hand be upon the man of Thy right hand, and upon the Son of man whom Thou madest strong for Thyself, and we will not depart from Thee."[11] This certainly is not the first Adam, in whom we departed from Him, but the second Adam, upon whom His hand is placed, so that we do not depart from Him. For Christ altogether with His members is — for the Church's sake, which is His body — the fulness of Him. When, therefore, God's hand is upon Him, that we depart not from God, assuredly God's work reaches to us (for this is God's hand); by which work of God we are caused to be abiding in Christ with God — not, as in Adam, departing from God. For "in Christ we have obtained a lot, being predestinated according to His purpose who worketh all things." This, therefore, is God's hand, not ours, that we depart not from God. That, I say, is His hand who said, "I will put my fear in their hearts, that they depart not from me."[12]

1 Ps. lxxxiv. 6.    2 Ps. lxvi. 9.    3 Ps. cxl. 8.
4 Matt. vi. 13.    5 Jas. i. 14.    6 Jas. i. 13.
7 Ps. xxvi. 2.    8 1 Thess. iii. 5.

9 Cyprian, On the Lord's Prayer, as above.
10 Eph. i. 11.    11 Ps. lxxx. 17, 18.    12 Jer. xxxii. 40.

CHAP. 15. — WHY GOD WILLED THAT HE SHOULD BE ASKED FOR THAT WHICH HE MIGHT GIVE WITHOUT PRAYER.

Wherefore, also He willed that He should be asked that we may not be led into temptation, because if we are not led, we by no means depart from Him. And this might have been given to us even without our praying for it, but by our prayer He willed us to be admonished from whom we receive these benefits. For from whom do we receive but from Him from whom it is right for us to ask? Truly in this matter let not the Church look for laborious disputations, but consider its own daily prayers. It prays that the unbelieving may believe; therefore God converts to the faith. It prays that believers may persevere; therefore God gives perseverance to the end. God foreknew that He would do this. This is the very predestination of the saints, "whom He has chosen in Christ before the foundation of the world, that they should be holy and unspotted before Him in love; predestinating them unto the adoption of children by Jesus Christ to Himself, according to the good pleasure of His will, to the praise of the glory of His grace, in which He hath shown them favour in His beloved Son, in whom they have redemption through His blood, the forgiveness of sins according to the riches of His grace, which has abounded towards them in all wisdom and prudence; that He might show them the mystery of His will according to His good pleasure which He hath purposed in Him, in the dispensation of the fulness of times to restore all things in Christ which are in heaven and which are in earth; in Him, in whom also we have obtained a lot, being predestinated according to His purpose who worketh all things."[1] Against a trumpet of truth so clear as this, what man of sober and watchful faith can receive any human arguments?

CHAP. 16 [VIII.] — WHY IS NOT GRACE GIVEN ACCORDING TO MERIT?

But "why," says one, "is not the grace of God given according to men's merits?" I answer, Because God is merciful. "Why, then," it is asked, "is it not given to all?" And here I reply, Because God is a Judge.[2] And thus grace is given by Him freely; and by His righteous judgment it is shown in some what grace confers on those to whom it is given. Let us not then be ungrateful, that according to the good pleasure of His will a merciful God delivers so many to the praise of the glory of His grace from such deserved perdition; as, if He should deliver no one therefrom, He would not be unrighteous. Let him, therefore, who is delivered love His grace. Let him who is not delivered acknowledge his due. If, in remitting a debt, goodness is perceived, in requiring it, justice — unrighteousness is never found to be with God.

CHAP. 17. — THE DIFFICULTY OF THE DISTINCTION MADE IN THE CHOICE OF ONE AND THE REJECTION OF ANOTHER.

"But why," it is said, "in one and the same case, not only of infants, but even of twin children, is the judgment so diverse?" Is it not a similar question, "Why in a different case is the judgment the same?" Let us recall, then, those labourers in the vineyard who worked the whole day, and those who toiled one hour. Certainly the case was different as to the labour expended, and yet there was the same judgment in paying the wages. Did the murmurers in this case hear anything from the householder except, Such is my will? Certainly such was his liberality towards some, that there could be no injustice towards others. And both these classes, indeed, are among the good. Nevertheless, so far as it concerns justice and grace, it may be truly said to the guilty who is condemned, also concerning the guilty who is delivered, "Take what thine is, and go thy way;"[3] "I will give unto this one that which is not due;" "Is it not lawful for me to do what I will? is thine eye evil because I am good?" And how if he should say, "Why not to me also?" He will hear, and with reason, "Who art thou, O man, that repliest against God?"[2] And although assuredly in the one case you see a most benignant benefactor, and in your own case a most righteous exactor, in neither case do you behold an unjust God. For although He would be righteous even if He were to punish both, he who is delivered has good ground for thankfulness, he who is condemned has no ground for finding fault.

CHAP. 18. — BUT WHY SHOULD ONE BE PUNISHED MORE THAN ANOTHER?

"But if," it is said, "it was necessary that, although all were not condemned, He should still show what was due to all, and so He should commend His grace more freely to the vessels of mercy; why in the same case will He punish me more than another, or deliver him more than me?" I say not this. If you ask wherefore; because I confess that I can find no answer to make. And if you further ask why is this, it is because in this matter, even as His anger is righteous and as His mercy is great, so His judgments are unsearchable.

CHAP. 19. — WHY DOES GOD MINGLE THOSE WHO WILL PERSEVERE WITH THOSE WHO WILL NOT?

Let the inquirer still go on, and say, "Why is

---

[1] Eph. i. 4-11.  [2] Rom. ix. 20.  [3] Matt. xx. 14, etc.

it that to some who have in good faith worshipped Him He has not given to persevere to the end?" Why except because he does not speak falsely who says, "They went out from us, but they were not of us ; for if they had been of us, doubtless they would have continued with us." [1]  Are there, then, two natures of men? By no means.  If there were two natures there would not be any grace, for there would be given a gratuitous deliverance to none if it were paid as a debt to nature.  But it seems to men that all who appear good believers ought to receive perseverance to the end.  But God has judged it to be better to mingle some who would not persevere with a certain number of His saints, so that those for whom security from temptation in this life is not desirable may not be secure. For that which the apostle says, checks many from mischievous elation: "Wherefore let him who seems to stand take heed lest he fall." [2] But he who falls, falls by his own will, and he who stands, stands by God's will.  "For God is able to make him stand ; " [3] therefore he is not able to make himself stand, but God.  Nevertheless, it is good not to be high-minded, but to fear.  Moreover, it is in his own thought that every one either falls or stands.  Now, as the apostle says, and as I have mentioned in my former treatise, "We are not sufficient to think anything of ourselves, but our sufficiency is of God." [4]  Following whom also the blessed Ambrose ventures to say, " For our heart is not in our own power, nor are our thoughts."  And this everybody who is humbly and truly pious feels to be most true.

### CHAP. 20. — AMBROSE ON GOD'S CONTROL OVER MEN'S THOUGHTS.

And when Ambrose said this, he was speaking in that treatise which he wrote concerning Flight from the World, wherein he taught that this world was to be fled not by the body, but by the heart, which he argued could not be done except by God's help.  For he says : "We hear frequent discourse concerning fleeing from this world, and I would that the mind was as careful and solicitous as the discourse is easy ; but what is worse, the enticement of earthly lusts constantly creeps in, and the pouring out of vanities takes possession of the mind ; so that what you desire to avoid, this you think of and consider in your mind.  And this is difficult for a man to beware of, but impossible to get rid of.  Finally, the prophet bears witness that it is a matter of wish rather than of accomplishment, when he says, ' Incline my heart to Thy testimonies, and not to covetousness.' [5]  For our heart and our thoughts are not in our own power, and these, poured forth

unexpectedly, confuse our mind and soul, and draw them in a different direction from that which you have proposed to yourself ; they recall you to worldly things, they interpose things of time, they suggest voluptuous things, they inweave enticing things, and in the very moment when we are seeking to elevate our mind, we are for the most part filled with vain thoughts and cast down to earthly things." [6]  Therefore it is not in the power of men, but in that of God, that men have power to become sons of God.[7] Because they receive it from Him who gives pious thoughts to the human heart, by which it has faith, which worketh by love ; [8] for the receiving and keeping of which benefit, and for carrying it on perseveringly unto the end, we are not sufficient to think anything as of ourselves, but our sufficiency is of God,[4] in whose power is our heart and our thoughts.

### CHAP. 21 [IX.] — INSTANCES OF THE UNSEARCHABLE JUDGMENTS OF GOD.

Therefore, of two infants, equally bound by original sin, why the one is taken and the other left ; and of two wicked men of already mature years, why this one should be so called as to follow Him that calleth, while that one is either not called at all, or is not called in such a manner, — the judgments of God are unsearchable. But of two pious men, why to the one should be given perseverance unto the end, and to the other it should not be given, God's judgments are even more unsearchable.  Yet to believers it ought to be a most certain fact that the former is of the predestinated, the latter is not.  "For if they had been of us," says one of the predestinated, who had drunk this secret from the breast of the Lord, "certainly they would have continued with us." [1]  What, I ask, is the meaning of, "They were not of us ; for if they had been of us, they would certainly have continued with us "?  Were not both created by God — both born of Adam — both made from the earth, and given from Him who said, " I have created all breath," [9] souls of one and the same nature?  Lastly, had not both been called, and followed Him that called them? and had not both become, from wicked men, justified men, and both been renewed by the laver of regeneration?  But if he were to hear this who beyond all doubt knew what he was saying, he might answer and say : These things are true.  In respect of all these things, they were of us.  Nevertheless, in respect of a certain other distinction, they were not of us, for if they had been of us, they certainly would have continued with us. What then is this distinction?  God's books lie

---

[1] 1 John ii. 19.     [2] 1 Cor. x. 12.     [3] Rom. xiv. 4.
[4] 2 Cor. iii. 5.     [5] Ps. cxix. 36.

[6] Ambrose, *On Flight from the World*, ch. i.
[7] John i. 12.     [8] Gal. v. 6.
[9] Isa. lvii. 16 [see LXX.].

open, let us not turn away our view; the divine Scripture cries aloud, let us give it a hearing. They were not of them, because they had not been "called according to the purpose;" they had not been chosen in Christ before the foundation of the world; they had not gained a lot in Him; they had not been predestinated according to His purpose who worketh all things. For if they had been this, they would have been of them, and without doubt they would have continued with them.

CHAP. 22.— IT IS AN ABSURDITY TO SAY THAT THE DEAD WILL BE JUDGED FOR SINS WHICH THEY WOULD HAVE COMMITTED IF THEY HAD LIVED.

For not to say how possible it may be for God to convert the wills of men averse and opposed to His faith, and to operate on their hearts so that they yield to no adversities, and are overcome by no temptation so as to depart from Him, — since He also can do what the apostle says, namely, not allow them to be tempted above that which they are able; — not, then, to say this, God foreknowing that they would fall, was certainly able to take them away from this life before that fall should occur. Are we to return to that point of still arguing how absurdly it is said that dead men are judged even for those sins which God foreknew that they would have committed if they had lived? which is so abhorrent to the feelings of Christians, or even of human beings, that one is even ashamed to rebut it. Why should it not be said that even the gospel itself has been preached, with so much labour and sufferings of the saints, in vain, or is even still preached in vain, if men could be judged, even without hearing the gospel, according to the contumacy or obedience which God foreknew that they would have had if they had heard it? Tyre and Sidon would not have been condemned, although more slightly than those cities in which, although they did not believe, wonderful works were done by Christ the Lord; because if they had been done in them, they would have repented in dust and ashes, as the utterances of the Truth declare, in which words of His the Lord Jesus shows to us the loftier mystery of predestination.

CHAP. 23.— WHY FOR THE PEOPLE OF TYRE AND SIDON, WHO WOULD HAVE BELIEVED, THE MIRACLES WERE NOT DONE WHICH WERE DONE IN OTHER PLACES WHICH DID NOT BELIEVE.

For if we are asked why such miracles were done among those who, when they saw them, would not believe them, and were not done among those who would have believed them if they had seen them, what shall we answer? Shall we say what I have said in that book [1]

wherein I answered some six questions of the Pagans, yet without prejudice of other matters which the wise can inquire into? This indeed I said, as you know, when it was asked why Christ came after so long a time: "that at those times and in those places in which His gospel was not preached, He foreknew that all men would, in regard of His preaching, be such as many were in His bodily presence, — people, namely, who would not believe on Him, even though the dead were raised by Him." Moreover, a little after in the same book, and on the same question, I say, "What wonder, if Christ knew in former ages that the world was so filled with unbelievers, that He was, with reason, unwilling for His gospel to be preached to them whom He foreknew to be such as would not believe either His words or His miracles"? Certainly we cannot say this of Tyre and Sidon; and in their case we recognise that those divine judgments had reference to those causes of predestination, without prejudice to which hidden causes I said that I was then answering such questions as those. Certainly it is easy to accuse the unbelief of the Jews, arising as it did from their free will, since they refused to believe in such great wonders done among themselves. And this the Lord, reproaching them, declares when He says, "Woe unto thee, Chorazin and Bethsaida, because if the mighty works had been done in Tyre and Sidon which have been done in you, they would long ago have repented in dust and ashes." [2] But can we say that even the Tyrians and Sidonians would have refused to believe such mighty works done among them, or would not have believed them if they had been done, when the Lord Himself bears witness to them that they would have repented with great humility if those signs of divine power had been done among them? And yet in the day of judgment they will be punished; although with a less punishment than those cities which would not believe the mighty works done in them. For the Lord goes on to say, "Nevertheless, I say unto you, it shall be more tolerable for Tyre and Sidon in the day of judgment than for you." [3] Therefore the former shall be punished with greater severity, the latter with less; but yet they shall be punished. Again, if the dead are judged even in respect of deeds which they would have done if they had lived, assuredly since these would have been believers if the gospel had been preached to them with so great miracles, they certainly ought not to be punished; but they will be punished. It is therefore false that the dead are judged in respect also of those things which they would have done if the gospel had reached them when they were

---

[1] Epistle 102, question 2; see the first volume of this series, p. 418.     [2] Luke x. 13.     [3] Matt. xi. 22.

alive. And if this is false, there is no ground for saying, concerning infants who perish because they die without baptism, that this happens in their case deservedly, because God foreknew that if they should live and the gospel should be preached to them, they would hear it with unbelief. It remains, therefore, that they are kept bound by original sin alone, and for this alone they go into condemnation; and we see that in others in the same case this is not remitted, except by the gratuitous grace of God in regeneration; and that, by His secret yet righteous judgment — because there is no unrighteousness with God — that some, who even after baptism will perish by evil living, are yet kept in this life until they perish, who would not have perished if bodily death had forestalled their lapse into sin, and so come to their help. Because no dead man is judged by the good or evil things which he would have done if he had not died, otherwise the Tyrians and Sidonians would not have suffered the penalties according to what they did; but rather according to those things that they would have done, if those evangelical mighty works had been done in them, they would have obtained salvation by great repentance, and by the faith of Christ.

CHAP. 24 [X.] — IT MAY BE OBJECTED THAT THE PEOPLE OF TYRE AND SIDON MIGHT, IF THEY HAD HEARD, HAVE BELIEVED, AND HAVE SUBSEQUENTLY LAPSED FROM THEIR FAITH.

A certain catholic disputant of no mean reputation so expounded this passage of the gospel as to say, that the Lord foreknew that the Tyrians and Sidonians would have afterwards departed from the faith, although they had believed the miracles done among them; and that in mercy He did not work those miracles there, because they would have been liable to severer punishment if they had forsaken the faith which they had once held, than if they had at no time held it. In which opinion of a learned and exceedingly acute man, why am I now concerned to say what is still reasonably to be asked, when even this opinion serves me for the purpose at which I aim? For if the Lord in His mercy did not do mighty works among them, since by these works they might possibly become believers, so that they might not be more severely punished when they should subsequently become unbelievers, as He foreknew that they would, — it is sufficiently and plainly shown that no dead person is judged for those sins which He foreknew that he would have done, if in some manner he were not helped not to do them; just as Christ is said to have come to the aid of the Tyrians and Sidonians, if that opinion be true, who He would rather should not come to the faith at all, than that by a much greater wickedness they should depart from the faith, as, if they had come to it, He foresaw they would have done. Although if it be said, "Why was it not provided that they should rather believe, and this gift should be bestowed on them, that before they forsook the faith they should depart from this life"? I am ignorant what reply can be made. For he who says that to those who would forsake their faith it would have been granted, as a kindness, that they should not begin to have what, by a more serious impiety, they would subsequently forsake, sufficiently indicates that a man is not judged by that which it is foreknown he would have done ill, if by any act of kindness he may be prevented from doing it. Therefore it is an advantage also to him who is taken away, lest wickedness should alter his understanding. But why this advantage should not have been given to the Tyrians and Sidonians, that they might believe and be taken away, lest wickedness should alter their understanding, he perhaps might answer who was pleased in such a way to solve the above question; but, as far as concerns what I am discussing, I see it to be enough that, even according to that very opinion, men are shown not to be judged in respect of those things which they have not done, even although they may have been foreseen as certain to have done them. However, as I have said, let us think shame even to refute this opinion, whereby sins are supposed to be punished in people who die or have died because they have been foreknown as certain to do them if they had lived; lest we also may seem to have thought it to be of some importance, although we would rather repress it by argument than pass it over in silence.

CHAP. 25 [XI.] — GOD'S WAYS, BOTH IN MERCY AND JUDGMENT, PAST FINDING OUT.

Accordingly, as says the apostle, "It is not of him that willeth, nor of him that runneth, but of God that showeth mercy,"[1] who both comes to the help of such infants as He will, although they neither will nor run, since He chose them in Christ before the foundation of the world as those to whom He intended to give His grace freely, — that is, with no merits of theirs, either of faith or of works, preceding; and does not come to the help of those who are more mature, although He foresaw that they would believe His miracles if they should be done among them, because He wills not to come to their help, since in His predestination He, secretly indeed, but yet righteously, has otherwise determined concerning them. For "there is no unrighteousness with God;"[2] but "His judgments are unsearchable, and His ways are past finding out; all the ways of the Lord are mercy and truth."[3]

---

[1] Rom. ix. 16.          [2] Rom. ix. 14.          [3] Ps. xxv. 10.

Therefore the mercy is past finding out by which He has mercy on whom He will, no merits of his own preceding; and the truth is unsearchable by which He hardeneth whom He will, even although his merits may have preceded, but merits for the most part common to him with the man on whom He has mercy. As of two twins, of which one is taken and the other left, the end is unequal, while the deserts are common, yet in these the one is in such wise delivered by God's great goodness, that the other is condemned by no injustice of God's. For is there unrighteousness with God? Away with the thought! but His ways are past finding out. Therefore let us believe in His mercy in the case of those who are delivered, and in His truth in the case of those who are punished, without any hesitation; and let us not endeavour to look into that which is inscrutable, nor to trace that which cannot be found out. Because out of the mouth of babes and sucklings He perfects His praise,[1] so that what we see in those whose deliverance is preceded by no good deservings of theirs, and in those whose condemnation is only preceded by original sin, common alike to both, — this we by no means shrink from as occurring in the case of grown-up people, that is, because we do not think either that grace is given to any one according to his own merits, or that any one is punished except for his own merits, whether they are alike who are delivered and who are punished, or have unequal degrees of evil; so that he who thinketh he standeth may take heed lest he fall, and he who glorieth may glory not in himself, but in the Lord.

CHAP. 26. — THE MANICHEANS DO NOT RECEIVE ALL THE BOOKS OF THE OLD TESTAMENT, AND OF THE NEW ONLY THOSE THAT THEY CHOOSE.

But wherefore is "the case of infants not allowed," as you write, "to be alleged as an example for their elders," by men who do not hesitate to affirm against the Pelagians that there is original sin, which entered by one man into the world, and that from one all have gone into condemnation?[2] This, the Manicheans, too, do not receive, who not only reject all the Scriptures of the Old Testament as of authority, but even receive those which belong to the New Testament in such a manner as that each man, by his own prerogative as it were, or rather by his own sacrilege, takes what he likes, and rejects what he does not like, — in opposition to whom I treated in my writings on Free Will, whence they think that they have a ground of objection against me. I have been unwilling to deal plainly with the very laborious questions that occurred, lest my work should become too

long, in a case which, as opposed to such perverse men, I could not have the assistance of the authority of the sacred Scriptures. And I was able, — as I actually did, whether anything of the divine testimonies might be true or not, seeing that I did not definitely introduce them into the argument, — nevertheless, by certain reasoning, to conclude that God in all things is to be praised, without any necessity of believing, as they would have us, that there are two co-eternal, confounded substances of good and evil.

CHAP. 27. — REFERENCE TO THE "RETRACTATIONS."

Finally, in the first book of the *Retractations*,[3] which work of mine you have not yet read, when I had come to the reconsidering of those same books, that is, on the subject of Free Will, I thus spoke: "In these books," I say, "many things were so discussed that on the occurring of some questions which either I was not able to elucidate, or which required a long discussion at once, they were so deferred as that from either side, or from all sides, of those questions in which what was most in harmony with the truth did not appear, yet my reasoning might be conclusive for this, namely, that whichever of them might be true, God might be believed, or even be shown, to be worthy of praise. Because that discussion was undertaken for the sake of those who deny that the origin of evil is derived from the free choice of the will, and contend that God, — if He be so, — as the Creator of all natures, is worthy of blame; desiring in that manner, according to the error of their impiety (for they are Manicheans), to introduce a certain immutable nature of evil co-eternal with God." Also, after a little time, in another place I say: "Then it was said, From this misery, most righteously inflicted on sinners, God's grace delivers, because man of his own accord, that is, by free will, could fall, but could not also rise. To this misery of just condemnation belong the ignorance and the difficulty which every man suffers from the beginning of his birth, and no one is delivered from that evil except by the grace of God. And this misery the Pelagians will not have to descend from a just condemnation, because they deny original sin; although even if the ignorance and difficulty were the natural beginnings of man, God would not even thus deserve to be reproached, but to be praised, as I have argued in the same third book.[4] Which argument must be regarded as against the Manicheans, who do not receive the holy Scriptures of the Old Testament, in which original sin is narrated; and whatever thence is read in the apostolic epistles, they contend was introduced

---

[1] Ps viii. 2.
[2] See the Letter of Hilary in Augustin's *Letters*, 226, ch. 8.
[3] *Retractations*, Book i. ch. 9.
[4] *Retractations*, Book i. ch. 20.

with a detestable impudence by the corrupters of the Scriptures, assuming that it was not said by the apostles. But against the Pelagians that must be maintained which both Scriptures commend, as they profess to receive them." These things I said in my first book of *Retractations,* when I was reconsidering the books on Free Will. Nor, indeed, were these things all that were said by me there about these books, but there were many others also, which I thought it would be tedious to insert in this work for you, and not necessary; and this I think you also will judge when you have read all. Although, therefore, in the third book on Free Will I have in such wise argued concerning infants, that even if what the Pelagians say were true, — that ignorance and difficulty, without which no man is born, are elements, not punishments, of our nature, — still the Manicheans would be overcome, who will have it that the two natures, to wit, of good and evil, are co-eternal. Is, therefore, the faith to be called in question or forsaken, which the catholic Church maintains against those very Pelagians, asserting as she does that it is original sin, the guilt of which, contracted by generation, must be remitted by regeneration? And if they confess this with us, so that we may at once, in this matter of the Pelagians, destroy error, why do they think that it must be doubted that God can deliver even infants, to whom He gives His grace by the sacrament of baptism, from the power of darkness, and translate them into the kingdom of the Son of His love?[1] In the fact, therefore, that He gives that grace to some, and does not give it to others, why will they not sing to the Lord His mercy and judgment?[2] Why, however, is it given to these, rather than to those, — who has known the mind of the Lord? who is able to look into unsearchable things? who to trace out that which is past finding out?

### CHAP. 28 [XII.] — GOD'S GOODNESS AND RIGHTEOUSNESS SHOWN IN ALL.

It is therefore settled that God's grace is not given according to the deserts of the recipients, but according to the good pleasure of His will, to the praise and glory of His own grace; so that he who glorieth may by no means glory in himself, but in the Lord, who gives to those men to whom He will, because He is merciful, what if, however, He does not give, He is righteous: and He does not give to whom He will not, that He may make known the riches of His glory to the vessels of mercy.[3] For by giving to some what they do not deserve, He has certainly willed that His grace should be gratuitous, and thus genuine grace; by not giving to all, He has shown what all deserve. Good in His goodness to some,

righteous in the punishment of others; both good in respect of all, because it is good when that which is due is rendered, and righteous in respect of all, since that which is not due is given without wrong to any one.

### CHAP. 29. — GOD'S TRUE GRACE COULD BE DEFENDED EVEN IF THERE WERE NO ORIGINAL SIN, AS PELAGIUS MAINTAINS.

But God's grace, that is, true grace without merits, is maintained, even if infants, when baptized, according to the view of the Pelagians, are not plucked out of the power of darkness, because they are held guilty of no sin, as the Pelagians think, but are only transferred into the Lord's kingdom: for even thus, without any good merits, the kingdom is given to those to whom it is given; and without any evil merits it is not given to them to whom it is not given. And this we are in the habit of saying in opposition to the same Pelagians, when they object to us that we attribute God's grace to fate, when we say that it is given not in respect to our merits. For they themselves rather attribute God's grace to fate in the case of infants, if they say that when there is no merit it is fate.[4] Certainly, even according to the Pelagians themselves, no merits can be found in infants to cause that some of them should be admitted into the kingdom, and others should be alienated from the kingdom. But now, just as in order to show that God's grace is not given according to our merits, I preferred to maintain this truth in accordance with both opinions, — both in accordance with our own, to wit, who say that infants are bound by original sin, and according to that of the Pelagians, who deny that there is original sin, and yet I cannot on that account doubt that infants have what He can pardon them who saves His people from their sins: so in the third book on Free Will, according to both views, I have withstood the Manicheans, whether ignorance and difficulty be punishments or elements of nature without which no man is born; and yet I hold one of these views. There, moreover, it is sufficiently evidently declared by me, that that is not the nature of man as he was ordained, but his punishment as condemned.

### CHAP. 30. — AUGUSTIN CLAIMS THE RIGHT TO GROW IN KNOWLEDGE.

Therefore it is in vain that it is prescribed to me from that old book of mine, that I may not argue the case as I ought to argue it in respect of infants; and that thence I may not persuade my opponents by the light of a manifest truth, that God's grace is not given according to men's merits. For if, when I began my books con-

---

[1] Col. i. 13.　　[2] Ps. c. 1.　　[3] Rom. ix. 23.

[4] See above, *Against Two Letters of the Pelagians,* Book ii. chs. 11, 12.

cerning Free Will as a layman, and finished them as a presbyter, I still doubted of the condemnation of infants not born again, and of the deliverance of infants that were born again, no one, as I think, would be so unfair and envious as to hinder my progress, and judge that I must continue in that uncertainty. But it can more correctly be understood that it ought to be believed that I did not doubt in that matter, for the reason that they against whom my purpose was directed seemed to me in such wise to be rebutted, as that whether there was a punishment of original sin in infants, according to the truth, or whether there was not, as some mistaken people think, yet in no degree should such a confusion of the two natures be believed in, to wit, of good and evil, as the error of the Manicheans introduces. Be it therefore far from us so to forsake the case of infants as to say to ourselves that it is uncertain whether, being regenerated in Christ, if they die in infancy they pass into eternal salvation; but that, not being regenerated, they pass into the second death. Because that which is written, " By one man sin entered into the world, and death by sin, and so death passed upon all men," [1] cannot be rightly understood in any other manner; nor from that eternal death which is most righteously repaid to sin does any deliver any one, small or great, save He who, for the sake of remitting our sins, both original and personal, died without any sin of His own, either original or personal. But why some rather than others? Again and again we say, and do not shrink from it, " O man, who art thou that repliest against God ? " [2] " His judgments are unsearchable, and His ways past finding out." [3] And let us add this, " Seek not out the things that are too high for thee, and search not the things that are above thy strength." [4]

CHAP. 31. — INFANTS ARE NOT JUDGED ACCORDING TO THAT WHICH THEY ARE FOREKNOWN AS LIKELY TO DO IF THEY SHOULD LIVE.

For you see, beloved, how absurd it is, and how foreign from soundness of faith and sincerity of truth, for us to say that infants, when they die, should be judged according to those things which they are foreknown to be going to do if they should live. For to this opinion, from which certainly every human feeling, on however little reason it may be founded, and especially every Christian feeling, revolts, they are compelled to advance who have chosen in such wise to be withdrawn from the error of the Pelagians as still to think that they must believe, and, moreover, must profess in argument, that the grace of God, through Jesus Christ our Lord,

by which alone after the fall of the first man, in whom we all fell, help is afforded to us, is given according to our merits. And this belief Pelagius himself, before the Eastern bishops as judges, condemned in fear of his own condemnation. And if this be not said of the good or bad works of those who have died, which they would have done if they had lived, — and thus of no works, and works that would never exist, even in the foreknowledge of God, — if this, therefore, be not said, and you see under how great a mistake it is said, what will remain but that we confess, when the darkness of contention is removed, that the grace of God is not given according to our merits, which position the catholic Church defends against the Pelagian heresy ; and that we see this in more evident truth especially in infants? For God is not compelled by fate to come to the help of these infants, and not to come to the help of those, — since the case is alike to both. Or shall we think that human affairs in the case of infants are not managed by Divine Providence, but by fortuitous chances, when rational souls are either to be condemned or delivered, although, indeed, not a sparrow falls to the ground without the will of our Father which is in heaven? [5] Or must we so attribute it to the negligence of parents that infants die without baptism, as that heavenly judgments have nothing to do with it ; as if they themselves who in this way die badly had of their own will chosen the negligent parents for themselves of whom they were born? What shall I say when an infant expires some time before he can possibly be advantaged by the ministry of baptism? For often when the parents are eager and the ministers prepared for giving baptism to the infants, it still is not given, because God does not choose ; since He has not kept it in this life for a little while in order that baptism might be given it. What, moreover, when sometimes aid could be afforded by baptism to the children of unbelievers, that they should not go into perdition, and could not be afforded to the children of believers? In which case it is certainly shown that there is no acceptance of persons with God ; otherwise He would rather deliver the children of His worshippers than the children of His enemies.

CHAP. 32 [XIII.] — THE INSCRUTABILITY OF GOD'S FREE PURPOSES.

But now, since we are now treating of the gift of perseverance, why is it that aid is afforded to the person about to die who is not baptized, while to the baptized person about to fall, aid is not afforded, so as to die before? Unless, perchance, we shall still listen to that absurdity by

---

[1] Rom. v. 12.　　[2] Rom. ix. 20.　　[3] Rom. xi. 33.
[4] Ecclus. iii. 21.

[5] Matt. x. 29.

which it is said that it is of no advantage to any one to die before his fall, because he will be judged according to those actions which God foreknew that he would have done if he had lived. Who can hear with patience this perversity, so violently opposed to the soundness of the faith? Who can bear it? And yet they are driven to say this who do not confess that God's grace is not bestowed in respect of our deservings. They, however, who will not say that any one who has died is judged according to those things which God foreknew that he would have done if he had lived, considering with how manifest a falsehood and how great an absurdity this would be said, have no further reason to say, what the Church condemned in the Pelagians, and caused to be condemned by Pelagius himself, — that the grace of God, namely, is given according to our merits, — when they see some infants not regenerated taken from this life to eternal death, and others regenerated, to eternal life; and those themselves that are regenerated, some going hence, persevering even to the end, and others kept in this life even until they fall, who certainly would not have fallen if they had departed hence before their lapse; and again some falling, but not departing from this life until they return, who certainly would have perished if they had departed before their return.

CHAP. 33. — GOD GIVES BOTH INITIATORY AND PERSEVERING GRACE ACCORDING TO HIS OWN WILL.

From all which it is shown with sufficient clearness that the grace of God, which both begins a man's faith and which enables it to persevere unto the end, is not given according to our merits, but is given according to His own most secret and at the same time most righteous, wise, and beneficent will; since those whom He predestinated, them He also called,[1] with that calling of which it is said, "The gifts and calling of God are without repentance."[2] To which calling there is no man that can be said by men with any certainty of affirmation to belong, until he has departed from this world; but in this life of man, which is a state of trial upon the earth,[3] he who seems to stand must take heed lest he fall.[4] Since (as I have already said before)[5] those who will not persevere are, by the most foreseeing will of God, mingled with those who will persevere, for the reason that we may learn not to mind high things, but to consent to the lowly, and may "work out our own salvation with fear and trembling; for it is God that worketh in us both to will and to do for His good pleasure."[6] We therefore will, but God worketh in us to will also. We there-

fore work, but God worketh in us to work also for His good pleasure. This is profitable for us both to believe and to say, — this is pious, this is true, that our confession be lowly and submissive, and that all should be given to God. Thinking, we believe; thinking, we speak; thinking, we do whatever we do;[7] but, in respect of what concerns the way of piety and the true worship of God, we are not sufficient to think anything as of ourselves, but our sufficiency is of God.[8] For "our heart and our thoughts are not in our own power;" whence the same Ambrose who says this says also: "But who is so blessed as in his heart always to rise upwards? And how can this be done without divine help? Assuredly, by no means. Finally," he says, "the same Scripture affirms above, 'Blessed is the man whose help is of Thee; O Lord,[9] ascent is in his heart.'"[10] Assuredly, Ambrose was not only enabled to say this by reading in the holy writings, but as of such a man is to be without doubt believed, he felt it also in his own heart. Therefore, as is said in the sacraments of believers, that we should lift up our hearts to the Lord, is God's gift; for which gift they to whom this is said are admonished by the priest after this word to give thanks to our Lord God Himself; and they answer that it is "meet and right so to do."[11] For, since our heart is not in our own power, but is lifted up by the divine help, so that it ascends and takes cognizance of those things which are above,[12] where Christ is sitting at the right hand of God, and not those things that are upon the earth, to whom are thanks to be given for so great a gift as this unless to our Lord God who doeth this, — who in so great kindness has chosen us by delivering us from the abyss of this world, and has predestinated us before the foundation of the world?

CHAP. 34 [XIV.] — THE DOCTRINE OF PREDESTINATION NOT OPPOSED TO THE ADVANTAGE OF PREACHING.

But they say that the "definition of predestination is opposed to the advantage of preaching,"[13] — as if, indeed, it were opposed to the preaching of the apostle! Did not that teacher of the heathen so often, in faith and truth, both commend predestination, and not cease to preach the word of God? Because he said, "It is God that worketh in you both to will and to

---

[1] Rom. viii. 30.   [2] Rom. xi. 29.   [3] Job vii. 1.
[4] 1 Cor. x. 12.   [5] Above, ch. xiv.   [6] Phil. ii. 12, 13.

[7] 2 Cor. iii. 5.
[8] Ambrose, *On Flight from the World*, ch. 1.
[9] Ps. lxxxiv. 5 [LXX.].
[10] LXX.: "In his heart he has purposed to go up."
[11] [An allusion to the *Sursum Corda* in the "Preface" of the Communion service. For its history see Smith and Cheetham's *Dictionary of Christian Antiquities*, p. 1693. Cyprian in his treatise on the Lord's Prayer already mentions it. It still has a place in the liturgies of the Church of England and the Protestant Episcopal Church in the United States. — W.]
[12] Col. iii. 1.   [13] In the Letters of Hilary and Prosper.

do for His good pleasure," [1] did he not also exhort that we should both will and do what is pleasing to God? or because he said, "He who hath begun a good work in you shall carry it on even unto the day of Christ Jesus," [2] did he on that account cease to persuade men to begin and to persevere unto the end? Doubtless, our Lord Himself commanded men to believe, and said, "Believe in God, believe also in me:" [3] and yet His opinion is not therefore false, nor is His definition idle when He says, "No man cometh unto me" — that is, no man believeth in me — "except it has been given him of my Father." [4] Nor, again, because this definition is true, is the former precept vain. Why, therefore, do we think the definition of predestination useless to preaching, to precept, to exhortation, to rebuke, — all which things the divine Scripture repeats frequently, — seeing that the same Scripture commends this doctrine?

## CHAP. 35. — WHAT PREDESTINATION IS.

Will any man dare to say that God did not foreknow those to whom He would give to believe, or whom He would give to His Son, that of them He should lose none? [5] And certainly, if He foreknew these things, He as certainly foreknew His own kindnesses, wherewith He condescends to deliver us. This is the predestination of the saints, — nothing else; to wit, the foreknowledge and the preparation of God's kindnesses, whereby they are most certainly delivered, whoever they are that are delivered. But where are the rest left by the righteous divine judgment except in the mass of ruin, where the Tyrians and the Sidonians were left? who, moreover, might have believed if they had seen Christ's wonderful miracles. But since it was not given to them to believe, the means of believing also were denied them. From which fact it appears that some have in their understanding itself a naturally divine gift of intelligence, by which they may be moved to the faith, if they either hear the words or behold the signs congruous to their minds; and yet if, in the higher judgment of God, they are not by the predestination of grace separated from the mass of perdition, neither those very divine words nor deeds are applied to them by which they might believe if they only heard or saw such things. Moreover, in the same mass of ruin the Jews were left, because they could not believe such great and eminent mighty works as were done in their sight. For the gospel has not been silent about the reason why they could not believe, since it says: "But though He had done such great miracles before them, yet they believed not on

Him; that the saying of Isaiah the prophet might be fulfilled which he spake, [6] Lord, who hath believed our report, and to whom hath the arm of the Lord been revealed? And, therefore, they could not believe, because that Isaiah said again, [7] He hath blinded their eyes and hardened their heart, that they should not see with their eyes, nor understand with their heart, and be converted, and I should heal them." [8] Therefore the eyes of the Tyrians and Sidonians were not so blinded nor was their heart so hardened, since they would have believed if they had seen such mighty works as the Jews saw. But it did not profit them that they were able to believe, because they were not predestinated by Him whose judgments are inscrutable and His ways past finding out. Neither would inability to believe have been a hindrance to them, if they had been so predestinated as that God should illuminate those blind eyes, and should will to take away the stony heart from those hardened ones. But what the Lord said of the Tyrians and Sidonians may perchance be understood in another way: that no one nevertheless comes to Christ unless it were given him, and that it is given to those who are chosen in Him before the foundation of the world, he confesses beyond a doubt who hears the divine utterance, not with the deaf ears of the flesh, but with the ears of the heart; and yet this predestination, which is plainly enough unfolded even by the words of the gospels, did not prevent the Lord's saying as well in respect of the commencement, what I have a little before mentioned, "Believe in God; believe also in me," as in respect of perseverance, "A man ought always to pray, and not to faint." [9] For they hear these things and do them to whom it is given; but they do them not, whether they hear or do not hear, to whom it is not given. Because, "To you," said He, "it is given to know the mystery of the kingdom of heaven, but to them it is not given." [10] Of these, the one refers to the mercy, the other to the judgment of Him to whom our soul cries, "I will sing of mercy and judgment unto Thee, O Lord." [11]

## CHAP. 36. — THE PREACHING OF THE GOSPEL AND THE PREACHING OF PREDESTINATION THE TWO PARTS OF ONE MESSAGE.

Therefore, by the preaching of predestination, the preaching of a persevering and progressive faith is not to be hindered; and thus they may hear what is necessary to whom it is given that they should obey. For how shall they hear without a preacher? Neither, again, is the preaching of a progressive faith which continues even to the end to hinder the preaching of predestination, so that he who is living faithfully and

---

[1] Phil. ii. 13.　　[2] Phil. i. 6.　　[3] John xiv. 1.
[4] John vi. 66.　　[5] John xviii. 9.

[6] Isa. liii. 1.　　[7] Isa. vi. 10.　　[8] John xii. 37 ff.
[9] Luke xviii. 1.　　[10] Matt. xiii. 11.　　[11] Ps. ci. 1.

obediently may not be lifted up by that very obedience, as if by a benefit of his own, not received ; but that he that glorieth may glory in the Lord. For " we must boast in nothing, since nothing is our own." And this, Cyprian most faithfully saw and most fearlessly explained, and thus he pronounced predestination to be most assured.[1] For if we must boast in nothing, seeing that nothing is our own, certainly we must not boast of the most persevering obedience. Nor is it so to be called our own, as if it were not given to us from above. And, therefore, it is God's gift, which, by the confession of all Christians, God foreknew that He would give to His people, who were called by that calling whereof it was said, " The gifts and calling of God are without repentance."[2] This, then, is the predestination which we faithfully and humbly preach. Nor yet did the same teacher and doer, who both believed on Christ and most perseveringly lived in holy obedience, even to suffering for Christ, cease on that account to preach the gospel, to exhort to faith and to pious manners, and to that very perseverance to the end, because he said, " We must boast in nothing, since nothing is our own ; " and here he declared without ambiguity the true grace of God, that is, that which is not given in respect of our merits ; and since God foreknew that He would give it, predestination was announced beyond a doubt by these words of Cyprian ; and if this did not prevent Cyprian from preaching obedience, it certainly ought not to prevent us.

CHAP. 37. — EARS TO HEAR ARE A WILLINGNESS TO OBEY.

Although, therefore, we say that obedience is the gift of God, we still exhort men to it. But to those who obediently hear the exhortation of truth is given the gift of God itself — that is, to hear obediently ; while to those who do not thus hear it is not given. For it was not some one only, but Christ who said, " No man cometh unto me, except it were given him of my Father ; "[3] and, " To you it is given to know the mystery of the kingdom of heaven, but to them it is not given."[4] And concerning continence He says, " Not all receive this saying, but they to whom it is given."[5] And when the apostle would exhort married people to conjugal chastity, he says, " I would that all men were even as I myself ; but every man hath his proper gift of God, one after this manner, another after that ; "[6] where he plainly shows not only that continence is a gift of God, but even the chastity of those who are married. And although these things are true, we still exhort to them as much as is given to any one of us to be able to exhort, because this also is His gift in whose hand are both ourselves and our discourses. Whence also says the apostle, " According to this grace of God which is given unto me, as a wise architect, I have laid the foundation."[7] And in another place he says, " Even as the Lord hath given to every man : I have planted, Apollos has watered, but God has given the increase. Therefore neither is he that planteth anything, nor he that watereth, but God that giveth the increase."[8] And thus as only he preaches and exhorts rightly who has received this gift, so assuredly he who obediently hears him who rightly exhorts and preaches is he who has received this gift. Hence is what the Lord said, when, speaking to those who had their fleshly ears open, He nevertheless told them, " He that hath ears to hear let him hear ; "[9] which beyond a doubt he knew that not all had. And from whom they have, whosoever they be that have them, the Lord Himself shows when He says, " I will give them a heart to know me, and ears to hear."[10] Therefore, having ears is itself the gift of obeying, so that they who had that came to Him, to whom " no one comes unless it were given to him of His Father." Therefore we exhort and preach, but they who have ears to hear obediently hear us, while in them who have them not, it comes to pass what is written, that hearing they do not hear, — hearing, to wit, with the bodily sense, they do not hear with the assent of the heart. But why these should have ears to hear, and those have them not, — that is, why to these it should be given by the Father to come to the Son, while to those it should not be given, — who has known the mind of the Lord, or who has been His counsellor ? Or who art thou, O man, that repliest against God ? Must that which is manifest be denied, because that which is hidden cannot be comprehended ? Shall we, I say, declare that what we see to be so is not so, because we cannot find out why it is so ?

CHAP. 38 [XV.] — AGAINST THE PREACHING OF PREDESTINATION THE SAME OBJECTIONS MAY BE ALLEGED AS AGAINST PREDESTINATION.

But they say, as you write : " That no one can be aroused by the incentives of rebuke if it be said in the assembly of the Church to the multitude of hearers : The definite meaning of God's will concerning predestination stands in such wise, that some of you will receive the will to obey and will come out of unbelief unto faith, or will receive perseverance and abide in the faith ; but others who are lingering in the delight of sins have not yet arisen, for the reason that the aid of pitying grace has not yet

1 Cyprian, *Testimonies,* iii. 4; see *The Ante-Nicene Fathers,* v. p. 528.
2 Rom. xi. 29.          3 John vi. 66.          4 Matt. xiii. 11.
5 Matt. xix. 11.          6 1 Cor. vii. 7.          7 1 Cor. iii. 10.          8 1 Cor. iii. 5.          9 Luke viii. 8.
10 Baruch ii. 31.

indeed raised you up. But yet, if there are any whom by His grace He has predestinated to be chosen, who are not yet called, ye shall receive that grace by which you may will and be chosen; and if any obey, if ye are predestinated to be rejected, the strength to obey shall be withdrawn from you, so that you may cease to obey." Although these things may be said, they ought not so to deter us from confessing the true grace of God, — that is, the grace which is not given to us in respect of our merits, — and from confessing the predestination of the saints in accordance therewith, even as we are not deterred from confessing God's foreknowledge, although one should thus speak to the people concerning it, and say: "Whether you are now living righteously or unrighteously, you shall be such by and by as the Lord has foreknown that you will be, — either good, if He has foreknown you as good, or bad, if He has foreknown you as bad." For if on the hearing of this some should be turned to torpor and slothfulness, and from striving should go headlong to lust after their own desires, is it therefore to be counted that what has been said about the foreknowledge of God is false? If God has foreknown that they will be good, will they not be good, whatever be the depth of evil in which they are now engaged? And if He has foreknown them evil, will they not be evil, whatever goodness may now be discerned in them? There was a man in our monastery, who, when the brethren rebuked him for doing some things that ought not to be done, and for not doing some things that ought to be done, replied, "Whatever I may now be, I shall be such as God has foreknown that I shall be." And this man certainly both said what was true, and was not profited by this truth for good, but so far made way in evil as to desert the society of the monastery, and become a dog returned to his vomit; and, nevertheless, it is uncertain what he is yet to become. For the sake of souls of this kind, then, is the truth which is spoken about God's foreknowledge either to be denied or to be kept back, — at such times, for instance, when, if it is not spoken, other errors are incurred?

## CHAP. 39 [XVI.] — PRAYER AND EXHORTATION.

There are some, moreover, who either do not pray at all, or pray coldly, because, from the Lord's words, they have learnt that God knows what is necessary for us before we ask it of Him. Must the truth of this declaration be given up, or shall we think that it should be erased from the gospel because of such people? Nay, since it is manifest that God has prepared some things to be given even to those who do not pray for them, such as the beginning of faith, and other things not to be given except to those who pray

for them, such as perseverance even unto the end, certainly he who thinks that he has this latter from himself does not pray to have it. Therefore we must take care lest, while we are afraid of exhortation growing lukewarm, prayer should be stifled and arrogance stimulated.

## CHAP. 40. — WHEN THE TRUTH MUST BE SPOKEN, WHEN KEPT BACK.

Therefore let the truth be spoken, especially when any question impels us to declare it; and let them receive it who are able, lest, perchance, while we are silent on account of those who cannot receive it, they be not only defrauded of the truth but be taken captive by falsehood, who are able to receive the truth whereby falsehood may be avoided. For it is easy, nay, and it is useful, that some truth should be kept back because of those who are incapable of apprehending it. For whence is that word of our Lord: "I have yet many things to say unto you, but ye cannot bear them now"?[1] And that of the apostle: "I could not speak unto you as unto spiritual, but as unto carnal: as if unto babes in Christ I have given you to drink milk, and not meat, for hitherto ye were not able, neither yet indeed now are ye able"?[2] Although, in a certain manner of speaking, it might happen that what is said should be both milk to infants and meat for grown-up persons. As "in the beginning was the Word, and the Word was with God, and the Word was God,"[3] what Christian can keep it back? Who can receive it? Or what in sound doctrine can be found more comprehensive? And yet this is not kept back either from infants or from grown-up people, nor is it hidden from infants by those who are mature. But the reason of keeping back the truth is one, the necessity of speaking the truth is another. It would be a tedious business to inquire into or to put down all the reasons for keeping back the truth; of which, nevertheless, there is this one, — lest we should make those who do not understand worse, while wishing to make those who do understand more learned; although these latter do not become more learned when we withhold any such thing on the one hand, but also do not become worse. When, however, a truth is of such a nature that he who cannot receive it is made worse by our speaking it, and he who can receive it is made worse by our silence concerning it, what do we think is to be done? Must we not speak the truth, that he who can receive it may receive it, rather than keep silence, so that not only neither may receive it, but that even he who is more intelligent should himself be made worse? For if he should hear and receive it, by his means also

---

[1] John xvi. 12.   [2] 1 Cor. iii. 1.   [3] John i. 1.

many might learn. For in proportion as he is more capable of learning, he is the more fitted for teaching others. The enemy of grace presses on and urges in all ways to make us believe that grace is given according to our deservings, and thus grace is no more grace ; and are we unwilling to say what we can say by the testimony of Scripture? Do we fear, forsooth, to offend by our speaking him who is not able to receive the truth? and are we not afraid lest by our silence he who can receive the truth may be involved in falsehood?

CHAP. 41. — PREDESTINATION DEFINED AS ONLY GOD'S DISPOSING OF EVENTS IN HIS FOREKNOWLEDGE.

For either predestination must be preached, in the way and degree in which the Holy Scripture plainly declares it, so that in the predestinated the gifts and calling of God may be without repentance ; or it must be avowed that God's grace is given according to our merits, — which is the opinion of the Pelagians ; although that opinion of theirs, as I have often said already, may be read in the Proceedings of the Eastern bishops to have been condemned by the lips of Pelagius himself.[1] Further, those on whose account I am discoursing are only removed from the heretical perversity of the Pelagians, inasmuch as, although they will not confess that they who by God's grace are made obedient and so abide, are predestinated, they still confess, nevertheless, that this grace precedes their will to whom it is given ; in such a way certainly as that grace may not be thought to be given freely, as the truth declares, but rather according to the merits of a preceding will, as the Pelagian error says, in contradiction to the truth. Therefore, also, grace precedes faith ; otherwise, if faith precedes grace, beyond a doubt will also precedes it, because there cannot be faith without will. But if grace precedes faith because it precedes will, certainly it precedes all obedience ; it also precedes love, by which alone God is truly and pleasantly obeyed. And all these things grace works in him to whom it is given, and in whom it precedes all these things. [XVII.] Among these benefits there remains perseverance unto the end, which is daily asked for in vain from the Lord, if the Lord by His grace does not effect it in him whose prayers He hears. See now how foreign it is from the truth to deny that perseverance even to the end of this life is the gift of God ; since He Himself puts an end to this life when He wills, and if He puts an end before a fall that is threatening, He makes the man to persevere even unto the end. But more marvellous and more manifest to believers is the largess of God's goodness, that this grace is given even to infants, although there is no obedience at that age to which it may be given. To whomsoever, therefore, God gives His gifts, beyond a doubt He has foreknown that He will bestow them on them, and in His foreknowledge He has prepared them for them. Therefore, those whom He predestinated, them He also called with that calling which I am not reluctant often to make mention of, of which it is said, " The gifts and calling of God are without repentance." [2] For the ordering of His future works in His foreknowledge, which cannot be deceived and changed, is absolute, and is nothing but, predestination. But, as he whom God has foreknown to be chaste, although he may regard it as uncertain, so acts as to be chaste, so he whom He has predestinated to be chaste, although he may regard that as uncertain, does not, therefore, fail to act so as to be chaste because he hears that he is to be what he will be by the gift of God. Nay, rather, his love rejoices, and he is not puffed up as if he had not received it. Not only, therefore, is he not hindered from this work by the preaching of predestination, but he is even assisted to it, so that although he glories he may glory in the Lord.

CHAP. 42. — THE ADVERSARIES CANNOT DENY PREDESTINATION TO THOSE GIFTS OF GRACE WHICH THEY THEMSELVES ACKNOWLEDGE, AND THEIR EXHORTATIONS ARE NOT HINDERED BY THIS PREDESTINATION NEVERTHELESS.

And what I said of chastity, can be said also of faith, of piety, of love, of perseverance, and, not to enumerate single virtues, it may be said with the utmost truthfulness of all the obedience with which God is obeyed. But those who place only the beginning of faith and perseverance to the end in such wise in our power as not to regard them as God's gifts, nor to think that God works on our thoughts and wills so as that we may have and retain them, grant, nevertheless, that He gives other things, — since they are obtained from Him by the faith of the believer. Why are they not afraid that exhortation to these other things, and the preaching of these other things, should be hindered by the definition of predestination? Or, perchance, do they say that such things are not predestinated? Then they are not given by God, or He has not known that He would give them. Because, if they are both given, and He foreknew that He would give them, certainly He predestinated them. As, therefore, they themselves also exhort to chastity, charity, piety, and other things which they confess to be God's gifts, and cannot deny that they are also foreknown by Him, and

---

[1] See above, *On the Proceedings of Pelagius*, ch. 30.

[2] Rom. xi. 24.

therefore predestinated; nor do they say that their exhortations are hindered by the preaching of God's predestination, that is, by the preaching of God's foreknowledge of those future gifts of His: so they may see that neither are their exhortations to faith or to perseverance hindered, even although those very things may be said, as is the truth, to be gifts of God, and that those things are foreknown, that is, predestinated to be given; but let them rather see that by this preaching of predestination only that most pernicious error is hindered and overthrown, whereby it is said that the grace of God is given according to our deservings, so that he who glories may glory not in the Lord, but in himself.

CHAP. 43. — FURTHER DEVELOPMENT OF THE FOREGOING ARGUMENT.

And in order that I may more openly unfold this for the sake of those who are somewhat slow of apprehension, let those who are endowed with an intelligence that flies in advance bear with my delay. The Apostle James says, " If any of you lack wisdom, let him ask of God, who giveth to all men liberally and upbraideth not, and it shall be given him."[1] It is written also in the Proverbs of Solomon, " Because the Lord giveth wisdom."[2] And of continency it is read in the book of Wisdom, whose authority has been used by great and learned men who have commented upon the divine utterances long before us; there, therefore, it is read, " When I knew that no one can be continent unless God gives it, and that this was of wisdom, to know whose gift this was."[3] Therefore these are God's gifts, — that is, to say nothing of others, wisdom and continency. Let those also acquiesce: for they are not Pelagians, to contend against such a manifest truth as this with hard and heretical perversity. " But," say they, " that these things are given to us of God is obtained by faith, which has its beginning from us; " and both to begin to have this faith, and to abide in it even to the end, they contend is our own doing, as if we received it not from the Lord. This, beyond a doubt, is in contradiction to the apostle when he says, " For what hast thou that thou hast not received?"[4] It is in contradiction also to the saying of the martyr Cyprian, " That we must boast in nothing, since nothing is our own."[5] When we have said this, and many other things which it is wearisome to repeat, and have shown that both the commencement of faith and perseverance to the end are gifts of God; and that it is impossible that God should not foreknow any of His future gifts, as

well what should be given as to whom they should be given; and that thus those whom He delivers and crowns are predestinated by Him; they think it well to reply, " that the assertion of predestination is opposed to the advantage of preaching, for the reason that when this is heard no one can be stirred up by the incentives of rebuke." When they say this, " they are unwilling that it should be declared to men, that coming to the faith and abiding in the faith are God's gifts, lest despair rather than encouragement should appear to be suggested, inasmuch as they who hear think that it is uncertain to human ignorance on whom God bestows, or on whom He does not bestow, these gifts." Why, then, do they themselves also preach with us that wisdom and continency are God's gifts? But if, when these things are declared to be God's gifts, there is no hindrance of the exhortation with which we exhort men to be wise and continent; what is after all the reason for their thinking that the exhortation is hindered wherewith we exhort men to come to the faith, and to abide in it to the end, if these also are said to be God's gifts, as is proved by the Scriptures, which are His witnesses?

CHAP. 44. — EXHORTATION TO WISDOM, THOUGH WISDOM IS GOD'S GIFT.

Now, to say nothing more of continency, and to argue in this place of wisdom alone, certainly the Apostle James above mentioned says, " But the wisdom that is from above is first pure, then peaceable, modest, easy to be entreated, full of mercy and good fruits, inestimable, without simulation."[6] Do you not see, I beseech you, how this wisdom descends from the Father of Lights, laden with many and great benefits? Because, as the same apostle says, " Every excellent gift and every perfect gift is from above, and comes down from the Father of Lights."[6] Why, then — to set aside other matters — do we rebuke the impure and contentious, to whom we nevertheless preach that the gift of God is wisdom, pure and peaceable; and are not afraid that they should be influenced, by the uncertainty of the divine will, to find in this preaching more of despair than of exhortation; and that they should not be stirred up by the incentives of rebuke rather against us than against themselves, because we rebuke them for not having those things which we ourselves say are not produced by human will, but are given by the divine liberality? Finally, why did the preaching of this grace not deter the Apostle James from rebuking restless souls, and saying, " If ye have bitter envying, and contentions are in your hearts, glory not, and be not liars against the truth. This is not

[1] Jas. i. 5.        [2] Prov. ii. 6.        [3] Wisd. viii. 21.
[4] 1 Cor. iv. 7.
[5] Cyprian, *Testimonies*, iii. 4; see *The Ante-Nicene Fathers*, v. 528.

[6] Jas. iii. 17.

the wisdom that cometh down from above, but is earthly, animal, devilish; for where envying and contention are, there are inconstancy and every evil work "? [1] As, therefore, the restless are to be rebuked, both by the testimony of the divine declarations, and by those very impulses of ours which they have in common with ourselves; and is it no argument against this rebuke that we declare the peaceful wisdom, whereby the contentions are corrected and healed, to be the gift of God; unbelievers are in such wise to be rebuked, as those who do not abide in the faith, without any hindrance to that rebuke from the preaching of God's grace, although that preaching commends that very grace and the continuance in it as the gifts of God. Because, although wisdom is obtained from faith, even as James himself, when he had said, "If any of you lack wisdom, let him ask of God, who giveth to all liberally and upbraideth not, and it shall be given," [2] immediately added, "But let him ask in faith, nothing wavering:" it is not, nevertheless, because faith is given before it is asked for by him to whom it is given, that it must therefore be said not to be the gift of God, but to be of ourselves, because it is given to us without our asking for it! For the apostle very plainly says, "Peace be to the brethren, and love with faith, from God the Father and the Lord Jesus Christ." [3] From whom, therefore, are peace and love, from Him also is faith; wherefore, from Him we ask not only that it may be increased to those that possess it, but also that it may be given to those that possess it not.

CHAP. 45. — EXHORTATION TO OTHER GIFTS OF GOD IN LIKE MANNER.

Nor do those on whose account I am saying these things, who cry out that exhortation is checked by the preaching of predestination and grace, exhort to those gifts alone which they contend are not given by God, but are from ourselves, such as are the beginning of faith, and perseverance in it even to the end. This certainly they ought to do, in such a way as only to exhort unbelievers to believe, and believers to continue to believe. But those things which with us they do not deny to be God's gifts, so as that with us they demolish the error of the Pelagians, such as modesty, continence, patience, and other virtues that pertain to a holy life, and are obtained by faith from the Lord, they ought to show as needing to be prayed for, and to pray for only, either for themselves or others; but they ought not to exhort any one to strive after them and retain them. But when they exhort to these things, according to their ability, and confess that men ought to be exhorted, — cer-

tainly they show plainly enough that exhortations are not hindered by that preaching, whether they are exhortations to faith or to perseverance to the end, because we also preach that such things are God's gifts, and are not given by any man to himself, but are given by God.

CHAP. 46. — A MAN WHO DOES NOT PERSEVERE FAILS BY HIS OWN FAULT.

But it is said, "It is by his own fault that any one deserts the faith, when he yields and consents to the temptation which is the cause of his desertion of the faith." Who denies it? But because of this, perseverance in the faith is not to be said not to be a gift of God. For it is this that a man daily asks for when he says, "Lead us not into temptation;" [4] and if he is heard, it is this that he receives. And thus as he daily asks for perseverance, he assuredly places the hope of his perseverance not in himself, but in God. I, however, am loth to exaggerate the case with my words, but I rather leave it to them to consider, and see what it is of which they have persuaded themselves — to wit, "that by the preaching of predestination, more of despair than of exhortation is impressed upon the hearers." For this is to say that a man then despairs of his salvation when he has learned to place his hope not in himself, but in God, although the prophet cries, "Cursed is he who has his hope in man." [5]

CHAP. 47. — PREDESTINATION IS SOMETIMES SIGNIFIED UNDER THE NAME OF FOREKNOWLEDGE.

These gifts, therefore, of God, which are given to the elect who are called according to God's purpose, among which gifts is both the beginning of belief and perseverance in the faith to the termination of this life, as I have proved by such a concurrent testimony of reasons and authorities, — these gifts of God, I say, if there is no such predestination as I am maintaining, are not foreknown by God. But they are foreknown. This, therefore, is the predestination which I maintain. [XVIII.] Consequently sometimes the same predestination is signified also under the name of foreknowledge; as says the apostle, "God has not rejected His people whom He foreknew." [6] Here, when he says, "He foreknew," the sense is not rightly understood except as "He predestinated," as is shown by the context of the passage itself. For he was speaking of the remnant of the Jews which were saved, while the rest perished. For above he had said that the prophet had declared to Israel, "All day long I have stretched forth my hands to an unbelieving and a gainsaying people." [7] And as if it were answered, What, then, has be-

---

[1] Jas. iii. 14.    [2] Jas. i. 5.    [3] Eph. vi. 23.

[4] Matt. vi. 13.    [5] Jer. xvii. 5.    [6] Rom. xi. 2.
[7] Rom. x. 21 et seq.

come of the promises of God to Israel? he added in continuation, " I say, then, has God cast away His people? God forbid! for I also am an Israelite, of the seed of Abraham, of the tribe of Benjamin." Then he added the words which I am now treating : " God hath not cast away His people whom He foreknew." And in order to show that the remnant had been left by God's grace, not by any merits of their works, he went on to add, " Know ye not what the Scripture saith in Elias, in what way he maketh intercession with God against Israel?"[1] and the rest. " But what," says he, " saith the answer of God unto him? 'I have reserved to myself seven thousand men, who have not bowed the knee before Baal.'"[2] For He says not, " There are left to me," or " They have reserved themselves to me," but, " I have reserved to myself." " Even so, then, at this present time also there is made a remnant by the election of grace. And if of grace, then it is no more by works; otherwise grace is no more grace." And connecting this with what I have above quoted, " What then?"[3] and in answer to this inquiry, he says, " Israel hath not obtained that which he was seeking for, but the election hath obtained it, and the rest were blinded." Therefore, in the election, and in this remnant which were made so by the election of grace, he wished to be understood the people which God did not reject, because He foreknew them. This is that election by which He elected those, whom He willed, in Christ before the foundation of the world, that they should be holy and without spot in His sight, in love, predestinating them unto the adoption of sons. No one, therefore, who understands these things is permitted to doubt that, when the apostle says, " God hath not cast away His people whom He foreknew," He intended to signify predestination. For He foreknew the remnant which He should make so according to the election of grace. That is, therefore, He predestinated them; for without doubt He foreknew if He predestinated; but to have predestinated is to have foreknown that which He should do.

CHAP. 48 [XIX.] — PRACTICE OF CYPRIAN AND AMBROSE.

What, then, hinders us, when we read of God's foreknowledge in some commentators on God's word, and they are treating of the calling of the elect, from understanding the same predestination? For they would perchance have rather used in this matter this word which, moreover, is better understood, and which is not inconsistent with, nay, is in accordance with, the truth which is declared concerning the predestination of grace. This I know, that no one has been able to dispute, except erroneously, against that predestination which I am maintaining in accordance with the Holy Scriptures. Yet I think that they who ask for the opinions of commentators on this matter ought to be satisfied with men so holy and so laudably celebrated everywhere in the faith and Christian doctrine as Cyprian and Ambrose, of whom I have given such clear testimonies; and that for both doctrines — that is, that they should both believe absolutely and preach everywhere that the grace of God is gratuitous, as we must believe and declare it to be; and that they should not think that preaching opposed to the preaching whereby we exhort the indolent or rebuke the evil; because these celebrated men also, although they were preaching God's grace in such a manner as that one of them said, " That we must boast in nothing, because nothing is our own; "[4] and the other, " Our heart and our thoughts are not in our own power; "[5] yet ceased not to exhort and rebuke, in order that the divine commands might be obeyed. Neither were they afraid of its being said to them, " Why do you exhort us, and why do you rebuke us, if no good thing that we have is from us, and if our hearts are not in our own power?" These holy men could by no means fear that such things should be said to them, since they were of the mind to understand that it is given to very few to receive the teaching of salvation through God Himself, or through the angels of heaven, without any human preaching to them; but that it is given to many to believe in God through human agency. Yet, in whatever manner the word of God is spoken to man, beyond a doubt for man to hear it in such a way as to obey it, is God's gift.

CHAP. 49. — FURTHER REFERENCES TO CYPRIAN AND AMBROSE.

Wherefore, the above-mentioned most excellent commentators on the divine declarations both preached the true grace of God as it ought to be preached, — that is, as a grace preceded by no human deservings, — and urgently exhorted to the doing of the divine commandments, that they who might have the gift of obedience should hear what commands they ought to obey. For if any merits of ours precede grace, certainly it is the merit of some deed, or word, or thought, wherein also is understood a good will itself. But he very briefly summed up the kinds of all deservings who said, " We must glory in nothing, because nothing is our own." And he who says, " Our heart and our

---

[1] Rom. xi. 4 *et seq.*     [2] Rom. xi. 5.     [3] Rom. xi. 7.

[4] Cyprian, *Testimonies*, iii. 4, as above.
[5] Ambrose, *On Flight from the World*, ch. 1.

thoughts are not in our own power," did not pass over acts and words also, for there is no act or word of man which does not proceed from the heart and the thought. But what more could that most glorious martyr and most luminous doctor Cyprian say concerning this matter, than when he impressed upon us that it behoves us to pray, in the Lord's Prayer, even for the adversaries of the Christian faith, showing what he thought of the beginning of the faith, that it also is God's gift, and pointing out that the Church of Christ prays daily for perseverance unto the end, because none but God gives that perseverance to those who have persevered? Moreover, the blessed Ambrose, when he was expounding the passage where the Evangelist Luke says, "It seemed good to me also," [1] says, "What he declares to have seemed good to himself cannot have seemed good to him alone. For not alone by human will did it seem good, but as it pleased Him who speaks in me, Christ, who effects that that which is good may also seem good to us: for whom He has mercy on He also calls. And therefore he who follows Christ may answer, when he is asked why he wished to become a Christian, ' It seemed good to me also.' And when he says this, he does not deny that it seemed good to God; for the will of men is prepared by God. For it is God's grace that God should be honoured by the saint." [2] Moreover, in the same work, — that is, in the exposition of the same Gospel, when he had come to that place where the Samaritans would not receive the Lord when His face was as going to Jerusalem, — he says, " Learn at the same time that He would not be received by those who were not converted in simpleness of mind. For if He had been willing, He would have made them devout who were undevout. And why they would not receive Him, the evangelist himself mentioned, saying, ' Because His face was as of one going towards Jerusalem.' [3] But the disciples earnestly desired to be received into Samaria. But God calls those whom He makes worthy, and makes religious whom He will." [4] What more evident, what more manifest do we ask from commentators on God's word, if we are pleased to hear from them what is clear in the Scriptures? But to these two, who ought to be enough, let us add also a third, the holy Gregory, who testifies that it is the gift of God both to believe in God and to confess what we believe, saying, " I beg of you confess the Trinity of one godhead; but if ye wish otherwise, say that it is of one nature, and God will be besought that a voice shall be given to you by the Holy Spirit;" that is, God will be

besought to allow a voice to be given to you by which you may confess what you believe. " For He will give, I am certain. He who gave what is first, will give also what is second." [5] He who gave belief, will also give confession.

CHAP. 50. — OBEDIENCE NOT DISCOURAGED BY PREACHING GOD'S GIFTS.

Such doctors, and so great as these, when they say that there is nothing of which we may boast as if of our own which God has not given us, and that our very heart and our thoughts are not in our own power; and when they give the whole to God, and confess that from Him we receive that we are converted to Him in such wise as to continue, — that that which is good appears also to us to be good, and we wish for it, — that we honour God and receive Christ, — that from undevout people we are made devout and religious, — that we believe in the Trinity itself, and also confess with our voice what we believe : — certainly attribute all these things to God's grace, acknowledge them as God's gifts, and testify that they come to us from Him, and are not from ourselves. But will any one say that they in such wise confessed that grace of God as to venture to deny His foreknowledge, which not only learned but unlearned men also confess? Again, if they had so known that God gives these things that they were not ignorant that He foreknew that He would give them, and could not have been ignorant to whom He would give them : beyond a doubt they had known the predestination which, as preached by the apostles, we laboriously and diligently maintain against the modern heretics. Nor would it be with any manner of justice said, nevertheless, to them because they preach obedience, and fervently exhort, to the extent of the ability of each one, to its practice, " If you do not wish that the obedience to which you are stirring us up should grow cold in our heart, forbear to preach to us that grace of God by which you confess that God gives what you are exhorting us to do."

CHAP. 51 [XX.] — PREDESTINATION MUST BE PREACHED.

Wherefore, if both the apostles and the teachers of the Church who succeeded them and imitated them did both these things, — that is, both truly preached the grace of God which is not given according to our merits, and inculcated by wholesome precepts a pious obedience, — what is it which these people of our time think themselves rightly bound by the invincible force of truth to say, " Even if what is said of the predestination of God's benefits be true, yet it

---

[1] Luke i. 3.
[2] Ambrose, *On Luke*, in the exposition of the prologue.
[3] Luke ix 53.          [4] Ambrose, *On Luke*, Book 7, ch. 27.

[5] Greg. of Nazianz. *Orat.* 44 *in Pentecosten*.

must not be preached to the people"?[1] It must absolutely be preached, so that he who has ears to hear, may hear. And who has them if he has not received them from Him who says, "I will give them a heart to know me, and ears to hear"?[2] Assuredly, he who has not received may reject; while, yet, he who receives may take and drink, may drink and live. For as piety must be preached, that, by him who has ears to hear, God may be rightly worshipped; modesty must be preached, that, by him who has ears to hear, no illicit act may be perpetrated by his fleshly nature; charity must be preached, that, by him who has ears to hear, God and his neighbours may be loved;—so also must be preached such a predestination of God's benefits that he who has ears to hear may glory, not in himself, but in the Lord.

CHAP. 52.—PREVIOUS WRITINGS ANTICIPATIVELY REFUTED THE PELAGIAN HERESY.

But in respect of their saying "that it was not necessary that the hearts of so many people of little intelligence should be disquieted by the uncertainty of this kind of disputation, since the catholic faith has been defended for so many years, with no less advantage, without this definition of predestination, as well against others as especially against the Pelagians, in so many books that have gone before, as well of catholics and others as our own;"[3]—I much wonder that they should say this, and not observe—to say nothing of other writings in this place—that those very treatises of mine were both composed and published before the Pelagians had begun to appear; and that they do not see in how many passages of those treatises I was unawares cutting down a future Pelagian heresy, by preaching the grace by which God delivers us from evil errors and from our habits, without any preceding merits of ours,—doing this according to His gratuitous mercy. And this I began more fully to apprehend in that disputation which I wrote to Simplicianus, the bishop of the Church of Milan, of blessed memory, in the beginning of my episcopate, when, moreover, I both perceived and asserted that the beginning of faith is God's gift.

CHAP. 53.—AUGUSTIN'S "CONFESSIONS."

And which of my smaller works has been able to be more generally and more agreeably known than the books of my *Confessions?* And although I published them before the Pelagian heresy had come into existence, certainly in them I said to my God, and said it frequently, "Give what Thou commandest, and command

what Thou willest."[4] Which words of mine, Pelagius at Rome, when they were mentioned in his presence by a certain brother and fellow-bishop of mine, could not bear; and contradicting somewhat too excitedly, nearly came to a quarrel with him who had mentioned them. But what, indeed, does God primarily and chiefly command, but that we believe on Him? And this, therefore, He Himself gives, if it is well said to Him, "Give what Thou commandest." And, moreover, in those same books, in respect of what I have related concerning my conversion, when God converted me to that faith which, with a most miserable and raging talkativeness, I was destroying, do you not remember that it was so narrated how I showed that I was granted to the faithful and daily tears of my mother, that I should not perish?[5] Where certainly I declared that God by His grace converted to the true faith the wills of men, which were not only averse to it, but even adverse to it. Further, in what manner I besought God concerning my growth in perseverance, you know, and you are able to review if you wish it. Therefore, that all the gifts of God which in that work I either asked for or praised, were foreknown by God that He would give, and that He could never be ignorant of the persons to whom He would give them, who can dare, I will not say to deny, but even to doubt? This is the manifest and assured predestination of the saints, which subsequently necessity compelled me more carefully and laboriously to defend when I was already disputing against the Pelagians. For I learnt that each special heresy introduced its own peculiar questions into the Church—against which the sacred Scripture might be more carefully defended than if no such necessity compelled their defence. And what compelled those passages of Scripture in which predestination is commended to be defended more abundantly and clearly by that labour of mine, than the fact that the Pelagians say that God's grace is given according to our merits; for what else is this than an absolute denial of grace?

CHAP. 54 [XXI.]—BEGINNING AND END OF FAITH IS OF GOD.

Therefore that this opinion, which is unpleasing to God, and hostile to those gratuitous benefits of God whereby we are delivered, may be destroyed, I maintain that both the beginning of faith and the perseverance therein, even to the end, are, according to the Scriptures—of which I have already quoted many—God's gifts. Because if we say that the beginning of faith is of ourselves, so that by it we deserve to receive

---

[1] In the Letters of Prosper and Hilary, printed among Augustin's *Letters*, Nos. 225 and 226.
[2] Baruch ii. 31.
[3] The Epistle of Hilary in Augustin's *Letters*, 226, ch. 8.

[4] *Confessions*, Book x. chs. 19, 31, and 37.
[5] *Confessions*, Book iii. chs. 11 and 12, Book ix. ch. 8.

other gifts of God, the Pelagians conclude that God's grace is given according to our merits. And this the catholic faith held in such dread, that Pelagius himself, in fear of condemnation, condemned it. And, moreover, if we say that our perseverance is of ourselves, not of God, they answer that we have the beginning of our faith of ourselves in such wise as the end, thus arguing that we have that beginning of ourselves much more, if of ourselves we have the continuance unto the end, since to perfect is much greater than to begin ; and thus repeatedly they conclude that the grace of God is given according to our merits. But if both are God's gifts, and God foreknew that He would give these His gifts (and who can deny this?), predestination must be preached, — that God's true grace, that is, the grace which is not given according to our merits, may be maintained with insuperable defence.

CHAP. 55. — TESTIMONY OF HIS PREVIOUS WRITINGS AND LETTERS.

And, indeed, in that treatise of which the title is, *Of Rebuke and Grace*,[1] which could not suffice for all my lovers, I think that I have so established that it is the gift of God also to persevere to the end, as I have either never before or almost never so expressly and evidently maintained this in writing, unless my memory deceives me. But I have now said this in a way in which no one before me has said it. Certainly the blessed Cyprian, in the Lord's Prayer, as I have already shown, so explained our petitions as to say that in its very first petition we were asking for perseverance, asserting that we pray for it when we say, " Hallowed be Thy name,"[2] although we have been already hallowed in baptism, — so that we may persevere in that which we have begun to be. Let those, however, to whom, in their love for me, I ought not to be ungrateful, who profess that they embrace, over and above that which comes into the argument, all my views, as you write, — let those, I say, see whether, in the latter portions of the first book of those two which I wrote in the beginning of my episcopate, before the appearance of the Pelagian heresy, to Simplicianus, the bishop of Milan,[3] there remained anything whereby it might be called in question that God's grace is not given according to our merits ; and whether I have not there sufficiently argued that even the beginning of faith is God's gift ; and whether from what is there said it does not by consequence result, although it is not expressed, that even perseverance to the end is not given, except by Him who has predestinated us to His kingdom and glory. Then, did not I many years

ago publish that letter which I had already written to the holy Paulinus,[4] bishop of Nola, against the Pelagians, which they have lately begun to contradict ? Let them also look into that letter which I sent to Sixtus, the presbyter of the Roman Church,[5] when we contended in a very sharp conflict against the Pelagians, and they will find it such as is that one to Paulinus. Whence they may gather that the same sort of things were already said and written several years ago against the Pelagian heresy, and that it is to be wondered at that these should now displease them ; although I should wish that no one would so embrace all my views as to follow me, except in those things in which he should see me not to have erred. For I am now writing treatises in which I have undertaken to retract my smaller works, for the purpose of demonstrating that even I myself have not in all things followed myself ; but I think that, with God's mercy, I have written progressively, and not begun from perfection ; since, indeed, I speak more arrogantly than truly, if even now I say that I have at length in this age of mine arrived at perfection, without any error in what I write. But the difference is in the extent and the subject of an error, and in the facility with which any one corrects it, or the pertinacity with which one endeavours to defend his error. Certainly there is good hope of that man whom the last day of this life shall find so progressing that whatever was wanting to his progress may be added to him, and that he should be adjudged rather to need perfecting than punishment.

CHAP. 56. — GOD GIVES MEANS AS WELL AS END.

Wherefore if I am unwilling to appear ungrateful to men who have loved me, because some advantage of my labour has attained to them before they loved me, how much rather am I unwilling to be ungrateful to God, whom we should not love unless He had first loved us and made us to love Him ! since love is of Him,[6] as they have said whom He made not only His great lovers, but also His great preachers. And what is more ungrateful than to deny the grace of God itself, by saying that it is given to us according to our merits ? And this the catholic faith shuddered at in the Pelagians, and this it objected to Pelagius himself as a capital crime ; and this Pelagius himself condemned, not indeed from love of God's truth, but yet for fear of his own condemnation. But whoever as a faithful catholic is horrified to say that the grace of God is given according to our merits, let him not withdraw faith itself from God's grace, whereby he obtained mercy that he should be faithful ; and thus let him attribute also perseverance to the

---

[1] *On Rebuke and Grace*, ch. 10.  [2] Matt. vi. 9.
[3] Two books to Simplicianus.
[4] *Letter to Paulinus*, 168.  [5] *Letter to Sixtus*, 194.
[6] 1 John iv. 7.

end to God's grace, whereby he obtains the mercy which he daily asks for, not to be led into temptation. But between the beginning of faith and the perfection of perseverance there are those means whereby we live righteously, which they themselves are agreed in regarding as given by God to us at the prayer of faith. And all these things — the beginning of faith, to wit, and His other gifts even to the end — God foreknew that He would bestow on His called. It is a matter, therefore, of too excessive contentiousness to contradict predestination, or to doubt concerning predestination.

CHAP. 57 [XXII.] — HOW PREDESTINATION MUST BE PREACHED SO AS NOT TO GIVE OFFENCE.

And yet this doctrine must not be preached to congregations in such a way as to seem to an unskilled multitude, or a people of slower understanding, to be in some measure confuted by that very preaching of it. Just as even the foreknowledge of God, which certainly men cannot deny, seems to be refuted if it be said to them, "Whether you run or sleep, you shall be that which He who cannot be deceived has foreknown you to be." And it is the part of a deceitful or an unskilled physician so to compound even a useful medicament, that it either does no good or does harm. But it must be said, "So run that you may lay hold;[1] and thus by your very running you may know yourselves to be foreknown as those who should run lawfully:" and in whatever other manner the foreknowledge of God may be so preached, that the slothfulness of man may be repulsed.

CHAP. 58. — THE DOCTRINE TO BE APPLIED WITH DISCRIMINATION.

Now, therefore, the definite determination of God's will concerning predestination is of such a kind that some from unbelief receive the will to obey, and are converted to the faith or persevere in the faith, while others who abide in the delight of damnable sins, even if they have been predestinated, have not yet arisen, because the aid of pitying grace has not yet lifted them up. For if any are not yet called whom by His grace He has predestinated to be elected, they will receive that grace whereby they may will to be elected, and may be so ; and if any obey, but have not been predestinated to His kingdom and glory, they are for a season, and will not abide in the same obedience to the end. Although, then, these things are true, yet they must not be so said to the multitude of hearers as that the address may be applied to themselves also, and those words of those people may be said to them which you have set down in your

letter, and which I have above introduced : "The definite determination of God's will concerning predestination is of such a kind that some of you from unbelief shall receive the will to obey, and come to the faith." What need is there for saying, "Some of you"? For if we speak to God's Church, if we speak to believers, why do we say that "some of them" had come to the faith, and seem to do a wrong to the rest, when we may more fittingly say the definite determination of the will of God concerning predestination is of such a kind that from unbelief you shall receive the will to obey, and come to the faith, and shall receive perseverance, and abide to the end?

CHAP. 59. — OFFENCE TO BE AVOIDED.

Neither is what follows by any means to be said, — that is, "But others of you who abide in the delight of sins have not yet arisen, because the aid of pitying grace has not yet lifted you up ;" when it may be and ought to be well and conveniently said, "But if any of you are still delaying in the delightfulness of damnable sins, lay hold of the most wholesome discipline ; and yet when you have done this be not lifted up, as if by your own works, nor boast as if you had not received this. For it is God who worketh in you both to will and to do for His good will,[2] and your steps are directed by the Lord, so that you choose His way.[3] But of your own good and righteous course, learn carefully that it is attributable to the predestination of divine grace."

CHAP. 60. — THE APPLICATION TO THE CHURCH IN GENERAL.

Moreover, what follows where it is said, "But yet if any of you are not yet called, whom by his grace He has predestinated to be called, you shall receive that grace whereby you shall will to be, and be, elected," is said more hardly than it could be said if we consider that we are speaking not to men in general, but to the Church of Christ. For why is it not rather said thus: "And if any of you are not yet called, let us pray for them that they may be called. For perchance they are so predestinated as to be granted to our prayers, and to receive that grace whereby they may will, and be made elected"? For God, who fulfilled all that He predestinated, has willed us also to pray for the enemies of the faith, that we might hence understand that He Himself also gives to the unbelievers the gift of faith, and makes willing men out of those that were unwilling.

CHAP. 61. — USE OF THE THIRD PERSON RATHER THAN THE SECOND.

But now I marvel if any weak brother among

---

[1] 1 Cor. ix. 24.

[2] Phil. i. 13.        [3] Ps. xxxvii. 23.

the Christian congregation can hear in any way with patience what is connected with these words, when it is said to them, " And if any of you obey, if you are predestinated to be rejected, the power of obeying will be withdrawn from you, that you may cease to obey." For what does saying this seem, except to curse, or in a certain way to predict evils? But if, however, it is desirable or necessary to say anything concerning those who do not persevere, why is it not rather at least said in such a way as was a little while ago said by me, — first of all, so that this should be said, not of them who hear in the congregation, but about others to them ; that is, that it should not be said, " If any of you obey, if you are predestinated to be rejected," but, " If any obey," and the rest, using the third person of the verb, not the second? For it is not to be said to be desirable, but abominable, and it is excessively harsh and hateful to fly as it were into the face of an audience with abuse, when he who speaks to them says, " And if there are any of you who obey, and are predestinated to be rejected, the power of obedience shall be withdrawn from you, that you may cease to obey." For what is wanting to the doctrine if it is thus expressed : " But if any obey, and are not predestinated to His kingdom and glory, they are only for a season, and shall not continue in that obedience unto the end"? Is not the same thing said both more truly and more fittingly, so that we may seem not as it were to be desiring so much for them, as to relate of others the evil which they hate, and think does not belong to them, by hoping and praying for better things ? But in that manner in which they think that it must be said, the same judgment may be pronounced almost in the same words also of God's foreknowledge, which certainly they cannot deny, so as to say, " And if any of you obey, if you are foreknown to be rejected you shall cease to obey." Doubtless this is very true, assuredly it is ; but it is very monstrous, very inconsiderate, and very unsuitable, not by its false declaration, but by its declaration not wholesomely applied to the health of human infirmity.

CHAP. 62. — PRAYER TO BE INCULCATED, NEVERTHELESS.

But I do not think that that manner which I have said should be adopted in the preaching of predestination ought to be sufficient for him who speaks to the congregation, except he adds this, or something of this kind, saying, " You, therefore, ought also to hope for that perseverance in obedience from the Father of Lights, from whom cometh down every excellent gift and every perfect gift,[1] and to

ask for it in your daily prayers ; and in doing this ought to trust that you are not aliens from the predestination of His people, because it is He Himself who bestows even the power of doing this. And far be it from you to despair of yourselves, because you are bidden to have your hope in Him, not in yourselves. For cursed is every one who has hope in man ;[2] and it is good rather to trust in the Lord than to trust in man, because blessed are all they that put their trust in Him.[3] Holding this hope, serve the Lord in fear, and rejoice unto Him with trembling.[4] Because no one can be certain of the life eternal which God who does not lie has promised to the children of promise before the times of eternity, — no one, unless that life of his, which is a state of trial upon the earth, is completed.[5] But He will make us to persevere in Himself unto the end of that life, since we daily say to Him, ' Lead us not into temptation.' "[6] When these things and things of this kind are said, whether to few Christians or to the multitude of the Church, why do we fear to preach the predestination of the saints and the true grace of God, — that is, the grace which is not given according to our merits, — as the Holy Scripture declares it? Or, indeed, must it be feared that a man should then despair of himself when his hope is shown to be placed in God, and should not rather despair of himself if he should, in his excess of pride and unhappiness, place it in himself ?

CHAP. 63 [XXIII.] — THE TESTIMONY OF THE WHOLE CHURCH IN HER PRAYERS.

And I wish that those who are slow and weak of heart, who cannot, or cannot as yet, understand the Scriptures or the explanations of them, would so hear or not hear our arguments in this question as to consider more carefully their prayers, which the Church has always used and will use, even from its beginnings until this age shall be completed. For of this matter, which I am now compelled not only to mention, but even to protect and defend against these new heretics, the Church has never been silent in its prayers, although in its discourses it has not thought that it need be put forth, as there was no adversary compelling it. For when was not prayer made in the Church for unbelievers and its opponents that they should believe ? When has any believer had a friend, a neighbour, a wife, who did not believe, and has not asked on their behalf from the Lord for a mind obedient to the Christian faith? And who has there ever been who has not prayed for himself that he might abide in the Lord? And who has dared, not only with his

---

[1] Jas. i. 17.

[2] Jas. xvii. 5.    [3] Ps. cxviii. 8.    [4] Ps. ii. 12.
[5] Job vii. 1.    [6] Matt. vi. 13.

voice, but even in thought, to blame the priest who invokes the Lord on behalf of believers, if at any time he has said, "Give to them, O Lord, perseverance in Thee to the end!" and has not rather responded, over such a benediction of his, as well with confessing lips as believing heart, "Amen"? Since in the Lord's Prayer itself the believers do not pray for anything else, especially when they say that petition, "Lead us not into temptation," save that they may persevere in holy obedience. As, therefore, the Church has both been born and grows and has grown in these prayers, so it has been born and grows and has grown in this faith, by which faith it is believed that God's grace is not given according to the merits of the receivers. For, certainly, the Church would not pray that faith should be given to unbelievers, unless it believed that God converts to Himself both the averse and adverse wills of men. Nor would the Church pray that it might persevere in the faith of Christ, not deceived nor overcome by the temptations of the world, unless it believed that the Lord has our heart in His power, in such wise as that the good which we do not hold save by our own will, we nevertheless do not hold except He worketh in us to will also. For if the Church indeed asks these things from Him, but thinks that the same things are given to itself by itself, it makes use of prayers which are not true, but perfunctory, — which be far from us! For who truly groans, desiring to receive what he prays for from the Lord, if he thinks that he receives it from himself, and not from the Lord?

CHAP. 64. — IN WHAT SENSE THE HOLY SPIRIT SOLICITS FOR US, CRYING, ABBA, FATHER.

And this especially since "we know not what to pray for as we ought," says the apostle, "but the Spirit Himself maketh intercession for us with groanings that cannot be uttered; and He that searcheth the hearts knoweth what is the mind of the Spirit, because He maketh intercession for the saints according to God."[1] What is "the Spirit Himself maketh intercession," but, "causes to make intercession," "with groanings that cannot be uttered," but "truthful," since the Spirit is truth? For He it is of whom the apostle says in another place, "God hath sent the Spirit of His Son into our hearts, "crying, Abba, Father!"[2] And here what is the meaning of "crying," but "making to cry," by that figure of speech whereby we call a day that makes people glad, a glad day? And this he makes plain elsewhere when he says, "For you have not received the Spirit of bondage again in fear, but you have received the Spirit of the

adoption of sons, in whom we cry, Abba, Father."[3] He there said, "crying," but here, "in whom we cry;" opening up, that is to say, the meaning with which he said "crying," — that is, as I have already explained, "causing to cry," when we understand that this is also itself the gift of God, that with a true heart and spiritually we cry to God. Let them, therefore, observe how they are mistaken who think that our seeking, asking, knocking is of ourselves, and is not given to us; and say that this is the case because grace is preceded by our merits; that it follows them when we ask and receive, and seek and find, and it is opened to us when we knock. And they will not understand that this is also of the divine gift, that we pray; that is, that we ask, seek, and knock. For we have received the spirit of adoption of sons, in which we cry, Abba, Father. And this the blessed Ambrose also said.[4] For he says, "To pray to God also is the work of spiritual grace, as it is written, No one says, Jesus is the Lord, but in the Holy Spirit."

CHAP. 65. — THE CHURCH'S PRAYERS IMPLY THE CHURCH'S FAITH.

These things, therefore, which the Church asks from the Lord, and always has asked from the time she began to exist, God so foreknew that He would give to His called, that He has already given them in predestination itself; as the apostle declares without any ambiguity. For, writing to Timothy, he says, "Labour along with the gospel according to the power of God, who saves us, and calls us with His holy calling, not according to our works, but according to His own purpose and grace, which was given us in Christ Jesus before the times of eternity, but is now made manifest by the coming of our Saviour Jesus Christ."[5] Let him, therefore, say that the Church at any time has not had in its belief the truth of this predestination and grace, which is now maintained with a more careful heed against the late heretics; let him say this who dares to say that at any time it has not prayed, or not truthfully prayed, as well that unbelievers might believe, as that believers might persevere. And if the Church has always prayed for these benefits, it has always believed them to be certainly God's gifts; nor was it ever right for it to deny that they were foreknown by Him. And thus Christ's Church has never failed to hold the faith of this predestination, which is now being defended with new solicitude against these modern heretics.

CHAP. 66 [XXIV.] — RECAPITULATION AND EXHORTATION.

But what more shall I say? I think that I

---

[1] Rom. iii. 26.        [2] Gal. iv. 6.

[3] Rom. viii. 15.        [4] Ambrose, *Commentary on Isaiah.*
[5] 2 Tim. i. 8, etc.

have taught sufficiently, or rather more than sufficiently, that both the beginning of faith in the Lord, and continuance in the Lord unto the end, are God's gifts. And other good things which pertain to a good life, whereby God is rightly worshipped, even they themselves on whose behalf I am writing this treatise concede to be God's gifts. Further, they cannot deny that God has foreknown all His gifts, and the people on whom He was going to bestow them. As, therefore, other things must be preached so that he who preaches them may be heard with obedience, so predestination must be preached so that he who hears these things with obedience may glory not in man, and therefore not in himself, but in the Lord; for this also is God's precept, and to hear this precept with obedience — to wit, that he who glories should glory in the Lord[1] — in like manner as the rest, is God's gift. And he who has not this gift, — I shrink not from saying it, — whatever others he has, has them in vain. That the Pelagians may have this we pray, and that our own brethren may have it more abundantly. Let us not, therefore, be prompt in arguments and indolent in prayers. Let us pray, dearly beloved, let us pray that the God of grace may give even to our enemies, and especially to our brethren and lovers, to understand and confess that after that great and unspeakable ruin wherein we have all fallen in one, no one is delivered save by God's grace, and that that grace is not repaid according to the merits of the receivers as if it were due, but is given freely as true grace, with no merits preceding.

CHAP. 67. — THE MOST EMINENT INSTANCE OF PREDESTINATION IS CHRIST JESUS.

But there is no more illustrious instance of predestination than Jesus Himself, concerning which also I have already argued in the former treatise;[2] and in the end of this I have chosen to insist upon it. There is no more eminent instance, I say, of predestination than the Mediator Himself. If any believer wishes thoroughly to understand this doctrine, let him consider Him, and in Him he will find himself also. The believer, I say; who in Him believes and confesses the true human nature that is our own, however singularly elevated by assumption by God the Word into the only Son of God, so that He who assumed, and what He assumed, should be one person in Trinity. For it was not a Quaternity that resulted from the assumption of man, but it remained a Trinity, inasmuch as that assumption ineffably made the truth of one person in God and man. Because we say that

Christ was not only God, as the Manichean heretics contend; nor only man, as the Photinian heretics assert; nor in such wise man as to have less of anything which of a certainty pertains to human nature, — whether a soul, or in the soul itself a rational mind, or flesh not taken of the woman, but made from the Word converted and changed into flesh, — all which three false and empty notions have made the three various and diverse parties of the Apollinarian heretics; but we say that Christ was true God, born of God the Father without any beginning of time; and that He was also true or very man, born of human mother in the certain fulness of time; and that His humanity, whereby He is less than the Father, does not diminish aught from His divinity, whereby He is equal to the Father. For both of them are One Christ — who, moreover, most truly said in respect of the God, "I and the Father are one;"[3] and most truly said in respect of the man, "My Father is greater than I."[4] He, therefore, who made of the seed of David this righteous man, who never should be unrighteous, without any merit of His preceding will, is the same who also makes righteous men of unrighteous, without any merit of their will preceding; that He might be the head, and they His members. He, therefore, who made that man with no precedent merits of His, neither to deduce from His origin nor to commit by His will any sin which should be remitted to Him, the same makes believers on Him with no preceding merits of theirs, to whom He forgives all sin. He who made Him such that He never had or should have an evil will, the same makes in His members a good will out of an evil one. Therefore He predestinated both Him and us, because both in Him that He might be our head, and in us that we should be His body, He foreknew that our merits would not precede, but that His doings should.

CHAP. 68. — CONCLUSION.

Let those who read this, if they understand, give God thanks, and let those who do not understand, pray that they may have the inward Teacher, from whose presence comes knowledge and understanding.[5] But let those who think that I am in error, consider again and again carefully what is here said, lest perchance they themselves may be mistaken. And when, by means of those who read my writings, I become not only wiser, but even more perfect, I acknowledge God's favour to me; and this I especially look for at the hands of the teachers of the Church, if what I write comes into their hands, and they condescend to acknowledge it.

---

[1] 1 Cor. i. 31.
[2] *On the Predestination of the Saints*, Book i. ch. 30.

[3] John x. 30.        [4] John xiv. 28.        [5] Prov. ii. 6.

# INDEXES.

# NOTE.

THE following indexes contain references to Augustin's writings included in this volume only; they contain no references to the notes, prefaces, or introductory essay.

The *Index of Subjects* is based upon that of Canon Bright's *Select Anti-Pelagian Treatises*. The frequent asterisk in the *Index of Texts* marks passages where the text is more or less fully explained.

554

# INDEX OF SUBJECTS.

# INDEX OF TEXTS.

## OLD TESTAMENT.

# NEW TESTAMENT.

# INDEX OF AUTHORS QUOTED.

230·14 SCH

X